Lecture Notes in Computer Science 4144

Commenced Publication in 1973
Founding and Former Series Editors:
Gerhard Goos, Juris Hartmanis, and Jan van Leeuwen

Thomas Ball   Robert B. Jones (Eds.)

Computer Aided Verification

18th International Conference, CAV 2006
Seattle, WA, USA, August 17-20, 2006
Proceedings

 Springer

Volume Editors

Thomas Ball
Microsoft Research
One Microsoft Way, Redmond, WA 98052, USA
E-mail: tball@microsoft.com

Robert B. Jones
Intel Corporation, RA2-459
2501 NW 229th Avenue, Hillsboro, OR 97124, USA
E-mail: robert.b.jones@acm.org

Library of Congress Control Number: 2006930415

CR Subject Classification (1998): F.3, D.2.4, D.2.2, F.4.1, I.2.3, B.7.2, C.3

LNCS Sublibrary: SL 1 – Theoretical Computer Science and General Issues

ISSN   0302-9743
ISBN-10   3-540-37406-X Springer Berlin Heidelberg New York
ISBN-13   978-3-540-37406-0 Springer Berlin Heidelberg New York

Springer is a part of Springer Science+Business Media

springer.com

© Springer-Verlag Berlin Heidelberg 2006
Printed in Germany

Typesetting: Camera-ready by author, data conversion by Scientific Publishing Services, Chennai, India
Printed on acid-free paper   SPIN: 11817963   06/3142   5 4 3 2 1 0

Preface

This volume contains the proceedings of the International Conference on Computer Aided Verification (CAV), held in Seattle, Washington, USA, July 16–20, 2006. CAV 2006 was the 18th in a series of conferences dedicated to the advancement of the theory and practice of computer-assisted formal analysis methods for software and hardware systems. The conference covers the spectrum from theoretical results to concrete applications, with an emphasis on practical verification tools and the algorithms and techniques that are needed for their implementation.

We received 121 regular paper submissions and 23 tool paper submissions. Of these, the Program Committee selected 35 regular papers and 10 tool papers. Each submission was reviewed by three members of the Program Committee. In addition, each regular paper was reviewed by at least one expert external to the Program Committee.

The CAV 2006 program included five invited talks:

- Manuvir Das (Microsoft) on "Formal Specifications on Industrial-Strength Code—From Myth to Reality"
- David Dill (Stanford University) on "I Think I Voted: E-voting vs. Democracy"
- David Harel (Weizmann Institute) on "Playing with Verification, Planning and Aspects: Unusual Methods for Running Scenario-Based Programs"
- Tony Hoare (Microsoft) on "The Ideal of Verified Software"
- Joe Stoy (Bluespec) on "Verification? Getting it Right the First Time"

The traditional CAV tutorial was replaced by a special symposium, "25 Years of Model Checking," organized by Orna Grumberg (Technion) and Helmut Veith (Technical University of Munich). The symposium consisted of 12 invited lectures delivered by leading researchers in the field of model checking.

This year, CAV was part of the Federated Logic Conference (FLoC 2006), and was jointly organized with ICLP (International Conference on Logic Programming), IJCAR (International Joint Conference on Automated Reasoning), LICS (Logic in Computer Science), RTA (Rewriting Techniques and Applications), and SAT (Theory and Applications of Satisfiability Testing). In particular, the invited talk by David Dill was a FLoC plenary talk, and the invited talk by David Harel was a FLoC keynote talk.

CAV 2006 had nine affiliated workshops:

- ACL2: 6th International Workshop on the ACL2 Theorem Prover and Its Applications (joint with IJCAR)
- BMC: 4th International Workshop on Bounded Model Checking
- CFV: Workshop on Constraints in Formal Verification
- FATES/FV: Formal Approaches to Testing and Runtime Verification (joint with IJCAR)

- GDV: Third Workshop on Games in Design and Verification
- SMT-COMP: Second Satisfiability Modulo Theories Competition
- TV: First Workshop on Multithreading in Hardware and Software: Formal Approaches to Design and Verification
- V&D: First International Workshop on Verification and Debugging
- VSTTE: Workshop on Verified Software: Theory, Tools, and Experiments

We gratefully acknowledge financial support for CAV 2006 from Cadence Design Systems, IBM, Intel Corporation, Microsoft Research, and NEC.

We thank the Program Committee members and the sub-referees for their work in evaluating the submissions. We appreciate the efforts of the Program Committee to attend the first physical PC meeting in the history of CAV. We thank Rance Cleveland and the University of Maryland for hosting the CAV PC meeting. We also thank the Steering Committee and the Chairs of CAV 2005 for their help and advice. Finally, we thank Andrei Voronkov for creating and supporting the outstanding EasyChair conference management system.

June 2006   Thomas Ball
                                                              Robert B. Jones

Conference Organization

Program Chairs

Thomas Ball (Microsoft Research, USA)
Robert B. Jones (Intel Corporation, USA)

Program Committee

Clark Barrett (New York University, USA)
Karthik Bhargavan (Microsoft Research, UK)
Per Bjesse (Synopsys, USA)
Ahmed Bouajjani (University of Paris 7, France)
Randy Bryant (Carnegie Mellon University, USA)
Rance Cleaveland (University of Maryland, USA)
Werner Damm (University of Oldenburg, Germany)
Steven German (IBM, USA)
Patrice Godefroid (Bell Labs, USA)
Ganesh Gopalakrishnan (University of Utah, USA)
Mike Gordon (University of Cambridge, UK)
Orna Grumberg (Technion, Israel)
Holger Hermanns (Saarland University, Germany)
Ranjit Jhala (University of California at San Diego, USA)
Roope Kaivola (Intel Corporation, USA)
Kenneth McMillan (Cadence Berkeley Labs, USA)
Tom Melham (Oxford University, UK)
Corina Pasareanu (NASA Ames, USA)
Amir Pnueli (New York University, USA)
Thomas Reps (University of Wisconsin, USA)
Sanjit Seshia (University of California at Berkeley, USA)
A. Prasad Sistla (University of Illinois at Chicago, USA)
Fabio Somenzi (University of Colorado, USA)

Steering Committee

Edmund M. Clarke (Carnegie Mellon University, USA)
Mike Gordon (University of Cambridge, UK)
Robert Kurshan (Cadence, USA)
Amir Pnueli (New York University, USA)

Corporate Sponsors

Cadence Design Systems
IBM
Intel Corporation
Microsoft Research
NEC

Referees

Fadi Aloul	Byron Cook	Ziyad Hanna
Flemming Anderson	Nathan Cooprider	John Harrison
Gilad Arnold	Jordi Cortadella	Klaus Havelund
Tamarah Arons	Patrick Cousot	Keijo Heljanko
Eugene Asarin	Pedro R. D'Argenio	Martijn Hendriks
Ittai Balaban	Alexandre David	Marc Herbstritt
Gogul Balakrishnan	Dan Deavours	Pei-Hsin Ho
Thomas Ball	Saumya Debray	Michael Hsiao
Roberto Barbuti	Salem Derisavi	Hardi Hungar
Sharon Barner	Jyotirmoy Deshmukh	Michael Huth
Robert Bauer	Henning Dierks	Sonjong Hwang
Jason Baumgartner	Yaniv Eitani	Radu Iosif
Peter Beerel	Allen Emerson	Franjo Ivancic
Gerd Behrmann	Michael Ernst	Himanshu Jain
Josh Berdine	Javier Esparza	Somesh Jha
Eyal Bin	Cormac Flanagan	Sven Johr
Jesse Bingham	Martin Fränzle	Rajeev Joshi
Roderick Bloem	Zhaohui Fu	Comon Jurski
Bernard Boigelot	Vinod Ganapathy	Vineet Kahlon
Dragan Bosnacki	Paul Gastin	Shmuel Katz
John Mark Bouler	Biniam Gebremichael	Zurab Khasidashvili
Patricia Boyer	Rajnish Ghughal	Nick Kidd
Aaron R. Bradley	Dimitra Giannakopoulou	Hyondeuk Kim
Guillaume Brat	Amit Goel	Mike Kishinevsky
Laura Brandan Briones	Dieter Gollmann	Christoph Koch
Glenn Bruns	Denis Gopan	Alfred Koelbl
Tevfik Bultan	Alexey Gotsman	Sava Krstic
Sebastian Burckhardt	Susanne Graf	Hillel Kugler
Doron Bustan	Radu Grosu	Jim Kukula
Luca Carloni	Jim Grundy	Viktor Kuncak
Arindam Chakrabarti	Sumit Gulwani	Orna Kupferman
Feng Chen	Arie Gurfinkel	Shuvendu K. Lahiri
Xiaofang Chen	Aarti Gupta	Akash Lal
Hana Chockler	Peter Habermehl	Robby Lampert
Alessandro Cimatti	Hyojung Han	Rom Langerak

Table of Contents

Invited Talks

Session 1. Automata

Session 2. Tools Papers

Session 3. Arithmetic

Session 4. SAT and Bounded Model Checking

Session 5. Abstraction/Refinement

Session 6. Tools Papers

Session 7. Symbolic Trajectory Evaluation

Session 8. Property Specification and Verification

Session 9. Time

Session 10. Tools Papers

Session 11. Concurrency

Session 12. Trees, Pushdown Systems and Boolean Programs

Session 13. Termination

Session 14. Tools Papers

Session 15. Abstract Interpretation

Session 16. Tools Papers

Session 17. Memory Consistency

Session 18. Shape Analysis

Formal Specifications on Industrial-Strength Code—From Myth to Reality

(Invited Talk)

Manuvir Das

Center for Software Excellence
Microsoft Corporation
manuvir@microsoft.com

Abstract. The research community has long understood the value of formal specifications in building robust software. However, the adoption of any specifications beyond run-time assertions in industrial software has been limited. All of this has changed at Microsoft in the last few years. Today, formal specifications are a mandated part of the software development process in the largest Microsoft product groups. Millions of specifications have been added, and tens of thousands of bugs have been exposed and fixed in future versions of products under development. In addition, Windows public interfaces are formally specified and the Visual Studio compiler understands and enforces these specifications, meaning that programmers anywhere can now use formal specifications to make their software more robust.

How did this happen? The key ingredients of success were picking a critical programming error that costs software companies real money (buffer overruns), and building an incremental solution in which programmers obtain value proportional to their specification effort. The key technical aspects of this incremental approach include SAL, a lightweight specification language for describing memory access behaviour of C/C++ programs; espX, a heavyweight modular checker that enforces consistency between the code and the specification and validates memory accesses; and SALinfer, a lightweight global analysis that infers and inserts a large fraction of the memory specifications automatically.

The goal of this talk is to share the technical story of the insights that enabled SAL, espX and SALinfer, as well as the social and practical story of how we were able to move organizations with thousands of programmers to an environment where the use of specifications is routine.

T. Ball and R.B. Jones (Eds.): CAV 2006, LNCS 4144, p. 1, 2006.
© Springer-Verlag Berlin Heidelberg 2006

I Think I Voted: E-Voting vs. Democracy
(FLoC Plenary Talk)

David Dill

Stanford University
dill@cs.stanford.edu

Abstract. Touch-screen voting machines store records of cast votes in internal memory, where the voter cannot check them. Because of our system of secret ballots, once the voter leaves the polls there is no way anyone can determine whether the vote captured was what the voter intended. Why should voters trust these machines?

In January 2003, I drafted a "Resolution on Electronic Voting" stating that every voting system should have a "voter verifiable audit trail," which is a permanent record of the vote that can be checked for accuracy by the voter, and which is saved for a recount if it is required. I posted the page with endorsements from many prominent computer scientists. At that point, I became embroiled in a nationwide battle for voting transparency that has continued now for three years.

In this talk, I'll explain the basic problems and solutions in electronic voting.

T. Ball and R.B. Jones (Eds.): CAV 2006, LNCS 4144, p. 2, 2006.
© Springer-Verlag Berlin Heidelberg 2006

Playing with Verification, Planning and Aspects: Unusual Methods for Running Scenario-Based Programs

(Abstract of FLoC Keynote Talk)

David Harel

The Weizmann Institute of Science
dharel@weizmann.ac.il

The talk first describes briefly the inter-object, scenario-based approach to programming that I've been working on with colleagues and students for the last eight years. It starts with the 1998 advent of the language of *live sequence charts*, or LSCs, jointly with Werner Damm. LSCs extend message sequence charts, or sequence diagrams with modalities, and thus can express possible, mandatory, forbidden and fragmented scenarios of behavior. Following this, together with my ex-PhD student Rami Marelly, we extended the language quite significantly, adding time, symbolic instances, forbidden elements and more. We also developed a convenient method for programming LSCs directly from a GUI, called *play-in*. The highlight of the work with Marelly, however, is *play-out*, a method for executing LSC specifications, and it is play-out that serves to turn the entire approach into a means for actually programming a system, and not just one for eliciting requirements. The entire approach we then implemented in a tool called the *Play-Engine*.

There is something very declarative about LSCs, and something akin to the execution mechanisms of constraint programming and logic programming in the play-out method, but for various reasons it is more subtle and therefore was considerably difficult to work out. Still, the basic play-out mechanism deals with the nondeterminism inherent in the LSC language in a naive way, just like the way most software development tools that execute models deal with racing conditions: it simply chooses one of the possible next things to do and does it. Of course, this may lead to violations of the constraints present in the LSC specification. Had another path been taken this could perhaps have been avoided.

The present talk discusses three more sophisticated ways to run LSCs, or, more generally, to execute scenario based models and programs. Interestingly, and somewhat unusually, the three methods use ideas from three quite separate fields of computer science: verification, AI and programming methods.

The first method, *smart play-out*, which was developed with ex-PhD student Hillel Kugler, translates the problem of finding a full non-violating superstep (i.e., a sequence of actions that the system takes in response to an external event) into a verification problem, and then employs model-checking to solve it. The resulting superstep is then promptly executed in a way that is transparent to

T. Ball and R.B. Jones (Eds.): CAV 2006, LNCS 4144, pp. 3–4, 2006.

the user. We thus, surprisingly, use hard-core verification not to prove properties of programs or check consistency, etc., but to run programs.

The second method, *planned play-out*, under development with MSc student Itai Segall, uses AI-style planning algorithms (we use one called Graphplan) to do essentially the same. The advantage over smart play-out is in the fact that we can find more than one possible superstep, and we have set-up a sort of user-guided exploration mechanism to allow the user to navigate among possibilities during execution.

While both these methods follow the original play-out mechanism in being an interpreter approach to execution, the third method is a compilation one. With PhD student Shahar Maoz, we exploit the similarities between aspect-oriented programming and the inter-object nature of LSCs, and have worked out a scheme for compiling LSCs directly into AspectJ. We use what we call scenario aspects to coordinate the simultaneous monitoring and direct execution of the LSCs.

All three methods still require lots of work. None work yet on the full extended LSC language, with time and symbolic instances being the main features that cause difficulties. There is also a lot of research still to be done in refining and strengthening the methods to scale up to large systems, and of course the jury is still not in on which of these will serve to be the best, and on whether there are other ideas for executing inter-object scenario-based programs. However, given our own excitement about the general approach, and the feedback we have been receiving, the topic seems to be deserving of the efforts needed.

The Ideal of Verified Software
(Invited Talk)

Tony Hoare

Microsoft Research
thoare@microsoft.com

Abstract. The ideal of verified software has long been the goal of research in Computer Science. This paper argues that the time is ripe to embark on a Grand Challenge project to construct a program verifier, based on a sound and complete theory of programming, and evaluated by experimental application to a large and representative sample of useful computer software.

1 Introduction

Computer Science owes its existence to the invention of the stored-program digital computer. It derives continuously renewed inspiration from the constant stream of new computer applications, which are still being opened up by half a century of continuous reduction in the cost of computer chips, and by spectacular increases in their reliability, performance and capacity. The Science of Programming has made comparable advances by the discovery of faster and more general algorithms, and by the development of a wide range of specific application programs, spreading previously unimaginable benefits into almost all aspects of human life.

These amazing advances in computer application can distract attention from the fact that Computer Science also has a central core of fundamental discoveries which are particular to itself as an independent intellectual discipline. Computing Research is driven, like research in other mature branches of pure science, by natural curiosity, exploring the basic foundations and limitations of the programmable computer, independent of any particular area of application. Because of its effective combination of pure knowledge and applied invention, Computer Science can reasonably be classified as a branch of Engineering Science.

Like all scientists, we are faced with the problem of complexity, both of computers and of the programs that control them. Many software systems in widespread and productive use today have grown and evolved over several decades. Although they are human artefacts, they are now comparable in complexity with the most complex known natural phenomena, for example the Human Genome, whose raw binary code (nearly a gigabyte) has recently been laboriously decoded and published. Geneticists are now engaged in the even more challenging task of understanding the complexity of this code. They too are driven by curiosity about the fundamental questions about the role of the genome as a blueprint

T. Ball and R.B. Jones (Eds.): CAV 2006, LNCS 4144, pp. 5–16, 2006.

for an entire human being. They want to find out firstly what the genes do, and secondly how they do it. They want to discover the basic chemical principles which govern genetic activity, and so to understand not only how but why the genome works as it does. And finally, they wish to support all their discoveries and generalisations by accumulation of sound scientific evidence. Even when the scientist has accomplished all these objectives, it remains for the engineer and the industrialist to find out how to exploit enlarged scientific understanding for commercial profit.

The challenge facing Computer Science is very similar to that facing genetics. Our first and entirely non-trivial task is to understand what a computer program does. As for other engineering artefacts, the externally visible aspects of program behaviour can be codified as a formal engineering specification, expressed in the relevant technical terminology. An explanation of how a program works can be formally expressed in terms of types, assertions, and other redundant annotations. They serve as internal specifications, attached at all the major and minor program interfaces. The correctness of the explanation can in principle be checked by a program analysis tool known as a program verifier. It uses automated logical and mathematical proof techniques to check consistency between a program and its internal and external specifications. A program verifier can play the same role in Software Engineering research as the automatic tools that are now essential or even obligatory in other branches of Engineering, to check the soundness and safety of engineering designs, long before they start construction. An adequately specified and annotated program, which has passed the scrutiny of an automatic program verifier, is said to be a verified program. It offers highly credible evidence that the program will work in accordance with its specification.

The ideal of verified software has been a long-standing inspiration to research in basic Computer Science, and has driven the development of a number of advanced tools performing many of the functions of a program verifier. The most widely used tools concentrate on the detection of programming errors, widely known as bugs. Foremost among these are modern compilers for strongly typed languages, which give warnings of potential anomalies in a program, insofar as those bugs that can be diagnosed without any knowledge of the program's specification. More advanced program analysers begin to take specifications into account. These have been applied by the computer hardware industry to verify programs that simulate the behaviour of computer chips, and they have averted expensive hardware design errors. Other program analysers are routinely used in the software industry to detect security risks and other errors in large-scale legacy code and in modifications to it.

It is expected that normal commercially motivated development of these tools will increase their power to detect more and more errors. This could be an unending task. There is evidence that in large-scale software there will always be more errors to detect, especially since correction of each error is itself prone to error. Eventually only the rarest errors will remain: each one that occurs in practice is extremely unlikely ever to occur again. Such errors are often not worth correcting, unless there is a risk that the error can be exploited by viruses, bugs, or worms. Unfortunately the analysis of each error is both expensive and error-prone. Like insects that carry disease, the least efficient way of eradicating program bugs is by squashing them one by one. A completely different approach is needed. The only sure safeguard against attack is to pursue the ideal of not making the errors in the first place.

That is the goal of more advanced program verification tools. They have been used in the design of critical embedded software applications, often to assist human reasoning in achievement of correctness by construction. They have also been used in support of academic teaching of the principles of programming. But program verification tools of the present day are a long way from the original vision of a program verifier described by Jim King in his Doctoral thesis in 1969. The more practical analysers in use today have made significant compromises, affecting the soundness of their guarantee of correctness as well as the expressive power of the language in which specifications and programs are written. The more idealistic tools are restricted in application by problems of scale, both in the size of the programs treated and in the complexity of the programming language accepted for analysis.

I suggest that the construction of a program verifier, with capabilities close to the original ideal, may be achieved in the foreseeable future by a co-ordinated long-term program of multi-national research, with three strands:

1. Theories: development and unification of the relevant general theories of programming, to cover programming languages in use today. It would have to include features of object orientation, inheritance, concurrency, etc.
2. Tools: incorporation of the theories into a coherent and co-ordinated toolset for program analysis, with evolving capabilities for program verification by a variety of techniques of constraint solving, model checking, and automatic theorem proving.
3. Experiments: evaluation of the tools by experimental application to a large and representative collection of real computer programs and their specifications, which are accumulated together with their specifications and proofs in a scientific repository. As a long-term target, we may hope to accumulate a million lines of verified code.

The project would employ computer scientists with varied specialist skills and experience drawn from around the world. We must combine long-term co-operation on strategic development with short-term scientific competition on methods and tactics. We must co-ordinate long-term planning of the eventual product with the setting of a hierarchy of intermediate goals. We must organise a division of labour to construct each of the tools of the verification toolset, and to verify each program in the expanding repository. We must ensure that intermediate results are accumulated in the repository, so that experiments can be repeated, and further research can build on their results. The broad scale, the long duration, and the high scientific ideals of this project are comparable to those of the Human Genome project; and maybe we too would be justified in appropriating the title of a Grand Challenge.

The methodology of the project derives its inspiration from the traditional practices of pure scientific research—the construction of theories, the exploration of their applicability by experiment, and (increasingly in the present day) the development and use of computer tools to confirm the match between theory and experimental result. The scientific understanding and technological advances arising from successful completion of the project will afford the opportunity for significant reduction in the direct and indirect costs currently associated with programming error.

2   The Ideals of Pure Science

Traditionally, the pure science of Physics claims the crown as the most advanced of the natural sciences. It satisfies a basic human curiosity by exploring the fundamental components and the structures of the material universe, and by giving an account of its origin and history and even its future. The most sophisticated mathematical concepts and theories have been developed, not just to describe but also to explain the behaviour and mutual interactions of all material objects, ranging is scale from quarks and elementary particles to clusters of galaxies and super-clusters. Like other branches of pure science, Physics invents its own language to ask its own abstruse questions, it sets its own agenda of investigation, and it engages in massive long-term collaborative projects to confirm its most general theories; a current example is the construction of high-energy particle accelerators, by which it is hoped to confirm existence of the theoretically predicted Higgs boson.

Computer Science is better known as an applied science, having more in common with other branches of Engineering Science than with a pure science like Physics. Its value has been fully demonstrated by the enormous contributions that have been made by computers and their software to almost every aspect of the modern technological world. And new opportunities for beneficial application are still repeatedly opened up by continuing improvements in the versatility and power and ubiquity and cheapness of computer hardware, reinforced by increases in the speed of computer-mediated communications. The success of any particular software product or project requires an understanding not only of computers and of their general-purpose software, but also of the domain in which they are to be applied. In this respect, applied Computer Science, like applied Mathematics and Statistics, is an inherently multi-disciplinary discipline.

Again like Mathematics and Statistics, Computer Science has a pure branch, in which research is motivated by curiosity and high scientific idealism. We pursue scientific ideals in the same way that Physicists to pursue the utmost accuracy of measurement, or chemists seek the utmost purity of their materials. For the computer scientist, the total correctness of computer programs is just such an ideal. Scientists seek such ideals for their own sake, going far beyond the current needs of the practicing engineer. The main daily concern of the engineer is to accommodate unavoidable impurities in materials and inaccuracies in measurement, just as computer users have to find workarounds for discovered errors in computer programs. Practical engineering is all about compromises that take into account the particular circumstances and timescales of the current project, and the particular interests of the current customer. For the engineer, good enough is always good enough; and fixed budgets and delivery dates are always an adequate excuse for imperfection. The scientist knows that only perfection will protect his work from being superseded by later work of other scientists.

In contrast to the particularities exploited by the good engineer, the pure scientist pursues generality of theory for its own sake. Although the success of any particular experiment may demand skilful compromise, the long-term goals are to transcend the particular circumstances of the current experiment, and to extend the boundaries of application of the current theory. The ultimate accolade goes to those who discover the most general concepts, explaining by the laws of a unified theory such highly disparate phenomena as the fall of an apple and the motion of the planets and moon.

Another ideal pursued by the scientist is certainty of knowledge, gained by accumulation of scientific evidence from widely varied sources. For the engineer, certainty is an irrelevance. His main concern is to make good decisions in the face of prevailing uncertainties that would take far too much time and money to remove.

Nevertheless, the scientist pursuing more abstract ideals, and accumulating knowledge in collaboration with the scientific community, will often make totally unexpected and unplanned contributions to the later success of the engineer and even to the monetary profits sought by the commercial entrepreneur. One day, the engineer realises that the purity and accuracy, which the pure scientist has shown to be achievable in the laboratory, can be exploited on an industrial scale in a deliverable product of a completely new kind. For example the silicon chip is now manufactured in a fabrication line that achieves levels of environmental purity that were only dreamed of in the scientific laboratories of twenty years ago. One day, the entrepreneur realises that a completely new market can be found for the product, and money can be made from it. Amazingly, the roles of scientist, engineer and entrepreneur are sometimes concentrated in a single person. But only because that person recognises how different the roles actually are.

The extra generality of theory sought by the pure scientist also offers long-term benefits for the engineer. It is a more general theory that allows the practical experience gained by the engineer on one project to be transferred to a later project which is not identical to it. It is generality of theory that allows the engineer to explore a range of product designs, and select the one that most fully satisfies the needs of a broad market of potential customers. Experience of modern technology reveals again and again the benefits of an understanding of general theories: initially, they seem to go far beyond the needs of any particular case, but in the long run they lead to continuous stream of new products which are more functional, more economic, and more reliable than anything that preceded them.

In summary, in the advancement of Engineering Science, the engineer and the pure scientist play distinct but closely related roles; their contributions are complementary to each other, and equally necessary. The role of the software engineer in extending the benefits of computer application can be immediately recognised and financially rewarded. But Computer Science also has a pure branch, which deserves equal recognition. It seeks answers to the same basic questions that inspire all branches of engineering science, no matter what their particular area of application.

3 The Five Basic Questions of an Engineering Science

There are five basic questions that are common to all branches of Engineering Science, whether the objects of study are ships, bridges, motor cars, genes or computer software. In summary, they are

1. What does it do?
2. How does it work?
3. Why does it work?
4. How do we know?
5. How can we exploit the knowledge to improve the product?

The third and fourth questions are primarily the domain of pure science, and the rest have more to do with engineering. The first engineering question is "Precisely what is the product for, and exactly what does it do to meet its goals?" The answer to this question is given in the form of an engineering specification of the product. Such a specification is usually drafted as a guide to design as well as the use of the product; it is therefore formulated at a high level of precision and detail.

Secondly, the engineer wants to understand exactly how the product works. This is described at varying levels of granularity and detail by the specifications of the internal interfaces of the product. These explain the functions of each component of the product, and how they interact. Often, the interface specifications are sufficiently complete and precise to permit mathematical calculations, guaranteeing that the joint working of all the components will lead to the correct operation of the product as a whole. In a mature branch of engineering, these calculations are implemented in a computer program, whose use is often obligated by standards of professional practice, and in some cases even by law.

The pure scientist asks two further questions, perhaps even more basic, about an engineering product. The first is the question "Why does the product work?" The explanation must appeal to general scientific principles that apply not just to a particular product, but to a general range of similar products, actual or hypothetical. The answers are found in the basic laws and fundamental theory of the relevant branches of pure Science. And finally, the scientist asks the most important question of all: "How do we know that the answers to the previous questions are actually right? How do we know that the theory corresponds to reality in general, as well as in each particular case?"

The answer is given by the experimental method, as recommended by Francis Bacon; it is on experiment that our confidence in the whole of modern Science is based. The desired connection between the theory and the observable experimental results often involves a long chain of mathematical reasoning and calculation. In earlier times, these calculations were performed by hand; but now the essence of the scientific theories is built into computer programs which analyse high volumes of experimental data, and check its conformity with theory.

The last engineering question, on how to exploit the accumulated knowledge for commercial advantage, is one which the scientist, pursuing knowledge for its own sake, should not be required to answer in advance. Pure knowledge is independent of application. That is why it is so valuable. There is plenty of experience that the first and most important application of new knowledge will be to meet needs that are entirely unpredicted when the research starts. Knowledge is what prepares us to meet the problems of an unknown future. So the fifth question is one that should not be answered until after the knowledge has been accumulated.

The general scientific questions described above are applied by Computer Scientists, to computer programs. The first question is "What does the program do?"; it is answered by a functional specification of the system, expressed as a formal description of the observable properties of its intended behaviour in action. The second question "How does it work?" is answered by specifications of the internal interfaces between components of the system, often expressed by technically redundant declarations and assertions sprinkled in the text of the program. The third question "Why does the program work?" is answered by the theory of programming, which formalises the semantics of the programming language in which the program is written: this provides a basis for the rules which define the correctness or conformity relation between a program and its accompanying documentation.

And the final question is "How do we know that the program is in fact correct?" The theory of programming tells us that this final assurance can in principle be given by mathematical reasoning and proof, guaranteeing that the specifications are a logical consequence of the text of the program. This theory has already been put into practice. Since the earliest times, proofs for small and critical programs have been constructed manually, and checked by human eye. In some cases, the proofs have been constructed as part of the development process for the software. More recently, the reliability and effectiveness of the verification has been increased by automation of the construction or the checking of the proofs. In analogy with other branches of science, consider the text of the program as the experimental data; consider the specifications of the external and internal interfaces of the program as a theory of how and why the program works. Now an automatic tool for program verification is one that checks the consistency of the theory with the actual text of the program, just like the analysis tools of other branches of science and engineering. Its application greatly increased confidence that the verified program when executed will conform to specification. That is the dream that has for over thirty years driven research in basic Computing Science.

The tool that realises this dream is called a program verifier. Unfortunately it does not yet exist.

4   Proposal for a Grand Challenge Project

A project to construct a program verifier will require the general support from the entire computer science research community, and especially from those who have the background, the skills and the experience to make a substantial contribution to its progress. The relevant topics of research include programming language semantics, programming principles, type theory, compiler construction, program analysis and optimisation, test case generation, mathematical modelling, programming methodology, design patterns, dependability, software evolution, and construction of programmer productivity tools. In addition there are various approaches to mechanical theorem proving, which include proof search, decision procedures, SAT solving, first-order induction, higher order logic, algebraic reduction, resolution, constraint solving, model checking, invariant abstraction, and abstract interpretation. These lists are not intended to be complete; new ideas are very necessary, and will be welcomed from any quarter.

The main challenge of a verification project will be to bring this wide range of skills to bear on the evolution of a coherent toolset. At least an equal effort must be devoted to exercise and evaluate the prototype tools on a realistic selection of actual computer programs and their specifications. The history of computing gives examples of amazing progress that can be made in the evolution of tools by their repeated application to a series of agreed challenges. And the success of the project would have an amazing impact on professional practice of programming, on the justified confidence which Society places in computers, and on the further progress of scientific research in consolidating and extending these benefits.

It is hoped that the majority of specialists in all these fields will welcome the prospect that a program verifier will exploit the results of their research, for the ultimate benefit of all programmers and users of computers. But most of them will not wish to commit their own efforts to such a long-term and laborious collaborative project. And rightly so. Most of scientific progress, and nearly all breakthroughs, are made by individual scientists, working by themselves or in a small local team; they need to preserve their freedom to pursue their own bright ideas in their own directions, and to communicate their research results by publication in the research literature. Other excellent engineering scientists may be discouraged by the long timescales of the project. They will prefer to grasp ever expanding opportunities for transfer of software verification technology into direct industrial and commercial exploitation, and they will enjoy the more significant and immediate benefits that can be achieved. The transfer of verification technology to the computer chip industry took just such a course. A balance between short-term opportunistic researches and a long-term co-ordinated research programme is essential. There should be a fruitful interchange of research skills, prototype tools and theoretical understanding between one style of research and another. Indeed, even after completion of the long-term project, the practical exploitation of a program verifier will be critically dependent on the continuing progress of research in such areas as system dependability and software evolution, programming methodology and software engineering.

In conclusion, we should not expect more than a small percentage of the relevant research communities to be engaged in a Grand Challenge project at any one time. Success of the project is far from a foregone conclusion, and to commit more than a small proportion of the world's scarce resources of scientific talent in any particular specialist area would be simply too great a risk.

The success of a Grand Challenge project depends on the agreement of a substantial community of the world's scientists, not only that the project is worth while, but also that the time is ripe to start it now. The project can hardly start without a measure of agreement on the following points:

1. Selection of an initial set of complementary tools, and allocation of responsibility for their development.
2. Establishment of a repository of representative programs and specifications, together with assertions, test cases, development histories, and other relevant formal material.
3. Planning for adaptation of the tools and representative programs, so that each tool applies to all programs.
4. Division of responsibility for supply of missing specifications, incomplete assertions or missing code for specifications and programs in the repository.
5. Experimental application of tools to the material in the repository.
6. Accumulation of the results of experiment for exploitation in subsequent research and development.
7. Identification of opportunities for improvement in the tools, and a planned programme for their implementation.
8. Design of internal interfaces behind which specialised tools can be combined, while preserving their freedom to evolve independently.
9. Election of an international guidance committee to oversee the progress and direction of the research.

In later phases, the project would develop by expanding the range and ambition of the representative programs in the repository, by implementation of new tools that combine technologies previously found successful on separate tests.

There is plenty of experience of large-scale, long-term collaborative projects in other branches of science. For example, in Astronomy and in Nuclear Physics, all new particle accelerators, satellites and telescopes are planned as long-term national or international collaborations. But such projects have so far been rare in Computer Science, and this may be a symptom of the immaturity of our subject. To embark on such a project now will need a fairly radical change to the culture and the daily practice of our research. We will have to accept that a worthy method of publication of new theoretical results will be to incorporate them in a set of tools that has been designed by others. We will have to accept that the best progress will be made by combining the technologies currently promoted in rival tools, each of which has hitherto aimed at universal applicability. And above all, we will have to give the highest scientific rewards to those who apply other peoples' theories and other peoples' toolsets to programs that have been written by yet some-one else. It is the users of telescopes and particle accelerators that win the Nobel prizes, not their builders. A broad division of labour among specialists is commonplace in all mature branches of science: no-one expected Einstein to test his own theories, and no-one expected Eddington to devise his own theories for experiment. But in our subject such division of labour would be a novelty. It is likely that successful conduct of a Grand Challenge project may require radical changes in current modes of refereeing, publication practices, administration of research funding, and even the criteria for promotion of academic researchers.

5 Costs and Benefits

Although the main goal of a Grand Challenge project is the advancement of Science, it would be unrealistic to embark on the project without some consideration of the costs and benefits for society as a whole.

The costs may be roughly estimated as between one and two thousand man-years of scientific effort, expended throughout the world over a period of ten to twenty years. This could be approaching ten percent of the world-wide availability of research skills of those currently engaged in the relevant areas of formally based research in Computer Science.

The benefits of program verification will be delivered in the form of reduction of the phenomenon of programming error, and a consequential increase of confidence in the dependability of software systems in widespread use. Fortunately, an estimate of the cost of programming errors is already available from an independent source, which attributes them to an inadequate infrastructure for program testing. Here is an extract from a recent report.

> Based on the software developer and user surveys, the national [US] annual costs of an inadequate infrastructure for software testing is estimated to range from $22.2 to $59.5 billion. Over half of these costs are borne by software users in the form of error avoidance and mitigation activities. The remaining costs are borne by software developers [The Economic Impacts of Inadequate Infrastructure for Software Testing, US Dept. of Commerce Planning Report 02-03, May 2002].

This figure should probably be doubled to cover the world-wide costs of programming error, and doubled again, if nothing is done about it, to cover the growth in computer usage in the next decade. The prospect of saving just one percent of this waste of resource for just one year would justify the allocation of more funds to a Grand Challenge project in program verification than it could ever find productive ways of spending. The limitation on the rate of progress will be the availability of researchers with the necessary background, skills and enthusiasm. Each year's delay in the delivery and exploitation of the results of the research will cost far more than the entire cost of the research project. Howevert, the project is a risky one and there is no guarantee of return on investment.

Of course, full exploitation of the ultimate benefits arising from the project will require more than simply the availability of a scientific prototype of a program verifier. It will require that software engineers as a profession must adopt a more scientific approach to the whole task of program development and evolution, from the elucidation of requirements and formalisation of specifications, to the design and testing of program changes to be installed in running software. It will require the development of re-usable libraries of useful concepts and specifications, covering all the major application areas for computers. It will require that the technology of verification developed in the project (though probably not the prototype verifier itself) should be incorporated into commercially marketed tool-sets. It will require the training and motivation of software engineers in the use of the tools; and when the technology is widely available, its use may be mandated, as in other branches of engineering, by official codes of engineering practice, reinforced perhaps by professional, legal or commercial sanctions. It is not the role of the scientist to predict or recommend such changes in law or society—only to make them possible. And without a program verifier, they will not be possible. In summary, the cost of technology transfer will be at least ten times the cost of the basic research. Fortunately, success in the original research project will greatly reduce the risk of this later and larger investment.

6   Public Esteem

In the present day, it must be admitted that the general public holds the profession of programming in rather low esteem. The newspapers delight in reporting examples of major projects that are over budget, late, and sometimes even cancelled before delivery. One of the many causes for these failures is the inadequacy, the instability, or even the total absence of timely specifications, agreed in advance with the informed consent of the customer. And even after delivery, the programs are full of annoying bugs, in some cases affecting many millions of users throughout the world. Sometimes these bugs provide a target for the entry and spread of viruses and worms in the computer network, which cause billions of dollars of damage to those whose business relies on the web.

The low esteem of the programming profession is confirmed by an examination of our normal every-day mode of working. Surely we are the only profession in the world that expends half of its working life detecting and removing mistakes committed in the other half. Our excuse is that without massive debugging efforts, the software delivered to customers would be even less reliable. But other professions have learnt that it pays to devote their main efforts to preventing the errors from occurring in the first place. If a program verifier can help us to do that, perhaps we can begin to earn the trust and respect of the public, and even our own self-respect. In the recognised professions such as medicine and law, as well as in established branches of engineering, professional practitioners strengthen their claim to the trust of the public, because they owe allegiance to principles and ideals that transcend considerations of personal, political, or financial advantage. It is important that Computer Scientists should insist on their right to pursue similar impersonal ideals.

One of the beneficial side-effects of the announcement of a Grand Challenge project is to raise public awareness and interest in the progress, the methods and the results of scientific research. Astronomy has gained enormous visibility from the spectacular achievements of the manned space programme, and the human genome project has attracted many clever and enthusiastic students into a scientific career in branches of biology. In general, young people are attracted to science and engineering by their idealism and their innate curiosity about the real world, or the workings of the products of engineering. A Grand Challenge in verified software may not have the same glamour as those in Genetics or Physics, but it makes the same kind of appeal to students who really want to understand how things work and why.

7   Conclusion

The long-term benefits of an improved understanding of the relationship between programs and their specifications are expressible as a vision of a future world in which

1. The education and training of software engineers is based on scientific principles.
2. Software engineers can be relied on to deliver new products on time, on budget, and to specification.
3. No design or implementation errors are found in delivered software.
4. Changes and improvements to working software are undertaken with equal confidence in their serviceability.
5. Computer software is always the most reliable component in any system which it controls.

These goals will be achieved by basic advances in our understanding of Computer Science. The advances are made by the normal scientific method of development of a comprehensive theory, the conduct of experiment to confirm its range of application, and the development of sophisticated computer programs to check the match between experiment and theory.

Antichains: A New Algorithm for Checking Universality of Finite Automata[*]

M. De Wulf[1], L. Doyen[1,**], T.A. Henzinger[2,3], and J.-F. Raskin[1]

[1] CS, Université Libre de Bruxelles, Belgium
[2] I&C, Ecole Polytechnique Fédérale de Lausanne (EPFL), Switzerland
[3] EECS, University of California at Berkeley, U.S.A.

Abstract. We propose and evaluate a new algorithm for checking the universality of nondeterministic finite automata. In contrast to the standard algorithm, which uses the subset construction to explicitly determinize the automaton, we keep the determinization step implicit. Our algorithm computes the least fixed point of a monotone function on the lattice of antichains of state sets. We evaluate the performance of our algorithm experimentally using the random automaton model recently proposed by Tabakov and Vardi. We show that on the difficult instances of this probabilistic model, the antichain algorithm outperforms the standard one by several orders of magnitude. We also show how variations of the antichain method can be used for solving the language-inclusion problem for nondeterministic finite automata, and the emptiness problem for alternating finite automata.

1 Introduction

The *universality problem* asks, given a nondeterministic finite automaton A over the alphabet Σ, if the language of A contains all finite words over Σ, that is, if $\mathsf{Lang}(A) = \Sigma^*$. This problem is fundamental in automata theory, and several important problems in verification reduce polynomially to this problem. The standard algorithm for universality is to first determinize the automaton using the *subset construction*, and then check for the reachability of a set containing only nonaccepting states. The subset construction may construct a deterministic automaton that is exponentially larger than the original automaton. This explosion is in some sense unavoidable, as the universality problem is known to be PSPACE-complete [MS72]. Explicit determinization via the subset construction is also useful to solve a wide range of other problems, such as checking the emptiness of alternating finite automata [CKS81, KV01], checking language inclusion and language equivalence for two nondeterministic finite automata [HMU01], and solving two-player safety games of incomplete information [Rei84].

[*] This research was supported in part by the NSF grants CCR-0234690 and CCR-0225610, and the Belgian FNRS grant 2.4530.02 of the FRFC project "Centre Fédéré en Vérification."

[**] Research fellow supported by the Belgian National Science Foundation (FNRS).

T. Ball and R.B. Jones (Eds.): CAV 2006, LNCS 4144, pp. 17–30, 2006.
© Springer-Verlag Berlin Heidelberg 2006

Recently, we showed that explicit determinization via the subset construction can be avoided when solving two-player safety games of incomplete information. To avoid the subset construction, we proposed in [DDR06] a *lattice-theoretic solution* that comes in the form of a monotone function on the lattice of antichains of state sets (an *antichain* is a set of $\subseteq$-incomparable sets). The greatest fixed point of this monotone function contains the solution to the strategy synthesis problem. The three main advantages of the antichain method over the subset construction are as follows. First, the new algorithm keeps determinization implicit. Second, the antichain algorithm takes into account the safety objective of the game and computes only what is necessary to establish the existence of a winning strategy for that particular objective. Third, antichains of state sets allow us to store only maximal subsets of states for which a winning strategy exists. This is because if Player I has a strategy to keep the game in safe states starting from a set s of states, then she also has such a strategy for all starting sets $s' \subseteq s$. We show in this paper that the idea of keeping determinization implicit using antichains can also be applied to important problems of automata theory, such as universality and language inclusion for nondeterministic automata, and emptiness for alternating automata.

First, we show that the universality problem for nondeterministic finite automata can be solved on the lattice of antichains of state sets using a variation of the monotone function proposed in our previous work. We reduce the universality problem to a two-player reachability game of incomplete information, which can be solved by computing the least fixed point of this monotone function. We implemented this solution using NuSMV [CCGR99] and the CUDD library [Som98]. To compare the performance of the antichain algorithm to the performance of various implementations of subset-construction based algorithms, we used a large set of examples generated in the probabilistic framework by Tabakov and Vardi [TV05]. This framework was proposed with the express purpose of comparing the performances of algorithms on finite automata. In their experiments, the authors conclude that explicit determinization as implemented in [Mø04] outperforms the algorithm of Brzozowski [BL80] as well as newer implementations, which use symbolic methods for the subset construction. Our experimental results show that our implementation of the antichain algorithm is considerably faster, on the entire parameter space of the probabilistic framework, than the most efficient implementation of the standard algorithm. In particular, on the most difficult instances of the probabilistic framework, the antichain algorithm outperforms [Mø04] by two orders of magnitude. For this comparison, we are limited to automata with approximately 175 states, which is the limit that the explicit-determinization approach can handle on the most expensive instances of the probabilistic framework. On these difficult instances, the antichain approach scales much better: we are able to successfully check universality for automata with several thousands of states in less than 10 seconds.

Second, to show the generality of the antichain approach, we also give new algorithmic solutions to the language-inclusion problem for nondeterministic automata, and to the emptiness problem for alternating automata. Again, no explicit determinization is performed. To solve the emptiness problem for alternating automata, we use the same lattice as for universality and only change the monotone function that operates on the lattice. To solve the language-inclusion problem for nondeterministic automata, we need a slightly richer lattice.

Structure of the Paper. In Section 2, we review some basic notions about finite automata. In Section 3, we introduce the lattice of antichains of state sets, and we present the antichain algorithm for the universality problem for nondeterministic automata. In Section 4, we report on two different symbolic implementations of the antichain algorithm, and we compare their performances with the classical algorithm that uses explicit determinization. In Section 5, we give antichain-based solutions for nondeterministic language inclusion and alternating emptiness.

2   Finite Automata

Definitions. A (*nondeterministic*) *finite automaton*, NFA for short, is a tuple $A = \langle \mathsf{Loc}, \mathsf{Init}, \mathsf{Fin}, \Sigma, \delta \rangle$, where Loc is a finite set of states (or locations), $\mathsf{Init} \subseteq \mathsf{Loc}$ is the set of initial states, $\mathsf{Fin} \subseteq \mathsf{Loc}$ is the set of accepting (or final) states, Σ is a finite alphabet, and $\delta \subseteq \mathsf{Loc} \times \Sigma \times \mathsf{Loc}$ is a (nondeterministic) transition relation. A *deterministic* finite automaton, DFA for short, is an NFA $A = \langle \mathsf{Loc}, \mathsf{Init}, \mathsf{Fin}, \Sigma, \delta \rangle$ such that for all states $\ell \in \mathsf{Loc}$ and all letters $\sigma \in \Sigma$, there exists a unique state $\ell' \in \mathsf{Loc}$ such that $\delta(\ell, \sigma, \ell')$. A *run* of the NFA $A = \langle \mathsf{Loc}, \mathsf{Init}, \mathsf{Fin}, \Sigma, \delta \rangle$ over a finite word $w = \sigma_1 \ldots \sigma_n$ is a sequence $r = \ell_0 \ell_1 \ldots \ell_n$ of states such that (1) $\ell_0 \in \mathsf{Init}$ and (2) $\delta(\ell_i, \sigma_{i+1}, \ell_{i+1})$ for all $0 \le i < n$. The run r is *accepting* iff $\ell_n \in \mathsf{Fin}$. The *language* $\mathsf{Lang}(A)$ accepted by A is the set of words $w \in \Sigma^*$ such that A has an accepting run over w.

Notations. Given a finite word $w = \sigma_1 \ldots \sigma_n$ of size $|w| = n$, we write $w(i) = \sigma_i$ for the i-th letter of w, and $w(0) = \varepsilon$ for the empty word. Given an NFA $A = \langle \mathsf{Loc}, \mathsf{Init}, \mathsf{Fin}, \Sigma, \delta \rangle$, a state set $s \subseteq \mathsf{Loc}$, and a letter $\sigma \in \Sigma$, we define $\mathsf{post}_\sigma^A(s) = \{\ell' \in \mathsf{Loc} \mid \exists \ell \in s : \delta(\ell, \sigma, \ell')\}$, $\mathsf{pre}_\sigma^A(s) = \{\ell \in \mathsf{Loc} \mid \exists \ell' \in s : \delta(\ell, \sigma, \ell')\}$, and $\mathsf{cpre}_\sigma^A(s) = \{\ell \in \mathsf{Loc} \mid \forall \ell' \in \mathsf{Loc} : \delta(\ell, \sigma, \ell') \rightarrow \ell' \in s\}$. Note that $\mathsf{Loc} \setminus \mathsf{cpre}_\sigma^A(s) = \mathsf{pre}_\sigma^A(\mathsf{Loc} \setminus s)$.

Operations. Given two NFAs A and B, we denote by $A \otimes B$ the synchronous product of the two automata, and by $A \oplus B$ the sum of the automata. The language accepted by the product is $\mathsf{Lang}(A \otimes B) = \mathsf{Lang}(A) \cap \mathsf{Lang}(B)$ and the language accepted by the sum is $\mathsf{Lang}(A \oplus B) = \mathsf{Lang}(A) \cup \mathsf{Lang}(B)$. Given a DFA A, we denote by $\overline{A}$ the complement of A, which accepts the language $\mathsf{Lang}(\overline{A}) = \Sigma^* \setminus \mathsf{Lang}(A)$.

Problems. The *emptiness problem* for NFAs is to decide, given an NFA A, if $\mathsf{Lang}(A) = \emptyset$. This problem is solvable in time linear in the size of A. The *universality problem* for NFAs is to decide, given an NFA A, if $\mathsf{Lang}(A) = \Sigma^*$. This problem is much harder than emptiness: it is complete for PSPACE [MS72]. The classical algorithm for deciding universality first determinizes A, and then checks emptiness of the complement. The difficult step is the determinization, as it may cause an exponential blow-up in the number of states of the automaton. The *language-inclusion problem* for NFAs is to decide, given two NFAs A and B, if $\mathsf{Lang}(A) \subseteq \mathsf{Lang}(B)$. This problem is also complete for PSPACE. The classical algorithm for deciding language inclusion checks emptiness of the product of A with the complement of B. In the next section, we propose a new approach to solve the universality problem, which does not involve explicit determinization, and later we extend the approach to solve also language inclusion.

3   A Fixed Point to Solve Universality

Two Lattices of Antichains. Let Loc be a set (in our case, a set of states of some automaton). An *antichain* over Loc is a set $q \subseteq 2^{\mathsf{Loc}}$ such that $\forall s, s' \in q :$ $s \not\subseteq s'$. Thus q is a set of pairwise incomparable subsets of Loc (with regard to set inclusion). We denote by L the set of antichains over Loc. We define the following partial orders: for two antichains $q, q' \in L$, let $q \sqsubseteq q'$ iff $\forall s \in q \cdot \exists s' \in q' : s \subseteq s'$, and let $q \mathrel{\widetilde{\sqsubseteq}} q'$ iff $\forall s' \in q' \cdot \exists s \in q : s \subseteq s'$. The two partial orders $\sqsubseteq$ and $\mathrel{\widetilde{\sqsubseteq}}$ yield complete lattices on the set L of antichains. This can be seen as follows. Given a set $q \subseteq 2^{\mathsf{Loc}}$ (not necessarily an antichain), a set $s \in q$ is *maximal* in q iff $\forall s' \in q : s \not\subset s'$. Similarly, $s \in q$ is *minimal* in q iff $\forall s' \in q : s' \not\subset s$. We write $\lceil q \rceil$ (resp. $\lfloor q \rfloor$) for the set of maximal (resp. minimal) elements of q. Given two antichains $q, q' \in L$, the $\sqsubseteq$-lub (least upper bound) of q and q' is the antichain $q \sqcup q' = \lceil \{s \mid s \in q \lor s \in q'\} \rceil$; the $\sqsubseteq$-glb (greatest lower bound) is the antichain $q \sqcap q' = \lceil \{s \cap s' \mid s \in q \land s' \in q'\} \rceil$. Similarly, the $\mathrel{\widetilde{\sqsubseteq}}$-lub is $q \mathbin{\widetilde{\sqcup}} q' = \lfloor \{s \cup s' \mid s \in q \land s' \in q'\} \rfloor$, and the $\mathrel{\widetilde{\sqsubseteq}}$-glb is $q \mathbin{\widetilde{\sqcap}} q' = \lfloor \{s \mid s \in q \lor s \in q'\} \rfloor$. These definitions can be extended to lub's and glb's of arbitrary (nonbinary) sets in the obvious way, yielding the operators $\bigsqcup$, $\bigsqcap$, $\widetilde{\bigsqcup}$, and $\widetilde{\bigsqcap}$. Adding suitable bottom and top elements, we obtain the following lemma.

Lemma 1. $\langle L, \sqsubseteq, \bigsqcup, \bigsqcap, \emptyset, \{\mathsf{Loc}\} \rangle$ *and* $\langle L, \mathrel{\widetilde{\sqsubseteq}}, \widetilde{\bigsqcup}, \widetilde{\bigsqcap}, \{\emptyset\}, \emptyset \rangle$ *are complete lattices.*

We call these two lattices the *lattice of antichains* and the *dual lattice of antichains*, respectively. We show how to solve the universality problem for nondeterministic finite automata using either lattice.

Game Interpretation of Universality. Consider the following game played by a protagonist and an antagonist. The protagonist wants to establish that a given NFA A does not accept the language Σ^*. The protagonist has to provide a finite word w such that, no matter which run of A over w the antagonist chooses, the run does not end in an accepting state. This game is a one-shot game. However, to obtain a fixed point solution to the universality problem, we can consider a multi-round game interpretation of this problem: in each round of the game, the protagonist provides a single letter σ, and the antagonist decides how to update the state of A on input σ according to the nondeterministic transition relation. To be equivalent to the one-shot game, the protagonist must not be able to observe the state of the automaton, which is chosen by the antagonist. So, we have to consider a game where the protagonist cannot distinguish between states of the automaton: this is a *game of imperfect information*. We can solve the universality problem by looking for the existence of winning strategies in such games. In a recent paper, we showed that safety games of imperfect information can be solved by computing the greatest fixed point of a monotone function on the lattice of antichains [DDR06]. We show here that reachability games of imperfect information can be solved by computing a least fixed point on this lattice. This gives a new algorithm for checking universality.

Using the Lattice of Antichains to Solve Universality. Given an NFA $A = \langle \mathsf{Loc}, \mathsf{Init}, \mathsf{Fin}, \Sigma, \delta \rangle$, we define the following monotone function on the lattice L of antichains over Loc. For an antichain $q \in L$, let

$$\mathsf{CPre}^A(q) = \lceil \{ s \mid \exists s' \in q \cdot \exists \sigma \in \Sigma : s = \mathsf{cpre}^A_\sigma(s') \} \rceil.$$

So, a set s of states belongs to the antichain $\mathsf{CPre}^A(q)$ iff it is maximal and there exist a state set $s' \in q$ and a letter $\sigma \in \Sigma$ such that for all states $\ell \in s$, the set of states ℓ' with $\delta(\ell, \sigma, \ell')$ is in s'. This monotone function can be used to solve the universality problem for NFAs. This is formalized in the next theorem.

Theorem 2. *Let $A = \langle \mathsf{Loc}, \mathsf{Init}, \mathsf{Fin}, \Sigma, \delta \rangle$ be an NFA, and let $\mathcal{F} = \bigsqcap \{ q \mid q = \mathsf{CPre}^A(q) \sqcup \{\overline{\mathsf{Fin}}\} \}$. Then $\mathsf{Lang}(A) \neq \Sigma^*$ iff $\{\mathsf{Init}\} \sqsubseteq \mathcal{F}$.*

Proof. First, assume that $\mathsf{Lang}(A)$ is not universal. Let $w \in \Sigma^* \setminus \mathsf{Lang}(A)$ be a word of size $|w| = n$. Consider the sequence $s_0, s_1, \ldots, s_n$ of state sets such that (1) $s_0 = \mathsf{Init}$, (2) $s_i = \mathsf{post}^A_{w(i)}(s_{i-1})$ for all $1 \leq i \leq n$, and (3) $s_n \subseteq \overline{\mathsf{Fin}}$ (recall that A has no accepting run over w). We prove by induction on k that $\{s_{n-k}\} \sqsubseteq \mathcal{F}$. For $k = 0$, since $s_n \subseteq \overline{\mathsf{Fin}}$, we obtain immediately $\{s_n\} \sqsubseteq \mathcal{F}$. For the inductive case, assume that $\{s_{n-k}\} \sqsubseteq \mathcal{F}$ for all $0 \leq k < i$, and let us show that $\{s_{n-i}\} \sqsubseteq \mathcal{F}$. Observe that by definition, for $\sigma = w(n - i + 1)$ we have $\mathsf{post}^A_\sigma(s_{n-i}) = s_{n-i+1}$. Therefore $\{s_{n-i}\} \sqsubseteq \mathsf{CPre}^A(\{s_{n+1-i}\})$, and by the monotonicity of CPre^A and the induction hypothesis, we get $\{s_{n-i}\} \sqsubseteq \mathsf{CPre}^A(\mathcal{F})$ and $\{s_{n-i}\} \sqsubseteq \mathsf{CPre}^A(\mathcal{F}) \sqcup \{\overline{\mathsf{Fin}}\}$, which is equivalent to $\{s_{n-i}\} \sqsubseteq \mathcal{F}$, as $\mathcal{F}$ is a fixed point. In particular, we have $\{s_0\} \sqsubseteq \mathcal{F}$, that is, $\{\mathsf{Init}\} \sqsubseteq \mathcal{F}$.

Second, assume that $\{\mathsf{Init}\} \sqsubseteq \mathcal{F}$. We construct a word $w \notin \mathsf{Lang}(A)$. Consider the infinite sequence $q_0, q_1, q_2, \ldots$ of antichains defined by (1) $q_0 = \emptyset$ and (2) $q_i = \mathsf{CPre}^A(q_{i-1}) \sqcup \{\overline{\mathsf{Fin}}\}$ for all $i \geq 1$. By Tarski's fixed point theorem, we know that $\mathcal{F} = q_n$ for some $n \in \mathbb{N}$. We construct an integer $k < n$, a sequence $s_0, s_1, \ldots, s_k$ of $k + 1$ state sets, and a word w of size k such that $\{s_i\} \sqsubseteq \mathsf{CPre}^A(q_{n-i-1})$ and $\mathsf{post}^A_{w(i+1)}(s_i) \subseteq s_{i+1}$ for all $0 \leq i < k$. We start with $s_0 = \mathsf{Init}$ so that $\{s_0\} \sqsubseteq q_n$. Then, we have either $\{s_0\} \sqsubseteq \{\overline{\mathsf{Fin}}\}$ or $\{s_0\} \sqsubseteq \mathsf{CPre}^A(q_{n-1})$ (because $\{s_0\}$ is a singleton). In the first case, we stop the construction with $k = 0$ and $w = \varepsilon$. In the second case, we continue the construction inductively. Assume that we have constructed $\{s_{i-1}\} \sqsubseteq \mathsf{CPre}^A(q_{n-i})$ for some $i \geq 1$. By the definition of CPre^A, we know that there are $\sigma_i \in \Sigma$ and $s_i \in q_{n-i}$ such that $\mathsf{post}^A_{\sigma_i}(s_{i-1}) \subseteq s_i$. We choose $w(i) = \sigma_i$. Then $\{s_i\} \sqsubseteq q_{n-i}$, and thus either $\{s_i\} \sqsubseteq \{\overline{\mathsf{Fin}}\}$ and we stop with

$k = i$ and $w = \sigma_1 \ldots \sigma_i$, or $\{s_i\} \sqsubseteq \mathsf{CPre}^A(q_{n-i-1})$. This construction stops for some $k < n$, as $q_1 = \{\overline{\mathsf{Fin}}\}$ and $\{s_k\} \sqsubseteq \{\overline{\mathsf{Fin}}\}$. The sequence $s_0, s_1, \ldots, s_k$ shows that A has no accepting run over w, because (1) $s_0 = \mathsf{Init}$, (2) $\mathsf{post}^A_{w(i)}(s_{i-1}) \subseteq s_i$ for all $1 \leq i \leq k$, and (3) $s_k \subseteq \overline{\mathsf{Fin}}$. Hence $w \notin \mathsf{Lang}(A)$.   ∎

The algorithm that consists in computing the least fixed point $\mathcal{F}$ from Theorem 2 through the successive approximation sequence $q_0 \sqsubseteq q_1 \sqsubseteq q_2 \sqsubseteq \cdots$ (as defined in the proof) is called the *backward antichain algorithm*. The computation is similar to the subset construction used in the backward determinization of A, with the essential difference that it maintains only sets of states that are *maximal* in the subset-inclusion order.

Using the Dual Lattice of Antichains to Solve Universality. In the previous algorithm, the automaton is traversed backward starting from the set of nonaccepting states. Using the dual lattice of antichains, we can formulate a solution that traverses the automaton forward starting from the set of initial states. Given an NFA $A = \langle \mathsf{Loc}, \mathsf{Init}, \mathsf{Fin}, \Sigma, \delta \rangle$ and an antichain $q \in L$, let

$$\mathsf{Post}^A(q) = \lfloor \{s \mid \exists s' \in q \cdot \exists \sigma \in \Sigma : s = \mathsf{post}^A_\sigma(s')\} \rfloor.$$

This function is monotone on the dual lattice of antichains. We can solve the universality problem for NFAs by iterating Post as follows, defining a *forward antichain algorithm*.

Theorem 3. *Let* $A = \langle \mathsf{Loc}, \mathsf{Init}, \mathsf{Fin}, \Sigma, \delta \rangle$ *be an NFA, and let* $\tilde{\mathcal{F}} = \widetilde{\bigsqcap} \{q \mid q = \mathsf{Post}^A(q) \; \tilde{\sqcap} \; \{\mathsf{Init}\}\}$. *Then* $\mathsf{Lang}(A) \neq \Sigma^*$ *iff* $\tilde{\mathcal{F}} \; \tilde{\sqsubseteq} \; \{\overline{\mathsf{Fin}}\}$.

The computation of the least fixed point $\tilde{\mathcal{F}}$ is similar to the standard, forward subset construction used in the determinization of A, with the essential difference that it maintains only *minimal* sets of states.

Relationship Between Forward and Backward Algorithms. Given an NFA $A = \langle \mathsf{Loc}, \mathsf{Init}, \mathsf{Fin}, \Sigma, \delta \rangle$, the *reverse* of A is the NFA $B = \langle \mathsf{Loc}, \mathsf{Fin}, \mathsf{Init}, \Sigma, \delta' \rangle$, where for all states $\ell, \ell' \in \mathsf{Loc}$ and all letters $\sigma \in \Sigma$, we have $\delta'(\ell, \sigma, \ell')$ iff $\delta(\ell', \sigma, \ell)$. Note that for all $\sigma \in \Sigma$ and all $s \subseteq \mathsf{Loc}$, we have $\mathsf{pre}^A_\sigma(s) = \mathsf{post}^B_\sigma(s)$. For a set $s \subseteq \mathsf{Loc}$, let $\overline{s}$ be the complement of s relative to Loc, that is, $\overline{s} = \mathsf{Loc} \setminus s$. For a set $q \subseteq 2^{\mathsf{Loc}}$, let $\tilde{q} = \{\overline{s} \mid s \in q\}$. Note that $\tilde{q}$ is an antichain iff q is an antichain, and $\widetilde{\lfloor q \rfloor} = \lceil \tilde{q} \rceil$.

Lemma 4. *Let* $A = (\mathsf{Loc}, \mathsf{Init}, \mathsf{Fin}, \Sigma, \delta)$ *be an NFA, let* B *be its reverse, and let* q *be an antichain over* Loc. *Then* $q' = \mathsf{CPre}^A(q)$ *iff* $\tilde{q}' = \mathsf{Post}^B(\tilde{q})$.

From this lemma, it follows that the forward and backward approaches are equivalent in the following sense: for every instance A of the universality problem that is difficult for the forward antichain algorithm, there is an equally difficult instance (namely, the reverse of A) for the backward antichain algorithm, and

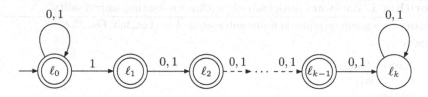

Fig. 1. A family of NFAs A_k, $k \geq 2$, for Theorem 5

vice versa. Indeed, let $q_0 \sqsubseteq q_1 \sqsubseteq q_2 \sqsubseteq \cdots$ be the sequence of antichains that are constructed when computing the least fixed point $\mathcal{F}$ from Theorem 2 (as defined in the proof of the theorem); and let $q'_0 \tilde{\sqsubseteq} q'_1 \tilde{\sqsubseteq} q'_2 \tilde{\sqsubseteq} \cdots$ be the sequence of antichains that are constructed when computing the least fixed point $\tilde{\mathcal{F}}$ from Theorem 3, defined as follows: (1) $q'_0 = \emptyset$ and (2) $q'_i = \mathsf{Post}^B(q'_{i-1}) \tilde{\sqcap} \{\overline{\mathsf{Fin}}\}$ for all $i \geq 1$. Using Lemma 4 and induction, we can prove that $q_i = \tilde{q}'_i$ for all $i \geq 0$.

Comparison with Explicit Determinization. We call the classical algorithm for solving the universality problem for NFAs the *subset algorithm*: it first determinizes the NFA using a subset construction, and then checks if every reachable state in the resulting DFA is accepting. The determinization is stopped whenever a rejecting state is encountered. Usually, the DFA is constructed in a breadth-first forward search, but it can also be done in a backward fashion.

Theorem 5. *For checking universality, there exists an infinite family of NFAs A_k, with $k \geq 2$ states, for which the forward subset algorithm is exponential, and the (forward and backward) antichain algorithms are polynomial. There also exists an infinite family of NFAs B_k for which the backward subset algorithm is exponential, and the antichain algorithms are polynomial.*

Proof. Consider the family of NFAs A_k, $k \geq 2$, over the alphabet $\Sigma = \{0,1\}$ shown in Fig. 1. The automaton A_k has $k + 1$ states, $\ell_0, \ldots, \ell_k$, all accepting except ℓ_k. There is only one initial state: $\mathsf{Init} = \{\ell_0\}$. Every A_k is universal, as the initial state has a self-loop labeled with Σ. The forward determinization of A_k has 2^k states. Hence the forward subset algorithm is exponential on the family A_k, $k \geq 2$. However, the backward antichain algorithm terminates in polynomial time, as the sequence $q_0 = \{\{\ell_k\}\}$, and $q_{i+1} = \mathsf{CPre}^{A_k}(q_i) \sqcup \{\{\ell_k\}\}$ for $i \geq 0$, stabilizes after k iterations with $q_i = \{\{\ell_{k-i}, \ldots, \ell_k\}\}$ for $i < k$, and $q_k = q_{k-1}$. The test $\{\mathsf{Init}\} \sqsubseteq q_i$ requires linear time. The forward antichain algorithm terminates after a single iteration with $\tilde{\mathcal{F}} = \{\mathsf{Init}\}$, and the test $\tilde{\mathcal{F}} \tilde{\sqsubseteq} \{\{\ell_k\}\}$ is done in constant time.

A similar proof holds for the second part of the theorem: for the family B_k, $k \geq 2$, choose each B_k to be the reverse of A_k. ∎

Algorithm 1. Backward antichain algorithm for testing universality

Data : a nondeterministic finite automaton $A = \langle \mathsf{Loc}, \mathsf{Init}, \mathsf{Fin}, \Sigma, \delta \rangle$.

begin

1 | Start $\leftarrow \{\mathsf{Init}\}$;
2 | $F \leftarrow \{\overline{\mathsf{Fin}}\}$;
3 | Frontier $\leftarrow F$;
4 | **while** (Frontier $\neq \emptyset$) $\wedge$ (Start $\not\sqsubseteq$ Frontier) **do**

5 | $\quad\lceil$ Frontier $\leftarrow \{q \in \mathsf{CPre}^A(\text{Frontier}) \mid q \not\sqsubseteq F\}$;
6 | $\quad\lfloor$ $F \leftarrow F \sqcup$ Frontier ;

7 | **return** (Start $\not\sqsubseteq$ Frontier);

end

---

4 Implementation and Practical Evaluation

Two Symbolic Implementations of Antichains. We implemented our new algorithm for testing universality on top of NuSMV [CCGR99] and the BDD library CUDD [Som98]. We considered two encodings of NFAs in NuSMV, and correspondingly, two encodings of antichains of state sets using BDDs.

Fully Symbolic Encoding. In the first encoding, we associate a boolean variable with each state of an NFA. A valuation of the variables corresponds to a state set, and a BDD represents a set of state sets. Two valuations v_1 and v_2 for a set X of variables are incomparable iff there exist $x, y \in X$ such that $v_1(x) > v_2(x)$ and $v_1(y) < v_2(y)$. If the BDD contains only valuations that are incomparable, then it symbolically represents an antichain of state sets. We call this encoding *fully symbolic*.

Semi-symbolic Encoding. In the second encoding, we associate an integer with each state of the automaton. Then a single integer counter is used to encode the current state. A BDD represents a set of integer values and so a set of states. An antichain of state sets is represented by a set of BDDs that are incomparable for valuation inclusion. We call this encoding *semi-symbolic*.

Algorithm. For both encodings, we use the backward Algorithm 1 to check universality. To avoid computing CPre twice for the same set, the algorithm computes iteratively CPre only on the frontier sets, which are the sets that were added to the approximation F of the least fixed point $\mathcal{F}$ in the previous iteration. When the automaton is not universal, then $\mathcal{F}$ is not fully computed, because we stop the computation as soon as one of the sets in F contains all initial states.

The Randomized Model. To evaluate the antichain algorithm and compare with the subset algorithm, we use a random model to generate NFAs. This model was recently proposed by Tabakov and Vardi to compare the efficiency of some algorithms for automata [TV05]. In the model, the input alphabet is fixed to $\Sigma = \{0,1\}$, and for each letter $\sigma \in \Sigma$, a number k_σ of different state pairs $(\ell, \ell') \in \mathsf{Loc} \times \mathsf{Loc}$ are chosen uniformly at random before the corresponding transitions (ℓ, σ, ℓ') are added to the automaton. The ratio $r_\sigma = \frac{k_\sigma}{|\mathsf{Loc}|}$ is called the *transition density* for σ. This ratio represents the average outdegree of each state for σ. In all experiments, we choose $r_0 = r_1$, and denote the transition density by r. The model contains a second parameter: the *density f of accepting states*. There is only one initial state, and the number m of accepting states is linear in the total number of states, as determined by $f = \frac{m}{|\mathsf{Loc}|}$. The accepting states themselves are chosen uniformly at random. Observe that since the transition relation is not always total, automata with $f = 1$ are not necessarily universal.

Tabakov and Vardi have studied the space of parameter values for this model and argue that "interesting" automata are generated by the model as the two parameters r and f vary. They have run large tests to evaluate the probability for an automaton to be universal as a function of the parameters. We reproduced those experiments for a greater space of parameter values and obtained a similar distribution (Fig. 2). To generate each sample point, we checked the universality of 200 random automata with 30 states.

Performance Comparison. We compare the performance of the backward antichain algorithm with the tool dk.brics.automaton developed by Møller [Mø04], which implements the forward subset algorithm and stops determinization whenever a rejecting state is encountered. According to the experiments of Tabakov and Vardi, this tool, which uses explicit state representation, is the most efficient one for checking universality [TV05]. For the comparison, we use the semi-symbolic encoding of antichains, as that turns out to be much more efficient than the fully symbolic encoding. The comparison is carried out on the whole parameter space of the randomized model. All experiments are conducted on a biprocessor Linux station (two 3.06Ghz Intel Xeons with 4GB of RAM). We only measure the execution times for the universality test in both approaches, not the time for parsing the input files and constructing the initial data structures.

In Fig. 3, Fig. 4, and Fig. 5, we present the execution times for checking universality by the explicit subset algorithm and the semi-symbolic antichain algorithm. To generate each sample point, we check the universality of 100 random automata with $|\mathsf{Loc}| = 175$ (this is roughly the largest size that the subset algorithm is able to handle on the entire parameter space with the available memory). In Fig. 3, we present the median execution times for testing universality by the subset approach as a function of r (transition density) and f (density of accepting states). The figure shows that the universality test is most difficult when $r = 2$ and $f = 1$. For the same instances, the median execution time of our algorithm is always less than the time unit of the system clock (1ms).

In Fig. 4 and Fig. 5, we present the average execution times for testing universality by the subset approach and the semi-symbolic antichain approach, respectively. Both figures exhibit similar peaks, showing that the difficult instances are roughly the same for both approaches. However, the antichain algorithm is much

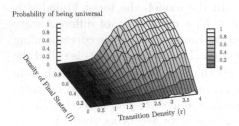

Fig. 2. Probability of universal automata ($|\mathsf{Loc}| = 30$)

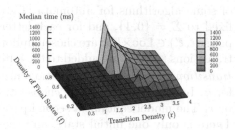

Fig. 3. Median execution time for the subset algorithm ($|\mathsf{Loc}| = 175$)

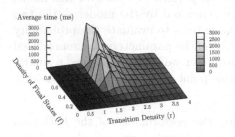

Fig. 4. Average execution time for the subset algorithm ($|\mathsf{Loc}| = 175$)

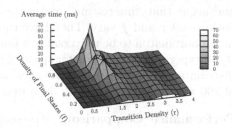

Fig. 5. Average execution time for the semi-symbolic antichain algorithm ($|\mathsf{Loc}| = 175$)

faster. For the most difficult parameter values ($r = 2$ and $f = 1$), the antichain algorithm is 165 times faster than the subset algorithm. Intuitively, these instances are difficult for both algorithms for the following two reasons. First, the probability to be universal for these parameter values is around 50 percent, and we believe that most of these instances are neither trivially universal nor trivially nonuniversal. Second, when an automaton is universal, the subset method has to build the entire deterministic automaton, and the antichain method has to complete the computation of the least fixed point.

In Fig. 6 we present the ratio of the average time for the subset approach and the average time for the antichain approach as a function of the densities. The comparison for $r \leq 1.4$ and $f \leq 0.2$ is not very significant, because the execution times are very close to the precision of the system clock (1ms). For the rest of the parameter space, the antichain algorithm performs always better (up to 200 times better). Finally, in Fig. 7, we show that the semi-symbolic antichain approach scales well when the size of the automaton increases, in contrast to the subset approach. For the experiments we generated randomly 100 automata per sample point for automaton sizes under 200 states, and 30 automata per sample point for sizes over 200 states. The densities are again $r = 2$ and $f = 1$. The antichain algorithm is able to handle random automata with 4000 states in the average time of 12s. The average size of the final antichain (for universal

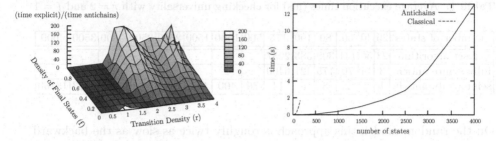

Fig. 6. Average execution time ratio (|Loc| = 175)

Fig. 7. Average execution times for the subset and semi-symbolic antichain algorithms (transition density 2; accepting-states density 1)

automata) is 217 state sets for automata with 4000 states. We did not pursue experiments with larger automata, because we would have had to modify the automaton generator, as it is not designed for such large automaton sizes. The subset algorithm quickly exceeds the memory limit when the number of states nears 200, so the curve is quite short in the left corner of Fig. 7.

As mentioned above, the semi-symbolic antichain encoding gives far better performances on the random model than the fully symbolic encoding, as shown in Table 1 for the difficult instances ($r = 2$ and $f = 1$). It also turns out that the fully symbolic encoding does not scale well when the size of the automaton increases. Each sample point is computed on a set of 50 random automata with less than 100 states. For 175 states, the sample size is 100, and for more states, the sample size is 30. The number of boolean variables of the BDDs that encode antichains seems to be the reason for the difference in performances: the number of boolean variables grows linearly with the number of states in the fully symbolic encoding, but logarithmically in the semi-symbolic encoding. We have also implemented the forward antichain algorithm with the semi-symbolic encoding.

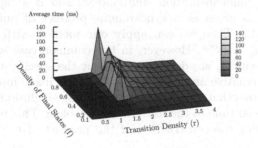

Fig. 8. Average execution time for the forward semi-symbolic antichain algorithm (|Loc|=175)

Table 1. Average execution times (ms) for checking universality with $r = 2$ and $f = 1$

number of states	20	40	60	80	100	175	500	1000	1500	2000	2500	3000	3500	4000
subset algorithm	23	50	141	309	583	2257	-	-	-	-	-	-	-	-
fully symb. antich.	3	14	70	175	421	6400	-	-	-	-	-	-	-	-
semi-symb. antich.	1	2	2	3	5	14	76	400	973	1741	2886	5341	9063	13160

On the random model, this approach is roughly twice as slow as the backward antichain algorithm, which is still better by several orders of magnitude than the subset algorithm. See Fig. 8 for the experimental results.

5   Beyond Universality

Language Inclusion. We show that language inclusion can be checked using an antichain algorithm based on a slightly richer lattice. Consider two NFAs $A = \langle \mathsf{Loc}_A, \mathsf{Init}_A, \mathsf{Fin}_A, \Sigma, \delta_A \rangle$ and $B = \langle \mathsf{Loc}_B, \mathsf{Init}_B, \mathsf{Fin}_B, \Sigma, \delta_B \rangle$ over the same alphabet. We wish to check whether $\mathsf{Lang}(A) \subseteq \mathsf{Lang}(B)$. An *antichain* over $\mathsf{Loc}_A \times 2^{\mathsf{Loc}_B}$ is a set $q \in 2^{\mathsf{Loc}_A \times 2^{\mathsf{Loc}_B}}$ such that for all $(\ell_1, s_1), (\ell_2, s_2) \in q$ with $\ell_1 = \ell_2$ and $s_1 \neq s_2$, we have neither $s_1 \subseteq s_2$ nor $s_2 \subseteq s_1$. Given a set $q \in 2^{\mathsf{Loc}_A \times 2^{\mathsf{Loc}_B}}$, an element $(\ell, s) \in q$ is *maximal* iff for every s' with $s' \supset s$, we have $(\ell, s') \notin q$. We denote by $\lceil q \rceil$ the set of maximal elements of q. Given two antichains q and q', we define

$$q \sqsubseteq_l q' \text{ iff } \forall (\ell, s) \in q \cdot \exists (\ell, s') \in q' : s \subseteq s';$$
$$q \sqcup_l q' = \lceil \{(\ell, s) \mid (\ell, s) \in q \vee (\ell, s) \in q'\} \rceil;$$
$$q \sqcap_l q' = \lceil \{(\ell, s \cap s') \mid (\ell, s) \in q \wedge (\ell, s') \in q'\} \rceil.$$

Let $\mathsf{CPre}_l(q) = \lceil \{(\ell, s) \mid \exists \sigma \in \Sigma \cdot \exists (\ell', s') \in q : \ell' \in \delta_A(\ell, \sigma) \wedge \mathsf{post}^B_\sigma(s) \subseteq s'\} \rceil$.

Theorem 6. *Let A and B be two finite automata, and let $\mathcal{F}_l = \bigsqcap_l \{q \mid q = \mathsf{CPre}_l(q) \sqcup_l (\mathsf{Fin}_A \times \{\overline{\mathsf{Fin}_B}\})\}$. Then $\mathsf{Lang}(A) \not\subseteq \mathsf{Lang}(B)$ iff there exists a state $\ell \in \mathsf{Init}_A$ such that $\{(\ell, \mathsf{Init}_B)\} \sqsubseteq_l \mathcal{F}_l$.*

Typically, A is an "implementation" automaton, and B a "specification" automaton. Often A is given as a synchronous product of automata, that is, $A = A_1 \otimes \cdots \otimes A_n$. Then we can apply our method with antichains over $\mathsf{Loc}_{A_1} \times \cdots \times \mathsf{Loc}_{A_n} \times 2^{\mathsf{Loc}_B}$. However, in the common case where the implementation components A_i are deterministic (but the specification B is nondeterministic), an alternative approach is possible, and likely more efficient. The following lemma shows that in this case, the language-inclusion problem can be reduced in polynomial time to the universality problem. This reduction has the advantage of avoiding the construction of the product of the implementation components.

Lemma 7. *For a set $A_1, \ldots, A_n$ of DFAs and an NFA B, we define the sum $C = \overline{A_1} \oplus \cdots \oplus \overline{A_n} \oplus B$. Then $\mathsf{Lang}(A_1) \cap \ldots \cap \mathsf{Lang}(A_n) \subseteq \mathsf{Lang}(B)$ iff $\mathsf{Lang}(C) = \Sigma^*$.*

Emptiness of Alternating Automata. The antichain algorithm for checking the universality of NFAs can be generalized to checking the emptiness of alternating automata, using the same lattice with a slight modification of the function CPre. In alternating automata, the transitions are given by boolean formulas. For example, $\rho(\ell, \sigma) = \ell_1 \vee (\ell_2 \wedge \ell_3)$ means that in state ℓ, a word of the form $\sigma \cdot w$ is accepted if either w is accepted in ℓ_1, or w is accepted in both ℓ_2 and ℓ_3. Our formal definitions follow [KV01]. Let $\mathcal{B}^+(\mathsf{Loc})$ be the set of monotone boolean formulas over Loc, defined by the grammar $\varphi ::= \mathsf{true} \mid \ell \mid \varphi \wedge \varphi \mid \varphi \vee \varphi$, where $\ell \in \mathsf{Loc}$. A set $s \subseteq \mathsf{Loc}$ of states *satisfies* a formula $\varphi \in \mathcal{B}^+(\mathsf{Loc})$ (denoted $s \models \varphi$) iff φ is equivalent to true when the states in s are replaced by true, and the states in $\mathsf{Loc} \setminus s$ by false.

An *alternating finite automaton*, or AFA, is a tuple $A = \langle \mathsf{Loc}, \mathsf{Init}, \mathsf{Fin}, \Sigma, \rho \rangle$, where Loc, Init, Fin, and Σ are as for NFAs, and $\rho: \mathsf{Loc} \times \Sigma \to \mathcal{B}^+(\mathsf{Loc})$ is a transition function. The NFAs can be seen as a subclass of the AFAs: the transition relation δ of an NFA can be translated into the transition function ρ of AFA such that $\rho(\ell, \sigma) = \ell_1 \vee \ldots \vee \ell_n$ for $\{\ell_1, \ldots, \ell_n\} = \{\ell' \in \mathsf{Loc} \mid (\ell, \sigma, \ell') \in \delta\}$. A *run* of the AFA A over a finite word w is a tree $T = (N, \Rightarrow)$, whose nodes are a prefix-closed set $N \subseteq \mathsf{Loc}^+$ of nonempty sequences of states. The level of a node $x = \ell_1 \ldots \ell_n$ in N is its size $|x| = n$, and the last element of x is $\mathsf{last}(x) = \ell_n$. The set N contains a single node at level 1, the root, which is a state in Init. We require that for all $x \in N$, we have $|x| \leq |w| + 1$. The child relation $\Rightarrow \subseteq N \times N$ satisfies the following condition: for all nodes $x \in N$, we have (1) if $x \Rightarrow x'$, then $x' = x \cdot \ell$ for some $\ell \in \mathsf{Loc}$, and (2) if $|x| \leq |w|$, then the set $s = \{\mathsf{last}(x') \mid x \Rightarrow x'\}$ is such that $s \models \rho(\mathsf{last}(x), w(|x|))$. A leaf of T is a node x of level $|x| = |w| + 1$. A run T is *accepting* iff $\mathsf{last}(x) \in \mathsf{Fin}$ for all leaves x of T. The *language* $\mathsf{Lang}(A)$ accepted by A is the set of words $w \in \Sigma^*$ such that A has an accepting run over w.

The *emptiness problem* for AFAs is to decide, given an AFA A, whether $\mathsf{Lang}(A) = \emptyset$. Since complementation of AFAs is easy (by dualizing the transition function and complementing the set of accepting states), the universality problem for AFAs (to decide, given an AFA A, if $\mathsf{Lang}(A) = \Sigma^*$) is polynomially equivalent to emptiness. Given an AFA $A = \langle \mathsf{Loc}, \mathsf{Init}, \mathsf{Fin}, \Sigma, \rho \rangle$, consider the following monotone function on the lattice L of antichains over Loc: for an antichain $q \in L$, let

$$\mathsf{CPre}_a(q) = \lceil \{s \mid \exists s' \in q \cdot \exists \sigma \in \Sigma \cdot \forall \ell \in s : s' \models \rho(\ell, \sigma)\} \rceil.$$

This monotone function on L can be used to decide the emptiness problem for AFAs, as shown in the following theorem.

Theorem 8. *Let $A = \langle \mathsf{Loc}, \mathsf{Init}, \mathsf{Fin}, \Sigma, \delta \rangle$ be an AFA, and let $\mathcal{F}_a = \bigsqcap \{q \mid q = \mathsf{CPre}_a(q) \sqcup \{\mathsf{Fin}\}\}$. Then $\mathsf{Lang}(A) \neq \emptyset$ iff $\{\mathsf{Init}\} \sqsubseteq \mathcal{F}_a$.*

6   Conclusions

We showed that explicit determinization can be avoided when solving several problems related to NFAs on finite words. Our new solutions to the universality

and language-inclusion problems for NFAs, and to the emptiness problem for
AFAs, evaluate the least fixed point of simple monotone functions on lattices of
antichains. They are goal-directed and leave determinization implicit. We implemented the new algorithm for the universality problem and compared its performance to that of the classical algorithm (which uses explicit determinization).
Our method outperforms the classical one dramatically on the entire parameter space of a randomized model. On the difficult instances of the randomized
model, our algorithm is several orders of magnitude faster than the classical one.

We plan to pursue several future directions. First, as the performance of the
new algorithm on the randomized model is very encouraging, we want to apply
antichain algorithms to practical problems. Second, the antichain method does
not extend trivially to automata over infinite words. We need further research
to see if our results can be extended to such cases.

Acknowledgements. We thank Deian Tabakov for his code and helpful answers
about the randomized model.

References

[BL80]   J.A. Brzozowski and E.L. Leiss. On equations for regular languages,
             finite automata, and sequential networks. *Theoretical Computer Science*,
             10:19–35, 1980.
[CCGR99]   A. Cimatti, E.M. Clarke, F. Giunchiglia, and M. Roveri. NuSMV: A
             new symbolic model verifier. In *Computer Aided Verification*, LNCS
             1633, pages 495–499. Springer, 1999.
[CKS81]   A.K. Chandra, D. Kozen, and L.J. Stockmeyer. Alternation. *J. ACM*,
             28:114–133, 1981.
[DDR06]   M. De Wulf, L. Doyen, and J.-F. Raskin. A lattice theory for solving
             games of imperfect information. In *Hybrid Systems—Computation and
             Control*, LNCS 3927, pages 153–168. Springer, 2006.
[HMU01]   J.E. Hopcroft, R. Motwani, and J.D. Ullman. *Introduction to Automata
             Theory, Languages, and Computation*. Addison-Wesley, 2001.
[KV01]   O. Kupferman and M.Y. Vardi. Weak alternating automata are not that
             weak. *ACM Trans. Computational Logic*, 2:408–429, 2001.
[Mø04]   A. Møller. dk.brics.automaton. http://www.brics.dk/automaton, 2004.
[MS72]   A.R. Meyer and L.J. Stockmeyer. The equivalence problem for regular
             expressions with squaring requires exponential space. In *Symp. Foun-
             dations of Computer Science*, pages 125–129. IEEE Computer Society,
             1972.
[Rei84]   J.H. Reif. The complexity of two-player games of incomplete informa-
             tion. *J. Computer and System Sciences*, 29:274–301, 1984.
[Som98]   F. Somenzi. CUDD: CU Decision Diagram Package Release 2.3.0. Uni-
             versity of Colorado at Boulder, 1998.
[TV05]   D. Tabakov and M.Y. Vardi. Experimental evaluation of classical au-
             tomata constructions. In *Logic for Programming, Artificial Intelligence,
             and Reasoning*, LNCS 3835, pages 396–411. Springer, 2005.

Safraless Compositional Synthesis*

Orna Kupferman[1,**], Nir Piterman[2], and Moshe Y. Vardi[3,***]

[1] Hebrew University
[2] Ecole Polytechnique Fédéral de Lausanne (EPFL)
[3] Rice University and Microsoft Research

Abstract. In automated synthesis, we transform a specification into a system that is guaranteed to satisfy the specification. In spite of the rich theory developed for system synthesis, little of this theory has been reduced to practice. This is in contrast with model-checking theory, which has led to industrial development and use of formal verification tools. We see two main reasons for the lack of practical impact of synthesis. The first is algorithmic: synthesis involves determinization of automata on infinite words, and a solution of parity games with highly complex state spaces; both problems have been notoriously resistant to efficient implementation. The second is methodological: current theory of synthesis assumes a single comprehensive specification. In practice, however, the specification is composed of a set of properties, which is typically evolving – properties may be added, deleted, or modified.

In this work we address both issues. We extend the Safraless synthesis algorithm of Kupferman and Vardi so that it handles LTL formulas by translating them to nondeterministic generalized Büchi automata. This leads to an exponential improvement in the complexity of the algorithm. Technically, our algorithm reduces the synthesis problem to the emptiness problem of a nondeterministic Büchi tree automaton $\mathcal{A}$. The generation of $\mathcal{A}$ avoids determinization, avoids the parity acceptance condition, and is based on an analysis of runs of universal generalized co-Büchi tree automata. The clean and simple structure of $\mathcal{A}$ enables optimizations and a symbolic implementation. In addition, it makes it possible to use information gathered during the synthesis process of properties in the process of synthesizing their conjunction.

1 Introduction

One of the most significant developments in the area of program verification over the last two decades has been the development of algorithmic methods for verifying temporal specifications of *finite-state* programs; see [5]. A frequent criticism against this approach, however, is that verification is done *after* significant resources have already

---

* A full version with full proofs can be downloaded from www.cs.huji.ac.il/~ornak/cav06.pdf.
** Supported in part by BSF grant 9800096, and by a grant from Minerva.
*** Supported in part by NSF grants CCR-9988322, CCR-0124077, CCR-0311326, and ANI-0216467, by BSF grant 9800096, and by Texas ATP grant 003604-0058-2003. Part of this work was done while the author was visiting the Isaac Newton Institute for Mathematical Science, as part of a Special Programme on Logic and Algorithm.

T. Ball and R.B. Jones (Eds.): CAV 2006, LNCS 4144, pp. 31–44, 2006.

been invested in the development of the program. Since programs invariably contain errors, verification simply becomes part of the debugging process. The critics argue that the desired goal is to use the specification in the program development process in order to guarantee the design of correct programs. This is called *program synthesis*.

In the late 1980s, several researchers realized that the classical approach to program synthesis, where a program is extracted from a proof that the specification is satisfiable, is well suited to *closed* systems, but not to *open* (also called *reactive*) systems [1,6,23]. In reactive systems, the program interacts with the environment, and a correct program should then satisfy the specification with respect to all environments. These researchers argued that the right way to approach synthesis of reactive systems is to consider the situation as a (possibly infinite) game between the environment and the program. A correct program can be then viewed as a winning strategy in this game. It turns out that satisfiability of the specification is not sufficient to guarantee the existence of such a strategy. Abadi et al. called specifications for which a winning strategy exists *realizable*. Thus, a strategy for a program with inputs in I and outputs in O maps finite sequences of inputs (words in $(2^I)^*$ – the actions of the environment so far) to an output in 2^O – a suggested action for the program. A strategy can then be viewed as a labeling of a tree with directions in 2^I by labels in 2^O. The traditional algorithm for finding a winning strategy transforms the specification into a parity automaton over such trees such that a program is realizable precisely when this tree automaton is nonempty, i.e., it accepts some infinite tree [23]. A finite generator of an infinite tree accepted by this automaton can be viewed as a finite-state program realizing the specification. This is closely related to the approach taken, e.g., in [25], to solve Church's *solvability problem* [4]. Several works during the 1990s showed how this approach to program synthesis can be carried out in a variety of settings.

In spite of the rich theory developed for program synthesis, little of this theory has been reduced to practice. In fact, the main approaches to tackle synthesis are either to use heuristic approaches (e.g., [12]) or to restrict the kind of allowed specification (e.g., [22]). Some people argue that this is because the realizability problem for linear-temporal logic (LTL) specifications is 2EXPTIME-complete [23,26], but this argument is not compelling. First, experience with verification shows that even nonelementary algorithms can be practical, since the worst-case complexity does not arise often (cf., the model-checking tool MONA [7]). Furthermore, in some sense, synthesis is not harder than verification. This may seem to contradict the known fact that while verification is "easy" (linear in the size of the model and at most exponential in the size of the specification [16]), synthesis is hard (2EXPTIME-complete). There is, however, something misleading in this fact: while the complexity of synthesis is given with respect to the specification only, the complexity of verification is given with respect to the specification and the program, which can be much larger than the specification. In particular, it is shown in [26] that there are temporal specifications for which every realizing program must be at least doubly exponentially larger than the specifications. Clearly, the verification of such programs is doubly exponential in the specification, just as the cost of synthesis.

We believe that there are two reasons for the lack of practical impact of synthesis theory. The first is algorithmic and the second is methodological. Consider first the algorithmic problem. First, constructing tree automata for realizing strategies uses determinization of Büchi automata. Safra's determinization construction has been notoriously resistant to efficient implementations [2,29] (An alternative construction is equally hard [2]. Piterman's improvement of Safra includes the tree structures that proved hard to implement [21].) Second, determinization results in automata with a very complicated state space. The best-known algorithms for parity-tree-automata emptiness [13] are nontrivial already when applied to simple state spaces. Implementing them on top of the messy state space that results from determinization is awfully complex, and is not amenable to optimizations and a symbolic implementation.

Another major issue is methodological. The current theory of program synthesis assumes that one gets a comprehensive set of temporal assertions as a starting point. This cannot be realistic in practice. A more realistic approach would be to assume an *evolving* formal specification: temporal assertions can be added, deleted, or modified. Since it is rare to have a complete set of assertions at the very start of the design process, there is a need to develop *compositional* synthesis algorithms. Such algorithms can, for example, refine designs when provided with additional temporal properties.

In this paper we address both issues. We focus on the case where forbidden behaviors are described by nondeterministic generalized Büchi automata on infinite words, which are Büchi automata with multiple acceptance sets (corresponding to the *impartiality* fairness condition of [17]). Our interest in specifying forbidden behaviors and in using the generalized Büchi condition is motivated by the fact that LTL formulas (and their negation) can be conveniently translated to nondeterministic generalized Büchi automata [9]. Equivalently, one can specify allowed behavior by universal generalized co-Büchi automata. Following [15], we offer an alternative to the standard automata-theoretic approach. The crux of our approach is avoiding the use of determinization constructions and of nondeterministic parity tree automata. In the approach described here, one checks whether the specification ψ is realizable using the following steps: (1) construct a universal generalized co-Büchi tree automaton $\mathcal{A}_\psi$ that accepts all realizing strategies for ψ, (2) reduce[1] $\mathcal{A}_\psi$ to an alternating weak tree automaton $\mathcal{A}_\psi^w$, (3) translate $\mathcal{A}_\psi^w$ to a nondeterministic Büchi tree automaton $\mathcal{A}_\psi^n$, and (4) check that the language of $\mathcal{A}_\psi^n$ is nonempty. The key is avoiding determinization, by using universal generalized co-Büchi automata instead of deterministic parity automata.[2]

The difference between our approach here and the approach in [15] is that here we use *generalized* co-Büchi automata, unlike the co-Büchi automata used there. This leads to an exponential improvement in the complexity of our algorithm, as we describe below. Extending the framework of [15] to generalized co-Büchi automata requires two key technical steps. First, as our Safraless approach used a "Safraful" bound on the size

---

[1] We use "reduce A_1 to A_2", rather than "translate A_1 to A_2" to indicate that A_2 accepts a subset of the language of A_1, yet the language of A_1 is empty iff the language of A_2 is empty.

[2] A note to readers who are discouraged by the fact our method goes via several intermediate automata: it is possible to combine the reductions into one construction, and in fact we describe here also a direct translation of universal generalized co-Büchi automata into nondeterministic Büchi automata. In practice, however, it is beneficial to have many intermediate automata, as each intermediate automaton undergoes optimization constructions that are suitable for its particular type, cf. [11].

of the realizing strategies, we need to extend Safra's construction to nondeterministic generalized Büchi automata, obtaining an exponential improvement (with respect to an approach that first translates the generalized Büchi automaton to a Büchi automaton) in that construction. Second, we need to show how the co-Büchi ranks devised in [14] for the analysis of runs of universal automata on words can be applied to the analysis of runs of universal automata on finitely generated trees.

Beyond the improvement in complexity, the advantage of the Safraless approach is that we get tree automata with cleanly described state spaces, which enables the application of symbolic algorithms for Büchi tree automata emptiness. Further, we can now obtain a *compositional* algorithm. Given a specification ψ, we first check its realizability. Suppose now that we get an additional specification ψ'. We can, of course, simply check the realizability of $\psi \wedge \psi'$ from scratch. Instead, we suggest to first check also the realizability of ψ'. We then show how, thanks to the simple structure of the tree automata, much of the work used in checking the realizability of ψ and ψ' in isolation can be reused in checking the realizability of $\psi \wedge \psi'$. The compositional algorithm we suggest can be combined with an *incremental* algorithm, in which we iteratively increase the bound on the size of the realizing strategy. As demonstrated in [11] for the linear setting, the bound that is needed in practice is usually much smaller than the worst-case bound. In addition, we explain how the incremental and compositional algorithm can be implemented symbolically.

2   Preliminaries

We assume familiarity with the basic notions of alternating automata on infinite trees, cf. [10].

Given an alphabet Σ and a set D of directions, a Σ-*labeled D-tree* is a pair $\langle T, \tau \rangle$, where $T \subseteq D^*$ is a tree over D and $\tau : T \to \Sigma$ maps each node of T to a letter in Σ. A *transducer* is a labeled finite graph with a designated start node, where the edges are labeled by D and the nodes are labeled by Σ. A Σ-labeled D-tree is *regular* if it is the unwinding of some transducer. More formally, a transducer is a tuple $\mathcal{T} = \langle D, \Sigma, S, s_{in}, \eta, L \rangle$, where D is a finite set of directions, Σ is a finite alphabet, S is a finite set of states, $s_{in} \in S$ is an initial state, $\eta : S \times D \to S$ is a deterministic transition function, and $L : S \to \Sigma$ is a labeling function. We define $\eta : D^* \to S$ in the standard way: $\eta(\varepsilon) = s_{in}$, and for $x \in D^*$ and $d \in D$, we have $\eta(x \cdot d) = \eta(\eta(x), d)$. Intuitively, A Σ-labeled D-tree $\langle D^*, \tau \rangle$ is regular if there exists a transducer $\mathcal{T} = \langle D, \Sigma, S, s_{in}, \eta, L \rangle$ such that for every $x \in D^*$, we have $\tau(x) = L(\eta(x))$. We then say that the size of the regular tree $\langle D^*, \tau \rangle$, denoted $\|\tau\|$, is $|S|$, the number of states of $\mathcal{T}$.

We denote an alternating tree automaton by a tuple $\mathcal{A} = \langle \Sigma, D, Q, q_{in}, \delta, \alpha \rangle$, where Σ is the input alphabet, D is a set of directions, Q is a finite set of states, $\delta : Q \times \Sigma \to \mathcal{B}^+(D \times Q)$ is a transition function, $q_{in} \in Q$ is an initial state, and α specifies the acceptance condition A run of $\mathcal{A}$ is accepting if all its infinite paths satisfy the acceptance condition. For a path π, we denote the set of automaton states visited infinitely often along this path by $inf(\pi)$. We consider here four acceptance conditions defined as follows

- A path π satisfies a *generalized Büchi* condition $\alpha = \{F_1, F_2, \ldots, F_k\} \subseteq 2^Q$ iff for all $1 \leq i \leq k$ we have $inf(\pi) \cap F_i \neq \emptyset$. The number k of sets in α is called the *index* of the automaton. If $|\alpha| = 1$ we call α a *Büchi* condition.
- A path π satisfies a *generalized co-Büchi* condition $\alpha = \{F_1, F_2, \ldots, F_k\} \subseteq 2^Q$ iff for some $1 \leq i \leq k$ we have $inf(\pi) \cap F_i = \emptyset$. The number k of sets in α is called the *index* of the automaton. If $|\alpha| = 1$ we call α a *co-Büchi* condition.
- A path π satisfies a *parity* condition $\alpha = \langle F_0, \ldots, F_k \rangle$ where $F_0, \ldots F_k$ form a partition of Q iff for some even i we have $inf(\pi) \cap F_i \neq \emptyset$ and forall $i' < i$ we have $inf(\pi) \cap F_{i'} = \emptyset$. We call k the number of *priorities* of α.

For the three conditions, an automaton accepts a tree iff there exists a run that accepts it. We denote by $\mathcal{L}(\mathcal{A})$ the set of all Σ-labeled trees that $\mathcal{A}$ accepts. We also refer to a fourth condition, which is a special case of the Büchi condition, and is referred to as the *weak* condition [20].

Below we discuss some special cases of alternating automata. The alternating automaton $\mathcal{A}$ is *nondeterministic* if for all the formulas that appear in δ, if (d_1, q_1) and (d_2, q_2) are conjunctively related, then $d_1 \neq d_2$. (i.e., if the transition is rewritten in disjunctive normal form, there is at most one element of $\{d\} \times Q$, for each $d \in D$, in each disjunct). The automaton $\mathcal{A}$ is *universal* if all the formulas that appear in δ are conjunctions of atoms in $D \times Q$, and $\mathcal{A}$ is *deterministic* if it is both nondeterministic and universal. The automaton $\mathcal{A}$ is a *word* automaton if $|D| = 1$. Then, we can omit D from the specification of the automaton and denote the transition function of $\mathcal{A}$ as $\delta : Q \times \Sigma \rightarrow \mathcal{B}^+(Q)$. If the word automaton is nondeterministic or universal, then $\delta : Q \times \Sigma \rightarrow 2^Q$.

We denote each of the different types of automata by an acronym in $\{D, N, U, A\} \times \{B, GB, C, GC, P\} \times \{W, T\}$, where the first letter describes the branching mode of the automaton (deterministic, nondeterministic, universal, or alternating), the second letter describes the acceptance condition (Büchi, generalized Büchi, co-Büchi, generalized co-Büchi, or parity), and the third letter describes the object over which the automaton runs (words or trees). For example, APT are alternating parity tree automata and UGCT are universal generalized co-Büchi tree automata.

3 Synthesis

Consider an UGCW $\mathcal{S}$ over the alphabet $2^{I \cup O}$, for sets I and O of input and output signals. The *realizability problem* for $\mathcal{S}$ [23] is to decide whether there is a *strategy* $f : (2^I)^* \rightarrow 2^O$, generated by a transducer[3] such that all the computations of the system generated by f are in $L(\mathcal{S})$. We call such a strategy, a *good* strategy. A computation $\rho \in (2^{I \cup O})^\omega$ is *generated by* f if $\rho = (i_0 \cup o_0), (i_1 \cup o_1), (i_2 \cup o_2), \ldots$ and for all $j \geq 1$, we have $o_j = f(i_0 \cdot i_1 \cdots i_{j-1})$.

In practice, the UGCW $\mathcal{S}$ originates from an LTL formula ψ that specifies the desired properties of the program we synthesize. In order to get $\mathcal{S}$, we first translate $\neg\psi$ to an NGBW $\mathcal{A}_{\neg\psi}$, and then dualize $\mathcal{A}_{\neg\psi}$ by viewing it as a UGCW. By [31,9], $\mathcal{A}_{\neg\psi}$, and thus

---

[3] As $\mathcal{S}$ recognizes an ω-regular language, if some transducer that generates f exists, then there is also a finite-state transducer.

also S, have $2^{O(|\psi|)}$ states and index $O(|\psi|)$. Alternatively, one can define properties directly using UGCW, as done, for example, in the framework of Generalized Symbolic Trajectory Evaluation [32], by means of *fair assertion graphs*.

Theorem 1. *The realizability problem for a UGCW can be reduced to the nonemptiness problem of a UGCT with the same state space and index.*

Proof: A strategy $f : (2^I)^* \to 2^O$ can be viewed as a 2^O-labeled 2^I-tree. Given a UGCW S, we define a UGCT S' such that S' accepts a 2^O-labeled 2^I-tree $\langle T, \tau \rangle$ iff τ is a good strategy for S.

Let $S = \langle 2^{I \cup O}, Q, q_{in}, \delta, \alpha \rangle$. Then, $S' = \langle 2^O, 2^I, Q, q_{in}, \delta', \alpha \rangle$, where for every $q \in Q$ and $o \in 2^O$, we have $\delta'(q, o) = \bigwedge_{i \in 2^I} \bigwedge_{q' \in \delta(q, i \cup o)} (i, q')$. Thus, from state q, reading the output assignment $o \in 2^O$, the automaton S' branches to each direction $i \in 2^I$, with all the states q' to which δ branches when it reads $i \cup o$ in state q. It is not hard to see that S' accepts a 2^O-labeled 2^I-tree $\langle T, \tau \rangle$ iff for all the paths $\{\varepsilon, i_0, i_0 \cdot i_1, i_0 \cdot i_1 \cdot i_2, \ldots\}$ of T, the infinite word $(i_0 \cup \tau(\varepsilon)), (i_1 \cup \tau(i_0)), (i_2 \cup \tau(i_0 \cdot i_1)), \ldots$ is accepted by the UGCW S as required. □

We now describe an emptiness preserving translation of UGCT to NBT. The correctness proof of the construction is given in Sections 4.1 and 4.2. There, we also suggest to use ABT as an intermediate step in the construction. While this adds a step to our chain of reductions, it enables further optimizations of the result.

For an integer c, let $[c]$ denote the set $\{0, 1, \ldots, c\}$, and let $[c]^{odd}$ and $[c]^{even}$ denote the set of odd and even members of $[c]$, respectively. Also, let $R_k(c) = [2c]^{even} \cup ([2c]^{odd} \times \{1, \ldots, k\})$, and $\leq$ be the lexicographical order on the elements of $R_k(c)$. We refer to the members of $R_k(c)$ in $[2c]^{even}$ as *even ranks* and refer to the members of $R_k(c)$ in $[2c]^{odd} \times \{j\}$ as *odd ranks with index j*. Note that the size of $R_k(c)$ is $c(k+1) + 1$. Our construction refers to a function $Det(n, k)$, which, as we show later, is bounded from above by $n^{2n+2}k^n$.

Theorem 2. *Let A be a UGCT with n states and index k. There is an NBT A' over the same alphabet such that all the following hold.*
- *$\mathcal{L}(A') \subseteq \mathcal{L}(A)$,*
- *$\mathcal{L}(A) \neq \emptyset$ implies $\mathcal{L}(A') \neq \emptyset$, and*
- *the number of states in A' is $2^{O(n^2(\log n + \log k))}$.*

Proof: Let $A = \langle \Sigma, D, Q, q_{in}, \delta, \{F_1, \ldots, F_k\} \rangle$, and let $c = Det(n, k)$. Note that c is $2^{O(n(\log n + \log k))}$. Let $\mathcal{R}_k(c)$ be the set of functions $f : Q \to R_k(c)$ in which $f(q)$, for all $q \in F_j$, is not odd with index j. For $g \in \mathcal{R}_k(c)$, let $odd(g) = \{q : g(q) \text{ is odd}\}$. We define $A' = \langle \Sigma, D, Q', q'_{in}, \delta', \alpha' \rangle$, where
- $Q' = 3^Q \times \mathcal{R}_k(c)$. For technical convenience, we refer to the states of Q' as triples $\langle S, O, f \rangle$ with $O \subseteq S \subseteq Q$ and $f \in \mathcal{R}_k(c)$.
- $q'_{in} = \langle \{q_{in}\}, \emptyset, g_0 \rangle$, where g_0 maps all states to $2c$.
- For $q \in Q$, $\sigma \in \Sigma$, and $d \in D$, let $\delta(q, \sigma, d) = \{q' \mid (d, q') \in \delta(q, \sigma)\}$. For $S \subseteq Q$, $\sigma \in \Sigma$, and $d \in D$ we define $\delta(S, \sigma, d)$ in the natural way. For two functions g and g' in $\mathcal{R}_k(c)$, a letter σ, and direction $d \in D$, we say that g' *covers* $\langle g, \sigma, d \rangle$ if for all q and q' in Q, if $q' \in \delta(q, \sigma, d)$, then $g'(q') \leq g(q)$. Let $g' \preceq \langle g, \sigma, d \rangle$ denote that g' covers $\langle g, \sigma, d \rangle$. Then, for all $\langle S, O, g \rangle \in Q'$ and $\sigma \in \Sigma$, we define δ as follows.

- If $O \neq \emptyset$, then

$$\delta'(\langle S,O,g\rangle, \sigma) = \bigwedge_{d \in D} \bigvee_{g_d \preceq \langle g,\sigma,d\rangle} (d, \langle \delta(S,\sigma,d), \delta(O,\sigma,d) \setminus odd(g_d), g_d\rangle)$$

- If $O = \emptyset$, then

$$\delta'(\langle S,O,g\rangle, \sigma) = \bigwedge_{d \in D} \bigvee_{g_d \preceq \langle g,\sigma,d\rangle} (d, \langle \delta(S,\sigma,d), \delta(S,\sigma,d) \setminus odd(g_d), g_d\rangle)$$

- $\alpha' = 2^Q \times \{\emptyset\} \times \mathcal{R}_k(c)$.

In Section 4 we sketch the proof that this automaton indeed satisfies the conditions of the theorem. □

In fact, $\mathcal{A}'$ accepts every regular tree in the language of $\mathcal{A}$ that is produced by a "small" transducer. We show that whenever $\mathcal{A}$ accepts some regular tree, there exists some "small" regular tree that is accepted by $\mathcal{A}'$. Thus, if $\mathcal{A}$ accepts some regular tree, it accepts a regular tree produced by a small transducer, and this regular tree is also accepted by $\mathcal{A}'$.

Corollary 1. *The realizability problem for an NGBW with n states and index k can be reduced to the nonemptiness problem of an NBT with $2^{O(n^2(\log n + \log k))}$ states.*

These bounds are exponentially better than those established in [15]. There, the NGBW is converted to an NBW with nk states and the overall resulting complexity is $2^{O((nk)^2(\log k + \log n))}$.[4]

The *synthesis problem* for S is to find a transducer that generates a strategy realizing S. Known algorithms for the nonemptiness problem can be easily extended to return a transducer [24]. The algorithm we present here also enjoys this property, thus it can be used to solve not only the realizability problem but also the synthesis problem. (For a comparison of the Safraless and the Safraful approaches to synthesis from the perspective of program size, see [15].)

4   From UGCT to NBT

Recall that runs of alternating tree automata are labeled trees. By merging nodes that are roots of identical subtrees, it is possible to maintain runs in graphs. In Section 4.2, we prove a bounded-size run graph property for UGCT. In Section 4.2, we show how the bounded-size property enables a simple translation of UGCT to ABT, which we then translate to an NBT. Combining the translations results in the UGCT to NBT construction described in Theorem 2. While our construction avoids using the determinization construction, the proof of the bounded-size run-graph property makes use of the bound the construction provides to the blow-up involved in determinization. Since we handle the generalized co-Büchi construction, we need a bound on the blow-up involved in the determinization of NGBW. We provide such a bound in Section 4.1.

---

[4] We can use the improved bound on determinization established in [21] to improve the bounds in [15]. This, however, reduces only the constants in the exponent.

4.1 NGBW to DPW

There are two known approaches to determinization of NGBW. The first is to convert the NGBW to an NBW [3] and then use determinization [27,21]. The second is to view the NGBW as a Streett automaton and apply determinization of Streett automata [28,21]. Both approaches produce automata with $(nk)^{O(nk)}$ states. In this section we show how to extend the determinization construction for the case of generalized Büchi automata. Our construction below produces a DPW with $(nk)^{O(n)}$ states, exponentially fewer states than the approaches described.

We offer here a succinct description of the improvement. The basis of our construction is Safra's determinization [27], as improved by Piterman [21]. The key is to augment compact Safra trees with an indexing function. In Piterman's construction, the DPW refers to a visit in the set of accepting states as a good event. In our extension, a good event occurs only after visits to all the sets in the generalized Büchi condition. Thus, the idea is similar to the indexing used in the translation of NGBW to NBW [9], but the challenge is to combine this indexing in the state space of the DPW in a way that minimizes the blow-up in terms of k. the improved construction is used only to generate the improved bound. The synthesis algorithm uses this bound but it does *not* use the determinization construction.

Theorem 3. *Given an NGBW with n states and index k, we can construct an equivalent DPW with at most $n^{2n+2}k^n$ states and $2n$ priorities.*

Proof: Let $\mathcal{N} = \langle \Sigma, S, \delta, s_0, \alpha \rangle$ be an NGBW with $|S| = n$ and $\alpha = \{F_1, \ldots, F_k\}$. Let $V = [n]$. We construct the DPW $\mathcal{D}$ equivalent to $\mathcal{N}$. Let $\mathcal{D} = \langle \Sigma, D, \rho, d_0, \alpha' \rangle$, where the components of $\mathcal{D}$ are as follows.

- A *generalized compact Safra tree* t is $\langle N, 1, p, l, h, r, g \rangle$ where $N \subseteq V$ is a set of nodes, $1 \in N$ is the root node, $p : N \to N$ is the parenthood function, $l : N \to 2^S$ is a labeling of the nodes with subsets of S, $h : N \to [k]$ is an indexing function associating with every node an index in $[k]$, and $r, g \in [n+1]$ are used to define the parity condition. In addition, the label of every node is a proper superset of the union of the labels of its children. The labels of two siblings are disjoint. The set of nodes is always consecutive and includes the first $|N|$ elements in V (i.e., $1, \ldots, |N|$). The set D of states is the set of *generalized compact Safra trees* over S and k.
- $d_0 \in D$ has a unique node 1 where $l(1) = \{s_0\}$, $h(1) = 1$, $r = 2$, and $g = 1$.
- The parity acceptance condition is $\alpha' = \{F'_0, \ldots, F'_{2n-1}\}$ where
  - $F'_0 = \{d \in D \mid g = 1\}$
  - $F'_{2i+1} = \{d \in D \mid r = i + 2 \text{ and } g \geq r\}$
  - $F'_{2i+2} = \{d \in D \mid g = i + 2 \text{ and } r > g\}$
- For every tree $d \in D$ and letter $\sigma \in \Sigma$ the transition $d' = \rho(d, \sigma)$ is the result of the following transformations on d. (1) For every node v with label S' replace S' by $\delta(S', \sigma)$. (2) For every node v with label S' such that $h(v) = i$ and $S' \cap F_i \neq \emptyset$, create a son v' such that v' is the minimal value in V that is greater than all other nodes. Set its label to $S' \cap F_i$ and its index to 1. We may use temporarily nodes in the range $[(n+1)..(2n)]$. (3) For every node v with label S' and state $s \in S'$ such that s belongs also to some sibling v' of v such that $v' < v$, remove s from the label of

v and all its descendants. (4) For every node v whose label is equal to the union of the labels of its children, remove all descendants of v. If $h(v) = k$, change $h(v)$ to 1 and call v *green*. If $h(v) < k$, increase $h(v)$ by one. Set g to the minimum of $n+1$ and the green nodes. (5) Remove all nodes with empty labels. Set r the minimum of $n+1$ and all the nodes removed during all stages of the transformation. (6) Let Z denote the set of nodes removed during all previous stages of the transformation. For every node v let $rem(v)$ be $|\{v' \in Z \mid v' < v\}|$. For every node v such that $l(v) \neq \emptyset$ we replace v by $v-rem(v)$.   □

Let $Det(n, k)$ be the number of generalized compact Safra trees for NGBW with n states and index k. By Theorem 3, $Det(n, k)$ is bounded from above by $n^{2n+2}k^n$.

4.2   From UGCT to NBT

A Bounded-Size Run Graph Property for UGCT. Let $\mathcal{A} = \langle \Sigma, D, Q, q_{in}, \delta, \alpha \rangle$ be a UGCT with $\alpha = \{F_1, \ldots, F_k\}$. Recall that a run $\langle T_r, r \rangle$ of $\mathcal{A}$ on a Σ-labeled D-tree $\langle T, \tau \rangle$ is a $(T \times Q)$-labeled tree in which a node y with $r(y) = \langle x, q \rangle$ stands for a copy of $\mathcal{A}$ that visits the state q when it reads the node x. Assume that $\langle T, \tau \rangle$ is regular, and is generated by a transducer $T = \langle D, \Sigma, S, s_{in}, \eta, L \rangle$. For two nodes y_1 and y_2 in T_r, with $r(y_1) = \langle x_1, q_1 \rangle$ and $r(y_2) = \langle x_2, q_2 \rangle$, we say that y_1 and y_2 are *similar* iff $q_1 = q_2$ and $\eta(x_1) = \eta(x_2)$. By merging similar nodes into a single vertex, we can represent the run $\langle T_r, r \rangle$ by a finite graph $G = \langle V, E \rangle$, where $V = S \times Q$ and $E(\langle s, q \rangle, \langle s', q' \rangle)$ iff there is $c \in D$ such that $(c, q') \in \delta(q, L(s))$ and $\eta(s, c) = s'$. We restrict G to vertices reachable from the vertex $\langle s_{in}, q_{in} \rangle$. We refer to G as the *run graph of $\mathcal{A}$ on T*. A run graph of $\mathcal{A}$ is then a run graph of $\mathcal{A}$ on some transducer T. We say that G is accepting iff every infinite path of G has only finitely many F_j-vertices (vertices in $S \times F_j$), for some $1 \leq j \leq k$. Since $\mathcal{A}$ is universal and T is deterministic, the run $\langle T_r, r \rangle$ is *memoryless* in the sense that the merging does not introduce to G paths that do not exist in $\langle T_r, r \rangle$, and thus, it preserves acceptance. Formally, we have the following:

Lemma 1. *Consider a UGCT $\mathcal{A}$. Let $\langle T, \tau \rangle$ be a tree generated by a transducer T. The run tree $\langle T_r, r \rangle$ of $\mathcal{A}$ on $\langle T, \tau \rangle$ is accepting iff the run graph G of $\mathcal{A}$ on T is accepting.*

Note that G is finite, and its size is bounded by $S \times Q$. We now bound S and get a bounded-size run-graph property for UGCT. The bound on S depends on the blow-up involved in NGBW determinization, which we studied in Section 4.1. Essentially, the bound depends on the size of an NPT equivalent to the UGCT, and in order to get such an NPT we have to determinize an NGBW that accepts bad paths in runs of the UGCT.

Theorem 4. *A UGCT $\mathcal{A}$ with n states and index k is not empty iff $\mathcal{A}$ has an accepting run graph with at most $Det(n, k) \cdot n$ vertices.*

From UGCT to NBT via ABT. Consider a graph $G' \subseteq G$. We say that a vertex $\langle s, q \rangle$ is *finite* in G' iff all the paths that start at $\langle s, q \rangle$ are finite. For $1 \leq j \leq k$, we say that a vertex $\langle s, q \rangle$ is *F_j-free* in G' iff all the vertices in G' that are reachable from $\langle s, q \rangle$ are not F_j-vertices. Note that, in particular, an F_j-free vertex is not an F_j-vertex.

Given a run $\langle T_r, r \rangle$, we define an infinite sequence of graphs $G_0 \supseteq G_1^1 \supseteq G_1^2 \supseteq \ldots G_1^k \supseteq G_1^{k+1} \supseteq G_3^1 \supseteq \ldots G_3^{k+1} \supseteq G_5^1 \ldots$ as follows. To simplify notations, we sometimes refer to G_{2i+1}^1 as G_{2i+1} and to G_{2i+1}^{k+1} as G_{2i+2}. Thus, $G_1 = G_1^1$, $G_2 = G_1^{k+1}$, $G_3 = G_3^1$, $G_4 = G_3^{k+1}$, and so on.

- $G_0 = G$.
- $G_{2i+1}^1 = G_{2i} \setminus \{\langle s, q \rangle \mid \langle s, q \rangle \text{ is finite in } G_{2i}\}$.
- $G_{2i+1}^{j+1} = G_{2i+1}^j \setminus \{\langle s, q \rangle \mid \langle s, q \rangle \text{ is } F_j\text{-free in } G_{2i+1}^j\}$, for $1 \leq j \leq k$.

Lemma 2. *A run graph $G = \langle V, E \rangle$ is accepting iff there is $i \leq |V|$ for which G_{2i} is empty.*

Let G be an accepting run graph. Given a vertex $\langle s, q \rangle$ in G, the *rank* of $\langle s, q \rangle$, denoted $rank(s, q)$, is defined as follows:

$$rank(s, q) = \begin{bmatrix} 2i & \text{If } \langle s, q \rangle \text{ is finite in } G_{2i}. \\ \langle 2i + 1, j \rangle & \text{If } \langle s, q \rangle \text{ is } F_j\text{-free in } G_{2i+1}^j. \end{bmatrix}$$

Recall that, for an integer c, we have defined $R_k(c) = [2c]^{even} \cup ([2c]^{odd} \times \{1, \ldots, k\})$, as a set of $c(k+1)$ ranks, and defined $\leq$ as the lexicographical order on the elements of $R_k(c)$. For an odd rank $\rho = \langle 2i + 1, j \rangle$, we refer to G_{2i+1}^j as G_ρ. Let $c = |V|$. By Lemma 2, there is $i \leq c$ for which G_{2i} is empty. Therefore, every vertex gets a well-defined rank in $R_k(c)$.

Lemma 3. *In every infinite path in an accepting run graph G, there exists a vertex $\langle s, q \rangle$ with an odd rank such that all the vertices $\langle s', q' \rangle$ on the path that are reachable from $\langle s, q \rangle$ have $rank(s', q') \leq rank(s, q)$.*

We can now use the analysis of ranks in order to translate UGCT to NBT. In order to enable further optimizations, we use ABT as an intermediate step in the construction.

Theorem 5. *Let $\mathcal{A}$ be a UGCT with n states and index k. There is an ABT $\mathcal{A}'$ over the same alphabet such that all the following hold.*
- *$\mathcal{L}(\mathcal{A}') \subseteq \mathcal{L}(\mathcal{A})$,*
- *$\mathcal{L}(\mathcal{A}) \neq \emptyset$ implies $\mathcal{L}(\mathcal{A}') \neq \emptyset$, and*
- *the number of states in $\mathcal{A}'$ is $2^{O(n(\log n + \log k))}$.*

As detailed in the proof of the Theorem, the ABT $\mathcal{A}'$ accepts all the regular trees $\langle T, \tau \rangle \in \mathcal{L}(\mathcal{A})$ that are generated by a transducer $\mathcal{T} = \langle D, \Sigma, S, s_{in}, \eta, L \rangle$ with at most $Det(n, k)$ states. Note that the run graph of $\mathcal{A}$ on such $\langle T, \tau \rangle$ is accepting and is of size most $Det(n, k) \cdot n$. By Theorem 4, we have that $\mathcal{L}(\mathcal{A}') \neq \emptyset$ iff $\mathcal{L}(\mathcal{A}) \neq \emptyset$.

The state space of $\mathcal{A}'$ is $Q' = Q \times R_k(c)$. Intuitively, when $\mathcal{A}'$ is in state $\langle q, \rho \rangle$ as it reads the node $x \in T$, it guesses that the rank of the vertex $\langle \eta(x), q \rangle$ of G is ρ. The transitions of $\mathcal{A}'$ allows the guessed ranks to decrease, but makes sure that if a state is in F_j, the guessed rank for it cannot be odd with index j. By Lemma 3, the guessed ranks should eventually converge to some odd rank, which is checked by the acceptance condition of $\mathcal{A}'$.[5]

---

[5] Readers familiar with weak automata [20], would note that our automaton is in fact an alternating weak tree automaton. It is the special structure of weak automata that enables some of the optimizations we describe below.

In [18], Miyano and Hayashi describe a translation of ABW to NBW. In Theorem 6 below (see also [19]), we present (a technical variant of) their translation, adapted to tree automata,

Theorem 6. *Let $\mathcal{A}$ be an ABT with n states. There is an NBT $\mathcal{A}'$ with $2^{O(n)}$ states, such that $\mathcal{L}(\mathcal{A}') = \mathcal{L}(\mathcal{A})$.*

Combining Theorems 5 and 6, one can reduce the nonemptiness problem for UGCT to the nonemptiness problem for NBT. Consider a UGCT $\mathcal{A}$ with n states and index k. If we translate $\mathcal{A}$ to an NBT by going through the ABT we have obtained in Theorem 5, we end up with an NBT with $2^{2^{O(n(\log n + \log k))}}$ states, as the ABT has $2^{O(n(\log n + \log k))}$ states. In order to complete the construction, and get the NBT described in the proof of Theorem 2, we exploit the special structure of the ABT and show that only $2^{O(n^2(\log n + \log k))}$ states of the NBT constructed in Theorem 6 may participate in an accepting run.

5 Compositional Synthesis

A serious drawback of current synthesis algorithms is that they assume a comprehensive set of temporal assertions as a starting point. In practice, however, specifications are evolving: temporal assertions are added, deleted, or modified during the design process. In this section we describe how our synthesis algorithm can support *compositional* synthesis, where the temporal assertions are given one by one. We show how the Safraless approach enables us, when we check the realizability of $\psi \wedge \psi'$, to use much of the work done in checking the realizability of ψ and ψ' in isolation. Devising compositional synthesis algorithms to other forms of composition, e.g., $\psi' \rightarrow \psi$, is an interesting research problem.

Our compositional algorithm extends the *incremental-synthesis* algorithm described in [15]. Essentially, we show that when we construct and check the emptiness of the NBT to which realizability of $\psi \wedge \psi'$ is reduced, we can use much of the work done in the process of checking the emptiness of the two (much smaller) NBTs to which realizability of ψ and ψ' is reduced (in isolation).

We first review the incremental-synthesis idea from [15]. Recall that our construction is based on the fact we can bound the maximal rank that a vertex in an accepting run graph G gets. Often, the sequence $G_0, G_1, G_2, \ldots$ of graphs described in Section 4.2 converges to the empty graph very quickly, making the bound on the maximal rank much smaller (see [11] for an analysis and experimental results for the case of UCW). Accordingly, one can regard the bound c as a parameter in the construction: start with a small parameter, and increase it if necessary.

To see how this is done, consider the combined construction described in Theorem 2. Starting with a UGCT $\mathcal{A}$ with state space Q of size n, we took $c = Det(n, k) \cdot n$ (an upper bound on the size of the minimal accepting run graph of $\mathcal{A}$), and constructed an NBT $\mathcal{A}'$ with state space $3^Q \times \mathcal{R}_k(c)$, where $\mathcal{R}_k(c)$ is the set of functions $f : Q \rightarrow R_k(c)$ in which $f(q)$ is not odd with index j for all $q \in F_j$. For $l \leq c$, let $\mathcal{R}_k[l]$ be the restriction of $\mathcal{R}_k$ to functions with range $R_k(l)$, and let $\mathcal{A}'[l]$ be the NBT $\mathcal{A}'$ resulting from replacing the functions $\mathcal{R}_k[c]$ by $\mathcal{R}_k[c]$. Recall that the NBT $\mathcal{A}'[l]$ is empty iff all the run graphs of $\mathcal{A}$ of size at most l are not accepting. Thus, coming to check the emptiness of $\mathcal{A}$, the incremental approach proceeds as follows: start with a small l and check the nonemptiness of $\mathcal{A}'[l]$. If $\mathcal{A}'[l]$ is not empty, then $\mathcal{A}$ is not empty, and we can terminate with a "nonempty" output. Otherwise, increase l, and repeat the procedure. When $l = c$ and $\mathcal{A}'[l]$ is still empty, we can terminate with an "empty" output.

As argued for UCTs in [15], it is possible to take advantage of the work done during the emptiness test of $\mathcal{A}'[l_1]$, when testing emptiness of $\mathcal{A}'[l_2]$, for $l_2 > l_1$. To see this, note that the state space of $\mathcal{A}'[l_2]$ consists of the union of $3^Q \times \mathcal{R}_k[l_1]$ (the state space of $\mathcal{A}'[l_1]$) with $3^Q \times (\mathcal{R}_k[l_2] \setminus \mathcal{R}_k[l_1])$ (states whose $f \in \mathcal{R}_k[l_2]$ has a state that is mapped to a rank greater than l_1). Also, since ranks can only decrease, once the NBT $\mathcal{A}'[l_2]$ reaches a state of $\mathcal{A}'[l_1]$, it stays in such states forever. So, if we have already checked the nonemptiness of $\mathcal{A}'[l_1]$ and have recorded the classification of its states to empty and nonempty, the additional work needed in the nonemptiness test of $\mathcal{A}'[l_2]$ concerns only states in $3^Q \times (\mathcal{R}[l_2] \setminus \mathcal{R}_k[l_1])$.

We now describe how the incremental approach can be extended to a compositional one. Let $\mathcal{S} = \langle \Sigma, Q, \delta, q_{in}, \{F_1, \ldots, F_k\}\rangle$ and $\mathcal{S}' = \langle \Sigma, Q', \delta', q'_{in}, \{F'_1, \ldots, F'_{k'}\}\rangle$ be UGCWs specifying required behaviors. Let $n = |Q|$ and $n' = |Q'|$. Without loss of generality, assume that the state spaces Q and Q' are disjoint. We can define the intersection of $\mathcal{S}$ and $\mathcal{S}'$ as the UGCW P obtained by putting $\mathcal{S}$ and $\mathcal{S}'$ "side by side"; thus[6] $P = \langle \Sigma, Q \cup Q', \delta \cup \delta', \{q_{in}, q'_{in}\}, \{F_1 \cup Q', \ldots, F_k \cup Q', F'_1 \cup Q, \ldots, F'_{k'} \cup Q\}\rangle$. Note that it is indeed the case that P has an accepting run on a word w iff both $\mathcal{S}$ and $\mathcal{S}'$ has an accepting run on w.

Let $\mathcal{A}$ and $\mathcal{A}'$ be the NBTs to which realizability of $\mathcal{S}$ and $\mathcal{S}'$ is reduced, respectively. A non-compositional approach generates the NBT that corresponds to P. By Theorem 2, this results in an NBT $\mathcal{U}$ with state space $3^{Q \cup Q'} \times R_{k+k'}(p)^{Q \cup Q'}$, for $p = Det(n + n', k + k') \cdot (n + n')$. On the other hand, the state spaces of $\mathcal{A}$ and $\mathcal{A}'$ are much smaller, and are $3^Q \times R_k(c)^Q$ and $3^{Q'} \times R_{k'}(c')^{Q'}$, for $c = Det(n, k) \cdot n$ and $c' = Det(n', k') \cdot n'$. respectively.

Let us examine the structure of the state space of $\mathcal{U}$ more carefully. Each of its states can be viewed as a triplet $\langle S \cup S', O \cup O', f\rangle$, for $O \subseteq S \subseteq Q$, $O' \subseteq S' \subseteq Q'$, and $f : Q \cup Q' \to R_{k+k'}(p)$. For f as above, let $f_{|Q}$ and $f_{|Q'}$ denote the restrictions of f to Q and Q', respectively. Note that if f maps the states in S to ranks in $R_k(c)$ and maps states in S' to ranks in $R_{k'}(c')$, then the state $\langle S \cup S', O \cup O', f\rangle$ corresponds to the states $\langle S, O, f_{|Q}\rangle$ of $\mathcal{A}$ and $\langle S', O', f_{|Q'}\rangle$ of $\mathcal{A}'$. Moreover, if one of these states is empty, so is $\langle S \cup S', O \cup O', f\rangle$. This observation is the key to our compositional algorithm.

For $l \leq c$ and $l' \leq c'$, let $\mathcal{U}[l, l']$ denote the NBT $\mathcal{U}$ restricted to states $\langle S \cup S', O \cup O', f\rangle$ in which $f(q)$, for $q \in S$, is in $R_k(l)$ and $f(q')$, for $q' \in S'$, is in $R_{k'}(l')$. We check the emptiness of $\mathcal{U}$ incrementally and compositionally as follows. We start with small l_1 and l'_1 and check the emptiness of $\mathcal{U}[l_1, l'_1]$. Doing so, we first mark as empty all states $\langle S \cup S', O \cup O', f\rangle$ for which either $\langle S, O, f_{|Q}\rangle$ is empty in $\mathcal{A}$ or $\langle S', O', f_{|Q'}\rangle$ is empty in $\mathcal{A}'$, and continue the emptiness check only in the (expectedly much smaller) state space. If $\mathcal{U}[l_1, l'_1]$ is not empty, we are done. Otherwise, we increase our parameters

---

[6] For technical simplicity, we allow P to have two initial states. This can be easily avoided by adding a new initial state whose transitions are the union of the transitions from q_{in} and q'_{in}.

to l_2 and l'_2, with $l_2 \geq l_1$ and $l'_2 \geq l'_1$. Note that we need not increase both parameters. Checking the emptiness of $\mathcal{U}[l_2, l'_2]$, we make use of the information gathered in the emptiness checks of $\mathcal{A}[l_2]$, $\mathcal{A}'[l'_2]$, as well as $\mathcal{U}[l_1, l'_1]$. The procedure continues until we either reach l_j and l'_j for which $\mathcal{U}[l_j, l'_j]$ is not empty, in which case the specification is realizable, or we find that $\mathcal{U}[p, p]$ is empty, in which case the specification is not realizable.

We note that, as with the incremental approach, the significant advantage of the compositional approach is when the specification is realizable, and especially when $\mathcal{U}[l, l']$ is not empty for l and l' smaller than c and c' – thus we can use information about $\mathcal{A}$ and $\mathcal{A}'$ all the way to the positive response. We also note that the incremental approach is possible due to the simple structure of the state spaces of the NBTs to which we have reduced the realizability problem. This simple structure also makes it easy to implement our approach symbolically: the state space of the NBT consists of sets of states and a ranking function, it can be encoded by Boolean variables, and the NBT's transitions can be encoded by relations on these variables and a primed version of them. The fixpoint solution for the nonemptiness problem of NBT (c.f., [30]) then yields a symbolic solution to the original UGCT nonemptiness problem. Moreover, checking the emptiness of $\mathcal{U}[l_j, l'_j]$, we can use BDDs for the empty states in $\mathcal{A}[l_j]$, $\mathcal{A}[l'_j]$, and $\mathcal{U}[l_{j-1}, l'_{j-1}]$. Finally, as discussed in [15], the BDDs that are generated by the symbolic nonemptiness procedure can be used to generate a symbolic witness strategy, from which we can synthesize a sequential circuit implementing the strategy.

References

1. M. Abadi, L. Lamport, and P. Wolper. Realizable and unrealizable concurrent program specifications. In *16th ICALP*, LNCS 372, pp 1–17. Springer-Verlag, 1989.
2. C. S. Althoff, W. Thomas, and N. Wallmeier. Observations on determinization of büchi automata. In *10th CIAA*, LNCS. Springer-Verlag, 2005.
3. Y. Choueka. Theories of automata on ω-tapes: A simplified approach. *JCSS*, 8:117–141, 1974.
4. A. Church. Logic, arithmetics, and automata. In *ICM, 1962*, pp 23–35, 1963.
5. E.M. Clarke, O. Grumberg, and D. Peled. *Model Checking*. MIT Press, 1999.
6. D.L. Dill. *Trace theory for automatic hierarchical verification of speed independent circuits*. MIT Press, 1989.
7. J. Elgaard, N. Klarlund, and A. Möller. Mona 1.x: new techniques for WS1S and WS2S. In *10th CAV*, LNCS 1427, pp 516–520. Springer-Verlag, 1998.
8. E.A. Emerson. Automata, tableaux, and temporal logics. In *WLP*, LNCS 193, pp 79–87. Springer-Verlag, 1985.
9. R. Gerth, D. Peled, M.Y. Vardi, and P. Wolper. Simple on-the-fly automatic verification of linear temporal logic. In *Protocol Specification, Testing, and Verification*, pp 3–18. 1995.
10. E. Grädel, W. Thomas, and T. Wilke. *Automata, Logics, and Infinite Games: A Guide to Current Research*. LNCS 2500. Springer-Verlag, 2002.
11. S. Gurumurthy, O. Kupferman, F. Somenzi, and M.Y. Vardi. On complementing nondeterministic Büchi automata. In *12th CHARME*, LNCS 2860, pp 96–110. Springer-Verlag, 2003.
12. A. Harding, M. Ryan, and P.Y. Schobbens. A new algorithm for strategy synthesis in ltl games. In *11th TACAS*, LNCS 3440, pp 477–492. Springer-Verlag, 2005.
13. M. Jurziński. Small progress measures for solving parity games. In *17th STACS*, LNCS 1770, pp 290–301. Springer-Verlag, 2000.

14. O. Kupferman and M.Y. Vardi. From complementation to certification. In *10th TACAS*, LNCS 2988, pp 591–606. Springer-Verlag, 2004.
15. O. Kupferman and M.Y. Vardi. Safraless decision procedures. In *46th FOCS*, 2005.
16. O. Lichtenstein and A. Pnueli. Checking that finite state concurrent programs satisfy their linear specification. In *12th POPL*, pp 97–107, 1985.
17. Z. Manna and A. Pnueli. *The Temporal Logic of Reactive and Concurrent Systems: Specification*. Springer-Verlag, 1992.
18. S. Miyano and T. Hayashi. Alternating finite automata on ω-words. *TCS*, 32:321–330, 1984.
19. A.W. Mostowski. Regular expressions for infinite trees and a standard form of automata. In *CT*, LNCS 208, pp 157–168. Springer-Verlag, 1984.
20. D.E. Muller, A. Saoudi, and P.E. Schupp. Alternating automata, the weak monadic theory of the tree and its complexity. In *13th ICALP*, LNCS 226. Springer-Verlag, 1986.
21. N. Piterman. From nondeterministic Büchi and Streett automata to deterministic parity automata. In *25th LICS*, 2006. to appear.
22. N. Piterman, A. Pnueli, and Y. Saar. Design synthesis in action: Solving a 2exptime-complete problem in n^3. In *7th VMCAI*, LNCS 3855, pp 364–380. Springer-Verlag, 2006.
23. A. Pnueli and R. Rosner. On the synthesis of a reactive module. In *16th POPL*, pp 179–190, 1989.
24. M.O. Rabin. Weakly definable relations and special automata. In *Symp. Math. Logic and Foundations of Set Theory*, pp 1–23. 1970.
25. M.O. Rabin. Automata on infinite objects and Church's problem. *AMS*, 1972.
26. R. Rosner. *Modular Synthesis of Reactive Systems*. PhD thesis, Weizmann Institute of Science, 1992.
27. S. Safra. On the complexity of ω-automata. In *29th FOCS*, pp 319–327, 1988.
28. S. Safra. Exponential determinization for ω-automata with strong-fairness acceptance condition. In *24th STOC*, 1992.
29. S. Tasiran, R. Hojati, and R.K. Brayton. Language containment using non-deterministic omega-automata. In *8th CHARME*, LNCS 987, pp 261–277, 1995. Springer-Verlag.
30. M.Y. Vardi and P. Wolper. Automata-theoretic techniques for modal logics of programs. *JCSS*, 32(2):182–221, 1986.
31. M.Y. Vardi and P. Wolper. Reasoning about infinite computations. *IC*, 115(1):1–37, 1994.
32. J. Yang and C.J.H. Seger. Introduction to generalized symbolic trajectory evaluation. In *19th DAC*, pp 360–367. IEEE, 2001.

Minimizing Generalized Büchi Automata

Sudeep Juvekar[1] and Nir Piterman[2]

[1] Indian Institute of Technology Bombay
[2] Ecole Polytechnique Fédéral de Lausanne (EPFL)

Abstract. We consider the problem of minimization of generalized Büchi automata. We extend fair-simulation minimization and delayed-simulation minimization to the case where the Büchi automaton has multiple acceptance conditions. For fair simulation, we show how to efficiently compute the fair-simulation relation while maintaining the structure of the automaton. We then use the fair-simulation relation to merge states and remove transitions. Our fair-simulation algorithm works in time $O(mn^3k^2)$ where m is the number of transitions, n is the number of states, and k is the number of acceptance sets. For delayed simulation, we extend the existing definition to the case of multiple acceptance conditions. We show that our definition can indeed be used for minimization and give an algorithm that computes the delayed-simulation relation. Our delayed-simulation algorithm works in time $O(mn^3k)$. We implemented the two algorithms and report on experimental results.

1 Introduction

In recent years algorithmic methods for verifying temporal-logic properties of *finite-state* systems have been discovered (cf. [CGP99]). The development of symbolic methods to reason about large state spaces [McM93, BCC+99] have led to the acceptance of model checking in hardware industry [BLM01, CFF+01]. The standard approach to linear temporal logic (LTL) model checking is to translate the given specification to a nondeterministic Büchi automaton [Var96]. By now, there are many algorithms that take an LTL formula (or formalisms that extend LTL, cf. [AFF+02, IEE05]) and construct an equivalent Büchi automaton [GPVW95, SB00, GO01]. The resulting automata may be exponentially larger than the original LTL formula.

To improve model-checking efficiency we would like to produce the minimal possible automata. Unfortunately, finding the minimal automaton equivalent to a given nondeterministic automaton is computationally expensive. Thus, we usually resort to computationally cheap methods that are not guaranteed to produce the best automata.

One such approach is to use simulation [Mil71]. A state t simulates a state s if it has the same observations and for every successor s' of s there exists a successor t' of t that simulates s'. If s and t are *simulation equivalent,* i.e., t simulates s and s simulates t, then we can merge s and t to a single state. Similarly, if s has transitions to both t and t' such that t' simulates t, then the transition to t is redundant. Simulation considers only the transition structure of the automaton and not its acceptance condition. Thus, simulation is inadequate for minimization of Büchi automata.

T. Ball and R.B. Jones (Eds.): CAV 2006, LNCS 4144, pp. 45–58, 2006.
© Springer-Verlag Berlin Heidelberg 2006

There have been several suggestions how to extend simulation to include the acceptance condition [DHW91, GL94, HKR97, EWS01]. The simplest of these, is *direct simulation* where in addition to agreement on observations of states, we demand agreement on acceptance [DHW91]. A variant is *reversed simulation* which checks the edges entering a state [SB00]. Both can be applied to automata on infinite objects [SB00, GBS02]. Agreement on acceptance makes direct and reversed simulation very restrictive.

Fair-Simulation is a more relaxed notion of simulation [HKR97]. According to this notion, simulation comes equipped with a strategy. The strategy instructs us which successor t' of t to choose. We demand in addition that by following the strategy a fair computation on one side produces a fair computation on the other side. That is, if we have an infinite sequence of states that starts from the simulated state we can use the strategy to produce an infinite sequence of simulating states. Furthermore, if the first sequence is fair so is the second. Etessami et al. show how to efficiently compute fair simulation for the case of Büchi automata [EWS01]. They show also that fair simulation is too relaxed and cannot be used to merge states. Gurumurthy et al. show that it is still worthwhile to try minimizing with fair simulation [GBS02]. They show that by checking every merge and edge removal for soundness, fair simulation can still be used for minimization. The total complexity of all successful soundness checks is bounded by the complexity of checking fair simulation.

Etessami et al. provide an intermediate simulation notion called *delayed simulation* [EWS01]. The simulation again includes a strategy but this time whenever one computation visits an accepting state the other computation must visit an accepting state later. They show that delayed simulation can be used to merge states. That is, if s and t are delayed-simulation equivalent, then the automaton in which s and t are merged into one state is equivalent to the original. By now most LTL to Büchi conversions use some form of simulation to minimize the size of the automaton.

Translation of LTL to Büchi automata results naturally in *generalized Büchi automata*, that is, Büchi automata with multiple acceptance sets (cf. [GPVW95, SB00]). A generalized Büchi automaton with k acceptance conditions and n states can be easily converted to a simple Büchi automaton with nk states (and one acceptance condition) [Cho74]. This conversion is natural (and even required) when explicit state model checking is used [CVWY92].[1] However, when using symbolic model checking this conversion is undesirable and unnecessary. Symbolic algorithms for checking emptiness of automata easily handle the generalized Büchi condition without loosing efficiency. On the other hand, converting generalized Büchi to simple Büchi results in model checking a problem that may be k times larger. Counter examples may be significantly longer (even more than a factor of k as the order between the acceptance sets may be important). A similar situation arises when considering complementation of generalized Büchi automata; handling generalized Büchi directly is exponentially

---

[1] In the case that a simple Büchi automaton is required it would be best to apply first the conversion to a simple Büchi automaton. The conversion from generalized Büchi to a simple Büchi involves the addition of a deterministic part; this implies that simulation on the generalized automaton translates to simulation on the simple automaton. It follows that every modification done using our techniques on the generalized automaton would be done on the simple automaton.

more efficient [KV04]. Also when we use LTL in the context of synthesis, handling the generalized Büchi condition directly produces algorithms that are exponentially better than converting them to simple Büchi [KPV06]. Thus, it is extremely important to be able to further minimize generalized Büchi automata without first converting them to simple Büchi automata.

The notions of direct and reversed simulation are extended naturally to generalized Büchi automata (though they are even more restrictive in this case) [EH00, SB00]. This is not the case for fair and delayed simulation. The definition of fair simulation does not rely on a specific acceptance condition. Indeed, it applies naturally to generalized Büchi automata. It is not clear, however, how to solve efficiently fair simulation with respect to generalized Büchi automata and how to extend the efficient soundness check. In the case of delayed simulation it is not even clear how to extend the definition to the case of generalized Büchi automata. As mentioned, generalized Büchi automata that are used for symbolic model checking are not converted to simple Büchi automata. As we do not know how to use fair-simulation minimization and delayed-simulation minimization on these automata, we use only the simple optimization techniques. Here we show how the more advanced minimization techniques can be applied to generalized Büchi automata.

In the context of fair simulation, the efficient computation of fair simulation for Büchi automata relies on Jurdziński's ranking for parity games [Jur00, EWS01]. We show how to define a ranking for this type of fair simulation, how to compute this ranking efficiently, and how to check efficiently whether fair-simulation minimization is sound. The overall complexity of the fair-simulation minimization for all successful merges / edge removals is $O(mn^3k^2)$ where m is the number of transitions of the automaton, n the number of states, and k the number of acceptance sets.

The definition of delayed simulation is tailored specifically for simple Büchi automata [EWS01]. We show how to extend this definition to the case of generalized Büchi automata. We prove that our definition, while seemingly very relaxed, has the power needed in order to be used to minimize generalized Büchi automata. We also show how to efficiently check delayed simulation for this case. The complexity of the delayed simulation minimization is $O(mn^3k)$ where m is the number of transitions of the automaton, n the number of states, and k the number of acceptance sets.

Finally, we have implemented both these extensions in Wring [SB00]. We report on the results of testing our implementation on 500 randomly generated LTL formulae.

2 Preliminaries

2.1 Games

A *game* is a tuple $G = \langle V, V_0, V_1, \rho, W \rangle$ where V is the set of locations of the game, V_0 and V_1 are a partition of V to locations of player 0 and player 1 respectively, $\rho \subseteq V \times V$ is the transition relation, and $W \subseteq V^\omega$ is the winning set of G.

A *play* in G is a maximal sequence of locations $\pi = v_0 v_1 \cdots$ such that for all $i \geq 0$ we have $(v_i, v_{i+1}) \in \rho$. A play π is winning for player 0 if $\pi \in W$ or π is finite and the last location in π is in V_1 (i.e., player 1 cannot move from the last location in π). Otherwise, player 1 wins. For an infinite play π we denote by $inf(\pi)$ the set of locations that recur infinitely often in π. Formally, $inf(\pi) = \{v \in V \mid v = v_i \text{ for infinitely many } i\}$.

A *strategy* for player 0 is a partial function $f : V^* \cdot V_0 \rightarrow V$ such that whenever $f(\pi v)$ is defined $(v, f(\pi v)) \in \rho$. We say that a play $\pi = v_0 v_1 \cdots$ is f-*conform* if whenever $v_i \in V_0$ we have $v_{i+1} = f(v_0 \cdots v_i)$. The strategy f is *winning from* v if every f-conform play that starts in v is winning for player 0. We say that *player 0 wins* from v if she has a winning strategy. The *winning region* of player 0, is the set of states from which player 0 wins. We denote the winning region of player 0 by W_0. A strategy, winning strategy, win, and winning region are defined dually for player 1. We *solve* a game by computing the winning regions W_0 and W_1. For the kind of games handled by this paper W_0 and W_1 form a partition of V [GH82].

In this paper we are interested in two types of winning conditions. In order to define the first winning conditions we use two sets $P = \{P_1, \ldots, P_k\}$ and $Q = \{Q_1, \ldots, Q_l\}$ of subsets of the states in G. The *generalized Streett[1]* condition on P and Q is the set of sequences $\pi \in V^\omega$ such that either there exists i such that $inf(\pi) \cap P_i = \emptyset$ or forall j we have $inf(\pi) \cap Q_j \neq \emptyset$. That is, either there exists some set in P that appears finitely often in π, or every set in Q appears infinitely often in π. Notice that when P and Q are singletons then the generalized Streett[1] condition on P and Q is in fact a Streett[1] condition [Str82] or a parity[3] condition [EJ91]. The second winning condition is *generalized response*. We use a set $P = \{\langle P_1, Q_1 \rangle, \ldots, \langle P_k, Q_k \rangle\}$ of pairs of subsets of V. In order to define the winning condition we add to the game a counter that ranges over $\{1, \ldots, k\}$. The counter is controlled by player 1 and before every move of player 1 she may change this counter arbitrarily. Player 0 wins the generalized response condition on P if either player 1 changes the counter infinitely often, or if eventually the counter is set to i and along the suffix of the play along which the counter is i every visit to P_i is followed by a visit to Q_i. That is, player 1 chooses a pair $\langle P_i, Q_i \rangle \in P$. While playing according to this pair a visit to P_i should be followed later by a visit to Q_i. At every given point in time player 1 may decide to change the target pair to j and start following $\langle P_j, Q_j \rangle$. If player 1 changes her mind infinitely often she looses. Notice that this is very different from ensuring that for every $j \in \{1, \ldots, k\}$ every visit to P_j is followed by a visit to Q_j. In our setting player 0 can work with each of the pairs separately. She does not care about other pairs while playing according to one pair (at least not directly). From every state in the winning region of player 0, she has a strategy to win the delayed game with respect to every one of the pairs. This strategy cannot leave the region from which she can win with respect to the other pairs. In order to ensure that forall $j \in \{1, \ldots, k\}$ every visit to P_j is followed by a visit to Q_j, player 0 has to memorize to which pairs she owes a visit. This is not necessary in our case. Notice that in the case that P is a singleton $\{\langle P_1, Q_1 \rangle\}$, this game is exactly the game defined in [EWS01] for delayed simulation. We explain below the motivation for these two conditions and in Section 3 show how to solve these two types of games.

2.2 Nondeterministic Büchi Automata

A *nondeterministic Büchi automaton* (or *NBW* for short) is $N = \langle \Sigma, S, S_0, \delta, T, \mathcal{F} \rangle$, where $\Sigma = \{-1, 0, 1\}^P$ for some set of propositions P is a finite alphabet, S is a finite set of states, $S_0 \subseteq S$ is a set of initial states, $\delta \subseteq S \times S$ is a transition relation, $T : S \rightarrow \Sigma$ is a labeling function, and $\mathcal{F} = \{F_1, \ldots, F_k\} \subseteq 2^S$ is a set of winning conditions. We call $F \in \mathcal{F}$ a winning set or acceptance set. For $v \in V$ we denote

$\delta(v) = \{w \mid (v, w) \in \delta\}$ and $\delta^{-1}(v) = \{w \mid (w, v) \in \delta\}$ the set of successors and predecessors of v. A *run* of N is an infinite sequence of states $s_0, s_1, \ldots \in S^\omega$ such that $s_0 \in S_0$ and forall $j \geq 0$ we have $(s_j, s_{j+1}) \in \delta$. For a run $r = s_0, s_1, \ldots$, let $inf(r) = \{s \in S \mid s = s_i$ for infinitely many i's$\}$ be the set of all states occurring infinitely often in the run. A run r is *accepting* if for every $1 \leq i \leq k$ we have $inf(r) \cap F_i \neq \emptyset$. Usually, we distinguish between Büchi automata where $|\mathcal{F}| = 1$ and *generalized Büchi* automata where $|\mathcal{F}| > 1$. In this paper we are interested mainly in generalized Büchi automata. Unless mentioned explicitly, all NBW have more than one acceptance set.

Given two labels $\sigma, \sigma' \in \{-1, 0, 1\}^P$, we say that σ' abstracts σ ($\sigma \sqsubseteq \sigma'$) if for every $q \in P$ such that $\sigma'(q) = 1$ we have $\sigma(q) = 1$ and for every q such that $\sigma'(q) = -1$ we have $\sigma(q) = -1$. It is simple to see that the abstraction relation is reflexive and transitive. An *infinite word* over P is an infinite sequence $w = w_0 w_1 \cdots \in \{-1, 1\}^P$ of truth assignments to the propositions in P. A run $r = s_0, s_1, \ldots$ *induces* an infinite word $w = w_0 w_1 \cdots$ if for every $i \geq 0$ we have that $T(s_i)$ abstracts w_i (notice that a single run may induce many different words). A word w is *accepted* by N if it is induced by some accepting run. The *language* of N, denoted $L(N)$, is the set of words accepted by N. We say that two automata are *equivalent* if they have the same language.

Another way to characterize sets of sequences of propositions is by LTL formulas [Pnu77, Eme90]. For every LTL formula φ, there exists an NBW N_φ with $2^{O(|\varphi|)}$ states, such that $L(N_\varphi) = L(\varphi)$ [VW94]. We would like the produced NBW to have a minimal number of states, transitions, and acceptance sets.

2.3 Simulation

A natural way of comparing automata is by considering language equivalence and language containment. However, these problems are computationally expensive and impractical. In many cases, we resort to using simulation, an equivalence criterion that implies language containment and is easy to compute.

Simulation does not consider the acceptance condition. We use the extensions *fair simulation* [HKR97] and *delayed simulation* [EWS01] that consider acceptance. Both simulations are defined via games. Consider two NBW $N = \langle \Sigma, S, S_0, \delta, T, \mathcal{F} \rangle$ and $N' = \langle \Sigma, R, R_0, \eta, T', \mathcal{F}' \rangle$. Let $G_{N,N'} = \langle V_0 \cup V_1, V_0, V_1, \rho, W \rangle$ be the *simulation game* where (a) $V_0 = S \times R \times \{0\}$ (b) $V_1 = \{(s, t, 1) : s \in S, t \in R,$ and $T(s) \sqsubseteq T'(t)\}$ (c) $\rho = \{((s, t, 1), (s', t, 0)) : (s, s') \in \delta\} \cup \{((s, t, 0), (s, t', 1)) \mid (t, t') \in \eta\}$ Note that the game has $O(|S| \cdot |R|)$ states and $O(|\delta| \cdot |R| + |\eta| \cdot |S|)$ transitions. In order to define the winning conditions we define sets of subsets of the locations that depend on the winning conditions of N and N'. Let $\mathcal{F} = \{F_1, \ldots, F_k\}$ and $\mathcal{F}' = \{F'_1, \ldots, F'_l\}$. We define the sets $P_1, \ldots, P_k$ and $Q_1, \ldots, Q_l$. The set P_i contains all locations $(s, t, 1)$ such that $s \in F_i$. The set Q_i contains all locations $(s, t, 1)$ such that $t \in F'_i$.

In order to consider *fair simulation* we consider the generalized Streett[1] game $G_{N,N'}$ over $P = \{P_1, \ldots, P_k\}$ and $Q = \{Q_1, \ldots, Q_l\}$. It follows that player 0 wins an infinite play if the projection of the play on the first component is fair implies that the projection of the play on the second component is fair. We call this game the *fair-simulation game* or just the *fair game*. If player 0 wins the fair game from state $(s, t, 1)$ then t *fair simulates* s, denoted $s \leq_f t$. We call $H = \{(s, t) \mid (s, t, 1) \in W_0\}$ the *simulation relation*. From every pair $(s, t) \in H$ player 0 has a strategy so that the play remains in H and if the projection of an infinite outcome on the first component is fair then so is the projection on the second component. We say that s and t are *fair equivalent*, denoted $s=_f t$ if both $s\leq_f t$ and $t\leq_f s$. Fair simulation implies language containment [HKR97]. Gurumurthy et al. show how to use fair simulation to reduce the number of states and transitions of an NBW where $|\mathcal{F}| = 1$ [GBS02].

In order to consider *delayed simulation* we require that $|\mathcal{F}| = |\mathcal{F}'|$ (i.e., $k = l$). Consider the generalized response game $G_{N,N'}$ over $P = \{\langle P_1, Q_1\rangle, \ldots, \langle P_k, Q_k\rangle\}$. We call this game the *delayed-simulation game* or just the *delayed game*. As before, if player 0 wins from $(s,t,1)$ then t *delayed simulates* s. That is, $H = \{(s,t) \mid (s,t,1) \in W_0\}$ is the simulation relation. From every pair $(s,t) \in H$ and for every pair $\langle P_i, Q_i\rangle \in P$ player 0 has a strategy so that the play remains in H and if the projection of an infinite outcome on the first component visits P_i then the projection on the second component visits Q_i sometime later. The notations $\leq_d$ and $=_d$ are defined like for fair simulation. We consider delayed simulation between an automaton and itself. When $|\mathcal{F}| = 1$ our definition is equivalent to the definition in [EWS01]. Etessami et al. study delayed simulation for the case where $|\mathcal{F}| = 1$. They show that delayed simulation is implied by direct simulation (which we do not define here) and it implies fair simulation. These two claims are true also for the general definition above. The first claim is immediate and the second can be proved much like Theorem 8.

We note that the generalization of delayed simulation to the case of generalized Büchi automata is not straight forward. The most straight forward extension would be to consider a play winning if for every $\langle P_i, Q_i\rangle \in P$ we have that every visit to P_i is followed by a visit to Q_i. In Section 4 we show that our definition is strong enough to be used for minimization of NBW. Having different strategies for every one of the pairs is exactly what is needed to establish correctness of delayed-simulation minimization (as long as the strategies remain in the winning region of player 0).

We use simulation to reduce the number of states and transitions of an automaton. We usually compute simulation between an NBW and itself. In order to reason about the changes done to an automaton, we consider simulation between two different automata.

3   Solving Games

3.1   Generalized Streett[1] Games

In [EWS01] and [GBS02], fair games are solved using a reduction to parity[3] games. Then Jurdziński's algorithm for solving parity games is used [Jur00]. Here we generalize this approach to our case.

Let $G = \langle V, \rho\rangle$ be a generalized Streett[1] game over $P = \{P_1, \ldots, P_k\}$ and $Q = \{Q_1, \ldots, Q_l\}$. We define a set of ranking functions $R = \langle r_1, \ldots, r_l\rangle$. The ranking r_i measures what is the minimum over j of the maximal number of visits to P_j until a visit to Q_i is enforced by player 0. If the rank of some state is finite, it means that either for some j we have P_j is visited finitely often or within a finite number of steps player 0 forces a visit to Q_i. We use the ranking to define a winning strategy for player 0 and show that whenever player 0 wins, such a ranking system exists.

We now define formally the range of the ranking functions and the ranking functions themselves. We denote by $|P_i - Q_j|$ the number of states in $P_i - Q_j$. For $j \in [k]$, let

$|j| = max_i\{|P_i - Q_j|\}$. We set $D_j = ([0..|j|] \times [1..k]) \cup \{\infty\}$. We order D_j according to the lexicographic order with ∞ as maximal element. This induces a well order on D_j and we define increment by one in the natural way according to this order. Namely $(r, i) + 1$ is $(r, i + 1)$ if $i < k$ and $(r + 1, 1)$ if $i = k$ and $r < |j|$. We set $(|j|, k) + 1 = \infty = \infty + 1$. Let $j \oplus 1$ denote $(j \bmod l) + 1$. Consider a set of ranking functions $R = \langle r_1, \ldots, r_l \rangle$ such that $r_j : V \to D_j$. We define $best_j(v)$ to be the rank of the minimal successor of v in case $v \in V_0$ and the maximal successor in case $v \in V_1$. If $v \in Q_j$ we take the minimal / maximal according to $r_{j \oplus 1}$, otherwise according to r_j. Formally,

$$best_j(v) = \begin{cases} min_{(v,w) \in \rho}\{r_{j \oplus 1}(w)\} & v \in V_0 \text{ and } v \in Q_j \\ min_{(v,w) \in \rho}\{r_j(w)\} & v \in V_0 \text{ and } v \notin Q_j \\ max_{(v,w) \in \rho}\{r_{j \oplus 1}(w)\} & v \in V_1 \text{ and } v \in Q_j \\ max_{(v,w) \in \rho}\{r_j(w)\} & v \in V_1 \text{ and } v \notin Q_j \end{cases}$$

A ranking is *good* if for every $v \in V$ and for every $j \in [1..l]$ all the following hold.
- If $v \in Q_j$ and $best_j(v) < \infty$ then $r_j(v) = (0, 1)$.
- If $v \notin Q_j$, $best_j(v) = (r, i)$, and $v \in P_i$ then $r_j(v) > best_j(v)$.
- Otherwise $r_j(v) \geq best_j(v)$.

Notice that there is a circular dependency between all the rankings through the definition of $best_j(v)$ when $v \in Q_j$. We claim that given a good ranking, every state v such that $r_1(v) < \infty$ is winning for player 0.

The ranking defines a winning strategy for player 0. More accurately, every ranking $([1..l])$ defines a different strategy. Player 0 chooses one such strategy and tries to decrease it. When playing according to strategy j and the play reaches a state v for which $r_j(v) = (0, 1)$ and $v \in Q_j$ she starts playing according to the $j \oplus 1$ strategy. If player 0 changes her strategy infinitely often then forall $1 \leq i \leq l$ we have Q_i is visited infinitely often and player 0 wins. If player 0 eventually plays according to some fixed strategy i, it follows that the rank eventually remains constant (r, i). It follows that P_i is not visited again and player 0 wins.

We say that a ranking is *tight* if it is good and in addition for every winning state v of player 0 we have $r_1(v) < \infty$. In [KPP05] we give a symbolic algorithm for the solution of generalized Streett[1] games. The algorithm consists of a μ-calculus formula that characterizes the set of winning states of player 0. In the full version we prove that the strategy proposed above is winning and use the algorithm of [KPP05] to prove that whenever there exists a winning strategy for player 0 a tight ranking system exists.

If we can produce a tight ranking system, it provides a partition of the states of the game to W_0 and W_1. In order to efficiently compute tight ranking system, we generalize Jurdziński's rank lifting algorithm [Jur00] to our case. For a state $v \in V$ and a ranking function $r_j : V \to D_j$, let $incr_v^j(i, o)$ be $(0, 1)$ in the case that $v \in Q_j$ and $(i, o) < \infty$, $(i, o) + 1$ in the case that $v \notin Q_j$ and $v \in P_o$, and (i, o) otherwise[2]. Let $update_j(r_j, v)$ be the ranking r'_j such that $r'_j(v') = r_j(v')$ for $v' \neq v$ and $r'_j(v) = max\{r_j(v), incr_v^j(best(v))\}$. The *lifting* algorithm that computes the good ranking is:

1 Let $R := \forall v, j : r_j(v) = (0, 1)$
2 While $(\exists v, j \text{ s.t. } r_j(v) \neq update_j(r_j, v))$ do
3   Let $r_j := update_j(r_j, v)$

---

[2] Notice that in the case that $v \in Q_j$ and $(i, o) = \infty$ then $incr_v^j(i, o) = \infty$.

Theorem 1. *Given a generalized Streett[1] game G, player 0 wins from a location v iff after the lifting algorithm $r_1(v) \neq \infty$.*

Etessami et al. give an efficient implementation that computes Jurdziński's ranking for parity[3] games [EWS01]. In Fig. 1 we generalize their approach to our ranking.

```
1   foreach v ∈ V and j ∈ [n] do
2       Bⱼ(v) := 0; Cⱼ(v) := |{w : (v, w) ∈ δ}|; rⱼ(v) := (0, 1);
3   L := {(v, j) ∈ V | qⱼ ∉ L(v) and p₁ ∈ L(v)};
4   while L ≠ ∅ do
5       let (v, j) ∈ L; L := L \ {(v, j)};
6       t := rⱼ(v);
7       Bⱼ(v) := bestⱼ(v); Cⱼ(v) := cntⱼ(v);
8       rⱼ(v) := incrⱼᵥ(bestⱼ(v));
9       P := {w ∈ V | (w, v) ∈ ρ};
10      foreach w ∈ P such that (w, j) ∉ L do
11          if w ∈ V₀ and t = Bⱼ(w) and Cⱼ(w) > 1 then Cⱼ(w)--;
12          if w ∈ V₀ and t = Bⱼ(w) and Cⱼ(w) = 1 then L := L ∪ {(w, j)};
13          if w ∈ V₁ and t = Bⱼ(w) then Cⱼ(w)++;
14          if w ∈ V₁ and t > Bⱼ(w) then L := L ∪ {(w, j)};
15      endforeach
16  endwhile
```

Fig. 1. Efficient solution of generalized Streett[1] games

Theorem 2. *We can solve a generalized Streett[1] game in time $O(tgkl)$ where t is the number of transitions, g the number of locations, $k = |P|$, and $l = |Q|$.*

When we use this algorithm to compute the fair simulation relation (i.e., solve $G_{N,N}$) we get the bounds stated in the following corollary.

Corollary 1. *We can compute the fair simulation on an NBW N in time proportional to $O(mn^3k^2)$ where m is the number of transitions of N, n is the number of states of N, and k is the size of $\mathcal{F}$.*

We note that if P and Q are singletons then our ranking and Jurdziński's ranking for parity[3] are one and the same. In this case the two algorithms are identical.

3.2   Generalized Response Games

In [EWS01], delayed games with one pair are solved using a reduction to parity[3] games. In order to remember whether the play owes a visit to the acceptance set they add a Boolean flag. We prefer to take the view of player 1. This allows us to remove the Boolean flag. The treatment of delayed games becomes completely different from the treatment of fair games.

Let $G = \langle V, V_0, V_1, \rho, W \rangle$ be the delayed game over $P = \{\langle P_1, Q_1 \rangle, \ldots, \langle P_k, Q_k \rangle\}$. In Fig. 2 we give an algorithm that solves delayed games. Intuitively, player 1 wins 'immediately' from P_i states from which player 1 can avoid Q_i states. Additional winning states are states from which player 1 can force the game to immediate wins or to previously recognized winning states. The algorithm computes the immediate winning according to some pair and the states from which player 1 can force visits to them. Then it proceeds to do the same thing for other pairs until no new winning states for player 1 are discovered. Here $\ominus$ and $\oplus$ denote cyclic subtraction and addition in $[1..k]$. The function $back\_reach(X)$ computes the set of states from which player 1 can force the play to X. The function $avoid\_set(X, Y)$ computes the set of states from which player 1 can avoid X or reach Y.

```
1  foreach ⟨Pᵢ, Qᵢ⟩ ∈ P do
2      winᵢ = ∅; old_winᵢ = V;
3      i := 1;
4      while winᵢ ≠ old_winᵢ do
5          old_winᵢ := winᵢ₍ᵢ₎;
6          avoid := avoid_set(Qᵢ, old_winᵢ);
7          imm_win := (avoid ∩ Pᵢ) ∨ old_winᵢ;
8          winᵢ := back_reach(imm_win);
9          i := i ⊕ 1;
10 endwhile
```

Fig. 2. Efficient solution of generalized response games

Theorem 3. *The algorithm in Fig. 2 computes W_1 in generalized response games.*

We prove soundness by showing that every state collected by the algorithm has some winning strategy for player 1. We prove completeness by showing that the winning region of player 1 can be partitioned to regions winning by each of the pairs.

Theorem 4. *We can solve generalized response games in time proportional to $O(tgk)$ where t is the number of transitions, g the number of locations, and k the size of P.*

When we use this algorithm to compute the delayed simulation relation we get the bounds stated in the following corollary.

Corollary 2. *We can compute the delayed simulation on an NBW N in time proportional to $O(mn^3k)$ where m is the number of transitions of N, n is the number of states of N, and k is the size of $\mathcal{F}$.*

4 Simulation Minimization

4.1 Modifications to NBW and Games

Given an automaton $N = \langle \Sigma, S, S_0, \delta, T, \mathcal{F} \rangle$ and two states $s, t \in S$ we would like to merge states s and t. We denote by $N(t \leftarrow s)$ the automaton N where state s is merged with state t. That is, we remove state s from the automaton, replace every occurrence of s in S_0, δ, and $\mathcal{F}$ by t. Formally, $N(t \leftarrow s) = \langle \Sigma, S', S_0', \delta', T, \mathcal{F}' \rangle$ with the following components.

- $S' = S - \{s\}$ - remove s from the set of states.
- If $s \in S_0$ then $S'_0 = (S_0 \cup \{t\}) - \{s\}$, otherwise $S'_0 = S_0$ - replace s by t in the set of initial states if necessary.
- $\delta' = (\delta \cup \{(t, s') : (s, s') \in \delta\} \cup \{(s', t) : (s', s) \in \delta\}) - (\{s\} \times S \cup S \times \{s\})$ - replace transitions entering or leaving s by the respective transition from / to t.
- For every $F \in \mathcal{F}$, if $s \in F$ add $(F \cup \{t\}) - \{s\}$ to $\mathcal{F}'$, otherwise add F to $\mathcal{F}'$.

In the case where $|\mathcal{F}| = 1$, Etessami et al. use delayed simulation to merge states [EWS01]. They show that if s and t are delayed equivalent then N and $N(t \leftarrow s)$ agree on their languages. Formally, we have the following.

Theorem 5. [EWS01] *For an NBW N such that $|\mathcal{F}| = 1$, and s, t such that $s =_d t$ we have $L(N) = L(N(t \leftarrow s))$.*

Etessami et al. show that in the case of NBW with one acceptance set, delayed simulation can be used for minimization. We show that this is the case also with our definition and NBW with multiple acceptance sets.

Merging two fair-equivalent states may result in automata that are not equivalent [EWS01]. Gurumurthy et al. show that it is still worthwhile to try and merge fair-equivalent states, however, every such merge has to be verified to make sure that it has not changed the automaton [GBS02]. We show how to extend the efficient algorithm for computing fair-simulation to the case of NBW with multiple acceptance sets.

Let $N = \langle \Sigma, S, S_0, \delta, T, \mathcal{F} \rangle$ and $N' = \langle \Sigma, R, R_0, \eta, L, \mathcal{F}' \rangle$ be two NBW such that $R = S$. Let $\Delta \subseteq S \times S$ be a set of transitions. We define $rem(N, \Delta) = \langle \Sigma, S, S_0, \delta - \Delta, T, \mathcal{F} \rangle$ and $add(N, \Delta) = \langle \Sigma, S, S_0, \delta \cup \Delta, T, \mathcal{F} \rangle$. Let $G_{N,N'} = \langle V, V_0, V_1, \rho, W \rangle$ be the simulation game for N and N'. We define $rem(G_{N,N'}, \Delta) = \langle V, V_0, V_1, \rho', W \rangle$ where $\rho' = \rho - \{((s, t, 0), (s, t', 1)) \mid (t, t') \in \Delta\}$. That is, we restrict the moves of player 0 by removing the moves in Δ. We define $add(G_{N,N'}) = \langle V, V_0, V_1, \rho'', W \rangle$ where $\rho'' = \rho \cup \{((s, t, 1), (s', t, 0)) \mid (s, s') \in \Delta\}$. That is, we add options to player 1 by adding the moves in Δ. Intuitively, if we add transitions to an automaton we know that the new automaton simulates the old one. We only check that the old automaton simulates the new one. Dually, when we remove transitions we know that the old automaton simulates the new one. We have to check only the other direction.

Theorem 6. [GBS02] *Let N be an NBW and Δ a set of transitions. All the following are true.*

- $G_{N, rem(N, \Delta)} = rem(G_{N,N}, \Delta)$.
- $rem(rem(G_{N,N}, \Delta), \Delta') = rem(G_{N,N}, \Delta \cup \Delta')$.
- $G_{add(N, \Delta), N} = add(G_{N,N}, \Delta)$.
- $add(add(G_{N,N}, \Delta), \Delta') = add(G_{N,N}, \Delta \cup \Delta')$.

According to this theorem it does not matter whether we handle the game graph directly or build it from scratch from the modified automata. Furthermore, a series of transitions can be removed one at a time without rebuilding the game. This theorem is used to efficiently check whether merging of fair equivalent states is allowed [GBS02].

4.2 Fair-Simulation Minimization

As mentioned fair simulation cannot be used for merging states. Gurumurthy et al. show that it is still worthwhile to try to merge using fair simulation provided that all merges are checked [GBS02]. Their algorithm is efficient in the sense that it does not start the fair simulation computation anew for every merge. In a similar way, if there exists a state s such that s has transition to both t and t' where $t \leq_f t'$ they try to remove the transition from s to t. In such a case, they say that t is a *little brother* of t'. Again, they show how to check efficiently all the edge removals. In this section we extend their approach to the case of generalized Büchi automata.

In order to use fair-simulation for minimization we have to check whether the changes done to the automaton are sound, i.e., the new automaton accepts the same language. We change the automaton by adding or removing transitions. In order to check soundness of changes we try to prove that the original automaton and the modified automaton are fair-simulation equivalent. In order to check a series of additions / removals efficiently, we show how to reuse the ranks computed in previous stages.

Consider an NBW $N = \langle \Sigma, S, S_0, \delta, T, \mathcal{F} \rangle$. It induces the fair game $G_{N,N} = \langle V, V_0, V_1, \rho, W \rangle$. Let $R = \{r_1, \ldots, r_k\}$ be the ranking computed by the algorithm in Section 3. We say that R is the ranking of a game G when R is the result of applying the rank computation algorithm. Given two ranking systems R and R', we say that R is *at least* R' if for every location v and every $1 \leq j \leq k$ we have $r_j(v) \geq r'_j(v)$. The following lemma is stated and proved in [GBS02] for NBW with $|\mathcal{F}| = 1$. The lemma and its proof are identical for the case of NBW where $|\mathcal{F}| > 1$.

Lemma 1. *For every set of transitions Δ, the ranking of $rem(G_{N,N}, \Delta)$ is at least the ranking of $G_{N,N}$ and the ranking of $add(G_{N,N}, \Delta)$ is at least the ranking of $G_{N,N}$.*

Intuitively, if we want to add transitions to the automaton, we add these transitions to the locations of player 1. If we want to remove transitions we remove these transitions from the locations of player 0. When we do that, the game becomes easier for player 1 and harder for player 0. It follows that the ranking in the modified game increases. This means, that if we start from the ranks computed in previous stages and only increase them we are safe. However, the ranks are bounded by values that are not changed by addition / removal of edges. When we measure the amount of work done in all stages of the algorithm (that include several lifting rounds) it cannot be more than $O(mn^3k^2)$ total. Essentially, we do the extra lifting rounds for free.

We would like to be able to merge fair equivalent states of N and check if the resulting automaton is equivalent to the original. We would like to use only addition / removal of transitions to do that. In order to check if a merge is possible, we create an automaton with two states with the same predecessors and the same successors. That is, if $s =_f t$ we add all outgoing / incoming transitions from /to s to t and vice versa. We show now that if we have two states with equivalent incoming / outgoing transitions, one of them can be removed.

Theorem 7. *Let $N = \langle \Sigma, S, S_0, \rho, T, \mathcal{F} \rangle$ be an NBW. Given s and t in S such that $\rho(s) = \rho(t)$ and $\rho^{-1}(s) = \rho^{-1}(t)$ then $L(N) = L(N(t \leftarrow s))$.*

Suppose that we have the game $G_{N,N}$ and the ranking R resulting from running our algorithm. This gives us the fair-simulation relation H. Consider two states s and t such that $s =_f t$. We would like to check whether we can merge s and t. In order to do that we make s and t have the same incoming edges and the same outgoing edges. Formally, let

$\Delta = \{(v,t) \mid (v,s) \in \delta\} \cup \{(v,s) \mid (v,t) \in \delta\} \cup \{(t,v) \mid (s,v) \in \delta\} \cup \{(s,v) \mid (t,v) \in \delta\}$. We consider the game $add(G_{N,N}, \Delta)$. We update the ranking according to the addition. If the new automaton fair simulates the old automaton we conclude the merge to be successful and continue. If the new automaton does not fair simulate the old automaton we conclude the merge to be unsuccessful and revert to the ranking before considering $add(G_{N,N}, \Delta)$. We then proceed to the next pair of candidates to merge. As explained we can now consider the game $add(add(G_{N,N}, \Delta), \Delta')$ where Δ' is the set of transitions that relate to the new pair of states to be merged. Little brothers are handled similarly.

4.3 Delayed-Simulation Minimization

Delayed simulation as defined for NBW with single acceptance condition can be used for minimization [EWS01]. That is, if $s=_d t$ then $L(N(t \leftarrow s)) = L(N)$. Our definition extends delayed simulation for the case of NBW with multiple acceptance conditions. We show that also under our definition $s=_d t$ implies $L(N(t \leftarrow s)) = L(N)$. Although our definition is weaker than the straight forward extension of delayed simulation it is strong enough. When considering an infinite fair computation of one automaton, there are infinitely many visits to every one of the acceptance sets. We use delayed simulation on every set separately. When the first automaton visits some acceptance set we force a visit to the same acceptance set in the second automaton. Until this goal is achieved we ignore accepting states belonging to other sets. Once this goal is achieved we consider the next acceptance set in cyclic order.

Theorem 8. *Given an NBW N and states s, t s.t. $s=_d t$ then $L(N(t \leftarrow s)) = L(N)$.*

We show that if there exists a run r of $N(t \leftarrow s)$ that starts with a fair state according to F_i we can find a run segment r' or N that simulates the prefix of r and ends with a fair state from F_i. Given an accepting run of $N(t \leftarrow s)$ every fair set is visited infinitely often. So we create a run of N that visits each fair set in turn. While going for a visit in F_i we ignore other sets in $\mathcal{F}$.

In a similar way we can prove that delayed simulation implies fair simulation (which in turn implies trace containment). As delayed simulation implies fair simulation, every delayed equivalent states are also fair equivalent. This means, that if we try delayed minimization after fair minimization, the only candidates for merging are the states that we try merging but fail to pass the fair simulation test.

5 Experimental Results

In this section, we present experimental results for our algorithms. We have implemented the approach described in Section 4 in Wring [SB00]. In order to test the efficiency of our application we tested it on randomly generated LTL formulas.

In Wring, the sequence of optimization steps applied to an NBW starts with a pruning step that removes states that cannot reach a fair cycle. This is followed by a minimization step that includes direct, reverse, fair, and delayed simulation minimization. Finally, there is another pruning step. Obviously, on NBW with multiple acceptance conditions only direct and reverse simulation are applied (in the original Wring).

We compare our extension to generalized Büchi automata, with the previously implemented algorithms. We have generated 537 random LTL formulas which produce NBW with more than one acceptance condition (that is, for these formulas direct and reversed simulation leave an NBW with more than one acceptance set). We report on the results of running our application on these formulas. We compare the original version of Wring, which applies direct and reverse minimization, to our version, which adds fair minimization, delayed minimization, or both fair and delayed minimization. The results are given in Table 1. For each option we give the total number of states, transitions, initial states, fairness conditions, and CPU time.

Table 1. Experimental results for 537 random LTL formulae

Method	States	Trans	Fair	Init	Time	Method	States	Trans	Fair	Init	Time
original	26836	104605	1213	3586	3006	delayed	26776	104236	1204	3585	3732
fair	26262	100912	1153	3518	6107	fair+delayed	26070	99672	1141	3518	6666

The results above show that our algorithm can improve generalized Büchi automata that have already undergone optimization. We save approximately 3% of the states of the automata, which is comparable to the 1% saved by the original implementation of fair and delayed simulation to NBW with one acceptance set [GBS02]. In the case of fair simulation the CPU time is considerable. We note that our automata are larger by a factor of 10 than the automata used in [GBS02] (where in average an NBW has 55 states and 100 transitions). When combined, delayed and fair simulation may produce better results. On one example (not included above), starting from 183 states, each separately hardly reduced the automaton while together they reduced about 90 states. On this example alone, our application requires about 2000 seconds while original Wring requires about 200. Out of 537 NBW, only on 70 our algorithm saves more than 2 states. On these automata it reduced the number of states from 4234 to 3572 and the number of transitions from 17029 to 13077 (about 15% of the states and 25% of the transitions).

Acknowledgments

We thank F. Somenzi for the opportunity to use Wring and for supplying us with the most up to date sources. We thank R. Bloem for his help in acquiring Wring sources and S. Toneta for his help in connecting Wring with lbtt. We thank C. Fritz for spotting an error in an earlier version.

References

[AFF+02]   R. Armoni, L. Fix, A. Flaisher, R. Gerth, B. Ginsburg, T. Kanza, A. Landver, S. Mador-Haim, E. Singerman, A. Tiemeyer, M.Y. Vardi, and Y. Zbar. The ForSpec temporal logic: A new temporal property-specification logic. In *8th TACAS*, LNCS 2280, pp. 296–211, 2002.

[BCC+99]   A. Biere, A. Cimatti, E.M. Clarke, M. Fujita, and Y. Zhu. Symbolic model checking using SAT procedures instead of BDDs. In *36th DAC*, pp. 317–320. IEEE, 1999.

[BLM01]   P. Biesse, T. Leonard, and A. Mokkedem. Finding bugs in an alpha microprocessors using satisfiability solvers. In *13th CAV*, LNCS 2102, pp. 454–464. 2001.

[CFF⁺01]   F. Copty, L. Fix, R. Fraer, E. Giunchiglia, G. Kamhi, A. Tacchella, and M.Y. Vardi. Benefits of bounded model checking at an industrial setting. In *13th CAV*, LNCS 2102, pp. 436–453. Springer-Verlag, 2001.

[CGP99]   E.M. Clarke, O. Grumberg, and D. Peled. *Model Checking*. MIT Press, 1999.

[Cho74]   Y. Choueka. Theories of automata on ω-tapes: A simplified approach. *JCSS*, 8:117–141, 1974.

[CVWY92]   C. Courcoubetis, M.Y. Vardi, P. Wolper, and M. Yannakakis. Memory efficient algorithms for the verification of temporal properties. *FMSD*, 1:275–288, 1992.

[DHW91]   D.L. Dill, A.J. Hu, and H. Wong-Toi. Checking for language inclusion using simulation relations. In *3rd CAV*, LNCS 575, pp. 255–265. Springer-Verlag, 1991.

[EH00]   K. Etessami and G. Holzmann. Optimizing büchi automata. In *11th Concur*, LNCS 1877, pp. 153–167. Springer-Verlag, 2000.

[EJ91]   E.A. Emerson and C. Jutla. Tree automata, μ-calculus and determinacy. In *Proc. 32nd FOCS*, pp. 368–377, 1991.

[Eme90]   E.A. Emerson. Temporal and modal logic. In *Handbook of TCS*, 1990.

[EWS01]   K. Etessami, Th. Wilke, and R. A. Schuller. Fair simulation relations, parity games, and state space reduction for Büchi automata. In *28th ICALP*, LNCS 2076, 2001.

[GBS02]   S. Gurumurthy, R. Bloem, and F. Somenzi. Fair simulation minimization. In *14th CAV*, LNCS 2404, pp. 610–623. Springer-Verlag, 2002.

[GH82]   Y. Gurevich and L. Harrington. Trees, automata, and games. In *14th STOC*, 1982.

[GL94]   O. Grumberg and D.E. Long. Model checking and modular verification. *ACM TOPLAS*, 16(3):843–871, 1994.

[GO01]   P. Gastin and D. Oddoux. Fast LTL to büchi automata translation. In *13th CAV*, LNCS 2102, pp. 53–65. Springer-Verlag, 2001.

[GPVW95]   R. Gerth, D. Peled, M.Y. Vardi, and P. Wolper. Simple on-the-fly automatic verification of linear temporal logic. In *PSTV*, pp. 3–18, 1995.

[HKR97]   T.A. Henzinger, O. Kupferman, and S. Rajamani. Fair simulation. In *8th Concur*, LNCS 1243, pp. 273–287. Springer-Verlag, 1997.

[IEE05]   IEEE. IEEE standard for property specification language (PSL), October 2005.

[Jur00]   M. Jurziñski. Small progress measures for solving parity games. In *17th STACS*, LNCS 1770, pp. 290–301. Springer-Verlag, 2000.

[KPP05]   Y. Kesten, N. Piterman, and A. Pnueli. Bridging the gap between fair simulation and trace containment. *IC*, 200(1):35–61, 2005.

[KPV06]   O. Kupferman, N. Piterman, and M.Y. Vardi. Safraless compositional synthesis. In *18th CAV*, LNCS. Springer-Verlag, 2006.

[KV04]   O. Kupferman and M.Y. Vardi. From complementation to certification. In *10th TACAS*, LNCS 2988, pp. 591–606. Springer-Verlag, 2004.

[McM93]   K.L. McMillan. *Symbolic Model Checking*. Kluwer, 1993.

[Mil71]   R. Milner. An algebraic definition of simulation between programs. In *Proc. 2nd International Joint Conference on Artificial Intelligence*, pp. 481–489. 1971.

[Pnu77]   A. Pnueli. The temporal logic of programs. In *18th FOCS*, pages 46–57, 1977.

[SB00]   F. Somenzi and R. Bloem. Efficient Büchi automata from LTL formulae. In *12th CAV*, LNCS 1855, pp. 248–263. Springer-Verlag, 2000.

[Str82]   R.S. Streett. Propositional dynamic logic of looping and converse. *IC*, 54, 1982.

[Var96]   M.Y. Vardi. An automata-theoretic approach to linear temporal logic. In *Logics for Concurrency: Structure versus Automata*, LNCS 1043, Springer-Verlag, 1996.

[VW94]   M.Y. Vardi and P. Wolper. Reasoning about infinite computations. *IC*, 115(1), 1994.

Ticc: A Tool for Interface Compatibility and Composition[*]

B. Thomas Adler[1], Luca de Alfaro[1], Leandro Dias Da Silva[2], Marco Faella[3], Axel Legay[1,4], Vishwanath Raman[1], and Pritam Roy[1]

[1] School of Engineering, University of California, Santa Cruz, USA
[2] EE Department, Federal University of Campina Grande, Paraiba, Brasil
[3] Dipartimento di Scienze Fisiche, Università di Napoli "Federico II", Italy
[4] Department of Computer Science, University of Liège, Belgium

Abstract. We present the tool Ticc (*Tool for Interface Compatibility and Composition*). In Ticc, a component interface describes both the behavior of a component, and the component's assumptions on the environment's behavior. Ticc can check the compatibility of such interfaces, and analyze their emergent behavior, via a symbolic implementation of game-theoretic algorithms.

1 Overview

Open systems are systems whose behavior is jointly determined by their internal structure, and by the inputs that they receive from their environment. In previous work, it has been argued that *games* constitute a natural model for open systems [1,6,7,4,2]. We use games to represent the interaction between the behavior originating within a component, and the behavior originating from the component's environment. In particular, we model components as Input-Output games: the moves of Input represent the behavior the component can accept from the environment, while the moves of Output represent the behavior the component can generate.

Unlike component models based on transition systems, models based on games provide a notion of *compatibility* [6,7,4]. When two components P and Q are composed, we can check whether the output behavior of P satisfies the input requirements of Q, and vice-versa. However, we do not define P and Q to be compatible only if their input requirements are *always* satisfied. Rather, we recognize that the output behavior of P and Q can still be influenced by their residual interaction with the environment (unless the composition of P and Q is closed). Thus, we define P and Q to be compatible if there is *some* environment under which their input assumptions are mutually satisfied, and we associate with their composition $P\|Q$ the *weakest* (most general) assumptions about the environment that guarantee mutual compatibility. In game-theoretic terms, P

[*] This research was supported in part by the NSF grants CCR-0132780 and CCR-0234690, the ARP grants SC20050553 and SC20051123, and a F.R.I.A grant.

and Q are compatible if, in their joint model, Input has a strategy to guarantee that all outputs from P to Q can be accepted by Q, and vice-versa; the environment assumption of $P\|Q$ is simply the most general such Input strategy.

These game-based component models have been called *interface theories,* and two tools for interface theories predate TICC. The asynchronous, action-based interface theories of [6] are implemented as part of the Ptolemy toolset [8]. The tool CHIC implements synchronous, variable-based interface theories closely modeled after [7]. Our goal in developing TICC was to provide an asynchronous model where components have rich communication primitives that facilitate the modeling of software and distributed systems.

In TICC, variables encode both the local state of the components (called *modules*) and the global state of the system. Modules synchronize on shared actions, and the occurrence of actions can cause variables to be updated. Each global variable can be updated by more than one module, so that it is both read and write-shared; restrictions ensure that variable updates are free from race-conditions. An action can appear in a module both as input and as output. If an action a occurs in a module P as output, but not as input, then P can generate a, but not accept it from other modules. If a occurs in P both as input and as output, then P can both generate a, and accept it from other modules. This enables the encoding of rich communication schemes, including exclusive, and many-to-many schemes, and differentiates the modules of TICC from other modules with more restrictive communication primitives, such as I/O Automata [10] and Reactive Modules [3]. The theory behind TICC has been presented in [5]; here, we describe the tool itself.

2   The TICC Tool

TICC parses interfaces, called *modules*, encoded in a guarded-command language, and builds symbolic representations for these interfaces that are used for compatibility checking and composition. TICC is written in OCaml [9], and the symbolic algorithms rely on the MDD/BDD Glue and Cudd packages [11]. The code of TICC is freely available and can be downloaded from *http://dvlab.cse.ucsc.edu/dvlab/Ticc*. This web site is an open Wiki that also contains the documentation for the tool, and several additional examples.

We illustrate the modeling language of TICC by means of a simple example: a fire detection system. The system is composed of a control unit and several smoke detectors. When a detector senses smoke (action *smoke*), it reports it by emitting the action *fire*. When the control unit receives action *fire* from any of the detectors, it emits the action *call_fd*, corresponding to a call to the fire department. Additionally, an input *disable* disables both the control unit and the detectors, so that the smoke sensors can be tested without triggering an alarm.

We provide the code for the control unit module (`ControlUnit`), for one of the (several) fire detectors (`FireDetector1`), as well as for a faulty detector that ignores the *disable* messages (`Faulty_FireDetector2`):

The body of each module starts with the list of its local variables; TICC supports Boolean and integral range variables. The transitions are specified using guarded commands *guard* ⇒ *command*, where *guard* and *command* are boolean expressions over the local and global variables; as usual, primed variables refer to the values after a transition is taken. For instance, the output transition *fire* in module `FireDetector1` can be taken only when s has value 1; the transition leads to a state where $s = 2$.

```
module ControlUnit:
    var s: [0..3] // 0=waiting, 1=alarm raised, 2=fd called, 3=disabled
    input fire:     { local: s = 0 | s = 1 ==> s' := 1
                      else  s = 2        ==>            }
    input disable:  { local: true ==> s' := 3 }
    output call_fd: { s = 1 ==> s' = 2 }
endmodule


module FireDetector1:
    var s: [0..2] // 0=idle, 1=smoke detected, 2=inactive
    input smoke1:  { local: s = 0 | s = 1 ==> s' := 1
                     else  s = 2 ==>            } // do nothing if inactive
    output fire:   { s = 1          ==> s'  = 2 }
    input fire:    { } // accepts (and ignores) fire inputs
    input disable: { local: true  ==> s' := 2 }
endmodule

module Faulty_FireDetector2:
    var s: [0..2] // 0=idle, 1=smoke detected, 2=inactive
    input smoke2:  { local: s = 0 | s = 1 ==> s' := 1
                     else  s = 2 ==>           } // do nothing if inactive
    output fire:   { s = 1          ==> s'  = 2 }
    input fire:    { } // accepts (and ignores) fire inputs
    // does not listen to disable action
endmodule
```

When modules `ControlUnit` and `FireDetector1` are composed, they synchronize on the shared actions *fire* and *disable*. First, input transitions in a module synchronize with the corresponding output transitions in the other module. Thus, the output transition labeled with *fire* in `FireDetector1` synchronizes with the input transitions labeled with *fire* in `ControlUnit`. Moreover, input transitions associated to a shared action in different modules also synchronize. For instance, the input transitions associated with *fire* in `FireDetector1` and `ControlUnit` synchronize, so that the composition `FireDetector1` || `ControlUnit` can also accept *fire* as input, and can therefore be composed with other fire detectors.

The composition of `ControlUnit` and `Faulty_FireDetector2` goes less smoothly. When the composition receives a *disable* action, the control unit shuts down ($s = 3$), while the faulty detector remains in operation. When the faulty detector senses smoke (input *smoke2*), it will emit *fire*: if the control unit has been disabled by the *disable* action, this causes an incompatibility. TICC diagnoses this incompatibility by synthesizing the following input restrictions:

- A restriction preventing the input *disable* if the faulty detector is in state $s = 1$, that is, it has detected smoke and is about to issue *fire*.
- A restriction preventing the input *smoke2* when `ControlUnit` is at $s = 3$ (disabled).

Since the actions *disable* and *smoke2* should be acceptable at any time, the new input restrictions for these actions are a strong indication that the composition `ControlUnit || Faulty_FireDetector2` does not work properly.

3   Using TICC

TICC is implemented as a set of functions that extends the capabilities of the OCaml command-line. The incompatibility mentioned in the previous section is exposed by the following series of OCaml commands:

```
# open Ticc;;
# parse "fire-detector-disable.si";;
# let controlunit = mk_sym "ControlUnit";;
# let wfire2 = mk_sym "Faulty_FireDetector2";;
# print_input_restriction (compose controlunit wfire2) "disable";;
# print_input_restriction (compose controlunit wfire2) "smoke2";;
```

The `mk_sym` function builds a symbolic representation of a module, given the module name. The last two lines print how the input actions have been restricted in the composition.

References

1. S. Abramsky. Semantics of interaction. In *Trees in Algebra and Programming – CAAP'96*, LNCS 1059, Springer-Verlag, 1996.
2. S. Abramsky, D. Ghica, A. Murawski, and L. Ong. Applying game semantics to compositional software modeling and verification. In *Proceedings of TACAS 04*, LNCS, Springer-Verlag, 2004.
3. R. Alur and T.A. Henzinger. Reactive modules. *Formal Methods in System Design*, 15:7–48, 1999.
4. L. de Alfaro. Game models for open systems. In *Proceedings of the International Symposium on Verification (Theory in Practice)*, LNCS 2772, Springer-Verlag, 2003.
5. L. de Alfaro, L. Dias da Silva, M. Faella, A. Legay, P. Roy, and M. Sorea. Sociable interfaces. In *Procedings of FROCOS 05*, LNAI 3717, Springer-Verlag, 2005.
6. L. de Alfaro and T.A. Henzinger. Interface automata. In *Proceedings of the 8th European Software Engineering Conference and the 9th ACM SIGSOFT Symposium on the Foundations of Software Engineering (ESEC/FSE)*. ACM Press, 2001.
7. L. de Alfaro and T.A. Henzinger. Interface theories for component-based design. In *Proceedings of EMSOFT 01*, LNCS 2211. Springer-Verlag, 2001.
8. E. A. Lee and Y. Xiong. A behavioral type system and its application in Ptolemy II. *Formal Aspect of Computing Journal*, 2003.
9. Xavier Leroy. Objective caml. http://www.ocaml.org.
10. N.A. Lynch. *Distributed Algorithms*. Morgan-Kaufmann, 1996.
11. Fabio Somenzi. Cudd: Cu decision diagram package. http://vlsi.colorado.edu/~fabio/CUDD/cuddIntro.html.

FAST Extended Release
(Tool Paper)

Sébastien Bardin[1], Jérôme Leroux[2], and Gérald Point[2]

[1] LSV: ENS de Cachan & CNRS,
61, av. Pdt. Wilson, 94235 Cachan Cedex, France
bardin@lsv.ens-cachan.fr
[2] LABRI: Uni. Bordeaux 1 & CNRS,
351, cours de la Libération
F-33405 Talence cedex, France
{leroux, point}@labri.fr

Abstract. FAST is a tool designed for the analysis of counter systems, i.e. automata extended with unbounded integer variables. Despite the reachability set is not recursive in general, FAST implements several innovative techniques such as acceleration and circuit selection to solve this problem in practice. In its latest version, the tool is built upon an open architecture: the Presburger library is manipulated through a clear and convenient interface, thus any Presburger arithmetics package can be plugged to the tool. We provide four implementations of the interface using LASH, MONA, OMEGA and a new *shared automata* package with computation cache. Finally new features are available, like different acceleration algorithms.

Keywords: counter systems verification, acceleration, generic Presburger interface, automata with cache computation.

1 Introduction

The automatic verification of reactive systems is a major field of research. A popular way of modeling such systems is by means of (synchronized) automata extended with variables. The automata represent the control structure of the system, while variables encode data. FAST is a tool for the analysis of systems manipulating unbounded integer variables. We check *safety properties* by computing the reachability set of the systems. Even if this reachability set is not necessarily recursive, we use innovative techniques (*acceleration, flattening, reduction*) to increase convergence. FAST relies heavily on Presburger arithmetics for both system/properties specification and symbolic representation of infinite sets of states. FAST theoretical background is described in [7,2,1,3].

In our opinion, the following facts make FAST a valuable tool for counter system analysis. (1) Since counter systems and Presburger constraints are very expressive, FAST can be applied to a large spectrum of applications and the tool is not tied to a particular specific case-study. (2) Despite the inherent theoretical

T. Ball and R.B. Jones (Eds.): CAV 2006, LNCS 4144, pp. 63–66, 2006.
© Springer-Verlag Berlin Heidelberg 2006

limitations, the analysis succeeds in most practical cases. (3) FAST design is fully based on a clear theoretical framework. Abilities and limits of the tool are identified: the tool is complete relatively to the class of flattable systems [3]. Since many decidable subclasses of counter systems are flattable [8], FAST provides a unified and efficient verification algorithm for many well-studied classes of counter systems. (4) Finally the user can guide the tool via a script language, which is useful since termination cannot be guaranteed.

Experimentations. FAST has been tested over a pool of 40 infinite-state systems, and the computation succeeded in around 80% of the tests [2,1]. In [5] FAST is used to prove properties of a class of communication protocols manipulating *counters and queues.* A comparison of FAST and other tools in [3] shows that FAST provides a very efficient engine for (forward) reachability set computation of counter systems.

Extended Release. This new version provides the following improvements: (1) an open architecture based on an analysis engine and a convenient interface (API) for Presburger arithmetics. We provide adaptations of the standard packages LASH [9], MONA [10] and OMEGA [11] to the API; (2) a new Presburger package implementing the API via shared automata [6] equipped with a *computation cache*; (3) various add-ons both in the analysis engine and in the interface.

2   Open Architecture

The architecture of the tool has been redesigned, and the tool is now divided in two parts: on the one side, a counter system analysis engine built upon a generic Presburger API; on the other side various implementations of this API. These different libraries can be re-used easily in various applications, independently of FAST and counter system analysis, corresponding to a recurrent demand.

*The Generic Presburger Programming Interface (*GENEPI*).* The API requires only basic operations on Presburger formulas such as conjunction, disjunction, negation, (inverse) projection and satisfiability testing. The API is easy to use, and it is also quite easy to adapt existing Presburger packages to the API.

Implementations of the API. We provide three implementations of the API based upon standard packages LASH, MONA and OMEGA. The MONA implementation corresponds to the former version of FAST.

Potential Applications. People concerned with Presburger packages can take advantage of our open architecture and API in at least two ways. *(1) Presburger developers.* People interested in developing a Presburger package can easily linked it to FASTER and use the tool and the 40 case-studies as *intensive benchmarking* for their package. *(2) Presburger users.* People interested in developing any application requiring Presburger arithmetics can use our generic Presburger API, and then select through the set of implementations which one fits most their application.

3   The Shared Automata Package

We have also developed from scratch an implementation of the API using shared automata introduced by Couvreur in [6]. These automata share their strongly connected components in a bdd-like manner. It allow to implement important features for intensive computation, such as cache computation and constant-time equality testing. Our library is functional, but the computation cache is not yet well optimized. However it has already permitted to speed up computation time by a factor 3. The shared automata package is called PRESTAF.

4   New Features in Analysis

The tool has been extended with new capacities, both in the analysis engine and in the interface. (1) One can specify the acceleration algorithm, choosing between standard acceleration and convex acceleration [1]. The last one considers restricted functions but is more efficient. Different search heuristics are also available. (2) One can specify some circuits to be used during the analysis. (3) Finally we developed a tool to transform a Petri net in PNML format into a FAST model. The language PNML [4] describes various extensions of Petri nets and it is under standardization.

5   Comparison of Presburger libraries

We present in figure 1 the performances (time spent in seconds) of FASTER depending on our different implementations of Presburger arithmetics. Columns V and T denote respectively the number of variables and transitions in the system. All these systems have infinite reachability sets, except Dekker.

System	V	T	MONA*	LASH	PRESTAF**	OMEGA
Central Server system	13	8	5.94	91.1	7.20	43.3
Consistency Protocol	12	8	77.4	2400	140	50.3
Producer/Consumer Java	18	14	446	2520	57.6	≥ 3600
CSM - N	13	13	13.1	241	12.5	616
Dekker ME	22	22	11.4	287	12.8	≥ 3600
Last-in First-served	17	10	0.65	8.12	1.13	13.9
Multipoll	17	20	7.25	283	8.55	295
SWIMMING POOL	9	6	44.1	993	48.6	≥ 3600

* This implementation corresponds to the former version of FAST.
** A computation cache is available, but not yet optimized.

Fig. 1. Comparison of different Presburger implementations

Even though the computation cache implemented in PRESTAF is not fully optimized, figure 1 shows that PRESTAF and MONA have significantly the same execution time. LASH seems outperformed by the two previous libraries. Recall that (1) LASH provides Presburger implementation for negative and non-negative integers, thanks to more complex algorithms, and (2) LASH does not implement any computation cache. OMEGA is also outperformed. The tool appears to compute unduly complicated Presburger formulas (even with the simplification method provided by the package), while LASH, MONA and PRESTAF benefit from canonical representations of formulas.

In the previous table, the memory used is not given because, due to cache computation, this value is not representative. Without computation cache, since the internal representations of LASH, MONA and PRESTAF are slightly the same, the three implementations require slightly the same amount of memory.

Availability. FASTER, GENEPI and PRESTAF are available at http://altarica. labri.fr/. The tool, the API and the libraries are freely available under the GPL license. The analysis engine is written in C++ and the different implementations of the API are written in C. FASTER has been tested on an Intel PC running Linux and **gcc 4.0.2**.

Acknowledgments. We are grateful to Jean-Michel Couvreur for providing us advices on the implementation of shared automata, and to Ales Smrcka for adapting OMEGA source code to recent compilers.

References

1. S. Bardin, A. Finkel, and J. Leroux. Faster acceleration of counter automata. In *TACAS'2004*. LNCS 2988. Springer, 2004.
2. S. Bardin, A. Finkel, J. Leroux, and L. Petrucci. FAST: Fast Acceleration of Symbolic Transition systems. In *CAV'2003*. LNCS 2725. Springer, 2003.
3. S. Bardin, A. Finkel, J. Leroux, and P. Schnoebelen. Flat acceleration in symbolic model checking. In *ATVA'2005*. LNCS 3707. Springer, 2005.
4. J. Billington, S. Christensen, K. van Hee, E. Kindler, O. Kummer, L. Petrucci, R. Post, C. Stehno, and M. Weber. The Petri Net Markup Language: Concepts, technology and tools. In *ICATPN'2003*. LNCS 2679. Springer, 2003.
5. J. Billington, G. E. Gallasch, and L. Petrucci. FAST verification of the class of stop-and-wait protocols modelled by coloured Petri nets. *Nordic Journal of Computing*. To appear.
6. J.-M. Couvreur. A bdd-like implementation of an automata package. In *CIAA'2004*. LNCS 3317. Springer, 2004.
7. A. Finkel and J. Leroux. How to compose Presburger-accelerations: Applications to broadcast protocols. In *FST&TCS'2002*. LNCS 2556. Springer, 2002.
8. J. Leroux and G. Sutre. Flat counter automata almost everywhere! In *ATVA'2005*. LNCS 3707. Springer, 2005.
9. LASH homepage. http://www.montefiore.ulg.ac.be/~boigelot/research/lash/
10. MONA homepage. http://www.brics.dk/mona/index.html
11. OMEGA homepage. http://www.cs.umd.edu/projects/omega/

Don't Care Words with an Application to the Automata-Based Approach for Real Addition*
(Extended Abstract)**

Jochen Eisinger[1] and Felix Klaedtke[2]

[1] Albert-Ludwigs-Universität Freiburg, Faculty of Applied Sciences, Germany
[2] ETH Zurich, Department of Computer Science, Switzerland

Abstract. Automata are a useful tool in infinite-state model checking, since they can represent infinite sets of integers and reals. However, analogous to the use of BDDs to represent finite sets, the sizes of the automata are an obstacle in the automata-based set representation. In this paper, we generalize the notion of "don't cares" for BDDs to word languages as a means to reduce the automata sizes. We show that the minimal weak deterministic Büchi automaton (WDBA) with respect to a given don't care set, under certain restrictions, is uniquely determined and can be efficiently constructed. We apply don't cares to improve the efficiency of a decision procedure for the first-order logic over the mixed linear arithmetic over the integers and the reals based on WDBAs.

1 Introduction

As Büchi observed almost 50 years ago [8, 9], automata can be used to decide arithmetical theories, like Presburger arithmetic. Roughly speaking, a Presburger arithmetic formula defines a regular language, for which one can build the automaton recursively over the structure of the formula. So, automata are used to represent sets of integers that are definable in Presburger arithmetic. More recently, model checkers for systems with unbounded integers, like FAST [1] and ALV [19] have been developed that use such an automata-based set representation. The use of automata in these model checkers can be compared to the use of BDDs in model checkers for finite state systems, like SMV [17]: automata describe sets of system states. Moreover, automata constructions can be used for computing or overapproximating the set of all reachable states.

Sets of reals can be represented by ω-automata. Boigelot, Jodogne, and Wolper [5] have shown recently that even weak deterministic Büchi automata (WDBAs) suffice to represent the first-order definable sets in $(\mathbb{R}, Z, +, <)$, where Z is the unary predicate stating whether a number is an integer. This result paves the way for a more effective automata-based decision procedure for the

---

* This work was supported by the German Research Foundation (DFG) and the Swiss National Science Foundation (SNF).
** Due to space limitations, proofs are omitted. Details are in the technical report [10].

T. Ball and R.B. Jones (Eds.): CAV 2006, LNCS 4144, pp. 67–80, 2006.
© Springer-Verlag Berlin Heidelberg 2006

first-order logic over $(\mathbb{R}, Z, +, <)$. WDBAs can be handled algorithmically almost as efficiently as automata over finite words. For instance, in contrast to Büchi automata, they can be efficiently minimized [16] and they are easy to complement. WDBAs and this logic have a wide range of applications, such as the symbolic verification of linear hybrid automata [3,4]. The automata library LASH [15] provides implementations of all the needed operations for implementing a decision procedure for the first-order logic over $(\mathbb{R}, Z, +, <)$ based on WDBAs.

However, analogous to BDDs, it turns out that a limiting factor in the automata-based representation of potential infinite sets of integers or reals is the size of the automata. In fact, our first results of an automata-based decision procedure for the first-order theory over $(\mathbb{R}, Z, +, <)$ were rather discouraging; even for medium sized formulas the minimal WDBAs were often huge. An analysis of the constructed automata lead to the results presented in this article.

For BDDs, many algorithms and methods have been developed to reduce the BDD sizes, which have improved the performance BDD-based model-checkers. One of these techniques is the use of *don't cares* [12]. Roughly speaking, don't cares are inputs of a combinational circuit for which the circuit output is not specified or irrelevant. The BDD representation of a circuit can be reduced by choosing appropriate output values for the don't care inputs. In this paper, we generalize the notion of don't cares for BDDs to languages. In the most general sense, a don't care set is a language over some alphabet. The set chosen depends on the application domain. The intuition of a don't care word is that it is irrelevant whether this word belongs to a language or not. Adding or removing don't care words to languages can result in smaller automata. A trivial example is where the don't care set consists of all words. In this case we can either add or remove all words and obtain an automaton with a single state. However, usually a don't care set is a proper subset of all words and it is not obvious which of these words must be added or removed to obtain smaller automata. Furthermore, the order in which we add and remove words might lead to different (minimal) automata accepting the same language *modulo* the don't care set. We prove that under certain restrictions on the don't care set, the minimal WDBA is uniquely determined and can be efficiently constructed.

To demonstrate the effectiveness of don't cares for automata, we apply it to the approach for representing and manipulating sets of integers and reals by WDBAs. First, we define a straightforward don't care set when encoding reals by ω-words. Second, we present an automata construction for handling the existential quantification, which becomes more complicated when using don't cares. Third, we show by experiments that introducing don't care sets can reduce the automata sizes significantly in computing and representing sets of integers and reals.

We proceed as follows. In 2, we give preliminaries. In §3, we introduce don't care words and present our general results about don't care sets. In §4, we present an automata construction for projecting sets of reals that are represented by WDBAs modulo a specific set of don't cares. In §5, we report on experimental results. Finally, in §6, we draw conclusions.

2   Preliminaries

We assume that the reader is familiar with the basics of automata theory and first-order logic. The purpose of this section is to recall some background in these areas, and fix the notation and terminology used in the remainder of the text.

2.1   Languages and Deterministic Automata

Let Σ be an alphabet. We denote the set of all finite words over Σ by Σ^* and Σ^+ denotes the set $\Sigma^* \setminus \{\varepsilon\}$, where ε is the empty word. Σ^ω is the set of all ω-words over Σ. The *concatenation* of words is written as juxtaposition. We write $|w|$ for the *length* of $w \in \Sigma^*$. We often write a word $w \in \Sigma^*$ of length $\ell \geq 0$ as $w(0) \ldots w(\ell - 1)$ and an ω-word $\alpha \in \Sigma^\omega$ as $\alpha(0)\alpha(1)\alpha(2)\ldots$, where $w(i)$ and $\alpha(i)$ denote the ith letter of w and α, respectively.

A *deterministic finite automaton* (DFA) $\mathcal{A}$ is a tuple $(Q, \Sigma, \delta, q_\mathrm{I}, F)$, where Q is a finite set of states, Σ is an alphabet, $\delta : Q \times \Sigma \to Q$ is the transition function, $q_\mathrm{I} \in Q$ is the initial state, and $F \subseteq Q$ is the set of accepting states. A state not in F is a *rejecting* state. The *size* of $\mathcal{A}$ is the cardinality of Q. We write $\mathcal{A}_q$ for the DFA that is identical to $\mathcal{A}$ except that $q \in Q$ is the initial state. We extend δ to the function $\hat{\delta} : Q \times \Sigma^* \to Q$ defined as $\hat{\delta}(q, \varepsilon) := q$ and $\hat{\delta}(q, bu) := \hat{\delta}(\delta(q, b), u)$, where $q \in Q$, $b \in \Sigma$, and $u \in \Sigma^*$. The DFA $\mathcal{A}$ defines the language $L_*(\mathcal{A}) := \{w \in \Sigma^* : \hat{\delta}(q_\mathrm{I}, w) \in F\}$.

The state $q \in Q$ is *reachable* from $p \in Q$ if there is a word $w \in \Sigma^*$ such that $\hat{\delta}(p, w) = q$. In the remainder of the text, we assume that every state in an automaton is reachable from its initial state. A *strongly connected component* (SCC) of $\mathcal{A}$ is a set $S \subseteq Q$ such that every $p \in S$ is reachable from every $q \in S$ and S is maximal. For $q \in Q$, $\mathrm{SCC}(q)$ denotes the SCC $S \subseteq Q$ with $q \in S$. We call an SCC S *accepting* if $S \subseteq F$, and *rejecting* if $S \cap F = \emptyset$.

We can view a DFA as a *deterministic Büchi automaton* (DBA). A *run* of the DBA $\mathcal{A}$ on the ω-word $\alpha \in \Sigma^\omega$ is an ω-word $\vartheta \in Q^\omega$ such that $\vartheta(0) = q_\mathrm{I}$ and $\vartheta(i + 1) = \delta(\vartheta(i), \alpha(i))$, for all $i \in \mathbb{N}$. The run ϑ is *accepting* if $\mathrm{Inf}(\vartheta) \cap F \neq \emptyset$, where $\mathrm{Inf}(\vartheta)$ is the set of states that occur infinitely often in ϑ. The DBA $\mathcal{A}$ defines the ω-language $L_\omega(\mathcal{A}) := \{\alpha \in \Sigma^\omega : \text{the run of } \mathcal{A} \text{ on } \alpha \text{ is accepting}\}$. The DBA $\mathcal{A}$ is *weak* if every SCC of $\mathcal{A}$ is either accepting or rejecting. We use the initialism WDBA for "weak deterministic Büchi automaton." Similarly, we can view a DFA as a *deterministic co-Büchi automaton* (CO-DBA). Runs of CO-DBAs are defined as for DBAs. A run ϑ of a CO-DBA $\mathcal{C}$ is *accepting* if $\mathrm{Inf}(\vartheta) \cap F = \emptyset$, where F is the set of "accepting" states of $\mathcal{C}$. We define $\overline{L}_\omega(\mathcal{C}) := \{\alpha \in \Sigma^\omega : \text{the run of } \mathcal{C} \text{ on } \alpha \text{ is accepting (in the co-Büchi sense)}\}$.

2.2   Representing Sets of Reals with Automata

Let $\mathfrak{R}$ be the structure $(\mathbb{R}, Z, +, <)$, where $+$ and $<$ are as expected and Z is the unary predicate such that $Z(x)$ is true iff x is an integer. For a formula $\varphi(x_1, \ldots, x_r)$ and $a_1, \ldots, a_r \in \mathbb{R}$, we write $\mathfrak{R} \models \varphi[a_1, \ldots, a_r]$ if φ is true in $\mathfrak{R}$ when the variable x_i is interpreted as a_i, for $1 \leq i \leq r$.

Boigelot, Jodogne, and Wolper have shown in [5] that for every first-order definable set $X \subseteq \mathbb{R}^r$ in $\mathfrak{R}$, there is a WDBA $\mathcal{A}$ that describes X. Moreover, they have shown that $\mathcal{A}$ can be effectively constructed from a formula $\varphi(x_1, \ldots, x_r)$ that defines X, i.e., $X = \{\bar{a} \in \mathbb{R}^r : \mathfrak{R} \models \varphi[\bar{a}]\}$. We recall the precise correspondence between subsets of $\mathbb{R}^r$ and ω-languages from [5]. In the remainder of the text, let $\varrho > 1$ and $\Sigma := \{0, \ldots, \varrho - 1\}$ be fixed. ϱ is called the *base*.

Definition 1. *Let $r \geq 1$.*
1. *V_r denotes the set of all ω-words over the alphabet $\Sigma^r \cup \{\star\}$ of the form $v \star \gamma$, where $v \in (\Sigma^r)^+$ with $v(0) \in \{0, \varrho - 1\}^r$ and $\gamma \in (\Sigma^r)^\omega$.*
2. *An ω-word $v \star \gamma \in V_r$ represents the vector of reals with r components*

$$\langle\!\langle v \star \gamma \rangle\!\rangle := \sum_{0 < i < |v|} \varrho^{|v|-i-1} \cdot v(i) + \sum_{i \geq 0} \varrho^{-i-1} \cdot \gamma(i) + \begin{cases} 0 & \text{if } v(0) = 0, \\ -\varrho^{|v|-1} & \text{if } v(0) = \varrho - 1, \end{cases}$$

where vector addition and scalar multiplication are componentwise.[1]
3. *For a formula $\varphi(x_1, \ldots, x_r)$, we define $L(\varphi) := \{\alpha \in V_r : \mathfrak{R} \models \varphi[\langle\!\langle \alpha \rangle\!\rangle]\}$.*

Note that the encoding $v \star \gamma \in V_1$ of a real is based on the ϱ's complement representation. The symbol $\star$ plays the role of a decimal point, separating the integer part v from the fractional part γ. Moreover, note that every vector in $\mathbb{R}^r$ can be represented by an ω-word in V_r. However, the representation is not unique. First, we can repeat the first letter arbitrary often without changing the represented vector. Second, a vector that contains in a component a rational whose denominator has only prime factors that are also factors of the base ϱ, has distinct representations, e.g., in base $\varrho = 2$, $\langle\!\langle 0 \star 10^\omega \rangle\!\rangle = \langle\!\langle 0 \star 01^\omega \rangle\!\rangle = \frac{1}{2}$, where b^ω denotes the infinite repetition of the letter b.

Additional Notation. Let $r \geq 1$ and $s, t \in \{1, \ldots, r\}$ with $s \leq t$. We denote the tth coordinate of $b \in \Sigma^r$ by $b_{\restriction t}$ and $b_{\restriction s,t} := (b_{\restriction s}, b_{\restriction s+1}, \ldots, b_{\restriction t})$. We write $\alpha_{\restriction t}$ for the tth *track* of $\alpha \in (\Sigma^r \cup \{\star\})^\omega$, i.e., $\alpha_{\restriction t}$ is the ω-word $\gamma \in (\Sigma \cup \{\star\})^\omega$ defined as $\gamma(i) := \star$ if $\alpha(i) = \star$, and $\gamma(i) := \alpha(i)_{\restriction t}$ otherwise, for $i \in \mathbb{N}$. Analogously, $\alpha_{\restriction s,t}$ denotes the ω-word consisting of the tracks $s, s + 1, \ldots, t$ of α. For $m, n \geq 1$ and ω-words $\alpha \in (\Sigma^m \cup \{\star\})^\omega$ and $\beta \in (\Sigma^n \cup \{\star\})^\omega$, we write (α, β) for the ω-word $\gamma \in (\Sigma^{m+n} \cup \{\star\})^\omega$ with $\gamma_{\restriction 1,m} = \alpha$ and $\gamma_{\restriction m+1,m+n} = \beta$. Here, we make the assumption that $\alpha(i) = \star$ iff $\beta(i) = \star$, for all $i \in \mathbb{N}$. We use the same notation for finite words, which is defined analogously.

3 Don't Cares for Optimizing the Real Representation

In this section, we define our optimized representation of the reals as ω-words, which leads us to the general concept of don't care words for ω-languages. We first give a motivating example.

Example 2. Consider the formula $\varphi(x, y) := x \neq 0 \land x + y = 0$. The minimal WDBA accepting $L(\varphi)$ in base $\varrho = 2$ is shown in Figure 1(a). This WDBA is rather

---

[1] Note that we do not distinguish between vectors and tuples.

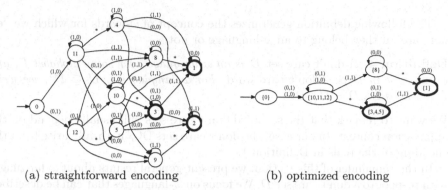

(a) straightforward encoding   (b) optimized encoding

Fig. 1. Minimal WDBAs for the formula $x \neq 0 \wedge x + y = 0$. For the sake of readability, we have omitted the rejecting sink states and their incoming transitions.

complex as it must either accept or reject all ω-words that represent the same pair of reals. For instance, the ω-words $\alpha := (1,0) \star (1,0)^\omega$ and $\beta := (0,1) \star (0,1)^\omega$ represent the pair $(0,0)$ of reals, which does not satisfy φ and thus, the WDBA must reject them. In the optimized encoding we exploit that already the ω-word $\gamma := (0,0) \star (0,0)^\omega$ takes care of the fact that the pair of reals $(0,0)$ is not in the represented set. That means, we can add α and β to the ω-language. More general, an ω-word that has a suffix in which at least one of its tracks is of the form 1^ω is treated as a *don't care*, i.e., we can freely chose whether the automaton should accept or reject this ω-word. Observe that for every don't care representing the pair (x,y) of reals, there is an ω-word that also represents (x,y) and is not a don't care.

Consider again the ω-words α and β, which are don't cares. When reading these ω-words, we eventually loop in the states 4 and 5, respectively. Note that all runs that eventually stay in one of these states are don't cares. Making the states 4 and 5 accepting clearly alters the ω-language of the WDBA. However, we only add ω-words that are don't cares, like α and β. If the states 4 and 5 are accepting we can merge them with state 3. Analogously, we can make state 2 rejecting. Then, we can merge the states 2 and 9 with the rejecting sink state. We could also make the states 11 or 12 accepting. However, this would not be beneficial since it will prevent us from merging the states 10, 11, and 12. The resulting minimized automaton is depicted in Figure 1(b).

In the context of encoding reals by ω-words we use the following don't cares.

Definition 3. *Let $r \geq 1$. An ω-word $\alpha \in (\Sigma^r \cup \{\star\})^\omega$ is a don't care word if there are $t \in \{1, \ldots, r\}$ and $k \in \mathbb{N}$ such that $\alpha(i) \in \Sigma^r$ and $\alpha(i)_{\upharpoonright t} = \varrho - 1$, for all $i \geq k$. DC_r denotes the set of all don't care words in $(\Sigma^r \cup \{\star\})^\omega$.*

Instead of constructing a WDBA that accepts the ω-language $L(\varphi)$ for a formula φ, we are interested in constructing a WDBA that accepts an ω-language that coincide on all the ω-words in $L(\varphi)$ that are not don't care words. Note that removing or adding *all* don't care words to $L(\varphi)$ does not necessarily result in a smaller automaton. Also note that by removing or adding all don't care words we can obtain ω-languages that are not recognizable by WDBAs.

The following definition generalizes the concept of ω-words for which we "do not care" if they belong to an ω-language or not.

Definition 4. *A don't care set D is an ω-language over some alphabet Γ, and an ω-word in D is a* don't care word. *For ω-languages $L, L' \subseteq \Gamma^\omega$, we write $L \equiv_D L'$ if $L \setminus D = L' \setminus D$.*

We want to remark that the so-called don't care sets will usually depend on the application context. In our case, the don't care sets DC_r naturally arise from the encoding of the reals in Definition 1.

In the remainder of this section, we present general results about ω-languages with respect to a don't care set D. We focus on ω-languages that can be described by Büchi automata, in particular by WDBAs. In §3.1 and §3.2, we establish some straightforward facts. Namely, in §3.1, we observe that standard automata constructions carry over to handle the Boolean operations when using don't care sets, and in §3.2, we show how to solve the emptiness problem for Büchi automata with respect to an ω-regular don't care set $D \subseteq \Gamma^\omega$. In §3.3, we describe minimization of WDBAs with respect to a don't care set $D \subseteq \Gamma^\omega$, where we assume that D fulfills the two properties: (1) $D \neq \Gamma^\omega$ and (2) $\alpha \in D \Leftrightarrow u\alpha \in D$, for all $u \in \Gamma^*$ and $\alpha \in \Gamma^\omega$. In particular, we show that the minimal WDBA is uniquely determined (up to isomorphism) and we give an efficient algorithm for constructing it under the assumption that D is ω-regular.

3.1   Boolean Operations

The automata construction for Boolean operations, like union and complementation of ω-languages, need not to be changed when using a don't care set $D \subseteq \Gamma^\omega$. For instance, for complementation, if we have that $L \equiv_D L'$, for ω-languages $L, L' \subseteq \Gamma^\omega$, then we have that $\Gamma^\omega \setminus L \equiv_D \Gamma^\omega \setminus L'$. Note that it is irrelevant whether L and L' differ on D, i.e., $L \cap D \neq L' \cap D$.

For WDBAs, we can use the standard product construction for the intersection and union. Let $\mathcal{A} = (Q, \Gamma, \delta, q_\mathrm{I}, F)$ and $\mathcal{B} = (Q', \Gamma, \delta', q'_\mathrm{I}, F')$ be WDBAs. For the intersection, we define $\mathcal{D} := (Q \times Q', \Gamma, \eta, (q_\mathrm{I}, q'_\mathrm{I}), F \times F')$, where $\eta((q, q'), b) := (\delta(q, b), \delta'(q', b))$, for $q \in Q$, $q' \in Q'$, and $b \in \Gamma$. The construction for the union is similar. Complementing WDBAs is done by flipping accepting and rejecting states of a WDBA. We define $\mathcal{C} := (Q, \Gamma, \delta, q_\mathrm{I}, Q \setminus F)$.

Proposition 5. *(a) For the WDBA $\mathcal{D}$, it holds that $L_\omega(\mathcal{D}) \equiv_D L_\omega(\mathcal{A}) \cap L_\omega(\mathcal{B})$.*
(b) For the WDBA $\mathcal{C}$, it holds that $L_\omega(\mathcal{C}) \equiv_D \Gamma^\omega \setminus L_\omega(\mathcal{A})$.

3.2   Emptiness Check

The emptiness problem for Büchi automata modulo a don't care set D is to check whether a Büchi automaton $\mathcal{A}$ accepts an ω-word that is not in D. If D is ω-regular, then we can solve this problem by constructing the Büchi automaton accepting $L_\omega(\mathcal{A}) \setminus D$ and check whether the resulting Büchi automaton accepts an ω-word. The complexity is in $O(n)$, where n is the number of states of $\mathcal{A}$. Note that D is fixed and hence, the size of the Büchi automaton for D is a constant.

3.3   Minimizing WDBAs with Don't Cares

Löding showed in [16] that the minimal WDBA can be constructed in two steps. In the first steps, the WDBA is put in linear time into a normal form by determining a suitable set of accepting states. This step does not change the accepted ω-language, since it only alters the acceptance types of states (rejecting or accepting) that cannot occur infinitely often in a run. In the second step, the WDBA in normal form is minimized by a standard DFA minimization algorithm, like that of Hopcroft [13]. We extend Löding's algorithm to WDBAs such that it takes a don't care set D over the alphabet Γ into account, where we require that (1) $D \neq \Gamma^\omega$ and (2) $\alpha \in D \Leftrightarrow u\alpha \in D$, for all $u \in \Gamma^*$ and $\alpha \in \Gamma^\omega$.

Definition 6. *Let $A = (Q, \Gamma, \delta, q_I, F)$ be a WDBA.*
1. *A is D-minimal if there is no smaller WDBA B such that $L_\omega(A) \equiv_D L_\omega(B)$.*
2. *A state $q \in Q$ is D-recurrent if $L_\omega(A') \setminus D \neq \emptyset$, where A' is the WDBA $(Q, \Gamma, \delta, q, \mathrm{SCC}(q))$. A state is D-transient if it is not D-recurrent. An SCC is D-recurrent if it contains a D-recurrent state, otherwise, it is D-transient.*

Note that an SCC without loops is D-transient. Moreover, note that for the ω-words not in D, it is irrelevant whether a D-transient SCC is accepting or rejecting. Thus, we can make D-transient SCCs accepting or rejecting without altering the accepted ω-language modulo the don't care set D.

Similar to Löding's algorithm, we construct first a suitable set of accepting states by determining the acceptance types of D-transient states optimal in the sense that applying a minimization algorithm for DFAs yields the minimal WDBA with respect to the don't care set D. We need the following definitions.

Definition 7. *Let $A = (Q, \Gamma, \delta, q_I, F)$ be a WDBA.*
1. *A mapping $c : Q \to \mathbb{N}$ is a D-coloring for A if the two conditions hold:*
   - *$c(q)$ is even $\Leftrightarrow q \in F$, for every D-recurrent state $q \in Q$, and*
   - *$c(p) \leq c(q)$, for all $p, q \in Q$ and $b \in \Gamma$ with $\delta(p, b) = q$.*
   The D-coloring c is k-maximal, where $k \in \mathbb{N}$, if $c(q) \leq k$ and $c'(q) \leq c(q)$, for every $q \in Q$ and every D-coloring $c' : Q \to \mathbb{N}$ for A.
2. *A is in D-normal form if for some even $k \in \mathbb{N}$, there is a k-maximal D-coloring $c : Q \to \mathbb{N}$ such that $F = F_c$, where $F_c := \{q \in Q : c(q) \text{ is even}\}$.*[2]

The algorithm in Figure 2 computes the D-normal form of a given WDBA $A = (Q, \Gamma, \delta, q_I, F)$. The main task of the algorithm is to compute a k-maximal coloring for A, where k is even and large enough. This is done by looking at the acyclic SCC graph of A, which the algorithm traverses in a reversed topological ordering (lines 4–19). The SCC graph and the topological ordering can be computed in linear time. Observe that the states in an SCC have the same color in a D-coloring. In the ith traversal of the for-loop (lines 4–19), we color the states in the ith SCC with respect to the reversed topological ordering, where the states in the successor SCCs are already colored. If there are no successor SCCs,

---

[2] Alternatively, we could require that k has to be odd. But we must fix some parity in order to obtain a canonical form for D-minimal WDBAs in D-normal form.

1: Compute the SCC graph G of $\mathcal{A}$.
2: Compute a topological ordering $v_1, \ldots, v_m$ on the vertices of G. To simplify notation, we identify a vertex v_i with its corresponding SCC, i.e., a set of states.
3: Let $k \geq m$ be an even number.
4: **for** $i = m$ **downto** 1 **do**   /* Compute a k-maximal D-coloring $c : Q \to \mathbb{N}$ */
5:    **if** v_i has no successors **and** v_i is accepting **then**
6:       Define $c(q) := k$, for all $q \in v_i$.
7:    **else if** v_i has no successors **and** v_i is rejecting **then**
8:       Define $c(q) := k - 1$, for all $q \in v_i$.
9:    **else**
10:       Let $\ell := \min\{c(q) : v_j$ is a successor of v_i and $q \in v_j\}$.
11:       **if** v_i is D-transient **then**
12:          Define $c(q) := \ell$, for all $q \in v_i$.
13:       **else if** (ℓ is even **and** v_i is accepting) **or** (ℓ is odd **and** v_i is rejecting) **then**
14:          Define $c(q) := \ell$, for all $q \in v_i$.
15:       **else**
16:          Define $c(q) := \ell - 1$, for all $q \in v_i$.
17:       **end if**
18:    **end if**
19: **end for**
20: Return the WDBA $\mathcal{A}' := (Q, \Gamma, \delta, q_\mathrm{I}, F_c)$.

Fig. 2. Algorithm for computing the D-normal form of a WDBA $\mathcal{A} = (Q, \Gamma, \delta, q_\mathrm{I}, F)$

we assign the maximal color to the states depending on k and their acceptance type (lines 5–8). Note that an SCC with no successors cannot be D-transient, since $D \neq \Gamma^\omega$. If the SCC has successors, the maximal color for the states in this SCC depends on the minimal color ℓ of the successor SCCs (line 10). If the SCC is D-transient (lines 11–12) then ℓ is the maximal color we can assign to these states. Depending on ℓ, the states in the SCC will then be either accepting or rejecting in the resulting WDBA. If the SCC is D-recurrent, the coloring has to preserve the acceptance type of the states in the SCC. Depending on ℓ, we assign the maximal possible color to the states in the SCC (lines 13–15).

In line 11 of the algorithm, we must check whether an SCC S is D-transient. This can be done by checking whether $L_\omega(\mathcal{C}) \subseteq D$ holds, where $\mathcal{C}$ is the WDBA $(Q, \Sigma, \delta, q, S)$ and q is an arbitrarily chosen state in S. Note that $L_\omega(\mathcal{C}) \subseteq D$ iff $L_\omega(\mathcal{C}) \cap (\Gamma^\omega \setminus D) = \emptyset$. Under the assumption that D is ω-regular, it is easy to see that $L_\omega(\mathcal{C}) \cap (\Gamma^\omega \setminus D) = \emptyset$ can be checked in time $O(|S|)$, since D is fixed and we can construct a Büchi automaton for the ω-language $\Gamma^\omega \setminus D$ in a preprocessing step. In summary, the checks performed in line 11 take time $O(\sum_{S \text{ SCC of } \mathcal{A}} |S|) = O(|Q|)$. So, if D is ω-regular, the algorithm in Figure 2 computes a k-maximal coloring in linear time.

Lemma 8. *For a given* WDBA *$\mathcal{A} = (Q, \Gamma, \delta, q_\mathrm{I}, F)$, there is a set $F' \subseteq Q$ such that the* WDBA *$\mathcal{A}' := (Q, \Gamma, \delta, q_\mathrm{I}, F')$ is in D-normal form and $L_\omega(\mathcal{A}) \equiv_D L_\omega(\mathcal{A}')$. The set F' can be constructed in time $O(|Q|)$ if D is ω-regular.*

Our minimization algorithm for WDBAs with the don't care set D is as follows: First, we put the given WDBA into D-normal form. Second, we apply to the WDBA in D-normal form the classical DFA minimization algorithm [13]. The overall complexity is in $O(n \log n)$, where n is the size of $\mathcal{A}$. This algorithm returns the unique minimal WDBA for the don't care set D.

Theorem 9. *For a given* WDBA $\mathcal{A} = (Q, \Gamma, \delta, q_1, F)$, *there is a D-minimal* WDBA $\mathcal{A}'$ *with* $L_\omega(\mathcal{A}) \equiv_D L_\omega(\mathcal{A}')$. $\mathcal{A}'$ *can be constructed in time* $O(|Q| \log |Q|)$ *if D is ω-regular. Furthermore, every D-minimal* WDBA $\mathcal{B}$ *in D-normal form with* $L_\omega(\mathcal{A}) \equiv_D L_\omega(\mathcal{B})$ *is isomorphic to* $\mathcal{A}'$.

Remark 10. Similar to Definition 3, we can define for $r \geq 1$, the set I_r that consists of the ω-words over $\Sigma^r \cup \{\star\}$ that are not periodic in at least one track. Note that such a periodic track, if it is also in V_1, corresponds to an irrational number. Obviously, I_r has the properties (1) and (2). The decision procedure for the first-order logic over $\mathfrak{R}$ using WDBAs given in [5] can be understood as an automata-based decision procedure for the first-order logic over $(\mathbb{Q}, Z, +, <)$ using WDBAs with the don't care sets I_r. Note that the ω-languages definable in the first-order logic over $(\mathbb{Q}, Z, +, <)$ are in general not ω-regular using the encoding in Definition 1.2. From this point of view, we see that WDBAs modulo don't care sets can describe non-ω-regular languages and in this case, they even have a canonical minimal form (Theorem 9). Analogously, WDBAs with the don't care sets DC_r can describe ω-regular languages that are not in the Borel class $F_\sigma \cap G_\delta$, which exactly captures the expressive power of WDBAs [18]. Furthermore, by Theorem 9, the ω-words in DC_r that have to be added to or removed from the ω-language are uniquely determined in order to obtain the minimal WDBA for the ω-language modulo the don't care set DC_r.

4   Quantification for the Reals

In this section, we give an automata construction for WDBAs that handles the quantification in the first-order logic over $\mathfrak{R}$ when using the don't care sets DC_r.

Roughly speaking, for the straightforward encoding, the existential quantification is done by eliminating the track of the quantified variable in the transitions of the WDBA.[3] Intuitively, this nondeterministic automaton guesses the digits of the quantified variable. As explained in [5], we can determinize this automaton by using the breakpoint construction for weak co-Büchi automata (see [14]). The construction for handling the existential quantification that we present in this subsection for the optimized encoding is also based on the breakpoint construction. However, the construction is more subtle because of the following problem: Assume that $\mathcal{A}$ is a WDBA for the formula $\varphi(x_1, \ldots, x_r)$, i.e., $L_\omega(\mathcal{A}) \equiv_{\mathsf{DC}_r} L(\varphi)$. Eliminating the track of the variable x_r results in a nondeterministic Büchi automaton that might accept ω-words $\alpha \notin \mathsf{DC}_{r-1}$ for which there is only an ω-word $\gamma \in \mathsf{DC}_1$ such that $(\alpha, \gamma) \in L_\omega(\mathcal{A})$. A WDBA for $\exists x_r \varphi$ must not accept such ω-words α. A concrete instance of this problem is given in the example:

Example 11. Consider again the formula $\varphi(x, y) := x \neq 0 \wedge x + y = 0$ and the WDBA in Figure 1(b) from Example 2. Eliminating the x-track, i.e., the

---

[3] Some additional work is needed for the sign bit, see, e.g., [6, 5] for details.

first track, yields a nondeterministic Büchi automaton that accepts the ω-word $0 \star 0^\omega$, since we can infinitely loop in state $q := \{3, 4, 5\}$ by reading the letter 0. However, $\mathfrak{R} \not\models \exists x \varphi[\langle\!\langle 0 \star 0^\omega \rangle\!\rangle]$. Here, the problem is that the only ω-word γ such that $(\gamma, 0 \star 0^\omega)$ is accepted by the WDBA in Figure 1(b) is the don't care word $1 \star 1^\omega$. On the one hand, for the ω-word $0 \star 0^\omega$ the state q has to be rejecting. On the other hand, for the ω-word $0 \star (10)^\omega$ the state q has to be accepting.

Before we present our construction, we remark that removing all don't care words from the ω-language of the given WDBA before applying the construction in [5] for handling the existential quantification does not work. The reason is that the resulting DBA is not necessarily *weak* and hence, we cannot longer apply the breakpoint construction after eliminating the track of the quantified variable.

Assume that $\mathcal{A} = (Q, \Sigma^r \cup \{\star\}, \delta, q_\mathrm{I}, F)$ is a WDBA for the formula φ with r free variables, i.e., $L_\omega(\mathcal{A}) \equiv_{\mathrm{DC}_r} L(\varphi)$. We divide the construction of the WDBA for $\exists x_i \varphi$ into two steps. First, we construct from $\mathcal{A}$ a co-DBA $\mathcal{B}$ that accepts an ω-language for $\exists x_i \varphi$, i.e., $\overline{L}_\omega(\mathcal{B}) \equiv_{\mathrm{DC}_{r-1}} L(\exists x_i \varphi)$. Second, we show that $\mathcal{B}$ can be easily turned into a WDBA. To simplify notation, we assume without loss of generality that $i = r$ and $L_\omega(\mathcal{A}) \subseteq \mathsf{V}_r$.

To define $\mathcal{B}$'s transition function, we need the following definitions. For $u \in \Sigma^+$ with $u(0) \in \{0, \varrho - 1\}$, we define

$$
\overline{u} := \begin{cases}
0^n & \text{if } u = (\varrho - 1)^n \text{ with } n > 0, \\
010^n & \text{if } u = 0(\varrho - 1)^n \text{ with } n \geq 0, \\
v(c + 1)0^n & \text{if } u = vc(\varrho - 1)^n \text{ with } v \in \Sigma^+, c \in \Sigma \setminus \{\varrho - 1\}, \text{ and } n \geq 0.
\end{cases}
$$

Note that $\langle\!\langle u(\varrho - 1)^n \star (\varrho - 1)^\omega \rangle\!\rangle = \langle\!\langle \overline{u}0^n \star 0^\omega \rangle\!\rangle$, for all $n \geq 0$ and $u \in \Sigma^+$ with $u(0) \in \{0, \varrho - 1\}$. We define the relation $M \subseteq Q \times Q$ by pMq iff $p \in F$ and for every $\alpha \in (\Sigma^{r-1})^\omega \setminus \mathrm{DC}_{r-1}$, it holds that $(\alpha, (\varrho - 1)^\omega) \in L_\omega(\mathcal{A}') \Rightarrow (\alpha, 0^\omega) \in L_\omega(\mathcal{A}_q)$, where $\mathcal{A}'$ is the WDBA $(Q, \Sigma^r \cup \{\star\}, \delta, p, \mathrm{SCC}(p))$.

Intuitively, the construction works as follows. As in the breakpoint construction, $\mathcal{B}$ has states of the form (R, S). Roughly speaking, in the first component we collect $\mathcal{A}$'s states that are reached by guessing the digits of the variable x_r. The second component checks whether we eventually stay in an accepting SCC of $\mathcal{A}$. In contrast to the breakpoint construction, R and S are not only subsets of Q but sets of pairs of states of $\mathcal{A}$. The reason for using pairs of states is the following. Assume that we reach the pair (R, S) from $\mathcal{B}$'s initial state by reading a finite prefix of an ω-word $\gamma \in \mathsf{V}_{r-1} \setminus \mathrm{DC}_{r-1}$. For $(p, q) \in R$, we have that p is reached by guessing a finite prefix of the digits of a real number for the quantified variable x_r. However, the guessed digits u could be a finite prefix of a don't care word $\alpha \in \mathrm{DC}_1 \cap \mathsf{V}_1$. Suppose that we visit p infinitely often when reading (γ, α). If p is accepting, $\mathcal{A}$ accepts (γ, α). However, since (γ, α) is a don't care word, $\langle\!\langle \alpha \rangle\!\rangle$ is not necessarily a real number such that $\mathfrak{R} \models \varphi[\langle\!\langle \gamma \rangle\!\rangle, \langle\!\langle \alpha \rangle\!\rangle]$. In order to detect such a case, we use the state q and the relation M. The state q is the state that is reached when guessing the corresponding digits for u of the ω-word $\beta \in \mathsf{V}_1 \setminus \mathrm{DC}_1$ such that $\langle\!\langle \alpha \rangle\!\rangle = \langle\!\langle \beta \rangle\!\rangle$. If pMq holds, then we know that $\mathfrak{R} \models \varphi[\langle\!\langle \gamma \rangle\!\rangle, \langle\!\langle \alpha \rangle\!\rangle]$, since $\langle\!\langle \alpha \rangle\!\rangle = \langle\!\langle \beta \rangle\!\rangle$ and $\mathcal{A}$ also accepts β. Hence, p is rightly an accepting state for the prefix of γ we have read so far. In the case where pMq does not hold, we have to treat p as a rejecting state.

Formally, $\mathcal{B}$ is the co-DBA $(\{q'_I\} \cup (K \times K), \Sigma^{r-1} \cup \{\star\}, \eta, q'_I, K \times \{\emptyset\})$, where $K := \mathcal{P}(Q \times Q)$, q'_I is a fresh state and η is defined as follows. For the initial state, we define $\eta(q'_I, b) := (\emptyset, \emptyset)$, for $b \notin \{0, \varrho-1\}^{r-1}$, and for $b \in \{0, \varrho-1\}^{r-1}$, we define $\eta(q'_I, b) := (I(b), \emptyset)$, where

$$I(b) := \left\{ \left(\hat{\delta}(q_I, (b^{|u|}, u)), \hat{\delta}(q_I, (b^{|\overline{u}|}, \overline{u}))\right) \,:\, u \in \Sigma^+ \text{ with } u(0) \in \{0, 1\} \right\}.$$

For a state $(R, S) \in K \times K$ and $b \in \Sigma^{r-1}$, we define

$$\eta((R, S), b) := \begin{cases} (R', R' \cap M) & \text{if } S = \emptyset, \\ (R', S' \cap M) & \text{if } S \neq \emptyset, \end{cases}$$

where

$$\begin{aligned}
R' &:= \left\{ \left(\delta(p, (b, \varrho-1)), \delta(q, (b, 0))\right) \,:\, (p, q) \in R \right\} \cup \\
&\quad \left\{ \left(\delta(p, (b, c)), \delta(p, (b, c+1))\right) \,:\, (p, q) \in R \text{ and } c \in \Sigma \setminus \{\varrho-1\} \right\}, \text{ and} \\
S' &:= \left\{ \left(\delta(p, (b, \varrho-1)), \delta(q, (b, 0))\right) \,:\, (p, q) \in S \right\} \cup \\
&\quad \left\{ \left(\delta(p, (b, c)), \delta(p, (b, c+1))\right) \,:\, (p, q) \in S \text{ and } c \in \Sigma \setminus \{\varrho-1\} \right\}.
\end{aligned}$$

Finally, $\eta((R, S), \star) := (R', R' \cap M)$, where $R' := \{(\delta(p, \star), \delta(q, \star)) \,:\, (p, q) \in R\}$.

Lemma 12. *It holds that* $\overline{L}_\omega(\mathcal{B}) \equiv_{\mathsf{DC}_{r-1}} L(\exists x_r \varphi)$.

An SCC of $\mathcal{B}$ might contain accepting and rejecting states. The next lemma shows that if an SCC of $\mathcal{B}$ contains accepting and rejecting states then we can make all states in this SCC accepting. Given this, it is easy to turn the co-DBA $\mathcal{B}$ into a WDBA $\mathcal{A}'$ for $L(\exists x_r \varphi)$, i.e., $L_\omega(\mathcal{A}') \equiv_{\mathsf{DC}_{r-1}} L(\exists x_r \varphi)$.

Lemma 13. *Let* $\psi(y_1, \ldots, y_s)$ *be a formula and let* $\mathcal{C} = (P, \Sigma^s \cup \{\star\}, \mu, p_I, E)$ *be a co-DBA with* $\overline{L}_\omega(\mathcal{C}) \equiv_{\mathsf{DC}_s} L(\psi)$. *If* $S \subseteq P$ *is an SCC with* $S \cap E \neq \emptyset$ *then* $\overline{L}_\omega(\mathcal{C}') \equiv_{\mathsf{DC}_s} L(\psi)$, *where* $\mathcal{C}'$ *is the co-DBA* $(P, \Sigma^s \cup \{\star\}, \mu, p_I, E \cup S)$.

The above given construction yields a WDBA that has $1 + 2^{2 \cdot |Q|^2}$ states. However, some of the states are not reachable from the initial state q'_I, e.g., the states $(R, S) \in K \times K$ with $S \not\subseteq R$ are never reachable from q'_I. Next, we briefly discuss the auxiliary computations involved in the construction.

For the transitions from the initial state q'_I, we need to compute the sets $I(b)$, for every $b \in \Sigma^{r-1}$. Computing $I(b)$ separately for each $b \in \Sigma^{r-1}$, yields an algorithm that is exponential in r and is not practical. The algorithm described in [6] for determining the initial transitions of DFAs for quantifying Presburger arithmetic formulas, can be adopted to our construction and it works well in practice, although it has exponential worst case complexity in r.

For computing the relation M, we define the WDBAs $\mathcal{G} := (Q, \Sigma^{r-1}, \delta_1, q_I, F)$ and $\mathcal{H} := (Q, \Sigma^{r-1}, \delta_2, q_I, F)$, where $\delta_1(q, b) := \delta(p, (b, \varrho-1))$ and $\delta_2(q, b) := \delta(p, (b, 0))$, for $q \in Q$ and $b \in \Sigma^{r-1}$. For states $p, q \in Q$, we have that pMq iff (1) $p \in F$ and (2) $L_\omega(\mathcal{G}') \cap L_\omega(\mathcal{H}_q)$ contains an ω-word not in DC_{r-1}, where $\mathcal{G}'$ is the WDBA $(Q, \Sigma^{r-1}, \delta_1, p, \mathrm{SCC}(p))$. Since the SCC of p consists of at most $|F|$ states, condition (2) can be checked in time $O(|Q| \cdot |F|)$, see §3.1 and §3.2. An upper bound for computing M is $O(|Q|^2 \cdot |F|^2)$, since the first component in M has to be a state in F.

5   Experimental Results

In this section, we report on experimental results obtained from our prototype implementation of an automata-based decision procedure for the first-order logic over $\mathfrak{R}$.[4] We want to point out that in our implementation we only used the don't care sets DC_r (Definition 3). We have carried out tests on two different classes of problems: (1) randomly generated formulas and (2) the iterative computation of the reachable states of infinite-state systems. In the later case, we mainly focus on the sizes of the automata, as our prototype is not intended to compete with optimized tools for solving the reachability problem.

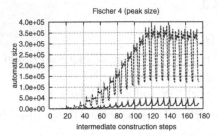 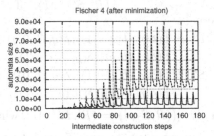

Fig. 3. Automata sizes encountered during the computation for Fischer's protocol with 4 processes. The solid (dashed) lines correspond to the optimized (straightforward) encoding. The intermediate construction steps correspond to the flows and jumps of the processes in Fischer's protocol. We obtain similar results for the other protocols.

Random Formulas. We have applied our prototype to randomly generated formulas. For a test set of 100 formulas with 4 variables with about 10 disjunctions and conjunctions each, the savings in terms of automata sizes encountered during the construction are observable (on average 8.4%), although moderate. Our new construction for the quantification generates larger automata (on average 40.1%), however, after normalization and minimization the resulting automata with don't care sets are smaller (on average 7.7%). Our prototype requires up to one order of magnitude more runtime for the quantification when using don't care words. When restricting the 4 variables to the integer domain, the savings due to the don't care set become more substantial (on average 48.5%), as every integer has encodings that are in the don't care set. In comparison to an implementation based on LASH [15] without don't cares, our prototype is faster. The marginal difference in performance on small quantifier free formulas grows rapidly when the formulas contain quantifiers or have more variables.

Reachability Analysis. Infinite-state systems, like systems with unbounded integers or linear hybrid automata can be analyzed symbolically in the first-order logic over $\mathfrak{R}$. We have analyzed the Bakery protocol, Fischer's protocol, and the

---

[4] Our prototype is publicly available online at http://www.informatik. uni-freiburg.de/~eisinger/research/rva.html.

	iterations	with don't cares			without don't cares		
		peak	final	runtime	peak	final	runtime
Fischer 2	9	238	53	43.98s	2,318	182	49.52s
Fischer 3	15	44,631	405	164.75s	90,422	2,045	184.59s
Fischer 4	21	51,676	4,377	2,739.58s	417,649	27,548	4,353.66s
Fischer 5	27	145,629	55,885	20,972.79s	1625,141	430,727	53,940.37s
Railroad	8	152,826	7,735	1,594.32s	365,004	9,411	1,080.24s
Bakery 2	30	107	-	52.42s	557	-	63.64s
Bakery 3	30	314	-	107.74s	2,010	-	121.09s
Bakery 4	30	909	-	201.41s	8,883	-	272.70s

Fig. 4. Iterations required to reach the fixpoint of the reachable state set for several infinite-state systems, construction times, and peak and final automata sizes. Note that the fixpoint for Bakery cannot be reached using our naive fixpoint computation.

railroad crossing example [11]. Using don't care words, the automata constructed during the iterative computation of the reachable states become smaller by an order of magnitude (see Figures 3 and 4). This saving can be explained by the following two observations. First, the formulas that describe the transitions of a system contain many variables (the formulas for Fischer's protocol with 5 processes have 34 variables). Note that the don't care sets contain more words if the formula contains many free variables. Second, the construction of the reachable state set requires a large number of automata constructions. Although the saving in a single automata construction might be small, the overall saving grows with the number of automata constructions.

6 Conclusions

We generalized the concept of *don't cares* for BDDs to automata and demonstrated that don't cares are effective in reducing the automata sizes. On the one hand, we were able to prove rather general results about don't cares sets, like the minimization of WDBAs. On the other hand, we presented an automata construction for the quantification in the first-order logic $\Re$, which depends on the used don't care set. We demonstrated the potential of don't cares by a prototype.

Related to our work is [2] on widening sets of integers that are represented by automata. In order to obtain always an overapproximation of a set, widening an automaton represented set only adds words to the language. In contrast, we allow words to be removed, and adding or removing don't care words still yields an exact automata-based representation of a set. Moreover, for the sets of vectors of reals, we used a don't care set for which the automata-based set representation is still unique. We want to point out that the widening method [2] is complementary to don't care words and hence, they can be combined in infinite-state model checkers that use an automata-based representation for the reachable states of a system. Analogously, don't care words are complementary to acceleration techniques like [7]. However, further work is needed in combining these techniques, since the automata constructions might need some adjustment to work also for don't care words (see, e.g., the automata construction in §4).

Future work also includes improving the mechanization of the automata construction for handling the existential quantification in the first-order logic over $\mathfrak{R}$, which is currently the bottleneck in our prototype. Another direction we want to pursue is to exploit don't cares further. For example, for carrying out the quantification of x in the second disjunct of the formula $\psi(\overline{y}) \vee \exists x \varphi(x, \overline{y})$, we can use the language of the automaton for ψ as a don't care set for making the automaton for φ smaller before we apply the construction for the existential quantification. Overall, we believe that don't care words have a large potential for making automata-based model checking more effective.

References

1. S. BARDIN, A. FINKEL, J. LEROUX, AND L. PETRUCCI, *FAST: Fast acceleration of symbolic transition systems*, in CAV'03, LNCS 2725, pp. 118–121.
2. C. BARTZIS AND T. BULTAN, *Widening arithmetic automata*, in CAV'04, LNCS 3114, pp. 321–333.
3. B. BOIGELOT, L. BRONNE, AND S. RASSART, *An improved reachability analysis method for strongly linear hybrid systems*, in CAV'97, LNCS 1254, pp. 167–178.
4. B. BOIGELOT, F. HERBRETEAU, AND S. JODOGNE, *Hybrid acceleration using real vector automata*, in CAV'03, LNCS 2725, pp. 193–205.
5. B. BOIGELOT, S. JODOGNE, AND P. WOLPER, *An effective decision procedure for linear arithmetic over the integers and reals*, ACM ToCL, 6 (2005), pp. 614–633.
6. B. BOIGELOT AND L. LATOUR, *Counting the solutions of Presburger equations without enumerating them*, TCS, 313 (2004), pp. 17–29.
7. B. BOIGELOT, A. LEGAY, AND P. WOLPER, *Omega-regular model checking*, in TACAS'04, LNCS 2988, pp. 561–575.
8. J. BÜCHI, *Weak second-order arithmetic and finite automata*, Zeitschrift der mathematischen Logik und Grundlagen der Mathematik, 6 (1960), pp. 66–92.
9. ———, *On a decision method in restricted second order arithmetic*, in Logic, Methodology and Philosophy of Science, Stanford University Press, 1962, pp. 1–11.
10. J. EISINGER AND F. KLAEDTKE, *Don't care words with an application to the automata-based approach for real addition*, Tech. Rep. 223, Institut für Informatik, Albert-Ludwigs-Universität Freiburg, 2006.
11. T. HENZINGER, *The theory of hybrid automata*, in LICS'96, pp. 278–292.
12. Y. HONG, P. A. BEEREL, J. R. BURCH, AND K. L. McMILLAN, *Safe BDD minimization using don't cares*, in DAC'97, ACM Press, pp. 208–213.
13. J. E. HOPCROFT, *An $n \log n$ algorithm for minimizing the states in a finite automaton*, in Theory of Machines and Computations, 1971, pp. 189–196.
14. O. KUPFERMAN AND M. VARDI, *Weak alternating automata are not that weak*, ACM ToCL, 2 (2001), pp. 408–429.
15. LASH, *The Liège Automata-based Symbolic Handler*. http://www.montefiore.ulg.ac.be/~boigelot/research/lash/.
16. C. LÖDING, *Efficient minimization of deterministic weak ω-automata*, IPL, 79 (2001), pp. 105–109.
17. K. L. McMILLAN, *Symbolic Model Checking*, Kluwer Academic Publishers, 1993.
18. L. STAIGER AND K. WAGNER, *Automatentheoretische und automatenfreie Charakterisierungen topologischer Klassen regulärer Folgenmengen*, Elektronische Informationsverarbeitung und Kybernetik, 10 (1974), pp. 379–392.
19. T. YAVUZ-KAHVECI, C. BARTZIS, AND T. BULTAN, *Action language verifier, extended*, in CAV'05, LNCS 3576, pp. 413–417.

A Fast Linear-Arithmetic Solver for DPLL(T)*

Bruno Dutertre and Leonardo de Moura

Computer Science Laboratory, SRI International,
333 Ravenswood Avenue, Menlo Park, CA 94025, USA
{bruno, demoura}@csl.sri.com

Abstract. We present a new Simplex-based linear arithmetic solver that can be integrated efficiently in the DPLL(T) framework. The new solver improves over existing approaches by enabling fast backtracking, supporting a priori simplification to reduce the problem size, and providing an efficient form of theory propagation. We also present a new and simple approach for solving strict inequalities. Experimental results show substantial performance improvements over existing tools that use other Simplex-based solvers in DPLL(T) decision procedures. The new solver is even competitive with state-of-the-art tools specialized for the difference logic fragment.

1 Introduction

Decision procedures for quantifier-free linear arithmetic determine whether a boolean combination of linear equalities, inequalities, and disequalities is satisfiable. Several tools for solving this problem rely on the DPLL(T) approach [1]: they combine boolean satisfiability solvers based on the Davis-Putnam-Logemann-Loveland (DPLL) procedure, and arithmetic solvers capable of deciding the satisfiability of conjunctions of linear constraints. Results of a first satisfiability modulo theories (SMT) competition, comparing several of these tools, are presented in [2]. Several tools (e.g., Barcelogic [21] or Slice [20]) are specialized for the *difference-logic* fragment of linear arithmetic and rely on graph algorithms. For general linear arithmetic, existing tools rely either on Fourier-Motzkin elimination [3] (used by CVClite [4], CVC [5], SVC [6]) or on Simplex methods [7] (used by MathSat [8], ICS [9], Simplics, Yices, ARIO [10]). Fourier-Motzkin elimination explodes on many problems and Simplex is generally superior.

The common methods for integrating a Simplex solver with DPLL rely on incremental versions of Simplex such as described in [11,12,13,14]. A tableau is constructed and updated incrementally: rows are added as DPLL proceeds and are later removed when DPLL backtracks. These frequent addition and removal of rows and the related bookkeeping have a significant cost. For example, backtracking may require pivoting operations. This paper presents a simpler and more efficient solver that considerably reduces this overhead. The approach relies on transforming the original formula Φ into

---

* This material is based upon work supported by the Defense Advanced Research Projects Agency (DARPA) under Contract No. NBCHD030010. Any opinions, findings, and conclusions or recommendations expressed in this material are those of the authors and do not necessarily reflect the views of DARPA or the Department of Interior National Business Center (DOI-NBC).

T. Ball and R.B. Jones (Eds.): CAV 2006, LNCS 4144, pp. 81–94, 2006.
© Springer-Verlag Berlin Heidelberg 2006

an equisatisfiable Φ' such that the satisfiability of Φ' is decided by solving a series of problems of the form

$$\text{find } x \in \mathbb{R}^n \text{ such that } Ax = 0 \text{ and } l_i \leq x_i \leq u_i \text{ for } i = 1, \ldots, n,$$

where the matrix A is fixed and l_i and u_i are bounds on x_i that may vary with each problem. Variants of Simplex can efficiently solve problems in this form. Section 4 presents such a variant designed to be efficient in the DPPL(T) context, and Section 5 shows how to extend it to problems with strict inequalities. Since A is fixed, no row is ever added or removed from the tableau, and backtracking is very cheap. The new solver has additional advantages: it is possible to simplify the problem a priori by eliminating irrelevant variables, and a simple but useful form of theory propagation can be implemented cheaply.

2 Background

Given a quantifier-free theory T, a T-*solver* is a procedure for deciding whether a finite set of atoms of T is satisfiable. If Φ is a formula built by boolean combination of atoms of T, then the satisfiability of Φ can be decided by combining a boolean satisfiability solver and a T-solver. The DPLL(T) approach is an efficient method for such integrations that relies on the DPLL procedure.

2.1 Solvers for DPPL(T)

In the DPLL(T) framework, a T-solver maintains a state that is an internal representation of the atoms asserted so far. This solver must provide operations for updating the state by asserting new atoms, checking whether the state is consistent, and backtracking. Optionally, the solver may also implement *theory propagation*, that is, identify atoms that are implied by the current state. To interact with the DPLL search, the solver must produce *explanations* for conflicts and propagated atoms. In an inconsistent state S, an explanation is any inconsistent subset of the atoms asserted in S. Similarly, an explanation for an implied atom γ is a subset Γ of the asserted atoms such that $\Gamma \models \gamma$. An explanation Γ is *minimal* if no proper subset of Γ is an explanation.

The solver is assumed initialized for a fixed formula Φ and we denote by $\mathcal{A}$ the set of atoms that occur in Φ. The set of atoms asserted so far is denoted by α. The solver also maintains a stack of *checkpoints* that mark consistent states to which the solver can backtrack. We assume that a T-solver implements the following API.[1]

- *Assert*(γ) asserts atom γ in the current state. It returns either ok or unsat$\langle \Gamma \rangle$ where Γ is a subset of α. In the first case, γ is inserted into α. In the latter case, $\alpha \cup \{\gamma\}$ is inconsistent and Γ is the explanation.
- *Check*() checks whether α is consistent. If so, it returns ok, otherwise it returns unsat$\langle \Gamma \rangle$. As previously $\Gamma \subseteq \alpha$ is an explanation for the inconsistency. A new checkpoint is created when ok is returned.

---

[1] This is similar to the API proposed in [1].

- *Backtrack*() backtracks to the consistent state represented by the checkpoint on the top of the stack.
- *Propagate*() performs theory propagation. It returns a set $\{\langle \Gamma_1, \gamma_1 \rangle, \ldots, \langle \Gamma_t, \gamma_t \rangle\}$ where $\Gamma_i \subseteq \alpha$ and $\gamma_i \in \mathcal{A} \setminus \alpha$. For every pair $\langle \Gamma_i, \gamma_i \rangle$ produced, γ_i is an atom not already asserted that is implied by Γ_i, and Γ_i is a subset of α.

Assert must be sound but is not required to be complete: *Assert*(γ) may return ok even if $\alpha \cup \{\gamma\}$ is inconsistent. Similarly, *Propagate* must be sound but does not have to be exhaustive. On the other hand, function *Check* is required to be sound and complete: if *Check*() = ok then α must be consistent. This model enables several atoms to be asserted in a single "batch", using several calls to *Assert* followed by a single call to *Check*. *Assert* can then implement only inexpensive (and possibly incomplete) consistency checks while *Check* implements a complete (and possibly expensive) consistency-checking procedure. The state S' after executing *Backtrack* must be logically equivalent to the state S when the checkpoint was created, but S' may be different from S.

2.2 Existing Simplex Solvers for DPLL(T)

A quantifier-free linear arithmetic formula is a first-order formula whose atoms are either propositional variables of equalities, disequalities, or inequalities of the form

$$a_1 x_1 + \ldots + a_n x_n \bowtie b,$$

where $a_1, \ldots, a_n$ and b are rational numbers, $x_1, \ldots, x_n$ are real (or integer) variables, and $\bowtie$ is one of the operators $=$, $\leq$, $<$, $>$, $\geq$, or $\neq$. In the DPLL(T) framework, deciding the satisfiability of such formulas requires a linear-arithmetic solver. A common approach is to use incremental forms of Simplex similar to the algorithms described in [11,12,13,14]. Tools based on this approach include our own tools, Yices and Simplics, and others such as MathSat [8].

In these algorithms, a solver state includes a Simplex tableau that is derived from all equalities and inequalities asserted so far. A tableau can be written as a set of equalities of the form

$$x_i = b_i + \sum_{x_j \in \mathcal{N}} a_{ij} x_j, \quad x_i \in \mathcal{B} \tag{1}$$

where $\mathcal{B}$ and $\mathcal{N}$ are disjoint sets of variables. Elements of $\mathcal{B}$ and $\mathcal{N}$ are called *basic* and *nonbasic* variables, respectively. Additional constraints are imposed on some variables of $\mathcal{B} \cup \mathcal{N}$. So-called *slack variables* are required to be non-negative, and the tableau may also contain *zero variables*, which are all implicitly equal to 0. Zero variables are used to generate explanations (cf. [11]).

A pivoting operation $pivot(x_r, x_s)$ swaps a basic variable x_r and a nonbasic variable x_s such that $a_{rs} \neq 0$. After pivoting, x_s becomes basic and x_r becomes nonbasic. The tableau is updated by replacing equation $x_r = b_r + \sum_{x_j \in \mathcal{N}} a_{rj} x_j$ with

$$x_s = -\frac{b_r}{a_{rs}} + \frac{x_r}{a_{rs}} - \sum_{x_j \in \mathcal{N} \setminus \{x_s\}} \frac{a_{rj} x_j}{a_{rs}} \tag{2}$$

and then equation (2) is used to eliminate x_s from the rest of the tableau by substitution.

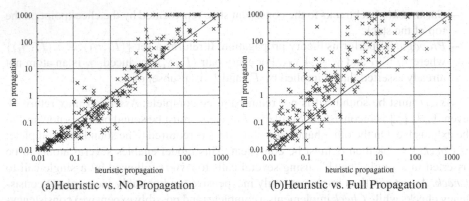

(a)Heuristic vs. No Propagation   (b)Heuristic vs. Full Propagation

Fig. 1. Impact of theory propagation in Simplics

Assertion of equalities or inequalities adds new equations to the tableau. For example, let γ be an atom of the form $t \geq 0$ where t is an arithmetic term. The operation $Assert(\gamma)$ involves three steps. First, γ is normalized by substituting any basic variable x_i occurring in t with the term $b_i + \sum_{x_j \in \mathcal{N}} a_{ij}x_j$. The solver checks then whether the resulting inequality $t' \geq 0$ is satisfiable. This step uses the Simplex algorithm to maximize t' subject to the tableau constraints. If t' has a maximum M and M is negative, then $t' \geq 0$ is not satisfiable and an explanation is generated. Otherwise, a fresh slack variable s_k is created and a row of the form $s_k = t''$ is added to the tableau. Some bookkeeping is required to record that s_k is nonnegative and is associated with atom γ. Processing of equalities and strict inequalities follows the same general principles. Backtracking removes rows from the tableau. For example, to retract γ, the solver retrieves the slack variable s_k associated with γ. If s_k is a basic variable in the current state then the corresponding equation is removed from the tableau. Otherwise, a pivoting operation is applied first to make s_k basic.

Disequalities are treated separately since they cannot be incorporated into the tableau. When a disequality $t \neq 0$ is asserted, it is first normalized as before, and then the solver must check whether the current tableau implies $t = 0$. This can be implemented via the *zero-detection procedure* described in [11] for example.

2.3 Performance

Assertions and backtracking have a significant cost in solvers based on incremental Simplex algorithms. Part of this cost (e.g., the pivoting involved in *Assert* operations) cannot be avoided, but there is also significant overhead in the frequent additions and removals of rows, creations and deletions of slack variables, and associated bookkeeping. The remainder of the paper describes a different type of solver, still based on the Simplex method, which significantly reduces this overhead. The new approach is simpler and more uniform than incremental Simplex. It is also more economical as irrelevant variables can be eliminated a priori and fewer slack variables are necessary.

Some of the simplifications are based on lessons we learned from experiments with our previous tools Simplics and Yices:[2]

---

[2] Both use incremental Simplex and zero detection.

- *Minimal explanations are critical.* Dramatic improvements were observed when comparing Simplics and Yices, which generate minimal explanations, and their predecessor ICS, which does not.
- *Theory propagation is useful if it can be done cheaply.* Figure 1 compares the results of Simplics on the real-arithmetic subset of the SMT-LIB benchmarks [15] using different levels of theory propagation. By default, Simplics uses a heuristic form of propagation that is relatively inexpensive but incomplete (no pivoting is used). This is compared in Figure 1(a) with Simplics running with no propagation at all, and in Figure 1(b) with Simplics running with complete propagation (where pivoting is used). On these benchmarks, full propagation is just too expensive, but no propagation is also a poor choice. Heuristic propagation is clearly superior.
- *Zero detection is expensive and can be avoided.* On a few examples in the SMT-LIB benchmarks, Simplics spends as much as 30% of its time in the zero-detection procedure. A simpler alternative is to rewrite a disequality $t \neq 0$ as the disjunction of two strict inequalities $(t < 0) \vee (t > 0)$. This transformation may seem wasteful since it may entail additional case splits, but it works well in practice. After this transformation, Simplics can solve six problems of the SMT-LIB benchmarks that it cannot solve otherwise.

3 Preprocessing

Incremental Simplex algorithms can be avoided by rewriting a linear arithmetic formula Φ into an equisatisfiable formula of the form $\Phi_A \wedge \Phi'$, where Φ_A is a conjunction of linear equalities, and all the atoms occurring in Φ' are *elementary atoms* of the form $y \bowtie b$, where y is a variable and b is a rational constant. The transformation is straightforward. For example, let Φ be the formula

$$x \geq 0 \wedge (x + y \leq 2 \vee x + 2y - z \geq 6) \wedge (x + y = 2 \vee x + 2y - z > 4).$$

We introduce two variables s_1 and s_2 and rewrite Φ to $\Phi_A \wedge \Phi'$ as follows.

$$(s_1 = x + y \wedge s_2 = x + 2y - z) \wedge$$
$$(x \geq 0 \wedge (s_1 \leq 2 \vee s_2 \geq 6) \wedge (s_1 = 2 \vee s_2 > 4))$$

Clearly, this new formula and Φ are equisatisfiable. In general, starting from a formula Φ, the transformation introduces a new variable s_i for every linear term t_i that is not already a variable and occurs as the left side of an atom $t_i \bowtie b$ of Φ. Then Φ_A is the conjunction of all the equalities $s_i = t_i$ and Φ' is obtained by replacing every term t_i by the corresponding s_i in Φ.

Let $x_1, \ldots, x_n$ be the arithmetic variables of $\Phi_A \wedge \Phi'$, that is, all the variables originally in Φ and m-additional variables $s_1, \ldots, s_m$ introduced by the previous transformation ($m \leq n$). Then formula Φ_A can be written in matrix form as $Ax = 0$, where A is a fixed $m \times n$ rational matrix and x is a vector in $\mathbb{R}^n$. The rows of A are linearly independent so A has rank m. Checking whether Φ is satisfiable amounts to finding an x such that $Ax = 0$ and x satisfies Φ'. In other words, checking the satisfiability of Φ in linear arithmetic is equivalent to checking the satisfiability of Φ' in *linear arithmetic modulo* $Ax = 0$. Since all atoms of Φ' are elementary, this requires a solver for deciding the consistency of a set of elementary atoms Γ modulo the constraints $Ax = 0$. If Γ contains only equalities and (nonstrict) inequalities, this reduces to searching for $x \in \mathbb{R}^n$ such that

$$Ax = 0 \text{ and } l_j \leq x_j \leq u_j \text{ for } j = 1, \ldots, n \qquad (3)$$

where l_j is either $-\infty$ or a rational number, and u_j is either $+\infty$ or a rational number.

Since the elementary atoms of Φ' are known in advance, we can immediately simplify the constraints $Ax = 0$ by removing any variable x_i that does not occur in any elementary atom of Φ'. This is done by Gaussian elimination. In practice, this presimplification can reduce the matrix size significantly (cf. [16]).

The variables s_i introduced during the transformation play the same role as the slack variables of standard Simplex. However, the presence of both lower and upper bounds is beneficial. For example, incremental Simplex algorithms need two slack variables to represent a constraint such as $1 \leq x + 3y \leq 4$, whereas a single s_k is sufficient if the general form (3) is used. Overall, rewriting Φ into $\Phi_A \wedge \Phi'$ and relying on the general form leads to problems with fewer variables than the algorithms discussed previously.

4   Basic Solver

We first describe a basic solver that handles equalities and nonstrict inequalities with real variables. Extensions to strict inequalities and integer variables are presented in the next sections. The basic solver decides the satisfiability of problems in form (3) and implements the API of Section 2.1 for integration with a DPLL-based SAT solver.

The solver state includes a tableau derived from the constraint matrix A. We will write such a tableau in the form:

$$x_i = \sum_{x_j \in \mathcal{N}} a_{ij} x_j \quad x_i \in \mathcal{B},$$

where $\mathcal{B}$ and $\mathcal{N}$ denote the set of basic and nonbasic variables, respectively.[3] Since all rows of this tableau are linear combinations of rows of the original matrix A, the equality $x_i = \sum_{x_j \in \mathcal{N}} a_{ij} x_j$ is satisfied by any x such that $Ax = 0$.

In addition to this tableau, the solver state stores upper and lower bounds l_i and u_i for every variable x_i and a mapping β that assigns a rational value $\beta(x_i)$ to every variable x_i. The bounds on nonbasic variables are always satisfied by β, that is, the following invariant is maintained

$$\forall x_j \in \mathcal{N}, \ l_j \leq \beta(x_j) \leq u_j. \qquad (4)$$

Furthermore, β satisfies the constraint $Ax = 0$. In the initial state, $l_j = -\infty, u_j = +\infty$, and $\beta(x_j) = 0$ for all j.

Figure 2 describes two auxiliary procedures that modify β. Procedure *update*(x_i, v) sets the value of a nonbasic variable x_i to v and adjusts the value of all basic variables so that all equations remain satisfied. Procedure *pivotAndUpdate*(x_i, x_j, v) applies pivoting to the basic variable x_i and the nonbasic variable x_j; it also sets the value of x_i to v and adjusts the values of all basic variables to keep all equations satisfied.

---

[3] This is the same as (1) with $b_i = 0$ for all $x_i \in \mathcal{B}$.

procedure update(x_i, v)
   for each $x_j \in \mathcal{B}$, $\beta(x_j) := \beta(x_j) + a_{ji}(v - \beta(x_i))$
   $\beta(x_i) := v$

procedure pivotAndUpdate(x_i, x_j, v)
   $\theta := \frac{v - \beta(x_i)}{a_{ij}}$
   $\beta(x_i) := v$
   $\beta(x_j) := \beta(x_j) + \theta$
   for each $x_k \in \mathcal{B} \setminus \{x_i\}$, $\beta(x_k) := \beta(x_k) + a_{kj}\theta$
   pivot(x_i, x_j)

Fig. 2. Auxiliary procedures

4.1 Main Algorithm

The main procedure of our algorithm is based on the dual Simplex and relies on Bland's pivot-selection rule to ensure termination. It relies on a total order on the variables. Assuming an assignment β that satisfies the previous invariants, but where $l_i \leq \beta(x_i) \leq u_i$ may not hold for some basic variables x_i, procedure *Check* searches for a new β that satisfies all constraints. The procedure is shown in Figure 3. It either terminates with a new assignment and basis that satisfy all lower and upper bounds (line 4), or finds the constraints to be unsatisfiable (lines 8 and 13). The body of the main loop selects a basic variable x_i that does not satisfy its bounds (line 3). If x_i is below l_i, then it looks for a variable x_j in the row $x_i = \sum_{x_j \in \mathcal{N}} a_{ij}x_j$ that can compensate the gap in x_i (lines 6-7). If no such x_j exists the problem is unsatisfiable (line 8) because the value of x_i is maximal and is below the lower bound l_i. Otherwise, the procedure pivots x_i and x_j, and x_i is set to l_i (line 9). The case where x_i is above its upper bound (lines 10-14) is symmetrical.

The following property implies the correctness of *Check*; a proof is given in [16].

Theorem 1. *Procedure Check always terminates.*

4.2 Generating Explanations

An inconsistency may be detected by *Check* at line 8 or 13. Let us assume a conflict is detected at line 8. There is then a basic variable x_i such that $\beta(x_i) < l_i$ and for every nonbasic variable x_j we have $a_{ij} > 0 \Rightarrow \beta(x_j) \geq u_j$ and $a_{ij} < 0 \Rightarrow \beta(x_j) \leq l_j$. Let $\mathcal{N}^+ = \{x_j \in \mathcal{N} \mid a_{ij} > 0\}$ and $\mathcal{N}^- = \{x_j \in \mathcal{N} \mid a_{ij} < 0\}$. Since β satisfies all bounds on nonbasic variables, we have $\beta(x_j) = l_j$ for every $x_j \in \mathcal{N}^-$ and $\beta(x_j) = u_j$ for every $x_j \in \mathcal{N}^+$. It follows that

$$\beta(x_i) = \sum_{x_j \in \mathcal{N}} a_{ij}\beta(x_j) = \sum_{x_j \in \mathcal{N}^+} a_{ij}u_j + \sum_{x_j \in \mathcal{N}^-} a_{ij}l_j.$$

The equation $x_i = \sum_{x_j \in \mathcal{N}} a_{ij}x_j$ holds for any x such that $Ax = 0$. Therefore, for any such x, we have

$$\beta(x_i) - x_i = \sum_{x_j \in \mathcal{N}^+} a_{ij}(u_j - x_j) + \sum_{x_j \in \mathcal{N}^-} a_{ij}(l_j - x_j),$$

```
1. procedure Check()
2.   loop
3.     select the smallest basic variable xᵢ such that β(xᵢ) < lᵢ or β(xᵢ) > uᵢ
4.     if there is no such xᵢ then return satisfiable
5.     if β(xᵢ) < lᵢ then
6.       select the smallest nonbasic variable xⱼ such that
7.         (aᵢⱼ > 0 and β(xⱼ) < uⱼ) or (aᵢⱼ < 0 and β(xⱼ) > lⱼ)
8.       if there is no such xⱼ then return unsatisfiable
9.       pivotAndUpdate(xᵢ, xⱼ, lᵢ)
10.    if β(xᵢ) > uᵢ then
11.      select the smallest nonbasic variable xⱼ such that
12.        (aᵢⱼ < 0 and β(xⱼ) < uⱼ) or (aᵢⱼ > 0 and β(xⱼ) > lⱼ)
13.      if there is no such xⱼ then return unsatisfiable
14.      pivotAndUpdate(xᵢ, xⱼ, uᵢ)
15.  end loop
```

Fig. 3. Check procedure

from which one can derive the following implication:

$$\bigwedge_{x_j \in \mathcal{N}^+} x_j \le u_j \;\wedge\; \bigwedge_{x_j \in \mathcal{N}^-} l_j \le x_j \;\Rightarrow\; x_i \le \beta(x_i).$$

Since $\beta(x_i) < l_i$, this is inconsistent with $l_i \le x_i$. The explanation for the conflict is then the following set of elementary atoms:

$$\Gamma = \{x_j \le u_j \mid j \in \mathcal{N}^+\} \cup \{x_j \ge l_j \mid j \in \mathcal{N}^-\} \cup \{x_i \ge l_i\}.$$

It is easy to see that Γ is minimal. Explanations for conflicts at line 13 are generated in the same way.

4.3 Assertion Procedures

The *Assert* function relies on two procedures shown in Figure 4 for updating the bounds l_i and u_i. Procedure *AssertUpper*($x_i \le c_i$) has no effect if $u_i \le c_i$ and returns unsatisfiable if $c_i < l_i$; otherwise the current upper bound on x_i is set to c_i. If variable x_i is nonbasic, then β is updated to maintain invariant (4). If an immediate conflict is detected at line 3 then generating a minimal explanation is straightforward.

Procedure *AssertLower*($x_i \ge c_i$) does the same thing for the lower bound. An equality $x_i = c_i$ is asserted by calling both *AssertUpper* and *AssertLower*.

4.4 Backtracking

Efficient backtracking is important since the number of backtracks is often very large. In our approach, backtracking can be efficiently implemented. We just need to save the value of u_i (l_i) on a stack before it is updated by the procedure *AssertUpper* (*AssertLower*). This information is used to restore the old bounds when backtracking is performed. Backtracking does not require saving the successive βs on a stack. Only

1. **procedure** AssertUpper($x_i \leq c_i$)
2.   **if** $c_i \geq u_i$ **then return** *satisfiable*
3.   **if** $c_i < l_i$ **then return** *unsatisfiable*
4. $u_i := c_i$
5.   **if** x_i is a nonbasic variable and $\beta(x_i) > c_i$ **then** update(x_i, c_i)
6.   **return** *ok*

1. **procedure** AssertLower($x_i \geq c_i$)
2.   **if** $c_i \leq l_i$ **then return** *satisfiable*
3.   **if** $c_i > u_i$ **then return** *unsatisfiable*
4. $l_i := c_i$
5.   **if** x_i is a nonbasic variable and $\beta(x_i) < c_i$ **then** update(x_i, c_i)
6.   **return** *ok*

Fig. 4. Assertion procedures

one assignment β needs to be stored, namely, the one corresponding to the last success-ful *Check*. After a successful *Check*, the assignment β is a model for the current set of constraints and for the set of constraints asserted at any previous checkpoint. Since no pivoting or other expensive operation is used, backtracking is very cheap.

4.5 Theory Propagation

Given a set of elementary atoms $\mathcal{A}$ from the formula Φ', then *unate propagation* is very cheap to implement. For example, if bound $x_i \geq c_i$ has been asserted then any unas-signed atom of $\mathcal{A}$ of the form $x_i \geq c'$ with $c' < c_i$ is immediately implied. Similarly, the negation of any atom $x_i \leq u$ with $u < c_i$ is implied. This type of propagation is useful in practice. It occurs frequently in several SMT-LIB benchmarks.

Another method is based on *bound refinement*. Given a row of a tableau, such as $x_i = \sum_{x_j \in \mathcal{N}} a_{ij} x_j$, one can derive a lower or upper bound on x_i from the lower or upper bounds on the nonbasic variables x_j. These computed bounds may imply unas-signed elementary atoms with variable x_i. This is a heuristic technique as the computed bounds may be weaker than the current bounds asserted on x_i (for example, the com-puted bounds may be $-\infty$ or $+\infty$). However, bound refinement is quite general. It is applicable with any equality $a_1 x_1 + \ldots + a_n x_n = 0$ derived by linear combination of rows of A, not just with rows of a tableau.

4.6 Example

Figure 5 illustrates the algorithm on a small example. Each row represents a state. The columns contain the tableaux, bounds, and assignments. The first row contains the ini-tial state. Suppose $x \leq -4$ is asserted. Then the value of x must be adjusted, since $\beta_0(x) > -4$. Since s_1 and s_2 depend on x, their values are also modified. No pivoting is required since the basic variables do not have bounds, so $A_1 = A_0$. Next, $x \geq -8$ is asserted. Since $\beta_1(x)$ satisfies this bound, nothing changes: $A_2 = A_1$ and $\beta_2 = \beta_1$.

$A_0 = \begin{cases} s_1 = -x + y \\ s_2 = x + y \end{cases}$		$\beta_0 = (x \mapsto 0, y \mapsto 0, s_1 \mapsto 0, s_2 \mapsto 0)$
$A_1 = A_0$	$x \leq -4$	$\beta_1 = (x \mapsto -4, y \mapsto 0, s_1 \mapsto 4, s_2 \mapsto -4)$
$A_2 = A_1$	$-8 \leq x \leq -4$	$\beta_2 = \beta_1$
$A_3 = \begin{cases} y = x + s_1 \\ s_2 = 2x + s_1 \end{cases}$	$-8 \leq x \leq -4$ $s_1 \leq 1$	$\beta_3 = (x \mapsto -4, y \mapsto -3, s_1 \mapsto 1, s_2 \mapsto -7)$

Fig. 5. Example

Next, $s_1 \leq 1$ is asserted. The current value of s_1 does not satisfy this bound, so *Check* must be invoked. *Check* pivots s_1 and y to decrease s_1. The resulting state S_3 is shown in the last row; all constraints are satisfied.

If $s_2 \geq -3$ is asserted in S_3 and *Check* is called then an inconsistency is detected: Tableau A_2 does not allow s_2 to increase since both x and s_1 are at their upper bound. Therefore, $s_2 \geq -3$ is inconsistent with state S_3.

5   Strict Inequalities

The previous method generalizes to strict inequalities using a simple observation.

Lemma 1. *A set of linear arithmetic literals Γ containing strict inequalities $S = \{p_1 > 0, \ldots, p_n > 0\}$ is satisfiable iff there exists a rational number $\delta > 0$ such that $\Gamma_\delta = (\Gamma \cup S_\delta) \setminus S$ is satisfiable, where $S_\delta = \{p_1 \geq \delta, \ldots, p_n \geq \delta\}$.*

This lemma says that we can replace all strict inequalities by nonstrict ones if a small enough δ is known. Rather than computing an explicit value for δ, we treat it symbolically, as an *infinitesimal parameter*. Bounds and variable assignments now range over the set $\mathbb{Q}_\delta$ of pairs of rationals. A pair (c, k) of $\mathbb{Q}_\delta$ is denoted by $c + k\delta$ and the following operations and comparison are defined in $\mathbb{Q}_\delta$:

$$(c_1, k_1) + (c_1, k_2) \equiv (c_1 + c_2, k_1 + k_2)$$
$$a \times (c, k) \equiv (a \times c, a \times k)$$
$$(c_1, k_1) \leq (c_2, k_2) \equiv (c_1 < c_2) \vee (c_1 = c_2 \wedge k_1 \leq k_2),$$

where a is a rational. Strict bounds in $\mathbb{Q}$ are converted to nonstrict bounds in $\mathbb{Q}_\delta$: inequality $x_i > l_i$ is converted to $x_i \geq l_i + \delta$, and $x_i < u_i$ is converted to $x_i \leq u_i - \delta$. Then all updates to β used in the previous algorithm can be performed in $\mathbb{Q}_\delta$. The matrix A does not change; all its coefficients are rational numbers.

By this process, a problem S with strict bounds in the rational is converted into a problem S' in the general form (3) but where the bounds l_i and u_i, and the variables x_i are elements of $\mathbb{Q}_\delta$. If an assignment β' satisfies S' then it can be converted into a rational assignment β that satisfies S. This relies on substituting the symbolic parameter δ with a small enough positive rational number $\delta_0 \in \mathbb{Q}$, which can always be done since there is a finite number of inequalities in S' (cf. [16]). If S' is unsatisfiable in $\mathbb{Q}_\delta$, then by Lemma 1, S is also unsatisfiable in the rationals.

6 Extensions

The previous solver is sound and complete for the reals. If some or all of the variables x_i are required to be integer, the algorithm is not complete. Nothing ensures that the assignment β constructed by *Check* gives an integer value to integer variables. To be complete in the integer or mixed integer case, we employ a *branch and cut* strategy, that is, the combination of branch-and-bound with a cutting plane generation algorithm [17,18]. The branch-and-bound algorithm works when problems are solved in $\mathbb{Q}_\delta$ rather than $\mathbb{Q}$. In other words, it can be used when strict inequalities are present. The cutting-plane method we use is based on mixed integer Gomory cuts. Such a cutting-plane algorithm is critical as it dramatically accelerates the convergence of branch-and-cut in several cases.

Also, it is possible to integrate the linear-arithmetic solver presented in this paper with solvers for other theories. The simplest method is to perform case-splits on equalities between variables that are shared between different theories. In most cases, the number of such shared variables is small in comparison with the total number of variables and this method is quite efficient. This approach is described in detail at [19]. It can be extended with an opportunistic equality-propagation method [16].

7 Experiments

Figure 6 compares a prototype SMT solver that uses the previous algorithms with other tools that participated in last year's SMT competition. The comparison uses all the SMT-LIB benchmarks in the QF_RDL (real difference logic), QF_IDL (integer difference logic), QF_LRA (linear real arithmetic), and QF_LIA (linear integer arithmetic) divisions. The experiments were conducted on identical PCs, all equipped with a 32bit Pentium 4 processor running at 3 GHz. The timeout was set to 1 hour and the memory usage was limited to 1 GB. With these timing and memory constraints, running all the benchmarks required approximately 60 CPU days.

Each point on the graphs represents a benchmark: + denotes a difference logic problem and × denotes a problem outside the difference-logic fragment. The axes correspond to the CPU time taken by the new solver (y-axis) or the other solver (x-axis) on each benchmark. CPU times are measured in seconds. Points below the diagonal are then SMT-LIB benchmarks where our new solver is faster. Points on the leftmost vertical edge are problems where a solver aborted, typically by running out of memory. The graphs comparing our new solver with Barcelogic and Simplics have fewer points, because Barcelogic supports only difference logic and Simplics does not support integer problems.

Table 1 summarizes the results. For each tool, it lists the number of instances solved and unsolved, and the total runtime. As can be seen, the new algorithm largely outperforms the other solvers. It is even faster on problems in the difference logic fragment

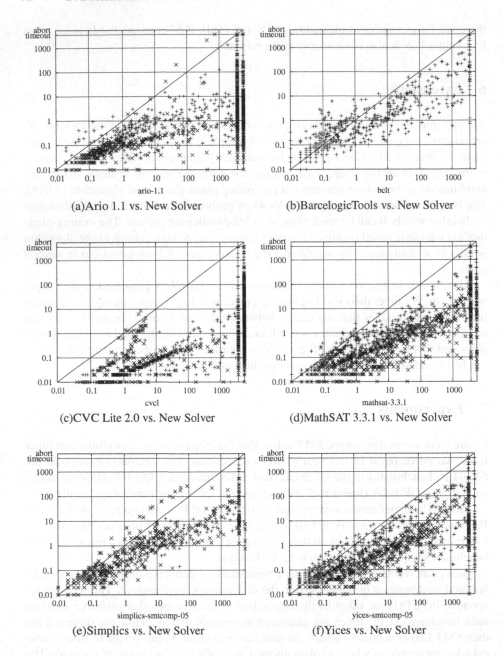

Fig. 6. Experimental results

than tools that are specialized for this fragment. The performance improvement is due to efficient backtracking and to the presimplification enabled by our approach, efficient theory propagation based on bound refinement also has a big impact.

Table 1. Experimental results: Summary

	sat	unsat	failed	time (secs)
Ario 1.1	186	640	517	1218371
BarcelogicTools	153	417	92	401842
CVC Lite	117	454	772	1193747
MathSAT 3.3.1	330	779	234	739533
Yices	358	756	229	702129
Simplics	240	351	110	476940
New Solver	**412**	**869**	**62**	**267198**

8 Conclusion

We have presented a new Simplex-based solver designed for efficiently solving SMT problems involving linear arithmetic. The main features of the new approach include the possibility to presimplify the input problem by eliminating variables, a reduction in the number of slack variables, and fast backtracking. A simple but useful form of theory propagation can also be implemented cheaply. Another result of the paper is a simple approach for solving strict inequalities that does not require modification of the basic Simplex algorithm. This approach is more generally applicable to other forms of solvers, such as graph-based solvers for difference logic.

Experimental results show that the new Simplex-based solver outperforms the most competitive solvers from SMT-COMP'05, including specialized solvers on difference logic problems.

Applications for the algorithm presented in this paper go beyond SMT. We are currently extending the solver to support a form of weighted MAX-SMT, that is, the search for an assignment to an SMT problem that maximizes a linear objective function. This MAX-SMT solver will be integrated to SRI's CALO system[4], as part of a module that combines learning and deductive algorithms.

References

1. Ganzinger, H., Hagen, G., Nieuwenhuis, R., Oliveras, A., Tinelli, C.: DPLL(T): Fast Decision Procedures. In Alur, R., Peled, D., eds.: Int. Conference on Computer Aided Verification (CAV'04). Volume 3114 of LNCS., Springer (2004) 175–188
2. Barrett, C., de Moura, L., Stump, A.: Design and Results of the 1st Satisfiability Modulo Theories Competition (SMT-COMP 2005). To appear in Journal of Automated Reasoning (2006)
3. Dantzig, G., Curtis, B.: Fourier-Motzkin Elimination and its Dual. Journal of Combinatorial Theory (1973) 288–297
4. Barrett, C., Berezin, S.: CVC Lite: A New Implementation of the Cooperating Validity Checker. In: Int. Conf. on Computer-Aided Verification (CAV). Volume 3114 of LNCS., Springer (2004)
5. Stump, A., Barrett, C., Dill, D.: CVC: A Cooperating Validity Checker. In: Int. Conference on Computer Aided Verification (CAV'02). Volume 2404 of LNCS., Springer (2002)

---

[4] http://caloproject.sri.com/

6. Barrett, C., Dill, D., Levitt, J.: Validity Checking for Combinations of Theories with Equality. In: Int. Conference on Formal Methods in Computer-Aided Design (FMCAD). Volume 1166 of LNCS. (1996) 187–201

7. Chvatal, V.: Linear Programming. W. H. Freeman (1983)

8. Bozzano, M., Bruttomesso, R., Cimatti, A., Junttila, T., van Rossum, P., Schulz, S., Sebastiani, R.: The MathSAT 3 system. In: Int. Conference on Automated Deduction (CADE). Volume 3632 of LNCS., Springer (2005)

9. Filliâtre, J.C., Owre, S., Rueß, H., Shankar, N.: ICS: Integrated Canonization and Solving. In: Proc. of CAV'01. Volume 2102 of LNCS. (2001)

10. Sheini, H.M., Sakallah, K.A.: A Scalable Method for Solving Satisfiability of Integer Linear Arithmetic Logic. In: SAT'05. Volume 3569 of LNCS., Springer (2005) 241–256

11. Rueß, H., Shankar, N.: Solving Linear Arithmetic Constraints. Technical Report SRI-CSL-04-01, SRI International (2004)

12. Detlefs, D., Nelson, G., Saxe, J.B.: Simplify: A Theorem Prover for Program Checking. Technical Report HPL-2003-148, HP Labs (2003)

13. Necula, G.: Compiling with Proofs. Technical Report CMU-CS-98-154, School of Computer Science, Carnegie Mellon University (1998)

14. Badros, G., Borning, A., Stuckey, P.: The Cassowary Linear Arithmetic Constraint Solving Algorithm. ACM Transactions on Computer-Human Interaction (TOCHI) 8(4) (2001) 267–306

15. Ranise, S., Tinelli, C.: The satisfiability modulo theories library (smt-lib) (2006) Available at http://goedel.cs.uiowa.edu/smtlib.

16. Dutertre, B., de Moura, L.: Integrating Simplex with DPLL(T). Technical report, CSL-06-01, SRI International (2006)

17. Schrijver, A.: Theory of Linear and Integer Programming. Wiley, New York (1986)

18. Nemhauser, G., Wosley, L.: Integer and Combinatorial Optimization. Wiley (1999)

19. Bozzano, M., Bruttomesso, R., Cimatti, A., Junttila, T., van Rossum, P., Ranise, S., Sebastiani, R.: Efficient Satisfiability Modulo Theories via Delayed Theory Combination. In: Int. Conf. on Computer-Aided Verification (CAV). Volume 3576 of LNCS., Springer (2005)

20. Wang, C., Ivancic, F., Ganai, M., Gupta, A.: Deciding Separation Logic Formulae with SAT and Incremental Negative Cycle Elimination. In: Logic for Programming Artificial Intelligence and Reasoning (LPAR). (2005)

21. Nieuwenhuis, R., Oliveras, A.: DPLL(T) with Exhaustive Theory Propagation and its Application to Difference Logic. In: Int. Conference on Computer Aided Verification (CAV'05), Springer (2005) 321–334

Bounded Model Checking for Weak Alternating Büchi Automata

Keijo Heljanko[1,*], Tommi Junttila[1], Misa Keinänen[1,**],
Martin Lange[2], and Timo Latvala[3,***]

[1] Laboratory for Theoretical Computer Science
Helsinki University of Technology
P.O. Box 5400, FI-02015 TKK, Finland
{Keijo.Heljanko, Tommi.Junttila, Misa.Keinanen}@tkk.fi
[2] Institut für Informatik Ludwig-Maximilians-Universität München, Germany
Martin.Lange@ifi.lmu.de
[3] Department of Computer Science, University of Illinois at Urbana-Champaign, USA
tlatvala@uiuc.edu

Abstract. We present an incremental bounded model checking encoding into propositional satisfiability where the property specification is expressed as a weak alternating Büchi automaton (WABA). The encoding is linear in the specification, or, more exactly $O(|I| + k \cdot |T| + k \cdot |\delta|)$, where $|I|$ is the size of the initial state predicate, k is the bound, $|T|$ is the size of the transition relation, and $|\delta|$ is the size of the WABA transition relation. Minimal length counterexamples can also be found by increasing the encoding size to be quadratic in the number of states in the largest component of the WABA. The proposed encoding can be used to implement more efficient bounded model checking algorithms for ω-regular industrial specification languages such as Accellera's Property Specification Language (PSL). Encouraging experimental results on a prototype implementation are reported.

Keywords: Weak Alternating Büchi Automata, Bounded Model Checking, PSL, NuSMV.

1 Introduction

Large and demanding verification efforts require that the property specification language used is up to the task. Linear temporal logic (LTL), the property specification language implemented in many model checkers, has been criticised for the lack of expressive power [1,2]. Expressing certain properties in LTL is cumbersome at best, and writing assumptions for compositional reasoning can even be impossible. Most of these shortcomings are in one way or another related to the fact that LTL cannot express all ω-regular languages. This has been recognised by many key players in the hardware industry and Accellera's Property Specification Language (PSL) [3,4] has been proposed

* Supported by the Academy of Finland (projects 112016, 213113).
** Supported by the Academy of Finland (project 211025) and Helsinki Graduate School in Computer Science and Engineering (HeCSE).
*** Supported by the Academy of Finland (project 109539) and the Emil Aaltonen Foundation.

T. Ball and R.B. Jones (Eds.): CAV 2006, LNCS 4144, pp. 95–108, 2006.
© Springer-Verlag Berlin Heidelberg 2006

as a solution. PSL extends LTL in many ways, but perhaps most importantly PSL can express all ω-regular languages.[1]

Expressive specification languages require efficient model checking techniques to deliver on their promise. *Bounded model checking* (BMC) [5] is a symbolic model checking technique that focuses on searching for bounded counterexamples to the given property. By encoding the model checking problem to propositional satisfiability (SAT), bounded model checking can leverage the efficiency of modern SAT-solver technology. Encoding BMC to SAT is accomplished by writing a propositional formula that models all executions of the system of certain length. Additional constraints ensure that the final formula is satisfiable if some execution is a counterexample. There are also methods for concluding that current reached depth is enough to prove that the given property holds [6,7,8,9]. BMC has established itself as an important tool among current verification techniques. A very important question is therefore, can BMC *efficiently* model check *all* ω-regular properties, especially those expressed in PSL.

This work explores different possibilities of implementing BMC for PSL by using the automata theoretic approach to model checking. The PSL property can first be converted into an alternating Büchi automaton (ABA) with the help of an external translation procedure, such as the one described by the Prosyd project (see [10]). This procedure can create so called *weak alternating automata* (WABA) which have certain restrictions on the structure of the automaton but are still able to express all ω-regular properties. A large subset of core PSL can be converted into a WABA with a linear number of states with a few exceptions [10].

In the rest of the paper we explore different options of creating an efficient BMC encoding for WABAs. With an exponential blow-up ($O(2^a + 3^b)$, where a is the number of accepting states and b is the number of non-accepting states) the WABA can be converted to an explicit state nondeterministic Büchi automaton using the Miyano-Hayashi construction [11]. This explicit state Büchi automaton could be used but the size of the encoding is in the worst case exponential in the size of the WABA.

A significantly better option would be to implement a symbolic version (SAT encoding) of the Miyano-Hayashi construction [10]. However, this approach does not exploit the weakness of the ABAs and might thus not be an optimal approach for WABAs. We have also experimentally observed that neither the symbolic nor the explicit state versions of the approach preserve minimal length counterexamples.

We present a new efficient BMC encoding specialised for model checking WABAs. The size of the encoding is *linear* in the specification as WABA and the system model. By increasing the size of the encoding to be quadratic in the number of states in the largest component of the WABA, we can guarantee that it detects minimal length counterexamples for all WABAs. The encoding utilises the incremental SAT encoding framework developed in [9].

We have experimentally evaluated our new BMC encoding for WABAs. Compared to BMC based on explicit state Büchi automata, the new WABA encoding is much more robust because the exponential blow-up in the explicit state Miyano-Hayashi construction is avoided. The new linear size encoding is clearly faster than a symbolic BMC

---

[1] PSL can also express properties of finite words, for simplicity only ω-words are considered here.

encoding of the Miyano-Hayashi construction. In addition, the minimal counterexample variant of our new encoding produces shorter counterexamples in some cases. On LTL formulas the new encoding generates minimum length counterexamples and is as compact (within a constant factor) as the most compact specialised LTL encodings known [9]. Furthermore, the performance on LTL is quite similar.

There is some earlier work on bounded model checking for subclasses of alternating Büchi automata and for all ω-regular properties. Sheridan [12] describes a *non-incremental* BMC encoding for very weak alternating Büchi automata. This encoding captures only the LTL subset of ω-regular properties since very weak alternating Büchi automata exactly correspond to LTL properties [13,14]. A BMC encoding for alternation-free μTL, a temporal logic that can express all ω-regular properties, has been developed by Jehle et al. [15]. The encoding is cubic in the used bound k and thus not as efficient as the new encoding presented in this work.

2 Alternating Büchi Automata

In this section we cover the technical definitions needed to introduce our BMC encoding for WABAs. The set of positive Boolean formulas over X, denoted by $\mathcal{B}^+(X)$, is the smallest set of formulas which contains all elements from X and is closed under disjunction and conjunction. A subset S of X is a model of $\theta \in \mathcal{B}^+(X)$, denoted by $S \models \theta$, iff the truth assignment that assigns true to the elements of S and false to the elements of $X \setminus S$ satisfies θ.

As alphabet Σ of alternating automata we restrict ourselves to only considering valuations of atomic propositions. More precisely, for a given non-empty finite set AP of atomic propositions we define the set of atomic proposition complements $\overline{AP} = \{\overline{p} \mid p \in AP\}$ and let Σ be the largest set $\Sigma \subseteq 2^{AP \cup \overline{AP}}$ such that for all $p \in AP$ exactly one element of $\{p, \overline{p}\}$ is contained in each member of Σ.

An alternating Büchi automaton (ABA) is of the form $A = (Q, \Sigma, q_0, \delta, F)$, where Q is a finite set of states, Σ is a finite alphabet, $q_0 \in Q$ is the initial state, $\delta : Q \to \mathcal{B}^+(AP \cup \overline{AP} \cup Q)$ is the transition relation and $F \subseteq Q$ is the set of accepting states. We use $\mathcal{B}^+(A)$ to denote the set of Boolean formulas that occur in A's transition function.

Given an infinite word $w \in \Sigma^\omega$, w_i denotes the i-th letter of w (i.e. $w = w_0 w_1 w_2 \ldots$). A run of $A = (Q, \Sigma, q_0, \delta, F)$ on w is a directed acyclic graph (dag) $G = (V, E)$ with the following properties:

- $V \subseteq Q \times \mathbb{N}$,
- $E \subseteq \bigcup_{i \geq 0}((Q \times \{i\}) \times (Q \times \{i+1\}))$,
- $(q_0, 0) \in V$,
- if $(q, i) \in V$ then $(w_i \cup \{q' \mid ((q, i), (q', i+1)) \in E\}) \models \delta(q)$, and
- if $((q, i), (q', i+1)) \in E$ then both $(q, i) \in V$ and $(q', i+1) \in V$.

For technical convenience this definition of a run allows for states which are unreachable from the initial state. Let σ be an infinite path in a run in G, i.e. an infinite sequence of nodes $(v_0, v_1, v_2, \ldots)$ such that $(v_i, v_{i+1}) \in E$ for all $i \geq 0$. Let $Inf(\sigma)$ be the set of states that consists of all automaton states appearing infinitely often in the nodes of σ. An infinite path σ is accepting iff $F \cap Inf(\sigma) \neq \emptyset$. A run G is accepting iff every infinite path through G is accepting. An ABA $A = (Q, \Sigma, q_0, \delta, F)$ accepts a word $w \in \Sigma^\omega$

iff there is an accepting run G of the automaton A on w. The definition of a run allows a state to have no successors and a path through the run (as well as the whole run) to be finite. In effect all such finite paths ending in a state with no successors are "accepting". Alternatively the existence of states with no successors could be easily ruled out by placing additional constraints on $\delta(\cdot)$.

Example 1. For instance, $\delta(q_1) = ((p \wedge q_1) \vee (\overline{p} \wedge ((r \wedge (q_2 \wedge q_3)) \vee \overline{r})))$ means that from state $(q_1, i) \in V$ with valuation $w_i = \{p, r\}$ move to a state set at $i + 1$ containing $\{q_1\}$ (this also happens with valuation $\{p, \overline{r}\}$), while with valuation $\{\overline{p}, r\}$ we will move to a state set containing $\{q_2, q_3\}$. With valuation $\{\overline{p}, \overline{r}\}$ the transition relation of q_1 becomes true, which means that we do not require q_0 to have any successors.

A weak alternating Büchi automaton (WABA) is an ABA $A = (Q, \Sigma, q_0, \delta, F)$ whose states Q can be partitioned into *components* $Q_1 \uplus \cdots \uplus Q_m$ such that:[2]

- for all $j, k \in \{1, \ldots, m\}$, $q_j \in Q_j$, $q_k \in Q_k$: if q_k appears syntactically in $\delta(q_j)$ then $k \leq j$; and
- for all $1 \leq j \leq m$: $Q_j \subseteq F$ or $Q_j \cap F = \emptyset$.

A WABA is a *very* weak alternating Büchi automaton (VWABA) if no component Q_j contains more than one state. For a component Q_j, $|\delta_j|$ denotes the sum of the sizes of the transition relations $\delta(q)$, where $q \in Q_j$.

Let A be a WABA with state set Q partitioned into components $Q_1 \uplus \cdots \uplus Q_m$ and final state set F. We next define the *component unrolling depth* d_j needed to detect minimal length counterexamples in our BMC encoding for each component Q_j. For any $j \in \{1, \ldots, m\}$ let

$$d_j = \begin{cases} 0 & \text{, if } Q_j \subseteq F \\ |Q_j| & \text{, if } Q_j \cap F = \emptyset \end{cases}$$

3 Incremental Bounded Model Checking for Weak Alternating Büchi Automata

Our incremental encoding for weak alternating automata is based on the simple BMC encodings [16,17,9] for LTL. The approach to incrementality used here is exactly the same as in [9]. First of all, the encoding needs to be formulated so that it is easy to derive the encoding for bound $k = i + 1$ from the encoding for bound $k = i$. This is done by separating the encoding to a k-invariant part and a k-dependent part. The information learned by the SAT solver from the k-invariant constraints can be reused when the bound is increased while the k-dependent constraints and all the information learned from them needs to be discarded. Thus we try to minimise the use of k-dependent constraints in our encoding. The so called *Base constraints* are also k-invariant, but they are conditions that are constant for all $0 \leq i \leq k$.

---

[2] Given an ABA the sets $Q_1, \ldots, Q_m$ can be easily computed by using an algorithm for computing the maximal strongly connected components (MSCCs) in a graph induced by the ABA transition relation as follows: the states are the nodes, and there is an edge from q_j to q_k iff q_k appears syntactically in $\delta(q_j)$.

As in earlier works, paths of length k are encoded using k-invariant *model constraints* $|[M]|_k$. They encode initialised finite paths of the model M of length k:

$$|[M]|_k \Leftrightarrow I(s_0) \wedge \bigwedge_{i=1}^{k} T(s_{i-1}, s_i),$$

where $I(s)$ is the initial state predicate and $T(s, s')$ is a total transition relation. Let $\pi = s_0 s_1 s_2 \ldots$ be an initialised infinite path through M. The corresponding word $w = w_0 w_1 w_2 \ldots \in \Sigma^\omega$ is obtained by concatenating the sets of valuations of atomic propositions in the states s_i. We say that π is a (k,l)-loop if $\pi = (s_0 s_1 \ldots s_{l-1})(s_l \ldots s_k)^\omega$ such that $0 < l \leq k$ and $s_{l-1} = s_k$.

The *loop constraints* also closely follow [9] by employing $k+1$ fresh *loop selector variables* $l_0, \ldots, l_k$. They constrain the finite path of the system to always be a (k,i)-loop for exactly one i, in which case the variable l_i is true and all other l_j variables are false. Many k-dependent constraints are avoided by introducing a new special system state s_E with fresh (unconstrained) state variables acting as a *proxy state* for the endpoint of the path. In the k-dependent part the proxy state s_E is constrained to be equivalent to s_k. The variable InLoop_i is true iff the state s_i belongs to the loop part of a (k,l)-loop. These are encoded by conjuncting the constraints below and denoted by $|[LoopConstraints]|_k$:

Base	$l_0 \Leftrightarrow \bot$
	$\text{InLoop}_0 \Leftrightarrow \bot$
$k-$invariant	$l_i \Rightarrow (s_{i-1} = s_E)$
$1 \leq i \leq k$	$\text{InLoop}_i \Leftrightarrow \text{InLoop}_{i-1} \vee l_i,$
	$\text{InLoop}_{i-1} \Rightarrow \neg l_i$
$k-$dependent	$\text{InLoop}_k \Leftrightarrow \top$
	$s_E \Leftrightarrow s_k$

We will first give an encoding that detects minimal length counterexamples for *all* WABAs, and later on show an optimisation that makes the encoding linear in the size of the WABA if this requirement is dropped. Given a WABA A, in our new encoding the state variables of the system are split at each time i to the actual state variables s_i of the system, to the set of variables for all automata states $|[s_q]|_i^d$ (one for $0 \leq i \leq k+1$ and each pair (q,d), where $q \in Q_j$ and $0 \leq d \leq d_j$). The encoding also contains a few additional variables which will be referred to explicitly. The rules of the encoding are given as a set of Boolean constraints.

The *WABA constraints* $|[A_{WABA}]|_k$ are new to this work and restrict the bounded paths defined by the model constraints and loop constraints to infinite words accepted by WABA A. One intuition for understanding the encoding is given by the fact that for (k,l)-loops the semantics of branching and linear time coincide. We will in fact employ algorithmic ideas similar to those used in branching time logic CTL model checkers.

The transition relation of A is encoded in a straightforward manner. For each component Q_j and for each state $q \in Q_j$ the following constraints are created:

	$0 \leq d \leq d_j$
Base	$|[s_{q_0}]|_0^0 \Leftrightarrow \top$, where q_0 is the initial state
$k-$invariant, $0 \leq i \leq k$	$|[s_q]|_i^d \Leftrightarrow |[\delta(q)]|_i^d$

where the $k-$invariant encoding $|[\delta(q)]|_i^d$ for each component Q_j, and for each state $q \in Q_j$ is the following:

$|[\delta(q)]|_i^d$	$0 \leq i \leq k, 0 \leq d \leq d_j$
$|[p]|_i^d$	$|[p]|_i^d \Leftrightarrow p_i$
$|[\overline{p}]|_i^d$	$|[\overline{p}]|_i^d \Leftrightarrow \neg p_i$
$|[q']|_i^d$	$|[q']|_i^d \Leftrightarrow |[s_{q'}]|_{i+1}^d$, if $q' \in Q_j$
	$|[q']|_i^d \Leftrightarrow |[s_{q'}]|_{i+1}^0$, if $q' \notin Q_j$
$|[\psi_1 \wedge \psi_2]|_i^d$	$|[\psi_1 \wedge \psi_2]|_i^d \Leftrightarrow |[\psi_1]|_i^d \wedge |[\psi_2]|_i^d$
$|[\psi_1 \vee \psi_2]|_i^d$	$|[\psi_1 \vee \psi_2]|_i^d \Leftrightarrow |[\psi_1]|_i^d \vee |[\psi_2]|_i^d$

In the encoding above p_i denotes the variable holding the value of the atomic proposition p in the state s_i. Notice how for state $q \in Q_j$ the successor states q' inside Q_j get the values from the current unrolling d while the successor states q' outside Q_j get their values from the unrolling $d = 0$. The intuition for this will be explained below.

We use a *proxy loop state* indexed with L with associated (free) automaton variables $|[s_q]|_L^d$ to act as the loop state in order to make as many constraints k-invariant as possible. For non-accepting components the k-dependent rules bind the truth values of $|[s_q]|_{k+1}^d$ to $|[s_q]|_L^{d+1}$ (jump to the next unrolling level $d + 1$), while for accepting components they bind the values of $|[s_q]|_{k+1}^0$ to the value of $|[s_q]|_L^0$, i.e. to the values at the loop point state of the same unrolling. This is encoded by conjuncting the following constraints for each component Q_j and for each state $q \in Q_j$:

	$0 \leq d \leq d_j$
Base	$|[s_q]|_L^{d_j+1} \Leftrightarrow \bot$, if $q \notin F$
$k-$invariant, $1 \leq i \leq k$	$l_i \Rightarrow \left(|[s_q]|_L^d \Leftrightarrow |[s_q]|_i^d \right)$
$k-$dependent	$|[s_q]|_{k+1}^d \Leftrightarrow |[s_q]|_L^{d+1}$, if $q \notin F$
	$|[s_q]|_{k+1}^0 \Leftrightarrow |[s_q]|_L^0$, if $q \in F$

The intuitive idea behind the encoding is as follows. Our encoding can be seen as a SAT implementation of an automata theoretic *branching time* model checker using WABAs such as [18] but specialised for models induced by (k,l)-loops. Because of the component structure of the WABA, each component Q_j can assume that all other components and atomic propositions it refers to have already been evaluated, and the results are available. This is all that is needed to evaluate the component Q_j by iteratively substituting these subresults.[3]

Similarly to [18] we want to compute the effect of these substitutions in terms of a fixpoint evaluation procedure. Consider a non-accepting component Q_j first. We want $|[s_q]|_L^1$ to evaluate to whether at the loop point L starting from a state $q \in Q_j$ the automaton has some run which accepts the ω-word induced by the loop. Because we do not want to allow accepting runs to be trapped forever in a non-accepting component, the fixpoint required is the least fixpoint, and gives us the initial approximation values $|[s_q]|_L^{d_j+1} \Leftrightarrow \bot$. By running through the loop once in the *backward direction* making substitutions of known results along the way, we can get a better approximation of the final value, namely $|[s_q]|_L^{d_j}$. Either we have already reached a fixpoint, or at least one of states $q' \in Q_j$ has obtained the value $|[s_{q'}]|_L^{d_j} = \top$, in which case we have to resubstitute this value by running through the loop a second time in the backward direction. Clearly after $d_j = |Q_j|$ rounds the fixpoint is guaranteed to be reached, and the values of $|[s_q]|_L^1$ are exact results of the fixpoint iteration. Finally, an extra fixpoint iteration is done with $|[s_q]|_i^0$ variables to get the correct final values for indices to the right of the loop point.

We could do the obvious dual greatest fixpoint iteration for the accepting components. However, we will use the optimisation trick of employing *any fixpoint* instead of the greatest fixpoint. The intuitive reason why this is sound is that any fixpoint will in our encoding cautiously underapproximate the greatest fixpoint, (see the soundness proof, Lemma 1 in Appendix A which never uses the fact that the fixpoint obtained for accepting components is the greatest fixpoint). The completeness part is trivial, as the any fixpoint enforcing constraints are strictly less constraining that the constraints that would be needed for enforcing the exact greatest fixpoint.

We can optionally add constraints based on the monotonicity of the fixpoint approximations of non-accepting components. These $k-$invariant propagation constraints are as follows. For each non-accepting component Q_j, and for each state $q \in Q_j$, $0 \leq i \leq k+1$, $1 \leq d \leq d_j$:

$k-$invariant	$|[s_q]|_i^d \Rightarrow |[s_q]|_i^{d-1}$

Conjuncting all the constraints above the encoding $|[M, A_{WABA}]|_k$ becomes:

$$|[M, A_{WABA}]|_k \Leftrightarrow |[M]|_k \wedge |[LoopConstraints]|_k \wedge |[A_{WABA}]|_k.$$

Theorem 1. *Given a finite Kripke structure M and a WABA A, M has a path π accepted by A iff there exists a $k \in \mathbb{N}$ such that $|[M, A_{WABA}]|_k$ is satisfiable. More specifically, if $\pi = s_0 s_1 s_2 \ldots$ is a (k,l)-loop accepted by A then $|[M, A_{WABA}]|_k$ is satisfiable.* [4]

Proof. Immediate by Lemmas 1 and 2 in Appendix A.   □

---

[3] Notice the similarity to evaluating CTL formulas by substituting subformula results and propagating these in the backward transition relation direction. See for example the WABA based CTL model checking algorithm [18] as well as similar algorithms for the alternation free μ-calculus [19]. The main difference is that we aim for an easy encoding into SAT instead of optimal running time as in the algorithms mentioned above.

[4] A direct corollary of this is that minimal length (k,l)-loop witnesses can be detected.

The exact size of the encoding is $O(|I| + k \cdot |T| + k \cdot |\delta| + k \cdot \sum_{j=1}^{m}(d_j \cdot |\delta_j|))$. Note that the size is bounded from above by $O(|I| + k \cdot |T| + k \cdot |Q| \cdot |\delta|)$, and becomes $O(|I| + k \cdot |T| + k \cdot |\delta|)$ when the WABA is a very weak alternating Büchi automaton (as produced by most LTL to WABA translations). Combined with a linear size translation from an LTL formula into a VWABA (for example a state acceptance based variant of [20] with a symbolically encoded transition relation), bounded LTL model checking using this approach is as compact as the approaches of [16,17,9]. In fact, by doing so the encoding would for LTL formulas effectively become an optimised incremental variant of [16].

Trading Minimal Length Witnesses for a Smaller Encoding. Instead of quantifying d over $0 \le d \le d_j$ in the encoding above, for any non-accepting component Q_j we can instead use $0 \le d \le c_j$, where $1 \le c_j \le d_j$. Now c_j is the number of fixpoint iterations made[5], and we need the following constraints to guarantee correctness of the approach. For each non-accepting component Q_j, and for each state $q \in Q_j$ the following fixpoint-enforcing constraints are added:

Base	$|[s_q]|_L^0 \Leftrightarrow |[s_q]|_L^1$

The constraints intuitively check that the fixpoint iteration has reached a fixpoint after c_j iterations. Thus the approach will be sound. The reason why the approach is still complete is that by going through the loop part of a (k, l)-loop d_j times one can with $c_j = 1$ simulate the d_j fixpoint iterations done by going through the loop part only once but with d_j unrollings. Thus increasing the bound by roughly a factor of d_j can compensate for the lack of d_j unrollings. By changing the quantification to, for example, always use $c_j = 1$ (as used in our experiments) the resulting encoding is of size $O(|I| + k \cdot |T| + k \cdot |\delta|)$, i.e. linear in the size of the WABA. The correctness of the encoding is preserved in the sense that every witness will eventually be detected when the bound is increased large enough (albeit with a non-minimal bound).

4 Experimental Results

We have implemented a prototype of the proposed WABA BMC encoding on top of a development version of the NuSMV tool [21]. We use the "Sugar" tool (obtained from http://www.prosyd.org/), by C. J. Kargl of TU Graz, as a translator from PSL to ABAs and reuse our previous incremental SAT encoding techniques [9]. As the SAT solver we use ZChaff version 2004.11.15 in the experiments. In order to evaluate and validate the proposed encoding, we have also implemented two other BMC approaches for WABAs on top of the same software platform: (i) translate the WABA to an explicit state Büchi automaton by using the Miyano-Hayashi algorithm of the "Sugar" tool and then do BMC by using the explicit state Büchi automaton, (ii) take the Miyano-Hayashi translation from (W)ABA to Büchi automata given in [10, page 38] and derive a *symbolic* BMC encoding from it.

---

[5] The encoding of $|[s_q]|_i^d$ with $d = 0$ can be seen as an "extra" fixpoint iteration. It is needed in order to also obtain correct $|[s_q]|_i^0$ values for indices i to the "right" of the loop point. We use it here to also check that the fixpoint has been reached.

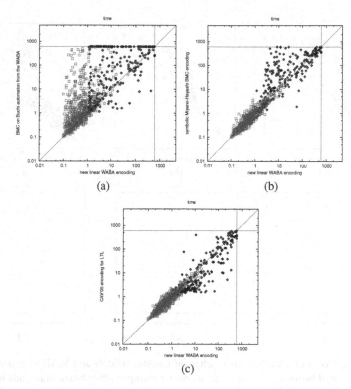

Fig. 1. A comparison of encoding approaches on random models and VWABAs generated from LTL formulae. Red boxes mark cases with a counterexample while black diamonds mark cases where none was found.

These two BMC encodings are linear in the bound k and the sizes of the transition relations of the corresponding automata (Büchi and WABA, resp.). Unfortunately we do not have space to explain them in more detail here. The prototype implementation as well as the experiments are available at `http://www.tcs.hut.fi/~timo/cav2006`. The implementation also contains a (W)ABA input path, allowing alternative PSL to (W)ABA translations to be used.

Figures 1 and 2 show a comparison of encoding schemes for randomly generated models (Kripke structures of 100 states and a single justice fairness requirement) and WABAs generated from LTL and PSL formulae (of parse tree sizes between 3 and 14). The time limit for each run was 10 minutes and the memory limit 1.5GiB.

In Fig. 1(a), 1(b) and 1(c), we benchmark our new algorithm on 1200 random LTL formulae. We plot the total execution time of each run to either find a counterexample for the property or to reach the bound limit of 50. In the plots, cases where a counterexample was found are denoted by red boxes while black diamonds denote cases where none of the approaches found a counterexample. The scales are logarithmic. Based on Fig. 1(a), it is easy to see that the "WABA to Büchi" approach is not very competitive: it suffers from the automata size blow-up occurring during the WABA to explicit state Büchi automata translation. We can see that the proposed WABA BMC encoding is

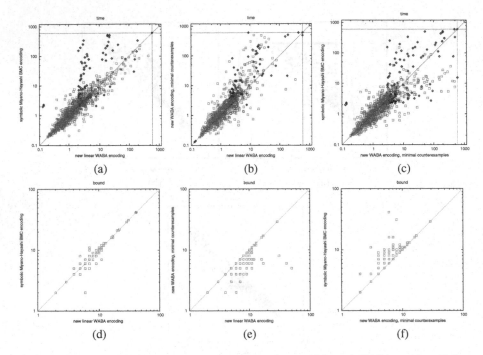

Fig. 2. A comparison of encoding approaches on random models and WABAs generated from PSL formulae. Red boxes mark cases with a counterexample while black diamonds mark cases where none was found.

competitive against the symbolic Miyano-Hayashi approach (Fig. 1(b)). As expected, the specialised LTL encoding of [9] performs slightly better than the new, more general encoding but the difference is not large: the new encoding seems to be a reasonably good BMC algorithm for LTL, too.

In Fig. 2, we compare the encodings on 1000+ WABAs obtained by generating random PSL formulas, translating them to ABAs using the "Sugar" tool, and picking those instances which are WABAs that are *not* very weak. It is known that in the version of the "Sugar" tool used by us there are some discrepancies with respect to the semantics of PSL, but that does not effect our use of it as a random WABA generator. The bound and other parameters of the setup, as well as plot point encoding, are identical to the LTL case. We also plot the *bound reached*, i.e. the counterexample length, for the runs that found one. The scales are logarithmic.

The new linear encoding performs better than the symbolic Miyano-Hayashi encoding, as shown in Fig. 2(a), with comparable counterexample lengths, as can be observed from Fig. 2(d). Comparing the two new encodings in Fig. 2(b), the linear encoding is clearly faster but may generate significantly longer counterexamples as shown in Fig. 2(e). If we were to model check systems with a larger transition relation, the increased counterexample length as seen here might sometimes translate into a slower running time. Comparing the new encoding that can find minimal counterexamples to the symbolic Miyano-Hayashi encoding in Figures 2(c) and 2(f) we see that there is no clear winner in speed but that the new encoding produces shorter counterexamples.

To sum up, these results show that the proposed WABA BMC is a competitive encoding for WABAs generated from PSL formulas, and quite close to a state-of-the-art BMC encoding specialised for LTL.

5 Conclusions

Our new BMC encoding for WABAs seems very competitive. With BMC using explicit state Büchi automata, it is obvious that for complicated properties the potentially exponential conversion from a WABA will become a bottleneck. The reason why our encoding performs better than a symbolic Miyano-Hayashi encoding is not completely clear to us. We speculate that the more deterministic nature of our encoding generates easier problems for the SAT solver. The fact that the new encoding can exploit the structure of WABAs unlike Miyano-Hayashi, which works for all alternating automata, may also help. Both are linear size in the specification, but if we use a version that is in the worst case quadratic in the number of states in the largest component of the WABA, our new encoding is guaranteed to find minimal length counterexamples.

The proposed WABA BMC encoding can be made complete (in the sense that it can also prove properties, not only find counterexamples) by modifying and applying the simple-path constrains of [9] in a straightforward way.

We would like to investigate whether it is possible to modify Miyano-Hayashi to generate tight Büchi automata. We believe that the BMC encoding of this work can be adapted to also generate a symbolic WABA to Büchi automaton conversion procedure (an alternative to Miyano-Hayashi for WABAs) which generates tight Büchi automata and thus detects minimal length counterexamples along the lines of [22]. This intuition is based on the fact that [22] is an adaptation of the PLTL BMC encoding [17] to the symbolic Büchi automaton setting and the implementation techniques used here are quite similar to those of [17].

Other potential future directions of research are related to succinctness. One possibility would be to devise new direct BMC encodings for general, non-weak ABAs or for alternating parity automata. Generalising the encoding to temporal logics with past operators (e.g. PSL extended with past) may potentially involve handling of two-way alternating automata.

Acknowledgements. The authors would like to thank I. Niemelä and H. Tauriainen for interesting discussions and pointers on the topic. Thanks also to R. Bloem and other contributors of the Prosyd project for their freely available PSL translation tool as well as A. Cimatti, M. Roveri, and the rest of the NuSMV team for assistance and providing us with a development version of NuSMV.

References

1. Lichtenstein, O., Pnueli, A., Zuck, L.D.: The glory of the past. In: Logic of Programs. Volume 193 of LNCS., Springer (1985) 196–218
2. Vardi, M.: Branching vs. linear time: Final showdown. In: TACAS. Volume 2031 of LNCS., Springer (2001) 1–22

3. Accellera: Property specification language: Reference manual – version 1.1 (2004)
   http://www.eda.org/vfv/docs/PSL-v1.1.pdf.
4. IEEE: IEEE Standard 1850 - Property Specification Language (PSL) (2005)
5. Biere, A., Cimatti, A., Clarke, E., Zhu, Y.: Symbolic model checking without BDDs. In:
   TACAS. Volume 1579 of LNCS., Springer (1999) 193–207
6. Sheeran, M., Singh, S., Stålmarck, G.: Checking safety properties using induction and a
   SAT-solver. In: FMCAD. Volume 1954 of LNCS., Springer (2000) 108–125
7. McMillan, K.L.: Interpolation and SAT-based model checking. In: CAV. Volume 2725 of
   LNCS., Springer (2003) 1–13
8. Awedh, M., Somenzi, F.: Proving more properties with bounded model checking. In: CAV.
   Volume 3114 of LNCS. (2004) 96–108
9. Heljanko, K., Junttila, T., Latvala, T.: Incremental and complete bounded model checking
   for full PLTL. In: CAV. Volume 3576 of LNCS., Springer (2005) 98–111
10. Ben-David, S., Bloem, R., Fisman, D., Griesmayer, A., Pill, I., Ruah, S.: Automata con-
    structon algorithms optimized for PSL. Technical Report Deliverable 3.2/4, ProdSyd project
    (2005) Available from: http://www.prosyd.org/.
11. Miyano, S., Hayashi, T.: Alternating finite automata on ω-words. Theoretical Computer
    Science 32 (1984) 321–330
12. Sheridan, D.: Bounded model checking with SNF, alternating automata, and Büchi automata.
    Electronic Notes in Theoretical Computer Science 119 (2005) 83–101
13. Rohde, G.S.: Alternating Automata and the Temporal Logic of Ordinals. PhD thesis, Uni-
    versity of Illinois at Urbana-Champaign (1997)
14. Löding, C., Thomas, W.: Alternating automata and logics over infinite words. In: IFIP
    TCS2000. Volume 1872 of LNCS., Springer (2000) 521–535
15. Jehle, M., Johannsen, J., Lange, M., Rachinsky, N.: Bounded model checking for all regular
    properties. Electronic Notes in Theoretical Computer Science 144 (2006) 3–18
16. Latvala, T., Biere, A., Heljanko, K., Junttila, T.: Simple bounded LTL model checking. In:
    FMCAD. Volume 3312 of LNCS., Springer (2004) 186–200
17. Latvala, T., Biere, A., Heljanko, K., Junttila, T.: Simple is better: Efficient bounded model
    checking for past LTL. In: VMCAI. Volume 3385 of LNCS., Springer (2005) 380–395
18. Kupferman, O., Vardi, M.Y., Wolper, P.: An automata-theoretic approach to branching-time
    model checking. J. ACM 47 (2000) 312–360
19. Cleaveland, R., Steffen, B.: A linear-time model-checking algorithm for the alternation-free
    modal mu-calculus. Formal Methods in System Design 2 (1993) 121–147
20. Gastin, P., Oddoux, D.: Fast LTL to Büchi automata translation. In Berry, G., Comon, H.,
    Finkel, A., eds.: CAV. Volume 2102 of LNCS., Springer (2001) 53–65
21. Cimatti, A., Clarke, E.M., Giunchiglia, E., Giunchiglia, F., Pistore, M., Roveri, M., Sebas-
    tiani, R., Tacchella, A.: NuSMV 2: An OpenSource tool for symbolic model checking. In:
    CAV. Volume 2404 of LNCS., Springer (2002) 359–364
22. Schuppan, V., Biere, A.: Shortest counterexamples for symbolic model checking of LTL with
    past. In: TACAS. Volume 3440 of LNCS., Springer (2005) 493–509

Appendix A - Proofs

Here we prove the soundness and completeness of the encoding.

Lemma 1. *Given a finite Kripke structure M, a WABA A and a $k \in \mathbb{N}$, if $|[M, A_{WABA}]|_k$ is satisfiable then there is an initialised infinite path π through M such that the induced word w is accepted by A.*

Proof. Suppose $\|[M, A_{WABA}]\|_k$ has a satisfying truth assignment β for its variables. Since β satisfies $\|[M]\|_k$ there are states $s_0 s_1 \ldots s_k$ that form an initialised finite path in M. Note that $\|[LoopConstraints]\|_k$ requires that there is $0 < l \leq k$ such that $s_k = s_{l-1}$. Let π now be the initialised infinite path $s_0 \ldots s_{l-1}(s_l \ldots s_k)^\omega$ through M. It remains to be seen that the corresponding word w is accepted by A.

We will prove the following stronger statement from which the claim of the theorem follows because of the base constraint for the initial state q_0. For a word $w = w_0 w_1 w_2 \ldots \in \Sigma^\omega$ let $w^{(i)}$ denote the suffix of w starting from w_i. We use A_q to denote the WABA that results from A by making q the initial state. *For all components Q_j of A, all $0 \leq d \leq d_j$, all $q \in Q_j$, and all $0 \leq i \leq k$: if $\beta(\|[s_q]\|_i^d) = \top$ then $w^{(i)}$ is accepted by A_q.*

Note that the topological order on A's components is well-founded. Hence, we can use Noetherian induction assuming that the statement has been proved for all lower components already.

Let Q_j be a final component. Take any $q \in Q_j$ and assume $\beta(\|[s_q]\|_i^0) = \top$ for some $0 \leq i \leq k$. It is straightforward to construct a run dag for A_q and $w^{(i)}$ starting with the node (q, i). The constraints for δ then require $\beta(\|[\delta(q)]\|_i^0) = \top$.[6] Since Boolean connectives in δ are uniformly translated in the constraints for δ, there must be a model Q' of $\delta(q)$. The construction of the run dag is then iterated on the next level with nodes $(q', i+1)$ for some $q' \in Q'$. Note that the constraints always ensure that there are models of $\delta(q)$ for each q that occurs in this construction. This continues on each infinite path of the run ad infinitum or until a state q' is reached such that $q' \notin Q_j$. But then, by weakness, q' must belong to some component for which an accepting run dag has already been constructed by the induction hypothesis. Note that all the states on such infinite paths that remain in component Q_j are final. Hence, the run dag is accepting, and we have $w^{(i)}$ is accepted by A_q.

Now let Q_j be a non-final component. Again, take any $q \in Q_j$ but now assume $\beta(\|[s_q]\|_i^d) = \top$ for some $0 \leq i \leq k$ and some $0 \leq d \leq d_j$. Again, we construct a run dag for A_q and $w^{(i)}$ starting with the node (q, i). As above, the constraints for δ always ensure the existence of a model for a node on some level of this run which creates the nodes on the following level. But note that the index d is increased in each transition from s_k to s_l. Since $\beta(\|[s_q]\|_L^{d_j+1}) = \bot$ is ensured by the constraints of the encoding, each infinite path in this run dag will eventually leave the component Q_j. By weakness, each infinite path proceeds into another component for which an accepting run dag has already been created by the induction hypothesis. Since a finite prefix of non-final states on any such an infinite path does not harm the acceptance condition, this run dag is accepting, too, and we have $w^{(i)}$ is accepted by A_q. $\square$

Lemma 2. *Given a finite Kripke structure M and a WABA A, if there is an initialised infinite path π through M such that the corresponding word w is accepted by A then there is a $k \in \mathbb{N}$ such that $\|[M, A_{WABA}]\|_k$ is satisfiable.*

---

[6] According to this, implications from left to right instead of bi-implications in the constraints for δ would already suffice. It is also not hard to see that this does not destroy completeness: if there is an assignment satisfying the bi-implications then this assignment would also satisfy the weaker implications.

Proof. Suppose there is an infinite path π such that the corresponding word w is accepted by A. Since the class of languages accepted by weak alternating Büchi automata are the ω-regular languages we can without loss of generality assume π to be a (k,l)-loop for some $0 < l \leq k$. Furthermore, without loss of generality we can assume that π is minimal in the following sense. There is no infinite path π' through M such that the corresponding word w' is accepted by A and π' is a (k',l')-loop for some $k' < k$ and some l'.

It remains to be seen that $\|[M, A_{WABA}]\|_k$ is satisfiable. Hence, we need to construct a truth assignment β to the variables $s_0 s_1 \ldots s_k$, InLoop$_i$ for each $0 \leq i \leq k$ as well as $\|[s_q]\|_i^d$ for each component Q_j of A, each $q \in Q_j$, each $0 \leq d \leq d_j$, and each $0 \leq i \leq k+1$. Note that the values of the other variables are determined by the values of these.

The values for the former are immediately given by the (k,l)-loop w. This shows satisfaction of the conjuncts $\|[M]\|_k$ and $\|[LoopConstraints]\|_k$.

For the rest of the variables we only give a proof sketch due to space considerations. After fixing w we can see A as a WABA *tree automaton* running on word (degenerate tree) w. Simplifying the encoding of δ with the values given by w to variables in the first phase above implements the tree WABA product construction in similar fashion as in Section 3.2 of [18] and thus the rest of the encoding solves the 1-letter WABA emptiness problem of a 1-letter product WABA induced by w. Now the rest of the encoding is basically a SAT implementation of a variant of the fixpoint computation algorithm of Theorem 4.7 in [18] to solve the 1-letter emptiness problem for WABAs. The non-accepting components correspond to least fixpoints and the accepting components correspond to greatest fixpoints. We can do an induction which processes one component at a time as in the proof of soundness above.

For an accepting component Q_j the values $\|[s_q]\|_i^0$ can be set to be identical to the final values computed by the algorithm of Theorem 4.7 in [18], thus obtaining a fixpoint which is easily checked to be a satisfying truth assignment.

For a non-accepting component Q_j the values $\|[s_q]\|_i^0$ can also be set to be identical to the final values computed by the algorithm of Theorem 4.7 in [18]. However, the values of $\|[s_q]\|_i^d$ with $1 \leq d \leq d_j$ are set to be the values obtained by a fixpoint approximation procedure which starts from the initial values given by $\beta(\|[s_q]\|_L^{d_j+1}) = \perp$ and for all i,d pairs proceeds for i from $k+1$ towards 0, and for d from d_j towards 1. It is easy to check that after at most $d_j = |Q_j|$ iterations through the loop in the backward direction final values have been obtained at the loop point $i = l, d = 1$ (recall that w is fixed and thus also the simplified form of δ is monotone and fixed according to w at each point of computing the fixpoint approximations), and thus we obtain a satisfying truth assignment for all the constraints concerning non-accepting components.

By the above and the fact that the algorithm of Theorem 4.7 in [18] computes $\top$ to the initial state iff w is accepted by A, we finally obtain $\beta(\|[s_{q_0}]\|_0^0) = \top$, and thus all constraints of the encoding are satisfied. $\square$

As a consequence of the proof, the encoding detects witnesses π that are (k,l)-loops at minimal parameter k.

Deriving Small Unsatisfiable Cores with Dominators

Roman Gershman, Maya Koifman, and Ofer Strichman

Technion, Haifa, Israel
ofers@ie.technion.ac.il

Abstract. The problem of finding a small unsatisfiable core of an unsatisfiable CNF formula is addressed. The proposed algorithm, *Trimmer*, iterates over each internal node d in the resolution graph that 'consumes' a large number of clauses M (i.e. a large number of original clauses are present in the unsat core only for proving d) and attempts to prove them without the M clauses. If this is possible, it transforms the resolution graph into a new graph that does not have the M clauses at its core. *Trimmer* can be integrated into a fixpoint framework similarly to Malik and Zhang's fix-point algorithm (RUN_TILL_FIX). We call this option TRIM_TILL_FIX. Experimental evaluation on a large number of industrial CNF unsatisfiable formulas shows that TRIM_TILL_FIX doubles, on average, the number of reduced clauses in comparison to RUN_TILL_FIX. It is also better when used as a component in a bigger system that enforces short timeouts.

1 Introduction

Given an unsatisfiable CNF formula, an *unsatisfiable core* (UC) is any subset of these clauses that is still unsatisfiable. The problem of finding a *minimum*, *minimal* or just a *small* UC has been addressed rather frequently in the last few years [2,10,16,11,6], partially due to its increasing importance in formal verification.

The decision problem corresponding to finding the *minimum* UC is a Σ_2-complete problem [5] and we are not aware of an algorithms for finding it that scales. Finding a *minimal* UC (any subset of clauses such that the removal of any one of them makes the formula satisfiable), according to Papadimitriou and Wolfe [12], is D^P-complete[1].

It is questionable whether finding a minimal UC has a practical value, however, since a non-minimal UC can be smaller than a minimal one, as long as it is not contained in it. Therefore heuristics that do not guarantee minimality, can be both faster and better than those that guarantee minimality. The latter are useful only when their result is compared to the core from which they started,

---

[1] D^P is the class containing all languages that can be considered as the difference between two languages in NP, or equivalently, the intersection of a language in NP with a language in co-NP.

T. Ball and R.B. Jones (Eds.): CAV 2006, LNCS 4144, pp. 109–122, 2006.

and thus can be used, for example, after another, faster algorithm, has already extracted a small core and cannot find a smaller one.

Typically UCs are needed as part of a larger system (such as an abstraction/refinement loop as we will soon describe), and the influence of the size of the UC on the other parts of the system is only vaguely known. Hence, although more computation time can lead to finding smaller cores, it is not clear whether it is cost-effective in the overall system. This suggests once again that minimality per-se is not so important in practice. Algorithms for extracting small cores should be measured instead by their *velocity*: how many clauses they remove from the initial formula per time unit, on average. They should also be measured by how small they can make the core within a time limit, in comparison with other algorithms, and whether they can contribute to a setting in which several of these algorithms are run sequentially or even in parallel. In Section 6 we measure our suggested technique, called *Trimmer*, with these criteria.

Before we describe previous work on this problem, let us mention some of the typical usages of UCs. A small unsatisfiable core reflects a more precise and focused explanation of the unsatisfiability of a given formula. In verification, it is used in several contexts, some of which are the following. Amla and McMillan [1] suggest to use UCs for a proof-based abstraction-refinement model-checking process: the UC of an unsatisfiable BMC instance contains information on the state variables that are sufficient for proving that no bug can be found up to a given depth; based on these state variables they build a refined abstract model and continue to iterate. Kroening et al. [8] use unsatisfiable cores for an iterative process of solving Presburger formulas: the UC is used for checking whether certain under-approximating restrictions on the solution space were used in the proof of unsatisfiability. If the answer is yes, these restrictions should be relaxed. A similar usage of UCs is by Grumberg et al. [4], in a process of under-approximation and widening of BMC formulas corresponding to a multi-threaded process. Outside verification, the identification of an inconsistent kernel can be important for solving the inconsistency in any constraints satisfaction problem. Further, looking beyond the Propositional world, finding a small unsatisfiable set of constraints is important for the efficiency of decision procedures like MathSat and CVC[15] that rely on explanations of the reason of unsatisfiability in order to prune the search space. The techniques we will discuss in this paper are equally relevant to such systems as they are for systems based on propositional reasoning.

Related Work. Lynce and Silva [10] suggested an approach for finding a minimal UC, in which a new 'clause selector' variable cs_i, $1 \leq i \leq m$, is added to each of the m clauses of the formula (for example, the ith clause $(l_1 \vee l_2)$ is replaced with $(cs_i \vee l_1 \vee l_2)$). The cs variable is set to TRUE iff the clause is not selected. They then use a SAT solver that decides first on the cs variables. If all the clauses become satisfied, it backtracks to the most recent cs variable set to true. If the solver reaches a conflict and consequently backtracks to the cs variables, it means that an unsatisfiable core was found. In such a case it records the size of the core and continues to search for a smaller one, after adding a clause over the cs variables that blocks the solver from repeating the same core. A similar process was suggested also by Oh et al. [11] (the 'Amuse' algorithm), although they modify the backtracking mechanism so it performs a bottom-up search for a UC instead of searching for a satisfying assignment. Different decision heuristics result in different UCs, which are not necessarily minimal.

Huang suggests the 'MUP' (Minimal Unsatisfiability Prover) algorithm in [6]. Rather than using m clause selector variables, he suggests to augment the clauses with minterms over $\log(m + 1)$ variables. The augmented formula, he proves, is minimally unsatisfiable iff there are exactly m models over the y variables (because in this case every clause that is removed makes the formula satisfiable). Hence, the problem of proving that an existing set is minimal is reduced to that of model-counting, which MUP performs with a variable elimination technique over BDDs. This technique can be taken one step further towards finding a minimal core, by running it not more than m times. MUP shows better experimental results than RUN_TILL_FIX (see below), but only, apparently, on hand-made and relatively small formulas, like the pigeonhole problem. None of the benchmarks reported in [6] has more than several thousand clauses, and it is not clear how it scales to industrial problems.

A more practical approach is to find a small core without guaranteeing minimality, while attempting to be efficient and produce intermediate valuable results in case the external process does not wish to wait for the final result. Zhang and Malik [16] were the first in the verification community, as far as we know, to address this problem from a practical point of view. They suggested a simple and effective iterative procedure for deriving a small unsatisfiable core: they extract an unsatisfiable core from an unsatisfiability proof of the formula provided by a SAT solver and then they run the SAT solver again starting from this core, which may result in an even smaller core. Their script RUN_TILL_FIX repeats this process until the core is equal to a core derived in the previous iteration, or, in other words, until it reaches a fixpoint. The solution and its implementation seem to be the most practical one available, and is indeed widely used. The experimental results that we present in Section 6 are compared against RUN_TILL_FIX.

What Is This Article About? We describe a new heuristic, called *Trimmer*, for finding a small UC. *Trimmer* takes the role of zVerify in RUN_TILL_FIX. It can be either applied once (and generate a core smaller or equal to that generated by zVerify) or as part of a fixpoint computation, in an algorithm we call TRIM_TILL_FIX. We will concentrate on *Trimmer* from hereon and return to TRIM_TILL_FIX in the description of the experimental results.

We assume from here on that the reader is familiar with the basic inner-workings of modern DPLL-based SAT solvers, and hence describe those parts of the solver that our algorithm relies on only in general, abstract terms.

New conflict clauses are derived in a process called Conflict Analysis, by (conceptually) traversing backwards the conflict graph and locating the reason for the conflict. This process can be interpreted as a series of resolution steps [16]. The SAT solver can output a graph reflecting the resolution steps, known as the *resolution graph*. The nodes of a resolution graph represent clauses, and the single sink node of this graph represents the empty clause. Each internal node has two parents, which represent the clauses from which it was resolved. In practice this graph can represent *Hyper-resolution* (a result of several resolution steps) and hence each node can have more than two parents. The general idea of the *Trimmer* algorithm, described in detail in Section 4, is the following. *Trimmer* locates internal nodes in the resolution graph that *dominate* other nodes, called the *minions* (i.e., all the paths from a minion node to the sink node go through the dominator), and checks whether they can be proved without their minions. If the answer is yes, the minions can be removed, and consequently the size of the UC is decreased. In such a case the resolution graph has to be transformed so it reflects the new proof. This transformation is the subject of Section 4.1. *Trimmer* repeats this process until no changes in the graph can be made. Experimental results show that integrating this procedure in a fixpoint script in the style of RUN_TILL_FIX, is better than RUN_TILL_FIX, at least with the relatively short timeouts we tried (30 and 60 minutes). *Trimmer* has the advantage that it generates intermediate results rather fast. Hence, while in many cases RUN_TILL_FIX times out (i.e. it cannot finish the first iteration after the initial core within the time limit), *Trimmer* almost always finishes several iterations by that time, even if in the long run RUN_TILL_FIX produces smaller cores.

2   Preliminaries

Resolution is a proof system for CNF formulas with one inference rule:

$$\frac{(A \vee x)\ (B \vee \neg x)}{(A \vee B)}$$

where A,B are disjunctions of literals (possibly with 0 disjuncts, i.e. the constant FALSE). The clause $(A \vee B)$ is the *resolvent*, and $(A \vee x)$ and $(B \vee \neg x)$ are the *resolving clauses*. The resolvent of the clauses (x) and $(\neg x)$ is the empty clause ($\perp$). Each application of the resolution rule is called a *resolution step*.

Lemma 1. *A Propositional CNF formula is unsatisfiable if and only if there exists a finite sequence of resolution steps ending with the empty clause.*

A sequence of resolution steps, each one uses the result of the previous step as one of the resolving clauses of the current step, is called *Hyper-resolution*. For example, from

$$(x_1 \vee x_2 \vee x_3)(\neg x_1 \vee x_4)(\neg x_2 \vee x_5)$$

we can derive $(x_3 \vee x_4 \vee x_5)$ by two resolution steps (first over x_1, then over x_2), or by one hyper-resolution step.

The hyper-resolution steps leading to the derivation of the empty clause can be depicted in a *Hyper-resolution graph* (or, simply, a resolution graph). From hereon, we use the terms *node* and *clause* interchangeably, since every node represents a clause.

Definition 1. *A* Hyper-resolution graph *corresponding to an unsatisfiability proof by resolution, is a Directed acyclic Graph $G(V, E, s)$ with a single sink node $s \in V$, in which the nodes represent CNF clauses: the leaf nodes (the sources) represent original clauses, the inner nodes represent clauses derived by resolution, and the sink represents the empty clause. Each node can be inferred from its parent nodes by some sequence of resolution steps.*

Modern DPLL-based SAT solvers can output a Hyper-resolution proof of unsatisfiability. The intermediate clauses in this proof are the conflict clauses that were generated during the run, and that are on a path from the leafs to the empty clause.

We now generalize resolution graphs to *Clause Implication Graphs*:

Definition 2 (Clause Implication Graph). *A* Clause-Implication Graph *(CIG) $G(V, E, s)$ is a directed acyclic graph with a single sink node $s \in V$, in which the nodes represent CNF clauses, and each node is logically implied by the conjunction of clauses represented by its parents.*

A CIG is less restrictive than hyper-resolution graphs. They can have edges such as

- *Subsumption* $((\Phi), (\Phi \vee x))$
- *Reflexive implication* $((\Phi), (\Phi))$
- *Resolution + Subsumption* $((\Phi_1 \vee x), (\Phi_1 \vee \Phi_2 \vee p))$ together with
                                $((\Phi_2 \vee \neg x), (\Phi_1 \vee \Phi_2 \vee p))$

where Φ_1, Φ_2 are disjunctions of literals, and p, x are variables. Other implications forbidden by hyper-resolution are also possible. Figure 1 (left) depicts an example of a Clause Implication Graph.

Let L denote the leaf nodes of a CIG, and assume that s represents the empty clause. By definition of CIG, the conjunction of the L clauses is unsatisfiable, and hence there exists a corresponding resolution proof of unsatisfiability starting from the same nodes. Therefore, for the purpose of finding small UCs, CIGs are sufficient for the analysis. Our construction will begin from the hyper-resolution graph, which can be derived from the resolution trace given to us by the SAT solver, but will transform it to a CIG as the algorithm progresses.

3   Dominators

Prosser [13] introduced the notion of dominance in the context of Flowgraph analysis (originally a term related to code analysis and compilers).

A Flowgraph $G = (V, E, r)$ is a directed graph such that every vertex is reachable from a distinguished root vertex $r \in V$. A vertex $d \in V$ *dominates* $v \in V, v \neq d$, if every path from r to v includes d. d *immediately dominates* v if it dominates v and there is no other node on the path between them that dominates v. We name v a *minion* of d. The set of minions of d is denoted by $M(d)$. A node is called a *dominator* if it dominates at least one node.

In order to adapt the notion of dominators to CIGs, we conceptually reverse the edges of the CIG. Thus, the sink node now becomes the root. Figure 1 (right) presents a *Dominator Tree*, which represents the immediate dominance relation, of a CIG.

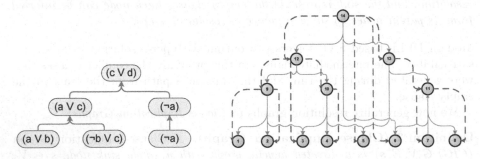

Fig. 1. (Left) A Conflict Implication Graph (CIG) (Right) A Dominator Tree over a reversed CIG. Solid edges belong to the CIG, dashed edges belong to the Dominator Tree. There is a dashed arrow from clause c to c' in Dominator Tree if c is the immediate dominator of c'.

For each vertex in a flowgraph $v \in V$, the set of all vertices dominated by v can be found in polynomial time.

Dominators in a Clause-Implication Graph. We will refer from hereon to a clause set and the formula obtained by conjoining the clauses in the set as the same thing, when the meaning is clear from the context.

Let $LM(d) \subseteq L$ denote the leaf minions of some dominator d. By definition of a CIG, $\bigwedge_{l \in L} l \models s$. The significance of a dominator $d \in V$ in a CIG is that if $L \setminus LM(d) \models d$, then $\bigwedge_{l \in (L \setminus LM(d))} l \models s$. In other words, if d is implied by the leafs which are not its minions, then $LM(d)$ are redundant in the Unsatisfiable Core. Yet removing $LM(d)$ from the CIG is not sufficient, if we want to repeat this process. The problem is that such a removal does not leave us with a valid CIG. The *Trimmer* algorithm, presented in the next section, iterates over dominators in the CIG, and substitutes whenever possible (i.e. when $L \setminus LM(d) \models d$) the old proof of the dominator d with a proof of $L \setminus LM(d) \models d$.

4 The *Trimmer* Algorithm

Our algorithm for decreasing the size of the UC is sketched in Figure 2.

Until Step 5 *Trimmer* is self explanatory. Step 6 Checks whether a dominator d has an alternative proof without $LM(d)$, which amounts to checking the satisfiability of $\varphi' : ((L \setminus LM(d)) \cup \{\neg d\})$, where $\{\neg d\}$ denotes the set of unit clauses corresponding to the negation of the clause d. For example, if $d = (z_1 \vee \ldots \vee z_n)$ is a dominator, then $\{\neg d\}$ are the clauses $(\neg z_1) \ldots (\neg z_n)$, which, for a reason that will soon be clear, we refer to as the *assumptions*. If φ' is satisfiable, the

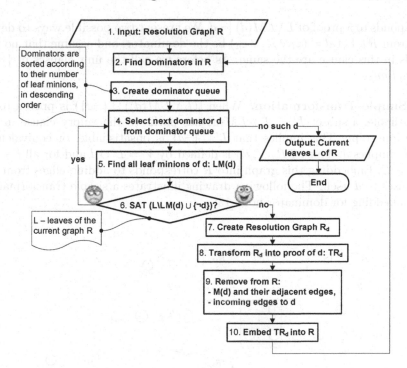

Fig. 2. The *Trimmer* algorithm

attempt failed and it proceeds to the next dominator in the queue. Otherwise, relying on the equivalence

$$((L \setminus LM(d)) \cup \{\neg d\}) \models \perp \qquad \Longleftrightarrow \qquad L \setminus LM(d) \models d,$$

in Step 8 *Trimmer* transforms the hyper-resolution graph R_d into a proof of d, and builds a corresponding CIG TR_d. A transformation is needed because the proof of φ''s unsatisfiability, as generated by the SAT solver, is a proof of the empty clause that uses assumptions. We have to transform it into a proof of d without the assumptions. We discuss two different methods for performing this transformation in Section 4.1. In step 9 *Trimmer* removes from R the graph elements corresponding to the old proof of d and replaces it with the new one, TR_d, in step 10. That is, it removes all the minions of d together with their adjacent edges and incoming edges to d, and *embeds* TR_d into R instead.

Definition 3 (Graph embedding). *The embedding of a graph $G(V, E)$ in a graph $G'(V', E')$, is a graph $G''(V'', E'')$ such that $V'' = V \cup V'$ and $E'' = E \cup E'$.*

After the old proof is replaced with the new one, the new graph is still a CIG, but has fewer leafs, and hence a smaller unsatisfiable core than the original graph.

4.1 Transforming the Resolution Graph

Recall that in Step 8 *Trimmer* is required to transform the resolution graph R_d, corresponding to a proof of $((L \setminus LM(d)) \cup \{\neg d\}) \models \perp$, into a CIG TR_d that corresponds to a proof of $L \setminus LM(d) \models d$. We present two possible ways to derive TR_d from R_d. Let $d = (z_1 \vee \ldots \vee z_n)$ be the dominator, and assume that no two literals in this clause are the same. As before we call the unit clauses in $\{\neg d\}$, *assumptions*.

The Simple Transformation. When $((L \setminus LM(d)) \cup \{\neg d\})$ is proven to be unsatisfiable, a subset $L' \subseteq L \setminus LM(d)$ has paths to the empty clause in the resolution graph. This implies that $L' \cup \{\neg d\}$ is unsatisfiable, or equivalently, that L' implies d. Thus, $TR_d(V, E)$ is defined by $V = L' \cup d$ and for all $l' \in L'$, $(l', d) \in E$. Embedding this graph into R corresponds to adding edges from the L' clauses to d itself. The following drawing illustrates a simple transformation and embedding for dominator node 13:

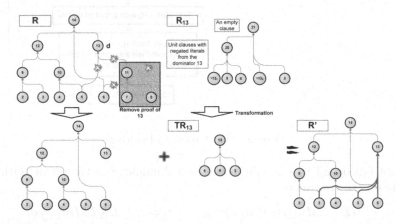

The disadvantage of the simple transformation is that it is too coarse. Since it disregards the conflict clauses, it loses the information about the way these original clauses imply the dominator. Consequently it provides little opportunity for removing more dominators in the main resolution graph. On the other hand, we cannot simply add the conflict clauses, because some of them are derived from the assumptions. What we need is a method for deriving a resolution proof of d from L'. We suggest the *Bubble transformation* method for this derivation.

The Bubble Transformation. For a given clause $d = \{z_1, \ldots, z_k\}$ and clauses $\{c_1, \ldots, c_n\}$ we build an assumption set $A = \{(\neg z_1), \ldots, (\neg z_k)\}$ and a new formula $F = \{c_1, \ldots, c_n\} \cup A$.

The *Convert* recursive transformation, which appears below, converts a resolution proof Π of the unsatisfiability of F provided by a SAT solver, to a new proof of d. It is initially called with the empty clause. Note that *Convert* is never called with an assumption leaf (these are taken care of in lines 3 and 4), and that the assumption leaves do not participate in the transformed graph. The *Resolve* step resolves between two transformed clauses on the same variable as the original resolution variable, if it still exists in both clauses in different polarity. In the end of this section we give an intuitive description of an implementation of this procedure, while for now we concentrate on correctness. The relevance of this general procedure to our case is clear: d is the dominator, A is $\{\neg d\}$ and $\{c_1, \ldots, c_n\}$ are the clauses of $L \setminus LM(d)$.

```
1: procedure CONVERT(Node: n )
2:     if n is leaf then return NewNode( n )
3:     if left(n) = (¬z_i) then return Convert(right(n))
4:     if right(n) = (¬z_i) then return Convert(left(n))
5:     return NewNode( Resolve(Convert(right(n), Convert(left(n)))) )
```

The following drawing demonstrates a bubble transformation with *Convert*, where $z \in d$:

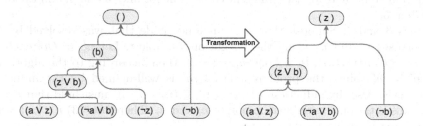

Fig. 3. A bubble proof transformation, where $z \in d$

The following drawing illustrates a bubble transformation and embedding for dominator node 13:

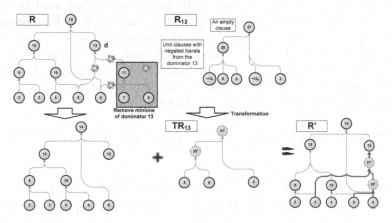

Proposition 1. *Let $\perp$ denote the empty clause of the proof Π (the proof of F's unsatisfiability). Then Convert($\perp$) returns a valid resolution proof Π' of $\{c_1, \ldots, c_n\} \models d'$, s.t. literals($d'$) $\subseteq$ literals(d).*

Proof. We use the term *proof of unsatisfiability* in order to emphasize that our proof is based on a resolution graph, not a hyper-resolution graph. The information provided by the SAT solver is enough for reconstructing any of these graphs. In order to simplify presentation of the proof even more, we use set notation for clauses to represent their literal sets.

Let $n' = Convert(n)$. We will prove the proposition by induction on the resolution graph structure using the following invariant:

- n' is well-defined
- $n \subseteq n' \subseteq (n \cup d)$.

<u>Base step</u>: if n is a leaf then $n' = n$, which is well-defined and, trivially,

$$n \subseteq n' \subseteq (n \cup d)$$

<u>Induction step</u>: there are two different cases - one for lines 3 and 4, and the other - for line 5.

Lines 3 and 4: Suppose that n is an inner node that was resolved by the two clauses n_l and n_r using the resolution variable t. Let $n'_r = Convert(n_r)$ and $n'_l = Convert(n_l)$. If, w.l.o.g. $n_l = (\neg z_i)$, then, according to the algorithm: (1) $n' = n'_r$. Since the proof is a DAG, n' is well-defined by the induction hypothesis. Also, by induction: (2) $n_r \subseteq n'_r \subseteq (n_r \cup d)$. It must hold that $t = z_i$, since this is the only variable common to n_l and n_r. Therefore: (3) $n \cup \{z_i\} = n_r$. Combining these expressions we get

$$n \overset{(3)}{\subseteq} n_r \overset{(2)}{\subseteq} n'_r \overset{(2)}{\subseteq} (n_r \cup d) \overset{(3)}{=} (n \cup \{z_i\}) \cup d \overset{z_i \in d}{=} (n \cup d)$$

Therefore

$$n \subseteq n'_r \overset{(1)}{=} n' \subseteq (n \cup d)$$

Line 5: Assuming that the invariant holds for n'_r and n'_l, we need to prove that a resolution step is valid on clauses n'_r and n'_l, i.e. that, they have opposite literals of at least one variable. Now, since Π was a valid proof, it must hold that there exists a literal t so that w.l.o.g $t \in n_r$ and $\neg t \in n_l$. Since $n_r \subseteq n'_r$ and $n_l \subseteq n'_l$, it holds that $t \in n'_r$ and $\neg t \in n'_l$. Therefore n' can be derived by resolution between n'_l and n'_r on the same t, and n' is well-defined. We need to prove that $n \subseteq n' \subseteq (n \cup d)$. Indeed,

$$n \overset{Resolution}{=} ((n_r \cup n_l) \setminus \{t, \neg t\}) \overset{Induction}{\subseteq} ((n'_r \cup n'_l) \setminus \{t, \neg t\}) \overset{Resolution}{=} n'$$

$$n' = ((n'_r \cup n'_l) \setminus \{t, \neg t\}) \overset{Induction}{\subseteq} (((n_r \cup d) \cup (n_l \cup d)) \setminus \{t, \neg t\})$$
$$= (((n_r \cup n_l) \setminus \{t, \neg t\}) \cup (d \setminus \{t, \neg t\})) = (n \cup (d \setminus \{t, \neg t\})) \subseteq (n \cup d)$$

Specially, the invariant implies that for the empty clause $\bot$:

$$Convert(\bot) \subseteq (\bot \cup d) = d \qquad \square$$

It is easy to show that the resulting graph is a CIG (a resolution graph, actually).

Convert can also be implemented with the following, more intuitive procedure:

1: **for** each assumption $(\neg z_i)$, $1 \leq i \leq n$ in R_d **do**
2:     Add z_i to all clauses on all the paths from $(\neg z_i)$ to the sink node.
3:     Remove the assumption $(\neg z_i)$ from the graph.

It can be proven that the two procedures are equivalent up to reflexive implications, although this is beyond the scope of this article.

5   Optimizations

Our tool includes the following optimizations.

1. In step 6 of the algorithm (Figure 2) rather than checking $((L \setminus LM(d)) \cup \{\neg d\})$, *Trimmer* conjoins with this formula all the conflict clauses in R that are not on any path from the minions to the sink node. This addition does not change the satisfiability of the formula, because these clauses are logically implied by $L \setminus LM(d)$. But they make the SAT solving stage incremental[14], and hence far more efficient.
2. In step 8, if none of the assumptions participate in the proof, *Trimmer* takes a different route. In this case R_d, which is the proof of unsatisfiability of $((L \setminus LM(d)) \cup \{\neg d\})$, can also be seen as the proof of unsatisfiability of $L \setminus LM(d)$, which are a subset of the clauses in the original formula. Let $L' \subseteq L \setminus LM(d)$ be the leafs of R_d. L' is a UC of $L \setminus LM(d)$, but also of the original formula, and it is smaller than the smallest core known so far (because the core of the current R is L). So, *Trimmer* assigns $R = R_d$ and returns to line 2.

6   Experimental Results

The implementation of the dominator algorithm in our tool TRIMMER is the SLT variant of the Lengauer-Tarjan algorithm[9] (which runs in $O(|E| \log |V|)$ time), as provided by the authors of [3] and published on their web site. We used version 2004.11.15 of zChaff, zVerify and RUN_TILL_FIX for both the comparison and the extraction of the resolution traces.

The benchmark suite is composed of 75 unsatisfiable CNF instances from the industrial category of the SAT competitions in the last two years, from IBM formal verification benchmarks, and BMC instances from the Sun's PicoJava benchmarks that were used in [1]. We did not include benchmarks that timed-out with both TRIMMER and RUN_TILL_FIX. The initial number of clauses ranges from $1,300$ to $800,000$, and the largest initial core size, which is our starting point, has around 160,000 clauses.

We measured two parameters: core reduction (the difference between the final and the initial number of clauses) and average velocity (core reduction divided by the time spent on the reduction). We used two different timeouts - 1, 800 seconds and 3, 500 seconds. Since UCs are typically used within a larger system in which they are extracted many times, relatively short timeouts reflect what is practically done for best overall tuning. For such systems velocity seems to be more relevant, assuming the process of decreasing the size of the UC is interrupted after a while, without waiting for the smallest core possible. The timeouts do not include the time of the first run of the solver that extracts the first resolution trace, since this step is common to all tools.

The competing systems in our benchmark are:

(Z) RUN_TILL_FIX.

(A) TRIM_TILL_FIX: running TRIMMER until it terminates, then running zChaff on the new core, then rerunning (T) starting from the new resolution graph, and so on until either a fixpoint or a timeout is reached.

(A‖Z) Running (A) and (Z) in parallel (on different machines) until the first one stops or a timeout is reached. The smallest core produced by the two programs so far is the resulting core of (A‖Z). This approach can be useful if (A) and (Z) are sufficiently different, and neither one dominates the other.

(T) A single run of TRIMMER.

The following table summarizes our results with time out of 3500 sec. *Core reduction* measures the number of clauses removed from the initial core, hence a larger number is better. An intriguing result is the superiority of (A) over (A‖Z) when it comes to clause reduction. This is because the number of clauses counted for (A‖Z) is due to the system that finishes first, which may remove fewer clauses than the other system.

The comparison between (Z) and (A) reveals that TRIM_TILL_FIX removes twice as many clauses on average as RUN_TILL_FIX but RUN_TILL_FIX is 50% faster. Note, however, the medians: the median of TRIM_TILL_FIX is 5 times larger on core reduction and 14 times larger on velocity, which is important in the realm of short timeouts. In other words, if we ran these benchmarks with a shorter timeout, the results would favor TRIM_TILL_FIX much stronger. This is also evident from Figure 5: although (Z)'s velocity is typically better, it suffers from a large number of timeouts, which is counted as 0 velocity in our calculations.

System	Velocity		Core Reduction	
	Med.	Avg.	Med.	Avg.
(Z)	1.1	200.8	729	3126.8
(A)	14.5	130.3	3404	6212.1
(A‖Z)	14.6	239.3	3310	5985.3
(T)	33.0	160.8	1464	3863.1

We also ran a detailed statistical analysis on the results, with the *ordinary sign test* – see [7] for more details. The results, referring to the differences in the

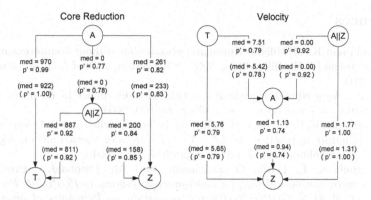

Fig. 4. Results summary of the statistical analysis of the difference in median values of velocity and core reduction. The nodes represent the competing systems, and an edge from a to b represents 99% confidence (i.e. $\alpha = 0.01$) in a's superiority over b. *med* is the median of the difference of values between the parent and its child. p' is the estimated probability of the parent's success (which is equal to the ratio of its success). The results without parentheses correspond to a timeout of 3, 500 sec., and within parentheses to 1, 800 sec. (A) is the ultimate leader in core reduction, and (T) and A$\|$Z are the fastest.

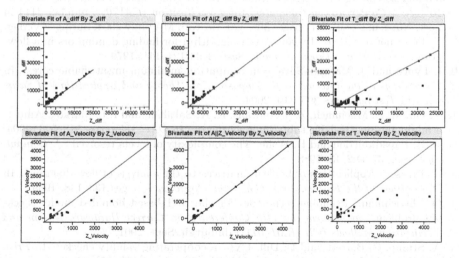

Fig. 5. Core Reduction (top) and Velocity (bottom) of A, A$\|$Z and T Compared to Z

medians of velocity and core reduction, are summarized in Figure 4. We see that there is a statistically significant difference between the competing programs both in velocity and in core reduction, with (A) and (A$\|$Z) being the winners. Note that this result is consistent with our previous conclusions.

As future work we plan to analyze *acceleration*, i.e. the velocity as a function of the elapsed time: this information can lead to new strategies and help choosing the best timeout.

References

1. N. Amla and K. McMillan. Automatic abstraction without counterexamples. In H. Garavel and J. Hatcliff, editors, *TACAS'03*, volume 2619 of *Lect. Notes in Comp. Sci.*, 2003.
2. R. Bruni. Approximating minimal unsatisfiable subformulae by means of adaptive core search. *Discrete Appl. Math.*, 130(2):85–100, 2003.
3. L. Georgiadis, R. F. Werneck, R. E. Tarjan, S. Triantafyllis, and D. I. August. Finding dominators in practice. In 12th *Annual European Symposium on Algorithms (ESA 2004)*, volume 3221 of *LNCS*, pages 677–688, 2004.
4. O. Grumberg, F. Lerda, O. Strichman, and M. Theobald. Proof-guided underapproximation-widening for multi-process systems. In *POPL '05: Proceedings of the 32nd ACM SIGPLAN-SIGACT sysposium on Principles of programming languages*, pages 122–131. ACM Press, 2005.
5. A. Gupta. *Learning Abstractions for Model Checking*. PhD thesis, Carnegie Mellon University, 2006. (to be published).
6. J. Huang. Mup: A minimal unsatisfiability prover. In *Proc. of the 10th Asia and South Pacific Design Automation Conference (ASP-DAC)*, pages 432–437, 2005.
7. M. Koifman. An approach to extracting a small unsatisfiable core. M.sc. thesis, Technion - I.I.T., Israel, Haifa, (to be published) 2006.
8. D. Kroening, J. Ouaknine, S. Seshia, and O. Strichman. Abstraction-based satisfiability solving of Presburger arithmetic. In R. Alur and D. Peled, editors, *Proc. 16th Intl. Conference on Computer Aided Verification (CAV'04)*, number 3114 in Lect. Notes in Comp. Sci., pages 308–320, Boston, MA, July 2004. Springer-Verlag.
9. T. Lengauer and R. E. Tarjan. A fast algorithm for finding dominators in a flowgraph. *ACM Trans. Program. Lang. Syst.*, 1(1):121–141, 1979.
10. I. Lynce and J. Marques-Silva. On computing minimum unsatisfiable cores. In *Proceedings of the International Symposium on Theory and Applications of Satisfiability Testing*, pages 305–310, 2004.
11. Y. Oh, M. N. Mneimneh, Z. S. Andraus, K. A. Sakallah, and I. L. Markov. Amuse: a minimally-unsatisfiable subformula extractor. In *DAC '04*, pages 518–523, 2004.
12. C. H. Papadimitriou and D. Wolfe. The complexity of facets resolved. *J. Comput. Syst. Sci.*, 37(1):2–13, 1988.
13. R. Prosser. Applications of boolean matrices to the analysis of flow diagrams. In *Proceedings of the Eastern Joint Computer Conference*, pages 133–138, 1959.
14. O. Shtrichman. Prunning techniques for the SAT-based bounded model checking problem. In *proc. of the 11th Conference on Correct Hardware Design and Verification Methods (CHARME'01)*, Edinburgh, Sept. 2001.
15. A. Stump, C. Barrett, and D. Dill. CVC: a cooperating validity checker. In *Proc. 14th Intl. Conference on Computer Aided Verification (CAV'02)*, 2002.
16. L. Zhang and S. Malik. Extracting small unsatisfiable cores from unsatisfiable boolean formula. In *Theory and Applications of Satisfiability Testing*, 2003.

Lazy Abstraction with Interpolants

Kenneth L. McMillan

Cadence Berkeley Labs

Abstract. We describe a model checker for infinite-state sequential programs, based on Craig interpolation and the lazy abstraction paradigm. On device driver benchmarks, we observe a speedup of up to two orders of magnitude relative to a similar tool using predicate abstraction.

1 Introduction

Craig interpolants derived from proofs have been shown to provide an efficient method of image approximation in finite-state symbolic model checking [10]. In this paper, we extend the interpolation-based model checking approach from finite- to infinite-state systems, in particular to the verification of sequential programs. The approach applies an interpolating prover [11] in the lazy abstraction paradigm [7]. Instead of iteratively refining an abstraction, lazy abstraction refines the abstract model on demand, as it is constructed. Up to now, this refinement has been based on predicate abstraction [12]. Here, we refine the abstraction using interpolants derived from refuting program paths. This avoids the high cost of computing the predicate image (or abstract "post") operator, yielding a substantial performance improvement.

To illustrate the algorithm, we will use the simple C fragment of Figure 1 (borrowed from [7]). We model the functions `lock` and `unlock` by setting and resetting a variable L representing the state of the lock. We would like to prove that L is always zero on entry to `lock`. A control-flow graph for the function is shown in the figure. We have initialized L to zero and added a transition to an error state when `lock` is called and L is non-zero. Our algorithm unwinds the control-flow graph of the program into a tree. Each vertex in the tree corresponds to a program control location, and is labeled with a fact about the program variables that is true at that point in the execution of the program. Each vertex is initially labeled TRUE. When we reach a vertex corresponding to the error location, we strengthen the facts along the path to that vertex, so as to prove the error vertex unreachable.

For example, suppose we first expand the path that branches to the error location on entering the loop (Figure 2a). We wish to label the error vertex FALSE, thus proving it unreachable. This is done by generating an *interpolant* for the path to the error state. An interpolant for a path is a sequence of formulas assigned to the vertices, such that each formula implies the next after executing the intervening program operation, and such that the initial vertex is labeled TRUE and the final vertex FALSE. Existence of an interpolant implies

T. Ball and R.B. Jones (Eds.): CAV 2006, LNCS 4144, pp. 123–136, 2006.

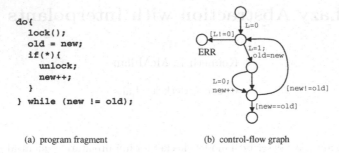

```
do{
    lock();
    old = new;
    if(*){
        unlock;
        new++;
    }
} while (new != old);
```

(a) program fragment   (b) control-flow graph

Fig. 1. A simple example program

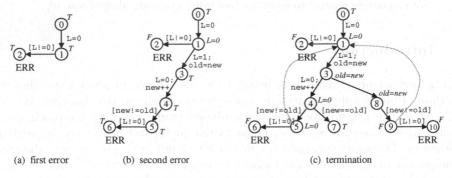

(a) first error   (b) second error   (c) termination

Fig. 2. Stages of the unwinding (vertex labels in italics)

that the final (error) vertex is unreachable. An interpolant can be derived from a refutation of the path generated by a theorem prover [11,6]. In Figure 2a, an interpolant would be: TRUE,$L = 0$,FALSE. In Figure 2b, we have strengthened the labeling on the error path with this interpolant (ruling out the error) and backtracked to explore the non-error branch. We pass through the loop, calling lock and unlock, then return to the top, taking the error branch again. In this case, our interpolant labels vertices 4 and 5 with $L = 0$ (again labeling the error vertex FALSE). Notice that vertices 5 and 1 correspond to the same location (the top of the loop) and that the label of vertex 5 implies the label of vertex 1. We say that vertex 1 *covers* vertex 5, and we cease expanding descendants of the covered vertex. However, if vertex 1 were to be strengthened in the future, it might cease to cover vertex 5, and we would have to continue expanding it.

Figure 2c shows the remainder of the unwinding, indicating coverings with dotted lines. We backtrack, expanding the path that falls out of the loop, and then the path that skips the call to unlock. In the latter case, we again reach an error state, strengthening the path. This labels vertex 9 with FALSE, thus it is also covered by vertex 1. At this point all unexpanded states are covered, so the procedure terminates. At termination, the disjunction of the labels for a given location is an invariant for that location. Notice also that the labels use the atomic predicates $L = 0$ and *old = new*, but are not the strongest facts expressible using those predicates (as we would obtain with predicate abstraction).

Rather, they are just strong enough to allow us to label the error vertices FALSE. Notice that we could also strengthen a path by computing strongest postconditions or weakest preconditions along the path (these are, in fact, the strongest and weakest interpolants respectively). However, by deriving interpolants from proofs, we exploit the prover's ability to focus on relevant facts, and thus avoid deducing irrelevant information that could complicate the analysis, or even lead to divergence.

Related Work. The most closely related technique is predicate abstraction [12]. This is implemented using the lazy paradigm in the BLAST model checker [7], and in a number of software model checkers [2,4,3] using a counterexample-based refinement loop. The advantage of the present method over predicate abstraction is that it avoids computing the abstract "post" operator. That is, in predicate abstraction, computing the set of successors of a set of abstract states requires an exponential number of calls to a decision procedure in the worst case. Because of this, weak approximations are typically used, such as the Cartesian or "Boolean Programs" approximations [1], with the associated need for refinement in case of failures. Even with approximations, computing the abstract post operator (or abstract transition relation) is still the dominant cost. By contrast, the present method requires just one call to a decision procedure for each error vertex reached, and one for each covering test.

The method is also closely related to the interpolation-based model checking method of [10]. That work only treated finite-state systems. In principle the method could be generalized to infinite-state programs, however it would require applying a decision procedure to an unfolding of the entire program up to some depth k. This would almost certainly be impractical. Using the lazy abstraction method, we only apply the decision procedure to individual program paths leading to error locations, greatly reducing the burden on the prover.

Outline of the Paper. In section 2, we will formalize the lazy interpolation-based model checking procedure, proving some results about soundness and termination. Then in section 3, we describe an implementation of the procedure in a software model checking tool called IMPACT, and compare the performance of this tool to the lazy predicate abstraction approach implemented in BLAST. Experiments using a small set of device driver benchmarks show a performance improvement of one to two orders of magnitude using the new method. Finally in section 4, we conclude and consider some future directions for research.

2   Lazy Interpolant-Based Model Checking

Throughout this paper, we will use standard first-order logic (FOL) and the notation $\mathcal{L}(\Sigma)$ to denote the set of well-formed formulas (*wff*'s) of FOL over a vocabulary Σ of non-logical symbols. For a given formula or set of formulas ϕ, we will use $\mathcal{L}(\phi)$ to denote the *wff*'s over the vocabulary of ϕ.

For every non-logical symbol s, we presume the existence of a unique symbol s' (that is, s with one prime added). We think of s with n primes added as representing the value of s at n time units in the future. For any formula or term ϕ, we will use the notation $\phi^{\langle n \rangle}$ to denote the addition of n primes to every symbol in ϕ (meaning ϕ at n time units in the future). For any set Σ of symbols, let Σ' denote $\{s' \mid s \in \Sigma\}$ and $\Sigma^{\langle n \rangle}$ denote $\{s^{\langle n \rangle} \mid s \in \Sigma\}$.

Modeling Programs. We use FOL formulas to characterize programs. To this end, let S, the state vocabulary, be a set of individual variables and uninterpreted n-ary functional and propositional constants. A *state formula* is a formula in $\mathcal{L}(S)$ (which may also include various interpreted symbols, such as $=$ and $+$). A *transition formula* is a formula in $\mathcal{L}(S \cup S')$.

For our purposes, a *program* is a tuple $(\Lambda, \Delta, l_i, l_f)$, where Λ is a finite set of program locations, Δ is a set of *actions*, $l_i \in \Lambda$ is the initial location and $l_f \in \Lambda$ is the error location. An *action* is a triple (l, T, m), where $l, m \in \Lambda$ are respectively the entry and exit locations of the action, and T is a transition formula. A *path* π of a program is a sequence of transitions of the form (l_0, T_0, l_1) $(l_1, T_1, l_2) \cdots (l_{n-1}, T_{n-1}, l_n)$. The path is an *error path* when $l_0 = l_i$ and $l_n = l_f$. The *unfolding* $\mathcal{U}(\pi)$ of path π is the sequence of formulas $T_0^{\langle 0 \rangle}, \ldots, T_n^{\langle n-1 \rangle}$, that is, the sequence of transition formulas $T_0 \ldots T_{n-1}$, with each T_i shifted i time units into the future.

We will say that path π is *feasible* when $\bigwedge \mathcal{U}(\pi)$ is consistent. We can think of a model of $\bigwedge \mathcal{U}(\pi)$ as a concrete program execution, assigning a value to every program variable at every time $0 \ldots n$. A program is said to be *safe* when every error path of the program is infeasible. An *inductive invariant* of a program is a map $I : \Lambda \to \mathcal{L}(S)$, such that $I(l_i) \equiv \text{TRUE}$ and for every action $(l, T, m) \in \Delta$, $I(l) \wedge T$ implies $I(m)'$. A *safety invariant* of a program is an inductive invariant such that $I(l_f) \equiv \text{FALSE}$. Existence of a safety invariant of a program implies that the program is safe.

To simplify presentation of the algorithms, we will assume that every location has at least one outgoing action. This can be made true without affecting program safety by adding self-loops.

Interpolants from Proofs. Given a pair of formulas (A, B), such that $A \wedge B$ is inconsistent, an *interpolant* for (A, B) is a formula $\hat{A}$ with the following properties:

- A implies $\hat{A}$,
- $\hat{A} \wedge B$ is unsatisfiable, and
- $\hat{A} \in \mathcal{L}(A) \cap \mathcal{L}(B)$.

The Craig interpolation lemma [5] states that an interpolant always exists for inconsistent formulas in FOL. To handle program paths, we generalize this idea to sequences of formulas. That is, given a sequence of formulas $\Gamma = A_1, \ldots, A_n$, we say that $\hat{A}_0, \ldots \hat{A}_n$ is an *interpolant* for Γ when

- $\hat{A}_0 = \text{TRUE}$ and $\hat{A}_n = \text{FALSE}$ and,
- for all $1 \leq i \leq n$, $\hat{A}_{i-1} \wedge A_i$ implies $\hat{A}_i$ and
- for all $1 \leq i < n$, $\hat{A}_i \in (\mathcal{L}(A_1 \ldots A_i) \cap \mathcal{L}(A_{i+1} \ldots A_n))$.

That is, the i-th element of the interpolant is a formula over the common vocabulary the prefix $A_0 \ldots A_i$ and the suffix $A_{i+1} \ldots A_n$, and each interpolant implies the next, with A_i. If Γ is quantifier-free, we can derive a quantifier-free interpolant for Γ from a refutation of Γ, in certain interpreted theories [11].

Program Unwindings. We now give a definition of a program unwinding, and an algorithm to construct a complete unwinding using interpolants. For two vertices v and w of a tree, we will write $w \sqsubset v$ when w is a proper ancestor of v.

Definition 1. *An* unwinding *of a program* $\mathcal{A} = (\Lambda, \Delta, l_i, l_f)$ *is a quadruple* (V, E, M_v, M_e), *where* (V, E) *is a directed tree rooted at* ϵ, $M_v : V \to \Lambda$ *is the vertex map, and* $M_e : E \to \Delta$ *is the edge map, such that:*

- $M_v(\epsilon) = l_i$
- *for every non-leaf vertex* $v \in V$, *for every action* $(M_v(v), T, m) \in \Delta$, *there exists an edge* $(v, w) \in E$ *such that* $M_v(w) = m$ *and* $M_e(v, w) = T$.

Definition 2. *A* labeled unwinding *of a program* $\mathcal{A} = (\Lambda, \Delta, l_i, l_f)$ *is a triple* $(U, \psi, \triangleright)$, *where*

- $U = (V, E, M_v, M_e)$ *is an unwinding of* $\mathcal{A}$
- $\psi : V \to \mathcal{L}(S)$ *is called the vertex labeling, and*
- $\triangleright \subseteq V \times V$ *is called the covering relation.*

A vertex $v \in V$ *is said to be* covered *iff there exists* $(w, x) \in \triangleright$ *such that* $w \sqsubseteq v$. *The unwinding is said to be* safe *iff, for all* $v \in V$, $M_v(v) = l_f$ *implies* $\psi(v) \equiv$ FALSE. *It is* complete *iff every leaf* $v \in V$ *is covered.*

Definition 3. *A labeled unwinding* $(U, \psi, \triangleright)$ *of a program* $\mathcal{A} = (\Lambda, \Delta, l_i, l_f)$, *where* $U = (V, E, M_v, M_e)$, *is said to be* well-labeled *iff:*

- $\psi(\epsilon) \equiv$ TRUE, *and*
- *for every edge* $(v, w) \in E$, $\psi(v) \wedge M_e(v, w)$ *implies* $\psi(w)'$, *and*
- *for all* $(v, w) \in \triangleright$, $\psi(v) \Rightarrow \psi(w)$, *and* w *is not covered.*

Notice that, if a vertex is covered, all its descendants are also covered. Moreover, we do not allow a covered vertex to cover another vertex. To see why, consider the unwinding of Figure 3. Here, vertex y covers x, but is itself covered, since its ancestor v is covered by w. This might seem acceptable, since any states reachable from y should be reachable from w through its descendant z. However, this is not the case. Because the vertex labels are approximate, it may be that $\psi(y) \not\Rightarrow \psi(z)$. Thus, z may not reach all states reachable from x.

Theorem 1. *If there exists a safe, complete, well-labeled unwinding of program* $\mathcal{A}$, *then* $\mathcal{A}$ *is safe.*

Proof. Let U be the set of uncovered vertices, and let function M map location l to $\bigvee\{\psi(v) \mid M_v(v) = l, v \in U\}$. M is a safety invariant for $\mathcal{A}$. $\square$

We now describe a semi-algorithm for building a complete, safe, well-labeled unwinding of a program. The algorithm terminates if the program is unsafe,

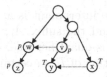

Fig. 3. Example showing why covered vertices must not cover others

global variables: V a set, $E \subseteq V \times V$, $\rhd \subseteq V \times V$ and $\psi : V \to \mathit{wff}$

procedure EXPAND($v \in V$):
    if v is an uncovered leaf then
        for all actions $(M_v(v), T, m) \in \Delta$
            add a new vertex w to V and a new edge (v, w) to E;
            set $M_v(w) \leftarrow m$ and $\psi(w) \leftarrow$ TRUE;
            set $M_e(v, w) \leftarrow T$

procedure REFINE($v \in V$):
    if $M_v(v) = l_f$ and $\psi(v) \not\equiv$ FALSE then
        let $\pi = (v_0, T_0, v_1) \cdots (v_{n-1}, T_{n-1}, v_n)$ be the unique path from ϵ to v
        if $\mathcal{U}(\pi)$ has an interpolant $\hat{A}_0, \ldots, \hat{A}_n$ then
            for $i = 0 \ldots n$:
                let $\phi = \hat{A}_i^{\langle -i \rangle}$
                if $\psi(v_i) \not\models \phi$ then
                    remove all pairs $(\cdot, v_i)$ from $\rhd$
                    set $\psi(v_i) \leftarrow \psi(v_i) \wedge \phi$
        else abort (program is unsafe)

procedure COVER($v, w \in V$):
    if v is uncovered and $M_v(v) = M_v(w)$ and $v \not\sqsubseteq w$ then
        if $\psi(v) \models \psi(w)$ then
             add (v, w) to $\rhd$;
             delete all $(x, y) \in \rhd$, s.t. $v \sqsubseteq y$;

Fig. 4. Three basic unwinding steps

but may not terminate if it is safe (which is expected, since program safety is undecidable). We first outline a non-deterministic procedure with three basic steps: EXPAND, which generates the successors of a leaf vertex, REFINE, which refines the labels along a path, labeling an error vertex FALSE, and COVER, which expands the covering relation. These steps are shown in Figure 4.

The interpolant in REFINE can be generated from a refutation of $\mathcal{U}(\pi)$, by the method of [11]. Each of the three steps preserves well-labeledness of the unwinding. In REFINE, the first two well-labeledness conditions are guaranteed by the properties of interpolants (*i.e.*, $\hat{A}_0 =$ TRUE and each interpolant formula implies the next). When we strengthen $\psi(v)$, we remove all arcs $(\cdot, v)$ in the covering relation, since a vertex covered by v may no longer be covered after strengthening v. In COVER, if a vertex v becomes covered, then all descendants of v are also covered. This means that any existing covering arcs (x, y) where $v \sqsubseteq y$ must be removed to maintain well-labeledness. If REFINE succeeds, then $\psi(v)$ must be FALSE (since $\hat{A}_n$ is always FALSE). Thus, to make the unwinding safe, we have only to apply REFINE to every error vertex. Finally, when none of the three steps can produce any change, the unwinding is both safe and complete, so we know the original program is safe.

```
procedure CLOSE(v ∈ V):
    for all w ∈ V s.t. w ≺ v and M_v(w) = M_v(v):
        COVER(v, w)

recursive procedure DFS(v ∈ V):
    CLOSE(v)
    if v is uncovered then
        if M_v(v) = l_f then
            REFINE(v);
            for all w ⊑ v: CLOSE(w)
        EXPAND(v);
        for all children w of v: DFS(w)

procedure UNWIND:
    set V ← {ε}, E ← ∅, ψ(ε) ← TRUE, ▷ ← ∅
    while there exists an uncovered leaf v ∈ V:
        for all w ∈ V s.t. w ⊏ v: CLOSE(w);
        DFS(v)
```

Fig. 5. DFS unwinding strategy

To build a well-labeled unwinding, we now have only to choose a strategy for applying the three unwinding rules. The most difficult question is when to apply COVER. Covering one vertex can result in uncovering others. Thus, applying COVER non-deterministically may not terminate. To avoid this possibility, we define a total order $\prec$ on the vertices. This order must respect the ancestor relation. That is, if $v \sqsubseteq w$ then $v \prec w$. For example, we could define $\prec$ by a pre-order traversal of the tree, or by numbering the vertices in order of creation. We then restrict COVER to pairs (v, w) such that $w \prec v$. Now suppose that in adding a covering arc (v, w), we remove (x, y), where $v \sqsubseteq y$. Then by transitivity, we must have $v \prec x$. Thus, covering a vertex v can only result in uncovering vertices greater than v. This implies that we cannot apply COVER infinitely.

We will say that a vertex v is *closed* if either it is covered, or no arc (v, w) can be added to $\triangleright$ (while maintaining well-labeledness). The procedure CLOSE of Figure 5 closes a vertex. We would like to guarantee that when a vertex is expanded, all of its ancestors are closed, thus we do not expand a vertex that could be covered instead. We could, of course, call CLOSE on all the ancestors of a vertex v before expanding it. This would be costly, however. A more efficient strategy is shown in Figure 5. The procedure UNWIND locates an uncovered leaf, then performs a local depth-first search around that leaf. During the search, it maintains the invariant that all ancestors of the currently visited leaf vertex v are closed. Moreover, all the vertices on the DFS stack are children of ancestors of v. Thus, when we pop a vertex off of the stack, we have only to call CLOSE on the new vertex to re-establish the invariant. After calling REFINE on an error vertex, the procedure calls CLOSE on all of the ancestors v. This can be improved somewhat by only re-closing those vertices that were actually strengthened by REFINE.

Theorem 2. *If procedure* UNWIND *terminates without aborting on program* $\mathcal{A}$, *then* $\mathcal{A}$ *is safe.*

Proof. Since only the operations EXPAND, REFINE and COVER alter the unwinding, and these preserve well-labeledness, the resulting unwinding is well-labeled.

Further, since all error vertices are refined, the unwinding is safe. Since the procedure terminates only when there are no uncovered leaves, the final unwinding is complete. Thus, by Theorem 1, program $\mathcal{A}$ is safe.   □

Termination. Due to decidability considerations, we do not expect the unwinding to terminate in all cases. However, in the finite-state case, or in general when the language $\mathcal{L}(S)$ has bounded ascending chains, we can show termination. A finite ascending chain is a sequence of formulas $\phi_0, \phi_1, \ldots, \phi_n$ such that for all $0 \leq i < j \leq n$, $\phi_j \not\Rightarrow \phi_i$. We will say that a language L is k-bounded, for integer k, if all ascending chains in L have length at most k. For example, the Boolean formulas over n variables are $2^n + 1$-bounded.

Theorem 3. *If $\mathcal{L}(S)$ is k-bounded, then procedure* UNWIND *terminates or aborts.*

Proof. Procedure DFS maintains the invariant that all ancestors of v are closed. Thus, there are no $x \sqsubset w \sqsubseteq v$ such that $M_v(x) = M_v(w)$ and $\psi(w) \Rightarrow \psi(x)$ (else w would not be closed). Thus, for any location l, the formulas $\phi(w)$ where $M_v(w) = l$ and $w \sqsubseteq v$ form an ascending chain. Since $\mathcal{L}(S)$ is k-bounded, it follows that the path from ϵ to v contains at most $|\Lambda| \cdot k$ vertices. Thus the depth of the tree is bounded. As argued above, COVER cannot continue to cover vertices infinitely. Thus, in the main loop, always eventually CLOSE fails to cover a new vertex, or the loop terminates. In the former case, vertex v remains uncovered, and is thus expanded in procedure DFS. However, we cannot expand vertices infinitely, since the tree depth is bounded. Thus, the loop must terminate (or abort in REFINE).   □

A Weak Notion of Completeness. In general, the FO formulas over a given vocabulary S have infinite ascending chains. Thus, the above termination result is not generally applicable. However, by restricting the language of the interpolants, we can force termination (perhaps without deciding safety). That is, given a language L, an L-restricted interpolant for a sequence Γ is an interpolant for Γ in which all formulas are contained in L. Techniques for computing L-restricted interpolants are described in [9]. Given a language L, let us define an unwinding procedure UNWIND(L) that differs from UNWIND only in that "interpolant" in procedure REFINE is replaced by "L-restricted interpolant". If language L is k-bounded, then UNWIND(L) must terminate or abort. Moreover, in [9] it is shown that if program $\mathcal{A}$ has an inductive invariant expressible in L, then every error path of $\mathcal{A}$ has an L-restricted interpolant. Thus UNWIND(L) cannot abort, and must terminate proving safety.

We can use this idea to create a procedure that is complete in the limited sense that it eventually verifies all programs that have inductive invariants expressible as quantifier-free formulas in a suitable FO theory. That is, we define an infinite chain of k-bounded, quantifier-free restriction languages $L_0 \subseteq L_1 \cdots$, such that every formula is contained in some L_k.[1] If a program has a quanti-

---

[1] Quantifier-freeness is required so that the entailment tests in REFINE and CLOSE are decidable. Otherwise completeness is relative to an oracle for the theory.

```
procedure FORCECOVER(v, w ∈ V)
    let x be the nearest common ancestor of v and w
    let π = (v₀, T₀, v₁) ··· (vₙ₋₁, Tₙ₋₁, vₙ) be the unique path from x to v
    let Γ = ψ(x) · U(π) · ¬ψ(w)⟨ⁿ⟩
    if Γ has an interpolant Â₀, ..., Âₙ₊₂ then
        for i = 0 ... n:
            let φ = Â₍ᵢ₊₁₎^⟨−i⟩
            if ψ(vᵢ) ⊭ φ then
                remove all pairs (·, vᵢ) from ▷
                set ψ(vᵢ) ← ψ(vᵢ) ∧ φ
```

Fig. 6. Procedure to force covering of one vertex by another

fier free safety invariant in the theory, then it has an invariant in some L_k. We start with L_0 and each time UNWIND(L_i) aborts, we move on to L_{i+1}. When we reach L_k, the UNWIND(L_k) must terminate. Thus, our approach is complete in the limited sense that it verifies (eventually) any program with a quantifier-free safety invariant in the theory (this is precisely the set of programs that we can verify with predicate abstraction *if* we can guess the right atomic predicates). Of course, in practice we must choose the restriction languages L_k carefully, so that termination occurs for a small value of k.

Forced Covering. To speed convergence of the unwinding procedure, we can use interpolant-based refinement to force a vertex v to be covered by some other vertex w. We will call this a *forced covering*. Suppose that v and w have nearest common ancestor x in the unwinding. We construct the characteristic formula for the path from x to v, asserting $\psi(x)$ at the beginning, and $\neg\psi(w)$ at the end. If this is infeasible (meaning $\psi(w)$ must hold at v) we strengthen all the vertices on the path from x to v by the corresponding interpolant formulas. Thus, we ensure that w covers v. This procedure is depicted in Figure 6. Clearly, attempting all possible forced coverings could be costly. In practice, before expanding a vertex we attempt a forced covering by a few recently generated vertices representing the same program location. This substantially reduces the part of the unwinding that we must explore.

Other Optimizations. As in other work using interpolants [6,8], we generate the characteristic formula of a path in static single-assignment (SSA) form. That is, we create a new instance of a program variable only when that variable is modified. This eliminates a large number of constraints of the form $x^{\langle i+1 \rangle} = x^{\langle i \rangle}$ that occur when a variable is unmodified by a program statement. When refining a program path, we also use a simple slicing (or "cone-of-influence" reduction) to remove from the program path any assignments that cannot affect the feasibility of the path. Slicing typically removes a large fraction of the assignments in the path, especially initializations of global variables that are not referenced. It should be noted, however, that slicing can affect completeness, since it is possible that a variable that is not referenced is nonetheless necessary to express an inductive invariant (it might even be an auxiliary variable added by the user for this purpose). In practice, however, this has not been observed to occur, and slicing yields a substantial performance improvement.

Finally, in the REFINE and COVER steps, we must test whether one formula entails another, using a decision procedure. Since the same test tends to occur many times, it pays to memoize the decision procedure calls.

3   Experiments

The lazy interpolation-based unwinding procedure is implemented in a software model checking tool called IMPACT[2] (carrying on the tradition of violent acronyms for software model checkers). In this section, we compare the interpolant-based method of IMPACT with the predicate abstraction approach of BLAST. The benchmarks we use are device drivers from the Microsoft Windows DDK, written in C. They were used as test cases in [6]. Each driver is provided with a test harness (*i.e.*, a main program that calls the driver functions appropriately in a non-deterministic manner) and is instrumented with auxiliary variables and safety assertions that test whether whether certain rules are obeyed in calling the kernel API functions.[3] All six of the example programs are safe. To check the implementation of IMPACT, however, we inserted three errors into each example program. IMPACT detected all 18 errors, each in at most a few seconds. Performance data are reported only for the safe versions.

IMPACT is based on the interpolating prover of [9]. This prover supports a first-order theory with equality, uninterpreted function symbols, and integer difference-bound arithmetic (*i.e.*, predicates of the form $x - y \leq c$, $x \leq c$ or $x \geq c$, where c is a constant). It also supports first-order arrays, with interpreted "select" and "store" functions. Support for full linear arithmetic is also possible, but currently not for integer models.

To handle C programs, we first reduce them to Simple Goto Programs (SGP's). These are programs containing only conditional goto statements, assignments and assertions, and whose only data types are unbounded integers and arrays of unbounded integers. Pointers and records are eliminated by this translation, and function calls are in-lined. This reduction was done using a modified version of the SATABS infrastructure [4]. Unfortunately, space does not permit a description of the translation process here.

Once a C program has been translated to a simple goto program, we can model it formally in the logic of the prover. The logic contains operations on arrays, as well as limited arithmetic. We model the unsupported integer operations (such as the bit-wise operators) with uninterpreted functions (thus we may fail to prove safety if it depends on properties of these operators). An assertion in the program is modeled by a conditional branch to the error state l_f. Transitions in the model correspond to basic blocks in the goto program. Having modeled the program, we can then verify safety using procedure UNWIND(L), where L is the restriction language for interpolation. We use the same sequence of restriction languages L_k as in [9]. This restricts the constants in arithmetic formulas to fall in a certain finite set that depends on k, and also restricts depth of function

---

[2] Interpolating software Model checker without Predicate abstrACTion.
[3] Benchmarks available from the author.

Table 1. Performance statistics on device driver benchmarks

name	source loc	SGP loc	BLAST time(s)	IMPACT time(s)	speedup	BLAST preds	BLAST post(s)	IMPACT interp(s)	BLAST vtcs	IMPACT vtcs
kbfiltr	12K	2.3K	26.3	3.15	8.3	25	23.3	2.2	1651	744
diskperf	14K	3.9K	102	20.0	5.1	84	92.2	19.3	3232	3885
cdaudio	44k	6.3K	310	19.1	16.2	108	265	11.9	5253	3257
floppy	18K	8.7K	455	17.8	25.6	105	404	16.9	9573	2518
parclass	138K	8.8K	5511	26.2	210	162	5302	22.9	8612	3720
parport	61K	13K	8084	37.1	218	224	7965	31.0	63.5K	12.7K

symbol nesting as a function of k. In fact, all of the example programs can be verified with restriction language L_0.

For comparison to predicate abstraction approach, we use the BLAST software model checker [7]. This tool is in some ways a good comparison, since it is also based on the "lazy abstraction" paradigm (using predicate abstraction instead of interpolation to refine paths). In addition, it uses the same interpolating prover to generate atomic predicates that IMPACT uses for path refinement. Thus in principle both tools should be able to construct the same class of safety invariants. On the other hand, the implementations are independent, so observed performance differences may be due in part to implementation efficiencies. In principle the closest comparison could be obtained by running both programs on the same SGP. However, as it turns out the performance of BLAST was significantly better when run on the original C source code. This may be because the elimination of pointers prevented the use of some pointer-based optimizations in BLAST. For this reason, we present performance numbers for BLAST as run on the original source code. We use the standard BLAST option that assigns to each new vertex all of the predicates that have been used for program locations in the same function scope. This tends to increase the number of predicates at each vertex, but reduces the number of refinements needed, thus yielding better performance.[4]

Table 1 compares the run time performance of BLAST and IMPACT on the six device driver examples. The first three columns show the name of the example, the number of textual lines in the source code, and the number of lines in the SGP. The last probably provides a better representation of the code size, since the source code contains much white space and many redundant declarations. The next two columns provide the run times for BLAST and IMPACT. Both are run on a 3GHz Intel Xeon processor. These times represent only the model checking process, and do not include time for parsing or translation to an SGP. The next column shows the speedup of IMPACT relative to BLAST. For the small examples, IMPACT has about an order of magnitude advantage, which increases to two orders of magnitude for the large examples.

The explanation for the performance difference may lie in the fact that the abstract post computation becomes increasingly expensive as the programs get

---

[4] The BLAST options used were -msvc -nofp -dfs -tproj -cldepth 1 -predH 6 -scope -nolattice -clock.

Table 2. Performance statistics for revised BLAST

name	source loc	SGP loc	BLAST time(s)	IMPACT time(s)	speedup	BLAST preds	BLAST post(s)	IMPACT interp(s)	BLAST vtcs	IMPACT vtcs
kbfiltr	12K	2.3K	11.9	3.15	3.8	38	6.6	2.2	1009	744
diskperf	14K	3.9K	117	20.0	5.9	119	49.8	19.3	1855	3885
cdaudio	44k	6.3K	202	19.1	10.6	180	114	11.9	3400	3257
floppy	18K	8.7K	164	17.8	9.2	154	77.9	16.9	2856	2518
parclass	138K	8.8K	463	26.2	17.7	242	175	22.9	5003	3720
parport	61K	13K	324	37.1	8.7	280	156	31.0	10.4K	12.7K

larger and the number of predicates increases. The table shows some run-time statistics that bear this out. Columns 7–9 show the number of atomic predicates used by BLAST, the amount of time spent by BLAST in the predicate image computation, and the amount of time spent by IMPACT in computing interpolants for path refinement. It is clear that avoiding the predicate image computation provides a significant advantage. The last two columns of the table show the number of vertices in the final unwinding for both BLAST and IMPACT. BLAST expands more vertices (though not enough to fully account for the performance difference). This may be because the predicate images computed by BLAST are stronger than necessary. Thus BLAST distinguishes states that need not be distinguished, resulting in a larger unwinding.

After this paper was originally submitted, Ranjit Jhala improved the performance of BLAST by making it less "lazy". In this version, each new vertex in the unwinding is assigned all the predicates seen thus far for the same program location, or if there are none, then predicates of its parent. This slightly "eager" approach greatly reduces the number of refinement steps. The reduction in refienements makes it practical to use only the predicates from the same *location*, rather than the same function scope, which reduces the number of predicates per vertex and thus speeds the predicate image computation substantially. Table 2 shows comparison data for this new version.[5] The performance gap between BLAST and IMPACT is now considerably smaller (only one order of magnitude). It could be that computing some state information in an eager manner would reduce the number of refinement steps of IMPACT as well. We leave this question for future research.

4   Conclusion

We have described a method that uses interpolation rather than predicate abstraction in the lazy abstraction paradigm. This avoids the most costly operation of predicate abstraction, the abstract image computation. In contrast to the interpolation-based model checking method of [10], it avoids constructing and refuting an unfolding of the entire program. Instead, the interpolating prover is

---

[5] BLAST options for this experiment were -msvc -nofp -craig 2 -scope -cldepth 1 -bfs except for cdaudio, which also required -clock. No single set of options was able to verify all the examples.

applied only to individual program paths, greatly lessening the burden on the prover. This makes it possible to apply the interpolation-based approach to the verification of infinite-state sequential programs. For a small collection of device driver examples, a run-time improvement of one to two orders of magnitude was obtained, relative to the lazy predicate abstraction approach. Although a greater variety of examples is clearly needed to study the trade-offs between the two methods, the experiments show that the interpolation method has the potential to provide a substantial performance improvement.

There are several potentially interesting topics for future research. Consider, for example, the following simple C program fragment:

```
for(i = 0; i < n; i++) x[i] = 0;
for(i = 0; i < n; i++) assert(x[i] == 0);
```

A safety invariant of this program requires a universal quantifier over the index of the array. Thus, predicate abstraction methods that use atomic predicates cannot verify this program. However, in [11] it is shown that an interpolating prover can be used to generate interpolants with quantifiers. This opens the possibility of generating quantified inductive invariants with the present method. There are several challenges involved in this. First the decision procedure must handle quantified formulas. Since the validity of quantified formulas is undecidable, we must have heuristics to instantiate quantifiers. Second, we must somehow prevent the number of quantifiers in the interpolants from increasing without bound. Although these problems remain to be solved, using a naïve approach to quantifier instantiation it is possible to verify simple programs like the above. Thus, it may be possible to use the method to verify properties that depend, for example, on the contents of arrays.

It also seems possible that the interpolation approach can be made to scale better by using function summaries, in an approach that might be called "summaries on demand". If we refute a program path that contains the expansion of a procedure call, we can derive an interpolant that is an over-approximation of the transition relation of the procedure (in the same way that transition relation approximations are derived in [8]). This approximation can be used as an abstraction (summary) of the procedure. When an error path is found not to be refutable, it might be refined by expanding one or more summarized functions, which would strengthen the summaries of the expanded functions. Thus, there seems to be scope for both enriching the class of properties that can be verified, and for improving the performance of the method on large programs.

Acknowledgments. Thanks to Daniel Kröning for providing the SATABS tool infrastructure used in this work, to Ranjit Jhala for help with BLAST, and to the anonymous reviewers for useful comments and corrections.

References

1. T. Ball, A. Podelski, and S. K. Rajamani. Boolean and Cartesian abstraction for model checking C programs. In T. Margaria and W. Yi, editors, *TACAS*, volume 2031 of *LNCS*, pages 268–283. Springer, 2001.

2. T. Ball and S. K. Rajamani. The SLAM project: debugging system software via static analysis. In *POPL*, pages 1–3, 2002.
3. S. Chaki, E. M. Clarke, A. Groce, S. Jha, and H. Veith. Modular verification of software components in C. In *ICSE*, pages 385–395. IEEE Computer Society, 2003.
4. E. Clarke, D. Kroening, N. Sharygina, and K. Yorav. SATABS: SAT-based predicate abstraction for ANSI-C. In *TACAS*, volume 3440 of *LNCS*, pages 570–574. Springer Verlag, 2005.
5. W. Craig. Three uses of the Herbrand-Gentzen theorem in relating model theory and proof theory. *J. Symbolic Logic*, 22(3):269–285, 1957.
6. T. A. Henzinger, R. Jhala, R. Majumdar, and K. L. McMillan. Abstractions from proofs. In *POPL*, pages 232–244, 2004.
7. T. A. Henzinger, R. Jhala, R. Majumdar, and G. Sutre. Lazy abstraction. In *POPL*, pages 58–70, 2002.
8. R. Jhala and K. L. McMillan. Interpolant-based transition relation approximation. In K. Etessami and S. K. Rajamani, editors, *CAV*, volume 3576 of *LNCS*, pages 39–51. Springer, 2005.
9. R. Jhala and K. L. McMillan. A practical and complete approach to predicate refinement. In H. Hermanns and J. Palsberg, editors, *TACAS*, volume 3920 of *LNCS*, pages 459–473. Springer, 2006.
10. K. L. McMillan. Interpolation and SAT-based model checking. In *CAV*, pages 1–13, 2003.
11. Kenneth L. McMillan. An interpolating theorem prover. *Theor. Comput. Sci.*, 345(1):101–121, 2005.
12. H. Saïdi and S. Graf. Construction of abstract state graphs with PVS. In *CAV*, pages 72–83, 1997.

Using Statically Computed Invariants Inside the Predicate Abstraction and Refinement Loop

Himanshu Jain[1,2], Franjo Ivančić[1], Aarti Gupta[1], Ilya Shlyakhter[1], and Chao Wang[1]

[1] NEC Laboratories America, 4 Independence Way, Suite 200, Princeton, NJ 08540
[2] Carnegie Mellon University, 5000 Forbes Avenue, Pittsburgh, PA 15213

Abstract. Predicate abstraction is a powerful technique for extracting finite-state models from often complex source code. This paper reports on the usage of statically computed invariants inside the predicate abstraction and refinement loop. The main idea is to *selectively strengthen* (conjoin) the concrete transition relation at a given program location by efficiently computed invariants that hold at that program location. We experimentally demonstrate the usefulness of transition relation strengthening in the predicate abstraction and refinement loop. We use invariants of the form $\pm x \pm y \leq c$ where c is a constant and x, y are program variables. These invariants can be discovered efficiently at each program location using the octagon abstract domain. We observe that the abstract models produced by predicate abstraction of strengthened transition relation are more precise leading to fewer spurious counterexamples, thus, decreasing the total number of abstraction refinement iterations. Furthermore, the length of relevant fragments of spurious traces needing refinement shortens. This leads to an addition of fewer predicates for refinement. We found a consistent reduction in the total number of predicates, maximum number of predicates tracked at a given program location, and the overall verification time.

1 Introduction

Predicate abstraction [13] is a powerful technique for extracting finite-state models from often complex source code. It abstracts data by keeping track of certain predicates on the data. Each predicate is represented by a Boolean variable in the abstract program, while the original data variables are eliminated. In most predicate abstraction and refinement based tools [4,14,6,17], spurious behavior in the abstract model is removed by adding new predicates or making the relationships between existing predicates more precise. Thus, even the information that can be discovered efficiently using other abstract domains (e.g., numerical abstract domains [10,22]) is learned only through multiple refinement iterations in the form of new predicates.

A large number of predicates poses a problem as both the predicate abstraction computation and the model checking of the abstraction are exponential in the number of predicates. In the SLAM [4] toolkit, this problem is handled by generating coarse abstractions using techniques such as *Cartesian approximation* and the *maximum cube length approximation*. These techniques limit the number of predicates in each theorem prover query. The refinement of the abstraction is carried out by adding new predicates.

T. Ball and R.B. Jones (Eds.): CAV 2006, LNCS 4144, pp. 137–151, 2006.

If no new predicates are found, the spurious behavior is due to inexact predicate relationships. Such spurious behavior is removed by making the relationships between existing predicates more precise.

The BLAST toolkit [14] introduced the notion of *lazy abstraction*, where the abstraction refinement is completely demand-driven to remove spurious behaviors. When refining an infeasible (spurious) sequence of program statements, BLAST adds new predicates only to basic blocks occurring in the infeasible trace [15]. We refer to this as *localization of predicates*. While BLAST makes use of interpolation, localization of predicates can also be carried out using weakest pre-conditions [17]. On average the number of predicates tracked at each program location is small and thus, the localization of predicates enables predicate abstraction to scale to larger programs.

The techniques described above employ over-approximations of the most precise abstract models to ensure scalability of the individual steps in the abstraction refinement loop. However, over-approximations introduce more spurious counterexamples resulting in an increase in the number of refinement iterations. Even though the refinement process is completely automatic, a large number of refinement iterations can make the entire predicate abstraction and refinement loop inefficient, and often intractable.

This paper makes the following contributions:

- Our main idea is to *strengthen* the *concrete transition relation* at a given program location l using invariants that hold at l. In standard predicate abstraction approaches (not using invariants) each program location is abstracted in isolation, that is, no relationships are assumed between the variables read at that location. Strengthening of the concrete transition relation using invariants provides additional relationships between the variables read at a program location. Thus, the abstract model produced using the strengthened transition relation can be more precise leading to fewer spurious counterexamples as compared to standard approaches.

- We show the efficacy of the above idea by incorporating an abstract domain, namely the *octagon abstract domain* [21,22], into the predicate abstraction and refinement loop. Octagonal invariants are invariants of the form $\pm x \pm y \leq c$, where x and y are numerical program variables and c is a numerical constant. These invariants can be computed efficiently by the octagon abstract domain. The octagon abstract domain has been used within Astrée [11], and was shown instrumental in reducing the number of false alarms when detecting runtime errors in critical embedded software [22]. The following ideas are needed to make strengthening using octagonal invariants beneficial in practice.

- *Invariant Generation:* Tracking octagonal relationships between a large number of program variables is expensive. In Astrée, the set of program variables is *clustered* into various sets of related variables known as *octagon packs*. The octagonal relationships between all octagon pack variables are computed separately for each octagon pack. The size of each octagon pack is kept small, so that the computation of octagonal relationships between the variables of an octagon pack does not become a bottleneck. We describe a new clustering strategy which attempts to create octagon packs containing program variables which may likely appear in predicates and their weakest pre-conditions through abstraction refinement.

- *Invariant Selection:* After invariant generation there can be many octagonal relationships that hold at each program location. Using all invariants that hold at program location l to strengthen the transition relation at program location l may not be beneficial. This is because providing too many additional relationships in form of invariants can potentially increase the burden on the decision procedure used for abstraction computation and simulation of abstract counterexamples. We describe a heuristic for *selecting* the invariants that are used for strengthening the transition relation at a given program location.

Further Related Work: The idea of using statically computed invariants during abstraction has been mentioned before [5,9,23]. Both Bensalem et al. [5] and Saïdi [23] note that using invariants during abstraction can produce abstract models with fewer transitions and less reachable states. However, in [5,9] the invariants to be used during abstraction need to be supplied by the user. An invariant generation technique is proposed in [23] which produces quantified invariants at each program location. However, the tradeoffs involved in efficiently using the computed invariants in the abstraction refinement loop are not discussed.

Constraints of the form $\pm x \pm y \leq c$ arise frequently in software verification. Seshia et al. [24] observe that most of the linear arithmetic constraints arising in software verification have the form $x - y < c$. Ball et al. [3] report that most of the queries that arise during the refinement process of SLAM are of the form $\pm x \pm y \leq c$. However, to the best of our knowledge none of the predicate abstraction and refinement tools for C code [4,14,6,17] use (octagonal) invariants during verification. Fischer et al. [12] describe a technique for obtaining a path sensitive version of any data flow analysis by using predicated lattices. Instead, we use transition relation strengthening as a means of incorporating information from other data flow analysis into the predicate abstraction and refinement loop.

2   Motivating Example

We use the counterexample-guided abstraction and refinement loop [19,7,4] to check safety properties (such as unreachability of error labels) in C programs. Consider the C program shown in Fig. 1(a) with variables x, y, z considered as integers. Assume that the statements not shown do not affect the variables x, y, z. Predicate abstraction of the C program with respect to an empty set of predicates is shown in Fig. 1(b). Observe that the control flow in both the abstract model and the C program is the same. Since the initial set of predicates is empty we cannot track the value of the conditions at program locations 1 and 10 in the abstract model precisely. Thus, the conditions at program locations 1 and 10 in the C program are replaced by non-deterministic choice (represented as * in the figure) in the abstract model. All assignments in the C program are replaced by `skip` statements in the abstract model. A skip statement at a program location l in the abstract model means that the statement at program location l in the C program has no effect on the predicates being tracked in the abstract model. The ERROR label in the C program is preserved in the abstract model.

Model checking of the abstraction in Fig. 1(b) produces an *abstract counterexample* which goes through all program locations starting from 1 to 11 (ERROR). Since the abstract counterexample may or may not correspond to a real bug in the C program, it is

```
PC                          PC                          PC
1: if (x > y) {             1: if (*) {                 1: assume (x > y);
2:     y = y + 1;           2:     skip;                2: y = y + 1;
...                         ...                         ...
5:     z = y;               5:     skip;                5: z = y;
...                         ...                         ...
10:  if (x < z)             10:  if (*)                 10: assume (x < z);
11:      ERROR:;            11:      ERROR:;
12: }                       12: }
```

| (a) | (b) | (c) |

```
PC  Invariants              PC
1:                          1: if (*) {
2:  x>y                     2:     skip;
..  x>y-1                   ...
5:  x>y-1                   5:     skip;
..  x>y-1, z=y, x>z-1       ...
10: x>y-1, z=y, x>z-1       10:  if (b)     [(PC = 10) → ¬b]
11:                         11:      ERROR:;
12:                         12: }
```

| (d) | (e) |

Fig. 1. PC stands for program counter. (a) C program. (b) Abstraction of C program with respect to an empty set of predicates. (c) Infeasible program trace corresponding to abstract counterexample in (b). (d) The computed invariants at every program location. (e) Refined abstraction with the use of invariants. This abstract model has no path to the ERROR label.

checked if there is a *feasible* sequence of statements in the original C program leading to the ERROR label and having the same control flow as the abstract counterexample. The feasibility check is carried out using a decision procedure. For the abstract counterexample produced by model checking the abstraction in Fig. 1(b), the corresponding sequence of statements in the C program is shown in Fig. 1(c). The assume statement shows which branch of the if statement was taken in the abstract counterexample.

Consider the program trace shown in Fig. 1(c). The relationship $x > y$ holds at the program location 2 (before y=y+1 is executed). Variable y is incremented at program location 2, thus, $x > y - 1$ holds after program location 2 (after y=y+1). Variable z is assigned y at location 5, so $x > z - 1$ holds after program location 5. Since x, y, z are integers, we have $x \geq z$ after program location 5. The relationship $x \geq z$ contradicts with the assume statement at location 10 ($x < z$). Thus, the trace in Fig. 1(c) is an infeasible trace. In order to eliminate the infeasible trace shown in Fig. 1(c) the refined abstract model needs to track the value of the condition $x < z$ at program location 10 precisely, as it guards the ERROR label. This is done by introducing new predicates in most tools.

Using the technique described in [15,17] the infeasible trace shown in Fig. 1(c) can be removed by tracking exactly one predicate at each program location from 1 to 10. The technique of [17] will track the following relationships in the abstract model: $x < y + 1$ is false at program location 2 (before y=y+1), $x < y$ is false from location 3 till 5, $x < z$ is false from location 6 to location 10. Note that even though three new predicates ($x < z, x < y, x < y + 1$) are introduced only the value of one predicate needs to be tracked at each program location. The drawback of these techniques is that predicate relationships need to be tracked for the entire infeasible trace, even at the program locations (3,4,6,7,8,9) not directly involved in the infeasibility of the program trace.

Next we show how the use of efficiently computable invariants (such as *octagonal invariants*) can improve the above techniques. The two variable invariants that hold at various program locations of the program in Fig. 1(a) are shown as annotations in Fig. 1(d). For example, at the program location 10 the relationships $x > y - 1, x > z - 1, y = z$ hold. The invariants shown can be written as conjunctions of octagonal invariants and can be computed using the octagon abstract domain [21,22]. For example, $x > y - 1$ can be written as $-x + y \leq 2$, and $y = z$ is equivalent to a conjunction of two octagonal invariants $y - z \leq 0$ and $-y + z \leq 0$. The advantages of using the invariants in the predicate abstraction and refinement loop are given below.

- *Reduction in the length of infeasible trace fragments needing refinement:* Let us consider the use of invariants during the detection of infeasible traces. Consider the program trace in Fig. 1(c). Without the use of invariants the trace is infeasible due to statements at location 1, 2, 5, 10. The refinement procedure generates new predicates by looking at all four statements. However, with the aid of invariants the statement at location 10 is itself infeasible because the invariant $x > z - 1$ holds at location 10 (see Fig. 1(d)). Thus, the refinement procedure only needs to look at a fragment of the trace consisting of only the statement at program location 10.

- *Reduction in the number of predicates needed for refinement:* Without the use of invariants, the refinement schemes of [15,17] track the value of at least one predicate at each program location from 1 to 10. Using invariants the refinement procedure only looks at program location 10 (PC=10) and the invariants that hold at that location. The condition $x < z$ of the assume statement at location 10 of the infeasible trace is introduced as a predicate and its value is tracked only at PC=10 in the refined abstract model shown in Fig. 1(e). The Boolean variable b represents the predicate $x < z$ in the abstract model. The constraint $\neg b$ holds at PC=10 as the invariant $x > z - 1$ holds at PC=10 in C program. With the aid of the constraint $(PC = 10) \rightarrow \neg b$ the abstract model of Fig. 1(e) has no path to the ERROR label.

Octagon abstract domain alone is precise enough to show that ERROR label is unreachable in Fig. 1(a). However, this is not always the case. If the condition at PC=10 in Fig. 1(a) is $2x < z + y$ (not in octagonal form), then the octagon abstract domain cannot show that ERROR label is unreachable. Predicate abstraction and refinement loop can still use the octagonal invariants and show the unreachability of ERROR label using the abstract model shown in Fig. 1(e), with b representing the predicate $2x < z + y$.

One reason to combine invariants with predicate abstraction, especially in the context of weakest pre-condition based refinement as in [6,17], is the problem of handling loops efficiently. Often, these techniques model multiple loop unwindings through the use of several related predicates that correspond to different loop unwindings. Instead, certain classes of loop invariants can be computed efficiently [11], and their usage inside the abstraction refinement loop can lead to quicker convergence in presence of loops.

Example: In the C code below we wish to verify the assert statement. The use of the loop invariant $x = y$ in the abstraction refinement loop can eliminate the need of numerous predicates of the form $x = 200, y = 200, \ldots, x = 0, y = 0$ which arise when using the weakest pre-condition based refinement. The invariant $x = y$ can be discovered using the octagon abstract domain.

```
1. int x = 200, y = 200;
2. while (x !=0) { x = x - 1; y = y - 1; }
3. assert (y==0);
```

In the above example, interpolant based refinement [15] may or may not succeed in finding $x = y$ as a predicate, due to its dependence on a proof of unsatisfiability of the infeasible trace. This problem is addressed in [18] where a specialized split prover is used to restrict the language of interpolants to avoid divergence and provide a (relatively) complete method for finding predicates. However, the impact of such restrictions and the practical efficiency of a split solver on large examples are not addressed.

3   Transition Relation Strengthening

We operate on a control flow graph of the given program, after various pre-processing steps performed by the F-SOFT tool [16]. Let b denote a basic block in the control flow graph. It can contain multiple assignments or an assume statement describing which branch of a condition is taken. Let $T_b(V,V')$ denote the transition relation of basic block b, where V, V' denote the state of program variables before and after executing b, respectively. An *invariant* I_b at basic block b is a Boolean formula over V. Invariant I_b evaluates to true whenever the program counter is at b in any execution of the program. Suppose we have pre-computed a particular set of invariants at each basic block. Let $CI_b(V)$ denote the conjunction of various invariants that hold at basic block b. The idea of *transition relation strengthening* is to use $CI_b(V) \wedge T_b(V,V')$ instead of $T_b(V,V')$ when analyzing b. We refer to $CI_b(V) \wedge T_b(V,V')$ as the *strengthened transition relation* of basic block b and denote it by $ST_b(V,V')$. Invariants over V' are not needed for strengthening the transition relation of b as they are implied by $ST_b(V,V')$. The strengthened transition relation $ST_b(V,V')$ can be used inside the predicate abstraction and refinement loop by using $ST_b(V,V')$ in place of $T_b(V,V')$. We describe this process in more detail below.

Predicate Abstraction Computation: In predicate abstraction, the variables of the concrete program are replaced by Boolean variables that correspond to a predicate on the variables in the concrete program. These predicates are functions that map a concrete state $V \in S$ into a Boolean value, where S denotes the set of program states. Let $P = \{\pi_1, \ldots, \pi_k\}$ be the set of predicates over the program variables. When applying all predicates to a specific concrete state, one obtains a vector of Boolean values, which represents an abstract state W. We denote this function by $\alpha(V)$. It maps each concrete state into an abstract state and is called an *abstraction function*.

The predicate abstraction of a basic block b is carried out using existential abstraction, i.e., the abstract model can make a transition from an abstract state W to W' iff there is a transition from V to V' after executing basic block b and V is abstracted to W and V' is abstracted to W'. We denote the abstract transition relation obtained by predicate abstraction of basic block b with respect to predicates in P as $\hat{T}_b(W,W')$.

$$\hat{T}_b := \{(W,W') \mid \exists V, V' \in S : (\alpha(V) = W) \wedge T_b(V,V') \wedge (\alpha(V') = W')\} \quad (1)$$

Note that the above equation computes the abstraction of b with respect to predicates in P in *isolation*. The term isolation means that no relationships are assumed between the variables in V during abstraction. However, certain relationships may hold between the variables in V when the program execution reaches b. In current predicate abstraction tools, such relationships will be discovered on-demand through multiple refinement iterations, in the form of new predicate relationships in the abstract model. Many of these relationships can however be computed efficiently in the form of invariants. The aim of strengthening is to provide such relationships in the concrete program itself, rather than discovering them in form of predicate relationships in the abstract model. Let $\hat{ST}_b(W, W')$ denote the abstract transition relation obtained by using the strengthened transition relation for basic block b, that is, replacing $T_b(V, V')$ by $ST_b(V, V')$ in Equation 1. The following claim states that predicate abstraction using the strengthened transition relation for b can be more precise than predicate abstraction of b in isolation.

Claim. $\forall b : \hat{ST}_b(W, W') \subseteq \hat{T}_b(W, W')$

The above claim follows from the definition of strengthened transition relation and Equation 1. Consider a concrete program C. Using the strengthened transition relation for each basic block in C during verification does not add any new behaviors to C or remove any existing behaviors from C. This is because strengthening provides invariants which are implicit in C. Let $\hat{C}$ denote the predicate abstraction of C obtained by using $\hat{ST}_b(W, W')$ for every basic block b in C. The following claim then states the soundness of predicate abstraction obtained using the strengthened transition relation.

Claim. Abstraction soundness: $\hat{C}$ is a conservative over-approximation of C.

Simulation of Program Traces: If the property is violated in the abstract model, we obtain an abstract counterexample from the model checker. In order to check if an abstract counterexample corresponds to a concrete counterexample, a *simulation* step is performed. By ensuring that the control flow in the concrete program is preserved in the abstract model, an abstract counterexample can be mapped back to a sequence Tr of basic blocks $b_1, \ldots, b_k$ in the concrete program, where b_1 is the entry block and b_k contains the ERROR label in the given program. Let V_i, V_{i+1} denote the state of program variables before and after executing the basic block b_i, respectively. We say Tr is *feasible* iff there is a real execution of the concrete program which follows the same sequence of basic blocks as Tr. The simulation step checks the feasibility of Tr by checking the satisfiability of the following equation:

$$Sim(Tr) := T_{b_1}(V_1, V_2) \wedge T_{b_2}(V_2, V_3) \wedge \ldots \wedge T_{b_k}(V_k, V_{k+1}) \qquad (2)$$

Claim. The trace Tr is feasible iff $Sim(Tr)$ is satisfiable.

Let $STsim(Tr)$ denote the simulation equation when the strengthened transition relation is used.

$$STsim(Tr) := ST_{b_1}(V_1, V_2) \wedge ST_{b_2}(V_2, V_3) \wedge \ldots \wedge ST_{b_k}(V_k, V_{k+1}) \qquad (3)$$

The following claim states that using the strengthened transition relation for simulation of abstract counterexamples is sound. That is, if Tr is a real counterexample (feasible), then $STsim(Tr)$ is satisfiable, and if Tr is infeasible, then $STsim(Tr)$ is unsatisfiable.

Claim. Simulation soundness: Tr is feasible iff $STsim(Tr)$ is satisfiable.

Let Tr be an infeasible trace when no invariants are used, then Tr is also infeasible when the strengthened transition relation is used (above claim). However, with strengthening it is possible that a sub-sequence Tr' of Tr is itself infeasible. In this case the refinement can be done by looking at only Tr' and the invariants that hold along Tr'. In Section 2 we presented an example where the length of infeasible trace is reduced from 10 to 1 by using the strengthened transition relation. This in turn allows refinement with fewer predicates per program location.

4   Invariants for Transition Relation Strengthening

The octagon abstract domain [21,22] allows the representation and manipulation of *octagonal invariants*, which have the form $\pm x \pm y \leq c$, where x, y are numerical variables and c is a numerical constant. The octagon abstract domain allows the representation of octagonal relationships between n program variables with $O(n^2)$ memory cost. In order to compute octagonal relationships various *abstract* operators (transfer functions) are needed. The octagon abstract domain provides all the required operators with worst case $O(n^3)$ time cost. We selected octagonal invariants for transition relation strengthening because they can be computed efficiently and are expressive enough to capture many commonly occurring variable relationships [24,3] and simple loop invariants, important for checking standard properties such as array bounds violation [21]. However, strengthening can also be carried out using other more expressive classes of invariants. Issues involved in the generation and usage of octagonal invariants are discussed below.

4.1   Octagon Packing for Invariant Generation

Computing octagonal relationships between n variables has $O(n^2)$ memory cost per program location and $O(n^3)$ time cost per transfer function. This can become prohibitive when n is large. In Astrée [11] the set of program variables is clustered into various sets of related variables, known as *octagon packs*. The octagonal relationships are computed separately for each octagon pack. The size of each octagon pack is kept small so that the computation of octagonal relationships between the variables in an octagon pack is fast. Octagon packing trades off accuracy of generated invariants for speed, and thus, choosing a right packing strategy is important for the generated invariants to be useful. We have experimented (Section 5.2) with the following octagon packing techniques.

- *Basic block based packing:* We implemented the octagon packing technique used in Astrée as described in [22] (Chapter 8). An octagon pack is associated with each basic block of the control flow graph. All the variables occurring in a basic block (excluding non-linear terms) are made a part of the octagon pack associated with the basic block. If the basic block is a part of a `while`, or `if-then-else` structure, then the variables appearing in the condition of the `while` or `if-then-else` structure are made a part of the octagon pack.
- *Control flow based packing:* We propose a new packing technique that associates an octagon pack with each condition in the control flow graph. Let $oct(c)$ denote the octagon pack corresponding to a condition c at program location l. All numerical

variables occurring in c are made a part of $oct(c)$. Then a backward traversal of the control flow graph is done starting from l. Whenever any variable in $oct(c)$ is updated through an assignment, the variables appearing in the assigned expression are added to $oct(c)$. Thus, the variables in $oct(c)$ affect the value of condition c either directly or indirectly. In the above packing techniques a user specified bound can be used to control the size of an octagon pack.

4.2 Invariant Selection for Strengthening

In general the expectation is that adding invariants would provide a performance improvement for the abstraction computation due to additional pruning of the search space. However, for the same pruning power, a smaller number of invariants is better since that would burden the decision procedure less. On the other hand, the invariants are redundant when we are checking the feasibility of an abstract counterexample. But using invariants can still speed up the feasibility check by providing facts that will otherwise need to be derived by the decision procedure. Using invariants also helps in obtaining smaller infeasible traces for refinement. Therefore, our heuristic is to use fewer invariants so that we get benefit from additional/quicker pruning, without incurring too much overhead due to additional constraints in the decision procedure calls.

For each octagon pack the relationships between the variables appearing in it are tracked at every basic block. This can result in a large number of invariants at every basic block. We apply a heuristic to filter out invariants that are not deemed important for checking the given property. Let I be an invariant that holds at the entry to a basic block b. Let $needed(b, E)$ denote the set of variables whose values need to be tracked at basic block b for checking the reachability of a given error label E. We compute $needed(b, E)$ at each basic block b by performing a syntactic cone-of-influence computation starting from E. We use the following heuristic for selecting the invariants:
InvSelect: Use I to strengthen the basic block b only if all variables appearing in I are present in $needed(b, E)$.

5 Experimental Results

We have implemented these techniques in NEC's F-SOFT [16] verification tool. F-SOFT allows checking the C code for user specified (assert statements) or standard properties (array bound violations, NULL pointer dereferences, use of uninitialized variables). Details about the software modeling in F-SOFT can be found in [16]. We used a 2.8 GHz dual-processor Linux machine with 4GB of memory for experiments. Before the abstraction refinement loop starts, we pre-compute the octagonal relationships using the octagon abstract domain library [2]. We use a SAT solver for computing the predicate abstraction [20,8] and simulation of counterexamples. We report results on TCAS and internal benchmarks. TCAS (Traffic Alert and Collision Avoidance System) is an aircraft conflict detection and resolution system. We used an ANSI-C version of a TCAS component available from Georgia Tech. Even though the preprocessed program has only 224 reachable basic blocks, the number of predicates needed to verify the properties is non-trivial for both F-SOFT and BLAST [1]. We checked 10 different safety properties of the TCAS system using predicate abstraction. None of these properties

Table 1. Comparison between three implementations of predicate abstraction and refinement loop. 1) Default: uses the localization of predicates [17]. 2) Strengthen: Uses the strengthened transition relation in the same framework as [17]. 3) BLAST: Results of running BLAST with Craig interpolation options. All times are reported in seconds. "Abs", "MC", "SR" sub-columns give the abstraction computation, model checking, simulation and refinement time, respectively. "Preds" gives the total number and the maximum number of predicates tracked at any program location. "I" sub-column gives the number of abstraction refinement iterations.

Bench	Default							Strengthen							BLAST		
-mark	Time	Abs	MC	SR	Preds	Cex	I	Time	Abs	MC	SR	Preds	Cex	I	Time	Preds	I
tcas1a	87	19	40	28	93/31	11	38	**51**	15	12	24	65/21	7.4	28	102	81/24	35
tcas1b	386	49	266	71	137/56	20	54	333	58	177	98	126/49	16	50	**278**	108/36	69
tcas2a	87	18	41	30	94/36	11.3	38	**48**	15	11	22	57/18	7.1	26	112	97/29	38
tcas2b	**95**	20	41	34	99/34	13.1	39	100	26	27	47	78/27	11.6	37	177	106/31	52
tcas3a	164	25	96	43	113/48	13.4	40	**131**	27	51	53	89/31	11.4	36	217	130/37	57
tcas3b	**56**	11	26	19	82/27	9.9	28	69	18	19	32	64/21	8.9	28	92	99/26	33
tcas4a	334	51	199	84	122/45	14.7	40	**167**	33	70	64	97/33	13	40	515	158/48	104
tcas4b	130	27	54	49	88/28	11.2	32	**90**	25	24	41	77/22	10.6	32	303	127/36	47
tcas5a	113	26	40	47	96/28	10.3	32	**27**	9	6	12	46/12	6.6	17	100	87/21	29
tcas5b	149	29	69	51	98/29	10.4	30	**87**	23	27	37	75/22	9.2	25	139	102/27	39

can be verified by using the octagonal invariants alone. We also analyzed 45 internal industrial benchmarks SW-1, ..., SW-45 for standard property violations. Some of these benchmarks have more than 1000 reachable basic blocks.

5.1 Use of Octagonal Invariants During Predicate Abstraction and Refinement

Table 1 presents a comparison between three different implementations of the predicate abstraction and refinement loop. The "Default" column uses the localization of predicates as described in [17]. This means that instead of maintaining a global set of predicates, localized predicates relevant to various basic blocks of the program are discovered by weakest pre-condition propagation along infeasible program traces.

The "Strengthen" column uses the same framework as the "Default" technique. However, it uses the strengthened transition relation for each basic block in the abstraction refinement loop. The strengthening is carried out using the octagonal invariants, which are pre-computed using the octagon abstract domain. We use control flow based packing for invariant generation and InvSelect heuristic for invariant selection (Section 4). Generation of octagonal invariants took five seconds for the TCAS benchmark. The "BLAST" column presents the results of running the BLAST [1] software model checker with the Craig interpolation [15] options craig2 and predH7.

The "Time" sub-column presents the total time taken by the abstraction and refinement loop when checking a given property. For the "Default" and "Strengthen" techniques the breakup of total time ("Time") is presented in the "Abs", "MC", and "SR" sub-columns. The "Abs" sub-column gives the total time spent in computing the predicate abstraction, the "MC" sub-column is the total time spent in model checking the abstracted program, the "SR" sub-column is the total time spent on the simulation of abstract counterexamples and refinement. The "Preds" sub-column provides two numbers separated by a slash: 1) Total number of predicates present in the last iteration of

Table 2. Results on some industrial examples. Refer Table 1 for the meaning of various columns.

Benchmark	Default						Strengthen					
	Time	Abs	MC	SR	Preds	I	Time	Abs	MC	SR	Preds	I
SW-1	29.1	8.3	2.3	18.5	53/17	14	**9.3**	2.9	0.5	5.9	16/4	6
SW-2	42.4	10.5	3.5	28.4	53/17	14	**9.1**	2.8	0.5	5.8	16/4	6
SW-3	**1.9**	0.8	0.3	0.8	16/14	5	3.0	0.8	0.3	1.9	16/14	5
SW-4	109.4	94	4.8	10.6	58/22	11	**6.3**	2.6	0.0	3.7	11/4	3

abstraction refinement loop. 2) Maximum number of predicates tracked at a given program location. The "Cex" sub-column provides the average length of infeasible traces that were given to the refinement procedure for generating new predicates. The "I" sub-column gives the total number of abstraction refinement iterations.

Reduction in the Number of Predicates: Observe that the strengthened transition relation ("Strengthen") allows checking the given properties with fewer predicates (first number in "Preds" column) on 9 out of 10 properties. Since all the three implementations use localization of predicates, the size of the abstract models produced can be exponential in the maximum number of predicates tracked at any program location. This is the second number in "Preds" column and it is smallest for the "Strengthen" column on 9 out of 10 properties as compared to both "Default" and "BLAST". As a result, the total time spent on model checking the abstractions ("MC") is smaller by 55% on average when using the strengthened transition relation as compared to the "Default" technique.

Reduction in the Length of Infeasible Traces: The "Cex" column shows the average length of infeasible traces that were given to the refinement procedure. This number is consistently smaller when using the strengthened transition relation as compared to the "Default" technique. When refining an infeasible trace consisting of basic blocks $b_1, \ldots, b_k$, new predicates are discovered at each basic block b_i by the refinement procedure [15,17]. Smaller infeasible traces were refined in the "Strengthen" case leading to fewer predicates as compared to the "Default" case.

Impact on Running Time: The significant reduction in the model checking time, enables "Strengthen" to outperform other techniques ("Default" and "BLAST") in terms of total time ("Time") on a majority of properties.

Results on SW-* *Benchmarks:* We checked these benchmarks for standard property violations using "Default" and "Strengthen" techniques. Since the standard property checks are added automatically through control flow graph modification, a comparison with BLAST was not possible. The results on some SW-* benchmarks are summarized in Table 2. The meaning of the various columns in Table 2 is the same as in Table 1. We observed a reduction in the total number of abstraction refinement iterations, predicates needed, overall runtime as compared to "Default" on many SW-* benchmarks.

5.2   Generation of Invariants

We describe results for the two different octagon packing techniques discussed in Section 4.1. For both basic block based packing and control flow based packing we limit the size of each octagon pack to 10. That is no more variables are added to an octagon pack

Table 3. Comparison between octagon packing techniques and their impact on invariant generation

Bench -mark	BB	Prop	Block				Control flow			
			Time	PackStats	Done	NumInv	Time	PackStats	Done	NumInv
tcas	224	10	18s	72/10/4.9	0	11196/5121	5s	49/5/2.7	0	3992/3456
SW-5	1587	295	190s	252/8/4.1	76	83478/38654	87s	180/6/1.5	90	35042/23431
SW-6	1986	592	264s	256/10/4.4	111	72972/50973	132s	203/6/1.5	131	58801/48612
SW-7	2440	542	576s	472/9/4.2	82	167738/87738	270s	310/9/1.5	82	105184/66130
SW-8	1472	402	237s	226/10/4.2	64	115254/90541	59s	132/8/2	64	98514/83096

once its size exceeds 10. Table 3 presents the comparison between the basic block based packing and control flow based packing and their impact on the invariant generation. Only the results for some SW-* benchmarks are reported in this table.

The "BB" column gives the total number of basic blocks in the benchmark, the "Prop" column gives the total number of safety properties (reachability of labeled error statements, or automatically generated standard property monitors) in a benchmark. The "Block" column presents the results for the basic block based packing and the "Control flow" column presents results for the control flow based packing. The subcolumn "Time" gives the total time required to compute the invariants for the octagon packs generated using a given packing technique. The "PackStats" column presents three numbers separated by a slash (/): total number of distinct octagon packs, maximum number of variables in an octagon pack, and average number of variables in an octagon pack. The "Done" column shows the number of safety properties ("Prop" column) that can be proved by using the octagon invariants only. The "NumInv" column presents two numbers separated by a slash (/): total number of invariants generated, and the total number of non-redundant invariants as computed by the octagon library [2].

Discussion of Octagon Packing Results: The control flow based packing produces consistently less number of octagon packs as compared to the basic block based packing. This is expected as the number of octagon packs is proportional to the number of basic blocks in basic block based packing, and proportional to the number of conditions in the program in control flow based packing. The maximum and the average number of variables tracked in an octagon pack is smaller in the control flow based packing technique. Thus, the time taken to compute invariants using the control flow based packing is smaller (by 2.8× on average) as compared to the basic block based packing.

In order to compare the quality of invariants generated using the two packing techniques we did two experiments: First, we looked at the number of safety properties shown correct by the use of octagonal invariants themselves. This number is shown in the "Done" column. We observed that the number of safety properties proved correct by basic block based packing was always a subset of or the same as those proved correct using control flow based packing.

Second, we used the generated invariants inside the predicate abstraction and refinement loop by transition relation strengthening. We found the addition of octagonal invariants generated (using either packing technique) to enable checking a given property with fewer predicates, as compared to not using the invariants. However, the addition of invariants generated using basic block based packing increased the predicate abstraction

Table 4. Application of InvSelect heuristic for selecting the invariants used for strengthening

Bench	Default			InvSelect		
-mark	Tot	Max	Avg	Tot	Max	Avg
tcas	3456	24	15.4	441	12	1.9
SW-5	23431	43	18	2825	14	2.2
SW-6	48612	34	20.7	3307	8	1.4
SW-7	66130	58	23.4	5068	14	1.8
SW-8	83096	73	56.5	14844	31	10.1

computation and simulation times significantly causing an overall increase in runtimes, as compared to not using invariants. For the TCAS benchmark after invariant generation and selection, an average of 8.6 invariants were added to each basic block when using the basic block based packing, as compared to an average of 1.9 invariants when using control flow based packing. As fewer invariants are added to each basic block with control flow based packing, the increase in abstraction computation and refinement times is much less as compared to using the basic block based packing. Overall, the addition of invariants generated using control flow based packing reduces the total runtime as compared to not using the invariants as discussed in Table 1, 2.

Why control flow based packing is useful: In many tools the generation of new predicates for abstraction refinement is done by computing the weakest pre-conditions of the conditions present in the control flow graph. Suppose the weakest pre-condition of a condition c for a certain number of steps results in predicates $p_1, \ldots, p_n$. Let $pvars$ denote the set of variables appearing in the predicates $p_1, \ldots, p_n$ and condition c. Let $vars(c)$ denote the octagon pack corresponding to condition c in the control flow based packing. If the size of $vars(c)$ is not restricted, then it is the case that $pvars \subseteq vars(c)$. Thus, the octagon packs computed using control flow based packing tend to cluster those variables for which relationships will be discovered later (through refinement) as new predicates and their weakest pre-conditions. Eagerly computing the relationships for such clusters and using them in the predicate abstraction and refinement loop, thus, attempts to get most benefit out of the efficiently computable invariants.

5.3   Invariant Selection for Strengthening

After invariant generation there can be many octagonal invariants that hold at each program location. As argued in Section 4.2, using all invariants that hold at program location l to strengthen the transition relation at l may not be beneficial. We apply a heuristic to filter out invariants that are not deemed important for checking a given property. The impact of the invariant selection heuristic InvSelect (Section 4.2) on the number of invariants that get selected for strengthening is summarized in Table 4. The "Default" column shows the statistics before InvSelect selection heuristic is applied. The "InvSelect" column gives the statistics after InvSelect selection heuristic is applied. The sub-column "Tot" gives the total number of invariants that get selected, the "Max" sub-column gives the maximum number of invariants selected at a basic block, and the "Avg" sub-column gives the average number of invariants selected at a basic block.

The invariant selection heuristic InvSelect (Section 4.2) helps in reducing the number of invariants that get selected at each basic block for transition relation strengthening.

For the TCAS benchmark, application of the InvSelect heuristic reduces the average number of invariants available for strengthening a given basic block from 15.4 to 1.9.

6 Conclusion

In this paper we presented how efficiently computable invariants can be used to improve the counterexample-guided abstraction refinement flow such as used in software verification tools using predicate abstraction. The invariants at program location l are *selectively* added to the concrete transition relation at l to obtain a *strengthened* transition relation at l. Using a strengthened transition relation in the predicate abstraction and refinement loop can lead to the creation of more precise abstract models leading to fewer and shorter infeasible traces. This can allow checking a given property with fewer predicates. More importantly, this technique can help in checking properties where using the standard predicate abstraction and refinement loop alone will take too long to converge (for example, properties depending on loop invariants). In our experiments we found a consistent reduction in the total number of predicates, maximum number of predicates tracked at a given program location, and the overall verification time.

Acknowledgment. We thank Antoine Miné for answering questions about the octagon abstract domain library, and Ranjit Jhala, Rupak Majumdar for their help with BLAST.

References

1. BLAST tool, http://embedded.eecs.berkeley.edu/blast/.
2. Octagon abstract domain library, http://www.di.ens.fr/~mine/oct/.
3. T. Ball, B. Cook, S.K. Lahiri, and L. Zhang. Zapato: Automatic theorem proving for predicate abstraction refinement. In *Computer-Aided Verification (CAV)*, pages 457–461, 2004.
4. T. Ball and S. K. Rajamani. Automatically validating temporal safety properties of interfaces. In *SPIN*, pages 103–122, 2001.
5. S. Bensalem, Y. Lakhnech, and S. Owre. Computing abstractions of infinite state systems compositionally and automatically. In *CAV*, pages 319–331, 1998.
6. S. Chaki, E. Clarke, A. Groce, S. Jha, and H. Veith. Modular verification of software components in C. In *ICSE*, pages 385–395, 2003.
7. E. Clarke, O. Grumberg, S. Jha, Y. Lu, and Veith H. Counterexample-guided abstraction refinement. In *CAV*, pages 154–169. Springer-Verlag, 2000.
8. E. Clarke, D. Kroening, N. Sharygina, and K. Yorav. Predicate abstraction of ANSI-C programs using SAT. *Formal Methods in System Design*, 25:105–127, Sep–Nov 2004.
9. M. Colón and T. E. Uribe. Generating finite-state abstractions of reactive systems using decision procedures. In *CAV*, pages 293–304, 1998.
10. P. Cousot and R. Cousot. Abstract interpretation: a unified lattice model for static analysis of programs by construction or approximation of fixpoints. In *POPL*, pages 238–252, 1977.
11. P. Cousot, R. Cousot, J. Feret, L. Mauborgne, A. Miné, D. Monniaux, and X. Rival. The Astreé analyzer. In *ESOP*, pages 21–30, 2005.
12. J. Fischer, R. Jhala, and R. Majumdar. Joining dataflow with predicates. In *FSE*, 2005.
13. S. Graf and H. Saïdi. Construction of abstract state graphs with PVS. In *CAV*, 1997.
14. T. A. Henzinger, R. Jhala, R. Majumdar, and G. Sutre. Lazy abstraction. In *Symposium on Principles of Programming Languages*, pages 58–70, 2002.

15. T.A. Henzinger, R. Jhala, R. Majumdar, and K.L. McMillan. Abstractions from proofs. In *POPL*, pages 232–244, 2004.
16. F. Ivančić, I. Shlyakhter, A. Gupta, Malay K. Ganai, V. Kahlon, C. Wang, and Z. Yang. Model checking C programs using F-SOFT. In *ICCD*. IEEE, 2005.
17. H. Jain, F. Ivančić, A. Gupta, and M.K. Ganai. Localization and register sharing for predicate abstraction. In *TACAS*, pages 397–412, 2005.
18. R. Jhala and K. L. McMillan. A practical and complete approach to predicate refinement. In *TACAS*, volume 3920, pages 459–473. Springer, 2006.
19. R.P. Kurshan. *Computer-aided verification of coordinating processes: the automata-theoretic approach.* Princeton University Press, 1994.
20. S. K. Lahiri, R. E. Bryant, and B. Cook. A symbolic approach to predicate abstraction. In W. A. Hunt and F. Somenzi, editors, *CAV*, number 2725 in LNCS, pages 141–153, 2003.
21. A. Miné. The octagon abstract domain. In *AST 2001 in WCRE 2001*, IEEE, pages 310–319. IEEE CS Press, October 2001. http://www.di.ens.fr/~mine/publi/article-mine-ast01.pdf.
22. A. Miné. *Weakly Relational Numerical Abstract Domains.* PhD thesis, December 2004.
23. H. Saïdi. Modular and incremental analysis of concurrent software systems. In *ASE*, 1999.
24. S. A. Seshia and R. E. Bryant. Deciding quantifier-free presburger formulas using parameterized solution bounds. In *LICS*, pages 100–109, 2004.

Counterexamples with Loops
for Predicate Abstraction*

Daniel Kroening and Georg Weissenbacher**

Computer Systems Institute, ETH Zurich, 8092 Zurich, Switzerland
{daniel.kroening, georg.weissenbacher}@inf.ethz.ch

Abstract. Predicate abstraction is a major abstraction technique for
the verification of software. Data is abstracted by means of Boolean
variables, which keep track of predicates over the data. In many cases, the
technique suffers from the fact that it requires at least one predicate for
each iteration of a loop construct in the program. We propose to extract
looping counterexamples from the abstract model, and to parameterize
the simulation instance in the number of loop iterations.

1 Introduction

Software Model Checking [1] promises an automatic way to discover flaws in large
computer programs. Despite of this promise, software model checking techniques
are applied rarely, as software verification tools lack scalability due to the state-
space explosion problem.

Abstraction techniques map the original, concrete set of states to a smaller set
of states in a way that preserves the property of interest. Predicate abstraction is
one of the most popular and widely applied methods for systematic state-space
reduction of programs [2]. This technique is promoted by the success of the SLAM
project [3,4]. SLAM is used to show lightweight properties of Windows device
drivers, and predicate abstraction enables SLAM to scale to large instances.

In predicate abstraction, data is abstracted by keeping track of certain predicates over the data. Each predicate is represented by a Boolean variable in the
abstract program, while the original data variables are eliminated. The resulting
Boolean program is an over-approximation of the original program. One starts
with a coarse abstraction, and if it is found that an error-trace reported by the
model checker is not realistic, the error trace is used to refine the abstract program, and the process proceeds until no spurious error traces can be found [5].
The actual steps of the loop follow the *abstract-verify-refine* paradigm [6]. A
second well-known implementation of this method is the software model checker
BLAST [7].

In many cases, the technique suffers from the fact that it requires at least one
predicate for each iteration of a loop construct in the program. This is due to the
fact that the simulation and refinement phases are ignorant of program loops.

---

* This research is supported in part by an award from IBM Research.
** Supported by a Microsoft Research European PhD scholarship.

T. Ball and R.B. Jones (Eds.): CAV 2006, LNCS 4144, pp. 152–165, 2006.
© Springer-Verlag Berlin Heidelberg 2006

The existing simulation techniques exactly simulate as many loop iterations as contained in the abstract trace. Most of the existing refinement techniques correspond to performing one more unwinding of the loop.

The information about looping structures is actually contained within the abstract model $\hat{M}$. However, the model checkers for $\hat{M}$ never output error traces with loops, as they aim at counterexamples that are as short as possible.

Contribution. We propose a novel predicate abstraction algorithm that makes two contributions:

1. We extend the abstraction refinement framework with the concept of abstract counterexamples that contain (possibly nested) loops. We add the capability to compute such counterexamples to BOPPO [8], a symbolic model checker for Boolean programs. The computation is done by means of a propositional SAT solver.
2. We describe a two-phase algorithm for simulating such a *looping counterexample* on the concrete model. The first phase attempts to compute a number n that corresponds to the number of loop iterations necessary to reach an error state. It is built using closed form solutions of recurrences and over-approximates the program. The second phase is a conventional simulation with n unwindings of the loop, which rules out spurious counterexamples. The predicates contained in the equation built for the first phase are used to improve the refinement in case the trace is spurious.

We report experimental results, which demonstrate that that our algorithm improves the performance significantly for benchmarks where a conventional abstraction refinement implementation has to perform repeated refinement steps to unroll the loop.

Related Work. The NEWTON tool is used by the SLAM toolkit to decide the feasibility of counterexamples and to generate new predicates in order to refine the abstraction [9]. NEWTON is limited to finite counterexamples without loops. Therefore, SLAM suffers from the problem described above.

Path Slicing is an approach that shortens counterexamples by dropping statements that have no impact on the reachability of the program location in question [10]. The statements and branches that can be bypassed are eliminated by backward slicing: For each program location, the set of relevant variables whose valuations at that point determine whether or not the error location is reachable is computed. The feasibility of a path slice implies the feasibility of the original counterexample, but assumes termination of the omitted code sequences.

Path slicing eliminates loops during the symbolic simulation if and *only* if they do *not* contribute to the reachability of the error location. Therefore, path slicing is orthogonal to the approach that we present, since it prevents expensive unrolling of loops that are not related to the error.

Linear programs have been proposed by Armando as an alternative, finer grained formalism for abstractions of sequential programs [11]. Due to the higher expressiveness of linear programs (in comparison to Boolean programs), this approach may yield a smaller number of spurious execution traces. However, the abstraction algorithm is restricted to a pointer-less subset of the C programming language that employs linear arithmetics and arrays [12].

Rybalchenko and Podelski present a complete method for detecting linear ranking functions of unnested program loops [13]. The inferred ranking function poses an upper bound for the iterations of the loop. This bound is not necessarily tight. Combined with abstraction-refinement, this approach enables proofs of program termination [14]. A proof of termination is insufficient to show the feasibility of counterexamples with loops, since the violation of the property usually depends on the number of iterations. Therefore, we utilize an incomplete method that provides the exact number of loop iterations necessary to reach the error state.

Linear algebra can be used for an inter-procedural program analysis that computes all affine relations which are valid at a program point [15]. The analysis presented by Müller-Olm interprets all assignment statements with affine expressions on the right hand side, while all other assignments are considered to be non-deterministic. It infers all linear and polynomial relations (up to a given degree). The approach is control-flow insensitive and cannot be used to decide reachability. The relations over the induction variables of a loop could aid the computation of the number of loop iterations that makes a counterexample feasible.

Zhang provides a sufficient condition for infinite looping and uses constraint solving techniques to detect infinite loops [16]. The method is sound, but not complete, since it is based on deciding theorems that involve non-linear integer arithmetic. The only goal of this approach is the detection of infinite loops. Feasibility of terminating loops is not discussed. Furthermore, nested loops are not considered.

Van Engelen presents an analysis method for dependence testing in the presence of nonlinear and non-closed array index expressions and pointer references [17]. His work is discussed in more detail in context with our loop simulation algorithm in Section 4. Van Engelen's approach targets compiler optimization, while our approach aims at feasibility checking and refinement.

Outline. The paper is organized as follows. Section 2 provides background on predicate abstraction refinement for software programs. The contribution of this paper is in Sections 3 to 4. Section 3 describes the syntax and semantics of looping abstract counterexamples. The simulation of such counterexamples on the concrete program is illustrated in Section 4. Experimental results are provided in Section 5.

2   Background

2.1   Predicate Abstraction and Refinement

Figure 1 shows an overview of counterexample-guided abstraction refinement. We provide background on each of the four steps of the loop.

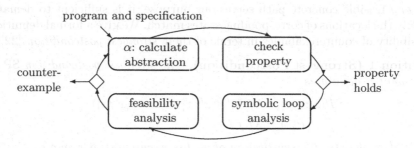

Fig. 1. Counterexample-guided abstraction refinement with two-phase simulation

Abstraction. The concrete model M is mapped to an abstract model $\hat{M}$ by means of an abstraction function α. The abstraction function α maps concrete states $s \in S$ to abstract states $\hat{s} \in \hat{S}$. We use γ to denote α^{-1}, which maps an abstract state back to a set of corresponding concrete states. Existential abstraction [18] is a reachability preserving transformation that guarantees that the abstract transition relation $\xrightarrow{a}$ is an over-approximation of $\xrightarrow{c}$, the transition relation of the original program. For reasons of efficiency, most implementations also over-approximate $\xrightarrow{a}$.

Given a set of predicates P, a *predicate abstraction* $\alpha_P(\varphi)$ is the strongest Boolean combination $\hat{\varphi}$ of these predicates such that φ implies $\hat{\varphi}$. The variables of the abstract state $\hat{s} \in \hat{S}$ correspond to the predicates in P, and their valuation is determined by $\hat{\varphi}$.

Verifying $\hat{M}$. The model checker for $\hat{M}$ searches the state space of $\hat{M}$ for states that violate a given specification. If no such state exists, the property holds on M, and the algorithm terminates. If an error state $\hat{s}_n$ exists, the model checker reports a counterexample that is a sequence of states $\hat{s}_1, \ldots, \hat{s}_n$ s.t. $\hat{s}_1$ is an initial state, $\hat{s}_i \xrightarrow{a} \hat{s}_{i+1}$ for each $i, 1 \leq i < n$, and $\hat{s}_n$ is an error state.

BEBOP is a symbolic model checker for Boolean programs that is used in SLAM to check the abstract model [19]. Boolean programs provide the same control flow constructs (including function calls) as C programs. BEBOP uses BDDs as internal representation for states and features function summarization.

MOPED is a BDD-based model checker for pushdown systems [20], which are as expressive as Boolean programs. ZING [21], an explicit-state model checker for concurrent programs, is used in an experimental version of SLAM that provides support for the verification of concurrent programs [8].

BEBOP, MOPED, and ZING produce counterexamples $\hat{s}_1, \ldots, \hat{s}_n$ with the property $\hat{s}_i \neq \hat{s}_j$ for all $i \neq j$, since they aim at providing the shortest counterexample possible.

Simulation. An abstract counterexample $\hat{s}_1, \hat{s}_2, \ldots, \hat{s}_n$ is feasible in M iff there exists a corresponding sequence of concrete states $s_1, s_2, \ldots, s_n$ such that $s_i \in \gamma(\hat{s}_i)$ for $1 \leq i \leq n$ and there is a concrete transition $s_i \xrightarrow{c} s_{i+1}$ for $1 \leq i < n$.

Since *any* feasible concrete path serves our purpose, it is sufficient to demand that only the locations of corresponding states match. We give a formal definition of feasibility of counterexamples in terms of their *strongest postcondition* [22].

Definition 1 (Strongest Postcondition). *The strongest postcondition* SP *of a statement is defined as*

$$SP(x := e) = \lambda f. \exists x'. f[x'/x] \wedge (x = e[x'/x])$$
$$SP(e) = \lambda f. f \wedge e$$

where $e[x'/x]$ *denotes the substitution of all free occurences of* x *in* e *by* x'.

Let $\ell(\hat{s}_i)$ denote the program location that is part of the abstract state $\hat{s}_i$, and let σ_i denote the concrete statement corresponding to $\ell(\hat{s}_i)$. The strongest postcondition for the sequence of statements $\sigma_1, \ldots, \sigma_n$ is $SP(\sigma_1, \ldots, \sigma_n) := SP(\sigma_n) \circ SP(\sigma_{n-1}) \circ \ldots \circ SP(\sigma_1)$. The resulting quantifiers can be eliminated by means of skolemization. Intuitively, this corresponds to a transformation of the path into *single static assignment* form (SSA) [23]. The formula $SP(\sigma_1, \ldots, \sigma_n)(\mathtt{true})$ represents all states that are reachable by executing the statements on the path $s_1, \ldots, s_n$.

Definition 2 (Feasibility of Counterexamples). *A counterexample is feasible iff* $SP(\bar{\sigma})(\mathtt{true})$ *is satisfiable for the corresponding sequence* $\bar{\sigma}$ *of concrete statements. A counterexample is* spurious *if it has an infeasible prefix.*

NEWTON uses a general purpose Nelson-Oppen style theorem prover to determine the feasiblity of counterexamples. Our model checker SATABS [24] translates the strongest postconditions into Boolean formulas and uses an incremental SAT solver to decide the SAT instances that result from unwinding the path.

Refinement. If the simulation yields a spurious counterexample p, $\hat{M}$ is refined such that p is removed from $\hat{M}$. This is done by adding an appropriate set of predicates. NEWTON uses heuristics to extract such predicates from $SP(p)$. McMillan observed that for each cut point of the path there exists a formula ψ (called the *Craig interpolant*) that represents precisely the facts that need to be known between σ_i to σ_{i+1} to prove infeasibility [25]. This approach is implemented in BLAST. A preliminary analysis identifies a number of promising cut points. The resulting interpolants are then used as new predicates. Both NEWTON and BLAST are unaware of loops and handle unrolled loops the same way as counterexamples that do not contain iterations.

2.2   Abstracting Programs with Loops

The traditional abstraction-refinement scheme with predicate abstraction performs poorly on programs that contain loops as shown in Figure 2. SLAM, BLAST, and previous versions of SATABS need at least 1000 refinement steps that successively add predicates over the loop counter (as indicated in Figure 3) to produce a feasible counterexample. We present a detection algorithm for loops contained in the abstract model in Section 3 and a novel two-phased simulation approach in Section 4.

```
int i, s = 0;
int a[1000];
for (i = 0; i ≤ 1000; i = i + 1) {
    assert(i < 1000);
    s = s + a[i]; }
```

Fig. 2. A simple program with a buffer overflow

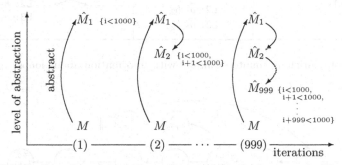

Fig. 3. Iterative abstraction refinement for the program in Figure 2

3   Abstract Counterexamples with Loops

Counterexamples with Loops. Consider the Boolean Program in Figure 4(a): It is the abstraction of the program in Figure 2 with respect to the assertion predicate $(i < 1000)$ and the loop condition $(i \leq 1000)$. For this program, all model checkers listed in Section 2 report the spurious counterexample 4(b). An inspection of the abstract model reveals that $\hat{M}$ contains a path with a potential iteration that traverses the same program locations as the spurious counterexample. Figure 4(c) shows a variant of the counterexample. The *repetition signs* ‖: and :‖ indicate that the sequence of enclosed states can be iterated arbitrarily often. The sequence of states to the right of the loop denotes the path that can be taken to reach the error state.

Figure 5 shows the structure of the counterexample 4(c). Each iteration of the loop visits the same program locations. Due to the non-deterministic assignment at location L5, the final iteration traverses a different sequence of states than the previous iterations. The counterexample in Figure 5 represents an *infinite set* of conventional counterexamples, one of which corresponds to the feasible path that violates the assertion in Figure 2 after 1000 iterations.

We define the semantics of a counterexample with loops in terms of the infinite set of conventional counterexamples it represents (Figure 6). We use the following notation: The double square brackets $[\![path]\!]$ denote the *expansion* of a path. The state indicated by $path[i]$ is the ith element of *path*. The function length(*path*) returns the number of states in a *path* without loops. The expression $(path_r)^*path$ denotes *all* paths that contain an arbitrary number of repetitions of $path_r$ followed by the postfix *path*. The concatenation operation $A^\frown B$ denotes all concatenations of each path p_a in set A with each path p_b in set B for which

(a) Boolean program	(b) Counterexample	(c) Counterexample with loop
bool b_1; /* $i < 1000$ */ bool b_2; /* $i \leq 1000$ */ L1: b_1, b_2 :=1,1; L2: if (!b_2) goto L7; L3: assert (b_1); L4: skip; L5: b_1, b_2 :=*,*; L6: goto L2; L7: skip;	L1: $b_1 \, b_2$ L2: $b_1 \, b_2$ L3: $b_1 \, b_2$ L4: $b_1 \, b_2$ L5: $\bar{b}_1 \, b_2$ L6: $\bar{b}_1 \, b_2$ L2: $\bar{b}_1 \, b_2$ L3: $\bar{b}_1 \, b_2$	L1: $b_1 \, b_2$ ‖: L2: $b_1 \, b_2$ L2: $b_1 \, b_2$ L3: $b_1 \, b_2$ L3: $b_1 \, b_2$ L4: $b_1 \, b_2$ L4: $b_1 \, b_2$ L5: $b_1 \, b_2$ L5: $\bar{b}_1 \, b_2$ L6: $b_1 \, b_2$:‖ L6: $\bar{b}_1 \, b_2$ L2: $\bar{b}_1 \, b_2$ L3: $\bar{b}_1 \, b_2$

Fig. 4. Enriching counterexamples with information about loops

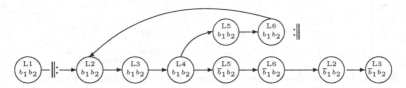

Fig. 5. Counterexample with loop for Figure 4(a)

there is an abstract transition from the last state of p_a to the first state of p_b. Note that the recursive syntax definition enables nested loops.

Definition 3 (Feasibility of counterexamples with loops). *An abstract counterexample p with loops is feasible iff $[\![p]\!]$ contains a path that is feasible according to Definition 2.*

Detection of Loops. A counterexample with loops can be constructed from a conventional counterexample $p = \hat{s}_1, \ldots, \hat{s}_n$ by performing a symbolic simulation of the abstract model along the locations $\ell(\hat{s}_1), \ldots, \ell(\hat{s}_n)$. At each location $\ell(\hat{s}_i)$ in p we search for a state $\hat{s}_j, j < i$ that allows us to fork a path that traverses the locations $\ell(\hat{s}_j), \ldots, \ell(\hat{s}_i)$ and then returns to $\hat{s}_j$. Figure 7 shows the pseudo code for this algorithm. The number of decision problems generated by this algorithm is quadratic in the length of the original path.

This loop detection algorithm obviously fails to compute all loops along p that are contained in $\hat{M}$. It misses loops that do not repeatedly visit the same state at the head of the loop. Furthermore, it (intentionally) does not detect loops that traverse different locations (e.g., branches of a conditional statement) in each iteration. Note that the latter kind of loop does not conform to the semantics given in Figure 6.

In both cases, the abstraction-refinement scheme is still sound. Any feasible counterexample that our loop detection misses is eventually found in a later iteration. Refinement boils down to successive unrolling of loops that are not detected. Thus, we either obtain a conventional counterexample, or the repetitive concatenation of the loop body results in an abstract loop that matches the criteria of the loop detection algorithm.

Syntax	Semantics
$path \to$ **state** $\mid$ '$\|$:' $path$ ':$\|$' $\mid$ $path\ path$	$[\![\|\!:path\!:\|]\!] = [\![(path_r)^* path_p]\!]$, foreach $path_p \in [\![path]\!]$ with $path_r$ such that length($path_r$)=length($path_p$)$\wedge$ $\forall i \in \{1,\ldots,$length($path_r$)$\}$. $\ell(path_r[i]) = \ell(path_p[i])$ $[\![path_1\,path_2]\!] = [\![path_1]\!] \frown [\![path_2]\!]$, where $[\![A]\!] \frown [\![B]\!]$ denotes $\{p_a p_b \mid p_a \in [\![A]\!] \wedge p_b \in [\![B]\!] \wedge$ $p_a[$length(p_a)$] \xrightarrow{a} p_b[1]\}$

Fig. 6. Syntax and semantics of abstract counterexamples with loops

FindLoops($\hat{s}_1,\ldots,\hat{s}_n$)
1 **foreach** $i \in \{1,\ldots,n\},\ j < i$:
2   **if** $\exists \hat{s}'_j,\ldots,\hat{s}'_i.\ \forall k \in \{j,\ldots,i\}.\ell(\hat{s}'_k) = \ell(\hat{s}_k)\wedge$
3          $\forall k \in \{j,\ldots,i-1\}.\hat{s}'_k \xrightarrow{a} \hat{s}'_{k+1}\wedge\ \hat{s}'_j = \hat{s}_j \wedge \hat{s}'_i \xrightarrow{a} \hat{s}'_j$
4   **then** insert $\|$: $\hat{s}'_j,\ldots,\hat{s}'_i$:$\|$
5 **return** counterexample $\hat{s}_1,\ldots,\hat{s}_n$ with loops

Fig. 7. Pseudo code for loop detection

Our approach does not necessarily benefit from a more agressive loop detection algorithm. Our experiments indicate that it is advantageous to keep the number of loops in a counterexample small, since the simulation of concrete loops is expensive.

We have implemented the algorithm of Figure 7 in Boppo. Boppo is a symbolic model checker for asynchronous Boolean programs. The Boolean program is translated to a propositional formula (function calls are inlined) and a SAT solver is used to perform reachability checking. Each decision problem of the loop detection algorithm corresponds to a SAT instance. The average overhead of the loop detection compared to the model checking run itself is below one percent[1].

4 Simulation and Refinement with Loops

The strongest postcondition presented in Definition 2 gives us only a semi-decision procedure for the feasibility of counterexamples with loops (namely, successive enumeration of all corresponding conventional counterexamples). We propose a new two-phase simulation semi-decision procedure for feasibility (see

---

[1] This number is based on benchmarking 489 typical Boolean programs between 26 and 656 lines of code that were generated by Slam.

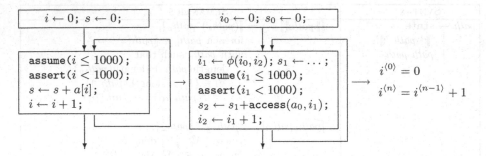

Fig. 8. Transforming a simple loop into a recurrent equation via SSA

Figure 1) of a counterexample p with loops. In the first phase, a heuristic is applied to pick a promising conventional counterexample p_c out of $[\![p]\!]$. In the second phase we check the feasibility of p_c using the traditional approach.

Simulation. The *symbolic loop analysis* phase provides a candidate n for the number of feasible iterations for each loop in the counterexample. The path is infeasible if no such n exists. The converse does not hold. Starting with the innermost loop, we parameterize each loop body with a fresh variable n using following algorithm:

1. Transform the loop into SSA form.
2. Generate a recurrence equation for each variable that is updated by a ϕ function.
3. Calculate the closed form of the recurrence equation (if possible). Substitute its right-hand-side for the corresponding occurrences of the variable (this step is known as *induction variable substitution* [17]). If unable to compute the closed form, assign the variable non-deterministically.
4. Generate the strongest postcondition of the loop body and existentially quantify n in the resulting formula.

Example 1. Consider once more the program in Figure 2. The loop in Figure 8 represents the set of concrete paths that corresponds to the looping counterexample in Figure 4. We transform the loop into SSA and obtain the recurrent equation in Figure 8. The closed form[2] of this recurrence is $i^{\langle n \rangle} = i^{\langle 0 \rangle} + 1 \cdot n$.

Therefore, SATABS replaces every occurrence of i_1 with $i_0 + 1 \cdot n$. By applying SP and quantifying n we obtain

$$SP(loop) = \lambda f.\exists n.\exists s_0'.i_2'.f[s_0'/s_0][i_2'/i_2]$$
$$\wedge ((i_0 + 1 \cdot n) \leq 1000) \wedge \neg((i_0 + 1 \cdot n) < 1000)$$
$$\wedge (s_0 = a_0[(i_0 + 1 \cdot n)]) \wedge (i_2 = (i_0 + 1 \cdot n) + 1)$$

---

[2] The closed form for a recurrent equation $i^{\langle 0 \rangle} = \alpha, i^{\langle n \rangle} = i^{\langle n-1 \rangle} + \beta + \gamma n, n > 0$ (where α, β, γ are numeric constants or loop invariant symbolic expressions) is $i^{\langle n \rangle} = \alpha + \beta n + \gamma \frac{n \cdot (n+1)}{2}$.

Solving the SAT instance that corresponds to $(SP(loop) \circ SP(i_0 = 0))(\texttt{true})$ yields $n = 1000$. Note that there is only one valid solution for n, since $(i \leq 1000)$ is a sufficiently strong loop invariant. The weakest loop condition that does not change the program semantics is $(i \neq 1001)$ and gives us the choice $n \in \{1000, 1002, 1003, \ldots\}$. In our current implementation we have no influence on the n that the SAT solver reports in such a case. We consider to use an optimizing solver like PBS [26] in future versions of our tool to obtain the minimal values of n.

Our approach is not restricted to simple loop counters. Van Engelen provides a framework for handling affine, polynomial, and geometric index expressions composed over linear and non-linear induction variables [17]. These analysis methods and our simulation algorithm also cope with pointer arithmetic and arrays. However, our current implementation supports only a fixed simple recurrence scheme (namely the one presented in Example 1). We treat recurrences that have no closed form equivalent (e.g., $k^{\langle n \rangle} = i \cdot k^{\langle n-1 \rangle} + 1$, where i is a linear induction variable) conservatively by introducing non-determinism (as explained in step 3 of our algorithm). The subsequent traditional simulation of the potentially spurious counterexample (see below) preserves soundness.

Example 2. Consider a function (e.g., as part of a library of combinatorial functions) that calculates the factorial m of a variable k by iterating over $i = \{0, \ldots, k\}$, $m = m \cdot (i + 1)$. Assume that the program contains a user-supplied assertion that the computation does not overflow. By substituting the right hand side of the closed form $i^{\langle n \rangle} = i^{\langle 0 \rangle} + n$ for i one obtains $m^{\langle n \rangle} = m^{\langle n-1 \rangle} \cdot (i^{\langle 0 \rangle} + n + 1)$. The resulting recurrence is $m^{\langle n \rangle} = m^{\langle 0 \rangle} \cdot \frac{i^{\langle 0 \rangle} + n!}{i^{\langle 0 \rangle}!}$.

On a 32 bit architecture, the overflow occurs at $k = 13$. This number is sufficiently small to use a bounded model checker (like CBMC [27]) to simulate the counterexample. For this reason, our current implementation ignores recurrence equations with a closed form that is a fast-growing monotonic function of n (e.g., $n!$ as in our example, or exponentiation with positive integer exponent or base). In this case, SATABS uses the standard abstraction-refinement algorithm instead of computing a solution for n. The bit-level accurate simulation algorithm of SATABS guarantees that an eventual overflow will be detected.

Generating Concrete Counterexamples. The symbolic loop analysis is followed by a traditional feasibility analysis (see Figure 1). Each loop of the counterexample is unrolled according to the results of the previous step. As usual, feasible counterexamples are reported to the user. The fact that they are annotated with information about loops makes them more readable. Spurious counterexamples are subject to refinement.

Refinement. We distinguish two causes of infeasibility of the spurious counterexample p:

- There is no such n that satisfies the recurrence, i.e., phase I reports the corresponding SAT instance to be unsatisfiable. Then we can refine $\hat{M}$ using a set of predicates that remove all paths $[\![p]\!]$ from $\hat{M}$. The unsatisfiability of formula $\varphi_1 \wedge \varphi_2^{\langle n \rangle} \wedge \varphi_3$ (where φ_1 corresponds to the prefix, $\varphi_2^{\langle n \rangle}$ to the parameterized loop body, and φ_3 to the tail of p) is an explanation for the infeasibility of p. Since no n satisfies the formula, setting n to 0 yields an infeasible counterexample from which we can extract a set of refinement predicates using the traditional methods presented in Section 2.

- The traditional feasibility analysis (phase II) refutes $\varphi_1 \wedge \varphi_2^{\langle c \rangle} \wedge \varphi_3$ for the particular constant $n = c$ obtained from phase I. That means that the recurrences $\varphi_2^{\langle n \rangle}$ are not sufficiently strong to show the infeasibility of all paths $[\![p]\!]$. Therefore, we compute a set of refinement predicates from the unrolled path that corresponds to $\varphi_1 \wedge \varphi_2^{\langle c \rangle} \wedge \varphi_3$. This guarantees that the execution of c iterations of the loop is infeasible in $\hat{M}$ and that the same loop is not detected again. We expect that the recurrences are loop invariants that make spurious counterexamples other than p abstractly infeasible, too. Therefore, we consider adding the corresponding predicates even if they have no effect on the feasibility of p.

5   Experimental Results

As expected, our implementation detects the buffer overflow in Figure 2 after only one iteration. The attempt to run BLAST and SATABS without loop detection on the same problem did not yield any results in reasonable time, but exposed an exponential increase of the runtime in every refinement step.

Figure 9 shows a buffer overflow in the Linux mail transfer agent AEON 0.02a. This bug allows local users to gain administrator privileges by executing malicious byte code with help of an overly long HOME environment variable (US-CERT CVE-2005-1019). The function getConfig is called immediately after the program is started and copies the string returned by getenv to a buffer of (fixed)

```
  /* reading rc file, handling missing options */
1 int getConfig(char settings[MAX_SETTINGS][MAX_LEN]) {
2      char home[MAX_LEN];
3      FILE *fp;                        /* .rc file handler */
4      int numSet = 0;                  /* number of settings */
5      strcpy(home, getenv("HOME"));    /* get home path */
6      strcat(home, "/.aeonrc");        /* full path to rc file */

1 char* strcpy (char *t, const char* s) {
2      for (i = 0 ;; i++) { assert (!(t == &home)||!(i>=MAX_LEN));
3          t[i] = s[i]; if (s[i] == '\0') break; }}
```

Fig. 9. Buffer overflow in AEON 0.2a

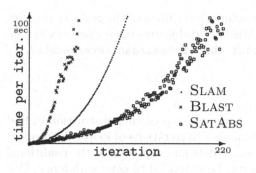

MAX_LEN	BLAST	SLAM	SATABS	+loops
25	161.1	44.0	57.7	25.0
50	1477.4	294.9	182.9	28.0
75	-	993.6	402.9	32.8
100	-	2446.0	765.0	34.1
150	-	9130.2	2241.9	50.3
200	-	23803.5	5402.9	55.8
300	-	-	18702.4	97.6
512	-	-	-	254.5

Runtime per iteration (AEON)

Total runtime (in sec)
for given MAX_LEN

Fig. 10. Runtime of BLAST, SLAM, SATABS and SATABS with loop detection (AEON)

size MAX_LEN without checking its bound (see line 5). This error is representative for many buffer overflows and is detected by SATABS with loop detection in one iteration.

The automatic verification condition generator of SATABS adds the assertion !(t == &home)||!(i>=MAX_LEN) to the loop body of strcpy (see line 2 in Figure 9). Note that SATABS does not specifically target buffer overflows, but aims at verifying arbitrary assertions in C programs. We manually added a corresponding assertion to the AEON sources to make a comparison with BLAST and SLAM possible. Our attempts to detect the bug with BLAST, SLAM and SATABS without loop detection failed despite a generous timeout of 25000 seconds. Therefore, we reduced the value of MAX_LEN (which is 512 in the original program) and compared the performance of BLAST, SLAM, SATABS without loop detection, and SATABS with loop detection. The results of this benchmark[3] are given in Figure 10. The table gives the runtime of all four tools for various values of MAX_LEN. As expected, the runtime of SLAM grows exponentially with the size of the buffer. BLAST crashes for MAX_LEN= 75. We did not further investigate this problem. SATABS performs slightly better than SLAM[4], but the runtime still increases exponentially with the number of iterations. The diagram in Figure 10 illustrates the exponential increase of the runtime in each abstraction-refinement iteration. We compared the runtime of all iterations that took less than 100 seconds.

SATABS *with* loop detection spends most of the time in the simulation of the unrolled counterexample. This is because SATABS performs SAT-based bit-level accurate simulation (unlike SLAM and BLAST, which model integer variables as unbounded integers). We listed the results for all four tools in the table in Figure 10.

---

[3] All our experiments were done on an Intel Pentium 4 with 3 GHz and 2 GB RAM.
[4] We adapted the refinement strategy of SATABS (with respect to spurious paths and spurious transitions [28]) to match the behaviour of SLAM and BLAST.

We refrain from presenting other benchmarks in favor of the in depth description of the AEON example. The SATABS executable and more examples can be downloaded from http://www.inf.ethz.ch/personal/daniekro/satabs/.

6   Conclusion

This paper presents a novel approach that enables predicate abstraction to find bugs that emerge as a result of a high number of iterations of loops. We propose an algorithm to detect loops in abstract models and explain how the traditional simulation and refinement algorithms can be extended to cope with loops. Our implementation outperforms the abstraction-refinement based verification tools BLAST and SLAM on typical buffer overflow examples.

Currently, our implementation recognizes only basic recurrences that are sufficient to find the most common bugs. An integration of the recurrence solving algorithms of van Engelen [17] can lift this limitation.

References

1. Clarke, E., Grumberg, O., Peled, D.: Model Checking. MIT Press (1999)
2. Graf, S., Saïdi, H.: Construction of abstract state graphs with PVS. In: CAV, Springer (1997) 72–83
3. Ball, T., Rajamani, S.: Boolean programs: A model and process for software analysis. Technical Report 2000-14, Microsoft Research (2000)
4. Ball, T., Cook, B., Levin, V., Rajamani, S.K.: SLAM and Static Driver Verifier: Technology transfer of formal methods inside Microsoft. In: IFM, Springer (2004)
5. Clarke, E.M., Grumberg, O., Jha, S., Lu, Y., Veith, H.: Counterexample-guided abstraction refinement. In: CAV, Springer (2000) 154–169
6. Kurshan, R.: Computer-Aided Verification of Coordinating Processes. Princeton University Press (1995)
7. Henzinger, T.A., Jhala, R., Majumdar, R., Sutre, G.: Lazy abstraction. In: POPL, ACM Press (2002) 58–70
8. Cook, B., Kroening, D., Sharygina, N.: Symbolic model checking for asynchronous Boolean programs. In: SPIN, Springer (2005) 75–90
9. Ball, T., Rajamani, S.: Generating Abstract Explanations of Spurious Counterexamples in C Programs. Technical Report MSR-TR-2002-09, Microsoft Research, Redmond (2002)
10. Jhala, R., Majumdar, R.: Path slicing. In: PLDI, ACM Press (2005) 38–47
11. Armando, A., Castellini, C., Mantovani, J.: Software model checking using linear constraints. In: IFCEM 2004: 6th Int. Conference on Formal Engineering Methods. (2004) 209–223
12. Armando, A., Benerecetti, M., Mantovani, J.: Model checking linear programs with arrays. In: SoftMC, Elsevier (2006) 79–94
13. Podelski, A., Rybalchenko, A.: A complete method for the synthesis of linear ranking functions. In: VMCAI, Springer (2004) 239–25
14. Cook, B., Podelski, A., Rybalchenko, A.: Abstraction-refinement for termination. In: SAS, Springer (2005) 87–101
15. Müller-Olm, M., Seidl, H.: Precise interprocedural analysis through linear algebra. In: POPL, ACM Press (2004) 330–341

16. Zhang, J.: A path-based approach to the detection of infinite looping. In: APAQS: Asia-pacific conference on quality software, IEEE Computer Society (2001) 88–96
17. van Engelen, R.A., Birch, J., Shou, Y., Walsh, B., Gallivan, K.A.: A unified framework for nonlinear dependence testing and symbolic analysis. In: ICS: International conference on Supercomputing, ACM Press (2004) 106–115
18. Clarke, E.M., Grumberg, O., Long, D.E.: Model checking and abstraction. In: POPL, ACM Press (1992) 343–354
19. Ball, T., Rajamani, S.K.: Bebop: A symbolic model checker for Boolean programs. In: SPIN, Springer (2000) 113–130
20. Esparza, J., Hansel, D., Rossmanith, P., Schwoon, S.: Efficient algorithms for model checking pushdown systems. In: CAV, Springer (2000) 232–247
21. Andrews, T., Qadeer, S., Rajamani, S.K., Xie, Y.: Zing: Exploiting program structure for model checking concurrent software. In: CONCUR, Springer (2004) 1–15
22. Gries, D.: The Science of Programming. Springer (1987)
23. Cytron, R., Ferrante, J., Rosen, B.K., Wegman, M.N., Zadeck, F.K.: Efficiently computing static single assignment form and the control dependence graph. ACM Transactions on Programming Languages and Systems 13 (1991) 451–490
24. Clarke, E., Kroening, D., Sharygina, N., Yorav, K.: Predicate abstraction of ANSI–C programs using SAT. FMSD 25 (2004) 105–127
25. Henzinger, T.A., Jhala, R., Majumdar, R., McMillan, K.L.: Abstractions from proofs. In: POPL, ACM Press (2004) 232–244
26. Aloul, F., Ramani, A., Markov, I., Sakallah, K.: PBS: A backtrack search pseudo-Boolean solver. In: Theory and Appl. of Satisfiability Testing. (2002) 346–353
27. Clarke, E., Kroening, D., Lerda, F.: A tool for checking ANSI-C programs. In: TACAS, Springer (2004) 168–176
28. Ball, T., Podelski, A., Rajamani, S.K.: Boolean and cartesian abstraction for model checking C programs. In: TACAS, London, UK, Springer-Verlag (2001) 268–283

Cascade: C Assertion Checker and Deductive Engine

(Tool Paper)

Nikhil Sethi and Clark Barrett

New York University, New York, NY, USA
{nsethi, barrett}@cs.nyu.edu

Abstract. We present a tool, called Cascade, to check assertions in C programs as part of a multi-stage verification strategy. Cascade takes as input a C program and a *control file* (the output of an earlier stage) that specifies one or more assertions to be checked together with (optionally) some restrictions on program behaviors. For each assertion, Cascade produces either a concrete trace violating the assertion or a deduction (proof) that the assertion cannot be violated.

1 Introduction

Software verification is an active area of research [2,3,5,6,9,10]. Tools have been developed which can find bugs in real applications with large code bases. However, in order to analyze large programs, these tools often make approximations. As a result, some of the errors reported by such tools can be false.

A promising alternative approach is the idea of two-stage verification [2,7,8]. In two-stage verification, a light-weight analysis capable of scaling to large programs is run first to identify potential bugs. This is followed by a more detailed analysis of the potential errors identified in the first stage. Cascade provides a generic back-end for two-stage verification of C programs which can be easily integrated with any initial stage. Cascade can handle most C constructs including loops, functions (including recursive functions), structs, pointers, and dynamic memory allocation.

2 System Description

Cascade consists of about 6000 lines of C++ code. Its overall design is shown in Fig. 1. The core module takes as input an abstract syntax tree representing a C program and a *control file* that specifies one or more potential errors to be checked. The core module uses symbolic simulation over the abstract syntax tree to build verification conditions corresponding to the assertions specified in the control file. The semantics of C statements are hard-coded into the translation rules that the core module uses to convert C statements into logic formulas. Cascade uses a bounded model-checking approach to handle loops (and recursive functions). Loops are unrolled a fixed number of times (this number can be specified by the user). Cascade models all pointers and addresses in the heap precisely. The *data* stored in memory is represented abstractly as integers.

T. Ball and R.B. Jones (Eds.): CAV 2006, LNCS 4144, pp. 166–169, 2006.
© Springer-Verlag Berlin Heidelberg 2006

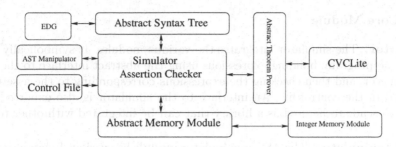

Fig. 1. Cascade: System design

2.1 Abstract Interfaces

Cascade is designed to be easily customizable. Major components are hidden behind abstract interfaces. This makes it easy to provide and experiment with a variety of configurations based on the same basic architecture. The core module depends on implementations of three generic abstract interfaces: an abstract syntax tree, a memory module, and a theorem prover.

Abstract Syntax Tree. Cascade has a simple internal representation of programs as an abstract syntax tree. All operations are done on this internal representation, completely separating it from the front end which is responsible for building the abstract syntax tree. Cascade currently has an implementation using EDG [4], an industrial-strength parser for C programs, as a front end to create the abstract syntax tree.

Abstract Theorem Prover. Cascade uses an abstract theorem proving interface. The interface provides an abstract `ExprNode` object which corresponds to logical expressions in the underlying theorem prover. It also specifies some standard operations on `ExprNodes` like arithmetic operations, Boolean operations and array operations. Any theorem prover which can support these operations can easily be used with Cascade. An unsupported operation can be set to return *unknown*. Cascade currently uses CVC Lite[1] as its theorem prover. CVC Lite can produce proofs and concrete counter-examples. An additional advantage of using CVC Lite is our in-house expertise on using and modifying the theorem prover.

Abstract Memory Module. All memory operations during simulation are handled by an abstract interface modeling heap memory. Memory is a mapping from addresses to values where both of them are `ExprNode` objects. Functions like allocate, deallocate, read and write are supported. The memory module also provides a `check_valid_address` function which checks if a given address is valid or not. This function can be used in assertions. The current implementation of the abstract memory module uses an array of integers to model memory. We expect to provide a more precise model of the data in memory using bit-vectors (which are supported in the latest version of CVC Lite) in the near future.

2.2   Core Module

Simulator. The simulator integrates the various modules. It symbolically simulates the program, building expressions using the abstract interface to the theorem prover, and then checking the expressions corresponding to the assertions specified in the control file. An interface to the simulator is also exported, enabling Cascade to be used as a library that can be integrated with other tools.

AST Manipulator. The AST manipulator module has various functions which can modify the AST. For example, unrolling of the loops is handled by this module. This module also interfaces with the control file and integrates the restrictions on execution paths and variables with the AST.

2.3   The Control File

Execution of the tool is guided by a **Control File**. A control file specifies the assertion(s) to be checked. In addition, a control file can be used to constrain the search for a violating trace by restricting the program paths to be explored or giving constraints on program variables. The control file allows important information about feasible violations (perhaps gathered by an earlier stage) to be communicated to Cascade.

The control file has a simple XML format. It begins with `SourceFile` sections which give the paths to C source files. It then has one or more `Run` sections, each defining a constrained run of the program. Each run starts with a single `StartPosition` and ends with a single `EndPosition` section. These give respectively the start point and end point of the simulation to be run. A `Run` may optionally specify one or more `WayPoint` sections. A `WayPoint` indicates that Cascade should consider only those program paths which pass through the `WayPoint`. Each position (start, end, or waypoint) can also include a command. Commands include: `cascade_assume`, which takes a Boolean C expression and adds it as an assumption to the theorem prover; `cascade_check`, which takes a Boolean C expression and checks whether it is valid at the given position; and `cascade_check_valid_address`, which takes a C expression as its argument and checks if the address represented by the expression is a valid address in memory.

3   An Example

Table 1 gives a small C function which has a `NULL` pointer access if its argument is negative. Suppose that a suitable first-stage tool [6,7,10] has flagged Line 9 as a potential error. With no further information, Cascade finds a violating trace in which the argument is negative. However, suppose the first-stage tool knows from its analysis that the function f is only called with a positive argument. Using the control file, the first-stage can constrain the search to only those cases when $a > 0$. In this case, Cascade can verify that the assertion cannot be violated. The code and control file for this example are shown below.

Table 1. Control file example

```
1   int* f(int a) {
2     int *p, *x, *y;
3     x = (int*) malloc(sizeof(int));
4     y = NULL;
5     if(a>=0)
6       p = x;
7     else
8       p = y;
9     *p = 5;
10    return p;
11  }
```

```
<ControlFile>
  <SourceFile>
    <Name>~/ex/f.c</Name><FileId>1</FileId>
  </SourceFile>
  <Run><StartPosition><Position>
    <FileId>1</FileId><LineNum>1</LineNum>
    </Position><Command>
      <CascadeFunction>cascade_assume
      </CascadeFunction>
      <Argument>a>0</Argument>
    </Command></StartPosition>
    <EndPosition><Position>
      <FileId>1</FileId><LineNum>9</LineNum>
    </Position><Command>
      <CascadeFunction>
        cascade_check_valid_address
      </CascadeFunction>
      <Argument>p</Argument>
    </Command></EndPosition></Run>
</ControlFile>
```

4 Conclusion

Cascade has been successfully run on programs of up to a few hundred lines of code. For a 400 line example, without any constraints in the control file, the run-time on a P4 2GHz is less than 1 minute. We expect that with suitably constrained control files, Cascade will scale to much larger code bases. Although it is still under development, we hope it will be of use and interest to a broader community. In addition, we hope to receive feedback and suggestions for further improvement. For further information on Cascade, including downloads, examples and documentation, see http://www.cs.nyu.edu/acsys/cascade/.

References

1. C. Barrett and S. Berezin. CVC Lite: A new implementation of the cooperating validity checker. In *Proceedings of CAV*, pages 515–518, July 2004.
2. D. Beyer, T. A. Henzinger, R. Jhala, and R. Majumdar. Checking memory safety with blast. In *FASE*, pages 2–18, 2005.
3. B. Blanchet, P. Cousot, R. Cousot, J. Feret, L. Mauborgne, A. Miné, D. Monniaux, and X. Rival. A static analyzer for large safety-critical software. In *Proceedings of PLDI*, pages 196–207, 2003.
4. Edison design group. http://www.edg.com.
5. S. Hallem, B. Chelf, Y. Xie, and D. Engler. A system and language for building system-specific, static analyses. In *Proceedings of PLDI*, pages 69–82, 2002.
6. G. J. Holzmann. Static source code checking for user-defined properties. In *Proc. IDPT 2002*, Pasadena, CA, USA, 2002.
7. Orion. http://cm.bell-labs.com/cm/cs/what/orion/index.html.
8. X. Rival. Understanding the origin of alarms in ASTRÉE. In *SAS*, volume 3672 of *LNCS*, pages 303–319, London (UK), Sept. 2005. Springer.
9. Y. Xie and A. Aiken. Saturn: A sat-based tool for bug detection. In *CAV*, pages 139–143, 2005.
10. Y. Xie, A. Chou, and D. Engler. Archer: using symbolic, path-sensitive analysis to detect memory access errors. In *Proceedings of ESEC/FSE*, pages 327–336, 2003.

YASM: A Software Model-Checker for Verification and Refutation
(Tool Paper)

Arie Gurfinkel, Ou Wei, and Marsha Chechik

Department of Computer Science, University of Toronto
{arie, owei, chechik}@cs.toronto.edu

1 Motivation

This paper presents YASM: a (yet another) software model-checker based on the Counter-Example Guided Abstraction Refinement (CEGAR) [6] framework. A number of well-engineered software model-checkers are available, e.g., SLAM [1] and BLAST [12]. Why build another one?

Traditional software model-checkers build over-approximating abstractions of the programs they analyze and typically bias their analysis towards proving that a (safety) property of interest holds (verification). On the other hand, since model-checkers are widely known for their bug-finding abilities, they are often used for refutation. In this case, the above approach seems unreasonable: why introduce spurious behaviour and make it more difficult to find a real bug? For such circumstances, one would just want to prove that the property is false (refutation). No witness for that is required.

A number of techniques for creating and combining over- and under-approximating abstractions have been proposed, e.g., [7,9,3,15,16]. In these approaches, model-checking yields either true or false, which are deemed to be conclusive, or maybe, in which case the abstraction needs to be refined. While all aspects of the CEGAR framework for such abstractions have been described theoretically [9,3,10,15,16], these ideas have not yet been implemented.

In this paper, we present YASM, which we believe to be the first symbolic software model-checker based on combining over- and under-approximating abstractions, which we refer to as *exact* [11]. It can prove and disprove properties with equal effectiveness. Our experiments [11] show that performance of the tool is comparable with standard over-approximating model-checkers. Moreover, we found that exact abstractions can become part of the standard CEGAR framework virtually without modifications and, more importantly, minor modifications of the framework enable an array of useful analyses, e.g., reasoning about the entire CTL, reusing previously computed abstractions, and many others.

The rest of the paper is organized as follows: Sec. 2 describes the design and the current state of the tool. Sec. 3 discusses the above observations. We conclude in Sec. 4.

2 Design and Implementation

YASM is based on the standard CEGAR loop.

T. Ball and R.B. Jones (Eds.): CAV 2006, LNCS 4144, pp. 170–174, 2006.

Abstractions. Following SLAM, abstractions are represented by Boolean Programs. Unlike SLAM, the semantics of these programs is given via a variant of Mixed Transition Systems (MixTS) [7,11]. Compared to Modal and 3-valued TSs, MixTSs allow for a monotonic refinement of abstractions, yet are simpler to encode symbolically than disjunctive (or hyper-) TSs [16,8]. We employ the standard technique for extracting an abstraction of a program by approximating weakest precondition of program statements. However, to allow for analysis of concurrent systems, we differentiate between program non-determinism and abstraction-induced non-determinism, both syntactically, in the Boolean Programs, and semantically, in MixTSs [11].

Model-Checking. YASM uses a specialized BDD-based symbolic model-checker, described in [4,3]. The May and Must transition relations of a MixTS are encoded in a single BDD, and each 3-valued predicate is represented by two BDD variables.

Counter-examples. When a property is inconclusive, the model-checker generates a proof of this fact that is mined for new predicates. For safety properties, this proof, described in [10,5], can be expanded into a standard counter-example – making all standard predicate discovery techniques applicable. However, unlike standard approaches, it does not need to be simulated in order to determine its feasibility.

Architecture and Implementation. The tool is written in Java (around 30K lines of code not including third-party components). It makes use of several tools including: CIL [13] for parsing and simplifying C code, CUDD BDD library [17] for decision diagrams, and CVCLite [2] for theorem proving, and we are currently working on the integration with Eclipse IDE.

YASM has been in operation for about a year and a half, and since that time has been used to check C programs up to 35K lines of code: network protocols, programs from the OpenSSH package, parts of Linux file system, etc. The tool is publicly available from http://www.cs.toronto.edu/~arie/yasm.

3   YASM with CEGAR Framework

The main advantage of exact (or even under-approximating) abstraction is its ability to refute properties. Consider abstracting a program shown in Fig. 1(a). Its abstraction using predicates b1, b2, b3 (See Fig. 1(b)) is sufficient for YASM to conclude that ERROR is reachable. However, this abstraction is insufficient for an over-approximating model-checker: the shortest path to ERROR (line 9), the one typically found by a model-checker, is spurious.

YASM succeeds because it partitions the abstract states into: (a) states from which ERROR is unavoidable (A), (b) states from which ERROR is unreachable (B), and (c) states that have a (potentially spurious) path to ERROR (C). If the initial state belongs to either A or B, the result is conclusive; otherwise, a path to ERROR is available to guide the refinement process. Note that an over-approximating analysis combines A and C, and under-approximating combines B and C.

In the remainder of this section, we show how knowing the set A changes the dynamics of the CEGAR framework.

Aggressive Abstraction. Compared to an over-approximating model-checker, YASM's bug-detecting ability is preserved even in the face of a very aggressive abstraction.

```
      1: int p1,p2,p3,x,y;                      1: bool b1,b2,b3;
      2:   p1=p2=p3=x=y=5;                       2:   b1=b2=b3=1;
      3:   if(p3<=0) return;                     3:   if (b3) return;
      4:   if(y<0)                               4:   if(*)
      5:      {if(x>2){                          5:      {if(*){
      6:         if(y>10)                        6:         if(*)
      7:            {if(p2>0)                     7:            {if(b2)
      8:               ERROR;}}                   8:               ERROR;}}
  (a) 9:      if(p1>0) ERROR;              (b)   9:      if(b1) ERROR;
     10: } else {                               10: } else {
     11: if(p2>0)                               11: if(b2)
     12:    {if(p1>0)  x = x+1;                 12:    {if(b1) ;
     13:     if(p2>0)  x = x+2;                 13:     if(b2) ;
     14:     if(p3<=0) x = x+3;                 14:     if(b3) ;
     15:     if(x>40)                           15:     if(*)
     16:        if(p1>0) ERROR;                 16:        if(b1) ERROR;
     17:     if(p1>0) ERROR;}}                  17:     if(b1) ERROR;}}
```

Fig. 1. (a) A C program. (b) An abstraction of (a) using predicates b1 : {p1>0}, b2 : {p2>0}, b3 : {p3<=0}.

For example, when conditions of the if-statements at lines 12–14 are abstracted away, i.e., replaced by *, the resulting abstraction has more spurious paths, and yet YASM is still able to conclude that ERROR is reachable. This allows us to augment the CEGAR framework to prefer a more aggressive (and computationally cheaper) abstraction and employ heuristics during the refinement stage to decide between increasing precision of the abstraction and adding new predicates.

Shallow Counterexamples. If we restrict our abstraction to predicates b1 and b2, YASM can show that ERROR is unavoidable from line 4. Yet the overall analysis is inconclusive due to a spurious counterexample: a path to ERROR on line 9. This path can be eliminated using new predicates y<0 and x>2. Using the fact that error is unavoidable from line 4, we can instead: (a) only generate the counterexample up to that line, and (b) discover that we need the predicate b3 : {p3<=0} to finish the analysis.

Reusing Previous Results. The set A can also be reused between successive iterations of the CEGAR loop. Once an abstraction is refined, we can check for reachability of A, instead of ERROR. For example, after analyzing an abstraction restricted to the predicate b1, we know that ERROR is unavoidable from $A = (pc \in \text{ERROR}) \vee (pc = 12 \wedge p1>0)$, and can use the property $EF\ A$ instead of $EF(pc \in \text{ERROR})$ in all successive iterations.

Note that a combination of an aggressive abstraction and reuse of previous results achieves a similar effect to Lazy Abstraction employed by BLAST– only the parts of the program relevant to the analysis are actively refined. Furthermore, by changing the property at each refinement step, we can guide the refinement process to the *least spurious* execution, instead of the shortest one.

4   Conclusion

At each step of the abstraction/refinement loop, all abstractions get refined: either by removing possible behaviours for over-approximation, or by adding them to under-approximation. Clearly, combining both approaches allows substantial reuse of the analysis infrastructure and may lead to faster convergence of the analysis, since each step improves abstraction either towards truth, or towards falsity. This interplay also leads to many interesting analyses, some of which we've described in this paper.

The use of the exact abstraction further allows us to check arbitrary CTL properties. For example, we have successfully used YASM to prove non-termination (i.e., EG true), and response (i.e., $AG(p \Rightarrow AFq)$) properties of C programs.

Finally, exact abstractions can precisely capture non-determinism present in concurrent programs. We have used YASM to check properties of the Bakery mutual exclusion protocol and error detection in RAX [14]. Our experiments look promising, yet more work is required to make YASM applicable to real-life concurrent programs written in fully-fledged programming languages such as C or Java.

Acknowledgments

We are grateful to Xin Ma, Kelvin Ku and Shiva Nejati for their help implementing, evaluating and improving YASM. Financial support provided by NSERC and an IBM Ph.D. Fellowship are acknowledged.

References

1. T. Ball, A. Podelski, and S. Rajamani. "Boolean and Cartesian Abstraction for Model Checking C Programs". *STTT*, 5(1):49–58, 2003.
2. C. Barrett and S. Berezin. "CVC Lite: A New Implementation of the Cooperating Validity Checker". In *CAV'04*, volume 3114 of *LNCS*, pages 515–518, 2004.
3. M. Chechik, B. Devereux, S. Easterbrook, and A. Gurfinkel. "Multi-Valued Symbolic Model-Checking". *ACM TOSEM*, 12(4):1–38, 2003.
4. M. Chechik, B. Devereux, and A. Gurfinkel. "XChek: A Multi-Valued Model-Checker". In *CAV'02*, volume 2404 of *LNCS*, pages 505–509, 2002.
5. M. Chechik and A. Gurfinkel. "A Framework for Counterexample Generation and Exploration". In *FASE'05*, volume 3442 of *LNCS*, pages 217–233, 2005.
6. E. Clarke, O. Grumberg, S. Jha, Y. Lu, and H. Veith. "Counterexample-Guided Abstraction Refinement for Symbolic Model Checking". *JACM*, 50(5):752–794, 2003.
7. D. Dams, R. Gerth, and O. Grumberg. "Abstract Interpretation of Reactive Systems". *ACM TOPLAS*, 2(19):253–291, 1997.
8. D. Dams and K.S. Namjoshi. "The Existence of Finite Abstractions for Branching Time Model Checking". In *LICS'04*, pages 335–344, 2004.
9. P. Godefroid, M. Huth, and R. Jagadeesan. "Abstraction-based Model Checking using Modal Transition Systems". In *CONCUR'01*, volume 2154 of *LNCS*, pages 426–440, 2001.
10. A. Gurfinkel and M. Chechik. "Proof-like Counterexamples". In *TACAS'03*, volume 2619 of *LNCS*, pages 160–175, 2003.
11. A. Gurfinkel and M. Chechik. "Why Waste a Perfectly Good Abstraction?". In *TACAS'06*, volume 3920 of *LNCS*, pages 212–226, 2006.
12. T. Henzinger, R. Jhala, R. Majumdar, and G. Sutre. "Lazy Abstraction". In *POPL'02*, pages 58–70, 2002.
13. G. Necula, S. McPeak, S. Rahul, and W. Weimer. "CIL: Intermediate Language and Tools for Analsysis and Transformation of C Programs". In *CC'02*, volume 2304 of *LNCS*, pages 213–228, 2002.

14. C. Pasareanu, R. Pelanek, and W. Visser. "Concrete Model Checking with Abstract Matching and Refinement". In *CAV'05*, volume 3576 of *LNCS*, pages 52–66, 2005.

15. S. Shoham and O. Grumberg. "A Game-Based Framework for CTL Counter-Examples and 3-Valued Abstraction-Refinement". In *CAV'03*, volume 2725 of *LNCS*, pages 275–287, 2003.

16. S. Shoham and O. Grumberg. "Monotonic Abstraction-Refinement for CTL". In *TACAS'04*, volume 2988 of *LNCS*, pages 546–560, 2004.

17. F. Somenzi. "CUDD: CU Decision Diagram Package Release", 2001.

SAT-Based Assistance in Abstraction Refinement for Symbolic Trajectory Evaluation

Jan-Willem Roorda and Koen Claessen

Chalmers University of Technology, Sweden
{jwr, koen}@chalmers.se

Abstract. We present a SAT-based algorithm for assisting users of Symbolic Trajectory Evaluation (STE) in manual abstraction refinement. As a case study, we demonstrate the usefulness of the algorithm by showing how to refine and verify an STE specification of a CAM.

1 Introduction

Symbolic Trajectory Evaluation (STE) [12] is a well-known simulation-based model checking technique. It combines three-valued simulation (using the standard values 0 and 1 together with the extra value X, "unknown") with symbolic simulation (using symbolic expressions to drive inputs). STE has been extremely successful in verifying properties of circuits containing large data paths (such as memories, fifos, floating point units) that are beyond the reach of traditional symbolic model checking [1,11,7].

In STE, specifications are *assertions* of the form $A \implies C$, where A is called the *antecedent* and C the *consequent*. Both A and C are formulas in a restrictive temporal logic, in which only statements about a finite number of time points can be made. The only variables in the logic are time-independent Boolean variables, called *symbolic variables*.

The power of STE comes from the use of *abstraction*. The abstraction is induced by the antecedent of the assertion; when the antecedent does not specify a value for a certain node, the value of the node is abstracted away by using the unknown value X. Thus, the antecedent plays two different roles in STE; it is the logical antecedent as well as a specification of what abstraction should be used in the verification. Because of the abstraction, the values of circuit nodes during simulation can be represented by BDDs in terms of the symbolic variables occurring in the assertion, providing an efficient means of checking an STE assertion.

A drawback of STE is that the user needs to spend time on finding the *right* abstraction. Often, just the right mix between symbolic variables and X's has to be used to make sure that the property holds in the abstraction induced, and the BDDs used in the verification do not blow up.

Abstraction Refinement. A common initial result in an STE verification attempt is that the model-checker cannot prove the assertion because the simulation using the antecedent yields X's at nodes that are required to have a particular Boolean value by

T. Ball and R.B. Jones (Eds.): CAV 2006, LNCS 4144, pp. 175–189, 2006.

the consequent. This indicates that the used abstraction was too coarse, leading to a so-called *spurious counter-model*. In contrast, a *real counter-model* is a simulation run that satisfies the antecedent but yields a 0 for a node for which the consequent requires a 1, or vice-versa. A *model* of an assertion is a simulation run that satisfies both the antecedent and the consequent.

When an STE model-checking run produces spurious counter-models but no real counter-models, we say that the result of the verification is *unknown*. In this case, the assertion must be refined (usually by introducing more symbolic variables in the antecedent) until the property is proved, or until a real counter-model is found. Often, a great deal of time is spent on such manual *abstraction refinement* [14,2].

Contribution. We have invented the concept of a *strengthening*, which is a particular piece of useful information that can help STE-users with manual abstraction refinement; given an STE assertion and a circuit, a strengthening indicates which extra inputs of the circuit need to be given a Boolean (non-X) value in order for relevant outputs to also get a Boolean value. We have also designed a SAT-based algorithm that calculates strengthenings, which we have implemented in a tool called STAR (SAT-based Tool for Abstraction Refinement in STE). STAR has two modes; the first mode calculates strengthenings that satisfy the assertion (corresponding to models), and the second mode calculates strengthenings that contradict the assertion (corresponding to real counter-models).

By inspecting a weakest satisfying strengthening, the user can gain intuition about how to refine the assertion by introducing a *minimal* number of extra symbolic variables. On the other hand, a weakest contradicting strengthening gives a *minimal* set of reasons for the failure of the assertion, which can be used to gain intuition about why the circuit does not satisfy the assertion. In the next section, we look at examples of satisfying and contradicting strengthenings in more detail.

Related Work. There exists a large body of work in the field of automatic abstraction refinement for model-checking techniques for hardware other than STE, for an overview see for example [5]. Most of these abstractions are state-based, focusing on how to represent the state space of a circuit, which is not applicable to STE. In [6] an algorithm providing an easy interface to abstraction in STE is described. The algorithm does, however, not help in finding a right abstraction.

In another paper [13] presented at this conference, the tool *AutoSTE* is described. This tool can automatically refine STE assertions that result in a spurious counter-model, until either the assertion is proved, a real counter-model is found (or resources are exhausted). We believe that STAR and AutoSTE are complementary, in the following sense. AutoSTE can automatically find certain refinements of a specific kind (namely where some nodes become driven by fresh symbolic variables under certain conditions). STAR assists the user in manually finding refinements of a much more general kind, for example when sophisticated symbolic indexing schemes [6,7] are needed. We show, for instance, in the next section, how the method can be used to derive a symbolic indexing scheme for the verification of Content-Addressable Memories.

2   A Case Study

Content-Addressable Memories (CAMs) are hardware implementations of lookup tables. A CAM stores a number of *tags*, each of which is linked to a specific *data-entry*. The basis of a CAM circuit consists usually of two memory blocks, one containing tag entries, and the other the same number of corresponding data entries, see Fig. 1. Given an input tag, the associative-read operation consists of searching all tags in the CAM to determine if there is a match to the input tag, and if so sending the associated data-entry to the output. Verifying this operation is non-trivial [7].

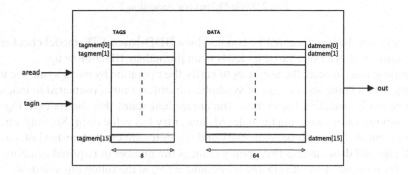

Fig. 1. A Content-Addressable Memory Circuit

What follows is a constructed, but realistic, account of how a verification engineer might use our method to derive an STE assertion for verifying the associative-read operation of a CAM. How to verify CAMs using STE is now well-known [7]. The STE assertion needed for the verification is however quite complex. We show how a user who is ignorant of the above mentioned work on CAM verification can derive the required assertion with help of the STAR-tool. We believe that this convincingly illustrates the usefulness of our method.

In the case-study, we assume that the verification engineer uses the BDD-based STE model-checker in Intel's verification toolkit Forte[4]. The CAM under verification is taken from Intel's GSTE tutorial.

An obvious way of verifying the associative-read operation using STE is to introduce symbolic variables for each tag- and data-entry. When doing so, the antecedent of the assertion specifies that each tag-entry tagmem[i] has symbolic value $tagmem_i$, and each data-entry datmem[i] has symbolic value $datmem_i$. The consequent checks that, for each i, when the input-tag is equal to $tagmem_i$ the output is equal to $datmem_i$.

$$
\begin{aligned}
&(\text{aread is } 1) \text{ and } (\text{tagin is } tagin) \\
&\text{and } (\text{tagmem}[0] \text{ is } tagmem_0) \text{ and } \ldots \text{ and } (\text{tagmem}[15] \text{ is } tagmem_{15}) \\
&\text{and } (\text{datmem}[0] \text{ is } datmem_0) \text{ and } \ldots \text{ and } (\text{datmem}[15] \text{ is } datmem_{15}) \\
&\qquad\qquad\qquad \Longrightarrow \\
&\qquad ((tagin = tagmem_0) \rightarrow (\text{out is } tagmem_0)) \\
&\qquad\qquad\qquad\qquad \vdots \\
&\text{and } ((tagin = tagmem_{15}) \rightarrow (\text{out is } tagmem_{15}))
\end{aligned}
\tag{1}
$$

```
Warning: Consequent failure at time 0 on node out[63]
Current value:data[63] + X(!data[63])
Expected value:data[63]
Weak disagreement when:!data[63]
----WARNING: Some consequent errors not reported

data[16]&data[21]&data[61]&data[34]&data[2]&data[7]&data[47]&data[52]&data[20]&
data[60]&data[33]&data[38]&data[6]&data[46]&data[51]&data[19]&data[59]&data[56]&
data[24]&data[32]&data[29]&data[37]&data[5]&data[45]&data[13]&data[42]&data[53]&
data[10]&data[50]&data[18]&data[58]&data[15]&data[26]&data[55]&data[23]&data[63]&
data[31]&data[28]&data[39]&data[36]&data[43]&data[44]&data[40]&data[12]&data[41]&
data[27]&data[49]&data[17]&data[57]&data[14]&data[25]&data[54]&data[22]&data[62]&
data[30]&data[9]&data[35]&data[3]&data[4]&data[0]&data[11]&data[1]&data[8]&data[48]
```

Fig. 2. Forte Output for Assertion 2

This assertion, however, cannot be handled by a BDD-based STE-model checker. The large number of symbolic variables leads to an immediate BDD-blow up.

Suppose that, instead, the user tries to verify the operation by using symbolic indexing [6]. When doing so, a vector of symbolic variables, $index$, is created to index over the potentially matching tag-entries. The antecedent states that the indexed tag-entry has symbolic value $tagin$ and the indexed data-entry has value $data$. So, only variables for the content of the indexed data-entry and tag-entry are created, instead of variables for all tag- and data-entries. This greatly reduces the number of required symbolic variables. Using symbolic indexing, the user could arrive at the following assertion.

$$
\begin{aligned}
&(\text{aread is } 1) \text{ and } (\text{tagin is } tagin) \\
\text{and } &((index = 0000) \rightarrow ((\text{tagmem}[0] \text{ is } tagin) \text{ and } (\text{datmem}[0] \text{ is } data))) \\
\text{and } &((index = 0001) \rightarrow ((\text{tagmem}[1] \text{ is } tagin) \text{ and } (\text{datmem}[1] \text{ is } data))) \\
&\vdots \qquad\qquad\qquad\qquad\qquad\qquad\qquad\qquad \vdots \\
\text{and } &((index = 1111) \rightarrow ((\text{tagmem}[15] \text{ is } tagin) \text{ and } (\text{datmem}[15] \text{ is } data))) \\
&\qquad\qquad\qquad\qquad\Longrightarrow \\
&\qquad\qquad\qquad \text{out is } data
\end{aligned}
$$

(2)

When the user tries to verify this assertion with the model-checker, the result is "unknown". The output of the model-checker is given in Fig. 2: the simulated value for node out[63] is $(data[63] + (\mathsf{X}\ \&\ \neg data[63]))$, while the required value is $data[63]$. When the symbolic variable $data[63]$ has value 0, the simulated value of out[63] evaluates to X, indicating a spurious counter-model. The expression $data[16]\ \&\ ....\ \&\ data[48]$ indicates that only when the data-entry consists of only high bits no spurious counter-model exists. So, the STE model-checker does not give much help with refining the assertion. This is where our tool STAR comes in.

STAR can be used to calculate a weakest contradicting strengthening of Assertion 2, see Fig. 3. The table presents an assignment of the symbolic variables, and a weakest strengthening of the antecedent that together contradict the consequent. Here, only bold-faced values (**0** or **1**) in the table represent strengthened nodes. A normal-faced 0 or 1 represents a node that has received the value 0 or 1 because it was required by the (original) antecedent. For instance, tagmem[12] is required to have value 00000000 by the antecedent, but tagmem[1] is required to have the same value by the strengthening. To increase readability, X's are represented by a dash –; entries for which all values are X have been left out of the table completely. The table states that

Symbolic Variables	
$index$	$= 1100$
$tagin$	$= 00000000$
$data$	$= 1111111111111111111111111111111111111111111111111111111111111111111100$
Inputs at time 0	
aread	$= 1$
tagin	$= 00000000$
Initial Values	
tagmem[1]	$= 00000000$
tagmem[12]	$= 00000000$
datmem[1]	$= --1-$
datmem[12]	$= 1111111111111111111111111111111111111111111111111111111111111111111100$
Outputs	
out	$= 111111111111111111111111111111111111111111111111111111111111111111111-$

Fig. 3. A Weakest Contradicting Strengthening of Assertion (2)

- the value of $index$ vector is 1100, so, tag- and data-entry 12 are indexed,
- not only the indexed tag 12 is equal to the input tag $tagin$ but also tag 1,
- data-entry 1 differs from the indexed data-entry 12, at the second-last position; data-entry 1 has value 1 at this position, while the indexed data-entry has value 0,
- the value of the output of the CAM at the second-last position is 1 instead of 0 as required by the consequent.

From this, the user can deduce that the assertion in fact does not hold for the circuit because the assertion does not consider the case in which two tag-entries are equal to the input tag. Also, the user can conclude that, apparently, the CAM contains a *bus* that, when given both a 0 and 1 value, chooses the 1 value over the 0 value.

An obvious way of circumventing this problem is to introduce symbolic variables for all tag-entries, and to add the constraint that there is at most one tag-entry equal to the input tag. To do so, many extra symbolic variables are needed; one for each bit of each tag-entry. Therefore, it is not surprising that the resulting assertion yields, again, a BDD blow-up.

To obtain an intuition on how to, instead, refine the assertion by introducing a very small number of extra symbolic variables, the user can calculate a weakest satisfying strengthening of the assertion. The user knows from the output of the model-checker that when all of the data-entries have value 1 no spurious counter-model exists. Therefore, the constraint that at least one of the data-entries has value 0 is given to STAR as well.

In Fig. 4, a weakest satisfying strengthening calculated by STAR is given. In this strengthening, for each non-indexed tag-entry *either* (1) the tag-entry differs at one position from the input tag, *or* (2) the tag-entry consist only of X's (tag-entries 5 and 11), and the corresponding data-entry contains a zero at the position where the indexed data-entry has a zero, and X's at each of the positions where the indexed data-entry contains a 1.

This can be explained as follows. There are two ways of making sure that a non-indexed data-entry does not corrupt the output: (1) making the tag-entry differ at at-least one position from the input tag, or (2) as the bus in the CAM favors a 1 over a 0, for each tag that potentially matches, having a 0 in the data-entry at each position where the indexed data-entry contains a 0.

Symbolic Variables	
index	= 0000
tagin	= 00000010
data	= 0100000000000000000000000000000000000000000000000000000000000000

Inputs at time 0	
aread	= 1
tagin	= 00000010

Initial Values	
tagmem[0]	= 00000010
tagmem[1]	= 1-------
tagmem[2]	= 1-------
tagmem[3]	= --1-----
tagmem[4]	= ------0-
tagmem[5]	= --------
tagmem[6]	= -1------
tagmem[7]	= --1-----
tagmem[8]	= -1------
tagmem[9]	= 1-------
tagmem[10]	= 1-------
tagmem[11]	= --------
tagmem[12]	= ---1----
tagmem[13]	= ----1---
tagmem[14]	= ------0-
tagmem[15]	= -1------
datmem[0]	= 0100000000000000000000000000000000000000000000000000000000000000
datmem[5]	= 0-00000000000000000000000000000000000000000000000000000000000000
datmem[11]	= 0-00000000000000000000000000000000000000000000000000000000000000

Fig. 4. A Weakest Satisfying Strengthening of Assertion (2)

As for the verification of the associative read property, no assumptions on the content of the data-entries in the CAM are wanted, the user can ask STAR to generate a weakest satisfying strengthening of Assertion (2) that does not strengthen the requirements on the values of data-entries. This strengthening, given in Fig. 5, makes each non-indexed tag-entry differ at one position from the input tag.

Inspired by this strengthening, the user can modify the assertion by introducing, for each tag-entry i, a vector of symbolic variables p_i that specifies at which position the tag-entry differs from the input tag when the tag-entry is not indexed. The formula expressing that tag i differs from the input tag $tagin$ at the position encoded by p_i is:

$$
\begin{aligned}
\mathrm{mismatch}(i) = \quad & ((p_i = 000) \rightarrow (\mathsf{tagmem}[i][0] \textbf{ is } \neg tagin[0])) \\
\textbf{and} \quad & ((p_i = 001) \rightarrow (\mathsf{tagmem}[i][1] \textbf{ is } \neg tagin[1])) \\
& \quad\vdots \qquad\qquad \vdots \qquad\qquad \vdots \\
\textbf{and} \quad & ((p_i = 111) \rightarrow (\mathsf{tagmem}[i][7] \textbf{ is } \neg tagin[7]))
\end{aligned}
$$

The formula expressing that each of the non-indexed tag-entries differs at at-least one place from $tagin$ is:

$$
\begin{aligned}
A' = \quad & ((index \neq 0000) \rightarrow \mathrm{mismatch}(0)) \\
\textbf{and} \quad & ((index \neq 0001) \rightarrow \mathrm{mismatch}(1)) \\
& \quad\vdots \qquad\qquad \vdots \qquad\qquad \vdots \\
\textbf{and} \quad & ((index \neq 1111) \rightarrow \mathrm{mismatch}(15)))
\end{aligned}
$$

Symbolic Variables	
$index$	= 1111
$tagin$	= 11111110
$data$	= 0100000000000000000000000000000000000000000000000000000000000000
Inputs at time 0	
aread	= 1
tagin	= 11111110
Initial Values	
tagmem[0]	= -------1
tagmem[1]	= ------0-
tagmem[2]	= ---0----
tagmem[3]	= ---0----
tagmem[4]	= ------0-
tagmem[5]	= -------1
tagmem[6]	= -------1
tagmem[7]	= 0-------
tagmem[8]	= ------0-
tagmem[9]	= --0-----
tagmem[10]	= ------0-
tagmem[11]	= --0-----
tagmem[12]	= -----0--
tagmem[13]	= ---0----
tagmem[14]	= 0-------
tagmem[15]	= 11111110
datmem[15]	= 0100000000000000000000000000000000000000000000000000000000000000

Fig. 5. A Weakest Satisfying Strengthening of Ass. (2) without extra assumptions on data-entries.

The assertion obtained by adding A' to the antecedent of assertion (2) is exactly the assertion described in [7] and is easily proved by an STE model-checker.

3   STE-Theory Revisited

Here, we briefly revisit the STE-theory needed to describe the algorithm in STAR.

Circuits and Values. A circuit is modeled by a set of node names $\mathcal{N}$ connected by logical gates and delay elements. $\mathcal{S} \subseteq \mathcal{N}$ is the set of output nodes of delay elements. In STE, we abstract away from specific Boolean values of a node taken from the set $\mathbb{B} = \{0, 1\}$, by using the value X, which stands for *unknown*. Furthermore, the *over-constrained value* T is introduced; a node assumes value T when it is both required to take on value 0 and value 1, leading to the set of *quaternary signal values*, denoted $\mathbb{V} = \{0, 1, X, T\}$. On this set an *information-ordering* $\leq$ is introduced. The unknown value X contains the least information, so $X \leq 0$ and $X \leq 1$, while 0 and 1 are incomparable. The overconstrained value T contains the most information, so $0 \leq T$ and $1 \leq T$. If $v \leq w$ it is said that v is *weaker* than w.

A *circuit state*, written s : State, is a function from $\mathcal{N}$ to $\mathbb{V}$, assigning a value from $\mathbb{V}$ to each node in the circuit. A *sequence* $\sigma : \mathbb{N} \to$ **State** is a function from points in time to circuit states, describing the behaviour of a circuit over time. The set of all sequences σ is written **Seq**. The set of sequences that do not assign the overconstrained value T to any node at any time-point is written $\mathbf{Seq_3}$.

Trajectory Evaluation Logic. STE assertions have the form $A \implies C$. Here A and C are formulas in *Trajectory Evaluation Logic* (TEL). The only variables in the logic are time-independent Boolean variables taken from the set V of *symbolic variables*. The language is given by the following grammar:

$$f ::= n \text{ is } 0 \mid n \text{ is } 1 \mid f_1 \text{ and } f_2 \mid P \to f \mid \mathbf{N}f$$

where $n \in \mathcal{N}$ and P is a Boolean propositional formula over the set of symbolic variables V. The notation n is P, where P is a Boolean formula over the set of symbolic variables V, is used to abbreviate the formula: $(\neg P \to n \text{ is } 0)$ and $(P \to n \text{ is } 1)$. The *depth* of a TEL-formula f is the maximal degree of nestings of $\mathbf{N}$ in f. The depth of an STE-assertion $A \Longrightarrow C$ is the maximum of the depth of A and the depth of C.

The meaning of a TEL formula is defined by a satisfaction relation that relates valuations of the symbolic variables and sequences to TEL formulas. Here, the following notation is used: The time shifting operator σ^1 is defined by $\sigma^1(t)(n) = \sigma(t+1)(n)$. Standard propositional satisfiability is denoted by $\models_{\text{Prop}}$. Satisfaction of a TEL-formula f, by a sequence $\sigma \in \mathbf{Seq}$, and a valuation $\phi : V \to \mathbb{B}$ (written $\phi, \sigma \models f$) is defined by

$$\begin{aligned}
\phi, \sigma &\models n \text{ is } b &\equiv&\ b \le \sigma(0)(n) \ ,\ b \in \{0,1\} \\
\phi, \sigma &\models f_1 \text{ and } f_2 &\equiv&\ \phi, \sigma \models f_1 \text{ and } \phi, \sigma \models f_2 \\
\phi, \sigma &\models P \to f &\equiv&\ \phi \models_{\text{Prop}} P \text{ implies } \phi, \sigma \models f \\
\phi, \sigma &\models \mathbf{N}f &\equiv&\ \phi, \sigma^1 \models f
\end{aligned}$$

Trajectories. In STE, three abstractions are used: (1) the value X can be used to abstract from a specific Boolean value of a circuit node, (2) information is only propagated forwards through the circuit (i.e. from inputs to outputs of gates) and through time (i.e. from time t to time $t+1$), (3) the initial value of all delay elements is assumed to be X. Given a circuit c, a *trajectory* is a sequence that meets the constraints of the circuit c, taking these abstractions into account. How to obtain the set of trajectories of a circuit c is described, for instance, in [10,8,9,6,1,12].

A circuit c *satisfies* a trajectory assertion $A \Longrightarrow C$, written $c \models A \Longrightarrow C$ iff for every valuation $\phi \in V \to \mathbb{B}$ of the symbolic variables, and for every trajectory τ of c such that $\tau \in \mathbf{Seq}_3$, it holds that: $\phi, \tau \models A \Rightarrow \phi, \tau \models C$.

STE-Model Checking. The theory of STE guarantees that for every TEL-formula A, circuit c and valuation ϕ, there exists an unique weakest trajectory that satisfies A. This trajectory is called the *defining trajectory of A w.r.t.* ϕ, written $\overset{\phi}{c}[\![\ A\ ]\!]$. Furthermore, for every TEL-formula C, and valuation ϕ there exists an unique weakest sequence that satisfies C. This sequence is called the *defining sequence of C w.r.t.* ϕ, written $\overset{\phi}{}[\,C\,]$.

The *Fundamental Theorem of STE* states that in order to check that an assertion is true, only the defining trajectories of the antecedent need to be considered (instead of all trajectories). That is, to check that $c \models A \Longrightarrow C$, we only need to check that for every valuation of the symbolic variables ϕ, such that $\overset{\phi}{c}[\![\ A\ ]\!] \in \mathbf{Seq}_3$, holds $\overset{\phi}{}[\,C\,] \le \overset{\phi}{c}[\![\ A\ ]\!]$.

Given a circuit description and an STE-assertion, an STE-simulator calculates a symbolic representation of the set of defining trajectories of the antecedent of the assertion. In *BDD-based STE*, BDDs are used to represent the defining trajectories. In *SAT-based STE*, non-canonical *Boolean expressions* are used. In both cases a *dual-rail encoding* is used to encode a quaternary value by two Boolean values [12].

After simulation, it is checked whether the symbolic representation of the defining trajectories of the antecedent satisfies the requirements of the consequent. In BDD-based STE this check is trivial because of the canonicity of BDDs. In SAT-based STE, a SAT-solver is called to perform this check.

4 Finding Satisfying and Contradicting Strengthenings

The job of the main algorithm in STAR is to, given a circuit and an STE-assertion, find a weakest satisfying strengthening (respectively weakest contradicting strengthening) of the assertion. In order to do so, the algorithm employs an STE-simulator on Boolean expressions. After simulation, a SAT-problem is generated whose solutions represent all satisfying (respectively contradicting) strengthenings of the assertion. Finally, an incremental SAT-solver [3] is iteratively called to find a weakest such strengthening. Before describing the algorithm in more detail, we make the concept of strengthenings more precise.

4.1 Satisfying Strengthenings

A strengthening of an STE-assertion gives extra Boolean requirements on nodes of the circuit over time. The set of the nodes and corresponding time-points that potentially can be strengthened is called the *set of strengthening candidates*, written $SC \subseteq \mathbb{N} \times \mathcal{N}$. Given an assertion of depth d, the set of strengthening candidates commonly consists of the input nodes $\mathcal{I}$ of the circuit over time-points $\{0, \ldots, d\}$ and the initial values of delay elements. That is, in that case: $SC = (\{0, \ldots, d\} \times \mathcal{I}) \cup (\{0\} \times S)$. However, sometimes, we might want to restrict the set of strengthening candidates as we did in the case-study.

Given a set of strengthening candidates, a *strengthening* is a function $\gamma : SC \to \{0, 1, X\}$ from nodes and time points to the values $0, 1$, and X, giving extra requirements on the nodes of a circuit. For example, if $\gamma(0, \mathsf{p}) = 1$, $\gamma(2, \mathsf{q}) = 0$, and $\gamma(t, n) = X$ for all other t and n, then node p is strengthened to have value 1 at time-point 0, and node q is strengthened to value 0 at time-point 2.

A strengthening can easily be transformed into a TEL-formula with the same meaning, denoted by $\mathsf{TEL}(\gamma)$, which is defined to be the conjunction of all $\mathbf{N}^t(n \text{ is } \gamma(t, n))$ with $(t, n) \in SC$ and for which $\gamma(t, n) \neq X$. For example, if γ is defined as in the above example, then $\mathsf{TEL}(\gamma) = ((\mathsf{p} \text{ is } 1) \text{ and } \mathbf{N}^2(\mathsf{q} \text{ is } 0))$. The TEL-formula $(A \text{ and } \mathsf{TEL}(\gamma))$ is called the *strengthening of A w.r.t.* γ, and is written $\mathsf{Str}(A, \gamma)$.

Given a circuit c and an assignment of symbolic variables $\phi : V \to \{0, 1\}$, a *satisfying strengthening* of an assertion $A \implies C$ is a strengthening γ such that simulating using γ and A does not yield overconstrained nodes and makes the consequent true, i.e. $_c^\phi[\![\mathsf{Str}(A, \gamma)]\!] \in \mathsf{Seq}_3$ and $\phi, _c^\phi[\![\mathsf{Str}(A, \gamma)]\!] \models C$.

Strengthenings can be compared by extending the information order $\leq$ point-wise to functions, arriving at the concept of a *weakest satisfying strengthening*, which is a satisfying strengthening weaker than all other satisfying strengthenings of an assertion. Note that weakest strengthenings are not unique; there can for example be several, but incomparable, weakest satisfying strengthenings.

4.2   Generation of the SAT-Problem

A SAT-problem consists of a set of *variables* W and a *Boolean formula* P. An *assignment* is a mapping $a : W \to \{0,1\}$. A SAT-problem S is satisfied by an assignment a, written $a \models S$, if a makes P evaluate to 1.

For calculating a strengthening of an STE-assertion of depth d, only the first d time-points of the simulation matter. Therefore, the concept of a *truncated* sequence is introduced, which is a function from the time-points $\{0, .., d\}$ to circuit states.

We will define a *SAT-problem for all satisfying strengthenings*, written SS$(A \Longrightarrow C, c, \mathcal{SC})$, whose solutions represent precisely those truncated sequences σ, valuations ϕ, and strengthenings γ such that γ is a satisfying strengthening of $A \Longrightarrow C$ w.r.t. ϕ.

For an STE-assertion of depth d, the SAT-problem contains a SAT-variable v for each variable v in the set of symbolic variables V. Furthermore, for each node n in the set of nodes $\mathcal{N}$ of the circuit c, and for each time point $0 \le t \le d$ *two* SAT-variables are introduced, written n_t^0 and n_t^1. The two variables n_t^0 and n_t^1 encode the value of node n at time t using a standard dual-rail encoding; the function mapping a dual-rail encoded quaternary value to the quaternary value itself, written quat, is defined by: $\mathrm{quat}(0,0) = \mathsf{X}$, $\mathrm{quat}(1,0) = 0$, $\mathrm{quat}(0,1) = 1$, and $\mathrm{quat}(1,1) = \mathsf{T}$.

Finally, for each time-point/node pair (t, n) in the set of strengthening candidates $\mathcal{SC}$, the SAT-problem contains a pair of SAT-variables $\hat{n}_t^0$ and $\hat{n}_t^1$ representing a possible requirement of a strengthening on node n at time t. Again, the dual-rail encoding is used; if $\hat{n}_t^0$ and $\hat{n}_t^1$ are both 0, there is no requirement on node n at time t, if $\hat{n}_t^0 = 1$ and $\hat{n}_t^1 = 0$ the node is required to have value 0, if $\hat{n}_t^0 = 0$ and $\hat{n}_t^1 = 1$ the node is required to have value 1. The SAT-problem is constructed such that $\hat{n}_t^0$ and $\hat{n}_t^1$ are not allowed to both have value 1.

A satisfying assignment a of the SAT-problem can thus be mapped to a assignment of symbolic variables ϕ_a defined by $\phi_a(v) = a(v)$, to a truncated sequence σ_a defined by $\sigma_a(t)(n) = \mathrm{quat}(a(n_t^0), a(n_t^1))$, and to a strengthening γ_a defined by $\gamma_a(t, n) = \mathrm{quat}(a(\hat{n}_t^0), a(\hat{n}_t^1))$.

Constructing the SAT-Problem.   The SAT-problem for all satisfying strengthenings SS$(A \Longrightarrow C, c, \mathcal{SC})$ is defined as the conjunction of two SAT-problems: (1) A SAT-problem that restricts the sequences σ, assignments ϕ and strengthenings γ such that σ is the defining trajectory of Str(A, γ) w.r.t. ϕ, and (2) A SAT-problem that restricts the sequences σ and assignments ϕ such that they together satisfy the consequent C. Below, we define both SAT-problems.

However, first we need to define the SAT-problem for the defining trajectory of a TEL-formula. It is well-known how to use an STE-simulator on Boolean expressions to generate a SAT-problem whose satisfying assignments correspond to the set of defining trajectories of the antecedent of the assertion [8,9,2,14]. We denote this SAT-problem by DTA(A, c, d), and we assume that its solutions represent exactly those valuations ϕ and truncated sequences σ such that $\sigma = {}_c^\phi[\![A]\!] \restriction \{0, .., d\}$ and $\sigma \in \mathbf{Seq}_3$.

SAT-Problem for the Antecedent.   We now define the SAT-problem for *the defining trajectory of a symbolically strengthened antecedent*, written DTSA$(A, c, d, \mathcal{SC})$ whose solutions represent precisely those truncated sequences σ, valuations ϕ, and strengthenings γ such that σ is the (truncated) defining trajectory of Str(A, γ) w.r.t. ϕ.

In order to do so, we first introduce the concept a *symbolically strengthened antecedent*, written $\mathsf{SymStr}(A, \mathcal{SC})$. The symbolically strengthened antecedent contains for each time-point/node pair in the set of strengthening candidates $\mathcal{SC}$ a pair of symbolic variables $\hat{n}_t^0$ and $\hat{n}_t^1$, representing a possible requirement of strengthening γ on node n at time t, and is defined by:

$$\mathsf{SymStr}(A, \mathcal{SC}) = A \text{ and } (\mathbf{and}_{(t,n)\in\mathcal{SC}} \, \mathbf{N}^t(\hat{n}_t^0 \to n \text{ is } 0 \text{ and } \hat{n}_t^1 \to n \text{ is } 1))$$

The SAT-problem for the defining trajectory of the symbolically strengthened antecedent is defined by: $\mathsf{DTSA}(A, c, d, \mathcal{SC}) = \mathsf{DTA}(\mathsf{SymStr}(A, \mathcal{SC}), c, d)$.

SAT-Problem for the Consequent. The SAT-problem for satisfaction of a consequent C, written $\mathsf{SAT}(C)$, is constructed such that its set of solutions contains precisely those sequences σ and assignments of the symbolic variables ϕ that together satisfy consequent C. (i.e. $\phi, \sigma \models C$).

In order to build this SAT-problem, we need to define the concept of *defining formula*. Given a consequent C, a node name n, a Boolean value $b \in \mathbb{B}$, and a time point t, we can construct a propositional formula that is true exactly when C requires the node n to have value b at time point t. This formula is called the *defining formula of $n = b$ at t*, and is denoted by $\langle C \rangle(t)(n = b)$.

For example, if the consequent C is defined as $(a \wedge b) \to \mathsf{p}$ is 0, then $\langle C \rangle(0)(\mathsf{p} = 0)$ is the formula $a \wedge b$, since only when $a \wedge b$ holds, does C require node p to be 0. However, $\langle C \rangle(0)(\mathsf{p} = 1)$ is the false formula 0, since C never requires the node p to be 1.

The *defining formula* is defined recursively as follows:

$$\langle m \text{ is } b' \rangle(t)(n = b) \quad = \begin{cases} 1, & \text{if } m = n, b' = b \text{ and } t = 0 \\ 0, & \text{otherwise} \end{cases}$$

$$\langle f_1 \text{ and } f_2 \rangle(t)(n = b) = \langle f_1 \rangle(t)(n = b) \vee \langle f_2 \rangle(t)(n = b)$$

$$\langle P \to f \rangle(t)(n = b) \quad = P \wedge \langle f \rangle(t)(n = b)$$

$$\langle \mathbf{N}f \rangle(t)(n = b) \quad = \begin{cases} \langle f \rangle(t - 1)(n = b), & \text{if } t > 0 \\ 0, & \text{otherwise} \end{cases}$$

Note that for an antecedent of the form f_1 **and** f_2 to require that a node n has a value b, it is enough that only one of the formulas f_1 or f_2 requires that n is b. The SAT-problem for the satisfaction of the consequent is now defined by:

$$\mathsf{SAT}(C) = \bigwedge_{(n,t)\in C} (\langle C \rangle(t)(n = 0) \to n_t^0) \wedge (\langle C \rangle(t)(n = 1) \to n_t^1)$$

Here, $(n, t) \in C$ means that C refers to node n at time-point t.

SAT-Problem for All Satisfying Strengthenings. Given an assertion $A \Longrightarrow C$ of depth d for a circuit c and a set of strengthening candidates $\mathcal{SC}$, the *SAT-problem for all satisfying strengthenings*, written $\mathsf{SS}(A \Longrightarrow C, c, \mathcal{SC})$, is defined by:

$$\mathsf{SS}(A \Longrightarrow C, c, \mathcal{SC}) = \mathsf{DTSA}(A, \mathcal{SC}, c, d) \wedge \mathsf{SAT}(C)$$

The solutions to the above SAT-problem represent exactly those valuations ϕ and strengthenings γ such that γ is a satisfying strengthening of $A \Longrightarrow C$ w.r.t. ϕ.

4.3 Finding a Weakest Assignment

Calling a SAT-solver on the SAT-problem for all satisfying strengthenings, $SS(A \implies C, c, SC)$, yields a satisfying strengthening (if one exists). This satisfying strengthening, however, is not necessarily a *weakest* satisfying strengthening. To find a weakest satisfying strengthening, iteratively "blocking constraints" are added to the SAT-problem that block the last found strengthening and allow only strictly weaker strengthenings. This process is repeated until the SAT-problem becomes unsatisfiable; the last found satisfying strengthening is then guaranteed to be a weakest satisfying strengthening. As said earlier, weakest strengthenings are not neccessarily unique; the result of this process is an arbitrary weakest satisfying strengthening.

Given a strengthening $\gamma : SC \rightarrow \{0,1\}$, the blocking constraint consists of four parts: (1) for every node n that is assigned value X at time t by γ, we require that it is assigned value X in any weaker strengthening, (2) any node that is assigned value 0 at time t is allowed to assume values 0 and X in a weaker strengthening, but not value 1, (3) any node that is assigned value 1 at time t is allowed to assume values 1 and X in a weaker strengthening, but not value 0, and (4) at least one of the nodes should change value. This yields the following blocking constraint $B(\gamma)$:

$$
\begin{aligned}
B(\gamma) = \quad &(\textstyle\bigwedge_{(t,n)\in SC, \gamma(t,n)=X} (\neg \hat{n}_t^0 \,\&\, \neg \hat{n}_t^1) \quad) \\
\wedge \;&(\textstyle\bigwedge_{(t,n)\in SC, \gamma(t,n)=0} \neg \hat{n}_t^1 \quad) \\
\wedge \;&(\textstyle\bigwedge_{(t,n)\in SC, \gamma(t,n)=1} \neg \hat{n}_t^0 \quad) \\
\wedge \;&((\textstyle\bigvee_{\gamma(t,n)=0} \neg \hat{n}_t^0) \vee (\textstyle\bigvee_{\gamma(t,n)=1} \neg \hat{n}_t^1))
\end{aligned}
$$

The solutions to the SAT-problem $B(\gamma)$ represent exactly those strengthenings γ' such that $\gamma' < \gamma$. This finishes the description of the algorithm for finding a weakest satisfying strengthening.

4.4 Contradicting Strengthenings

Given a circuit c and an assignment of symbolic variables $\phi : V \rightarrow \{0,1\}$, a *contradicting strengthening* of an assertion $A \implies C$ is a strengthening γ such that such that there exists a node n, time-point t, and Boolean value b, such that simulating using γ and A yields b for n at time t (i.e. $\phi_c[\![\, \mathrm{Str}(A,\gamma) \,]\!](t)(n) = b$), but the consequent requires n to be $\neg b$ (i.e. $\phi[\![\, C \,]\!](t)(n) = \neg b$). Again, we require that the strengthened antecedent does not yield overconstrained nodes, i.e. $\phi_c[\![\, \mathrm{Str}(A,\gamma) \,]\!] \in \mathbf{Seq_3}$.

The SAT-problem for finding a weakest contradicting strengthening has the same structure as the SAT-problem for the weakest satisfying strengthening; one part for the antecedent, and one part for the consequent. The SAT-problem for the contradiction of a consequent C, written $\mathrm{CON}(C)$, is constructed such that at least one node differs in its Boolean value from what is required by C:

$$
\mathrm{CON}(C) = \bigvee_{(n,t)\in C} ((\langle C \rangle)(t)(n=0) \wedge n_t^1) \vee ((\langle C \rangle)(t)(n=1) \wedge n_t^0)
$$

The *SAT-problem for all contradicting strengthenings*, written $\mathrm{CS}(A \implies C, c, SC)$ is defined by: $\mathrm{CS}(A \implies C, c, SC) = \mathrm{DTSA}(A, SC, c, d) \wedge \mathrm{CON}(C)$. We find an actual *weakest* contradicting strengthening in exactly the same way as described in the previous subsection.

5   Discussion

We have introduced the novel concept of strengthenings, that can greatly assist in performing manual abstraction refinement for STE. Furthermore, we have developed a SAT-based algorithm for finding weakest strengthenings using an incremental SAT-solver to minimise the strengthening. We have implemented the algorithm in a tool called STAR, and have shown how it can be used to assist in abstraction refinement in a non-trivial case-study.

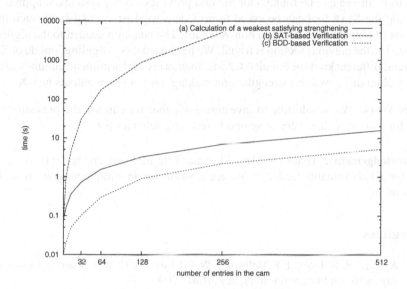

Fig. 6. Experimental results for CAMs with a tag-width of 16 bits, a data-width of 64 bits, and a varying number of entries, using a PC with a Pentium IV processor at 3GHz and 2GB of memory

As far as we believe, the information provided by our method cannot be calculated by BDD-based techniques, because too many BDD-variables would be needed.

Scalability.   We believe that our method scales well. To illustrate this, we compare the running times[1] of three different experiments for CAMs with a varying number of entries[2] in Fig. 6: (a) finding a weakest satisfying strengthening of CAM assertion 2 using STAR, (b) proving the corrected assertion using a SAT-based STE model-checker (as described in [9]), and (c) proving the corrected assertion with BDDs using Forte.

As the figure shows, when the right abstraction has been found, BDD-based STE is superior over SAT-based STE for proving properties. As discussed before, finding

---

[1] For the SAT-based methods we only show the time spent by SAT-solving. Overhead in simulating the circuit is not counted since this was implemented inefficiently. Efficient symbolic simulators (like the one in Forte) can perform symbolic simulation with Boolean expressions in negligible time.

[2] We provide the netlists of the CAMs used at http://www.cs.chalmers.se/~jwr/CAV2006.

the right abstraction is, however, highly non-trivial. Here, STAR can help by finding weakest strengthenings. The graph shows that this can be done in reasonable time.

Another Application. In practical uses of STE, often the first step in a verification attempt is the *wiggling* phase [1]. The goal of this phase is to find out what minimal set of inputs and initial values of registers should be driven to make non-X values appear at designated circuit outputs. Commonly, wiggling is performed by using the STE-model checker as a scalar (that is, non-symbolic) simulator; the simulator is iteratively fed with vectors of Boolean values and X's, in the hope that, by trial-and-error, a minimal set of nodes to be driven can be found. Our method provides a more systematic approach to wiggling; the STAR tool can be asked to provide a weakest strengthening such that a given set of output nodes takes on non-X values. The adaption needed to the algorithm presented in the previous section is trivial. We have used this "wiggling"-mode of STAR on several different kinds of circuits (CAMs, memories, and arithmetic circuits), always quickly obtaining a weakest strengthening making a set of given outputs non-X.

Future Work. We would like to investigate whether we can use the presented technique for automatic discovery of symbolic indexing schemes [6].

Acknowledgements. Thanks to Mary Sheeran, Tom Melham, and the anonymous referees for giving valuable feedback. We are grateful for an equipment grant from Intel Corporation.

References

1. M. Aagaard, R. B. Jones, T. F. Melham, J. W. O'Leary, and C.-J. H. Seger. A methodology for large-scale hardware verification. In *FMCAD*, 2000.
2. P. Bjesse, T. Leonard, and A. Mokkedem. Finding bugs in an Alpha microprocessor using satisfiability solvers. In *CAV 2001*, volume 2102 of *LNCS*. Springer-Verlag, 2001.
3. N. Eén and N. Sörensson. An extensible SAT-solver. In *Proceedings of the 6th International Conference on Theory and Applications of Satisfiability Testing (SAT2003)*, 2003.
4. FORTE. http://www.intel.com/software/products/opensource/tools1/verification.
5. B. Li, C. Wang, and F. Somenzi. Abstraction refinement in symbolic model checking using satisfiability as the only decision procedure. *Journal on STTT*, 7(2):143–155, Apr. 2005.
6. T. F. Melham and R. B. Jones. Abstraction by symbolic indexing transformations. In *Formal Methods in Computer-Aided Design FMCAD*, volume 2517 of *LNCS*, 2002.
7. M. Pandey, R. Raimi, R. E. Bryant, and M. S. Abadir. Formal verification of content addressable memories using symbolic trajectory evaluation. In *DAC'97*, 1997.
8. J.-W. Roorda. Symbolic trajectory evaluation using a satisfiability solver. Licentiate thesis, Computing Science, Chalmers University of Technology, 2005.
9. J.-W. Roorda and K. Claessen. A new SAT-based Algorithm for Symbolic Trajectory Evaluation. In *Correct Hardware Design and Verification Methods (CHARME)*, 2005.
10. J.-W. Roorda and K. Claessen. Explaining Symbolic Trajectory Evaluation by Giving it a Faithful Semantics. In *International Computer Science Symposium in Russia (CSR)*, volume 3967 of *LNCS*, 2006.
11. T. Schubert. High level formal verification of next-generation microprocessors. In *Proceedings of the 40th conference on Design automation*, pages 1–6. ACM Press, 2003.

12. C.-J. H. Seger and R. E. Bryant. Formal verification by symbolic evaluation of partially-ordered trajectories. *Formal Methods in System Design*, 6(2), 1995.
13. R. Tzoref and O. Grumberg. Automatic Refinement and Vacuity Detection for Symbolic Trajectory Evaluation. In *Computer Aided Verification (CAV)*, 2006.
14. J. Yang, R. Gil, and E. Singerman. satGSTE: Combining the abstraction of GSTE with the capacity of a SAT solver. In *Designing Correct Circuits (DCC'04)*, 2004.

Automatic Refinement and Vacuity Detection for Symbolic Trajectory Evaluation

Rachel Tzoref[1,2] and Orna Grumberg[1]

[1] Computer Science Department, Technion, Haifa, Israel
[2] IBM Haifa Research Laboratory, Israel
{rachelt, orna}@cs.technion.ac.il

Abstract. Symbolic Trajectory Evaluation (STE) is a powerful technique for model checking. It is based on 3-valued symbolic simulation, using 0,1 and X ("unknown"). The X value is used to abstract away parts of the circuit. The abstraction is derived from the user's specification. Currently the process of abstraction and refinement in STE is performed manually. This paper presents an automatic refinement technique for STE. The technique is based on a clever selection of constraints that are added to the specification so that on the one hand the semantics of the original specification is preserved, and on the other hand, the part of the state space in which the "unknown" result is received is significantly decreased or totally eliminated. In addition, this paper raises the problem of vacuity of passed and failed specifications. This problem was never discussed in the framework of STE. We describe when an STE specification may vacuously pass or fail, and propose a method for vacuity detection in STE.

1 Introduction

Symbolic Trajectory Evaluation (STE) [11] is a powerful technique for hardware model checking. STE is based on combining 3-valued simulation with symbolic simulation. It is applied to a circuit M, described as a graph over *nodes* (gates and latches). The specification consists of assertions in a restricted temporal language. The assertions are of the form $A \Longrightarrow C$, where the *antecedent* A expresses constraints on nodes n at different times t, and the *consequent* C expresses requirements that should hold on such nodes (n, t). STE computes a symbolic representation for each node (n, t). The size of this representation depends on the size of A, rather than on the circuit size. *Abstraction* in STE is derived from the specification by initializing all inputs not appearing in A to the X ("unknown") value. A forth value, $\perp$, represents a contradiction between the constraint of A on some node (n, t) and its actual behavior. A *refinement* amounts to changing the assertion in order to present nodes values more accurately.

STE assertions may either pass or fail on M. In [5], a 4-valued truth domain $\{0, 1, X, \perp\}$ is defined for the temporal language of STE, corresponding to the 4-valued domain of the values of the circuit nodes. The motivation for a 4-valued semantics is to distinguish between different causes for the pass or fail of an STE assertion. The X truth value distinguishes the case in which the STE assertion fails due to partial information about the state space from the case in which it is actually violated by M. In the latter

T. Ball and R.B. Jones (Eds.): CAV 2006, LNCS 4144, pp. 190–204, 2006.
© Springer-Verlag Berlin Heidelberg 2006

case a *counterexample* is produced, representing an execution of M that satisfies A but contradicts C. The X truth value stems from a too coarse antecedent which underspecifies the circuit. The $\perp$ truth value indicates that the STE assertion passes vacuously due to a contradiction between A and M.

Generalized STE (GSTE) [19] is a significant extension of STE that can verify all ω-regular properties. Manual refinement methods for GSTE are presented in [18]. In [16], SAT-based STE is used for manual refinement of GSTE assertion graphs.

(G)STE has been in active use in the industry, and has been very successful in verifying huge circuits containing large data paths [12,10,17]. Its main drawback, however, is the need for manual abstraction and refinement, which can be very labor-intensive.

Our Contribution. We propose a technique for automatic refinement of assertions in STE. In our technique, the initial abstraction is derived, as usual in STE, from the given specification. The refinement is an iterative process, which stops when a truth value other than X is achieved. In case of a 0 truth value, a counterexample is presented to the user. Our automatic refinement is applied when the STE specification results with X. We compute a set of input nodes, whose refinement is sufficient for eliminating the X truth value. We further suggest heuristics for choosing a small subset of this set.

Selecting a "right" set of inputs has a crucial role in the success of the abstraction and refinement process: selecting too many inputs will add many variables to the computation of the symbolic representation, and may result in memory and time explosion. On the other hand, selecting too few inputs or selecting inputs that do not affect the result of the verification will lead to many iterations with an X truth value.

We point out that, as in any automated verification framework, we are limited by the following observations. First, there is no automatic way to determine whether the provided specification is correct. Therefore, we assume it is, and we make sure that our refined assertion passes on the concrete circuit iff the original assertion does. Second, bugs cannot automatically be fixed. Thus, counterexamples are analyzed by the user.

Abstraction-Refinement is a well known methodology in model checking [4,6] for fighting the state explosion problem. In [3], it is shown that the abstraction in STE is an abstract interpretation via a Galois connection. [9] presents a SAT-based algorithm to assist in manual refinement of STE assertions. However, automatic refinement has never been suggested before for STE. The work that is closest to ours is [15], which suggests an automatic abstraction-refinement for symbolic simulation. However, the suggested heuristics are significantly different from ours.

Another important contribution of our work is identifying that STE results may hide vacuity. This possibility was never raised before. Hidden vacuity may occur since an abstract execution of M on which the truth value of the specification is 1 or 0, might not correspond to any concrete execution of M. In such a case, a pass is *vacuous*, while a counterexample is *spurious*. We propose a method for detecting these cases.

We implemented our automatic refinement technique within Intel's Forte environment [12]. We ran it on two nontrivial circuits with several assertions. Our experimental results show success in automatically identifying a set of inputs that are crucial for reaching a definite truth value. Thus, a small number of iterations were needed.

2 Basic Definitions

A circuit M consists of a set of nodes $\mathcal{N}$, connected by directed edges. The nodes consist of inputs and internal nodes. Internal nodes consist of latches and combinational nodes. Each combinational node is associated with a Boolean function. We say that a node n_1 enters a node n_2 if there exists a directed edge from n_1 to n_2. The nodes entering a certain node are its *source nodes*, and the nodes to which a node enters are its *sink nodes*. The value of a latch at time t can be expressed as a Boolean expression over its source nodes at times t and $t - 1$, and over the latch value at time $t - 1$. The directed graph induced by M may contain loops but no combinational loops. Throughout the paper we refer to a node n at a specific time t as (n, t).

The *bounded cone of influence* (**BCOI**) of a node (n, t) contains all nodes (n', t') with $t' \leq t$ that may influence the value of (n, t), and is defined recursively as follows: the BCOI of a combinational node at time t is the union of the BCOI of its source nodes at time t, and the BCOI of a latch at time t is the union of the BCOI of its source nodes at times t and $t - 1$ according to the latch type.

Usually, the circuit nodes receive Boolean values. In STE, a third value, X ("unknown"), is introduced. Attaching X to a certain node represents lack of information regarding the truth value of that node. A forth value, $\perp$, is added to represent the over-constrained value, in which a node is

AND	X	0	1	$\perp$		OR	X	0	1	$\perp$		NOT	
X	X	0	X	$\perp$		X	X	X	1	$\perp$		X	X
0	0	0	0	$\perp$		0	X	0	1	$\perp$		0	1
1	X	0	1	$\perp$		1	1	1	1	$\perp$		1	0
$\perp$	$\perp$	$\perp$	$\perp$	$\perp$		$\perp$	$\perp$	$\perp$	$\perp$	$\perp$		$\perp$	$\perp$

Fig. 1. Quaternary operations

forced both to 0 and to 1. This value indicates that contradiction exists between external assumptions on the circuit and its actual behavior. The set of values $\mathcal{Q} \equiv \{0, 1, X, \perp\}$ forms a complete lattice with the partial order $0 \sqsubseteq X, 1 \sqsubseteq X, \perp \sqsubseteq 0$ and $\perp \sqsubseteq 1$. This order corresponds to set inclusion, where X represents the set $\{0, 1\}$, and $\perp$ represents the empty set. As a result, the *greatest lower bound* $\sqcap$ corresponds to set intersection and the *least upper bound* $\sqcup$ corresponds to set union. The Boolean operations AND, OR and NOT are extended to the domain $\mathcal{Q}$ as shown in Figure 1.

A *state* s of the circuit M is an assignment of values from $\mathcal{Q}$ to all circuit nodes, $s : \mathcal{N} \to \mathcal{Q}$. Given two states s_1, s_2, we say that $s_1 \sqsubseteq s_2 \iff ((\exists n \in \mathcal{N} : s_1(n) = \perp) \vee (\forall n \in \mathcal{N} : s_1(n) \sqsubseteq s_2(n)))$. A state is *concrete* if all nodes are assigned with values out of $\{0, 1\}$. A state s is an abstraction of a concrete state s_c if $s_c \sqsubseteq s$.

A *sequence* σ is any infinite series of states. We denote by $\sigma(i), i \in \mathbb{N}$, the state at time i in σ, and by $\sigma(i)(n), i \in \mathbb{N}, n \in \mathcal{N}$, the value of node n in the state $\sigma(i)$. $\sigma^i, i \in \mathbb{N}$, denotes the suffix of σ starting at time i. We say that $\sigma_1 \sqsubseteq \sigma_2 \iff ((\exists i \geq 0, n \in \mathcal{N} : \sigma_1(i)(n) = \perp) \vee (\forall i \geq 0 : \sigma_1(i) \sqsubseteq \sigma_2(i)))$. Note that we refer to states and sequences that contain $\perp$ values as least elements w.r.t $\sqsubseteq$.

Let V be a set of symbolic Boolean variables over the domain $\{0, 1\}$. A *symbolic expression* over V is an expression consisting of quaternary operations, applied to $V \cup \mathcal{Q}$. A *symbolic state* over V is a mapping which maps each node of M to a symbolic expression. Each symbolic state represents a set of states, one for each assignment to the variables in V. A *symbolic sequence* over V is a series of symbolic states. It represents a set of sequences, one for each assignment to V. Given a symbolic sequence σ and an assignment ϕ to V, $\phi(\sigma)$ denotes the sequence that is received by applying ϕ to all symbolic expressions in σ. Given two symbolic sequences σ_1, σ_2 over V, we say that $\sigma_1 \sqsubseteq \sigma_2$ if for all assignments ϕ to V, $\phi(\sigma_1) \sqsubseteq \phi(\sigma_2)$.

A **Trajectory Evaluation Logic** (TEL) formula is defined recursively over V as follows:

$$f ::= n \text{ is } p \mid f_1 \wedge f_2 \mid p \rightarrow f \mid \mathbf{N}f$$

where $n \in \mathcal{N}$, p is a Boolean expression over V and $\mathbf{N}$ is the next time operator. Note that TEL formulas can be expressed as a finite set of constraints on values of specific nodes at specific times. N^t denotes the application of t next time operators. The constraints on (n, t) are those appearing in the scope of N^t. The **maximal depth** of a TEL formula f, denoted depth(f), is the maximal time t for which a constraint exists in f on some node (n, t), plus 1.

Usually, the satisfaction of a TEL formula f on a symbolic sequence σ is defined in the 2-valued truth domain [11], i.e., f is either satisfied or not satisfied. In [5], $\mathcal{Q}$ is used also as a 4-valued truth domain for an extension of TEL. Our 4-valued semantics definition is different from [5] w.r.t $\perp$ values. In [5], a sequence σ containing $\perp$ values could satisfy f with a truth value different from $\perp$. In our definition this is not allowed. We believe that our definition captures better the intent behind the specification w.r.t contradictory information about the state space. Given a TEL formula f over V, a symbolic sequence σ over V, and an assignment ϕ to V, we define the satisfaction of f as follows:

$[\phi, \sigma \models f] = \perp \;\leftrightarrow\; \exists i \geq 0, n \in \mathcal{N} : \phi(\sigma)(i)(n) = \perp.$ Otherwise:

$[\phi, \sigma \models n \text{ is } p] = 1 \;\leftrightarrow\; \phi(\sigma)(0)(n) = \phi(p)$

$[\phi, \sigma \models n \text{ is } p] = 0 \;\leftrightarrow\; \phi(\sigma)(0)(n) \neq \phi(p)$ and $\phi(\sigma)(0)(n) \in \{0, 1\}$

$[\phi, \sigma \models n \text{ is } p] = X \;\leftrightarrow\; \phi(\sigma)(0)(n) = X \qquad \phi, \sigma \models p \rightarrow f = (\neg\phi(p) \vee \phi, \sigma \models f)$

$\phi, \sigma \models f_1 \wedge f_2 = (\phi, \sigma \models f_1 \wedge \phi, \sigma \models f_2) \qquad \phi, \sigma \models \mathbf{N}f = \phi, \sigma^1 \models f$

Note that given an assignment ϕ to V, $\phi(p)$ is a constant (0 or 1). In addition, the $\perp$ truth value is determined only according to ϕ and σ, regardless of f. It is proven in [5] that the satisfaction relation is monotonic, i.e., for all TEL formulas f, symbolic sequences σ_1, σ_2 and assignments ϕ to V, if $\phi(\sigma_2) \sqsubseteq \phi(\sigma_1)$ then $[\phi, \sigma_2 \models f] \sqsubseteq [\phi, \sigma_1 \models f]$. This also holds for our satisfaction definition. We define the truth value of $\sigma \models f$ as follows:

$[\sigma \models f] = 0 \;\leftrightarrow\; \exists\phi : [\phi, \sigma \models f] = 0$

$[\sigma \models f] = X \;\leftrightarrow\; \forall\phi : [\phi, \sigma \models f] \neq 0$ and $\exists\phi : [\phi, \sigma \models f] = X$

$[\sigma \models f] = 1 \;\leftrightarrow\; \forall\phi : [\phi, \sigma \models f] \notin \{0, X\}$ and $\exists\phi : [\phi, \sigma \models f] = 1$

$[\sigma \models f] = \perp \;\leftrightarrow\; \forall\phi : [\phi, \sigma \models f] = \perp$

It is proven in [5] that every TEL formula f has a **defining sequence**, which is a symbolic sequence σ^f so that $[\sigma^f \models f] = 1$ and for all σ, $[\sigma \models f] \in \{1, \perp\}$ iff $\sigma \sqsubseteq \sigma^f$. For example, $\sigma^{q \rightarrow (n \text{ is } p)}$ is the sequence $s_{(n,q \rightarrow p)} s_x s_x s_x \ldots$, where $s_{(n,q \rightarrow p)}$ is the state in which n equals $(q \rightarrow p) \wedge (\neg q \rightarrow X)$, and all other nodes equal X, and s_x is the state in which all nodes equal X. σ^f may be incompatible with the behavior of M. A **(symbolic) trajectory** π is a (symbolic) sequence that is compatible with the behavior of M [8]: let $val(n, t)$ be the value of a node (n, t) as computed according to its source nodes values in π. It is required that for all nodes (n, t), $\pi(t)(n) \sqsubseteq val(n, t)$

(strict equality is not required in order to allow external assumptions on nodes values to be embedded into π). A trajectory is **concrete** if all its states are concrete. A trajectory π is an abstraction of a concrete trajectory π_c if $\pi_c \sqsubseteq \pi$.

The **defining trajectory** π^f of M and f is a symbolic trajectory so that $[\pi^f \models f] \in \{1, \perp\}$ and for all trajectories π of M, $[\pi \models f] \in \{1, \perp\}$ iff $\pi \sqsubseteq \pi^f$ (Similar definitions for σ^f and π^f exist in [11] w.r.t a 2-valued truth domain). Given σ^f, π^f is computed as follows: $\forall i$, $\pi^f(i)$ is initialized to $\sigma^f(i)$, and the nodes values from time i and $i - 1$ are propagated forward to nodes at time i until no new values are derived. The $\sqcap$ operator is used to incorporate a propagated value into the current value of a node (n, i).

STE assertions are of the form $A \Longrightarrow C$, where A (the antecedent) and C (the consequent) are TEL formulas. A expresses constraints on circuit nodes at specific times, and C expresses requirements that should hold on circuit nodes at specific times. $M \models (A \Longrightarrow C)$ iff for all concrete trajectories π of M and assignments ϕ to V, $[\phi, \pi \models A] = 1$ implies that $[\phi, \pi \models C] = 1$.

A natural verification algorithm for an STE assertion $A \Longrightarrow C$ is to compute the defining trajectory π^A of M and A and then compute the truth value of $\pi^A \models C$. If $[\pi^A \models C] \in \{1, \perp\}$ then it holds that $M \models (A \Longrightarrow C)$. If $[\pi^A \models C] = 0$ then it holds that $M \not\models (A \Longrightarrow C)$. If $[\pi^A \models C] = X$, then it cannot be determined whether $M \models (A \Longrightarrow C)$. The case in which there is ϕ so that $\phi(\pi^A)$ contains $\perp$ is known as an **antecedent failure**. The default behavior of most STE implementations is to consider antecedent failures

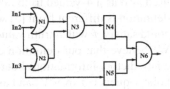

Fig. 2. A Circuit

as illegal, and the user is required to change A in order to eliminate any $\perp$ values. For lack of space, in the rest of the paper, we take the same approach. The alternative approach of STE implementations that supports occurrences of $\perp$ in π^A is described in [13]. Note that although π^A is infinite, it is suffice to examine only a bounded prefix of length depth(A) in order to detect $\perp$ in π^A. The first $\perp$ in π^A is the result of the $\sqcap$ operation on some node (n, t), where both operands have contradicting assignments 0 and 1. Since $\forall i > \text{depth}(A) : \sigma^A(i) = s_x$, it must hold that $t \leq \text{depth}(A)$. In order to compute $\pi^A \models C$ (assuming π^A does not contain $\perp$), π^A is compared to σ^C, the defining sequence of C. If $\pi^A \sqsubseteq \sigma^C$, then $[\pi^A \models C] = 1$. If there are $\phi, i \geq 0, n \in \mathcal{N}$ so that $\phi(\pi^A)(i)(n) \not\sqsubseteq \phi(\sigma^C)(i)(n)$ and $\phi(\pi^A)(i)(n) \not\sqsupseteq \phi(\sigma^C)(i)(n)$, then $[\pi^A \models C] = 0$. Otherwise, $[\pi^A \models C] = X$. Note that although π^A and σ^C are infinite, it is suffice to examine only a bounded prefix of length depth(C), since $\forall i > \text{depth}(C) : \sigma^C(i) = s_x$.

Example 1. Consider the circuit M in Figure 2, containing three inputs In1, In2 and In3, two OR nodes N1 and N2, two AND nodes N3 and N6, and two latches N4 and N5. For simplicity, the latches clocks were omitted and at each time t the latches sample their data source node from time $t - 1$. Note the negation on the source node In2 of N2. Also consider the STE assertion $A \Longrightarrow C$, where $A = (\text{In1 is } 0) \wedge (\text{In3 is } v_1) \wedge (\text{N3 is } 1)$, and $C = \mathbf{N}(\text{N6 is } 1)$. Figure 3 describes the defining trajectory π^A of M and A, up to time 1. It contains the symbolic expression of each node at time 0 and 1. The state $\pi^A(i)$ is represented by row i. The notation $v_1?1 : X$ stands for "if v_1 holds then 1 else X". σ^C is the sequence in which all nodes at all times are assigned X, except for node N6 at time 1, which is assigned 1. $[\pi^A \models C] = 0$ due to those assignments in which $v_1 = 0$. We will return to this example in Section 5.

STE implementations use a specific encoding called **dual rail** in order to represent the nodes (n, t) in sequences. The dual rail of a node (n, t) in π^A consists of two functions defined from V to $\{0, 1\}$: $f^1_{n,t}$

Time	In1	In2	In3	N1	N2	N3	N4	N5	N6
0	0	X	v_1	X	$v_1?1:X$	1	X	X	X
1	X	X	X	X	X	X	1	v_1	v_1

Fig. 3. The Defining Trajectory π^A

and $f^0_{n,t}$, where V is the set of variables appearing in A. For each assignment ϕ to V, if $f^1_{n,t} \wedge \neg f^0_{n,t}$ holds under ϕ, then (n, t) equals 1 under ϕ. Similarly, $\neg f^1_{n,t} \wedge f^0_{n,t}$, $\neg f^1_{n,t} \wedge \neg f^0_{n,t}$ and $f^1_{n,t} \wedge f^0_{n,t}$ stand for 0, X and $\perp$ under ϕ, respectively. Likewise, $g^1_{n,t}$ and $g^0_{n,t}$ is the dual rail representation of (n, t) in σ^C. Note that $g^1_{n,t} \wedge g^0_{n,t}$ never holds, since we always assume that C is not self-contradicting.

3   Choosing Our Automatic Refinement Methodology

Intuitively, the defining trajectory π^A of a circuit M and an antecedent A is an abstraction of all concrete trajectories of M on which the consequent C is required to hold. This abstraction is directly derived from A. If $[\pi^A \models C] = X$, then A is too coarse, that is, contains too few constraints on the values of circuit nodes. Our goal is to automatically refine A (and subsequently π^A) in order to eliminate the X truth value.

In this section we examine the requirements that should be imposed on automatic refinement in STE. We then describe our automatic refinement methodology, and formally state the relationship between the two abstractions, derived from the original and refined antecedent. We refer only to STE implementations that compute π^A. We assume that antecedent failures are handled as described in Chapter 2.

Traditionally, the abstraction and refinement process in STE works as follows: the user writes an STE assertion $A \implies C$ for M, and receives a result from STE. If $[\pi^A \models C] = 0$, then the set of all ϕ so that $[\phi, \pi^A \models C] = 0$ is provided to the user. This set, called the **symbolic counterexample**, is given by the Boolean expression over V: $\bigvee_{(n,t) \in C} ((g^1_{n,t} \wedge \neg f^1_{n,t} \wedge f^0_{n,t}) \vee (g^0_{n,t} \wedge f^1_{n,t} \wedge \neg f^0_{n,t}))$. It stems from either an illegal behavior of the circuit, or an erroneous specification. The user decides which of these possibilities the counterexample displays. If $[\pi^A \models C] = X$, then the set of all ϕ so that $[\phi, \pi^A \models C] = X$ is provided to the user. This set, called the **symbolic incomplete trace**, is given by: $\bigvee_{(n,t) \in C} ((g^1_{n,t} \vee g^0_{n,t}) \wedge \neg f^1_{n,t} \wedge \neg f^0_{n,t})$. The user decides how to refine the specification in order to eliminate the partial information that causes the X truth value. Otherwise, $[\pi^A \models C] = 1$ and the verification completes successfully.

As mentioned before, we must assume that the given specification is correct. Thus, automatic refinement of A must preserve the semantics of $A \implies C$: Let $A_{new} \implies C$ denote the refined assertion. Let $runs(M)$ denote the set of all concrete trajectories of M. We require that $A_{new} \implies C$ holds on $runs(M)$ iff $A \implies C$ holds on $runs(M)$.

In order to achieve the above preservation, we chose our automatic refinement as follows. Whenever $[\pi^A \models C] = X$, we add constraints to A that force the value of input nodes at certain times (and initial values of latches) to the value of *fresh symbolic variables*, that is, symbolic variables that do not already appear in V. By initializing an input (in, t) with a fresh symbolic variable instead of X, we represent the value of (in, t) accurately and add knowledge about its effect on M. However, we do not constrain input behavior that was allowed by A, nor do we allow input behavior that was forbidden by A. Thus, the semantics of A is preserved. In Section 4, a small but significant addition is made to our refinement technique.

We now formally state the relationship between the abstractions derived from the original and the refined antecedents. Let A be the antecedent we want to refine. Let A_{org} be the original antecedent written by the user. Let V_{new} be a set of symbolic variables so that $V \cap V_{new} = \emptyset$. Let PI_{ref} be the set of inputs at specific times, selected for refinement. Let A_{new} be a refinement of A over $V \cup V_{new}$, where A_{new} is received from A by attaching to each input $(in, t) \in PI_{ref}$ a unique variable $v_{in,t} \in V_{new}$ and adding conditions to A as follows: $A_{new} = A \wedge \bigwedge_{(in,t) \in PI_{ref}} N^t(p \to (in \text{ is } v_{in,t}))$, where $p = \neg q$ if (in, t) has a constraint $N^t(q \to (in \text{ is } e))$ in A_{org} for some Boolean expressions q and e over V, and $p = 1$ otherwise $((in, t)$ has no constraint in $A_{org})$. The reason we consider A_{org} is to avoid a contradiction between the added constraints and the original ones, due to constraints in A_{org} of the form $q \to f$.

Let $\pi^{A_{new}}$ be the defining trajectory of M and A_{new}, over $V \cup V_{new}$. Let ϕ be an assignment to V. Then $runs(A_{new}, M, \phi)$ denotes the set of all concrete trajectories π for which there is an assignment ϕ' to V_{new} so that $(\phi \cup \phi')(\pi^{A_{new}})$ is an abstraction of π. Since for all concrete trajectories π, $[(\phi \cup \phi'), \pi \models A_{new}] = 1 \iff \pi \sqsubseteq (\phi \cup \phi')(\pi^{A_{new}})$, we get that $runs(A_{new}, M, \phi)$ are exactly those π for which there is ϕ' so that $[(\phi \cup \phi'), \pi \models A_{new}] = 1$.

Theorem 1. *1. For all assignments ϕ to V, $runs(A, M, \phi) = runs(A_{new}, M, \phi)$.*
2. If $[\pi^{A_{new}} \models C] = 1$ then $\forall \phi$ it holds that $\forall \pi \in runs(A, M, \phi) : [\phi, \pi \models C] = 1$.
3. If there is ϕ' to V_{new} and $\pi \in runs(A_{new}, M, \phi \cup \phi')$ so that $[(\phi \cup \phi'), \pi \models A_{new}] = 1$ but $[(\phi \cup \phi'), \pi \models C] = 0$ then $\pi \in runs(A, M, \phi)$ and $[\phi, \pi \models A] = 1$ and $[\phi, \pi \models C] = 0$.

Theorem 1 implies that if $A_{new} \implies C$ holds on all concrete trajectories of M, then so does $A \implies C$. Moreover, if $A_{new} \implies C$ yields a concrete counterexample ce, then ce is also a concrete counterexample w.r.t $A \implies C$.

4   Selecting Inputs for Refinement

In this section we describe how exactly the refinement process is performed. We assume that $[\pi^A \models C] = X$, and thus automatic refinement is activated. Our goal is to add a small number of constraints to A forcing inputs to the value of fresh symbolic variables, while eliminating as many assignments ϕ as possible so that $[\phi, \pi^A \models C] = X$. The refinement process is incremental - inputs (in, t) that are switched from X to a fresh symbolic variable will not be reduced to X in subsequent iterations.

Choosing Our Refinement Goal. Assume that $[\pi^A \models C] = X$, and the symbolic incomplete trace is generated. This trace contains all assignments ϕ for which $[\phi, \pi^A \models C] = X$. For each such assignment ϕ, the trajectory $\phi(\pi^A)$ is called an ***incomplete***

trajectory. In addition, this trace may contain multiple nodes that are required by C to a definite value (either 0 or 1) for some assignment ϕ, but equal X. We refer to such nodes as **undecided nodes**. We want to keep the number of added constraints small. Therefore, we choose to eliminate one undecided node (n, t) in each refinement iteration, since different nodes may depend on different inputs. A motivation for eliminating only part of the undecided nodes is that an eliminated X value may be replaced in the next iteration with a definite value that contradicts the required value (a counterexample). We suggest to choose an undecided node (n, t) with minimal number of inputs in its BCOI. Out of those, we choose a node with minimal number of nodes in its BCOI. Our experimental results support this choice. The chosen undecided node is our **refinement goal** and is denoted $(root, tt)$. We also choose to eliminate at once all incomplete trajectories in which $(root, tt)$ is undecided. These trajectories are likely to be eliminated by similar sets of inputs. Thus, by considering them all at once we can considerably reduce the number of refinement iterations, without adding too many variables.

The Boolean expression $(\neg f^1_{root,tt} \wedge \neg f^0_{root,tt} \wedge (g^1_{root,tt} \vee g^0_{root,tt}))$ represents the set of all ϕ for which $(root, tt)$ is undecided in $\phi(\pi^A)$. Our goal is to add a small number of constraints to A so that $(root, tt)$ will not be X whenever $(g^1_{root,tt} \vee g^0_{root,tt})$ holds.

Eliminating Irrelevant Inputs. Once we have a refinement goal $(root, tt)$, we need to choose inputs (in, t) for which constraints will be added to A. Naturally, only inputs in the BCOI of $(root, tt)$ are considered, but some of these inputs can be safely eliminated.

Consider an input (in, t), an assignment ϕ to V and the defining trajectory π^A. We say that (in, t) is **relevant** to $(root, tt)$ under ϕ, if there is a path of nodes P from (in, t) to $(root, tt)$ in M, so that for all nodes (n, t') in P, $\phi(\pi^A)(t')(n) = X$. (in, t) is **relevant** to $(root, tt)$ if there exists ϕ so that (in, t) is relevant to $(root, tt)$ under ϕ.

For each (in, t), we compute the set of assignments to V for which (in, t) is relevant to $(root, tt)$. The computation is performed recursively starting from $(root, tt)$. $(root, tt)$ is relevant when it is X and is required to have a definite value: $(\neg f^1_{root,tt} \wedge \neg f^0_{root,tt} \wedge (g^1_{root,tt} \vee g^0_{root,tt}))$. A source node (n, t) of $(root, tt)$ is relevant whenever $(root, tt)$ is relevant and (n, t) equals X. Let $out(n, t)$ return the sink nodes of (n, t) that are in the BCOI of $(root, tt)$. Proceeding recursively, we compute for each node (n, t) the set of assignments relevant$_{n,t}$ given by the Boolean expression $(\bigvee_{(m,t') \in out(n,t)} \text{relevant}_{m,t'}) \wedge \neg f^0_{n,t} \wedge \neg f^1_{n,t}$, until we reach the input nodes (in, t).

For all ϕ that are not in relevant$_{in,t}$, changing (in, t) from X to 0 or to 1 in $\phi(\pi^A)$ can never change the value of $(root, tt)$ in $\phi(\pi^A)$ from X to 0 or to 1. Thus, if (in, t) is chosen for refinement, a possible optimization is to constrain it to a fresh symbolic variable only when relevant$_{in,t}$ holds, as follows: relevant$_{in,t} \rightarrow \mathbf{N}^t(in$ is $v_{in,t})$. If (in, t) is chosen in a subsequent iteration for refinement of a new refinement goal $(root', tt')$, then the previous constraint is extended by disjunction to include the condition under which (in, t) is relevant to $(root', tt')$. Theorem 1 holds also for the optimized refinement. Let PI be the set of inputs of M. The set of all inputs that are relevant to $(root, tt)$ is $PI_{(root,tt)} \equiv \{(in, t) \mid in \in PI \wedge \text{relevant}_{in,t} \not\equiv 0\}$. Adding constraints to A for all relevant inputs (in, t) will result in a refined antecedent A_{new}. In $\pi^{A_{new}}$, it is guaranteed that $(root, tt)$ will not be undecided. Note that $PI_{(root,tt)}$ is sufficient but not minimal for elimination of all undesired X values from $(root, tt)$. Namely, adding constraints for all inputs in $PI_{(root,tt)}$ will eliminate all cases in which $(root, tt)$ is undecided. However, adding constraints for only a subset of $PI_{(root,tt)}$ may still eliminate all such cases. The set $PI_{(root,tt)}$ may be valuable to the user even if automatic refinement does not take place, since it excludes inputs that are in the BCOI of $(root, tt)$ but will not change the verification results w.r.t $(root, tt)$.

Heuristics for Selection of Important Inputs. We now propose heuristics for selecting a subset of $PI_{(root,tt)}$ for refinement. A motivation for this is that a 1 or 0 truth value may be reached even without adding constraints for all relevant inputs.

We apply the following heuristics: each node (n, t) selects a subset of $PI_{(root,tt)}$ as candidates for refinement. The final set of inputs for refinement is selected out of the candidates of $(root, tt)$. Each input in $PI_{(root,tt)}$ selects itself as a candidate. Other inputs have no candidates for refinement. $sourceCand_{n,t}$ denotes the sets of candidates of the source nodes of a node (n, t), excluding the source nodes that do not have candidates. The candidates of (n, t) are determined as follows:

1. If there are candidate inputs that appear in all sets of $sourceCand_{n,t}$, then they are the candidates of (n, t).
2. Otherwise, if (n, t) has source nodes that can be classified as control and data, then the candidates of (n, t) are the union of the candidates of its control source nodes, if this union is not empty. For example, a latch has one data source node and at least one control source node - its clock. The identity of control source nodes is automatically extracted from the netlist representation of the circuit.
3. If none of the above holds, then the candidates of (n, t) are the inputs with the largest number of occurrences in $sourceCand_{n,t}$.

We prefer to refine inputs that affect control before those that affect data since the value of control inputs has usually more affect on the verification result. Moreover, the control inputs determine when data is sampled. Therefore, if the value of a data input is required for verification, it can be restricted according to the value of previously refined control inputs. In the final set of candidates, sets of nodes that are entries of the same vector are treated as one candidate. Since the heuristics could not prefer one entry of the vector over the other, then probably only their joint value can change the verification result. Additional heuristics choose a fixed number of l candidates out of the final set.

5   Detecting Vacuity and Spurious Counterexamples

In this section we raise the problem of hidden vacuity and spurious counterexamples that may occur in STE. This problem was never addressed before in the context of STE.

In STE, A functions both as determining the level of the abstraction of M, and as determining the trajectories of M on which C is required to hold. An important point is that the constraints imposed by A are applied (using the $\sqcap$ operator) to *abstract* trajectories of M. If for some node (n, t) and assignment ϕ to V, there is a contradiction between $\phi(\sigma^A)(t)(n)$ and the value propagated through M to (n, t), then $\phi(\pi^A)(t)(n) = \bot$, indicating that there is no concrete trajectory π so that $[\phi, \pi \models A] = 1$.

In this section we point out that due to the abstraction in STE, it is possible that for some assignment ϕ to V, there are no concrete trajectories π so that $[\phi, \pi \models A] = 1$, but still $\phi(\pi^A)$ does not contain $\perp$ values. This is due to the fact that an abstract trajectory may represent more concrete trajectories than the ones that actually exist in M. Consequently, it may be that $[\phi, \pi^A \models C] \in \{1, 0\}$, and there is no indication that this result is vacuous, i.e., for all concrete trajectories π, $[\phi, \pi \models A] = 0$. Note that this problem may only happen if A contains constraints on internal nodes of M. Given a constraint a on an input, there always exists a concrete trajectory that satisfies a (unless a itself is a contradiction, which can be easily detected). This problem exists also in STE implementations that do not compute π^A, such as [8].

Example 2. We return to Example 1 from Section 2. Note that the defining trajectory π^A does not contain $\perp$. In addition, $[\pi^A \models C] = 0$ due to the assignments to V in which $v_1 = 0$. However, A never holds on concrete trajectories of M when $v_1 = 0$, since N3 at time 0 will not be equal to 1. Thus, the counterexample is spurious, but we have no indication of this fact. The problem occurs when calculating the value of (N3,0) by computing $X \sqcap 1 = 1$. If A had contained a constraint on the value of In2 at time 0, say (In2 is v_2), then the value of (N3,0) in π^A would have been $(v_1 \wedge v_2) \sqcap 1 = (v_1 \wedge v_2?1 : \perp)$, indicating that for all assignments in which $v_1 = 0$ or $v_2 = 0$, π^A does not correspond to any concrete trajectory of M.

Vacuity may also occur if for some ϕ to V, C under ϕ imposes no requirements. This is due to constraints of the form $p \rightarrow f$ where $\phi(p)$ is 0.

An STE assertion $A \Longrightarrow C$ is **vacuous** in M if for all concrete trajectories π of M and assignments ϕ to V, either $[\phi, \pi \models A] = 0$, or C under ϕ imposes no requirements. This definition is compatible with the definition in [1] for ACTL.

We say that $A \Longrightarrow C$ **passes vacuously** on M if $A \Longrightarrow C$ is vacuous in M and $[\pi^A \models C] \in \{\perp, 1\}$. A counterexample π is **spurious** if there is no concrete trajectory π_c of M so that $\pi_c \sqsubseteq \pi$. Given π^A, the symbolic counterexample ce is **spurious** if for all assignments ϕ to V in ce, $\phi(\pi^A)$ is spurious. $A \Longrightarrow C$ **fails vacuously** on M if $[\pi^A \models C] = 0$ and ce is spurious.

As explained before, vacuity detection is required only when A constrains internal nodes. It is performed only if $[\pi^A \models C] \in \{0, 1\}$ (if $[\pi^A \models C] = \perp$ then surely $A \Longrightarrow C$ passes vacuously). In order to detect non-vacuous results in STE, we need to check whether there exists an assignment ϕ to V and a concrete trajectory π of M so that C under ϕ imposes some requirement and $[\phi, \pi \models A] = 1$. In case $[\pi^A \models C] = 0$, we also require that $[\phi, \pi \models C] = 0$. Since A can be expressed as an LTL formula, we can translate A and M into a Bounded Model Checking (BMC) [2] problem. Note that in this BMC problem we search for a satisfying assignment for A, not for its negation. Additional constraints should be added to the BMC formula as follows.

For detection of vacuous pass, the BMC formula is constrained as follows: Recall that $(g_{n,t}^1, g_{n,t}^0)$ denotes the dual rail representation of (n, t) in σ^C. The Boolean expression $g_{n,t}^1 \vee g_{n,t}^0$ represents all assignments ϕ to V under which C imposes a requirement on (n, t). Thus, $\bigvee_{(n,t) \in C} g_{n,t}^1 \vee g_{n,t}^0$ represents all assignments ϕ under which C imposes some requirement, and is added as an additional constraint to the BMC formula. A satisfying assignment to the resulting formula constitutes a witness for $A \Longrightarrow C$.

For detection of vacuous fail, the BMC formula is constrained by conjunction with the symbolic counterexample $ce = \bigvee_{(n,t) \in C} ((g_{n,t}^1 \wedge \neg f_{n,t}^1 \wedge f_{n,t}^0) \vee (g_{n,t}^0 \wedge f_{n,t}^1 \wedge \neg f_{n,t}^0))$.

ce represents all assignments ϕ for which $[\phi, \pi^A \models C] = 0$. A satisfying assignment to the resulting formula constitutes a concrete counterexample for $A \Longrightarrow C$.

If BMC finds a satisfying assignment to the resulting formula, then the original truth value of $[\pi^A \models C]$ is returned. Otherwise, we conclude that the STE result is vacuous. In [13], we suggest an alternative vacuity detection algorithm that uses STE and present an additional vacuity problem that arises in constraint-based STE [8].

6   Experimental Results

We implemented our automatic refinement algorithm **AutoSTE** on top of STE in Intel's FORTE environment [12]. **AutoSTE** receives a circuit M and an STE assertion $A \Longrightarrow C$. When $[\pi^A \models C] = X$, it chooses a refinement goal $(root, tt)$ out of the undecided nodes, as described in Section 4. Next, it computes the set of relevant inputs (in, t). The Heuristics described in Section 4 are applied in order to choose a subset of those inputs. In our experimental results we restrict the number of refined candidates in each iteration to 1. A is changed as described in Section 4 and STE is rerun on the new assertion.

We ran **AutoSTE** on two different circuits, which are challenging for Model Checking: the Content Addressable Memory (CAM) from Intel's GSTE tutorial, and IBM's Calculator 2 design [14]. The latter has a complex specification.Therefore, it constitutes a good example for the benefit the user can gain from automatic refinement in STE. All runs were performed on a 3.2 GHz Pentium 4 computer with 4 GB memory.

Content Addressable Memory. The CAM shown in Figure 4 contains 16 entries, has a data size of 64 bits and a tag size of 8 bits. It contains 1152 latches, 83 inputs and 5064 combinational gates. CAMs use bit fields called tags to identify particular data entries stored in an array. The associative read operation (aread) of CAMs consists of searching in parallel all tags in the CAM tag memory to find

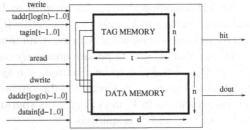

Fig. 4. Content Addressable Memory. Tag size=t, Number of entries=n, Data size=d.

a match to an input tag (tagin). If a match is found, the CAM outputs the associated data entry to dout. The verification of the aread operation using STE is described in [7]. The assertions in [7] contain assumptions on the internal state of the tag memory. The user may want to check the aread operation after a write operation to the tag memory. In STE such cases can be checked by bounding the time that passed between the writing and the reading of the tag. We present the results of **AutoSTE** on 3 such assertions. Figure 5 reports the final result, number of refinement iterations, run-time in seconds and peak BDD nodes for each assertion. Table 1 reports the refinement goal and added constraint in each refinement iteration. $v_{n,t}$ denotes a fresh symbolic variable for node (n, t). $\overrightarrow{v}_{n,t}$ denotes a vector of fresh symbolic variables for a vector of nodes (n, t).

Assertion 1 checks that if a tag value $\overrightarrow{TAG}$ is written to an address $\overrightarrow{A}$ in the tag memory at time 0 (where $\overrightarrow{TAG}$ and $\overrightarrow{A}$ are vectors of symbolic variables over $\{0, 1\}$), and at time 1 $\overrightarrow{TAG}$ is read, then it should be found in the tag memory and hit should be 1: (tagin is $\overrightarrow{TAG}$)∧(taddr is $\overrightarrow{A}$)∧(twrite is 1)∧$\mathbf{N}$(($areadis1$)∧($taginis\overrightarrow{TAG}$)) $\Longrightarrow$ $\mathbf{N}(hitis1)$. Assertion 1 should pass: if at time 1 there is no write operation to the tag memory (twrite is 0), then $\overrightarrow{TAG}$ should be found in address $\overrightarrow{A}$. If at time 1 twrite is 1, $\overrightarrow{TAG}$ should be found since it is writ-

ten again to the tag memory. However, $[\pi^A \models C] = X$. Since twrite and taddr at time 1 are X, the CAM cannot determine whether to write the value of tagin at time 1 to the tag memory, and to which tag entry to write it. As a result, the entire tag memory at time 1 is X.Thus, hit at time 1 is X.

Assertion	result	Total Iter.	Time	BDD Nodes
1	pass	2	3	4768
2	fail	7	20	57424
3	fail	3	17	29006

Fig. 5. Automatic Refinement Performance on CAM Assertions

After two refinements, **AutoSTE** returns a pass result. Note that only constraints necessary for obtaining the pass result were added. $\overrightarrow{TAG} \neq 0$ appears in the constraint since in this CAM implementation, the default value of the data source nodes of the tag memory is 0. Thus, when $\overrightarrow{TAG} = 0$, even without knowing if and to which entry a tag is written at time 1, the CAM determines that a tag that equals 0 exists in the tag memory.

Assertion 2 is an extension of Assertion 1. We add a constraint to the antecedent that at time 0, datamem$[\overrightarrow{A}]$ is $\overrightarrow{D}$. We also add a requirement to the consequent that at time 1, dout is $\overrightarrow{D}$. The first two refinements are the same as for assertion 1. The next refinement goal is dout[0]. In iterations 3-4, twrite and taddr at time 1 are added to A when $\overrightarrow{TAG} = 0$, since they are required in order to determine the value of dout[0] at time 1. The relevant inputs for refinement in iterations 5-7 were dwrite, daddr and din[0], all at times 0 and 1, the initial values of all tag memory entries and of bit number 0 of all data memory entries. The final iteration yields a counterexample in which dwrite at time 1 equals 1, daddr at time 1 equals taddr at time 0, and din[0] at time 1 is different from D[0]. This counterexample stems from an erroneous specification. If new data is written at time 1 to the data entry associated with $\overrightarrow{TAG}$, then dout at time 1 will be equal to the new data. Note that only constraints relevant to this counterexample were added.

Assertion 3 is as follows: (tagin is $\overrightarrow{TAG}$)∧(taddr is $\overrightarrow{A}$)∧(twrite is 1)∧(datamem$[\overrightarrow{A}]$ is $\overrightarrow{D}$) ∧$\mathbf{N}$((twrite is 0) ∧ (dwrite is 0)) ∧ $\mathbf{N}^2$((aread is 1) ∧ (tagin is $\overrightarrow{TAG}$) ∧

Table 1. Automatic Refinement of CAM Assertions

Assertion	Iteration	Goal	Added Constraint
1,2	1	hit,1	$\mathbf{N}(\overrightarrow{TAG} \neq 0 \rightarrow$ twrite is $v_{twrite,1})$
1,2	2	hit,1	$\mathbf{N}((\overrightarrow{TAG} \neq 0 \wedge v_{twrite,1} = 1) \rightarrow$ taddr is $\overrightarrow{v}_{taddr,1})$
2	3	dout[0],1	$\mathbf{N}(\overrightarrow{TAG} = 0 \rightarrow$ twrite is $v_{twrite,1})$
2	4	dout[0],1	$\mathbf{N}((\overrightarrow{TAG} = 0 \wedge v_{twrite,1} = 1) \rightarrow$ taddr is $\overrightarrow{v}_{taddr,1})$
2	5	dout[0],1	$\mathbf{N}($dwrite is $v_{dwrite,1})$
2	6	dout[0],1	$\mathbf{N}(v_{dwrite,1} = 1 \rightarrow$ daddr is $\overrightarrow{v}_{daddr,1})$
2	7	dout[0],1	$\mathbf{N}(((v_{dwrite,1} = 1) \wedge (\overrightarrow{v}_{daddr,1} = \overrightarrow{A})) \rightarrow$ din[0] is $v_{din[0],1})$
3	1	dout[0],2	$D[0] \neq 0 \rightarrow$ dwrite is $v_{dwrite,0}$
3	2	dout[0],2	$(D[0] \neq 0 \wedge v_{dwrite,0} = 1) \rightarrow$ daddr is $\overrightarrow{v}_{daddr,0}$
3	3	dout[0],2	$(D[0] \neq 0 \wedge \overrightarrow{A} \neq 0) \rightarrow$ tagmem0 is $\overrightarrow{v}_{tagmem0,0}$

(twrite is 0) $\wedge$ (dwrite is 0)) $\implies$ $\mathbf{N}^2$((hit is 1) $\wedge$ (dout is $\vec{D}$)). This assertion should fail since the tag memory may already hold at time 0 a tag that equals $\overline{\text{TAG}}$. Though usually it is assumed that the CAM environment will not write the same tag to two different entries, most CAM implementations do not assume so. **AutoSTE** generates a counterexample after 3 refinement iterations. In the counterexample, tag entry 0 equals $\overline{\text{TAG}}$, and the address $\vec{A}$ to which $\overline{\text{TAG}}$ is written is different from 0. The data associated with tag entry 0 appears in dout, rather than the one written to address $\vec{A}$. This assertion demonstrates the case in which there is a need for refinement of initial values of latches (tagmem0 at time 0). Since our heuristics prefer inputs that influence control, the constraint on tagmem0 was added after constraints were added on dwrite and $\overrightarrow{\text{daddr}}$ at time 0.

Calculator Design. Calculator 2 design [14] shown in Figure 6 is used as a case study design in simulation based verification. It contains 2781 latches, 157 inputs and 56960 combinational gates. The calculator supports 4 types of commands: add, sub, shift right and shift left. *none* stands for no command. Any other command is invalid. It has two internal arithmetic pipelines: one for add/sub and one for shifts. The first argument of the command is sent at the same cycle as the command. The second argument is sent in the next cycle. The tag is a unique identifer for each of the commands from each of the 4 ports. It is sent at the same cycle as the command. The commands may be executed out of order. However, commands from the same port that use the same pipeline must return in order. The response is 1 for good, 2 for underflow, overflow or invalid command, 3 for an internal error and 0 for no response. Reset is 1 for the first 3 cycles.

We present the results of **AutoSTE** on 4 assertions. Figure 7 reports the final result, number of refinement iterations, run-time in seconds and peak BDD nodes for each assertion. For lack of space, the description of assertion 4 exists in [13]. Table 2 reports the refinement goal and added constraint in each refinement iteration for assertions 1-3.

Assertion 1 checks whether after reset, if a port sends an add or sub command, and the other ports send no command or a command other than add and sub, then the port that sent the add/sub command receives a good response with the appropriate tag at the first

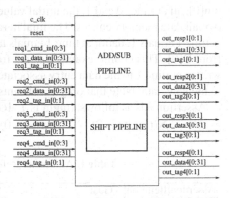

Fig. 6. Calculator

available time (4 cycles after the commands were sent). A vector $\vec{P}$ of symbolic variables is used to determine which port is sending the add or sub command.

In the counterexample, a data overflow occurs for an add command sent by port 1, which triggers an invalid response at cycle 7. The BCOI of out_resp1[0] contains all command, tag and data inputs of all ports at different times. However, the set of relevant inputs contains only all entries of req1_data_in at cycles 3 and 4. req1_data_in[31] at cycles 3 and 4 is the minimal subset that is suffice to produce a counterexample, and is indeed the one chosen by our heuristics.

Assertion 2 constrains the command sent by port i to add. The msb bits of the sent data are constrained to 0 to avoid a possible overflow. The requirement is that the output data for port i should match the expected data. No constraints exist on the commands sent by other ports. In the counterexample, both ports 1 and 2 send an add command. Port 1 is answered before port 2. The assertion fails due to an erroneous specification: since port 1 has priority over port 2, port 2 may not receive a response at the first possible cycle. Due to the implementation of the priority queue, the value of an additional port had to be definite. The BCOI of (out_resp2[0],7) contains cmd, data and tag inputs of all ports at cycles 3 and 4. Out of them, only the cmd and data inputs are relevant inputs.

Assertion 3 presents the following constraints: after reset, a port sends an add or sub command, followed by an add command with a certain tag and data arguments, while limiting the msb of the data to 0 to avoid a possible overflow. All other ports do not send an add or sub command during this time. The requirements are: the port that sent the add command receives a

Assertion	result	Total Iter.	Time	BDD Nodes
1	fail	2	87	6241
2	fail	2	100	20134
3	fail	1	220	530733
4	pass	11	494	17323

Fig. 7. Automatic Refinement Performance on Calculator Assertions

response with the appropriate tag value and expected output data. There was one refinement iteration. The BCOI of resp_out1[0] includes all data and tag inputs of all ports. However, only the tags of all ports at cycles 3-5 are relevant inputs. Our heuristics chose the tag of port 1 at cycle 3. Choosing any other input would require additional iterations in order to produce a counterexample. In the counterexample, the tag values of port 1 at cycles 3 and 4 are not consecutive. This counterexample stems from a planted design bug documented in [14]. There is supposed to be no restriction on tag ordering. However, commands whose tags are out of order are treated as invalid.

Table 2. Automatic Refinement of Calculator Assertions

Assert.	Iteration	Goal	Added Constraint
1	1	out_resp1[0],7	$N^3 \overrightarrow{P} = 1 \rightarrow$ req1_data_in[31] is $v_{req1\_data\_in[31],3}$
1	2	out_resp1[0],7	$N^4 \overrightarrow{P} = 1 \rightarrow$ req1_data_in[31] is $v_{req1\_data\_in[31],4}$
2	1	out_resp2[0],7	$N^3 \overrightarrow{P} = 2 \rightarrow$ req1_cmd_in is $\overrightarrow{v}_{req1\_cmd\_in,3}$
2	2	out_resp2[0],7	$N^3(\overrightarrow{P} = 2 \wedge \overrightarrow{v}_{req1\_cmd\_in,3} = (add \vee sub)) \rightarrow$ req3_cmd_in is $\overrightarrow{v}_{req3\_cmd\_in,3}$
3	1	out_resp1[0],9	$N^3 \overrightarrow{P} = 1 \rightarrow$ req1_tag_in is $\overrightarrow{v}_{req1\_tag\_in,3}$

Acknowledgement. We thank Eli Singerman for introducing us to STE and to the Forte environment.

References

1. I. Beer, S. Ben-David, C. Eisner, and Y. Rodeh. Efficient detection of vacuity in ACTL formulas. In *CAV*, 1997.
2. A. Biere, A. Cimatti, E. M. Clarke, and Y. Zhu. Symbolic model checking without BDDs. In *TACAS*, 1999.

3. C-T. Chou. The mathematical foundation of symbolic trajectory evaluation. In *CAV*, 1999.
4. E. M. Clarke, O. Grumberg, S. Jha, Y. Lu, and H. Veith. Counterexample-guided abstraction refinement. In *CAV*, 2000.
5. S. Hazelhurst and C.-J. H. Seger. Model checking lattices: Using and reasoning about information orders for abstraction. *Logic journal of IGPL*, 7(3), 1999.
6. R. P. Kurshan. *Computer-Aided Verification of coordinating processes - the automata theoretic approach*. 1994.
7. M. Pandey, R. Raimi, R. E. Bryant, and M. S. Abadir. Formal verification of content addressable memories using symbolic trajectory evaluation. In *DAC*, 1997.
8. J.-W. Roorda and K. Claessen. A new SAT-based algorithm for symbolic trajectory evaluation. In *CHARME*, 2005.
9. J.-W. Roorda and K. Claessen. SAT-based assistance in abstraction refinement for symbolic trajectory evaluation. In *CAV*, 2006.
10. T. Schubert. High level formal verification of next-generation microprocessors. In *DAC'03*.
11. C.-J. H. Seger and R. E. Bryant. Formal verification by symbolic evaluation of partially-ordered trajectories. *Formal Methods in System Design*, 6(2), 1995.
12. C.-J. H. Seger, R. B. Jones, J. W. O'Leary, T. F. Melham, M. Aagaard, C. Barrett, and D. Syme. An industrially effective environment for formal hardware verification. *IEEE Trans. on Computer-Aided Design of Integrated Circuits and Systems*, 24(9), 2005.
13. R. Tzoref. Automatic refinement and vacuity detection for symbolic trajectory evaluation. Master's thesis, Department of Computer Science, Technion, Israel, 2006.
14. B. Wile, W. Roesner, and J. Goss. *Comprehensive Functional Verification: The Complete Industry Cycle*. Morgan-Kaufmann, 2005.
15. J.C. Wilson. *Symbolic Simulation Using Automatic Abstraction of Internal Node Values*. PhD thesis, Stanford University, Dept. of Electrical Engineering, 2001.
16. J. Yang, R. Gil, and E. Singerman. satGSTE: Combining the abstraction of GSTE with the capacity of a SAT solver. In *DCC*, 2004.
17. J. Yang and A. Goel. GSTE through a case study. In *ICCAD*, 2002.
18. J. Yang and C.-J. H. Seger. Generalized symbolic trajectory evaluation - abstraction in action. In *FMCAD*, 2002.
19. J. Yang and C.-J. H. Seger. Introduction to generalized symbolic trajectory evaluation. *IEEE Trans. Very Large Scale Integr. Syst.*, 11(3), 2003.

Some Complexity Results
for SystemVerilog Assertions

Doron Bustan and John Havlicek

Freescale Semiconductor, Inc.

Abstract. SystemVerilog Assertions (SVA) is a linear temporal logic within the recently approved IEEE 1800 SystemVerilog standard. The complexities of the satisfiability and model-checking problems are studied for a basic subset of SVA and for extensions of the basic subset obtained by adding each of the following features: local variables, regular expression intersection, quantified variables, and property declarations with arguments. It is shown that the complexities for the basic subset are PSPACE-complete, while the complexities increase to EXPSPACE-complete [1] in each of the extensions. Alternating Büchi automata constructions provide the upper bounds, while reductions from PSPACE and EXPSPACE tiling problems provide the lower bounds.

1 Introduction

SystemVerilog Assertions, abbreviated SVA, is the assertion sublanguage of the recently approved IEEE 1800 SystemVerilog standard [14]. It is a linear temporal logic that is intended to be used to represent correctness properties and functional coverage events for the validation and verification of SystemVerilog designs. Prior to revision in the IEEE P1800 committee, development of SystemVerilog was carried out within the Accellera Organization, culminating in Accellera SystemVerilog 3.1a [1]. Industrial interest in SVA has been growing, as evidenced by its support in electronic design automation (EDA) tools, its discussion among verification engineers [19], and its deployment by semiconductor companies.

SVA has been developed in parallel with another recently approved standard assertion language, IEEE 1850 Property Specification Language (PSL) [15]. The two languages share a common core based on regular expressions. The common core includes temporal properties built using implication with regular expression antecedent and the standard logical boolean operators. While SVA and PSL have syntactic differences, there has been substantial work within Accellera and IEEE committees to ensure that the languages are aligned on the semantics of the common core. The two languages differ more substantially outside the common core.

---

[1] EXPCACE is defined us $\bigcup_{k \in \natural} \mathsf{DSPACE}(2^{n^k})$.

T. Ball and R.B. Jones (Eds.): CAV 2006, LNCS 4144, pp. 205–218, 2006.
© Springer-Verlag Berlin Heidelberg 2006

PSL provides the standard LTL operators, which are not in SVA, quantified variables, and numerous derived operators.[2] PSL, similar languages, such as For-Spec, and academic simplifications have also received attention in recent literature [5,4,9,6]. However, there remain gaps in the analysis of the complexity of these languages for model checking. SVA, on the other hand, provides local variables as one of its distinguishing features. A local variable is used to capture the value of an expression at one point within a property and hold it for later reference, after which the local variable may be reassigned. Without local variables, complex auxiliary state machines are often required to represent temporal properties of practical interest. This makes local variables extremely useful for an industrially deployed temporal logic. The semantics of local variables has been studied in the committees [10], but SVA with local variables has received little attention in the literature and the expressiveness and complexity of the logic have not been studied before. This theoretical deficit has resulted in a certain amount of confusion in the industrial verification community. EDA companies disagree on what part of SVA should be supported in model checking, and verification engineers do not know whether properties that run in simulation can reasonably be expected to be supported in formal verification.

In this paper, we fill some of the theoretical gaps by studying the expressiveness and complexity of a basic subset of SVA and several of its extensions. The basic subset is obtained from the common core by eliminating the intersection operator on regular expressions. Previous work shows that the basic subset can express all omega-regular languages [4] and that the satisfiability and model-checking problems for the basic subset are in PSPACE [7,8]. We prove a matching lower bound, hence these problems for the basic subset are PSPACE-complete.

We prove that extending the basic subset of SVA with either local variables or intersection of regular expressions increases the complexity of satisfiability and model-checking from PSPACE-complete to EXPSPACE-complete. For each of these extensions, we present a construction of alternating Büchi automata that gives an algorithm with tight complexity for the satisfiability and model-checking problems. These constructions also prove that the extensions do not increase expressiveness. Adding both local variables and intersection, the complexity of these problems in the combined extension remains EXSPACE-complete. We also study extension of the basic subset with quantified variables analogous to those in PSL. The satisfiability and model-checking problems for this extension are EXSPACE-complete. Finally, we study extension of the basic subset with declared properties and arguments. Their addition also results in EXPSPACE-complete complexity for satisfiability and model checking. With the exception of those involving local variables, each of the results also holds for the corresponding subset of PSL.

Our lower bounds imply that, from the point of view of complexity classes, addition to the basic subset of any one of local variables, regular expression intersection, quantified variables, or declared properties with arguments is not harder

---

[2] PSL also offers a branching subset with CTL-like syntax and semantics. In this paper we consider only the linear subset of PSL.

than another. Statements like "local variables cannot be used in model checking" and "local variables can be used in model checking only if they are restricted to analogues of PSL quantified variables" are not justified by our complexity analysis. The jump from PSPACE-hard to EXPSPACE-hard is significant, though, and model checking of arbitrary properties in these extensions is not generally considered practical. This does not mean that such features should not be supported in model-checking tools. Consider the simple use of integer constant parameters in operators, such as [*n] (repeat n times). This feature also makes the model-checking problem EXPSPACE-hard because integers have logarithmic representation [2]. We do not conclude that parameters should be written in unary or that declaration and instantiation of properties with arguments should be disallowed for formal verification. Such features are considered indispensable in industrially deployed languages. Similarly, local variables, regular expression intersection, and quantified variables are in the standardized assertion languages because they have proven to be very useful for writing properties in industrial practice. By understanding how the various language features contribute to the complexity, verification engineers can make more informed decisions about trade-offs in coding styles for properties and can better estimate their tractability in formal verification. Tool builders also can better target the sources of hardness for model checking while providing a richer feature set in the property language that is supported. Hopefully, the automata constructions from this paper will provide a starting point for broader EDA tool support for formal verification using SVA.

2   Preliminaries

Given a set A, A^* denotes the set of finite words over A, A^ω denotes the set of infinite words over A, and A^∞ denotes the union $A^* \cup A^\omega$. The length of word $u \in A^\infty$ is denoted $|u|$. The empty word is denoted ε. The letters of u are indicated by superscripts and are indexed consecutively beginning at zero. If $|u| > 0$, then the first letter of u is denoted u^0; if $|u| > 1$, then the second letter of u is denoted u^1; and so forth.

SVA has four language layers: boolean, sequence, property, and statement. The *boolean* layer consists of boolean expressions in which each variable referenced is either a design variable or a local variable of the assertion. Σ denotes the finite alphabet of valuations of the design variables. The *sequence* layer consists of regular expressions over the boolean layer. Every regular language of finite words over Σ can be represented by a suitably chosen sequence. The *property* layer combines sequences to create temporal logic formulas. The *statement* layer defines whether a property is to be evaluated as an obligation, an assumption, or a coverage goal. SVA statements are not discussed further in this paper.

For simplicity, we restrict each local variable to have a single-bit, boolean type (i.e., type bit in SystemVerilog). For a given finite set of sequences and properties, there is a finite set V of local variables that appear therein. The set of valuations of these local variables is 2^V. It is understood that V is disjoint from the set of design variables. The set of semantic equivalence classes of boolean expressions can be identified with $2^{\Sigma \times 2^V}$. The constant "true" is denoted 1, and the constant "false" is denoted 0.

For the rest of this document we use the following notations: σ denotes a letter in Σ; w, x, y, z denote finite or infinite words over Σ; v denotes a one-bit local variable; b and e denote boolean expressions; R denotes a sequence; P denotes a property; and L denotes a local variable valuation in 2^V. Primes, subscripts, and superscripts are also added to these notations. The grammar for SVA sequences is

$$R ::= b \mid (1, v = e) \mid (R) \mid R \#\#0\ R \mid R \#\#1\ R \mid R \text{ or } R \mid$$
$$R \text{ intersect } R \mid R[*0] \mid R[*1:\$]$$

$R[*0:\$]$ is an abbreviation for $R[*0]$ or $R[*1:\$]$, and, for $n > 0$, $R[*n]$ is an abbreviation for the concatenation $R \#\#1 \cdots \#\#1\ R$ (n copies of R).

The grammar for SVA properties is

$$P ::= R \mid (P) \mid P \text{ or } P \mid P \text{ and } P \mid R \mathbin{|\text{->}} P \mid \text{not } P$$

$R \text{ seq } P$ is an abbreviation for $\text{not}(R \mathbin{|\text{->}} (\text{not } P))$. The operator seq is the dual of $\mathbin{|\text{->}}$.[3]

Tight Satisfaction of Sequences. *Tight satisfaction* is a four-way relation, denoted $w, L_0, L_1 \models R$, that defines when a finite word w together with input local variable valuation L_0 satisfies a sequence R and yields output local variable valuation L_1. Determination of whether the relation holds can be thought of as evaluation of R over w starting with local variable valuation L_0. As R is evaluated, its local variables may be assigned, reassigned, and referenced at various points. In order for the result of the evaluation to be well-defined, a reference to a local variable must not be made unless the structure of R ensures that the local variable holds a well-defined value at that point. There is some subtlety to this requirement. For example, a local variable may be assigned inconsistently in the two operands of intersect, after which a well-defined value cannot be guaranteed.

The IEEE 1800 standard addresses this problem by restricting syntactically the places within a sequence or property at which a given local variable can be referenced.[4] These restrictions ensure that references to local variables yield well-defined values [10]. For example, if a local variable is assigned in both operands of an intersect, then the local variable cannot be referenced after the intersect until it has been reassigned a well-defined value. We assume that all top-level properties satisfy the restrictions (e.g., as checked by a compiler). This allows us to simplify the definition of tight satisfaction from that given in [14].

For a boolean expression b and $(\sigma, L) \in \Sigma \times 2^V$, let $b[\sigma, L]$ denote the boolean value obtained by evaluating the expression b using the valuation (σ, L) of the design and local variables. The tight satisfaction relation is defined as follows:

---

[3] "seq" is not an explicit operator of SVA. It is equivalent to the the *follows_by* operator of ForSpec [4].

[4] See the recursive functions *flow*, *sample*, and *block* defined in Annex E of [14].

- $w, L_0, L_1 \models b$ iff $|w| = 1$ and $b[w^0, L_0] = 1$ and $L_1 = L_0$.
- $w, L_0, L_1 \models$ (1, $v = e$) iff $|w| = 1$ and L_1 results from L_0 by assigning $e[w^0, L_0]$ to v.
- $w, L_0, L_1 \models$ (R) iff $w, L_0, L_1 \models R$.
- $w, L_0, L_1 \models R_1$ ##0 R_2 iff there exist x, y, z, L' such that $w = xyz$ and $|y| = 1$ and $xy, L_0, L' \models R_1$ and $yz, L', L_1 \models R_2$.
- $w, L_0, L_1 \models R_1$ ##1 R_2 iff there exist x, y, L' such that $w = xy$ and $x, L_0, L' \models R_1$ and $y, L', L_1 \models R_2$.
- $w, L_0, L_1 \models R_1$ or R_2 iff either $w, L_0, L_1 \models R_1$ or $w, L_0, L_1 \models R_2$.
- $w, L_0, L_1 \models R_1$ intersect R_2 iff there exist L', L'' such that $w, L_0, L' \models R_1$ and $w, L_0, L'' \models R_2$ and $L_1(v) = L'(v)$ if v is assigned in R_1, and $L_1(v) = L''(v)$ otherwise.
- $w, L_0, L_1 \models R$[*0] iff $|w| = 0$ and $L_1 = L_0$.
- $w, L_0, L_1 \models R$[*1:$] iff there exist $j \geq 1$ and $L_{(0)} = L_0, w_1, L_{(1)}, w_2, L_{(2)}, \ldots, w_j, L_{(j)} = L_1$ such that $w = w_1 w_2 \cdots w_j$ and for every i such that $1 \leq i \leq j$, $w_i, L_{(i-1)}, L_{(i)} \models R$.

The asymmetry of the definition of L_1 in the case of intersect is justified as follows. If v is assigned in both R_1 and R_2, then the syntactic restrictions bar its reference after the intersect until it is reassigned. Therefore, we are free to let v take either the value from L' or the value from L''.

Satisfaction of Properties. *Satisfaction* is a three-way relation, denoted $w, L \models P$, that defines when an infinite word w together with input local variable valuation L satisfies a property P

- $w, L \models R$ iff there exist x, y, L' such that $w = xy$, $|x| > 0$, and $x, L, L' \models R$.
- $w, L \models$ (P) iff $w, L \models P$.
- $w, L \models P_1$ or P_2 iff either $w, L \models P_1$ or $w, L \models P_2$.
- $w, L \models P_1$ and P_2 iff both $w, L \models P_1$ and $w, L \models P_2$.
- $w, L \models R$ |-> P iff for all x, y, z, L' such that $w = xyz$ and $|y| = 1$ and $xy, L, L' \models R$, $yz, L' \models P$.
- $w, L \models$ not P iff $w, L \not\models P$.

Let P be a top-level property. The syntactic restrictions on references to local variables guarantee that for any $L, L', w, L \models P$ iff $w, L' \models P$. We write $w \models P$ iff for some (equivalently, for all) $L \in 2^V$, $w, L \models P$, and we let $\mathcal{L}(P)$ denote the set $\{w \in \Sigma^\omega \mid w \models P\}$. A model satisfies P iff each of its infinite computation traces satisfies P.

An SVA property is in *positive normal form (PNF)* if it does not contain any not operator. Positive normal form can be achieved by using DeMorgan's laws and the duality of |-> and seq to push all not operators down until they apply only to the boolean layer, where they can be absorbed into the boolean expressions. The case of not R is handled by using the fact that, as property, R is equivalent to R seq 1.

Automata. A *nondeterministic finite word automaton (NFW)* is a tuple $N = \langle \Sigma, S, S_0, \rho, F \rangle$, where Σ is a finite alphabet, S is a finite set of states, $\rho \subseteq S \times \Sigma \times S$ is a transition relation,[5] $S_0 \subseteq S$ is a set of initial states, and $F \subseteq S$ is a set of accepting states. A sequence $\xi = \xi^0 \xi^1 \cdots \xi^k \in S^*$ $(k \geq 0)$ is a *run* of N over the finite word $w \in \Sigma^*$ provided $k = |w|$, $\xi^0 \in S_0$, and for every $0 \leq i < |w|$, $(\xi^i, w^i, \xi^{i+1}) \in \rho$. The run ξ is *accepting* if $\xi^{|w|} \in F$. An NFW N accepts a word w if there exists an accepting run of N over w. We use $\mathcal{L}(N)$ to denote the set of words in Σ^* that are accepted by N.

A *nondeterministic Büchi automaton (NBW)* is a tuple $\langle \Sigma, S, S_0, \rho, F \rangle$ defined similarly to NFW. The automaton accepts an infinite word w iff it has an infinite run over w which contains infinitely many accepting states.

For a given set X, let $\mathsf{Bool}^+(X)$ be the set of positive Boolean formulas over X (i.e., Boolean formulas built from elements in X using $\land$ and $\lor$), where we also allow the formulas **true** and **false**. Let $Y \subseteq X$. We say that Y *satisfies* a formula $\theta \in \mathsf{Bool}^+(X)$ if the truth assignment that assigns *true* to the members of Y and assigns *false* to the members of $X \setminus Y$ satisfies θ. A *tree* is a prefix-closed subset $X \subseteq \mathbb{N}^*$.

An *alternating Büchi word automaton (ABW)* is a tuple $B = \langle \Sigma, Z, z_0, \delta, A \rangle$, where Σ, Z, and A are as Σ, S, and F (respectively) in the definition of NFW, $z_0 \in Z$ is a single initial state, and $\delta : Z \times \Sigma \to \mathsf{Bool}^+(Z)$ is a transition function. A *run tree* of B on an infinite word $w \in \Sigma^\omega$ is a pair (X, τ) where X is a (possibly infinite) tree and $\tau : X \to Z$ is a labeling function such that $\tau(\varepsilon) = z_0$ and such that the following holds: if $x \in X$, $|x| = i$, $\tau(x) = z$, and $\delta(z, w^i) = \theta$, then x has k children $x_1, \ldots, x_k$ in X for some $0 \leq k \leq |Z|$ and $\{\tau(x_1), \ldots, \tau(x_k)\}$ satisfies θ. The run tree (X, τ) is *accepting* if every infinite branch in X has infinitely many labels in A. Note that the run tree can also have finite branches: if $|x| = i$, $\tau(x) = z$, and $\delta(z, w^i) = \mathbf{true}$, then x need not have any children. B accepts a word $w \in \Sigma^\omega$ if there exists an accepting run tree of B over w. We use $\mathcal{L}(B)$ to denote the set of words in Σ^ω that are accepted by B.

An *alternating transition system (ATS)* is a tuple $B = \langle \Sigma, Z, Z_0, \delta, A \rangle$, where Σ, Z, δ, and A are as in the definition of ABW and $Z_0 \subseteq Z$ is a set of initial states. For $z \in Z_0$, $B^{(z)}$ is the ABW that results from B by replacing Z_0 by z.

SVA Subsets. The *basic subset* of SVA, denoted SVA^b, is obtained by limiting the sequence operators to ##1, ##0, or, [*0], and [*1:$]. All SVA property operators are allowed, but local variables and **intersect** are excluded. Every operator in SVA^b has an equivalent operator in PSL. We consider the following extensions to the basic subset: (1) SVA^{b+l}, obtained by adding local variables; (2) SVA^{b+i}, obtained by adding the intersect operator; (3) SVA^{b+d}, obtained by adding declared properties with arguments; and (4) SVA^{b+q}, obtained by adding quantified variables analogous to those in PSL.[6] SVA^{b+l+i} denotes the extension of SVA^b by adding both local variables and the **intersect** operator. The quantified variables feature is defined as follows. Let P be a property with

---

[5] ρ can also be given as a function $S \times \Sigma \to 2^S$.

[6] SVA does not have quantified variables, so SVA^{b+q} is not, strictly speaking, a subset of SVA. However, SVA^{b+q} is equivalent to a subset of PSL.

free variable x. Then "for x in S: and P" is equivalent to "$\text{and}_{s \in S} P|_{x \leftarrow s}$" and "for x in S: or P" is equivalent to "$\text{or}_{s \in S} P|_{x \leftarrow s}$". $P|_{x \leftarrow s}$ results from P by replacing every occurrence of x by s.

3   Automata Constructions for SVA

In [7] it is shown how to construct an ABW for each formula from a subset of PSL. The size of the ABW is linear in the size of the formula. Every operator in SVA^b has an equivalent operator in this subset of PSL. Thus, for every property P in SVA^b there exists an ABW with size linear in the size of P that accepts $\mathcal{L}(P)$. For every property P in SVA^{b+q} or in SVA^{b+d} there is a simple exponential translation to a property in SVA^b. Therefore, there exists an ABW with size exponential in the size of P that accepts $\mathcal{L}(P)$.

The construction presented in [7] first builds particular NFWs for the sequences and then uses these NFWs to construct the ABW. The construction of the ABW can take any NFW in place of the particular ones given for sequences, and the size of the ABW is linear in the sizes of the NFWs plus the number of property operators. While the PSL subset considered in [7] does not include intersection, an exponential construction for NFWs for regular expressions with the intersect operator is given in [13]. Using this construction, it follows that for every property P in SVA^{b+i} there exists an ABW with size exponential in the size of P that accepts $\mathcal{L}(P)$. In the rest of this section we present exponential ABW constructions for the SVA^{b+l} and SVA^{b+l+i} subsets.

NFW for Sequences with Local Variables. Let R be a sequence in SVA^{b+l}. We present an inductive construction of an NFW $N(R)$ for R. The construction will arrange a function λ mapping the set of states of $N(R)$ to 2^V. The base cases are as follows.

- $N(b) = \langle \Sigma, \{0,1\} \times 2^V, \{0\} \times 2^V, \rho, \{1\} \times 2^V \rangle$, where ρ is the set of $((0,L), \sigma, (1,L))$ such that $b[\sigma, L] = 1$. $\lambda((0,L)) = \lambda((1,L)) = L$.
- $N(R[*0]) = \langle \Sigma, \{0\} \times 2^V, \{0\} \times 2^V, \emptyset, \{0\} \times 2^V \rangle$. $\lambda((0,L)) = L$.
- $N((1, v = e)) = \langle \Sigma, \{0,1\} \times 2^V, \{0\} \times 2^V, \rho, \{1\} \times 2^V \rangle$, where ρ is the set of $((0,L), \sigma, (1,L'))$ such that L' results from L by assigning $e[\sigma, L]$ to v. $\lambda((0,L)) = \lambda((1,L)) = L$.

For the inductive cases, assume that we have constructed NFWs $N(R_1) = \langle \Sigma, S_1, I_1, \rho_1, F_1 \rangle$ and $N(R_2) = \langle \Sigma, S_2, I_2, \rho_2, F_2 \rangle$ and associated functions λ_1, λ_2. The sets S_1 and S_2 are assumed to have been made disjoint.

- $N((R_1)) = N(R_1)$. $\lambda = \lambda_1$.
- $N(R_1 \;\#\#0\; R_2) = \langle \Sigma, S_1 \cup S_2, I_1, \rho_1 \cup \rho_2 \cup \rho, F_2 \rangle$, where ρ is the set of (s_1, σ, s_2) such that there exist $s' \in F_1$ and $s'' \in I_2$ such that $(s_1, \sigma, s') \in \rho_1$ and $(s'', \sigma, s_2) \in \rho_2$ and $\lambda_1(s') = \lambda_2(s'')$. $\lambda = \lambda_1 \cup \lambda_2$.
- $N(R_1 \;\#\#1\; R_2) = \langle \Sigma, S_1 \cup S_2, I, \rho_1 \cup \rho_2 \cup \rho, F_2 \rangle$, where $I = I_1 \cup I_2$ if $I_1 \cap F_1 \neq \emptyset$, $I = I_1$ otherwise, and ρ is the set of (s_1, σ, s_2) such that $s_2 \in I_2$ and there exists $s' \in F_1$ such that $(s_1, \sigma, s') \in \rho_1$ and $\lambda_1(s') = \lambda_2(s_2)$. $\lambda = \lambda_1 \cup \lambda_2$.

- $N(R_1 \text{ or } R_2) = \langle \Sigma, S_1 \cup S_2, I_1 \cup I_2, \rho_1 \cup \rho_2, F_1 \cup F_2 \rangle.$ $\lambda = \lambda_1 \cup \lambda_2.$
- $N(R_1 [\ast 1 : \$]) = \langle \Sigma, S_1, I_1, \rho_1 \cup \rho, F_1 \rangle$, where ρ is the set of (s, σ, s') such that $s \in F_1$ and there exists $s'' \in I_1$ such that $(s'', \sigma, s') \in \rho_1$ and $\lambda_1(s) = \lambda_1(s'')$. $\lambda = \lambda_1.$

By $N(R)|_L$ we mean the automaton obtained from $N(R)$ by eliminating from the set of initial states those that are not mapped by λ to L.

Lemma 1. *Let R be a sequence in* SVA^{b+l}*, and let* $w \in \Sigma^*$*. $w, L_0, L_1 \models R$ iff $N(R)|_{L_0}$ has an accepting run over w that ends in a state mapped by λ to L_1.*

Lemma 2. *Let R be a sequence in* SVA^{b+l}*, let V be the set of local variables in R, and let $S(R)$ be the set of states in the NFW $N(R)$. Then $|S(R)| = O(|R| \cdot 2^{|V|})$.*

ABW for Properties with Local Variables. Let P be a property in SVA^{b+l}. We present an inductive construction of an ATS $B(P)$ for P, which extend the construction presented in [7]. The construction will arrange a function λ mapping the set of states of $B(P)$ to 2^V in such a way that λ induces a bijection when restricted to the set of initial states. For $L \in 2^V$, $B(P)|_L$ is the ABW that results from $B(P)$ by restricting to the single initial state that is mapped by λ to L.

We assume that the properties are in PNF. Wherever a sequence R other than 1 or 0 appears as a property, we understand it to be replaced by R **seq** 1. The base cases of the construction are as follows.

- $B(1) = \langle \Sigma, \{0\} \times 2^V, \{0\} \times 2^V, \delta, \emptyset \rangle$, where $\delta((0, L), \sigma) = \mathbf{true}$. $\lambda((0, L)) = L$.
- $B(0) = \langle \Sigma, \{0\} \times 2^V, \{0\} \times 2^V, \delta, \emptyset \rangle$, where $\delta((0, L), \sigma) = \mathbf{false}$. $\lambda((0, L)) = L$.

For the inductive cases, assume that we have constructed the NFW $N(R) = \langle \Sigma, S, I, \rho, F \rangle$ and function λ_R for sequence R and, for $i = 1, 2$, the ATS $B_i = \langle \Sigma, Z_i, Z_{i0}, \delta_i, A_i \rangle$ and function λ_i for property P_i. Let ρ be given as a function $2^S \times \Sigma \to 2^S$, where $\rho(S', \sigma) = \cup_{s \in S'} \rho(s, \sigma)$ for $S' \subseteq S$. Assume also that the state sets S, Z_1, Z_2 have been made disjoint and are disjoint from $\{0\} \times 2^V$. Let $I|_L = I \cap \lambda_R^{-1}(L)$ and, for $i = 1, 2$, let $z_{i0,L}$ be the unique state of Z_{i0} mapped by λ_i to L.

- $B((P_1)) = B(P_1)$. $\lambda = \lambda_1$.
- $B(R \mathrel{|->} P_1) = \langle \Sigma, (\{0\} \times 2^V) \cup S \cup Z_1, \{0\} \times 2^V, \delta \cup \delta_1, S \cup A_1 \rangle$, where δ is defined over $((\{0\} \times 2^V) \cup S) \times \Sigma$ as follows.
  - $\delta((0, L), \sigma) = \bigwedge \rho(I|_L, \sigma) \wedge \bigwedge \delta_1(Z, \sigma)$, where Z is the set of $z \in Z_{10}$ such that $\lambda_1(z) \in \lambda_R(\rho(I|_L, \sigma) \cap F)$.
  - $\delta(s, \sigma) = \bigwedge \rho(s, \sigma) \wedge \bigwedge \delta_1(Z, \sigma)$, where Z is the set of $z \in Z_{10}$ such that $\lambda_1(z) \in \lambda_R(\rho(s, \sigma) \cap F)$.

  $\lambda = \lambda' \cup \lambda_R \cup \lambda_1$, where λ' maps $\{0\} \times 2^V$ by $((0, L)) \mapsto L$.
- $B(R \text{ \textbf{seq} } P_1) = \langle \Sigma, (\{0\} \times 2^V) \cup S \cup Z_1, \{0\} \times 2^V, \delta \cup \delta_1, A_1 \rangle$, where δ is defined over $((\{0\} \times 2^V) \cup S) \times \Sigma$ as follows.
  - $\delta((0, L), \sigma) = \bigvee \rho(I|_L, \sigma) \vee \bigvee \delta_1(Z, \sigma)$, where Z is the set of $z \in Z_{10}$ such that $\lambda_1(z) \in \lambda_R(\rho(I|_L, \sigma) \cap F)$.
  - $\delta(s, \sigma) = \bigvee \rho(s, \sigma) \vee \bigvee \delta_1(Z, \sigma)$, where Z is the set of $z \in Z_{10}$ such that $\lambda_1(z) \in \lambda_R(\rho(s, \sigma) \cap F)$.

$\lambda = \lambda' \cup \lambda_R \cup \lambda_1$, where λ' maps $\{0\} \times 2^V$ by $((0, L)) \mapsto L$.

- $B(P_1 \text{ or } P_2) = \langle \Sigma, (\{0\} \times 2^V) \cup Z_1 \cup Z_2, \{0\} \times 2^V, \delta \cup \delta_1 \cup \delta_2, A_1 \cup A_2 \rangle$, where δ is defined over $(\{0\} \times 2^V) \times \Sigma$ by $\delta((0, L), \sigma) = \delta_1(z_{10,L}, \sigma) \vee \delta_2(z_{20,L}, \sigma)$.
  $\lambda = \lambda' \cup \lambda_1 \cup \lambda_2$, where λ' maps $\{0\} \times 2^V$ by $((0, L)) \mapsto L$.

- $B(P_1 \text{ and } P_2) = \langle \Sigma, (\{0\} \times 2^V) \cup Z_1 \cup Z_2, \{0\} \times 2^V, \delta \cup \delta_1 \cup \delta_2, A_1 \cup A_2 \rangle$, where δ is defined over $(\{0\} \times 2^V) \times \Sigma$ by $\delta((0, L), \sigma) = \delta_1(z_{10,L}, \sigma) \wedge \delta_2(z_{20,L}, \sigma)$.
  $\lambda = \lambda' \cup \lambda_1 \cup \lambda_2$, where λ' maps $\{0\} \times 2^V$ by $((0, L)) \mapsto L$.

Lemma 3. *Let P be a property in* SVA^{b+l} *in PNF, and let $w \in \Sigma^\omega$. $w, L \models P$ iff $w \in \mathcal{L}(B(P)|_L)$.*

Lemma 4. *Let P be a property in* SVA^{b+l} *in PNF, let V be the set of local variables in P, and let $Z(P)$ be the set of states in the ATS $B(P)$. Then $|Z(P)| = O(|P| \cdot 2^{|V|})$.*

The Intersect Operator. In this section we extend the construction of ABWs for properties in SVA^{b+l} to SVA^{b+l+i}. Assume that for the sequences R_1 and R_2 we have constructed the NFWs $N_1 = \langle \Sigma, S_1, I_1, \rho_1, F_1 \rangle$ with mapping $\lambda_1 \colon S_1 \to 2^V$ and $N_2 = \langle \Sigma, S_2, I_2, \rho_2, F_2 \rangle$ with mapping $\lambda_2 \colon S_2 \to 2^V$, respectively. We define $N(R_1 \text{ intersect } R_2) = \langle \Sigma, S_1 \times S_2, I, \rho, F_1 \times F_2 \rangle$, where $I = \{(i_1, i_2) \in I_1 \times I_2 \mid \lambda_1(i_1) = \lambda_2(i_2)\}$ and

$$\rho = \{((s_1, s_2), \sigma, (s_1', s_2')) \mid (s_1, \sigma, s_1') \in \rho_1 \text{ and } (s_2, \sigma, s_2') \in \rho_2\}$$

and we define $\lambda \colon S_1 \times S_2 \to 2^V$ by $\lambda((s_1, s_2))(v) = \lambda_1(s_1)(v)$ if v is assigned in R_1 and $\lambda((s_1, s_2))(v) = \lambda_2(s_2)(v)$ otherwise. The following lemma extends the result of Lemma 1 to SVA^{b+l+i}.

Lemma 5. *Let R be a sequence in* SVA^{b+l+i}, *and let $w \in \Sigma^*$. $w, L_0, L_1 \models R$ iff $N(R)|_{L_0}$ has an accepting run over w that ends in a state mapped by λ to L_1.*

Lemma 6. *Let R be a sequence in* SVA^{b+l+i}, *let V be the set of local variables in R, and let $S(R)$ be the set of states in the NFW $N(R)$. If V is non-empty, then $|S(R)| = O(2^{|R| \cdot |V|})$. Otherwise $|S(R)| = O(2^{|R|})$.*

Lemma 7. *Let P be a property in* SVA^{b+l+i} *in PNF, let V be the set of local variables in P, and let $Z(P)$ be the set of states in the ATS $B(P)$. If V is non-empty, then $|Z(P)| = O(2^{|P| \cdot |V|})$. Otherwise $|Z(P)| = O(2^{|P|})$.*

Upper Bound Complexity. Following the automata-theoretic approach of [17], the satisfiability and model-checking problems for linear temporal logics are solved by representing the property by an ABW and then translating the ABW into an exponentially larger NBW [12]. Satisfiability is solved by checking for emptiness of the NBW, and model-checking is solved by checking for emptiness of the product of the model with the NBW for the negation of the property. Since the emptiness problem for NBWs is in NLOGSPACE [18], the complexity of these problems is in PSPACE with respect to the number of states of the ABW [17]. These observations and the automata constructions of the preceding sections lead to the following theorem.

Theorem 1

- *The satisfiability and model-checking problems for properties in any of the extensions* SVA^{b+i}, SVA^{b+q}, SVA^{b+d} *are in EXPSPACE with respect to* $|P|$.
- *The satisfiability and model-checking problems for properties in* SVA^{b+l} *are in EXPSPACE with respect to* $|V|$ *and in PSPACE with respect to* $|P|$.
- *The satisfiability and model-checking problems for properties in* SVA^{b+l+i} *are in EXPSPACE with respect to* $|V| \cdot |P|$.

4   Lower Bounds

In this section we explore some of the "sources of hardness" of SVA satisfiability and model-checking. In the previous section we showed that the satisfiability and model checking problems for properties in SVA^b are in PSPACE. A reduction from the PSPACE tiling problem [20,11,16] can be used to prove the following.

Proposition 1. *The satisfiability and model checking problems for properties in* SVA^b *are PSPACE-hard.*

When SVA^b is extended by local variables, regular expression intersection, declared properties with arguments, or quantified variables, the complexity of the model-checking and satisfiability problems become EXPSPACE-hard.

Theorem 2. *The satisfiability and model checking problems for properties in* SVA^{b+l}, SVA^{b+i}, SVA^{b+d}, *and* SVA^{b+q} *are EXPSPACE-hard.*

We present a proof sketch by outlining a reduction from a version of the EX-PSPACE tiling problem [20,11,16] to each of the subsets. In the *EXPSPACE tiling problem*, the following are given: a finite set T of "tiles", vertical and horizontal restrictive relations $\mathcal{V} \subseteq T \times T$ and $\mathcal{H} \subseteq T \times T$, an initial tile $\tau_0 \in T$, a final tile $\tau_a \in T$, and an integer $n > 0$. The problem is to decide whether there exists $m > 0$ such that there exists a tiling of a $2^n \times m$ grid such that the following hold: (1) τ_0 is in the bottom left corner; (2) the first occurrence of τ_a is in the top left corner; (3) every pair of horizontally neighboring tiles is in $\mathcal{H}$; and (4) every pair of vertically neighboring tiles is in $\mathcal{V}$.

Given an EXPSPACE tiling problem $\mathcal{T} = \langle T, \mathcal{V}, \mathcal{H}, \tau_0, \tau_a, n \rangle$, we define for each subset a property P, polynomial[7] in n, such that there exists an infinite word w that satisfies P iff there exists a tiling for $\mathcal{T} = \langle T, \mathcal{V}, \mathcal{H}, \tau_0, \tau_a, n \rangle$. The idea is to partition w into substrings of length n called "blocks" such that every block represents one tile. The n letters in a block provide a binary encoding of a number between 0 and $2^n - 1$, inclusive. We refer to this number as the *counter value* of the block. The blocks are enumerated in the order of increasing counter values modulo 2^n, starting from 0. Pairs of consecutive blocks (except those enumerated $(2^n - 1, 0)$) must satisfied $\mathcal{H}$, and pairs of blocks whose counter values are equal and are separated by $2^n - 1$ intermediate blocks must satisfy $\mathcal{V}$.

---

[7] Quadratic for SVA^{b+i} and SVA^{b+d}, linear for the other extensions.

We construct the properties for the reductions to the different subsets in two parts. The *shared part* is common to all the properties and is in SVA^b. For each subset we construct its *specific part* using the extending feature of the subset.

The alphabet for all properties is $2^{\{\clubsuit,\Diamond,c,z\}} \times T$, where $\clubsuit$ is a special signal that marks the beginning of a block, $\Diamond$ is a special signal that is first high one letter after the last block of the tiling, c is a one-bit signal used to represent the counter value of the block, and z is an auxiliary variable used to represent the carry over when incrementing the counter value. We use the convention that the value of c in the first (resp., last) letter of a block is the least (resp., most) significant bit of the counter value. The set T of tiles is of constant size. The T component of a letter is referenced by the signal t. The tile represented by a block is understood to be the value of t in its last letter.

For lack of space, we do not present the shared part. It is obtained by creating properties in SVA^b of size $O(n)$ requiring that (1) a prefix of w be partitioned into blocks of length n, the first letter of each being indicated by $\clubsuit$; (2) the counter values of the blocks increment modulo 2^n starting at 0; (3) $\Diamond$ appear for the first time after a block with counter value $2^n - 1$ and mark the first letter after the end of the prefix; (4) the first block's tile value be τ_0; (5) the tile value of the first block in the last row be τ_a; and (6) every two consecutive blocks in the same row be in $\mathcal{H}$. It remains to construct for each of the extensions the specific part of the property requiring that a pair of blocks with the same counter value that are separated by $2^n - 1$ intermediate blocks be in $\mathcal{V}$.

For the local variable extension, we let $R_{c \neq v}$ denote a sequence that is tightly satisfied by a block iff the counter value of the block is different than the binary value represented by the local variables $v_0, v_1, \ldots, v_{n-1}$. Such a sequence can be created with size $O(n)$. Also, we let $R_{c=v}$ denote the sequence

$$c == v_0 \ \texttt{\#\#1} \ c == v_1 \ \texttt{\#\#1} \ \cdots \ \texttt{\#\#1} \ c == v_{n-1},$$

which is tightly satisfied by a block iff the counter value of the block is equal to the binary value represent by $v_0, v_1, \ldots, v_{n-1}$. The specific part $P_{\mathcal{V}}^l$ for the local variable extension is as follows:

```
(1[*n] ##0 t!=τₐ)[*0:$] ##1
(1,v₀=c) ##1 (1,v₁=c) ##1 ··· ##1 (1,vₙ₋₁=c) ##0 t!=τₐ |->
```
$\text{and}_{\tau_1 \in T} \ (t == \tau_1 \ \texttt{|->} \ 1 \ \texttt{\#\#1} \ R_{c \neq v}[*1:\$] \ \texttt{\#\#1} \ R_{c=v} \ \texttt{\#\#0} \ ||_{\mathcal{V}(\tau_1,\tau_2)} t == \tau_2)$

After any number of blocks with tile other than τ_a, the counter value is stored in $v_0, v_1, \ldots, v_{n-1}$. Then a conjunction over $\tau_1 \in T$ of implications whose antecedents test $t == \tau_1$ ensures that $(\tau_1, \tau_2) \in \mathcal{V}$, where τ_2 is the tile of the next block at which the counter value equals the binary value saved in $v_0, v_1, \ldots, v_{n-1}$. The size of $P_{\mathcal{V}}^l$ is $O(n)$.

The specific part for the extension by quantified variables is similar:

```
for v₀,...,vₙ₋₁ in bit: and
(1[*n] ##0 t!=τₐ)[*0:$] ##1 R_{c=v} ##0 t!=τₐ |->
```
$\text{and}_{\tau_1 \in T} \ (t == \tau_1 \ \texttt{|->} \ 1 \ \texttt{\#\#1} \ R_{c \neq v}[*1:\$] \ \texttt{\#\#1} \ R_{c=v} \ \texttt{\#\#0} \ ||_{\mathcal{V}(\tau_1,\tau_2)} t == \tau_2)$

Instances of properties with arguments can be used to universally quantify the arguments. In this way, we can adapt the specific part with quantified variables to serve as the specific part using declared properties with arguments. Here is an example to illustrate. Let $P(a, b, c)$ be a declared property with arguments. Define $P_1(b, c) = P(1, b, c)$ and $P(0, b, c)$, $P_2(c) = P_1(1, c)$ and $P_1(0, c)$, $P_3 = P_2(1)$ and $P_2(0)$. The property P_3 is equivalent to $\forall a \forall b \forall c : P(a, b, c)$. The adaptation involves n declared properties, each of size $O(n)$, so the specific part is of size $O(n^2)$.

For the specific part using intersect, we assume that the following auxiliary sequences of size $O(n)$ have been constructed. For $0 \leq i \leq n - 2$, R_i is a sequence that is tightly satisfied by a series of two or more blocks provided the ith bits of the counters of the first and last blocks are equal. R_{n-1} is a sequence that is tightly satisfied by a series of two or more blocks provided the $(n-1)$st bits of the counters of the first and last blocks are equal and, in addition, counter bit $n - 1$ changes its value exactly twice in the intermediate blocks. The minimum number of intermediate blocks is 2^{n-1}, and the maximum number is $3 \cdot 2^{n-1} + 2$. Inside these boundaries, distinct blocks have distinct counter values. The sequence $R_{\text{tiles in } \mathcal{V}}$ is tightly satisfied by a series of blocks provided the pair formed by the tiles of the first and last blocks is in $\mathcal{V}$. From these auxiliary sequences, we construct $R_{\text{next}} = R_0 \text{ intersect} \cdots \text{ intersect } R_{n-1}$, which is tightly satisfied by a series of blocks provided the first and last blocks have the same counter value and there are exactly $2^n - 1$ intermediate blocks. R_{next} is of size $O(n^2)$. The specific part $P_{\mathcal{V}}^i$ is as follows:

```
(1[*n − 1] ##1 t!=τ_a)[*0:$] ##1 1 |->
(1[*n − 1] ##1 t==τ_a) or (R_next intersect R_tiles in ν)
```

The consequent is tightly satisfied by a series of two or more blocks provided that either the tile of the first block is τ_a or the first and last blocks have the same counter value, their tiles are in $\mathcal{V}$, and there are exactly $2^n - 1$ intermediate blocks. The property $P_{\mathcal{V}}^i$ requires the consequent for every block before τ_a occurs.

5   Conclusions and Related Work

There has been some prior work on the complexity of satisfiability and model checking of PSL and similar languages. In [4], the complexity of the ForSpec language is shown to be PSPACE-complete. In [3] there is a discussion of the complexity of the *reset operator* in Sugar and ForSpec. Symbolic verification of PSL properties restricted to negated sequences is explored in [6]. A construction of alternating Büchi automata for a large subset of PSL is presented in [7]. The automata from this construction run over both finite and infinite words, and the construction accounts for the neutral semantic variant for finite words.

In this paper we have explored the complexity of SVA. We have shown that when features like local variables, regular expression intersection, and declared properties with argument are used, the complexity of the language becomes EXPSPACE-complete. These results invite further investigation of the practical usage of these features and the performance of model-checking algorithms that support them. Other theoretical gaps in the complexity analysis remain. For example, the expressiveness and complexity of SVA with recursive properties and the complexity of checking SVA in simulation are still open.

References

1. Accellera. *SystemVerilog 3.1a Language Reference Manual: Accellera's Extensions to Verilog.* 2004. www.eda.org/sv/SystemVerilog_3.1a.pdf.
2. R. Alur and T. Henzinger. Real-time logics: complexity and expressiveness. In *Proc. 5th Symp. on Logic in Computer Science*, pages 390–401, June 1990.
3. R. Armoni, D. Bustan, O. Kupferman, and M. Y. Vardi. Resets vs. aborts in linear temporal logic. In *Proc. 9th Int'l Conf. on Tools and Algorithms for the Construction and Analysis of Systems*, volume 2619 of *LNCS*, pages 65–80, 2003.
4. R. Armoni, L. Fix, R. Gerth, B. Ginsburg, T. Kanza, A. Landver, S. Mador-Haim, A. Tiemeyer, E. Singerman, M.Y. Vardi, and Y. Zbar. The ForSpec temporal logic: A new temporal property-specification language. In *Proc. 8th Int'l Conf. on Tools and Algorithms for the Construction and Analysis of Systems*, volume 2280 of *LNCS*, pages 296–311, 2002.
5. I. Beer, S. Ben-David, C. Eisner, D. Fisman, A. Gringauze, and Y. Rodeh. The temporal logic Sugar. In *Proc. 13th Int'l Conf. on Computer Aided Verification*, volume 2102 of *LNCS*, pages 363–367, 2001.
6. S. Ben-David, D. Fisman, and S. Ruah. Embedding finite automata within regular expressions. In *Int'l Symp. on Leveraging Applications of Formal Methods*, 2004.
7. D. Bustan, D. Fisman, and J. Havlicek. Automata construction for PSL. Technical Report MCS05-04, The Weizmann Institute of Science, May 2005.
8. D. Bustan, A. Flaisher, O. Grumberg, O. Kupferman, and M.Y. Vardi. Regular vacuity. In *13th Advanced Research Working Conf. on Correct Hardware Design and Verification Methods*, volume 3725 of *LNCS*, pages 191–206, 2005.
9. M. J. C. Gordon. Validating the PSL/Sugar semantics using automated reasoning. *Formal Aspects of Computing*, 15(4):406 – 421, December 2003.
10. J. Havlicek, K. Shultz, R. Armoni, S. Dudani, and E. Cerny. Notes on the semantics of local variables in Accellera SystemVerilog 3.1 concurrent assertions. Technical Report 2004.01, Accellera, May 2004. Available from www.accellera.org.
11. H.R. Lewis. Complexity of solvable cases of the decision problem for the predicate calculus. In *Foundations of Computer Science*, volume 19, pages 35–47, 1978.
12. S. Miyano and T. Hayashi. Alternating finite automata on ω-words. *Theoretical Computer Science*, 32:321–330, 1984.
13. M.O. Rabin and D. Scott. Finite automata and their decision problems. *IBM Journal of Research and Development*, 3:115–125, 1959.
14. IEEE Computer Society. *1800: IEEE Standard for SystemVerilog–Unified Hardware Design, Specification, and Verification Language.* IEEE, 2005.
15. IEEE Computer Society. *1850: IEEE Standard for Property Specification Language (PSL).* IEEE, 2005.
16. P. van Emde Boas. The convenience of tilings. In *Complexity, Logic and Recursion Theory*, volume 187 of *Lecture Notes in Pure and Applied Mathematics*, pages 331–363, 1997.
17. M.Y. Vardi. An automata-theoretic approach to linear temporal logic. In F. Moller and G. Birtwistle, editors, *Logics for Concurrency: Structure versus Automata*, volume 1043 of *Lecture Notes in Computer Science*, pages 238–266, 1996.

18. M.Y. Vardi and P. Wolper. Reasoning about infinite computations. *Information and Computation*, 115(1):1–37, November 1994.
19. Verification guild: A community of verification professionals. `http://verificationguild.com`.
20. H. Wang. Dominoes and the AEA case of the decision problem. In *Symposium on the Mathematical Theory of Automata*, pages 23–55, 1962.

Check It Out: On the Efficient Formal Verification of Live Sequence Charts[*]

Jochen Klose[3], Tobe Toben[1], Bernd Westphal[1], and Hartmut Wittke[2]

[1] Fak. II, Dept. für Informatik, Carl von Ossietzky Universität Oldenburg,
26111 Oldenburg, Germany
{toben, westphal}@informatik.uni-oldenburg.de
[2] OSC – ES AG, Industriestr. 11, 26121 Oldenburg, Germany
wittke@osc-es.de
[3] Bombardier Transportation, Wolfenbüttler Str. 86/Obergstr. 5,
38102 Braunschweig, Germany
jochen.klose@de.transport.bombardier.com

Abstract. Live Sequence Charts (LSCs) are an established visual formalism for requirements in formal, model-based development, in particular aiming at formal verification of the model. The model-checking problem for LSCs is principally long solved as each LSC has an equivalent LTL formula, but even for moderate sized LSCs the formulae grow prohibitively large. In this paper we elaborate on practically relevant subclasses of LSCs, namely bonded and time bounded, which don't require the full power of LTL model-checking. For bonded LSCs, a combination of observer automaton and fixed small liveness property and for additionally time bounded LSCs reachability checking is sufficient.

1 Introduction

Scenario-based approaches in general and Live Sequence Charts (LSCs) [1] in particular have shown adequate for the formal specification of inter-object requirements on distributed systems in formal, model-based development(cf. [2] for references). That is, requirements on a system under design are formally specified by LSCs before a model of the system is built. Model-checking can then automatically check whether the model satisfies the requirements to find errors early, before the actual implementation.

The model-checking problem of LSCs vs. Kripke structures is principally solved since universal LSCs translate to equivalent LTL formulae [3] and existential LSCs translate to observer automata, i.e. 1-acceptance [4], or CTL* thus corresponding model-checkers can directly be employed. Accordingly there are proof-of-concept results for the formal verification of LSCs against Statemate [5,6] and UML [7,8] models. In particular with the industrial case study considered in [5] it turned out that the LTL formulae grow large even for LSCs of moderate size. That is, formal verification becomes expensive due to the size

---

[*] Partly supported by DFG, grants SFB/TR 14 AVACS and DA 206/7-3, SPP 1064.

T. Ball and R.B. Jones (Eds.): CAV 2006, LNCS 4144, pp. 219–233, 2006.

of the *requirements* (for details cf. [3,9]). Our subject is *efficient* formal verification of LSCs. We identify two sub-classes of LSCs for which techniques that are faster but less powerful than LTL model-checking are sufficient, or help in finding errors fast.

Related Work. Model-checking LSCs against system models has been first investigated by [10]. They manually derive a selection of small, local LTL properties from an LSC and check whether they hold for a model of a bus protocol. The limited size of the checked properties didn't raise the need to consider more efficient procedures. In [11], model-checking is used as a technique to obtain satisfying paths for a set of LSCs in the context of playing-out LSCs [12]. Their representation of LSCs employs one automaton per instance-line. Similarly, [13] check a set of LSCs for consistency using a CSP semantics of LSCs, namely one CSP process per instance line, and the FDR model-checker. Both are particularly tailored for checking LSCs against each other and don't discuss the relation to general system model. Furthermore, both discuss only a limited subset of the dialect [5], in particular excluding time. We use the term "LSC verification" similar to, for instance, "LTL verification" which means checking a formula against a model. The observer based approach for LSC model-checking has been introduced in [14] and further studied in the context of Symbolic Timing Diagrams (STDs) in [15]. Our results slightly extend [15] since we have to discuss the case of non-deterministic automata which are needed for non-bonded LSCs while deterministic automata are sufficient for the scope of [15].

The remainder of the paper is structured as follows. In Sect. 2 we briefly recall LSCs. Section 3 introduces Timed Symbolic Automata (TSA), the semantical foundation of LSCs, together with the notions of determinism and time boundedness. It provides the basic strategy for efficient verification of TSAs. The application to LSC model-checking is discussed in Sect. 4. Section 5 supplies experimental results and Sect. 6 concludes.

2   Live Sequence Charts

The visual formalism LSCs has been introduced in [1] to overcome several shortcomings of the well-known Message Sequence Charts (MSC) wrt. a formal usage.

Table 1. Modalities of LSC elements and their semantics

	mandatory/hot/universal	possible/cold/existential
chart	... each activating system run suffix adheres to scenario	... there is an activating and adhering system run suffix
location	progress enforced	progress not enforced
condition/ local invar.	system violates LSC if condition doesn't hold	system satisfies LSC if condition doesn't hold
message	reception has to be observed	reception needn't be observed

It is a conservative extension of basic MSCs that gains increased expressive power by adding *modalities* to charts, locations, and elements (cf. Table 1).

The mode of a chart can be either *existential* or *universal*. An existential LSC is satisfied by a system if there is at least one system run adhering to the LSC. Conversely, a universal LSC is satisfied if all runs of the system adhere to it. A location's mode, either *hot* or *cold*, expresses liveness requirements. An element following a hot location has to be observed *finally* in order to satisfy the LSC. A cold location doesn't enforce progress. Conditions are, in contrast to MSCs, semantically relevant in LSCs and have a mode. If a *mandatory* (or *hot*) condition isn't satisfied when supposed to according to the scenario, the chart is violated. If a *possible* (or *cold*) condition isn't satisfied, the whole chart is immediately considered satisfied. It is *legally exited*. This interpretation applies alike to *local invariants*. They have been introduced in [5] to state requirements on spans of time instead of only single points in time as with conditions. The mode of a message, either mandatory (hot) or possible (cold), denotes whether the message may get lost. The reception of a hot message has to be observed to satisfy the LSC, for a cold message it needn't be observed.

In addition to modes, LSCs add to MSCs means that characterise the situations to which the scenario applies, i.e. its *activation*. Activation in general is characterised by a prefix of the LSC called *pre-chart* meaning whenever the pre-chart is observed then the system shall adhere to the rest of the LSC, the *main-chart*. The *activation condition* is a shortcut for pre-charts with a single condition only. For formal verification, [5] adds the activation mode – one of *initial*, *invariant*, or *iterative* – to further restrict activation. Initial LSCs may only be activated in initial system states. Iterative LSCs disregard violations of reactivating LSCs, i.e. LSCs that comprise a sequence that adheres to the LSC's own pre-chart again. Furthermore, both [5,12] have added the notion of *strict* vs. *tolerant* (or *weak*) interpretation. The strict interpretation requires that messages used in the chart don't occur at other points in time than the ones given by the LSC. The tolerant interpretation ignores additional messages. For example, a system sending *red_on* once again before expiration of the timer would not satisfy the LSC from Fig. 1 strictly.

Fig. 1(a) is a simplified requirement on a level crossing controller. It is activated when the crossing controller receives an asynchronous message '*secreq*' from the environment. The crossing controller shall finally, as indicated by the solid segment of its instance line, start the lights and barrier controllers by synchronous messages '*lights_on*' and '*barrier_down*'. The timing interval [5, 15] requires lowering the barrier to take between 5 and 15 units of time and the hot local invariant ¬*MvUp* requires the barrier not to move up from '*barrier_down*' reception up to and including the point in time where '*barrier_ok*' is sent. If the traffic lights controller is not operational when receiving '*lights_on*', the LSC is legally exited at the cold condition '*Operational*'. Otherwise timer t is started. Timeout of t shall occur when sending '*lights_ok*', i.e. switching on the lights shall take exactly 7 units of time. The order of '*lights_ok*' and '*barrier_ok*' is explicitly relaxed by enclosing them in a *coregion* as indicated by the dotted line.

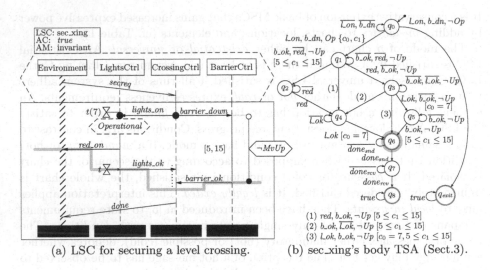

(a) LSC for securing a level crossing.　　　(b) sec_xing's body TSA (Sect.3).

Fig. 1. For brevity, overlining denotes negation and comma denotes conjunction in Fig. 1(b). E.g. q_0's loop fires if neither '*lights_on*' nor '*barrier_down*' are observed.

The messages may occur in any order, even simultaneously. When both have been received, the crossing controller *may* send '*done*' back to the environment as no hot location *enforces* progress at this position.

We postpone recalling the formal semantics of LSC following [5] to Sect. 4, thus after the introduction of Timed Symbolic Automata in Sect. 3. Note that we discuss the LSC dialect of [5] which is tailored for the application domain of formal verification in contrast to the play-engine dialect of [12]. This is not an exclusive choice as both share a large common sublanguage. LSC specifications may well be played in following [12] and then strengthened for formal verification using the features from [5]. Furthermore we assume *well-formed* LSCs [2], i.e. LSCs without internal contradictions.

3   Efficient TSA Model-Checking

3.1   Preliminaries

We use $Expr_S$ to denote the propositional logic formulae over signature S, and $\mathcal{I} \models \psi$ to denote that interpretation $\mathcal{I}$ satisfies $\psi \in Expr_S$ with fixed non-empty universe $\mathcal{U}$. Let C be a set of clocks. A *clock valuation* is a mapping $\tau : C \to \mathbb{N}_0$, and $T(C)$ denotes the set of all clock valuations. The update of a time valuation $\tau \in T(C)$ by a value $x \in \mathbb{N}_0$, written $\tau + x$, is pointwise defined as $(\tau + x)(c) := \tau(c) + x$ for all $c \in C$. The set of *clock constraints* $\Phi(C)$ is defined by the grammar $\phi ::= true \mid c \leq x \mid c \geq x$, $\varphi ::= \phi \mid \varphi_1 \wedge \varphi_2 \mid \varphi_1 \vee \varphi_2$, $c \in C$, $x \in \mathbb{N}_0$. We write $\tau \models \varphi$ to denote that the clock valuation $\tau \in T(C)$ satisfies the clock constraint $\varphi \in \Phi(C)$. The definition of satisfaction is standard.

3.2   Timed Symbolic Automata

Timed Symbolic Automata (TSA) are a variant of timed Büchi automata where transitions are labelled by expressions from $Expr_S$ instead of just an element of an alphabet (cf. [15] for references). The new notion of *default transitions* significantly eases the formal definition of the clock propagation introduced below.

Formally, a TSA over a signature S is a tuple $A = (Q, q_s, C, \leadsto, D, F)$ with a finite set of states Q, initial state $q_s \in Q$, a finite set of clocks C, transition relation $\leadsto \subseteq Q \times Expr_S \times \Phi(C) \times 2^C \times Q$, default transitions $D \subseteq Q \times Q$, and accepting states $F \subseteq Q$. We define $\to \subseteq Q \times Q$ as $\to := D \cup \{(q, q') \mid \exists (q, \psi, \varphi, \rho, q') \in \leadsto\}$. A TSA is called *Partially Ordered TSA* (POTSA) if the reflexive transitive closure of $\to$ is a partial order, i.e. $\to^*$ is anti-symmetric. Note that all loops in a POTSA are consequently self-loops.

Let S be a signature and U a fixed universe. A *timed interpretation sequence* is a sequence $r = ((\iota_i, t_i))_{i \in \mathbb{N}_0}$ with ι_i an interpretation of S and $t_i \in \mathbb{N}_0$ a timestamp such that $t_i < t_{i+1}$, $i \in \mathbb{N}_0$. Let $((q_i, \tau_i))_{i \in \mathbb{N}_0}$ be a sequence with $q_i \in Q$ a state and $\tau_i \in T(C)$ a valuation of the clocks, $i \in \mathbb{N}_0$. It is called *timed run* of A over r iff it starts in the initial state, i.e. $q_0 = q_s$, the clocks initially have value zero, i.e. $\tau_0(c) = 0$, $c \in C$, and states are A-successors. That is, for $i \in \mathbb{N}_0$ either there is a transition $(q_i, \psi_i, \varphi_i, \rho_i, q_{i+1}) \in \leadsto$ such that the boolean and clock constraints hold, $\iota_i \models \psi_i$ and $(\tau_i + (t_{i+1} - t_i)) \models \varphi_i$, and the clock valuations are updated according to ρ_i, i.e. $\tau_{i+1}|_{\rho_i} = 0$ and $\tau_{i+1}|_{C \setminus \rho_i} = (\tau_i + (t_{i+1} - t_i))|_{C \setminus \rho_i}$, or there is a default transition $(q_i, q_{i+1}) \in D$ and $\tau_{i+1} = \tau_i + (t_{i+1} - t_i)$. A timed run $((q_i, \tau_i))_{i \in \mathbb{N}_0}$ is called *accepting* if $q_i \in F$ for infinitely many $i \in \mathbb{N}_0$. The *language accepted* by A, denoted by $\mathcal{L}(A)$, is the set of timed interpretation sequences for which an accepting run exists.

In the following we introduce two subclasses of TSAs, namely deterministic and time-bounded ones. In Sect. 3.4 we will see how membership in these classes determines the efficiency of the model-checking procedure.

We call a state $q \in Q$ *determinstic* if the constraints on all outgoing transitions are mutually disjoint, i.e. for each two transitions $(q, \psi_1, \varphi_1, \rho_1, q_1)$, $(q, \psi_2, \varphi_2, \rho_2, q_2) \in \leadsto$ with $q_1 \neq q_2$ we have $(\iota \models \psi_1 \wedge \tau \models \varphi_1) \to \neg(\iota \models \psi_2 \wedge \tau \models \varphi_2)$ for any ι and τ. It is called *reaching-deterministic* if all $q' \in Q$ with $q' \to^* q$ are deterministic. We call A *determinstic* iff all its states are deterministic.

Given a set of clocks C, the set of upper bounded clock constraints $\Phi_\triangleleft(C) \subseteq \Phi(C)$ is defined by the grammar $\phi ::= x_1 \leq c \wedge c \leq x_2$, $\varphi ::= \phi \mid \varphi_1 \wedge \varphi_2 \mid \varphi_1 \vee \varphi_2$, $c \in C$, $x_1, x_2 \in \mathbb{N}_0$. We call a state $q \in Q$ *time bounded* iff the clock constraints on all outgoing transitions are from $\Phi_\triangleleft(C)$. We call A time bounded iff all states from $Q \setminus F$ are time bounded. Now let A be a POTSA and q a state of it s.t. all outgoing transitions impose a finite upper bound on clock c. Let q' be a state from which an accepting state is only reached by visiting q and let c not be reset along the path from q' to q. Then the boundedness of c transitively induces bounds on all transitions between q' and q, including self-loops [15]. For example, clock constraint $c_0 = 7$ at the transition from state q_4 to q_6 in Fig. 1(b) propagates to the transition from q_2 to q_4 and to the self-loops at q_4 and q_2. Consequently, the number of time bounded states can be increased by propagating clock constraints backwards through the automaton, i.e. making the implicit constraints explicit. In [15] we give an algorithm which performs *clock propagation* on POTSAs and yields a language-equivalent POTSA.

Another operation of interest is the *failure state completion* [15] of $\mathcal{A}$. For each reaching-deterministic state in Q, it adds a default transition to a designated failure state 'q_{fail}', i.e. it yields the language equivalent [15] TSA $(Q \dot\cup \{q_{fail}\}, q_s, C, \leadsto, D', F)$ with $D' := D \cup \{(q, q_{fail}) \mid q$ is reaching-deterministic$\}$. Then reaching 'q_{fail}' with sequence r is a sufficient criterion for $r \notin \mathcal{L}(\mathcal{A})$.

3.3 Timed Symbolic Automata as Specification

A *Kripke Structure* is a tuple $K = (AP, S, S_0, R, L)$ with atomic propositions AP, states S, initial states $S_0 \subseteq S$, transition relation $R \subseteq S \times S$, and labelling function $L : S \to 2^{AP}$, AP and S finite. As TSAs are defined using interpretation sequences, we assume that each subset $\ell \subseteq AP$ defines an interpretation ι_ℓ of S. The TSA and the model are then called *compatible*. A run $s_0, s_1, \dots$ of K induces the timed interpretation sequence $((\iota_i, t_i))_{i \in \mathbb{N}_0}$ with $\iota_i = L(s_i)$, $t_i = i$. The set of all timed interpretation sequences induced by the runs of K is denoted by $R(K)$.

Using a TSA $\mathcal{A}$ as a specification on K means relating $R(K)$ to $\mathcal{L}(\mathcal{A})$. To increase precision of the specification, here we always consider an *activation condition* $\nu \in Expr_S$ and an activation mode of *initial*, *invariant*, and *iterative* together with $\mathcal{A}$. We say K satisfies $\mathcal{A}$ initially wrt. ν, denoted by $K \models_{\nu, init} \mathcal{A}$, iff all $((\iota_i, t_i))_{i \in \mathbb{N}_0} \in R(K)$ with $\iota_0 \models \nu$ are in $\mathcal{L}(\mathcal{A})$. It satisfies $\mathcal{A}$ invariantly wrt. ν, denoted by $K \models_{\nu, inv} \mathcal{A}$, iff $\iota_i \models \nu$ implies that the suffix $(\bar\iota_{i+1}, \bar t_{i+1})(\bar\iota_{i+n}, \bar t_{i+n}) \cdots$ is in $\mathcal{L}(\mathcal{A})$. Iterative satisfaction, denoted by $K \models_{\nu, iter} \mathcal{A}$, is special to POTSAs. It is similar to invariant but excludes overlapping activations of $\mathcal{A}$. The motivation to introduce this mode was to ease the understanding of counter-examples. It is easier to uniquely identify where activation takes place if there are no overlapping activations. But this mode has the serious drawback that if it is used for a TSA that actually *has* an overlapping activation, a violation may be shadowed. Checking whether a TSA doesn't have an overlapping activation (it is then called *non-reactivating*) or not is an additional non-trivial task.

Note that by the definition above we choose model steps as time units. In general, other notions of time have to be supported, for instance, the supersteps of Statemate models. In [15], the approach presented here has been extended to support two notions of time by assuming that the passing of time is observable on the model, for instance by a special signal of the model which is raised whenever a superstep is completed. To keep the discussion focused and to adhere to space restrictions, we only consider step time. Adding the more general treatment of time following [15] is actually straightforward.

3.4 Efficient POTSA Model-Checking

Each non-iterative POTSA with step clocks has an equivalent LTL formula [16] in negative normal form, thus LTL model-checking can be applied to decide whether K satisfies $\mathcal{A}$. For all POTSAs, there is an additional approach based on composing in parallel to the model a number of time counters, one for each

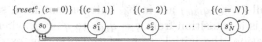

$$\{reset^c,(c=0)\}\quad\{(c=1)\}\qquad\{(c=2)\}\qquad\qquad\{(c=N)\}$$

$$s_0 \longrightarrow s_1^c \longrightarrow s_2^c \dashrightarrow \cdots \dashrightarrow s_N^c$$

Fig. 2. Kripke structure of timer c with upper bound $N+1$

clock, and a kind of transition system view of the TSA, i.e. dismissing the Büchi criterion. This parallel composition is then checked for reachability of certain states or for a small fixed liveness formula. In this section we introduce the parallel composition of K with observers. Section 3.4.3 discusses when to apply which approach.

3.4.1 Timer Extension

In model-checking timed TSA properties, we can't directly employ the sequences from $R(K)$ as the time stamps are unbounded. By [15] it is sufficient for the observer approach to consider finite time counters for each clock of the (not necessarily time bounded) TSA and these bounds are effectively computable. These time counters are transition systems that count model steps until their finite upper bound is reached and that may reset themselves any time and then set a reset flag (cf. Fig. 2). They are composed in parallel to the model. More formally, let c be a clock with upper bound $N+1$, and $S_c = \{s_0^c, \ldots, s_N^c\}$ a set of fresh states wrt. S. The *timer extension* of K for c is $K^c = (AP^c, S^c, S_0^c, R^c, L^c)$ with

- $AP^c = AP \dot{\cup} \{reset^c, (c=0), \ldots, (c=N)\}$, $S^c = S \times S_c$, $S_0^c = S_0 \times \{s_0^c\}$,
- $R^c = \{((s, s_i^c), (s', s_0^c)), ((s, s_N^c), (s', s_N^c)) \mid (s, s') \in R\}$
  $\cup \{((s, s_i^c), (s', s_{i+1}^c)) \mid (s, s') \in R, 0 \le i < N\}$
- $L^c((s, s_i^c)) = L(s) \cup \{reset^c \mid i = 0\} \cup \{(c = i)\}$.

The timer extension K^c is by the same procedure extended to $K^{c,c'}$ for a second clock. We use $K^C := K^{c_1, \ldots, c_n}$ to denote the timer extension of K for all clocks from C. A state $s \in K^C$ canonically defines a clock valuation τ_s as $\tau_s(c) := i$ if $(c = i) \in L(s)$. The clocks reset in s are $\rho_s := \{c \mid reset^c \in L(s)\}$.

3.4.2 Observer Extension

Let $\mathcal{A} = (Q, q_s, C, \rightsquigarrow, D, F)$ be a TSA compatible with K and K^C the timer extension of K. Using s_C to denote the components of states that are introduced by the timer extension, the observer extension of K for activation expression ν and initial activation $\mathcal{A}$ is $K^{\mathcal{A}}/init = (AP^{\mathcal{A}}, S^{\mathcal{A}}, S_0^{\mathcal{A}}, R^{\mathcal{A}}, L^{\mathcal{A}})$ with

- $AP^{\mathcal{A}} = (AP^C \dot{\cup} \{fair, fail\})$, $S^{\mathcal{A}} = S^C \times (Q \dot{\cup} \{q_{idle}\})$,
- $S_0^{\mathcal{A}} = \{(s, s_C, q_s) \mid (s, s_C) \in S_0^C, \iota_{L(s)} \models \nu\}$
  $\cup \{(s, s_C, q_{idle}) \mid (s, s_C) \in S_0^C, \iota_{L(s)} \not\models \nu\}$,
- $((s, s_C, q), (s', s_C', q')) \in R^{\mathcal{A}}$ iff $((s, s_C), (s', s_C')) \in R^C$ and $q = q' = q_{idle}$ or
  - either there is a regular transition $(q, \psi, \varphi, \rho, q') \in \rightsquigarrow$ with
    $\iota_{L(s)} \models \psi$, $\tau(s', s_C') \models \varphi$, and $\rho_s = \rho$
  - or there is a default transition $(q, q') \in D$ and $\rho_s = \emptyset$,
- $L^{\mathcal{A}}((s, s_C, q)) = L^C((s, s_C)) \cup \{fair \mid q \in F\} \cup \{fail \mid q = q_{fail}\}$.

For invariant activation, the observer K^A/inv is activated non-deterministically thus additionally all (s, s_C, q_{idle}) are in S_0^A independent from satisfaction of ν. Furthermore there is a transition from $q = q_{idle}$ to $q' = q_s$ whenever $\iota_{L(s)} \models \nu$. For iterative activation, the initial states of the observer extension are as in $K^A/init$. $K^A/iter$ remains in q_{idle} only if ν is not satisfied and takes the transition to q_s whenever possible. In addition there are transitions back to q_{idle} and q_s from each accepting state with only a self-loop. The transition is to q_s if ν is satisfied and to q_{idle} otherwise. Thus $K^A/iter$ is slightly smaller than K^A/inv. Note that K^A/m, m a mode, restricts the behaviour of the clocks, but not the behaviour of the model. In K^A/m, clocks are only reset if there is a transition in the TSA with a corresponding reset set. K^A/m sets the flag '*fail*' iff the failure state of the TSA is reached and '*fair*' iff the TSA is in an accepting state. We call a state $s^A \in S^A$ a *failure state* iff $fail \in L^A(s^A)$ and *fair state* iff $fair \in L^A(s^A)$.

3.4.3   Putting It All Together

Now we can devise a strategy for deciding whether a given Kripke structure satisfies a failure state completed POTSA using four different standard model-checking procedures of different worst-case complexity, namely reachability checking with safety observer, ACTL model-checking with and without observer, and LTL model-checking. The following Lemma states that the less powerful techniques are helpful for finding violations early and that they are sufficient for deterministic (time bounded) POTSAs.

Lemma 1. *Let A be a POTSA, K a Kripke structure, ν a condition, m a mode.*

1. [15] *If a failure state of K^A/m is reachable, then $K \not\models_{\nu,m} A$. If A is deterministic and time bounded then $K \not\models_{\nu,m} A$ implies reachability of a failure state.*
2. [15] *If $K^A/m \models$ AG AF fair, then $K \models_{\nu,m} A$. If A is deterministic then $K \models_{\nu,m} A$ implies $K^A/m \models$ AG AF fair.*
3. *If A is non-deterministic, then there is no LTL formula λ using only atomic proposition 'fair' s.t. $K^A/m \not\models_{\nu,m} \lambda$ implies $K \not\models_{\nu,m} A$.* $\Diamond$

Proof. (1.3) Assuming such a formula λ, exploit non-determinism in observer to construct a Kripke structure K s.t. K^A/m doesn't satisfy λ but $K \models_{\nu,m} A$. $\square$

Note that Lemma 1.3 implies that there is no known procedure to decide satisfaction of iterative non-deterministic TSAs because within an LTL formula we cannot, as with observer extensions, refer to the own state of activation.

Using that the ACTL formula obtained from an LTL formula in negative normal form by prefixing all modal operators by 'A' implies the LTL formula, we devise the strategy depicted in the following control flow diagram for the verification of POTSA specifications. The idea is to apply the procedure with the best worst-case complexity first to find contradictions early. Only if no errors are unveiled *and* the procedure is too weak for the POTSA, the next expensive procedure is applied. The increasing prevalence of multi-processor or multi-core hosts allows to apply the procedures in parallel and stop all other procedures once a significant result is obtained.

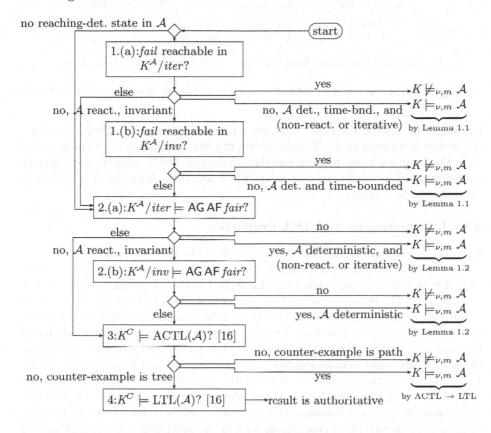

The refinement of steps 1 and 2 into (a) and (b) is a minor optimisation using the expectation that checking $\mathcal{A}$ iteratively is less expensive (cf. 3.4.2). An initial TSA is treated like an interative one, as the time of activation is then uniquely determined to be an initial state.

Note that the time and space resource consumption of certain observer based tasks can be reduced by applying a POTSA version of the decomposition algorithm presented in [9] and conducting the decomposed, smaller tasks in parallel.

4   Efficient LSC Model-Checking

The following transfer of the results from the previous section to the domain of LSCs is effective as most practically used LSCs yield deterministic POTSAs. Furthermore, unbounded liveness requirements typically only occur in early and rather abstract parts of a system's LSC specification and are restricted by bounds in later, more detailed versions thus most LSCs yield time-bounded TSAs.

Section 4.1 briefly recalls the LSC semantics in terms of TSA and relates the TSA classes identified in Sect. 3 to LSCs. For a complete definition of the LSC

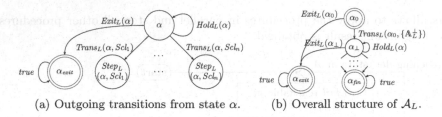

(a) Outgoing transitions from state α.   (b) Overall structure of $\mathcal{A}_L$.

Fig. 3. Structure of the LSC body automaton. Double lined states are in F.

language, its abstract syntax, and the semantics-giving unwinding procedure the reader is referred to [5]. The discussion of LSC verification starts in Sect. 4.2 with the simplest case, namely invariant universal LSCs without pre-chart or assumptions. The additional features of LSCs are then discussed in isolation in the subsequent sections.

4.1   LSC Semantics and TSA Properties

The central concept of the LSC semantics [5] is the notion of the *cut*, i.e. a set of at least one location per instance line (more than one for coregions). The gray line in Fig. 1(a) indicates a cut. Each TSA state corresponds to one cut of the LSC, e.g. the example cut in Fig. 1(a) corresponds to state q_6 in Fig. 1(b). Intuitively, a system satisfies the LSC if for each system run suffix with a prefix in the language of the pre-chart TSA, the rest of the run is in the language of the main-chart TSA. The algorithm of [5] translates the pre- and main-chart of each commitment and assumption LSC of a requirement into separate TSAs. Fig. 3(a) schematically shows a state of the TSA obtained by the unwinding procedure [5]. It has a self-loop awaiting the subsequent LSC elements and one transition for each combination of occurrence and non-occurrence of awaited elements. Violations of cold conditions lead to the accepting state α_{exit}. Fig. 3(b) shows the overall structure of the TSA. The state $\alpha_\perp$ corresponds to the cut with all instance heads and α_{fin} to complete traversal. Fig. 1(b) gives the TSA of the main-chart from Fig. 1(a). (The initial TSA state α_0 is omitted for brevity.)

Following [3], each TSA of an LSC is a POTSA. The timer propagation algorithm of [15] applies directly. In [3], we have introduced a sufficient criterion on LSCs that implies determinism of the corresponding TSAs. The TSAs are deterministic if all conditions and local invariants occur *bonded* in the LSCs. That is, if they are in a simultaneous region with at least one message, timeout, or instance head. Then the evaluation time for the condition is well-defined. This criterion is easily [2] checkable on the abstract syntax of the LSC. The observer automaton construction of [15] as introduced in Sect. 3 applies directly as LSCs share activation modes initial, invariant, and iterative with TSAs.

4.2   LSC Model-Checking

Note that an LSC's strict or tolerant interpretation is mostly orthogonal to the issues discussed below. In the TSA, strictness is expressed by strenghtening the transition annotations. Each expression is additionally conjoined with a term that excludes all messages that are not referred to by the expression. Thus the strict TSA doesn't introduce new non-determinism and as it only considers messages, non-determism is not resolved except for few pathological cases. Consequently we needn't treat the interpretation explicitly below.

4.2.1 Universal, No Pre-chart or Assumption

In the easiest case, we only have to consider the TSA $\mathcal{A}$ of the main-chart and an activation condition. Then the algorithm from Sect. 3.4.3 applies directly.

4.2.2 Pre-chart

For the pre-chart of an LSC, a separate TSA is constructed. The slightly different algorithm adjusts transitions to the special interpretaton of pre-charts which don't have a notion of violation. Using the ACTL/LTL way there are two options for checking an LSC with pre-chart. Let φ_{pc} and φ_L be the LTL formulae corresponding to the pre-chart and the *whole* LSC, i.e. pre- and main-chart together. Following [17], we can check $G(\varphi_{pc} \to \varphi_L)$. This formula tends to grow large since the pre-chart part occurs twice, even if the more compact formulae also presented in [17] is usable.

As the semantics of the pre-chart is indication of complete traversal of its scenario, the Büchi criterion is actually not needed. Finite automaton acceptance is sufficient. This can be exploited by composing in parallel with the observer extension of a model a (non-deterministically activating) observer for the pre-chart that drives an additional proposition 'pc' which holds iff the pre-chart has just been observed. By changing the main-chart observer such that its activation expression is 'pc' the algorithm from Sect. 3.4.3 still applies directly.

If the observer way is too weak, then $G(pc \to \varphi_{mc})$ (or the ACTL correspondence) is checked in steps 3 and 4; φ_{mc} being the main-chart's LTL formula.

4.2.3 Assumptions

The semantics of LSC assumptions is standard. A system satisfies a universal LSC with assumptions iff all runs satisfying all assumptions also satisfy the commitment. Thus, iff

$$(G(\varphi_{a_1} \wedge \cdots \wedge \varphi_{a_m})) \to (G(pc \to \varphi_{mc})), \tag{1}$$

with $\varphi_{a_1}, \ldots, \varphi_{a_m}$ the LTL formulae for the assumptions, 'pc' the pre-chart observer from Sect. 4.2.2, and φ_{mc} the main-chart's LTL formula.

To avoid representing the assumption part as (again large) formulae, we can start with properties which are stronger than (1), i.e. that imply (1), but are easier to check. On the downside, obtaining a counter-example is then no longer *directly* significant as the counter-example may be a false negative. It has to be checked not to be spurious, for example by simulation.

An approach stronger than (1) is to consider the tableau of the parallel composition of all assumptions as an additional observer, i.e. parallel composed to the observer extension. The formula to check is then $(AG\,AF\,afair) \to (AG\,AF\,fair)$ (2)

where '*afair*' holds iff the tableau is in an accepting state. If (2) passes and if the LSC and all assumptions are bonded, then the system satisfies the LSC. A failure may be a false negative.

An approach stronger than (2) is to check for reachability of a state with ¬*afail* ∧ *fail* in the parallel composition of K^A with one iteratively activated observer automaton per assumption, i.e. not the tableaux. If such a state isn't reachable and if the LSC and all assumptions are bonded and time-bounded and no assumption is invariant, then the system satisfies the LSC.

With these three (non exhaustive) options, the algorithm from Sect. 4.2.1 can be extended as follows. Pragmatically we don't consider *all* of the possible combinations with procedures for the commitment. In step 1, only the first option is used for assumptions in order to obtain a reachability property. In each substep of 2, the first option for assumptions can be tried first, followed by the second option from above. In steps 3 and 4, all three options can be tried subsequently, trading size of the formula for size of the model.

Note that a non-bonded assumption is typically easily violated by "clever choice" of transitions in the TSA. Therefore non-bonded assumptions in general are of limited use as an easily violated assumption excludes too many system runs from consideration; the requirement may even be trivially satisfied if all system runs are excluded. As a consequence, all LSCs used in assumption/guarantee style verification should be bonded.

4.2.4   Existential LSCs

Recall from Sect. 2 that an existential LSC is satisfied by a system iff there is at least one system run that adheres to the LSC. Using CTL*, we obtain an equivalent formula by prefixing the LTL formula with the existential quantifiers 'E' or 'EF' [3].

But the existential mode is different from the universal mode in that one wants to obtain a *witness* if the formula is satisfied. That is, similar to pre-charts, the Büchi criterion isn't used and thus the ACTL/LTL way is practically not relevant. Furthermore, in practice one is typically interested in an example system run that traverses the LSC *completely* [18] instead of taking a legal exit on a cold condition. To achieve all this, the states of the main-chart TSA are turned into non-accepting states except for the state corresponding to the final cut. If the LSC has a pre-chart, the main-chart TSA is again activated by the pre-chart observer '*pc*' as discussed in Sect. 4.2.2. Verifying the existential LSC is then equivalent to reachability of the remaining unique accepting state under all given assumptions.

5   Figures, Please

Table 2 supports our claims with exemplary experimental results. It lists pure model-checking time, i.e. without constructing and loading the transition relation BDD, and without counter-example post processing, for all techniques discussed in Sect. 4 (VIS 2.0 [Brayton et al.], Intel Xeon 3.06GHz, 4GByte). The

Table 2. Experimental Results. Model-checking time in seconds.

	rch/iter	rch/inv	AGAF/iter	AGAF/inv	ACTL	LTL
Fig.1/tb	36.3s/✗*	48.6s/✗	303.4s/✗	294.9s/✗	755.2s/✗	–
Fig.1/tb	37.3s/✔*	45.0s/✔	41.0s/✔	31.5s/✔	698.8s/✔	–
Fig.1	72.7s/✔	82.2s/✔	81.8s/✔*	57.4s/✔	468.1s/✔	–
Fig.1/as	359.3s/✔	49.2s/✔	47.2s/✔*	29.0s/✔	757.7s/✔	–
Fig.1/nd	56.9s/✔	48.7s/✔	134.2s/✗	128.4s/✗	–	–
[9]/2	31.0s/✔	44.5s/✔	96.3s/✔*	37.5s/✔	258.1s/✔	–
[9]/3	43.6s/✔	121.6s/✔	60.7s/✔*	87.5s/✔	–	–

(✔= passed, ✗= failed, – = terminated after 1h, * = first significant result.)

pre-chart is always an observer and the tableau is used for assumptions. The implementation is taken from [5] and [15]. To isolate the effects under discussion, all experiments use a model that first solves a puzzle to provide some complexity and then adds one or two paths relevant for the LSC.

All experiments use a model which first solves a puzzle to provide some complexity and then adds one or two paths relevant for the LSC.

The first (singleton) group is a time bounded version of the LSC from Fig. 1 on a model not satisfying it due to a condition violation. From the table we can see that the reachability-based approach is significantly faster than the others.

The second group uses a model satisfying the LSC. Its first row is the LSC from Fig. 1, 'as' is a variant with an assumption, and 'nd' is a non-deterministic variant where the condition *Operational* is moved downwards such that it is no longer bonded. In this group, the table indicates that the reachability approach is not always faster, in particular if the property actually holds. In case 'nd' we remain inconclusive whether the system satisfies the LSC or not. The '✔' results of the reachability way only indicate that there is no safety violation. The following two '✗' results only indicate that it's possible to avoid a fair state.

The last group is the example from [9], an untimed but highly concurrent LSC with extraordinary large corresponding formulae. It uses only 6 (9) messages to require that 2 (3) agents are started concurrently, then work concurrently, and then report back concurrently. This LSC is bonded, but not time bounded. From the table we can see that the observer approach allows to establish the property in the given amount of time and space while the formula doesn't.

Noticeable in the table is that the LTL way is always terminated prematurely, even if the preceding puzzle is removed. If the model has only a single trace and the LSC is changed s.t. it comprises no timing requirements and no concurrency, the task completes within ~1h, thus the LTL way seems rather impractical.

6   Conclusion

Although LSC model-checking is basically solved as each LSC has an equivalent temporal logic formula, in practice direct model-checking of the formula is prohibitively expensive due to its size. Our results indicate that full model-checking power is only necessary for non-bonded LSCs which occur seldom in practice. In contrast, bonded, time-bounded LSCs are as easy as a reachability problem. To the practically most relevant class of bonded, non-time-bounded LSCs, an approach *in between* both techniques applies that uses an observer automaton and a small fixed liveness formula. Experimental data indicates that it's beneficial to apply the reachability approach even to non-time-bounded LSCs as contradictions are found faster.

Although our criteria classify most practically occurring LSCs correctly, it is of academic interest to have an algorithm *deciding* time boundedness. It would be a minor improvement to identify more states as deterministic by more sophisticated procedures.

References

1. Damm, W., Harel, D.: LSCs: Breathing Life into Message Sequence Charts. Formal Methods in System Design **19** (2001) 45–80
2. Westphal, B., Toben, T.: The good, the bad and the ugly: Well-formedness of Live Sequence Charts. In Baresi, L., Heckel, R., eds.: Proc. FASE 2006. Volume 3922 of LNCS. (2006) 230–246
3. Toben, T., Westphal, B.: On the expressive power of LSCs. In Wiedermann, J., et al., eds.: Proc. SOFSEM 2006. Volume 2., Inst. of CS, AS, Prague (2006) 33–43
4. Thomas, W.: Automata on infinite objects. In van Leeuwen, J., ed.: Handbook of theor. comp. sc. (vol. B): Formal Models And Semantics. MIT (1990) 133–191
5. Klose, J.: Live Sequence Charts: A Graphical Formalism for the Specification of Communication Behavior. PhD thesis, C. v. O. Universität Oldenburg (2003)
6. Bohn, J., Damm, W., Wittke, H., Klose, J., Moik, A.: Modelling and validating train system applications using statemate and live sequence charts. In: Proc. IDPT 2002, Society for Design and Process Science (2002)
7. Schinz, I., Toben, T., Mrugalla, C., Westphal, B.: The Rhapsody UML Verification Environment. In Cuellar, J.R., Liu, Z., eds.: Proc. SEFM 2004. (2004) 174–183
8. Westphal, B.: LSC verification for UML models with unbounded creation and destruction. In Byron Cook, Scott Stoller, W.V., ed.: Proc. SoftMC 2005. Volume 144:3 of ENTCS., Elsevier B.V. (2005) 133–145
9. Toben, T., Westphal, B.: Concurrent LSC verification. In Lazic, R., ed.: Proc. AVoCS 2005. Volume 145 of ENTCS., Elsevier B. V. (2006) 95–111
10. Bunker, A., Gopalakrishnan, G., Slink, K.: Live sequence charts applied to hardware requirements specification and verification: A VCI bus interface model. Software Tools for Technology Transfer **7** (2004) 341–350
11. Harel, D., Kugler, H., Marelly, R., Pnueli, A.: Smart play-out of behvioral requirements. In: Proc. FMCAD'02. (2002) 378–398
12. Harel, D., Marelly, R.: Come, Let's Play. Springer (2003)
13. Sun, J., Dong, J.S.: Model checking Live Sequence Charts. In: ICECCS, IEEE Computer Society (2005) 529–538
14. Grégoire, B.: Automata oriented program verification. Master's thesis, Facultés Universitaires Notre-Dame de la Paix, Namur (2002)
15. Wittke, H.: A Framework for Specification Verification for Complex Embedded Systems. PhD thesis, C. v. O. Universität Oldenburg (2005)

16. Schlör, R.C.: Symbolic Timing Diagrams: A Visual Formalism for Model Verification. PhD thesis, C. v. O. Universität Oldenburg (2000)
17. Kugler, H., et al.: Temporal logic for scenario-based specifications. In Halbwachs, N., Zuck, L.D., eds.: Proc. TACAS 2005. Volume 3440 of LNCS. (2005)
18. Brill, M., et al.: Formal verification of LSCs in the development process. In Ehrig, H., et al., eds.: SoftSpez. Number 3147 in LNCS. Springer-Verlag (2004) 494–516

Symmetry Reduction for Probabilistic Model Checking*

Marta Kwiatkowska, Gethin Norman, and David Parker

School of Computer Science, University of Birmingham,
Birmingham B15 2TT, United Kingdom
{mzk, gxn, dxp}@cs.bham.ac.uk

Abstract. We present an approach for applying symmetry reduction
techniques to probabilistic model checking, a formal verification method
for the quantitative analysis of systems with stochastic characteristics.
We target systems with a set of non-trivial, but interchangeable, components such as those which commonly arise in randomised distributed
algorithms or probabilistic communication protocols. We show, for three
types of probabilistic models, that symmetry reduction, similarly to the
non-probabilistic case, allows verification to instead be performed on a
bisimilar quotient model which may be up to factorially smaller. We
then propose an efficient algorithm for the construction of the quotient
model using a symbolic implementation based on multi-terminal binary
decision diagrams (MTBDDs) and, using four large case studies, demonstrate that this approach offers not only a dramatic increase in the size
of probabilistic model which can be quantitatively analysed but also a
significant decrease in the corresponding run-times.

1 Introduction

Probabilistic model checking is a formal verification technique for the analysis
of systems which exhibit stochastic behaviour. It has been successfully applied
to case studies from a wide range of application domains, including randomised
distributed algorithms, communication and security protocols, dynamic power
management schemes and biological systems. The key strength of the technique
is the ability to automatically compute precise quantitative results based on an
exhaustive analysis of a formal model. This allows reasoning about, for example,
"the worst-case probability of system failure within T seconds" or "the minimum
expected power consumption over all possible schedulings".

As with conventional model checking, the principal limiting factor with such
techniques is the size of the models to be analysed. Although the development
of symbolic implementations, which use binary decision diagrams (BDDs) and
related data structures, have provided a significant increase in the applicability
of the techniques, model size remains a major issue. In this paper we employ

---

* Supported in part by EPSRC grants GR/S11107 and GR/S46727 and Microsoft
Research Cambridge contract MRL 2005-44.

T. Ball and R.B. Jones (Eds.): CAV 2006, LNCS 4144, pp. 234–248, 2006.

symmetry reduction, a way of exploiting the presence of replication in a model which has yielded considerable success in non-probabilistic verification. In fact, this is particularly appealing in the context of probabilistic model checking since one of its more common, and indeed promising, applications is for the analysis of randomised distributed algorithms. These algorithms, which use electronic coin-flipping or random number generation, are increasingly used to provide elegant and efficient *symmetric* solutions to distributed coordination problems, as evidenced by the fact that they represent crucial components of many modern communication protocols such as Firewire, Bluetooth and Zeroconf.

We consider the case of *component symmetry*, in which any pair from a set of symmetric components in a model can be exchanged with no effect on the overall behaviour. We show that the key ideas of symmetry reduction in this case, namely that verification of a model can instead be performed on a bisimilar quotient model which is up to factorially smaller, carry across with relative ease to the probabilistic verification of three types of models: discrete-time Markov chains, continuous-time Markov chains and Markov decision processes.

We then propose an efficient algorithm for the construction of these quotient models which builds on the existing efficient symbolic implementations of probabilistic model checking in the tool PRISM [15, 24], based on the MTBDD (multi-terminal BDD) data structure [9, 3]. In doing so, we use ideas from the *dynamic symmetry reduction* technique of Emerson and Wahl [13]. Once the quotient model has been constructed, it can be analysed with existing algorithms and their implementations. Using experimental results from four large case studies, we show that our approach results in significant increases in both the size of models which can be verified and the speed with which this can be performed.

2 Background

2.1 Symmetry Reduction

Symmetry reduction is a way of exploiting the occurrence of replication in a model. Consider a transition system $M = (S, R)$ comprising a (finite) set S of states and a transition relation $R \subseteq S \times S$. A permutation $\pi : S \to S$ on the state space is called an *automorphism* when it preserves the transition relation R, i.e. if $(s, s') \in R$, then $(\pi(s), \pi(s')) \in R$. Given a group G of such automorphisms under function composition, there is a corresponding equivalence relation θ on the set of states S where $(s, s') \in \theta$ if there is a permutation in G mapping s to s', i.e. if s and s' are symmetric. This relation θ is known as the *orbit relation* and its equivalence classes are called *orbits*.

If we then choose a set $\overline{S}$ containing a unique representative state for each equivalence class, we can define a function $rep : S \to \overline{S}$ which selects the corresponding unique representative $rep(s) \in \overline{S}$ for each state $s \in S$ and use this to induce a new transition relation $\overline{R} = \{(rep(s), rep(s')) \mid (s, s') \in R\}$. Since all permutations in G preserve the transition relation R, this *quotient transition system* $(\overline{S}, \overline{R})$ is bisimilar to the original transition system (S, R).

In many cases, this means that an analysis of the full system can instead be performed on the (smaller) quotient model. For example, if the states of the transition system (S, R) are labelled with atomic propositions from some set AP and we wish to model check a formula in the temporal logic CTL, then provided the atomic propositions in AP are preserved by the orbit relation, model checking can safely be carried out on the reduced model [11, 8].

In this paper, we consider *component symmetry* in which a model contains N symmetric components, any pair of which can be exchanged without any effect on the behaviour of the system. For a (global) state s of the model, we denote the local states of the N components by $s_1, \ldots, s_N$, respectively. A permutation π of S operates by mapping s to s' in which the values $s_1, \ldots, s_N$ are themselves permuted. Applying symmetry reduction to such a model where each of the N symmetric components has M local states provides, in the best case, a reduction in state space size from M^N to $\binom{M+N-1}{N}$, which tends towards $N!$ as M increases.

In the case of component symmetry, one way to define a unique representative for each set of symmetric states is to select the lexicographically least (given some ordering of the local states). This can be obtained by sorting the elements of the state. An alternative is to count the number of processes which are in each possible local state. Consider the case of 4 symmetric processes each with two local states A and B (where $A < B$). The states (A, B, A, A) and (A, A, B, A) are equivalent. Using the two schemes described above, they would both be mapped to (A, A, A, B) and $(A = 3, B = 1)$, respectively.

2.2 Symmetry Reduction for Symbolic Model Checking

The practicalities of exploiting symmetry reduction in the context of model checking have been studied at some length in the literature. Given a method of computing the representative $rep(s)$ for any state s it is possible, as shown by Ip and Dill [17], to compute the quotient transition system directly with a simple modification of a conventional, explicit state-space exploration algorithm: at every step of the exploration, each newly discovered state is immediately converted to its unique representative.

Clearly it would be desirable to combine *symbolic* model checking techniques, which have proven very successful for improving the efficiency of model checking, with symmetry reduction. Early results were discouraging: in [8], it was proved that for common types of symmetry, including component symmetry, the size of the BDD representing the orbit relation θ is exponential in either the number N of symmetric processes or the number M of local states that each can occupy. Progress was made in this area with several ways of reducing BDD sizes by, for example, allowing multiple representatives for each state [8], or attempting an under-approximation of reachability (aimed principally at falsification rather than verification) [5].

Recently, a promising approach known as *dynamic symmetry reduction* was proposed by Emerson and Wahl [13]. Their technique bypasses the construction of the orbit relation by only computing representatives for the set of states that are found during the process of model exploration (which, depending on the property, may not even be the set of all reachable states). This is achieved by sorting the components of all the currently explored states at each step. This procedure works using a bubble sort algorithm, applied directly to a BDD representation of the state set.

An alternative approach to symmetry reduction for systems exhibiting component symmetry, which is amenable to both explicit and symbolic model checking techniques, is *counter abstraction* [23] or *generic representatives* [12]. This is based on the idea of counting the number of processes in each local state, a process which in many cases can be carried out with a conversion of the model in the context of the high-level formalism in which it is described. Counter abstraction has been shown to perform particularly well, especially in situations where there are a large number of processes with a relatively small number of local states. For larger local state spaces, however, the exponential blow-up in variables required makes it very inefficient.

It should be noted that the work described above represents only a fraction of the available literature on symmetry reduction, the focus being on techniques for component symmetry and those targeted at a symbolic implementation.

2.3 Probabilistic Model Checking

Probabilistic model checking is an extension of model checking that is applied to transition systems augmented with information about the likelihood that each transition will occur. For a model with set of states S, its behaviour is specified not by a transition relation on S but a *transition function*. We most commonly deal with three types of probabilistic model: discrete-time Markov chains (DTMCs), continuous-time Markov chains (CTMCs) and Markov decision processes (MDPs). See e.g. [25] for an overview.

DTMCs are defined by a function $P : S \times S \to [0,1]$ satisfying $\sum_{s' \in S} P(s, s') = 1$ for each $s \in S$. This function, known as the *transition probability matrix*, gives the probability $P(s, s')$ of making a transition from each state s to any other state s'. DTMCs are typically used to represent synchronous systems with a discrete model of time. CTMCs, on the other hand, are defined by a *transition rate matrix* $R : S \times S \to \mathbb{R}_{\geq 0}$ giving the rate $R(s, s')$ at which transitions between state pairs (s, s') occur. This rate is interpreted as the parameter of a negative exponential distribution, resulting in a dense model of time. Lastly, MDPs are defined by a function $Steps : S \to 2^{Dist(S)}$ mapping each state s to a finite, non-empty set $Steps(s)$ of probability distributions over the state space S. Intuitively, this is interpreted as a nondeterministic choice between several probabilistic behaviours, and is thus useful for example to represent the asynchronous parallel composition of several stochastic processes.

Probabilistic model checking is applied to DTMCs, CTMCs and MDPs by formulating properties in the temporal logics PCTL and CSL which are probabilistic extensions of the logic CTL. This allows reasoning about, for example, "the probability of the algorithm terminating in error", "the probability that k packets are successfully transmitted within t seconds" or "the expected number of rounds for the protocol to complete". Because these are quantitative in nature, probabilistic model checking algorithms must perform numerical computation (typically iterative solution of linear equation systems or linear optimisation problems) in addition to the usual reachability-based algorithms.

Probabilistic model checking has been successfully applied to a large number of case studies from a wide range of application domains; see for example [20, 24]. In this paper, we have implemented our techniques using the open-source probabilistic model checker PRISM [15, 24].

2.4   Symbolic Techniques for Probabilistic Model Checking

Symbolic model checking techniques, i.e. those using BDDs or similar data structures have been successfully adapted to the field of probabilistic model checking. As in the non-probabilistic case, the key idea is that, by exploiting high-level structure and regularity in a model, it is possible to derive a very compact representation which can be efficiently manipulated. A popular data structure for this purpose, and the one used in the probabilistic model checker PRISM upon which our implementation is based, is multi-terminal BDDs (MTBDDs) [9, 3].

An MTBDD M is a directed acyclic graph, the nodes of which are labelled with Boolean variables from some set $\underline{x} = \{x_1, \ldots, x_n\}$. The MTBDD represents a real-valued function $f_M(x_1, \ldots, x_n) : \{0,1\}^n \to \mathbb{R}$. A BDD is thus a special case of an MTBDD which only maps to the two values 0 and 1. Given an encoding of the state space S of a probabilistic model into n Boolean variables, and two disjoint sets of n such variables $\underline{x} = \{x_1, \ldots, x_n\}$ and $\underline{y} = \{y_1, \ldots, y_n\}$, the transition probability/rate matrix of a DTMC or a CTMC can be represented as an MTBDD over these $2n$ variables. An MDP, although defined as a mapping to sets of probability distributions, can also be represented as a non-square $k \cdot |S| \times |S|$ matrix (where there are $k = \max_{s \in S} |Steps(s)|$ rows corresponding to each state) and represented in similar fashion [14].

Given a high-level description of a probabilistic model in some formalism, e.g. a stochastic process algebra or, as in our case, the PRISM modelling language, it is possible to construct the corresponding MTBDD directly, in a compositional fashion [14], often resulting in a very compact representation. Subsequently, we usually implement probabilistic model checking in one of two ways: (a) entirely with MTBDDs; or (b) using a combination of MTBDDs and explicit data structures such as sparse matrices and arrays [19]. In the PRISM tool, these are referred to as the "MTBDD" and "hybrid" engines, respectively. The former, where applicable, has successfully been applied to huge probabilistic models (see e.g. [21]) but this is highly dependent on model regularity and in many cases, where irregularities introduced during numerical solution become a factor, has infeasible time and/or memory usage. The "hybrid" approach is usually faster but, due to storage requirements linear in the size of the state space, is generally limited to models of approximately 10^7–10^8 states. It is frequently the case that compact symbolic representations can be constructed for extremely large probabilistic models, but that verification, in particular via numerical computation, of these models is prohibitively expensive, both in terms of time and space.

3   Symmetry Reduction for Probabilistic Model Checking

The notion of symmetry in DTMCs, CTMCs and MDPs can be formulated analogously to the non-probabilistic case, described in Section 2.1. We consider permutations $\pi : S \rightarrow S$ on the state space which preserve the transition function. For DTMCs, we require that $P(\pi(s), \pi(s')) = P(s, s')$ for all $s, s' \in S$. Similarly, for CTMCs, we need $R(\pi(s), \pi(s')) = R(s, s')$ for all $s, s' \in S$. In the case of MDPs, for each $s \in S$ and each distribution $\mu \in Steps(s)$, there must be a distribution $\mu' \in Steps(\pi(s))$ such that $\mu'(\pi(s')) = \mu(s')$ for all $s' \in S$.

As before, we consider a group G of such permutations on S and the corresponding orbit relation θ. From the equivalence classes of the latter we define a reduced state space $\overline{S}$ containing a unique representative for each orbit and a function $rep : S \rightarrow \overline{S}$ which computes the representative for each state. Construction of the quotient model can then be carried out as follows. For a DTMC (S, P), we build $(\overline{S}, \overline{P})$ where for each pair of states $\overline{s}, \overline{s}' \in \overline{S}$:

$$\overline{P}(\overline{s}, \overline{s}') = \sum_{\{s' \in S \mid rep(s') = \overline{s}'\}} P(\overline{s}, s') . \tag{1}$$

For a CTMC (S, R), the quotient model is $(\overline{S}, \overline{R})$ where for $\overline{s}, \overline{s}' \in \overline{S}$:

$$\overline{R}(\overline{s}, \overline{s}') = \sum_{\{s' \in S \mid rep(s') = \overline{s}'\}} R(\overline{s}, s') . \tag{2}$$

Finally, for an MDP $(S, Steps)$, the quotient model is $(\overline{S}, \overline{Steps})$ where if $\overline{s} \in \overline{S}$, then $\overline{Steps}(\overline{s})$ contains a distribution $\overline{\mu}$ if and only if there exists $\mu \in Steps(\overline{s})$ such that for each $\overline{s}' \in \overline{S}$:

$$\overline{\mu}(\overline{s}') = \sum_{\{s' \in S \mid rep(s') = \overline{s}'\}} \mu(s') . \tag{3}$$

Constructed in such a way, the quotient model in each of the three cases can easily be shown to be equivalent to the original unreduced model in the context of (strong) probabilistic bisimulation, which is well understood for DTMCs [22], CTMCs [6] and MDPs [26]. Furthermore, from results in [2, 4, 26], we can hence deduce that for formulas in the temporal logics PCTL (for DTMCs or MDPs) and CSL (for CTMCs) using a set of atomic propositions AP which is preserved by symmetry, probabilistic model checking can be performed equivalently on the quotient model rather than the original, unreduced model. Additionally, quantitative analysis of cost- and reward-based specifications are similarly preserved.

3.1   Example

We now consider a simple illustrative example: an MDP representing two symmetric processes with three states (0, 1 and 2) which interact as follows. Initially, both are in state 0. First, one moves randomly to state 1 or 2 (each with probability 0.5). The other then does likewise. If, in the second step, state 2 is chosen and a process is already in state 2, the one which moved first moves to state 1.

Figure 1(a) shows the MDP. States are denoted by circles labelled ij, where i and j represent the state of process 1 and 2, respectively. Each of the possible probability distributions from a state is denoted by a set of probability-labelled transitions (arrows) grouped by an arc. Figure 1(b) gives the function rep which maps each state from the MDP to a unique symmetric representative and Figure 1(c) shows the resulting quotient model over the reduced state space.

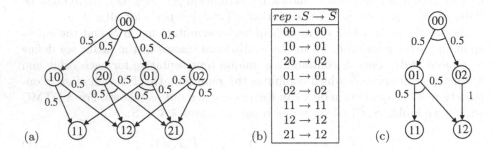

Fig. 1. A simple example: (a) full MDP (b) state representatives (c) quotient MDP

4   A Symbolic Implementation

We now consider in more detail how to exploit symmetry reduction for probabilistic model checking. More precisely, we consider the problem of constructing, for a DTMC, CTMC or MDP exhibiting component symmetry, the corresponding quotient model upon which probabilistic model checking can instead be performed. Although the method of Ip and Dill [17] can readily be adapted for this purpose, it is only applicable only to the construction of models in an explicit fashion. As stated earlier, we wish to instead build upon the efficient *symbolic* model checking framework that already exists.

One way that this could be achieved is to use counter abstraction, which works by applying symmetry reduction at a higher level: on the language description of the model. Preliminary results for the application of such techniques to probabilistic model checking can be found in [10]. An advantage of this is that existing efficient methods for the construction of a symbolic model can be used unmodified; however it is known, from applications of this to non-probabilistic model checking, that performance is typically poor for examples where symmetric processes have many local states.

Previous experience with symbolic methods for probabilistic model checking suggests that the most desirable way of constructing an MTBDD representing the quotient model would be to do so directly from a high-level model description and in a compositional manner. Unfortunately, there is no obvious way of achieving this due to the implicit introduction, during symmetry reduction, of a large number of inter-component dependencies. Hence, our approach proceeds by first building a symbolic representation for the full model and then reducing it to the quotient model. Working in an explicit context, this would negate any benefit of symmetry reduction, since constructing and storing the model itself represents the bottleneck. In a symbolic setting, though, this is not so: it is very often the case that it is possible to build the MTBDD representing extremely large models but that model checking cannot be carried out, either in a fully symbolic fashion (because irregularity in the computation causes a blow-up in MTBDD sizes) or with the use of explicit data structures (because of excessive memory requirements). It is in such cases that symmetry reduction has the potential to be very useful. In Section 5 we will demonstrate exactly this on a number of large case studies.

4.1   The Algorithm

We now present our algorithm for converting a probabilistic model with N symmetric components to its reduced quotient form which is applicable to all three model types: DTMCs, CTMCs and MDPs. In the following we shall refer to the *transition matrix*, which corresponds to P, R and *Steps*, respectively, for the three models. As described in Section 2.4, for an MDP, *Steps* can be thought of as non-square matrix where there are multiple rows corresponding to each state.

Our algorithm proceeds in three steps. Firstly, we identify the quotient state space: the set $\overline{S}$. Secondly, every row in the transition matrix corresponding to states not in $\overline{S}$ is removed (replaced with a row of zeros). Thirdly, we modify each of the remaining rows, moving entries in column s' to column $rep(s')$. More precisely, since a row may contain multiple non-zero entries which move to the same column, we replace each element of row s of the matrix with the sum of the values from columns s' for which $s = rep(s')$. Note that this corresponds precisely to our three definitions of the quotient model in Section 3.

The full algorithm, expressed in terms of the operations on BDDs and MTBDDs, is shown in Figure 2. The inputs to the algorithm are a BDD reach over set of variables $\underline{x}$ representing the set of reachable states S and an MTBDD trans over the variable sets $\underline{x}$ and $\underline{y}$ representing the transition matrix (see Section 2.4). Since this MTBDD is constructed in a compositional fashion, the variable sets $\underline{x}$ and $\underline{y}$ are conveniently partitioned into subsets $\underline{x}_i$ and $\underline{y}_i$ for $1 \leq i \leq N$, one for each of the N symmetric processes. We can illustrate this as follows. Let us assume that the state space S of the model is simply the product of the (identical) local state spaces $\hat{S}$ of each of the N symmetric components, i.e. $S = \hat{S}^N$. We have both an encoding $\alpha : S \to \{0,1\}^n$ of the whole state space S into n Boolean variables and an encoding $\hat{\alpha} : \hat{S} \to \{0,1\}^{n/N}$ of the local state space $\hat{S}$ into Boolean variables. Consider for example an MTBDD M over variables $\underline{x} = \{x_1, \ldots, x_n\}$. This MTBDD represents a real-valued function over the state space S which, for a state $s = (s_1, \ldots, s_N)$ in S, can be defined either as $f_M(\alpha(s))$ or, equivalently, $f_M(\hat{\alpha}(s_1), \ldots, \hat{\alpha}(s_N))$.

The output of the algorithm is a modified copy of the trans MTBDD representing the quotient transition matrix. This MTBDD is also over the variable sets $\underline{x}$ and $\underline{y}$, meaning that we retain the same encoding of the state space and

---

// *Step 1: Identify quotient state space, i.e. all representative states*
1. repr := reach
2. **for** ($i := 1..N - 1$)
3. sorted_i := VARIABLESLESSTHANEQUALS($\underline{y}_i$, $\underline{y}_{i+1}$) $\wedge$ reach
4.   repr := repr $\wedge$ sorted_i

// *Step 2: Remove rows corresponding to non-representative states*
5. trans := APPLY($\times$, trans, SWAPVARIABLES(repr, $\underline{y}$, $\underline{x}$))

// *Step 3: Construct matrix for quotient model via bubble sort*
6. **for** ($i := N, \ldots, 2$)
7.   trans_ prev := trans
8.   **for** ($j := 1, \ldots, i-1$)
9.   good := APPLY($\times$, trans, sorted_j)
10.   bad := APPLY($\times$, trans, $\neg \text{sorted}_j$)
11.   fixed := SWAPVARIABLES(bad, y_j, y_{j+1})
12.   trans := APPLY($+$, good, fixed)
13.   **if** (trans = trans_prev) **return** trans
14. **return** trans

Fig. 2. MTBDD-based algorithm for computing the quotient model

remove (set to zero) all entries of rows and columns of the matrix corresponding to states not in $\overline{S}$, rather than select a new encoding for the set $\overline{S}$. This is important in order to preserve the regularity of the original data structure.

In the first step of the algorithm (lines 1-4) we compute the BDD repr representing the set $\overline{S}$. This is in fact relatively easy. Since our unique representative function *rep* simply sorts the values of symmetric components, $\overline{S}$ is the subset of S containing states s in which $s_1 \leq s_2 \leq \cdots \leq s_N$. Hence symm is formed from the conjunction of reach and $N-1$ BDDs, the ith of which, denoted sorted_i, encodes all states in which $s_i \leq s_{i+1}$. Given the BDD variable sets $\underline{y}_i$ and $\underline{y}_{i+1}$, encoding the ith and $(i+1)$th processes, the latter are small (linear in the size of $\underline{y}_i$) and easy to construct (in the CUDD library which we use, there is a built-in function to do so).

The second step of the algorithm (line 5) requires a single application of the APPLY function, a fundamental MTBDD operation which performs a pointwise application of a binary function on two MTBDDs. We use a pointwise multiplication of the BDD (0-1 valued MTBDD) repr and MTBDD trans. Since we are removing rows from the matrix, not columns, we first swap the variables in repr from $\underline{y}$ to $\underline{x}$.

The third and most important step (lines 6-14) permutes and sums matrix elements to compute the MTBDD for the quotient matrix. Essentially, each element in column s of the matrix needs to move to column s' where the latter can be determined by sorting the components $(s_1, \ldots, s_N)$ of s into ascending numerical order. We do this using a standard bubble sort algorithm comprising $N-1$ passes, the ith of which compares s_j and s_{j+1} for all $j < i$ and swaps the

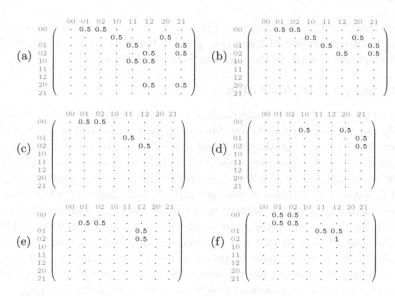

Fig. 3. Executing the algorithm from Figure 2 on the MDP from Figure 1(a): (a) trans (initially) (b) trans (after step 2) (c) good (d) bad (e) fixed (f) trans (finally)

two values if $s_j > s_{j+1}$. The novelty is that we perform this sorting process for all elements of each row simultaneously and, furthermore, for all rows simultaneously. This concurrent approach to algorithm design is typical of symbolic, i.e. BDD-based, implementations.

In terms of MTBDDs, each iteration of bubble sort, as described above, is achieved as follows. We partition the current copy of the matrix trans into two parts, good and bad, the latter containing all columns of the matrix for which in the column index s, $s_j > s_{j+1}$. We can then use the primitive MTBDD operation SWAPVARIABLES and the variable sets y_j and y_{j+1} to convert bad to an equivalent MTBDD fixed in which s_j and s_{j+1} have been swapped for all column indices. Summing (using APPLY) the MTBDDs good and fixed gives the new version of trans for this iteration.

A feature of bubble sort is that, if no swaps are performed in an entire outer iteration, then we can deduce that the sort has been completed early. Thanks to the canonicity property of MTBDDs, it is trivial to compare two MTBDDs for equality. Hence, for each outer iteration of our algorithm, we check whether the MTBDD trans has been modified (lines 7 and 13), terminating early if not.

4.2   Example

We now return to our example of Section 3.1 (Figure 1). Figure 3 illustrates the execution of the algorithm from Figure 2 on the MDP from Figure 1(a). Figure 3(a) shows the matrix trans for the full MDP. Figure 3(b) shows trans after step 2 (line 5 of Figure 2). Since this example comprises just two processes, we require only a single iteration of bubble sort. The matrices good, bad and fixed from this iteration are shown in Figures 3(c), 3(d) and 3(e), respectively. The final resulting version of trans (i.e. good + fixed) is shown in Figure 3(f) which corresponds exactly to the quotient MDP in Figure 1(c).

4.3   Efficiency of the Algorithm

Clearly, the most costly part of our method is the sorting process. As mentioned previously our decision to use the bubble sort algorithm for this is motivated by [13], where it is argued that, despite being a poor choice in general, bubble sort is well suited for a BDD-based implementation. Firstly, it allows each step of the algorithm to be applied in parallel to several separate sorting problems: in the case of [13], values for all states in a set are sorted simultaneously, whereas in our case we take this a step further, sorting values in all rows and columns of an entire real-valued matrix. Secondly, the most costly operation at the BDD or MTBDD level is the permutation of two sets of Boolean variables, the performance of which worsens with an increase in the distance between the two sets in the variable ordering. Bubble sort has the advantage that it only swaps the variables corresponding to adjacent processes which are very close in the ordering.

The complexity of bubble sort is $O(N^2)$. Since model sizes are typically exponential in the number of processes they contain, N will usually be comparatively small. More crucial from a performance point of view will be the effect that the sorting process will have on the size of the MTBDD representation of the matrix. The unavoidable loss in regularity associated with this process would be expected to have at least some detrimental effect in this respect but, as is always the case with BDD and MTBDD-based implementations, the exact effect is hard to predict. We will give an analysis based on empirical data in the next section.

5   Results

We now present experimental results to illustrate the performance of our approach, which has been implemented as a prototype extension of the PRISM probabilistic model checker [15, 24] using the CUDD BDD/MTBDD library [27]. For this, we have used four case studies: the IEEE 802.3 CSMA/CD communication protocol [16], the shared coin component of Aspnes and Herlihy's randomised consensus protocol [1], studied in [21]; the randomised Byzantine agreement protocol of Cachin, Kursawe and Shoup [7], studied in [18]; and a simple peer-to-peer (P2P) protocol based on BitTorrent. The first three have been modelled as MDPs, the latter as a CTMC. In all cases, we model check a single quantitative property. All PRISM models and properties are available [24]. At this stage, symmetry has been identified manually; future work will involve modifying the PRISM input language to facilitate automation of this process.

The table in Figure 4 summarises the results of our experiments, which were executed on a 2.80GHz Pentium 4 PC with 1GB RAM running Linux. The first two columns show the range of values of N (number of symmetric processes) for which we have obtained results with each case study. The next three columns show the sizes of the full and symmetry-reduced state spaces (i.e. $|S|$ and $|\overline{S}|$)

Case study	N	State space			MTBDD size (nodes)		Time (sec.)			
		Size		Reduct. factor			Model build	Model sort	Model checking	
		Normal	Symm.		Normal	Symm.			Normal*	Symm.*
CSMA	4	678,831	35,270	19.2	64,857	37,653	9.25	1.05	134 (H)	26.5 (H)
	5	1.7e+7	203,271	81.9	207,837	105,768	45.3	4.17	1,988 (H)	131 (H)
	6	3.2e+8	813,520	392	538,931	244,970	158	13.1	21,511 (M)	491 (H)
	7	5.7e+9	2.8e+6	2,073	1.1e+6	510,618	499	31.5	Mem. out	1,934 (H)
	8	1.0e+11	8.4e+6	11,962	2.1e+6	1.1e+6	1,831	76.8	Mem. out	5,281 (H)
Cons-ensus	8	6.1e+7	46,482	1,313	15,529	15,883	1.41	0.46	5,447 (M)	74.6 (H)
	10	2.8e+9	136,708	20,198	29,419	29,939	3.01	1.02	27,668 (M)	412 (H)
	12	1.2e+11	339,729	352,407	50,037	50,741	5.71	2.11	> 24 hrs	2,047 (H)
	14	5.0e+12	747,243	6.7e+6	78,171	79,123	9.59	5.05	> 24 hrs	6,816 (H)
	16	2.1e+14	1.5e+6	1.4e+8	115,385	116,691	19.0	7.56	> 24 hrs	19,168 (H)
Byza-ntine	8	6.4e+8	298,993	2,142	713,143	167,587	21.0	5.15	111 (M)	10.8 (M)
	12	3.6e+12	3.3e+6	1.1e+6	2.6e+6	529,619	86.0	23.9	1,430 (M)	56.6 (M)
	16	1.9e+16	1.2e+7	9.3e+8	6.6e+6	1.2e+6	241	75.3	Mem. out	186 (M)
	20	9.5e+19	9.1e+7	1.0e+12	1.3e+7	2.3e+6	1,503	237	Mem. out	740 (M)
P2P	4	1.0e+6	52,360	20.0	2,735	28,684	0.10	0.34	34.1 (H)	8.75 (H)
	5	3.4e+7	376,992	89.0	12,230	67,764	0.08	0.88	1,756 (H)	70.1 (H)
	6	1.1e+9	2.3e+6	462	26,555	134,641	0.16	1.77	Mem. out	547 (H)
	7	3.4e+10	1.3e+7	2,723	40,880	233,068	0.28	3.38	Mem. out	3,556 (H)

* (M) denotes use of MTBDD engine, (H) denotes use of hybrid engine

Fig. 4. Experimental results for the four case studies

and the factor of reduction achieved. In the next two columns, we give the size of the MTBDD (number of nodes) representing the transition matrix for the original model and the reduced quotient model.

We first note that, as expected, we can obtain large (several orders of magnitude) reductions in state space size using component symmetry and that these reductions improve with an increase in N, Of equal importance, however, is the size of the MTBDD representation of the quotient model. Our result shows that in some cases this is actually smaller (approximately half the size for CSMA, even smaller for Byzantine), in others there is little change (Consensus) but that there can also be a significant increase in size (P2P). There are two contrasting factors which influence this. Firstly, the removal of a large number of rows decreases MTBDD size. The BDD representing the set of representative states (repr in Figure 2) is normally quite regular, unlike for example the set of all reachable states. On the other hand, the permutation of a large number of matrix elements during sorting destroys a great deal of the matrix's regularity and hence increases MTBDD size. This is confirmed by a more detailed analysis of the MTBDD size during the process of constructing the quotient model which usually exhibits an initial decrease followed by a steady increase.

We thus observe that the example exhibiting the most regularity before symmetry, P2P (compare the MTBDD size and state space), suffers the highest increase. Although the Consensus and Byzantine examples are also regular, the fact that we can work with larger values of N results in a greater reduction in state space and hence the gain from removal of rows outweighs the loss in structure. Similarly, we can see that the effect of loss in regularity (increase in MTBDD size) decreases with increasing N on the P2P example.

The last four columns in Figure 4 show the times taken for each part of our experiments: building the original full model (including reachability), construction of the quotient model via bubble sort and performing model checking on each of the two models. In the latter case we use the fastest PRISM engine which can complete the task: either the MTBDD (M) or hybrid (H) engine. All experiments requiring more than 24 hours were discounted.

We see that the times for constructing the quotient model (i.e. to run the algorithm in Figure 2), although slower on the CSMA and Byzantine examples for which the MTBDDs are larger, are generally fast, certainly with respect to the time required for model checking. More significantly, we observe that using symmetry reduction we can obtain a dramatic increase in the size of models that can be successfully verified. Note that this is true even on the P2P example for which the MTBDD sizes increase. For three of our case studies, this is because the large reduction in state space makes use of the hybrid engine possible after symmetry reduction. Another consequence of this is that we also observe a significant improvement in run-time using symmetry reduction. On the Consensus case study, the total time required for solution drops from several weeks to a few hours. For the Byzantine case study, where we use the MTBDD engine both before and after reduction, the decrease in MTBDD size means that we still obtain huge improvements in both state space and run-time.

6 Conclusion

We have presented an efficient approach for the exploitation of component symmetry in three types of probabilistic models: discrete-time Markov chains, continuous time Markov chains and Markov decision processes. Our algorithm, based on multi-terminal BDDs and implemented in the PRISM tool, has been applied to four large case studies and demonstrates that the technique performs extremely well. In comparison to existing state-of-the-art implementations, it allows quantitative verification to be performed on models many orders of magnitude larger and results in significantly faster run-times.

Our work can be extended in several directions. Following ideas put forward in [13], we hope to able to apply our technique to a wider range of symmetric systems, including those based on rotational, rather than component, symmetry (i.e. rings). We would also like to extend the PRISM modelling language with a notion of scalarsets [17] in order to facilitate the automation of detecting and exploiting symmetry. Finally, we hope to undertake a comparison with symmetry reduction methods based on counter abstraction [10].

References

[1] J. Aspnes and M. Herlihy. Fast randomized consensus using shared memory. *Journal of Algorithms*, 15(1):441–460, 1990.
[2] A. Aziz, V. Singhal, F. Balarin, R. Brayton, and A. Sangiovanni-Vincentelli. It usually works: The temporal logic of stochastic systems. In *Proc. CAV'95*, 1995.
[3] I. Bahar, E. Frohm, C. Gaona, G. Hachtel, E. Macii, A. Pardo, and F. Somenzi. Algebraic decision diagrams and their applications. *Formal Methods in System Design*, 10(2/3):171–206, 1997.

[4] C. Baier, B. Haverkort, H. Hermanns, and J.-P. Katoen. Model checking continuous-time Markov chains by transient analysis. In *Proc. CAV'00*, 2000.

[5] S. Barner and O. Grumberg. Combining symmetry reduction and under-approximation for symbolic model checking. In *Proc. CAV'02*, 2002.

[6] P. Buchholz. Markovian process algebra: Composition and equivalence. In *Proc. PAPM'94*, pages 11–30, 1994.

[7] C. Cachin, K. Kursawe, and V. Shoup. Random oracles in Constantinople: Practical asynchronous Byzantine agreement using cryptography (extended abstract). In *Proc. Symposium on Principles of Distributed Computing*, pages 123–132, 2000.

[8] E. Clarke, R. Enders, T. Filkorn, and S. Jha. Exploiting symmetry in temporal logic model checking. *Formal Methods in System Design*, 9(1/2):77–104, 1996.

[9] E. Clarke, M. Fujita, P. McGeer, K. McMillan, J. Yang, and X. Zhao. Multi-terminal binary decision diagrams: An efficient data structure for matrix representation. *Formal Methods in System Design*, 10((2/3):149–169, 1997.

[10] A. Donaldson and A. Miller. Symmetry reduction for probabilistic systems. In *Proc. 12th workshop on Automated Reasoning*, pages 17–18, 2005.

[11] E. Emerson and A. Sistla. Symmetry and model checking. *Formal Methods in System Design*, 9(1/2):105–131, 1996.

[12] E. Emerson and R. Trefler. From asymmetry to full symmetry: New techniques for symmetry reduction in model checking. In *Proc. CHARME'99*, 1999.

[13] E. Emerson and T. Wahl. Dynamic symmetry reduction. In *Proc. TACAS'05*, volume 3440 of *LNCS*, pages 382–396. Springer, 2005.

[14] H. Hermanns, M. Kwiatkowska, G. Norman, D. Parker, and M. Siegle. On the use of MTBDDs for performability analysis and verification of stochastic systems. *Journal of Logic and Algebraic Programming*, 56(1-2):23–67, 2003.

[15] A. Hinton, M. Kwiatkowska, G. Norman, and D. Parker. PRISM: A tool for automatic verification of probabilistic systems. In *TACAS'06*, volume 3920 of *LNCS*, pages 441–444. Springer, 2006.

[16] IEEE 802.3-2002. IEEE Standard for Carrier Sense Multiple Access with Collision Detection (CSMA/CD). http://standards.ieee.org/getieee802/802.3.html, 2002.

[17] C. Ip and D. Dill. Better verification through symmetry. *Formal Methods In System Design*, 9(1-2):41–75, 1996.

[18] M. Kwiatkowska and G. Norman. Verifying randomized Byzantine agreement. In *Proc. FORTE'02*, volume 2529 of *LNCS*, pages 194–209. Springer, 2002.

[19] M. Kwiatkowska, G. Norman, and D. Parker. Probabilistic symbolic model checking with PRISM: A hybrid approach. *International Journal on Software Tools for Technology Transfer (STTT)*, 6(2):128–142, 2004.

[20] M. Kwiatkowska, G. Norman, and D. Parker. Probabilistic model checking in practice: Case studies with PRISM. *ACM SIGMETRICS Performance Evaluation Review*, 32(4):16–21, 2005.

[21] M. Kwiatkowska, G. Norman, and R. Segala. Automated verification of a randomized distributed consensus protocol using Cadence SMV and PRISM. In *Proc. CAV'01*, volume 2102 of *LNCS*, pages 194–206. Springer, 2001.

[22] K. Larsen and A. Skou. Bisimulation through probabilistic testing. *Information and Computation*, 94:1–28, 1991.

[23] A. Pnueli, J. Xu, and L. Zuck. Liveness with $(0, 1, \infty)$-counter abstraction. In *Proc. CAV'02*, pages 107–122, 2002.

[24] PRISM web site. http://www.cs.bham.ac.uk/~dxp/prism/.

[25] J. Rutten, M. Kwiatkowska, G. Norman, and D. Parker. *Mathematical Techniques for Analyzing Concurrent and Probabilistic Systems,* P. Panangaden and F. van Breugel (eds.). American Mathematical Society, 2004.

[26] R. Segala and N. Lynch. Probabilistic simulations for probabilistic processes. In *Proc. CONCUR'94),* volume 836 of *LNCS,* pages 481–496. Springer, 1994.

[27] F. Somenzi. CUDD: Colorado University decision diagram package. Public software, Colorado Univeristy, Boulder, http://vlsi.colorado.edu/~fabio/.

Communicating Timed Automata:
The More Synchronous, the More
Difficult to Verify*

Pavel Krcal and Wang Yi

Uppsala University, Sweden
{pavelk, yi}@it.uu.se

Abstract. We study channel systems whose behaviour (sending and receiving messages via unbounded FIFO channels) must follow given timing constraints specifying the execution speeds of the local components. We propose Communicating Timed Automata (CTA) to model such systems. The goal is to study the borderline between decidable and undecidable classes of channel systems in the timed setting. Our technical results include: (1) CTA with one channel without shared states in the form $(A_1, A_2, c_{1,2})$ is equivalent to one-counter machine, implying that verification problems such as checking state reachability and channel boundedness are decidable, and (2) CTA with two channels without sharing states in the form $(A_1, A_2, A_3, c_{1,2}, c_{2,3})$ has the power of Turing machines. Note that in the untimed setting, these systems are no more expressive than finite state machines. This shows that the capability of synchronizing on time makes it substantially more difficult to verify channel systems.

1 Introduction

FIFO channels (i.e., unbounded buffers) are widely used as a communication mechanism in concurrent systems. In many applications, channels are a critical element for the correct functioning of such systems. In this work, we study timed systems whose components communicate through (unbounded) channels. An example of such systems is illustrated in Figure 1, where A_1 is a producer (or sender) which generates messages and puts them into the buffer $c_{1,2}$ and A_2 is a consumer (or receiver) which gets messages from the buffer. Assume that the production and consumption of messages must follow given timing constraints (specifying the relative execution speeds of the producer and the consumer). A relevant question to ask is whether the channel is bounded, and if it is, what is the maximal size of the buffer. This is a typical scenario in designing embedded systems, where it is desirable to know a priori the maximal size of a buffer needed to avoid buffer overflow and over-allocation of memory blocks in the final implementation.

---

* Partially supported by the European Research Training Network GAMES.

T. Ball and R.B. Jones (Eds.): CAV 2006, LNCS 4144, pp. 249–262, 2006.

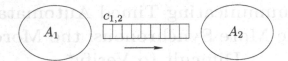

Fig. 1. A schema of a CTA with one channel

In the literature, channel systems have been studied intensively in the un-timed setting, within the context of verification of infinite state systems (see below for related work which provides a brief summary of known results). To our best knowledge, this is the first attempt to study channel systems in the timed setting. The existing works address mainly channel systems that are a fi-nite set of Communicating Finite State Machines (CFSMs). In the CFSM model, no notion of time is assumed and systems run in a fully asynchronous manner in the sense that any local move of a machine is allowed at any time. We observe that for systems modeled as CFSMs, the source of infiniteness is in not only *unbounded channels* but also the capability of *synchronization* or exchanging in-formation between the machines. In fact, asynchronous systems – as illustrated in Figure 1 and 2 with only one-directional communication, where the receivers are not allowed to inform directly or indirectly the senders about the receipt of messages – are no more expressive than finite state machines [Pac03, CF05], and thus all properties such as reachability and channel boundedness are decid-able. Roughly speaking, synchronization within CFSMs may be achieved through either shared states [BZ83], or two-direction communication [FM97] or combina-tion of accepting conditions and doubled one-direction channels [Pac03, Pac82]. The synchronization features together with the unboundedness of channels are the essential source of undecidability for channel systems in the untimed setting.

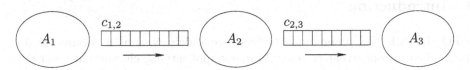

Fig. 2. A schema of a CTA with two channels

As a model for timed systems communicating via channels, we propose and study Communicating Timed Automata (CTA), i.e., networks of timed automata extended with (unbounded) channels. A CTA is a channel system where the sending and receiving transitions of machines are constrained with clock con-straints. We shall show that channel systems (with one channel) as illustrated in Figure 1, which accept only regular languages in the untimed setting, are expressive enough to simulate one-counter machines in the timed setting. How-ever, the density of time adds no more expressive power (than discrete time), and many questions of interests such as reachability and channel boundedness are still decidable for CTA with one channel. As a main technical contribution, we present a novel proof showing that CTAs with one channel without sharing states are no more expressive than one-counter machines. The proof uses the notion of CDR (Clock Difference Relations) developed in [KP05]. To study the borderline of decidability and undecidability for CTA, we have shown that CTAs with two channels, as illustrated in Figure 2, can simulate Turing machines. By this we show the theoretical limits of analysis of timed systems with unbounded channels.

Related Work. Channel systems, i.e., networks of communicating finite state machines (*CFSMs*) have been widely studied in the untimed setting, as a model for communication protocols, in which no global notion of time is assumed and any local move of FSMs at any time is allowed. The first undecidability results for the untimed setting were presented in [BZ83] showing that two FSMs with shared states and one channel can simulate Turing machines. Further results consider even more restricted settings, showing that two identical simple FSMs with one channel in both directions are powerful enough to simulate a Turing machine [FM97]. A suprising result due to [Pac03, Pac82] is that two FSMs connected by two channels going in the same direction can simulate Initial Post's Correspondence Problem, and therefore have the power of Turing machines. Classes of CFSMs with decidable reachability problems have been identified in [CF05] (half-duplex systems), [Pac03] (cyclic systems with one channel bounded), and [PP92] (cyclic systems with one-type messages). Abstractions of CFSMs for acceleration in reachability analysis are presented in [FPS03]. Another recent work [GMK04] shows the equivalence of several formalisms when the communication is existentially bounded. Apart from work on systems with perfect channels, systems with unreliable channels have been studied in [AJ96a, AJ96b]. An excellent survey on work in this direction can be found in [CFP96].

2 Communicating Timed Automata

We assume that the reader is familiar with timed automata [AD94]. A network of Communicating Timed Automata (*CTA*) is a tuple $(A_1, A_2, \ldots, A_n, c_{i_1,j_1}, c_{i_2,j_2}, \ldots, c_{i_m,j_m})$ where each $A_i = (Q_i, \mathcal{A}ct, \mathcal{C}_i, E_i, q_i^0, F_i)$ is a timed automaton and each $c_{i,j}, i, j \in \{1 \ldots n\}$ is an unidirectional unbounded channel containing messages sent from A_i to A_j. Mutually disjoint finite sets $Q_1, \ldots Q_n$ contain locations of A_i's. A finite set $\mathcal{A}ct$ denotes a communication alphabet common for all A_i's. In addition, we assume that automata may perform an internal transition denoted by ϵ. $\mathcal{C}_i$ is a finite set of real-valued clocks ($\mathcal{C}_i, \mathcal{C}_j$ are disjoint for $i \neq j$), $q_i^0 \in Q_i$ is an initial location, and $F_i \subseteq Q_i$ is a set of accepting locations. $E_i \subseteq Q_i \times (\{1 \ldots n\} \times \{?, !\} \times \mathcal{A}ct) \cup \{\epsilon\} \times \mathcal{G}(\mathcal{C}) \times 2^{\mathcal{C}} \times Q_i$ is the set of transitions of A_i, where $\mathcal{G}(\mathcal{C})$ and $2^{\mathcal{C}}$ are timed automata guards and resets, respectively. Transitions are labeled by not only a letter from $\mathcal{A}ct$, but also information about whether a letter is sent or received (! or ?, respectively) and to or from which channel. We write $q_i \xrightarrow{k!a, g, r} q_i'$ when $(q_i, k!a, g, r, q_i') \in E$. Channels are assumed to be perfect. We denote the contents of a channel by finite words over $\mathcal{A}ct$.

Let $\nu_i : \mathcal{C}_i \mapsto \mathcal{R}_{\geq 0}$ denote a valuation of clocks in A_i. Let $\nu_i \models g$ denote that the guard g is satisfied by ν_i and $r(\nu_i), r \subseteq \mathcal{C}_i$ denote a valuation where all clocks from r are reset and other clocks keep their values. A state of the system is a tuple $(q_1, \nu_1, \ldots, q_n, \nu_n, w_1, \ldots, w_m)$, where $q_i \in Q_i$ is a location of A_i and $w_k \in \mathcal{A}ct^*$ is the content of channel c_{i_k, j_k}. We define the semantics of CTA based on Labeled Transition System (LTS).

Definition 1 (Synchronized Semantics). *The semantics of a CTA* $(A_1, \ldots, A_n, c_{i_1, j_1}, \ldots, c_{i_m, j_m})$ *is a labeled transition system with initial state* $(q_1^0, \nu_1^0, q_2^0, \nu_2^0, \ldots, q_n^0, \nu_n^0, \epsilon, \ldots, \epsilon)$, *where* $\nu_i^0(x) = 0$ *for all* $x \in \mathcal{C}_i$ *and two types of transitions – time pass and discrete transition – defined as follows. Let* $s = (q_1, \nu_1, \ldots, q_n, \nu_n, w_1, \ldots, w_m)$ *and* $s' = (q_1', \nu_1', \ldots, q_n', \nu_n', w_1', \ldots, w_m')$.

- $s \xrightarrow{t} s'$ *if* $\nu_i' = \nu_i + t$, $q_i' = q_i$ *and* $w_j' = w_j$ *for all* $1 \leq i \leq n$ *and* $1 \leq j \leq m$.
- $s \xrightarrow{(a,i,k,!)} s'$ *if* $q_i \xrightarrow{k!a,g,r} q_i'$, $w_l' = a \cdot w_l$, *where* w_l *is the content of* $c_{i,k}$, $\nu_i \models g$, $\nu_i' = r(\nu_i)$, *and* $q_j' = q_j, \nu_j' = \nu_j, w_k' = w_k$ *for all* $j \neq i, k \neq l$,
- $s \xrightarrow{(a,i,k,?)} s'$ *if* $q_i \xrightarrow{k?a,g,r} q_i'$, $a \neq \epsilon$, $w_l' \cdot a = w_l$, *where* w_l *is the content of* $c_{k,i}$, $\nu_i \models g$, $\nu_i' = r(\nu_i)$, *and* $q_j' = q_j, \nu_j' = \nu_j, w_k' = w_k$ *for all* $j \neq i, k \neq l$, *and*
- $s \xrightarrow{(\epsilon,i)} s'$ *if* $q_i \xrightarrow{\epsilon,g,r} q_i'$, $\nu_i \models g$, $\nu_i' = r(\nu_i)$, $q_j' = q_j, \nu_j' = \nu_j, w_k' = w_k$ *for all* $j \neq i, k \in \{1, \ldots, m\}$, *and there is no* $q_i \xrightarrow{k?a,\bar{g},\bar{r}} q_i''$ *such that* $\nu_i \models \bar{g}$ *and* $w_l = w_l'' \cdot a$, *where* w_l *is the content of* $c_{k,i}$.

All automata move synchronously; time passes at the same pace for all of them. The automata read from the channels in an *urgent* manner, an automaton is not allowed to take an ϵ-transition if it can take a receiving a-transition and a is at the head of the corresponding channel. Another possibility is to define reading as non-urgent, i.e., there are no restrictions on taking ϵ transitions. In Section 3, we show by an example that CTA's even with non-urgent reading from the channels have strictly more expressive power than CFSMs in the untimed setting.

Let S be a CTA and T_S be its corresponding LTS. By ρ we denote a finite path in T_S, by $[\rho]$ a sequence of labels occurring along ρ, and by $[\rho]_i^!$ $([\rho]_i^?)$ a sequence of letters from $\mathcal{A}ct$ which is a projection of $[\rho]$ to letters sent (received) by an automaton A_i. If the location vector $(q_1, \ldots, q_n)$ of the last global state of ρ is accepting (i.e., $\forall i.q_i \in F_i$) then we say that the run is accepting, denoted $\rho \triangleright T_S$. A language accepted by a CTA S is a set $L_S(S) = \{[\rho]_1^! \mid \rho \triangleright T_S\}$.

Note that we can model CFSMs by CTA. Therefore, all negative results proved for CFSMs apply also to our model. In the following, we study the expressive power of the model by identifying decidable and undecidable classes of CTA.

3   CTA with One Channel

Let us first consider a system $(A_1, A_2, c_{1,2})$ schematically depicted in Figure 1. It has been shown that CFSMs with such topology accept regular languages and reachability and boundedness problems are decidable [Pac03, CF05]. We show that CTA of this form can accept also some non-regular context-free languages. Moreover, we show that for such a CTA there is a one-counter machine which accepts the same language. Therefore, state reachability and channel boundedness problems are decidable, which follows from the decidability of emptiness and infiniteness for context-free languages.

To establish the proof, we propose an alternative (*desynchronized concrete*) semantics for CTA which resembles the reordering technique [Pac03] for CFSMs and the local time semantics for timed systems [BJLY98]. However, states in this semantics still contain concrete valuations of clocks. Therefore, we define a (*desynchronized symbolic*) semantics where the continuous part of the state has a finite symbolic representation. This symbolic semantics can be easily simulated by a one-counter machine. We also show that instructions of a one-counter machine can be simulated by a CTA of the form $(A_1, A_2, c_{1,2})$ and thus the expressive power of CTA with this topology is equivalent to one-counter machine.

Intuitively, we let the automata to desynchronize so that there is at most one message in the channel during the first part of the computation and that only the producing automaton runs during the second part of the computation. Local time (time from the beginning of the computation) can be different in A_1 and A_2. We keep track of the difference between local times of automata in a real valued variable. The acceptance condition is extended by a requirement that the system should be synchronized, i.e., the value of this variable is equal to 0.

In the following, we denote A_1 as A and A_2 as B. We also write $!a$ instead of $2!a$ and $?a$ instead of $1?a$. Without loss of generality, we assume that there is a clock t_i in each A_i which is never reset. The reason is to simplify the notation later. A state in the concrete desynchronized semantics is a tuple $(q_A, \nu_A, q_B, \nu_B, w, T)$, where $q_A \in Q_A, q_B \in Q_B, w \in Act^*$, valuations ν_A, ν_B are as in the original semantics, and $T \in \mathcal{R}$ is the lag of B behind A (it is negative if B is ahead). By $(q_A, \nu_A) \xrightarrow{lab} (q'_A, \nu'_A)$ we mean that there is a transition from (q_A, ν_A) to (q'_A, ν'_A) labeled by lab in the standard timed automata semantics LTS. We need to take special care about reading – a letter should not be read before it has been produced.

We let the automata to alternate in running as long as the size of the channel content does not exceed 1. When it contains at least two letters then only A can move. We assume $a \in Act$ and $w \in Act^*$ in the following definition.

Definition 2 (Desynchronized Concrete Semantics). *The* desynchronized concrete semantics *of a CTA* $(A, B, q_{A,B})$ *is a labeled transition system with initial state* $(q_A^0, \nu_A^0, q_B^0, \nu_B^0, \epsilon, 0)$ *and transitions induced by the following rules:*

- $(q_A, \nu_A, q_B, \nu_B, w, T) \xrightarrow{t}_{dc} (q_A, \nu_A + t, q_B, \nu_B, w, T + t)$ *if* $(q_A, \nu_A) \xrightarrow{t} (q_A, \nu_A + t)$,

- $(q_A, \nu_A, q_B, \nu_B, w, T) \xrightarrow{(a,1,2,!)}_{dc} (q'_A, \nu'_A, q_B, \nu_B, a \cdot w, T)$ *if* $(q_A, \nu_A) \xrightarrow{!a} (q'_A, \nu'_A)$,

- $(q_A, \nu_A, q_B, \nu_B, w, T) \xrightarrow{t}_{dc} (q_A, \nu_A, q_B, \nu_B + t, w, T - t)$ *if* $(q_B, \nu_B) \xrightarrow{t} (q_B, \nu_B + t)$ *and* $|w| \leq 1$,

- $(q_A, \nu_A, q_B, \nu_B, a, T) \xrightarrow{(a,2,1,?)}_{dc} (q_A, \nu_A, q'_B, \nu'_B, \epsilon, T)$ *if* $(q_B, \nu_B) \xrightarrow{?a} (q'_B, \nu'_B)$ *and* $T \leq 0$,

$-\ (q_A, \nu_A, q_B, \nu_B, w, T) \xrightarrow{\epsilon}_{dc} (q_A, \nu_A, q'_B, \nu'_B, w, T)$ if $(q_B, \nu_B) \xrightarrow{\epsilon} (q'_B, \nu'_B)$,
$|w| \leq 1$, if $T \geq 0$ then $(w = a \Rightarrow (q_B, \nu_B) \overset{?a}{\nrightarrow})$, and if $T < 0$ then $(w =$
$a \wedge (q_B, \nu_B) \overset{?a}{\nrightarrow})$.

A run with the last state $(q_A, \nu_A, q_B, \nu_B, w, T)$ is accepting if $q_A \in F_A, q_B \in F_B$, and $T = 0$. Definition of the accepted language $L_{DC}(S)$ for a given CTA S is the same as for synchronized semantics. The set of reachable states of a given CTA is equal to the set of states reachable in its desynchronized concrete semantics where $T = 0$. Also, the language accepted by a CTA is the same in both semantics.

Lemma 1. *For a given CTA S of the form $(A, B, c_{A,B})$, the reachability set $\{(q_A, \nu_A, q_B, \nu_B, w) \mid (q^0_A, \nu^0_A, q^0_B, \nu^0_B, \epsilon) \rightarrow^* (q_A, \nu_A, q_B, \nu_B, w)\}$ is equal to the set $\{(q_A, \nu_A, q_B, \nu_B, w) \mid (q^0_A, \nu^0_A, q^0_B, \nu^0_B, \epsilon, 0) \longrightarrow_{dc}^* (q_A, \nu_A, q_B, \nu_B, w, 0)\}$. Moreover, $L_S(S) = L_{DC}(S)$.*

The basic idea of the proof of this lemma is the same as in [Pac03]. Desynchronized concrete semantics cannot reach more states where $T = 0$ or accept more words because the counter gives us a possibility to check the following conditions on the transitions of B. A letter can be read only after it has been produced and ϵ-transitions can be taken only when no enabled transition is labeled by the head of the buffer.

The desynchronization semantics shows how to avoid necessity to remember the whole content of the buffer during the run of a CTA. Note that one does not have to remember the content of the channel when its size exceeds 1, because it will never be read. The price we have to pay is an additional real number as a part of the state. In case of discrete time, T is an integer and therefore one can replace such a system by a language equivalent (in fact, bisimilar) one-counter machine. To be able to prove that there is a one-counter machine which is language equivalent to such a system in the dense time, we need to handle real valued clocks and T in a symbolic way, such that we get a finite state control unit and one counter.

The first step is to use regions [AD94] instead of valuations for each automaton. We denote regions by D, D_A, D_B. When D is a region over clocks of two automata A and B then by $(\nu_A, \nu_B) \in D$ we mean that $\nu \in D$ where $\nu(x) = \nu_A(x)$ for all $x \in C_A$ and $\nu(y) = \nu_B(y)$ for all $y \in C_B$. We write $D \Rightarrow D_A$ if D is a region over clocks of A, B, D_A is a region over clocks of A, and for all $(\nu, \nu') \in D$ it holds that $\nu \in D_A$.

Now we need to take care of T. There are two sources of infinity in T – its integral part, which can grow arbitrarily large, and its fractional part. We remember the integral part of T in a counter, denoted N. To remember the fractional part of T, we use the extra local clocks t_A and t_B of A and B. We observe that the difference of their fractional parts is equal to the fractional part of T (we do not use their integral parts). More precisely, if $(q_A, \nu_A, q_B, \nu_B, w, T)$ is reachable and $N = \lceil T \rceil$ then $T = N + (\mathrm{fr}(\nu_A(t_A)) - \mathrm{fr}(\nu_B(t_B)))$ if $\nu_A(t_A) \geq \nu_B(t_B)$ and $T = N + (1 - (\mathrm{fr}(\nu_B(t_B)) - \mathrm{fr}(\nu_A(t_A))))$ if $\nu_A(t_A) < \nu_B(t_B)$.

The fractional parts of t_A and t_B are then symbolically represented by regions and we remember their relative order as a constraint of the form $t_A \bowtie t_B$, where $\bowtie \in \{<, =, >\}$. Assume that local regions D_A, D_B were reached during the standard reachability analysis. For two given local regions D_A, D_B, our goal is to find a global region D which contains only valuations reachable in the desynchronized concrete semantics. We can define D as an ordering of the fractional parts of clocks which is consistent with D_A, D_B ($D \Rightarrow D_A, D \Rightarrow D_B$), and with $t_A \bowtie t_B$.

However, such constraints on global regions are not sufficient. There are CTA for which symbolic analysis reaches $D_A, D_B, t_A \bowtie t_B$, but there is a global region D consistent with $D_A, D_B, t_A \bowtie t_B$ which contains unreachable valuations.

To eliminate such global regions, we will remember also relations between clock differences. We use the fact that t_A and t_B are never reset and relate all other clocks to them. The concept of *clock difference relations* has been used before in [KP05] to characterize reachability relations. Here we give a slightly modified definition which suits our purposes better. To differentiate this definition from the original one, we call it *desynchronized* clock difference relations here, but later we will use only an abbreviation CDR or clock difference relation.

Definition 3. *A* desynchronized clock difference relation *(CDR) is a set of (in)equalities of the form $exp \bowtie exp$ or $exp \bowtie 1 - exp$ where exp is a clock difference (over the clocks of either A or B) in the form: $t_A - x$, $x - t_A$, $t_B - y$ or $y - t_B$, x is a clock of A, y is a clock of B, and $\bowtie \in \{<, >, =\}$.*

Definition 4. *The semantics of a CDR is defined as follows. Assume C is a CDR. We say that a pair of valuations (ν, ν') satisfies C $((\nu, \nu') \vDash C)$ if:*

- *if $x - y \bowtie u - v \in C$ then $\mathsf{fr}(\nu(x)) - \mathsf{fr}(\nu(y)) \bowtie \mathsf{fr}(\nu'(u)) - \mathsf{fr}(\nu'(v))$,*
- *if $x - y \bowtie 1 - (u - v) \in C$ then $\mathsf{fr}(\nu(x)) - \mathsf{fr}(\nu(y)) \bowtie 1 - (\mathsf{fr}(\nu'(u)) - \mathsf{fr}(\nu'(v)))$,*

Additionally, we require that for each $x - y$ (or $u - v$), $\mathsf{fr}(\nu(x)) - \mathsf{fr}(\nu(y)) > 0$.

We will use clock difference relations to restrict possible merges of regions over clocks of A and B. The merged regions represent only reachable concrete desynchronized valuations now.

States of the desynchronized symbolic system $(q_A, D_A, q_B, D_B, C, t_A \bowtie t_B,$ $w, N)$ consist of locations and regions of A and B, respectively, clock difference relations, relation of t_A and t_B, $w \in Act^*$ is a content of the buffer, and N is an integer used to remember the difference between the integral parts of t_A and t_B.

We need some more technical definitions before the definition of the semantics. By $D \models C$ where D is a global region we mean that there exists $(\nu_A, \nu_B) \in D$ such that $(\nu_A, \nu_B) \models C$. We write e for a clock difference relation (a single (in)equality). We define a predicate $\mathsf{Consistent}(D_A, D_B, C, t_A \bowtie t_B) = \exists D.D(t_A)$ $\bowtie D(t_B), D \models C, D \Rightarrow D_A, D \Rightarrow D_B$.

Definition 5 (Desynchronized Symbolic Semantics). *The desynchronized symbolic semantics of a CTA $(A, B, q_{A,B})$ is a labeled transition system with initial state $(q_A^0, D_A^0, q_B^0, D_B^0, \emptyset, t_A = t_B, \epsilon, 0)$, transition rules are given in Table 1, Table 2, and Table 3.*

Table 1. Rules for symbolic transitions induced by the region graph of A. For clarity, we omit locations in the rules for time pass.

Time Pass:		
$D_A \to D'_A,\ \exists x \in integral(D_A)$		
$(D_A, D_B, C, t_A < t_B, w, N)$	$\longrightarrow_{ds}$	$(D'_A, D_B, C, t_A < t_B, w, N)$
$(D_A, D_B, C, t_A = t_B, w, N)$	$\longrightarrow_{ds}$	$(D'_A, D_B, C, t_A > t_B, w, N)$
$(D_A, D_B, C, t_A > t_B, w, N)$	$\longrightarrow_{ds}$	$(D'_A, D_B, C, t_A > t_B, w, N)$
$D_A,\ \nexists x \in integral(D_A)$		
$(D_A, D_B, C, t_A < t_B, w, N)$	$\longrightarrow_{ds}$	$(D_A, D_B, C, t_A = t_B, w, N + 1)$ if Consistent$(D_A, D_B, C, t_A = t_B)$
$(D_A, D_B, C, t_A = t_B, w, N)$	$\longrightarrow_{ds}$	$(D_A, D_B, C, t_A > t_B, w, N)$
$D_A \to D'_A,\ \exists x \in integral(D'_A)$		
$(D_A, D_B, C, t_A < t_B, w, N)$	$\longrightarrow_{ds}$	$(D'_A, D_B, C', t_A = t_B, w, N + 1)$ if Consistent$(D'_A, D_B, C', t_A = t_B)$
$(D_A, D_B, C, t_A < t_B, w, N)$	$\longrightarrow_{ds}$	$(D'_A, D_B, C', t_A < t_B, w, N)$ if Consistent$(D'_A, D_B, C', t_A < t_B)$
$(D_A, D_B, C, t_A > t_B, w, N)$	$\longrightarrow_{ds}$	$(D'_A, D_B, C', t_A < t_B, w, N)$ if $t_A \in integral(D'_A), t_B \notin integral(D_B)$
$(D_A, D_B, C, t_A > t_B, w, N)$	$\longrightarrow_{ds}$	$(D'_A, D_B, C', t_A = t_B, w, N + 1)$ if $t_A \in integral(D'_A), t_B \in integral(D_B)$
Discrete Transition:		
$(q_A, D_A) \to (q'_A, D'_A),\ x$ is reset		
$(q_A, D_A, q_B, D_B, C, t_A \bowtie t_B, w, N) \xrightarrow{(a,1,2,!)}_{ds} (q'_A, D'_A, q_B, D_B, C', t_A \bowtie t_B, a \cdot w, N)$ if $a \in Act \cup \{\epsilon\}$ is the label on the corresponding edge of A		
$(q_A, D_A) \to (q'_A, D_A),\ $ no clock is reset		
$(q_A, D_A, q_B, D_B, C, t_A \bowtie t_B, w, N) \xrightarrow{(a,1,2,!)}_{ds} (q'_A, D_A, q_B, D_B, C, t_A \bowtie t_B, a \cdot w, N)$ if $a \in Act \cup \{\epsilon\}$ is the label on the corresponding edge of A		

A run with the last state $(q_A, D_A, q_B, D_B, C, t_A \bowtie t_B, w, N)$ is accepting if $q_A \in F_A, q_B \in F_B, N = 0$, and $t_A = t_B$. Definition of the accepted language $L_{DS}(S)$ for a given CTA S is the same as for synchronized semantics. Now we state that the desynchronized symbolic semantics is language equivalent to the desynchronized concrete one.

Lemma 2. *For a given CTA S, $L_{DS}(S) = L_{DC}(S)$.*

Proof. Proof is given in the full version of this paper [KY06].

Obviously, this system can be replaced by a one-counter machine accepting the same language (actually, a bisimilar one-counter machine).

Theorem 1. *State reachability and channel boundedness problems are decidable for CTA of the form $(A_1, A_2, c_{1,2})$.*

Table 2. Rules for symbolic transitions induced by the region graph of B. All transitions are constrained by $|w| \leq 1$. Transitions for time pass are the same as for A except for that N is never incremented, but it is decremented when $t_A = t_B$ changes to $t_A < t_B$ and inequality signs in $t_A \bowtie t_B$ are inverted. Complete table is given in the full version of this paper [KY06].

Discrete Transition:
$(q_B, D_B) \to (q'_B, D'_B)$, x is reset
$(q_A, D_A, q_B, D_B, C, t_A \bowtie t_B, a, N) \xrightarrow{(a,2,1,?)}_{ds} (q_A, D_A, q'_B, D'_B, C', t_A \bowtie t_B, \epsilon, N)$ if $?a$, $a \in \mathcal{A}ct$ is the label on the corresponding   edge of B, and $N < 0 \vee (N = 0 \wedge t_A = t_B)$
$(q_A, D_A, q_B, D_B, C, t_A \bowtie t_B, w, N) \xrightarrow{t}_{ds} (q_A, D_A, q'_B, D'_B, C', t_A \bowtie t_B, w, N)$ if ϵ is the label on the corresponding edge of B,   if $N \geq 0$ then $(w = a \Rightarrow (q_B, \nu_B) \xrightarrow{?a})$ and   if $N < 0$ then $(w = a \wedge (q_B, \nu_B) \xrightarrow{?a})$

Similarly when no clock is reset.

Proof. Follows from Lemma 1, Lemma 2, and basic language theory.

Now we show that the instructions of a one-counter machine can be encoded in a CTA with one channel. The counter is encoded as the number of a's in the channel. Figure 3 shows how to encode incrementation of the counter q_i: C:=C+1; goto q_j and conditional decrementation of the counter q_i: if C=0 then goto q_j else C:=C-1; goto q_k. Each transition takes exactly one time unit. We omit clocks and guards on all other edges (they are labeled by $x = 1, x := 0$). Test for zero is performed by a nondeterministic choice for A. To check that the choice was correct, A produces b. If it was wrong then b is not consumed by the corresponding transition of B, stays in the channel and eventually blocks the computation of B. At the end of the computation, B has to check whether there is any b in the channel. If it is the case then it moves to an error location.

To illustrate the expressive power of CTA, Figure 4 shows a (schematic description of a) CTA which accepts a non-regular context-free language $a^n b a^n b$. Again, each transition takes exactly one time unit and we omit $x = 1, x := 0$ from all edges. The number of a's is remembered in the size of the channel content and we use different speed of production/consumption to maintain the correct number of a's in the channel. At the beginning, A produces twice faster than B reads. There are $n/2$ a's in the channel when B reads the first b and from this moment B reads twice faster then A produces.

From the point of view of the desynchronized semantics, the number of a's in the channel corresponds to the level of desynchronization. After reading the first n letters a the lag of B is $2n$ time units. Then it reads a dividing letter b and reads a's again. If there are n letters a then A and B get synchronized again and the accepting configuration is reachable after two more steps. If there are more a's then B gets stuck reading them, because it reads faster than A produces. If there are less a's then B can read b immediately and it has to go down to the error state. All locations of A are accepting, but the only accepting location of B is the next to the last one.

Table 3. Updates of the clock difference relations according to the type of the transition of the desynchronized symbolic system. We write e for a clock difference relation (a single (in)equality). We write exp for an expression of the form $x - y$ or $1 - (x - y)$ where x, y are clock from the automaton given by the context.

C'	Condition, A moves
$D_A \to D'_A, \exists x \in integral(D'_A)$	
e	$e \in C$, e does not contain any $x \in integral(D'_A)$
$y - x \bowtie^{-1} 1 - (exp)$	$x - y \bowtie exp \in C, x \in integral(D'_A)$
$D_A \to D'_A, x$ is reset	
e	$e \in C$, e does not contain x
$t_A - x > exp$	$t_A - y \geq exp \in C$
$t_A - x < 1 - exp$	$z - t_A \geq exp \in C$
$t_A - x < t_B - y$	$t_A < t_B, y \in integral(D_B)$
$t_A - x < 1 - (y - t_B)$	$t_A < t_B, D_B(y) > D_B(t_B)$
$t_A - x = t_B - y$	$t_A = t_B, y \in integral(D_B)$
$t_A - x > t_B - y$	$t_A = t_B, y \notin integral(D_B), D_B(y) < D_B(t_B)$
$t_A - x < 1 - (y - t_B)$	$t_A = t_B, D_B(y) > D_B(t_B)$
$t_A - x > t_B - y$	$t_A > t_B, D_B(y) < D_B(t_B)$

C'	Condition, B moves
$D_B \to D'_B, \exists x \in integral(D'_B)$	
e	$e \in C$, e does not contain any $x \in integral(D'_B)$
$exp \bowtie y - x$	$exp \bowtie 1 - (x - y) \in C, x \in integral(D'_B)$
$exp \bowtie 1 - (y - x)$	$exp \bowtie x - y \in C, x \in integral(D'_B)$
$D_B \to D'_B, x$ is reset	
e	$e \in C$, e does not contain x
$exp < t_B - x$	$exp \leq t_B - y \in C$
$exp < 1 - (t_B - x)$	$exp \leq z - t_B \in C$
$t_A - y > t_B - x$	$t_A > t_B, y \in integral(D_A)$
$y - t_A < 1 - (t_B - x)$	$t_A > t_B, D_A(y) > D_A(t_A)$
$t_A - y = t_B - x$	$t_A = t_B, y \in integral(D_A)$
$t_A - y < t_B - x$	$t_A = t_B, y \notin integral(D_A), D_A(y) < D_A(t_A)$
$y - t_A < 1 - (t_B - x)$	$t_A = t_B, D_A(y) > D_A(t_A)$
$t_A - y < t_B - x$	$t_A < t_B, D_A(y) < D_A(t_A)$

This automaton accepts the same language also in discrete time. It also shows the expressive power of CTA with one channel without urgency in the semantics, i.e., ϵ-transitions of B are not restricted. The language accepted by the CTA in Figure 4 remains the same even for non-urgent semantics when the only accepting location of A is the location m.

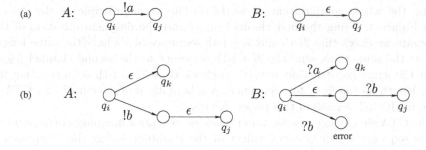

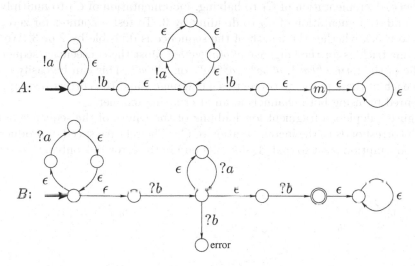

Fig. 3. A CTA encoding instructions of a one-counter machine. (a) encodes incrementation of the counter and (b) encodes conditional decrementation of the counter.

Fig. 4. A CTA accepting the language $a^n b a^n b$

4 CTA with Two Channels

Now we consider systems of the form $(A_1, A_2, A_3, c_{1,2}, c_{2,3})$ shown in Figure 2. We show that such CTA have the Turing power. This contrasts with the CFSMs, where systems of this form can accept only regular languages. The notion of the global time changes substantially the expressive power.

We cannot encode counters in the number of a's as we did it for one-counter machine, because there is no way how to verify nondeterministic choice of A_1 when deciding whether $c_{2,3}$ is empty. We will build on the construction from Figure 4. Again, we use different speed of production/consumption to maintain number of a's in the channels.

To show the simulation of a two-counter machine by a CTA with two channels we first notice that there is a system which accepts a language $a^n (a^n b a^n b)^*$. Therefore, there is a system which can keep the number of a's at the same level during the whole computation. It works on the same principle as the system from Figure 4. Using the first channel ($c_{1,2}$) and the desynchronization of the automata we check that $2i$-th and $2i + 1$-th sequence of a's have the same length and, at the same time, send the $2i + 1$-th sequence to the second channel ($c_{2,3}$). Then the same construction is used to check that $2i + 1$-th sequence has the same length as the $2i + 2$-th sequence. A schematic description of this CTA is given in the full version of this paper [KY06].

The CTA simulating a two-counter machine accepts a language corresponding to the sequence of the encoded values of the counters during the computation of this machine. The values m, n of the two counters C_1, C_2 are encoded by the length of the sequence of a's – the corresponding sequence is $a^{2^n 3^m}$. Therefore, incrementation of the counter C_1 corresponds to doubling of the length of the sequence, decrementation of C_1 to halving, incrementation of C_2 to multiplying by 3, and decrementation of C_2 to dividing by 3. To test a counter for zero, we need to check whether the length of the sequence is divisible by 2 or 3. We use the same trick as for the language $a^n b(a^n b a^n b)^*$. Just the consecutive sequences can be of the form $a^n b a^{2n}$, $a^n b a^{3n}$, $a^{2n} b a^n$, or $a^{3n} b a^n$. This can be easily done, since each of these pairs are context-free languages, and the correct overlapping is secured by using both channels in an alternating manner.

Figure 5 depicts a fragment for doubling of the length of the sequence of a's, which corresponds to the incrementation of C_1. The relative speed of production and consumption is set so that A_2 does not end in the error sink only if the second

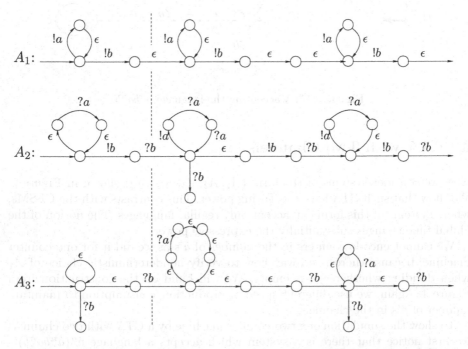

Fig. 5. A widget for doubling of the number of a's – incrementation of C_1

sequence is twice as long as the first one. The third sequence is as long as the second one (otherwise, A_3 ends up in the error sink), but A_2 gets desynchronized at the same time. This is a preparation for the next operation. Therefore, the simulation of the next instruction does not start with the first loop, but it goes directly to the second loop (behind the dashed line). This is to ensure overlapping of the length checking. Each transition takes one time unit, we omit guards and resets ($x = 1, x := 0$). All these constructions also work in the discrete time, but they do not work for non-urgent semantics. The encodings for halving and test for zero are given in the full version of this paper [KY06].

Theorem 2. *Reachability for networks of communicating timed automata of the form* $(A_1, A_2, A_3, c_{1,2}, c_{2,3})$ *is undecidable.*

5   Conclusions

To the best of our knowledge, this is the first attempt to study channel systems in the timed setting. We have proposed CTA as a general framework for modeling of channel systems in which the relative speeds of message production and consumption by local components must meet given timing constraints. Our goal is to mark the basic ground by identifying decidable and undecidable problems for such systems and raise relevant questions for future work. Our technical results can be summarized as follows: (1) CTA with one channel without sharing states in the form $(A_1, A_2, c_{1,2})$ (as shown in Figure 1) is equivalent to one-counter machine and therefore questions such as state reachability and channel bound-edness are decidable for such systems, and (2) CTA with two channels without sharing states in the form $(A_1, A_2, A_3, c_{1,2}, c_{2,3})$ (as shown in Figure 2) has the power of Turing machines.

An interesting question related to the timed setting is whether one can synthesize the clock constraints of a CTA (or a controller for a CTA in general) under given liveness requirements such that the channel content remains bounded. As future work, we will also study and develop abstraction techniques for efficient analysis of timed channel systems.

References

[AD94]   Rajeev Alur and David L. Dill. A theory of timed automata. *Theoretical Computer Science*, 126(2):183–235, 1994.

[AJ96a]   Parosh Aziz Abdulla and Bengt Jonsson. Undecidable verification problems for programs with unreliable channels. *Information and Computation*, 130(1):71–90, 1996.

[AJ96b]   Parosh Aziz Abdulla and Bengt Jonsson. Verifying programs with unreliable channels. *Information and Computation*, 127(2):91–101, 1996.

[BJLY98]   Johan Bengtsson, Bengt Jonsson, Johan Lilius, and Wang Yi. Partial order reductions for timed systems. In *Proc. of CONCUR'98*, volume 1466 of *LNCS*, pages 485–500. Springer, 1998.

[BZ83]   Daniel Brand and Pitro Zafiropulo. On communicating finite-state ma-
            chines. *J. ACM*, 30(2):323–342, 1983.
[CF05]   Gérard Cécé and Alain Finkel. Verification of programs with half-duplex
            communication. *Information and Computation*, 202(2):166–190, 2005.
[CFP96]   Gérard Cécé, Alain Finkel, and S. Purushothaman Iyer. Unreliable chan-
            nels are easier to verify than perfect channels. *Information and Compu-
            tation*, 124(1):20–31, 1996.
[FM97]   Alain Finkel and Pierre McKenzie. Verifying identical communicating
            processes is undecidable. *Theoretical Computer Science*, 174(1-2):217–
            230, 1997.
[FPS03]   Alain Finkel, S. Purushothaman Iyer, and Grégoire Sutre. Well-abstracted
            transition systems: Application to FIFO automata. *Information and
            Computation*, 181(1):1–31, 2003.
[GMK04]   Blaise Genest, Anca Muscholl, and Dietrich Kuske. A Kleene theorem for
            a class of communicating automata with effective algorithms. In *Proc. of
            DTL'04*, volume 3340 of *LNCS*, pages 30–48. Springer, 2004.
[KP05]   Pavel Krčál and Radek Pelánek. On sampled semantics of timed systems.
            In *Proc. of FSTTCS'05*, volume 3821 of *LNCS*, pages 310–321. Springer,
            2005.
[KY06]   Pavel Krcal and Wang Yi. Communicating timed automata. Technical
            Report 2006-008, Uppsala University, 2006.
[Pac82]   Jan K. Pachl. Reachability problems for communicating finite state ma-
            chines. Technical Report CS-82-12, Department of Computer Science,
            University of Waterloo, 1982.
[Pac03]   Jan K. Pachl. Reachability problems for communicating finite state ma-
            chines. *ArXiv Computer Science e-prints*, arXiv:cs/0306121, 2003.
[PP92]   Wuxu Peng and S. Purushothaman Iyer. Analysis of a class of communi-
            cating finite state machines. *Acta Informatica*, 29(6/7):422–499, 1992.

Allen Linear (Interval) Temporal Logic – Translation to LTL and Monitor Synthesis

Grigore Roşu[1],[*] and Saddek Bensalem[2]

[1] Department of Computer Science, University of Illinois at Urbana-Champaign, USA
[2] VERIMAG, 2 Avenue de Vignate, 38610 Gieres, France

Abstract. The relationship between two well established formalisms for temporal reasoning is first investigated, namely between Allen's interval algebra (or Allen's temporal logic, abbreviated ATL) and linear temporal logic (LTL). A discrete variant of ATL is defined, called Allen linear temporal logic (ALTL), whose models are ω-sequences of timepoints. It is shown that any ALTL formula can be linearly translated into an equivalent LTL formula, thus enabling the use of LTL techniques on ALTL requirements. This translation also implies the NP-completeness of ATL satisfiability. Then the problem of monitoring ALTL requirements is investigated, showing that it reduces to checking satisfiability; the similar problem for unrestricted LTL is known to require exponential space. An effective monitoring algorithm for ALTL is given, which has been implemented and experimented with in the context of planning applications.

1 Introduction

Allen's interval algebra, also called Allen's temporal logic (ATL) in this paper, is one of the best established formalisms for temporal reasoning [5]. It is frequently used in AI, especially in planning. Linear temporal logic (LTL) [8] is successfully applied in program verification, temporal databases, and related domains. Despite the widespread use of both ATL and LTL, there is no formal and systematic investigation of their relationship. This paper makes a step in this direction. To have a semantic basis for such a relationship, we define a discrete variant of ATL, called Allen linear temporal logic (ALTL), whose syntax and complexity of satisfiability are the same as for ATL, but whose models resemble those of LTL.

We show that ALTL can be linearly encoded into a subset of LTL. This encoding yields the NP-completeness of the satisfiability problem for an ATL (proposed in [4]) slightly richer than the original one proposed by Allen. On the practical side, this result allows us to use the plethora of techniques and analysis tools developed for LTL on requirements (or compatibilities) expressed using ATL. Since ATL is *the* logic of planning, and since validation and verification (V&V) of complex plans for systems with decisional autonomy is highly desirable, if not crucial, in many applications, this automated translation into LTL

---
[*] Supported by NSF grants CCF-0234524, CCF-0448501, and CNS-0509321.

T. Ball and R.B. Jones (Eds.): CAV 2006, LNCS 4144, pp. 263–277, 2006.
© Springer-Verlag Berlin Heidelberg 2006

potentially enables us to use well-understood V&V techniques and tools in a domain lacking (but in need of) them. Further, it may also support the suggestion made in [2] that LTL can be itself seriously regarded as a suitable formalism for temporal reasoning in AI, and particularly in planning. There are, however, complexity aspects that cannot be ignored (some of them pointed in this paper).

The importance of monitoring in planing cannot be overestimated. For example, an autonomous rover whose execution plans have been rigorously verified may still fail for reasons such as hardware or operating system failures, unexpected terrain in an unknown environment, etc. Having monitors to check online the execution of plans step by step and to trigger recovery code in case of violations is of crucial importance. It is the challenge of generating efficient monitors from planning requirements that motivated the work in this paper. We argue that a blind use of monitoring algorithms for LTL to monitor ALTL formulae is not feasible even on small ALTL formulae; then we give a special-purpose monitoring algorithm for ALTL which only needs to call a boolean satisfiability checker at each step if synchronous monitoring is desired, or at the end of the monitoring session if asynchronous monitoring is acceptable, or anywhere in between, for example at specific relevant events, such as synchronization points. Since checking satisfiability of a formula is a simpler problem than synchronous monitoring (a synchronous monitor should report violation right away if the formula is not satisfiable), the algorithm proposed in this paper is asymptotically optimal. This result is particularly interesting because, for unrestricted LTL, it is known that any monitor (synchronous or not) needs exponential space [10]. The proposed monitoring algorithm has been implemented and experimented with in the context of planning for autonomous rovers.

Preliminaries. We assume the reader familiar with Linear Temporal Logic (LTL) [8]. We here only recall some basics and introduce our notation. LTL is interpreted in "flows of time", modeled as strict linear orders $(T, <)$, where T is a nonempty set of "time points".The LTL language consists of propositional symbols $(p_0, p_1, \cdots)$, boolean operators ($\neg$ and $\wedge$), and temporal operators $\mathcal{U}$ ("until") and $\circ$ ("next"), and LTL formulae follow the common syntax $\varphi ::= p \mid \neg\varphi \mid \varphi_1 \wedge \varphi_2 \mid \varphi_1 \, \mathcal{U} \, \varphi_2 \mid \circ\varphi$. LTL models are triples $M = (T, <, v)$ such that $(T, <)$ is a strict total order (a flow of time) and v is a map called valuation associating with each variable p a set $v(p) \subseteq T$ of time points (where p is supposed to be true). The satisfaction relation $M \models \varphi$ is defined as in [8]. Other important temporal operators, such as $\Diamond$(eventually) and $\Box$ (always), are expressible using $\mathcal{U}$ as $\Diamond\varphi = \text{true} \, \mathcal{U} \, \varphi$ (φ will eventually hold) and $\Box\varphi = \neg\Diamond\neg\varphi$ (φ will always hold). $\Diamond$ can also be expressed in terms of $\Box$, namely $\Diamond\varphi = \neg\Box\neg\varphi$. In this paper we only need the $\{\Box, \Diamond\}$-fragment of LTL (without $\circ$ and $\mathcal{U}$). Since $\Diamond$ and $\Box$ can be defined in terms of each other, we take the liberty to call this fragment LTL$_\Box$ (could have also called it LTL$_\Diamond$). The "satisfiability problem" for a formula φ is concerned with whether there is some model M such that $M \models \varphi$. The satisfiability problem of LTL formulae is PSPACE-complete, while the satisfiability of LTL$_\Box$ is NP-complete [11].

2   Allen (Linear) Temporal Logic - **ATL (ALTL)**

Allen Temporal Logic (ATL). [1] is specified as a framework to deal with incomplete relative temporal information, such as "event A is before or overlaps event B". Allen takes the *interval* as the primitive temporal quantity and introduces 13 (mutually exclusive) basic binary relations between any two intervals, with the following intuitive meaning: $Equals(i, j)$ holds iff i and j consist of the same time points; $Meets(i, j)$ (or $MetBy(j, i)$) holds iff j starts *immediately* after i; $Before(i, j)$ (or $After(j, i)$) holds iff i starts and ends before j, but there is also some proper time elapsed between the end of i and the beginning of j; $Overlaps(i, j)$ (or $OverlappedBy(j, i)$) holds iff i starts strictly before j starts, they have some common time points, and i ends strictly before j ends; $Contains(i, j)$ (or $During(j, i)$) holds iff j starts strictly after i starts and terminates strictly before i terminates; $Starts(i, j)$ (or $StartedBy(j, i)$) holds iff i and j start together but j continues (strictly) after i ends; dually, $Ends(i, j)$ (or $EndedBy(j, i)$) holds iff i and j terminate together but j starts strictly before i starts. Constraints among intervals, also called requirements or *compatibilities*, are given as boolean combinations of such relations on intervals. In (model-)theoretical works on ATL, time is assumed to flow continuously, typically *not* at an enumerable rate (e.g., timepoints can be rational or real numbers). Following this model, we formally define the semantics of these interval relations in Definition 4; then we propose a time-discrete variant of ATL, in which the time-points are enumerable.

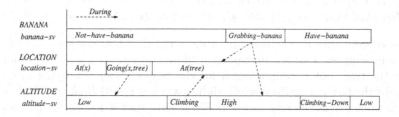

Fig. 1. Attributes and compatibilities

ATL is extensively used in AI planing to formalize and reason about concurrency and temporal extent. In AI planning, intervals can represent both action instances and the states of various attributes or components of a system. Attributes whose states change over time are called *state variables*, each being possibly regarded as a concurrent thread. The history of states of a state variable over a period of time is called a *timeline* and is typically partitioned into *intervals*, where an interval is a set of contiguous timepoints in which the corresponding state variable satisfies some property of interest. A *compatibility* then determines necessary correlations among various behaviors of parts of the system in order for a plan to be legal. One appealing aspect of ATL in this domain is that compatibilities can be elegantly depicted using an intuitive graphical notation (see Figure 1), that allows planning specialists to develop surprisingly large and complex specifications in a short time.

Example 1. We use McCarthy's classic monkey/banana planning problem as a running example. A monkey is at location "x", the banana is hanging from the tree. The monkey is at height "Low", but if it climbs the tree then it will be at height "High", same as the banana. Available actions are: "Going" from a place to another, "Climbing" (up) and "Climbing Down", and "Grabbing" banana.

Attributes. BANANA has one state variable *"Banana-sv"* saying if the monkey has the banana or not. LOCATION has one variable *"Location-sv"* for the location of the monkey. ALTITUDE has one variable *"Altitude-sv"* for the height.

Compatibilities. Now we can consider some *compatibilities* for the intervals corresponding to these attributes, also depicted in Figure 1:

- *Have-banana* ("H_b") requires *Grabbing-banana* ("G_b") which requires *Not-have-banana* ("N_{hb}"). *Grabbing-banana* is performed while *High* and *At(tree)*.
- *At(tree)* ("*@(tree)*") requires going from the location *"x"* to the tree which requires *At(x)* ("*@(x)*"). *Going(x,tree)* ("$G(x, tree)$") is performed while *Low*.
- *High* ("*H*") requires *Climbing* ("*C*") which requires *Low* ("*L*"), and *Climbing-Down* ("C_D") requires *High*. *Climbing* is performed while *At(tree)*.

These compatibilities can be formally specified in ATL as follows:

$Meets(N_{hb}, G_b) \wedge Meets(G_b, H_b) \wedge During(G_b, @(tree)) \wedge During(G_b, H) \wedge$
$Meets(@(x), G(x, tree)) \wedge Meets(G(x, tree), @(tree)) \wedge During(G(x, tree), L) \wedge$
$Meets(L, C) \wedge Meets(C, H) \wedge Meets(H, C_D) \wedge Meets(C_D, L) \wedge During(C, @(tree)).$

Let us consider the subformula consisting of the first four conjuncts above (first line), and suppose that an unexpected "flying monkey" wants the banana. It climbs the tree, but it cannot reach for the banana. Being a flying monkey, it jumps for the banana, grabs it while gliding when it is still *High* and *At(tree)*, but as it glides it leaves the tree location. Supposing that it leaves the tree location at the same time it changes the status from *Grabbing-banana* to *Have-banana*, one can notice that the third conjunct is violated. Indeed, G_b must hold *during* *@(tree)*, meaning that there must be some (non-zero) periods of time in which the monkey was at the tree location before and after grabbing the banana.

It is often useful to state that some propositions hold all the time or eventually *during* an interval. For example, assume one more state predicate, *hungry*, saying whether the monkey is hungry or not, and assume that we want to state that monkeys should grab and have bananas only if they are hungry and do not already have bananas. This can be done with the following additional conjunct:

$Occurs(hungry, N_{hb}) \wedge Holds(hungry, G_b) \wedge Holds(hungry, H_b)$ □

There are different views on how intervals should be modeled in different time flows. A common interpretation is that the intervals are ordered pairs of distinct points in $\mathbb{Q}$ or $\mathbb{R}$. For simplicity, it is convenient to use semantics where intervals are arbitrary convex non-empty subsets of time points of an arbitrary time flow.

Definition 1. *If* $\mathcal{P}$ *is a set of* **atomic propositions** *and* $\mathcal{I}$ *is a set of* **intervals**, *then an* **Allen temporal logic formula over** $\mathcal{P}$ **and** $\mathcal{I}$, *or an* **ATL**$(\mathcal{P},\mathcal{I})$**-formula** *or even just a* **formula** *when* $\mathcal{P}$ *and* $\mathcal{I}$ *are understood from context, is any boolean combination of* **basic formulae** *of the form Equals*(i,j), *Before*(i,j), *After*(i,j), *Overlaps*(i,j), *OverlappedBy*(i,j), *Meets*(i,j), *MetBy*(i,j), *Contains*(i,j), *During*(i,j), *Starts*(i,j), *StartedBy*(i,j), *Ends*(i,j), *EndedBy*(i,j), *Holds*(p,i), *Occurs*(p,i), *where* $i,j \in \mathcal{I}$ *and* $p \in$ *Bool*$(\mathcal{P})$.

Bool$(\mathcal{P})$ is the set of boolean propositions over variables in $\mathcal{P}$. Interestingly, the original formulation of ATL [1] did not include *Holds* and *Occurs*; motivated by practical reasons, they were added later in [4]. To define a formal semantics of ATL we need to first define an appropriate notion of model.

Definition 2. *Let* $(T,<)$ *be a strict total order. The relation* $<$ *is tacitly extended to a strict partial order on subsets of* T, *namely* $X < Y$ *iff* $x < y$ *for all* $x \in X$ *and* $y \in Y$. *Also, by abuse of notation, we may write just* x *instead* $\{x\}$; *thus,* $x < Y$ *means that* $x < y$ *for all* $y \in Y$. *For* $x,y \in T$ *let* (x,y) *be the set* $\{z \in T \mid x < z < y\}$. *A subset* C *of* T *is* $<$-**convex**, *or simply* **convex**, *iff* $(x,y) \subseteq C$ *for any* $x,y \in C$.

In $\mathbb{R}$, for example, the convex sets are precisely the intervals. Recall that intervals in $\mathbb{R}$ can be open or closed on any of their ends, and that they may be bound by $-\infty$ or $+\infty$ at their left or right ends, respectively.

Definition 3. *A* $(\mathcal{P},\mathcal{I})$-**interval model** *(or simply an* **interval model** *when* $\mathcal{P}$ *and* $\mathcal{I}$ *are understood) is a structure* $\mathcal{M} = (T,<,v,\sigma)$, *where* $(T,<)$ *is a strict total order (modeling the intended flow of time),* $v : \mathcal{P} \rightarrow 2^T$ *is a valuation map assigning to each atomic proposition* $p \in \mathcal{P}$ *a set of time points* $v(p)$ *(in which the proposition is assumed to be true), and* σ *is a map that associates with every interval* $i \in \mathcal{I}$ *a non-empty convex subset* $\sigma(i)$ *of* T. *We may also refer to* $(\mathcal{P},\mathcal{I})$-*interval models as models of* ATL$(\mathcal{P},\mathcal{I})$.

We are now ready to give the formal semantics of ATL.

Definition 4. *An interval model* $\mathcal{M} = (T,<,v,\sigma)$ **satisfies**: *Equals*(i,j) *iff* $\sigma(i) = \sigma(j)$; *Before*(i,j) *or After*(j,i) *iff there is some* $t \in T$ *such that* $\sigma(i) < t < \sigma(j)$; *Overlaps*$(i,j)$ *or OverlappedBy*(j,i) *iff* $\sigma(i) \cap \sigma(j) \neq \emptyset$ *and there are some* $t_i \in \sigma(i)$ *and* $t_j \in \sigma(j)$ *such that* $t_i < \sigma(j)$ *and* $\sigma(i) < t_j$; *Meets*(i,j) *or MetBy*(j,i) *iff* $\sigma(i) < \sigma(j)$ *and there is no* $t \in T$ *such that* $\sigma(i) < t < \sigma(j)$; *Contains*$(i,j)$ *or During*(j,i) *iff there are some* $t_i, t_i' \in \sigma(i)$ *such that* $t_i < \sigma(j) < t_i'$; *Starts*(i,j) *or StartedBy*(j,i) *iff* $\sigma(i) \subset \sigma(j)$, *there is no* $t_j \in \sigma(j)$ *such that* $t_j < \sigma(i)$, *but there is some* $t_j \in \sigma(j)$ *such that* $\sigma(i) < t_j$; *Ends*(i,j) *or EndedBy*(j,i) *iff* $\sigma(i) \subset \sigma(j)$, *there is no* $t_j \in \sigma(j)$ *such that* $\sigma(i) < t_j$, *but there is some* $t_j \in \sigma(j)$ *such that* $t_j < \sigma(i)$; *Holds*(p,i) *iff* $\sigma(i) \subseteq v(p)$; *and Occurs*(p,i) *iff* $\sigma(i) \cap v(p) \neq \emptyset$ *iff* $\neg$*Holds*$(\neg p,i)$. *Satisfaction is defined as usual on boolean combinations of* ATL *formulae. We use the notation* $\mathcal{M} \models_{ATL} \varphi$ *to denote the fact that the interval structure* $\mathcal{M}$ *satisfies the* ATL *formula* φ.

Therefore, $Holds(p, i)$ is satisfied iff p holds at any time point in i, while $Occurs(p, i)$ is satisfied iff p holds at some time point in i. The propositions p used in $Holds$ and $Occurs$ may hold at various random timepoints, so they cannot be replaced by intervals. The NP-completeness of the satisfiability problem for ATL without $Holds$ [12] gives us immediately the NP-hardness of our ATL with $Holds$ above. We will show in the next section that it is actually NP-complete.

In many practical applications of interest, time elapses at a discrete and enumerable rate. We next define a variant of Allen temporal algebra in which the support of the interval models are ω-sequences of time points, that is, linear (infinite) sequences $t_1 < t_2 < t_3 < \cdots < t_n < \cdots$. We write these strict total orders compactly as $t_1 t_2 t_3 \ldots t_n \ldots$. We call the new logic **Allen Linear Temporal Logic** (ALTL). Note that ALTL has the same syntax as ATL and its satisfaction relation is defined like in ATL, but that its models are structures of the form $\mathcal{M} = (t_1 t_2 \ldots, v, \sigma)$, where $t_1 t_2 \ldots$ are ω-sequences of time points and σ maps intervals in $\mathcal{I}$ into non-empty convex sets $\sigma(i)$ of $T = \{t_1, t_2, \ldots\}$ (with the expected strict total ordering $<$ defined as $t_m < t_n$ iff $m < n$). It is easy to see that the convex sets of T are either finite sets of the form $\{t_m, t_{m+1}, \ldots, t_n\}$ for some $0 < m \leq n$, or infinite sets of the form $\{t_m, t_{m+1}, \ldots\}$ for some $0 < m$.

3   Linear Translation of **ALTL** into **LTL**

We next define an automatic encoding of ALTL into LTL$_\square$. Note that the models of ALTL differ from those of LTL in that they contain a concrete interpretation for each interval. Therefore, in order to establish a semantic relationship between the models of the two logics, we need to first add syntactic support for "intervals" to LTL. A simple way to do this is to add an atomic propositional symbol $\in_i$ to the syntax of LTL for each interval $i \in \mathcal{I}$, with the intuition that a time point is in the interval i in a model of ALTL if and only if the proposition $\in_i$ holds in that time point in the corresponding model of LTL. Moreover, we need to also capture, via corresponding LTL formulae, the fact that intervals are interpreted into non-empty convex sets in ALTL models.

Definition 5. Let $\mathcal{P}_\mathcal{I}$ be the set of atomic propositions $\mathcal{P} \cup \{\in_i \mid i \in \mathcal{I}\}$ and let $\Psi_\mathcal{I}$ be the set of LTL formulae $\{\psi_i \mid i \in \mathcal{I}\}$ over propositions in $\mathcal{P}_\mathcal{I}$, where ψ_i is the formula $\Diamond \in_i \land \neg \Diamond(\in_i \land \Diamond(\neg \in_i \land \Diamond \in_i))$ for each $i \in \mathcal{I}$.

The following establishes the relationship between models of ALTL and of LTL:

Proposition 1. There is a bijection between $(\mathcal{P}, \mathcal{I})$-interval models and models of $LTL(\mathcal{P} \cup \{\in_i \mid i \in \mathcal{I}\})$ that satisfy $\Psi_\mathcal{I}$.

Proof. Let $\mathcal{M} = (T, <, v, \sigma)$ be a tuple where $(T, <)$ is an ω-sequence, v is a map $\mathcal{P} \to 2^T$, and σ is a map $\mathcal{I} \to 2^T$; what $\mathcal{M}$ is missing to be a model of ALTL$(\mathcal{P}, \mathcal{I})$ is the requirements that $\sigma(i)$ is non-empty and convex for any $i \in \mathcal{I}$. Then we can build a model $\mathcal{N} = (T, <, u)$ of $LTL(\mathcal{P} \cup \{\in_i \mid i \in \mathcal{I}\})$, where $u(p) = v(p)$ for all $p \in \mathcal{P}$ and $u(\in_i) = \sigma(i)$ for all $i \in I$. Conversely, for any model $\mathcal{N} = (T, <, u)$

of LTL($\mathcal{P} \cup \{\in_i \mid i \in \mathcal{I}\}$) one can build a tuple $\mathcal{M} = (T, <, v, \sigma)$, where v is the restriction of u to $\mathcal{P}$ and $\sigma(i)$ is defined as $u(\in_i)$ for any $i \in \mathcal{I}$. What is left to prove is that $\sigma(i)$ is non-empty and convex for any $i \in \mathcal{I}$ if and only if $\mathcal{N} \models_{\text{LTL}} \Psi_{\mathcal{I}}$. First, note that, for any $i \in \mathcal{I}$, $\sigma(i) \neq \emptyset$ is equivalent to $\mathcal{N} \models_{\text{LTL}} \Diamond \in_i$. Second, since $\sigma(i)$ is convex if and only if there are no time points t_m, t_n, t_k with $0 < m < n < k$ such that $t_m, t_k \in \sigma(i)$ and $t_n \notin \sigma(i)$, one deduces that $\sigma(i)$ is convex if and only if $\mathcal{N} \models_{\text{LTL}} \neg\Diamond(\in_i \wedge \Diamond(\neg\in_i \wedge \Diamond\in_i))$. Therefore, $\sigma(i)$ is non-empty and convex for each $i \in \mathcal{I}$ if and only if $\mathcal{N} \models_{\text{LTL}} \Psi_{\mathcal{I}}$.   □

Definition 6. *We let* $[\cdot]$ *define the bijection above, that is, if* $\mathcal{M}$ *is a* $(\mathcal{P}, \mathcal{I})$-*interval model then* $[\mathcal{M}]$ *is the corresponding model of* LTL($\mathcal{P} \cup \{\in_i \mid i \in \mathcal{I}\}$) *satisfying* $\Psi_{\mathcal{I}}$, *defined as in the proof of Proposition 1.*

We are now ready to define the first part of our syntactic encoding of ALTL formulae into LTL formulae.

Definition 7. *Let* $[\cdot]$ *be the function taking formulae* φ *in* ALTL($\mathcal{P}, \mathcal{I}$) *into formulae* $[\varphi]$ *in* LTL($\mathcal{P} \cup \{\in_i \mid i \in \mathcal{I}\}$) *defined inductively as follows:* $[\neg\varphi]$ *is* $\neg[\varphi]$; $[\varphi_1 \wedge \varphi_2]$ *is* $[\varphi_1] \wedge [\varphi_2]$; $[Equals(i,j)]$ *is* $\Box(\in_i \Leftrightarrow \in_j)$; $[Before(i,j)]$ *and* $[After(j,i)]$ *are* $\Diamond(\in_i \wedge \Diamond(\neg\in_i \wedge \neg\in_j \wedge \Diamond\in_j))$; $[Meets(i,j)]$ *and* $[MetBy(j,i)]$ *are* $\Diamond(\in_i \wedge \Diamond\in_j \wedge \neg\Diamond(\in_i \wedge \in_j) \wedge \neg\Diamond(\neg\in_i \wedge \neg\in_j \wedge \Diamond\in_j))$; $[Overlaps(i,j)]$ *and* $[OverlappedBy(j,i)]$ *are* $\Diamond(\in_i \wedge \neg\in_j \wedge \Diamond(\in_i \wedge \in_j \wedge \Diamond(\neg\in_i \wedge \in_j)))$; $[Contains(i,j)]$ *and* $[During(j,i)]$ *are* $\Diamond(\in_i \wedge \neg\in_j \wedge \Diamond(\in_i \wedge \in_j \wedge \Diamond(\in_i \wedge \neg\in_j)))$; $[Starts(i,j)]$ *and* $[StartedBy(j,i)]$ *are* $\Box(\in_i \Rightarrow \in_j) \wedge \neg\Diamond(\in_j \wedge \neg\in_i \wedge \Diamond\in_i) \wedge \Diamond(\in_j \wedge \neg\in_i)$; $[Ends(i,j)]$ *and* $[EndedBy(j,i)]$ *are* $\Box(\in_i \Rightarrow \in_j) \wedge \Diamond(\in_j \wedge \neg\in_i) \wedge \neg\Diamond(\in_j \wedge \in_i \wedge \Diamond(\in_j \wedge \neg\in_i))$; $[Holds(p,i)]$ *is* $\Box(\in_i \Rightarrow p)$; *and* $[Occurs(p,i)]$ *is* $[\neg Holds(\neg p, i)]$, *that is,* $\Diamond(\in_i \wedge p)$.

Example 2. Let us consider again the subformula

$$Meets(N_{hb}, G_b) \wedge Meets(G_b, H_b) \wedge During(G_b, @(tree)) \wedge During(G_b, H)$$

of the formula that characterizes the compatibilities of the monkey/banana problem (see Example 1), to illustrate how to encode an ALTL formula into an equivalent LTL$_\Box$ one. Its encoding is:

$$\Diamond(\in_{N_{hb}} \wedge \Diamond\in_{G_b} \wedge \neg\Diamond(\in_{N_{hb}} \wedge \in_{G_b}) \wedge \neg\Diamond(\neg\in_{N_{hb}} \wedge \neg\in_{G_b} \wedge \Diamond\in_{G_b})) \wedge$$
$$\Diamond(\in_{G_b} \wedge \Diamond\in_{H_b} \wedge \neg\Diamond(\in_{G_b} \wedge \in_{H_b}) \wedge \neg\Diamond(\neg\in_{G_b} \wedge \neg\in_{H_b} \wedge \Diamond\in_{H_b})) \wedge$$
$$\Diamond(\in_{@(tree)} \wedge \neg\in_{G_b} \wedge \Diamond(\in_{@(tree)} \wedge \in_{G_b} \wedge \Diamond(\in_{@(tree)} \wedge \neg\in_{G_b}))) \wedge$$
$$\Diamond(\in_H \wedge \neg\in_{G_b} \wedge \Diamond(\in_H \wedge \in_{G_b} \wedge \Diamond(\in_H \wedge \neg\in_{G_b}))) \wedge (\bigwedge_{i \in \mathcal{I}} \psi_i),$$

where $\mathcal{I} = \{N_{hb}, H_b, H, G_b, @(tree)\}$ and ψ_i is $\Diamond\in_i \wedge \neg\Diamond(\in_i \wedge \Diamond(\neg\in_i \wedge \Diamond\in_i))$. As expected, the LTL encoding of the entire formula in Example 1 is very large.   □

The companion report [9] shows a rewriting implementation of this encoding.

Theorem 1. *Given an* ALTL($\mathcal{P}, \mathcal{I}$) *formula* φ *and a* $(\mathcal{P}, \mathcal{I})$-*interval model* $\mathcal{M}$, *then* $\mathcal{M} \models_{\text{ALTL}} \varphi$ *iff* $[\mathcal{M}] \models_{\text{LTL}} [\varphi]$.

Proof. Structural induction on φ. If φ has the form $\neg\varphi_1$ then $\mathcal{M} \models_{\text{ALTL}} \varphi$ is equivalent to saying that it is *not* the case that $\mathcal{M} \models_{\text{ALTL}} \varphi_1$, which, by the induction hypothesis and Definition 7, is equivalent to saying that $[\mathcal{M}] \models_{\mathsf{LTL}} [\varphi]$. The case where φ has the form $\varphi_1 \wedge \varphi_2$ is similar. What is left to show is that the property holds when φ is any of the interval relations. Let us discuss only one of them, for example $Meets(i,j)$. Suppose that $\mathcal{M} = (T, <, v, \sigma)$ and recall that $\sigma(i)$ is non-empty for any interval i. By Definition 4, $\mathcal{M} \models_{\mathsf{ALTL}} Meets(i,j)$ iff $\sigma(i) < \sigma(j)$ and there is so $t \in T$ such that $\sigma(i) < t < \sigma(j)$. By the way $[\mathcal{M}]$ is built and because ψ_i and ψ_j ensure the non-emptiness and the convexity of the trace fragments in which $\in_i$ and $\in_j$ hold, This is equivalent to saying that $\in_j$ holds *strictly* after $\in_i$, i.e., the $\Diamond(\in_i \wedge \Diamond \in_j \wedge \neg \Diamond(\in_i \wedge \in_j) \wedge ...)$; part of $[Meets(i,j)]$, and that there is no period of time following $\in_i$ that appears before $\in_j$ in which neither $\in_i$ nor $\in_j$ holds, i.e., the $\Diamond(... \neg \Diamond(\neg \in_i \wedge \neg \in_j \wedge \Diamond \in_j))$ part of $[Meets(i,j)]$. The result can be proved similarly for the other intervals. $\qquad\square$

Our goal next is to reduce the satisfiability problem for ALTL to LTL$_\square$ satisfiability, known to be an NP-complete problem [11]. Theorem 1 gives us only half of the result, namely that if a formula φ is satisfiable in ALTL then the formula $[\varphi]$ is satisfiable in LTL$_\square$. To get the other half, one could define a slightly different translation of ALTL formulae, namely one that would also include the conjunction of the formulae in $\Psi_{\mathcal{I}}$. The problem with that is, however, that $\mathcal{I}$ can be infinite, meaning that the generated LTL formula would be infinite. Fortunately, only the intervals that explicitly appear in φ need to be taken into account, thus making our transformation finite:

Definition 8. *For an $ALTL(\mathcal{P}, \mathcal{I})$ formula φ, let $\mathcal{I}_\varphi$ be the finite set of intervals appearing in φ and let $\langle \varphi \rangle$ be the formula $[\varphi] \wedge \bigwedge \Psi_{\mathcal{I}_\varphi}$ in $LTL(\mathcal{P} \cup \{\in_i \mid i \in \mathcal{I}_\varphi\})$.*

Corollary 1. *Given a formula φ in $ALTL(\mathcal{P}, \mathcal{I})$, the following are equivalent: (1) φ is satisfiable in $ALTL(\mathcal{P}, \mathcal{I})$; (2) $\langle \varphi \rangle$ is satisfiable in $LTL(\mathcal{P} \cup \{\in_i \mid i \in \mathcal{I}_\varphi\})$; and (3) $\langle \varphi \rangle$ is satisfiable in $LTL(\mathcal{P} \cup \{\in_i \mid i \in \mathcal{I}\})$.*

Proof. Since a model over more atomic propositions can be also regarded as a model over fewer propositions, it is immediate that *3.* implies *2.*. By Theorem 1, any model of φ in $ALTL(\mathcal{P}, \mathcal{I})$ yields a model of $[\varphi]$ in $LTL(\mathcal{P} \cup \{\in_i \mid i \in \mathcal{I}\})$ that satisfies $\Psi_{\mathcal{I}}$. Therefore, *1.* implies *3.*. To show that *2.* implies *1.*, by Proposition 1 it suffices to show that any model in $LTL(\mathcal{P} \cup \{\in_i \mid i \in \mathcal{I}_\varphi\})$ satisfying $\Psi_{\mathcal{I}_\varphi}$ can be extended, by just adding appropriate valuations for the additional atomic propositions to assure that the satisfaction of φ is not affected, to a model in $LTL(\mathcal{P} \cup \{\in_i \mid i \in \mathcal{I}\})$ satisfying $\Phi_{\mathcal{I}}$. This can be done many different ways. One straightforward model extension is to require that each proposition in $\{\in_i \mid i \in \mathcal{I} - \mathcal{I}_\varphi\}$ holds in precisely one (arbitrary) time point.

Corollary 2. *The satisfiability problem for ALTL is NP-complete.*

Proof. By Corollary 1, an ALTL formula φ is satisfiable iff $\langle \varphi \rangle$ is satisfiable as an LTL formula. Since $\langle \varphi \rangle$ can be generated linearly in the size of the φ and since LTL-satisfiability is NP-complete, ALTL-satisfiability is also NP-complete.

4   Monitoring ALTL

It is known that *any* monitoring algorithm for LTL-formulae requires space exponential in the size of the monitored formula [10] in the worst case. Can we find better monitoring algorithms for ALTL? We first argue empirically that a blind use of monitoring algorithms for LTL may be unfeasible in large applications and then propose an ALTL-specific monitoring algorithm which avoids the exponential-space complexity of monitoring LTL-formulae. More precisely, we give a monitoring algorithm for ALTL which only requires space (it needs to store its current state only) that is linear in the size of the input formula and whose most expensive task is to check the satisfiability of a *boolean* formula that is incrementally smaller (in the sense that some of its variables are irreversibly replaced by true or false) with each event received from the monitored system, and which initially has precisely the size of the original ALTL formula.

Let us first describe informally the "monitoring problem" for a logic whose models are (finite or infinite) traces. Given a formula ξ of size n and a "running system" abstracted by its incrementally emitted events (or abstract states encoded by the atomic propositions that "hold" in them) t_1, t_2, ..., the problem is to report when a bad prefix is reached, that is, when a finite trace $t_1 t_2 .. t_m$ is encountered such that there is no infinite trace $t_1 t_2 ... t_m t_{m+1} ...$ that satisfies ξ. We here assume that storing the events is *not* an option, because their number can grow arbitrarily large. Indeed, m can be large enough so that even an algorithm that is linear in the continuously increasing execution trace at each emitted event (e.g., one that traverses the trace backwards, like the one in [10]) can become easily more impractical than one just exponential in the formula but constant in the trace (e.g., when one generates an automata monitor from it, like in [3]). One can (non-trivially) formalize the monitoring problem for a logic as a decision problem, but this is rather intricate and beyond our scope here. Here we limit ourselves to the informal problem description above and conclude that ALTL-monitoring is asymptotically as expensive as ALTL-satisfiability:

(a) in any logic, monitoring is a harder problem than satisfiability;
(b) for any ALTL-formula ξ, we give a monitoring algorithm which is not more expensive than checking the satisfiability of ξ.

One can readily see that monitoring is harder than satisfiability: a monitor for ξ reports violation on the empty trace iff ξ is not satisfiable. Since ALTL-satisfiability is NP-complete (Corollary 2), any monitoring algorithm for ALTL is expected to be worst-case exponential in practice. However, as in many other similar situations, this does not necessarily mean that the problem of monitoring ALTL formulae is not practical. We next briefly discuss an immediate algorithm based on the translation to LTL, and then give an algorithm specific to ALTL that avoids the complexity of monitoring LTL and which seems quite efficient in practice. The next section discusses an experiment where the ALTL formula is large enough that the LTL-based monitoring algorithms cannot handle it.

The transformation in Section 3 suggests using a general purpose monitoring algorithm for LTL (e.g., the one in [3]), to monitor the LTL formula obtained linearly from the ALTL formula. We have experimented with this technique and have succeeded to generate, unfortunately huge, LTL monitors only for relatively small ALTL formulae. For example, for the ALTL formula in Example 2, which is a subformula of the ALTL formula in Example 1, the generated monitor had more than 60,000 edges, while the algorithm ran out of memory trying to generate an LTL monitor for the entire ALTL formula in Example 1; and that is just a toy example. The reason for our failure to generate monitors following this approach is the intermediate Büchi automata generator from LTL formulae; the LTL monitors in [3] are obtained pruning the corresponding Büchi automata (which can be exponential), by removing portions of them related to liveness – only the safety fragment of a formula is monitorable. The interested reader is encouraged to check [9] for more details on this unsuccessful approach.

We next give a monitoring algorithm for ALTL *not* based on general monitoring algorithms for LTL. The idea is to regard the ALTL formula φ as a *boolean proposition* in which the interval relations are regarded as special "dynamic" variables. For each interval relation we generate a little state machine, which has two special states, true and false. These state machines are shown in Figure 2. We also add a top-level conjunct consisting of precisely one special variable for each interval that appears in φ; these latter variables correspond, intuitively, to the formulae ψ_i in Definition 5. The monitoring algorithm works as follows: (1) generate all the state machines in Figure 2 (left-top state is initial); (2) let ξ be the boolean proposition obtained from φ as above; (3) run a *boolean* satisfiability checker on ξ and stop with "error" if ξ not satisfiable; (4) otherwise, for the next event t received from the monitored system, run all the state machines one step according to t (take that deterministic edge which is satisfied by t); (5) modify the formula ξ by replacing each variable whose corresponding state machine is in a state true or false by the corresponding truth value; (6) goto step (3).

Let us briefly discuss the state machines. The ones for ψ_i ensure that intervals are contiguous (convex); some intervals can be unbounded. The next seven state machines correspond to the relations on intervals. Let us discuss the one for $Meets(i, j)$. One starts with the initial state $\widehat{(i, j)}$ (neither in i nor in j), and there it stays as far as one does not enter any of the intervals. If while in this state the monitored program enters the interval j, that is, if $\in_j$ holds, then the relation $Meets(i, j)$ is obviously violated (interval i cannot be empty). Otherwise, if the interval i but not j is entered, then the machine moves to state $(i, \overline{j})$ where it waits until either i is left and j is entered in which case it returns true, or otherwise until i is left without entering j or i and j overlap, when it returns false. The machine for $Holds(p, i)$ checks that p holds during the interval i.

Example 3. Let us consider again the monkey/banana formula in Example 2,

$$(Meets(N_{hb}, G_b) \wedge Meets(G_b, H_b) \wedge During(G_b, @(tree)) \wedge During(G_b, H)),$$

and consider an execution trace which starts with the abstract events $t_1 = \{\in_{N_b}\}$, $t_2 = \{\in_{N_b}, \in_{@(tree)}\}$, $t_3 = \{\in_{G_b}, \in_{@(tree)}, \in_H\}$, $t_4 = \{\in_{H_b}, \in_H\}$, ..., where an abstract event formed of a set of atomic propositions is an event in which all those, and only those propositions hold. This execution trace corresponds to the "flying monkey" scenario at the end of Example 1.

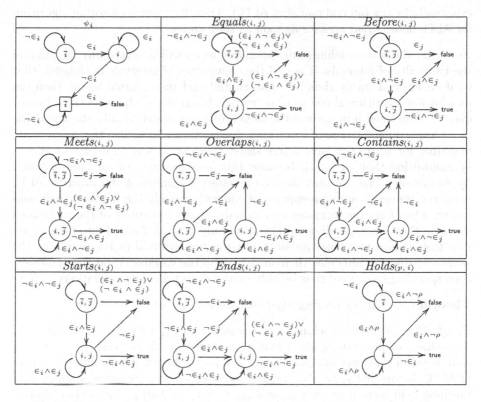

Fig. 2. State machines are run synchronously by the monitor with each event

Let us simulate the execution of the ALTL monitoring algorithm above on this example. There are nine state machines like in Figure 2 necessary, four corresponding to each of the four interval relations and five corresponding to each interval appearing in the formula. The boolean formula ξ is just a conjunction of the corresponding nine variables. All one needs to do is to run the nine state machines on the execution trace, update the boolean proposition and then check for satisfiability after each event. After the first three events, the five ψ_i formulae will be in some intermediate (not false) states, and the four machines corresponding to the interval relations will be in the states true, $(G_b, \overline{H_b})$, $(@(tree), G_b)$, and (G_b, H), respectively, so the formula is still satisfiable. However, when the event t_4 is processed, the machine corresponding to $During(G_b, @(tree))$, or to $Contains(@(tree), G_b)$, transits to false, invalidating the boolean proposition. $\square$

Example 4. Consider now the ALTL formula $\neg Before(i,j)$ and a two-event trace $\{\in_i\}\{\}$. The monitoring algorithm above sets the machine corresponding to $Before(i,j)$ to state $(i, \bar{j})$ after processing $\{\subset_i\}$ and then to state true after processing $\{\}$, causing the monitor to report "error" before any event containing $\in_j$ is seen. Note that $\{\in_i\}\{\}$ is indeed a bad prefix for $\neg Before(i,j)$ ($\in_j$ must hold eventually in any interval model of ALTL). Therefore, our monitoring algorithm for ALTL detects bad prefixes as soon as they appear.   □

Note that the state machines corresponding to ψ_i will intercept any violation of the convexity of intervals. If any of the convexities of intervals is violated, that is, if an interval starts, then it is interrupted and then started again, then the monitoring algorithm above returns "error", because the observed trace cannot even be continued into an interval model; one can easily modify the algorithm to return a different type of error in such situations. Note also that these state machines for ψ_i do not have a true state: there is no way to decide by means of monitoring that ψ_i holds, because this is a property of an infinite trace; by monitoring, one can only detect the safety fragment of the inherent ALTL property "intervals are non-empty and convex", namely the break of their convexity. Therefore, the formulae ψ_i can only detect violations of the monitored formula: their corresponding variables can only be transformed into false, never into true. If in a particular application there are external factors implying the well-formedness of intervals, then one can drop the variables (and the machines) corresponding to ψ_i (and thus be able to also detect formula validations online).

Theorem 2. *The monitoring algorithm for ALTL above is correct.*

Proof. Thanks to the machines corresponding to ψ_i, we can assume the well-formedness of intervals in the proof. Consider some finite trace $\tau = t_1 t_2 ... t_m$ that is well-formed wrt intervals, i.e., it can be the prefix of some interval model of ALTL. Let us first prove that for any interval relation, its corresponding state machine is in state false after processing τ iff τ is a bad prefix of that interval relation. We only show it for one relation, say $Before(i, j)$; the others are similar. Note that τ is a bad prefix of $Before(i, j)$ iff τ contains (some event satisfying) $\in_j$ before or at the same time with $\in_i$. Since the state machine of $Before(i, j)$ reaches the state false iff $\in_j$ is seen before in_j or if $\in_j$ and $\in_i$ are seen together as part of an event, and since the machines corresponding to ψ_i ensure the contiguity of intervals, we can conclude that τ is a bad prefix of $Before(i, j)$ iff the corresponding machine of $Before(i, j)$ is in state false after processing τ.

Let us next prove that for any interval relation, the corresponding machine is in state true after processing τ iff τ is a good prefix of that relation, in the sense that for any infinite trace ϕ such that $\tau\pi$ is an interval model of ALTL, it is the case that $\tau\pi$ satisfies that relation. As above, let us just prove it for $Before(i, j)$. Note that the machine of $Before(i, j)$ can be in state true after processing τ iff τ contains no event satisfying $\in_j$ and contains some event satisfying $\in_i$ followed by one which does not satisfy $\in_i$. This is equivalent to saying that any interval model of the form $\tau\pi$ (recall that intervals have non-empty interpretations in interval models) satisfies $Before(i, j)$.

Let us now consider any ALTL formula φ and a finite trace τ as above such that the ξ formula maintained by the algorithm is satisfiable after processing τ. If φ has the form $\varphi_1 \wedge \varphi_2$ then τ is a bad (good) prefix of φ iff it is a bad (good) prefix of φ_1 or (and) φ_2. If φ has the form $\neg\varphi_1$ then τ is a bad (good) prefix of φ iff it is a good (bad) prefix of φ_1. Therefore, in order to test whether τ is a bad prefix of φ one only needs to know whether it is a bad prefix of φ's interval relations, that is, if their corresponding state machines are in their corresponding false or true states after processing τ. The satisfiability checking of ξ after each event ensures that violations are reported as early as possible.   □

If one is not interested in reporting ALTL property violations as early as possible, then one can run the satisfiability checker less frequently, say once every 100 events, or even just once at the end of the monitoring session, and thus significantly reduce the runtime overhead. If minimal runtime overhead is highly desirable, since the formula ξ to check for satisfiability changes incrementally by irreversibly transforming some of its variables into true or false, to achieve a minimal runtime overhead one can use an incremental SAT solver.

5 Experiment

Implementation. We have implemented a prototype monitor generation tool, called ALTL2Monitor. It implements the monitoring algorithm presented in the previous section using the SAT solver zChaff [7] for satisfiability checking.

Case Study. Our case study is a simplified version of an exploration rover (Gromit, at Nasa Ames). The mission of the robot is to visit a number of waypoints, into an initially unknown rough environment, while monitoring interesting targets on its path. The robot continuously takes pictures of the terrain in front of it, performs a stereo correlation to extract a cloud of 3D points, merges these points in its model of environment and starts this process again. In parallel, it continuously considers its currents position, the next waypoint to visit, the obstacles in the model of the environment built and produces a trajectory. These two interdependent cyclic processes are synchronized. Last, a third process interrupts whenever an interesting rock has been detected. The functional layer of Gromit is implemented using functional modules (for more details see [6]). For each of them we shall consider the "visible" state variables of interest:

- RFLEX is the module interfaced with the low-level speed controller. It has a state variable for the position of the robot, each interval representing a specific robot position, and another one for the speed passed to the wheels controller.
- CAMERA shoots a pair of stereo calibrated images and saves them. It has one state variable representing the camera status (taking picture, or idle).
- SCORREL produces and stores a stereo correlated image. It has a state variable representing the SCORREL process (performing stereo correlation, or idle).
- LANE builds a model of the environment by aggregating clouds of 3D points produced by SCORREL. It services two requests: read in an internal buffer and fuse the read. LANE has one state variable for the model building process.
- P3D is a rover navigation software. It produces an arc trajectory which is translated in a speed reference, to try to reach a waypoint. P3D has a variable for its state (idle or computing the speed) and one for the waypoints to visit.
- SCIENCE. This module monitors a particular condition of interest to scientist (such as detecting a rock with particular features). When such a condition arises

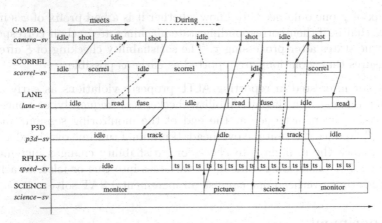

Fig. 3. Partial Gromit Model: Attributes and compatibilities

while the robot is moving toward a waypoint, it stops and takes a picture of the rock. It has one state variable for its state (monitoring interesting rock or idle).

Figure 3 shows some temporal relations representing a simplified version of the actual Gromit Rover.

Results. Due to intellectual property restrictions, we did not have access to the execution platform of the Gromit Rover. However, the CNRS Laboratory LAAS (at Toulouse, France) provided[1] us with a file formalizing some of the compatibilities as an ATL formula of more than 100 interval relations, as well as with a set of one hundred traces generated by Gromit Rover execution platform. We applied our prototype ALTL2Monitor off-line to check these traces; the checking took negligible time. However, the satisfiability checker was applied only once at the end of the monitoring session of each trace, because we expected the traces to be correct, which was indeed the case.

6   Conclusion

We presented Allen linear temporal logic (ALTL), an automated translation of ALTL into LTL, a monitor synthesis algorithm for ALTL, as well as a real-life experiment. While LTL can be a suitable logic for AI and planning, we also believe that ALTL can be a suitable logic for certain program verification efforts. Its simplicity, neutrality and visual interpretation cannot be ignored. We plan to apply our ALTL monitoring prototype to the autonomous embedded system iRobot ATRV of the LAAS Laboratory.

References

1. J. Allen. Towards a general theory of actions and time. *Artificial Intelligence*, 23(2):123–154, 1984.

---

[1] We warmly thank Felix Ingrand for help.

2. D. Calvanese, G. De Giacomo, and M. Y. Vardi. Reasoning about actions and planning in LTL action theories. In *KR*, pages 593–602, 2002.
3. M. D'Amorim and G. Roşu. Efficient monitoring of omega-languages. In *CAV'05*, volume 3576 of *LNCS*, pages 364–378. Springer, July 2005.
4. M. Ghallab and A.M. Alaoui. Managing efficiently temporal relations through indexed spanning trees. In *IJCAI*, pages 1297–1303, 1989.
5. A.A. Krokhin, P. Jeavons, and P. Jonsson. Reasoning about temporal relations: The tractable subalgebras of Allen's interval algebra. *J. ACM*, 50(5):591–640, 2003.
6. S. Lacroix, A. Mallet, D. Bonnafous, G. Bauzil, S. Fleury, M. Herrb, and R. Chatila. Autonomous rover navigation on unknown terrains, functions and integration. *International Journal of Robotics Research*, 2003.
7. M. Moskewicz, C. Madigan, Y. Zhao, L. Zhang, and S. Malik. Chaff: Engineering an efficient SAT solver. In *Design Automation Conference (DAC'01)*, June 2001.
8. A. Pnueli. The temporal logic of programs. In *Proceedings of the 18th Annual Symposium on Foundations of Computer Science*, New York, 1977. IEEE.
9. G. Roşu and S. Bensalem. Allen linear (interval) temporal logic – translation to LTL and monitor synthesis. Technical Report UIUCDCS-R-2006-2681, University of Illinois at Urbana-Champaign, January 2006.
10. G. Roşu and K. Havelund. Rewriting-based techniques for runtime verification. *J. of Automated Software Engineering*, 12(2):151–197, 2005.
11. A. P. Sistla and E. M. Clarke. The complexity of propositional linear temporal logics. *J. ACM*, 32(3):733–749, 1985.
12. M. Vilain, H. Kautz, and P. van Beek. Constraint propagation algorithms for temporal reasoning: a revised report. In *Readings in Qualitative Reasoning about Phisical Systems*. Morgan Kaufmann, Los Altos, CA, 1989.

DiVinE – A Tool for Distributed Verification*
(Tool Paper)

Jiří Barnat, Luboš Brim, Ivana Černá, Pavel Moravec,
Petr Ročkai, and Pavel Šimeček

Faculty of Informatics, Masaryk University, Brno, Czech Republic

Abstract. We present a tool for cluster-based LTL model-checking and reachability analysis. The tool incorporates several novel distributed-memory algorithms and provides a unique interface to use them. We describe the basic structure of the tool, discuss the main architecture decisions made, and briefly explain how the tool can be used.

1 Introduction

A few enumerative verification tools have been developed to support engineers in their verification needs. Despite significant improvements in model-checking techniques, their verification capabilities are in the case of real-life industrial models limited by the amount of data a *single* state-of-the-art computer is able to handle efficiently.

In recent years, extensive research has been conducted in parallel and distributed model-checking with the aim to push forward the frontiers of enumeratively verifiable systems [1,3,4,6,8]. Consequently, several distributed verification prototype tools emerged. The deployment and usage of a distributed tool is significantly more demanding compared to the sequential one. It assumes a cluster with properly installed message passing software and also some programming skills are required in the case the tool has to be compiled from its source codes. These are some of the reasons why distributed verification tools are used rarely, although their verification capabilities are undoubtedly bigger in comparison to the sequential tools.

The goal of Distributed Verification Environment project (DiVinE) is to provide an extensible framework to support distributed verification on clusters. DiVinE offers three means to achieve this goal: First, a library of common functions (DiVinE LIBRARY) on top of which various distributed verification algorithms can be implemented. Second, a collection of state-of-the-art distributed verification algorithms incorporated into a single software product (DiVinE TOOL) which is as easy to install as most sequential tools. And third, a ready-to-use cluster for users of sequential tools in case they need to run experiments using DiVinE TOOL without having access to their own cluster. In this paper we report on DiVinE TOOL only.

* This work has been partially supported by the Grant Agency of Czech Republic grant No. 201/06/1338 and the Academy of Sciences grant No. 1ET408050503.

T. Ball and R.B. Jones (Eds.): CAV 2006, LNCS 4144, pp. 278–281, 2006.

2 DiVinE Tool

DiVinE Tool is a parallel, distributed-memory enumerative model-checking tool for verification of concurrent systems. The tool employs aggregate power of network-interconnected workstations to verify systems whose verification is beyond capabilities of sequential tools.

DiVinE modelling language is rich enough to describe systems made of synchronous and asynchronous processes communicating via shared memory and buffered or unbuffered channels. System properties can be specified either directly in Linear Temporal Logic (LTL) or alternatively as processes describing undesired behaviour of systems under consideration (negative claim automata). Thanks to the DivSPIN project [2], DiVinE Tool is also capable of verifying models written in ProMeLa.

From the algorithmic point of view, the tool is quite unique. In automata-based approach to LTL model-checking, the verification problem is reduced to problem of accepting cycle detection in the graph of Büchi automaton. Two algorithms are typically used for solving the problem: Nested Depth-First Search algorithm and Tarjan's algorithm for decomposition of the graph into strongly connected components. Unfortunately, they both strongly rely on depth-first search postorder that is known to be difficult to be computed in parallel. Therefore, new, principally different, parallel algorithms for accepting cycle detection had to be designed. These are, namely, algorithm for cycle detection using additional dependency data structure, algorithm based on negative cycles, algorithms for forward and backward elimination of trivial and non-accepting strongly connected components, algorithm for cycle detection based on breadth-first search, and algorithm based on propagation of the value of maximal accepting predecessor(see [1] for an overview). Besides these, DiVinE Tool includes also an algorithm for distributed state space generation and an algorithm that performs sequential NestedDFS in a distributed-memory setting. More details on algorithms can be found on DiVinE project web pages [5].

DiVinE Tool can be deployed either as a complete software package to be installed on a separate Linux cluster or as a small Java application to access a pre-installed clusters. In the first case, basic Linux administrator skills are required to install the tool, but the user is in the full control of environment settings under which distributed algorithms are to be executed and can control the tool from a command line. In the second case, the tool can be used employing DiVinE pre-installed clusters and accessed remotely via a graphical user interface. The graphical user interface (GUI) requires properly installed Java Runtime Environment. Both versions are available on DiVinE project web page [5] together with a few models determined for initial acquaintance with the tool.

An important part of the DiVinE project is the maintenance of a *public* server together with a limited number of DiVinE dedicated clusters. For security reasons registered users are allowed to connect to DiVinE public server only. New users can be registered by following instructions given on DiVinE project web pages.

3   Interacting with DiVinE by Using GUI

The description of command line interface is beyond the scope of this paper. Therefore, we focus on controlling DiVinE Tool with GUI only. GUI is implemented as a client-server application where the server part is responsible for the control of the tool. This means the server maintains currently verified models, executes distributed algorithms, monitors cluster load, etc.

The client window is divided into three parts. In the main working area, models and properties are specified, and outputs of distributed algorithms are displayed. Another part of the client window has a tree-like structure and is used to browse currently loaded models including corresponding properties and verification results. The third part displays messages reporting changes in the status of running algorithms.

A new *verification project* is started by pressing the *New model* button. The system to be verified can be written directly into the main window or imported from a local file. Having specified a model of the system the user is expected to provide properties the system should meet using the button *Add property*. Besides distributed state space generation, the tool is capable of verifying full range of LTL formulae over state-based atomic propositions. Atomic propositions are specified using the keyword #define, e.g. #define p x>3, the formula is specified using the keyword #property, e.g. #property FG(p). Property specification can also be imported from a local file. The pair model-property is called a *task*. User can assign several distributed algorithms to be run for a given task. The number of workstations to be used can be specified for every algorithm as well. Individual algorithms are initiated with the button *Execute*.

Each algorithm produces two different types of output that can be accessed with the client: the standard output and log files. While the standard output is used to report progress in the computation and final verification results, logs are used to generate multiple statistics to support the performance analysis. For each computer participating in the computation, the logged values include the amount of memory currently allocated by the algorithm, number of sent and received messages, time spent in user and kernel space, size of queue of unexplored states, etc. Client displays the last logged values with refresh rate around five seconds, which allows the user to monitor the status of the computation in almost real time.

All specified models, properties and verification results are stored on the server until they are explicitly removed. Therefore, the user can disconnect from the server, while initiated algorithms are still running, and reconnect later to collect the verification results. It is also possible to specify and initiate new tasks during computation of others. Hence, several tasks can be computed in parallel.

4   Conclusion

DiVinE is a tool for enumerative model checking of LTL properties on a cluster of workstations. We performed numerous experiments that clearly demonstrates the tool is capable to handle systems intractable by a single machine. E.g. for some classical verification problems the results on a cluster with 20 workstations were: Anderson's mutual exclusion problem – space required was 10GB of memory/verification took about 40 minutes, Dining Philosophers – 9GB/20 minutes, Leader Election – 17GB/46 minutes. For more examples see the tool web page. Another interesting performance characteristic is the scalability. The figure shows typical behaviour of algorithms with respect to the number of workstations involved.

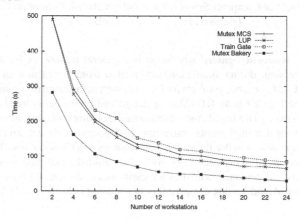

References

1. J. Barnat, L. Brim, and I. Černá. Distributed Analysis of Large Systems. In *Proc. of the 4th International Symposium on Formal Methods for Components and Objects (FMCO 05)*, LNCS. Springer, 2006.
2. J. Barnat, V. Forejt, M. Leucker, and M. Weber. DivSPIN – A SPIN compatible distributed model checker. In *Proc. 4th International Workshop on Parallel and Distributed Methods in verifiCation*, pages 95–100, 2005.
3. G. Behrmann, T. S. Hune, and F. W. Vaandrager. Distributed timed model checking — how the search order matters. In *Proc. of the 12th International Conference on Computer Aided Verification*, volume 1855 of *LNCS*, pages 216–231. Springer, 2000.
4. B. Bollig, M. Leucker, and M. Weber. Parallel model checking for the alternation free μ-calculus. In *Proc. of the 7th International Conference on Tools and Algorithms for the Construction and Analysis of Systems (TACAS'01)*, volume 2031 of *LNCS*, pages 543–558. Springer, 2001.
5. DiVinE project web page: http://anna.fi.muni.cz/divine/.
6. H. Garavel, R. Mateescu, and I.M Smarandache. Parallel State Space Construction for Model-Checking. In *Proc. of the 8th International SPIN Workshop on Model Checking of Software (SPIN'01)*, volume 2057 of *LNCS*, pages 200–216. Springer, 2001.
7. F. Holmen, M. Leucker, and M. Lindstrom. Uppdmc: A distributed model checker for fragments of the mu-calculus. *Electronic Notes in Theoretical Computer Science*, 128(3):91–105, 2005.
8. F. Lerda and R. Sisto. Distributed-memory model checking with SPIN. In *Proc. of the 5th International SPIN Workshop*, volume 1680 of *LNCS*, pages 22–39. Springer, 1999.

EverLost: A Flexible Platform for Industrial-Strength Abstraction-Guided Simulation[*]
(Tool Paper)

Flavio M. de Paula and Alan J. Hu

Department of Computer Science, University of British Columbia, Canada
{depaulfm, ajh}@cs.ubc.ca

Abstract. *Abstraction-guided simulation* is a general framework for automatically harnessing, during simulation, information from abstraction and model checking. EverLost is our platform for industrial-strength abstraction-guided simulation. EverLost takes an RTL Verilog design and preimage/abstraction information from any BDD-based abstraction/model-checking tool, and automatically generates code that implements abstraction-guided simulation and directly compiles with the design under the widely-used Synopsys VCS simulator. The platform enables flexible exploration of abstraction-guided simulation — different formal tools and guidance heuristics are easily inserted — while providing the capacity, speed, and Verilog compatibility of a leading industry-standard tool.

1 Abstraction-Guided Simulation

Automatic formal hardware verification continues to progress, through advances such as model checking [5,8], symbolic model checking [3], bounded model checking [1,2], and counterexample-guided abstraction refinement [7], which have greatly expanded the capacity of automatic verification tools. Conventional simulation, however, remains the primary workhorse for industrial hardware validation. Simulation provides unparalleled capacity for handling design size and complexity, but (or because) it performs no analysis of the design. Abstraction and model checking, on the other hand, derive considerable information about the structure of the state space of the design, but (therefore) suffer from capacity limitations.

Abstraction-guided simulation[1] is a general framework for automatically harnessing, during simulation, information obtained by model checking and abstraction of the design. Briefly, abstraction-guided simulation consists of the following:

– We assume the goal of verification is to find an execution sequence that reaches a specified set of states, e.g., error states or a hard-to-reach coverage target.

---

[*] Supported by an NSERC Discovery Grant. We would also like to thank Daniel Kroening and Himanshu Jain for their help with the *vcegar* tool.

[1] The idea of guiding state exploration via abstraction has been independently invented several times, e.g., as "tracks" [10], "abstraction database" [6], and "distance-guided simulation" [9]. Unlike other work, our emphasis is on working with the capabilities and limits of real, industrial simulation tools. We prefer the nomenclature "abstraction-guided" to "distance-guided" because the analysis of the abstract model gives not true distances, but only lower bounds on distances, and the challenge for good guidance heuristics is precisely to handle this inaccuracy.

T. Ball and R.B. Jones (Eds.): CAV 2006, LNCS 4144, pp. 282–285, 2006.
© Springer-Verlag Berlin Heidelberg 2006

- Any conservative abstraction technique is used to create a model small enough for symbolic model checking. The abstract model preserves existence of any paths to the error states, but may introduce paths that don't correspond to any concrete path.
- If formal verification succeeds (either finding no abstract error paths, or successfully concretizing an abstract error path), we are done. The interesting case for simulation is when formal verification fails (and attempts at abstraction refinement fail to create a tractable model), as can occur typically with large hardware designs.
- The model checker has computed a series of pre-images from the error states in the abstract model. From these pre-images, we can dump a sequence of BDDs, representing sets of abstract states whose shortest (abstract) path to an error state is i abstract states long. Visualize these sets as concentric "rings" around the error states. A concrete state that abstracts to an abstract state in ring i is at least i clock cycles away from an error state.
- During directed random simulation, the simulator can consult the abstraction information for guidance by periodically computing the abstraction of the current simulation state and querying which ring it is in. Thus, the simulator can benefit from considerable information computed by model checking the abstract model.

An analogy is to driving with a GPS navigation device: one's concrete location (GPS coordinates) goes into the device, which contains an abstract model of the terrain and provides optimum routing for the abstract model; problems arise when the abstract model is inaccurate (e.g., due to construction); in those cases, the user wanders semi-lost until the device computes a usable new route. The name "EverLost" is a play on a pioneering, widely-deployed in-car GPS navigation system.

Abstraction-guided simulation is a broad and flexible framework, so research is needed to explore trade-offs. Hence, we have created EverLost, as a flexible, yet industrial-strength platform for exploring abstraction-guided simulation. The key features of EverLost are:

- Direct connection into Synopsys VCS, one of the most widely used Verilog simulators, giving true industrial capacity, simulation speed, and language compatibility.
- Simple interfacing to any BDD-based abstraction/model-checking tool. All we need are the concrete state variables, the abstraction functions, and the BDD rings.
- Easy exploration of different guidance heuristics. Currently, we have implemented a simple parameterized stochastic search; this is an active research area.

2   EverLost Architecture

The three major components for using EverLost are the logic simulator, the abstraction/model-checking engine, and the EverLost tool itself (Fig. 1). For tight integration and highest performance, we had to target a specific logic simulator, although the tool could be retargeted easily. We chose Synopsys VCS, one of the most widely used industrially. For the interface with the abstraction/model-checking engine, we designed for maximum flexibility: all we require are a list of the design's latches, the abstraction map, and the BDD pre-images that are a by-product of model checking.

Given the needed inputs, EverLost generates a simulation guidance driver in C, the abstraction function in C, and a C interface in Verilog, which are passed to VCS along

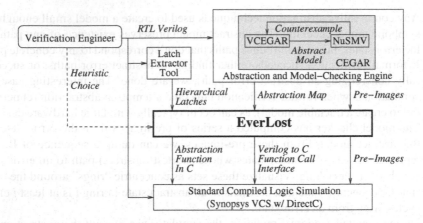

Fig. 1. Overall Tool Flow with EverLost

with the Verilog files and the BDD pre-images. The user can specify different simulation guidance heuristics via EverLost options.

The code generated by EverLost is compiled with VCS into a single executable. Internally, the simulator calls the EverLost driver every clock cycle. The EverLost code can read the current simulation state, possibly save it, and possibly evaluate it using the abstraction information. The EverLost code can then allow the simulation to continue, or it can force the simulator to jump to a particular state. In our current guidance heuristic, from a given state, the simulator explores n different traces for k cycles and picks the best state (i.e., the state that abstracts to the pre-image closest to the target states) from which to continue; one more parameter controls when to resort to a random walk to try to get around dead-ends.

3 Sample Results and Performance Overhead

We report some results from two publicly available designs: a USB 1.1 PHY [11] interface, and a full USB 2.0 Function Core [12]. We used VCEGAR [7] with NuSMV [4] as our formal engine; these tools are state-of-the-art, freely available, and support Verilog. When the designs were too big, the formal engine did not produce useful abstract models, so in some experiments, we used only a few sub-modules. VCS and EverLost, of course, had no capacity problems, including for the full Function Core.

When the formal engine provided enough pre-image rings, EverLost was able to guide simulation towards a target using up to an order of magnitude fewer simulation clock cycles than random simulation. For example, while verifying two usb_rx_phy coverage points, the formal engine generated 27 and 23 pre-images for (1) acknowledging receiving data and (2) proper synchronization. For (1), over 30 simulation trials, random simulation averaged 206K clock cycles and 2.1 seconds CPU time versus 5.3K clock cycles and 4 seconds for EverLost. For (2), also over 30 trials, random simulation averaged 1.4M clock cycles and 13 seconds versus 0.5M clock cycles and 1.25 seconds for EverLost.

Table 1. Simulation Overhead. The columns show, from left to right: the design, the number of latches, the length of each random trace, and the CPU times for the simulation when EverLost is absent, when only the C-Interface calls are added, and when both C-Interface calls and guiding heuristics are present, and the total overhead ratio

Module	Latches	Cycles	Standard	No-Op C-Calls	C-Calls+Heuristic	Overhead Ratio
usb_rx_phy	56	5M	96.3s	145.2s	490.0s	5.1
usbf_pl	696	250K	38.2s	232.3s	333.7s	8.7
usb	1785	15K	25.5s	379.5s	421.6s	16.5

Simulation overhead has two components: the overhead of calling/returning from the Verilog test bench to the C interface, and the time required by the heuristic to evaluate concrete states and choose an action. To measure the overhead, we ran extended random simulations on variously sized designs. Table 1 shows the results, averaged over 5 random runs each, with negligible standard deviations. Notice that as the design size increases, the predominant overhead is due to the interface between Verilog and C, rather than the guidance heuristic.

Future work includes reducing overhead and exploring guidance heuristics.

References

1. A. Biere, A. Cimatti, E. M. Clarke, Y. Zhu. Symbolic model checking without BDDs. *Tools and Algorithms for Construction and Analysis of Systems*, LNCS 1579, pp. 193–207, 1999.
2. V. Boppana, S. P. Rajan, K. Takayama, M. Fujita. Model checking based on sequential ATPG. *Computer-Aided Verification: 11th Intl Conf*, LNCS 1633, pp. 418–430, 1999.
3. J. R. Burch, E. M. Clarke, K. L. McMillan, D. L. Dill, L. J. Hwang. Symbolic model checking: 10^{20} states and beyond. *Conf on Logic in Computer Science*, pp. 428–439, 1990.
4. A. Cimatti, E. Clarke, E. Giunchiglia, F. Giunchiglia, M. Pistore, M. Roveri, R. Sebastiani, A. Tacchella. NuSMV 2: An OpenSource tool for symbolic model checking. *Computer-Aided Verification: 14th Intl Conf*, LNCS 2404, pp. 359–364, 2002.
5. E. M. Clarke, E. A. Emerson. Design and synthesis of synchronization skeletons using branching time temporal logic. *Workshop on Logics of Programs*, LNCS 131, pp. 52–71, May 1981.
6. S. Edelkamp, A. Lluch-Lafuente. Abstraction in directed model checking. *Workshop on Connecting Planning Theory and Practice*, pp. 7–13, 2004.
7. H. Jain, D. Kroening, N. Sharygina, E. Clarke. Word level predicate abstraction and refinement for verifying RTL verilog. *42nd Design Automation Conf*, pp. 445–450, 2005.
8. J.-P. Queille, J. Sifakis. Specification and verification of concurrent systems in Cesar. *5th Intl Symp on Programming*, LNCS 137, pp. 337–351, 1981.
9. S. Shyam, V. Bertacco. Distance-guided hybrid verification with GUIDO. *Design Automation and Test in Europe*, pp. 1211–1216, 2006.
10. C. H. Yang, D. L. Dill. Validation with guided search of the state space. *35th Design Automation Conf*, pp. 599–604, 1998.
11. USB 1.1 PHY. http://www.opencores.org/projects.cgi/web/usb_phy/overview.
12. USB 2.0 Function Core. http://www.opencores.org/projects.cgi/web/usb/overview.

Symbolic Model Checking of Concurrent Programs Using Partial Orders and On-the-Fly Transactions

Vineet Kahlon[1], Aarti Gupta[1], and Nishant Sinha[2]

[1] NEC Laboratories America, Princeton, NJ 08540, USA
[2] Carnegie Mellon University, Pittsburgh, PA 15213, USA

Abstract. The state explosion problem is one of the core bottlenecks in the model checking of concurrent software. We show how to ameliorate the problem by combining the ability of partial order techniques to reduce the state space of the concurrent program with the power of symbolic model checking to explore large state spaces. Our new verification methodology involves translating the given concurrent program into a circuit-based model which gives us the flexibility to then employ any model checking technique of choice – either SAT or BDD-based – for verifying a broad range of linear time properties, not just safety. The reduction in the explored state-space is obtained by statically augmenting the symbolic encoding of the program by additional constraints. These constraints restrict the scheduler to choose from a minimal *conditional stubborn set* of transitions at each state. Another key contribution of the paper, is a new method for detecting transactions *on-the-fly* which takes into account patterns of lock acquisition and yields better reductions than existing methods which rely on a lockset based analysis. Moreover unlike existing techniques, identifying on-the-fly transactions does not require the program to follow a lock discipline in accessing shared variables. We have applied our techniques to the Daisy test bench and shown the existence of several bugs.

1 Introduction

The widespread use of concurrent software in modern day computing systems necessitates the development of effective verification methodologies for multi-threaded programs. However, subtle interactions between threads makes multi-threaded software behaviorally complex and hard to analyze necessitating the use of formal methodologies for their debugging. It is not surprising then that the use of model checking – both symbolic and explicit state – for the verification of concurrent software has recently been an active area of research.

Explicit state model checkers, such as Verisoft [God97] rely on exploring an enumeration of the states and transitions of the concurrent program at hand. Additional techniques such as state hashing for compaction of state representations, and partial order methods are typically used to avoid exploring all interleavings of transitions of the constituent threads. While these techniques are powerful tools for state space reduction, they still do not fully address the scalability issues that arise due to state explosion when model checking large-scale concurrent programs.

Symbolic model checkers, on the other hand, avoid an explicit enumeration of the state space by using symbolic representations of sets of states and transitions. One of

T. Ball and R.B. Jones (Eds.): CAV 2006, LNCS 4144, pp. 286–299, 2006.
© Springer-Verlag Berlin Heidelberg 2006

the first successful approaches in this regard was the use of BDDs to succinctly represent large state spaces for the purpose of model checking [McM93]. More recently, SAT-based techniques [BCCY99] have become popular both for finding bugs using SAT-based Bounded Model Checking (BMC) and for generating proofs via SAT-based Unbounded Model Checking (UMC).

One of the contributions of this paper is that we have proposed a new methodology to leverage the synergy that results from combining the ability of partial order techniques to reduce the state space of the system to be explored with the power of symbolic model checking techniques to explore large state spaces that has many advantages over existing techniques that attempt to achieve the same goals. Indeed, methods different from ours that combine partial order reductions with the use of BDDs were given in [ABH+01, LST03]. However, the use of BDDs requires one to first symbolically encode the entire state space of the given concurrent program thereby running into the state explosion problem. Our technique gives us the freedom to use any technique of choice, either SAT or BDD-based. This is crucial as SAT-based BMC techniques tend to be much more scalable on larger programs than the ones based on the use of BDDs.

We start by translating a given concurrent program into a circuit-based (finite-state) model. Building upon the F-Soft framework [ISGG05] for translating sequential programs with bounded data and bounded recursion into circuits, we first obtain a finite model for each individual thread wherein each variable of the thread is represented in terms of a vector of binary-valued *latches* and a boolean next-state function (or relation) for each latch. Then using a scheduler, we compose the circuits for the individual threads into one single circuit for the entire concurrent program. Verification is then carried out on this circuit. Partial order techniques are incorporated into the framework by statically augmenting the circuit-based boolean encoding of the given concurrent program with additional constraints. These constraints restrict the transitions explored from each global state to a minimal *conditional stubborn set* of that state.

Another contribution of this paper is that we have proposed a new provably better method for identifying transactions *on-the-fly* that is based on analyzing patterns of lock acquisition as opposed to existing techniques [Sto02, FQ03] which rely on a lockset based analysis. Lockset based methods for state space reduction essentially exploit the ability of locks to enforce mutually exclusive access to regions of code encapsulated between the locking and unlocking operations on the same lock. They rely on the assumption that the given concurrent program follows a *lock discipline* in accessing shared variables, i.e., all accesses to a shared variable sh are protected by the same lock l_{sh} [Sto02, FQ03]. Then we can cut down on the number of interleavings that need to be explored by essentially allowing context switches only before the acquire and after the release operations on l_{sh} and prohibiting them before access to sh. Disallowing context switches increases the granularity of transitions and cuts down on the number of possible interleavings resulting in a reduced state space to be explored.

On the other hand, by analyzing concurrent programs for patterns of lock acquisition rather than for locksets, we can identify not only those transactions which lockset based method do but also some that they don't. This makes our new technique provably better. In fact, the lockset based technique for identifying transactions turns out to be a special case of the one based on lock acquisition patterns that we propose here.

Moreover, our technique does not rely on the given concurrent program following a locking discipline in accessing shared variables. An important advantage of the non-reliance of our method on lock discipline is that one of the main reasons for the existence of data races in threads is an unprotected/wrongly protected access to a shared variable. The requirement of lock discipline precludes the application of these powerful reductions to programs where such commonly occurring bugs are present. Thus our method enables the use of lock-based reductions for a broader class of concurrent programs, viz., that need not follow lock discipline, to catch a frequently occurring class of bugs.

Another, important feature of the lock-pattern based transactions is that they can be transparently incorporated into partial order reduction by improved conditional dependency detection via addition of extra constraints that are incorporated into the transition relation not a priori but dynamically while unrolling the executions of the threads. We show that the increased granularity of transitions due to transactions can be captured as a reduction in the sizes of the conditional stubborn sets of states.

We believe that our decision to build circuit-based models for concurrent programs gives us many unique advantages. Indeed, in this sense, the work most closely resembling ours are the approaches presented in [RG05, CKS05] that involve translating a C program directly into a SAT formula for model checking using SAT-based BMC. However [RG05] does not incorporate partial order reductions and neither technique leverages on-the-fly transactions. Circuit based models make it easy to incorporate static space reduction techniques like partial order reductions, on-the-fly-transactions as well as lightweight static analysis techniques like range analysis to reduce model sizes. Another advantage of our approach lies in the separation of the model building and verification phases. Once we have built a circuit for the concurrent program at hand, it affords us the flexibility to tackle the verification problem using any model checking technique of choice for a broad range of linear time temporal properties, not just safety. Unlike [RG05, CKS05], we can employ a suite of model checking tools for a rich class of *linear-time* temporal properties, which can be used *both* for finding bugs and generating proofs. These include SAT-based BMC and UMC as well as BDD based model checking. We believe this flexibility is important as software generated circuits are not as well structured as hardware circuits and hence no one strategy can be expected to be universally effective. Thus we have presented a new approach for model checking concurrent programs that combines the power of symbolic techniques with partial order reduction and on-the-fly transactions while at the same time retaining the flexibility to employ a broad arsenal of model checking techniques – both SAT and BDD-based – for checking not just reachability but a richer classes of linear-time temporal properties.

In the rest of the paper, Section 2 introduces the system model while on-the-fly transactions are defined in section 3. The details for modeling concurrent programs as circuits are provided in section 4 and the Daisy case study in section 5. Finally, we conclude with some remarks in section 6 along with a comparison with related work.

2   System Model

We consider concurrent systems comprised of a finite number of processes or threads where each thread is a deterministic sequential program written in a language such as

C. Threads interact with each other using communication/synchronization objects like shared variables, locks and semaphores.

Formally, we define a concurrent program CP as a tuple $(\mathcal{T}, \mathcal{V}, \mathcal{R}, s_0)$, where $\mathcal{T} = \{T_1, ..., T_n\}$ denotes a finite set of threads, $\mathcal{V} = \{v_1, ..., v_m\}$ a finite set of shared variables and synchronization objects with v_i taking on values from the set V_i, $\mathcal{R}$ the transition relation and s_0 the initial state of CP. Each thread T_i is represented by the control flow graph of the sequential program it executes, and is denoted by the pair (C_i, R_i), where C_i denotes the set of control locations of T_i and R_i its transition relation. A global state s of CP is a tuple $(s[1], ..., s[n], v[1], ..., v[m]) \in \mathcal{S} = C_1 \times ... \times C_n \times V_1 \times ... \times V_m$, where $s[i]$ represents the current control location of thread T_i and $v[j]$ the current value of variable v_j. The global state transition digram of CP is defined to be the standard interleaved composition of the transition diagrams of the individual threads. Thus each global transition of CP results by firing a local transition of the form (a_i, g, u, b_i), where a_i and b_i are control locations of some thread $T_i = (C_i, R_i)$ with $(a_i, b_i) \in R_i$; g is a guard which is a Boolean-valued expression on the values of local variables of T_i and global variables in $\mathcal{V}$; and u is function that encodes how the value of each global variable and each local variable of T_i is updated. A transition $t = (a_i, g, u, b_i)$ of thread T_i is enabled in state s iff $s[i] = a_i$ and guard g evaluates to true in s. If $s[i] = a_i$ but g need not be true in s, then we simply say that t is *scheduled* in s. We write $s \xrightarrow{t} s'$ to mean that the execution of t leads from state s to s'. Given a transition $t \in \mathcal{T}$, we use $proc(t)$ to denote the process executing t. Finally, we note that each concurrent program CP with a global state space $\mathcal{S}$ defines the global transition system $A_G = (\mathcal{S}, \Delta, s_0)$, where $\Delta \subseteq \mathcal{S} \times \mathcal{S}$ is the *transition relation* defined by $(s, s') \in \Delta$ iff $\exists t \in \mathcal{T} : s \xrightarrow{t} s'$; and s_0 is the initial state of CP.

3   Lock Synchronization Based Reductions

We start by using some examples to motivate our technique. Consider the concurrent program CP shown in figure 1. Here x, which is the only variable shared among the threads, is unprotected at control location 5b and protected by lock lk at all other locations. Since x is not protected at all locations where it is accessed, it does not satisfy lock discipline in the sense of [Sto02, FQ03], which will therefore force a context switch before locations 3a and 3b. Consider, however, a global state s of CP with threads T_1 and T_2 at control locations 3a and 1b, respectively. The key observation is that starting at global state s of CP, 3a does not interfere with 3b and 5b even though 5b is unprotected. This is because for T_2 to execute 3b it has to acquire lk currently

```
1a:  a = 0;            1b:  z = 5;
2a:  lock(lk);         2b:  lock(lk);
3a:  x = 1;            3b:  x = 2;
4a:  unlock(lk);       4b:  unlock(lk);
5a:  a = 4;            5b:  x = 6;
         (a)                    (b)
```

Fig. 1. Threads T_1(a) and T_2(b) with unprotected access to x

held by T_1. But in order for T_1 to release 1k, it has to first execute 3a. Thus starting at s, CP is forced to execute 3a before 3b. As a result no context switch is required before 3a. However, in the global state s' with T_1 and T_2 at control locations 3a and 5b, respectively, the transitions 3a and 5b do interfere with each other thus forcing a context switch before 3a. The bottom line is that even when shared variables do not follow locking discipline globally, we can still identify local portions of the state space where locking discipline is followed. Thus a context driven analysis allows us to define transactions locally *on-the-fly* where existing methods [Sto02, FQ03], because of their reliance on a global analysis, fail to do so.

```
1a: a = 1;          1b: b = 0;
2a: lock(lk1);      2b: lock(lk2);
3a: lock(lk2);      3b: lock(lk1);
4a: y = 1;          4b: z = 2;
5a: unlock(lk2);    5b: unlock(lk1);
6a: x = 0;          6b: x = 1;
7a: unlock(lk1);    7b: unlock(lk2);
       (a)                 (b)
```

Fig. 2. Threads T_1(a) and T_2(b) with unprotected access to x

Taking the above discussion further, we next show that transactions can be identified even in the absence of lock discipline–local or global. Let CP be the concurrent program comprised of the two threads T_1 and T_2 sharing variable x shown in figure 2. Consider a global state s of CP with threads T_1 and T_2 in control locations 6a and 1b, respectively. Observe that starting at s, the transitions at control locations 6a and 6b cannot interfere with each other even though they access the same shared variable x. This is because in order for thread T_2 to reach location 6b from 1b it has to traverse the local path 1b, 2b, 3b, 4b, 5b, along which it has to acquire (and release) lock 1k1 currently held by T_1. In order for that to happen, T_1 must release 1k1 for which it must execute transition 6a. This forces transition 6a to be executed before 6b. Thus no context switch is required before location 6a. The key observation is that even though disjoint sets of locks were held at locations 6a and 6b, it was the set of locks that needed to be acquired by T_2 in order to transit from 1b to 6b (even though some of these locks were released before reaching 6b) that prevented 6a and 6b from interfering with each other. A traditional lockset based analysis as given in [Sto02, FQ03] would treat 6a and 6b as conflicting transitions (as x does not follow locking discipline) and force a context switch before these locations. Thus a conflict analysis based on lock acquisition patterns is more refined than one based on locksets. Indeed, a lockset based analysis is a special case of lock-pattern based analysis since the set of locks held at a location would have to be acquired and thus would be tracked in the lock acquisition pattern.

Transactions Via Persistent Sets. We now show how to integrate lock-pattern based on-the-fly transactions with partial order reduction in a transparent fashion by capturing the increased granularity of transitions due to transactions as a reduction in the sizes of the conditional stubborn sets of states. This is accomplished by ensuring that if in a global state s, a thread T_i is in the process of executing a transaction, then in the persistent set of s, we include only one transition, viz., the transition of T_i that fires next along the transaction being executed. This ensures that once the first transition of a transaction is executed, by a thread T_i then no other process can be scheduled unless all transitions of the transaction finish firing.

State space reduction using partial order techniques is obtained by exploring from each state only those transitions that belong to a persistent set of that state instead of all the enabled transitions. Although there are many ways to compute persistent sets, the method of computing conditional stubborn sets usually generates those with small cardinality. In this paper, we use standard terminology from the theory of partial order reductions and the algorithm for computing conditional stubborn sets from [God96], which we denote by $Algo_1$. We recall the following definition from [God96].

Might-be-first-to-interfere. *Let op and op′ be two operations on the same object O and s be a reachable state. The relation op $\triangleright_s$ op′ holds if there exists a sequence $s = s_1 \xrightarrow{t_1} s_2 \xrightarrow{t_2} \ldots \xrightarrow{t_n} s_{n+1}$ of transitions in A_G such that $\forall 1 \leq i < n : \forall op''$ on O used by t_i: op and op″ are independent in state s_i, t_n uses op′, and op and op′ are dependent in s_n.*

For each local transition $a \xrightarrow{g} b$ of a thread, we let $used(t)$ denote the set of operations on variables and synchronization objects executed during the execution of t. A conditional stubborn set of state s of A_G can then be calculated as follows:

1. Initialize $T_s = \{t\}$, where t is some enabled transition in s.
2. For each $t = a \xrightarrow{g} b \in T_s$
   (a) If t is disabled in s,
       i. if $T_j = proc(t)$ and $s[j] \neq a$, then add to T_s all transitions t' of T_j of the form $c \xrightarrow{g'} a$, or
       ii. choose a condition c_j in the guard g of t that evaluates to false in s; then, for all operations op used by t to evaluate c_j, add to T_s all transitions t' such that $\exists op' \in used(t') : op \triangleright_s op'$.
   (b) If t is enabled in s add to T_s all transitions t' such that
       i. $proc(t) \neq proc(t')$ and $\exists op \in used(t), \exists op' \in used(t') : op \triangleright_s op'$.
3. Repeat step 2 until no more transitions can be added in T_s. Then return all transitions in T_s that are enabled in s.

Fig. 3. $Algo_1$ for Computing Conditional Stubborn sets

In $Algo_1$ dependencies between transitions, arising out of operations on shared communication objects are captured using the $\triangleright_s$ relation which captures for each operation op used by a transition in a state s which other operations *might be first to interfere with op from the current state s*. In practice, to avoid exploration of the state space of the program at hand, static analysis is employed in order to compute a relation, $\triangleright_s^{st}$, which is an over-approximation of $\triangleright_s$. Towards that end, we say that two operations op and op' are *statically dependent* if they access a common shared variable such that at least one of the accesses is a write operation. Then $\triangleright_s^{st}$, is defined as follows.

Definition. *Let op and op′ be two operations on a common shared variable and s a reachable state of A_G. The relation op $\triangleright_s^{st}$ op′ holds iff there exist distinct threads T_i*

and T_j such that there exists (1) a transition of T_i scheduled (not necessarily enabled) at s using op, and (2) a local path $x : p_0 \xrightarrow{t_1} ... \xrightarrow{t_n} p_n$ of T_j such that p_0 is the local state of T_j in s, $\forall 1 \leq k < n : \forall op''$ used by t_k: op and op'' are not statically dependent, t_n uses op', and op and op' are statically dependent.

To incorporate on-the-fly transactions, we modify the above definition of $\triangleright_s^{st}$ to get a new relation $\triangleright_s^{lp} \subseteq \triangleright_s^{st}$ by adding (in accordance with our discussion above), the extra constraint that none of the locks held by T_i in s is acquired (and possibly released) by T_j along x. Note that since $\triangleright_s^{lp}$ is more constrained it enforces fewer dependencies between operations than $\triangleright_s^{st}$ thus resulting in smaller conditional stubborn sets. The effect is to weed out certain interleavings to get the effect of executing transactions. Indeed, in the example given in fig 2, in global state s, if op and op' are the operations $x = 0$ and $x = 1$ at locations 6a and 6b, respectively, then $op \triangleright_s^{st} op'$ but $\neg(op \triangleright_s^{lp} op')$. Thus, using $\triangleright_s^{lp}$ instead of $\triangleright_s^{st}$ to compute conditional stubborn sets removes transition 1b from the conditional stubborn set of s thus preventing a context switch before 6a. Formally, $\triangleright_s^{lp}$ is defined as follows.

Definition (might-be-the-first-to-interfere-modulo-lock-acquisition). *Let op and op' be two operations on a common shared variable and s a reachable state of A_G. The relation $op \triangleright_s^{lp} op'$ holds iff there exist distinct threads T_i and T_j such that there exists (1) a transition of T_i scheduled (not necessarily enabled) at s using op, and (2) a local path $x : p_0 \xrightarrow{t_1} ... \xrightarrow{t_n} p_n$ of T_j such that $\forall 1 \leq k < n : \forall op''$ used by t_k: op and op'' are not statically dependent, t_n uses op', and op and op' are statically dependent and no lock held by T_i in s is acquired by T_j along x.*

Let $Algo_2$ be the result of replacing $\triangleright_s$ in $Algo_1$ by $\triangleright_s^{st}$ and $Algo_3$ the result of replacing $\triangleright_s^{st}$ in line 2.(b).i of $Algo_2$ by $\triangleright_s^{lp}$. Then the following two results state that $Algo_3$ does indeed compute a conditional stubborn set and that, in fact, it computes smaller conditional stubborn sets than $Algo_2$. Note that although we used a specific relation $\triangleright_s^{st}$ for computing dependencies statically, one can, of course, incorporate on-the-fly-transactions with any other *implementation* of $\triangleright_s$ by merely adding the extra condition regarding lock acquisition patterns, as above.

Theorem 1. *All sets T_s that are computed by $Algo_3$ are conditional stubborn sets of s.*

Proof Sketch. Let $t = a \xrightarrow{g} b$ executed by thread T_i belong to T_s. Let $w = s_1 \xrightarrow{t_1} s_2 \xrightarrow{t_2} ... \xrightarrow{t_n} s_{n+1}$ be a sequence of transitions of A_G such that t is dependent with t_n in s_n. We need to show that at least one of $t_1,...,t_n$ is in T_s. Without loss of generality, we may assume that for $1 \leq i < n$, t is independent with t_i in s_i and t_n is dependent with t in s_n, else we can pick an appropriate prefix of w.

First assume that t is disabled in s. Since t is disabled in s and s_n is the first state along w in which t is dependent (with t_n), we have that t is enabled in s_{n+1}. Since t is disabled in s, either $s[i] \neq a$, or a condition c in guard g evaluates to false in s. In the first case, since t is enabled in s_{n+1}, there exists a transition t_j fired along w, of the form $d \rightarrow a$ labeled with some guard g'. But then executing step 2.(a).i of $Algo_3$, would cause t_j to be included in T_s. In the second case, there exists a transition t_j, that changes the value of c from false to true by changing the output of an operation op used to evaluate c, i.e., by performing an operation op' dependent with op in s_j. Let t_j be the first such transition occurring along w. Clearly op' is statically dependent with op. By definition of $\rhd_s^{st}$, we have $op \rhd_s^{st} op'$, and so $t_j \in T_s$ by step 2.a.(ii).

Consider now the case when t is enabled in s. From the facts that (i) for $1 \leq j \leq n-1$, t is independent with t_j in s_j, and (ii) t is enabled in s, we have that for $1 \leq j \leq n-1$, t is enabled in s_j. This implies that thread T_i does not execute any transition along w, for otherwise since T_i is deterministic, we can conclude that t is the first transition that T_i executes along w. This which would force T_i out of it current local state thereby disabling t thus contradicting the above observation. Note that here we assumed that executing a transition takes a process out of its current local state, i.e., there are no self loops in a program thread, a reasonable assumption for software programs Now, since t and t_n are dependent in s_n, it implies that $\exists op \in used(t), \exists op' \in used(t_n)$: op and op' are dependent in s_n and hence are also statically dependent. Let t_j be the first transition along w that uses an operation op'' dependent op. Note also that there does not exist a lock l held by T_i at s such that l has to be acquired before t_j is executed along w. For otherwise, l must first be released by T_i thus forcing T_i to execute a transition contradicting our observation above that T_i does not execute any transition along w. Thus we have $op \rhd_s^{lp} op''$. Hence $t_j \in T_s$ by step 2.b.(i). This completes the proof. □

Theorem 2. *For all transitions t that are enabled in s, for all persistent sets $Algo_2(t)$ that can be returned by $Algo_2$, there exists a run of $Algo_3$ that returns a persistent set $Algo_3(t) \subseteq Algo_2(t)$.*

Proof Sketch. From the definition of relation $\rhd_s^{lp}$, it follows that $\rhd_s^{lp}$ is included in $\rhd_s^{st}$. Thus the set T_s returned by $Algo_3$ is always a subset of the one returned by $Algo_2$, provided the same choices are made in case of nondeterminism. □

Note that since $Algo_3$ computes smaller persistent sets than existing lockset-based techniques, it is guaranteed to improve the performance of explicit state model checkers. Even for symbolic model checkers, since the reduction in the number of scheduled transitions results in a pruning of the state space, it leads to a performance boost which, however, may not be directly proportional to the decrease in the size of the state space being explored.

4 Software Modeling for Concurrent C Programs

4.1 Translating Individual Threads into Circuits

In this section we briefly describe how, using the F-Soft machinery, we first obtain a circuit-based model of each thread, under the assumption of bounded data and bounded control (recursion) (see [ISGG05] for more details).

We begin with full-fledged C and apply a series of source-to-source transformations to simplify complex C expressions into smaller but equivalent subsets of C . We flatten all arrays and structs by replacing them with collections of simple scalar variables, and build an internal memory representation of the program by assigning to each scalar variable a unique number representing its memory address. Variables that are adjacent in C program memory are given consecutive memory addresses in our model; this facilitates modeling of pointer arithmetic. We model the heap as a finite array, adding a simple implementation of malloc() that returns pointers into this array. For handling pointer accesses, we first perform a points-to analysis to determine the set of variables that a pointer variable can point to. Then, we convert each indirect memory access, through a pointer or an array reference, to a direct memory access. For example, if we determine that pointer p can point to variables a,b,...,z at a given program location, we rewrite a pointer read *(p+i) as a conditional expression of the form ((p+i)==&a ? a : ((p+i)==&b ? b : ...)), where &a,&b,... are the numeric memory addresses we assigned to the variables a,b,..., respectively. Non-recursive function calls are handled by inlining exactly once, and replacing the function return by a set of goto-s conditioned upon the unique call site id stored on function entry. Bounded recursive functions are modeled by introducing a bounded call stack. While we aim for accurate modeling of all C, practical modeling requires making approximations. We truncate large arrays: writes to elements above a certain index are ignored, and reads from these elements yield non-deterministic values. We currently approximate floating-point values by modeling their integral parts only.

The simplified program consists of scalar variables of simple types (Boolean, enumerated, integer). This is compiled using standard techniques into its control flow graph (CFG). The CFG representation can be viewed as a finite state machine with state vector (pc,V), where pc denotes an encoding of the basic blocks, and V is a vector of integer-valued program variables. We then construct symbolic transition relations for pc, and for each data variable appearing in the program. For pc, the transition relation reflects the guarded transitions between basic blocks in the CFG. For a data variable, the transition relation is built from expressions assigned to the variable in various blocks. Finally, we construct a symbolic representation of these transition relations resembling a hardware circuit. For the pc variable, we allocate $\lceil \log N \rceil$ latches, where N is the total number of basic blocks. For each C program variable, we allocate a vector of n latches, where n is the bit width of the variable. At the end, we obtain a circuit-based model of each thread of the given concurrent program, where each variable of the thread is represented in terms of a vector of binary-valued *latches* and a Boolean next-state function (or relation) for each latch.

4.2 Building the Circuit for the Concurrent Program

Given the circuit C_i for each individual thread T_i, we now show how to get the circuit C for the concurrent program CP comprised of these threads. In the case where local variables with the same name occur in multiple threads, to ensure consistency we prefix the name of each local variable of thread T_i with thread_i. Next, for each thread T_i we introduce a gate execute_i indicating whether P_i has been scheduled to execute in the next step of CP or not.

For each latch 1, let *next-state$_i$*(1) denote the next state function of 1 in circuit C_i. Then in circuit C, the next state value of latch thread_i_1 corresponding to a local variable of thread T_i, is defined to be *next-state$_i$*(thread_i_1) if execute_i is true, and the current value of thread_i_1, otherwise. If, on the other hand, latch 1 corresponds to a shared variable, then *next-state*(1) is defined to be *next-state$_i$*(1), where execute_i is true. Note that we need to ensure that execute_i is true for exactly one thread T_i. Towards that end, we implement a scheduler which determines in each global state of $\mathcal{CP}$ which one of the signals execute_i is set to *true* and thus determines the semantics of thread composition.

Conditional Stubborn Sets Based Persistent Sets. To incorporate partial order reduction, we need to ensure that from each global state s, only transitions belonging to a conditional stubborn set of s are explored. Let $\mathcal{R}$ and R_i denote the transitions relations of $\mathcal{CP}$ and T_i, respectively. If $\mathcal{CP}$ has n threads, we introduce the n-bit vector $cstub$ which identifies a conditional stubborn set for each global state s, i.e., in s, $cstub_i$ is *true* for exactly those threads T_i such that the (unique) transition of T_i enabled at s belongs to the same minimal conditional stubborn set of s. Then

$$\mathcal{R}(s, s') = \bigvee_{1 \leq i \leq n} ((\texttt{execute\_i}) \land cstub_i(s) \land R_i(s, s')).$$

The $cstub$ vector can be computed in the following way:

1. For each shared variable x and thread T_i, we introduce a latch *touch-now*(T_i, x) which is true at control location pc_i of T_i iff T_i accesses x at control location pc_i. This can be done via a static analysis of the CFG of T_i by determining at which control locations x was accessed and taking a disjunction for those values of pc_i.

2. For each shared variable x and thread T_j, introduce the latch *touch-now-later* (T_j, x), which is true at control location pc_j of T_j if T_j accesses x at some location pc'_j reachable from pc_j. Thus computing *touch-now-later*(T_j, x) involves deciding the reachability of pc'_j, and since we cannot compute it exactly without exploring the entire state space A_G of $\mathcal{CP}$, we over-approximate it by doing a context-sensitive analysis of the control-flow graph of T_j. We set *touch-now-later-pair* (T_j, x) to *true* in control pc_j if for some control pc'_j reachable from pc_j in the control flow graph of T_j, x is accessed at pc'_j.

3. For distinct threads T_i and T_j, the relation $conflict_i(j)$ is then defined as $\bigvee_{x \in \mathcal{V}_{sh}}$ (*touch-now*$(T_i, x)(pc_i) \land$ *touch-now-later*$(T_j, x)(pc_j)$), where pc_i and pc_j are the control locations of T_i and T_j, respectively, in the current global state and $\mathcal{V}_{sh}$ is the set of shared variables of $\mathcal{CP}$.

4. Using a circuit to compute transitive closures, for each i, starting with $J_i = \{i\}$ we compute the closure of J_i under the *conflict* relation defined above.

5. We build a circuit to compute the index min such that the cardinality of J_{min} is the least among the sets $J_1, ..., J_n$. Finally $\forall 1 \leq i \leq n$, set $cstub_i = 1$ iff $i \in J_{min}$. Note that in the implementation we need to pick only one set with the least cardinality.

Cycle Detection. We first identify *sticky* transitions [KLM+98] for all potential global cycles. We then force a conflict for the process containing the sticky locations with all other processes via the encoding below. Let $sticky(pc)$ be a predicate evaluating to true iff location pc has been marked sticky. Then, for global state s, we define $conflict_i(j)$ = $sticky(pc_i) \lor$ (*touch-now*$(T_i, x)(pc_i) \land$ *touch-now-later*$(T_j, x)(pc_j)$), where pc_m is the current control location of T_m in s. In other words, if pc_i is sticky then thread T_i is said to conflict with all other threads. This implies that either a thread T_k, with smaller conflict set J_k, would be chosen for the persistent set computation or a full expansion forced.

This reduction is sound, since (as was shown in [KLM⁺98]) any cycle in the global state space can be projected on to one or more local cycles in the control flow graph of the individual threads. By forcing a full expansion inside each (potential) local cycle with the help of sticky transitions, we ensure that there is no global cycle such that a thread transition is postponed at each state of the cycle. Therefore this encoding allows the model checker to explore a conservative over-approximation of the representative (minimal) set of interleavings of the given threads. Although the reduced model remains sound, the number of interleavings considered may decrease dramatically with the number of annotated sticky transitions.

So far, we have implemented sticky transitions only for special cases in which cycles can occur locally in threads. In fact, as was noted in [FG05], our experience also has been that acyclic state spaces are very common in software implementations for the purpose of model checking and cycle detection becomes more critical when one is using an abstraction (which introduces cycles) refinement framework. However since (i) we put a lot of effort in modeling programs concretely, (ii) do not use abstraction refinement, and (iii) introduce sticky transitions to cover common trivial cases, the impact of the existence of cycles is reduced. Nevertheless, we are currently in the process of extending the implementation of sticky transitions to the general case.

Encoding Lock Pattern Based Reductions. In order to incorporate transactions *on-the-fly*, we augment the predicate *touch-now-later*, to generate the new predicate *touch-now-later-LS* that also includes lock acquisition pattern information. For control locations pc_i and pc_i', of thread T_i, let $paths(pc_i, pc_i')$ denote the set of paths in the CFG of T_i starting from pc_i that may reach pc_i'. For each $\pi \in paths(pc_i, pc_i')$ of T_i, let $lockPred(\pi)$ be a formula denoting the set of locks acquired (and possibly released) along π, e.g., $lk_1 = T_i \wedge lk_2 = T_i$. Let $touch-now-later-pair(T_j, x)(pc_j, pc_j')$ encode all possible sets of locks that can potentially be acquired along local paths in T_i from pc_i to pc_i' accessing x, i.e., $touch-now-later-pair(T_j, x)(pc_j, pc_j') = touch-now(T_j, x)(pc_j') \wedge AP_x(pc_j, cp_j')$, where $AP_x(pc_i, pc_i') = \bigvee_{\pi \in paths(pc_i, pc_i')} lockPred(\pi)$. Let $CLP(T_i, s)$ denote a formula encoding the ownership of locks by T_i in global state s. Then the relation $touch-now-LS(T_i, x)$ is obtained from $touch-now-later-pair(T_i, x)$ by quantifying out pc_i' and conjoining with the $CLP(T_i, s)$, i.e., $touch-now-LS(T_i, x)(pc_i) = (\exists pc_i' \ touch-now-later-pair(T_i, x)(pc_i, pc_i')) \wedge CLP(T_i, s)$. Thus $touch-now-LS(T_i, x)(pc_i)$ is true if there is a location pc_i' accessing shared variable x that is reachable from pc_i via a local path π in T_i such that no lock held in s is acquired along π. We evaluate $lockPred(\pi)$ using a context sensitive static analysis of the CFG of T_i.

5   The Daisy Case Study

We have used our technique to find bugs in the Daisy file system which is a benchmark for analyzing the efficacy of different methodologies for verifying concurrent programs [dai]. Daisy is a 1KLOC Java implementation of a toy file system where each file is allocated a unique inode that stores the file parameters and a unique block which stores data. An interesting feature of Daisy is that it has fine grained locking in that access to each file, inode or block is guarded by a dedicated lock. Moreover, the acquire and release of each of these locks is guarded by a 'token' lock. Thus control locations in the program might possibly have multiple open locks and furthermore the acquire and release of a given lock can occur in different procedures.

Currently F-Soft only accepts programs written in C and so we first manually translated the Daisy code which is written in Java into C. Furthermore, to reduce the model sizes, we truncated the sizes of the data structures modeling the disk, inodes, blocks, file names, etc., which were not relevant to the race conditions we checked, resulting in a sound and complete *small-domain* reduction. We have shown the existence of the race conditions described below also noted by other researchers (cf. [dai]). The efficacy of our techniques can be judged from the fact that our model checking methodology has been able to detect these race conditions in Daisy in a fully automatic fashion directly on the source code without any code structuring/abstractions beyond redefining the constants as discussed above.

1. Daisy maintains an allocation area where for each block in the file system a bit is assigned 0 or 1 accordingly as the block has been allocated to a file or not. But each disk operation reads/writes an entire byte. Two threads accessing two different files might access two different blocks. However since bytes are not guarded by locks in order to set their allocation bits these two different threads may access the same byte in the allocation block containing the allocation bit for each of these locks thus setting up a race condition. Note that the race condition occurs for any pair of blocks with numbers i and j where $floor(i/8) = floor(j/8)$.

The verification statistics are as follows: We ran our experiments on a machine with an Intel Pentium4 3.20GHz processor and 2GB RAM. Each run was given a timeout of 2 days and had a memout of 2GB. Witnesses for the above race condition were found in two cases, WW_1–corresponding to blocks 0 and 1, and WW_2–due to blocks 1 and 2. Using purely interleaved scheduling, we failed to find either witness because of a memout at depth 15. When only partial order reduction was employed WW_1 was found using SAT-based BMC at unroll depth 122 in 36707 sec and 999MB while incorporating on-the-fly transactions drastically reduced the time and memory usage to 1283sec and 122MB, respectively. The second witness WW_2 was found at depth 151. Using partial order reduction alone took 145176 sec and 1870 MB, while adding transactions reduced it to 5925 sec and 902 MB.

2. In Daisy reading/writing a particular byte on the disk is broken down into two operations: a seek operation that mimics the positioning of the head and a read/write operation that transfers the actual data. Due to this separation between seeking and data transfer a race condition may occur. For example, reading two disk locations, say n and m, we must make sure that $seek(n)$ is followed by $read(n)$ without $seek(m)$ or $read(m)$ scheduled in between. In this case a witness was found at depth 48. Using partial order reduction alone took 2.99 sec and 5.7 MB while adding transactions reduced it to 2.89 sec and 5.5 MB. For this example also BMC on the completely interleaved model failed to find a witness because of a memout at depth 20.

The bottom line is that, for deep bugs techniques that leverage the use of on-the-fly transactions combined with partial order reduction greatly outperform those which use only partial order reduction – both in terms of time taken and memory used.

6 Concluding Remarks and Related Work

A comparison of our work with [RG05, CKS05], to which it is most closely related, was presented in the introduction. Partial order reduction has been used before for symbolic model checking using BDDs [ABH+01, LST03]. On the other hand, by separating the modeling and verification phases, our methodology gives us the ability to combine partial order reductions with any symbolic model checking technique of choice, either SAT or BDD based. An interesting approach for the verification of concurrent programs using proof-guided under-approximation-widening methodology was presented in [GLST05]. Here constraints are added to the BMC model instance so that only a subset of behaviors of the concurrent system are explored. These constraints are iteratively removed during the widening phase as a result of which, in the worst case, one might end up exploring the entire state space of the concurrent program at hand. In contrast, we add constraints so that we explore a conditional stubborn set at each global state thereby yielding considerable state space reduction. Moreover, [GLST05] does not leverage the use of transactions.

There has also been interesting work ([FQ03, Sto02, SC03, AQR+04, LPQR05]) on the use of lockset based transactions for verifying software and combining it with partial order reductions. These techniques first compute the valid set of transactions in each of the processes and then perform partial order reduction-based state-space exploration. As noted before, such a two-step combination technique may overlook potential reductions related to shared variables which do not always follow a locking discipline. The key reason is that in these approaches a thread-wise global analysis is done to look for potential dependencies between transitions. In contrast, our approach adds information to the model while exploring the state space by detecting dependencies *on-the-fly* via an analysis of patterns of lock acquisition. Our more refined method generates fewer dependencies between transitions resulting in a lesser number of context switches. This gives us better state space reduction than existing lockset based techniques.

To sum up, we have presented a new approach for verifying concurrent programs that combines the power of symbolic model checking with partial order reduction and on-the-fly transactions while at the same time retaining the flexibility to employ a variety of error trace generation/proof techniques – both SAT and BDD-based – for checking not just safety but a broad class of linear time temporal properties. The use of lock acquisition patterns rather than locksets to identify transactions *on-the-fly* is not only a powerful technique in its own right but can also be used in a synergistic manner with both explicit state and BDD-based exploration of concurrent programs as also with dynamic partial order reduction techniques [FG05].

References

[ABH+01]   R. Alur, R. K. Brayton, T. A. Henzinger, S. Qadeer, and S. K. Rajamani. Partial-order reduction in symbolic state-space exploration. *Form. Methods Syst. Des.*, 18(2):97–116, 2001.

[AQR+04]   T. Andrews, S. Qadeer, S. K. Rajamani, J. Rehof, and Y. Xie. Zing: Exploiting program structure for model checking concurrent software. In *CONCUR*, 2004.

[BCCY99]   A. Biere, A. Cimatti, E.M. Clarke, and Y.Zhu. Symbolic model checking without BDDs. In *TACAS*, 1999.

[CKS05]   Byron Cook, Daniel Kroening, and Natasha Sharygina. Symbolic model check-
            ing for asynchronous boolean programs. In *SPIN 2005*, pages 75–90, 2005.
[dai]   Joint CAV/ISSTA Special Event on Specification, Verification, and Testing of
            Concurrent Software. In *http://research.microsoft.com/ qadeer/cav-issta.htm*.
[FG05]   Cormac Flanagan and Patrice Godefroid. Dynamic partial-order reduction for
            model checking software. In *POPL '05*, pages 110–121, 2005.
[FQ03]   C. Flanagan and S. Qadeer. Transactions for software model checking. In *SoftMC
            03*, 2003.
[GLST05]   O. Grumberg, F. Lerda, O. Strichman, and M. Theobald. Proof-guided underap-
            proximation widening for multi process systems. In *POPL '05*, pages 122–131,
            2005.
[God96]   P. Godefroid. *Partial-order methods for the verification of concurrent systems:
            an approach to the state-explosion problem*. LNCS 1032. Springer-Verlag, 1996.
[God97]   Patrice Godefroid. Model checking for programming languages using verisoft.
            In *POPL '97*, pages 174–186, 1997.
[ISGG05]   F. Ivančić, I. Shlyakhter, A. Gupta, and M. Ganai. Model checking c programs
            using F-Soft. In *ICCD*, 2005.
[KLM$^+$98] Robert P. Kurshan, Vladimir Levin, Marius Minea, Doron Peled, and Hüsnü
            Yenigün. Static partial order reduction. In *TACAS '98*, 1998.
[LPQR05]   V. Levin, R. Palmer, S. Qadeer, and S. K. Rajamani. Sound transaction-based
            reduction without cycle detection. In *SPIN '05*, 2005.
[LST03]   F. Lerda, N. Sinha, and M. Theobald. Symbolic model checking of software.
            Electr. Notes Theor. Comput. Sci., 89(3), 2003.
[McM93]   K.L. McMillan. *Symbolic model checking: an approach to the state explosion
            problem*. Kluwer Academic Publishers, 1993.
[RG05]   I. Rabinovitz and O. Grumberg. Bounded model checking of concurrent pro-
            grams. In *CAV '05*, pages 82–97, 2005.
[SC03]   Scott D. Stoller and Ernie Cohen. Optimistic synchronization-based state-space
            reduction. In *TACAS '03*, LNCS, pages 489–504, April 2003.
[Sto02]   Scott D. Stoller. Model-checking multi-threaded distributed Java programs. *In-
            ternational Journal on Software Tools for Technology Transfer*, 4(1):71–91, Oc-
            tober 2002.

Model Checking Multithreaded Programs with Asynchronous Atomic Methods

Koushik Sen and Mahesh Viswanathan

Department of Computer Science,
University of Illinois at Urbana-Champaign
{ksen, vmahesh}@cs.uiuc.edu

Abstract. In order to make multithreaded programming manageable, programmers often follow a design principle where they break the problem into tasks which are then solved asynchronously and concurrently on different threads. This paper investigates the problem of model checking programs that follow this idiom. We present a programming language SPL that encapsulates this design pattern. SPL extends simplified form of sequential Java to which we add the capability of making asynchronous method invocations in addition to the standard synchronous method calls and the ability to execute asynchronous methods in threads atomically and concurrently. Our main result shows that the control state reachability problem for finite SPL programs is decidable. Therefore, such multithreaded programs can be model checked using the counterexample guided abstraction-refinement framework.

1 Introduction

Multithreaded programming is often used in software as it leads to reduced latency, improved response times of interactive applications, and more optimal use of processing power. Multithreaded programming also allows an application to progress even if one thread is blocked for an I/O operation. However, writing correct programs that use multiple threads is notoriously difficult, especially in the presence of a shared mutable memory. Since threads can interleave, there can be unintended interference through concurrent access of shared data and result in software errors due to data race and atomicity violations.

Therefore, programmers writing multithreaded code, often adhere to a design idiom where the computational problem is broken up into *tasks* which are then assumed to be finished asynchronously, concurrently, and atomically. Specifically, threads during their execution may send tasks or events or asynchronous messages to other threads. If a thread is busy completing a task, the messages sent to it get added to a pool of tasks associated with the thread. When the thread has completed the current task, it takes out a task from its pending pool and starts processing it concurrently with other threads. If the pool is empty the thread waits for a new task or event or message. Even though these asynchronous tasks are executed concurrently on different threads, an underlying assumption is that these tasks will be executed atomically. This is often ensured through various synchronization primitives, such as locks, mutexes, semaphores, etc.

For example, in the Swing/AWT subsystem of Java, a non-GUI thread is not allowed to make any direct changes to the user interface represented by a Swing

T. Ball and R.B. Jones (Eds.): CAV 2006, LNCS 4144, pp. 300–314, 2006.

object. Instead such a thread submits the request to the EventQueue by calling SwingUtilities.invokeLater(runnable). The thread associated with the Swing event queue handles these requests one by one atomically. This ensures that the user interface operations are performed in a non-interfering way and the user interface has a consistent state and look. Another context where this design paradigm is widely prevalent is multithreaded web servers. When a page request is sent to a web server, the web server posts the request to a request queue. If there is a free thread in the finite thread pool of the web server, the free thread removes a request from the request queue and starts processing the request. The use of threads ensures that multiple requests to the web-server can be served concurrently. Moreover, synchronization primitives are used to ensure that the threads do not interfere with each other. Another application area where this paradigm is used is embedded software which is naturally event-driven. Finally, multithreaded transaction servers for databases also view transactions as asynchronous requests that are served by the different threads of the server concurrently. Since requests in this context are transactions, the server ensures that the service of a transaction satisfies the ACID (atomicity, consistency, isolation, durability) property.

The prevalence of this design idiom has also been observed by Allen Holub [17] in his book "Taming Java Threads". In this book, Holub points out that programmers classify method invocations or messages into two categories: synchronous messages and asynchronous messages. The handler for synchronous messages doesn't return until the processing of the message is complete. On the other hand, asynchronous messages are processed possibly by a different thread in the background some time after the message is received. However, the handler for asynchronous messages returns immediately, long before the message is processed.

In this paper, we investigate the verification of programs written adhering to this design principle. We introduce a simple programming language, called SPL, that encapsulates this design goal. It is a simplified form of sequential Java to which we add the capability of making asynchronous method invocations in addition to the standard synchronous method calls and the ability to dynamically create threads. We define its semantics in terms of concurrently executing threads. We then observe that the requirement that asynchronous methods execute atomically, allows us to reason about the program using a new semantics wherein the threads service these asynchronous method invocations serially.

The analysis of SPL programs with respect to the serialized semantics can then proceed by following the popular methodology of software model checking [29,2,15], where the program is first automatically abstracted using boolean predicates into one that has finitely many global states, and the abstracted program is then model checked. The results of the model checking are then used to either demonstrate a bug/correctness of the program, or used to refine the abstraction.

The success of the software model checking framework depends upon the model checking problem for SPL programs with finitely many global states being decidable. We first observe that the serial semantics ensures that the local stack of at most one thread is non-empty at any time during the execution; the semantics of such programs can thus be defined using only one stack. We introduce *multi-set pushdown systems* (MPDS) to model such finite SPL programs. MPDSs have finitely many control states, one unbounded stack to execute recursive, synchronous methods, and one unbounded bag to store the asynchronous method invocations. The main restriction that is imposed on such systems is that messages from the bag be serviced only when the stack is empty, a consequence of our atomicity requirements. Our main result is that the problem of control state reachability of MPDSs is decidable, thus demonstrating that SPL programs can be analyzed in the counterexample guided abstraction-refinement framework.

The rest of the paper is organized as follows. Next, we discuss closely related work and place our results in context. Section 2 introduces notation, definitions and classical results used in proving our results. The simple parallel language (SPL) for multithreaded programming is presented along with its semantics in Section 3. We investigate the verification problem in Section 4 and conclude by giving a lower bound. Due to lack of space, we defer some of the proofs to [31].

Related Work. Model-checking algorithms and tools [29,2,15] for single-threaded programs with procedures based on predicate abstraction have been developed. These model checkers use the fact that the reachable configurations of pushdown systems are regular [1,13]. Ramalingam [28] showed that verification of concurrent boolean programs is undecidable. As a consequence, approximate analysis techniques that over-approximate [4] and under-approximate [26,3] the reachable states have been considered, as have semi-decision procedures [25]. Note that the algorithm in [25] can be shown to terminate if the whole execution of a thread is assumed to be a transaction. Other techniques [7,16,8] try verifying each thread compositionally, by automatically abstracting the environment. Finally, the KISS checker [27] for concurrent programs simulates the executions of a concurrent program by the executions of a sequential program, where the various threads of the concurrent program are scheduled by the single stack of the sequential program. It is worth mentioning [27] first proposed the use of a single stack to model executions of multithreaded software. Though complete, the KISS checker is not sound.

There has also been considerable effort in characterizing concurrent systems with finitely many global states for which the reachability analysis is unknown to be decidable. Starting from the work of Caucal [6] and Moller [22], where purely sequential and purely parallel processes were considered, hierarchies of systems have been defined. Mayr [21] gave many decidability and undecidability results based on a unified framework. Among the models that allow both recursion and dynamic thread creation, most disallow any form of synchronization between the threads [11,30,20,23]. More recently, the model of *constrained dynamic pushdown networks* (CDPN) [5] was introduced which allowed for thread creation and limited forms of synchronization. CDPNs have a more sophisticated means to synchronize, but they limit synchronization only between a parent thread and its descendants. Our model of MPDS, allows dynamic thread creation and limits context switches to happen only when asynchronous methods have finished execution. Thus, MPDSs and CDPNs are incomparable and apply to different multi-threaded programs.

2 Preliminaries

Multi-sets and Strings. Given a finite set Σ, the collection of all finite multi-sets with elements in Σ will be denoted by $M_\omega[\Sigma]$. We say $a \in M$ if a is an element of multi-set

M. For multi-sets M and M', $M \cup M'$ is the multi-set union of M and M', and $M \setminus M'$ the multi-set difference between M and M'. We use $\emptyset$ to denote the empty multi-set. Recall that Σ^* is the collection of all finite strings over the alphabet Σ, with ϵ being the empty string. Given two finite strings w and w', we will denote their concatenation by ww'. For a string w, $\mathbb{M}(w)$ will denote the multi-set formed from the symbols of w. For example, if $w = aaba$, then $\mathbb{M}(w) = \{a, a, a, b\}$. Finally, for $L \subseteq \Sigma^*$, $\mathbb{M}(L) = \{\mathbb{M}(w) \mid w \in L\}$.

Well-quasi-orderings. Recall that a *quasi-ordering* $\leq$ over a set X, is a binary relation that is reflexive and transitive. Given a quasi-ordering $\leq$, an *upward closed set* $U \subseteq X$ is a set such that if $x \in U$ and $x < y$ then $y \in U$. For a set $S \subseteq X$, the smallest upward closed set containing S will be denoted by $\text{CL}(S)$, i.e., $\text{CL}(S) = \{x \mid \exists y \in S. \, y \leq x\}$. For a set S, the minimal elements in S is $\text{MIN}(S) = \{x \mid \forall y \in S. \, y \not\leq x\}$.

A quasi-ordering $\leq$ over X is said to be a *well-quasi-ordering* (wqo) if for any infinite sequence $x_1, x_2, x_3, \ldots$ of elements in X, there exist indices i, j such that $i < j$ and $x_i \leq x_j$. We now recall some well-known observations about well-quasi-orderings [18,12].

Proposition 1. *For a wqo $\leq$ and any set $S \subseteq X$, $\text{MIN}(S)$ is finite.*

Proposition 2. *For a wqo $\leq$, any infinite increasing sequence $U_0 \subseteq U_1 \subseteq U_2 \subseteq \cdots$ of upward closed sets eventually stabilizes, i.e., there is a $k \in \mathbb{N}$ such that for all $i \geq k$ $U_i = U_k$.*

Pushdown Systems. A *pushdown system* (PDS) is $\mathcal{P} = (Q, \Gamma, \delta, q_0, \gamma_0)$, where Q is a finite set of states, Γ is a finite set of stack alphabets, $q_0 \in Q$ is the initial state, $\gamma_0 \in \Gamma$ is the initial stack configuration, and $\delta \subseteq (Q \times \Gamma) \times (Q \times \Gamma^*)$ is the transition relation. The execution of a PDS can be described in terms of a transition system over configurations, which are $(q, w) \in Q \times \Gamma^*$. We say $(q_1, w_1\gamma) \longrightarrow (q_2, w_1w_2)$ if there is a transition $((q_1, \gamma), (q_2, w_2)) \in \delta$. We say a configuration (q, w) is reachable iff $(q_0, \gamma_0) \longrightarrow^* (q, w)$, where $\longrightarrow^*$ is the reflexive, transitive closure of $\longrightarrow$, and that a control state q is reachable iff (q, w) is reachable for some $w \in \Gamma^*$. It is well-known that the problem of control state reachability is decidable (see [13,1]); this is the content of the next theorem.

Theorem 1. *Given a PDS $\mathcal{P}$, checking if a control state q is reachable is decidable in $O(n^3)$ time, where n is the size of the PDS $\mathcal{P}$.*

3   Programming Language

We describe a simple parallel language SPL, which captures the essential concepts of multithreaded programs with asynchronous atomic methods. The SPL language is a simplified form of the sequential Java language. Similar to Java, the SPL language supports objects. In addition to definition of classes, we allow the definition of a special type called **thread**. Instances of a **class** is called an object and instances of a **thread** is called a thread object. A thread of control is associated with every thread object. The objects in SPL behave similarly as in Java. A method invocation of an object is *synchronous* and its execution is carried out using a stack. However, for thread objects we introduce a new semantics for method invocation. Specifically, we assume that an invocation of a method of a thread object is *asynchronous* and *atomic*. If a thread of control invokes a method of a thread object, then the method call returns immediately and the call is added as a message to a global message bag. If the thread of control associated with the callee object is not busy processing a message, then it takes out a message (i.e., a call to one of its methods) targeted to it from the global bag and starts executing it atomically and concurrently with other threads. Note that in an execution of a SPL program, several threads can execute concurrently. The atomicity condition requires that for every possible interleaved execution of a SPL program, there exists an equivalent execution with the same overall behavior where the methods of the thread objects are executed serially, that is, the execution of a thread object method is not interleaved with actions of other threads. This particular restriction ensures that the execution of a method of a thread object is not interfered by other threads through shared objects.

$$
\begin{aligned}
P &::= \mathit{defn}^* \; (\textbf{new } T).\mathit{md}(c^*) \\
\mathit{defn} &::= \textbf{class } C \; \{\mathit{field}^* \; \mathit{meth1}^*\} \mid \textbf{thread } T \; \{\mathit{field}^* \; \mathit{meth2}^*\} \\
\mathit{field} &::= \mathit{type} \; \mathit{fd} \\
\mathit{meth1} &::= (\mathit{type} \mid \textbf{void}) \; \mathit{md}(\mathit{arg}^*)\{\mathit{local}^* \; \mathit{stmt}^*\} \\
\mathit{meth2} &::= \textbf{void } \mathit{md}(\mathit{arg}^*)\{\mathit{local}^* \; \mathit{stmt}^*\} \\
\mathit{stmt} &::= l: S; \\
S &::= x = e \mid x.\mathit{fd} = y \mid x.\mathit{md}(y^*) \mid \textbf{if } x \textbf{ goto } l' \mid \textbf{return } x \\
e &::= \textbf{new } \mathit{type} \mid \textbf{null} \mid \textbf{this} \mid c \mid x \mid x.\mathit{fd} \mid x.\mathit{md}(y^*) \mid f(x^*) \\
\mathit{arg} &::= \mathit{type} \; x \\
\mathit{local} &::= \mathit{type} \; y \\
\mathit{type} &::= C \mid T \mid \text{primitive types such as int, float, boolean, etc.} \\
l &::= \mathit{label} \\
x, y &::= \text{variable name} \\
C &::= \text{class name} \\
T &::= \text{thread name} \\
\mathit{fd} &::= \text{a field name} \\
\mathit{md} &::= \text{a method name} \\
f &::= \text{pre-defined functions such as } +, -, *, /, \text{etc.} \\
c &::= \text{constants such as } 1, 2, \text{true, etc.}
\end{aligned}
$$

Fig. 1. SPL Syntax

3.1 Syntax of SPL

The formal syntax of SPL is given in Figure 1. A program in SPL consists of a sequence of definitions of **classes** and **threads** followed by an asynchronous method invocation of a newly created thread object. Observe that the execution of a statement can access at most one shared memory location. This allows us to treat the execution of a statement as an atomic operation. Branching and looping constructs are imitated using the statement **if** x **goto** l, where l is the label of a statement in the method that contains the **if** statement. We assume that a program in SPL is properly typed.

3.2   Semantics of SPL

In the semantics of SPL, we assume that actions of multiple threads can interleave in any way; however, we impose the restriction that the execution of an asynchronous method must be *atomic*. We call this semantics the concurrent semantics of SPL.

The concurrent semantics of SPL is given by augmenting more rules to the standard semantics of Java. Instantaneous snapshot of the execution of a SPL program is called a *configuration*. Formally, a configuration C is a 3-tuple (q, S, M), where

- q is the global state containing the value of every object and thread object currently in use in the program and the program counter of each thread associated with every thread object.
- S is a map from a thread object to an execution stack. The stack for each thread is used in the usual way to execute an asynchronous method sequentially. Note that the invocation of an object method is always synchronous and the method is executed by the caller thread by creating a new stack frame in its stack.
- M is a multi-set or bag of messages. Whenever, a thread invokes a method of a thread object, the target thread object, the method name, and the values of the arguments passed to the method are encoded into a message and placed in the bag. We use $M \cup e$ to represent the multi-set obtained by adding the element e to the multi-set M.

Let C be set of all configurations. We define a transition relation $C \leadsto_t^s C'$ (see Figure 2) for the concurrent semantics. Such a relation represents the transition from the configuration C to C' due to the execution of the statement s by the thread t. Henceforth, if t is a thread object, then we will also use t to denote the thread of control associated with the thread t. The transition relations are described abstractly using a number of functions described, informally, below:

- THREADS(q) returns the set of thread objects that are created in the execution.
- GETNEXTSTATEMENT(q, t) returns the next statement to be executed by the thread t. The function uses the value of the program counter found in q for the thread t to determine the next statement. If the thread t is not executing any asynchronous method, then the function returns $\perp$.
- EXECUTENEXTSTATEMENT$(q, S(t), t)$ executes the next statement of the thread t following the standard sequential Java semantics and returns a pair containing the updated global state q' and the updated map S' in which the stack $S'(t)$ has possibly been modified. The program counter of the thread t is also updated appropriately in the global state q'.
- SETNEXTSTATEMENT$(q, S(t), t, t.md(v^*))$, where v denotes a value, creates a stack frame in the stack $S(t)$ to prepare for the invocation of the method *md* and sets the program counter of t in q to the first statement of the method *md* of t. The updated global state q' and the map S' is returned by the function.
- SKIPNEXTSTATEMENT(q, t) updates the program counter in q of the thread t, such that the thread t skips the execution of the next statement.
- $[\![x]\!]_{S(t)}$ returns the value of the local variable x, which is obtained from the topmost stack frame of the stack $S(t)$.

[JAVA SEMANTICS]

$$\frac{\begin{array}{l}\exists t \in \textsc{Threads}(q).(s = \textsc{getNextStatement}(q,t)\\ \wedge\ s \neq \perp \wedge \neg(s = x.md(y^*) \wedge [\![x]\!]_{S(t)} \in \textsc{Threads}(q)))\\ \wedge\ (q', S') = \textsc{executeNextStatement}(q, S(t), t)\end{array}}{(q,S,M) \rightsquigarrow_t^s (q',S',M)}$$

[CONSUME MESSAGE]

$$\frac{\begin{array}{l}\exists t \in \textsc{Threads}(q).(\textsc{getNextStatement}(q,t) = \perp\\ \wedge\ (q', S') = \textsc{setNextStatement}(q, S(t), t, t.md(v^*)))\end{array}}{(q,S,M \cup \{t.md(v^*)\}) \rightsquigarrow_t^{\perp} (q',S',M)}$$

[SEND MESSAGE]

$$\frac{\begin{array}{l}\exists t \in \textsc{Threads}(q).(s = \textsc{getNextStatement}(q,t)\\ \wedge\ (s = x.md(y^*) \wedge [\![x]\!]_{S(t)} \in \textsc{Threads}(q)))\end{array}}{(q,S,M) \rightsquigarrow_t^s (\textsc{skipNextStatement}(q,t), S, M \cup \{[\![x]\!]_{S(t)}.md([\![y]\!]^*_{S(t)})\})}$$

Fig. 2. Concurrent Semantics

The initial configuration of a SPL program $defn^*$ (**new** $T).md(c^*)$, given by $C_0 = (q_0, S_0, M_0)$, where q_0 contains the thread object, say t, created by the **new** T expression, S_0 maps t to an empty stack, and M_0 contains the only message $t.md(c^*)$. The program counter of t in q_0 is undefined. Thus the CONSUME MESSAGE is the only rule applicable to the initial configuration.

Atomicity Requirement. The concurrent semantics of SPL allows arbitrary interleaving of multiple threads. However, we want to impose the restriction on possible interleavings so that the execution of each asynchronous method is atomic. We next describe this atomicity requirement.

We abstractly represent a finite execution of the form $C_0 \rightsquigarrow_{t_1}^{s_1} C_1 \rightsquigarrow_{t_2}^{s_2} C_2 \cdots C_{n-1} \rightsquigarrow_{t_n}^{s_n} C_n$ of a SPL program following the concurrent semantics by the sequence $\tau = \rightsquigarrow_{t_1}^{s_1}\rightsquigarrow_{t_2}^{s_2} \cdots \rightsquigarrow_{t_n}^{s_n} C_n$. We use MSET$(\tau)$ to represent the multi-set $\{(t_1,s_1),(t_2,s_2),\ldots,(t_n,s_n)\}$. We restrict the set of executions that can be exhibited by a SPL program following the concurrent semantics by imposing the atomicity requirement on asynchronous method executions as follows. If a finite execution $\tau = \rightsquigarrow_{t_1}^{s_1}\rightsquigarrow_{t_2}^{s_2} \cdots \rightsquigarrow_{t_n}^{s_n} (q,S,M)$ be such that $\forall t \in \textsc{Threads}(q).(\textsc{getNextStatement}(q,t) = \perp)$, then τ is said to be a *valid* execution of the program following the concurrent semantics iff the following holds. There exists a finite execution $\tau' = \rightsquigarrow_{t'_1}^{s'_1}\rightsquigarrow_{t'_2}^{s'_2} \cdots \rightsquigarrow_{t'_n}^{s'_n} (q',S',M')$ of the program following the concurrent semantics such that

1. $(q, S, M) = (q', S', M')$,
2. $\text{MSET}(\tau) = \text{MSET}(\tau')$,
3. if for any two elements (t, s) and (t, s') in the $\text{MSET}(\tau)$, $\leadsto_t^s$ appears before $\leadsto_t^{s'}$ in the sequence τ, then $\leadsto_t^s$ also appears before $\leadsto_t^{s'}$ in the sequence τ', and
4. in the sequence τ', all transitions after a $\leadsto_t^\perp$ and before any $\leadsto_{t''}^\perp$ are of the form $\leadsto_{t'}^s$ such that $t = t'$ and $s \neq \perp$.

The above requirement ensures that the execution of an asynchronous method by a thread is atomic. In general, it has been shown that such atomicity requirements for multithreaded programs can be guaranteed statically by using a type system for atomicity [14] or dynamically through rollback [32]. We assume that the language SPL is augmented with an atomicity type system or implemented in a way such that an execution of a program in the language following the concurrent semantics is always valid.

Serialized Semantics. To effectively reason about the behavior of a SPL, we introduce the serialized semantics of SPL and show that for the reasoning purpose we can only consider the serialized semantics of SPL.

Similar to the concurrent semantics, in the serialized semantics, we assume that there is global state q, a global message bag or a multi-set of messages M, and a map S from thread objects to stacks. Then the following happens in a loop. If there is a message (i.e., an asynchronous method call along with values for its arguments) for a thread in the bag, then the thread removes the message from the bag and executes the method in the message. No other thread is allowed to interleave their executions till the execution of the method terminates. During the execution of the method, the executing thread can call asynchronous methods of any thread object. Those calls along with the values for their arguments are placed in the bag as messages. Note that a non-deterministic choice is associated with the picking of a message from the bag.

We define a transition relation $C \longrightarrow_t^s C'$ for the serialized semantics. The rules for transition in the serialized semantics is same as that in the concurrent semantics except for the rule [CONSUME MESSAGE] (see Figure 3). In the serialized semantics, the rule is applicable if none of the threads is executing an asynchronous method and there is a message in the bag. In the concurrent semantics, the rule is applicable if there exists a thread, which is not executing an asynchronous method, and there is a message for the thread in the bag. Note that the atomicity requirement trivially holds in the case of serialized semantics. We represent a finite execution of the form $C_0 \longrightarrow_{t_1}^{s_1}$ $C_1 \longrightarrow_{t_2}^{s_2} C_2 \cdots C_{n-1} \longrightarrow_{t_n}^{s_n} C_n$ following the serialized semantics by the sequence $\longrightarrow_{t_1}^{s_1} \longrightarrow_{t_2}^{s_2} \cdots \longrightarrow_{t_n}^{s_n} C_n$.

[CONSUME MESSAGE]

$$\frac{\forall t \in \text{THREADS}(q).(\text{GETNEXTSTATEMENT}(q, t) = \perp) \\ \land \quad (q', S') = \text{SETNEXTSTATEMENT}(q, S(t'), t', t'.md(v^*))}{(q, S, M \cup \{t'.md(v^*)\}) \longrightarrow_{t'}^\perp (q', S', M)}$$

Fig. 3. Serialized Semantics

Given that a program in SPL always exhibits valid executions following the concurrent semantics, the next result shows that any execution of the program following the concurrent semantics is *equivalent* to an execution of the program following the serialized semantics.

Proposition 3. *For any program execution* $\leadsto_{t_1}^{s_1} \leadsto_{t_2}^{s_2} \cdots \leadsto_{t_n}^{s_n} (q, S, M)$ *where* $\forall t \in$ THREADS(q).GETNEXTSTATEMENT$(q, t) = \bot$, *there is a serialized execution* $\longrightarrow_{t_1'}^{s_1'} \longrightarrow_{t_2'}^{s_2'} \cdots \longrightarrow_{t_n'}^{s_n'} (q', S', M')$ *such that* $(q, S, M) = (q', S', M')$.

The above result allows us to treat any valid execution of a program in SPL following the concurrent semantics in terms of an equivalent execution following the serialized semantics. Reasoning about a serialized execution is easier because in such an execution we have to consider a sequence of method invocations by different threads, where the execution of each method can be reasoned sequentially. In fact, in the next section we show that reachability of finite programs in SPL is decidable. It is worth mentioning that the reachability of a program in SPL following the concurrent semantics is not decidable if we do not impose the atomicity restriction.

4   Verifying SPL Programs

In this section we consider the problem of verifying SPL programs. Recall that for SPL programs restricted to valid concurrent executions, we observed (in Section 3.2) that reasoning about serialized executions is sufficient when answering questions about global state reachability. Further, during a serialized execution of a SPL program, at any point only one thread executes an asynchronous method up to completion without interleaving with any other thread. This implies that the stack of at most one thread is non-empty at any point in a serialized execution. As a result, we can define the (serialized) semantics using only one stack which is re-used by every active thread.

The verification of serialized SPL programs can proceed by following the familiar methodology of abstracting SPL programs, model checking, checking the validity of a counterexample, and then refining the abstraction if the counterexample if found to be invalid. Using standard predicate abstraction techniques, an SPL program over arbitrary data types can be abstracted into an SPL program all of whose variables are boolean. The steps of checking counterexamples and refining, again can be performed using well-known algorithms. In this section, we therefore focus our attention on model checking finite SPL programs. We first define the formal model of *multi-set pushdown systems* (MPDS) that have finitely many global states, one stack to execute recursive, synchronous method calls, and one message bag to store pending asynchronous method calls. Such MPDSs define the (serialized) semantics of finite SPL programs. We then show that the control state reachability problem for MPDSs is decidable. Finally, we conclude this section by showing that the control state reachability problem has a lower bound of EXPSPACE.

4.1   Multi-set Pushdown Systems

We present the formal definition and semantics of multi-set pushdown systems.

Definition 1. *A multi-set pushdown system (MPDS) is a tuple* $\mathcal{A} = (Q, \Gamma, \Delta, q_0, \gamma_0)$, *where Q is a finite set of global states, Γ is a finite set of stack and multi-set symbols, $\Delta \subseteq (Q \times \Gamma) \times (Q \times \Gamma^* \times \Gamma)$ is the transition relation, $q_0 \in Q$ is the initial state, and $\gamma_0 \in \Gamma$ is the initial method call.*

We let q to range over Q, γ to range over Γ, w to range over Γ^*, M to range over $M_\omega[\Gamma]$. The semantics of an MPDS $\mathcal{A}$ is defined in terms of a transition system as follows. A configuration $\mathcal{C}$ of $\mathcal{A}$ is a tuple $(q, w, M) \in Q \times \Gamma^* \times M_\omega[\Gamma]$. The initial configuration of $\mathcal{A}$ is $(q_0, \epsilon, \{\gamma_0\})$. The transition relation $\longrightarrow$ on configurations is $\longrightarrow_1 \cup \longrightarrow_2$, where $\longrightarrow_1$ and $\longrightarrow_2$ are defined as follows: $(q, w\gamma, M) \longrightarrow_1 (q', ww', M \cup \{\gamma'\})$ if and only if $((q, \gamma), (q', w', \gamma')) \in \Delta$; and $(q, \epsilon, M \cup \{\gamma\}) \longrightarrow_2 (q, \gamma, M)$. Observe that $\longrightarrow_1$ corresponds to the transition rules [Java Semantics] and [Send Message] and $\longrightarrow_2$ corresponds to the transition rule [Consume Message] in Figure 3. Also note that there is no transition from $(q, \epsilon, \emptyset)$ for any $q \in Q$; therefore, $\mathcal{A}$ halts when it reaches a configuration of the form $(q, \epsilon, \emptyset)$. Finally, $\longrightarrow^*$, $\longrightarrow_1^*$ denote the reflexive, transitive closure of $\longrightarrow$ and $\longrightarrow_1$, respectively.

Definition 2. *A configuration (q, w, M) is said to be* reachable *iff $(q_0, \epsilon, \{\gamma_0\}) \longrightarrow^* (q, w, M)$. A control state q is said to be* reachable *if for some $w \in \Gamma^*$ and $M \in M_\omega[\Gamma]$, (q, w, M) is reachable.*

4.2 Control State Reachability in MPDSs

We are interested in verifying if a certain global state (or set of global states) of a finite SPL program is reachable. This is the same as checking if a certain control state (or set of control states) is reachable in the MPDS associated with the SPL program. Let us fix an MPDS $\mathcal{A} = (Q, \Gamma, \Delta, q_0, \gamma_0)$. Recall that a control state q is reachable if for some w and M, $(q_0, \epsilon, \{\gamma_0\}) \longrightarrow^* (q, w, M)$. That means for some $q_1, q_2, \ldots q_n, \gamma_1, \gamma_2 \ldots \gamma_n$ and $M_1, M_2, \ldots M_n$, we have

$$(q_0, \epsilon, \{\gamma_0\}) \longrightarrow_2 (q_0, \gamma_0, \emptyset) \longrightarrow_1^* (q_1, \epsilon, M_1 \cup \{\gamma_1\}) \longrightarrow_2 (q_1, \gamma_1, M_1) \longrightarrow_1^* (q_2, \epsilon, M_2 \cup \{\gamma_2\})$$
$$\longrightarrow_2 (q_2, \gamma_2, M_2) \cdots \longrightarrow_1^* (q_n, \epsilon, M_n \cup \{\gamma_n\}) \longrightarrow_2 (q_n, \gamma_n, M_n) \longrightarrow_1^* (q, w, M)$$

Thus, the problem of checking whether a control state q is reachable, conveniently breaks up into two parts: for some q', w, γ, M and M', check whether $(q_0, \epsilon, \{\gamma_0\}) \longrightarrow^* (q', \epsilon, M' \cup \{\gamma\})$ and whether $(q', \gamma, M') \longrightarrow_1^* (q, w, M)$. Further observe that $(q', \gamma, \emptyset) \longrightarrow_1^* (q, w, M)$ for some w and M iff $(q', \gamma, M') \longrightarrow_1^* (q, w, M' \cup M)$ for every M'. Hence, we can further simplify our tasks as follows. For some q' and γ, check whether $(q_0, \epsilon, \{\gamma_0\}) \longrightarrow^* (q', \epsilon, M' \cup \{\gamma\})$ for M' and whether $(q', \gamma, \emptyset) \longrightarrow_1^* (q, w, M)$ for some M and w. We will call the first *coverability* problem and the second *control state reachability without context switches* problem. We will treat these problems one by one and show each to be decidable.

Reachability Without Context Switches. We will first consider the problem of checking if for some w, M, $(q', \gamma, \emptyset) \longrightarrow_1^* (q, w, M)$. Observe that since the messages in the bag do not play a role in the transition $\longrightarrow_1$, we can ignore the asynchronous method calls that are generated during a transition in order to decide this problem. Thus, this problem can be reduced to checking reachability in pushdown systems. More formally, consider the pushdown system $\mathcal{P} = (Q', \Gamma', \delta', q_0', \gamma_0')$ where $Q' = Q$ the states of the MPDS $\mathcal{A}$, $\Gamma' = \Gamma$, $q_0' = q'$, $\gamma_0' = \gamma$, and δ' is defined as follows: $((q_1, \gamma_1), (q_2, w_2)) \in \delta$ iff $((q_1, \gamma_1), (q_2, w_2, \gamma_2)) \in \Delta$ (transition relation of $\mathcal{A}$) for some γ_2. The MPDS $\mathcal{A}$ and the PDS $\mathcal{P}$ are related as follows.

Proposition 4. *A configuration* (q_1, w_1) *is reachable in* $\mathcal{P}$ *iff* $(q', \gamma, \emptyset) \longrightarrow_1^* (q_1, w_1, M)$ *for some* M.

The proof is straightforward and skipped in the interests of space. Hence based on Proposition 4 and Theorem 1, we can conclude that the control state reachability problem, without context switches is decidable in polynomial time for MPDSs.

Coverability. We now study the problem of coverability. Recall that, given a state q' and a stack symbol γ, we need to decide if for some $M' \in M_\omega[\Gamma]$, $(q_0, \epsilon, \{\gamma_0\}) \longrightarrow^*$ $(q', \epsilon, M' \cup \{\gamma\})$. We will introduce a new model of *regular multi-set systems* (RMS), which are slight generalization of *multi-set automata*, and show that the coverability problem can be reduced to a reachability problem on RMS. We will then show that the reachability problem for RMSs is decidable.

Definition 3. *A* regular multi-set system *(RMS) is a tuple* $\mathcal{R} = (Q, \Gamma, \delta, q_0, \gamma_0)$, *where* Q *is the set of the states of* $\mathcal{R}$, Γ *is the multi-set alphabet,* $q_0 \in Q$ *is the initial state, and* $\delta \subseteq ((Q \times \Gamma) \times (Q \times L))$ *is the transition relation with* $L \subseteq \Gamma^*$ *being a regular language. A configuration is the pair* (q, M), *where* $q \in Q$ *and* $M \in M_\omega[\Gamma]$ *and the initial configuration is* $(q_0, \{\gamma_0\})$. *The semantics of a RMS is given by the transition relation* $\hookrightarrow$ *over configurations. We say* $(q, M \cup \{\gamma\}) \hookrightarrow (q', M')$ *iff there is* $((q, \gamma), (q', L)) \in \delta$ *and* $w \in L$ *such that* $M' = (M \cup \mathbb{M}(w))$.

Regular multi-set systems are a generalization of multi-set automata, where instead of a transition adding the same multi-set to a bag every time, an RMS transition chooses a multi-set from among a collection described by a regular language and adds to the bag.

We will consider reachability problems for RMSs. A pair (q, γ) is said to be reachable iff there is some M such that $(q_0, \{\gamma_0\}) \hookrightarrow^* (q, M \cup \{\gamma\})$. We will show that the coverability problem of MPDS can be reduced to such a reachability problem. But for that we need to make an important observation about MPDSs.

Proposition 5. *For MPDS* $\mathcal{A}$, *and any states* q_1, q_2 *and stack symbol* γ_1 *define* $\mathcal{M}(q_1, q_2, \gamma_1) = \{M \mid (q_1, \gamma_1, \emptyset) \longrightarrow_1^* (q_2, \epsilon, M)\}$. *There is a regular language* $L(q_1, q_2, \gamma_1)$ *such that* $\mathbb{M}(L(q_1, q_2, \gamma_1)) = \mathcal{M}(q_1, q_2, \gamma_1)$.

Proof. Consider the following pushdown automaton $\mathcal{P} = (Q', \Sigma, \Gamma', \delta, q_0', \gamma_0', F)$ where $Q' = Q$ the states of $\mathcal{A}$, input alphabet $\Sigma = \Gamma$, stack alphabet $\Gamma' = \Gamma$, initial state $q_0' = q_1$, initial stack configuration $\gamma_0' = \gamma_1$, $F = \{q_2\}$, and the transition relation $\delta \subseteq Q \times \Gamma \times \Sigma \times Q \times \Gamma^*$ is defined as follows: $((p_1, \gamma_1'), \gamma_2', (p_2, w)) \in \delta$ iff $((p_1, \gamma_1'), (p_2, w, \gamma_2')) \in \Delta$. In other words, $\mathcal{P}$ has a transition on input γ_2' exactly if the corresponding transition in MPDS $\mathcal{A}$ asynchronously calls γ_2'. Let $L(\mathcal{P})$ be the language accepted by $\mathcal{P}$ simultaneously by empty stack and final state. It is easy to see that $\mathbb{M}(L(\mathcal{P})) = \mathcal{M}(q_1, q_2, \gamma_1)$.

We now recall an important observation due to Parikh [24].

Theorem 2 (Parikh). *For an context-free language L_1 there is a regular language L_2 such that $\mathbb{M}(L_1) = \mathbb{M}(L_2)$. Moreover, given a PDA recognizing L_1 we can effectively construct an automaton for L_2.*

Hence, there is a regular language $L(q_1, q_2, \gamma_1)$ such that $\mathbb{M}(L(q_1, q_2, \gamma_1)) = \mathbb{M}(L(\mathcal{P})) = \mathcal{M}(q_1, q_2, \gamma_1)$. $\qquad\qquad\square$

Lemma 1. *Given an MPDS $\mathcal{A}$, there is an RMS $\mathcal{R}$ with the same states and multi-set alphabet such that $(q_0, \epsilon, \{\gamma_0\}) \longrightarrow^* (q, \epsilon, M \cup \{\gamma\})$ for any M in the MPDS iff (q, γ) is reachable in $\mathcal{R}$.*

From Lemma 1 we observe that the coverability problem of MPDS is decidable provided checking if (q, γ) is reached in an RMS is decidable. We, therefore, focus on the reachability problem of RMSs. We will show that this problem is decidable by using properties about well-quasi-orderings (wqo) and performing backward reachability as in [12].

For the rest of this section let us fix an RMS $\mathcal{R} = (Q, \Gamma, \delta, q_0, \gamma_0)$. Let us define an ordering $\leq$ over the configurations of a RMS as follows: $(q, M) \leq (q', M')$ iff $q = q'$ and $M \subseteq M'$. An immediate consequence of Dickson's Lemma [9] is the fact that this ordering is a wqo. For a set of configurations S, define $\mathrm{PRE}(S) = \{(q, M) \mid \exists (q', M') \in S . (q, M) \hookrightarrow (q', M')\}$ to be the set of configurations that can reach some configuration in S in one step. Finally, let $\mathrm{PRE}^*(S) = \bigcup_{i \in \mathbb{N}} \mathrm{PRE}^i(S)$ be the set of all configurations that can reach some configuration in S in finitely many steps.

Recall that to check if (q, γ) is reachable, we need to see if some configuration in $V = \mathrm{CL}(\{(q, \{\gamma\})\})$ is reachable from the initial configuration of the RMS. Hence, we will compute $\mathrm{PRE}^*(V)$ and check if $(q_0, \{\gamma_0\}) \in \mathrm{PRE}^*(V)$. Observe that in an RMS, if $(q_1, M_1) \hookrightarrow (q_2, M_2)$ then for every M, $(q_1, M_1 \cup M) \hookrightarrow (q_2, M_2 \cup M)$. Thus, for an upward closed set U, $\mathrm{PRE}(U)$ is also upward closed. This suggests the following algorithm. Compute progressively the sets U_i, where $U_0 = V$ and $U_{i+1} = \mathrm{PRE}(U_i) \cup U_i$. The sequence $U_0, U_1, \ldots$ is an increasing sequence of upward closed sets, and so by Proposition 2 we know that this sequence stabilizes in finitely many iterations.

To prove decidability of the reachability problem, all we need to show is that we can compute a representation of U_{i+1}, given a representation of U_i. We can represent an upward closed set U by its minimal elements $\mathrm{MIN}(U)$ which will be finite (by Proposition 1). Thus, we need to describe how to compute $\mathrm{MIN}(U_{i+1})$ from $\mathrm{MIN}(U_i)$.

Consider any upward closed set U and $(q, M) \in \mathrm{MIN}(U)$. For a transition $t_q = ((q', \gamma), (q, L)) \in \delta$ (whose destination is state q) and $w \in L$ define $\mathrm{MIN}(\mathrm{PRE}_{t_q}^w(U))$ to be $(q', (M \setminus \mathbb{M}(w)) \cup \{\gamma\})$. In other words, $\mathrm{MIN}(\mathrm{PRE}_{t_q}^w(U))$ is the least configuration that can make a transition using t_q by pushing $\mathbb{M}(w)$ elements into the bag and reach a configuration in U. Let $S = \{\mathrm{MIN}(\mathrm{PRE}_{t_q}^w(U)) \mid \text{for every } w \in L, (q, M) \in \mathrm{MIN}(U) \text{ and transition } t_q\}$ Our first observation is that S can be represented using regular languages.

Lemma 2. *There are regular languages L_q such that $S = \bigcup_{q \in Q} \{q\} \times \mathbb{M}(L_q)$.*

Finally, we show that given an automaton representation of S, we can compute $\mathrm{MIN}(\mathrm{PRE}(U))$. From the definition of S it follows that $\mathrm{CL}(S) = \mathrm{PRE}(U)$. Thus

MIN(PRE(U)) = MIN(S). Our next observation is that given an automaton representation of S, MIN(S) is computable.

Lemma 3. *Given finite automata A_q for each L_q such that $S = \bigcup_{q \in Q} \{q\} \times \mathbb{M}(L_q)$, MIN($S$) is computable.*

4.3 EXPSPACE Lower Bound

We now show that the control state reachability problem is, in fact, computationally very difficult; we prove the problem is EXPSPACE-hard. The proof relies on ideas for showing the hardness of the reachability problem of Petri Nets due to Lipton [19]. Therefore, we first recall definitions needed to state Lipton's observation, and then sketch how they can be used to prove the lower bound.

Lipton's result can be seen as showing a lower bound for halting problem of special programs called *net programs* [10]. A net program is a finite sequence of labeled commands that manipulate finitely many counter variables. Each statement of a net program is labeled. The basic commands that constitute a net program are as follows: *incrementing* a counter x ($\ell : x = x + 1$); *decrementing* a counter x ($\ell : x = x - 1$); *unconditional branching* ($\ell :$ goto ℓ_1); *nondeterministic branching* ($\ell :$ goto ℓ_1 or goto ℓ_2); *subroutine call* ($\ell :$ gosub ℓ_1); *return from subroutine* ($\ell :$ return); and halt ($\ell :$ halt). So a net program is a sequence of distinctly labeled commands such that the targets of goto and gosub statements are correct labels. Lipton's result applies to *well-structured* net programs, which are programs that can be decomposed into a main program that only calls level 1 subroutines, which in turn only call level 2 subroutines, etc., and the jump commands in a subroutine only have other commands of the same subroutine as target. In terms of such programs Lipton's result can be stated as follows.

Theorem 3 (Lipton [19,10]). *Given a well-structured net program P the problem of checking if some computation ends in the statement halt is EXPSPACE-hard.*

We will prove an EXPSPACE lower bound for the control state reachability of MPDSs by showing that every well-structured net program can be simulated by an MPDS. More precisely, for any well-structured net program P, there is an MPDS $\mathcal{A}(P)$ such that some computation of P halts if and only if a special state q_{halt} is reachable in $\mathcal{A}(P)$. Unfortunately, due to lack of space, we cannot give all the details of the construction of $\mathcal{A}(P)$; instead we will only sketch the main ideas. Corresponding to each labeled statement $\ell : stmt$, we will have a control state q_ℓ. For each variable x, there will be a multi-set symbol x; the number of such symbols n the bag will denote the current value of x. The stack at all times will have only one symbol, which will be popped at times to remove a message from the multi-set store. We will now sketch the translation of each of the basic commands. The goto statements just involve a change of control state without changing either the stack or the multi-set store. Incrementing x involves making a new asynchronous call to x (i.e., adding x to the multi-set). Decrementing x is a two step process: first we pop the stack (to get to an empty stack) and reach a new control state q'. State q' has the property that if the new method serviced (i.e., removed from multi-set and put on stack) is anything other than x, then it simply makes the same asynchronous call again, pops the stack and goes back to q'; on the other hand if the new method to be serviced is x, it simply new moves to the control state corresponding to the next statement. The idea in simulating subroutine calls is to transfer control to the control state of the subroutine, and then at the same time make an asynchronous call that stores the return address. On a return, we do something similar to the decrement step, to only service the message storing the return address; based on the return address we go to the appropriate new control state. The resulting MPDS has the same order of control states as the net program, and the stack alphabet is also of the same size as the net program. Thus, based on all these observations, we have the following theorem.

Theorem 4. *The control state reachability problem for MPDSs EXPSPACE-hard.*

Acknowledgment

We would like to thank Gul Agha, Chandrasekhar Boyapati, Cormac Flanagan, Ranjit Jhala, and Shaz Quadeer for providing valuable comments on this work. This work is supported in part by the ONR Grant N00014-02-1-0715, the NSF Grants NSF CNS 05-09321, NSF CCF 04-29639, and NSF CAREER 04-48178.

References

1. J.-M. Autebert, J. Berstel, and L. Boasson. Context-free languages and pushdown automata. pages 111–174, 1997.
2. T. Ball and S. Rajamani. The SLAM Toolkit. In *Proceedings of CAV'2001 (13th Conference on Computer Aided Verification)*, volume 2102 of *LNCS*, pages 260–264, 2001.
3. A. Bouajjani, J. Esparza, S. Schwoon, and J. Strejcek. Reachability analysis of multithreaded software with asynchronous communication. In *Proc. Foundations of Software Technology and Theoretical Computer Science (FSTTCS'05)*, volume 3821 of *LNCS*, 2005.
4. A. Bouajjani, J. Esparza, and T. Touili. A generic approach to the static analysis of concurrent programs with procedures. In *Principles of Programming Languages (POPL'03)*, 2003.
5. A. Bouajjani, M. Mueller-Olm, and T. Touili. Regular symbolic analysis of dynamic networks of pushdown systems. In *Proc. 16th Intern. Conf. on Concurrency Theory (CONCUR'05)*, volume 3653 of *LNCS*, 2005.
6. D. Caucal. On the regular structure of prefix rewriting. *Theoretical Computer Science*, 106:61–86, 1992.
7. S. Chaki, E. Clarke, A. Groce, S. Jha, and H. Veith. Modular verification of software components in C. *IEEE Transactions on Software Engineering (TSE)*, 30(6):388–402, 2004.
8. J. M. Cobleigh, D. Giannakopoulou, and C. S. Pasareanu. Learning assumptions for compositional verification. In *Proc. of the 9th International Conference on Tools and Algorithms for the Construction and Analysis of Systems (TACAS)*, pages 331–346, 2003.
9. L. E. Dickson. Finiteness of the odd perfect and primitive abundant numbers with r distinct prime factors. *American Journal of Mathematics*, 35:413–422, 1913.
10. J. Esparza. Decidability and complexity of Petri net problems — An introduction. In *Lectures on Pteri Nets I: Basic Models. Adavnaces in Petri Nets*, number 1491 in Lecture Notes in Computer Science, pages 374–428. 1998.
11. J. Esparza and A. Podelski. Efficient algorithms for pre* and post* on interprocedural parallel flow graphs. In *Principles of Programming Languages (POPL'00)*, pages 1–11, 2000.
12. A. Finkel and P. Schnoebelen. Well-structured transition systems everywhere! *Theoretical Computer Science*, 256(1):63–92, 2001.

13. A. Finkel, B. Willems, and P. Wolper. A direct symbolic approach to model checking push-down systems. In *Proc. 2nd Int. Workshop on Verification of Infinite State Systems (INFIN-ITY'97)*, volume 9 of *Electronic Notes in Theor. Comp. Sci.* Elsevier, 1997.
14. C. Flanagan and S. Qadeer. A type and effect system for atomicity. In *Proc. of the ACM SIG-PLAN conference on Programming language design and implementation (PLDI'03)*, 2003.
15. T. Henzinger, R. Jhala, R. Majumdar, and G. Sutre. Lazy Abstraction. In *Proc. of the ACM Symposium on Principles of Programming Languages*, pages 58–70, 2002.
16. T. A. Henzinger, R. Jhala, R. Majumdar, and S. Qadeer. Thread-modular abstraction refinement. In *Proc. of the 15th International Conference on Computer-Aided Verification (CAV)*, volume 2725 of *LNCS*, pages 262–274. Springer, 2003.
17. A. Holub. *Taming Java Threads*. APress, 2000.
18. J. B. Kruskal. The theory of well-quasi-ordering: A frequently discovered concept. *Journal of Combinatorial Theory: Series A*, 13(3):297–305, 1972.
19. R. Lipton. The reachability problem requires exponential space. Technical Report 62, Yale University, 1976.
20. D. Lugiez and P. Schnoebelen. The regular viewpoint on PA-processes. *Theoretical Computer Science*, 274(1–2):89–115, 2002.
21. R. Mayr. *Decidability and Complexity of Model Checking Problems for Infinite-State Systems*. PhD thesis, Technical University Munich, 1998.
22. F. Moller. Infinite results. In *Proceedings of the Conference on Concurrency Theory*, pages 195–216, 1996.
23. M. Müller-Olm. Precise interprocedural dependence analysis of parallel programs. *Theoretical Computer Science*, 311(325–388), 2004.
24. R. Parikh. On context-free languages. *Journal of the ACM*, 13(4):570–581, 1966.
25. S. Qadeer, S. Rajamani, , and J. Rehof. Procedure summaries for model checking multi-threaded software. In *Principles of Programming Languages (POPL'04)*, 2004.
26. S. Qadeer and J. Rehof. Context-bounded model checking of concurrent software. In *11th International Conference on Tools and Algorithms for the Construction and Analysis of Systems*, volume 3440 of *LNCS*, pages 93–107, 2005.
27. S. Qadeer and D. Wu. KISS: keep it simple and sequential. In *ACM SIGPLAN 2004 conference on Programming language design and implementation*, pages 14–24, 2004.
28. G. Ramalingam. Context-sensitive synchronization-sensitive analysis is undecidable. *ACM Trans. Program. Lang. Syst.*, 22(2):416–430, 2000.
29. S. Graf and H. Saidi. Construction of abstract state graphs with PVS. In *Conference on Computer Aided Verification (CAV'97)*, volume 1254 of *LNCS*, pages 72–83, 1997.
30. H. Seidl and B. Steffen. Constraint-based inter-procedural analysis of parallel programs. In *European Symposium on Programming (ESOP'00)*, volume 1782 of *LNCS*, 2000.
31. K. Sen and M. Viswanathan. Model checking multithreaded programs with asynchronous atomic methods. Technical Report UIUCDCS-R-2006-2683, UIUC, 2006.
32. A. Welc, S. Jagannathan, and A. L. Hosking. Transactional monitors for concurrent objects. In *Proceedings of the European Conference on Object-Oriented Programming*, volume 3086 of *LNCS*, pages 519–542. Springer, 2004.

Causal Atomicity

Azadeh Farzan* and P. Madhusudan

Department of Computer Science,
University of Illinois at Urbana-Champaign
{afarzan, madhu}@cs.uiuc.edu

Abstract. Atomicity is an important generic specification that assures
that a programmer can pretend blocks occur sequentially in any execution. We define a notion of atomicity based on *causality*. We model the
control flow of a program with threads using a Petri net that naturally
abstracts data, and faithfully captures the independence and interaction
between threads. The causality between events in the partially ordered
executions of the Petri net is used to define the notion of *causal atomicity*. We show that causal atomicity is a robust notion that many correct
programs adopt, and show how we can effectively check causal atomicity
using Petri net tools based on unfoldings, which exploit the concurrency
in the net to yield automatic partial-order reduction in the state-space.

1 Introduction

Programs with multiple threads are a common paradigm in concurrent programming. Programming correctly with threads is particularly hard as one has
to consider the various interleavings of threads at run-time. Moreover, bugs that
manifest themselves because of interleavings are harder to detect using testing,
as they can be very infrequent in occurrence. A practical approach to programming threads is to develop techniques that allow the programmer to specify and
verify disciplined interaction between threads.

The lack of *race conditions* is such a discipline; a race condition occurs when
two threads simultaneously access a global variable, and one of the accesses is
a *write*. Depending on when the write event gets scheduled, the program could
take very different paths, which is a cause of concern. While the lack of races does
seem to be a natural discipline to adhere to, it has been observed and argued
that it is not a strong enough condition [10].

A stronger[1] discipline is to require methods or blocks of code to be *atomic*.
The general definition of atomicity is: *a code block is atomic [10] if for every interleaved execution of the program in which the code block is executed, there is an
equivalent run of the program where the code block is executed sequentially (without interleaving with other threads).* Intuitively, since for every interleaved execution t, there is an equivalent execution t' where the block occurs sequentially,

---

* Research supported by ONR grant N00014-02-1-0715.
[1] Atomicity is not a strictly stronger notion than race-freedom; see Figure 7 for an
example.

T. Ball and R.B. Jones (Eds.): CAV 2006, LNCS 4144, pp. 315–328, 2006.
© Springer-Verlag Berlin Heidelberg 2006

if the block had a logical error making t incorrect, then t' would be incorrect as well, arguing that the error in the block was not because of its interleaving with other threads. Consequently, a block being atomic greatly simplifies writing and understanding code: the programmer can *pretend* that the code block is executed sequentially, which simplifies its correctness argument. Note that the problem of checking atomicity of program blocks is obviously undecidable.

Atomicity is a well-argued principle of programming: in the database literature, it is known as *serializability* [6,19,2,1,21], and in the software analysis literature, it has been argued that many errors in threaded code can be traced back to blocks being non-atomic [10,9,7,23,13,8,22]. There has been extensive work on detecting atomicity of program blocks: static analysis techniques that use type-checking to detect *transactions* [15,10,9,23], where a transaction is a strong notion that implies atomicity; dynamic analysis that checks atomicity of tests of the program at run-time [8,22]; and model checking for atomicity where a monitor that detects non-atomic blocks runs in parallel with the system, which is then model checked [13,7].

In order to get effective algorithms, atomicity checkers aim for soundness (i.e. if the tool reports a block to be atomic, then the block should indeed be atomic), and the generic way to achieve this is to abstract the program in a sound fashion, as well as define a sound notion of *equivalence* between abstract traces. In other words, the equivalence relation between traces of the abstract model should imply that the concrete traces represented by them are equivalent as well.

While atomicity checkers in the literature do assure that their analyses are sound, they do not define precisely the abstraction they use, nor define precisely the notion of equivalence they assume. For example, static atomicity checking using types are based on transactions (transactions imply atomicity), but transactions require knowing what kind of "mover" each statement is, which is achieved using a separate race-checking analysis (which again is not precisely defined). The algorithm for checking for transactions is then implemented using types, and again it is not argued whether given the classification of statements as movers, the type-checking approach is *complete* or not. All in all, though every step is sound, and the soundness of the whole algorithm is assured, the precise abstraction and notion of equivalence used is not clear, making it hard to evaluate and compare the formalisms.

The main contribution of this paper is a new notion of atomicity for programs based on *causality*, and that has precise definitions of the abstraction mechanism and the notion of equivalence between abstract runs. Given a program P with multiple threads, we exhibit a clean *control* model of the program as a Petri net [18,16]. This modeling is aimed at capturing control and abstracting away the data values used in the program. Moreover, the Petri net explicitly captures the *independence* of execution of threads, and the interaction mechanism of the threads (using shared variables, locks, etc.). The model for the program is independent of any notion of atomicity, and captures just the dependence and independence of control in the threads of the program.

This model of a Petri net generates, in a standard way, partially-ordered runs of P that depict possible control interactions between threads [4]; we call these partially-ordered runs the *control traces* of P. The partially ordered control traces depict the set of events that have occurred and also define the *causal* relation between these events (such a causal structure is not evident in the *linear* runs of P). Moreover, the Petri net model is such that if one linearization σ of a partially ordered run Tr is feasible in the original program, then all linearizations of the Tr are feasible in the concrete program as well and are equivalent to r (in terms of the final state reached).

Causal atomicity is defined using the causal structure of the control traces generated by the program. We consider two sequential executions of a program to be *equivalent* if and only if they correspond to linearizations of the same partially-ordered trace of the program. Causal atomicity reduces to a very simple property on partially ordered traces: a block B of a thread is causally atomic if there is no control trace of the program where an event of another thread occurs *causally after* the beginning of B and *causally before* another event that is within the same block B.

Our notion of causal atomicity is simple and yet powerful enough to capture common interaction disciplines in correct programs. Our notion is certainly stronger than looking for patterns of *transactions* [15,10], and can handle programs that do not explicitly use locks.

Turning to algorithms for checking atomicity, we show how causal atomicity can be checked using *partial-order* techniques based on unfoldings of Petri nets. Our algorithm is sound *and* complete in checking for causal atomicity of the net. Given a Petri net model of P with a block marked to be checked for atomicity, we show how to reduce the problem of checking causal atomicity of P to a coverability problem for an associated *colored* Petri net Q [14]. The latter problem is decidable and there are several tools that can efficiently check coverability in colored Petri nets. In particular, the tools that use *unfolding* techniques [17,5] of nets are useful as they exploit the structure of the net to give automatic reduction in state-space (akin to partial-order reduction that has been exploited in model checking concurrent systems).

Finally, we show that causal atomicity is a common paradigm in many programs by considering several examples. We report on experiments that reduce checking causal atomicity to coverability, where the latter is solved using the PEP tool (Programming Environment based on Petri nets) [12]. The experiments show that causal atomicity lends itself to fast partial-order based model checking.

When there is only one block that is being checked for atomicity, our notion of atomicity is the same as the notion of *serializability* studied for database transactions [11,1]. However, when there are multiple blocks, serializability demands that for every execution, there is one execution where *all* the atomic blocks are executed serially, while our notion demands that for every execution and every block, there is some execution where *that* block occurs sequentially. We believe our notion is more appropriate for threaded software. Figure 1 shows an example

of a trace of a program with four threads and two blocks which intuitively ought
to be declared atomic. For instance, any pre-post condition of the block B (or
B') that depends only on the variables used in the block holds on all interleaved
runs provided it holds in runs where the block is executed sequentially. Note
a program with such a trace would be declared non-serializable, but declared
causally atomic.

While we believe the jury is still out
on which of these notions of atomicity is useful and accurate for checking
programs, note that our contributions
hold equally well for serializability: we
can define a notion of serializability
using the causal edges in the Petri net
model and check for it using unfolding algorithms (however, checking serializability seems more complex than
checking causal atomicity).

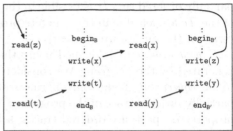

Fig. 1. Serializable but not causally atomic

The paper is structured as follows. Section 2 introduces a simple syntax for
a programming language with threads, and defines Petri nets and the partially
ordered traces they generate. Section 3 defines the modeling of a program as a
Petri net and defines causal atomicity based on the traces generated by this net.
Section 4 gives the generic translation of such a program model into a colored
Petri net, reducing causal atomicity to coverability. Section 5 gives experimental
results that show the efficacy of partial-order model checking tools in detecting
causal atomicity, and Section 6 contains concluding remarks.

2   Preliminaries

2.1   The Language for Programs

We base our formal development on the language SML (Simple Multithreaded
Language). Figure 2 presents the syntax of SML. The number of threads in an
SML program is fixed and preset. There are two kinds of variables: local and
global, respectively identified by the sets *LVar* and *GVar*. All variables that
appear at the definition list of the program are global and shared among all
threads. Any other variable that is used in a thread is assumed to be local to
the thread.

We assume that all variables are integers and are initialized to zero. We use
small letters (capital letters) to denote local (global, resp.) variables. *Lock* is a
global set of locks that the threads can use for synchronization purposes through
`acquire` and `release` primitives. The semantics of a program is the obvious one
and we do not define it formally.

`begin` and `end` primitives are used to mark the beginning and end of a block
that is intended to be checked for atomicity. The goal of the atomicity checker is
to check whether all such blocks are indeed atomic. Figure 5 shows two examples
of multithreaded programs written in SML.

P ::= defn thlist	(program)
thlist ::= null | stmt || thlist	(thread list)
defn ::= **int** Y | **lock** l | defn ; defn	(variable declaration)
stmt ::= $x := e$	
$\quad$ | **while** (b) { stmt } | **begin** stmt **end**	
$\quad$ | **if** (b) { stmt } **else** { stmt } | **skip**	
$\quad$ | **acquire**(l) | **release**(l) | stmt ; stmt	(statement)
$e ::= i \mid x \mid Y \mid e + e \mid e * e \mid e/e$	(expression)
$b ::=$ **true** | **false** | e op e | $b \vee b$ | $\neg b$	(boolean expression)

$$op \in \{<, \leq, >, \geq, =, ! =\}$$
$$x \in \text{LVar}, Y \in \text{GVar}, \quad i \in \text{Integer}, l \in \text{Lock}$$

Fig. 2. SML syntax

2.2   Petri Nets and Traces

Definition 1. *A Petri net is a triple $N = (P, T, F)$, where P is a set of places, T (disjoint from P) is a set of transitions, and $F \subseteq (P \times T) \cup (T \times P)$ is the flow relation.*

For a transition t of a (Petri) net, let ${}^\bullet t = \{p \in P | (p, t) \in F\}$ denote its set of pre-conditions and $t^\bullet = \{p \in P | (t, p) \in F\}$ its set of post-conditions.

A marking of the net is a subset M of positions of P.[2] A marked net is a structure (N, Init), where N is a net and Init is an initial marking. A transition t is *enabled* at a marking M if ${}^\bullet t \subseteq M$. The transition relation is defined on the set of markings: $M \xrightarrow{t} M'$ if a transition t is enabled at in M and $M' = (M \backslash {}^\bullet t) \cup t^\bullet$. Let $\xrightarrow{*}$ denote the reflexive and transitive closure of $\longrightarrow$. A marking M' *covers* a marking M if $M \subseteq M'$.

A *firing sequence* is a finite or infinite sequence of transitions $t_1 t_2 \ldots$ provided we have a sequence of markings $M_0 M_1 \ldots$ such that $M_0 = \text{Init}$ and for each i, $M_i \xrightarrow{t_{i+1}} M_{i+1}$. We denote the set of firing sequences of (N, Init) as $FS(N, \text{Init})$. A firing sequence can be viewed as a sequential execution of the Petri net. However, we are interested in the partially-ordered runs that the Petri net exhibits; we will define these using Mazurkiewicz traces.

Traces: A *trace alphabet* is a pair (Σ, I) where Σ is a finite alphabet of actions and $I \subseteq \Sigma \times \Sigma$ is an irreflexive and symmetric relation over Σ called the *independence* relation. The induced relation $D = (\Sigma \times \Sigma) \backslash I$ (which is symmetric and reflexive) is called the *dependence* relation. A Mazurkiewicz trace is a behavior that describes a partially-ordered execution of events in Σ (when $I = \emptyset$, it is simply a word).

Definition 2. *[4] A (Mazurkiewicz) trace over the trace alphabet (Σ, I) is a Σ-labeled poset $t = (\mathcal{E}, \preceq, \lambda)$ where $\mathcal{E}$ is a finite or a countable set of events, $\preceq$*

---

[2] Petri nets can be more general, but in this paper we restrict to 1-safe Petri nets where each place gets at most one token.

is a partial order on $\mathcal{E}$*, called the* causal order*, and* $\lambda : \mathcal{E} \longrightarrow \Sigma$ *is a labeling function such that the following hold:*

- $\forall e \in \mathcal{E}, \downarrow e$ *is finite.*   *Here,* $\downarrow e = \{e' \in E \mid e' \leq e\}$.
  So we demand that there are only finitely many events causally before e.
- $\forall e, e' \in \mathcal{E}, e \prec e' \Rightarrow \lambda(e)D\lambda(e')$.[3] *Events that are immediately causally related must correspond to dependent actions.*
- $\forall e, e' \in \mathcal{E}, \lambda(e)D\lambda(e') \Rightarrow (e \preceq e' \vee e' \preceq e)$. *Any two events with dependent labels must be causally related.*

$\mathcal{T}(\Sigma, I)$ denotes the set of all traces over (Σ, I). We identify traces that are isomorphic.

A *linearization* of a trace $t = (\mathcal{E}, \preceq, \lambda)$ is a linearization of its events that respects the partial order; in other words, it is a word structure $(\mathcal{E}, \preceq', \lambda)$ where $\preceq'$ is a linear order with $\preceq \subseteq \preceq'$.

Let us define an equivalence on words over Σ: $\sigma \sim \sigma'$ if and only if for every pair of letters $a, b \in \Sigma$, with aDb, $\sigma \downarrow \{a, b\} = \sigma' \downarrow \{a, b\}$, where $\downarrow$ is the projection operator that drops all symbols not belonging to the second argument. Then, σ and σ' are linearizations of the same trace iff $\sigma \sim \sigma'$. We denote the equivalence class that σ belongs to as $[\sigma]$.

Let (Σ, I) be a trace alphabet and $\sim$ be the associated relation. Let us now formally associate the (unique) trace that corresponds to a word σ over Σ.

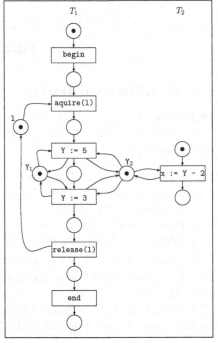

Fig. 3. Sample Net Model

A finite word σa is said to be *prime* if for every $\sigma' \sim \sigma a$, σ' is of the form $\sigma'' a$ (i.e. all words equivalent to σa end with a).

Let σ be a finite or infinite word over Σ. The trace associated with σ, $Tr(\sigma) = (\mathcal{E}, \preceq, \lambda)$ is defined as:

- $\mathcal{E} = \{[\sigma'] \mid \sigma' \text{ is prime}, \exists \sigma'' \sim \sigma, \sigma' \text{ is a prefix of } \sigma''\}$,
- $[\sigma] \preceq [\sigma']$ if there exists $\sigma_1 \in [\sigma], \sigma_1' \in [\sigma']$ such that σ_1 is a prefix of σ_1',
- $\lambda([\sigma' a]) = a$ for each $[\sigma' a] \in \mathcal{E}$.

It is easy to see that $Tr(\sigma)$ is a trace, and σ is a linearization of it.

Traces of a Petri Net: Let us now define the set of traces generated by a Petri net. Given a marked net (N, Init), $N = (P, T, F)$, we consider the trace alphabet

---

[3] $\prec$ is the immediate causal relation defined as: $e \prec e'$ iff $e \prec e'$ and there is no event e'' such that $e \prec e'' \prec e'$.

(Σ, I) where $\Sigma = T$, and $(t, t') \in I$ if and only if the neighborhoods of t and t' are disjoint, i.e. $({}^\bullet t \cup t^\bullet) \cap ({}^\bullet t' \cup t'^\bullet) = \emptyset$.

Now the traces generated by the net is is defined as $\{ Tr(\sigma) \mid \sigma \in FS(N, \mathrm{Init}) \}$. Note that a single trace represents several sequential runs, namely all its linearizations.

3   Causal Atomicity

Modeling Programs Using Petri Nets

We model the flow of control in SML programs by Petri nets. This modeling formally captures the concurrency between threads using the concurrency constructs of a Petri net, captures synchronizations between threads (e.g.. locks, accesses to global variables) using appropriate mechanisms in the net, and formalizes the fact that data is abstracted in a sound manner.

Figure 4 illustrates the function N that models statements using nets (inductively, for a fixed number of threads n). $N(\mathrm{S})$ is defined to have a unique *entry* place p_{in}^{S} and one or more *exit* transitions $tx_1^{\mathrm{S}}, \ldots, tx_m^{\mathrm{S}}$. In this natural way of modeling the control of a program, transitions correspond to program statements, and places are used to control the flow, and model the interdependencies and synchronization primitives. Figure 3 illustrates the Petri net model for the program in Figure 5(a).

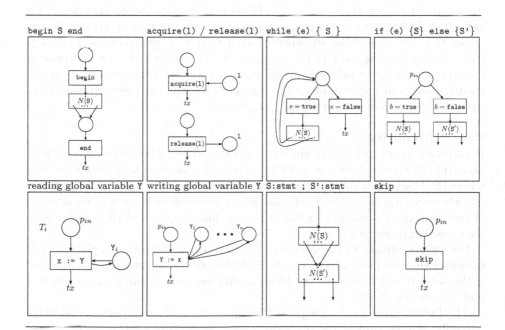

Fig. 4. Model Construction

There is a place l associated to each lock l which initially has a token in it. To acquire a lock, this token has to be available which then is taken and put back when the lock is released. This ensures that at most one thread can hold the lock at any time.

For each global variable Y, there are n places $Y_1, \ldots, Y_n$, one per thread. Every time the thread T_i reads the variable Y (Y appears in an expression), it takes the token from the place Y_i and puts it back immediately. If T_i wants to write Y (Y is on the left side of an assignment), it has to take one token from each place Y_j, $1 \leq j \leq n$ and put them all back. This is to ensure causality: two read operations of the same variable by different threads will be independent (as their neighborhoods will be disjoint), but a read and a write, or two writes are declared dependent. If $N_i = (P_i, T_i, F_i)$ is the Petri net model for statement S_i ($1 \leq i \leq n$), then the Petri net model for $S_1 \parallel \cdots \parallel S_n$ is the net ($P_1 \cup \cdots \cup P_n, T_1 \cup \cdots \cup T_n, F_1 \cup \cdots \cup F_n$), assuming T_i's are disjoint. Note the soundness of the abstraction: if a read and a write of two threads are simultaneously enabled (i.e. if there is a race condition), then the order on their accesses *may* be crucial. Since we are not keeping track of data in any manner, we declare them to be causally dependent and hence will consider the two runs inequivalent. The dependency relation defined in the model will lead to the appropriate notion of causality in the traces of the Petri net.

For a firing sequence σ of the net corresponding to a program, the sequence σ may not be feasible in the concrete program (because of the abstraction of data values). However, note that for every feasible sequence of the concrete program, its control trace is a trace of the net. Moreover, if σ is a firing sequence of the net which is feasible in the program (say by a concrete run r), then it is easy to see that for *each* firing sequence σ' such that $\sigma' \in [\sigma]$, there is a concrete run r' corresponding to it in the program that is equivalent to r (in terms of resulting in the same valuation of concrete variables). This property is key in ensuring that our entire approach is sound, as we will use trace equivalence as the equivalence over runs in defining atomicity.

Causal Atomicity

Recall the general notion of atomicity: a block is atomic if for for every sequential execution in which it is executed, there is another *equivalent* sequential execution where the block is executed without being interleaved with other threads. Given our abstraction using a Petri net, the only reasonable definition of equivalence of two sequential executions is that they are linearizations of the *same control trace* (see argument above).

Let us first illustrate the concept of causal atomicity by a simple example. Consider the two programs in Figure 5. Although the first thread (on the left) is the same in both versions, the block within **begin** and **end** is atomic in 5(b) and not atomic in 5(a).

The Petri net model of a program P induces the traces that correspond to the partially ordered runs of the program, which we call the *control traces*. *Causal atomicity* is defined as a property of these control traces. Figure 6 shows a control trace of the non-atomic program of Figure 5(a). Here labels of the events

T	T'		T	T'
`lock 1 ; int Y;`	`||`		`lock 1 ; int Y;`	`||`
`(1) begin`	`(1) x := Y - 2`		`(1) begin`	`(1) acquire(1)`
`(2)   acquire(1)`			`(2)   acquire(1)`	`(2) x := Y - 2`
`(3)     Y := 5;`			`(3)     Y := 5;`	`(3) release(1)`
`(4)     Y := 3`			`(4)     Y := 3`	
`(5)   release(1)`			`(5)   release(1)`	
`(6) end`			`(6) end`	
(a)			(b)	

Fig. 5. Two Programs

(transitions given by λ) are mentioned instead of the event names themselves to make the trace more readable. The arrows depict the immediate causality relation. The trace is a witness for non atomicity since `x:=Y-2` is causally after `Y:=5` and causally before `Y:=3`, and therefore in all linearizations of this trace, `x:=Y-2` has to appear in the middle of the block.

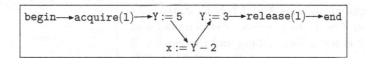

Fig. 6. Non-Atomic Trace

A notational remark: when we denote a transition as t^{T_i}, we mean that it belongs to the thread T_i.

Definition 3. *A code block $B =$ begin S end of the program P is **causally atomic** if and only if the Petri net model of the program P does not induce a trace $Tr = (mathcalE, \preceq, \lambda)$ for which the following holds:*

$$\exists e_1, e_2, f \in \mathcal{E} : e_1 \preceq f \preceq e_2 \qquad \text{where}$$
$$\lambda(e_1) = t^T_{\text{begin}}, \lambda(e_2) = t^T_2, \lambda(f) = t^{T'}_3 \quad \text{such that}$$
$$T \neq T' \text{ and } \nexists e \in \mathcal{E} : (\lambda(e) = t^T_{\text{end}} \land e_1 \preceq e \preceq e_2)$$

The above definition says that a block declared atomic is not causally atomic if the block begins, and there are two events, e_2 belonging to the same thread (and e_2 occurs before the block finishes) and f belonging to another thread such that f occurs causally between the beginning of the block and e_2. Note that traces that witness non-atomicity may not even execute the block completely (and we do not require any termination requirement for blocks).

The following theorem captures the intuition of why the above defines causal atomicity; it argues that if a trace of the program is not of the kind mentioned in the definition above, then there is indeed some linearization of events that executes the atomic block without interleaving. The proof is easy for finite traces, but more involved for the infinite ones; we skip the proofs.

Theorem 1. (a) *A code block* $B = $ begin S end *of the program* P *is causally atomic if and only if for all finite traces induced by the Petri net model of* P, *there is a linearization of the trace where all occurrences of block* B *occur sequentially (without interleaving with other threads).*

(b) *If a code block* $B = $ begin S end *of thread* T *in the program* P *is causally atomic then for all infinite traces induced by the Petri net model of* P, *there is a linearization of a causally downward closed subset of the events of the trace that contains all events belonging thread* T, *in which occurrences of block* B *occur sequentially.*

Note that the above theorems yield soundness of our approach: if a code block B is causally atomic, then by the above theorem and by the fact that either every linearization of a trace of the net is feasible in the concrete program or none are, it follows that the block B is atomic in the concrete program as well.

The program in Figure 7 distinguishes causal atomicity from other static notions of atomicity in the literature. The code block in thread T_2 is causally atomic. However, since there are races on both global variables X and Y, both statements X = 1 and Y = 1 are *non-mover* statements and this block is *not a transaction*, and therefore will not be detected as atomic by the method in [10]. Our notion of causal atomicity is also *behavioral*

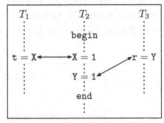

Fig. 7. Example

and more geared towards model checking as it depends on the partial-order executions of the program, not on the static structure of the code.

Commit-atomicity [7] is a dynamic notion of atomicity which is different from our static notion. The presence of data in commit-atomicity allows a more precise detection of atomicity according to the general definition of atomicity and there are examples (e.g. see Bluetooth3 in Section 5) that can be detected atomic by commit-atomicity, but they fail the causal atomicity check. On the other hand, the presence of data limits commit-atomicity to finite state space programs, and impedes scalability (specifically, in terms of number of threads). However, causal atomicity can deal with infinite data since the data is completely abstracted. Also, the commit-atomicity method requires the the atomic blocks to be terminating while we do not need such an assumption.

4   Checking Atomicity

In this section, we present how causal atomicity defined on traces can be reduced to coverability in a colored Petri net.

Colored Petri Nets

Colored Petri nets are subclass of *high level Petri nets* [14]. We explain how causal atomicity checks can be done by checking very simple properties on the colored nets. This does not imply any complications theoretically since the result in [14] shows that each colored net has an equivalent Petri net, and practically since most Petri net analysis tools today support high level nets.

We use a very simplified definition of colored Petri nets. We will not define them formally, but explain them intuitively. A colored Petri net has, as an underlying structure, a Petri net, but a token at a place can take a color c, which is drawn from a finite set of colors C. Transitions get enabled when their preconditions get marked, as before; but the transitions can now examine the colors of tokens and decide the colors of tokens on the post-conditions.

Given a model of a program P as a net $N = (P, T, F)$ and an initial marking Init, we define a colored Petri net that has the same underlying net N, but with colors $C = \{A, B, Y, R\}$. The initial marking is the initial marking Init, with all tokens colored A (achromatic).

The evolution of colors is determined by rules defined below. Note however that since the colored net has the same underlying net, it inherits the independence relation and generates the same traces as the net modeling the program.

Tokens are of one of the colors achromatic (A), blue (B), yellow (Y), and red (R), and we use them to monitor executions. The net nondeterministically chooses an occurrence of a block B of a thread T that is to be checked for atomicity, and at its **begin** event, turns the local control place of T to the color blue. Whenever an event has a local pre-condition marked blue, it taints all its post-conditions blue; hence the blue color spreads to all conditions causally after the **begin**-event of B. When a different thread reads a blue token, it transforms the token to yellow. Events that read any yellow-colored pre-condition taint their post-conditions to yellow as well, and hence propagate the yellow color to causal successors. If the thread T executes a statement of block B (before reaching the end of the block) and reads a pre-condition labeled yellow, it would detect violation of causal atomicity, and mark a special place red. If the end of block B is reached without detecting violation of causal atomicity, the net abruptly stops, as the occurrence of the block guessed to be non causal atomic was wrong.

Thus the problem of checking atomicity in the Petri net model of a program reduces to the problem of checking whether in the associated colored net, there is a reachable marking that covers a special place colored red (R).

Theorem 2. *The special place with a red (R) token is coverable in the colored Petri net constructed from the Petri net model of the program if and only if some marked block B is not causally atomic.*

5   Experiments

We have applied the method in Section 4 to check causal atomicity of several programs taken from [7]. This section presents a brief description of each program and the performance of our algorithm.

Dekker's Mutual Exclusion Algorithm: Dekker's algorithm is a classic algorithm for mutual exclusion between two threads that uses subtle synchronization. The mutual exclusion is modeled by means of two boolean variables. We check whether the critical sections of the threads are atomic, and they do turn out to be causally atomic.

Busy-Waiting Acquire Lock: In this example a busy waiting while loop is used to acquire a lock. There is a forever loop that acquires the mutex using this method, then a global variable data is updated, and the mutex is released. The correctness specification requires the updating of the data to be done atomically. We have checked two different versions of this example. In Acquire1 there is only one line modifying the data, while in Acquire2 there are several lines manipulating the data. Using our technique, there is negligible difference difference in the size of the unfolding between the two cases since the partial order semantics would not interleave the internal statements that modify the data. In contrast, the model checking algorithm in [7] uses interleavings, and they see a large increase in the time taken for Acquire2. One can make the block in Acquire1 non-atomic by adding an extra thread that manipulates the data without acquiring the mutex; nAcquire1 refers to this case.

In Acquire1* and Dekker*, multiple blocks (one per thread) are checked for causal atomicity. This is in contrast to the rest of the benchmarks where one block is checked at a time.

Bluetooth Device Driver: We used a simplified version of the Bluetooth device driver in Windows NT (Bluetooth), similar to the one used in [20,7]. There are two dispatch functions; let us call them Add and Stop. Any process that wants to use the driver calls Add, and any process that wants to stop the driver calls Stop. The correctness specification requires these two dispatch functions to run atomically. The Add function is not causally atomic which can be verified using only two threads where one calls Add and the other one calls Stop. This turns out to be a real cause for concern in the code, as interleaving events from other threads while executing Add does make the program behave unexpectedly; this was already reported in [20,7]. There is a fixed version of Bluetooth from [3] (Bluetooth3) which is still not causally atomic despite the fact that it is correct. However, *commit-atomicity* [7] can detect this as atomic since it can keep track of the value of the counter in the program.

Experimental Results

Table 1 shows the result of evaluating the above benchmarks using PEP [12]. Each program is modeled as a colored Petri net as described in Section 4. The unfolding of the colored net is generated. Then, with a simple query, we check whether the special place having a red token is coverable. The table reports the size of the unfolding, the time taken to check for causal atomicity (in seconds), and whether the atomicity checker detected causal atomicity. We performed these experiments under Linux on a 1.7GHz Pentium M laptop with 384MB of memory. The output time is reported with the precision of 10 milliseconds, and all experiments with 0 reported time were done in less than 10ms.

Note that in the Acquire1 example, the size of the unfolding grows only linearly with the number of threads; this reflects the space savings obtained through unfoldings. In contrast, the model checking algorithm in [7], which reasons using sequential traces, started to fail at around four threads. Note however that this isn't a fair comparison as the notion of atomicity (called *commit-atomicity*) in [7] is quite different, more accurate, and harder to check. However, in all the

Table 1. Programs and Performances

Benchmark	Causally Atomic?	#Threads	Unfolding #Places	Unfolding #Events	Time (sec)
Dekker	Yes	2	52	24	0
Dekker*	Yes	2	795	409	0.01
Acquire1	Yes	4	81	34	0
Acquire1	Yes	30	2135	1022	0.03
Acquire1	Yes	100	21105	10402	3.71
Acquire1	Yes	150	46655	23102	22.31
Acquire1*	Yes	4	146	56	0
Acquire1*	Yes	30	4202	1200	0.35
Acquire1*	Yes	50	10582	2985	5.02
Acquire1*	Yes	100	40486	10784	635.56
nAcquire1	No	4	97	43	0
nAcquire1	No	6	171	77	0
nAcquire1	No	8	261	119	0
Acquire2	Yes	4	73	30	0
Acquire2	Yes	6	146	74	0
Bluetooth	No	2	235	116	0
Bluetooth3	No	2	223	109	0

examples except Bluetooth3, their notion of atomicity agreed with ours. All the experiments can be found at: `http://peepal.cs.uiuc.edu/~azadeh/atomicity`.

6 Conclusions

We have defined a notion of atomicity based on the causal structure of events that occur in executions of programs. The causal structure is obtained using a straightforward data abstraction of the program that captures control interactions between threads using the concurrent model of Petri nets. We have demonstrated the usefulness of the notion of causal atomicity and shown that it can be effectively checked using unfolding based algorithms on Petri nets.

This work is part of a bigger project whose aim is to identify sound control abstractions for concurrent programs that can be used for static analysis (for example, dataflow analysis). We believe that true concurrent models (such as Petri nets) and true concurrent behaviors (like traces and event structures) would prove to be effective for this purpose. This paper demonstrates the efficacy of a truly concurrent behavior model (traces) in identifying atomicity.

There are several future directions. Our method of checking atomicity is a *global analysis* involving all threads simultaneously, while methods based on types and transactions work *locally* on each thread independently. Since local algorithms are likely to scale better, it would be interesting to find the weakest local property that ensures global causal atomicity. Also, finding *compositional* algorithms that derive information from each program locally and combine these to check for global atomicity would be interesting to study as they would scale better than global analysis and be more accurate than local analysis. Finally, we would also like to study extensions of atomicity defined in the literature (for example, *purity* [9]), in the causal setting.

References

1. R. Alur, K. McMillan, and D. Peled. Model-checking of correctness conditions for concurrent objects. *Inf. Comput.*, 160(1-2):167–188, 2000.
2. P. Bernstein, V. Hadzilacos, and N. Goodman. *Concurrency control and recovery in database systems*. Addison-Wesley Longman., 1987.
3. S. Chaki, E. Clarke, N. Kidd, T. Reps, and T. Touili. Verifying concurrent message-passing C programs with recursive calls. In *TACAS*, volume 3920 of *LNCS*, pages 334–349, 2006.
4. V. Diekert and G. Rozenberg. *The Book of Traces*. World Scientific Publishing Co., 1995.
5. J. Esparza, S. Romer, and W. Vogler. An improvement of McMillan's unfolding algorithm. In *TACAS*, volume 1055 of *LNCS*, pages 87 – 106, 1996.
6. K. Eswaran, J. Gray, R. Lorie, and I. Traiger. The notions of consistency and predicate locks in a database system. *Commun. ACM*, 19(11):624–633, 1976.
7. C. Flanagan. Verifying commit-atomicity using model-checking. In *SPIN*, pages 252–266, 2004.
8. C. Flanagan and S. Freund. Atomizer: a dynamic atomicity checker for multi-threaded programs. In *POPL*, pages 256–267, 2004.
9. C. Flanagan, S. Freund, and S. Qadeer. Exploiting purity for atomicity. *IEEE Trans. Software Eng.*, 31(4):275–291, 2005.
10. C. Flanagan and S. Qadeer. Types for atomicity. In *TLDI*, pages 1 – 12, 2003.
11. M. Flé and G. Roucairol. On serializability of iterated transactions. In *PODC*, pages 194–200, 1982.
12. B. Grahlmann. The PEP tool. In *CAV*, pages 440–443, 1997.
13. J. Hatcliff, Robby, and M. Dwyer. Verifying atomicity specifications for concurrent object-oriented software using model-checking. In *VMCAI*, pages 175–190, 2004.
14. K. Jensen. *Coloured Petri nets (2nd ed.): basic concepts, analysis methods and practical use: volume 1*. Springer-Verlag, London, UK, 1996.
15. R. Lipton. Reduction: A method of proving properties of parallel programs. *Commun. ACM*, 18(12):717–721, 1975.
16. K. Lodaya, M. Mukund, R. Ramanujam, and P. S. Thiagarajan. Models and logics for true concurrency. Technical Report TCS–90–3, School of Mathematics Internal, 1990.
17. K. McMillan. A technique of state space search based on unfolding. *Formal Methods in System Design*, 6(1):45–65, 1995.
18. M. Nielsen, G. Plotkin, and G. Winsker. Peri nets, event structures and domains — part i. *Theoretical Computer Science*, 13:85 – 108, 1981.
19. C. Papadimitriou. *The theory of database concurrency control*. Computer Science Press, Inc., New York, NY, USA, 1986.
20. S. Qadeer and D. Wu. KISS: keep it simple and sequential. In *PLDI*, pages 14–24, 2004.
21. A. Silberschatz, H. Korth, and S. Sudarshan. *Database Systems Concepts*. McGraw-Hill, 5th edition, 2005.
22. L. Wang and S. Stoller. Run-time analysis for atomicity. *Electr. Notes Theor. Comput. Sci.*, 89(2), 2003.
23. L. Wang and S. Stoller. Static analysis of atomicity for programs with non-blocking synchronization. In *PPOPP*, pages 61–71, 2005.

Languages of Nested Trees*

Rajeev Alur[1], Swarat Chaudhuri[1], and P. Madhusudan[2]

[1] University of Pennsylvania, USA
[2] University of Illinois at Urbana-Champaign, USA

Abstract. We study languages of *nested trees*—structures obtained by augmenting trees with sets of nested *jump-edges*. These graphs can naturally model branching behaviors of pushdown programs, so that the problem of branching-time software model checking may be phrased as a membership question for such languages. We define finite-state automata accepting such languages—these automata can pass states along jump-edges as well as tree edges. We find that the model-checking problem for these automata on pushdown systems is EXPTIME-complete, and that their alternating versions are expressively equivalent to NT-μ, a recently proposed temporal logic for nested trees that can express a variety of branching-time, "context-free" requirements. We also show that monadic second order logic (MSO) cannot exploit the structure: MSO on nested trees is too strong in the sense that it has an undecidable model checking problem, and seems too weak to capture NT-μ.

1 Introduction

Regular languages of infinite trees, accepted by finite-state tree automata, have been studied in detail and found many applications in the last thirty years. Such languages are known to be closed under all interesting operations and enjoy decidable membership and emptiness questions [10]. A cornucopia of other results are known: parity tree automata are equivalent to monadic second-order logic (MSO) on trees, their bisimulation-closed subclass is exactly captured by the modal μ-calculus [13], parity games and their zero-memory determinacy provide crucial steps that simplify the decidability proof, etc. [9,13,20,8,10]. Moreover, various decidability results for monadic logics on infinite graphs have been obtained using interpretations on the binary tree [7,10,24].

Our interest in regular tree languages stems from the application of these results to program verification. In its traditional phrasing, the branching-time model-checking problem is to determine, given a program P and a regular tree language S defining the specification, whether the execution tree of P is a member of S. Here, S may be given as a tree automaton or a formula in a temporal logic such as the μ-calculus [14]. In classical model checking, P is a finite state program modeling, for instance, hardware or network protocols. Recently, in order to analyze software, this problem was generalized to the case when P is a

---

* This research was partially supported by ARO URI award DAAD19-01-1-0473 and NSF award CCR-0306382.

T. Ball and R.B. Jones (Eds.): CAV 2006, LNCS 4144, pp. 329–342, 2006.

pushdown system. Such pushdown models can capture control flow in typical imperative programming languages with recursive calls, have a decidable model-checking problem against regular branching specifications, and are central to interprocedural dataflow analysis [22] and a number of software model-checking platforms [5,11]. In this paper, we fix them as our program models.

Here, our focus is on specification formalisms. The motivating observation is that regular tree languages are not expressive enough for many interesting specifications. For example, the μ-calculus cannot argue about the "matching" between calls and returns in a program, and, by implication, about pre/post-conditions, interprocedural dataflow requirements, and many access control properties involving the stack. While context-free specifications are expressive enough for these purposes, they are not closed under intersection or complement and have an undecidable model-checking problem on pushdown systems.

In this paper, we identify an alternative phrasing of the branching-time model-checking problem that is decidable but is capable of expressing "context-free" specifications as above. Inspired by recent work on automata on *nested words* [3,4], we model a program unfolding not by a tree, but by a directed acyclic graph known as a *nested tree* that is obtained by adding a set of properly nested *jump-edges* to a tree (see Fig. 1; the jump-edges are dashed). Based on the structure of jump-edges, we can classify nodes in a nested tree as *calls* (sources of jumps), *returns* (their targets), and *locals* (the remaining nodes). In nested trees generated from programs, calls and returns model call and return sites in the program, and jump-edges correspond to *summary edges*. Now we investigate finite-state automata and logics that define *regular languages* of such structures. Then the model-checking problem is to determine if the nested tree generated by a program belongs to a regular language of nested trees.

We begin our study by considering nondeterministic parity automata on infinite, ordered nested trees (NP-NTAs). An NP-NTA can send states along tree edges and jump edges, so that its state while reading a node depends on the states at its parent and the jump-predecessor (if one exists). Since there is an explicit jump-edge from a call to its matching return in a nested tree, these automata are naturally capable of matching calls with returns. Pleasantly, they are also closed under intersection. However, they are not closed under complement, so that they are unlikely to have an attractive logical characterization. This motivates us to consider *alternating* parity automata on nested trees (AP-NTAs). These automata, more naturally defined on unordered nested trees, are closed under all Boolean operations (though not under projection). While they have an undecidable emptiness problem, their model-checking problem is EXPTIME-complete, matching that for alternating *tree* automata on pushdown systems.

Our candidate for a canonical temporal logic for nested trees is $NT\text{-}\mu$, a fixpoint calculus introduced in our previous work [1] under the name VP-μ and a different but equivalent interpretation. The logic NT-μ is evaluated over subtrees of a nested tree summarizing procedural contexts and can reason about concatenation of such trees. Earlier, we established that it can express a variety of interesting requirements not expressible by regular tree languages, that its fixpoints naturally correspond to interprocedural summary computations, and that its model-checking problem on pushdown systems is EXPTIME-complete (and thus no more costly than that of weaker logics such as CTL). In this paper, we demonstrate that it defines a robust class of languages by proving that it has the same expressive power as AP-NTAs. Our proof[1] offers polynomial translations from AP-NTAs to NT-μ and vice versa, as well as insights about the connection between runs of AP-NTAs and the notion of summaries in NT-μ. This result is especially intriguing as the model-checking algorithms for NT-μ and AP-NTAs are very different in flavor—while the latter reduces to pushdown games, the former seems to have no connection to the various previously known results about trees, context-free languages, and pushdown graphs.

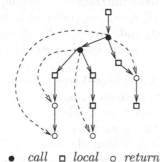

• *call* □ *local* ○ *return*

Fig. 1. A nested tree

Given the appealing trinity of automata, μ-calculus, and MSO for regular tree languages, we study *MSO-logic over nested trees*, which extends standard MSO-logic over trees with a predicate $(x \hookrightarrow y)$ that can check the existence of a jump-edge between two nodes. We show that MSO-logic is strictly more expressive than NP-NTAs, and that the matching predicate is too powerful leading to undecidable satisfiability and model checking problems. The undecidability proof shows that the difficulty lies with combining second-order existential quantification with the matching predicate. On the other hand, there seems to be no way to encode sets of summaries in MSO-logic over nested trees, and we conjecture that NT-μ cannot be translated to MSO-logic.

The paper is organized as follows. Sec. 2 defines nested trees and nested pushdown trees (nested trees generated by pushdown systems). In Sec. 3, we define and study NP-NTAs and AP-NTAs. Sec. 4 describes NT-μ and proves its expressive equivalence with AP-NTAs. In Sec. 5, we introduce MSO-logic over nested trees, prove it to be undecidable, and show that it cannot be captured by NT-μ. Sec. 6 has some concluding remarks.

2   Nested Trees

We now define nested trees, which are directed acyclic graphs obtained by augmenting a tree with a set of *jump-edges* representing non-trivial forward jumps. Jump-edges do not cross, and can capture the nesting of calls and returns in programs. We also model the intuition that if a call does not return, then neither does any of the calls pending up to it.

Formally, let $T = (S, r, \rightarrow)$ be an unordered infinite tree with node set S, root r and edge relation $\rightarrow \subseteq S \times S$. Let $\xrightarrow{+}$ denote the transitive (but not reflexive) closure of the edge relation, and let a *path* in T from node s_1 be a sequence $\pi = s_1 s_2 \ldots s_n \ldots$ over S, where $n \geq 2$ and $s_i \rightarrow s_{i+1}$ for all $1 \leq i$. In this paper, we only consider trees where all maximal paths are infinite.

---

[1] In the current version, we only offer proof sketches for the more important theorems. Full proofs are available in a technical report [2].

An *unordered nested tree* is a directed acyclic graph $(T, \hookrightarrow)$, where $\hookrightarrow \subseteq T \times T$ is a set of *jump-edges* satisfying:

1. if $s \hookrightarrow t$, then $s \xrightarrow{+} t$, and we do not have $s \to t$;
2. if $s \hookrightarrow t$ and $s \hookrightarrow t'$, then neither $t \xrightarrow{+} t'$ nor $t' \xrightarrow{+} t$;
3. if $s \hookrightarrow t$ and $s' \hookrightarrow t$, then $s = s'$;
4. if there is a path π such that for nodes s, t, s', t' lying on π we have $s \xrightarrow{+} s'$, $s \hookrightarrow t$, and $s' \hookrightarrow t'$, then either $t \xrightarrow{+} s'$ or $t' \xrightarrow{+} t$;
5. if $s \xrightarrow{+} t \xrightarrow{+} s'$, $s \hookrightarrow s'$, and $t \hookrightarrow t'$ for some t', then there is some t'' such that $t \hookrightarrow t''$ and $t'' \xrightarrow{+} s'$.

We are also interested in *ordered, binary nested trees* (although, by default, nested trees are assumed to be unordered). Let $T = (S, r, \to_1, \to_2)$ be an ordered binary tree, where S is a set of nodes, r is the root, and $\to_1, \to_2 \subseteq S \times S$ are the left and right edge relations. Then $(T, \hookrightarrow)$ is an ordered, binary nested tree if $((S, r, \to_1 \cup \to_2), \hookrightarrow)$ is an unordered nested tree.

For an alphabet Σ, a Σ-labeled (ordered or unordered) nested tree is a structure $\mathcal{T} = (T, \hookrightarrow, \lambda)$, where $(T, \hookrightarrow)$ is a nested tree with node set S, and $\lambda : S \to \Sigma$ is a node-labeling function. All nested trees in this paper are Σ-labeled.

A node s in a nested tree such that $s \hookrightarrow t$ ($t \hookrightarrow s$) for some t is a *call* (*return*) node; the remaining nodes are said to be *local*. We note that the sets of call, return and local nodes are disjoint. If $s \hookrightarrow t$, then we call s the *jump-predecessor* of t and t the *jump-successor* of s. Edges from a call node and to a return node are known as *call* and *return* edges; the remaining edges are *local*. The fact that an edge (s, t) exists and is a call, return or local edge is denoted by $s \xrightarrow{call} t$, $s \xrightarrow{ret} t$, or $s \xrightarrow{loc} t$. For an ordered or unordered nested tree $\mathcal{T} = (T, \hookrightarrow, \lambda)$ with edge set E, the *structured tree* of $\mathcal{T}$ is the node and edge-labeled tree $Struct(\mathcal{T}) = (T, \lambda, \eta : E \to \{call, ret, loc\})$, where $\eta(s, t) = a$ iff $s \xrightarrow{a} t$.

The *bisimulation relation* $\sim$ for nested trees is defined as: two (ordered, unordered) nested trees $\mathcal{T}_1$ and $\mathcal{T}_2$ are bisimilar (we write $\mathcal{T}_1 \sim \mathcal{T}_2$) if $Struct(\mathcal{T}_1)$ and $Struct(\mathcal{T}_2)$ are bisimilar by the usual definition of bisimulation on trees. The *bisimulation closure* of a set L of nested trees is the set $L_\sim = \{\mathcal{T}' : \mathcal{T}' \sim \mathcal{T} \text{ for some } \mathcal{T} \in L\}$. We call L *bisimulation-closed* if $L_\sim = L$.

A few observations: first, the sets of call, return and local edges define a partition of the set of tree edges. Second, if $s \xrightarrow{ret} s_1$ and $s \xrightarrow{ret} s_2$ for distinct s_1 and s_2, then s_1 and s_2 have the same jump-predecessor. Third, the jump-edges in a nested tree are completely captured by the edge labeling in the corresponding structured tree, so that we can *reconstruct* a nested tree $\mathcal{T}$ from $Struct(\mathcal{T})$.

Fig. 1 depicts part of a nested tree. The jump-edges are dashed, and call, return, and local nodes are drawn in different styles.

Nested Pushdown Trees. We are particularly interested in nested trees generated by *pushdown systems* (pushdown automata without accepting conditions), or, equivalently, recursive state machines or Boolean programs.

Consider a pushdown system $\mathcal{P}$ with a set of states V, a stack alphabet B, and initial state v_0. Transitions are of the form $v \longrightarrow v'$ (local moves),

$v \xrightarrow{push(b)} v'$ (pushes), and $v \xrightarrow{pop(b)} v'$ (pops). We assume that if there is a push-move (similarly, pop-move) from state v, then there are no local moves or pops (similarly, pushes) from v. Let $\kappa : V \to \Sigma$ label states by an alphabet Σ.

A *configuration* of $\mathcal{P}$ is a pair (v, w), where $v \in V$ is a state and $w \in B^*$ is the *stack*; let $C_{\mathcal{P}}$ be the set of configurations of $\mathcal{P}$. Let the configuration $c_0 = (v_0, \epsilon)$ be the *initial configuration*. The *configuration graph* of $\mathcal{P}$ has these configurations as vertices, and an edge relation $\dashrightarrow \subseteq C_{\mathcal{P}} \times C_{\mathcal{P}}$ that is the least relation satisfying: (1) $(v, w) \dashrightarrow (v', w)$, for $w \in B^*$, if $v \longrightarrow v'$ is a transition in $\mathcal{P}$, (2) $(v, w) \dashrightarrow (v', b.w)$ if $v \xrightarrow{push(b)} v'$, and (3) $(v, b.w) \dashrightarrow (v', w)$ if $v \xrightarrow{pop(b)} v'$. We assume that there is an outgoing edge from every $c \in C_{\mathcal{P}}$. The *configuration tree* of $\mathcal{P}$ is the unordered tree $T_{\mathcal{P}} = (S_{\mathcal{P}}, c_0, \longrightarrow_{\mathcal{P}})$, where $S_{\mathcal{P}} \subseteq C_{\mathcal{P}}^*$ and $\longrightarrow_{\mathcal{P}} \subseteq S_{\mathcal{P}} \subseteq S_{\mathcal{P}}$ are the least node set and edge relation constructed by the rules: (1) $c_0 \in S_{\mathcal{P}}$, and (2) if $s.c \in S_{\mathcal{P}}$ and $c \dashrightarrow c'$ for some $s \in C_{\mathcal{P}}^*$ and $c, c' \in C_{\mathcal{P}}$, then we have $s.c.c' \in S_{\mathcal{P}}$ and $s.c \longrightarrow_{\mathcal{P}} s.c.c'$. Also, let us define a map $Stack : S_{\mathcal{P}} \to B^*$ such that if a node is of the form $s = s'.(v, w)$ for $s' \in C_{\mathcal{P}}^*$, then $Stack(s) = w$.

The *nested pushdown tree* generated by $\mathcal{P}$ is the structure $CTree(\mathcal{P}) = (T_{\mathcal{P}}, \hookrightarrow \subseteq S_{\mathcal{P}} \times S_{\mathcal{P}}, \lambda : S_{\mathcal{P}} \to \Sigma)$, where λ is such that for any node $s = s'.(u, w)$, we have $\lambda(s) = \kappa(u)$, and the jump-edge relation $\hookrightarrow$ is such that $s \hookrightarrow t$ iff $Stack(s) = Stack(t)$ and there no node t' such that $s \xrightarrow{+} t' \xrightarrow{+} t$ and $Stack(t') = Stack(s)$. It is easily verified that $CTree(\mathcal{P})$ is a nested tree. Intuitively, the call and return nodes model push and pop sites in the branching behavior of the pushdown system, and the jump-edges model *summary edges* relating pushes with matching pops.

While nested trees generated by programs are naturally unordered, we will also consider the *ordered, binary nested pushdown tree* $CTree_{ord}(\mathcal{P})$ of $\mathcal{P}$. This tree may be obtained by ordering the moves of $\mathcal{P}$, lifting this order to the (bounded-degree) configuration tree of $\mathcal{P}$, encoding this ordered tree by a binary tree, and adding jump-edges in the natural way. We skip the details.

3   Automata on Nested Trees

In this section, we study finite-state automata operating on nested trees. Recall that for tree automata, the state while reading a (non-root) tree node depends on its state at the node's parent. The state of a *nested tree automaton* (NTA) at a node in a nested tree depends on its states at the node's parent and the node's jump-predecessor (if it exists). We define these automata in nondeterministic and alternating flavors; the natural semantics of these are respectively over ordered and unordered nested trees.

Formally, a (top-down) *nondeterministic parity nested tree automaton* (NP-NTA) over Σ is a structure $\mathcal{A} = (Q, q_0, \Delta, \Omega)$ where Q is a finite set of *states*, $q_0 \in Q$ is the initial state, $\Delta \subseteq Q \times \Sigma \times (TT \times TT)$, where $TT = Q \cup (Q \times Q) \cup \{\bot\}$, is a *transition relation*, and $\Omega : Q \to \{0, 1, \ldots, n\}$, for some $n \in \mathbb{N}$, is the *parity accepting condition* that assigns a *priority* to each automaton state.

A run of $\mathcal{A}$ on an ordered, binary nested tree $\mathcal{T} = ((S, r, \to_1, \to_2), \hookrightarrow, \lambda)$ is a labeling $\rho : S \to Q$ of nodes of $\mathcal{T}$ by automaton states such that: (1) $\rho(r) = q_0$, and (2) if for some s we have $\rho(s) = q$ and $\lambda(s) = \sigma$, and s_1 and s_2 are the left and right children of s (set s_1 or s_2 to $\bot$ if the left or right child does not exist), then for some $(q, \sigma, (\tau_1, \tau_2)) \in \Delta$, we have: (a) if s_i, for $i \in \{1, 2\}$, is a call or local node, then $\tau_i = \rho(s_i)$, (b) if s_i is a return node, then $\tau_i = (\rho(t), \rho(s_i))$, where $t \hookrightarrow s_i$, and (c) if $s_i = \bot$, then $\tau_i = \bot$.

Let π_i denote the i-th vertex in a path π in T. A run ρ of A on T is *accepting* if for all infinite paths π in T, $\theta' = \max\{\theta : \Omega(\rho(\pi_i)) = \theta$ for infinitely many $i\}$ is even. An ordered, binary nested tree T is *accepted* if A has an accepting run on it. The *language* $\mathcal{L}(A)$ of A is the set of nested trees it accepts.

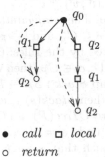

• *call* □ *local*
○ *return*

Fig. 2. A nested tree

Fig. 2 illustrates part of a run of an NP-NTA on a nested tree (assume that the label of every node is σ and that every node has a left child). Transitions include $(q_1, \sigma, ((q_0, q_2), \bot))$ and $(q_0, \sigma, (q_1, q_2))$.

Note that we can define an equivalent semantics of NP-NTAs by letting the automaton manipulate a stack rather than consult a node's jump-predecessor. In this case, A pushes the current state while taking a call edge, pops on a return edge, and leaves the stack unchanged on a local edge. As jump-edges are nested, the top of the automaton stack at a return node stores the state at the node's matching call.

As we shall see, NP-NTAs do not have robust closure properties, so that defining *alternating* nested tree automata will be worthwhile. It is more natural to interpret these automata on unordered nested trees. Also, their semantics are defined more easily if we let them manipulate stacks of states.

Formally, for a finite set Q, define the set $TT(Q)$ of *transition terms* whose members f are of the form $f := tt \mid ff \mid f \vee f \mid f \wedge f \mid \langle loc \rangle q \mid [loc]q \mid \langle call \rangle q \mid [call]q \mid \langle ret, q' \rangle q \mid [ret, q']q$, where $q, q' \in Q$. An *alternating parity nested tree automaton* (AP-NTA) over Σ is a structure $A = (Q, q_0, \Delta, \Omega, q_f)$, where Q is a finite set of states, $q_0 \in Q$ is the initial state, $\Delta : Q \times \Sigma \to TT(Q)$ is a transition function, and $\Omega : Q \to \{0, 1, \ldots, n\}$ is the parity accepting condition.

We define the semantics of an AP-NTA $A = (Q, q_0, \Delta, \Omega)$ via a parity game. The acceptance game $\mathcal{G}(A, T)$ of a Σ-labeled nested tree $T = (T, \hookrightarrow, \lambda)$ by A is played by two players A and E. The vertex set of the game graph is $V = T \times Q \times Q^* \times TT$, and the set of moves $\Rightarrow \subseteq V \times V$ is the least set such that:

- for all $v \in V$ of the form $(s, q, \alpha, f_1 \vee f_2)$ or $(s, q, \alpha, f_1 \wedge f_2)$ for some $v' \in V \cup \{\epsilon\}$, we have $v \Rightarrow (s, q, \alpha, f_1)$ and $v \Rightarrow (s, q, \alpha, f_2)$;
- for all $v \in V$ of the form $(s, q, \alpha, \langle loc \rangle q')$ or $(s, q, \alpha, [loc]q')$, and for all s' such that $s \xrightarrow{loc} s'$, we have $v \Rightarrow (s', q', \alpha, f)$, where $f = \Delta(q', \lambda(s'))$;
- for all $v \in V$ of the form $(s, q, \alpha, \langle call \rangle q')$ or $(s, q, \alpha, [call]q')$, and for all s' such that $s \xrightarrow{call} s'$, we have $v \Rightarrow (s', q', q.\alpha, f)$, where $f = \Delta(q', \lambda(s'))$;
- for all $v \in V$ of the form $(s, q, q''.\alpha, \langle ret, q'' \rangle q')$ or $(s, q, q''.\alpha, [ret, q'']q')$, and for all s' such that $s \xrightarrow{ret} s'$, we have $v \Rightarrow (s', q', \alpha, f)$, where $f = \Delta(q', \lambda(s'))$;

The vertex set V is partitioned into two sets V_E and V_A corresponding to the two players. The set V_A comprises vertices of the form (s, q, α, f), where s, q and α are arbitrary and f has the form tt, $[call]q$, $[loc]q$, $[ret, q']q$, or $(f_1 \wedge f_2)$. The remaining vertices constitute V_E. We also lift the priority map Ω to $\Omega_V : V \rightarrow \{0, 1, \ldots, n\}$ by defining $\Omega_V(s, q, \alpha, f) = \Omega(q)$ for all s, q, α, and f.

The two players A and E play on the graph starting from the initial position $v_{in} = (s_0, q_0, \epsilon, \Delta(q_0, \lambda(s_0)))$ by moving a token along edges of the game graph. Whenever the token is in a position v, the player who owns the vertex must move the token. Formally, a *play* of $\mathcal{G}$ is a non-empty, finite or infinite sequence $\alpha = v_1 v_2 \ldots$ that is a path in the game graph, where $v_1 = v_{in}$. A finite play is winning for player A if the last position is a player E vertex from which there is no move; analogously, we define winning finite plays for player E. An infinite play α is winning for player E if $\theta' = \max\{\theta : \Omega_V(v_i) = \theta \text{ for infinitely many } i\}$ is even; otherwise A wins the play. A *strategy* for player E (or A) is a subset of edges $Str \subseteq \Rightarrow$ such that all these edges originate in a vertex in V_E (or V_A)². A play is according to a strategy Str if all edges in the play are in Str. A strategy is winning if all maximal plays according to the strategy are winning.

An AP-NTA $\mathcal{A}$ *accepts* a nested tree $\mathcal{T}$ if E has a winning strategy in $G(\mathcal{A}, \mathcal{T})$. The *language* $\mathcal{L}(\mathcal{A})$ of $\mathcal{A}$ is the set of nested trees accepted by $\mathcal{A}$.

We also consider automata that accept by the weaker *final-state condition*. For nondeterministic versions of such automata, a nested tree is accepted if a special *final state* q_f is seen along every path in some run on it. In alternating versions, all infinite plays are won by A, and if a play reaches a game vertex (s, q_f, α, f) for some s, α, and f, then the game terminates and E is the winner.

Closure Properties. Easy constructions show that AP-NTAs are closed under union and intersection and that NP-NTAs are closed under union. A product construction suffices to show that NP-NTAs are also closed under intersection. Also, AP-NTAs are closed under complement since one can take the *dual* of the transition functions and add 1 to each priority, making the odd priorities even and vice versa. This automaton will accept the complement since parity games are *determined* (if a nested tree is not accepted by an AP-NTA, then player A has a winning strategy in the acceptance game that translates to a winning strategy for E in the dual game). Hence:

Theorem 1. *AP-NTAs are closed under union, intersection, and complement. NP-NTAs are closed under union and intersection.*

Observe that by our definition, languages accepted by AP-NTAs are closed under bisimulation, while those accepted by NP-NTAs are not in general. To compare the expressiveness of an AP-NTA and an NP-NTA meaningfully, we need to consider the language obtained by starting with the language L of the NP-NTA, stripping the order between tree edges off nested trees in L, and closing it under

---

² Strategies are often defined in a more general way that refer to the history of the play. This definition suffices as parity games always admit zero-memory strategies [10].

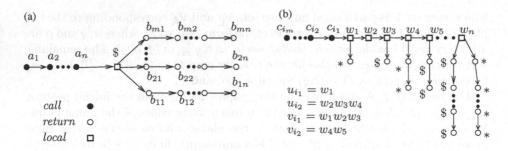

Fig. 3. (a) Expressiveness of AP-NTAs and NP-NTAs (b) Gadget for undecidability

bisimulation.[3] Formally, for a language L of ordered nested trees, we define $Unord(L)$ as the bisimulation closure of the set of nested trees $((S, r, \rightarrow), \hookrightarrow, \lambda)$ such that $\rightarrow = \rightarrow_1 \cup \rightarrow_2$ for some $((S, r, \rightarrow_1, \rightarrow_2), \hookrightarrow, \lambda) \in L$.

Now consider ordered nested trees of the form in Fig. 3-a, where $\Sigma = \{0, 1, \$\}$, and $a_i, b_{ij} \in \Sigma$ for all i, j (while the structure in the figure is not binary, it can be encoded as such; also, the jump-edges, omitted to keep the figure clean, can be reconstructed). Let L_{gap} be the language of such structures where for all $i \leq n$, there is some $k \leq m$ such that $a_{n-i+1} = b_{ki}$. First, we note that L_{gap} cannot be recognized by an NP-NTA $\mathcal{A}_N$ with N states. To see why, take a structure as above where $n = m > N$, and for each $1 \leq i \leq n$, there is a *distinct* branch k such that $a_{n-i+1} = b_{ki}$. In any run, $\mathcal{A}_N$ must enter two branches in the same state; also, the sequence of states at calls unmatched till these points are the same. We can replace one of these branches with the other to get an accepting run on a structure not in L_{gap}. Note that $Unord(L_{gap})$ is recognized by AP-NTA. Hence:

Theorem 2. *There is a language L of ordered, binary nested trees s.t. (1) there is no NP-NTA accepting L, and (2) there is an AP-NTA accepting $Unord(L)$.*

We note that the complement of the language L_{gap} is accepted by an NP-NTA $\mathcal{A}'_N$, which guesses the i such that a_i cannot be matched along any of the branches, and sends a state to each branch to check this is true. Hence:

Theorem 3. *NP-NTAs are not closed under complementation.*

The projection over Σ_1 of a language L of (ordered, unordered) nested trees over $\Sigma_1 \times \Sigma_2$ is the language obtained by replacing every label (a, b) in every nested tree $\mathcal{T} \in L$ by a. For NP-NTAs, closure under projection is easy; an NP-NTA can guess the second component of each label and mimic the moves. However, we can show that AP-NTAs are not closed under projection:

Theorem 4. *NP-NTAs are closed under projection, but AP-NTAs are not.*

---

[3] Alternatively, we could define AP-NTAs on ordered nested trees. Under this definition as well, AP-NTAs are strictly more powerful than NP-NTAs.

Decision Problems. The *model-checking* problem for AP-NTAs on pushdown systems is the problem of deciding, given an AP-NTA $\mathcal{A}$ and a pushdown system $\mathcal{P}$, whether $CTree(\mathcal{P}) \in \mathcal{L}(\mathcal{A})$. An EXPTIME-hardness result for this problem follows from the known hardness of the model-checking problem for alternating tree automata on pushdown systems [23].

We get an EXPTIME procedure for this problem via a reduction to a *pushdown parity game*. A two-player pushdown parity game is a parity game played on the configuration graph of a pushdown system. It is known that pushdown parity games are solvable in EXPTIME [23]. Now, given an AP-NTA $\mathcal{A}$ and $\mathcal{P}$, $CTree(\mathcal{P}) \in \mathcal{L}(\mathcal{A})$ iff player E wins the acceptance game of $\mathcal{A}$. Now recall that call-edges (or return-edges) in $CTree(\mathcal{P})$ encode push-moves (pops) of $\mathcal{P}$—however, these edges are also where the stack of states in the semantics of $\mathcal{A}$ is pushed (popped). Thus, the stack of $\mathcal{P}$ is "synchronized" with the implicit stack of $\mathcal{A}$, so that the graph of the acceptance game of $CTree(\mathcal{P})$ by $\mathcal{A}$ happens to be the configuration graph of a pushdown system that is roughly the "synchronized product" of $\mathcal{P}$ and $\mathcal{A}$. Using this, we get:

Theorem 5. *The model-checking problem for AP-NTAs on pushdown systems is EXPTIME-complete.*

While model-checking for alternating NTAs is decidable, emptiness is not[4]. This is proved by a reduction from the Post's Correspondence Problem (PCP) [12]. Consider a tuple $((u_1, \ldots, u_k), (v_1, \ldots, v_k))$, where the u_i's and v_i's are finite words over an alphabet A; the PCP is to determine if there is a sequence $i_1, \ldots, i_m$, where $i_j \leq k$, such that $u_{i_1} u_{i_2} \ldots u_{i_m} = v_{i_1} v_{i_2} \ldots v_{i_m} = w$. Now consider nested trees of the form in Fig. 3-b (again, jump-edges are omitted) such that the initial call-chain is of length m and is labeled by symbols from the alphabet $\{1, \ldots, k\}$, and the symbols w_i on the "stem" of local nodes succeeding this chain form the string w. Now suppose the sequence of input symbols on the call chain is $c_{i_m} \ldots c_{i_1}$. There are two kinds of return chains hanging from the stem—the ones marked with the symbol $*$ (similarly $\$$) are exactly at the points where w may be possibly factored into $u_{i_1}, u_{i_2}, \ldots, u_{i_m}$ (similarly $v_{i_1}, \ldots, v_{i_m}$). Also, the i-th return chain (counting from left) of either type is of length i. Then such a nested tree is a witness for an instance of PCP being positive. We can, however, show that there is an alternating NTA accepting by final state that accepts the set of nested trees bisimilar to such witnesses. In fact, we can show that there is a nondeterministic final-state NTA that accepts any nested tree *not* of the above form (under some ordering of edges). Hence:

Theorem 6. *Universality for nondeterministic NTAs and emptiness for alternating NTAs are undecidable problems, even for acceptance by final state.*

However, we can prove the emptiness problem of NP-NTAs to be solvable in EXPTIME by reducing it to that for pushdown tree automata [15].

---

[4] This result was obtained independently by Löding [16].

4   A Fixpoint Calculus for Nested Trees

Now we study a fixpoint calculus for nested trees, presented in our previous work [1] under the name VP-μ and a different but equivalent semantics as a specification language for procedural programs. This logic, which we call NT-μ, turns out to have the same expressive power as AP-NTAs.

Formally, let AP be a finite set of atomic propositions, Var be a finite set of *variables*, and $R_1, R_2, \ldots$ be a countable, ordered set of *markers*. For $p \in AP$, $X \in Var$, and $m \geq 0$, formulas φ of NT-μ are defined by:

$$\varphi, \psi_i := p \mid \neg p \mid X \mid \langle ret \rangle(R_i) \mid [ret](R_i) \mid \varphi \vee \varphi \mid \varphi \wedge \varphi \mid \mu X.\varphi \mid \nu X.\varphi \mid$$
$$\langle call \rangle(\varphi)\{\psi_1, \psi_2, \ldots, \psi_m\} \mid [call](\varphi)\{\psi_1, \psi_2, \ldots, \psi_m\} \mid \langle loc \rangle \varphi \mid [loc] \varphi.$$

The *arity* of a formula φ is the maximum m such that φ has a subformula $\langle call \rangle \varphi' \{\psi_1, \ldots, \psi_m\}$ or $[call]\varphi'\{\psi_1, \ldots, \psi_m\}$. Also, we define the constants *tt* and *ff* in the standard way.

Formulas are evaluated at structures known as *summaries*. Let $\mathcal{T} = (T, \hookrightarrow, \lambda)$ be an unordered nested tree labeled by $\Sigma = 2^{AP}$. A node t of $\mathcal{T}$ is said to be a *matching exit* of a node s if there is an s' such that $s' \xrightarrow{+} s$ and $s' \hookrightarrow t$, and there are no s'', t'' such that $s' \xrightarrow{+} s'' \xrightarrow{+} s \xrightarrow{+} t''$, and $s'' \hookrightarrow t''$. Intuitively, a matching exit of s is the first "unmatched" return along some path from s. The set of matching exits of s is denoted by $ME(s)$. For a non-negative integer k, a *summary* **s** in $\mathcal{T}$ is a tuple $\langle s, U_1, U_2, \ldots, U_k \rangle$, where $s \in T$, $k \geq 0$, and $U_1, U_2, \ldots, U_k \subseteq ME(s)$. The set of summaries in a structured tree $\mathcal{T}$ is denoted by $Summ^{\mathcal{S}}$.

Let the free variables in a formula φ be denoted by $Free(\varphi)$. Then φ is interpreted in an *environment* $\mathcal{E} : Free(\varphi) \to 2^{Summ^{\mathcal{S}}}$ that maps variables to sets of summaries. Some of the clauses that define the truth of a formula φ at a summary $\mathbf{s} = \langle s, U_1, \ldots, U_k \rangle$ are:

- $\mathbf{s}, \mathcal{E} \models p$ iff $p \in \lambda(s)$; $\mathbf{s}, \mathcal{E} \models X$ iff $\mathbf{s} \in \mathcal{E}(X)$
- $\mathbf{s}, \mathcal{E} \models \varphi_1 \vee \varphi_2$ iff $\mathbf{s}, \mathcal{E} \models \varphi_1$ or $\mathbf{s}, \mathcal{E} \models \varphi_2$
- $\mathbf{s}, \mathcal{E} \models \langle call \rangle(\varphi')\{\psi_1, \psi_2, \ldots, \psi_m\}$ iff there is a $t \in S$ such that $s \xrightarrow{call} t$, and also a summary $\mathbf{t} = \langle t, V_1, V_2, \ldots, V_m \rangle$ satisfying (1) $\mathbf{t}, \mathcal{E} \models \varphi'$, and (2) for all i and all $s' \in V_i$, $\langle s', U_1 \cap ME(s'), U_2 \cap ME(s'), \ldots, U_k \cap ME(s') \rangle, \mathcal{E} \models \psi_i$.
- $\mathbf{s}, \mathcal{E} \models \langle loc \rangle \varphi'$, iff there is a $t \in S$ such that $s \xrightarrow{loc} t$, and also a summary $\mathbf{t} = \langle t, V_1, V_2, \ldots, V_k \rangle$ such that (1) $V_i = ME(t) \cap U_i$, and (2) $\mathbf{t}, \mathcal{E} \models \varphi'$
- $\mathbf{s}, \mathcal{E} \models \langle ret \rangle(R_i)$ iff there is a $t \in S$ such that $s \xrightarrow{ret} t$ and $t \in U_i$
- $\mathbf{s}, \mathcal{E} \models \mu X.\varphi'$, iff $\mathbf{s} \in \mathbf{S}$ for all $\mathbf{S} \subseteq Summ^{\mathcal{S}}$ such that: for all $\mathbf{t}$ such that $\mathbf{t}, \mathcal{E}[X \mapsto \mathbf{S}] \models \varphi', \mathbf{t} \in \mathbf{S}$

Here $\mathcal{E}[X \mapsto \mathbf{S}]$ is the environment $\mathcal{E}'$ such that (1) $\mathcal{E}'(X) = \mathbf{S}$, and (2) $\mathcal{E}'(Y) = \mathcal{E}(Y)$ for all variables $Y \neq X$.

Consider the unique empty environment $\mathcal{E}_\perp : \emptyset \to Summ^{\mathcal{S}}$. A nested tree $\mathcal{T}$ with initial node s_0 *satisfies* a formula φ iff $\langle s_0, \emptyset, \ldots, \emptyset \rangle, \mathcal{E} \models \varphi$. The language of φ, denoted by $\mathcal{L}(\varphi)$, is the set of nested trees satisfying φ.

Now consider the problem of model-checking NT-μ over nested pushdown trees, i.e. determining, given a pushdown system $\mathcal{P}$ and an NT-μ formula φ, whether $CTree(\mathcal{P})$ satisfies φ. We previously gave an EXPTIME procedure for this problem [1]. Interestingly, this procedure involves a fixpoint computation over equivalence classes of summaries, mirroring symbolic model-checking algorithms for the μ-calculus, and has no direct connection to pushdown games. We also established that the satisfiability problem for NT-μ is undecidable.

Relation Between NT-μ and NTAs. We now establish our main theorems, which show that AP-NTAs are exactly as expressive as NT-μ.

Theorem 7. *Given any closed NT-μ formula φ, one can construct an AP-NTA $\mathcal{A}_\varphi$ such that for any nested tree T, $T \in \mathcal{L}(\varphi)$ iff $T \in \mathcal{L}(\mathcal{A}_\varphi)$. The size of $\mathcal{A}_\varphi$ is polynomial in the size of φ.*

Proof. (Sketch) The AP-NTA $\mathcal{A}_\varphi$ is over an input alphabet 2^{AP}. For every subformula ψ of φ, $\mathcal{A}_\varphi$ has a state q_ψ. The initial state is q_φ.

For any variable X in φ, let $\Psi(X)$ be the subformula of form $\mu X.\varphi'$ or $\nu X.\varphi'$ that binds X (we assume that each variable in φ is bound at most once). For instance, if $\varphi = \langle call \rangle(\mu X.(p \vee X))\{q\}$, then $\Psi(X) = \mu X.(p \vee X)$. For each bound variable X in φ, the state q_X is *identified* with the state $q_{\Psi(X)}$.

Let $p \in AP$, and $\sigma \in 2^{AP}$. The transition relation Δ of $\mathcal{A}_\varphi$ is defined inductively over the structure of φ:

$\Delta(q_p, \sigma) = tt$ if $p \in \sigma$, else ff

$\Delta(q_{\varphi_1 \wedge \varphi_2}, \sigma) = \Delta(q_{\varphi_1}, \upsilon) \wedge \Delta(q_{\varphi_2}, \sigma)$

$\Delta(q_{\varphi_1 \vee \varphi_2}, \sigma) = \Delta(q_{\varphi_1}, \sigma) \vee \Delta(q_{\varphi_2}, \sigma)$

$\Delta(q_{\mu X.\varphi'}, \sigma) = \Delta(q_{\varphi'}, \sigma)$

$\Delta(q_{\nu X.\varphi'}, \sigma) = \Delta(q_{\varphi'}, \sigma)$

$\Delta(q_{\langle call \rangle(\varphi')\{\psi_1,...,\psi_k\}}, \upsilon) = \langle call \rangle q_{\varphi'}$

$\Delta(q_{[call](\varphi')\{\psi_1,...,\psi_k\}}, \sigma) = [call] q_{\varphi'}$

$\Delta(q_{\langle loc \rangle \varphi'}, \sigma) = \langle loc \rangle q_{\varphi'}$

$\Delta(q_{[loc]\varphi'}, \sigma) = [loc] q_{\varphi'}$

$\Delta(q_{\langle ret \rangle R_i}, \sigma) = \bigvee_{\phi', \psi_{1 \leq j \leq k}}(\langle ret, q_{\langle call \rangle(\phi')\{\psi_1,...,\psi_k\}} \rangle q_{\psi_i} \vee \langle ret, q_{[call](\phi')\{\psi_1,...,\psi_k\}} \rangle q_{\psi_i})$

$\Delta(q_{[ret]R_i}, \sigma) = \bigvee_{\phi', \psi_{1 \leq j \leq k}}([ret, q_{\langle call \rangle \phi'\{\psi_1,...,\psi_k\}}] q_{\psi_i} \vee [ret, q_{[call]\phi'\{\psi_1,...,\psi_k\}}] q_{\psi_i})$

The proof is similar in spirit to a known translation from the μ-calculus to alternating tree automata [9]. The main difference, of course, is in the *call* and *ret* clauses. At a call in a nested tree, the state of $\mathcal{A}_\varphi$ contains information about the return conditions that φ asserts. When a matching return (jump-successor) is reached, $\mathcal{A}_\varphi$ consults this state and checks that the return assertions hold.

The priority of states of the form $q_{\mu X.\varphi}$ and $q_{\nu X.\varphi}$ are respectively odd and even, and roughly equal to the alternation depth of φ. The priority for all other states is 0. The correctness proof for parity acceptance is along the lines of [9].

Theorem 8. *Given any AP-NTA $\mathcal{A}$, one can construct an NT-μ formula $\varphi_\mathcal{A}$ such that for any nested tree T, $T \in \mathcal{L}(\varphi_\mathcal{A})$ iff $T \in \mathcal{L}(\mathcal{A})$. The size of $\varphi_\mathcal{A}$ is polynomial in the size of φ.*

Proof. (Sketch) We skip the full proof and establish the above for alternating nested tree automata $\mathcal{A}$ accepting by a final state q_f. We write the formula $\varphi_{\mathcal{A}}$ using a set of equations rather than in the standard form. Translation from this equational form to the standard form is as for the modal μ-calculus [10].

Let $Q = \{q_1, \ldots, q_n\}$ and TT respectively be the sets of states and transition conditions of $\mathcal{A}$. For each $q \in Q$, we have a marker R_q; for each pair of states $q, q' \in Q$, we have a variable $X_{q,q'}$. Intuitively, a summary $\langle s, U_{q_1}, \ldots, U_{q_n} \rangle$ is collected in $X_{q,q'}$ iff $\mathcal{A}$ has a way to start at node s at state q, and end up at a return $s' \in U_{q_j}$ in state q_j, having checked that q' was the state of the automaton in the current play at the jump-predecessor of s'. Now for each pair of states $q, q' \in Q$, we define a map $\mathcal{F}_{q,q'} : TT \to \Phi$, where Φ is the set of NT-μ formulas:

$$\mathcal{F}_{q,q'}(tt) = tt \qquad\qquad \mathcal{F}_{q,q'}(f\!f) = f\!f$$
$$\mathcal{F}_{q,q'}(f_1 \wedge f_2) = \mathcal{F}_{q,q'}(f_1) \wedge \mathcal{F}_{q,q'}(f_2)$$
$$\mathcal{F}_{q,q'}(f_1 \vee f_2) = \mathcal{F}_{q,q'}(f_1) \vee \mathcal{F}_{q,q'}(f_2)$$
$$\mathcal{F}_{q,q'}(\langle call \rangle q'') = \langle call \rangle (X_{q'',q})\{X_{q_1,q'}, \ldots, X_{q_n,q'}\}$$
$$\mathcal{F}_{q,q'}([call]q'') = [call](X_{q'',q})\{X_{q_1,q'}, \ldots, X_{q_n,q'}\}$$
$$\mathcal{F}_{q,q'}(\langle loc \rangle q'') = \langle loc \rangle X_{q'',q'} \qquad\qquad \mathcal{F}_{q,q'}([loc]q'') = [loc]X_{q'',q'}$$
$$\mathcal{F}_{q,q'}(\langle ret, q \rangle q'') = \langle ret \rangle (R_{q''}) \qquad\qquad \mathcal{F}_{q,q'}([ret, q]q'') = [ret]R_{q''}$$

Then the formula $\varphi_{\mathcal{A}}$ is the formula corresponding to X_{q_0,γ_0} when taking the least fixpoint of the following equations:

$$X_{q,q'} = \begin{cases} tt & \text{if } q = q_f \\ \bigvee_{\sigma \subseteq AP}((\wedge_{p \in \sigma} p) \wedge (\wedge_{p \notin \sigma} \neg p) \wedge \mathcal{F}_{q',q}(\Delta(q,\sigma) \vee \Delta_r(q,\sigma))) & \text{otherwise.} \end{cases}$$

5   Monadic Second-Order Logic on Nested Trees

We now study *monadic second-order (MSO) logic* interpreted on ordered nested trees. Formulas in MSO-logic are built over a set of first-order variables $(x, y \ldots)$ and a set of second-order variables $(X, Y, \ldots)$, ranging over nodes and sets of nodes in a nested tree $\mathcal{T}$. For each $\sigma \in \Sigma$, the signature of MSO-logic has a unary predicate Q_σ, where $Q_\sigma(s)$ is true at a node s iff s is labeled by σ; we also have a binary equality predicate $x = y$. There are also left and right edge predicates $x \to_1 y$ and $x \to_2 y$, and a jump-edge predicate $x \hookrightarrow y$.

The syntax of MSO-logic is: $\varphi := Q_\sigma(x) \mid \neg\varphi \mid \varphi \vee \varphi \mid x = y \mid x \to_1 y \mid x \to_1 y \mid x \hookrightarrow y \mid \exists x.\varphi \mid \exists X.\varphi \mid X(x)$. The semantics is the natural one on ordered nested trees. The language $\mathcal{L}(\varphi)$ of φ is the set of nested trees that satisfy it; φ is said to be bisimulation-closed if $\mathcal{L}(\varphi)$ is bisimulation-closed. The model-checking problem is: given φ and a pushdown system $\mathcal{P}$, does $CTree_{ord}(\mathcal{P})$ satisfy φ?

While MSO-logic over trees is decidable, MSO-logic over nested tree structures is not. To see why, note that the gadget $\mathcal{S}$ used to prove Theorem 6 (Fig. 3-b) may be embedded in the ordered nested pushdown tree $\mathcal{T}$ of a simple pushdown system. Using existential set quantification, MSO-logic can select $\mathcal{S}$ from $\mathcal{T}$, so that there is a φ that holds on $\mathcal{T}$ iff gadgets as above exist. Hence:

Theorem 9. *The model-checking problem for (even the bisimulation-closed fragment of) MSO-logic on nested pushdown trees is undecidable.*

The satisfiability problem for MSO on nested trees is also undecidable. Further:

Theorem 10. *There is a bisimulation-closed MSO-logic formula φ such that there is no AP-NTA $\mathcal{A}$ satisfying $\mathcal{L}(\mathcal{A}) = Unord(\mathcal{L}(\varphi))$.*

It is natural to ask if MSO-logic is more expressive than nested tree automata. It indeed turns out that runs of any NP-NTA $\mathcal{A}$ can be encoded by an MSO-logic formula $\varphi_{\mathcal{A}}$. The latter uses existential quantification over sets to "guess" a global labeling of the nodes of a nested tree by states of $\mathcal{A}$, and uses the predicates $\longrightarrow$ and $\hookrightarrow$ to check the consistency of this guess. We can show that:

Theorem 11. *For every NP-NTA $\mathcal{A}$, there is an MSO-logic formula $\varphi_{\mathcal{A}}$ such that $\mathcal{L}(\mathcal{A}) = \mathcal{L}(\varphi)$.*

However, a "jump-edge" predicate seems too weak to capture the interplay of recursion and Boolean closure in AP-NTAs; higher-order quantification seems necessary. We conjecture that there is a language L recognized by an AP-NTA such that there is no MSO formula φ that recognizes L_{ord}, where $Unord(L_{ord}) = L$, making MSO neither less nor more expressive than AP-NTAs.

6   Conclusions

This paper introduces *nested trees*, a class of graphs that naturally abstract branching behaviors of structured programs. Different ways to define languages over nested trees are explored. Of these, alternating automata and the logic NT-μ are found to have attractive closure and decidability properties. The central result, the equivalence of NT-μ and AP-NTAs, is the analog of the the well-known expressive equivalence between the μ-calculus and alternating parity tree automata. On the other hand, nondeterministic automata and MSO-logic turn out to be less robust here than in the classical setting.

It is interesting to contrast the benefits of modeling programs by nested structures rather than word or tree structures for linear-time and branching-time model-checking. In the linear-time case, model checking corresponds to language inclusion, and the frontier of checkable specifications expands from regular word languages to nested word languages [3,4]. In the branching-time case, model checking corresponds to membership, and the answer to this question changes from regular tree languages to languages of nested trees. This is because in the world of nested tree languages, alternation adds to the power of acceptors, and interacts with the ability to "jump" to create a new decidability frontier.

Open theoretical questions include establishing that MSO-logic on nested trees cannot capture the third-order fixpoints of NT-μ. Also, we believe that nested trees are conceptually fundamental and merit further study. Applications beyond program verification are possible: nested word structures are already known to have connections with XML query languages, since XML documents have a natural matching tag structure that can be modeled by jump-edges.

References

1. R. Alur, S. Chaudhuri, and P. Madhusudan. A fixpoint calculus for local and global program flows. In *Proc. of POPL '06*, pp. 153–165, 2006.
2. R. Alur, S. Chaudhuri, and P. Madhusudan. Languages of nested trees. University of Pennsylvania Technical Report MS-CIS-06-10, 2006.
3. R. Alur and P. Madhusudan. Visibly pushdown languages. In *Proc. of STOC '04*, pp. 202–211, 2004.
4. R. Alur and P. Madhusudan. Adding nesting structure to words. In *Proc. of DLT '06*, LNCS 4036, pp. 1–13, 2006.
5. T. Ball and S. Rajamani. The SLAM project: debugging system software via static analysis. In *Proc. of POPL '02*, pp. 1–3, 2002.
6. O. Burkart and B. Steffen. Model checking the full modal mu-calculus for infinite sequential processes. *Theoretical Computer Science*, 221, pp.251–270, 1999.
7. D. Caucal. On infinite transition graphs having a decidable monadic theory. *Theor. Comput. Sci.*, 290(1), pp.79–115, 2003.
8. H. Comon, M. Dauchet, R. Gilleron, D. Lugiez, S. Tison, and M. Tommasi. Tree automata techniques and applications. Draft, 2003.
9. E.A. Emerson and C.S. Jutla. Tree automata, mu-calculus, and determinacy. In *Proc. of FOCS '91*, pp. 368–377, 1991.
10. E. Grädel, W. Thomas, and T. Wilke, editors. *Automata, Logics, and Infinite Games: A Guide to Current Research*, LNCS 2500, 2002.
11. T.A. Henzinger, R. Jhala, R. Majumdar, G.C. Necula, G. Sutre, and W. Weimer. Temporal-safety proofs for systems code. *CAV '02*, LNCS 2404, pp. 526–538, 2002.
12. J.E. Hopcroft and J.D.Ullman. Introduction to automata theory, languages, and computation. Addison-Wesley, 1979.
13. D. Janin and I. Walukiewicz. On the expressive completeness of the propositional mu-calculus with respect to monadic second order logic. In *Proc. of CONCUR '96*, LNCS 1119, pp. 263–277, 1996.
14. D. Kozen. Results on the propositional mu-calculus. *Theoretical Computer Science*, 27:333–354, 1983.
15. O. Kupferman, N. Piterman, and M.Y. Vardi. Pushdown specifications. In *Proc. of LPAR '02*, LNCS 2514, pages 262–277. Springer, 2002.
16. C. Löding. Private communication.
17. C. Löding, P. Madhusudan, and O. Serre. Visibly pushdown games. In *Proc. of FSTTCS '04*, LNCS 3328, pp. 408–420, 2004.
18. K.L. McMillan. *Symbolic model checking: an approach to the state explosion problem*. Kluwer Academic Publishers, 1993.
19. D. E. Muller and P. E. Schupp. Alternating automata on infinite trees. *Theor. Comput. Sci.*, 54(2-3):267–276, 1987.
20. D.E. Muller and P.E. Schupp. The theory of ends, pushdown automata, and second-order logic. *Theoretical Computer Science*, 37:51–75, 1985.
21. M.O. Rabin. Decidability of second order theories and automata on infinite trees. *Transactions of the AMS*, 141:1–35, 1969.
22. T. Reps, S. Horwitz, and S. Sagiv. Precise interprocedural dataflow analysis via graph reachability. In *Proc. of POPL '95*, pp. 49–61, 1995.
23. I. Walukiewicz. Pushdown processes: Games and model-checking. *Information and Computation*, 164(2):234–263, 2001.
24. I. Walukiewicz. Monadic second-order logic on tree-like structures. *Theor. Comput. Sci.*, 275(1-2):311–346, 2002.

Improving Pushdown System Model Checking[*]

Akash Lal[1] and Thomas Reps[1,2]

[1] University of Wisconsin
[2] GrammaTech, Inc.
{akash, reps}@cs.wisc.edu

Abstract. In this paper, we reduce pushdown system (PDS) model checking to a graph-theoretic problem, and apply a fast graph algorithm to improve the running time for model checking. Several other PDS questions and techniques can be carried out in the new setting, including witness tracing and incremental analysis, each of which benefits from the fast graph-based algorithm.

1 Introduction

Pushdown systems (PDSs) have served as an important formalism for program analysis and verification because of their ability to concisely capture interprocedural control flow in a program. Various tools [6,18,12,10,4] use pushdown systems as an abstract model of a program and use reachability analysis on these models to verify program properties. Using PDSs provides an infinite-state abstraction for the control state of the program. Some of these tools [6,18,4], however, can only verify properties that have a finite-state data abstraction. Other tools [10,12] are based on the more generalized setting of weighted pushdown systems (WPDSs) [16] and are capable of verifying infinite-state data abstractions as well.

At the heart of all these tools is a PDS reachability-analysis algorithm that uses a chaotic-iteration strategy to explore all reachable states [2,7,17]. Even though there has been work to address the worst-case running time of this algorithm [5], to our knowledge, no one has addressed the issue of giving direction to the chaotic-iteration scheme to improve the running time of the algorithm in practice. In this paper, we try to improve the worst-case running time, as well as the running-time observed in practice. To provide a common setting to discuss most PDS model checkers, we use WPDSs to describe our improvements to PDS reachability.

An interprocedural control flow graph (ICFG) is a set of graphs, one per procedure, connected via special call and return edges [14]. A WPDS with a given initial query can also be decomposed into a set of graphs whose structure is similar. (When the underlying PDS is obtained by the standard encoding of an ICFG as a PDS for use in program analysis, these decompositions coincide.) Next, we use a fast graph algorithm, namely the Tarjan path-expression algorithm [19] to represent each graph as a regular expression. WPDS reachability can then be reduced to solving a set of regular equations. When the underlying PDS is obtained from a structured (reducible) control flow

[*] Supported by ONR (N00014-01-1-{0708,0796}) and NSF (CCR-9986308 and CCF-0524051).

T. Ball and R.B. Jones (Eds.): CAV 2006, LNCS 4144, pp. 343–357, 2006.

graph, the regular expressions can be found and solved very efficiently. Even when the control flow is not structured, the regular expressions provide a fast iteration strategy that improves over the standard chaotic-iteration strategy.

Our work is inspired by previous work on dataflow analysis of single-procedure programs [20]. There it was shown that a certain class of dataflow analysis problems can take advantage of the fact that a (single-procedure) CFG can be represented using a regular expression. We generalize this observation to multiple-procedure programs, as well as to WPDSs. The contributions of this paper can be summarized as follows:

- We present a new reachability algorithm for WPDSs that improves on previously known algorithms for PDS reachability. The algorithm is asymptotically faster when the PDS is *regular* (decomposes into a single graph), and offers substantial improvement in the general case as well.
- The algorithm is completely demand-driven, and computes only that information needed for answering a particular user query. It has an implicit slicing stage where it disregards parts of the program not needed for answering the user query.
- We show that several other PDS analysis questions and techniques, including witness tracing and incremental analysis, carry over to the new approach.

The rest of the paper is organized as follows: §2 provides background on PDSs and WPDSs. §3 presents the previously known algorithm and our new algorithm for solving reachability queries on WPDSs. In §4, we describe algorithms for witness tracing and incremental analysis. §5 presents experimental results. §6 describes related work.

2   PDS Model Checking

Definition 1. *A **pushdown system** is a triple* $\mathcal{P} = (P, \Gamma, \Delta)$ *where* P *is the set of states or control locations,* Γ *is the set of stack symbols, and* $\Delta \subseteq P \times \Gamma \times P \times \Gamma^*$ *is the set of pushdown rules. A **configuration** of* $\mathcal{P}$ *is a pair* $\langle p, u \rangle$ *where* $p \in P$ *and* $u \in \Gamma^*$. *A rule* $r \in \Delta$ *is written as* $\langle p, \gamma \rangle \hookrightarrow \langle p', u \rangle$ *where* $p, p' \in P$, $\gamma \in \Gamma$ *and* $u \in \Gamma^*$. *These rules define a transition relation* $\Rightarrow$ *on configurations of* $\mathcal{P}$ *as follows: If* $r = \langle p, \gamma \rangle \hookrightarrow \langle p', u \rangle$ *then* $\langle p, \gamma u' \rangle \Rightarrow \langle p', u u' \rangle$ *for all* $u' \in \Gamma^*$. *The reflexive transitive closure of* $\Rightarrow$ *is denoted by* $\Rightarrow^*$.

Without loss of generality, we restrict PDS rules to have at most two stack symbols on the right-hand side. The standard approach for modeling program control flow is as follows: Let $(\mathcal{N}, \mathcal{E})$ be an ICFG where each *call* node is split into two nodes: one has an interprocedural edge going to the entry node of the procedure being called; the second has an incoming edge from the exit node of the procedure. $\mathcal{N}$ is the set of nodes in this graph and $\mathcal{E}$ is the set of control-flow edges. Fig. 1(a) shows an example of an ICFG, Fig. 1(b) shows the pushdown system that models it. The PDS has a single state p, one stack symbol for each node in $\mathcal{N}$, and one rule for each edge in $\mathcal{E}$. We use rules with one stack symbol on the right-hand side to model intraprocedural edges, rules with two stack symbols on the right-hand side (*push* rules) for *call* edges, and rules with no stack symbols on the right-hand side (*pop* rules) for *return* edges. It is easy to see that a valid path in the program corresponds to a path in the pushdown system's transition system,

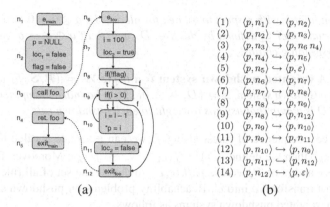

(a)   (b)

Fig. 1. (a) An ICFG. The e and *exit* nodes represent entry and exit points of procedures, respectively. flag is a global variable, loc_1 and loc_2 are local variables of main and foo, respectively. Dashed edges represent interprocedural control flow. (b) A pushdown system that models the control flow of the graph shown in (a).

and vice versa. Thus, PDSs can encode ordinary control flow graphs, but they also provide a convenient mechanism for modeling certain kinds of non-local control flow, such as setjmp/longjmp in C. At a setjmp, we push a special symbol on the stack, and at a longjmp with the same environment variable (identified using some preprocessing) we pop the stack until that symbol is reached. The longjmp value can be passed using the state of the PDS.

Because the number of configurations of a pushdown system is unbounded, it is useful to use finite automata to describe certain infinite sets of configurations.

Definition 2. *If* $\mathcal{P} = (P, \Gamma, \Delta)$ *is a pushdown system, then a* $\mathcal{P}$**-automaton** *is a finite automaton* $(Q, \Gamma, \rightarrow, P, F)$ *where* $Q \supseteq P$ *is a finite set of states,* $\rightarrow \subseteq Q \times \Gamma \times Q$ *is the transition relation,* P *is the set of initial states, and* F *is the set of final states of the automaton. We say that a configuration* $\langle p, u \rangle$ *is accepted by a* $\mathcal{P}$*-automaton if the automaton can accept* u *when it is started in the state* p *(written as* $p \xrightarrow{u}{}^* q$, *where* $q \in F$). *A set of configurations is called* **regular** *if some* $\mathcal{P}$*-automaton accepts it.*

A weighted pushdown system is obtained by supplementing a pushdown system with a weight domain that is a bounded idempotent semiring [16,3]. Such semirings are powerful enough to encode finite-state data abstractions such as the one required for Boolean program verification, as well as infinite-state data abstractions, such as copy-constant propagation and affine-relation analysis [12].

Definition 3. *A* **bounded idempotent semiring** *is a quintuple* $(D, \oplus, \otimes, \overline{0}, \overline{1})$, *where* D *is a set whose elements are called* **weights**, $\overline{0}$ *and* $\overline{1}$ *are elements of* D, *and* $\oplus$ *(the combine operation) and* $\otimes$ *(the extend operation) are binary operators on* D *such that*

1. $(D, \oplus)$ *is a commutative monoid with* $\overline{0}$ *as its neutral element, and where* $\oplus$ *is idempotent.* $(D, \otimes)$ *is a monoid with the neutral element* $\overline{1}$.
2. $\otimes$ *distributes over* $\oplus$, *i.e., for all* $a, b, c \in D$ *we have*
$$a \otimes (b \oplus c) = (a \otimes b) \oplus (a \otimes c) \text{ and } (a \oplus b) \otimes c = (a \otimes c) \oplus (b \otimes c).$$

3. $\overline{0}$ is an annihilator with respect to $\otimes$, i.e., for all $a \in D$, $a \otimes \overline{0} = \overline{0} = \overline{0} \otimes a$.

4. In the partial order $\sqsubseteq$ defined by $\forall a, b \in D$, $a \sqsubseteq b$ iff $a \oplus b = a$, there are no infinite descending chains.

Definition 4. A **weighted pushdown system** is a triple $\mathcal{W} = (\mathcal{P}, \mathcal{S}, f)$ where $\mathcal{P} = (P, \Gamma, \Delta)$ is a pushdown system, $\mathcal{S} = (D, \oplus, \otimes, \overline{0}, \overline{1})$ is a bounded idempotent semiring and $f : \Delta \to D$ is a map that assigns a weight to each pushdown rule.

Let $\sigma \in \Delta^*$ be a sequence of rules. Using f, we can associate a value to σ, i.e., if $\sigma = [r_1, \ldots, r_k]$, then we define $v(\sigma) \overset{\text{def}}{=} f(r_1) \otimes \ldots \otimes f(r_k)$. Moreover, for any two configurations c and c' of $\mathcal{P}$, we use $path(c, c')$ to denote the set of all rule sequences $[r_1, \ldots, r_k]$ that transform c into c'. Reachability problems on pushdown systems are generalized to weighted pushdown systems as follows.

Definition 5. Let $\mathcal{W} = (\mathcal{P}, \mathcal{S}, f)$ be a weighted pushdown system, where $\mathcal{P} = (P, \Gamma, \Delta)$, and let $C \subseteq P \times \Gamma^*$ be a regular set of configurations. The **generalized pushdown predecessor** (GPP) problem is to find for each $c \in P \times \Gamma^*$:

$$\delta(c) \overset{\text{def}}{=} \bigoplus \{ v(\sigma) \mid \sigma \in path(c, c'), c' \in C \}$$

The **generalized pushdown successor** (GPS) problem is to find for each $c \in P \times \Gamma^*$:

$$\delta(c) \overset{\text{def}}{=} \bigoplus \{ v(\sigma) \mid \sigma \in path(c', c), c' \in C \}$$

To illustrate the above definitions, let us encode Boolean programs as a WPDS. Consider the program shown in Fig. 1. It has one global variable flag. We ignore local variables for now, and details regarding their treatment can be found in [11]. Let G be the set of all valuations of global variables. In our case, $G = \{0, 1\}$ because we only have one global variable. Each ICFG edge can be associated with a transformer, which is a binary relation on G, and describes the effect of executing that edge on the global variables, e.g., the edge (n_2, n_3) will be associated with the relation $\{(0, 0), (1, 0)\}$ because flag is set to 0 (or false). Therefore, we use the weight domain $(2^{G \times G}, \cup, \circ, \emptyset, id)$, and for a PDS rule, we associate it with the transformer of the corresponding ICFG edge. Assertion checking in the program can be performed by seeing if a configuration c (or a set of configurations) can be reached with non-zero weight, i.e, $\delta(c) \neq \overline{0}$.

Boolean programs can also be encoded using PDSs by using the states of the PDS to encode valuations of global variables. However, WPDSs provide a more efficient representation of Boolean programs because the weights can symbolically encode transformers, for example, by using BDDs [17]. Moreover, WPDSs are strictly more powerful than PDSs because they can be used with *infinite-width* abstract domains to perform copy-constant propagation and affine relation analysis [12]. More details on the uses of PDSs for model checking, and their encoding as WPDSs can be found in [11].

3 Solving Reachability Problems

In this section, we review the existing algorithm for solving generalized reachability problems on WPDSs [16], which is based on chaotic iteration, and present our new algorithm, which uses Tarjan's path-expression algorithm [19]. We limit our discussion to GPP; GPS is similar but slightly more complicated.

3.1 Solving GPP Using Chaotic Iteration

Let $\mathcal{W} = (\mathcal{P}, \mathcal{S}, f)$ be a WPDS where $\mathcal{P} = (P, \Gamma, \Delta)$ is a pushdown system and $\mathcal{S} = (D, \oplus, \otimes, \bar{0}, \bar{1})$ is the weight domain. Let C be a regular set of configurations that is recognized by $\mathcal{P}$-automaton $\mathcal{A} = (Q, \Gamma, \to_0, P, F)$. GPP is solved by saturating this automaton with new weighted transitions (each transition t has a weight label $l(t)$), to create automaton $\mathcal{A}_{pre^*}$, such that $\delta(c)$ can be read-off efficiently from $\mathcal{A}_{pre^*}$: $\delta(\langle p, u \rangle)$ is the combine of weights of all accepting paths for u starting from p, where the weight of a path is the extend of the weight-labels of the transitions in the path in order. We present the algorithm for building $\mathcal{A}_{pre^*}$ based on its abstract grammar problem.

Definition 6. *[16] Let $(S, \sqcap)$ be a meet semilattice. An **abstract grammar** over $(S, \sqcap)$ is a collection of context-free grammar productions, where each production θ has the form $X_0 \to g_\theta(X_1, \dots, X_k)$. Parentheses, commas, and g_θ (where θ is a production) are terminal symbols. Every production θ is associated with a function $g_\theta : S^k \to S$. Thus, every string α of terminal symbols derived in this grammar denotes a composition of functions, and corresponds to a unique value in S, which we call $val_G(\alpha)$. Let $L_G(X)$ denote the strings of terminals derivable from a nonterminal X. The **abstract grammar problem** is to compute, for each nonterminal X, the value $\text{MOD}_G(X) = \bigsqcap_{\alpha \in L_G(X)} val_G(\alpha)$. This value is called the **meet-over-all-derivations** value for X.*

We define abstract grammars over the meet semilattice $(D, \oplus)$, where D is the set of weights as given above. An example is shown in Fig. 2. The non-terminal t_3 can derive the string $\alpha = g_4(g_3(g_1))$ and $val(\alpha) = w_4 \otimes w_3 \otimes w_1$.

(1) $t_1 \to g_1(\epsilon)$	$g_1 = w_1$	(3) $t_2 \to g_3(t_1)$	$g_3 = \lambda x.w_3 \otimes x$
(2) $t_1 \to g_2(t_2)$	$g_2 = \lambda x.w_2 \otimes x$	(4) $t_3 \to g_4(t_2)$	$g_4 = \lambda x.w_4 \otimes x$

Fig. 2. A simple abstract grammar with four productions

Production	for each
(1) $PopSeq_{(q,\gamma,q')} \to g_1(\epsilon)$	$(q, \gamma, q') \in \to_0$
$\quad g_1 = \bar{1}$	
(2) $PopSeq_{(p,\gamma,p')} \to g_2(\epsilon)$	$r = \langle p, \gamma \rangle \hookrightarrow \langle p', \varepsilon \rangle \in \Delta$
$\quad g_2 = f(r)$	
(3) $PopSeq_{(p,\gamma,q)} \to g_3(PopSeq_{(p',\gamma',q)})$	$r = \langle p, \gamma \rangle \hookrightarrow \langle p', \gamma' \rangle \in \Delta, q \in Q$
$\quad g_3 = \lambda x.f(r) \otimes x$	
(4) $PopSeq_{(p,\gamma,q)} \to g_4(PopSeq_{(p',\gamma',q')}, PopSeq_{(q',\gamma'',q)})$	$r = \langle p, \gamma \rangle \hookrightarrow \langle p', \gamma'\gamma'' \rangle \in \Delta, q, q' \in Q$
$\quad g_4 = \lambda x.\lambda y.f(r) \otimes x \otimes y$	

Fig. 3. An abstract grammar problem for solving GPP

The abstract grammar for solving GPP is shown in Fig. 3. The grammar has one non-terminal $PopSeq_t$ for each possible transition $t \in Q \times \Gamma \times Q$ of $\mathcal{A}_{pre^*}$. The productions describe how the weights on those transitions are computed. Let $l(t)$ be the weight label on transition t. Then we want $l(t) = \text{MOD}(PopSeq_t)$. The meet-over-all-derivation value is obtained as follows [16]: Initialize $l(t) = \bar{0}$ for all transitions t. If $PopSeq_t \rightarrow g(PopSeq_{t_1}, PopSeq_{t_2})$ is a production of the grammar (with possibly fewer non-terminals on the right-hand side) then update the weight label on t to $l(t) \oplus g(l(t_1), l(t_2))$. The existing algorithm for solving GPP is a worklist-based algorithm that uses chaotic iteration to choose (i) a transition in the worklist and (ii) all productions that have this transition on the right side, and updates the weight on the transitions on the left-hand side of the productions as described earlier. If the weight on a transition changes then it is added to the worklist. Defn. 3(4) guarantees convergence.

Such a chaotic-iteration scheme is not very efficient. Consider the abstract grammar in Fig. 2. The most efficient way of saturating weights on transitions would be to start with the first production and then keep alternating between the next two productions until $l(t_1)$ and $l(t_2)$ converge before choosing the last production. Any other strategy would have to choose the last production multiple times. Thus, it is important to identify such "loops" between transitions and to stay within a loop before exiting it.

3.2 Solving GPP Using Path Expressions

To find a better iteration scheme for GPP, we convert GPP into a hypergraph problem.

Definition 7. *A (directed) **hypergraph** is a generalization of a directed graph in which generalized edges, called **hyperedges**, can have multiple sources, i.e., the source of an edge is an ordered set of vertices. A **transition dependence graph** (**TDG**) for a grammar G is a hypergraph whose vertices are the non-terminals of G. There is a hyperedge from $(t_1, \cdots, t_n)$ to t if G has a production with t on the left-hand side and $t_1 \cdots t_n$ are the non-terminals that appear (in order) on the right-hand side.*

If we construct the TDG of the grammar shown in Fig. 3 when the underlying PDS is obtained from an ICFG, and the initial set of configurations is $\{\langle p, \varepsilon \rangle \mid p \in P\}$ (or $\rightarrow_0 = \emptyset$), then the TDG is identical to the ICFG (with edges reversed). Fig. 4 shows an example. This can be observed from the fact that except for the PDS states in Fig. 3, the transition dependences are almost identical to the dependences encoded in the pushdown rules, which in turn come from ICFG edges; e.g., the ICFG edge (n_1, n_2) corresponds to the transition dependence $((t_2), t_1)$ in Fig. 4, and the call-return pair (n_3, n_6) and (n_{12}, n_4) in the ICFG corresponds to the hyperedge $((t_4, t_6), t_3)$.

For such pushdown systems, constructing TDGs might seem unnecessary but it allows us to choose an initial set of configurations, which defines a region of interest in the program. Moreover, PDSs can encode much stronger properties than an ICFG, such as setjmp/longjmp in C programs. However, it is still convenient to think of a TDG as an ICFG. In the rest of this paper, we illustrate the issues using the TDG of the grammar in Fig. 3. We reduce the meet-over-all-derivation problem on the grammar to a meet-over-all-paths problem on its TDG.

Intraprocedural Iteration. We first consider TDGs of a special form: consider the intraprocedural case, i.e., there are no hyperedges in the TDG (and correspondingly no push rules in the PDS). As an example, assume that the TDG in Fig. 4 has only the part corresponding to procedure foo() without any hyperedges. In such a TDG, if an edge

$((t_1), t)$ was inserted because of the production $t \rightarrow g(t_1)$ for $g = \lambda x.x \otimes w$ for some weight w, then label this edge with w. Next, insert a special node t_s into the TDG and for each production of the form $t \rightarrow g(\epsilon)$ with $g = w$, insert the edge $((t_s), t)$ and label it with weight w. t_s is called a source node. This gives us a graph with weights on each edge. Define the weight of a path in this graph in the standard (but reversed) way: the weight of a path is the extend of weights on its constituent edges in the reverse order. It is easy to see that $\text{MOD}(t) = \bigoplus \{v(\eta) \mid \eta \in path(t_s, t)\}$, where $path(t_s, t)$ is the set of all paths from t_s to t in the TDG and $v(\eta)$ is the weight of the path η. To solve for MOD, we could still use chaotic iteration, but instead we will make use of Tarjan's path-expression algorithm [19].

Problem 1. Given a directed graph G and a fixed vertex s, the **single-source path expression** (SSPE) problem is to compute a regular expression that represents $path(s, v)$ for all vertices v in the graph. The syntax of regular expressions is as follows: $r ::= \emptyset \mid \varepsilon \mid e \mid r_1 \cup r_2 \mid r_1.r_2 \mid r^*$, where e stands for an edge in G.

We can use the SSPE algorithm to compute regular expressions for $path(t_s, t)$, which gives us a compact description of the set of paths we need to consider. Also, the Kleene-star operator identifies loops in the TDG. Let $\otimes^c$ be the reverse of $\otimes$, i.e., $w_1 \otimes^c w_2 = w_2 \otimes w_1$. To compute $\text{MOD}(t)$, we take the regular expression for $path(t_s, t)$ and replace each edge e with its weight, $\emptyset$ with $\overline{0}$, ε with $\overline{1}$, $\cup$ with $\oplus$, . with $\otimes^c$, and solve the expression. The weight w^* is computed as $\overline{1} \oplus w \oplus (w \otimes w) \oplus \cdots$; because of the bounded-height property of the semiring, this iteration converges. The two main advantages of using regular expressions to compute $\text{MOD}(t)$ are: First, loops are identified in the expression, and the evaluation strategy saturates a loop before exiting it. Second, we can compute w^* faster than normal iteration could. For this, observe that
$$(\overline{1} \oplus w)^n = \overline{1} \oplus w \oplus w^2 \oplus \cdots \oplus w^n$$
where exponentiation is defined using $\otimes$, i.e., $w^0 = \overline{1}$ and $w^i = w \otimes w^{(i-1)}$. Then w^* can be computed by repeatedly squaring $(\overline{1} \oplus w)$ until it converges. If $w^* = \overline{1} \oplus w \oplus \cdots \oplus w^n$ then it can be computed in $O(\log n)$ operations. A chaotic-iteration strategy would take $O(n)$ steps to compute the same value. In other words, having a closed representation of loops provides an exponential speedup.[1]

Tarjan's algorithm uses *dominators* to construct the regular expressions for SSPE. This has the effect of computing the weight on the dominators of a node before computing the weight on the node itself. This avoids unnecessary propagation of partial weights to the node (which is the case when you exit a loop too early). Given a graph with m edges (or m grammar productions in our case) and n nodes (or non-terminals), regular expressions for $path(t_s, t)$ can be computed for all nodes t in time $O(m \log n)$ when the graph is *reducible*. Evaluating these expressions will take an additional $O(m \log n \log h)$ semiring operations, where h is the height of the semiring.[2] Because most high-level

---

[1] This assumes that each semiring operation takes the same amount of time. In the absence of any assumption on the semiring being used, we aim to decrease the number of semiring operations. In some cases, e.g., BDD-based weight domains, repeated squaring may not reduce the overall running time. However, the user can supply a procedure for computing w^* whenever there is a more efficient way of computing it than by using simple iteration [13].

[2] The combined sizes of the regular expressions are bounded by the running time of the SSPE algorithm.

languages are well-structured, their ICFGs are mostly reducible. When the graph is not reducible, the running time degrades to $O((m \log n + k) \log h)$ semiring operations, where k is the sum of the cubes of the sizes of *dominator-strong components* of the graph. In the worst case, k can be $O(n^3)$. In our experiments, we seldom found irreducibility to be a problem: k/n was a small constant. A pure chaotic-iteration strategy would take $O(m\ h)$ semiring operations in the worst case. Comparing these complexities, we can expect the algorithm that uses path expressions to be much faster than chaotic iteration, and the benefit will be greater as the height of the semiring increases.

Interprocedural Iteration. We now generalize our algorithm to any TDG. For each hyperedge $((t_1, t_2), t)$, delete it from the graph and replace it with the edge $((t_1), t)$. This new edge is called a *summary edge*, and node t_2 is called an *out-node*. For example, in Fig. 4 we would delete the hyperedge $((t_4, t_6), t_3)$ and replace it with $((t_4), t_3)$. The new edge is called a summary edge because it crosses a call-site (from a return node to a call node) and will be used to summarize the effect of a procedure call. Node t_6 is an out-node and will supply the procedure summary weight. The resultant TDG is a collection of connected graphs, with each graph roughly corresponding to a procedure. In Fig. 4, the transitions that correspond to procedures main and foo get split. Each connected graph is called an *intragraph*. For each intragraph, we introduce a source node as before and add edges from the source node to all nodes that have ϵ-productions. The weight labels are also added as before. For a summary edge $((t_1), t)$ obtained from a hyperedge $((t_1, t_2), t)$ with associated production function $g = \lambda x.\lambda y.w \otimes x \otimes y$, label it with $w \otimes t_2$, or $t_2 \otimes^c w$.

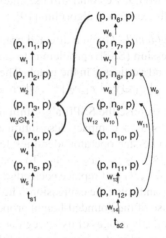

Fig. 4. TDG for the PDS shown in Fig. 1. A WPDS is obtained from the PDS by supplementing rule number i with weight w_i. Let t_j stand for the node (p, n_j, p). The thick bold arrows form a hyperedge. Nodes t_{s1} and t_{s2} are source nodes, and the dashed arrow is a summary edge. These, along with edge labels, are explained later in §3.2.

This gives us a collection of intragraphs with edges labeled with either a weight or a simple expression with an out-node. To solve for the MOD value, we construct a set of *regular equations*, which we call as out-node equations. For an intragraph G, let t_G be its unique source node. Then, for each out-node t_o in G, construct the regular expression for all paths in G from t_G to t_o, i.e., for $path(t_G, t_o)$. In this expression, replace each edge with its corresponding label. If the resulting expression is r and it contains out-nodes t_1 to t_n, add the equation $t_o = r(t_1, \cdots, t_n)$ to the set of out-node equations. Repeat this for all intragraphs. The resulting set of out-node equations describe all hyperpaths in the TDG to an out-node from the collection of all source nodes. The MOD value of the out-nodes is the greatest fix-point of these equations (with respect to $\sqsubseteq$ of Defn. 3(4)). For example, for the TDG shown in

Fig. 4, assuming that t_1 is also an out-node, we would obtain the following out-node equations.[3]

$$t_6 = w_{14}.(w_9 \oplus w_{13}.w_{11}.(w_{12}.w_{10})^*.w_8).w_7.w_6$$
$$t_1 = w_5.w_4.(t_6.w_3).w_2.w_1$$

Here we have used . as a shorthand for $\otimes^c$. One way to solve these equations is by using chaotic iteration: start by initializing each out-node with $\overline{0}$ (the greatest element in the semiring) and update the values of out-nodes by repeatedly solving the equations until they converge. We can give direction to this iteration by constructing a dependence graph of these equation, where an equation $t_o = r(t_1, \cdots, t_n)$ gives rise to dependences $t_i \to t_o, 1 \le i \le n$. We take a *strongly connected component* (SCC) decomposition of this graph and solve all equations in one component before moving to equations in next component (in a topological order). We could also use regular expressions to define an evaluation order on these equations (details are given in [11]), but we chose a simpler implementation because SCCs in this dependence graph, which correspond to mutually recursive procedures, tend to be quite small in practice.

Each regular expression in the out-node equations summarizes all paths in an intragraph and can be quite large. Therefore, we want to avoid evaluating them repeatedly while solving the equations. To this end, we incrementally evaluate the regular expressions: only that part of an expression is reevaluated that contains a modified out-node. (In the algorithm given in Fig. 5, the entire expression may be traversed, but reevaluations are performed selectively.) A regular expression is represented using its abstract-syntax tree, where leaves are weights or out-nodes, and internal nodes correspond to $\oplus$, $\otimes$, or *. As a further optimization, all regular expressions share common subtrees, and are represented as DAGs instead of trees. The incremental algorithm we use takes care of this sharing and also identifies modified out-nodes in an expression automatically. At each DAG node we maintain two integers, last_change and last_seen, as well as the weight weight of the subdag rooted at the node. We assume that all regular expressions share the same leaves for out-nodes. We keep a global counter update_count that is incremented each time the weight of some out-node is updated. For a node, the counter last_change records the last update count at which the weight of its subdag changed, and the counter last_seen records the update count at which the subdag was reevaluated. The evaluation algorithm is shown in Fig. 5. When the weight of an out-node is changed, its corresponding leaf node is updated with that weight, update_count is incremented, and the out-node's counters are set to update_count.

Once we solve for the values of the out-nodes, we can change the out-node labels on summary edges in the intragraphs and replace them with their corresponding weight. Then the MOD values for other nodes in the TDG can be obtained as in the intraprocedural version by considering each intragraph in isolation.

The time required for solving this system of equations depends on reducibility of the intragraphs. Let S_G be the time required to solve SSPE on intragraph G, i.e., $S_G = O(m \log n + k)$ where k is $O(n^3)$ in the worst-case, but is ignorable in practice. If the equations do not have any mutual dependences (corresponding to no recursion) then

---

[3] The equations might be different depending on how the SSPE algorithm was implemented, but all such equations would have the same solution.

the running time is $\sum_G S_G \log h$, where the sum ranges over all intragraphs, because each equation has to be solved exactly once. In the presence of recursion, we use the observation that the weight of each subdag in a regular expression can change at most h times while the equations are being solved because it can only decrease monotonically. Because the size of a regular expression obtained from an intragraph G is bounded by S_G, the worst-case time for solving the equations is $\sum_G S_G \ h$. This bound is very pessimistic and is actually worse than that of chaotic iteration. Here we did not make use of the fact that incrementally computing regular expressions is much faster than reevaluating them. For a regular expression with one modified out-node, we only need to perform semiring operations for each node from the out-node leaf to the root of the expression. For a nearly balanced regular expression tree, this path to the root can be as small as $\log S_G$. Empirically, we found that incrementally computing the expression required many fewer operations than recomputing the expression.

```
1    procedure evaluate(r)
2    begin
3        if r.last_seen == update_count then return
4        case r = w, r = t_o return
5        case r = op(r_1,r_2)
6            evaluate(r_1), evaluate(r_2)
7            m = max{r_1.last_change, r_2.last_change}
8            if m > r.last_seen then
9                w = op(r_1.weight, r_2.weight)
10               if r.weight ≠ w then
11                   r.last_change = m
12                   r.weight = w
13           r.last_seen = update_count
14   end
```

Fig. 5. Incremental evaluation algorithm for regular expressions. Here op is the prefix version of $\otimes$, $\oplus$, or $*$. When op is $*$, r_2 can be ignored.

Unlike the chaotic-iteration scheme, where the weights of all TDG nodes are computed, we only need to compute the weights on out-nodes. The weights for the rest of the nodes can be computed lazily by evaluating their corresponding regular expression only when needed. For applications that just require the weight for a few TDG nodes, this gives us additional savings. We also limit the computation of weights of out-nodes to only those intragraphs that contain a TDG node whose weight is required. This corresponds to slicing the out-node equations with respect to the user query, which rules out computation in procedures that are irrelevant to the query.

Handling Local Variables. WPDSs were recently extended to Extended-WPDSs to provide a more convenient mechanism for handling local variables [12]. Reachability problems in EWPDS are also based on abstract grammars similar to the ones for a WPDS. Thus, we can easily adapt our algorithm to EWPDSs as well. Details are given in [11]. We use EWPDSs in our experiments.

4 Solving Other PDS Problems

In this section, we give algorithms for some important PDS problems: witness tracing and incremental analysis. Our technical report [11] also gives an algorithm for differential weight propagation. Of these three, only witness tracing and differential propagation have been discussed before for WPDSs [16].

4.1 Witness Tracing

For program-analysis tools, if a program does not satisfy a property, it is often useful to provide a justification of why the property was not satisfied. In terms of WPDSs, it amounts to reporting a set of paths, or rule sequences, that together justify the reported weight for a configuration. Formally, using the notation of Defn. 5, the witness tracing problem for GPP is to find, for each configuration c, a set $\omega(c) \subseteq \bigcup_{c' \in C} path(c, c')$ such that $\bigoplus_{\sigma \in \omega(c)} v(\sigma) = \delta(c)$. This definition of witness tracing does not impose any restrictions on the size of the reported witness set because any compact representation of the set suffices for most applications. The algorithm for witness tracing for GPP [16] requires $O(|Q|^2 |\Gamma| h)$ memory. Our algorithm only requires $O(|ON| h)$ memory, where $|ON|$ is the number of out-nodes, which is expected to be much smaller than $|\Gamma|$.

In our new GPP algorithm, we already have a head start because we have regular expressions that describe all paths in an intragraph. In the intragraphs, we label each edge with not just a weight, but also the rule that justifies the edge. Push rules will be associated with summary edges and pop rules with edges that originate from a source node. Edges from the source node that were inserted because of production (1) in Fig. 3 are not associated with any rule (or with an empty rule sequence). After solving SSPE on the intragraphs, we can replace each edge with the corresponding rule label. This gives us, for each out-node, a regular expression in terms of other out-nodes that captures the set of all rule sequences that can reach that out-node. Next, while solving the regular equations, we record the weights on out-nodes; i.e., when we solve the equation $t_o = r(t_1, \cdots, t_n)$, we record the weights on $t_1, \cdots, t_n$ — say $w_1, \cdots, w_n$ — whenever the weight on t_o changes to, say, w_o. Then the set of rule sequences to create transition t_o with weight w_o is given by the expression r (where we replace TDG edges with their rule labels) by replacing each out-node t_i with the regular expression for all rule sequences used to create t_i with weight w_i (obtained recursively). This gives a regular expression for the witness set of each out-node. Witness sets for other transitions can be obtained by solving SSPE on the intragraphs by replacing out-node labels with their witness-set expression.

Here we only require $O(|ON| h)$ space for recording witnesses because we just have to remember the history of weights on out-nodes. For PDSs obtained from ICFGs and empty initial automaton, $|ON|$ is the number of procedures in the ICFG, which is very small compared to $|\Gamma|$.

4.2 Incremental Analysis

The first incremental algorithm for verifying finite-state properties on ICFGs was given by Conway et al. [4]. We can use the methods presented in this paper to generalize their algorithm to WPDSs. An incremental approach to model checking has the advantage of amortizing the verification time across program development or debugging time.

We consider two cases: addition of new rules and deletion of existing ones. In each case we work at the granularity of intragraphs. When a new rule is added, the fix-point solution of the out-node equations monotonically decreases and we can reuse all of the existing computation. We first identify the intragraphs that changed (have more edges) because of the new rule. Next, we recompute the regular expressions for out-nodes in those intragraphs and add them to the set of out-node equations.[4] Then we solve the equations as before, but set the initial weights of out-nodes to be their existing value. If new out-nodes were added, then set their initial value to $\overline{0}$.

Deletion of a rule requires more work. Again, we identify the changed intragraphs and recompute the out-node equations for them. We call out-nodes in these intragraphs as *modified* out-nodes. Next, we look at the dependence graph of the out-node equations as constructed in §3.2. We perform an SCC decomposition of this graph and topologically sort the SCCs. Then the weights for all out-nodes that appear before the first SCC that has a modified out-node need not be changed. We recompute the solution for other out-nodes in topological order, and stop as soon as the new values agree with previous values. We start with out-nodes in the first SCC that has a modified out-node and solve for their weights. If the new weight of an out-node is different from its previously computed weight, all out-nodes in later SCCs that are dependent on it are marked as modified. We repeat this procedure until there are no more modified out-nodes.

The advantage of doing incremental analysis in our framework is that very little information has to be stored between analysis runs: We only need to store weights on out-nodes.

5 Experiments

We are aware of two implementations of WPDSs: WPDS++ [8] and one used by nMoped [9]. We call the implementation of our algorithm as FWPDS (F stands for "fast"). It can be plugged-in as a back-end for each of the WPDS libraries. WPDS++ also supports an optimized iteration strategy where the user can supply a priority-ordering on stack symbols, which is used by chaotic iteration to choose the transition with least priority first. We refer to this version as BFS-WPDS++ and supply it with a breadth-first ordering on the ICFG obtained by treating it as a graph. BFS-WPDS++ almost always performs better than WPDS++.

To measure end-to-end performance, FWPDS only computes the weight on transitions required by the application. We also report the time taken to compute the weight on all transitions and refer to this as FWPDS-Full. A comparison with FWPDS-Full will give an indication of "application-independent" improvement provided by our approach because it computes the same amount of information as the previous WPDS algorithms. However, we measure speedups using FWPDS running times to show the potential of using lazy-evaluation in real settings. FWPDS-Full uses a left-associative evaluation order for computing weights of regular expressions. It is also worth noting that repeated

---

[4] There are incremental algorithms for SSPE as well, but we have not used them because solving SSPE for a single intragraph is usually very fast.

squaring for computing w^* did not cause any appreciable difference compared with using a simple iterative method.

We tested FWPDS on three applications that use WPDSs. In each, we perform GPS on the WPDS with the entry point of the program as the initial configuration. The first application performs affine-relation analysis (ARA) on x86 programs [12]. An x86 program is translated into a WPDS to find affine relationships between machine registers. The application only requires affine relationships at certain branch points [1]. Some of the results are shown in Table 1. Over all the experiments we performed, FWPDS provided an average speedup of 1.6 times (i.e., reduced running time by 38%) over BFS-WPDS++.

Table 1. Comparison of ARA results. The last column show the speedup (ratio of running times) of FWPDS versus BFS-WPDS++. The programs are common Windows executables, and the experiments were run on 3.2 Ghz P4 machine with 4GB RAM.

Prog	Insts	Procs	WPDS++	BFS-WPDS++	FWPDS-Full	FWPDS	Speedup
print	75539	697	1.23	1.02	0.77	0.41	2.48
finger	96123	893	11.14	7.94	7.13	4.44	1.79
winhlp32	157634	6491	25.51	19.61	17.32	11.00	1.78
regsvr32	225857	9625	58.70	38.83	37.15	24.65	1.57
cmd	230481	2317	69.19	46.33	52.38	34.87	1.33
notepad	239408	2911	54.08	40.8	41.85	26.50	1.54

The second application, BTRACE, is for debugging [10]. It performs path optimization on C programs: given a set of ICFG nodes, called critical nodes, it tries to find a shortest ICFG path that touches the maximum number of these nodes. The path starts at the entry point of the program and stops at a given failure point in the program. FWPDS only computes the weight at the failure point. As shown in Table 2, FWPDS performs much better than BFS-WPDS++ for this application, and the overall speedup was 4.3 times. Some experimental results on incremental analysis for BTRACE are presented in [11]: We observed a roughly 10-fold improvement by incrementally computing the solution after a deleted procedure was reinserted in the program.

Table 2. Comparison of BTRACE results. The last column shows speedup of FWPDS over BFS-WPDS++. The critical nodes were chosen at random from ICFG nodes and the failure site was set as the exit point of the program. The programs are common Unix utilities, and the experiments were run on 2.4 GHz P4 machine with 4GB RAM.

Prog	ICFG nodes	Procs	BFS-WPDS++	FWPDS-Full	FWPDS	Speedup
make	40667	204	15.1	7.7	5.8	2.58
indent	28155	104	19.6	28.2	15.9	1.24
less	33006	359	22.4	8.6	5.3	4.19
patch	27389	133	70.2	23.2	17.1	4.09
gawk	86617	401	72.7	64.5	45.1	1.61
wget	44575	399	318.4	58.9	27.0	11.77

Table 3. nMoped results. The last column shows speedup of FWPDS over nMoped. The programs were provided by S. Schwoon, and are not yet publically available.

Prog	nMoped	FWPDS-Full	FWPDS	Speedup
bugs5	13.11	13.03	7.25	1.81
slam-fixed	32.67	19.23	13.3	2.46
slam	6.32	5.21	3.27	1.93
unified-serial	37.10	19.65	12.46	2.98
iscsi1	29.15	27.12	14.08	2.07
iscsi10	178.22	59.63	31.29	5.70

The third application is nMoped [9], which is a model checker for Boolean programs. It uses a WPDS library for performing reachability queries. Weights are binary relations on valuations of Boolean variables, and are represented using BDDs. We measure the performance of FWPDS against this library using a set of programs (and an error configuration for each program) supplied by S. Schwoon. We compute the set of all variable valuations that can hold at the error configuration by computing its meet-over-all-paths weight. As shown in Table 3, FWPDS is 2 to 5 times faster than nMoped. Our technical report [11] gives some other set of experiments, but they were on much smaller programs and led to inconclusive results.

nMoped can also be asked to stop as soon as it finds out that the error configuration is reachable (instead of exploring all paths leading to the error configuration). In that case, when the error configuration was reachable, nMoped performed much better than FWPDS, often completing in less than a second. This is expected because the evaluation strategy used by FWPDS is oriented towards finding the complete weight (MOD value) on a transition. For example, it might be better to avoid saturating a loop completely and propagate partially computed weights in the hope of finding out if the error configuration is reachable. However, when the error configuration is unreachable, or when the abstraction-refinement mode in nMoped is turned on, it explores all paths in the program and computes the MOD value of all transitions. In such situations, it may be better to use FWPDS.

6   Related Work

The basic strategy of using a regular expression to describe a set of paths has been used previously for dataflow analysis [20] of single-procedure programs. The only work that we are aware of that uses this technique for multi-procedure programs is by Ramalingam [15]. However, he used regular expressions for a particular analysis (execution frequency analysis) and the technique was motivated by the special requirements of execution frequency analysis when creating procedure summaries, rather than efficiency. We have generalized the approach to apply to a much broader set of problems, namely anything that can be encoded as a WPDS, and showed how various enhancements (incremental recomputation of regular expressions, computing lazily, etc.) contribute to creating a faster analysis.

There has been a host of previous work on incremental program analysis as well as on interprocedural automaton-based analysis [4]. The incremental algorithm we have presented is similar to the algorithm in [4], but generalizes it to WPDSs and is thus applicable in domains other than finite-state property verification. A key difference with their algorithm is that they explore the property automaton on-the-fly as the program is explored. Our encoding into a WPDS requires the whole automaton before the program is explored. This difference can be significant when the automaton is large but only a small part of the automaton needs to be generated.

References

1. G. Balakrishnan and T. Reps. Analyzing memory accesses in x86 executables. In *CC*, 2004.
2. A. Bouajjani, J. Esparza, and O. Maler. Reachability analysis of pushdown automata: Application to model checking. In *Concurrency Theory (CONCUR)*, pages 135–150, 1997.
3. A. Bouajjani, J. Esparza, and T. Touili. A generic approach to the static analysis of concurrent programs with procedures. In *POPL*, pages 62–73, 2003.
4. C. L. Conway, K. S. Namjoshi, D. Dams, and S. A. Edwards. Incremental algorithms for inter-procedural analysis of safety properties. In *CAV*, pages 449–461, 2005.
5. J. Esparza, D. Hansel, P. Rossmanith, and S. Schwoon. Efficient algorithms for model checking pushdown systems. In *CAV*, pages 232–247, 2000.
6. J. Esparza and S. Schwoon. A BDD-based model checker for recursive programs. In *CAV*, pages 324–336, 2001.
7. A. Finkel, B. Willems, and P. Wolper. A direct symbolic approach to model checking pushdown systems. *Electronic Notes in Theoretical Computer Science*, 9, 1997.
8. N. Kidd, T. Reps, D. Melski, and A. Lal. WPDS++: A C++ library for weighted pushdown systems, 2005. http://www.cs.wisc.edu/wpis/wpds++.
9. S. Kiefer, S. Schwoon, and D. Suwimonteerabuth. nMoped, 2005. http://www.informatik.uni-stuttgart.de/fmi/szs/tools/moped/nmoped/.
10. A. Lal, J. Lim, M. Polishchuk, and B. Liblit. Path optimization in programs and its application to debugging. In *European Symposium On Programming*, pages 246–263, 2006.
11. A. Lal and T. Reps. Improving pushdown system model checking. Technical Report 1552, University of Wisconsin-Madison, Jan. 2006.
12. A. Lal, T. Reps, and G. Balakrishnan. Extended weighted pushdown systems. In *CAV*, pages 434–448, 2005.
13. Y. Matsunaga, P. C. McGeer, and R. K. Brayton. On computing the transitive closure of a state transition relation. In *Design Automation Conference (DAC)*, pages 260–265, 1993.
14. E. W. Myers. A precise interprocedural data flow algorithm. In *POPL*, pages 219–230, 1981.
15. G. Ramalingam. Data flow frequency analysis. In *PLDI*, pages 267–277, 1996.
16. T. Reps, S. Schwoon, S. Jha, and D. Melski. Weighted pushdown systems and their application to interprocedural dataflow analysis. *Science of Computer Programming*, 2005.
17. S. Schwoon. *Model-Checking Pushdown Systems*. PhD thesis, Technical Univ. of Munich, Munich, Germany, July 2002.
18. S. Schwoon. Moped, 2002. http://www.fmi.uni-stuttgart.de/szs/tools/moped/.
19. R. E. Tarjan. Fast algorithms for solving path problems. *J. ACM*, 28(3):594–614, 1981.
20. R. E. Tarjan. A unified approach to path problems. *J. ACM*, 28(3):577–593, 1981.

Repair of Boolean Programs with an Application to C

Andreas Griesmayer[1], Roderick Bloem[1], and Byron Cook[2]

[1] Graz University of Technology
[2] Microsoft Research

Abstract. We show how to find and fix faults in Boolean programs by extending
the program to a game. In the game, the protagonist can select an alternative implementation for an incorrect statement. If the protagonist can do so successfully
using a memoryless strategy that does not depend on the stack contents, we have
found a correction for the Boolean program. We present a symbolic algorithm
that localizes possibly faulty statements and provides corrections.

If the Boolean program is an abstraction of a C program, the repair for the
Boolean program suggests a repair for the original C program. This yields a correct but incomplete approach to repairing C programs. We have applied this approach to Boolean programs that are produced as abstractions by SLAM and have
thus successfully patched several faulty Windows device drivers.

1 Introduction

When a software model checker disproves a property, it typically returns a counterexample. A counterexample, however, is just an example of a failure, only a hint to the
root cause of the program's error. In order to fix the bug we must understand the counterexample, find its root cause, and then implement a fix. In this paper we describe a
method to automatically suggest repairs to source code based on the abstractions computed within a software model checker. With our method the programmer can either
simply implement one of the proposed repairs, or the programmer may find that the
proposed repairs lead to greater understanding of the root cause of the counterexample
returned by the software model checker.

The technical contribution of our work is a method to fix faulty Boolean programs
by computing a memoryless, stackless strategy. We assume that the software model
checker is based on predicate abstraction [11] to Boolean programs [5] (i.e., pushdown
automata), as is done in tools like SLAM [3]. The Boolean program can be converted
into a game between the system (protagonist) and the environment (antagonist). Given
a suspect expression, the system decides how the expression should behave, whereas
the environment resolves nondeterminism. Such a game can be regarded as the pushdown equivalent of a reactive module [1]. A winning strategy for this game is one
that ensures that the specification is adhered to by fixing the proper decisions for the
system. If such a strategy exists, we can fix the Boolean program by implementing
the decisions that the strategy prescribes. We are looking for a repair that changes the
program as little as possible, so that it remains amenable to further modification by the
programmer. The repair should depend only on global variables and the local variables
that are currently in scope, and not on the stack contents. A change that does not satisfy

T. Ball and R.B. Jones (Eds.): CAV 2006, LNCS 4144, pp. 358–371, 2006.

these constraints cannot be easily implemented in a Boolean program. Such a repair corresponds to a memoryless, stackless strategy [2]. Our choice to repair the program by replacing expressions works relatively well in practice, but is not the only possibility. Our technical approach is applicable to different fault models as well.

By replacing the Boolean predicates by the expressions they represent, we obtain a constraint describing a set of repairs for the original C program. Any such repair leads to a C program that adheres to its specification. The programmer then selects a repair that does not violate any implicit assumptions. Although a repair for the Boolean program guarantees the existence of a repair for the C program, the converse does not hold. The abstract program may contain spurious counterexamples as well as the real counterexample that corresponds to the bug and it may not be possible to repair all of these. In order to demonstrate the viability of our approach we have implemented the proposed method and used it to compute suggested repairs for several Microsoft Windows device drivers after analysis using SLAM [3].

Related Work. The work described here extends work done in [13, 17] on locating and correcting faults in finite-state systems.

Alur, La Torre, and Madhusudan [2] give a fixpoint computation algorithm for solving modular pushdown games that is similar to the algorithm we present in this paper. They do not apply it to repair and do not show an implementation. They further focus on complexity analysis for reachability in different settings of visibility: global memory, local memory and local but persistent memory.

Work by Walukiewicz [18] focuses on computing strategies for more general μ-calculus properties on pushdown systems. This work is not in the setting of repair and the strategies that are found are not in general memoryless. Basing a repair on them would significantly alter the program by adding a second concurrent thread. Bouajjani, Esparza, and Maler [6] give algorithms for reachability analysis in alternating pushdown systems. Their algorithm is polynomial, but the strategy it produces is an alternating automaton and may depend on the contents of the stack.

There has been considerable work in fault localization. Most of it is of heuristic nature and relies on similarities between incorrect traces of the program and their differences with similar, correct traces [4, 12, 19]. Unlike our approach, this work requires the existence of correct executions that are similar to the counterexamples found, but most importantly, none of this work addresses repair. The approach of [4], for instance, marks as suspect the statements that appear in different failure traces but not in traces that satisfy the specification, and thus works on the basic block level. There is no guarantee that the statements found can be used to repair the program or that a possible repair location is found, even if it exists. Nevertheless, the approach appears to be quite good at finding faulty statements. It would be interesting to see if it can be used as a preprocessing step to our algorithm to limit the number of statements that we attempt to repair.

In [8], fault localization is extended to abstract counterexamples. The authors argue that explanations of abstract counterexamples are more informative than explanations of concrete counterexamples, because the predicates used capture the important information in the program, but not more: it is an automatically generated high-level description of the program. For instance, the information that x should be greater than y may be much more informative that the information that x should be 8239 and not 4.

Demsky and Rinard [9] and Khurshid, García, and Suen [14] present work on repairing corrupt data structures without terminating the program. Their work is on recovering from a failure, not on fixing faults in the system.

2 Boolean Programs

2.1 Syntax and Semantics

Boolean programs [5] are similar to C programs: they have functions and recursion, global and local variables. The difference is that all variables are of Boolean domain and no additional storage is available. Boolean programs also support assertions, parallel assignments, and nondetermism. In the following, we give a short formalization. We will not give the details of the execution model, but it can easily be defined in terms of a virtual machine. Note that a Boolean program may have more than one execution, depending on nondeterminism.

A *Boolean program* is a tuple (R, main, V_g), where R is a set of routines, $\text{main} \in R$ is the *initial routine*, and V_g is a set of *global variables*. A *routine* $r \in R$ is a tuple (S_r, V_r), where $S_r = (s_{r,0}, \ldots, s_{r,f})$ is a sequence of statements and V_r is a set of local variables. Statement $s_{r,0}$ is the *initial statement* and $s_{r,f}$ is the *final statement*.

The set of variables visible in r is $V_r' = V_g \cup V_r$. A valuation $\xi \subseteq V_r'$ is the subset of the visible variables that is set to 1, and the set of valuations in routine r is $X_r = 2^{V_r'}$.

We will not define the statements in detail. For a formalization it suffices to define two functions: The control flow graph is given by $next(\xi, s, s')$ meaning that control may continue at $s' \in S_r$ after executing $s \in S_r$ with valuation $\xi \in X_r$. For conditional statements, s' depends on ξ. (Because of nondeterminism, a conditional statement may have multiple successors for one ξ.) In particular, if $s_{r,i}$ is a function call, it is followed by the statement $s_{r,i+1}$, not by the first statement of the called routine.

The change of the valuation that results from executing $s \in S_r$ is denoted by $\tau_s \subseteq X_r \times X_r$. For instance, if s assigns 1 to variable a, then $\tau_{(s)} = \{(\xi, \xi \cup \{a\}) \mid \xi \in X_r\}$. The expression `choose[v,w]` expresses nondeterminism. It evaluates to 1 if v is 1. Otherwise, it evaluates to 0 if w is 1, and nondeterministically otherwise. Thus, if statement s is `a := choose[v,w]` then $\tau_s = \{(\xi, \xi') \mid \xi \setminus \{a\} = \xi' \setminus \{a\} \wedge (v \in \xi \rightarrow a \in \xi') \wedge ((v \notin \xi \wedge w \in \xi) \rightarrow a \notin \xi')\}$. Since Boolean programs are usually abstractions of C programs, and the Boolean variables are predicates, not all valuations are possible. Nondeterminism can be limited to feasible valuations by an *enforce* statement. We will not take such statements into account in the formalization, but they are easily added and are handled by our implementation.

The set of *states* of a routine is $Q_r = S_r \times X_r$ and the set of *initial states* is $I_r = \{s_{r,0}\} \times X_r$. The set of states of a program is the (disjoint) union of the set of states of its routines. The initial states of the program are the initial states of main. A state (s, ξ) is a *bad state* if s is an assert statement and ξ is a valuation that violates the assertion.

For a call statement s from routine src to routine dst, we use a relation $\mu_s : X_{src} \times X_{dst}$. This mapping handles the assignment of the actual parameters to the formal parameters. The values of global variables remain unchanged and local variables that are not formal parameters are assigned nondeterministically. We use the function $\rho_s :$

$X_{src} \times X_{dst} \rightarrow X_{src}$ to compute the valuation after the call returns. It copies the values of the global variables from the called function, copies the values of the local variables from the values they had before the call, and assigns the value returned by dst.

Example. We give an example of a Boolean program in Fig. 1(a). It was generated by abstraction of the C program in Fig. 2, using the predicates shown in Fig. 3. We only have global variables and $V'_{\mathtt{main}} = V'_{\mathtt{f}} = \{p_1, p_2, p_3\}$, so $X_{\mathtt{main}} = X_{\mathtt{f}} = X = 2^{\{p_1, p_2, p_3\}}$. The first statement in Line 1 is a parallel assignment which simultaneously assigns values to all variables. Thus, $\tau_1 = \{(\xi, \{p_2, p_3\}) \mid \xi \in X\}$. (The subscript to τ refers to the line number.) Note that f does not have arguments or return results. Thus, $\mu_2 = \mu_8 = \{(\xi, \xi) \mid \xi \in X\}$ and $\rho_2(\xi_{\mathtt{main}}, \xi_{\mathtt{f}}) = \rho_8(\xi_{\mathtt{main}}, \xi_{\mathtt{f}}) = \xi_{\mathtt{f}}$.

Routine f assigns new values to all of the variables in Line 6 and calls itself until p2 = 0. In Line 3 of the main routine, an assertion checks that $p_1 = 1$. The program does not fulfill this requirement.   □

2.2   Model Checking of Boolean Programs

We review model checking of Boolean programs [5, 10]. Given a Boolean program $P = (R, \mathtt{main}, V_g)$, we associate with every routine $r \in R$ an *execution graph* $\mathcal{E}_r = \langle Q_r, E_r \rangle$, where Q_r is the set of states of r and $E_r \subseteq Q_r \times Q_r$ is a set of edges (to be defined). Intuitively, an edge represents a step in the execution and elements of E^* represent executions. ((The relation E^* is closely related to the *path edges* used in interprocedural dataflow analysis [15].)) We associate with P an execution graph $\mathcal{E} = \langle Q, E \rangle$, where $Q = \bigcup_{r \in R} Q_r$, $E = E_c \cup \bigcup_{r \in R} E_r$. The set E_c of *call edges* is defined below.

The definitions of the edge relations E_r and E_c are mutually recursive. First, we define an update relation τ'_s on the statements. If s is a statement other than a call, then $\tau'_s = \tau_s$. Otherwise τ'_s complies with the called routine dst: $\tau'_s = \{(\xi_1, \xi_2) \mid \exists \xi'_1, \xi'_2 : (\xi_1, \xi'_1) \in \mu_s \wedge ((s_{dst,0}, \xi'_1), (s_{dst,f}, \xi'_2)) \in E^*_{dst} \wedge \rho_s(\xi_1, \xi'_2) = \xi_2\}$.

Furthermore, we define the *reachable states* Rch and the sets of edges E_r and E_c as follows.

$$Rch = \{(s, \xi) \mid \exists \xi_0 : ((s_{\mathtt{main},0}, \xi_0), (s, \xi)) \in E^*\},$$
$$E_r = \{((s, \xi), (s', \xi')) \mid (s, \xi) \in Rch \wedge next(\xi, s, s') \wedge (\xi, \xi') \in \tau'_s\}, \text{ and}$$
$$E_c = \{((s_{src}, \xi), (s_{dst,0}, \xi')) \mid s_{src} \text{ calls } dst \wedge (s_{src}, \xi) \in Rch \wedge (\xi, \xi') \in \mu_{s_{src}}\}.$$

Thus, we start with the initial states of the program and add edges from states as they become reachable. In particular, edges from call statements are added as soon as paths through the called routine are calculated.

Theorem 1. *For $q, q' \in Q$, we have $(q, q') \in E^*$ iff there is an execution of the program that reaches q and subsequently reaches q'.*

Example. Fig. 1(b) gives the execution graph of the example. An example of an execution starts in Line 1 with $p_1 = p_2 = p_3 = 0$. (We denoted this state by $(1, (0, 0, 0))$.) Then it progresses to state $(2, (0, 1, 1))$ and calls f with the same valuation. Then, the

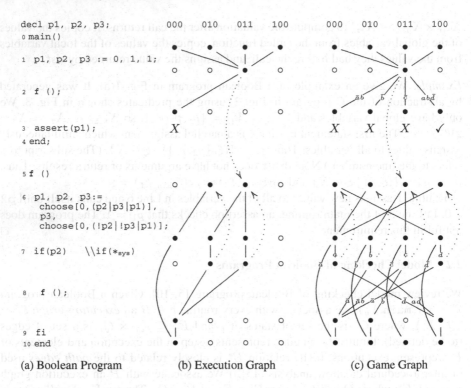

(a) Boolean Program   (b) Execution Graph   (c) Game Graph

Fig. 1. Boolean program and corresponding execution and game graph. There is one column for every consistent valuation. The valuation is given as a triplet $p_1p_2p_3$. Reached states are given by •, unreachable states by ○. Control flow goes from the top to the bottom, except for the dotted lines, which denote call edges.

```
1 static int x;

2 void main() {
3    x = 3;
4    f ();
5    assert(x == 0);
  }
6 void f () {
7    x = x - 1;
8    if (x > 1) {
9       f ();
     }
  }
```

Fig. 2. Faulty C program

p1: $x == 0$
p2: $x > 1$
p3: $x > 2$

Fig. 3. Predicates used for abstraction

a: $*_{sys}(000) = 1$ $\bar{a}$: $*_{sys}(000) = 0$
b: $*_{sys}(010) = 1$ $\bar{b}$: $*_{sys}(010) = 0$
c: $*_{sys}(011) = 1$ $\bar{c}$: $*_{sys}(011) = 0$
d: $*_{sys}(100) = 1$ $\bar{d}$: $*_{sys}(100) = 0$

Fig. 4. Abbreviations for the conditions on the implementation of $*_{sys}$

valuation nondeterministically becomes 010 or 011. It then recurs and, unless the recursion is infinite, finishes f with valuation 000. It returns to main in that state, showing that the assertion can be violated. □

3 Repair of Boolean Programs

Suppose a Boolean program contains executions that violate an assert statement. A *repair* is a replacement of an existing statement such that the resulting program can not reach a bad state. Such a replacement can involve the choose function, and thus be nondeterministic. In this case, the program does not reach a bad state for any behavior of the nondeterministic statement.

To find repairs, a proper *fault model* has to be used. In the following, we assume that the program contains one fault, viz. an incorrect expression. This is only one possible fault model. Our algorithm is independent of the used fault model and other models could be used, including changes to the left hand side of an assignment or insertion or deletion of statements at arbitrary positions. We can thus adjust our approach to different areas of application, but this is not in the scope of this paper.

3.1 Building the Game

To compute a correct replacement for an existing expression, we extend the model checking algorithm to compute games between the environment (the antagonist) and the system (the protagonist). We extend the set of expressions with the construct $*_{sys}$. This construct represents an arbitrary function controlled by the system. The environment controls nondeterminism through the choose function.

We replace a given expression by $*_{sys}$ and ask the following question: is there an implementation for $*_{sys}$ such that the bad states are avoided regardless of the choices of the environment? We do this by negating the question and computing under which implementations of $*_{sys}$ the bad states are reached. If we then replace $*_{sys}$ by any *other* implementation, the resulting Boolean program satisfies its specification. We allow the implementation of $*_{sys}$ to be an arbitrary expression in terms of the visible variables. Thus, $*_{sys}$ does not introduce extra memory, nor can the result of $*_{sys}$ depend on the content of the stack. Computation of $*_{sys}$ corresponds to the computation of a modular strategy in [2]. In Section 3.5 we show how to attempt repair on all expressions simultaneously.

3.2 Computing the Strategy

Let P be a Boolean program $(R, \mathtt{main}, V_g)$ that contains exactly one occurrence of $*_{sys}$. In order to compute a proper implementation of $*_{sys}$, we define the game graph of P. In this graph, we may progress from one state to another under one implementation of $*_{sys}$ and not under another. This holds both for statements in which $*_{sys}$ occurs and for call statements, because the behavior of the called routine may depend on the implementation of $*_{sys}$.

Suppose that $*_{sys}$ occurs in routine r. A set of valuations $c \subseteq X_r$ defines an implementation of $*_{sys}$: for $\xi \in X_r$ we have $*_{sys}(\xi) = 1$ if and only if $\xi \in c$. Let $C = 2^{X_r}$ be the set of possible implementations.

We associate with every routine $r \in R$ a *game graph* $\mathcal{G}_r = \langle Q_r, E_r \rangle$, where Q_r is the set of states of r and $E_r \subseteq Q_r \times C \times Q_r$ is a set of labeled edges (to be defined). The game graph of P is $\mathcal{G} = \langle Q, E \rangle$, where $Q = \bigcup_{r \in R} Q_r$, $E = E_c \cup \bigcup_{r \in R} E_r$. ($E_c \subseteq Q \times S \times Q$ is defined below.) We define the reflexive transitive closure of a labeled edge relation $E \subseteq Q \times C \times Q$ as $E^* = \{(q, c, q'') \mid q = q'' \vee \exists q' : (q, c, q') \in E^* \wedge (q', c, q'') \in E\}$.

For game graphs, $\tau'_s \subseteq X_r \times C \times X_r$ takes into account the implementation of $*_{\text{sys}}$. If s is a statement that does not include $*_{\text{sys}}$ and is not a call, we have $\tau'_s = \{(\xi, c, \xi') \mid c \in C \wedge (\xi, \xi') \in \tau_s\}$. We will use an example to show how $*_{\text{sys}}$ is handled. Given an implementation c, the statement $s = (a := *_{\text{sys}})$, assigns 1 to a in states ξ with $\xi \in c$. Thus, we have

$$\tau'_s = \{(\xi, c, \xi') \mid c \in C \wedge (\xi \in c \wedge \xi' = \xi \cup \{a\}) \vee (\xi \notin c \wedge \xi' = \xi \setminus \{a\}).$$

(If the set of valuations is limited using an enforce statement, we do not include edges to impossible valuations.) Finally, if s is a call to dst,

$$\tau'_s = \{(\xi_1, c, \xi_2) \mid \exists \xi'_1, \xi'_2 :$$
$$(\xi_1, \xi'_1) \in \mu_s, ((s_{dst,0}, \xi'_1), c, (s_{dst,f}, \xi'_2)) \in E^*_{dst} \wedge \rho_s(\xi_1, \xi'_2) = \xi_2\}.$$

Now we can define

$$R_c = \{(s, \xi) \mid \exists \xi_0 : ((s_{\text{main}, 0}, \xi_0), c, (s, \xi)) \in E^*\},$$
$$E_r = \{((s, \xi), c, (s', \xi')) \mid (s, \xi) \in R_c \wedge next(\xi, s, s') \wedge (\xi, c, \xi') \in \tau'_s\},$$
$$E_c = \{((s_{src}, \xi), c, (s_{dst, 0}, \xi')) \mid s_{src} \text{ calls } dst \wedge (s_{src}, \xi) \in R_c \wedge (\xi, \xi') \in \mu_{s_{src}}\}.$$

We have the following lemma.

Lemma 1. *For $c \in C$, let P'_c be the Boolean program in which $*_{\text{sys}}$ is replaced by the function described by c. There is an edge $(q, c, q') \in E^*$ iff P'_c contains an execution that reaches q and subsequently reaches q'.*

Symbolic Computation. Iterating over all possible implementation of $*_{\text{sys}}$ is very inefficient: there are 2^{X_r} such implementations. The algorithm can be implemented symbolically using binary decision diagrams (BDDs) [7]. For each valuation $\xi \in X_r$ we introduce a BDD variable x_ξ that we refer to as a *condition*: $x_\xi = 1$ (0) iff $*_{\text{sys}}(\xi) = 1$ (0, resp.). Thus, an assignment to the variables corresponds to an implementation $c \subseteq 2^{X_r}$. We construct a BDD for τ'_s for every s and use these BDDs to construct E^* symbolically. The algorithm is analogous to the explicit one, except that we handle all possible implementations simultaneously. The number of BDD variables is exponential in the number of variables in scope, which is the major bottleneck for efficiency. Thus, our algorithm is doubly exponential in the number of variables and exponential in the number of nodes in the graph, which matches the lower bound shown in [2].

Example. We attempt to repair the Boolean program by replacing the if statement in Line 7 by $*_{\text{sys}}$. (See Fig. 1(c) for the game graph.) The edges between the states are labeled with a Boolean function over X_r that represents all implementations for that edge. The conditions are given in Fig. 4. For instance, b represents all implementations such that $*_{sys}(0, 1, 0) = 1$.

Consider state $(6, (0, 1, 1))$ of routine f. From here, an execution may nondeterministically proceed to $(7, (0, 1, 0))$ and then to Line 10, provided that $*_{sys}(0, 1, 0) = 0$. Because the other edges on the path do not restrict the implementation of $*_{sys}$, the program can proceed, from state $(6, (0, 1, 1))$ to $(10, (0, 1, 0))$ if $*_{sys}(0, 1, 0) = 0$. This condition propagates to Line 2 of main, which calls f. Thus, in main, the program proceeds from $(2, (0, 1, 1))$ to $(3, (0, 1, 0))$ if $*_{sys}(0, 1, 0) = 0$, and then violates the assertion. Thus, a successful implementation of $*_{sys}$ cannot have $*_{sys}(0, 1, 0) = 0$.   □

3.3 Extracting a Repair

To extract a repair from the game graph, we select all paths $(v, c, v') \in E^*_{main}$ that connect an initial state with a bad state. Implementations that allow these paths are faulty. The set of correct implementations is thus $I = C \setminus \bigcup \{c \mid \exists (x, c, y) \in E^* \wedge x \in I_{main} \wedge y \in bad\}$, where bad is the set of bad states.

Theorem 2. *If we replace $*_{sys}$ with any implementation $c \in I$, the resulting program contains no execution that leads to a bad state.*

If I is given symbolically, each prime implicant of I corresponds to a repair. The BDD variables V_P that appear positively in the implicant denote the conditions under which the implementation must return 1 and the negative variables V_N denote conditions under which the implementation must return 0. Thus, $*_{sys}$ must return 1 (0) for implementations ξ such that $x_\xi \in V_P$ ($x_\xi \in V_N$, resp.) Identifying variables with the conditions they denote, the repair can be given as a set of statements choose $[\bigvee_{x \in V_P} x, \bigvee_{x \in V_N} x]$, one for each (irredundant) prime implicant.

Example. Consider again Fig. 1(c). There are paths from the initial states to error states for any implementation that satisfies $ab \vee \bar{b} \vee \bar{c}$, which can be simplified to $\bar{a} \vee \bar{b} \vee \bar{c}$. Thus, $I = abc$. Therefore, the suggested repair is choose$(a \vee b \vee c, 0)$, or, in terms of predicates, *choose*$(\neg p1 \wedge (p2 \vee \neg p3), 0)$.   □

3.4 Mapping Boolean Repairs to C

Suppose the Boolean program is a conservative abstraction of the C program. A repair for a Boolean program corresponds to a repair for the C program. If we substitute the meaning of the predicates in the repair for the Boolean program, we obtain a constraint for the C program. This constraint requires that in a given line a given predicate becomes true in some situations and false in others. Any implementation that satisfies this constraint is guaranteed satisfy the specification. Note that there may be more than one implementation that satisfies the constraint. It is up to the programmer to select a good repair, depending on the intended semantics.

Example. Recall that the Boolean program that we have repaired is an abstraction of the C program in Fig. 2. The meaning of the predicates p_1, p_2, and p_3 is given in Fig. 3. The repair that we have found says that the then branch should certainly be taken if $x \neq 0 \wedge (x > 1 \vee x \leq 2)$, which is equivalent to $x \neq 0$. Substituting $x \neq 0$ in Line 8 gives the correct behavior. Note that the suggestion allows us to take the then branch also in other cases. In particular, we could satisfy it by substituting true in Line 8. Although this satisfies the specification (the assertion is never violated), it is clearly undesirable, as it introduces an infinite loop. In general, user interaction is necessary to select the desired repair from the set of possible repairs given by the algorithm. We have observed, however, that the suggested repairs are typically quite good. They reduce the number of statements to be considered to just a few and give good hints on how to modify the statements. A more realistic example is found in the next section.   □

3.5 Localizing Faults

With the graphs we defined so far, we can localize the fault by successively replacing every expression in the program by $*_{sys}$ and computing the related game graph. Expressions for which a repair is found are potential fault locations. These games differ only in the implementation of one expression. To avoid redundant computations, we compute a combined game graph for all possible repairs at one time. To this end, we compute τ' for each statement once with the original expression, and a second time for its implementation with $*_{sys}$. The combined graph is built using labels identifying the different subgraphs for the repair of each statement. Using symbolic representation, this can be done quite efficiently.

4 Experimental Results

In order to demonstrate the viability of our approach, we have performed experiments on Boolean programs constructed by the SLAM-based Static Driver Verifier [3] , using our implementation based on CUDD [16]. We examined nine bugs in drivers from the Windows operating system. We used a representative set of drivers that implemented various functionalities, including storage, input, networking, etc. For this reason we believe that the results should be repeatable for other drivers and other code of similar size and complexity. The driver's code size ranged from 2,000 to 35,000 lines of C code. (Between 1,700 and 25,000 lines in the Boolean program.)

For verification, a driver is accompanied by a test harness and an automaton. The harness is the same in every test and contains a routine that nondeterministically calls functions in the drivers API. The automaton contains code to test if a given property holds.

Table 1 lists the results of the experiments. This table contains the following information: (1) the name of the driver, (2) the number of lines of code of the Boolean program, (3) the number of expressions examined for repair, (4) the number of repairs in the Boolean program, (5) the number of repairs in the C-code of the driver (all other repairs attempt to fix the bug by changing the test harness or the automaton), (6) the overall run time, (7) number of global variables and the maximum number of local variables, (8) the results of the approach (discussed below), and (9) the name of the tested property. Table 2 contains brief and informal descriptions of the properties that we used.

We examined the repairs computed for the Boolean program and checked if they can be used for the C code of the driver. Examples where the real fault was within the set of found repairs are marked with ✓. For the remaining examples we either found

Table 1. Results from experiments with Boolean programs produced by SLAM when checking properties of Windows device drivers

Driver	LoC	# Expr.	# Total	# in Driver	Time(s)	# vars	Results	Property
1394 diag	7223	273	57	8	1345	2/10	✓	MarkIrpPending
bulltlp3.1	4751	860	30	3	16482	13/15	X^1	IrpProcComplete
daytona	14364	305	2	0	379	2/0	X^1	StartIoRecursion
gameenum	4001	217	29	1	577	2/9	✓	MarkIrpPending
hidgame	3611	335	27	4	7132	9/17	X^2	LowerDriverReturn
mousefilter	1755	165	21	3	4035	7/33	✓	PendCompleteReq
parport	24379	1055	3	1	8334	2/0	✓	DoubleCompletion
pscr	4842	374	5	0	2797	6/7	X^1	IrqlReturn
sfloppy	2216	19	6	4	4	2/0	✓	AddDevice

Table 2. Informal summary of properties listed in Table 1

Property	Summary
AddDevice	Checks that a driver's AddDevice routine calls certain key APIs.
DoubleCompletion	Checks that drivers do not complete I/O request packets twice.
IrpProcComplete	Ensures that dispatch routines completely process I/O request packets.
IrqlReturn	Checks that a driver dispatch routine's thread priority is the same at function call and exit.
LowerDriverReturn	Checks that if a driver calls another driver lower in stack, the dispatch routine will return the same status as lower driver.
MarkIrpPending	Ensures that returns of STATUS_PENDING and calls to IoMarkIrpPending are correlated.
PendCompleteReq	Checks that drivers do not return STATUS_PENDING if IoCompleteRequest has been called during the execution of the dispatch routine.
StartIoRecursion	Checks for potential recursion in a driver's StartIo routines.

no repairs, or the approach suggested only "cheating" repairs such as avoiding a call to the erroneous routine or staying in a loop forever. Missing the repair can have two reasons:X^1 marks examples where the fault was a missing call or the wrong order of calls. These faults do not fit in our fault model and thus cannot be found. X^2 marks examples where the abstraction was too coarse to find a repair.

In the rest of the section, we describe adjustments to our approach that made our approach feasible for real device drivers and we present a case study of the Windows parallel port driver.

4.1 Adjustments for Checking Windows Device Drivers

Limiting the Number of Variables Considered for Repair: While the examples contain up to 40 predicates visible at one time, many of them are temporary local variables that are uninteresting. Global variables hold information from the test harness, which give informations about the driver's environment. By reducing the number of variables considered for the implementation of $*_{sys}$, we may drastically reduce the size of the BDD. On the other hand, we can miss results that are not expressible with the limited set. No incorrect repairs are generated. For five of the examples, this heuristic was necessary to be able to compute repairs.

Parallel Assignments: Parallel assignments are hard to handle: Repairing all expressions at the same time is very inefficient. Repairing only one is usually infeasible because the assignments are tightly related and because many valuations of the predicates

```
state ( bool CompletionAlreadyCalled = 0; )

IoCompleteRequest.entry
{
    if (SdvHarnessIrp==$1) {
        if (CompletionAlreadyCalled) { error(); }
        else { CompletionAlreadyCalled = 1; }
    }
}
```

```
133 NTSTATUS
134 PptDispatchClose(PDEVICE_OBJECT DevObj,PIRP Irp) {
135     PFDO_EXTENSION fdx = DevObj->DeviceExtension;
136     P5TraceIrpArrival( DevObj, Irp );
137     if( DevTypeFdo == fdx->DevType ) {
138         return PptFdoClose( DevObj, Irp );
139     } else {
140         return PptPdoClose( DevObj, Irp );
141 } }
```

Fig. 5. Temporal property *DoubleCompletion*   **Fig. 6.** Source code from dispatchRedirect.c in Parallel port device driver

are ruled out using an enforce statement. Therefore, we searched for a new implementation of one expression, while allowing the other predicates to take arbitrary values in accordance with the enforce rule. The repairs for *1394 diag* and *gameenum* suggest new values in parallel assignments which were not possible without this optimization.

Removing Nondeterministic Functions: The abstraction refinement process starts with a nondeterministic program and adds predicates when unfeasible paths are reported. In some cases, a feasible counterexample is found before any predicates for some of the functions are discovered. Such functions induce infeasible paths which make it impossible to repair the Boolean program. In two cases, *bulltlp3.1* and *hidgame*, we removed calls to such functions from the harness in order to find repairs. In contrast to the other heuristics, this one can produce repairs which are not valid in the original C program. Tighter integration of the approach with SLAM would instead trigger further abstraction in such cases.

4.2 Case Study: Windows Parallel Port Device Driver

We will now describe how we have used our approach to find a repair for a buggy Windows parallel port device driver. The relevant code is given in Figs. 6, 7, and 8. The code in Figure 5 describes a temporal property, *DoubleCompletion*. The driver violates this property, which ensures that the device driver dispatch routines do not call the kernel-level API function IoCompleteRequest more than once on the same I/O request packet. (This example originally appears in [3]) The Windows kernel function IoCompleteRequest frees up the space of a request packet, which may then be re-allocated and passed to another thread in the system. Calling IoCompleteRequest twice with the same parameter can have disastrous consequences to the system's stability.

When trying to prove that the device driver does not violate the rule, the test harness calls the device driver's dispatch routines nondeterministically, using an I/O request packet called SdvHarnessIrp. The erroneous execution is as follows. The test harness calls the parallel port device driver's *close* dispatch routine PptDispatchClose (Fig. 6, Line 134) on the I/O request packet SdvHarnessIrp. The function IoCompleteRequest will erroneously be called twice on this package. When PptFdoClose (Fig. 7, Line 4) is called, we enter the conditional statement at Line 14 and call P4CompleteRequest (Fig. 8, Line 1774). Then, in Line 1782, IoCompleteRequest is called on SdvHarnessIrp and the function returns to the call site. We then leave the conditional statement via the goto on Line 18. At Line 60 P4CompleteRequestReleaseRemLock (Fig. 8, Line 1786) is called, which itself calls P4CompleteRequest and thus makes the second call to IoCompleteRequest on SdvHarnessIrp.

```
04 NTSTATUS PptFdoClose(
05   IN  PDEVICE_OBJECT  DeviceObject,
06   IN  PIRP            Irp
07 ) {
08   PFDO_EXTENSION fdx=DeviceObject->DeviceExtension;
09   NTSTATUS       status;
10
11   PAGED_CODE();
12
13   // Verify that device was not SUPRISE_REMOVED.
14   if(fdx->PnpState & PPT_DEVICE_SURPRISE_REMOVED) {
15     // Our device has been SURPRISE removed, but
16     // since this is a CLOSE, SUCCEED anyway
17     status=P4CompleteRequest(Irp,STATUS_SUCCESS,0);
18     goto target_exit;
19   }
...
59   target_exit:
60   DD((PCE)fdx,DDT,"PptFdoClose - ........");
61   return P4CompleteRequestReleaseRemLock(
62        Irp, STATUS_SUCCESS, 0, &fdx->RemoveLock);
63 }
```

Fig. 7. Source code from fdoClose.c in Parallel port device driver

```
1774 NTSTATUS P4CompleteRequest(
1775   IN PIRP       Irp,
1776   IN NTSTATUS   Status,
1777   IN ULONG_PTR  Information
1778 ){
1779   P5TraceIrpCompletion(Irp);
1780   Irp->IoStatus.Status      = Status;
1781   Irp->IoStatus.Information = Information;
1782   IoCompleteRequest(Irp,IO_NO_INCREMENT);
1783   return Status;
1784 }
1785
1786 NTSTATUS P4CompleteRequestReleaseRemLock(
1787   IN PIRP       Irp,
1788   IN NTSTATUS   Status,
1789   IN ULONG_PTR  Information,
1790   IN PIO_REMOVE_LOCK RemLock
1791 ) {
1792   P4CompleteRequest(Irp,Status,Information);
1793   PptReleaseRemoveLock(RemLock,Irp);
1794   return Status;
1795 }
```

Fig. 8. Source code from util.c in Parallel port device driver

```
1 void P4CompleteRequest_2() begin
2   if( *sys ) then
3       goto L7;
4   else
5       goto L8;
6   fi
7 L8: SLIC_IoCompleteRequest_entry_51();
8 L7: IoCompleteRequest_1();
9   return ;
10 end
```

Fig. 9. Boolean routine from abstraction of P4-CompleteRequest (Fig. 8, line 1775)

```
if (SdvHarnessIrp==R) {
  if (CompletionAlreadyCalled) {}
  else {
    CompletionAlreadyCalled = 1;
    IoCompleteRequest(R);
  }
}
```

Fig. 10. Replacement for the call of Io-CompleteRequest in P4CompleteRequest

Our algorithm finds three repairs for the Boolean program, including Line 2 of routine P4CompleteRequest_2, shown in Fig. 9, which is the abstraction of the routine P4CompleteRequest. The abstraction of the driver contains two predicates: g0: CompletionAlreadyCalled $\neq 0$ and g1: done $\neq 0$. We know the predicate CompletionAlready-Called from the safety property. Variable done is defined by the SDV harness and is true iff we are still verifying the property (Irp is still equal to SdvHarnessIrp). The if statement in Line 2 decides whether or not to call SLIC_IoCompleteRequest_entry_51 which executed an abstracted version of the rule-checking code in Fig. 5. The original

Fig. 11. Tool for viewing the repairs. On the left, we can choose which repair to examine. The text fields give details on the repair and the corresponding parts of the Boolean program and C code.

routine, IoCompleteRequest_1(), is called in any case. The suggested repair for Line 2 is `if(choose[g0&&!g1,0])`, which means we may not enter IoCompleteRequest if we are still checking the property and CompletionAlreadyCalled is 0. A screen shot of the tool used to examine the repairs is given in Fig.11.

A possible implementation of this result in the driver is to add a new variable CompletionAlreadyCalled that is initialized to zero (as in the automaton) and a variable SdvHarnessIrp which is initialized to the value of the I/O request packet passed into the driver dispatch routine. Thus, we repair the driver by replacing the call to IoCompleteRequest in P4CompleteRequest by the code given in Fig. 10. Note that the repair of the Boolean program is memoryless because the automaton that implements the temporal property is included in the Boolean program. For the C program this is not the case, and we need to add a variable.

5   Conclusions

Modern software model checkers provide counterexamples when they disprove a property. While clearly useful, counterexamples are not what the programmer is eventually wants: *a correct program*. In this paper we have presented a method to automatically suggest repairs in Boolean program. Given a model checker for C that uses Boolean programs as an abstraction, we can use this method to fix faults in C programs. If a repair is found for the Boolean program, then there is a repair for the C program. Our approach often yields useful results, as shown by the application of our algorithm to buggy Windows device drivers.

Future research includes finding fixes for violations of liveness constraints such as infinite recursion. It would also be interesting to integrate repair and refinement more tightly, by adding new predicates when needed for repair. Our approach is inefficient when there are many Boolean variables in scope at the same time. One way to speed the algorithm up may be a preprocessing step by a fault localization tool to narrow down the set of suspect statements. Finally, our fault model may not be ideal. Instead of replacing existing expressions, we may need to consider other repairs, such as the insertion of statements. The theory presented here works regardless of the fault model.

Acknowledgments

The authors would like to thank Ranjit Jhala and the anonymous reviewers for their valuable comments. This work was supported in part by the European Commission under contract 507219 (PROSYD).

References

[1] R. Alur and T. A. Henzinger. Reactive modules. *Formal Methods in System Design*, 15:7–48, 1999.
[2] R. Alur, S. La Torre, and P. Madhusudan. Modular strategies for recursive game graphs. In *Tools and Algorithms for the Construction and the Analysis of Systems (TACAS'03)*, pages 363–378, 2003.

[3] T. Ball, E. Bounimova, B. Cook, V. Levin, J. Lichtenberg, C. McGarvey, B. Ondrusek, S. K. Rajamani, and A. Ustuner. Thorough static analysis of device drivers. In *European Systems Conference (EuroSys'06)*, 2006.

[4] T. Ball, M. Naik, and S. K. Rajamani. From symptom to cause: Localizing errors in counterexample traces. In *30th Symposium on Principles of Programming Languages (POPL 2003)*, pages 97–105, 2003.

[5] T. Ball and S. K. Rajamani. Bebop: A symbolic model checker for Boolean programs. In *SPIN 00: SPIN Workshop*, pages 113–130. 2000.

[6] A. Bouajjani, J. Esparza, and O. Maler. Reachability analysis of pushdown automata: Application to model checking. In *Proc. 8th Int. Conf. on Concurrency Theory (CONCUR'97)*, pages 135–150. 1997.

[7] R. E. Bryant. Symbolic boolean manipulation with ordered binary decision diagrams. *ACM Computing Surveys*, 24:293–318, 1992.

[8] S. Chaki, A. Groce, and O. Strichman. Explaining abstract counterexamples. In *Proc. of the International Symposium on Foundations of Software Engineering*, pages 73–82, 2004.

[9] B. Demsky and M. Rinard. Automatic detection and repair of errors in data structures. In *Conference on Object-Oriented Programming, Systems, Languages, and Applications (OOPSLA'03)*, pages 78–95, 2003.

[10] J. Esparza, D. Hansel, P. Rossmanith, and S. Schwoon. Efficient algorithms for model checking pushdown systems. In *Twelfth Conference on Computer Aided Verification (CAV'00)*, pages 324–336. Springer-Verlag, 2000.

[11] S. Graf and H. Saïdi. Construction of abstract state graphs with PVS. In *Ninth Conference on Computer Aided Verification (CAV'97)*, pages 72–83. 1997.

[12] A. Groce. Error explanation with distance metrics. In *Tools and Algorithms for Construction and Analysis of Systems (TACAS'04)*, pages 108–122, 2004.

[13] B. Jobstmann, A. Griesmayer, and R. Bloem. Program repair as a game. In *17th Conference on Computer Aided Verification (CAV'05)*, pages 226–238 2005.

[14] S. Khurshid, I. García, and Y. Suen. Repairing structurally complex data. In *SPIN Workshop on Model Checking of Software (SPIN'05)*, pages 123–138, 2005.

[15] T. Reps, S. Horwitz, and S. Sagiv. Precise interprocedural dataflow analysis via graph reachability. In *Symposium on Principles of Programming Languages*, pages 49–61, 1995.

[16] F. Somenzi. *CUDD: CU Decision Diagram Package*. University of Colorado at Boulder, ftp://vlsi.colorado.edu/pub/.

[17] S. Staber, B. Jobstmann, and R. Bloem. Finding and fixing faults. In *13th Conference on Correct Hardware Design and Verification Methods (CHARME '05)*, pages 35–49. 2005.

[18] I. Walukiewicz. Pushdown processes: Games and model-checking. *Information and Computation*, 157:234–263, 2000.

[19] A. Zeller. Isolating cause-effect chains from computer programs. In *10th Int. Symp. on the Foundations of Software Engineering (FSE-10)*, pages 1–10, November 2002.

Termination of Integer Linear Programs

Mark Braverman*

Department of Computer Science
University of Toronto

Abstract. We show that termination of a simple class of linear loops over the integers is decidable. Namely we show that termination of deterministic linear loops is decidable over the integers in the homogeneous case, and over the rationals in the general case. This is done by analyzing the powers of a matrix symbolically using its eigenvalues. Our results generalize the work of Tiwari [Tiw04], where similar results were derived for termination over the reals. We also gain some insights into termination of non-homogeneous integer programs, that are very common in practice.

1 Introduction

Termination analysis is one of the building blocks of automated verification. For a generic loop

    while (*conditions*)   { *commands* }

it is well known that the termination problem is undecidable in all but the most simple cases. Even when all the conditions and updates are given as piecewise linear functions, the problem of deciding termination of the loop remains undecidable since such programs can naturally simulate counter machines [Tiw04], and the problem of whether a counter machine terminates on all inputs is undecidable [BBK+01].

In view of the undecidability mentioned above, the efforts on practical termination analysis of loops have been concentrated on partial decision procedures. One approach is synthesizing a *ranking function*. Synthesis of ranking functions has been studied in [CSS03, BMP05a, BMP05b]. In some cases, one can even find a complete method for synthesis of *linear* ranking functions [PR04]. Even a complete synthesis method, however, can only establish existence of a certain way of proving termination, and not actually decide the termination problem itself. It is not hard to construct an example of a program that terminates but has no linear ranking function.

The termination problem appears to be much harder, and one can expect it to be decidable only in the simplest cases. In [Tiw04] termination has been shown to be decidable for loops of the form

    while $(Bx > b)$ { $x \leftarrow Ax + c$ }

where $Bx > b$ represents a conjunction of linear inequalities over the state variables x, and $x \leftarrow Ax + c$ represents a (deterministic) linear update of each

---

* Partially supported by an NSERC postgraduate scholarship.

T. Ball and R.B. Jones (Eds.): CAV 2006, LNCS 4144, pp. 372–385, 2006.

variable. The variables are interpreted over the reals $\mathbb{R}$, and there are no constraints on the initial conditions. Roughly speaking, [Tiw04] shows that only the subspace corresponding to eigenvectors of A with positive real eigenvalues is relevant to the termination problem. In the homogeneous case

while $(Bx > 0)$ $\{\; x \leftarrow Ax \;\}$

it is immediate to see that if there is an eigenvector v of A such that $Av = \lambda v$, $\lambda > 0$ and $Bv > 0$, then the loop is non-terminating on v. The decision procedure depends on the fact that the inequality $Bx > 0$ is strict. More importantly, it depends on the fact that the variables are interpreted over the *reals*. As the following example illustrates, a program may be terminating over the integers, but not over the reals.

Example 1. Consider the homogeneous loop

$$\textbf{while}\;\; (4x + y > 0)\;\; \left\{\; \begin{pmatrix} x \\ y \end{pmatrix} \leftarrow \begin{pmatrix} -2 & 4 \\ 4 & 0 \end{pmatrix} \begin{pmatrix} x \\ y \end{pmatrix} \;\right\}$$

The matrix has two eigenvectors, $(-1-\sqrt{17}, 4)$ and $(-1+\sqrt{17}, 4)$ corresponding to eigenvalues $-1 - \sqrt{17}$ and $-1 + \sqrt{17}$, respectively.

The eigenvector $(-1+\sqrt{17}, 4)$ satisfies the loop condition, and corresponds to a positive eigenvalue. Hence the loop does not terminate over $\mathbb{R}$. However, the line $(-1 + \sqrt{17}, 4)\alpha$ does not contain any rational points, and the loop outside this line is always dominated by the eigenvalue $-1 - \sqrt{17} < 0$ that is bigger in absolute value than the other eigenvalue. At the limit, the orbit of (x, y) will alternate between the directions $(-1 - \sqrt{17}, 4)$ and $(1 + \sqrt{17}, -4)$. Hence the loop terminates on all integers.   ∎

The example highlights the difference between the integer and the real case. In general, it is not unusual to have differences between hardness of decidability of problems over the reals $\mathbb{R}$ and problems over the integers $\mathbb{Z}$. One notorious example is *quantifier elimination*. Given a quantified formula

$$Q_1 x_1 Q_2 x_2 \ldots Q_n x_n \;\; f(x_1, \ldots, x_n),$$

there is an algorithm to decide its validity over $\mathbb{R}$ [Tar51], but not over $\mathbb{Z}$. In fact, by undecidability of Diophantine equations [Mat93], the formula above is undecidable even in the case when $Q_i = \exists$ for all i.

It has been conjectured in [Tiw04] that the termination of programs as above is still decidable when interpreted over the integers. In this paper we prove the following:

Theorem 1. *Let A, B_s, B_w be rational matrices and b_s, b_w, c be rational vectors. Then the termination problem of the loop*

while $(B_s x > b_s) \wedge (B_w x \geq b_w)$ $\{\; x \leftarrow Ax + c \;\}$

is decidable when the variables range over the reals $\mathbb{R}$ or the rationals $\mathbb{Q}$. It is decidable over the integers $\mathbb{Z}$ in the homogeneous case when $b_s, b_w, c = 0$.

Theorem 1 settles the termination problem over the rationals for a linear loop with a deterministic update and no initial conditions in the most general form.

Using Lemma 4 on linear combinations of sums of powers of complex units, we are able to deal with non-strict inequalities. Over the integers termination in the *non-homogeneous* case remains an intriguing open problem. We will return to it in Section 6.

In practice, the programs are usually specified over integer variables, and it is encouraging to know that the termination of homogeneous loops as above is still decidable in this setting. Most of the paper is dedicated to proving Theorem 1.

2   Proof Outline of Theorem 1

The main part of the proof is in deciding termination over $\mathbb{Q}$ for homogeneous programs (i.e. programs for which $b_s, b_w, c = 0$). Unlike the termination analysis over $\mathbb{R}$ [Tiw04], we cannot ignore the vectors corresponding to negative and complex eigenvalues. As illustrated in the following example, it is possible that there are no rational points on the non-terminating subspace S^+ corresponding to the positive eigenvalues of A, but there is a rational vector outside S^+ very close to it, and on which the loop is still non-terminating.

Example 2. Consider the loop

$$\textbf{while } (4x - 5y > 0) \ \left\{ \ \begin{pmatrix} x \\ y \end{pmatrix} \leftarrow \begin{pmatrix} 2 & 4 \\ 4 & 0 \end{pmatrix} \begin{pmatrix} x \\ y \end{pmatrix} \ \right\}$$

The matrix has two eigenvectors, $(1+\sqrt{17}, 4)$ and $(1-\sqrt{17}, 4)$ corresponding to eigenvalues $1+\sqrt{17}$ and $1-\sqrt{17}$, respectively. The only eigenvector in S^+ is $v_1 = (1+\sqrt{17}, 4)$, which satisfies the loop condition, but contains no rational points. However, the orbit of a rational perturbation q_1 of v_1 converges to the direction of v_1 at the limit. Hence it is possible to choose q_1 that is a nonterminating rational initial condition, and the loop is non-terminating over $\mathbb{Q}$ despite the fact that there are no rational points in S^+. The point $q_1 = (9,7)$ is an example of a specific such value. Note that $\left| \frac{9}{7} - \frac{1+\sqrt{17}}{4} \right| < 0.005$, which means that q_1 is a good rational approximation of v_1. ∎

We will see that the set N of real points for which the program is non-terminating is a convex cone. Hence it has a dimension and a unique minimal linear space S_{min} containing it. The rough outline of the procedure for finding a rational point in N (i.e. in $\mathbb{Q}^n \cap N$) is as follows:

Termination (*loop P*)
compute S_{min}
$Q_{min} \leftarrow S_{min} \cap \mathbb{Q}^n$
if $Q_{min} = \emptyset$
    return *terminating*
if $dim(Q_{min}) = dim(S_{min})$
    return *non-terminating*
else
    reduce the loop to a loop P' on the subspace Q_{min}
    run **Termination**(P')

At each iteration, S_{min} is the current feasible real subspace, and Q_{min} its rational subspace. We continuously update both until their dimensions match or until Q_{min} becomes empty. If the dimensions match, we know that Q_{min} is dense in N, and we can return *non-terminating*. If Q_{min} becomes empty, we can return *terminating*. At each iteration we reduce the dimension of the loop by at least 1, hence the algorithm terminates. The crucial step in the computation is the ability to compute S_{min} at each step of the iteration.

Running the procedure on Example 1 above, we would obtain that S_{min} is the one-dimensional space $span\{(-1 + \sqrt{17}, 4)\}$, and $Q_{min} = \{0\}$, thus outputting **terminating**. On the other hand, for Example 2 above we would obtain $S_{min} = \mathbb{R}^2$, and $Q_{min} = \mathbb{Q}^2$, thus $dim(Q_{min}) = dim(S_{min})$, and we output **non-terminating**.

3 Preliminaries

3.1 Linear Algebra

We will see that symbolically powering the matrix A is an essential step in deciding termination of the loop. If A is similar to some matrix D via $A = P^{-1}DP$ then

$$A^n = (P^{-1}DP)^n = (P^{-1}DP)(P^{-1}DP)\ldots(P^{-1}DP) = P^{-1}D^n P.$$

Hence powering the matrix A is as hard as powering the matrix D. We would like to make D as simple as possible. It is well known from linear algebra [HK71] that any A can be transformed into *Jordan canonical form*:

Lemma 2 (Jordan canonical form). *For any matrix $A \in \mathbb{C}^{n \times n}$ there is a matrix P, and a matrix D of the form $D = Diag(J_1, J_2, \ldots, J_N)$ with each block J_i having the form*

$$J_i = \begin{pmatrix} \lambda_i & 1 & 0 & \ldots & 0 \\ 0 & \lambda_i & 1 & \ldots & 0 \\ \vdots & \vdots & \vdots & \ddots & \vdots \\ 0 & 0 & 0 & \ddots & 1 \\ 0 & 0 & 0 & \ldots & \lambda_i \end{pmatrix},$$

where λ_i is an eigenvalue of A and $A = P^{-1}DP$. Moreover, if A is an algebraic matrix, then D and P are also algebraic matrices and their entries can be computed from the entries of A.

Next, we explicitly write the n-th power of the matrix D. The formula can be proved by induction on n.

Lemma 3. *For a matrix $D = Diag(J_1, \ldots, J_N)$ in Jordan canonical form, its n-th power is given by $D^n = Diag(J_1^n, J_2^n, \ldots, J_N^n)$, where*

$$
J_i^n = \begin{pmatrix}
\lambda_i^n & n\lambda_i^{n-1} & \binom{n}{2}\lambda_i^{n-2} & \cdots & \binom{n}{N_i-1}\lambda_i^{n-(N_i-1)} \\
0 & \lambda_i^n & n\lambda_i^{n-1} & \cdots & \binom{n}{N_i-2}\lambda_i^{n-(N_i-2)} \\
\vdots & \vdots & \ddots & \ddots & \vdots \\
0 & 0 & \ddots & \lambda_i^n & n\lambda_i^{n-1} \\
0 & 0 & \cdots & 0 & \lambda_i^n
\end{pmatrix},
$$

where N_i is the dimension of the block J_i, and $\binom{n}{k} = 0$ if $n < k$.

3.2 A Lemma About Complex Units

Let $\zeta \neq 1$ be a complex number on the unit circle, that is, $|\zeta| = 1$. It is easy to see that the orbit $\zeta, \zeta^2, \zeta^3, \ldots$ will visit the negative half of the complex plane infinitely often. We need a generalization of this fact to a linear combination of such ζ's.

Lemma 4. *Let $\zeta_1, \zeta_2, \ldots, \zeta_m \in \mathbb{C}$ be a collection of distinct complex numbers such that $|\zeta_i| = 1$ and $\zeta_i \neq 1$ for all i. Let $\alpha_1, \alpha_2, \ldots, \alpha_m$ be any complex numbers. Denote*

$$
z_n = \alpha_1 \zeta_1^n + \alpha_2 \zeta_2^n + \ldots + \alpha_m \zeta_m^n.
$$

Then one of the following is true:

1. *the real part $Re(z_n) = 0$ for all n; or*
2. *there is a $c < 0$ such that $Re(z_n) < c$ for infinitely many n's.*

We will be interested in the case when $z_n \in \mathbb{R}$ are all reals. In this case we have $Re(z_n) = z_n$ for all n, and the lemma applies directly to z_n.

Proof. Due to space constraints, we will only present a proof idea here. First of all, we can write

$$
y_n = 2Re(z_n) = z_n + \bar{z}_n = \alpha_1 \zeta_1^n + \ldots + \alpha_m \zeta_m^n + \bar{\alpha}_1 \bar{\zeta}_1^n + \ldots + \bar{\alpha}_m \bar{\zeta}_m^n \in \mathbb{R}.
$$

After collecting together terms where $\zeta_i = \bar{\zeta}_j$, we see that the claim for y_n is equivalent to the claim for the z_n, but now $y_n \in \mathbb{R}$ for all n. Hence it suffices to prove the lemma under the assumption $z_n \in \mathbb{R}$. We actually show that if z_n is not syntactically 0, then the second possibility above holds.

The two key claims of the proof are that

1. The cumulative sum of the z_n is bounded from above: $\left| \sum_{n=0}^{N} z_n \right| \leq C_1$, where $C_1 > 0$ is some explicit constant.

2. The sum of absolute values $|z_n|$ is bounded from below: $\sum_{n=N+1}^{N+m} |z_n| > C_2$ for each N for some explicit constant $C_2 > 0$.

Both claims are not too hard to prove, and together they yield the statement of the lemma: Choose an integer K such that $K \cdot C_2 > 4C_1$. Then for any N we have by the first claim

$$\sum_{n=N+1}^{N+Km} z_n = \sum_{n=0}^{N+Km} z_n - \sum_{n=0}^{N} z_n < 2C_1.$$

On the other hand, by the second claim we have

$$\sum_{n=N+1}^{N+Km} |z_n| = \sum_{i=0}^{K-1} \sum_{n=N+mi+1}^{N+mi+m} |z_n| > K \cdot C_2 > 4C_1.$$

These together imply that

$$\sum_{n=N+1,\, z_n<0}^{N+Km} z_n < -C_1.$$

Hence there is an $n \in \{N+1, \ldots, N+Km\}$ such that $z_n < -C_1/(Km)$.

Set $c = -C_1/(Km)$. We have just seen that there is a z_n satisfying $z_n < c$ among any Km consecutive elements. This completes the proof of Lemma 4.

Remark: It is also possible to give a less constructive proof of Lemma 4 using ergodic theory. ∎

4 Termination over $\mathbb{Q}$ and $\mathbb{R}$ in the Homogeneous Case

In this section we assume that the loop is homogeneous, that is $c, b_s, b_w = 0$. Let N be the set of nonterminating points of the program over $\mathbb{R}^n$. We are interested in determining whether N and $N \cap \mathbb{Q}^n$ are empty.

For a point $z \in \mathbb{R}^n$ we consider the evolution of the loop with initial variables vector z. We denote the value of the variables after i iterations by $z(i) = A^i z$. In particular $z(0) = z$. $z \in N$ if and only if $z(i)$ satisfies the loop conditions $B_s z(i) > 0$ and $B_w z(i) \geq 0$ for all $i \geq 0$.

First, we note that N is a convex cone.

Lemma 5. *Assuming $N \neq \emptyset$, N must be a convex cone. That is, for every $x, y \in N$ and $\lambda > 0$, $\lambda x \in N$, and the line segment connecting x to y belongs to N.*

Proof. Since the loop is homogeneous, the execution on x will run for exactly as long as the execution on λx. In particular if the loop does not terminate on x, it will not terminate on λx. Suppose that initially z is on the line segment connecting x with y. Then $z(0) = z = \alpha x + (1-\alpha)y$ for some $\alpha \in [0,1]$. On the n-th iteration we have

$$z(n) = \alpha x(n) + (1-\alpha)y(n),$$

is still on the line segment connecting $x(n)$ with $y(n)$, and

$$B_s z(n) = \alpha B_s x(n) + (1 - \alpha) B_s y(n) > 0,$$
$$B_w z(n) = \alpha B_w x(n) + (1 - \alpha) B_w y(n) \geq 0,$$

because the loop does not terminate on both x and y.   ∎

N is a convex body in $\mathbb{R}^n$ and as such, has a dimension d_N, which is the rank of the smallest subspace containing N. Determining the minimum linear space $S_{min} = span\{N\}$ containing N is central to the construction.

4.1   Finding the Minimum Space $S_{min} \supset N$

Intuition: N is a convex cone. If we consider N as a subset on S_{min}, we see that it has an interior $int(N)$, and for any point x in the interior small perturbations $x + \varepsilon v$ of x remain in N if and only if $v \in S_{min}$. The v's for which $x + \varepsilon v$ is in N span S_{min}. We first find such an x, we call z_{max}, and then generate all the small perturbations that leave z_{max} in N in order to get a linear basis for S_{min}.

We are interested in the behavior of the loop with initial condition $z(0)$. In particular, we would like to know whether $z(i) = A^i z(0)$ always satisfies the loop conditions. Since we know the Jordan canonical form of A, we can explicitly write the **while** condition after i steps as

$$\begin{cases} B_s A^i z(0) > 0 \\ B_w A^i z(0) \geq 0 \end{cases} \Leftrightarrow \begin{cases} B_s P^{-1} D^i P z(0) > 0 \\ B_w P^{-1} D^i P z(0) \geq 0 \end{cases} \tag{1}$$

where $D = PAP^{-1} = Diag(J_1, \ldots, J_N)$ is the Jordan canonical form of A.

Our next goal is to use (1) to write the conditions on $z(i)$ in an explicit form. Let $0 < \lambda_1 < \lambda_2 < \ldots < \lambda_r$ be the absolute values of the eigenvalues of A sorted in the increasing order. We only consider the nonzero eigenvalues here. Let $\{\zeta_{ij}\}$ be complex numbers on the unit circle, $|\zeta_{ij}| = 1$, and $\zeta_{ij} \neq 1$ such that the eigenvalues of A are a subset of

$$\{\lambda_1, \lambda_1\zeta_{11}, \lambda_1\zeta_{12}, \ldots, \lambda_1\zeta_{1m_1}, \lambda_2, \lambda_2\zeta_{21}, \lambda_2\zeta_{22}, \ldots, \lambda_2\zeta_{2m_2}, \ldots,$$
$$\lambda_r, \lambda_r\zeta_{r1}, \lambda_r\zeta_{r2}, \ldots, \lambda_r\zeta_{rm_r}\}.$$

The ζ_{ij} are the arguments of the corresponding eigenvalues. By Lemma 3, symbolically, D^i is a linear combination of

$$\{\lambda_1^i, \lambda_1^i\zeta_{11}^i, \lambda_1^i\zeta_{12}^i, \ldots, \lambda_1^i\zeta_{1m_1}^i, i\lambda_1^{i-1}, i\lambda_1^{i-1}\zeta_{11}^{i-1}, i\lambda_1^{i-1}\zeta_{12}^{i-1}, \ldots, i\lambda_1^i\zeta_{1m_1}^{i-1}, \ldots,$$

$$\binom{i}{n_1-1}\lambda_1^{i-(n_1-1)}, \binom{i}{n_1-1}\lambda_1^{i-(n_1-1)}\zeta_{11}^{i-(n_1-1)}, \ldots,$$

$$\binom{i}{n_1-1}\lambda_1^{i-(n_1-1)}\zeta_{1m_1}^{i-(n_1-1)}, \lambda_2^i, \lambda_2^i\zeta_{21}^i, \lambda_2^i\zeta_{22}^i, \ldots, \lambda_2^i\zeta_{2m_2}^i, \ldots$$

$$\lambda_r^i, \lambda_r^i\zeta_{r1}^i, \lambda_r^i\zeta_{r2}^i, \ldots, \lambda_r^i\zeta_{rm_r}^i, \ldots, \binom{i}{n_r-1}\lambda_r^{i-(n_r-1)},$$

$$\binom{i}{n_r-1}\lambda_r^{i-(n_r-1)}\zeta_{r1}^{i-(n_r-1)}, \ldots, \binom{i}{n_r-1}\lambda_r^{i-(n_r-1)}\zeta_{rm_r}^{i-(n_r-1)}\}$$

Thus we can rewrite (1) as a set of conditions on the initial $z(0)$ of the form

$$Cond_k(z(0), i) = \lambda_1^i (C_{k11} + \zeta_{11}^i N_{k111} + \zeta_{12}^i N_{k112} + \ldots + \zeta_{1m_1}^i N_{k11m_1}) z(0) +$$

$$i\lambda_1^{i-1}(C_{k12} + \zeta_{11}^{i-1} N_{k121} + \zeta_{12}^{i-1} N_{k122} + \ldots + \zeta_{1m_1}^{i-1} N_{k12m_1}) z(0) + \ldots +$$

$$\binom{i}{n_1 - 1} \lambda_1^{i-(n_1-1)} (C_{k1n_1} + \zeta_{11}^{i-(n_1-1)} N_{k1n_11} + \zeta_{12}^{i-(n_1-1)} N_{k1n_12} + \ldots +$$

$$\zeta_{1m_1}^{i-(n_1-1)} N_{k1n_1m_1}) z(0) + \ldots +$$

$$\lambda_r^i (C_{kr1} + \zeta_{r1}^i N_{kr11} + \zeta_{r2}^i N_{kr12} + \ldots + \zeta_{rm_1}^i N_{kr1m_r}) z(0) +$$

$$i\lambda_r^{i-1}(C_{kr2} + \zeta_{r1}^{i-1} N_{kr21} + \zeta_{r2}^{i-1} N_{kr22} + \ldots + \zeta_{rm_r}^{i-1} N_{kr2m_r}) z(0) + \ldots +$$

$$\binom{i}{n_r - 1} \lambda_r^{i-(n_r-1)} (C_{krn_r} + \zeta_{r1}^{i-(n_r-1)} N_{krn_r1} + \zeta_{r2}^{i-(n_r-1)} N_{krn_r2} + \ldots +$$

$$\zeta_{rm_r}^{i-(n_r-1)} N_{krn_rm_r}) z(0) \rhd 0,$$

where $\rhd \in \{>, \geq\}$. The coefficients $C_{kj\ell}$ and $N_{kj\ell t}$ are all algebraic vectors and can be computed explicitly. Moreover, in our case all the conditions and A are over the reals, hence every coefficient $\sum_{t=1}^{m_j} N_{kj\ell t} \zeta_{jt}^i$ will add up to a real number. A point $z(0)$ is in N if and only if the conditions $Cond_k(z(0), i)$ are satisfied for all k and for all $i = 0, 1, 2 \ldots$.

Using the Jordan canonical form of A, we can split the space $\mathbb{R}^n$ into the subspace S^+ corresponding to the positive eigenvalues of A, and the subspace S^o corresponding to the other eigenvalues. Each $v \in \mathbb{R}^n$ decomposes uniquely into a sum $v = v^+ + v^o$ such that $v^+ \subset S^+$ and $v^o \in S^o$. If we write $Cond_k(z(0)^+, i)$ we get all $N_{kj\ell t}$'s equal to zero, since there are no vectors in S^+ corresponding to the complex eigenvalues. Similarly, in $Cond_k(z(0)^o, i)$ we get all $C_{kj\ell}$'s equal to zero.

Observe that the magnitude of the terms

$$C_{kj\ell} + \zeta_{j1}^i N_{kj\ell 1} + \zeta_{j2}^i N_{kj\ell 2} + \ldots \zeta_{jm_j}^i N_{kj\ell m_j}$$

remains bounded by a constant independent of i throughout the iteration. Hence the magnitude of the components of $Cond_k(z(0))$ as i tends to ∞ is primarily dictated by the $\binom{i}{\ell - 1} \lambda_j^{i-(\ell-1)}$ terms of the products. These terms have a clear dominance order as $i \to \infty$. For higher j the terms grow geometrically faster, because $\lambda_{j_1}^i \ll \lambda_{j_2}^i$ for $j_1 < j_2$. For the same j, terms with higher ℓ grow polynomially faster, because $\binom{i}{\ell_1 - 1} \ll \binom{i}{\ell_2 - 1}$ for $\ell_1 < \ell_2$. This yields a natural lexicographic order $\prec$ on the pairs of indexes $j\ell$:

$$Ind = \{0 \prec 11 \prec 12 \prec \ldots \prec 1n_1 \prec 21 \prec \ldots \prec 2n_2 \prec \ldots \prec r1 \prec \ldots \prec rn_r\}.$$

The term 0 is the smallest term, it is introduced for completeness in the case of non-strict inequalities. It does not correspond to any actual index.

Our first step is very similar to [Tiw04]: we solve the problem over the positive eigenspace S^+.

Lemma 6. *For every vector $z \in S^+$ the program with initial conditions $A^q z$ is non-terminating for some integer $q \geq 0$ if and only if there is a function*

$$index_z : k \mapsto index_z(k) \in Ind$$

which maps the condition $Cond_k(z)$ to the highest ranking nonzero $C_{k,index_z(k)}$. All higher ranking coefficients must be zero. In other words, for each k,

$$\begin{cases} C_{k,ind} z = 0, & \text{if } ind \succ index_z(k) \\ C_{k,ind} z > 0, & \text{if } ind = index_z(k) \end{cases}$$

In the case that the k-th inequality is strict we must have $index_z(k) \succ 0$.

Proof. First of all note that since z is in S^+, only the $C_{k,ind}$ (and no $N_{k,ind,t}$'s) appear in the expressions for $Cond_k(z, i)$.

It is obvious that for $A^q z$ to be non-terminating for some q the conditions $Cond_k(z, i)$ must be satisfied as $i \to \infty$. In particular, the highest ranking coefficient, which dominates the behavior as i goes to infinity must be positive (or all of them may be 0 in the case of a non-strict inequality). Note that $index_z$ is a well-defined function for each such z.

Conversely, if the $index_z(k)$ function as in the statement of the lemma exists, then the dominating term in each $Cond_k(z, i)$ has a positive coefficient. Hence the conditions $Cond_k(z, i)$ are satisfied for sufficiently large i. In particular, there is a q such that they are satisfied for $i \geq q$, making the program non-terminating on $A^q z$.   ∎

We denote the set of z's for which $A^q z \in N$ for some q by N^e – "eventually non-terminating". Those are the points which might be terminating, but become non-terminating after finitely many applications of A. Lemma 6 gives a characterization of N^e, and associates a unique function $index_z$ with each $z \in N^e$. We claim that there is a maximum such function.

Lemma 7. *There is a $z_{max} \in N \cap S^+$ with an index function $index_{z_{max}} = index_{max}$ such that for any $z \in N \cap S^+$, for all k,*

$$index_z(k) \preceq index_{max}(k).$$

Proof. First we note that N^e is convex. If $z_1, z_2 \in N^e$, then there is a q such that $A^q z_1, A^q z_2 \in N$. N is convex, hence the line segment I connecting $A^q z_1$ to $A^q z_2$ is in N. The line segment connecting z_1 to z_2 is mapped to I by A^q, hence it is in N^e.

Denote $z = (z_1 + z_2)/2$. Then it is easy to see that

$$index_z = \max(index_{z_1}, index_{z_2}).$$

Thus, there can be only one maximal index function, which is the maximum index function for some $z'_{max} \in N^e \cap S^+$. We can take sufficiently many iterations of z'_{max} to obtain $z_{max} \in N \cap S^+$.

Note that it is easy to compute z_{max} and $index_{max}$ by considering the constraint satisfaction problem corresponding to each index function and choosing the maximum feasible function and a corresponding z_{max}. In fact, a generic element y of $N \cap S^+$ satisfies $index_y = index_{max}$. ∎

As mentioned in the beginning of the section, the main idea in finding the minimal space S_{min} containing N is that it is spanned by small perturbations of z_{max}. The claim is that a small perturbation of z_{max} is in N as long as we do not introduce any terms that are more dominant than the currently dominant ones.

Lemma 8. *For a vector $v \in \mathbb{R}^n$ there is an $\varepsilon \neq 0$ such that $z_{max} + \varepsilon v \in N$ if and only if for all k*

$$\begin{cases} C_{k,ind} v = 0, & for \ ind \succ index_{max}(k) \\ N_{k,ind,t} v = 0, & for \ ind \succ index_{max}(k), \ for \ all \ t \end{cases}$$

Proof. **The "if" direction.** $Cond_k(z_{max}, i)$ is dominated by the $C_{k,index_{max}(k)} z$ term for all i. It will remain positive if we add εv to it for some small ε. By the condition it will remain dominating, since no non-zero higher order terms are introduced by adding εv.

The "only if" direction. We first show by contradiction that the first condition must hold. Suppose that there is a v and ε such that

$$y = z_{max} + \varepsilon v \in N,$$

but $C_{k,ind} v \neq 0$ for some k and $ind \succ index_{max}(k)$. Decompose $y = y^+ + y^o$, so that $y^+ \in S^+$ and $y^o \in S^o$. Then $C_{k,ind} y = C_{k,ind} y^+$. There are two cases:

Case 1: For each k, the highest-ranking non-zero $C_{k,ind} y^+$ is positive. In this case $y^+ \in N^e$ by Lemma 6. By the definition of $index_{max}$ we get $C_{k,ind} y = C_{k,ind} y^+ = 0$ for all $ind \succ index_{max}$. Hence $C_{k,ind} v = (C_{k,ind} y)/\varepsilon = 0$, contradiction.

Case 2: There is a k such that the highest-ranking non-zero $C_{k,ind} y = C_{k,ind} y^+$ is negative. In this case the dominating term of $Cond_k(y, i)$ has the coefficient

$$C_{k,ind} y + \zeta_{k1}^i N_{k,ind,1} y + \zeta_{k2}^i N_{k,ind,2} y + \ldots + \zeta_{km_k}^i N_{k,ind,m_k} y.$$

By Lemma 4 the expression will be negative below $C_{k,ind} y$ infinitely often, hence $Cond_k(y, i)$ will be violated infinitely often, contradiction.

Now suppose that for some k and $ind \succ index_{max}(k)$ the second condition is violated. We already know that $C_{k,ind} y = 0$, and the dominating term of $Cond_k(y, i)$ has the coefficient

$$C(i) = \zeta_{k1}^i N_{k,ind,1} y + \zeta_{k2}^i N_{k,ind,2} y + \ldots + \zeta_{km_k}^i N_{k,ind,m_k} y,$$

which is not identically 0. By Lemma 4 we know that there is a $c < 0$ such that $C(i) < c$ infinitely often. Since this is a dominating term, it will cause $Cond_k(y, i)$ to be violated infinitely often, contradiction. ∎

Solving the constraint system from Lemma 8 gives us a linear basis for S_{min}. The computation is done entirely symbolically over algebraic numbers. Note that we do not need to know ε from Lemma 8, but merely that such an ε exists. This solves the termination problem over $\mathbb{R}$. Our goal now is to tackle the problem over $\mathbb{Q}$. If $S_{min} = \emptyset$, we can return **terminates**, otherwise we need to find the rational subspace of S_{min}.

4.2   Looking for Rational Points in S_{min}

If the parameters of the loop are given by rationals, then the spanning vectors of S_{min} can be produced as explicit algebraic numbers. Denote by L_S the base vectors for S_{min} presented as algebraic numbers in some finite degree extension $\mathbb{Q}(\alpha)$ of $\mathbb{Q}$. By viewing $\mathbb{Q}(\alpha)$ as a finite-dimensional vector space over $\mathbb{Q}$ we can find the maximum space Q_{min} of *rational vectors* spanned by L_S. For further details about computations with algebraic numbers see [Bhu93, Loos83, Yap00]. We illustrate finding the rational subspace with the following simple example.

Example 3. Consider the simple example when $\mathbb{Q}(\alpha) = \mathbb{Q}(\sqrt{2})$ and $L_S = \{v_1 = (1, 0, \sqrt{2}), v_2 = (-\sqrt{2}, 1, 0)\}$. We are looking for coefficients $\beta, \gamma \in \mathbb{Q}(\sqrt{2})$ for which $\beta v_1 + \gamma v_2 \in \mathbb{Q}^3$. By writing $\beta = \beta_1 + \beta_2\sqrt{2}$, $\gamma = \gamma_1 + \gamma_2\sqrt{2}$ with $\beta_1, \beta_2, \gamma_1, \gamma_2 \in \mathbb{Q}$ we obtain the conditions

$$\begin{cases} \beta + (-\sqrt{2})\gamma \in \mathbb{Q} \\ \gamma \in \mathbb{Q} \\ (\sqrt{2})\beta \in \mathbb{Q} \end{cases} \iff \begin{cases} \beta_2 - \gamma_1 = 0 \\ \gamma_2 = 0 \\ \beta_1 = 0 \end{cases}$$

Hence we must have $\gamma = \beta/\sqrt{2} \in \mathbb{Q}$, and the rational subspace of $span(L_S)$ is one dimensional, spanned by $\sqrt{2}v_1 + v_2 = (0, 1, 2)$.   ∎

There are three possible cases. The first one is that $dim(Q_{min}) = dim(S_{min})$. This means that the rational points are dense in the nonterminating set N, and hence there are nonterminating rational points, and we can return **nonterminating**.

If $dim(Q_{min}) = 0$, then the only potential nonterminating rational point is 0. It is trivial to check whether 0 is non-terminating in the homogeneous case: we just need to check whether it satisfies the loop conditions. If it does we return **non-terminating**, otherwise return **terminating**.

The more difficult and interesting case is when $0 < d = dim(Q_{min}) < dim(S_{min})$. In this case there are some rational points in S_{min}, but we can no longer guarantee that any of them are in N, since they all lie in a proper subspace of S_{min}. The only thing we know is that *all* potential rational non-terminating points lie in Q_{min}. Denote by R_{min} the space of *real* vectors spanned by Q_{min}. Obviously $dim(R_{min}) = dim(Q_{min})$. We prove the following.

Lemma 9. R_{min} *is invariant under* A, *that is* $Av \in R_{min}$ *for any* $v \in R_{min}$.

Proof. First of all, the non-terminating set N is invariant under A, since if the loop is nonterminating on x, it is also nonterminating on Ax. N contains a linear basis for S_{min}, hence S_{min} is invariant under A.

Let q be any rational vector in Q_{min}. Aq is rational, and $Aq \in S_{min}$ by the invariance of S_{min}. Hence by the definition of Q_{min} (as containing all the rational vectors in S_{min}), $Aq \in Q_{min}$. The rational vectors of R_{min} span it, hence R_{min} is invariant under A. ∎

R_{min} is a subspace invariant under A, and it has a rational basis $L_R=\{r_1, \ldots, r_d\}$. We can translate the action of A on R_{min} with respect to L_R, to obtain a $d \times d$ *rational* matrix A' such that

$$A : \alpha_1 r_1 + \ldots + \alpha_d r_d \mapsto \beta_1 r_1 + \ldots + \beta_d r_d,$$

where $(\beta_1, \ldots, \beta_d)^T = A'(\alpha_1, \ldots, \alpha_d)^T$. The conditions $B_s x > 0$ and $B_w x \geq 0$ can also be readily translated into *rational* conditions over the d-dimensional coefficient vector $(\alpha_1, \ldots, \alpha_d)$, where $x = \alpha_1 r_1 + \ldots + \alpha_d r_d \in R_{min}$. Thus we obtain a new loop, over d-dimensional vectors

while $(B'_s x > 0) \wedge (B'_w x \geq 0)$ $\{ x \leftarrow A'x \}$

and we need decide termination of the new loop over $\mathbb{Q}$. Note that we have reduced the dimension of the problem from n to $d < n$, and thus we will be able to decide termination over $\mathbb{Q}$ in the homogeneous case in at most n iterations.

5   The Integer and the Non-homogeneous Cases

In the case the program is interpreted over the reals or the rationals, the transition from general termination to the homogeneous case is done exactly as in [Tiw04] by adding an extra auxiliary variable z. The program

while $(B_s x > b_s) \wedge (B_w x \geq b_w)$ $\{ x \leftarrow Ax + c \}$

always terminates if and only if the program

while $(B_s x > b_s z) \wedge (B_w x \geq b_w z) \wedge (z > 0)$ $\{ x \leftarrow Ax + cz, \; z \leftarrow z \}$

terminates. This is true both over $\mathbb{Q}$ and $\mathbb{R}$. If the first program does not terminate, then the second does not terminate with the same initial condition and $z = 1$. In the opposite direction, we can scale a nonterminating starting point of the second program so that $z = 1$, and thus make it a nonterminating starting point for the first one.

Note that in the homogeneous case we can scale any nonterminating solution, and hence termination over $\mathbb{Q}$ is always equivalent to termination over $\mathbb{Z}$. This is not true in the non-homogeneous case: termination over $\mathbb{Q}$ implies termination over $\mathbb{Z}$, but not vice versa. Thus it can only be used as a partial termination test. The termination problem over $\mathbb{Z}$ as well as termination of loops with initial conditions appears to be much harder and will be discussed in next section.

6   Further Directions and Open Problems

We have seen that termination of deterministic loops with no initial conditions is decidable over $\mathbb{Q}$ and over $\mathbb{Z}$ in the homogeneous case. On the other hand, by allowing the linear loop to be general enough one can easily make the termination problem undecidable. For example, having k different update functions depending on different conditions

while one of the k conditions is met for $1 \leq i \leq k$
  if $B_i x > d_i \ \{ \ x \leftarrow A_i x + c_i \ \}$

is enough to make the termination problem undecidable, since this class of loops is sufficiently rich to allow encoding of counter machines [Tiw04].

This gives rise to natural open questions about termination of programs more general than the ones considered in this paper, but for which termination is still decidable. One such class are the programs discussed in [PR04]. They are similar to the ones described here, but have a nondeterministic inequality as an update:

while $(B_s x > b_s) \wedge (B_w x \geq b_w)$ $\{ \ x \leq Ax + c \ \}$

In [PR04] a complete linear ranking function generating algorithm is presented, but it still leaves the more general termination problem open over either $\mathbb{R}$, $\mathbb{Q}$ or $\mathbb{Z}$.

Another natural generalization is introducing initial conditions and the related problem of termination over $\mathbb{Z}$. It appears that to decide termination over $\mathbb{Z}$ it is necessary to be able to tell, given a point x_0, whether the program terminates on x_0 or not. Solving the termination problem on a given input would require a much sharper version of Lemma 4. In Lemma 4, we have shown that the expression $z_n = \sum_{i=1}^{m} \alpha_i \zeta_i^n$ always eventually falls below zero by at least some fixed amount c. It is even possible to compute the infimum of the expression using ergodic theory. However, this still falls short of solving the termination problem. Consider the following algebraic expression. Here $|\zeta| = 1$, $\zeta \neq 1$:

$$z(i) = Re(\zeta^i + 1 - 2^{-i}).$$

We would like to know whether $z(i)$ ever falls below 0. This depends on how close the orbit of ζ^i gets to -1. To answer this question some analysis of the continued fraction expansion of $\log \zeta$ seems to be needed.

We summarize the problems:

1. Given a deterministic linear loop P and an input x_0, does P terminate on x_0?
2. Given a deterministic linear loop P does it terminate on all integer inputs?
3. How much nondeterminism can be introduced in a linear loop with no initial conditions before termination becomes undecidable?

7   Conclusion

We have demonstrated a first termination decision procedure that works over the integers for simple homogeneous loop programs. Most programs in practice are specified over the integers, yet algorithms usually only work with the larger domain of real numbers because decision procedures are generally easier there.

We have gained new insights into termination of more general deterministic linear loops. We believe that techniques presented in the paper can be generalized using more refined analysis to obtain at least a good partial termination test over the integers for loops with initial constraints.

Acknowledgments. I would like to thank Marsha Chechik and Arie Gurfinkel for encouraging me to work on the problem. I am also grateful to Arie Gurfinkel for his many useful comment on preliminary versions of the paper. I would like to thank Ilia Binder for our useful discussions on applying the ergodic theorem. Finally, I would like to thank the anonymous referees for the many useful suggestions for improvements of the paper.

References

[BPR03]   S. Basu, R. Pollack, M.F. Roy, Algorithms in Real Algebraic Geometry, Springer, 2003.

[Bhu93]   M. Bhubaneswar, Algorithmic Algebra, Springer-Verlag, 1993.

[BBK+01] V.D. Blondel, O. Bournez, P. Koiran, C.H. Papadimitriou, J.N. Tsitsiklis, Deciding stability and mortality of piecewise affine dynamical system. Theoretical Computer Science, **255** (1-2), pp. 687696, 2001.

[BMP05a] A.R. Bradley, Z. Manna, H.B. Simpa, Linear ranking with reachability, in CAV 2005, pp. 491-504, 2005.

[BMP05b] A.R. Bradley, Z. Manna, H.B. Simpa, Termination analysis of integer linear loops, in CONCUR 2005, pp. 488-502, 2005.

[CSS03]   M.A. Colón, S. Sankaranarayanan, H.B. Simpa, Linear invariant generation using non-linear constraint solving, in CAV 2003, LNCS 2725, pp. 420-432, 2003.

[HK71]   K. Hoffman and R. Kunze, Linear Algebra, Prentice-Hall, 2nd ed., 1971.

[Loos83] R. Loos, Computing in Algebraic Extensions, in B. Buchberger, G.E. Collins et al. eds., Computer Algebra: Symbolic and Algebraic Computation, 2nd ed., Springer-Verlag, pp. 173-188, 1983.

[Mat93]   Y. Matiyasevich, *Hilbert's Tenth Problem*, The MIT Press, Cambridge, London, 1993.

[PR04]   A. Podelski, A. Rybalchenko, A complete method for synthesis of linear ranking functions, in B. Steffen and G. Levi (Eds.): VMCAI 2004, LNCS 2937, pp. 239-251, 2004.

[Tar51]   A. Tarski, A Decision Method for Elementary Algebra and Geometry, 2nd ed. Berkeley, CA: University of California Press, 1951.

[Tiw04]   A. Tiwari, Termination of linear programs, in R. Alur and D.A. Peled (Eds.): CAV 2004, LNCS 3114, pp. 70-82, 2004.

[Yap00]   C.K. Yap, Fundamental Problems of Algorithmic Algebra, Oxford University Press, 2000.

Automatic Termination Proofs for Programs with Shape-Shifting Heaps

Josh Berdine[1], Byron Cook[1], Dino Distefano[2], and Peter W. O'Hearn[1,2]

[1] Microsoft Research
[2] Queen Mary, University of London

Abstract. We describe a new program termination analysis designed to handle imperative programs whose termination depends on the mutation of the program's heap. We first describe how an abstract interpretation can be used to construct a finite number of relations which, if each is well-founded, implies termination. We then give an abstract interpretation based on separation logic formulæ which tracks the depths of pieces of heaps. Finally, we combine these two techniques to produce an automatic termination prover. We show that the analysis is able to prove the termination of loops extracted from Windows device drivers that could not be proved terminating before by other means; we also discuss a previously unknown bug found with the analysis.

1 Introduction

Consider the code fragment in Fig. 1, which comes from the source code of a Windows device driver. Does this loop guarantee termination? It's *supposed to*: failure of this loop to terminate would have catastrophic effects on the stability and responsiveness of the computer. Why would it be a problem if this loop didn't terminate? First of all, the device that this code is managing would cease to function. Secondly, due to the fact that this code executes at kernel-level priority, non-termination would cause it to starve other threads running on the system. Note that we cannot simply kill the thread, as it can be holding kernel locks and modifying kernel-level data-structures—forcibly killing the thread would leave the operating system in an inconsistent state. Furthermore, if the loop hangs, the machine might not actually crash.[1] Instead, the thread will likely just hang until the user resets the machine. This means that the bug cannot be diagnosed using post-crash analysis tools.

This example highlights the importance of termination in systems level code: in order to improve the responsiveness and stability of the operating system it is vital that we can automatically check the termination of loops like this one. In this case, in order to prove the termination of the loop, we need to show the following conditions:

1. `DeviceExtension->ReadQueue.Flink` is a pointer to a circular list of elements (via the `Flink` field).

---

[1] Although hanging kernel-threads can trigger other bugs within the operating system.

T. Ball and R.B. Jones (Eds.): CAV 2006, LNCS 4144, pp. 386–400, 2006.

```
for (entry = DeviceExtension->ReadQueue.Flink;
     entry != &DeviceExtension->ReadQueue;
     entry = entry->Flink) {
    irp = (IRP *)((CHAR *)(entry)-(ULONG *)(&((IRP *)0)->Tail.Overlay.ListEntry));
    stack = IoGetCurrentIrpStackLocation (irp);
    if (stack->FileObject == FileObject) {
        RemoveEntryList(entry);
        if (IoSetCancelRoutine (irp, NULL)) {
            return irp;
        } else {
            InitializeListHead (&irp->Tail.Overlay.ListEntry);
        }
    }
}
```

Fig. 1. Code from a Windows device driver which contains a termination bug found by the analysis described in this paper. The bug has catastrophic effects on the responsiveness of the computer when it occurs.

2. During the execution of this loop, entry is always getting closer to taking the value of &DeviceExtension->ReadQueue.
3. The loop will terminate when entry is finally assigned the value equaling &DeviceExtension->ReadQueue.
4. The assignments to other parts of the heap occurring during the loop's execution (*e.g.*, the side-effects from executing InitializeListHead) do not affect conditions 1, 2, and 3.

Unfortunately, there *is a termination bug* in Fig. 1: in some cases this loop may violate condition 4.

To date, automatically checking the termination of loops like this one has been beyond any known tool. This is because the termination argument is based on the semantics of imperative heap-mutation during the loop's execution. Today's termination analysis tools (that is: tools that both find *and* check termination arguments automatically) simply do not support an analysis at this level of depth; instead they only support arguments involving the values of arithmetic variables. Examples of such tools include TERMINATOR [5] and POLYRANK [2].

In this paper, we present a new termination prover which supports loops of this sort. In cases where loops have termination bugs the prover is able to provide information which can be used to automatically find a counterexample. The prover implements an abstract analysis, based on formulæ expressed in separation logic, which keeps track of the relative differences between heap objects while abstracting away the exact details. This analysis produces a finite collection of depth relations such that the program is well-founded if each individual relation is. The correctness of the termination argument relies on a result of Podelski & Rybalchenko [12]. The candidate depth relations constructed are checked for well-foundedness with the use of projection and the RANKFINDER tool [11].

Separation logic [14] is used as the basis of our analysis because it lets us symbolically carry around just enough information to prove that loops are *making*

MUTANT (P, I, ℓ) {
    $Y := \text{SONAR}^*_P[\{I\}]$
    if $\top \in Y$ return "Loop may crash", with $\top$
    foreach $y \in Y$ such that $\text{pc}(y) = \ell$ {
        $s := \text{SEED}(y)$
        $Z := \text{SONAR}^+_P[\{s\}]$
        foreach $z \in Z$ such that $\text{pc}(z) = \ell$ {
            if $\neg\text{WF}(z)$ return "Loop may diverge", with (y, z)
        }
    }
    return "Loop ℓ-terminates"
}

Fig. 2. MUTANT algorithm

progress while abstracting enough information such that the tool produces a compact over-approximation of the reachable states. Furthermore, separation logic mitigates the need for a global alias check when size information is changed: the alteration of the size of one piece of the heap does not affect any others that are held in different components of a separating conjunction. These characteristics are what make the new termination proof method powerful, yet still tractable.

This paper begins with a description of the algorithm, followed by the details of the separation logic analysis, and then experimental results. Our experiments include loops extracted from Windows device drivers that could not be handled using TERMINATOR [5] due to its overly-coarse model of heaps [13].

2 Termination Via Separation Analysis and Rank Synthesis

Our termination checking algorithm, MUTANT, is displayed in Fig. 2. The input is a program P, an abstract initial state expressed as a separation logic formula I, and a program location ℓ. The algorithm is designed to prove that the program P cannot visit location ℓ infinitely-often during its execution when started in states satisfying I. We call this condition ℓ-termination. If we wish to prove that P terminates, we can prove ℓ-termination for each program location. We can also optimize by focusing only on a subset of the locations (*i.e.*, a set of *cutpoints* [9]).

MUTANT first calls an analysis engine, SONAR (defined in Section 3), to calculate the finite set of reachable abstract states Y. For a program P, SONAR$_P$ is the binary transition relation on abstract states, and SONAR$^*_P$ denotes its reflexive transitive closure. SONAR$^*_P[\{I\}]$ denotes the post-image under the pre-state I. During this analysis SONAR also proves that P cannot commit any of a basic set of safety violations, such as an access to a deallocated heap object. If SONAR returns $\top$, then it cannot guarantee that P is safe from this class of errors—and our method cannot prove termination.

Next, for each reachable symbolic state y at program location ℓ, the algorithm constructs a new state with additional history variables that symbolically record a snapshot of the depths of pieces of y's heap. We call this step *seeding*, and use the notation SEED(y) to represent the output of this operation. If $s =$ SEED(y) then, when symbolically executing instructions starting from s, we can see how the effects of these operations relate to the original values from y.

MUTANT then calls SONAR again to compute the states reachable from SEED(y) in *at least one step* and which are at the same program location (*i.e.*, $\mathsf{pc}(y) = \mathsf{pc}(z) = \ell$). Each of the pairs (y, z) in the abstract semantics determines an over-approximation of transitions in the concrete semantics of the program, and together they over-approximate all transitions in the concrete semantics.

The SONAR analysis uses heap predicates together with certain auxiliary variables that describe heap depths. For example $\mathsf{ls}^k(a, b)$ describes a linked list of length k running from a to b. Seeding maps this formula to $k_s{=}k \wedge \mathsf{ls}^k(a, b)$, where k_s is a symbolic constant used to record the initial value of k. Running SONAR starting from this state can change k but not k_s. So, if the final state is $k_s{>}k \wedge \mathsf{ls}^k(a, b)$ then this indicates that the linked list has decreased in length (as can happen, *e.g.*, by removing an element from the list).

Because we seed y before running SONAR again to obtain z, the single abstract state z will actually contain information, in the form of an assertion, which relates initial (seeded) values of heap-depth variables to their final values (for this run of SONAR). In the above example it is just $k_s{>}k$. The WF(z) procedure extracts this information from z and treats it as a binary relation T_i, which relates the relative differences between the depths of pieces of heaps referenced by z. WF(z) then calls the RANKFINDER tool [11] to determine if this relation is well-founded. Note that the well-foundedness of each z is checked independently of the others.

In essence, MUTANT constructs a finite set $T_1, \ldots, T_n$ of binary relations, whose union over-approximates changes to the auxiliary variables that track heap depths. If one of the determined relations T_i is not well-founded, then MUTANT's attempted proof of ℓ-termination fails. However, if all of the found pairs denote well-founded relations, then ℓ-termination has been proved. The correctness of this assertion comes from [12], which shows that: to establish that ℓ is not visited infinitely often, it is sufficient to find a finite union of well-founded relations that over-approximates the transitions through location ℓ.

The algorithm is different from the one in the TERMINATOR tool [5]. As described in [3], TERMINATOR uses counterexample-guided abstraction refinement to add disjuncts to a collection $T_1, \ldots, T_n$ of well-founded relations, and then uses a *binary reachability analysis* [4] to check the subset inclusion. Checking the inclusion is the expensive part of TERMINATOR. In contrast, here we never do the inclusion check. Rather, SONAR produces a finite set of T_i's (determined by the (y, z) pairs), which together satisfy the inclusion by construction. As with TERMINATOR, we still have to check for well-foundedness of each T_i.

3   Tracking Depths of Abstracted Heaps

SONAR implements an analysis that is sound for safety properties of programs. It uses an abstract domain based on separation logic formulæ, and as a result, is set up to express deep properties (meaning properties that depend on areas of the heap not immediately referenced by program variables) of mutating heaps. Reachability between program states is computed using a fixed-point algorithm built from single-step symbolic execution (notationally: $\rightsquigarrow$) together with a case analysis or concretion step ($\rightarrow_E$) which incrementally reveals the pointer structure of abstracted or summarized heap objects, and an abstraction step ($\rightarrow$) which enables convergence to fixed-points.

SONAR is based on SPACEINVADER [7]. The difference between the two analysis engines is in SONAR's tracking of depths of inductive heap predicates. Depth does not necessarily refer to lengths of pointer chains in the heap, but instead refers to the number of inductive unfoldings a formula represents. For lists, this corresponds to length. In this section we describe the underlying fundamentals behind SONAR. We focus on linked lists in the exposition, but the method of proving ℓ-termination generalizes to data structures expressed using other inductive predicates in separation logic, such as trees, doubly-linked lists, etc.

Programs. SONAR supports a simple language of goto programs extended with the usual four heap operations: allocate, deallocate, load, and store. A program P is a function mapping a fixed finite subset of naturals $\{0, \ldots, end - 1\}$ to commands C, given by:

$$
\begin{aligned}
E &::= \mathsf{nil} \mid x \mid x' && \text{expressions} \\
S &::= \mathsf{skip} \mid x := E \mid x := \mathsf{new}() && \text{safe commands} \\
A(E) &::= \mathsf{dispose}(E) \mid x := [E] \mid [E] := E && \text{heap accessing commands} \\
B &::= E{=}E && \text{simple Boolean formulæ} \\
G &::= B \mid \neg B && \text{branch tests} \\
C &::= S \mid A(E) \mid \mathsf{goto}\, n \mid \mathsf{if}(G)\,\{\mathsf{goto}\, n\}\ \mathsf{else}\ \{\mathsf{goto}\, n\}
\end{aligned}
$$

where $n \in \{0, \ldots, end\}$; and variables $x, y, \ldots$ range over some infinite set Var; and primed variables $x', y', \ldots$ range over some disjoint infinite set Var$'$. Primed variables cannot appear in programs. They are included in expressions since these also appear in formulæ (below). For convenience of later definitions, commands S are syntactically distinguished from commands $A(E)$. The difference between the two is that for a command S, execution is always safe, while execution of a command $A(E)$ may be unsafe, due to access of heap location E.

Symbolic Heaps and Depths. SONAR operates over an abstract domain that represents sets of concrete program states as sets of separation logic formulæ called symbolic heaps. Note the inclusion of depth formulæ K, and depth variable annotations N on list segment predicates $\mathsf{ls}^N(E, E)$:

$$
\begin{aligned}
N &::= 1 \mid k \mid k' & \Pi &::= \mathsf{true} \mid B \mid K \mid \Pi \wedge \Pi \\
K &::= N{=}N \mid N{>}N & \Sigma &::= \mathsf{emp} \mid H \mid \Sigma * \Sigma \mid \mathsf{junk} \\
H &::= E{\mapsto}E \mid \mathsf{ls}^N(E, E) & Q &::= \Pi \wedge \Sigma
\end{aligned}
$$

Depth variables $k, l, \ldots, k', l', \ldots$ and primed depth variables $k', l', \ldots$ range over DVar and DVar$'$, respectively, and denote natural numbers. DVar is infinite and disjoint from Var and Var′, while DVar′ is an infinite subset of DVar. Note that formulæ are considered up to symmetry of =, permutations across $\wedge$ and $*$ (*e.g.*, $\Pi \wedge B_0 \wedge B_1$ and $\Pi \wedge B_1 \wedge B_0$ are equated), unit laws for true and emp, and idempotency of $-*$ junk (*e.g.*, junk $*$ junk and junk are equated).

Symbolic heap formulæ consist of two parts: a Boolean formula Π built from =, >, and $\wedge$ which is independent of the heap and has the usual classical arithmetic meaning; and a heap formula Σ which expresses heap shape. The meaning of a symbolic heap Q is the same as $\exists \vec{x'}, \vec{k'}. Q$ in the usual semantics of separation logic [14], where we existentially quantify all the primed variables. The empty heap, which contains no allocated cells at all, is described by emp. A heap consisting of a single cell at location E with contents F is described by $E \mapsto F$. The separating conjunction $*$ describes composition of disjoint heaps: heaps with shape $\Sigma_0 * \Sigma_1$ consist of two subheaps with no allocated locations in common, one with shape Σ_0 and the other with shape Σ_1. Non-empty heaps, usually consisting of unreachable cells, are described by junk. Finally, $\mathsf{ls}^N(E, F)$ describes acyclic singly-linked lists of length $N \geq 1$. Cyclic lists, such as that in the introductory example, can be expressed using multiple predicates: *e.g.*, $\mathsf{ls}^k(x, y') * \mathsf{ls}^j(y', x)$. Note that the ls^1 and $\mapsto$ predicates are not equivalent, since $x \mapsto x$ admits cycles (of length one), while $\mathsf{ls}^1(x, x)$ is inconsistent.

The definition of the abstract transition relation asks several types of questions about symbolic heaps: entailment of an equality ($Q \vdash E=F$), entailment of a disequality ($Q \vdash E \neq F$), or inconsistency ($Q \vdash$ false). We also sometimes ask the negations of these questions. Sound implementations of these queries can be obtained from those defined in [7].

Symbolic Execution ($\rightsquigarrow$). The symbolic execution relation captures the effect of executing a straight-line command from a symbolic heap. That is, $Q_0 \overset{C}{\rightsquigarrow} Q_1$ means that Q_1 over-approximates the concrete states which can result from executing C from states satisfying Q_0. We do not show the axioms which define symbolic execution of basic commands S and $A(E)$ as they are reported in [1, 7], but for illustration we show the axiom for loading the contents of a memory address E into x:

$$Q * E \mapsto F \overset{x:=[E]}{\rightsquigarrow} x=F[x'/x] \wedge (Q * E \mapsto F)[x'/x] \qquad (1)$$

where x' is globally fresh. This axiom says that if we load the contents of E into x in a state which looks like Q with a separate single heap cell at location E with contents F, then the resulting state will look the same except that now x will have the value of the contents of E in the pre-state, $F[x'/x]$. As usual [9], we think of x' as standing for the value of x that was overwritten, and the renaming is necessary to account for the changing value of x.

Rearrangement ($\rightarrow_E$). Symbolic execution does not operate on arbitrary pre-states. For instance, the axiom for load (1) requires that the source heap cell be explicitly known. In order to put symbolic heaps into the form required for symbolic execution of a command, we use a rearrangement relation $\rightarrow_E$, defined by the following axioms:

$$\frac{\text{SubstE}}{z'{=}E \wedge Q \;\to\; Q[E/z']} \qquad\qquad \frac{\text{SubstN}}{l'{=}N \wedge Q \;\to\; Q[N/l']}$$

$$\frac{\text{JunkGT}}{k'{>}N \wedge Q \;\to\; Q} \qquad \frac{\text{JunkLT}}{N{>}k' \wedge Q \;\to\; Q} \qquad \frac{\text{Transitivity}}{N{>}k' \wedge k'{>}N' \wedge Q \;\to\; N{>}N' \wedge Q}$$

$$\frac{\text{Junk}}{Q * H(x',E) \;\to\; Q * \mathsf{junk}} \qquad \frac{\text{JunkCycle}}{Q * H_0(x',y') * H_1(y',x') \;\to\; Q * \mathsf{junk}}$$

$$\frac{\text{AppendLsNil}}{Q * H_0(E,x') * H_1(x',F) \;\to\; Q * \mathsf{ls}^{k''}(E,\mathsf{nil})} \; Q \vdash F{=}\mathsf{nil}$$

$$\frac{\text{AppendLsGuard}}{Q * H_0(E,x') * H_1(x',F_0) * H_2(F_1,G) \;\to\; Q * \mathsf{ls}^{k''}(E,F_0) * H_2(F_1,G)} \; Q \vdash F_0{=}F_1$$

Here formulæ $H(E,F)$ are of form $E{\mapsto}F$ or $\mathsf{ls}^N(E,F)$; and k',x',y' do not occur other than where explicitly indicated; and k'' is fresh.

Fig. 3. Abstraction relation $(\to)$

$$
\begin{aligned}
Q * F{\mapsto}G &\;\to_E\; Q * E{\mapsto}G && \text{if } Q \vdash E{=}F && \text{Switch} \\
Q * \mathsf{ls}^1(F,G) &\;\to_E\; Q * E{\mapsto}G && \text{if } Q \vdash E{=}F && \text{SwitchLs} \\
Q * \mathsf{ls}^k(F,G) &\;\to_E\; k'{>}k \wedge k'{=}1 \wedge Q[k'/k] * E{\mapsto}G && \text{if } Q \vdash E{=}F && \text{Unroll1} \\
Q * \mathsf{ls}^k(F,G) &\;\to_E\; k'{>}k \wedge Q[k'/k] * E{\mapsto}x' * \mathsf{ls}^k(x',G) && \text{if } Q \vdash E{=}F && \text{Unroll>1}
\end{aligned}
$$

where k' and x' are globally fresh. Note that these axioms are directed toward a heap location of interest E, increasing the determinacy of symbolic execution.

Rearrangement reveals the pointer structure of heaps which are abstracted or summarized (by an ls predicate). This is achieved by performing case analysis: a symbolic heap rewrites to a set of symbolic heaps, each of which, modulo renaming k, is logically stronger (represents fewer concrete states). Given that we are proving ℓ-termination, it is also crucial for rearrangement to track the changing depths of list segment predicates. This is captured by the $k'{>}k$ in the right-hand side of Unroll>1, which indicates that the length of the list starting from x' in the post-state is less than that of the list starting from x in the pre-state.

Abstraction for Fixed-Point Computations $(\to)$. Abstraction is accomplished by certain separation logic implications that rewrite a symbolic heap to a logically weaker one. The abstraction relation on symbolic heaps $Q_0 \to Q_1$ is defined by the axioms shown in Fig. 3.

As opposed to rearrangement above, which takes lists apart and strengthens the individual symbolic heap formulæ in a symbolic state, abstraction constructs larger lists, weakening the symbolic heap formulæ. This step is very coarse for depth information since, in the examples we have investigated, *increasing* list lengths are not generally a progress measure for ℓ-termination—instead it is

CRASH

$$\dfrac{Q \overset{P(n)}{\rightsquigarrow} \top}{\langle n\,,Q\rangle \rightsquigarrow_P \top}$$

HEAP ACCESS

$$\dfrac{Q_0 \rightarrow_E Q_2 \quad Q_2 \overset{A(E)}{\rightsquigarrow} Q_3 \quad Q_3 \rightarrow^* Q_1}{\langle n\,,Q_0\rangle \rightsquigarrow_P \langle n+1\,,Q_1\rangle}\ P(n) \equiv A(E)$$

SAFE

$$\dfrac{Q_0 \overset{S}{\rightsquigarrow} Q_2 \quad Q_2 \rightarrow^* Q_1}{\langle n\,,Q_0\rangle \rightsquigarrow_P \langle n+1\,,Q_1\rangle}\ P(n) \equiv S$$

GOTO

$$\dfrac{}{\langle n\,,Q\rangle \rightsquigarrow_P \langle m\,,Q\rangle}\ P(n) \equiv \mathtt{goto}\ m$$

IF FALSE

$$\dfrac{}{\langle n\,,Q\rangle \rightsquigarrow_P \langle m\,,E{=}F \wedge Q\rangle}\quad \begin{array}{l} P(n) \equiv \mathtt{if}(E{\neq}F)\ \{\mathtt{goto}\,l\}\ \mathtt{else}\ \{\mathtt{goto}\,m\} \\ \text{and } Q \nvdash E{\neq}F \end{array}$$

Fig. 4. Transition relation ($\rightsquigarrow_P$)

decreasing list lengths, captured by the rearrangement relation, which furnish progress measures for ℓ-termination.

The Transition Relation ($\rightsquigarrow_P$). In the MUTANT algorithm, for a program P, SONAR$_P$ = $\rightsquigarrow_P$. The transition relation $\rightsquigarrow_P$ relates configurations consisting of a program location and a symbolic heap to another program location and a symbolic heap or crash (notationally $\top$): $\langle n\,,Q_0\rangle \rightsquigarrow_P \langle m\,,Q_1\rangle$ or $\langle n\,,Q_0\rangle \rightsquigarrow_P \top$ where $m \leq end$ and $n \leq end - 1$ are values of the program counter. The program stops when execution reaches end either by falling through an S or $A(E)$ instruction, or by a goto. That is, configurations $\langle end\,,Q_0\rangle$ are stuck.

The rules shown in Fig. 4 define the transition relation in terms of the symbolic execution relation $\rightsquigarrow$, the rearrangement relation $\rightarrow_E$, and the reflexive transitive closure of the abstraction relation $\rightarrow^*$. We have shown only one of the four axioms for conditional branches; the others can be defined similarly from [7].

The key rule is HEAP ACCESS, which says that when the current instruction will attempt to access a heap cell E, the symbolic state Q_0 is first rearranged to reveal the heap cell at E, yielding state Q_2, from which the current instruction is executed, yielding state Q_3, which is then abstracted, yielding the final state Q_1. The definition allows for flexibility regarding the amount of abstraction that is performed, and how often. By default, SONAR fully abstracts at each step, but when this strategy loses too much precision to prove memory safety, we abstract fully only at the program point ℓ in question.

The first call $Y := $ SONAR$_P^*[\{I\}]$ of the analysis in the MUTANT algorithm requires that the transition relation $\rightsquigarrow_P$ (*i.e.*, SONAR$_P$) be an over-approximation of the concrete semantics in the usual sense: that it over-approximates reachability. If σ_1 is a concrete state that is reachable from an initial state σ_0 satisfying initial symbolic heap I, then there is a reachable symbolic heap Q that is satisfied by σ_1. The concrete semantics does not operate on depth variables, and the relevant notion of satisfaction involves existentially quantifying *all* of the depth variables in Q. This sense of over-approximation follows essentially from the soundness result of [7].

The second call to SONAR in the algorithm requires a different notion of over-approximation for *transitions*, which we discuss in Section 4.

A Small Example. To see how this analysis tracks the progress of heap updates for ℓ-termination proofs we consider advancing a pointer to a list to the next node. The initial state $i_s{=}i \wedge j_s{=}j \wedge \mathsf{ls}^j(y, x) * \mathsf{ls}^i(x, \mathsf{nil})$ indicates that the heap shape is an acyclic singly-linked list of length $j + i$ starting from pointer y and ending with nil. The pointer x splits this list into two sublists of length j and i. Consider the program fragment: n: x = x->next;. In MUTANT's input format this is represented by a program P where $P(n) = x{:=}[x]$. For this example, $\leadsto_P$ contains two transitions, one for the case where the sublist $\mathsf{ls}^i(x, \mathsf{nil})$ is of length 1:

$$\langle n, i_s{=}i \wedge j_s{=}j \wedge \mathsf{ls}^j(y, x) * \mathsf{ls}^i(x, \mathsf{nil}) \rangle \tag{2}$$
$$\leadsto_P \langle n+1, x{=}\mathsf{nil} \wedge i_s{>}i \wedge i_s{=}1 \wedge j_s{=}j \wedge \mathsf{ls}^{k''}(y, \mathsf{nil}) \rangle$$

and one for the case where $\mathsf{ls}^i(x, \mathsf{nil})$ is of length greater than 1:

$$\langle n, i_s{=}i \wedge j_s{=}j \wedge \mathsf{ls}^j(y, x) * \mathsf{ls}^i(x, \mathsf{nil}) \rangle \tag{3}$$
$$\leadsto_P \langle n+1, i_s{>}i \wedge j_s{=}j \wedge \mathsf{ls}^{k''}(y, x) * \mathsf{ls}^i(x, \mathsf{nil}) \rangle$$

Here, we have seeded the initial state with $i_s{=}i$ and $j_s{=}j$ to keep track of the initial depths i_s and j_s so that we can observe that $i_s{>}i$. This indicates that the sublist $\mathsf{ls}^i(x, \mathsf{nil})$ in the post-state is shorter than that in the pre-state. It is inequalities like this which are the reason for well-foundedness of the computed transition relations.

In the derivations of the transitions (2) and (3), first the state $i_s{=}i \wedge j_s{=}j \wedge \mathsf{ls}^j(y, x) * \mathsf{ls}^i(x, \mathsf{nil})$ is rewritten to two intermediate states by the application of the rearrangement axioms UNROLL1 and UNROLL>1, respectively:

$$i_s{=}i \wedge j_s{=}j \wedge \mathsf{ls}^j(y, x) * \mathsf{ls}^i(x, \mathsf{nil}) \tag{4}$$
$$\rightarrow_x i_s{=}i' \wedge i'{>}i \wedge i'{=}1 \wedge j_s{=}j \wedge \mathsf{ls}^j(y, x) * x{\mapsto}\mathsf{nil}$$

$$i_s{=}i \wedge j_s{=}j \wedge \mathsf{ls}^j(y, x) * \mathsf{ls}^i(x, \mathsf{nil}) \tag{5}$$
$$\rightarrow_x i_s{=}i' \wedge i'{>}i \wedge j_s{=}j \wedge \mathsf{ls}^j(y, x) * x{\mapsto}x' * \mathsf{ls}^i(x', \mathsf{nil})$$

Now, in both of the resulting states, the heap cell at x is explicit, therefore the symbolic execution rules can be applied to the right-hand side of (4) and (5):

$$i_s{=}i' \wedge i'{>}i \wedge i'{=}1 \wedge j_s{=}j \wedge \mathsf{ls}^j(y, x) * x{\mapsto}\mathsf{nil}$$
$$\overset{x{:=}[x]}{\leadsto} x{=}\mathsf{nil} \wedge i_s{=}i' \wedge i'{>}i \wedge i'{=}1 \wedge j_s{=}j \wedge \mathsf{ls}^j(y, x') * x'{\mapsto}\mathsf{nil}$$

$$i_s{=}i' \wedge i'{>}i \wedge j_s{=}j \wedge \mathsf{ls}^j(y, x) * x{\mapsto}x' * \mathsf{ls}^i(x', \mathsf{nil})$$
$$\overset{x{:=}[x]}{\leadsto} x{=}x' \wedge i_s{=}i' \wedge i'{>}i \wedge j_s{=}j \wedge \mathsf{ls}^j(y, x'') * x''{\mapsto}x' * \mathsf{ls}^i(x', \mathsf{nil})$$

Finally, the resulting states are abstracted by $\rightarrow$. For the first state, we apply the SUBSTN and APPENDLSNIL rules to abstract as much as possible, and for the second state we apply SUBSTN, SUBSTE, and APPENDLSGUARD, yielding:

$$x{=}\mathsf{nil} \wedge i_s{=}i' \wedge i'{>}i \wedge i'{=}1 \wedge j_s{=}j \wedge \mathsf{ls}^j(y, x') * x'{\mapsto}\mathsf{nil} \tag{6}$$

$$\to^* x{=}\mathsf{nil} \land i_s{>}i \land i_s{=}1 \land j_s{=}j \land \mathsf{ls}^{k''}(y, \mathsf{nil})$$

$$x{=}x' \land i_s{=}i' \land i'{>}i \land j_s{=}j \land \mathsf{ls}^j(y, x'') * x''{\mapsto}x' * \mathsf{ls}^i(x', \mathsf{nil}) \qquad (7)$$

$$\to^* i_s{>}i \land j_s{=}j \land \mathsf{ls}^{k''}(y, x) * \mathsf{ls}^i(x, \mathsf{nil})$$

The right-hand sides of (6) and (7) are the resulting states of (2) and (3).

4   Checking Well-Foundedness of the Over-Approximation

Now that the abstract transition relation has been described, the remaining ingredients of the ℓ-termination proof method of Fig. 2 are SEED and WF.

Considering Fig. 2, we know that y is an element of Y (*i.e.*, of $\mathrm{SONAR}_P^*[\{I\}]$). SEED($y$) computes s, which is a new state in which the values of all the depth variables occurring in y are symbolically recorded:

$$\mathrm{SEED}(Q) \triangleq (\textstyle\bigwedge_{k \in fdv(Q)} k_s{=}k) \land Q$$

where $fdv(Q)$ denotes the (unprimed or primed) depth variables in Q. Each k_s is a fresh symbolic constant (*i.e.*, uninterpreted nullary function symbol), which we formally represent as an unprimed variable. Now assume, as is done in Fig. 2, that $z \in \mathrm{SONAR}_P^+[\{s\}]$.

The procedure WF(z) is used to try to prove that z represents a well-founded binary relation. Formally, this procedure proves well-foundedness of the relation that represents an over-approximation (determined by (y, z)) of all concrete executions that visit y and then visit z.

WF implements this procedure by first computing a representative set of arithmetic inequalities. Due to seeding and the fact that symbolic execution maintains the relationship between the seeded information and the updated information, the arithmetic component of the relation (y, z) represents an over-approximation of the changes in depths due to executing from y to z, and exists entirely in the symbolic state z. Hence we can extract them via a projection $\alpha(z)$:

$$\alpha(\mathsf{true} \land \Sigma) \triangleq \mathsf{true} \qquad\qquad \alpha(K \land \Sigma) \triangleq K$$
$$\alpha(B \land \Sigma) \triangleq \mathsf{true} \qquad\qquad \alpha(\Pi_0 \land \Pi_1 \land \Sigma) \triangleq \alpha(\Pi_0 \land \Sigma) \land \alpha(\Pi_1 \land \Sigma)$$

The formula resulting from this projection is interpreted as a binary relation over the naturals from the seed variables to the other variables. As an example, consider this abstraction applied to the post-state of the transition of the previous section (3): $\alpha(i_s{>}i \land j_s{=}j \land \mathsf{ls}^{k''}(y, x) * \mathsf{ls}^i(x, \mathsf{nil})) = i_s{>}i \land j_s{=}j$. We now take this as one of the disjuncts in the transition invariant from Section 2, $T_n = i_s{>}i \land j_s{=}j$, which clearly represents a well-founded relation from i_s, j_s to i, j, over the naturals.

After projecting out the inequalities, WF calls the RANKFINDER tool [11] to attempt to prove well-foundedness:

WF(z) { **return** (RANKFINDER($\alpha_k(z)$) reports "Rank function found") }

Checking well-foundedness relies on a second notion of over-approximation that is relevant to the second call $Z := \text{SONAR}_P^+[\{s\}]$ of the depth analysis in the MUTANT algorithm. The formulation and proof of this second sense of over-approximation is non-trivial, and for space reasons we can only give an outline of it here. It involves setting up an instrumented semantics which manipulates the depth variables k; the reason for the additional semantics is that the standard concrete semantics of heap mutation does not mention the auxiliary depth variables used in our analysis. The instrumented semantics mixes both concrete and abstract semantics. For example, an assignment statement $[x]:=y$ alters concrete heap cell x, but can also bump a depth variable down by one, corresponding to an application of the UNROLL>1 rearrangement rule. The crucial point is that the rearrangement rules ($\rightarrow_E$) are sound for the updates of depth variables in the instrumented semantics. Overall, what we require, first, is that if the projection $\alpha(Q)$ denotes a well-founded relation, then that implies well-foundedness of executions in the instrumented semantics starting from seeded states; in essence, α constrains the changes to depth variables. Then, the soundness of MUTANT requires a simulation argument connecting the instrumented semantics with a standard concrete semantics of heap mutation.

5   A Complete Example

To illustrate the analysis in action, we consider trying to prove ℓ-termination of the simple program in Fig. 5, where ℓ is location 5, and the initial state is $\mathsf{ls}^k(x, \text{nil})$. As in Fig. 2, the first step of MUTANT$(P, I, 5)$ is to compute SONAR$_P^*[I]$. First SONAR computes the transition relation:

$$\langle 3, \mathsf{ls}^k(x, \text{nil}) \rangle \rightsquigarrow_P^* \langle 5, y{=}x \wedge \mathsf{ls}^k(x, \text{nil}) \rangle$$

$$\langle 5, y{=}x \wedge \mathsf{ls}^k(x, \text{nil}) \rangle \rightsquigarrow_P^+ \langle 5, y{\mapsto}x * \mathsf{ls}^k(x, \text{nil}) \rangle$$

$$\langle 5, y{\mapsto}x * \mathsf{ls}^k(x, \text{nil}) \rangle \rightsquigarrow_P^+ \langle 5, \mathsf{ls}^{k'}(y, x) * \mathsf{ls}^k(x, \text{nil}) \rangle$$

$$\langle 5, \mathsf{ls}^{k'}(y, x) * \mathsf{ls}^k(x, \text{nil}) \rangle \rightsquigarrow_P^+ \langle 5, \mathsf{ls}^{k'}(y, x) * \mathsf{ls}^k(x, \text{nil}) \rangle$$

We show only those transitions in $\rightsquigarrow_P^+$ involving program location 5, since the algorithm will consider only those states. In this case:

C program	program in SONAR format

`1 void main()`
`2 {`
`3      y = x;`
`4      while (x!=NULL) {`
`5          x = x->next`
`6      }`
`7 }`
	$P(3) = y{:=}x$
	$P(4) = \text{if}(x{\neq}\text{nil})\ \{\text{goto}\ 5\}\ \text{else}\ \{\text{goto}\ 7\}$
	$P(5) = x{:=}[x]$
	$P(6) = \text{goto}\ 4$

Fig. 5. Simple example program: list traversal

$$Y = \{\langle 5, y{=}x \wedge \mathsf{ls}^k(x, \mathsf{nil})\rangle, \langle 5, y{\mapsto}x * \mathsf{ls}^k(x, \mathsf{nil})\rangle, \langle 5, \mathsf{ls}^{k'}(y, x) * \mathsf{ls}^k(x, \mathsf{nil})\rangle\} \cup Y'$$

where Y' contains the states not at program location 5. Note that $\top \notin Y$, meaning that executing P from I is guaranteed to be safe with respect to the basic set of (memory) safety properties we consider.

Of the three reachable states in Y, we need only to consider $q = \langle 5, \mathsf{ls}^{k'}(y, x) * \mathsf{ls}^k(x, \mathsf{nil})\rangle$ since execution from the other two states will result either in the state $\langle 5, \mathsf{ls}^{k'}(y, x) * \mathsf{ls}^k(x, \mathsf{nil})\rangle$ itself or in the loop exiting. The next step in Fig. 2 is to seed q, which yields: $s = \langle 5, k'_s{=}k' \wedge k_s{=}k \wedge \mathsf{ls}^{k'}(y, x) * \mathsf{ls}^k(x, \mathsf{nil})\rangle$. The variables k and k' are set equal to the fresh constants k_s and k'_s. Later, during the successive call to SONAR, we will be able to see how the values of k and k' change relative to k'_s and k_s.

The next step is to compute $(\text{SONAR}_P)^+[\{s\}]$, which equals:

$$\langle 5, k'_s{=}k' \wedge k_s{=}k \wedge \mathsf{ls}^{k'}(y, x) * \mathsf{ls}^k(x, \mathsf{nil})\rangle \; \leadsto^+_P \; \langle 5, k_s{>}k \wedge \mathsf{ls}^{k'}(y, x) * \mathsf{ls}^k(x, \mathsf{nil})\rangle$$

$$\langle 5, k_s{>}k \wedge \mathsf{ls}^{k'}(y, x) * \mathsf{ls}^k(x, \mathsf{nil})\rangle \; \leadsto^+_P \; \langle 5, k_s{>}k \wedge \mathsf{ls}^{k'}(y, x) * \mathsf{ls}^k(x, \mathsf{nil})\rangle$$

From this we see that the set of states at program location 5 reachable from s after executing the loop one or more times is $Z = \{\langle 5, k_s{>}k \wedge \mathsf{ls}^{k'}(y, x) * \mathsf{ls}^k(x, \mathsf{nil})\rangle\}$. Let r be the element in Z from Fig. 2: $r = \langle 5, k_s{>}k \wedge \mathsf{ls}^{k'}(y, x) * \mathsf{ls}^k(x, \mathsf{nil})\rangle$. All that remains is to prove $\mathrm{WF}(r)$, which we do by calculating: $\alpha_k(r) = k_s{>}k$ and then calling RANKFINDER($k_s{>}k$). In this case RANKFINDER reports that the relation is well-founded.

6   Experimental Results

In the experimental results described in [4], TERMINATOR [5] was used to try to prove that Windows device driver dispatch routines always return to their calling context. A number of false bugs were reported in those experiments due to TERMINATOR's inaccuracy with respect to heaps. In this section we revisit 21 loops from [4] in which ℓ-termination was not provable. Fig. 6 displays the results of these experiments (which were run on a 3.6GHz Pentium 4 machine). The symbol ✓ is used to indicate the 16 cases in which MUTANT was able to prove ℓ-termination. The symbol ⊘ is used to represent failed proof attempts.

Loop	1	2	3	4	5	6	7	8	9	10	11	12	13	14	15	16	17	18	19	20	21
Time (s)	0.0	0.0	8.0	0.3	1.7	13	296	0.1	5.4	0.0	8.2	821	0.0	1.6	152	0.0	2.6	3.5	58	32	261
Result	✓	⊘	✓	✓	✓	✓	✓	⊘	⊘	✓	✓	✓	✓	✓	✓	✓	⊘	✓	⊘	✓	✓
WF checks	1	4	16	3	5	9	15	2	4	1	6	39	1	3	16	1	28	9	85	20	37

Fig. 6. Results of experiments using MUTANT on loops from extracted from Windows device drivers falsely reported as non-terminating by TERMINATOR (see [4]). The symbol ✓ indicates that MUTANT was able to prove the loop ℓ-terminating; The symbol ⊘ means that a termination bug was found.

The number of disjuncts in the transition invariant, described in Section 2, is reported in the bottom row.

Each failed well-foundedness check leads directly to a counterexample in the code (the production of counterexamples could be automated but isn't in the current setup). Note that for now we have to extract each loop from a Windows device driver loop by hand: MUTANT currently does not support C functions and address-of (&) operator on stack variables, so some manual translation akin to a compiler front-end was required to construct equivalent programs. Furthermore, loop preconditions were inserted by hand. These preconditions could probably be automatically computed via the analysis like the one described in [7].

Example 19 is the code from Fig. 1. As we see from Fig. 6, this loop has a termination bug. The problem is that `InitializeListHead` creates a self-loop from `&irp->Tail.Overlay.ListEntry.Flink` to `&irp->Tail.Overlay.ListEntry` and that `irp->Tail.Overlay.ListEntry.Flink` aliases `entry`, meaning that after the call to `InitializeListHead`, `entry` equals `entry->Flink`. Example 18 is based on fixed code provided to us from the Windows kernel team after we reported the bug. These experiments reveal a strong difference in MUTANT's running time between analyzing terminating versus non-terminating loops.

Example 8 is the only false bug reported by MUTANT: the loop actually does ℓ-terminate, but our analysis is unable to prove it. This example amounts to reversing a panhandle list. The initial state describes such lists, which cycle back to a list node other than the head node, with the formula: $\mathsf{ls}^i(c, x') * \mathsf{ls}^j(x', y') * \mathsf{ls}^k(y', x')$. The program is essentially a common in-place list reversal algorithm. When the program is run starting from a panhandle list, first the handle is reversed in the usual way, then the cycle is reversed, and finally the handle is reversed once again. Notice, in particular, that the handle is walked twice, and so the quantity which is decreasing with each loop iteration is $2i + j + k$, which our analysis does not detect. Finally, note that MUTANT correctly proves the termination of list reversal when starting either with an acyclic or cyclic list.

7 Conclusion

In this paper we have introduced a novel method of automatically proving the termination of loops whose correctness depends on the mutation of the heap. As the experimental results demonstrate, MUTANT is able to prove the termination of loops that TERMINATOR was previously unable to handle. MUTANT is completely automatic (*e.g.*, it does not require the user to provide ranking functions). MUTANT provides information which may lead to concrete counterexamples when a termination proof fails.

Related Work. Our work differs from the previous research on termination proof methods in that we have proposed the first known tool to support entirely automatic termination proofs of imperative programs with deep heap updates. To the best of our knowledge, the experimental results in Section 6 represent the first known successful application of this type of tool to industrial systems with loops that imperatively construct or destruct heap-based data structures. Note that absolutely no user intervention is required (*i.e.*, ranking functions or proof hints). Yahav's dissertation [15] discusses experiments in which imperative list-processing loops are proved terminating (the programs come from [8]). This work is less automatic than MUTANT: for the reason that the user must first examine the loop and specify a single (possibly lexicographically ordered) ranking function. MUTANT/TERMINATOR automatically proves all of the examples from [8] in less than 10s total. Note that 6.5s of this 10s was spent solving the one arithmetic (non-heap) example using the standard TERMINATOR algorithm.

MUTANT also uses the relatively new TERMINATOR proof-rule (finding a disjunctively well-founded over-approximation), which was originally proposed in [12]. While this use is not an original contribution, it means that the flavor of the analysis is different from previous approaches (such as [16], [10] or [6]).

Our algorithm works in reverse order with respect to TERMINATOR's original method for arithmetic programs. TERMINATOR iteratively refines the set of well-founded relations based on false counterexamples to the termination property. The relations are well-founded by construction, the difficultly is proving that they over-approximate the meaning of the loop or recursive function. MUTANT first computes an over-approximation and proves that it is disjunctively well-founded. The over-approximation is given, the question is *are the disjuncts well-founded?*

Acknowledgments

We are grateful to Andreas Podelski, Andrey Rybalchenko, Moshe Vardi, Tal Lev-Ami, Roman Manevich, Noam Rinetzky, Mooly Sagiv, Eran Yahav, and Greta Yorsh for discussions, and the anonymous referees for helpful comments. Distefano and O'Hearn acknowledge support from the EPSRC.

References

[1] J. Berdine, C. Calcagno, and P. O'Hearn. Symbolic execution with separation logic. In *APLAS*, 2005.

[2] A. Bradley, Z. Manna, and H. Sipma. Termination of polynomial programs. In *VMCAI*, 2005.

[3] B. Cook, A. Podelski, and A. Rybalchenko. Abstraction refinement for termination. In *SAS*, 2005.

[4] B. Cook, A. Podelski, and A. Rybalchenko. Termination proofs for systems code. In *PLDI*, 2006.

[5] B. Cook, A. Podelski, and A. Rybalchenko. Terminator: Beyond safety. In *CAV*, 2006.

[6] D. Distefano, J.-P. Katoen, and A. Rensink. Who is pointing when to whom? on the automated verification of linked list structures. In *FSTTCS*, 2004.

[7] D. Distefano, P. W. O'Hearn, and H. Yang. A local shape analysis based on separation logic. In *TACAS*, 2006.

[8] N. Dor, M. Rodeh, and S. Sagiv. Checking cleanness in linked lists. In *SAS*, 2000.

[9] R. W. Floyd. Assigning meanings to programs. In *Proceedings of Symposia in Applied Mathematics*, 1967.

[10] C. S. Lee, N. D. Jones, and A. M. Ben-Amram. The size-change principle for program termination. In *POPL*, 2001.

[11] A. Podelski and A. Rybalchenko. A complete method for the synthesis of linear ranking functions. In *VMCAI*, 2004.

[12] A. Podelski and A. Rybalchenko. Transition invariants. In *LICS*, 2004.

[13] A. Podelski and A. Rybalchenko. Transition predicate abstraction and fair termination. In *POPL*, 2005.

[14] J. Reynolds. Separation logic: A logic for shared mutable data structures. In *LICS*, 2002.

[15] E. Yahav. *Property-Guided Verification of Concurrent Heap-Manipulating Programs*. PhD thesis, 2004.

[16] E. Yahav, T. Reps, M. Sagiv, and R. Wilhelm. Verifying temporal heap properties specified via evolution logic. In *ESOP*, 2003.

Termination Analysis with Calling Context Graphs*

Panagiotis Manolios and Daron Vroon

College of Computing, Georgia Institute of Technology, Atlanta, GA, 30332, USA
http://www.cc.gatech.edu/home/{manolios, vroon}

Abstract. We introduce *calling context graphs* and various static and theorem proving based analyses that together provide a powerful method for proving termination of programs written in feature-rich, first order, functional programming languages. In contrast to previous work, our method is highly automated and handles any source of looping behavior in such languages, including recursive definitions, mutual recursion, the use of recursive data structures, etc. We have implemented our method for the ACL2 programming language and evaluated the result using the ACL2 regression suite, which consists of numerous libraries with a total of over 10,000 function definitions. Our method was able to automatically detect termination of over 98% of these functions.

1 Introduction

Proofs of termination are a critical component of program correctness arguments. In the case of transformational systems, termination proofs allow us to extend partial correctness results to total correctness. In the case of reactive systems, they are used to prove liveness properties, *i.e.*, to show that some desirable behavior is not postponed forever. Unfortunately, besides being the quintessential undecidable problem [21], termination analysis is further exacerbated by modern programming language features such as recursion, mutual recursion, non-linear loop conditions, and loops that depend on recursive data structures.

Because of this, previous work has tended to focus on finding decidable fragments of the problem, or has been designed for simple languages that lack the complexity of actual programming languages. Within such restricted settings, much progress has been made, *e.g.*, there is work on analyzing the termination of semi-algebraic programs, toy functional languages, and term rewriting systems (see Section 6).

We present a new termination analysis based on calling context graphs (CCGs) for a fully featured class of modern functional programming languages. If a purely functional program is nonterminating, there exists a sequence of values $v_1, v_2, \ldots, v_n$ such that for some function f_1, $f_1(v_1, v_2, \ldots, v_n)$ leads to an infinite sequence of function calls, $f_2(\ldots), f_3(\ldots), \ldots$, where the call to f_i results in the call to f_{i+1}, for all i. CCGs are a data structure which can conservatively approximate all such possible sequences. In addition, we show that CCGs are amenable to various analyses, involving both static analysis and theorem proving, that enable us to construct surprisingly precise approximations of the actual function call sequences. The termination proof then involves

---

* This research was funded in part by NSF grants CCF-0429924, IIS-0417413, and CCF-0438871.

T. Ball and R.B. Jones (Eds.): CAV 2006, LNCS 4144, pp. 401–414, 2006.

assigning sets of calling context measures (CCMs) over well-founded domains to the calls and showing that for every possible infinite sequence there is a corresponding sequence of CCMs that is infinitely decreasing. We present an algorithm based on CCGs and CCMs that can automatically reason about any source of looping behavior in first order purely functional programming languages and which can automatically handle a much larger class of programs than previous approaches.

We have implemented our algorithm in the ACL2 theorem proving system, which consists of a feature-rich first-order functional programming language, a logic for that language, and an automatic theorem prover [11,10,9]. It has a large, worldwide user base, and has been used in a wide variety of industrial verification projects ranging from reasoning about modern processor designs to modeling programs written in imperative languages such as Java. ACL2 is part of the Boyer-Moore family of provers, for which its authors received the 2005 ACM Software System Award. Termination plays a key role in ACL2, as it is used to justify induction schemes and also every defined function must be shown to terminate. Therefore, users spend a significant amount of time reasoning about termination, and stand to greatly benefit from the work presented here.

In order to evaluate our work, we ran our implementation on the ACL2 regression suite, a collection of numerous libraries by a variety of authors covering topics such as commercial floating point verification (at AMD and IBM), JVM bytecode verification, term rewriting algorithm verification, the verification of a model checker, the verification of graph algorithms, etc. Our algorithm was able to automatically prove termination for over 98% of the more than 10,000 functions in the regression suite. This was accomplished with no user interaction.

The rest of the paper is organized as follows. In Section 2 we introduce the core of first-order functional languages. In Section 3, we introduce and develop the theory of calling context graphs. Our termination algorithm appears in Section 4, and experimental results are given in Section 5. Some readers may want to read Section 5 first. We end with related work and conclusions.

2   Semantics

While our method works for feature-rich, first-order functional programming languages including ACL2, such languages are quite complicated and we cannot fully describe them here. Instead, in Figure 1, we present the semantics of *FL*, a language that only contains the core features of first-order functional languages. The semantics are similar to what can be found in standard programming language texts. Some readers may want to skim this section initially, returning as needed later.

We are concerned with proving the termination of well-formed function definitions (members of the set *Defs*), which are of the form define $f(x_1, \ldots, x_n) = e$, where $f \in FName$ is a function name, $x_1, \ldots, x_n \in Var$ are variables, and $e \in Expr$ is an expression whose free variables are a subset of $\{x_1, \ldots, x_n\}$.

The universe of values over which *FL* is defined is *Val* and it includes symbols, strings, integers, rationals, and lists, but is otherwise unspecified. However, since this is a first order language, functions are not first class data objects, and are not included in *Val*. We use $\perp$ (which is not in *Val*) to denote nontermination, and $Val_\perp = Val \cup \{\perp\}$. An environment maps variables to values.

$$d \in Defs$$
$$f \in FName$$
$$x \in Var$$
$$e \in Expr$$
$$v \in Val$$
$$u \in Val_\perp = Val \cup \{\perp\}$$
$$\epsilon \in Env = Var \rightarrow Val$$
$$\phi \in Funct = Val^* \rightarrow Val_\perp$$
$$\psi \in TFunct = Val^* \rightarrow Val \subseteq Funct$$
$$h \in IHist = FName \rightarrow Val^* \rightarrow Val_\perp$$
$$H \in Hist = FName \rightarrow Val^* \rightarrow Val \subseteq IHist$$

$$[\![e]\!]^h \epsilon \ : \ Expr \times IHist \times Env \rightarrow Val_\perp$$
$$\mathcal{O} \ : \ Op \rightarrow TFunct$$
$$str \ : \ Funct \rightarrow Val_\perp^* \rightarrow Val_\perp$$
$$\mathcal{D}\,[\![d]\!]\,H \ : \ Defs \times Hist \rightarrow Funct^+$$
$$fix \ : \ (Funct^* \rightarrow Funct^*) \rightarrow Funct^*$$

$$str\,(\phi)\,\langle u_i \rangle_{i=1}^n = \begin{cases} \perp & \text{if } \langle \exists i \in [1..n] :: u_i = \perp \rangle \\ \phi\,(u_i)_{i=1}^n & \text{otherwise} \end{cases}$$

$$fix\,\xi = \lim_{j \to \infty} \xi^j\,\langle \lambda v_i . \perp \rangle_{i=1}^m$$

$$[\![x]\!]^h \epsilon = \epsilon.x \ , \quad [\![v]\!]^h \epsilon = v$$

$$[\![e_1\ op\ e_2]\!]^h \epsilon = str\,(\mathcal{O}\,[\![op]\!])\,\left\langle [\![e_i]\!]^h \epsilon \right\rangle_{i=1}^2$$

$$[\![f(e_1,\ldots,e_n)]\!]^h \epsilon = str\,(h.f)\,\left\langle [\![e_i]\!]^h \epsilon \right\rangle_{i=1}^n$$

$$\left[\!\!\left[\begin{array}{l} \texttt{let } x_1 = e_1 \\ \quad \cdots \\ \quad x_n = e_n \\ \texttt{in } e \end{array} \right]\!\!\right]^h \epsilon = str\,\left(\lambda(v_i)_{i=1}^n . [\![e]\!]^h \epsilon[v_i/x_i]_{i=1}^n \right)\,\left\langle [\![e_i]\!]^h \epsilon \right\rangle_{i=1}^n$$

$$[\![\texttt{if } e_1 \texttt{ then } e_2 \texttt{ else } e_3]\!]^h \epsilon = str\,\left(\lambda(v) . \left\{ \begin{array}{l} [\![e_2]\!]^h \epsilon \text{ if } v \neq \texttt{nil}, \\ [\![e_3]\!]^h \epsilon \text{ otherwise.} \end{array} \right. \right)\,\left\langle [\![e_1]\!]^h \epsilon \right\rangle$$

$$\mathcal{D} \left[\!\!\left[\begin{array}{l} \texttt{define } f_1(x_1^1,\ldots,x_{n_1}^1) = e_1 \\ \quad \cdots \\ \texttt{define } f_k(x_1^k,\ldots,x_{n_k}^k) = e_k \end{array} \right]\!\!\right] H = fix\,\left(\lambda(\phi_i)_{i=1}^k . \left\langle \lambda(v_j^i)_{j=1}^{n_j} . [\![e_i]\!]^{H[\phi_i/f_i]} [v_j^i/x_j^i]_{j=1}^{n_j} \right\rangle_{i=1}^k \right)$$

Fig. 1. Language Semantics of *FL*

Function definitions in *FL* denote mathematical functions, which can either be members of the set *Funct* or *TFunct*. *Funct* consists of a set of partial functions, which means that for some inputs, functions in *Funct* may return $\perp$, denoting nontermination. *TFunct* is the subset of *Funct* consisting of all the total (*i.e.*, terminating) functions. A *history* maps function names to total functions (of the appropriate arity) and an *intermediate history* maps function names to partial functions (of the appropriate arity).

The termination problem we consider is: given a history, H, and a set of mutually recursive definitions, d, show that the functions corresponding to the definitions in d are terminating. To do this, we need to refer not only to H, but also to the (possibly partial) functions corresponding to the definitions in d. This is accomplished by using an intermediate history, h, which is just H extended so that it includes the function names appearing in d and their corresponding functions, as given by the semantics of *FL* (which are given in Figure 1 and described in more detail in the next paragraph). We then attempt to prove that the functions defined in d terminate, which implies that the intermediate history, h, is actually a history. If so, we have a new history. Otherwise, we reject d, revert to H, and report the problem to the user. This allows the user to incrementally define programs, as is common in programming environments for functional languages, such as Lisp.

We use five functions to define the semantics of *FL*. The function $[\![e]\!]^h \epsilon$ defines how to evaluate an expression, e, given an intermediate history, h, and an environment, ϵ. The function $\mathcal{O}$ maps *FL*'s unspecified set of built-in operators (*Op*) to their corresponding functions. The set of built-in operators includes the usual Boolean and arithmetic operators, such as and, or, not, iff, implies, +, -, /, *, etc. The function *str* corresponds to strict application. As input, it takes a function and a vector of values (possibly including $\bot$, which indicates nontermination). It returns $\bot$ if any of the input values is $\bot$; otherwise, it returns the result of applying the function to the values (which could also be $\bot$). The definitions of the semantics functions for variables, values, built-in operators, function application, lets, and ifs are now straightforward.

Function definitions are handled with $\mathcal{D}\,[\![d]\!]\,H$, which defines what mathematical functions (elements of *Functs*) correspond to a set of function definitions, d, given history H. Its definition depends on the *fix* function, which is used to define the semantics of recursive function definitions using the standard fixpoint approach. The *fix* function takes as input ξ, a function from a vector of functions to a vector of functions, and returns the vector of functions obtained by taking the limit as j approaches infinity of applying ξ to the vector of functions returning $\bot$. The definition of $\mathcal{D}\,[\![d]\!]\,H$ uses *fix* to "unroll" the bodies of the definitions an unbounded number of times, which results in a vector of partial functions that corresponds to the semantics of the definitions.

Throughout the rest of this paper, unless otherwise specified, we assume a fixed history, H and a set of syntactically correct, mutually-recursive function definitions, d, such that none of the function names in d are the same as those in the domain of H. The intermediate history h is obtained by extending H with the semantics of the function definitions in d. To simplify the notation, we assume the uniqueness of subexpressions. That is, if expression e has two identical subexpressions, then we have some way of determining which is which. This can be accomplished by pairing each subexpression with its unique position within the base expression. We use "$e_1 \trianglelefteq e_2$" to denote that e_1 is a sub-expression of e_2.

We now give several definitions related to the semantics of *FL* that we will use throughout the paper. We begin by defining the set of *governors* under which a subexpression e' of e is reached, ignoring nontermination (for now). Our definition is synonymous with that in [12]. If e is an *FL* let statement and $e' \trianglelefteq e$, then we use $\sigma_{e'}^e$ to denote the substitution (a mapping from variables to expressions) corresponding to the let bindings of e that are visible in e'. For example, if $e = \text{let } x = e_1 \text{ in } e_2$, then $\sigma_{e_2}^e = \{\langle x, e_1 \rangle\}$ and $\sigma_{e_1}^e = \{\}$. We use $e\sigma$ to denote the expression obtained by applying substitution σ to e.

Definition 1. *Given expressions e', e such that $e' \trianglelefteq e$, the* set of governors of e' in e *is the set* $\{e_1\sigma_{e_1}^e \mid \text{if } e_1 \text{ then } e_2 \text{ else } e_3 \trianglelefteq e \wedge e' \trianglelefteq e_2\} \cup \{\text{not}(e_1\sigma_{e_1}^e) \mid \text{if } e_1 \text{ then } e_2 \text{ else } e_3 \trianglelefteq e \wedge e' \trianglelefteq e_3\}$.

The idea of the governors of e' in e is that the execution of e reaches e' exactly when the governors are true. We therefore define the more general notion of when expressions "hold":

Definition 2. *We say a set of expressions, E, holds for environment ϵ, denoted $\mathcal{H}^h\,[\![E]\!]\,\epsilon$, if $\bigwedge_{e \in E}([\![e]\!]^h\,\epsilon \notin \{\text{nil}, \bot\})$.*

3   Calling Context Graphs

In this section, we introduce calling context graphs (CCGs) and related notions. We also show how CCGs can be used reason about program termination.

```
define f(x) =
  if not(intp(x)) or x = 0
    then 0
    else if x < 0 then f(x+1)
                  else f(x-1)
define dec(n) =
  if not(intp(x)) or x ≤ 0
    then 255
    else n - 1

define foo(i, j) =
  if i = 1 then
    if j = 1 then 0
    else foo(dec(j), dec(j))
  else foo(dec(i), j)
```

1. $\langle$ f, $\{$intp(x), x $\neq$ 0, x $<$ 0$\}$, f(x+1)$\rangle$
2. $\langle$ f, $\{$intp(x), x $\neq$ 0, x $\geq$ 0$\}$, f(x-1)$\rangle$

1. $\langle$ foo, $\{$i = 1, j $\neq$ 1$\}$, foo(dec(j), dec(j))$\rangle$
2. $\langle$ foo, $\{$i $\neq$ 1$\}$, foo(dec(i), j)$\rangle$

Fig. 2. Definitions, contexts, and minimal CCGs for f and foo

Definition 3. *A* calling context *is a triple, $\langle f, G, e \rangle$, where f is the name of a function defined in d, G is a set of expressions whose free variables are all parameters of f, and e is a call of a function in d whose free variables are all parameters of f. This is a* precise *calling context if e is a subexpression in the body of f and G is the set of governors of e in the body of f.*

We sometimes refer to a calling context simply as a context. The definitions and contexts for two examples are given in Figure 2. We now introduce the notion of a well-formed sequence of contexts, a notion that is strongly related to termination in *FL*.

Definition 4. *Let $c = (\langle f_i, G_i, f_{i+1}(e_{i,1}, \ldots, e_{i,n_{i+1}}) \rangle)_i$ be a sequence of calling contexts, where n_i is the arity of f_i and $(x_{i,k})_{k=1}^{n_i}$ are the formals of f_i. For a given vector of values v, we define a sequence of environments where ϵ_1^v maps $x_{1,k}$ to v_k and ϵ_{i+1}^v maps $x_{i+1,k}$ to $[\![e_{i,k}]\!]^h \epsilon_i^v$. We say c is* well-formed *if there exists a witness for c: a vector of values, v, such that for every $i > 0$, $\mathcal{H}^h [\![G_i]\!] \epsilon_i^v$ and $\langle \forall j \leq n_i :: [\![e_{i,j}]\!]^h \epsilon_i^v \neq \bot$.*

We use the notation ϵ_i^v introduced in the above definition throughout the paper. Termination in *FL* can be expressed in terms of well-formed sequences, as we see in the next theorem. (Due to space considerations all proofs have been elided.)

Theorem 1. *The functions of d terminate on all inputs iff every well-formed sequence of precise contexts is finite.*

We now define the notion of a *calling context graph* and show that it is a conservative approximation of the well-formed sequence of contexts.

Definition 5. *A* calling context graph (CCG), *is a directed graph, $\mathcal{G} = (C, E)$, where C is a set of calling contexts, and for any pair of contexts $c_1, c_2 \in C$, if the sequence $\langle c_1, c_2 \rangle$ is well-formed, then $\langle c_1, c_2 \rangle \in E$. If C is the set of precise contexts of d, then $\mathcal{G}$ is called a* precise CCG *of d.*

The minimal precise CCG for function f in Figure 2 is shown in the same figure. Note that there is no edge between the two contexts. This is because if x is a positive integer, then decrementing x by 1 will not lead to a negative integer. Likewise, adding 1 to x if it is a negative integer cannot produce a positive integer. Notice that this mirrors the

```
define size(x) = if pairp(x) then size(first(x)) + size(rest(x)) + 1
                 else if intp(x) then abs(x) else 0
```

Fig. 3. Definition of `size`

looping behaviors of the function. Figure 2 also contains the minimal precise CCG for function `foo`. Notice that if the first context of `foo` is reached, `foo` calls itself, passing in $\langle \text{dec } j \rangle$ for both arguments. Since $\langle \text{dec } j \rangle$ cannot simultaneously be both equal to 1 and not equal to 1, it is impossible to immediately reach context 1 again. However both contexts can reach context 2, and context 2 can reach context 1.

Lemma 1. *Given a CCG, $\mathcal{G} = (C, E)$, every well-formed sequence of calling contexts of C is a path in $\mathcal{G}$.*

Note that the converse of the above lemma does not hold. This is because the definition of a CCG only requires local reachability whereas a well-formed sequence of contexts requires that the entire sequence correspond to a single computation. As a result, a CCG is an abstraction of the actual system. We use CCGs to perform a local analysis which if successful can determine that the definitions terminate. To do this, we start by assigning calling context measures to contexts in the CCG.

Definition 6. *Given a calling context, $c = \langle f, G, e \rangle$, and a set $S \subseteq Val$, a calling context measure (CCM) for c over S, s, is an expression whose free variables are parameters of f and for any environment, ϵ, $\mathcal{H}^h [\![G]\!] \epsilon \Rightarrow [\![s]\!]^h \epsilon \in S$.*

CCMs simply map the parameters of a function into some set. For our purposes, this set will have a well-founded ordering on it. Now we create a mechanism for comparing the CCM of two adjacent contexts in a CCG.

Definition 7. *Let $\mathcal{G} = (C, E)$ be a CCG with $e = \langle c_1, c_2 \rangle \in E$. Let $\langle S, \prec \rangle$ be a well-founded structure where S_{c_1} and S_{c_2} are sets of CCMs over S for c_1 and c_2, respectively. Then, the CCM function for e over $\prec, S_{c_1}$, and S_{c_2} is the function ϕ : $S_{c_1} \times S_{c_2} \to \{>, \geq, \times\}$ such that: (1) $\phi(s_1, s_2) = \ >$ only if for all witnesses v for $\langle c_1, c_2 \rangle$, we have $[\![s_1]\!]^h \epsilon_1^v \succ [\![s_2]\!]^h \epsilon_2^v$; (2) $\phi(s_1, s_2) = \ \geq$ only if for all witnesses v for $\langle c_1, c_2 \rangle$, we have $[\![s_1]\!]^h \epsilon_1^v \succeq [\![s_2]\!]^h \epsilon_2^v$; (3) $\phi(s_1, s_2) = \times$, otherwise.*

We represent CCM functions for $\langle c_1, c_2 \rangle$ graphically with a box containing the CCMs for c_1, c_2 on the left and right, respectively. An edge is drawn from s_1, a left CCM, to s_2, a right CCM, with the label $\phi(s_1, s_2)$ iff it is $>$ or $\geq$. If $\phi(s_1, s_2)$ is $\times$, no edge is drawn.

We now consider some examples. For the function `f` in Figure 2, we use the `size` function in Figure 3 applied to `f`'s parameter, `x`, as the only CCM for both contexts. The range of `size` is the set of natural numbers, and the function is designed to mirror common induction schemes, *e.g.*, induction on the size of a list. Notice that for each context in our example, the CCM decreases for all values of `x` that satisfy the governors of the context. The resulting CCM functions are shown in Figure 4a. For the function `foo` in Figure 2, we use different CCMs. Namely, we apply `dec` to the arguments; note that `dec` always returns a natural number, which is a well-founded domain under the

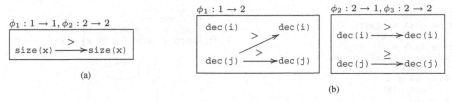

Fig. 4. (a) CCM function for f. (b) CCM functions for foo.

```
define ack (x, y) =
    if (not(intp(x)) or x ≤ 0) then 1
    else if (not(intp(y)) or y ≤ 0)
        then if x=1 then 2 else x+2
        else ack(ack(x-1, y), y-1)
```

$\phi_1 : 1 \rightarrow 1,$
$\phi_2 : 1 \rightarrow 2$

$x \xrightarrow{>} x$

$y \xrightarrow{\geq} y$

$\phi_3 : 2 \rightarrow 1,$
$\phi_4 : 2 \rightarrow 2$

$x \qquad x$

$y \xrightarrow{>} y$

1. $\langle \text{ack}, \{\text{intp(x)}, 0 < \text{x}, \text{intp(y)}, 0 < \text{y}\}, \text{ack(x-1, y)}\rangle$
2. $\langle \text{ack}, \{\text{intp(x)}, 0 < \text{x}, \text{intp(y)}, 0 < \text{y}\}, \text{ack(ack(x-1, y), y-1)}\rangle$

Fig. 5. Ackermann's function

$<$ relation. The result is shown in Figure 4b. The question of how to choose CCMs is addressed in Section 4.

We use CCM functions to show that certain infinite paths are not feasible and also to show that CCGs correspond to terminating functions.

Definition 8. *We say that a CCG, $\mathcal{G} = (C, E)$ is well-founded if there exists a well-founded structure, $\langle S, \prec \rangle$ and a mapping, m, from C into sets of CCMs over S such that $\mathcal{M}_{C, \prec, m}(c)$ for all infinite paths, $c = c_1, c_2, \ldots$, through $\mathcal{G}$. $\mathcal{M}_{C, \prec, m}$ is a CCM predicate and holds for an infinite sequence of contexts, c, iff there exists $i_0 \geq 1$ and a sequence $s_{i_0}, s_{i_0+1}, \ldots$ such that for all $i \geq i_0$, $s_i \in m(c_i)$ and $\phi_i(s_i, s_{i+1}) \in \{>, \geq\}$, and for infinitely many such i, $\phi_i(s_i, s_{i+1}) = >$, where ϕ_i denotes the CCM function for $\langle c_i, c_{i+1} \rangle$ with CCMs $m(c_i)$ and $m(c_{i+1})$.*

It is important to note here that we do not need to fix a CCM for each context in order to satisfy the CCM predicate. Rather, we can select from any of the CCMs for a given context each time it appears in a sequence. For example, consider Ackermann's function, given in Figure 5. Here, if a sequence contains context 2 infinitely often, then y decreases infinitely, and if it does not, then there is an infinite suffix of the sequence that is just context 1, which means that x decreases infinitely often. It is possible to create one measure that decreases in both cases, but this measure requires a well-founded structure more powerful and complex than the natural numbers.

It turns out that we only need to consider maximal SCCs (strongly connected components) to establish termination.

Theorem 2. *Let $\mathcal{G} = (C, E)$ be a CCG, s.t. C is the set of precise contexts of d. If every maximal SCC of $\mathcal{G}$ is well-founded, then all functions of d terminate on all inputs.*

Notice that the converse of Theorem 2 does not hold because the paths of a CCG are a superset of the well-formed sequences of contexts. For example, notice that when

```
define g(x) = f(x+1)
define h(x) = f(x-1)
define f(x) =
    if not(intp(x)) or x=0
        then 0
    else if x < 0
        then g(x)
    else h(x)
```

1. $\langle g, \{\}, f(x+1) \rangle$
2. $\langle h, \{\}, f(x-1) \rangle$
3. $\langle f, \{intp(x), x \neq 0, x < 0\}, g(x) \rangle$
4. $\langle f, \{intp(x), x \neq 0, 0 \leq x\}, h(x) \rangle$

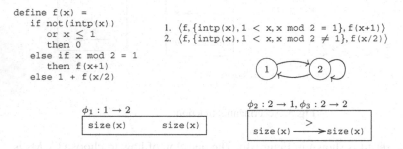

Fig. 6. Altered version of function defined in Figure 2

```
define f(x) =
    if not(intp(x))
        or x ≤ 1
        then 0
    else if x mod 2 = 1
        then f(x+1)
    else 1 + f(x/2)
```

1. $\langle f, \{intp(x), 1 < x, x \bmod 2 = 1\}, f(x+1) \rangle$
2. $\langle f, \{intp(x), 1 < x, x \bmod 2 \neq 1\}, f(x/2) \rangle$

$\phi_1 : 1 \to 2$

size(x)	size(x)

$\phi_2 : 2 \to 1, \phi_3 : 2 \to 2$

size(x)	$\xrightarrow{\ >\ }$	size(x)

Fig. 7. Example of the abstraction inherent in the infinite CCM relation

we split function f from Figure 2 into several functions, as in Figure 6, all the contexts now appear in the same SCC. Why? Consider the function, g. Note that g(2) results in the call f(3), which leads to context 4. A similar situation arises for h. Thus $1, 4, 2, 3, 1, 4, 2, 3, \ldots$ is a valid path through any CCG, even though it is not a well-formed sequence of contexts. Each time through the loop $1, 4, 2, 3$, the value of x stays the same, hence, the termination analysis presented so far fails.

Another source of imprecision is due to the local analysis used in determining if a CCG is well-founded. If a value decreases over several steps, but increases for one of those steps, the termination analysis presented so far will fail. Consider the example in Figure 7. When x is odd, 1 is added to x and when it is even, x is divided by 2. This continues until x is 1 (or not a positive integer). This results in an overall decrease of the value of x despite the initial increase.

In order to gain more accuracy and overcome many of the problems caused by the local nature of our analysis, we introduce the idea of context merging. This essentially enables us to consider multiple steps instead of single steps.

Definition 9. *The* call substitution *of* $e = f(e_1, e_2, \ldots, e_n)$, *denoted* σ_e, *maps* x_i *to* e_i *for all* $1 \leq i \leq n$, *where* $x_1, x_2, \ldots, x_n$ *are the parameters of f.*

Definition 10. *Let* $\langle c_1, c_2 \rangle$ *be a well-formed sequence of calling contexts, where* $c_1 = \langle f_1, G_1, e_1 \rangle$ *and* $c_2 = \langle f_2, G_2, e_2 \rangle$. *The* merging *of* c_1 *and* c_2, *denoted* $c_1; c_2$, *is the calling context* $\langle f_1, G_1 \cup \{p\sigma_{e_1} \mid p \in G_2\}, e_2\sigma_{e_1} \rangle$.

As an example, note that if in Figure 6 we merge context 3 with context 1 and context 4 with context 2, we get contexts 1 and 2 of Figure 2, respectively. This makes sense as

$1; 2 \ : \langle \text{f}, \{\text{intp(x)}, 0 \le \text{x}, \text{x} \ne 1, \text{x} \bmod 2 = 1, \text{intp(x+1)}, 0 \le \text{x+1}, (\text{x+1}) \bmod 2 \ne 1\}, \text{f((x+1)/2)}\rangle$
$2; 1 \ : \langle \text{f}, \{\text{intp(x)}, 0 \le \text{x}, \text{x} \ne 1, \text{x} \bmod 2 \ne 1, \text{intp(x/2)}, 0 \le \text{x/2}, (\text{x/2}) \bmod 2 = 1\}, \text{f(x/2+1)}\rangle$
$2; 2 \ : \langle \text{f}, \{\text{intp(x)}, 0 \le \text{x}, \text{x} \ne 1, \text{x} \bmod 2 \ne 1, \text{intp(x+1)}, 0 \le \text{x+1}, (\text{x+1}) \bmod 2 \ne 1\}, \text{f((x/2)/2)}\rangle$

Fig. 8. Merging and compaction results for Figure 7

the example in Figure 6 was obtained by splitting f into several functions and merging essentially recombines the contexts. For a more interesting example, in Figure 7 consider merging context 1 with context 2, context 2 with context 1, and context 2 with itself; the result appears in Figure 8.

We now use merging to define the notion of absorption and show that given a CCG, we can define an infinite sequence of CCGs such that if we can prove that at least one CCG in the sequence terminates, then so does the original CCG. This can greatly extend the applicability of our analysis.

Definition 11. *Given a CCG,* $\mathcal{G} = (C, E)$*, the result of* absorbing $c \in C$ *is a CCG* $\mathcal{G}' = (C', E')$ *where* $C' = C \backslash \{c\} \cup \{c; c' \mid \langle c, c' \rangle \in E\}$*.*

Theorem 3. *Let* $\mathcal{G}_0, \mathcal{G}_1, \dots$ *be a sequence of CCGs such that* $\mathcal{G}_0$ *is a precise CCG of* d*, and* $\mathcal{G}_{i+1}$ *is obtained from* $\mathcal{G}_i$ *by absorbing a context. If for some* i*, every maximal SCC of* $\mathcal{G}_i$ *is well-founded, then every function in* d *terminates on all inputs.*

4   Algorithm

The definitions given in Section 3 suggest the following algorithm for the termination analysis of a set of function definitions, d, using static analysis and theorem proving.

1. Using static analysis, construct the precise calling contexts of d.
2. Using theorem proving, build a precise CCG.
3. Absorb contexts that have only one successor.
4. Divide the CCG into SCCs
5. Choose a well-founded structure for each SCC, and a set of CCMs for each context.
6. Use theorem proving to construct safe approximations of the CCM functions.
7. Perform analysis to decide the CCM predicate for all paths through each SCC.

Step 1 is straightforward, and one can construct the algorithm from Definition 1. Step 2 involves building a CCG. We wish to construct as minimal a CCG as we can, in order to avoid spurious paths through the CCG, which complicate the rest of the algorithm and can lead to less accurate analysis. Therefore, for every pair of contexts, $c_1 = \langle f, G_1, e_1 \rangle$ and $c_2 = \langle g, G_2, e_2 \rangle$, such that e_1 is a call to g, we query the theorem prover to prove that $\langle c_1, c_2 \rangle$ is not well-formed, and therefore no edge needs to be added from c_1 to c_2. The corresponding theorem prover query is $\langle \forall v \in Val^* :: (\bigwedge_{p \in G_1} [\![p]\!]^h \epsilon_1^v \ne \text{nil}) \Rightarrow \neg(\bigwedge_{q \in G_2} [\![q \sigma_{e_1}]\!]^h \epsilon_1^v \ne \text{nil})\rangle$. If the proof is successful, we omit the edge $\langle c_1, c_2 \rangle$.

For this algorithm, we choose a simple absorption strategy. While absorbing a context in a CCG may result in a CCG that is more amenable to analysis, it may also increase the size of the CCG (by up to a factor of 2). However, if a context has only one successor in the CCG, absorbing it creates a CCG at most the size of the original. We therefore perform several passes through the graph, absorbing all such contexts with each pass. This simple absorption strategy is quite effective, *e.g.*, it allows us to automatically prove the termination of the functions in Figure 6. We plan to explore other strategies, such as looping from step 3 through step 7 and using the result of the previous failed termination analysis to guide absorption.

Once absorption is completed, we choose well-founded structures and CCMs. Currently, we always default to natural numbers for our well-founded structure. We use heuristics to automatically choose CCMs. Currently, these include the following.

- We use a version of the `size` function from Figure 3, called `acl2-count`, that is extended to deal with more types, adding the `size` of each parameter of a function to the CCMs of each context from that function.
- When $e_1 < e_2$ or $e_1 \leq e_2$ is a governor of a context, we add $e_1 - e_2$ as a CCM.
- When `intp(e)` and $0 < e$ are governors of the context, we add e as a CCM.

Finally, we propagate measures other than the `size` of the parameters through the rest of the contexts. That is, if we add a CCM s, to a context, then to each of its predecessors in the CCG we add the CCM $s\sigma_e$, where e is the call of the predecessor. We repeat this until the CCM is propagated to each of the contexts in the CCG.

In step 6, we approximate the CCM functions using the theorem prover. Given two adjacent contexts, $c_1 = \langle f, G_1, e_1 \rangle$ and $c_2 = \langle g, G_2, e_2 \rangle$, in an SCC, then for every CCM, s_1, for c_1 and every CCM, s_2, for c_2, we perform the following analysis. We first attempt to prove that for all ϵ, $[(\bigwedge_{p \in G_1} [\![p]\!]^h \epsilon \neq \texttt{nil}) \wedge (\bigwedge_{q \in G_2} [\![q\sigma_{e_1}]\!]^h \epsilon \neq \texttt{nil})] \Rightarrow [\![s_1]\!]^h \epsilon \prec [\![s_2\sigma_{e_1}]\!]^h \epsilon$. If this succeeds, we set $\phi(s_1, s_2)$ to be $>$. Otherwise, we attempt to prove that for all ϵ, $[(\bigwedge_{p \in G_1} [\![p]\!]^h \epsilon \neq \texttt{nil}) \wedge (\bigwedge_{q \in G_2} [\![q\sigma_{e_1}]\!]^h \epsilon \neq \texttt{nil})] \Rightarrow [\![s_1]\!]^h \epsilon \preceq [\![s_2\sigma_{e_1}]\!]^h \epsilon$. If this succeeds, we set $\phi(s_1, s_2)$ to be $\geq$. If neither proof succeeds, we set $\phi(s_1, s_2)$ to be $\times$.

The final step of the algorithm is to determine the value of the CCM predicate. In other words, we wish to determine that for every path through the graph, we can choose one of the CCMs from each context in the path such that they never increase in value, and infinitely decrease in value. A basic algorithm for doing this appears in [13].

5   Experimental Results

In this section, we experimentally evaluate the theory of calling context graphs we have introduced in this paper. As we saw in the previous section, our analysis is parameterized by the CCMs used and by the merging and absorption strategies employed. Our goal is to evaluate a simple, baseline version of the algorithms we have presented. Therefore, we use a simple absorption strategy and a small, simple collection of CCMs.

We have implemented our termination algorithm and used it on the ACL2 system, an industrial-strength theorem proving system that consists of a feature-rich functional programming language, a first-order logic for reasoning about this language, and a theorem prover for the automation of this reasoning. The ACL2 language can roughly be thought of as an applicative (pure, functional) subset of Common Lisp. The reality is more complicated because ACL2 has many advanced features such as single-threaded objects, which have been shown to enable execution at close to C speeds. ACL2 is actively used by a worldwide user-base to perform tasks as diverse as microprocessor modeling and simulation, the analysis of graph algorithms, algebraic reasoning, the analysis of imperative programs written in languages such as Java, etc. For more information on ACL2 see [11,10,9].

ACL2 is a good choice for us because termination arguments play a key role in its logic. First, every program admitted by the definitional principle must be shown to terminate before it is accepted by ACL2. This guarantees that definitions do not render ACL2 inconsistent. Second, inductive reasoning, ACL2's forte, is justified using termination arguments (to show that the induction is well-founded). Currently, termination in ACL2 is proven by providing an ordinal-valued measure and showing that it decreases on every recursive call. The ordinals are a transfinite extension of the natural numbers that form the basis of set theory; in fact, any well-founded argument can be phrased in terms of the ordinals. In recent work, we improved ACL2's handling of the ordinals, defined algorithms for ordinal arithmetic, and created a library of theorems for reasoning about the ordinals and ordinal arithmetic. The result was a significant improvement in ACL2's ability to reason about termination, once an ordinal measure is provided [14,15,16,17]. ACL2 tries to automate termination analysis by guessing a measure of the form `acl2-count(x)`, where x is some parameter of the function. Unfortunately, it is often the case that this simple heuristic fails and the user must discover and provide an appropriate ordinal measure.

Another advantage of using ACL2 is that it has a regression suite consisting of 137 MB of definitions and theorems. There are over 10,400 function definitions arising in the work of various researchers around the world and ranging from bit-vector libraries used by AMD (to prove the correctness of their floating point units) to set theory libraries to graph algorithms to model checkers, *etc.* The termination of all of these functions has already been proven with ACL2. In the cases where ACL2 does not automatically prove termination, human guidance is required. We distinguish two types of guidance.

Implicit guidance is given when users prove auxiliary lemmas which help ACL2 to complete the termination proof. While it is difficult to identify the theorems used solely to prove termination, it is clear that many termination proofs require auxiliary lemmas and substantial human effort. For example, in a recent posting to the ACL2 mailing list, an experienced ACL2 user asked whether a particular proof could be simplified. After some discussion, he simplified his proof and posted a proof challenge to see if anyone could simplify it further. The point was to establish the termination of function `fringep`. The simplified proof included a library for reasoning about arithmetic, seven lemmas, one theory command, and five function definitions. Two of the functions were needed to define `fringep`, but the other three functions were needed for the proof. The proof script also contained several hints, the use of the proof checker, and several theorems that were classified as `:linear` rules (which are handled in a special way by ACL2). The proof was simplified by another experienced ACL2 user, but it still required the library, five function definitions, and five theorems. Using our system, we proved termination directly in seconds, without using the library, without the extra definitions, without any lemmas, and most importantly, without thinking.

Explicit guidance is given when users provide the measure explicitly or when they provide hints on how to prove termination. Such guidance is easy to detect and of the

Table 1. Results of experiments on the regression suite

Which Functions	Total	# Correct	% Correct
All	10,442	10,308	98.7%
With Explicit Guidance	421	287	68.2%

10,442 functions in the regression suite, 404 required the user to provide explicit measures and 17 more requited hints. For example, here is a part of a function from the regression suite that specifies an explicit measure: an ordinal constructed using ordinal multiplication (o*), ordinal addition (o+), the first infinite ordinal ((omega)), and several auxiliary functions (*e.g.*, tuple-set-max-first).

```
(defun tuple-set->ordinal-partial-sum (k S i)
  (declare (xargs
            :measure (o+ (o* (omega) (nfix k))
                         (nfix (- (tuple-set-max-first S) i)))))
  ...)
```

The actual function definition is too long to list here, but discovering infinite measures requires some skill. Our system automatically proves that the above function terminates.

To quantitatively evaluate our work, we removed all sources of explicit hints and ran our termination method on the full regression suite. Since identifying the implicit guidance is difficult, we did not attempt to remove such lemmas, but we note that since our termination analysis is very different from ACL2's, such lemmas are not very likely to provide much help for us. The results of our experiments are presented in Table 1. Out of all 10,442 functions analyzed by our system, 10,308 (over 98%) were automatically proven to terminate. Included in these are 287 of the 421 functions which required the user to provide explicit measures or hints for ACL2 to prove termination. In other words, of the most difficult 4% of functions to analyze, our tool successfully and fully automatically analyzed almost 70% of them.

6   Related Work

Termination is one of the oldest problems in computing science and it has received a significant amount of attention. Here we will briefly review recent work on automating termination analysis.

One of the most often cited techniques for the proving termination of programs is called the *size change principle* [13]. This method involves using a well-order on function parameters, analyzing recursive calls to label any clearly decreasing or non-increasing parameters. Then, all infinite paths are analyzed to ensure that some parameter never increases and infinitely decreases over each path. We use this path analysis in step 7 of our algorithm. The size change principle has several limitations, *e.g.*, it does not show how to take governors into account and it does not provide any method for determining the sizes of the outputs of user-defined functions. Both of these considerations are almost always important for establishing termination in realistic programming languages.

Much work has gone into developing termination analyses for term rewriting systems and logic programs, *e.g.*, [2,8,4]. However, these methods do not scale to the complexity of functional programming languages. For example, the AProVE tool [8], cannot prove the termination of a function that takes two integer arguments, x and y, and increments x until it is greater than y, which is the behavior of a simple for loop.

There has been a significant amount of work on proving the termination of programs written in high-level imperative languages such as C. This work tends to focus on semi-algebraic functions, whose termination behavior is governed by integer arithmetic. Most of it has been even more narrowly defined than that, dealing only with systems whose behavior is linear [19,20]. Recently, this work has been extended to programs with polynomial behavior [3,6]. While successful in dealing with semi-algebraic programs, these methods are not applicable outside of this domain, *e.g.*, they cannot reason about data structures, which often play a crucial role in termination proofs, or non-polynomial arithmetic. A recent paper presents an abstraction-refinement algorithm for termination analysis. The algorithm deals with loops, but cannot currently handle recursion and was not implemented [5].

7   Conclusion

We introduced the notion of calling context graphs and various related static and theorem proving based analyses that together led to a powerful new method for proving termination of programs written in feature-rich, first-order, purely functional languages. We implemented our algorithm and were able to automatically detect the termination of over 98% of the more than 10,000 function definitions in the ACL2 regression suite. For future work, we are developing an abstraction-refinement framework that uses more advanced absorption and merging strategies to refine CCGs. We are also looking at extending our analysis to deal with imperative languages such as C by taking advantage of various static analyses (such as alias analysis, data-flow, and control-flow) and taking advantage of the fact that Static Single Assignment (SSA), a popular intermediate language used for the analysis and optimization of imperative programs, is essentially a pure functional language [1]. More generally, we are interested in exploring algorithms that combine static analysis methods with theorem proving [18].

References

1. Andrew W. Appel. SSA is functional programming. *SIGPLAN Not.*, 33(4):17–20, 1998.
2. Thomas Arts and Jürgen Giesl. Termination of term rewriting using dependency pairs. *Theoretical Computer Science*, 236:133–178, 2000.
3. Aaron R. Bradley, Zohar Manna, and Henny B. Sipma. Termination of polynomial programs. In Cousot [7], pages 113–129.
4. M. Codish and C. Taboch. A semantic basis for the termination analysis of logic programs. *The Journal of Logic Programming*, 41(1):103–123, 1999.
5. Byron Cook, Andreas Podelski, and Andrey Rybalchenko. Abstraction refinement for termination. In *Static Analysis: 12th International Symposium, SAS 2005*, volume 3672 of *LNCS*, pages 87–102, September 2005.
6. Patrick Cousot. Proving program invariance and termination by parametric abstraction, lagrangian relaxation and semidefinite programming. In Cousot [7], pages 1–24.

7. Radhia Cousot, editor. *Verification, Model Checking, and Abstract Interpretation, 6th International Conference, VMCAI 2005, Paris, France, January 17-19, 2005, Proceedings*, volume 3385 of *Lecture Notes in Computer Science*. Springer, 2005.

8. J. Giesl, R. Thiemann, P. Schneider-Kamp, and S. Falke. Automated termination proofs with AProVE. In *Proceedings of the 15th International Conference on Rewriting Techniques and Applications (RTA-04)*, volume 3091 of *LNCS*, pages 210–220. Springer–Verlag, 2004.

9. Matt Kaufmann, Panagiotis Manolios, and J Strother Moore, editors. *Computer-Aided Reasoning: ACL2 Case Studies*. Kluwer Academic Publishers, June 2000.

10. Matt Kaufmann, Panagiotis Manolios, and J Strother Moore. *Computer-Aided Reasoning: An Approach*. Kluwer Academic Publishers, July 2000.

11. Matt Kaufmann and J Strother Moore. ACL2 homepage. See URL http://www.cs.-utexas.edu/users/moore/acl2.

12. Matt Kaufmann and J. Strother Moore. Structured theory development for a mechanized logic. *J. Autom. Reason.*, 26(2):161–203, 2001.

13. Chin Soon Lee, Neil D. Jones, and Amir M. Ben-Amram. The size-change principle for program termination. In *ACM Symposium on Principles of Programming Languages*, volume 28, pages 81–92. ACM Press, 2001.

14. Panagiotis Manolios and Daron Vroon. Ordinal arithmetic: Algorithms and mechanization. *Journal Of Automated Reasoning*. To Appear.

15. Panagiotis Manolios and Daron Vroon. Algorithms for ordinal arithmetic. In Franz Baader, editor, *19th International Conference on Automated Deduction – CADE-19*, volume 2741 of *LNAI*, pages 243–257. Springer–Verlag, July/August 2003.

16. Panagiotis Manolios and Daron Vroon. Ordinal arithmetic in ACL2. In Matt Kaufmann and J Strother Moore, editors, *Fourth International Workshop on the ACL2 Theorem Prover and Its Applications (ACL2-2003)*, July 2003. See URL http://www.cs.utexas.edu/-users/moore/acl2/workshop-2003/.

17. Panagiotis Manolios and Daron Vroon. Integrating reasoning about ordinal arithmetic into ACL2. In *Formal Methods in Computer-Aided Design: 5th International Conference – FMCAD-2004*, LNCS. Springer–Verlag, November 2004.

18. Panagiotis Manolios and Daron Vroon. Integrating static analysis and general-purpose theorem proving for termination analysis. In *ICSE'06, The 28th international Conference on Softwar Engineering, Emerging Results*. ACM, May 2006.

19. Andreas Podelski and Andrey Rybalchenko. A complete method for the synthesis of linear ranking functions. In *VMCAI*, pages 239–251, 2004.

20. A. Tiwari. Termination of linear programs. In R. Alur and D. Peled, editors, *Computer-Aided Verification, CAV*, volume 3114 of *LNCS*, pages 70–82. Springer, July 2004.

21. Alan Turing. On computable numbers, with an application to the entscheidungsproblem. In *Proceedings of the London Mathematical Society*, volume 42 of *Series 2*, pages 230–265, 1936.

TERMINATOR: Beyond Safety
(Tool Paper)

Byron Cook[1], Andreas Podelski[2,3], and Andrey Rybalchenko[2,4]

[1] Microsoft Research
[2] Max-Planck-Institut für Informatik
[3] Universität Freiburg, Institut für Informatik
[4] EPFL

Abstract. Previous symbolic software model checkers (*i.e.*, program analysis tools based on predicate abstraction, pushdown model checking and iterative counterexample-guided abstraction refinement, etc.) are restricted to safety properties. TERMINATOR is the first software model checker for termination. It is now being used to prove that device driver dispatch routines always return to their caller (or return counterexamples if they if they fail to terminate).

1 Introduction

TERMINATOR is a program analysis and verification tool for termination. It supports large program fragments (*i.e.*, >20,000 LOC) together with C programming language features such as arbitrarily nested loops, arbitrarily nested recursive functions, pointer-aliasing and side-effects, function-pointers, etc. It is fully automatic; no annotations or auxiliary proof arguments (*e.g.*, ranking functions) need to be provided. It automatically synthesizes the termination argument. In the case where the proof cannot be refined TERMINATOR produces counterexamples in the form of (possibly nested) looping paths through the control flow graph. In program analysis terms, TERMINATOR is interprocedural, path sensitive and context-sensitive. Technically it is based on predicate abstraction, pushdown model checking and iterative counterexample-guided abstraction refinement, *i.e.*, on the ingredients of software model checkers such as BLAST [12], MAGIC [3], SLAM [1].

We have applied TERMINATOR to device drivers ranging in sizes from 5,000 to 35,000 LOC in order to prove that their dispatch routines always return to the operating system when called. These experiments were carried out using an integration of TERMINATOR and the Windows Static Driver Verifier[1,15] product. Overall, 8 termination bugs were found in 23 device drivers. The runtime ranged from 5 seconds to 44 hours. A full account of the results can be found in [8]. See also the TERMINATOR home page http://research.microsoft.com/TERMINATOR.

2 Termination Analysis for Software

Reactive systems such as operating systems, web servers, mail servers, and database engines are constructed from sets of components that we expect will

T. Ball and R.B. Jones (Eds.): CAV 2006, LNCS 4144, pp. 415–418, 2006.

always terminate. Cases where these functions unexpectedly do not return to their calling contexts leads to non-responsive systems and system crashes. Proving that these system components always terminate has been a challenge because, until now, no termination tool has ever been able to provide the necessary capacity (>20,000 LOC) together with accurate support for programming language features such as arbitrarily nested loops and recursive functions, pointers and side-effects, function-pointers, etc. TERMINATOR fills this gap.

In the context of program analysis and model checking, tools checking programs over infinite data spaces have been targeted at safety properties. These tools are usually based on abstraction. While the preservation of termination properties from the abstract to the concrete system is sound (if the abstract system terminates then so does the concrete one), it is also worthless in all but pathological cases (with classical abstraction techniques related to homomorphic abstraction or simulation, the abstraction to a finite graph will 'always' introduce a loop and thus it will *not* preserve the termination property).

There exist tools for proving termination for very specialized classes of programs and calculi, such as rewriting [11], logic and functional programming [5,13,14], and imperative programs with specific arithmetic operations [2,6,9]. None of these tools targets scalability and the features of practical programming languages.

3   Foundations Behind Terminator

TERMINATOR is the culmination of successive research, namely (i) a new proof rule for termination, (ii) an appropriate form of abstraction for the automation of the proof rule via abstract interpretation, (iii) a form of iterative counterexample-guided refinement not only of the abstraction but also of the candidate termination argument, and finally (iv) a practical algorithm for binary reachability analysis that is used for validation of candidate termination arguments. Below we highlight the theoretical foundations of TERMINATOR.

(i) Termination argument. The termination argument constructed by TERMINATOR is a union of well-founded relations that forms a transition invariant, *i.e.*, a binary relation over program states that contains the transitive closure of the transition relation of the program [17]. One distinguishing feature of transition invariants is that they can be constructed by abstract fixpoint computation. This fits well into the framework of abstract interpretation [10] and thus leads naturally to automatic methods.

(ii) Abstraction for termination. Transition predicate abstraction [18] overcomes the above-mentioned limitation of classical abstraction techniques to the verification of safety properties. Transition predicate abstraction induces a finite graph where nodes are labeled by abstract transitions. Termination is determined by the well-foundedness of those abstract transitions, and not the absence of loops. Transition predicate abstraction can be refined in the classical way, namely by adding more predicates [4].

(iii) Refinement for termination. As described in [7], TERMINATOR incrementally constructs a candidate transition invariant and thus iteratively *refines* the termination argument. This refinement is again guided by counterexamples. A counterexample is here a path that leads some state s to some state s' such that the pair (s, s') violates the candidate transition invariant (which does not yet fully contain the transitive closure of the transition relation). The path, a sequence of statements, may be viewed as a program. TERMINATOR uses the ranking function synthesis tool RANKFINDER [16] to compute a ranking function for this program. The corresponding ranking relation consists of all pairs of states with decreasing rank, including the pair (s, s'). The refinement of the termination argument amounts to adding this relation to the candidate transition invariant (a union of well-founded relations).

(iv) Binary reachability analysis. In the refinement loop described above, for each new candidate transition invariant, we need to check its validity (the fact that it contains the transitive closure of the transition relation). TERMINATOR implements this check, the *binary* reachability analysis, using a second kind of refinement, namely counterexample-guided *abstraction* refinement (viz. of transition predicate abstraction). In contrast, a safety property translates to one fixed invariant, whose validity is checked by (standard, *unary*) reachability analysis. The crux of TERMINATOR's implemenation of binary reachability analysis is to reduce each new binary reachability problem to a (unary) reachability problem for a new program constructed by a syntactic transformation from the given program [8]. After each transformation, TERMINATOR applies (unary) reachability analysis. In a sense, TERMINATOR implements a reduction of termination not to a safety property but to the *existence* of a certain safety property.

4   Beyond Termination

In some cases, termination depends on additional properties (such as: the repeated request will eventually be served) that can be modeled as *fairness* assumptions. Termination is an example of a basic *liveness* property. We are working on the next generation of TERMINATOR that will prove general liveness properties under fairness assumptions.

References

1. T. Ball, E. Bounimova, B. Cook, V. Levin, J. Lichtenberg, C. McGarvey, B. Ondrusek, S. K. Rajamani, and A. Ustuner. Thorough static analysis of device drivers. In *EuroSys'06: European Systems Conference*, pages 73–85, 2006.
2. A. Bradley, Z. Manna, and H. Sipma. Termination of polynomial programs. In *VM-CAI'05: Verification, Model Checking, and Abstract Interpretation*, volume 3385 of *LNCS*, pages 113–129. Springer, 2005.
3. S. Chaki, E. Clarke, A. Groce, S. Jha, and H. Veith. Modular verification of software components in C. In *ICSE'03: International Conference on Software Engineering*, pages 385–395. IEEE, 2003.

4. E. M. Clarke, O. Grumberg, S. Jha, Y. Lu, and H. Veith. Counterexample-guided abstraction refinement. In *CAV'00: Computer Aided Verification*, volume 1855 of *LNCS*, pages 154–169. Springer, 2000.

5. M. Codish and C. Taboch. A semantic basis for the termination analysis of logic programs. *The Journal of Logic Programming*, 41(1):103–123, 1999.

6. M. Colón and H. Sipma. Practical methods for proving program termination. In *CAV'02: Computer Aided Verification*, volume 2404 of *LNCS*, pages 442–454. Springer, 2002.

7. B. Cook, A. Podelski, and A. Rybalchenko. Abstraction refinement for termination. In *SAS'05: Static Analysis Symposium*, volume 3672 of *LNCS*, pages 87–101. Springer, 2005.

8. B. Cook, A. Podelski, and A. Rybalchenko. Termination proofs for systems code. In *PLDI'06: Programming Language Design and Implementation (to appear)*, 2006.

9. P. Cousot. Proving program invariance and termination by parametric abstraction, lagrangian relaxation and semidefinite programming. In *VMCAI'05: Verification, Model Checking, and Abstract Interpretation*, volume 3385 of *LNCS*, pages 1–24. Springer, 2005.

10. P. Cousot and R. Cousot. Systematic design of program analysis frameworks. In *POPL'79: Principles of Programming Languages*, pages 269–282. ACM Press, 1979.

11. J. Giesl, R. Thiemann, P. Schneider-Kamp, and S. Falke. Automated termination proofs with AProVE. In *RTA'04: Rewriting Techniques and Applications*, volume 3091 of *LNCS*, pages 210–220. Springer, 2004.

12. T. A. Henzinger, R. Jhala, R. Majumdar, and K. L. McMillan. Abstractions from proofs. In *POPL'04: Principles of Programming Languages*, pages 232–244. ACM Press, 2004.

13. C. S. Lee, N. D. Jones, and A. M. Ben-Amram. The size-change principle for program termination. In *POPL'01: Principles of Programming Languages*, volume 36, 3 of *ACM SIGPLAN Notices*, pages 81–92. ACM Press, 2001.

14. N. Lindenstrauss, Y. Sagiv, and A. Serebrenik. TermiLog: A system for checking termination of queries to logic programs. In *CAV'97: Computer-Aided Verification*, LNCS, pages 444–447. Springer, 1997.

15. Microsoft Corporation. Windows Static Driver Verifier. Available at www.microsoft.com/whdc/devtools/tools/SDV.mspx, July 2004.

16. A. Podelski and A. Rybalchenko. A complete method for the synthesis of linear ranking functions. In *VMCAI'04: Verification, Model Checking, and Abstract Interpretation*, pages 239–251, 2004.

17. A. Podelski and A. Rybalchenko. Transition invariants. In *LICS'04: Logic in Computer Science*, pages 32–41. IEEE, 2004.

18. A. Podelski and A. Rybalchenko. Transition predicate abstraction and fair termination. In *POPL'05: Principles of Programming Languages*, pages 132–144. ACM Press, 2005.

CUTE and jCUTE: Concolic Unit Testing and Explicit Path Model-Checking Tools

(Tool Paper)

Koushik Sen and Gul Agha

University of Illinois at Urbana-Champaign, USA
{ksen, agha}@cs.uiuc.edu

Abstract. CUTE, a Concolic Unit Testing Engine for C and Java, is a tool to systematically and automatically test sequential C programs (including pointers) and concurrent Java programs. CUTE combines concrete and symbolic execution in a way that avoids redundant test cases as well as false warnings. The tool also introduces a race-flipping technique to efficiently test and model check concurrent programs with data inputs.

1 Introduction

Software testing is the primary technique used in the software industry to improve reliability, safety, security, and robustness of software. Our research on concolic testing [1,6,4] shows that we can combine random testing and symbolic testing of a program to provide a scalable tool for automatically generating test cases, which improves test coverage and avoids redundant test cases as well as false warnings. Concolic testing involves *explicit path model-checking* in which our goal is to generate data inputs and schedules that would exercise all feasible execution paths of a program. We have developed two automated concolic testing tools: CUTE for C and jCUTE for Java programs.

We have used CUTE and jCUTE to find bugs in several real-world software systems including SGLIB, a popular C data structure library used in a commercial tool, implementations of the Needham-Schroeder protocol and the TMN protocol, the scheduler of Honeywell's DEOS real-time operating system, and the Sun Microsystems' JDK 1.4 collection framework.

2 Concolic Testing

We briefly describe the algorithm for concolic testing; details can be found in [6,5,4]. The algorithm executes a program both concretely and symbolically. The symbolic execution differs from traditional symbolic execution, in that the algorithm follows the path that the concrete execution takes. During the execution, the algorithm collects the constraints over the symbolic values at each branch point (i.e., the *symbolic constraints*). At the end of the execution, the algorithm has computed a sequence of symbolic constraints corresponding to each

T. Ball and R.B. Jones (Eds.): CAV 2006, LNCS 4144, pp. 419–423, 2006.

branch point. We call the conjunction of these constraints a *path constraint*. Observe that all input values that satisfy a given path constraint will explore the same execution path, provided that we follow the same thread schedule.

Apart from collecting symbolic constraints, the algorithm also computes the race condition (both data race and lock race) between various events in the execution of a program, where, informally, an event represents the execution of a statement in the program by a thread.

The algorithm first generates a random input and a schedule, which specifies the order of execution of threads. Then the algorithm does the following in a loop: it executes the code with the generated input and the schedule. At the same time the algorithm computes the race conditions between various events as well as the symbolic constraints. It backtracks and generates a new schedule or a new input, either by re-ordering the events involved in a race or by solving symbolic constraints, respectively, to explore all possible distinct execution paths using a depth first search strategy. Note that because the algorithm does concrete executions, it is sound, i.e. all bugs it finds are real.

There is one complication: for some symbolic constraints, our constraint solver may not be powerful enough to compute concrete values that satisfy the constraints. To address this difficulty, such symbolic constraints *are simplified by replacing some of the symbolic values with concrete values*. Because of this, our algorithm is complete only if given an oracle that can solve the constraints in a program, and the length and the number of paths is finite.

3   Tool Details

The tools, CUTE and jCUTE, consist of two main modules: an instrumentation module and a library to perform symbolic execution, to solve constraints, and to control thread schedules. The instrumentation module inserts code in the program under test so that the instrumented program calls the library at runtime for performing symbolic execution. jCUTE comes with a graphical user interface (a snapshot can be found in Figure 1).

CUTE and jCUTE uses CIL [3] and the SOOT compiler framework [8] to instrument C and Java programs, respectively. Instrumentation of jCUTE associates a semaphore with each thread and adds operations on these semaphores before each shared-memory access. These semaphores are used to control the schedule of the threads at runtime. To solve arithmetic inequalities, the constraint solver of CUTE uses lpsolve [2], a library for integer linear programming. CUTE and jCUTE save all the generated inputs and the schedules (in case of jCUTE) in the file-system. As such the users of CUTE and jCUTE can replay the program to reproduce the bugs. The replay can also be performed with the aid of a debugger. For sequential programs, jCUTE can generate JUnit test cases, which can be used by the user for regression testing as well as for debugging. jCUTE also allows the users to graphically visualize the multi-threaded execution.

CUTE provides a macro CUTE_input(x), which allows the user to specify that the variable x (of any type, including a pointer) is an input to the program. This

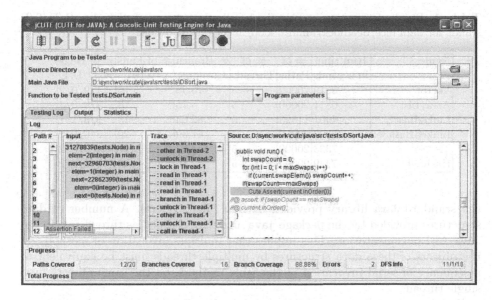

Fig. 1. Snapshot of jCUTE

comes in handy to replace any external user input, e.g., scanf(''%d'',&v) by
CUTE_input(v) (which also assigns a value to &v). Note that this macro can be
used anywhere in the program. jCUTE also provides a similar function to obtain
input from the external environment.

4   Case Studies

We briefly describe our experience with two of the case-studies we have done,
one is a data structure library in C and the other is the thread-safe Collection
framework provided with Sun Microsystems' Java 1.4.

SGLIB Library. We applied CUTE to unit test *SGLIB* [7] version 1.0.1, a
popular, open source C library for generic data structures, such as lists, hash
tables, red-black trees, and so on. The library has been extensively used to
implement the commercial tool Xrefactory.

We found *two bugs* in SGLIB using CUTE within 3 seconds of testing. The
first bug is a segmentation fault that occurs in the doubly-linked-list library
when a non-zero length list is concatenated with another zero-length list. The
second bug is an infinite loop, which CUTE discovered in the hash table library.
We reported these bugs to the SGLIB developers, who confirmed that these are
indeed bugs. Further details about this case study along with branch coverage,
runtime for testing, number of inputs generated, etc., can be found in [6].

Sun Microsystems' Java Collection Framework. We tested the thread-
safe Collection framework implemented as part of the java.util package of

Table 1. Results for testing synchronized Collection classes of JDK 1.4. R/D/L/E stands for data race/deadlock/infinite loop/uncaught exceptions

Name	Run time in seconds	# of Paths	# of Threads	% Branch Coverage	# of Funs Tested	# of Bugs R/D/L/E
Vector	5519	20000	5	76.38	16	1/9/0/2
ArrayList	6811	20000	5	75	16	3/9/0/3
LinkedList	4401	11523	5	82.05	15	3/3/1/1
LinkedHashSet	7303	20000	5	67.39	20	3/9/0/2
TreeSet	7333	20000	5	54.93	26	4/9/0/2
HashSet	7449	20000	5	69.56	20	19/9/0/2

the standard Java library provided by Sun Microsystems. A number of data structures provided by the package java.util are claimed as thread-safe in the Java API documentation. This implies that multiple invocation of methods on the objects of these data structures by multiple threads must be equivalent to a sequence of serial invocation of the same methods on the same objects by a single thread.

We chose this library as a case study primarily to evaluate the effectiveness of our jCUTE tool. As Sun Microsystems' Java is widely used, we did not expect to find potential bugs. Much to our surprise, we found several previously undocumented data races, deadlocks, uncaught exceptions, and an infinite loop in the library. Note that, although the number of potential bugs is high, these bugs are all caused by a couple of problematic design patterns used in the implementation. The details of this case study can be found in [5]. Here we briefly describe an infinite loop that jCUTE discovered in the synchronized LinkedList class. We present a simple scenario under which the infinite loop happens. We first create two synchronized linked lists l1 and l2 by calling Collections.synchronizedList(new LinkedList()) and add null to both of them. Then we concurrently allow a new thread to invoke l1.clear() and another new thread to invoke l2.containsAll(l1). jCUTE discovered an interleaving of the two threads that resulted in an infinite loop. However, the program never goes into an infinite loop if the methods are invoked in any order by a single thread. jCUTE also provided a trace of the buggy execution. This helped us to detect the cause of the bug. A summary of the results of testing various Java synchronized Collection classes is provided in Table 1.

Acknowledgment. This work is supported in part by the ONR Grant N00014-02-1-0715, the NSF Grant NSF CNS 05-09321, and the Motorola Grant RPF #23.

References

1. P. Godefroid, N. Klarlund, and K. Sen. DART: Directed automated random testing. In *Proc. of the ACM SIGPLAN 2005 Conference on Programming Language Design and Implementation (PLDI)*, 2005.

2. lp_solve. http://groups.yahoo.com/group/lp_solve/.
3. G. C. Necula, S. McPeak, S. P. Rahul, and W. Weimer. CIL: Intermediate Language and Tools for Analysis and transformation of C Programs. In *Proceedings of Conference on compiler Construction*, pages 213–228, 2002.
4. K. Sen and G. Agha. Automated systematic testing of open distributed programs. In *Fundamental Approaches to Software Engineering (FASE'06)*, volume 3922 of *LNCS*, pages 339–356. Springer, 2006.
5. K. Sen and G. Agha. Concolic testing of multithreaded programs and its application to testing security protocols. Technical Report UIUCDCS-R-2006-2676, UIUC, 2006.
6. K. Sen, D. Marinov, and G. Agha. CUTE: A concolic unit testing engine for C. In *5th meeting of the European Software Engineering Conference and ACM SIGSOFT Symposium on the Foundations of Software Engineering (ESEC/FSE)*. ACM, 2005.
7. SGLIB. http://xref-tech.com/sglib/main.html.
8. R. Vallee-Rai, L. Hendren, V. Sundaresan, P. Lam, E. Gagnon, and P. Co. Soot - a Java optimization framework. In *Proceedings of CASCON 1999*, pages 125–135.

SMT Techniques for Fast Predicate Abstraction

Shuvendu K. Lahiri[1], Robert Nieuwenhuis[2,*], and Albert Oliveras[2,*]

[1] Microsoft Research
research.microsoft.com/~shuvendu
[2] Technical Univ. of Catalonia, Barcelona
www.lsi.upc.es/~roberto|~oliveras

Abstract. Predicate abstraction is a technique for automatically extracting finite-state abstractions for systems with potentially infinite state space. The fundamental operation in predicate abstraction is to compute the best approximation of a Boolean formula φ over a set of *predicates P*. In this work, we demonstrate the use for this operation of a decision procedure based on the DPLL(T) framework for SAT Modulo Theories (SMT). The new algorithm is based on a careful generation of the set of all satisfying assignments over a set of predicates. It consistently outperforms previous methods by a factor of at least 20, on a diverse set of hardware and software verification benchmarks. We report detailed analysis of the results and the impact of a number of variations of the techniques. We also propose and evaluate a scheme for incremental refinement of approximations for predicate abstraction in the above framework.

1 Introduction

In many industrial verification problems, typical logical formulas consist of large sets of clauses such as:

$$p \quad \vee \quad \neg q \quad \vee \quad a{=}f(b-c) \quad \vee \quad read(s,\, f(b-c)\,){=}d \quad \vee \quad a - g(c) \leq 7$$

containing purely propositional atoms as well as atoms over (combined) theories, such as the integers, arrays, or Equality with Uninterpreted Functions (EUF). Deciding the satisfiability of such clause sets modulo the background theories is known as the *Satisfiability Modulo Theories* (SMT) problem, and the systems for doing so are called *SMT solvers*. Currently, SMT is a very active area of research, and efficient SMT solvers exist that can handle (combinations of) many such theories (see also the SMT problem library [TR05] and the SMT Competition [BdMS05]). One particular SMT solver used in this paper is the Barcelogic-Tools implementation of the DPLL(T) approach to SMT [GHN+04, NO05a]. It consists of a Davis-Putnam-Loveland-Logemann-based DPLL(X) engine, whose parameter X can be instantiated with a specialized solver $Solver_T$ for the given (possibly combined) T under consideration, thus producing a DPLL(T) system.

* Partially supported by Spanish Min. of Educ. and Science through the LogicTools project (TIN2004-03382, both), FPU grant AP2002-3533 (Oliveras) and personal research grant "SMT Solvers for High-Level Hardware Verification" from Intel Corporation (Nieuwenhuis).

T. Ball and R.B. Jones (Eds.): CAV 2006, LNCS 4144, pp. 424–437, 2006.
© Springer-Verlag Berlin Heidelberg 2006

Predicate abstraction [GS97] (an instance of the more general theory of *abstract interpretation* [CC77]) is a technique for constructing finite-state abstractions from large or infinite-state systems. The resulting finite-state abstraction can be analyzed efficiently using Boolean techniques. Predicate abstraction has been applied successfully in various verification tools to analyze software [BMMR01, HJMS02, CCG$^+$03, FQ02], hardware [CKSY04] and high-level protocols [DDP99, LBC03].

Predicate abstraction involves approximating a concrete transition system or a set of concrete states using a set P of formulas, also called *predicates*. The predicates usually denote properties of the state and are expressed as formulas, modulo some background theory, over the state variables. The abstraction is defined by the value of these predicates in any concrete state of the system. The fundamental operation in predicate abstraction can be summarized as follows:

> Given a formula φ and a set of predicates P in a theory T, generate the most precise approximation of φ using P.

Depending on the nature of the problem domain, one may either want to generate (i) the best underapproximation of φ, i.e., the *weakest* Boolean combination of P that implies φ (denoted by $\mathcal{F}_P(\varphi)$) or (ii) the best overapproximation of φ, i.e., the *strongest* Boolean combination of P that is implied by φ (denoted by $\mathcal{G}_P(\varphi)$). Here, the notions of weakness, strength and implication are with respect to entailment in the given theory T. These operations are dual of each other — $\mathcal{G}_P(\varphi)$ is the same as $\neg\mathcal{F}_P(\neg\varphi)$, and therefore it suffices to provide a procedure to compute only one of them.

Example 1. Let T be the theory of the integers, and let φ be $x < y - 2 \vee x > y$. Furthermore, let P be $\{p_1, p_2, p_3\}$ where p_1, p_2 and p_3 are $x < 0$ and $y = 2$ and $x \neq 4$, respectively.

W.l.o.g., we can express $\mathcal{F}_P(\varphi)$ as a DNF, i.e., as a disjunction of cubes. Here $\mathcal{F}_P(\varphi)$ is $p_1 p_2 \vee p_2 \overline{p_3}$. Clearly, both its cubes T-entail φ and hence their disjunction does too. Moreover it is as weak (modulo T) as possible: all other cubes that T-entail φ either contain one of these two or are T-inconsistent.

The need for efficient predicate abstraction has motivated a significant amount of work during the last years. For example, Clarke et al. [CKSY04], and Lahiri and Bryant [LBC03, LB04] perform predicate abstraction by Boolean quantifier elimination using SAT solvers for propositional and first-order logic respectively. The idea of using SMT solvers for predicate abstraction has also been explored repeatedly [DDP99, SS99, FQ02, BCLZ04], but differently from what we do here, in particular, concerning incrementality. The recent *symbolic decision procedure* approach of [LBC05] is a specialized method for predicate abstraction based on saturating a set of predicates; however, it imposes restrictions on the underlying theories, it requires an expensive transformation of the queries to a logically equivalent conjunctive normal form, and combination methods for non-convex theories would need to be devised for it.

In this paper, we show how to adapt SMT solvers to compute predicate abstraction efficiently. The key idea of the procedure is to use the SMT solver to enumerate all T-models over P of φ (or, sometimes, $\neg\varphi$). For this purpose, we have turned our DPLL(X) engine into an *AllSAT* engine, i.e., an engine that can enumerate all models. Several ways of doing so are discussed and compared experimentally in this paper, including some AllSAT techniques that are also useful for DPLL-based propositional SAT solvers. With no additional work one can now obtain an efficient tool for predicate abstraction modulo a theory T by simply instantiating our adapted DPLL(X) engine with the corresponding *Solver$_T$* as it is used for DPLL(T).

The key difference of our work with previous SMT solver-based predicate abstraction techniques is in the amount of incrementality achieved in enumerating all the solutions. We show that the incrementality, aggressive theory propagation and efficient conflict analysis present in the DPLL(T) framework are crucial for obtaining an efficient predicate abstraction engine.

In particular, according to our extensive experimental results on large sets of benchmarks from three completely different sources, using the BarcelogicTools SMT solver, we always obtain a speedup factor of at least 20 with respect to the method that was previously best on that benchmark family. This scheme of using SMT solvers for predicate abstraction is attractive because it allows us to leverage the advances in the development of SMT decision procedures for obtaining more efficient predicate abstraction procedures.

We also show how we can adapt the DPLL(T)-based *AllSAT* engine to compute a series of increasingly precise approximations of $\mathcal{G}_P(\varphi)$, where for some $k < n$, approximations only use cubes of size k. Given a fixed set of predicates P and a query φ, this allows a client of predicate abstraction to first explore coarser approximations (that can be generated fast) that might suffice for proving a desired property. In fact, our experiments reveal that (i) for small cube sizes, the computation times are extremely small, and that (ii) computing the full $\mathcal{G}_P(\varphi)$ in successive steps slightly increasing the cube size can be done almost as efficiently as computing it directly, if each step is done incrementally from the previous one. Although several approaches have been developed in recent years to compute coarser approximations [GS97, BMMR01, DD01], the process of refining the approximations is not incremental, and can sometimes be the main bottleneck in the verification [BCDR04].

The rest of the paper is structured as follows. We first give some background and definitions about SMT and DPLL(T) in Section 2. Section 3 is on the encoding in SMT of the under and upper approximation problems. Its Subsections 3.1 and 3.2 discuss the different ways of forcing the enumeration of all cubes over P and the variations with increasing cube sizes. Section 4 analyzes a large number of experiments on problems from three completely different applications. Finally, Section 5 lists future work and conclusions.

2 Background

2.1 Formal Preliminaries

A *theory* T is a set of closed first-order formulas. A formula φ is T-*satisfiable* or T-*consistent* if $\varphi \wedge T$ is satisfiable in the first-order sense. Otherwise, it is called *T-unsatisfiable* or *T-inconsistent*. In this paper we will deal with (partial) assignments M, where M is a set (conjunction) of ground literals. If M is a T-consistent partial assignment and φ is a ground formula such that M is a model of φ in the propositional sense, then we say that M *is a T-model of φ*. The SMT problem for a theory T is the problem of determining, given a formula φ, whether φ is T-satisfiable, or, equivalently, whether φ has a T-model. As usual in SMT, here we only consider the SMT problem for *ground* (and hence quantifier-free) CNF formulas φ. If φ and ψ are formulas, then φ *T-entails* ψ, written $\varphi \models_T \psi$, if $\varphi \wedge \neg\psi$ is T-inconsistent. A *theory lemma* is a clause C such that $\emptyset \models_T C$.

2.2 The DPLL(T) Approach to SMT

The so-called *lazy* approach to SMT, in its simplest form, initially considers each atom occurring in the input formula F simply as a propositional symbol, i.e., it "forgets" about the theory T. Then it sends the formula to a SAT solver. If the SAT solver reports propositional unsatisfiability, then F is also T-unsatisfiable. If it returns a propositional model of F, then this assignment is checked by a specialized T-solver that can only deal with conjunctions of literals. If the model is found T-consistent then it is a T-model of F. Otherwise, the T-solver builds a ground clause that is a logical consequence of T, i.e., a theory lemma, precluding that assignment. This lemma is added to F and the SAT solver is started again. This process is repeated until the SAT solver finds a T-model or returns unsatisfiable.

DPLL-based refinements of the lazy approach use *incremental T-solvers* that check the T-inconsistency of the partial models while they are being built. Moreover, the DPLL-based SAT solver is usually *on-line*: upon each T-inconsistent assignment it can then backjump to some point where the assignment was still T-consistent, instead of restarting the search from scratch.

DPLL(T) is such a new modular lazy-like approach for SMT. It is based on a general DPLL(X) engine, whose parameter X can be instantiated with a specialized *Solver$_T$* for conjunctions of (ground) atoms, thus producing a system DPLL(T). Once the DPLL(X) engine has been implemented, this approach becomes very flexible: a DPLL(T) system for a theory T is obtained by simply plugging in the corresponding *Solver$_T$*. In DPLL(T), a special attention is devoted to *theory propagation*, a refinement that can have a crucial impact on performance. The idea is that the T-solver tells the DPLL(X) engine which literals can be set to true because they are T-consequences of the current partial assignment. For example, if T is the theory of equality and the current assignment contains the literals $b{=}d$, $f(b){=}d$ and $f(d){=}a$, then the T-solver may report $a{=}b$ as a T-consequence instead of letting DPLL(X) guess a truth value for it.

3 Predicate Abstraction Using SMT

For us, a *predicate* will be any ground formula. If P is a set of finite predicates, a *cube* over P is a conjunction $p_1 \wedge \ldots \wedge p_k \wedge \neg p'_1 \wedge \ldots \wedge \neg p'_{k'}$, where all p_i and p'_j are distinct predicates of P and $k + k'$ is the *size* of the cube. A *minterm* over

P is a cube of size $|P|$. A *Boolean formula over* P is either a predicate of P or a conjunction, disjunction or negation of Boolean formulas over P.

Given a theory T, a set of predicates $P = \{p_1, \ldots, p_n\}$ and a ground formula φ, the central operation in predicate abstraction is to compute the weakest Boolean formula $\mathcal{F}_P(\varphi)$ over P that T-entails φ. Equally important is the dual operation, to compute the strongest Boolean formula $\mathcal{G}_P(\varphi)$ over P that is T-entailed by φ, but this operation can be reduced to the previous one, since it is not difficult to see that $\mathcal{F}_P(\varphi)$ is indeed $\neg\mathcal{G}_P(\neg\varphi)$.

$\mathcal{F}_P(\varphi)$ can be characterized as the disjunction of all the minterms over P that T-entail φ, that is:

$$\mathcal{F}_P(\varphi) \equiv \bigvee \{c \mid c \text{ is a minterm over } P \text{ and } c \models_T \varphi\}$$

Since each minterm T-entails φ, this formula clearly T-entails φ as well. Any other formula over P that T-entails φ, when expressed as a disjunction of minterms, consists only of minterms T-entailing φ, all of which belong to $\mathcal{F}_P(\varphi)$. Hence, $\mathcal{F}_P(\varphi)$ is also the weakest such formula. Now we can also easily characterize $\mathcal{G}_P(\varphi)$ by using its relation to $\mathcal{F}_P(\neg\varphi)$:

$$\begin{aligned}
\mathcal{G}_P(\varphi) &\equiv \neg\mathcal{F}_P(\neg\varphi) \\
&\equiv \neg\,(\bigvee\{c \mid c \text{ is a minterm over } P \text{ and } c \models_T \neg\varphi\}) \\
&\equiv \bigvee\{c \mid c \text{ is a minterm over } P \text{ and } c \not\models_T \neg\varphi\} \\
&\equiv \bigvee\{c \mid c \text{ is a minterm over } P \text{ and } c \wedge \varphi \text{ is } T\text{-satisfiable}\}
\end{aligned}$$

i.e., computing $\mathcal{G}_P(\varphi)$ amounts to enumerating all minterms over P that are T-satisfiable when conjoined with φ.

As in [LBC03, CKSY04], we can introduce a set B of n fresh propositional variables $\{b_1, \ldots b_n\}$ and consider the formula $\varphi \wedge \bigwedge_{i=1}^{n} b_i \Leftrightarrow p_i$. Given a T-model M of this formula, we collect the conjunction of all B-literals that are true in M, and replace each b_i by its corresponding formula p_i. The resulting minterm c, called the *projection of M onto P*, is over P and $c \wedge \varphi$ is T-satisfiable.

For enumerating *all* such c, in principle, *every* off-the-shelf SMT solver can be used, by adding, each time a T-model is found whose B-literals are $\{l_1, \ldots, l_n\}$, a *blocking clause* $\neg l_1 \vee \ldots \vee \neg l_n$ and then starting the SMT solver from scratch, and repeating this until no more T-models are found. The number of restarts is no more than the number of different minterms over P, that is, 2^n. Each model found can be stored, say, in a BDD, or in a file to be treated once the AllSAT procedure has finished. The computation of $\mathcal{F}_P(\varphi)$ can be done in a similar way.

3.1   AllSAT and AllSAT over *Important* Symbols

The complete black-box approach explained above is not very efficient. This is due to the restarts from scratch, where moreover the lemmas learned by the SMT solver are not re-used between restarts, and due to the worst-case exponential growth of the clause set (one additional blocking clause for each model found). We now show that these problems can be entirely overcome, without modifying the search behavior of the best DPLL implementations, i.e., using the best known conflict analysis techniques and conflict-driven backjumping, and without the need of keeping the blocking clauses or the learned lemmas.

In this section we focus on the propositional case, since all these results on AllSAT immediately extend to AllSAT in the SMT case, i.e., for enumerating all T-models using any of the modern DPLL-based SMT solvers, including DPLL(T).

For the general AllSAT problem, i.e., without considering a subset of important symbols, the idea is as follows. Each time a model $\{l_1, \ldots, l_n\}$ is found, store it and do (e.g., 1UIP) conflict-driven backjumping as if the blocking clause $\neg l_1 \vee \ldots \vee \neg l_n$ (which is conflicting in the current DPLL state) belonged to the clause set; see [ZMMM01, NO05a]. Keeping the *lemmas learned* in backjump steps (or the blocking clauses) is optional: as usual, they can be kept only as long as they are *active* pruning the search.

Property 1. This AllSAT procedure terminates and enumerates all models.

As pointed out in [JHS05], for Chaff's DPLL procedure this result easily follows from the proofs in [ZM03]. For essentially any practical DPLL strategy or variant, it follows from [NOT05], where the termination proof uses a well-founded ordering on DPLL search states, based on a lexicographic comparison of the number of literals in each *decision level*. Roughly, the intuition is that a search state is *more advanced* than another one if it has more information at lower decision levels, i.e., for some i, it has set more literals at decision level i, and it has the same number of literals at all decision levels lower than i.

An important variant of the AllSAT problem is, given a subset P of *distinguished* or *important* symbols (in this paper, the predicates), to enumerate all (sub)models over P that can be extended to total models over all symbols. This also has important applications to, e.g., model checking [GSY04]. For this, the same procedure applies by removing from the blocking clause the non-important literals, and the same correctness proof based on [NOT05] holds.

Property 2. This AllSAT procedure with distinguished symbols P terminates and enumerates all models over P that can be extended to total models over all symbols.

We have not found this observation elsewhere in the literature. E.g., [GSY04] does chronological backtracking on the important literals, and forces the decision heuristic to split on important literals first.

Quite surprisingly, if, as proposed here, not all blocking clauses or lemmas are kept, some model may be found more than once. However, according to our experiments, this phenomenon appears to be rare and has a very low impact on performance, see Section 4.

3.2   Incrementally Refining the Approximation

The approaches for predicate abstraction of [DDP99, SS99, FQ02] aim at explicitly asking an SMT solver for each cube c whether $\varphi \wedge c$ is T-satisfiable or not. For reducing the number of calls to the SMT solver, they work by starting with smaller cube sizes. For example, if P is $\{p_1, \ldots, p_n\}$, one can first send $\varphi \wedge p_1$ to the SMT solver, and only if this is T-satisfiable, try with $\varphi \wedge p_1 \wedge p_2$ and with $\varphi \wedge p_1 \wedge \neg p_2$, and so on. But this still leads to a large exponential number of independent calls to the SMT solver, without much incrementality to be exploited.

In this subsection we also work with increasing cube sizes, but in a completely different way and with a completely different purpose. Rather than directly computing the strongest overapproximation $\mathcal{G}_P(\varphi)$, we want to compute a sequence $\mathcal{G}_P^{k_1}(\varphi), \mathcal{G}_P^{k_2}(\varphi), \ldots, \mathcal{G}_P^{k_m}(\varphi)$ of successively stronger (i.e., each one T-entails the previous ones) overapproximations over P of φ, where the last one is $\mathcal{G}_P(\varphi)$. Here we will compute each $\mathcal{G}_P^k(\varphi)$ by collecting cubes of size k, and the sizes will be such that $k_1 < \ldots < k_m = |P|$.

The motivation for doing this is that for certain applications, some of the first few $\mathcal{G}_P^{k_i}(\varphi)$'s may already suffice. Moreover, our experiments reveal that for small k, computing $\mathcal{G}_P^k(\varphi)$ is very fast. In addition, computing the whole sequence with small increments of k can be done almost as efficiently as computing $\mathcal{G}_P(\varphi)$, if each step is done incrementally from the previous one.

In the following, let $restr$ be any function such that, given a minterm c over P and an integer k with $k \leq |P|$, $restr(c, k)$ returns a subcube of size k of c.

Theorem 1. *For every* $k_1 < \ldots < k_m = |P|$, *the sequence* $\mathcal{G}_P^{k_1}(\varphi), \ldots, \mathcal{G}_P^{k_m}(\varphi)$ *is such that*

- $\mathcal{G}_P^{k_i}(\varphi)$ *is T-entailed by φ for all i in $\{1, \ldots, m\}$,*
- $\mathcal{G}_P^{k_{i+1}}(\varphi) \models_T \mathcal{G}_P^{k_i}(\varphi)$ *for all i in $\{1, \ldots, m-1\}$, and*
- $\mathcal{G}_P^{k_m}(\varphi)$ *is $\mathcal{G}_P(\varphi)$.*

if, for all i in $\{1, \ldots, m\}$, the following two conditions hold:

1. $\mathcal{G}_P^{k_i}(\varphi) \equiv \bigvee \{restr(c, k_i) \mid c \text{ is a minterm over } P \text{ and } c \wedge \varphi \text{ is } T\text{-satisfiable}\}$
2. *For each minterm c over P with $c \wedge \varphi$ T-satisfiable there exists a minterm c' over P with $c' \wedge \varphi$ T-satisfiable such that $restr(c, k_i) \supset restr(c', k_{i-1})$.*

Proof. (sketch) Each $\mathcal{G}_P^{k_i}(\varphi)$ is T-entailed by φ, since the disjunction of all minterms c over P with T-satisfiable $c \wedge \varphi$ is T-entailed by φ, and for each one of these c there is some subcube in $\mathcal{G}_P^{k_i}(\varphi)$. The increasing strength follows in a similar way from the second condition, since each disjunct of $\mathcal{G}_P^{k_i}(\varphi)$ contains a disjunct of $\mathcal{G}_P^{k_{i-1}}(\varphi)$. Finally, $\mathcal{G}_P^{k_m}(\varphi)$ is $\mathcal{G}_P(\varphi)$ if k_m is $|P|$ due to the characterization of $\mathcal{G}_P(\varphi)$ given at the beginning of this section. $\square$

This theorem gives us a way to use our algorithm of the previous subsections for computing the successive $\mathcal{G}_P^{k_i}(\varphi)$'s. A difference is that, since here we collect cubes c_k of size k instead of the whole minterms, we can, after c_k has been collected, do the conflict analysis with the corresponding blocking clause $\neg c_k$ of size k. Note that this may preclude some minterms c extending c_k from later consideration, but we are still safe since for these c we can assume $restr(c, k)$ to be c_k. Again, as in Properties 1 and 2, termination follows from [NOT05].

In this algorithm, one could use a function *restr* such that $restr(c, k)$ always returns the subset of literals of c over $\{p_1, \ldots, p_k\}$, i.e., the first k elements of P. However, having in each $\mathcal{G}_P^k(\varphi)$ only predicates of $\{p_1, \ldots, p_k\}$ may not be very useful. This is because in most cases no subset of P will suffice to construct strong invariants of interest. We believe that it is much more useful to have most predicates of P appear in some of the k-size cubes. Therefore, in our implementation we use a random *restr* function. The second condition of Theorem 1 can be enforced as follows if one remembers the previous $\mathcal{G}_P^{k_{i-1}}(\varphi)$: for each minterm c considered in the computation of $\mathcal{G}_P^{k_i}(\varphi)$, we know that a subcube of c of size k_{i-1} must belong to $\mathcal{G}_P^{k_{i-1}}(\varphi)$. This subcube was added to $\mathcal{G}_P^{k_{i-1}}(\varphi)$ as the restriction $restr(c', k_{i-1})$ for some[1] minterm c'. The only thing we have to impose is that $restr(c, k_i)$ includes $restr(c', k_{i-1})$. This is all clearer in the example below:

Example 2. Let φ be the formula $x < y - 2$ $\vee$ $x > y$ and P be $\{p_1, p_2, p_3\}$ where p_1 is $x < 0$, p_2 is $y = 2$ and p_3 is $x = 4$. We will construct the sequence of approximations $\mathcal{G}_P^1(\varphi), \mathcal{G}_P^2(\varphi), \mathcal{G}_P^3(\varphi)$. For a better understanding of the algorithm, let us present the set of all minterms c such that $c \wedge \varphi$ is T-satisfiable: $\{p_1 p_2 \overline{p}_3, \ p_1 \overline{p}_2 \overline{p}_3, \ \overline{p}_1 p_2 p_3, \ \overline{p}_1 \overline{p}_2 p_3, \ \overline{p}_1 \overline{p}_2 p_3, \ \overline{p}_1 \overline{p}_2 \overline{p}_3\}$.

For the computation of $\mathcal{G}_P^1(\varphi)$, the AllSAT procedure first finds the minterm $p_1 p_2 \overline{p}_3$ and restricts it to $\overline{p}_3$. After adding the blocking clause p_3, the minterm $\overline{p}_1 p_2 p_3$ is found and restricted to $\overline{p}_1$. Then, p_1 is added as a blocking clause and since there are no more minterms to be found we finish with $\mathcal{G}_P^1(\varphi) \equiv \overline{p}_3 \vee \overline{p}_1$.

For $\mathcal{G}_P^2(\varphi)$ we start with the minterms already computed in the previous step. We can restrict $p_1 p_2 \overline{p}_3$ to $p_2 \overline{p}_3$ (note that, due to condition 2 of Theorem 1, $p_1 p_2$ would not have been a correct restriction), and similarly restrict $\overline{p}_1 p_2 p_3$ to $\overline{p}_1 p_2$. After adding the blocking clauses $\overline{p}_2 \vee p_3$ and $p_1 \vee \overline{p}_2$, the AllSAT procedure starts the search. First, it finds the minterm $p_1 \overline{p}_2 \overline{p}_3$, and restricts it to $p_1 \overline{p}_3$ (again due to condition 2 of Theorem 1, $p_1 \overline{p}_2$ would not have been a correct choice). Then, after the blocking clause $\overline{p}_1 \vee p_3$ is added, $\overline{p}_1 \overline{p}_2 p_3$ is found and restricted to $\overline{p}_1 \overline{p}_2$. Since the blocking clauses preclude any other possible minterm, $\mathcal{G}_P^2(\varphi)$ is $p_2 \overline{p}_3 \vee \overline{p}_1 p_2 \vee p_1 \overline{p}_3 \vee \overline{p}_1 \overline{p}_2$.

Finally, for $\mathcal{G}_P^3(\varphi)$ we start with the four minterms already computed and then the AllSAT procedure will compute the two missing ones, namely $\overline{p}_1 p_2 \overline{p}_3$ and $\overline{p}_1 \overline{p}_2 \overline{p}_3$.   □

The interesting aspect hereby is that, at each incremental step, we reuse from previous step(s):

1. all lemmas learned by DPLL(T) that are T-consequences of φ, which helps to speed up the search.
2. all minterms c already computed.

We finish this section with three remarks about the quality of these approximations. First, let us note that the strongest disjunction of cubes over P of

---

[1] Note that we cannot assume c' to be c because, due to the use of blocking clauses, c might not have been considered in the computation of $\mathcal{G}_P^{k_{i-1}}(\varphi)$.

size k that is T-entailed by φ does not always exist. Second, in CNF it does exist: the strongest conjunction of clauses over P of size k that is T-entailed by φ is a well-defined concept. Third, let us remark that there are formulas for which our algorithm would compute a stronger approximation than this CNF and viceversa.

4 Experimental Evaluation

4.1 Benchmarks and Their Source

The set of benchmarks for evaluating our technique has been generated from three completely different verification tasks:

1. **SLAM:** This category contains a set of 665 predicate abstraction queries generated from Windows device driver verification in SLAM [BMMR01]. In SLAM, predicate abstraction is used to abstract a Boolean program from a C program. This set has been previously used to evaluate the predicate abstraction technique in [LBC05].
2. **UCLID Suite:** This category contains $\mathcal{G}_P(\varphi)$ queries generated during the verification of high-level description of microprocessors, cache-coherence protocols and other distributed algorithms [LB04]. Each benchmark in this category contains around 6 to 19 predicate abstraction queries denoting the different image computation steps.
3. **Recursive Data Structures (RDS):** This is a set of benchmarks generated from the verification of programs manipulating linked lists inside UCLID [LQ06]. Each benchmark contains a set of $\mathcal{G}_P(\varphi)$ queries for different abstract image computation steps.

The theories used in all the three categories are combinations of EUF and difference logic (constraints of the form $x \leq y + c$). For the latter two classes of benchmarks for UCLID and RDS, more complex theories are axiomatized using quantifiers. However, these quantifiers are eliminated upfront using simple (but sufficient to prove the properties in the examples) quantifier instantiation within UCLID, to generate a quantifier-free predicate abstraction query.

4.2 Results and Analysis

We have implemented the procedure described in Section 3.1 on top of the BarcelogicTools implementation of the DPLL(T) approach for SMT. Each minterm was stored in a BDD immediately after finding it. For this, the CUDD [CUD] BDD package was used. The result was read from the BDD as a disjunction of prime implicants. This significantly reduced the number of disjuncts (see the table below) especially when many minterms were stored. For each of the benchmarks described above, our resulting system was compared with the best existing competitor by running experiments on a 2GHz 512 MB Pentium 4.

For the SLAM benchmarks we compared our system with the symbolic decision procedure approach of [LBC05]. This set of benchmarks posed little difficulty to our approach: the whole set of benchmarks (655 queries) was processed in less than 5 seconds, whereas the symbolic decision procedure implementation took 273 seconds. This is a first indication that our approach is superior, but, since the running time for each single query is negligible, we will concentrate on analyzing the results obtained from the other two families.

For the UCLID and Recursive Data Structures benchmarks, the table below lists the number of queries for each family, predicates each query consists of, and the total number of minterms of the $\mathcal{G}_P(\varphi)$'s to be computed. Finally, for UCLID [LBC03] we give the aggregated running time in seconds and for our BarcelogicTools implementation, we give the running time, the speedup factor w.r.t. UCLID, and the number of cubes in the answers. In order to be more confident about the results, we used CUDD to check whether the output of our tool was equivalent to UCLID's output.

Benchmark family	#queries	#prds.	#minterms	UCLID time	BCLT time	speedup	#cubes
UCLID Suite:							
aodv	7	21	2916	657	4.6	143x	458
bakery	19	32	426	245	11	22x	294
BRP	10	22	30	3.5	0.1	35x	24
cache_ibm	10	16	326	34	1.3	26x	123
cache_bounded	18	26	2238	1119	23	49x	1022
DLX	6	23	38080	335	13	26x	2704
OOO	10	25	10728	921	36	26x	242
Rec. Data Struct.:							
reverse_acyclic	7	16	91	20	0.6	33x	44
set_union	6	24	334	22	0.7	31x	60
simple_cyclic	5	15	110	3.7	0.11	34x	20
sorted_int	10	21	2465	765	19	40x	250

Independently of the benchmark, BCLT is always at least 20 times faster. Hence, it is also very robust, i.e. it is not tailored towards any specific type of benchmark.

As mentioned in Section 3.1, a possible drawback of our AllSAT approach is that the same minterm can be listed more than once. Therefore, we also tried a mixed approach where, in order to preclude most repeated minterms, blocking clauses were kept while they were active (as it is done with learned lemmas). This did not produce any observable improvement. This is probably due to the fact that even for the DLX and OOO families, where the number of minterms to be enumerated is significant, the number of repeated minterms did not account for more than 3 percent of the total.

Profiling shows that the BDD operations (including the computation of prime implicants) take negligible runtime compared to the rest of the procedure. A typical distribution of the running time for these benchmarks is to spend 50 percent of the total time in the Boolean reasoning part, 30 percent in the theory reasoning and the rest mainly on the branching heuristic.

4.3   Results on Alternative Settings and Analysis

In order to understand the reasons behind the performance of our Barcelogic-Tools implementation (called *good* in the table below), we also ran it with three different settings.

One of them, (*black-box* in the table) was to use the black-box approach explained at the beginning of Section 3, where each time a T-model is found a blocking clause is added and the search is restarted from scratch, with no possibility to reuse the lemmas already computed. This setting was modified by allowing the lemmas to be reused (*naive* in the table). Finally, in order to analyze the role of theory propagation [NO05b], we also ran BCLT with the more advanced enumeration algorithm but with theory propagation turned off (*noTP* in the table).

Benchmark family	#queries	#preds.	#minterms	BCLT			
				good	black-box	naive	no TP
UCLID Suite:							
aodv	7	21	2916	4.6	24	11	11
bakery	19	32	426	11	19	13	14
BRP	10	22	30	0.1	0.12	0.13	0.2
cache_ibm	10	16	326	1.3	2.3	2	2.5
cache_bounded	18	26	2238	23	63	31	32
DLX	6	23	38080	13	242	63	15
OOO	10	25	10728	36	176	57	615
Rec. Data Struct.:							
reverse_acyclic	7	16	91	0.6	0.7	0.7	1
set_union	6	24	334	0.7	1	0.8	1
simple_cyclic	5	15	110	0.11	0.16	0.13	0.2
sorted_int	10	21	2465	19	38	24	154

Clearly, the black-box approach is not very competitive. It significantly improves if we allow the reusability of lemmas among the enumeration of models (*naive*). In fact, it is not much slower than *good*: since the number of minterms is not too large, the useless restarts are not too frequent, and also the explosion in the formula size does not show up in its full extent. Only in the families with many minterms (DLX and OOO), one starts noticing the benefits of a better AllSAT algorithm.

Concerning the role of theory propagation in these benchmarks, we can see that in some families (OOO and `sorted_int`) it is crucial for the success of the method. This is interesting because these two families are the ones which use arithmetic symbols most heavily among all. Moreover, applying theory propagation never increases the runtime, because the overhead in time it produces is always compensated by a reduction in the search space. This confirms, in another application area, the results presented in [NO05b] with respect to the importance of theory propagation.

4.4   Results on the Incremental Refinements of the Approximation

The procedure presented in Section 3.2 has also been implemented in order to evaluate its feasibility. The table below includes, in its third column, the time (in seconds) needed to directly compute $\mathcal{G}_P(\varphi)$, as explained in Section 3.1. The other columns are in groups of two, using different increment steps, comparing the incremental version of the procedure (`incr` in the table), with a non-incremental version (`n-incr`, not reusing lemmas nor minterms from previous steps). For example, the column `incr` below `step` 2 contains the time needed to compute, with the incremental algorithm, the whole set of approximations $\mathcal{G}_P^2(\varphi), \mathcal{G}_P^4(\varphi), \mathcal{G}_P^6(\varphi), \ldots$, until finally computing the exact $\mathcal{G}_P(\varphi)$.

Benchmark family	#preds.	exact	step 1		step 2		step 5	
			incr.	n-incr.	incr.	n-incr.	incr.	n-incr.
UCLID Suite:								
aodv	21	4.6	15	47	10	24	7.2	13
bakery	32	11	28	159	21	86	16	40
BRP	22	0.1	1.1	1.7	0.6	1	0.3	0.5
cache_ibm	16	1.3	3	8.6	2.2	5.1	1.7	2.8
cache_bounded	26	23	71	333	51	185	40	88
DLX	23	13	37	84	26	42	18	21
OOO	25	36	67	368	50	193	43	102
Rec. Data Struct.:								
reverse_acyclic	16	0.6	1.1	2.4	0.9	1.5	0.7	1
set_union	24	0.7	1.7	4.8	1.2	2.7	0.9	1.6
simple_cyclic	15	0.11	0.4	0.7	0.3	0.4	0.2	0.3
sorted_int	21	19	25	113	20	63	19	36

The first important thing to note is that even when we use an increment of 1, which means that more than 20 approximations are computed on average, the time needed in the incremental version only increases by a factor of 2 or 3 with respect to the time required to directly compute $\mathcal{G}_P(\varphi)$. One can also notice that this factor is reduced when we use a bigger increment step. This shows that in a situation where one wants to use some of these approximations but they do not suffice, the time needed to compute $\mathcal{G}_P(\varphi)$ will not be much worse than if we had tried to directly compute it.

The other important conclusion is that it is essential to use an incremental algorithm, e.g., using an increment step of 1 and a non-incremental algorithm requires about 10 times as much time as directly computing $\mathcal{G}_P(\varphi)$.

5   Conclusions and Further Work

In this paper, we have demonstrated the use of an SMT solver based on the DPLL(T) framework for efficient predicate abstraction. The algorithm is based on a careful generation of the set of all satisfying assignments over a set of predicates, and we have illustrated the impact of the various factors such as theory propagation, backjumping and incrementality on this approach. We also show how the technique can be adapted to compute increasingly precise approximations with respect to a given set of predicates in an incremental fashion, which provides an alternate method for refining predicate abstractions with a fixed set of predicates [DD01, JM05].

We are currently investigating exploiting incrementality when computing an abstraction over an monotonically growing set of predicates, which can be useful for creating Boolean programs [BMMR01] incrementally. Another area of future work is to extend a minterm c over P to a larger cube *on-the-fly*, before starting the search for a new minterm — this could impact the performance of queries (e.g. OOO, DLX and `sorted_int`) that have a very large #minterms/#cubes ratio.

References

[BCDR04]   T. Ball, B. Cook, S. Das, and S. K. Rajamani. Refining Approximations in Software Predicate Abstraction. In *TACAS'04*, LNCS 2988, pages 388–403.

[BCLZ04]   T. Ball, B. Cook, S. K. Lahiri, and L. Zhang. Zapato: Automatic theorem proving for predicate abstraction refinement. In *CAV'04*, LNCS 3114, pages 457–461. Springer, 2004.

[BdMS05]   C. Barrett, L. de Moura, and A. Stump. SMT-COMP: Satisfiability Modulo Theories Competition. In *CAV'05*, LNCS 3576, pages 20–23. Springer, 2005.

[BMMR01]   T. Ball, R. Majumdar, T. Millstein, and S. K. Rajamani. Automatic predicate abstraction of C programs. In *PLDI'01, SIGPLAN Notices*, 36(5), May 2001.

[CC77]   P. Cousot and R. Cousot. Abstract interpretation : A Unified Lattice Model for the Static Analysis of Programs by Construction or Approximation of Fixpoints. In *POPL'77*. ACM Press, 1977.

[CCG+03]   S. Chaki, E. M. Clarke, A. Groce, S. Jha, and H. Veith. Modular Verification of Software Components in C. In *ICSE'03)*, pages 385–395. IEEE Computer Society 2003, May 2003.

[CKSY04]   E. Clarke, D. Kroening, N. Sharygina, and K. Yorav. Predicate abstraction of ANSI–C programs using SAT. *FMSD'04*, 25, 2004.

[CUD]   CUDD: CU Decision Diagram Package. Available at http://vlsi. colorado.edu/fabio/CUDD/cuddIntro.html.

[DD01]   S. Das and D. Dill. Successive approximation of abstract transition relations. In *LICS'01*, pages 51–60. IEEE Computer Society, June 2001.

[DDP99]   S. Das, D. L. Dill, and S. Park. Experience with predicate abstraction. In *CAV'99*, LNCS 1633, pages 160–171. Springer, 1999.

[FQ02]   C. Flanagan and S. Qadeer. Predicate abstraction for software verification. In *POPL'02*, pages 191–202. ACM, 2002.

[GSY04]   O. Grumberg, A. Schuster and A. Yadgar. Memory efficient all-solutions sat solver and its application for reachability analysis. In *FMCAD'04*, LNCS 3312, pages 275–289. Springer, 2004.

[GHN+04]   H. Ganzinger, G. Hagen, R. Nieuwenhuis, A. Oliveras, and C. Tinelli. DPLL(T): Fast Decision Procedures. In *CAV'04*, LNCS 3114, pages 175–188. Springer, 2004.

[GS97]   S. Graf and H. Saïdi. Construction of abstract state graphs with PVS. In *CAV'97*, LNCS 1254, pages 72–83. Springer, 1997.

[HJMS02]   T. A. Henzinger, R. Jhala, R. Majumdar, and G. Sutre. Lazy Abstraction. In *POPL'02*, pages 58–70. ACM Press, 2002.

[JHS05]   H. Jin, H. Han, and F. Somenzi. Efficient conflict analysis for finding all satisfying assignments of a boolean circuit. In *TACAS'05*, LNCS 3440, pages 287–300. Springer, 2005.

[JM05]   R. Jhala and K. L. McMillan. Interpolant-based transition relation approximation. In *CAV'05*, LNCS 3576, pages 39–51. Springer, 2005.

[LB04]   S. K. Lahiri and R. E. Bryant. Constructing Quantified Invariants via Predicate Abstraction. In *VMCAI'04*, LNCS 2937, pages 267–281, 2004.

[LBC03]   S. K. Lahiri, R. E. Bryant, and B. Cook. A symbolic approach to predicate abstraction. In *CAV'03*, LNCS 2725, pages 141–153. Springer, 2003.

[LBC05]   S. K. Lahiri, T. Ball, and B. Cook. Predicate abstraction via symbolic
           decision procedures. In *CAV'05*, LNCS 3576, pages 24–38. Springer,
           2005.

[LQ06]   S. Lahiri and S. Qadeer. Verifying properties of well-founded linked
           lists. In *POPL'06*, pages 115–126. ACM, 2006.

[NO05a]   R. Nieuwenhuis and A. Oliveras. Decision procedures for SAT, SAT
           Modulo Theories and Beyond. The BarcelogicTools. (Invited Paper).
           In *LPAR'05*, LNCS 3835, pages 23–46. Springer, 2005.

[NO05b]   R. Nieuwenhuis and A. Oliveras. DPLL(T) with Exhaustive Theory
           Propagation and its Application to Difference Logic. In *CAV'05* LNCS
           3576, pages 321–334. Springer, 2005.

[NOT05]   R. Nieuwenhuis, A. Oliveras, and C. Tinelli. Abstract DPLL and
           Abstract DPLL Modulo Theories. *LPAR'04*, LNCS 3452, pp. 36–50.
           Springer, 2005.

[SS99]   H. Saïdi and N. Shankar. Abstract and model check while you prove.
           In *CAV'99*, LNCS 1633, pages 443–454. Springer, 1999.

[TR05]   C. Tinelli and S. Ranise. SMT-LIB: The Satisfiability Modulo Theories
           Library, July 2005. http://goedel.cs.uiowa.edu/smtlib/.

[ZM03]   L. Zhang and S. Malik. Validating sat solvers using an independent
           resolution-based checker In *DATE 2003*, pages 10880–10885. IEEE
           Computer Society, 2003.

[ZMMM01]   L. Zhang, C. F. Madigan, M. W. Moskewicz, and S. Malik. Efficient
           conflict driven learning in a Boolean satisfiability solver. In *ICCAD'01*,
           pages 279–285, 2001.

The Power of Hybrid Acceleration

Bernard Boigelot[1,*] and Frédéric Herbreteau[2,**]

[1] Institut Montefiore, B28
Université de Liège
B-4000 Liège, Belgium
boigelot@montefiore.ulg.ac.be
[2] LaBRI
351, cours de la Libération
33405 Talence Cedex, France
frederic.herbreteau@labri.fr

Abstract. This paper addresses the problem of computing symbolically the set of reachable configurations of a linear hybrid automaton. A solution proposed in earlier work consists in exploring the reachable configurations using an *acceleration* operator for computing the iterated effect of selected control cycles. Unfortunately, this method imposes a periodicity requirement on the data transformations labeling these cycles, that is not always satisfied in practice. This happens in particular with the important subclass of *timed automata*, even though it is known that the paths of such automata have a periodic behavior.

The goal of this paper is to broaden substantially the applicability of hybrid acceleration. This is done by introducing powerful reduction rules, aimed at translating hybrid data transformations into equivalent ones that satisfy the periodicity criterion. In particular, we show that these rules always succeed in the case of timed automata. This makes it possible to compute an exact symbolic representation of the set of reachable configurations of a linear hybrid automaton, with a guarantee of termination over the subclass of timed automata. Compared to other known solutions to this problem, our method is simpler, and applicable to a much larger class of systems.

1   Introduction

Hybrid automata [Hen96] provide a convenient formalism for reasoning about systems that combine discrete and continuous features. A hybrid automaton is basically a finite-state machine extended with real variables, equipped with a dual semantics: A configuration can evolve either in a continuous way by spending some time at a control location (*time step*), or in a discrete way by following a transition (*discrete step*).

This paper considers *linear hybrid automata*, a subclass of hybrid automata with a semantics essentially defined in terms of linear constraints. Linear hybrid

---

*   The work of this author was done in part while visiting the LaBRI.
** The work of this author was supported by *Persée*, a project funded by the *ACI Sécurité Informatique* of the French Ministry of Scientific Research.

T. Ball and R.B. Jones (Eds.): CAV 2006, LNCS 4144, pp. 438–451, 2006.

automata are well suited for modeling discrete systems operating in a real-time environment. Indeed, their variables can be used not only as real-valued clocks for dealing with continuous time, but also as general-purpose integer counters.

In order to analyze the reachability properties of a linear hybrid automaton, a classical solution is to explore symbolically its state space [ACH+95]. This consists in starting from the initial configuration, and then repeatedly applying time steps and discrete steps to obtain new reachable configurations. Since a time step generally leads to an uncountable number of configurations, one groups such configurations into *regions* that can be manipulated implicitly, with the help of a suitable data structure.

The drawback of this approach is that state-space exploration terminates only if the reachable state space is covered by a finite number of regions, in which case the hybrid automaton is essentially equivalent to a finite-state *region automaton*. This prevents from analyzing models in which the expressive power of linear hybrid automata is used for describing unbounded discrete features. For instance, the model of an idealized communication protocol may define, in addition to the clocks dealing with the timed aspects, variables for representing unbounded message sequence numbers. A discrete variable may also be used as a parameter for reasoning about an infinite family of similar models.

However, techniques are known for exploring symbolically the state space of infinite discrete systems. A solution is to add to the semantics of a system *meta-transitions*, which are objects that capture the effect of iterating control cycles [Boi98]. With meta-transitions, state-space exploration algorithms are able to compute in one step the reachable configurations obtained by following arbitrarily many times some loops of the system under analysis. Meta-transitions thus *accelerate* state-space exploration, and can make it terminate in some cases.

In order to add meta-transitions to a linear hybrid automaton, one needs a data structure for representing sets of configurations, as well as a decision procedure for checking whether the unbounded iteration of a given loop can be computed over this data structure. For the former problem, a suitable representation system, the *Real Vector Automaton (RVA)* [BBR97, BJW05] has been developed. One can effectively represent with RVA all the sets that are definable in the first order additive theory of the integer and real numbers $\langle \mathbf{R}, \mathbf{Z}, +, \leq \rangle$. This covers linear constraints, but also discrete unbounded periodicities.

The latter problem has also been investigated in earlier work. In [BBR97], one adapts to linear hybrid automata the meta-transition computation algorithms known for unbounded integer systems. With this method, only cycles with a deterministic behavior can be turned into meta-transitions, which conflicts with the inherently branching nature of timed steps. Another technique is developed in [BHJ03], which characterizes precisely the data transformations that label paths of timed automata, and give a sufficient *periodicity* criterion for constructing meta-transitions corresponding to the iteration of such paths.

Unfortunately, this periodicity criterion is not always satisfied in practice. This happens in particular with *timed automata*, which are a restricted subclass of linear hybrid automata. However, it is known that the data transformations labeling the paths of timed automata have a periodic behavior [CJ98], and that their reachability set can be computed within $\langle \mathbf{R}, \mathbf{Z}, +, \leq \rangle$ [CJ99]. Moreover, the shortcomings of finite-state approaches to exploring timed automata [Bou03, BY03, BLR05] provide an incentive to develop alternate solutions.

In [BHJ03], a simple reduction rule was introduced for translating linear hybrid transformations into equivalent ones that satisfy the periodicity criterion. In this paper, we generalize this idea to a much broader class of transformations, by developing several new complementary reduction rules. In particular, we show that the iteration of the multiple-counters systems studied in [CJ98] can be systematically reduced to iterating periodic linear hybrid transformations. As a secondary contribution, we provide a simpler proof of the central result of [CJ98].

For the particular case of timed automata, our algorithms make it possible to carry out symbolic state-space exploration without resorting to abstraction, and with a guarantee of termination, which solves the problems reported in [Bou03, BY03, BLR05]. Although this result was already achievable as a consequence of [CJ99], our method is simpler, and applicable to a much larger class of systems.

2   Linear Hybrid Automata

2.1   Syntax and Semantics

We use the term *convex linear constraint* to denote a finite conjunction of linear constraints with integer coefficients, i.e., a set $\{x \in \mathbf{R}^n \mid Px \# q\}$, with $P \in \mathbf{Z}^{m \times n}$, $q \in \mathbf{Z}^m$, and $\# \in \{<, \leq, =, \geq, >\}^m$. The term *linear transformation* denotes a relation of the form $\{(x, x') \in \mathbf{R}^n \times \mathbf{R}^n \mid x' = Ax + b\}$, with $A \in \mathbf{Z}^{n \times n}$ and $b \in \mathbf{Z}^n$.

Definition 1. *A* Linear Hybrid Automaton (LHA) *[ACH+ 95, Hen96] is a tuple* $(x, V, E, v_0, X_0, G, A, I, R)$*, where*

- x *is a vector of n real-valued* variables, *or* clocks, *with $n > 0$;*
- (V, E) *is a finite directed* control graph, *the vertices of which are the* locations *of the automaton. The* initial location *is v_0;*
- X_0 *is an* initial region, *defined by a convex linear constraint;*
- G *and A respectively associate to each edge in E a* guard, *which is a convex linear constraint, and an* assignment, *which is a linear transformation;*
- I *and R respectively associate to each location in V an* invariant, *which is a convex linear constraint, and a* rectangular activity $(l, u) \in \mathbf{Z}^n \times \mathbf{Z}^n$, *which denotes the constraint $l \leq \dot{x} \leq u$, where $\dot{x}$ is the first derivative of x.*

The semantics of a LHA $(x, V, E, v_0, X_0, G, A, I, R)$ is defined by the transition system $(Q, Q_0, (\rightarrow_\delta \cup \rightarrow_\tau))$, where

- $Q = V \times \mathbf{R}^n$ is the set of *configurations*;
- $Q_0 = \{(v, x) \in Q \mid v = v_0 \wedge x \in X_0 \cap I(v_0)\}$ is the set of *initial configurations*;

- The *discrete-step* transition relation $\rightarrow_\delta \subseteq Q \times Q$ is such that $(v, \boldsymbol{x}) \rightarrow_\delta$ $(v', \boldsymbol{x}')$ iff $\boldsymbol{x}' \in I(v')$ and there exists $e \in E$ such that $e = (v, v')$, $\boldsymbol{x} \in G(e)$ and $(\boldsymbol{x}, \boldsymbol{x}') \in A(e)$. Such a transition can also be denoted $(v, \boldsymbol{x}) \xrightarrow{e}_\delta (v', \boldsymbol{x}')$ when one needs to refer explicitly to e;
- The *time-step* transition relation $\rightarrow_\tau \subseteq Q \times Q$ is such that $(v, \boldsymbol{x}) \rightarrow_\tau (v', \boldsymbol{x}')$ iff $v' = v$, there exists $t \in \mathbf{R}_{\geq 0}$ such that $\boldsymbol{x} + t\boldsymbol{l} \leq \boldsymbol{x}' \leq \boldsymbol{x} + t\boldsymbol{u}$, with $(\boldsymbol{l}, \boldsymbol{u}) = R(v)$, and $\boldsymbol{x}' \in I(v)$.

Let $\rightarrow$ denote the relation $(\rightarrow_\delta \cup \rightarrow_\tau)$, and let $\rightarrow^*$ be the reflexive and transitive closure of $\rightarrow$. A configuration $(v', \boldsymbol{x}') \in Q$ is *reachable from* a configuration $(v, \boldsymbol{x}) \in Q$ iff $(v, \boldsymbol{x}) \rightarrow^* (v', \boldsymbol{x}')$. A configuration is *reachable* iff it is reachable from some configuration in Q_0. The *reachability set* of a LHA is the set of its reachable configurations.

2.2   Linear Hybrid Relations

Let $\mathcal{H} = (\boldsymbol{x}, V, E, v_0, X_0, G, A, I, R)$ be a LHA, and let $\sigma = e_1; e_2; \ldots; e_p$, with $p > 0$ and $\forall i \in [1, \ldots, p] : e_i \in E$, be a path in its control graph. Let $v_1, v_2, \ldots, v_{p+1} \in V$ be the locations successively visited by σ.

Following σ from a configuration $(v_1, \boldsymbol{x})$ to a configuration $(v_{p+1}, \boldsymbol{x}')$, denoted $(v_1, \boldsymbol{x}) \xrightarrow{\sigma} (v_{p+1}, \boldsymbol{x}')$, amounts to performing a time step at location v_1, followed by a discrete step through e_1, then a time step at $v_2, \ldots$, ending with a time step at v_{p+1}. This can only be done provided that $\boldsymbol{x}$, $\boldsymbol{x}'$, and all intermediate clock values visited along σ, satisfy some linear constraints derived from the semantics of time steps and discrete steps. Projecting out all intermediate variables from these constraints, one obtains that $(v_1, \boldsymbol{x}) \xrightarrow{\sigma} (v_{p+1}, \boldsymbol{x}')$ iff $\boldsymbol{x}$ and $\boldsymbol{x}'$ are linked by a relation θ_σ that has the following form [BHJ03].

Definition 2. *A Linear Hybrid Relation (LHR) is a relation*

$$\theta = \left\{ (\boldsymbol{x}, \boldsymbol{x}') \in \mathbf{R}^n \times \mathbf{R}^n \,\Big|\, P \begin{bmatrix} \boldsymbol{x} \\ \boldsymbol{x}' \end{bmatrix} \preceq \boldsymbol{q} \right\},$$

with $n > 0, P \in \mathbf{Z}^{m \times 2n}, \boldsymbol{q} \in \mathbf{Z}^m, \preceq \in \{<, \leq\}^m, and\ m > 0.$

Note that a LHR is fully characterized by its linear system $(P, \boldsymbol{q}, \preceq)$, and that P can be decomposed into $[P_1; P_2]$, with $P_1, P_2 \in \mathbf{Z}^{m \times n}$. In the sequel, we will denote such a LHR as either $(P, \boldsymbol{q}, \preceq)$, or $(P_1, P_2, \boldsymbol{q}, \preceq)$. We will also write $\theta(S)$ as a shorthand for $\{\boldsymbol{x}' \mid \exists \boldsymbol{x} \in S : (\boldsymbol{x}, \boldsymbol{x}') \in \theta\}$.

3   Acceleration

3.1   Meta-transitions

The idea behind acceleration is to capture the effect of selected *cycles* in the control graph (V, E) of the LHA $\mathcal{H}$ being analyzed, i.e., paths that start and end in the same control location.

Let σ be such a cycle, starting from the location $v_1 \in V$. The *meta-transition* [Boi98] corresponding to σ is defined as the relation $\xrightarrow{\sigma^*}$ such that $(v, \boldsymbol{x}) \xrightarrow{\sigma^*} (v', \boldsymbol{x}')$ iff $v = v' = v_1$ and $(\boldsymbol{x}, \boldsymbol{x}') \in \theta_\sigma^*$, where $\theta_\sigma^* = \cup_{i \geq 0} \theta_\sigma^i$.

Intuitively, following a meta-transition once leads in one step to all the configurations that could be reached by iterating its underlying cycle arbitrarily many times. Adding meta-transitions to the transition relation of a system thus preserves its semantics, but speeds up, or *accelerates*, state-space exploration, making it possible to explore in finite time some infinite region automata (though not all of them).

The practical use of meta-transitions requires a decision procedure for checking whether the closure θ^* of a given transformation θ can effectively be constructed and computed over sets of data values that are symbolically representable. We describe in the next section a symbolic representation system suited for analyzing linear hybrid automata.

3.2   Real Vector Automata

In order to explore symbolically the state-space of a linear hybrid automaton, one needs a data structure for representing the sets of configurations that have to be handled. Since hybrid automata have a finite number of control locations, it is actually sufficient to represent symbolically sets of clock values, that is, subsets of $\mathbf{R}^n$.

When only time steps and discrete steps are performed, the sets to be represented are characterized by conjunctions of linear constraints, and thus correspond to convex polyhedra. However, following meta-transitions may produce sets that cannot be expressed as finite unions of polyhedra. For instance, think of a cycle that has the effect of adding a constant set of values S_0 to the current clock value. The meta-transition associated to this cycle would transform a set S of clock values into the set $\cup_{i \in \mathbf{N}} S + i S_0$. We say that sets of this form have a *periodic structure*.

Real Vector Automata (RVA) [BBR97] have been introduced as effective data structures for representing convex and non convex polyhedra, as well as sets with a periodic structure. A RVA is, essentially, a finite-state automaton recognizing the infinite-word encodings of real vectors in some base $r > 1$. It is shown in [BJW05] that RVA are able to represent all the sets that are definable in $\langle \mathbf{R}, \mathbf{Z}, +, \leq \rangle$, i.e., the first-order additive theory of integer and real numbers. It is known that these sets essentially correspond to those that have a periodic structure [Wei99]. Efficient algorithms have been developed for constructing and manipulating RVA, that do not rely on the costly mechanisms usually associated to infinite-word automata. An implementation of RVA is available in the framework of the LASH toolset [LASH].

3.3   Acceleration of Linear Hybrid Relations

Let σ be a cycle of a LHA $\mathcal{H}$, and let θ_σ be its associated LHR. This cycle can be turned into a meta-transition if unbounded iterations of θ_σ preserve the representable nature of sets. This property is formalized by the following definition.

Definition 3. *The LHR θ_σ is iterable iff, for each set $S \subseteq \mathbf{R}^n$ definable in $\langle \mathbf{R}, \mathbf{Z}, +, \leq \rangle$, the set $\theta_\sigma^*(S)$ is definable in the same theory.*

The following sufficient criterion for iterability is given in [BHJ03].

Theorem 1. *Let $\theta_\sigma = (P, q, \preceq)$. If the system $(P, q, \preceq)$ over x and x' is only composed of constraints of the form $p.x \# q$, $p.x' \# q$, and $p.(x' - x) \# q$, with $p \in \mathbf{Z}^n$, $q \in \mathbf{Z}$, and $\# \in \{<, \leq\}$, then θ_σ is iterable.*

LHR that satisfy the hypotheses of Theorem 1 are said to be *periodic*. Intuitively, if a LHR θ_σ is a conjunction of constraints of the form $p.(x'-x) \# q$, then its effect consists in adding a constant convex polyhedron Π to the current clock value, i.e., $\theta_\sigma(S) = S + \Pi$ for all sets $S \subseteq \mathbf{R}^n$. One thus has, for each $k \geq 0$, $\theta_\sigma^k(S) = S + k\Pi$, hence θ_σ^k is a conjunction of constraints of the form $p.(x' - x) \# kq$. One can then compute θ_σ^* within $\langle \mathbf{R}, \mathbf{Z}, +, \leq \rangle$ by quantifying k over the natural integers. For any set $S \subseteq \mathbf{R}^n$, we thus have $\theta_\sigma^*(S) = \cup_{i \in \mathbf{N}} S + i\Pi$, which has a periodic structure.

Constraints of the form $p.x \# q$ or $p.x' \# q$ are handled using a convexity argument. When a system of periodic constraints is iterated k times from a clock value x to a value x', one can always place the intermediate values $x_1, x_2, \ldots, x_{k-1}$ produced by the successive iterations onto the straight line joining x and x'. Since the constraints are convex, it is thus sufficient to enforce them on x_1 and x_{k-1}, which can be done by a simple construction [BHJ03].

4   Reduction Rules

The iterability criterion expressed by Theorem 1 is not sufficient for identifying all LHR θ such that $\theta^*(S)$ has a periodic structure for any $S \in \mathbf{R}^n$. This restriction is problematic in practice, since simple case studies such as the classical *leaking gas burner* [ACH+95] cannot be handled.

In this section, we develop *reduction rules* aimed at broadening substantially the scope of Theorem 1. The approach consists in considering LHR θ that are not periodic, such as those given in Figure 1, and then try to express their iterated effect in terms of that of a periodic LHR θ'. Precisely, we say that θ is *reducible to θ'* if $\theta^k(S)$ can be expressed in terms of $(\theta')^k(S)$ within $\langle \mathbf{R}, \mathbf{Z}, +, \leq \rangle$, for any $S \subseteq \mathbf{R}^n$ and $k > 0$. Concretely, that θ reduces to θ' entails that an algorithm for computing $(\theta')^*$ can straightforwardly be transformed into one computing θ^*.

We first generalize in Section 4.1 a reduction rule introduced in [BHJ03], and then propose new rules in Sections 4.2 and 4.3.

4.1   Subspace Reduction

Consider the non-periodic LHR θ_1 in Figure 1. This relation transforms $\mathbf{R}^2$ into a set of smaller dimension, namely $E_1 = \theta_1(\mathbf{R}^2) = \{(x, x - 1) \mid x \in \mathbf{R}\}$. Hence,

$\theta_1 \equiv \begin{cases} x_1' + x_2' = 2x_1 + 1 \\ x_1' - x_2' = 1 \end{cases}$	$\theta_2 \equiv \begin{cases} x_1' + x_2' = 2x_1 + 1 \\ x_1 - x_2 = 1 \end{cases}$	$\theta_3 \equiv \begin{cases} x_1' + x_2' = x_1 + x_2 + 1 \\ x_1' - x_2' \geq x_1 + x_2 \end{cases}$
$\theta_4 \equiv \begin{cases} x_1' + x_2' \leq 2x_1 + 1 \\ x_1' + x_2' \geq x_1 + x_2 \\ x_1' + x_2' \geq x_1 - x_2 \end{cases}$	$\theta_5 \equiv \begin{cases} x_1' + x_2' \leq 2x_1 + 1 \\ x_1' + x_2' \geq x_1 + x_2 \\ x_1' + x_2' \geq x_1 - x_2 \\ x_1' - x_2' \leq 2 \end{cases}$	$\theta_6 \equiv \begin{cases} x_1' + x_2' \leq 2x_1 + 1 \\ x_1' + x_2' \geq x_1 + x_2 \\ x_1' + x_2' \geq x_1 - x_2 \\ x_1 - x_2 \leq 2 \end{cases}$
$\theta_7 \equiv \begin{cases} x_1' \geq x_2 + 1 \\ x_2' \geq x_1 + 2 \end{cases}$	$\theta_8 \equiv \begin{cases} x_1' \geq x_2 + 1 \\ x_2' \geq x_1 + 2 \\ x_3' + x_4' \leq x_3 + x_4 + 3 \end{cases}$	$\theta_9 \equiv \begin{cases} x_1' + x_2' \geq x_1 - x_2 + 1 \\ x_1' - x_2' \geq x_1 + x_2 + 2 \\ x_1' + x_3' \leq x_1 + x_3 + 3 \end{cases}$

Fig. 1. Examples of non-periodic LHR

for any set $S \subseteq \mathbf{R}^2$, the images $\theta_1(S)$, $\theta_1^2(S)$, $\theta_1^3(S)$, ..., are all subsets of E_1. It is thus sufficient to study the iterations of θ_1 in this subspace, in which it turns out to be periodic.

Formally, restricting a LHR $\theta \subseteq \mathbf{R}^n \times \mathbf{R}^n$ to a subspace E such that $\dim(E) = m$, with $m < n$, is done by a variable change operation. Let $\boldsymbol{u}_0 \in \mathbf{Z}^n$ be an arbitrary element of E, let $\boldsymbol{u}_1, \boldsymbol{u}_2, \ldots, \boldsymbol{u}_m \in \mathbf{Z}^n$ be a vector basis of $E - \boldsymbol{u}_0$, and let $U \in \mathbf{Z}^{n \times m} = [\boldsymbol{u}_1; \ldots; \boldsymbol{u}_m]$. We introduce new variables $y_1, y_2, \ldots, y_m$ and $y_1', y_2', \ldots, y_m'$, such that $(x_1, \ldots, x_n) = U(y_1, \ldots, y_m) + \boldsymbol{u}_0$ and $(x_1', \ldots, x_n') = U(y_1', \ldots, y_m') + \boldsymbol{u}_0$. Adding these constraints to the underlying system of θ, and then projecting out the variables x_i and x_i' for all $i \in [1, \ldots, n]$, one obtains a transformation $\theta' \subseteq \mathbf{R}^m \times \mathbf{R}^m$ that has the same iterative behavior as θ. Indeed, for any $S \subseteq \mathbf{R}^n$ and $k > 0$, we have $\theta^k(S) = U(\theta')^{k-1}(S') + \boldsymbol{u}_0$, where $S' \subseteq \mathbf{R}^m$ is the solution of $\theta(S) = US' + \boldsymbol{u}_0$. It is worth emphasizing that computing S' from S and $\theta^k(S)$ from $(\theta')^{k-1}(S')$ can be done within $\langle \mathbf{R}, \mathbf{Z}, +, \leq \rangle$. We thus have the following rule.

Reduction Rule 1. *If a LHR $\theta \subseteq \mathbf{R}^n \times \mathbf{R}^n$ is such that $\dim(\theta(\mathbf{R}^n)) = m$ with $m < n$, then θ is reducible to a computable LHR $\theta' \subseteq \mathbf{R}^m \times \mathbf{R}^m$.*

In the case of our example θ_1, we have $\dim(E_1) = 1$, which prompts the definition of new variables y_1, y_1' such that $x_1 = y_1$, $x_2 = y_1 - 1$, $x_1' = y_1'$, and $x_2' = y_1' - 1$. The LHR θ_1 then translates into $\theta_1' \equiv y_1' = y_1 + 1$, which is periodic.

Rule 1 admits a dual form. The LHR θ_2 in Figure 1 is such that $\theta_2(\mathbf{R}^2) = \mathbf{R}^2$, hence Rule 1 does not apply. Notice however that θ_2 produces a nonempty result only when it is applied to values that belong to $E_2 = \theta_2^{-1}(\mathbf{R}^2) = \{(x, x-1) \mid x \in \mathbf{R}\}$. In order to study the iterations of θ_2, one can therefore ignore the values that are outside of this subspace. This leads to the following rule.

Reduction Rule 2. *If a LHR $\theta \subseteq \mathbf{R}^n \times \mathbf{R}^n$ is such that $\dim(\theta^{-1}(\mathbf{R}^n)) = m$ with $m < n$, then θ is reducible to a computable LHR $\theta' \subseteq \mathbf{R}^m \times \mathbf{R}^m$.*

Technically, the reduction of θ is performed in the following way. Let $E = \theta^{-1}(\mathbf{R}^n)$. We first transform θ into $\theta'' = \theta \wedge (\boldsymbol{x}' \in E)$, so as to systematically discard output values that do not belong to E. Then, we define a variable change $(x_1, \ldots, x_n) = U(y_1, \ldots, y_m) + \boldsymbol{u}_0$, with $U \in \mathbf{Z}^{n \times m}$ and $\boldsymbol{u}_0 \in \mathbf{Z}^n$, from

$\mathbf{R}^n$ to E. Applying this variable change to θ'' yields a LHR $\theta' \in \mathbf{R}^m \times \mathbf{R}^m$. For each $S \subseteq \mathbf{R}^n$ and $k > 0$, we then have $\theta^k(S) = \theta(U(\theta')^{k-1}(S') + \boldsymbol{u}_0)$, where S' is the solution of $S \cap E = US' + \boldsymbol{u}_0$.

4.2   Rank Reduction

Rules 1 and 2 are not able to capture all sources of periodicity. For instance, they cannot be applied to the LHR θ_3 in Figure 1, since $\theta_3(\mathbf{R}^2) = \theta_3^{-1}(\mathbf{R}^2) = \mathbf{R}^2$.

However, remark that applying θ_3 to two vectors (a_1, a_2) and (b_1, b_2) such that $a_1 + a_2 = b_1 + b_2$ produces identical output values. Therefore, the iterations of θ_3 can be studied with respect to a single variable $y_1 = x_1 + x_2$. Like in the previous case, this variable change transforms θ_3 into a LHR of smaller dimension.

Formally, consider a LHR $\theta \in \mathbf{R}^n \times \mathbf{R}^n$. The system of constraints $(P_1, P_2, \boldsymbol{q}, \preceq)$ of θ can be rewritten as $P_2 \boldsymbol{x}' \preceq -P_1 \boldsymbol{x} + \boldsymbol{q}$. Let $p = \rho(P_1)$ be the rank of P_1. If $p < n$, then the possible values of $P_1 \boldsymbol{x}$, and hence also of $\boldsymbol{x}'$, can be described in terms of only p independent variables. We express P_1 as a product $P_1 = P_1' U$, with $P_1' \in \mathbf{Z}^{m \times p}$ and $U \in \mathbf{Z}^{p \times n}$, and introduce new variables $y_1, \ldots, y_p, y_1', \ldots, y_p'$ such that $(y_1, \ldots, y_p) = U(x_1, \ldots, x_n)$ and $(y_1', \ldots, y_p') = U(x_1', \ldots, x_n')$. Adding these constraints to $(P_1, P_2, \boldsymbol{q}, \preceq)$, and then projecting out $x_1, \ldots, x_n$ and $x_1', \ldots, x_n'$, yields a LHR $\theta' \in \mathbf{R}^p \times \mathbf{R}^p$. For each $S \subseteq \mathbf{R}^n$ and $k > 0$, we have $\theta^k(S) = \theta''((\theta')^{k-1}(US))$, where $\theta'' \in \mathbf{R}^p \times \mathbf{R}^n \equiv P_2 \boldsymbol{x}' \preceq -P_1' \boldsymbol{y} + \boldsymbol{q}$. Thus, θ is reducible to θ', which leads to the following rule.

Reduction Rule 3. *If a LHR $\theta \subseteq \mathbf{R}^n \times \mathbf{R}^n = (P_1, P_2, \boldsymbol{q}, \preceq)$ is such that $\rho(P_1) = p$ with $p < n$, then θ is reducible to a computable LHR $\theta' \subseteq \mathbf{R}^p \times \mathbf{R}^p$.*

A similar reduction can also be applied if the rank of P_2 is less than the number of variables. Consider the LHR θ_4 in Figure 1. If the vector (a_1, a_2) belongs (resp. does not belong) to $\theta_4(S)$ for some $S \subseteq \mathbf{R}^2$, then for all $(b_1, b_2) \in \mathbf{R}^2$ such that $b_1 + b_2 = a_1 + a_2$, we have $(b_1, b_2) \in S$ (resp. $(b_1, b_2) \notin S$). Thus, the behavior of θ_4 can be studied with respect to a single variable defined as $y_1 = x_1 + x_2$.

More generally, let $\theta \in \mathbf{R}^n \times \mathbf{R}^n$ be a LHR, and let $(P_1, P_2, \boldsymbol{q}, \preceq)$ be its underlying system of constraints. If $p = \rho(P_2)$ is such that $p < n$, then we decompose P_2 into $P_2 = P_2' U$, with $P_2' \in \mathbf{Z}^{m \times p}$ and $U \in \mathbf{Z}^{p \times n}$, and introduce new variables $y_1, \ldots, y_p, y_1', \ldots, y_p'$ such that $(y_1, \ldots, y_p) = U(x_1, \ldots, x_n)$ and $(y_1', \ldots, y_p') = U(x_1', \ldots, x_n')$. This variable change transforms θ into a LHR $\theta' \in \mathbf{R}^p \times \mathbf{R}^p$. For each $S \subseteq \mathbf{R}^n$ and $k > 0$, we have $\theta^k(S) = \theta''((\theta')^{k-1}(U\theta(S)))$, where $\theta'' \in \mathbf{R}^p \times \mathbf{R}^n \equiv U\boldsymbol{x}' = \boldsymbol{y}$. We therefore have the following rule.

Reduction Rule 4. *If a LHR $\theta \subseteq \mathbf{R}^n \times \mathbf{R}^n = (P_1, P_2, \boldsymbol{q}, \preceq)$ is such that $\rho(P_2) = p$ with $p < n$, then θ is reducible to a computable LHR $\theta' \subseteq \mathbf{R}^p \times \mathbf{R}^p$.*

4.3   Static Reduction

None of the reduction rules obtained so far can handle the LHR θ_5 in Figure 1. One nevertheless observes that the linear system of θ_5 contains a constraint $x_1' - x_2' \leq 2$ that is solely expressed over the output variables. Requiring that the value produced at the end of an iteration of θ_5 satisfies this constraint is actually equivalent to imposing $x_1 - x_2 \leq 2$ on the input value of the next iteration. Hence, the LHR θ_6 in Figure 1, on which Rule 4 can be applied, has essentially the same iterative behavior as θ_5.

Formally, let θ be a LHR. We call a constraint of θ *static* if it involves only either $x_1, \ldots, x_n$, or $x'_1, \ldots, x'_n$, and *dynamic* otherwise. A static constraint is said to be *explicit* if it is not implied by the dynamic constraints of θ. We denote by $\overline{\theta}$ the conjunction of explicit static constraints in θ. The LHR obtained from θ by rewriting over $x_1, \ldots, x_n$ (resp $x'_1, \ldots, x'_n$) all constraints in $\overline{\theta}$ is denoted θ_x (resp. $\theta_{x'}$).

For all $S \subseteq \mathbf{R}^n$ and $k \geq 1$, we have $\theta^k(S) = (\theta \wedge \overline{\theta_x})((\theta_x)^{k-2}(\theta(S)))$ and $\theta^k(S) = \theta((\theta_{x'})^{k-2}(\theta(S) \wedge \overline{\theta_{x'}}))$. We thus have the following rule.

Reduction Rule 5. *Every LHR θ is reducible to θ_x and $\theta_{x'}$.*

In practice, Rule 5 is only useful when it can be followed by another reduction. A simple guideline consists of reducing systematically LHR θ to θ_x before attempting to apply Rules 2 and 4, and to $\theta_{x'}$ before Rules 1 and 3.

5 Multiple Counters Systems

The combination of Rules 1 to 5 suffices for many applications. However, these rules are unable to handle relations such as θ_7 in Figure 1. This LHR is actually an instance of a *Multiple Counters System (MCS)*. It is known [CJ98] that all such relations θ are iterable within $\langle \mathbf{R}, \mathbf{Z}, +, \leq \rangle$.

In this section, we give a simpler proof of that result, and use it to derive an expression of $\theta^k(S)$ in terms of $k \in \mathbf{N}$ and $S \subseteq \mathbf{R}^n$. We then show that the acceleration of MCS can be reduced to that of periodic LHR. MCS are formally defined as follows.

Definition 4. *A* Multiple Counters Systems (MCS) *[CJ98] is a relation $\theta(\boldsymbol{x}, \boldsymbol{x}')$ $\subseteq \mathbf{R}^n \times \mathbf{R}^n$, defined by a finite conjunction of constraints of the form $z_1 \# z_2 + c$, where $z_1, z_2 \in \{x_1, \ldots, x_n, x'_1, \ldots, x'_n\}$, $\# \in \{<, \leq, \geq, >\}$, and $c \in \mathbf{Z}$.*

5.1 Acceleration of MCS

Let $\theta \subseteq \mathbf{R}^n \times \mathbf{R}^n$ be a MCS. We assume w.l.o.g. that the explicit static constraints of θ are expressed over both $x_1, x_2, \ldots, x_n$ and $x'_1, x'_2, \ldots, x'_n$.

Our goal is to construct within $\langle \mathbf{R}, \mathbf{Z}, +, \leq \rangle$ an expression for $\theta^k(\boldsymbol{x}^0, \boldsymbol{x}^k)$ in terms of the variables $\boldsymbol{x}^0$, $\boldsymbol{x}^k$ and k. For a fixed value of k, such an expression can be obtained by projecting $\boldsymbol{x}^1, \boldsymbol{x}^2, \ldots, \boldsymbol{x}^{k-1}$ out of $\theta(\boldsymbol{x}^0, \boldsymbol{x}^1) \wedge \theta(\boldsymbol{x}^1, \boldsymbol{x}^2) \wedge \cdots \wedge \theta(\boldsymbol{x}^{k-1}, \boldsymbol{x}^k)$, which can be done by Fourier-Motzkin elimination.

In this operation, the dynamic constraints of $\theta^k(\boldsymbol{x}^0, \boldsymbol{x}^k)$ are all obtained as combinations of constraints in $\theta(\boldsymbol{x}^0, \boldsymbol{x}^1)$, $\theta(\boldsymbol{x}^1, \boldsymbol{x}^2)$, $\ldots$, $\theta(\boldsymbol{x}^{k-1}, \boldsymbol{x}^k)$. Each dynamic constraint of θ^k results from combining a sequence of constraints of θ that links a variable x_i^0 to a variable x_j^k, with $i, j \in [1, \ldots, n]$, hence it takes the form $x_j^k \# x_i^0 + c$, where $\# \in \{<, \leq, \geq, >\}$ and $c \in \mathbf{Z}$. Likewise, the static constraints of θ^k correspond to sequences of constraints of θ that link either x_i^0 to x_j^0, or x_i^k to x_j^k, for some $i, j \in [1, \ldots, n]$.

This leads to a simple way of characterizing the constraints of θ^k. Inspired by [Rev93, CJ98], we build two directed graphs $G_<^\theta$ and $G_>^\theta$ in the following way. The vertices of these graphs correspond to the variables $x_1, \ldots, x_n$. The edges of $G_<^\theta$ (resp. $G_>^\theta$) are labeled by tuples $(\#, c, d)$, where $\# \in \{<, \leq\}$ (resp. $\# \in \{>, \geq\}$) is a $strictness\ marker$, $c \in \mathbf{Z}$ is a $cost$, and $d \in \{-1, 0, 1\}$ is a $depth$. The edges of $G_<^\theta$ and $G_>^\theta$ are created as follows:

- For each constraint $x_j \preceq x_i + c$ in θ, with $\preceq \in \{<, \leq\}$, we add the edge $(x_i, (\preceq, c, 0), x_j)$ to $G_<^\theta$, and the edge $(x_j, (\succeq, -c, 0), x_i)$ to $G_>^\theta$;
- For each constraint $x_j' \preceq x_i + c$ in θ, we add the edge $(x_i, (\preceq, c, 1), x_j)$ to $G_<^\theta$, and the edge $(x_j, (\succeq, -c, -1), x_i)$ to $G_>^\theta$;
- For each constraint $x_j' \succeq x_i + c$ in θ, we add the edge $(x_j, (\preceq, -c, -1), x_i)$ to $G_<^\theta$, and the edge $(x_i, (\succeq, c, 1), x_j)$ to $G_>^\theta$.

For each path π in $G_<^\theta$ or $G_>^\theta$, we define its $strictness$ $s(\pi)$ as the strongest marker labeling the transitions followed by π, and its $cost$ $c(\pi)$ and $depth$ $d(\pi)$ as the sums of the individual cost and depth of all these transitions. The $absolute$ $depth$ of π is $|d(\pi)|$. The minimum (resp. maximum) depth $d_-(\pi)$ (resp. $d_+(\pi)$) of π is defined as the smallest (resp. largest) depth among all prefixes of π. Intuitively, a path π of $G_<^\theta$ or $G_>^\theta$ linking a variable x_i to a variable x_j represents constraints $x_j^{d'} \# x_i^d + c$, where $\#$ corresponds to the strictness of π, $d' - d$ to its depth, and c to its cost. The minimum and maximum depth of π then bound the superscripts of the intermediate variables that are visited by π, and that are thus projected out when the constraints of θ are combined.

Proposition 1. $Each\ dynamic\ constraint\ x_j^k \# x_i^0 + c\ of\ \theta^k(\boldsymbol{x}^0, \boldsymbol{x}^k),\ with\ \# \in \{<, \leq, \geq, >\}\ and\ c \in \mathbf{Z},\ corresponds\ to\ a\ path\ \pi\ from\ x_i\ to\ x_j\ in\ either\ G_<^\theta\ or\ G_>^\theta,\ such\ that\ s(\pi) = \#,\ c(\pi) = c,\ d(\pi) = k,\ d_-(\pi) = 0,\ and\ d_+(\pi) = k.$ $Similarly,\ static\ constraints\ x_j^0 \# x_i^0 + c\ correspond\ to\ paths\ \pi\ from\ x_i\ to\ x_j\ such\ that\ s(\pi) = \#,\ c(\pi) = c,\ d(\pi) = 0,\ d_-(\pi) = 0,\ and\ d_+(\pi) \leq k.\ Finally,\ static\ constraints\ x_j^k \# x_i^k + c\ correspond\ to\ paths\ \pi\ from\ x_i\ to\ x_j\ such\ that\ s(\pi) = \#,\ c(\pi) = c,\ d(\pi) = 0,\ d_-(\pi) \geq -k,\ and\ d_+(\pi) = 0.$

The problem of computing the constraints of $\theta^k(\boldsymbol{x}^0, \boldsymbol{x}^k)$ has thus been reduced to that of characterizing, in terms of k, the costs of the paths of depths 0 and k that link two given variables in $G_<^\theta$ and $G_>^\theta$, without exceeding some minimum and maximum depths. Note that, in the case of multiple paths, it is sufficient to consider the strongest constraints, which correspond to the paths with the minimal cost in $G_<^\theta$ and with the maximal cost in $G_>^\theta$.

We now show that this characterization can be carried out with a bounded construction. Let π be a path of $G_<^\theta$ (the graph $G_>^\theta$ is handled symmetrically).

- If π contains occurrences of a simple loop σ, i.e., $\pi = \pi_1 \sigma^{k_1} \pi_2$ with $k_1 > 0$, such that $d(\sigma) = 0$ and $c(\sigma) \geq 0$. Then the path $\pi' = \pi_1 \pi_2$ has the same depth as π, but a smaller or equal cost.

- If π *contains occurrences of a simple loop* σ *such that* $d(\sigma) = 0$ *and* $c(\sigma) < 0$. Then π represents an unsatisfiable constraint.
- If π *contains occurrences of two simple loops* σ_1 *and* σ_2, *i.e., we have* $\pi = \pi_1 \sigma_1^{k_1} \pi_2 \sigma_2^{k_2} \pi_3$ *or* $\pi = \pi_1 \sigma_2^{k_2} \pi_2 \sigma_1^{k_1} \pi_3$, *such that either* $d(\sigma_1) > 0$ *and* $d(\sigma_2) > 0$, *or* $d(\sigma_1) < 0$ *and* $d(\sigma_2) < 0$, *and* $c(\sigma_1)/|d(\sigma_1)| \leq c(\sigma_2)/|d(\sigma_2)|$. *Then, removing* $|d(\sigma_1)|/g$ *occurrences of* σ_2 *and adding* $|d(\sigma_2)|/g$ *occurrences of* σ_1, *with* $g = \gcd(|d(\sigma_1)|, |d(\sigma_2)|)$, *transforms* π *into a path with the same depth, but a smaller or equal cost.*
- If π *contains occurrences of two simple loops* σ_1 *and* σ_2 *such that* $d(\sigma_1) < 0$, $d(\sigma_2) > 0$, *and* $c(\sigma_1)/d(\sigma_1) \geq c(\sigma_2)/d(\sigma_2)$. *Then removing* $-d(\sigma_1)/g$ *occurrences of* σ_2 *and* $d(\sigma_2)/g$ *occurrences of* σ_1 *from* π, *where* $g = \gcd(-d(\sigma_1), d(\sigma_2))$, *yields a path that has the same depth as* π, *but a smaller or equal cost.*
- If π *contains occurrences of two simple loops* σ_1 *and* σ_2 *such that* $d(\sigma_1) < 0$, $d(\sigma_2) > 0$, *and* $c(\sigma_1)/d(\sigma_1) < c(\sigma_2)/d(\sigma_2)$. *For any* $l > 0$, *adding* $-l.d(\sigma_1)/g$ *occurrences of* σ_2 *and* $l.d(\sigma_2)/g$ *occurrences of* σ_1, *with* $g = \gcd(-d(\sigma_1), d(\sigma_2))$, *transforms* π *into a path that has the same depth, but a smaller or equal cost.* In this case, we thus obtain the strongest constraint by selecting the largest value of l for which the minimum and maximum path depths are not exceeded. The path π is then split into $\pi = \pi_1 \pi_2$, such that each subpath π_1 or π_2 contains only iterations of either σ_1 or σ_2, and the split point maximizes the depth of the subpath π_1 or π_2 that contains the iterations of σ_2. Since the constraints represented by π are implied by those corresponding to π_1 and π_2, these two paths can now be considered individually.

Let $l_<$ (resp. $l_>$) be the least common multiple of the absolute depths of the simple cycles in $G^\theta_<$ (resp. $G^\theta_>$). Applying repeatedly the above transformations, the paths of $G^\theta_<$ are eventually replaced by ones in which all occurrences of simple loops but one have an absolute depth less than $l_<$. We thus have a simple algorithm for iterating θ:

1. Compute $l = \mathrm{lcm}(l_<, l_>)$. Since l is fixed, θ is reducible to θ^l;
2. In order to obtain the constraints of $(\theta^l)^k(\boldsymbol{x}^0, \boldsymbol{x}^k)$, it is sufficient to consider the paths of $G^{\theta^l}_<$ and $G^{\theta^l}_>$ with a depth $d \in \{0, k\}$, that are either acyclic or of the form $\pi_1 \sigma^{d - d(\pi_1) - d(\pi_2)} \pi_2$, where π_1 and π_2 are acyclic, and σ is a simple cycle of absolute depth 1. These paths can be inspected in bounded time. For each of them, one must also ensure that the minimum and maximum depth constraints imposed by Proposition 1 are satisfied.

   Recall that σ represents a constraint of the form $x_i' \# x_i + c$, hence σ^{k-d_0}, with $d_0 = d(\pi_1) + d(\pi_2)$, corresponds to $x_i' \# x_i + (k - d_0)c$. The dynamic constraints of $(\theta^l)^k(\boldsymbol{x}^0, \boldsymbol{x}^k)$ are thus obtained in the form $k \geq q \Rightarrow x_j^k \# x_i^0 + k\delta + \gamma$, with $\delta, \gamma \in \mathbf{Z}$, and $q \in \mathbf{N}$.

5.2   MCS and Periodic LHR

The results of the previous section give an interesting insight into the iterative behavior of MCS. For any MCS θ, we now know that there exists $l > 0$ such that

$(\theta^l)^k$ can be decomposed into $(\theta^l)^k = \theta_0 \cup \bigcup_{1 \leq i \leq p} \theta_i \circ (\theta')^{k-k_i} \circ \theta'_i$, where $p \geq 0$, θ' is a periodic LHR, $\theta_0, \theta_1, \ldots, \theta_p, \theta'_1, \ldots, \theta'_p$ are LHR, and $k_1, \ldots, k_p \in \mathbf{N}$. We therefore have the following result.

Reduction Rule 6. *Every MCS θ is reducible to a periodic LHR θ'.*

In practice, we iterate a given LHR θ by first applying all possible reductions rules from 1 to 5, and then checking whether the resulting system forms a periodic LHR, a MCS, or a conjunction of both. In the last situation, we can iterate θ provided that the periodic LHR θ_P and the remaining MCS θ_M that compose θ are defined over distinct subsets of variables. Indeed, assuming w.l.o.g. that the variables of θ_P precede these of θ_M, we have $\theta^k(S) = \theta_P^k(S_P) \times \theta_M^k(S_M)$, for all $S \subseteq \mathbf{R}^n$ and $k > 0$, where S_P and S_M are the projections of S over the variables of θ_P and θ_M. The LHR θ_8 in Figure 1 provides an example of relation that can be handled in this way.

This approach has the shortcoming that the class of LHR that can be iterated is not closed under linear transformations, e.g., the LHR θ_9 in Figure 1, which is functionally equivalent to θ_8, cannot be handled. A method that lifts this restriction will be investigated in another paper.

6   Application to Timed Automata

Definition 5. *A Timed Automaton (TA) is a LHA $(\boldsymbol{x}, V, E, v_0, X_0, G, A, I, R)$ such that*

- *its initial region X_0, guard $G(e)$ of each edge $e \in E$, and invariant $I(v)$ of each location $v \in V$ are conjunctions of constraints of the form $x_i \# c$ and $x_i - x_j \# c$, with $\# \in \{<, \leq, =, \geq, >\}$ and $c \in \mathbf{Z}$;*
- *the assignment $A(e)$ of each edge $e \in E$ has the form $\bigwedge_{i=0}^{n} x'_i = d_i x_i$, with $\forall i \in [1, \ldots, n] : d_i \in \{0, 1\}$. In other words, a transition can either reset a clock, or leave it unchanged;*
- *the activity $R(v)$ of each location $v \in V$ equals $((1, \ldots, 1), (1, \ldots, 1))$, i.e., all clocks increase uniformly with time.*

It is shown in [Fri98, CJ98] that the LHR that label arbitrary paths of timed automata can be turned into MCS by a simple variable change operation. Let π be such a path. The idea consists in defining one new global clock t that is never reset, and that will serve as a reference for relating the values of other variables. Then, for each clock x_i of the TA that is reset along π, or that is evaluated without having been reset, one introduces a new variable t_i such that $x_i = t - t_i$. Let $t^0, t_1^0, t_2^0, \ldots$ denote the initial values, and $t', t'_1, t'_2, \ldots$ the final values, of $t, t_1, t_2, \ldots$ with respect to π. Intuitively, each t'_i gives the *date*, expressed with respect to the reference timeframe, at which the corresponding clock x_i has been last reset. Expressed over $t^0, t_1^0, t_2^0, \ldots$ and $t', t'_1, t'_2, \ldots$, the LHR induced by π takes the form of a MCS [Fri98, CJ98].

Together with Rule 6, this result gives an effective algorithm for turning any cycle of a TA into a meta-transition. We now recall a property established in [CJ99].

Theorem 2. *For any TA, there exists a finite choice of meta-transitions for which symbolic state-space exploration terminates.*

Algorithms are given in [Boi98, BLFP03] for discovering automatically such a choice of meta-transitions whenever one exists. It is thus possible to guarantee that exploring symbolically the state-space of timed automata with hybrid acceleration terminates.

7 Conclusions

The contribution of this paper is to show that, for a large class of linear hybrid relations θ, computing θ^* reduces to iterating the periodic relations considered in [BHJ03]. This broadens substantially the applicability of hybrid acceleration, and provides a powerful framework for reasoning about linear hybrid automata.

A secondary contribution is to provide a simpler proof of the acceleration result for multiple counters systems given in [CJ98]. We have established that the iterative behavior of such systems reduces to that of periodic relations, which brings their acceleration algorithm closer to an actual implementation.

For the particular case of timed automata, an exact state-space exploration algorithm was already known [CJ99]. Compared to this method, the advantage of our approach is to be applicable to a much larger class of systems (although obviously without a general guarantee of termination). For large systems, we also expect our technique to scale up much more nicely than [CJ99]. Indeed, iterating a periodic hybrid relation in $\langle \mathbf{R}, \mathbf{Z}, +, \leq \rangle$ is fundamentally very close to iterating a linear transformation within $\langle \mathbf{Z}, +, \leq \rangle$, as done by the NDD package of LASH [LASH]. Although this conjecture remains to be substantiated with actual experiments, we believe that adding timed constraints to the case studies performed with LASH will not significantly complicate their analysis.

Acknowledgments

We would like to thank the reviewers of this paper for their insightful comments on the MCS acceleration algorithm described in Section 5.1.

References

[ACH+95]   R. Alur, C. Courcoubetis, N. Halbwachs, T. A. Henzinger, P.-H. Ho, X. Nicollin, A. Olivero, J. Sifakis, and S. Yovine. The algorithmic analysis of hybrid systems. *Theoretical Computer Science*, 138(1):3–34, 1995.

[BBR97]   B. Boigelot, L. Bronne, and S. Rassart. An improved reachability analysis method for strongly linear hybrid systems. In *Proceedings of the 9th Int. Conf. on Computer-Aided Verification (CAV'97)*, volume 1254 of *Lecture Notes in Computer Science*, pages 167–177. Springer-Verlag, 1997.

[BHJ03]   B. Boigelot, F. Herbreteau, and S. Jodogne. Hybrid acceleration using real vector automata. In *Proc. of the 15th Int. Conf. on Computer-Aided Verification (CAV'03)*, volume 2725 of *Lecture Notes in Computer Science*, pages 193–205. Springer-Verlag, 2003.

[BJW05]   B. Boigelot, S. Jodogne, and P. Wolper. An effective decision procedure
            for linear arithmetic with integer and real variables. *ACM Transactions
            on Computational Logic (TOCL)*, 6(3):614–633, 2005.

[BLFP03]   S. Bardin, J. Leroux, A. Finkel, and L. Petrucci. FAST: Fast accel-
            ereation of symbolic transition systems. In *Proc. 15th Int. Conf. on
            Computer-Aided Verification*, volume 2725 of *Lect. Notes in Comp. Sc.*,
            pages 118–121, 2003.

[BLR05]   P. Bouyer, F. Laroussinie, and P.-A. Reynier. Diagonal constraints in
            timed automata: Forward analysis of timed systems. In *Proc. of the 3rd
            Int. Conf. on Formal Modelling and Analysis of Timed Systems*, volume
            3829 of *Lecture Notes in Computer Science*, pages 112–126. Springer-
            Verlag, 2005.

[Boi98]   B. Boigelot. *Symbolic Methods for Exploring Infinite State Spaces*. PhD
            thesis, Université de Liège, 1998.

[Bou03]   P. Bouyer. Untameable timed automata! In *Proc. of 20th Ann. Symp.
            Theoretical Aspects of Computer Science (STACS'03)*, Lecture Notes in
            Computer Science, Berlin, Germany, 2003. Springer-Verlag.

[BY03]   J. Bengtsson and W. Yi. On clock difference constraints and termination
            in reachability analysis of timed automata. In *Proc. of 5th Int. Conf. on
            Formal Engineering Methods (ICFEM'03)*, volume 2885 of *Lecture Notes
            in Computer Science*, pages 491–503, 2003.

[CJ98]   H. Comon and Y. Jurski. Multiple counters automata, safety analysis
            and Presburger arithmetic. In *Proc. of 10th Int. Conf. on Computer-
            Aided Verification (CAV'98)*, volume 1427 of *Lecture Notes in Computer
            Science*, pages 268–279. Springer-Verlag, 1998.

[CJ99]   H. Comon and Y. Jurski. Timed automata and the theory of real num-
            bers. In *Proc. 10th Int. Conf. Concurrency Theory (CONCUR'99)*,
            volume 1664 of *Lecture Notes in Computer Science*, pages 242–257.
            Springer-Verlag, 1999.

[Fri98]   L. Fribourg. A closed-form evaluation for extended timed automata.
            Research Report LSV-98-2, LSV, March 1998.

[Hen96]   T. A. Henzinger. The theory of hybrid automata. In *Proc. 11th An-
            nual Symp. on Logic in Computer Science (LICS)*, pages 278–292. IEEE
            Computer Society Press, 1996.

[LASH]   The Liège Automata-based Symbolic Handler (LASH). Available at :
            http://www.montefiore.ulg.ac.be/~boigelot/research/lash/.

[Rev93]   P. Z. Revesz. A closed-form evaluation for datalog queries with integer
            (gap)-order constraints. *Theor. Comp. Sc.*, 116(1&2):117–149, 1993.

[Wei99]   V. Weispfenning. Mixed real-integer linear quantifier elimination. In
            *ISSAC: Proceedings of the ACM SIGSAM Int. Symp. on Symbolic and
            Algebraic Computation*, pages 129–136, Vancouver, 1999. ACM Press.

Lookahead Widening[*]

Denis Gopan[1] and Thomas Reps[1,2]

[1] University of Wisconsin
[2] GrammaTech, Inc.
{gopan, reps}@cs.wisc.edu

Abstract. We present *lookahead widening*, a novel technique for using existing widening and narrowing operators to improve the precision of static analysis. This technique is both self-contained and fully-automatic in the sense that it does not rely on separate analyzes or human involvement. We show how to integrate lookahead widening into existing analyzers with minimal effort. Experimental results indicate that the technique is able to achieve sizable precision improvements at reasonable costs.

1 Introduction

Abstract interpretation is a general framework used for static analysis and verification of software [7,6]. In abstract interpretation, the collecting semantics of a program is expressed as a least fix-point of a set of equations. The equations are solved over some abstract domain chosen based on desired precision and cost. Typically, the equations are solved iteratively; that is, successive approximations of the solution are computed until they converge to a least fix-point. However, for many useful abstract domains (particularly those for analyzing numeric properties, such as intervals, octagons [11], and polyhedra [8,9]) such chains of approximations can be very long or even infinite. To make use of such domains, abstract interpretation uses an extrapolation technique, called *widening* [7].

Widening attempts to predict the fix-point based on the sequence of approximations computed on earlier iterations of the analysis. Typically, widening degrades the precision of the analysis; i.e., the obtained solution is a fix-point or a post-fix-point, but not necessarily the least fix-point. If the obtained solution is a post-fix-point, it can be refined by computing a *descending approximation sequence* that converges to a (not necessarily least) fix-point. Again, the chain of approximations can be very long or infinite. To ensure convergence, either a fixed, finite number of descending iterations is performed, or a counterpart of widening, called *narrowing* [7] is used. Such use of widening and narrowing is sufficient to get precise results for loops with regular[1] behavior. However, as we illustrate in §2, it loses precision for more complex loops.

---

[*] Supported by ONR(N00014-01-1-{0708,0796}) and NSF (CCR-9986308 and CCF-0524051).

[1] In this paper, we use the term *regular* in the sense of ordinary usage, i.e., consistent in action, orderly, predictable, etc. We do not use it in the mathematical sense of formal-language theory.

T. Ball and R.B. Jones (Eds.): CAV 2006, LNCS 4144, pp. 452–466, 2006.

In this paper, we present a novel approach to using existing widening and narrowing operators to improve the precision of numeric program analysis. The idea behind the approach is to separate loops into phases with simpler behavior, and apply existing analysis methods to the individual phases. This offers an opportunity to obtain better results when phases of a loop have regular behavior that is lost when they are considered simultaneously. In practice, we achieve this effect by propagating two abstract values. The first value is used to keep the analysis within the current loop phase: this value is used to decide "where to go" at program conditionals and is never widened. The second value is used to compute the solution for the current phase: both widening and narrowing are applied to it. When the second value stabilizes, it is promoted into the first value, thereby allowing the analysis to advance to the next phase.

We refer to the first value as the *main value*, because it contains the overall solution after the analysis converges, and to the second value as *the pilot value*, because it "previews" the behavior of the program along the paths to which the analysis is restricted.[2] The overall technique is called *lookahead widening*, because, from the point of view of the main value, the pilot value determines a suitable extrapolation for it by sampling the analysis future.

We show how to implement lookahead widening in practice so that it can be integrated into existing analyzers with minimal effort. The idea behind the implementation is to construct from an arbitrary abstract domain, such as intervals, octagons, or polyhedra, an abstract domain that implements our technique. The constructed domain can then be directly plugged into existing analyzers. However, to guarantee that such an analysis converges, we impose two minor restrictions: one on the iteration strategy employed by the analyzer, and one on the properties of the widening operator of the base domain. A major benefit of our implementation is that it can be directly used in analyzers that are not equipped for computing descending iteration sequences. Such a situation often arises when a capability to model numeric properties is added to an existing symbolic analyzer.

We present experimental results that we obtained by applying a prototype implementation of the technique to a handful of benchmarks that appeared recently in the literature on widening. Lookahead widening improves precision for half of the benchmarks. We also present experimental results from on-going work in which weighted pushdown systems are used for numeric program analysis. The use of lookahead widening in this framework allowed to establish tighter loop invariants for 4-40% of the loops in a selected set of benchmarks, with overheads ranging from 3% to 30%.

Contributions. In this paper we make the following contributions:

- We present a novel technique, lookahead widening, that uses existing widening and narrowing operators to improve the precision of static analysis. The technique is both self-contained and fully-automatic.
- We show how to implement lookahead widening in practice so that it can be integrated into existing analyzers with minimal effort.

---

[2] The word *pilot* is used in the sense of, e.g., a sitcom pilot in the television industry.

- We present experimental results that we obtained with two prototype implementations of lookahead widening. Our results suggest that lookahead widening improves analysis precision at modest cost.

Paper Organization. The paper is organized as follows: §2 introduces basic concepts and presents the running example; §3 describes lookahead widening; §4 addresses several implementation issues; §5 presents experimental results; §6 discusses related work.

2 Preliminaries

In this section, we briefly introduce several concepts that will be used throughout the paper. Due to space limitations, we assume that the reader is familiar with abstract interpretation and the standard use of widening and narrowing. For a thorough discussion of these topics, see [12, §4.2]. We assume that widening points are selected according to Bourdoncle's technique [4]. That is, we assume that a *weak topological order (WTO)* is computed for the nodes in the program's control-flow graph (CFG), and that widening is performed at the heads of the components that the WTO defines.[3] Another concept from [4] that is important for the paper is the *recursive iteration strategy*, which requires the analyzer to stabilize the currently analyzed WTO component before proceeding to CFG nodes outside of the component. The examples in the paper use the abstract domain of polyhedra [8,9].

Running Example. We use the program in Fig. 1(a) as a running example. Fig. 2 illustrates the results from applying a solver that incorporates standard widening techniques to the program. For brevity, only some of the program points are shown. Widening is performed at node n_1 on the second and third iterations. After the third iteration, the analysis converges to a post-fix-point. A descending iteration sequence converges in one iteration: it recovers the precision lost by the application of widening on the third iteration, but is not able to recover the precision lost by the application of widening on the second iteration.

3 Lookahead Widening

Let us start by explaining the weaknesses of the standard approach that our technique aims to overcome. The loop in Fig. 1(a) has two explicit phases: during the first phase (the first 51 iterations) both variables x and y are incremented; during the second phase (iterations 51 through 102) variable x is incremented, but variable y is decremented. While the loop's behavior during each phase is regular and could be captured precisely by standard use of widening and narrowing, the overall loop behavior is non-regular and, as was shown in §2, the standard approach yields an imprecise solution.

In particular, the limitation of the standard approach is manifested at the beginning of the second iteration. At that point in the analysis, an application

---

[3] In structured programs, components defined by a WTO correspond to program loops.

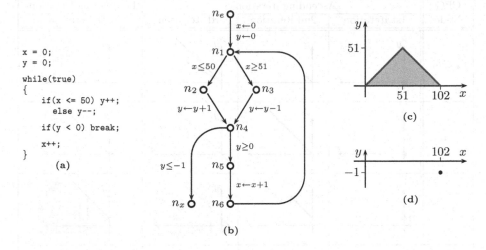

```
x = 0;
y = 0;
while(true)
{
    if(x <= 50) y++;
        else y--;

    if(y < 0) break;

    x++;
}
        (a)
```

Fig. 1. Running example: (a) a loop with non-regular behavior; (b) control-flow graph for the program in (a); (c) the set of program states at n_1: the points with integer coordinates that lie on the dark upside-down "v" are the precise set of concrete states; the gray triangle gives the best approximation of that set in the polyhedral domain; (d) the single program state that reaches n_x

of widening yields an overapproximation of the behavior of the first phase of the loop, i.e., no upper bounds are discovered for x and y. As a result, the analysis starts exploring the second phase of the loop with imprecise initial assumptions, in effect, propagating the precision loss incurred on the first phase. As the last column in Fig. 2 shows, the descending iteration sequence fails to recover the lost precision.

The general idea behind our technique is to improve the precision of the analysis by obtaining a more precise solution for each loop phase before proceeding to the next. Intuitively, this can be envisioned as applying standard analysis techniques to a (finite) sequence of *syntactic restrictions* of the analyzed program that eventually converge to the entire program. The result obtained for a particular program restriction is used as the starting point for the analysis of the next restriction in the sequence.

Fig. 3 illustrates this process for our running example. Fig. 3(a) shows the first program restriction that is considered. Note that this restriction corresponds to the first phase of the loop. Fig. 3(c) shows the solution at node n_1, obtained for this restriction with the standard method. Fig. 3(b) shows the second restriction of the program; this restriction encompasses both loop phases, but does not include edges that lead outside of the loop. The analysis starts with the values obtained from the first restriction, and, at n_1, yields the solution shown in Fig. 3(d), which is the precise invariant for the loop in the polyhedral domain. The final restriction consists of the entire program (Fig. 1(b)). Applying standard analysis methods to this restriction yields, at node n_x, the solution shown

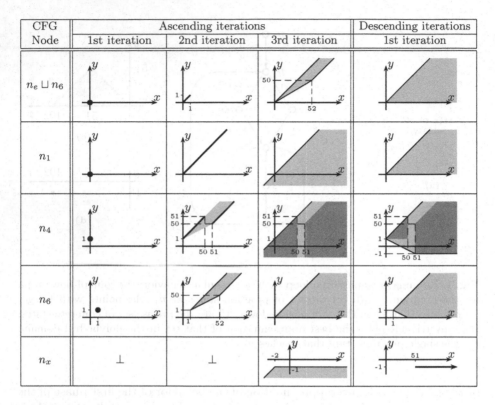

Fig. 2. Standard analysis trace. Widening is performed at node n_1. At the join point, n_4, the polyhedra that are joined are shown in dark gray and the result is shown in light gray.

in Fig. 3(e), which is the least fix-point, in the polyhedral domain, for the set of equations generated for the program in Fig. 1.

Although the above idea leads to superior results, it may seem to be hard to implement in practice. In particular, it is not obvious how to automatically derive program restrictions that correspond to loop phases. In the remainder of this section, we show how to implicitly confine the analysis to individual loop phases and how to implement our technique in a way that can be directly integrated into existing analyzers with only minor changes to their implementations.

3.1   Approximation of Loop Phases

Rather than explicitly derive syntactic program restrictions, as described above, our technique approximates this behavior by using a specially designed abstract value to guide the analysis through the program. That is, the analysis propagates a pair of abstract values: the first value (referred to as *the main value*) is used to decide at conditional points which paths are to be explored; the second value (referred to as *the pilot value*) is used to compute the solution along those paths. Widening and narrowing are only applied to the pilot value. Intuitively, the

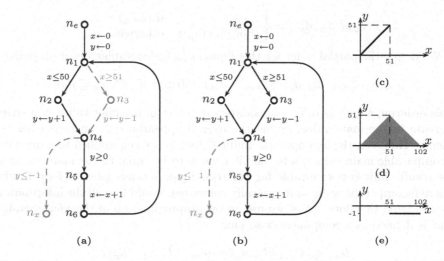

(a)   (b)   (c)
                                                (d)
                                                (e)

Fig. 3. Syntactic program restrictions for the program in Fig. 1: the omitted CFG nodes and edges are shown in gray and are dashed; (a) the first restriction corresponds to the first loop phase; (b) the second restriction consists of both loop phases, but not the loop exit edge; (c) solution (at n_1) for the first restriction; (d) solution (at n_1) for the second restriction; (e) solution (at n_x) for the third restriction (shown in Fig. 1(b))

main value restricts the analysis to a particular loop phase, while the pilot value computes the solution for it. After the pilot value stabilizes, it is used to update the main value, essentially switching the analysis to the next syntactic restriction in the sequence.

Let $\mathbb{D}$ be an arbitrary abstract domain: $\mathbb{D} = \langle D, \sqsubseteq, \sqcup, \top, \bot, \nabla, \Delta, \{\tau\}\rangle$, where D is a set of domain elements; $\sqsubseteq$ is a partial order on D; $\sqcup$, $\top$, and $\bot$ denote least upper bound operation, the greatest element, and the least element of D with respect to $\sqsubseteq$; ∇ and Δ are the widening operator and the narrowing operator; and $\{\tau\colon D \to D\}$ is the set of (monotonic) abstract transformers associated with the edges of program's CFG. We construct a new abstract domain:

$$\mathbb{D}_{LA} = \langle D_{LA}, \sqsubseteq_{LA}, \sqcup_{LA}, \top_{LA}, \bot_{LA}, \nabla_{LA}, \{\tau_{LA}\}\rangle,$$

each element of which is a pair of elements of $\mathbb{D}$: one for the main value and one for the pilot value. The pilot value must either equal the main value or overapproximate it. Also, the main value (and, consequently the pilot value) cannot be bottom. We add a special element to represent bottom for the new domain:

$$D_{LA} = \{\langle d_m, d_p\rangle \mid d_m, d_p \in D,\ d_m \sqsubseteq d_p,\ d_m \neq \bot\} \cup \{\bot_{LA}\}.$$

The top element for the new domain is defined trivially as $\top_{LA} = \langle \top, \top\rangle$.

Abstract transformers are applied to both elements of the pair. However, to make the main value guide the analysis through the program, if an application of the transformer to the main value yields bottom, we make the entire operation yield bottom:

$$\tau_{LA}(\langle d_m, d_p \rangle) = \begin{cases} \bot_{LA} & \text{if } \tau(d_m) = \bot \\ \langle \tau(d_m), \tau(d_p) \rangle & \text{otherwise} \end{cases}$$

We define the partial order for this domain as lexicographic order on pairs:

$$\langle c_m, c_p \rangle \sqsubseteq_{LA} \langle d_m, d_p \rangle \triangleq (c_m \sqsubset d_m) \vee [(c_m = d_m) \wedge (c_p \sqsubseteq d_p)].$$

This ordering allows us to accommodate a decrease in the pilot value by a strict increase in the main value, giving the overall appearance of an increasing sequence. However, the join operator induced by $\sqsubseteq_{LA}$, when applied to pairs with incomparable main values, sets the pilot value to be equal to the main value in the result. This is not suitable for our technique, because joins at loop heads, where incomparable values are typically combined, would lose all the information accumulated by pilots. Thus, we use an overapproximation of the join operator that is defined as a component-wise join:

$$\langle c_m, c_p \rangle \sqcup_{LA} \langle d_m, d_p \rangle = \langle c_m \sqcup d_m, c_p \sqcup d_p \rangle.$$

The definition of the widening operator encompasses the essence of our technique: the main value is left intact, while the pilot value first goes through an ascending phase, then through a descending phase, and is *promoted* into the main value after stabilization. Conceptually, the widening operator is defined as follows:

$$\langle c_m, c_p \rangle \nabla_{LA} \langle d_m, d_p \rangle = \begin{cases} \langle c_m \sqcup d_m, c_p \nabla d_p \rangle & \text{if the pilot value is ascending} \\ \langle c_m \sqcup d_m, c_p \Delta d_p \rangle & \text{if the pilot value is descending} \\ \langle d_p, d_p \rangle & \text{if the pilot value has stabilized} \end{cases}$$

The direct implementation of the above definition requires an analyzer to be modified to detect whether the pilot value is in ascending mode, descending mode, or whether it has stabilized. Also, for short phases, there is a possibility that the main value exits the phase before the pilot value stabilizes, in which case the pilot must be switched to ascending mode. These are global properties, and the modifications that are required depend heavily on the implementation of the analyzer. In our implementation, we took a somewhat different route, which we describe in the next section.

3.2   Practical Implementation

To simplify the integration of our technique into an existing analyzer, we impose on both the analyzer and the underlying abstract domain restrictions that allow us to check locally the global properties that are necessary for defining a widening operator:

- **R1. Analyzer restriction:** the analyzer must follow a *recursive iteration strategy* [4]; that is, the analysis must stay within each WTO component until the values within that component stabilize.
- **R2. Abstract domain restriction:** the abstract domain must possess a *stable widening operator* [4]; that is, $x \sqsubseteq y$ must imply that $y \nabla x = y$.

Furthermore, our implementation does not utilize narrowing operators, and only computes the equivalent of a single descending iteration for each loop phase. We believe that this simplification is reasonable because meaningful narrowing operators are only defined for a few abstract domains; also, in the experimental evaluation we did not encounter examples that would have significantly benefited from a longer descending-iteration sequences.

We define the widening operator as follows:

$$\langle c_m, c_p \rangle \nabla_{LA} \langle d_m, d_p \rangle = \begin{cases} \langle c_m, c_p \rangle & \text{if } \langle d_m, d_p \rangle \sqsubseteq_{LA} \langle c_m, c_p \rangle \\ \langle d_p, d_p \rangle & \text{if } d_p \sqsubseteq c_p \\ \langle c_m \sqcup d_m, c_p \nabla d_p \rangle & \text{otherwise} \end{cases}$$

The first case ensures that the widening operator is stable. The second case checks whether the pilot value has stabilized, and promotes it into the main value. Note that the pilot value that is promoted is not c_p, but the value d_p, which was obtained from c_p by propagating it through the loop to collect the effect of loop conditionals (i.e., one possibly-descending iteration is performed). The last case incorporates the pilot's ascending sequence: the main values are joined, and the pilot values are widened.

Soundness. It is easy to see that the results obtained with our technique are sound. Consider the operations that are applied to the main values: they precisely mimic the operations that the standard approach applies, except that widening is computed differently. Therefore, because the application of ∇_{LA} never decreases main values and because main values must stabilize for the analysis to terminate, the obtained results are guaranteed to be sound.

Convergence. We would like to show that a standard analyzer that is constructed in accordance with the principles outlined in §2 and that employs $\mathbb{D}_{LA}$ as an abstract domain converges. The use of the recursive iteration strategy (R1) allows us to limit our attention to a single WTO component: that is, if we show that the analysis converges for an arbitrary component, then it must converge for the entire program. Let us focus on the head of an arbitrary component: this is where both widening is applied and stabilization is checked.

First, we show that either the pilot value is promoted or the entire component stabilizes after a finite number of iterations. To do this, we rely on the property of the recursive-iteration strategy that the stabilization of a component can be detected by stabilization of the value at its head [4, Theorem 5]. The main value goes through a slow ascending sequence, during which time the analysis is restricted to a subset of the component's body. The pilot goes through an accelerated ascending sequence, which, if the underlying widening operator ∇ is defined correctly, must converge in a finite number of iterations. ∇_{LA} detects stabilization of the pilot's ascending sequence by encountering a first pilot value (d_p) that is less than or equal to the pilot value on the previous iteration (c_p): because the widening operator is stable (R2), application of widening will not change the previous pilot value. Note that c_p is a (post-)fix-point for the restricted component, and d_p is the result of propagating that (post-)fix-point through the same restricted component, and thus, is itself a (post-)fix-point. Two scenarios must now be considered: either the main value has also stabilized (i.e., $d_m \sqsubseteq c_m$), in which case $\langle d_m, d_p \rangle \sqsubseteq_{LA} \langle c_m, c_p \rangle$ and the entire component stabilizes (due to stability of ∇_{LA}); or the main value has not yet stabilized, in which case the (post-)fix-point d_p is promoted into the main value.

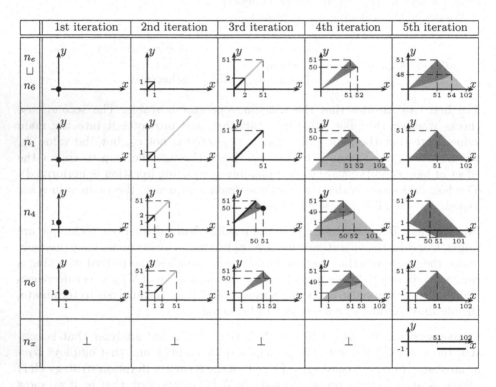

Fig. 4. Lookahead-widening analysis trace. Widening is applied at node n_1. Main values are shown in dark gray. Light gray indicates the extent of the pilot value beyond the main value. Pilot values are promoted on the 3rd and 5th iterations.

Next, we show that only a finite number of promotions can ever occur. The argument is based on the number of edges in the CFG. Depending on whether or not new CFG edges within the component's body are brought into consideration by the promotion of the pilot value into the main value, two scenarios are possible. If no new edges are brought into consideration, then the analysis stabilizes on the next iteration because both main value and pilot value are (post-)fix-points for this component. Alternatively, new CFG edges are taken into consideration. In this case, the process described in the previous paragraph starts anew, eventually leading to the next promotion. Because the body of the component is finite, new edges can only be brought into consideration a finite number of times. Thus, there can only be a finite number of promotions before the analysis of a component converges.

Revisiting the Running Example. We illustrate the technique of lookahead widening by applying it to our running example. Fig. 4 shows the trace of abstract operations performed by the analysis. Due to space constraints, we only show abstract values accumulated at program points of interest. The first iteration is identical to the standard approach shown in Fig. 2. Differences are manifested on the second iteration: the widening operator propagates the unmodified main value, but applies widening to the pilot value. At node n_4, note that the pilot value has been filtered by the conditional on the edge (n_1, n_2). In contrast, in Fig. 2, the abstract state at n_4 on the second iteration has an unbounded band running off to the northeast. On the third iteration, the pilot value that reaches node n_1 is smaller than the pilot value stored there on the second iteration. Thus, this pilot value is promoted into the main value. This corresponds to the solution of the first loop phase from Fig. 3(a). As the third iteration progresses, the analysis starts exploring new CFG edges that were brought into consideration by the promotion, in essence, analyzing the program restriction from Fig. 3(b).

On the fourth iteration, at n_1, the widening operator is applied to the pilot value. At n_6, note that the pilot value has been filtered through the conditional on the edge (n_4, n_5). On the fifth iteration, the pilot value is promoted again. From here on the analysis proceeds in the same fashion as the standard analysis would, and converges on the next iteration. The analysis obtains more precise abstract values at all program points, except for n_2 (not shown in the figure).

4   Implementation Notes

"Accumulating" Analyzers. In some analyzers, rather than computing the abstract value for a CFG node n as the join of the values coming from predecessors (i.e., $V(n) = \bigsqcup_{(m,n) \in E} \tau_{(m,n)}(V(m))$), such analyzers *accumulate* the abstract value at n by joining the (single) abstract value contributed by a given predecessor m_i to the value stored at n (i.e., $V(n) = V(n) \sqcup \tau_{(m_i,n)}(V(m_i))$). In particular, the WPDS++ implementation of weighted pushdown systems [10], which was our main target for integrating our technique, follows this model.

The challenge that such an analyzer design poses to lookahead widening is that the pilot value cannot be promoted directly into the main value by applying ∇_{LA} of the previous section. That is, it is not sound to update n's value by $V(n) = V(n)\nabla_{LA}\tau_{(m_i,n)}(V(m_i))$ because if the pilot value of $\tau_{(m_i,n)}(V(m_i))$ is promoted to be the main value at n, this can lose the contribution of one or more of n's other predecessors.[4] For instance, in Fig. 4, on the third iteration, an accumulating analyzer would attempt to widen the value at n_1 with the value at n_6. (The identity transformation is associated with edge (n_6, n_1).) The pilot value at n_6 is strictly smaller than the pilot value at n_1, and thus qualifies to be

---

[4] In contrast, in analyzers that update n with the join of the values from all predecessors, any promotion of the pilot in $V(n) = V(n)\nabla_{LA}\bigsqcup_{(m,n) \in E} \tau_{(m,n)}(V(m))$ does account for the contributions from all predecessors.

promoted. However, promoting it would result in an unsound main value: the point $(0,0)$ would be excluded.

To allow lookahead widening to be used in such a setting, we slightly redefine the widening operator for accumulating analyzers. In particular, before making decisions about promotion, we join the new pilot value with the main value that is stored at the node. This makes the pilot value account for the values propagated along other incoming edges. The new widening operator is defined as follows:

$$
\langle c_m, c_p \rangle \, \nabla_{LA} \, \langle d_m, d_p \rangle = \begin{cases} \langle c_m, c_p \rangle & \text{if } \langle d_m, d_p \rangle \sqsubseteq_{LA} \langle c_m, c_p \rangle \\ \langle d_p \sqcup c_m, d_p \sqcup c_m \rangle & \text{if } d_p \sqcup c_m \sqsubseteq c_p \\ \langle d_m \sqcup c_m, c_p \nabla (d_p \sqcup c_m) \rangle & \text{otherwise} \end{cases}
$$

Runaway Pilots. In loops (or loop phases) that consist of a small number of iterations, it is possible for the analysis to exit the loop (or phase) before the pilot value has stabilized. For instance, if the condition of the if-statement in the running example is changed to $x < 1$, the pilot value will be widened on the second iteration, but will not be effectively filtered through the conditionals because of the contribution from the path through node n_3, which is now enabled by the main value. As a result, the analysis will propagate a pilot value that is larger than desired, which can lead to a loss of precision at future promotions. We refer to this as the problem of *runaway pilots*.

One possible approach to alleviating this problem is to perform a promotion indirectly: that is, instead of replacing the main value with the pilot value, apply widening "up to" [9] to the main values using the symbolic concretization [13] of the pilot value as the set of "up to" constraints.

Memory Usage. The abstract states shown in Fig. 4 suggest that the main value and the pilot value are often equal to each other: in our running example, this holds for abstract states that arise on the first, third, and fifth iterations of the analysis (more than half of all abstract states that arise). In our implementation, to improve memory usage, we detect this situation and store a single value instead of a pair of values when the pilot value is equal to the main value.

Delayed Widening. Another interesting implementation detail is the interaction of lookahead widening with a commonly used technique called *delayed widening*. The idea behind delayed widening is to avoid applying the widening operator during the first k iterations of the loop, where k is some predefined constant. This allows the abstract states to accumulate more explicit constraints that will be used by the widening operator to generalize the loop behavior. We found it useful in practice to reset the delayed-widening counter after each promotion of the pilot value. Such resetting allows the analysis to perform k widening-free iterations at the beginning of each phase.

5   Experimental Results

We experimented with two implementations of lookahead widening: the first implementation was built into a small intraprocedural analyzer; the second im-

Table 1. Intraprocedural implementation results. Columns labeled *steps* indicate the number of node visits performed; *LFP* indicates whether the analysis obtains the least-fix-point solution ('-' indicates that we were not able to determine the least fix-point for the benchmark); *Improved precision* reports the percentage of *important* program points at which the analysis that used lookahead widening yielded smaller values ('-' indicates no increase in precision). Important program points include loop heads and exit nodes.

Program	Vars	Loops	Depth	Standard+		Lookahead		Overhead	Improved
				steps	LFP	steps	LFP	(% steps)	precision (%)
test1	1	1	1	19	yes	19	yes	-	-
test2	2	1	1	24	yes	24	yes	-	-
test3	3	1	1	16	-	19	-	18.8	-
test4	5	5	1	79	-	97	-	22.8	33.3
test5	2	2	2	84	yes	108	yes	28.6	-
test6	2	2	2	110	-	146	-	32.7	100.0
test7	3	3	2	93	no	104	**yes**	11.8	25.0
test8	3	3	3	45	yes	45	yes	-	-
test9	3	3	3	109	yes	142	yes	30.3	-
test10	4	4	3	227	no	266	no	17.2	20.0
astree1	1	1	1	16	no	19	**yes**	18.8	50.0
astree2	1	1	1	27	-	33	-	22.2	-
phase	2	1	1	46	no	58	**yes**	26.1	100.0
merge	3	1	1	63	no	64	**yes**	1.6	100.0

plementation was built into an off-the-shelf weighted-pushdown-system solver, WPDS++ [10]. In both cases, incorporation of lookahead widening required no changes to the analysis engine.[5] Both implementations used polyhedral abstract domains built with the Parma Polyhedral Library [2].

Intraprocedural Implementation. We applied the first implementation to a number of small benchmarks that appeared in recent papers about widening. The benchmarks `test*` come from work on policy iteration [5]. The `astree*` examples come from [3], where they were used to motivate *threshold widening*: a human-assisted widening technique. `Phase` is our running example, and `merge` is a program that merges two sorted arrays.

Because lookahead widening essentially makes use of one round of descending iteration for each WTO component, we controlled for this effect in our experiments by comparing lookahead widening to a slight modification of the standard widening approach: in Standard+, after each WTO component stabilizes, a single descending iteration is applied to it. This modified analysis converged for all of our benchmarks, and yielded solutions that were at least as precise and often more precise than the ones obtained by the standard analysis. The only exception was `test10`, where the results at some program points were incomparable to the standard technique.

---

[5] Weighted pushdown systems, by default, do not support widening. Certain changes had to be made to the engine to make it widening-aware.

Tab. 1 shows the results we obtained. To determine least-fix-points, we ran the analysis without applying widening. The results indicate that lookahead widening achieved higher precision than the strengthened standard approach on half of the benchmarks. Also, the cost of running lookahead widening was not extremely high, peaking at about 33% extra node visits for test6.

Space constraints limit us to discussing just one of the benchmarks. In astree1, an inequation is used as the loop condition: i = 0; while(i != 100) i++;. We assume that the inequation '$i \neq 100$', which is hard to express in abstract domains that rely on convexity, is modeled by replacing the corresponding CFG edge with two edges: one labeled with '$i < 100$', the other labeled with '$i > 100$'. The application of widening extrapolates the upper bound for i to $+\infty$; the descending iterations fail to refine this bound. In contrast, lookahead widening is able to obtain the precise solution: the main value, to which widening is not applied, forces the analysis to always follow the '$i < 100$' edge, and thus the pilot value picks up this constraint before being promoted.

Table 2. WPDS implementation results. *Instr* lists the number of x86 instructions in the program. *Coverage* indicates what portion of each program was analyzed. *Stack symbols* correspond to program points: there are (roughly) two stack symbols per basic block. *Same-level* rules correspond to intraprocedural CFG edges between basic blocks; *push* rules correspond to procedure calls; *pop* rules correspond to procedure returns. Reported times are for the WPDS *poststar* operation. Precision improvement is given as the percentage of loop heads at which the solution was improved by the lookahead-widening technique.

Name	Program		Push-down System				Time (sec)		Overhead	Improved
	instr	coverage (%)	stack sym	same level	push	pop	std	look ahead	(%)	precision (%)
speex	22364	7.9	517	483	26	20	1.13	1.33	17.4	40.0
gzip	13166	29.0	1815	2040	76	20	5.70	7.32	28.4	38.2
grep	30376	22.0	9029	10733	201	39	18.62	20.61	10.7	3.3
diff	142959	24.7	9516	11147	217	67	28.41	32.87	15.7	7.5
plot	119910	27.5	15536	15987	1050	159	44.08	45.41	3.0	20.3
graph	129040	26.0	16610	17800	824	155	53.92	56.67	5.1	19.8
calc	178378	18.7	26829	28894	1728	241	85.33	92.23	9.3	5.2

WPDS Implementation. We used the WPDS++ implementation to determine linear relations over registers in x86 executables. CodeSurfer/x86 was used to extract a pushdown system from the executable. The contents of memory were not modeled and reads from memory were handled conservatively. Also, we chose to ignore unresolved indirect calls and jumps: as the result, only a portion of each program was analyzed. We applied this implementation to a number of GNU Linux programs that were compiled under Cygwin. The lookahead-widening technique was compared to standard widening. No descending iteration sequence was applied, because it would have required a major redesign of the WPDS++ solver. Tab. 2 presents the results obtained: lookahead widening improves the precision of the analysis on all of the benchmarks, and runs with an overhead of at most 30%.

6 Related Work

Improving Widening Operators [1]. One research direction is the design of more precise widening operators—that is, widening operators that are better at capturing the constraints that are present in their arguments. This approach is orthogonal to our technique: lookahead widening would benefit from the availability of more precise (base-domain) widening operators.

Widening "up to" [9] (a.k.a. *limited widening*). In this technique, each widening point is augmented with a fixed set of constraints, M. The value that is obtained from the application of the standard widening operator is further restricted by those constraints from M that are satisfied by both arguments of the widening operator. Given a well-chosen set of constraints, this technique is very powerful. A number of heuristics are available for deriving these constraint sets. In principle, the propagation of the pilot value by our technique can be viewed as an automatic way to collect and propagate such constraints to widening points. Alternatively, whenever such constraint sets are available (e.g., are derived by some external analysis or heuristic), lookahead widening can utilize them by applying widening "up to" to the pilot values. This will be beneficial when the lookahead widening is not able to break a loop into simpler phases (for instance, if a loop contains a non-deterministic conditional).

"New-Control-Path" Heuristic [9]. This heuristic addresses imprecision that is due to new loop behaviors that appear on later loop iterations: it detects whether new paths through the loop body were explored by the analysis on its last iteration—in which case the application of widening is delayed (to let captured relationships evolve before widening is applied). While this heuristic handles the introduction of new loop behaviors well, it does not seem to be able to cope with complete changes in loop behavior, e.g., it will not improve the analysis precision for our running example. The lookahead-widening technique can be viewed as an extension of the new-control-path heuristic: not only the application of widening is delayed when the new control paths become available, but also the solution for the already explored control paths is refined by computing a descending iteration sequence.

Policy iteration [5]. This technique abandons chaotic iteration altogether in favor of different equation-solving strategies. While this technique is guaranteed to find the most precise solution, the search carried out in policy space appears to be quite expensive, and the approach requires building dedicated analyzers. In contrast, our technique can be easily integrated into existing analyzers.

References

1. R. Bagnara, P. M. Hill, E. Ricci, and E. Zaffanella. Precise widening operators for convex polyhedra. In *SAS*, 2003.
2. R. Bagnara, E. Ricci, E. Zaffanella, and P. M. Hill. Possibly not closed convex polyhedra and the Parma Polyhedra Library. In *SAS*, 2002.
3. B. Blanchet, P. Cousot, R. Cousot, J. Feret, L. Mauborgne, A. Miné, D. Monniaux, and X. Rival. Design and implementation of a special-purpose static program analyzer for safety-critical real-time embedded software. In *The Essence of Computation: Complexity, Analysis, Transformation.* Springer-Verlag, 2002.
4. F. Bourdoncle. Efficient chaotic iteration strategies with widenings. In *Formal Methods in Prog. and their Appl.*, 1993.
5. A. Costan, S. Gaubert, E. Goubault, M. Martel, and S. Putot. A policy iteration algorithm for computing fixed points in static analysis of programs. In *CAV*, 2005.
6. P. Cousot. Verification by abstract interpretation. In *Symp. on Verification*, 2003.
7. P. Cousot and R. Cousot. Abstract interpretation: A unified lattice model for static analysis of programs by construction of approximation of fixed points. In *POPL*, 1977.
8. P. Cousot and N. Halbwachs. Automatic discovery of linear constraints among variables of a program. In *POPL*, 1978.
9. N. Halbwachs, Y.-E. Proy, and P. Roumanoff. Verification of real-time systems using linear relation analysis. *FMSD*, 1997.
10. N. Kidd, T. Reps, D. Melski, and A. Lal. WPDS++: A C++ library for weighted pushdown systems, 2004. http://www.cs.wisc.edu/wpis/wpds++/.
11. A. Mine. The Octagon abstract domain. In *WCRE*, 2001.
12. F. Nielson, H.R. Nielson, and C. Hankin. *Principles of Program Analysis*. Springer-Verlag, 1999.
13. T. Reps, M. Sagiv, and G. Yorsh. Symbolic implementation of the best transformer. In *VMCAI*, pages 252–266, 2004.

The Heuristic Theorem Prover: Yet Another SMT Modulo Theorem Prover

(Tool Paper)

Kenneth Roe

kendroe@fordocsys.com

1 Introduction

HTP is an SMT Modulo theorem prover similar to many others.[2,3,4,5,6,9,11] As input, HTP accepts problems using the SMT-LIB format[8]. As output, HTP will answer either *SAT*, *UNSAT* or *UNKNOWN*. Alternatively, HTP can be run in a preprocessing mode in which the output is the simplified problem in SMT-LIB format. An evidence file showing the derivation in a human readable form can be produced. There is a *Treeview* application which shows this derivation in a tree widget making it convenient to navigate a complex proof.

The main contribution of HTP is the introduction of a preprocessor that includes algorithms for detecting unate predicates, eliminating variables, symmetry breaking and boolean encoding. The other algorithms of HTP are similar to other systems. HTP implements a DPLL(T) similar to BarcelogicTools[6]. There are domain theories for equality of uninterpreted function symbols, real difference logic, linear inequality and array logic.

2 The Preprocessor

HTP has a preprocessor that applies a number of algorithms to incrementally simplify problems before handing them off to the DPLL(T) solver. There are command line switches to turn on and off some of the algorithms.

2.1 Rewriting

Before anything else is done with a problem, HTP rewrites it using a number of algebraic simplification rules for arithmetic and boolean equations. As an example, the system will rewrite a+b=2*a+1 to b=a+1 and it will rewrite 1+1+1+1+1+a<1+1+b to a+3<b. Boolean expressions are also simplified. For example, a and a is rewritten to a.

HTP also implements a simple contextual rewriting mechanism. The idea is that certain subterms can be assumed to be true or false while rewriting others. For example, for the expression a<b and not(a=b), when simplifying not(a=b), the system can assume a<b is true. This reduces not(a=b) to true and hence the whole expression reduces to a<b.

T. Ball and R.B. Jones (Eds.): CAV 2006, LNCS 4144, pp. 467–470, 2006.

2.2 The Unate Detection Algorithm

For any boolean expression E (which HTP is trying to satisfy), if asserting a predicate P is guaranteed to make E false, then we know that for any assignment to the predicates satisfying E, we know that P has to be false. P is thus a *unate* predicate. The theorem can be simplified by making not(P) an assumption and then simplifying E. HTP can detect unate predicates efficiently.

The algorithm is most easily described through the use of an example, (a<b) and (if b=c then a+1=b else a<b+1). This expression has four atomic predicates, a<b, b=c, a+1=b and a<b+1. The goal is to figure out which are unate.

The system creates a table with all pairwise implications between the atomic predicates. Then the system annotates each boolean subterm of the expression with four sets, the set of atomic predicates that when asserted make that subterm true, the set of atomic predicates which when asserted make that subterm false, the set of atomic predicates which when denied make that subterm true and the set of atomic predicates which when denied make that subterm false.

The system starts by computing these sets for each of the atomic predicate subterms in the theorem. Then these sets are combined with simple set operations (union or intersection) to create the sets for each of the non-atomic terms. The table below shows these computations for the example above.

	Assert makes true	Deny makes false
b=c	b=c	b=c
a<b	a<b,a+1=b	a<b,a<b+1
a+1=b	a+1=b	a+1=b,a<b,a<b+1
a<b+1	a<b,a<b+1,a+1=b	a<b+1
if b=c then a+1=b else a<b+1	a+1=b	a<b+1
(a<b) and (if b=c (then a+1=b else a<b+1)	a+1=b	a<b,a<b+1

HTP stores all expressions as DAGs. Hence, the work in computing these sets only needs to be done once for each unique subterm. Also, the sets are represented as bit vectors making the computations very efficient.

Variable elimination is a special case of unate detection. If it is found that denying a predicate of the form v=e, where v is a variable, makes the theorem false, then we know any satisfying assignment must have v=e as true. Hence, within our theorem, we can replace all instances of v with e and simplify. We do not need to enter v=e as an assumption.

2.3 Symmetry Breaking

Symmetry breaking in HTP is an extension of the idea studied in the context of SAT problem solving.[7]. The algorithm works through the following steps. First, all symmetric pairs of variables are detected. A pair of variables (a,b) are said to be a symmetric pair if in the theorem T (the theorem HTP is trying to prove) when replacing all instances of a with b and b with a, the resulting theorem is exactly the same as T. The current algorithm for finding pairs simply tests all possible pairs of variables of the same type to see if swapping them produces the same theorem. From this set of symmetric pairs of variables, symmetric pairs of atomic predicates are identified. P1 and P2 are said to be symmetric if there is a set of symmetric variable pairs $\{(a_1, b_1) \ldots (a_n, b_n)\}$ such that P1 can be transformed to P2 by simply replacing each a_i with b_i and each b_i with a_i for each of the pairs in the set of symmetric variables. Next we calculate groups of symmetric predicates. A group of symmetric predicates is a set of two or more atomic predicates such that any two predicates in the group are symmetric. Finally, symmetry breaking disjuncts are added in a manner similar to [7].

2.4   Boolean Encoding

HTP implements an algorithm for doing boolean encoding of difference logic built on ideas from [10]. More information on this algorithm is available on the author's website at **www.fordocsys.com/htp.htm**.

3   Current State of the Implementation

The system is implemented in C and compiled both on Windows and Linux. The Treeview program for viewing outputs is only available on Windows. The author's website contains detailed tables with results and a downloadable executable. HTP has been run in stand alone mode on the entire QF_UF problem set as well as the scheduling problems in QF_RDL[1] giving results which are competitive with other top systems. The preprocessing mode has been run on all SMT-COMP'05 problems except the QF_UFIDL and QF_AUFLIA sections.

The preprocessor was evaluated by running the output in MathSat[2], YICES[3], Simplics[4] and BarcologicTools[6]. Using symmetry breaking, the preprocessor substantially improved the performance of problems in the QF_UF section. However, the current algorithm cannot be applied to other sections. Combining the preprocessor with YICES yields a combined theorem proving tool that can solve 40 problems from SMT-COMP'05. BarcelogicTools, the top system from the competition, only solved 39 problems. Unate detection and rewriting improved the performance of the QF_LRA/spider_benchmarks, the QF_LIA/sal and the QF_LRA/sal sections. For many of these problems, rewriting and unate detection were sufficient to solve the problems. Rewriting also improved the performance of the QF_LIA/wisa benchmarks. This was due to many expressions of the form 1+1+1+...+x=y being simplified to n+x=y. The unate detection and rewriting had little impact for the other sections. In some cases applying the preprocessor changed the performance of other tools by as much as a factor of five either way. This variance has also been seen with minor permutations of problems in many SMT Modulo solvers. The difference logic encoding was quite effective in improving performance when it was applicable.

4   Conclusion and Future Work

Good preprocessing techniques are the most promising direction for finding performance improvements. Future work will also include expansion of the stand alone mode to handle problems from all divisions of SMT-COMP'05[1] as well as adding bit vector and quantifier logic. The two most promising preprocessing directions for creating additional performance enhancements are that of developing boolean encoding algorithms and symmetry breaking. Boolean encoding routines are being extended beyond difference logic. Symmetry breaking is being extended to handle problems outside the QF_UF division.

Acknowledgement. The author thanks Leonardo de Moura from SRI for his feedback on this paper.

References

1. Clark Barrett, Leonardo de Moura, and Aaron Stump. Smt-comp: Satisfiability modulo theories competition. In *CAV*, volume 3576 of *LNCS*, pages 20–23. Springer, 2005.
2. Marco Bozzano, Roberto Bruttomesso, Alessandro Cimatti, Tommi Junttila, Peter van Rossum, Stephan Schulz, and Roberto Sebastiani. The mathsat 3 system. In *CADE-20, Int. Conference on Automated Deduction*, volume 3632 of *Lecture Notes in Computer Science*. Springer, July 2005.
3. Leonardo de Moura. System description: Yices 0.1. Technical report, Computer Science Laboratory, SRI International, 333 Ravenswood Ave., Menlo Park, CA 94062, July 2005. http://fm.csl.sri.com/yices.
4. Bruno Dutertre and Leonardo de Moura. Simplics: Tool description. Technical report, Computer Science Laboratory, SRI International, 333 Ravenswood Ave., Menlo Park, CA 94062, July 2005. http://fm.csl.sri.com/simplics.
5. Jean-Christophe Filliâtre, Sam Owre, Harald Rueß, and N. Shankar. ICS: integrated canonizer and solver. In *CAV*, volume 2102 of *LNCS*, 2001.
6. Robert Nieuwenhuis and Albert Oliveras. DPLL(T) with Exhaustive Theory Propagation and its Application to Difference Logic. In *CAV*, volume 3576, pages 321–334, 2005.
7. Arathi Ramani, Fadi A. Aloul, Igor L. Markov, and Karem A. Sakallah. Dynamic symmetry-breaking for improved boolean optimization. In *Asia and South Pacific Design Automation Conference (ASP-DAC)*, Januray 2005.
8. Silvio Ranise and Cesare Tinelli. The smt-lib standard: Version 1.1. Technical report, Department of Computer Science, The University of Iowa, 2005. Available at goedel.cs.uiowa.edu/smtlib.
9. Sanjit A. Seshia, Shuvendu K. Lahiri, , and Randal E. Bryant. A hybrid sat-based decision procedure for separation logic with uninterpreted functions. In *Proc. 40th Design Automation Conference (DAC)*, pages 425–430, June 2003.
10. Ofer Strichman, S. Seshia, and R. Bryant. Deciding separation formulas with sat. In *Proc. of Computer Aided Verification*, 2002.
11. A. Stump, C. Barrett, and D. Dill. CVC: a Cooperating Validity Checker. In *14th International Conference on Computer-Aided Verification*, 2002.

LEVER: A Tool for Learning Based Verification
(Tool Paper)

Abhay Vardhan[1],* and Mahesh Viswanathan[2],**

[1] Google Inc.
abhayv@google.com
[2] University of Illinois at Urbana-Champaign
vmahesh@cs.uiuc.edu

1 Introduction

Software systems are often modeled using infinite structures such as unbounded integers, infinite message queues and call stacks, and unbounded number of processes. This makes verification of these systems hard- in fact, for most common classes of infinite state systems, the verification problem is undecidable.

In the *Learning-to-Verify* [12,13,11,10] project, we have developed a new paradigm for verification of systems (possibly infinite state) which is based on using techniques from *computational learning theory*. Verification of systems usually entails computing either the set of states reachable from the initial states or certain *fixpoints* associated with logical formulas. To see our main idea, consider the problem of identifying the set of reachable states which is needed for verifying safety properties. Instead of computing this set by iteratively applying the transition relation, we view it as a target set to be learned by answering certain queries (such as membership and equivalence queries). In general, these queries cannot be answered for the reachable states directly. To solve this problem, instead of learning the reachable states, we learn a richer set of state-witness pairs where a pair consists of a reachable state and a witness which demonstrates how that state is reachable. We have shown that the additional information in the witness allows both membership and equivalence queries to be answered. Once the set of state-witness pairs is learned, the reachable states are easily computed which can in turn be used to check the safety property. We have also extended the learning technique to verify liveness properties using either *Computational Tree Logic* with fairness or ω-regular languages (see [12,13]).

The learning based verification method enjoys several nice properties. First, the running time of the verification algorithm depends not on the time taken to converge to the fixpoint (which may not even be achievable in a finite number of steps) but on the size of the symbolic representation of the fixpoint. Second, it avoids the space overhead of computing intermediate approximations to the fixpoint. Finally, the learning based verification method is sound (it never

---

* Supported in part by ONR N00014-02-1-0715. Part of this work was done while the author was at the University of Illinois.
** Supported in part by NSF CAREER 0448178 and NSF CCF 0429639.

T. Ball and R.B. Jones (Eds.): CAV 2006, LNCS 4144, pp. 471–474, 2006.
© Springer-Verlag Berlin Heidelberg 2006

gives an incorrect answer) and if the fixpoint set is representable in the symbolic representation used by the learner, it is also complete (it is guaranteed to terminate).

In this paper, we present a tool called LEVER which implements some of the techniques developed in the *Learning-to-Verify* project. We give some details about the tool and discuss results of running LEVER on some interesting examples. We also compare LEVER with some other tools that are available for verification of infinite state systems.

Related Work. Independently of our work, Habermehl *et al.* [4] have also proposed a learning based method for verification of systems. However, their work assumes that the transition system is length-preserving which is a restrictive assumption in the case of verification of liveness properties. Learning has also been used for verification in other contexts such as learning assumptions in compositional reasoning and mining specifications. This is different than our approach because we are learning the fixpoints needed for verification. Apart from learning based verification, some other tools used for verification of infinite state systems are: FAST [3] which uses acceleration techniques to compute the effect of infinite iteration of certain loops, BRAIN [8] which does a backward search from the "unsafe states" and uses Hilbert's bases for symbolic representation of integer sets and ALV [1] which uses *widening* and can also employ acceleration techniques. For a more detailed treatment of the related work, the reader is referred to [14,9].

2   Overview of Lever

LEVER is currently targeted towards systems with unbounded natural numbers and parameterized systems with unbounded number of processes. The input to LEVER consists of a description of the system model to be analyzed in terms of its variable declarations, transition guards and actions, initial states, the labeling of states with atomic propositions and the property to be verified. The syntax used for the input is similar to FAST [3]. If LEVER terminates on the given system, the output is simply whether the system satisfies the given property or not. In future, a negative answer may be extended to providing a counterexample trace demonstrating the property violation.

Motivated by the practical success demonstrated by *regular model checking*, the states of the system are represented as strings and *regular sets* (encoded as *Deterministic Finite Automata*) are used for the symbolic representation of the fixpoints to be computed for verification. More precisely, we encode a vector $(x_1, x_2, \ldots, x_n)$ of natural numbers as a string s over an alphabet $\Sigma = \{0, 1\}^n$. The value of x_i is given in binary by a string formed by s by projecting each of its letters to its ith component. This representation is similar to Boigelot's Number Decision Diagrams and is known to be expressive enough to encode any Presburger set.

We use the automata library from MONA [6]. MONA keeps the states of the automata explicitly but the transition relation is encoded as a multi-terminal shared BDD. This allows a compact representation of the automata even when the alphabet is of large size. The transducer representing the transition relation is also encoded as an automaton in MONA with a set of new variables added to represent the values taken by system variables after application of a transition.

As mentioned earlier, LEVER uses learning to find the fixpoints needed for verification. We use a learning framework that allows the learner to make two kinds of queries: a membership query asking if a particular element is a member of the target set and an equivalence query asking if a proposed hypothesis is equal to the target set. Since regular sets are used as the underlying symbolic representation for sets of states, we need an algorithm for learning regular sets using membership and equivalence queries. For this, we use a modified version of the algorithm described in Kearns and Vazirani [5] which in turn is inspired by the classical Angluin's [2] algorithm for learning regular sets. One major change we have made in the Kearns-Vazirani algorithm is to use the idea of analyzing counterexamples in a binary-search manner as described in Rivest et. al. [7]. For efficiency, we also use a symbolic way of answering certain kinds of membership queries as described in [14].

3   Results

We have used LEVER to analyze over 30 different examples. These include various cache coherence protocols such as *Dragon, Firefly, Illinois, MESI, MOESI, Berkeley, Futurebus* and *Synapse*; mutual exclusion protocols such as *peterson, lamport, ticket* and *bakery*; broadcast protocols such as *consistency*, and *producer-consumer*; petri nets such as *lastinfirstservcd protocol, Espurza-Finkel-Mayr Counter Machine, RTP* and *manufacturing*; and counter machines such as *lift* and *barber*. We have used LEVER to analyze some safety properties, some simple branching time properties and some more complicated liveness properties which also need fairness constraints. All these examples are available for download along with the LEVER tool.

In order to evaluate the performance of our tool, we have compared our LEVER tool with three other tools popular for verifying safety properties of infinite state systems: FAST [3], BRAIN [8] and ALV [1]. In Table 1, we present a few of the examples we have analyzed (space constraints prevent us from presenting the full results but these are available in [9]). All analysis was done on Intel Xeon based Linux machine running at 1.70GHz with 1GB memory. For some examples, the analysis could not be completed either because the tool did not terminate in two hours, or it exhausted available memory, or (in the case of ALV) it reported that it cannot provide an answer. For these cases, the table shows an entry of ↑.

The overall comparison of the performance of the various tools is mixed. No single tool is able to outperform all others for all the examples. There are also examples in which some tools are unable to give an answer within a given period of time while others are successful. However, the important observation is that the performance of LEVER is comparable to the other tools and for some examples it is significantly better. Another significant advantage of using LEVER is that, given enough time and memory, the learning based technique gives is guaranteed to terminate as long as the set being learned is regular.

Table 1. Running times for safety properties. Due to space constraints only a few examples are presented; full results can be obtained from [9].

	LEVER	FAST	BRAIN	ALV
noaccel	0.031s	↑	0.004s	0.025s
flatcounter	0.153s	↑	0.004s	0.052s
manufacturing	0.821s	2.422s	10.974s	↑
ticket2i	0.585s	0.679s	↑	↑
consistency	0.932s	142.814s	0.057s	571.473s
kanban	3.952s	7.081s	↑	↑

We have also used LEVER to do a case study on the verification of a model of the *Read-Copy-Update* mechanism in the Linux kernel. The interested reader is referred to [9] for details.

References

1. ALV. Action language verifier. http://www.cs.ucsb.edu/~bultan/composite/, 2004.
2. D. Angluin. Learning regular sets from queries and counterexamples. *Inform. Comput.*, 75(2):87–106, Nov. 1987.
3. S. Bardin, A. Finkel, J. Leroux and L. Petrucci. FAST: Fast Accelereation of Symbolic Transition systems. In *Proc. 15th Conf. on Computer Aided Verification*, 2003.
4. P. Habermehl and T. Vojnar. Regular model checking using inference of regular languages. In *Proc. of Infinity'04, London, UK*, 2004.
5. M. J. Kearns and U. V. Vazirani. *An Introduction to Computational Learning Theory*. The MIT Press, Cambridge, Massachusetts, 1994.
6. N. Klarlund and A. Møller. Mona. http://www.brics.dk/mona/, 2004.
7. R. L. Rivest and R. E. Schapire. Inference of finite automata using homing sequences. *Inform. Comput.*, 103(2):299–347, Apr. 1993.
8. T. Rybina and A. Voronkov. Brain : Backward reachability analysis with integers. In *AMAST*, pages 489–494, 2002.
9. A. Vardhan. *Learning to Verify Systems*. PhD thesis, Dep. of Computer Science, University of Illinois at Urbana Champaign, 2006.
10. A. Vardhan, K. Sen, M. Viswanathan, and G. Agha. Actively learning to verify safety for FIFO automata. In *LNCS 3328, Proc. of FSTTCS'04, Chennai, India*, pages 494–505, 2004.
11. A. Vardhan, K. Sen, M. Viswanathan, and G. Agha. Learning to verify safety properties. In *LNCS 3308, Proc. of ICFEM'04, Seattle, USA*, pages 274–288, 2004.
12. A. Vardhan, K. Sen, M. Viswanathan, and G. Agha. Using language inference to verify omega-regular properties. In *Proceedings of the Eleventh International Conference on Tools and Algorithms for the Construction and Analysis of Systems (TACAS'05)*, volume 3440, pages 45–60, Edinburgh, UK, April 2005. Springer.
13. A. Vardhan and M. Viswanathan. Learning to verify branching time properties. In *Proc. of the Twentieth IEEE/ACM International Conference on Automated Software Engineering, Long Beach, California, USA*, 2005.
14. A. Vardhan and M. Viswanathan. Learning to verify branching time properties. Technical Report UIUCDCS-R-2005-2630, ftp://ftp.cs.uiuc.edu/pub/dept/tech_reports/2005/UIUCDCS-R-2005-2630.pdf.gz, Department of Computer Science, University of Illinois at Urbana-Champaign, 2005.

Formal Verification of a Lazy Concurrent List-Based Set Algorithm

Robert Colvin[1], Lindsay Groves[2], Victor Luchangco[3], and Mark Moir[3]

[1] ARC Centre for Complex Systems, School of Information Technology and
Electrical Engineering, University of Queensland, Australia
[2] School of Mathematics, Statistics and Computer Science,
Victoria University of Wellington, New Zealand
[3] Sun Microsystems Laboratories, 1 Network Drive, Burlington, MA 01803, USA

Abstract. We describe a formal verification of a recent concurrent list-based set algorithm due to Heller *et al.* The algorithm is optimistic: the *add* and *remove* operations traverse the list without locking, and lock only the nodes affected by the operation; the *contains* operation uses no locks and is wait-free. These properties make the algorithm challenging to prove correct, much more so than simple coarse-grained locking algorithms. We have proved that the algorithm is linearisable using simulation between input/output automata modelling the behaviour of an abstract set and the implementation. The automata and simulation proof obligations are specified and verified using PVS.

1 Introduction

Concurrent algorithms are notoriously difficult to design correctly, and high performance algorithms that make little or no use of locks even more so. Formal verification of such algorithms is challenging because their correctness often relies on subtle interactions between processes that heavier use of locks would preclude. These proofs are too long and complicated to do (and check) reliably "by hand", so it is important to develop techniques for mechanically performing, or at least checking, such proofs.

In this paper we describe a formal verification of *LazyList*, a recent concurrent list-based set algorithm due to Heller *et al.* [1]. Our proof shows that the algorithm is linearisable to an abstract set object supporting *add*, *remove*, and *contains* methods. Linearisability [2] is the standard correctness condition for concurrent shared data structures. Roughly, it requires that each operation can be assigned a unique *linearisation point* during its execution at which the operation appears to take effect atomically.

The LazyList algorithm is optimistic: *add* and *remove* operations attempt to locate the relevant part of the list without using locks, and only use locks to validate the information read and perform the appropriate insertion or deletion. The *contains* operation uses no locks, and is simple, fast, and wait-free. Heller *et al.* present performance studies showing that this algorithm outperforms well known algorithms in the literature, especially on common workloads in which the *contains* method is invoked significantly more often than *add* and *remove* [1].

The simplicity and efficiency of the *contains* method is achieved by avoiding all checks for interactions with concurrent *add* and *remove* operations. As a result, a *contains* operation can decide that the value it is seeking is not in the set at a moment when

T. Ball and R.B. Jones (Eds.): CAV 2006, LNCS 4144, pp. 475–488, 2006.

in fact the value is in the set. The main challenge in proving that the algorithm is linearisable is to show that this happens only if the sought-after value was absent from the set *at some point* during the execution of the *contains* operation.

We have proved that the algorithm is linearisable using simulation between input/output automata modelling the abstract behaviour of the set and the implementation. Our proof uses a combination of forward and backward simulations, and has the interesting property that a single step of the implementation automaton can correspond to steps by an arbitrary number of different processes in the specification automaton. We modelled the automata and encoded the proof obligations for simulations in the PVS specification language [3], and used the PVS system to check our proofs.

Apart from presenting the first complete and formal verification of an important new algorithm, a contribution of this paper is to describe our ongoing work towards making proof efforts like these easier and more efficient. The proof presented in this paper builds on earlier work in which we proved (and in some cases disproved and/or improved) a number of nonblocking implementations of concurrent stacks, queues and deques [4,5,6,7]. While we still have work to do in this direction, we have made a lot of progress in understanding how to model algorithms and specifications, and how to approach proofs. In this paper, we briefly describe some of the lessons learned. We have made our proof scripts available at http://www.mcs.vuw.ac.nz/research/SunVUW/, so that others may examine our work in detail and benefit from our experience.

The rest of the paper is organised as follows. We describe the LazyList algorithm in Section 2, and our verification of it in Section 3. We discuss our experience with using PVS for this project in Section 4, and conclude in Section 5.

2 The LazyList Algorithm

The LazyList algorithm implements a concurrent set supporting three operations:

- *add(k)* adds k to the set and "succeeds" if k is not already in the set.
- *remove(k)* removes k from the set and "succeeds" if k is in the set.
- *contains(k)* "succeeds" if k is in the set.

Each operation returns *true* if it succeeds; otherwise it "fails" and returns *false*.

The algorithm uses a linked-list representation. In addition to *key* and *next* fields, each list node has a *lock* field, used to synchronise *add* and *remove* operations, and a *marked* field, used to logically delete the node's key value (see Figure 1). The list is maintained in ascending key order, and there are two sentinel nodes, *Head* and *Tail*, with keys $-\infty$ and $+\infty$ respectively. We assume that the list methods are invoked only with integer keys k (so that $-\infty < k < +\infty$).

As explained in more detail below, a successful *add(k)* operation inserts a new node containing k into the list, and a successful *remove(k)* operation logically removes k from the set by marking the node containing k (i.e., setting its *marked* field to *true*), before cleaning up by removing the node from the list. Thus, at any point in time, the abstract set is exactly the set of values stored in the *key* fields of the unmarked nodes in the list.

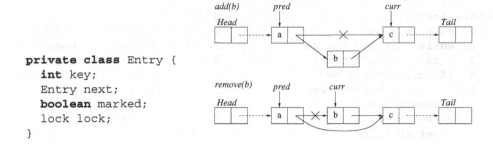

```
private class Entry {
    int key;
    Entry next;
    boolean marked;
    lock lock;
}
```

Fig. 1. Declaration of list node type   **Fig. 2.** Inserting and removing list nodes

The *add(k)* and *remove(k)* methods (see Figure 3) use a helper method *locate(k)*, which sets *curr* to point to the first node with a key greater than or equal to *k* and *pred* to point to that node's predecessor in the list—the values in *Head* and *Tail* ensure that these both exist. The *locate* method optimistically searches the list without using locks, and then locks the nodes pointed to by *curr* and *pred*. If both nodes are unmarked (i.e., their *marked* fields are *false*) and *pred.next* is equal to *curr*, the *add* or *remove* operation can proceed; otherwise, the locks are released and the search is restarted.

An *add(k)* operation calls *locate*, then compares *curr.key* to *k*. If *curr.key* is not equal to *k*, then *k* is not in the list, so *add* creates a new node, setting its *key* field to *k* and its *next* field to point to *curr* (see Figure 2). It then sets the *next* field of *pred* to point to this new node, releases the locks on *curr* and *pred*, and succeeds. If *curr.key* is equal to *k*, then *k* is already in the list, so the *add* operation fails.

A *remove(k)* operation also calls *locate*, then compares *curr.key* to *k*. In this case, if *curr.key* equals *k*, then *remove* removes the node at *curr* from the list and succeeds; otherwise, *k* is not in the list, so *remove* fails. A successful removal is done in two stages: first the key is logically removed from the set by setting the *marked* field of *curr*; then it is physically removed by setting the *next* field of its predecessor (*pred*) to its successor (*curr.next*) (see Figure 2). Separating the logical removal of the key from the set and the physical removal of the node from the list is crucial to the simplicity and efficiency of the algorithm: because nodes are not removed before they are marked, observing an unmarked node is sufficient to infer that its key is in the set.

A *contains(k)* operation makes a single pass through the list, starting from *Head*, searching for a node with a key not less than *k*. If this node contains *k* and is not marked, the *contains* operation succeeds; otherwise it fails. This operation requires no locks and is wait-free (i.e., it is guaranteed to complete within a finite number of its own steps, even if processes executing other operations are delayed or stop completely).

Linearisation Points. A common way to prove that an algorithm is linearisable is to identify a particular step of each operation as the linearisation point of that operation. With some simple invariants showing there are no duplicate keys in the list, it is straightforward to assign linearisation points in this way for *add* and *remove* operations, and for successful *contains* operations. We can linearise a successful *add* operation when it inserts its node into the list (line 6), a successful *remove* operation at the point at which

```
contains(k) :                        add(k) :
 1   curr := Head;                     1   pred, curr := locate(k);
 2   while curr.key < k do             2   if curr.key != k then
 3      curr := curr.next;             3      entry := new Entry();
 4   if curr.key = k and               4      entry.key := k;
 5         ~curr.marked then           5      entry.next := curr;
        return true                    6      pred.next := entry;
     else                              7      res := true
        return false                      else
locate(k) :                            8      res := false;
     while true do                     9   pred.unlock();
 1      pred := Head;                  10   curr.unlock();
 2      curr := pred.next;                 return res
 3      while curr.key < k do         remove(k) :
 4         pred := curr;               1   pred, curr := locate(k);
 5         curr := curr.next;          2   if curr.key = k then
 6      pred.lock();                   3      curr.marked := true;
 7      curr.lock();                   4      entry := curr.next;
 8      if ~pred.marked and            5      pred.next := entry;
 9         ~curr.marked and            6      res := true
10         pred.next = curr then          else
11         return pred, curr           7      res := false;
        else                           8   pred.unlock();
12         pred.unlock();              9   curr.unlock();
13         curr.unlock()                  return res
```

Fig. 3. Pseudocode for LazyList algorithm

it marks the node (line 3), and a successful *contains* operation at the point at which it reads the *marked* field of a node containing its key (line 5). An unsuccessful *add* or *remove* can be linearised anywhere between acquiring the lock on *curr* and releasing the lock on *pred*.

Things are not so simple for failed a *contains* operation, however. If the node found by the loop at lines 2 and 3 contains a key greater than k, or it is marked, *contains*(k) returns *false*. But there is no step of the *contains* operation at which k is guaranteed not to be in the set. In particular, when its *key* or *marked* field is checked, the node may have already been removed from the list, and another process may have added a new node with key k, so that k is in the abstract set at that time. Thus the simple approach of proving linearisability by defining a linearisation point for each operation at one of its steps does not work for this algorithm.

The key to proving that LazyList is linearisable is to show that, for any failed *contains*(k) operation, k is absent from the set at *some* point during its execution. Our proof shows that if a *contains*(k) operation fails, then either k is absent from the set when the operation begins or some successful *remove*(k) operation marks a node containing k during the execution of the *contains*(k) operation. Because there may be many *contains*(k) operations executing concurrently, it is sometimes necessary to linearise multiple failed *contains* operations after the same *remove(k)* operation. We found this interesting, because our previous proofs have not required this.

3 Verification

To prove that LazyList is a linearisable implementation of a set supporting *add*, *remove*, and *contains* operations, we define two input/output automata (IOA) [8,9]: a *concrete automaton ConcAut*, which models the behaviour of the LazyList algorithm, and a simple *abstract automaton AbsAut*, which specifies all correct behaviours of a linearisable set. We use *simulation* proof techniques [10] to prove that *ConcAut* implements *AbsAut*.

3.1 I/O Automata and Simulation Proofs

We now informally describe the IOA model and simulation proofs. In our verification, we use a simplified version of IOAs, which is sufficient for this verification. See [8,9,10] for a more detailed and formal discussion.

An IOA consists of a set of states and a set of actions. Each action has a *precondition*, which determines the set of states from which it can be executed, and an *effect*, which determines the next state after the action has been executed. The actions are partitioned into *external* actions, which define the interface of the automaton, and *internal* actions, which represent internal details. An automaton C *implements* an automaton A if for every execution of C, there exists an execution of A with the same external actions, implying that C and A are indistinguishable to an external observer.

One way to prove that C implements A is by *forward simulation*. Given an arbitrary execution of C, we inductively construct an equivalent execution for A by working forwards from the beginning of C's execution, choosing a (possibly empty) sequence of actions of A for each step in C's execution. That is, we start from some initial state of A, choose a sequence of actions of A for the first step of C, execute those actions, resulting in a new state of A, and then choose and execute a sequence of actions corresponding to the next step of C, and so on. In a forward simulation proof, we must choose the action(s) of A for a given step of C based on the step and the state of A thus far in the simulation; we cannot use steps of C later in the execution to make this choice.

The goal is for the constructed execution of A to have the same external behaviour as the execution of C. To guarantee that it does, we insist that the sequence of actions chosen for an internal action of C contains no external actions, and the sequence of actions chosen for an external action of C contains that external action and no other external action. We must also ensure that the sequence of actions we choose for A can be executed from the state of A resulting from the sequence of actions corresponding to the previous step of C.

To ensure that we can successfully carry out this process over the entire execution of C, we must choose actions for A in a way that keeps A "in step" with C. We capture our intuition about what "in step" means by defining a relation, called a *forward simulation*, between states of C and states of A, and we choose actions for A so as to "preserve" the simulation relation. Often the biggest challenge lies in precisely capturing our intuition about why C implements A so that we can define a simulation relation that makes this possible.

For some algorithms and their specifications, however, there is no way to define such a forward simulation because for some action of C, the actions of A that we should choose depend on future actions (i.e., actions that appear later in the execution). As we explain later, LazyList is one such algorithm. In such circumstances, we use a *backward simulation*. Instead of starting from the initial state and working forwards along an execution of C, in a backward simulation we start at the *last* state of an arbitrary execution, and work backwards towards the initial state. (Because we are only concerned with safety properties in this work, it suffices to consider only finite executions.)

Apart from the direction of the induction, there are some additional differences between forward and backward simulations. First, in a forward simulation, the sequence of actions we choose for A (together with the current state of A) uniquely determines the poststate for A (at least for automata with deterministic actions like the ones we use). But in a backward simulation, for a given action of C, we are given a *poststate* of A, and we must choose not only a sequence of actions for A, but also a *prestate* such that executing the chosen action(s) from this prestate brings us to the given poststate *and* the prestate of C's action is related by the simulation relation to the chosen prestate for A.

Second, we must ensure that when we reach the beginning of C's execution, A is in an initial state too. Therefore, a backward simulation relation must ensure that every state of A that is related to an initial state of C is an initial state of A. Forward simulation has no such proof obligation.

When a backward simulation is necessary, it is often convenient to develop the proof in two stages by defining an "intermediate" automaton, and proving (i) that the concrete automaton implements the intermediate automaton using a forward simulation and (ii) that the intermediate automaton implements the abstract one using a backward simulation. We took this approach for this verification, as we had used it successfully in previous verifications, e.g. [5].

3.2   The Abstract and Concrete Automata

We now describe informally the abstract and concrete IOAs that we use in this verification; more detailed descriptions of the way we use IOAs to model specifications and implementations can be found in [4,5,6,7].

The abstract automaton *AbsAut* models a set of processes operating on an abstract set, in which each process is either "idle", in which case it can invoke any operation on the set, or is in the midst of executing an operation.

Each operation is modelled in *AbsAut* using four actions: two external actions modelling the operation's invocation and response, and two internal actions modelling successful and unsuccessful application of the operation. For example, for the *add* operation (see Figure 4), the *addInv*(k, p) action models the invocation of the *add*(k) operation by process p, and the *addResp*(r, p) action models the operation returning boolean value r to process p. The precondition of the *doAddT* action requires that k is not in the abstract set, and its effect adds k to the set; the precondition of the *doAddF* action requires that k is in the set, and its effect does not modify the set.

Per-process *program counter* variables constrain the order in which actions are performed, ensuring that each operation consists of an invocation action, a *do* action, and a

Action	Precondition	Effect
addInv(k, p)	pc(p) = idle	pc(p) := pcDoAdd(k)
doAddT(k, p)	pc(p) = pcDoAdd(k) AND NOT member(k, keys)	pc(p) := pcAddResp(true) keys := add(k, keys)
doAddF(k, p)	pc(p) = pcDoAdd(k) AND member(k, keys)	pc(p) := pcAddResp(false)
addResp(r, p)	pc(p) = pcAddResp(r)	pc(p) := idle

Fig. 4. *AbsAut* actions for the *add* operation

response action. These variables also connect the return value of the response action to the *do* action. For example, the *doAddT*(*p*) action sets process *p*'s program counter to *pcAddResp*(*true*). Thus each operation is guaranteed to return a value consistent with applying the operation atomically at the point at which the *do* action is executed. Because each operation "takes effect" atomically at the execution of its internal *do* action, all executions of *AbsAut* are behaviours of a linearisable set. Thus, proving that *ConcAut* implements *AbsAut* proves that LazyList is a linearisable set implementation.

The concrete automaton *ConcAut* models a set of processes operating on a set implemented by the LazyList algorithm. It has the same external actions as *AbsAut* (i.e invocations and responses for each operation), and has an internal action for each step of the algorithm corresponding to a labelled step in the pseudocode shown in Figure 3, which are assumed to be atomic. In fact, conditional steps in the algorithm have two associated actions, one for each outcome of the step. For example, the precondition of the *cont2T*(*p*) action (which models an execution by process *p* of line 2 of the *contains* method when the test succeeds) requires that *p*'s program counter is *pcCont2* and *curr.key$_p$* < *k$_p$*, and its effect sets *p*'s program counter to *pcCont3*. The compound tests in *contains* (lines 4 and 5) and *locate* (lines 8 to 10) are each treated as a sequence of (two and three, respectively) atomic tests. We also assume that allocation of a new node (*add* line 3) is atomic.

3.3 An Intermediate Automaton

As mentioned earlier, we cannot prove that *ConcAut* implements *AbsAut* using a forward simulation proof. The reason is that, to do so, we must identify a point at which each operation "takes effect" and choose the corresponding *do* action in *AbsAut* at that point. However, as explained in Section 2, a failed *contains* operation may not take effect at the point that it determines it has failed: the point at which the sought-after key is absent from the set may be earlier. A correct forward simulation proof would have to choose the *doContF* action at a point that the key is absent from the set. However, at that point, it is still possible that the *contains* operation will return *true*, so choosing *doContF* would make it impossible to complete the proof because when *ConcAut* executes the external *contResp*(*true*) action, the precondition for this action would not hold in the *AbsAut* state (recall that we are required to choose the same action for *AbsAut* when the *ConcAut* action is external).

Thus, we introduce an intermediate automaton *IntAut* that eliminates the need to "know the future" when choosing appropriate actions to prove that *ConcAut* implements

IntAut using a forward simulation, and we show that *IntAut* implements *AbsAut* using a backward simulation. Because backward simulations are generally more difficult than forward ones, we prefer to keep the intermediate automaton as close as possible to the abstract one. We achieved this by modifying *AbsAut* slightly so that the *contains* operation can decide to return *false* if the key it is seeking was absent from the set at some time since its invocation (though it may still return *true* if it finds its key in the set). We now explain how we achieved this.

The state of *IntAut* is the same as that of *AbsAut*, except that we augment each process p with a boolean flag *seen_out_p*. When process p is executing a *contains*(k) operation, *seen_out_p* indicates whether k has been absent from the set at any time since the invocation of the operation.

The transitions of *IntAut* are the same as those of *AbsAut*, except that:

- The *contInv*(p, k) action sets *seen_out_p* to *false* if k is in the abstract set, and to *true* otherwise.
- The *doRemT*(q, k) action, in addition to removing k from the set, also sets *seen_out_p* for every process p that is executing *contains*(k).
- The precondition of the *doContF*(k, p) action requires *seen_out_p* to be true instead of k being absent from the set.

Thus the *doContF*(p) action is enabled if k was not in the set when *contains*(k) was invoked, or if it was removed later by some other process q performing *doRemT*(q, k). Therefore, in this automaton, a *contains*(k) operation can decide to return *false* even when k is in the set, provided k was absent from the set sometime during the operation. This is what we need in order to prove a forward simulation from *ConcAut* to *IntAut*.

3.4   The Backward Simulation

Because *IntAut* is so close to *AbsAut*, the backward simulation is relatively straightforward: it requires that the sets of keys in *IntAut* and *AbsAut* are identical, and that each process p in *AbsAut* stays "in step" with process p in *IntAut*, with one exception. In *AbsAut*, p may have already executed *doContF*, indicating that it will subsequently return *false*, whereas in *IntAut*, p has not yet decided to return *false*. This is allowed only if *seen_out_p* is *true*, indicating that either k was absent from the abstract set at the invocation *contInv*(k, p), or was present at the invocation but was subsequently removed before *doContF* is performed. The PVS definition of our backward simulation between *IntAut* state i and *AbsAut* state a is shown below.

```
bsr(i, a): bool = i'keys = a'keys AND
                  FORALL p: (i'pc(p) = a'pc(p) OR
                            (i'pc(p) = pcDoCont AND
                             a'pc(p) = pcContResp(false) AND
                             i'seen_out(p)))
```

Below we briefly describe how we choose an action sequence for *AbsAut* for a given step of *IntAut* in our backward simulation proof. Readers interested in details of how we choose a prestate for *AbsAut*, and how we discharge the various proof obligations for a backward simulation (including proving that our choices result in a valid execution of *AbsAut*) can examine our files and step through the proofs.

In the backward simulation, for most actions in *IntAut*, we choose the same action for *AbsAut*. However, as discussed above, we cannot simply choose *doContF* in *AbsAut* when a *doContF* action occurs in *IntAut* because the sought-after key may be in the set at that point. Instead, we choose *doContF* actions as follows:

– For a *contInv*(k, p) action in *IntAut*, if p is enabled to return *false* in the poststate of *AbsAut*, we choose *contInv*(k, p) followed by *doContF*(k, p).
– For a *doRemT*(k, p) action in *IntAut* (which removes k from the abstract set), we choose a sequence of actions for *AbsAut* consisting of *doRemT*(k, p) followed by a *doContF*(k, p) action for each process p that is executing a *contains*(k) operation and is enabled to return *false* in the poststate of *AbsAut*.

3.5 The Forward Simulation

When defining the relationship between the states of *IntAut* and *ConcAut*, one option is to represent the relationship directly in the forward simulation. However, because in this case the relationship is quite complex, we instead reflect the state of *IntAut* within *ConcAut* by introducing two auxiliary variables, *aux_keys* and *aux_seen_out*. Then, rather than constructing the forward simulation to directly relate the *ConcAut* state and the *IntAut* state, we capture this relation as invariants of *ConcAut*, and simply require, for the forward simulation, that the auxiliary variables equal their counterparts in *IntAut*. This makes it easier to test properties using a model checker before we attempt to prove them.

ConcAut is augmented with the auxiliary variables in a straightforward manner: *aux_keys* is updated when a node is inserted into the list at line 6 of the *add* method, or is marked for deletion at line 3 of the *remove* method; and *aux_seen_out$_p$* is updated when the *contains* method is invoked by process p, and when another process executes line 3 of the *remove* method to remove the same value p is seeking.

With the addition of the auxiliary variables, the simulation relation is quite simple. Like the backward simulation relation, it has two components, one relating data and one relating program counters of processes. The first component simply requires that the auxiliary variables of *ConcAut* equal their counterparts in *IntAut*. The second component is more complicated than in the backward simulation relation, because we must relate each program counter of *ConcAut* to a program counter value in *IntAut*.

The proof for the forward simulation is also quite straightforward: almost all of the cases of the proof were dispatched automatically using PVS strategies. The only proofs that required user interaction were those to show that whenever we choose a *do* action for *IntAut* for a given *ConcAut* action, that action's precondition holds in *IntAut*. These proofs required the introduction of high-level invariants of the concrete automaton— one for each action corresponding to a *do* action in the intermediate automaton—that show that at the point that we choose these actions in the simulation, their preconditions hold in *IntAut*.

For one interesting example, we must show that when we choose *doContF*(k, p) as the action for *IntAut*, *seen_out$_p$* is *true*. More specifically, we show that *aux_seen_out$_p$* is *true* in the *ConcAut* state, and then use the simulation relation's requirement that *aux_seen_out* and *seen_out* are equal to infer that the *IntAut* action is enabled.

3.6   Invariants

To prove the invariants required to show that an *IntAut* action's precondition holds when we choose it in the simulation, we needed over a hundred supporting invariants and lemmas. Proving these properties was the bulk of the proof effort. We do not have room to discuss all these properties, but we invite the interested reader to consult our PVS theory files and proof scripts.

Many of these properties are "obvious": In an informal proof, we might say that some follow "by inspection" (e.g., a local variable of a process is changed only by an action of that process; the *key* field of a node is changed only by line 4 of the *add* method). Others follow immediately given that nodes are not modified unless they are locked or newly allocated (e.g., the *pred* node of a process at lines 2–9 of the *add* method is not marked). One "obvious" invariant that was more difficult to prove than we expected is that a node pointed to by *curr* is *public*, which means that it was placed into the list at some time in the past (i.e., it was allocated by some process that is not still at lines 4–6 of the *add* method with that node pointed to by *entry*). Proving this required jointly proving that *pred* is public, that the successor of any public node is public, that *entry* is public for a process at line 5 of the *remove* method, and that *entry.next* = *curr* for a process at line 6 of the *add* method. These five properties mutually depend on each other, and are expressed in the public_nodes invariant.

The locate_works invariant captures properties that are guaranteed by the *locate* method because it locks the nodes and then validates the desired properties before returning to *add* or *remove*. Specifically, locate_works says that after returning from a call to *locate*, the process has locks on adjacent *live nodes* (i.e., public and unmarked nodes) such that the key of the first node is less than the sought-after key, and the key of the second is greater or equal. The locate_works invariant ensures, for example, that, before the *next* field of the *pred* node is set at line 5 of the *remove* method, that field still points to the *curr* node. The entry_unchanged_in_rem invariant ensures that the value written to that field is the value in the *next* field of the *curr* node, so that exactly one node (the *curr* node) is removed.

The aux_keys_accurate invariant states that *aux_keys* is exactly the set of keys for which there is a live node. The proof of this property is mostly straightforward because a key is inserted into *aux_keys* each time a new node containing that key is inserted into the list (thus becoming live), and removed from *aux_keys* each time a node containing the key is marked (thus ceasing to be live). The difficult case in this proof is showing that marking a node with a certain key ensures that no live node with that key exists. This case uses several additional invariants: live_nodes_in_list says that all live nodes are reachable from *Head*; one_from_other says that if two different nodes are both reachable from *Head* then one of them is reachable from the other; and later_nodes_greater_and_public says that if one node is reachable from another, then it has a higher key. Together these three properties imply that there is at most one live node with a given key at any time, and therefore marking one falsifies the existence of any such node, as required.

Given the aux_keys_accurate invariant, and the simulation relation's requirement that *ConcAut*'s *aux_keys* equals *IntAut*'s *keys*, it is easy to see that we can choose the *doContT* action when a *contains(k)* operation finds an unmarked node with key k, and therefore decides to return *true*. A *contains*(k) operation that returns *false* is more interesting. First, note that if *seen_out*$_p$ is set to *true* during a *contains*(k) operation of process p, then it remains *true* for the duration of the operation, so we are justified in choosing the *doContF* action for *IntAut* if *ConcAut* decides to return *false*.

Otherwise, assume *seen_out*$_p$ is set to *false* by *contInv*(k, p) and remains *false* throughout the operation until it decides to return *false*. This implies that there is a live node containing k when *contInv*(k, p) is executed. Because nodes are marked before being removed from the list, the node remains live throughout the operation unless it is marked. If it is marked, the action sequence chosen for *IntAut* corresponding to the marking action in *ConcAut* sets *seen_out*$_p$ to *true*, contradicting the assumption. Therefore, the node remains live throughout the operation, implying that, immediately after the *cont1* action reads *Head* into *curr*$_p$, the live node is reachable from the node indicated by *curr*$_p$. As explained below, this remains true as p walks down the list towards the live node unless the node is marked (again, this contradicts the assumption). Thus, the *contains*(k) operation finds this live node, and does not return *false* as assumed.

The above reasoning is captured in part by the `cont_val_still_in` invariant, which states that as p executes the loop at lines 2 and 3 of the *contains*(k) method, either *aux_seen_out*$_p$ is *true*, or there is a path from *curr*$_p$ to a live node m containing k. The path property is expressed as `leadsfrom`($curr_p, m$), which states that there is a non-zero-length path from *curr*$_p$ to m. `leadsfrom` is defined using `leadsfromsteps` as follows to allow us to prove to PVS that inductive proofs over it are finite.

```
leadsfromsteps(c, n, m, w): INDUCTIVE bool =
  n /= Tail AND ((w=1 AND c'nextf(n) = m) OR
               (w>1 AND c'nextf(n) /= m AND
                           leadsfromsteps(c,c'nextf(n),m,w-1)))
leadsfrom(c, n, m): bool = EXISTS w: leadsfromsteps(c, n, m, w)
```

A challenging part of the proof is proving that `leadsfrom`($curr_p, m$) is falsified only from a state in which node m is marked, and therefore `cont_val_still_in` is not falsified by `leadsfrom`($curr_p, m$) becoming false (because the invariant implies that m is unmarked). The intuition for this property is clear: changes outside the path between *curr*$_p$ and m have no effect, and inserting or removing a node from the list between *curr*$_p$ and m preserves the `leadsfrom`($curr_p, m$) property. Thus, only removing a link to m can falsify `leadsfrom`($curr_p, m$), and it is easy to prove that this occurs only after m has been marked. While the intuition for this property is straightforward, the proof is somewhat involved because it requires various inductions over the `leadsfrom` property to capture the effects of inserting and removing nodes in the middle of the list. Our decision to represent the path property using the recursive `leadsfrom` predicates was driven by our desire to minimise the size of the state space to accommodate model checking work by our colleagues (see below). Explicitly encoding the paths in auxiliary variables would simplify the proof considerably.

4 Experience with PVS

We used PVS [3] to verify all the proofs discussed in this paper. As we are not experts in the use of PVS, and we had no special support, our experience may be relevant both to others considering using PVS to verify similar proofs, and as a comparison to others' experience with different formal tools. In addition to our work with PVS, we collaborated with David Friggens and Ray Nickson, who developed models for this algorithm for use in the model checkers Spin and SAL [11,12]. As well as model checking the entire algorithm for small numbers of threads and small bounds on the queue size, which gave us some confidence that our proof attempt would eventually be successful, they used these models to test some of the putative invariants we used in our proofs before we actually proved them.

In approaching this verification, we worked mostly "top-down", starting with the simulation proofs and then proceeding with the invariants. We did not develop the basic proof using PVS; rather, we figured out the top-level invariants informally, and prepared a fairly detailed proof sketch of these invariants, and some of their supporting lemmas and invariants, before formalizing them in PVS. We did not, however, work out all the low-level lemmas and invariants that we knew would be helpful for the proofs, leaving many of them to be stated and proved as necessary.

As mentioned earlier, introducing auxiliary variables in the concrete automaton pushed the bulk of the work for this proof into the verification of invariants. The complete verification contains 165 PVS proofs: 32 typecheck constraints, 30 lemmas for the simulation proofs, and 103 invariants and supporting lemmas. Pushing most of the work into the invariants reduced the state that had to be managed within a PVS proof, because invariants are about a single automaton, while simulations are relations between two automata. Also, unlike simulation relations, invariants are straightforward to check using model checkers, so this reduced the gap between our work and that of our colleagues working with Spin and SAL.

PVS includes support for proof management, tracking which proofs have been done, and marking lemmas as proven but "incomplete" if they depend on earlier lemmas that have not yet been proved completely. This support helped us to work independently on different lemmas, which was especially helpful as the authors were spread over three countries. However, PVS manages changes at the file level—any change in a file invalidates all proofs for lemmas in that file—so we often had to rerun proofs that were unchanged. Finer-grained dependency tracking would have saved us considerable time.

PVS supports the creation of user-defined rules, called *strategies*, by combining built-in rules. These strategies can be saved and used in other proofs (or used again in a single proof). We used strategies extensively, for example, to set up the beginning of invariant proofs, which almost always begin assuming the invariant holds on an arbitrary reachable state and setting up as a goal that it holds after executing any action; to extract parts of the precondition or effect of an action; and to handle the many "trivial" cases in the forward simulation proof for concrete actions that did not correspond to any action in the intermediate automaton.

As useful as strategies are, we found that in many cases it was better to define a lemma that captured a desired property than to design a strategy to prove it. There are two advantages: First, PVS doesn't have to do the proof each time—it just uses the lemma. Second, often the way you state a property makes a significant difference in how you are able to use it. With a lemma, you can easily control how a property is stated.

One challenge in this verification was making proofs that PVS could check quickly. In particular, in an invariant proof, we typically show that the property is preserved by every action. Usually, only a few actions affect any of the variables mentioned by the property, and only those actions need to be considered; the rest obviously preserve the property. However, PVS must check all of those actions, and even a couple of seconds for each action turns into minutes for 52 actions. Thus, we stated and proved several "does not modify" lemmas, one for each variable, stating which actions actually modified that variable, and we used those lemmas extensively to avoid having PVS consider each of the other actions separately.

We also found it helpful to define functions to describe things that we wanted to refer to frequently, and especially that we might want to use in a strategy. For example, in the forward simulation proof, we defined the *action_corr* function to return, for any transition of the concrete automaton, the corresponding sequence of actions of the intermediate automaton. We also defined *pcin* and *pcout* to return, for each action, the program counters corresponding to the prestate and poststate respectively.

5   Concluding Remarks

We have developed the first complete and formal correctness proof for the LazyList algorithm of Heller *et al.* [1]. We model the algorithm and specification as I/O Automata in the PVS specification language, and proved that the algorithm implements the specification using simulation proofs developed in and checked by the PVS system.

As in previous algorithms we have verified [4,5,6,7], we found that the outcome of an operation cannot always be determined before it takes effect. Our proof uses a combination of backward and forward simulations to deal with this problem. An interesting aspect of the proof, which we have not encountered in our previous proofs, is the need for an arbitrary number of operations to be linearised after an action of a different operation.

In a related manual verification effort, Vafeiadis *et al.* [13] also present a verification of the LazyList algorithm. They add the abstract set as an auxiliary variable and add actions that perform the abstract operation and record the abstract result at the linearisation point of each operation. They then use the Rely-Guarantee proof method [14,15] to show that the implementation and the abstract set behave the same way in every execution of this augmented algorithm. Because it is impossible to correctly linearise a failed *contains* operation without knowledge of the future, this approach cannot be used to prove the linearisability of failed *contains* operations, and [13] only considers this case informally. It is noteworthy that this case accounted for a large proportion of the complexity and the effort involved in our completely machine-checked proof.

We have made our proof scripts available so that others may benefit from our experience (see http://www.mcs.vuw.ac.nz/research/SunVUW/). We also plan to test our hypothesis that substantial parts of our proof can be reused to verify several optimised versions of LazyList. In the longer term, we plan to continue refining our proof methodology to make it easier and more efficient to develop fully machine-checked proofs for concurrent algorithms.

Acknowledgements. We are grateful to David Friggens and Ray Nickson for useful conversations and for model checking various proposed properties.

References

1. Heller, S., Herlihy, M., Luchangco, V., Moir, M., Scherer, W., Shavit, N.: A lazy concurrent list-based set algorithm. In: 9th International Conference on Principles of Distributed Systems (OPODIS). (2005)
2. Herlihy, M.P., Wing, J.M.: Linearizability: a correctness condition for concurrent objects. TOPLAS **12**(3) (1990) 463 – 492
3. Crow, J., Owre, S., Rushby, J., Shankar, N., Srivas, M.: A tutorial introduction to PVS. In: Workshop on Industrial-Strength Formal Specification Techniques, Boca Raton, Florida (1995)
4. Doherty, S.: Modelling and verifying non-blocking algorithms that use dynamically allocated memory. Master's thesis, School of Mathematical and Computing Sciences, Victoria University of Wellington (2003)
5. Doherty, S., Groves, L., Luchangco, V., Moir, M.: Formal verification of a practical lock-free queue algorithm. In de Frutos-Escrig, D., Núñez, M., eds.: Formal Techniques for Networked and Distributed Systems — FORTE 2004, 24th IFIP WG 6.1 International Conference, Madrid Spain, September 27-30, 2004, Proceedings. Volume 3235 of Lecture Notes in Computer Science., Springer (2004) 97–114
6. Colvin, R., Doherty, S., Groves, L.: Verifying concurrent data structures by simulation. In Boiten, E., Derrick, J., eds.: Proc. Refinement Workshop 2005 (REFINE 2005). Volume 137(2) of Electronic Notes in Theoretical Computer Science., Guildford, UK, Elsevier (2005)
7. Colvin, R., Groves, L.: Formal verification of an array-based nonblocking queue. In: ICECCS 2005: Proceedings of the 10th IEEE International Conference on Engineering of Complex Computer Systems, Shanghai, Chin (2005) 507–516
8. Lynch, N., Tuttle, M.: An Introduction to Input/Output automata. CWI-Quarterly **2**(3) (1989) 219–246
9. Lynch, N.A.: Distributed Algorithms. Morgan Kaufmann (1996)
10. Lynch, N.A., Vaandrager, F.W.: Forward and backward simulations – part I: untimed systems. Information and Computation **121**(2) (1995) 214 – 233
11. Holzmann, G.J.: The model checker SPIN. IEEE Trans. Softw. Eng. **23**(5) (1997) 279–295
12. de Moura, L., Owre, S., Rueß, H., Rushby, J., Shankar, N., Sorea, M., Tiwari, A.: SAL 2. In Alur, R., Peled, D., eds.: Computer-Aided Verification, CAV 2004. Volume 3114 of Lecture Notes in Computer Science., Boston, MA, Springer-Verlag (2004) 496–500
13. Vafeiadis, V., Herlihy, M., Hoare, T., Shapiro, M.: Proving correctness of highly-concurrent linearisable objects. In: PPoPP '06: Proc. 11th ACM SIGPLAN Symposium on Principles and Practice of Parallel Programming, New York, NY, USA, ACM Press (2006) 129–136
14. Jones, C.B.: Specification and design of (parallel) programs. In: 9th IFIP World Computer Congress (Information Processing 83). Volume 9 of FIP Congress Series., IFIP, North-Holland (1983) 321–332
15. Xu, Q., de Roever, W.P., He, J.: The rely-guarantee method for verifying shared variable concurrent programs. Formal Aspects of Computing **9**(2) (1997) 149–174

Bounded Model Checking of Concurrent Data Types on Relaxed Memory Models: A Case Study*

Sebastian Burckhardt, Rajeev Alur, and Milo M.K. Martin

Department of Computer Science
University of Pennsylvania
{sburckha, alur, milom}@cis.upenn.edu

Abstract. Many multithreaded programs employ concurrent data types to safely share data among threads. However, highly-concurrent algorithms for even seemingly simple data types are difficult to implement correctly, especially when considering the relaxed memory ordering models commonly employed by today's multiprocessors. The formal verification of such implementations is challenging as well because the high degree of concurrency leads to a large number of possible executions. In this case study, we develop a SAT-based bounded verification method and apply it to a representative example, a well-known two-lock concurrent queue algorithm. We first formulate a correctness criterion that specifically targets failures caused by concurrency; it demands that all concurrent executions be observationally equivalent to some serial execution. Next, we define a relaxed memory model that conservatively approximates several common shared-memory multiprocessors. Using commit point specifications, a suite of finite symbolic tests, a prototype encoder, and a standard SAT solver, we successfully identify two failures of a naive implementation that can be observed only under relaxed memory models. We eliminate these failures by inserting appropriate memory ordering fences into the code. The experiments confirm that our approach provides a valuable aid for designing and implementing concurrent data types.

1 Introduction

Shared-memory multiprocessor architectures dominate the server and scientific computing market today and are even finding their way into desktop, laptop and gaming machines. Nevertheless, programming such systems remains a challenge [1]. To cope with the subtleties of concurrent program executions, software architects often introduce abstraction layers in the form of *concurrent data types*.

Concurrent data types provide familiar data abstractions (such as queues, hash tables, or trees) to client programs that have concurrently executing threads. The interface of the data type specifies the operations. The implementation provides the actual code for the operations; it hides the concurrency from the client program, using lower-level synchronization primitives such as locks or semaphores as needed. To allow for more concurrency and better performance, optimized implementations use fine-grained locking or even avoid locks altogether by using lock-free synchronization techniques [2, 3, 4].

---

* Supported partially by NSF awards CCR 0306352 and CNS 0524059 and donations from Intel Corporation.

T. Ball and R.B. Jones (Eds.): CAV 2006, LNCS 4144, pp. 489–502, 2006.
© Springer-Verlag Berlin Heidelberg 2006

Writing correct and efficient code for concurrent data types is challenging. To make matters worse, many contemporary shared-memory architectures use *relaxed memory ordering models* [5]. For example, a processor may execute memory accesses in a different order than specified by the program, and stores may take effect locally before becoming visible to remote processors. Although regular "fully synchronized" programs are not sensitive to the memory model, implementations that contain concurrency optimizations (such as intentional data races or lock-free synchronization) become exposed to such ordering and atomicity relaxations. Because the resulting executions are counterintuitive and nondeterministic, even highly skilled engineers are likely to make programming errors when relying on informal reasoning and conventional testing only, which motivates the use of formal verification.

The operations of the concurrent data type are invoked by a multi-threaded client program and may execute concurrently on a multiprocessor. Our correctness criterion is *operation-level sequential consistency*. It requires that all concurrent executions be observationally equivalent to a *serial* execution, that is, an execution in which the operations execute atomically and in the order they are invoked by each thread. As we assume that all serial executions reflect the semantics of the abstract data type correctly (which can be verified independently using standard techniques for sequential programs), correctness in our sense implies that client programs always observe the correct semantics. In particular, the data type is guaranteed to appear sequentially consistent to the client program even if the underlying multiprocessor executions are not sequentially consistent [6] on the instruction level.

To bound the number of threads, the state space, and the depth of the execution, we consider client programs that make a fixed number of operation calls only. We call these bounded instances *symbolic tests*. Furthermore, the user must specify *commit points* [7], that is, single out an instruction within each operation such that the logical order of the operations always matches the execution order of their commit points. We qualify soundness and completeness of our approach as follows: (a) it can prove correctness for all executions of the given symbolic test, and (b) it generates counterexamples that are sound with respect to the chosen memory model and commit point specification.

We encode the existence of a violating execution as a CNF instance that can be solved or refuted by a standard SAT solver (corresponding to cases (b) and (a) above). Our encoding combines several ideas that appear in prior work, such as loop unrolling and SSA transformations [8] and axiomatic memory model encodings [9, 10].

We successfully applied our method to an example that represents optimized implementations of concurrent data types, the two-lock concurrent queue by Michael and Scott [11]. First, we verified that the implementation code is correct for all symbolic tests in our suite when executed on a sequentially consistent memory model. Next, our prototype found two failures that can occur when the same code is executed on a relaxed memory model. Guided by the counterexamples, we identified the problematic instruction reorderings and prevented them by inserting two memory ordering fences. Finally, we verified that with these fences, the code executes correctly on a relaxed memory model for all symbolic tests in the suite.

1.1   Related Work

Most prior work on formal verification of concurrent data types assumes a sequentially consistent memory model [12, 13, 14]. In that context, linearizability [15] is the correctness criterion of choice. Unfortunately, its definition assumes that an execution globally orders the operation invocations and returns, which is not well defined on relaxed memory models because instructions may be reordered across operation boundaries.

Model checking of assembly code snippets for relaxed memory models was first attempted with explicit state enumeration [16, 17] using an operational memory model and interleaving concurrency. More recently, constraint-based encodings of axiomatic memory models have been proposed for memory-model sensitive race detection [9]. Our approach differs because we specifically target concurrent data types and because we use operation-level sequential consistency as our correctness criterion.

2   The Challenge

Our verification target is the two-lock FIFO queue implementation [11] by Michael and Scott (Fig. 1). We chose this example because of its optimized use of locks: the enqueue and dequeue operations can proceed concurrently because they use independent locks. This concurrency improves performance, but it also introduces a race condition if the queue is empty. Race conditions sometimes indicate an improper locking discipline [18], but as we see here, they may also be a side effect of concurrency optimizations.

We encountered several challenges in the course of our case study:

Avoiding State Explosion. An interleaving model of concurrency can lead to large state spaces; relaxed memory models exacerbate this effect because they introduce additional concurrency at the instruction level. Therefore, we decided against unrolling the transition relation and representing executions as global state sequences. Instead, we represent the program executed by each thread as a linear symbolic instruction stream, and we encode the relative order of instructions using SAT variables.

Defining Memory Models. We compared the memory model specifications for the IBM PowerPC [19], Sun SPARC v9 TSO/PSO/RMO [20], Alpha [21], and IBM zArchitecture [22]. Although there are many differences, the specifications use similar rules (axioms) to describe the valid memory orderings. By comparing the axioms, we derived a generic relaxed memory model (to be defined in section 3.4) that provides a common conservative approximation and abstracts unneeded details.

Encoding Memory Models. We can encode the memory model axioms directly because we have explicit representations of the instruction streams for each thread [9, 23]. In contrast, classic interleaving models based on labeled transition systems require a prior conversion of the axiomatic specification into an operational style [16, 17].

Bounding Instances. To achieve a bounded formulation, we approximate admissible client programs using a manually constructed suite of symbolic tests. Each test specifies a fixed, finite sequence of symbolic operation invocations for each thread. Unlike deterministic tests, a symbolic test covers all possible instruction interleavings and

```
structure node_t {                    structure queue_t {
    value: value_t;                       head: ptr to node_t;
    next: ptr to node_t                   tail: ptr to node_t;
}                                         headlock: lock_t;
                                          taillock: lock_t;
                                      }
1  initialize(Q: ptr to queue_t)
2    // Make dummy node             27  dequeue(Q: ptr to queue_t,
3    node = new_node()              28         pvalue: ptrto value_t)
4    node->next = NULL              29         : boolean
5    Q->head = Q->tail = node       30    lock(&Q->headlock)
6    Q->headlock = FREE             31    node = Q->head
7    Q->taillock = FREE             32    new_head = node->next
8                                   33    if new_head == NULL
9  enqueue(Q: ptr to queue_t,       34    // queue empty
10        value: value_t)           35      unlock(&Q->headlock)
11    node = new_node()             36      return false
12    node->value = value           37    endif
13    node->next = NULL             38    *pvalue = new_head->value
14    lock(&Q->taillock)            39    Q->head = new_head
15      Q->tail->next = node        40    unlock(&Q->headlock)
16      Q->tail = node              41    free(node)
17    unlock(&Q->taillock)          42    return true
```

Fig. 1. Michael and Scott's two-lock queue implementation [11]. The queue is represented by a dynamically allocated singly linked list with head and tail pointers, each protected by a separate lock. To simplify the empty queue case, the first node of the linked list is a "dummy" element: its value is not part of the queue.

reorderings and all possible call arguments and return values. The total number of instructions executed during a test is bounded because the operations do not contain loops. As a result, each test has a finite (albeit exponential) number of possible executions, which explains how we avoid the undecidability of sequential consistency [24].

Representing Parameters. The implementation is parameterized by (a) the number of threads, (b) the size of the queue, (c) the size of the instruction reordering window, and (d) the number of distinct data values. As our formulation targets individual symbolic tests with finitely many executions, we can easily find static bounds. For instance, the number of threads is explicitly specified by the test, the queue size and the number of data values never exceed the number of "enqueue" calls, and the instruction reorder window need not be larger than the total number of instructions.

Avoiding Mixed Quantifiers. Our correctness criterion contains alternating quantifiers (we ask if there exists a observationally equivalent serial execution for each concurrent execution), which can not be directly encoded in SAT. We avoid this problem (at the expense of some generality and automation) by asking the user to designate one instruction for each operation to be the *commit point*. If correctly specified, the order in which the commit points execute matches the logical order of the operations. With this additional information, we can construct a deterministic serial reference execution for each concurrent execution. If the two executions are observationally equivalent in all cases, we have shown that the implementation is sequentially consistent. If not, our tool provides a counterexample trace that shows both executions, which may point out an actual defect in the implementation or an incorrect commit point specification.

Making Memory Accesses Explicit. The original algorithm (Fig. 1) uses a pseudo-code notation similar to C. To accurately model synchronization instructions and the effects of the memory model, we require a lower-level representation that makes the loads and stores explicit. Our back-end prototype accepts a loop-free imperative intermediate language that has (a) a small syntax, (b) a well-defined semantics even for weak memory models, and (c) supports modelling of spin loops, atomic blocks, and assertions.

Translating the Code. We envision a tool that includes a front end that accepts a subset of C and performs the translation automatically. However, for this case study, we used a straightforward manual translation of the pseudo-code into our tool's intermediate language.

Modelling Locks and Detecting Deadlocks. The code for the two-lock queue makes calls to `lock()` and `unlock()` without fully specifying their memory ordering semantics. For reference, we use a lock implementation from an architecture manual [20] that contains a spin loop, an atomic load-store primitive, and (partial) memory ordering fences. We use a reduction for side-effect free spin loops that allows us to model a single iteration of the spin loop only, while still covering all executions and detecting all deadlocks caused by an improper locking discipline in the implementation.

Modelling Dynamic Memory Management. To model dynamic memory allocation, we create an array of blocks, each with its own lock. The allocation call nondeterministically selects a free block and locks it. The deallocation call unlocks it again. The array size is bounded by the number of "enqueue" calls in the symbolic test.

3 Solution

In this section, we formalize symbolic tests and our correctness criterion, we show how to prove correctness or provide a counterexample for a given commit point specification, and we formally define our memory model.

3.1 Symbolic Tests

A symbolic test $T(A, B)$ specifies a finite sequence of operation invocations for each thread. A is a set of symbolic variables that represents argument values passed to the

$T(A, B)$		Meaning of the operations:
thread 1:	thread 2:	— *enqueue*(v)
$(b_1, b_2) = dequeue()$	$enqueue(a_2)$	adds value v to the queue
$enqueue(a_1)$	$(b_5, b_6) = dequeue()$	— *dequeue*() returns values (r, v)
$(b_3, b_4) = dequeue()$		if queue is empty, returns $r = false$;

$A = \{a_1, a_2\}$ and $B = \{b_1, \ldots, b_6\}$ otherwise, returns $r = true$ and the dequeued value v

Fig. 2. An example for a symbolic test $T(A, B)$

operations, and B similarly represents values returned by the operations. For our queue example, a symbolic client program $T(A, B)$ may look as in in Fig. 2.

For a given symbolic test $T(A, B)$, let V_A be the set of valuations to the variables in A, and let V_B the set of valuations to the variables in V_B. Given an implementation I, a memory model Y, and a symbolic test $T(A, B)$, we define the set $R_{T,I,Y} \subset V_A \times V_B$ to consist of all tuples (a, b) such that it is possible to observe the output values b when executing the test T with implementation I and input values a on a machine with memory model Y.

Let Π_T be the set of all total orders on the invocations in T. We say an order $o \in \Pi_T$ is *consistent* with T (written *consistent* $_T(o)$) if and only if for all invocations made by the same thread, the order in T matches the order o. Define the function $g_{I,T} : \Pi_T \times V_A \to V_B$ such that $g_{I,T}(o, a)$ describes the return values that result from executing the invocations appearing in T in a single thread, in the order specified by o, and with input values a. We guarantee that $g_{I,T}$ is a well-defined function as follows:

1. We admit only implementations I whose single-threaded executions are deterministic. Where we want nondeterminism (such as for modelling memory allocation), we express it by declaring additional symbolic input values.
2. We assume that executions never deadlock. However, because deadlocks are well possible in practice, we discharge this assumption separately by performing a prior check for deadlocks using an independent SAT instance (which we do not describe further here).

With the formalism introduced above we can now precisely define operation-level sequential consistency for a given test T.

Formulation. The implementation I is correct for a given symbolic test T and a memory model Y if and only if for all $(a, b) \in R_{T,I,Y}$, there exists an invocation order $o \in \Pi_T$ such that o is consistent with T and $b = g_{I,T}(o, a)$.

If an implementation is correct for all symbolic tests T, it is guaranteed to be free of defects that are caused by concurrency; if it contains any other errors, those are guaranteed to manifest themselves in some serial execution, and can therefore be easily covered with conventional verification methods.

3.2   Encoding Concurrent Executions

Our first subgoal is to encode the concurrent executions in a way that is suitable for SAT solving. We show in this section how to define auxiliary variables C, M and a formula $\Phi_{T,I,Y}(A, B, C, M)$ such that for all $(a, b) \in V_A \times V_B$ the following holds:

$$(a, b) \in R_{T,I,Y} \quad \Leftrightarrow \quad \exists C : \exists M : \Phi_{T,I,Y}(a, b, C, M) \tag{1}$$

The variable M represents the memory order; different valuations to M correspond to different instruction interleavings (and possibly reorderings). C is a set of variables that represent intermediate values of the computation. Each variable that represents an input, intermediate, or return value is local to a thread k, and we partition $A = \bigcup_k A_k$, $B = \bigcup_k B_k$, $C = \bigcup_k C_k$ accordingly. The formula $\Phi_{T,I,Y}$ then decomposes

(a) Implementation code for the operation *func*	(b) Symbolic instruction stream for the expanded invocation $y = func(x)$

```var arr : array[8] of int```
 	
```op func(int index) returns int```
  ```if (index < 0) then```
    ```return 0```
  ```else```
    ```return arr[index]```
  ```endif```
```endop```
	``` move (x < 0), c```
	```[+c] move 0, r1```
	```[-c] load arr[x], r2```
	``` move (c ? r1 : r2), y```

(c) Corresponding formula over $A_k = \{x\}$, $B_k = \{y\}$, $C_k = \{c, r1, r2\}$
$\Delta(A_k, B_k, C_k) \;\equiv\; (c = (x < 0)) \;\wedge\; (r1 = 0) \;\wedge\; ((c \wedge (y = r1)) \vee (\neg c \wedge (y = r2)))$

Fig. 3. Example of the thread-local encoding

into subformulas that represent the communication and the thread-local components separately:

$$\Phi_{T,I,Y}(A, B, C, M) \;\equiv\; \Theta_{T,I,Y}(M, C) \;\wedge\; \bigwedge_k \Delta_{T,I,k}(A_k, B_k, C_k) \qquad (2)$$

The Thread-Local Formulas. For each thread k, the formula $\Delta_{T,I,k}$ captures the connection among input values A_k, intermediate values C_k, and return values B_k: the solutions to $\Delta_{T,I,k}(A_k, B_k, C_k)$ correspond to all possible executions of thread k in an unspecified environment (that is, for arbitrary values returned by the load instructions). We obtain the encoding as follows (see Fig. 3 for an example):

- Expand the invocation sequence for thread k specified in $T(A, B)$ by inlining the implementation code I.
- Unroll loop iterations. We can skip this step for this case study (and avoid the associated loss of precision) because the implementation code is already loop-free.
- Compile the code into a linear, finite instruction sequence consisting of loads, stores, fences, and instructions that capture the thread-local computations. We call the latter *move* instructions.
- Create a variable in C_k for each intermediate value produced by a load or move.
- For each move instruction, create constraints on the source and destination values that express the nature of the computation. Take the conjunction of these constraints to get the formula $\Delta_{T,I,k}$.
- If the code contains conditionals, use *predicates* to express conditional execution of instructions. For each instruction i, define the predicate $\pi(i)$ to be a boolean formula over variables in C_k that captures the condition(s) under which this instruction gets executed. Fig. 3 illustrates how to use predicates; we skip the further details of the compilation algorithm here.

The Communication Formula. The formula $\Theta_{T,I,Y}(M,C)$ encodes the valid interactions between the threads as they execute load, store, and fence instructions. It thus captures the shared memory semantics of the multiprocessor, which is defined by the memory model Y.

To encode $\Theta_{T,I,Y}$, we first create predicated instruction streams for each thread as described in section 3.2. Let X be the set of all loads and stores appearing in these streams. Let Π_X be the set of all total orders on X. Define the *memory order* variable M to range over Π_X. We can now encode $\Theta_{T,I,Y}$ such that its solutions have the following properties: (a) the value loaded by a load matches the last value stored to the same address (where "last" is interpreted in terms of the memory order M), and (b) the memory order M follows the ordering axioms of the memory model.

We give a full definition for the formula $\Theta_{T,I,Relaxed}$ describing our relaxed memory model in section 3.4; in the remainder of this section we discuss the similar but somewhat simpler case of a sequentially consistent multiprocessor only. For each memory access $x \in X$, let $\pi(x)$ be its predicate (a boolean formula over the variables in C that captures the condition under which x gets executed), and let $a_x, v_x \in C$ be the variables that represent the address and data value of x, respectively. Let $L \subset X$ be the set of loads, and $S \subset X$ be the set of stores. Let $<_p$ be the program order; that is, $<_p$ is a partial order on X such that $x <_p y$ if and only if x, y are appear in the same stream, and x comes before y. Then

$$\Theta_{T,I,SeqCons}(M,C) \quad \equiv \tag{3}$$
$$\forall x, y \in X : \ (\pi(x) \wedge \pi(y) \wedge x <_p y) \Rightarrow x <_M y$$
$$\wedge \ \forall l \in L : \forall s \in S : \ sees\,(l, s) \Rightarrow [\, v_l = v_s \vee (\exists s' \in S : sees\,(l, s') \wedge s <_M s')\,]$$

$$\text{where} \quad sees\,(l, s) \equiv (\pi(l) \wedge \pi(s) \wedge (a_s = a_l) \wedge (s <_M l))$$

The second line of (3) expresses that the memory order may not contradict the program order, which is the essence of sequential consistency. The third line of (3) specifies that a load gets the last value "seen", that is, the last value stored to the same address. It uses the subformula *sees* (l, s), which is defined on the last line of (3) and says that a load "sees" a store if and only if it succeeds it in the memory order M, goes to the same address, and both predicates are true.

The formula (3) still contains non-boolean variables and quantifiers. To obtain a CNF representation, we (a) encode non-boolean variables in A, B, or C as bitvectors, (b) expand quantifiers into finite conjunctions or disjunctions, and (c) break M down into boolean variables $\{M_{xy} \mid x, y \in X\}$ such that M_{xy} represents $x <_M y$ and add clauses to express transitivity, antisymmetry and non-reflexivity. The number of variables and clauses is then quadratic and cubic in $|X|$, respectively.

3.3 Encoding Correctness

We now show how to construct a formula Ψ such that (a) Ψ can be solved by a SAT solver, (b) unsatisfiability of Ψ implies correctness, and (c) given a satisfying assignment for Ψ, we can construct a counterexample trace. Such a trace shows a concurrent execution for which the serial reference execution is not observationally equivalent.

For a given test T and implementation I, a commit point specification h is understood as a function $\Pi_X \to \Pi_T$ that maps a given memory order m to the invocation order $h(m)$ that reflects how m orders the commit points. Now we can define

$$\Psi_{T,I,Y,h} \equiv \exists A : \exists B : \exists C : \exists M : \quad \Phi_{T,I,Y}(A, B, C, M) \wedge \quad (4)$$
$$(g_{I,T}(h(M), A) \neq B \quad \vee \quad \neg\, consistent_T(h(M)))$$

To encode the subformula $g_{I,T}(h(M), A) \neq B$ in (4), we create a copy $T'(A, B')$ of $T(A, B)$ in which we put each invocation in a separate thread, and we define a special "memory model" *Atomic*, which is similar to sequential consistency but executes each thread atomically. Then $g_{I,T}(h(m), A) \neq B$ if and only if

$$\exists B' : \exists C' : \exists M' : \Phi_{T',I,Atomic}(A, B', C', M') \wedge h(M') = h(M) \wedge B \neq B' \quad (5)$$

After substituting (5) into (4), we can move all existential quantifiers to the front as required for SAT solving.

If the SAT solver determines that $\Psi_{T,I,Y,h}$ is unsatisfiable, it follows directly from the definitions that the implementation I is correct for the test T and memory model Y (regardless of h). However, if the SAT solver provides a satisfying assignment for $\Psi_{T,I,Y,h}$, our prototype presents the corresponding concurrent and serial executions to the user. The user can then analyze the counterexample and determine whether there is a defect in the implementation or a mistake in the commit point specification h.

3.4 Encoding Relaxed Memory Models

Relaxed memory models impose fewer ordering restrictions on the instruction streams than sequential consistency; therefore $R_{T,I,SeqCons} \subset R_{T,I,L}$ for all relaxed models L. Finding a uniform specification framework for the puzzling variety of memory models is a challenge of its own [25, 26]. For this case study, we restricted our attention to a selection of memory models (listed in the next paragraph) that are commonly used by hardware. Moreover, we are content with a *conservative approximation*, that is, a model *Relaxed* such that $R_{T,I,Y} \subset R_{T,I,Relaxed}$ for all memory models Y in our selection.

We compared the memory model specifications for the IBM PowerPC [19], Sun SPARC v9 TSO/PSO/RMO [20], Alpha [21], and IBM zArchitecture [22]. Although there are many differences, all of the specifications are based on a similar axiomatic style: they consist of a collection of rules that describe the valid instruction orderings and how values may flow from stores to loads. This non-operational style suits our purpose well; it allows us to compare the different models and derive a common approximation *Relaxed*, which we now describe in detail.

First, let us describe the relaxations with respect to sequential consistency informally. We use the symbols X, M, C, S, L, $\pi(x)$, a_x, v_x, and $<_p$ as defined in section 3.2.

- Accesses to different locations by the same thread may be executed out of order: If $x, y \in X$ and $x <_p y$ and $a_x \neq a_y$, we may have $y <_M x$.
- Loads to the same location by the same thread may be executed out of order: If $l, l' \in L$ and $l <_p l'$ and $a_l = a_{l'}$, we may have $l' <_M l$.

- Stores may be non-atomic: the stored value may be held in a thread-local buffer before becoming visible to other threads. We use $<_M$ to express the time at which a store commits globally, and we adjust the definition of *sees* (l, s) to allow a load to see stores in the buffer. For example, if $s \in S$ and $l \in L$ and $s <_p l$ and $a_s = a_l$, we may have $l <_M s$ and *sees* (l, s).

Our formalization is similar to the Sparc RMO memory model axioms [16]. In fact, our generic model is equivalent to the latter if we remove the RMO-specific axiom (m1) that defines how value and control dependencies influence the memory order.

If a memory ordering fence instruction appears in between two memory accesses in the code, they must execute in order. Fences affect only instructions in the same thread, and there exist specific variations (such as load-load, load-store, store-load or store-store fences) that target a subset of instructions only. Formally, let F to be the set of memory fences appearing in all instruction streams, and for each fence $f \in F$, let $X_f \subset X$ be the set of accesses affected by f. For example, if f is a store-load fence, then $X_f = \{s \in S \mid s <_p f\} \cup \{l \in L \mid f <_p l\}$.

Now we are ready to define *Relaxed* formally. We do so by directly specifying

$$\Theta_{T,I,Relaxed}(M, C) \quad \equiv \tag{6}$$
$$\forall x \in X : \forall s \in S : \quad (\pi(x) \wedge \pi(s) \wedge a_x = a_s \wedge x <_p s) \Rightarrow x <_M s$$
$$\wedge \; \forall l \in L : \forall s \in S : \quad sees\,(l, s) \; \Rightarrow \; v_l = v_s \vee (\exists s' \in S : sees\,(l, s') \wedge s <_M s')$$
$$\wedge \; \forall f \in F : \forall x, y \in X_f : \quad (\pi(f) \wedge \pi(x) \wedge \pi(y) \wedge (x <_p f <_p y)) \Rightarrow x <_M y$$

$$\text{where} \quad sees\,(l, s) \equiv \pi(l) \wedge \pi(s) \wedge (a_s = a_l) \wedge (s <_M l \vee s <_p l)$$

The second line of (6) specifies the conditions under which the memory order may not contradict the program order. When compared with the formula (3) for sequential consistency, we see that this line has been weakened to reflect the ordering relaxations we described earlier. The third line specifies that a load gets the last value "seen", that is, the last value stored to the same address. It is the same as for sequential consistency (3), but the definition of *sees* (l, s) on the last line has been modified to allow forwarding. The fourth line of (6) defines the effect of memory fences on the valid memory orderings.

The memory model *Relaxed* is simpler than most memory models used for actual hardware because (a) it consistently relaxes the order, for example, even data- or control-dependent instructions may be reordered, and no special measures are taken to prevent circular value flow, (b) it uses a single, generic memory ordering fence construct, (c) it does not contain specific synchronization primitives, but allows them to be expressed as atomic blocks (we omitted atomic blocks from the formalization above, but they can introduced easily by adding suitable constraints on $<_M$), and (d) it omits unneeded details such as the behavior of instruction caches and I/O, special flushing operations, or unaligned and non-atomic memory accesses.

This (relative) simplicity makes *Relaxed* a good model for studying the algorithms: even though it may exhibit executions that are not possible on a specific target architecture, we are made aware of all issues by verifying our code on *Relaxed*. Once we understand which instructions need to stay in order, it is comparatively easy to pick the right fences for a specific target architecture.

Specialized algorithms to insert memory fences automatically during compilation have been proposed [27, 28]. However, these methods are based on a conservative program analysis, and they enforce sequential consistency on the instruction level rather than the operation level. These characteristics make them unattractive for optimized implementations, because redundant fences imply suboptimal performance [29].

4 Results

We implemented a prototype that encodes SAT instances as described in the previous chapter, solves them using zChaff [30], and converts satisfying assignments into human-readable execution traces. We first tested our prototype on some smaller examples (including the spinlock [16]). Then we hand-translated the pseudo-code (Fig. 1) into the intermediate language accepted by our back-end prototype. Next, we created a suite of symbolic tests (Fig. 4) and made an initial guess at the commit points (lines 15 and 31 in Fig. 1).

Running our prototype, we found five problems (numbered 1–5 below). First, we ran T0 on a sequentially consistent memory model, finding problem 1. Then, we ran T0 on our relaxed memory model, finding problems 2–4. Next, we ran on T1 on the relaxed model and found problem 5. After that, no more problems were found. The tests T0 and T1 alone (neither of which took more than a few seconds) therefore uncovered all the bugs found.

1. **Incorrect commit point specification.** We had guessed line 31 to be the commit point. The tool produced a counterexample revealing a race between the store on line 15 and the load on line 32. The outcome of this race determines the logical order of the operations, so we changed the commit point for the dequeue to be line 32 instead of line 31.

2. **Incorrect modelling of dynamic memory.** Our initial model for dynamic memory allocation was incorrect for relaxed memory models: the trace showed a load from a storage location inside a dynamically allocated block that took effect only after the block was freed, re-allocated by another thread, and then overwritten. This situation caused the load to get the wrong value. We fixed this problem by inserting fences into the alloc() and free() calls.

Program name	T0	T1	T5-3	T5-4	T5-5	T5-6	Tpc4	Tpc6
Thread 1 sequence	e	e	e e e e	e e e	e e	e	e e e e	e e e e e e
Thread 2 sequence	d	e	d	e	e	e	d d d d	d d d d d d
Thread 3 sequence		d	d	d	e	e		
Thread 4 sequence		d		d	d	e		
Thread 5 sequence					d	d		
Thread 6 sequence						d		

Fig. 4. A selection of the symbolic tests we used. The letters e and d represent calls to the enqueue and dequeue operation (with symbolic arguments). All calls operate on the same queue object.

	Program Characteristics				SAT encoding		Requirements	
	threads	operations	instructions	loads	stores	variables	clauses	memory [kB]	time [s]
T0	2	2	65	12	18	551	4,081	332	0.004
T1	4	4	119	23	30	1,514	44,479	4,165	0.87
T5-3	3	6	163	31	44	3,380	160,516	16,246	9.33
T5-4	4	6	163	31	44	3,400	167,456	16,308	21.1
T5-5	5	6	163	31	44	3,413	173,324	16,357	35.4
T5-6	6	6	163	31	44	3,419	179,109	16,401	42.8
Tpc2	2	4	119	23	30	1,504	42,829	4,151	0.139
Tpc3	2	6	173	34	42	3,717	170,116	16,320	5.23
Tpc4	2	8	227	45	54	5,797	430,445	33,372	45.7
Tpc5	2	10	281	56	66	8,315	877,624	100,462	300.0
Tpc6	2	12	335	67	78	11,271	1,549,090	131,087	886.3
Tpc7	2	14	389	78	90	12,394	2,438,721	n/a	> 1000

Fig. 5. Some experimental data. All resource requirements are reported by the zChaff solver (version 2004/11/15) and refer to unsatisfiable instances using a relaxed memory model. The tests were run on a 3 GHz Pentium 4 desktop Linux PC.

3. **Missing store-store fence.** On a relaxed model, the store instruction that updates the queued value (line 12) may be ordered after the load that is supposed to read it (line 38). To force the store to take effect by the time the node is linked into the list, we insert a store-store fence before the store on line 15.

4. **Missing load-load fence.** Symmetrically, we need to make sure that the load of the queued value (line 38) does not take effect before the load of its address on line 32. This may seem automatic — but some weak memory models (such as Alpha [21]) do not enforce in-order execution of loads, even if there is a value dependency [31]. Therefore, we insert a load-load memory fence after the load on line 32.

5. **Incorrect modelling of locks.** During the translation, we had misplaced one of the fences within the code for `unlock()`. It appeared after instead of before the committing store, where it is useless. Without proper fences in `lock()` and `unlock()`, memory accesses can "escape" from the critical section.

Analysis. The results indicate that our method is efficient at finding errors in highly concurrent programs, but does not scale to long program executions. As expected, zChaff was much quicker at solving satisfiable instances than at refuting unsatisfiable ones, but the choice of the memory model seemed to have a negligible effect on the runtime. We show some statistics about the programs and the resources required (for unsatisfiable instances and the relaxed memory model) in Fig. 5. The results show that making the programs longer (Tpc series, see Fig. 4 for definition) is more challenging for the solver than making them more concurrent (T5 series). This result is not surprising because we chose an encoding that specializes on highly concurrent executions.

5   Conclusions

Verifying the sequential consistency of a concurrent data type implementation on a relaxed memory model presents a challenge because of the high degree of concurrency at the instruction level and the infinite state space. In this case study, we developed a new SAT-based method that can solve a bounded formulation of this problem (using finite symbolic tests and commit point annotations) and demonstrated its practical value by applying it successfully to Michael and Scott's two-lock queue implementation.

Future work includes exploring more example data structure implementations, eliminating the need for commit point specifications, automating the creation of a symbolic test suite, improving the scalability with more efficient or incremental SAT encodings, and developing a front end for the tool that would accept a subset of C as the specification of the implementation.

References

[1] H. Sutter and J. Larus. Software and the concurrency revolution. *ACM Queue*, 3(7):54–62, 2005.

[2] M. Herlihy. Wait-free synchronization. *ACM Trans. Program. Lang. Syst.*, 13(1):124–149, 1991.

[3] G. L. Peterson. Concurrent reading while writing. *ACM Trans. Program. Lang. Syst.*, 5(1):46–55, 1983.

[4] L. Lamport. Concurrent reading and writing. *Commun. ACM*, 20(11):806–811, 1977.

[5] S. V. Adve and K. Gharachorloo. Shared memory consistency models: a tutorial. *Computer*, 29(12):66–76, 1996.

[6] L. Lamport. How to make a multiprocessor computer that correctly executes multiprocess programs. *IEEE Trans. Comp.*, C-28(9):690–691, 1979.

[7] T. Elmas, S. Tasiran, and S. Qadeer. VYRD: verifying concurrent programs by runtime refinement-violation detection. In *Programming Language Design and Implementation (PLDI)*, pages 27–37, 2005.

[8] E. Clarke, D. Kroening, and F. Lerda. A tool for checking ANSI-C programs. In *Tools and Algorithms for the Construction and Analysis of Systems (TACAS)*, LNCS 2988, pages 168–176. Springer, 2004.

[9] Y. Yang, G. Gopalakrishnan, and G. Lindstrom. Memory-model-sensitive data race analysis. In *International Conference on Formal Engineering Methods (ICFEM)*, LNCS 3308, pages 30–45. Springer, 2004.

[10] G. Gopalakrishnan, Y. Yang, and H. Sivaraj. QB or not QB: An efficient execution verification tool for memory orderings. In *Computer-Aided Verification (CAV)*, LNCS 3114, pages 401–413, 2004.

[11] M. M. Michael and M. L. Scott. Simple, fast, and practical non-blocking and blocking concurrent queue algorithms. In *Principles of Distributed Computing (PODC)*, pages 267–275, 1996.

[12] V. Vafeiadis, M. Herlihy, T. Hoare, and M. Shapiro. Proving correctness of highly-concurrent linearisable objects. In *Principles and Practice of Parallel Programming (PPoPP)*, pages 129–136, 2006.

[13] I. Rabinovitz and O. Grumberg. Bounded model checking of concurrent programs. In *Computer-Aided Verification (CAV)*, LNCS 3576, pages 82–97. Springer, 2005.

[14] E. Yahav and M. Sagiv. Automatically verifying concurrent queue algorithms. *Electr. Notes Theor. Comput. Sci.*, 89(3), 2003.

[15] M. P. Herlihy and J. M. Wing. Linearizability: a correctness condition for concurrent objects. *ACM Trans. Program. Lang. Syst.*, 12(3):463–492, 1990.

[16] S. Park and D. L. Dill. An executable specification, analyzer and verifier for RMO (relaxed memory order). In *Symposium on Parallel Algorithms and Architectures (SPAA)*, pages 34–41, 1995.

[17] D. L. Dill, S. Park, and A. G. Nowatzyk. Formal specification of abstract memory models. In *Symposium on Research on Integrated Systems*, pages 38–52. MIT Press, 1993.

[18] S. Savage, M. Burrows, G. Nelson, P. Sobalvarro, and T. Anderson. Eraser: A dynamic data race detector for multithreaded programs. *ACM Trans. Comp. Sys.*, 15(4):391–411, 1997.

[19] B. Frey. *PowerPC Architecture Book v2.02*. International Business Machines Corporation, 2005.

[20] D. L. Weaver and T. Germond, editors. *The SPARC Architecture Manual Version 9*. PTR Prentice Hall, 1994.

[21] Compaq Computer Corporation. *Alpha Architecture Reference Manual*, 4th edition, January 2002.

[22] International Business Machines Corporation. *z/Architecture Principles of Operation*, first edition, December 2000.

[23] Y. Yang, G. Gopalakrishnan, G. Lindstrom, and K. Slind. Analyzing the Intel Itanium memory ordering rules using logic programming and SAT. In *Correct Hardware Design and Verification Methods (CHARME)*, LNCS 2860, pages 81–95. Springer, 2003.

[24] R. Alur, K. McMillan, and D. Peled. Model-checking of correctness conditions for concurrent objects. In *Logic in Computer Science (LICS)*, pages 219–228, 1996.

[25] R. C. Steinke and G. J. Nutt. A unified theory of shared memory consistency. *J. ACM*, 51(5):800–849, 2004.

[26] Y. Yang, G. Gopalakrishnan, G. Lindstrom, and K. Slind. Nemos: A framework for axiomatic and executable specifications of memory consistency models. In *International Parallel and Distributed Processing Symposium (IPDPS)*, 2004.

[27] D. Shasha and M. Snir. Efficient and correct execution of parallel programs that share memory. *ACM Trans. Program. Lang. Syst.*, 10(2):282–312, 1988.

[28] X. Fang, J. Lee, and S. P. Midkiff. Automatic fence insertion for shared memory multiprocessing. In *International Conference on Supercomputing (ICS)*, pages 285–294, 2003.

[29] C. von Praun, T. Cain, J. Choi, and K. Ryu. Conditional memory ordering. In *International Symposium on Computer Architecture (ISCA)*, 2006.

[30] M. Moskewicz, C. Madigan, Y. Zhao, L. Zhang, and S. Malik. Chaff: Engineering an efficient SAT solver. In *Design Automation Conference (DAC)*, pages 530–535, 2001.

[31] M. Martin, D. Sorin, H. Cain, M. Hill, and M. Lipasti. Correctly implementing value prediction in microprocessors that support multithreading or multiprocessing. In *International Symposium on Microarchitecture (MICRO)*, pages 328–337, 2001.

Fast and Generalized Polynomial Time Memory Consistency Verification

Amitabha Roy, Stephan Zeisset, Charles J. Fleckenstein, and John C. Huang

Intel Corporation
{amitabha.roy, stephan.zeisset, chuck.fleckenstein}@intel.com,
jhuangtw@umich.edu

Abstract. The problem of verifying multi-threaded execution against the memory consistency model of a processor is known to be an NP hard problem. However polynomial time algorithms exist that detect almost all failures in such execution. These are often used in practice for microprocessor verification. We present a low complexity and fully parallelized algorithm to check program execution against the processor consistency model. In addition our algorithm is general enough to support a number of consistency models without any degradation in performance. An implementation of this algorithm is currently used in practice to verify processors in the post silicon stage for multiple architectures.

1 Introduction

Verifying processor execution against its stated memory consistency model is an important problem in both design and silicon system verification. Verification teams for a microprocessor are often concerned with the memory consistency model visible to external customers such as system programmers. In the context of multi-threading, both in terms of Simultaneous Multi Threading(SMT) and Chip Multi Processing(CMP), Intel®[1] and other CPU manufacturers are increasingly building complex processors and SMP platforms with a large number of execution threads. In this environment the memory consistency model of microprocessors will come under close scrutiny, particularly by developers of multi-threaded applications and operating systems. Allowing any errors in implementing the consistency model to show up as customer visible is thus unacceptable. The problem we are concerned with is that of matching the result of executing a random set of load store memory operations distributed across processors, on a set of shared locations, against a memory consistency model. The algorithm should flag an error if the consistency model does not allow the observed execution results. This forms the basis for Random Instruction Test(RIT) generators such as TSOTOOL[2] [1] and Intel's Multi Processor(MP) RIT environment. The Intel MP RIT Tool incorporates the algorithm in this paper. Formally, we concentrate on variations of the VSC (Verifying Sequential Consistency) problem [2]. The VSC problem is exactly the problem described above, when restricted to sequential consistency. The general

---

[1] Intel® is a trademark or registered trademark of Intel Corporation or its subsidiaries in the United States and other countries.

[2] Other names and brands may be claimed as the property of others.

T. Ball and R.B. Jones (Eds.): CAV 2006, LNCS 4144, pp. 503–516, 2006.
© Springer-Verlag Berlin Heidelberg 2006

VSC problem is NP complete [3]. The general coherence problem has also been shown to be NP complete [4]. A formulation of VSC for more general memory consistency models was done in [1] where a polynomial time algorithm was presented for verifying a memory consistency model at the cost of correctness, although the incorrect executions missed were shown to be insignificant for the purpose of CPU verification. That work focused almost exclusively on the Total Store Order(TSO) memory consistency model and presented a worst case $O(n^5)$ algorithm. In this work, we present an efficient implementation of the basic algorithm in [1]. Our key contribution is to reduce the worst case complexity to $O(n^4)$ for *any* memory consistency model using $\Theta(n^2)$ space. Although the work in [5] has reduced the complexity to $O(kn^3)$ where k is the number of processors, that algorithm assumes the TSO memory consistency model and does not generalize to other models. Our motivation for generalizing and improving it is Intel's complex verification environment, where microprocessors support as many as five different consistency models at the same time. The primary objectives of our algorithm design are simplicity, performance and seamless extendibility in the implementation to any processor environment, including the Itanium®[3]. Another goal is enhanced support for debugging reported failures, which is crucial to reducing time to market for complex multi processors.

The algorithm we have developed is currently implemented in Intel's in house random test generator and is used by both the IA-32 and Itanium verification teams. We also present scalability results and a processor bug that was caught by the tool using this algorithm.

2 Memory Consistency

Consider a set of processors each of which executes a stream of loads and stores. These are done to a set of locations shared across the processors. We are concerned with a global ordering of all the loads and stores, which when executed serially leads to the same result. The strictest consistency model is the sequential consistency (SC) model which insists that the only valid orderings are those that do not relax per processor program order between the memory operations. Relaxing restrictions between operations such as stores and loads leads to progressively weaker models such as Total Store Order (TSO) and Release Consistency (RC). All these are surveyed in [6]. We point out that in these orderings we refer to load executions and store executions. A load is considered performed(or executed) if no subsequent store to that location(on any processor) can change the load return value. A store is considered performed(or executed) if any subsequent load to that location (on any processor) returns its value. These are definitions from [7]. Any instruction on a modern pipelined processor has a number of phases and some, such as instruction fetch and retirement, occur in strict program order without regard to the memory consistency model. We are concerned only with ordering the load and store execution phases for instructions referring to memory.

---

[3] Itanium® is a trademark or registered trademark of Intel Corporation or its subsidiaries in the United States and other countries.

2.1 Formalism

The terminology used in this paper is similar to [1]. We use ; to denote program order and $\leq$ to denote global order. Thus $A; B$ and $A \leq B$ mean that B follows A in program order and global order respectively. The fundamental operations in our test consist of L_a^i and S_a^i which are loads and stores respectively to location a by processor i. We also consider $[L_a^i; S_a^i]$ which is an atomic load store operation. Examples are XCHG in IA-32 [8] and FETCHADD in Itanium [9]. We use $val(L_a^i)$ to denote the load return value of a load operation and $val(S_a^i)$ to denote the value stored by a store operation.

For any location a we define the type of a location to be
$Type(a) \in \{WB, WT, WP, UC, WC\}$. The type of a location is the *memory* type of the location. IA-32 [8] supports all five memory types, Write Back (WB), Write Through (WT), Write Protect (WP), Write Combining(WC) and Uncacheable. Itanium [9] supports only three, WB, WC and UC. In addition to cacheability and write through implications of these memory types, they also affect the consistency model.

2.2 Axioms and Orders

Both $\leq$ and ; are transitive, reflexive and antisymmetric orders. The program order is limited to operations on the same processor while the global order covers all operations across all processors. We also define $A < B$ to mean $A \leq B$ and $A \neq B$.

We define the following axiom to support atomic operations.

Axiom 1 (Atomic Operations). $[L_a^i; S_a^i] \Rightarrow (L_a^i \leq S_a^i) \bigwedge (\forall S_b^j : (S_b^j \leq L_a^i) \bigvee (S_a^i \leq S_b^j))$

As a result of this, we can treat atomic operations as a single operation for verification. We assume the following two axioms to hold, the bare minimum to be able to use the basic algorithm proposed in [1].

Axiom 2 (Value Coherence). $val[L_a^i] \in \{val[\overset{Max}{\leq} S_a^k | S_a^k < L_a^i], val[\overset{Max}{;} S_a^i | S_a^i; L_a^i]\}$

The value returned by a read is from either the most recent store in program order or the most recent store in global order. This is intuitive for a cache coherent system. Note that the most recent store in program order may not be a preceding store in global order. This is because many architectures including Intel ones can support the notion of store forwarding, which allows a store to be forwarded to local loads before it is made globally visible. Also, in the test a load may occur before any store to that location in which case it returns the initial value of that location. Such cases are handled by assuming a preliminary set of stores that write initial values to locations. The store values to a location and initial value of the location are chosen to be unique by the test generator. This allows the axiom to be applied after the test is completed to link a load to the store that it reads.

Axiom 3 (Total Store Order). $\forall S_a^i, S_b^j((S_a^i \leq S_b^j) \bigvee (S_b^j \leq S_a^i))$.

Unlike [1], we have avoided imposing any additional constraints between operations on the same processor. Rather, we allow these constraints to be dynamically specified. This allows us to parameterize the same algorithm to work across CPU architectures (Itanium and IA-32) and processor generations (Intel NetBurst®[4] and P6 in the case of IA-32).

Define $Ops = \{L, S, X\}$ to be the allowed types of an operation. Thus we can define $Type(L_a^i) = L$, $Type(S_a^i) = S$ and $Type([L_a^i; S_a^i]) = X$. We also define $Loc(Op)$ to return the memory location used by the operation. For example $Loc(L_a^i) = a$.

We can then define the constraint function
$f : (OpsX\{WB, WP, WT, WC, UC\})^2 \rightarrow \{0, 1\}$. This is used to impose the dynamic set of constraints:

Definition 1 (Local Ordering). $[O_1; O_2$ and
$f((Type(O_1), Type(Loc(O_1)), (Type(O_2), Type(Loc(O_2))))) = 1] \Rightarrow O_1 \leq O_2$
If the LHS of the implication is satisfied we call O_1 and O_2 as locally ordered memory operations.

As an example, from [8] we know that Write back stores do not bypass each other. Hence f((S, WB),(S,WB))=1. However, write combining stores are allowed to bypass each other and hence f((S, WC), (S,WC))=0. There are other more subtle orderings which vary between processor generations and in this case we obtain appropriate ordering functions from the CPU architects or designers.

3   Algorithm

Our objective is an algorithm that takes in the result of an execution and flags violation of the memory consistency model. The basic algorithm in [1] that we extend uses constraint graphs to model the execution. There have been similar approaches in the past too, such as [10] and an approach to the same problem using Boolean satisfiability solvers [11], which models write atomicity accurately, but can handle only much shorter executions than our method can handle. We model the execution as a directed graph G=(V, E) where the nodes represent memory operations and the edges represent the $\leq$ global order. However, as in [1], we do not put self edges although the relation is reflexive. Thus if $O_1 \leq O_2$ then we add an edge from the node for O_1 to that for O_2. For brevity, we refer to operations and their corresponding nodes by the same name. $A \rightarrow B$ means there is an edge from A to B while $A \rightarrow_P B$ means there is a path from A to B.

Based on the per processor ordering imposed by our ordering function f, we can immediately add static edges to the graph.

Rule 1 (Static Edges). For every pair of nodes O_1 and O_2 such that they are locally ordered by definition 1, add the edge $O_1 \rightarrow O_2$.

---

[4] Intel NetBurst® is a trademark or registered trademark of Intel Corporation or its subsidiaries in the United States and other countries.

After execution of the test, we determine a function $Reads$ in a preprocessing step (operating on loads) such that $Reads(L_a^i) = S_a^j$ if L_a^i reads S_a^j. Otherwise (the case where the initial value for the location is read), $Reads(L_a^i) = Sentinel$, a special sentinel node. We add edges from $Sentinel$ to all other store nodes in the graph. This is the same construction as described in [1]. From the value axiom we know that any read that returns the value of a remote write must have occurred after the remote write has been globally observed. This allows us to add observed edges to the graph based on the values returned by the loads in the test. Note that for the rules below we treat an atomic operation as both a load and a store.

Rule 2 (Observed Edge). *For every load L_a^i, if $Reads(L_a^i) = S_a^j$ where $i \neq j$, or if $Reads(L_a^i) = Sentinel$, add the edge $Reads(L_a^i) \to L_a^i$. Note that since stores to the same location write unique values and all locations are initialized to hold unique values, value equivalence means that the load must have read that store.*

The next few set of edges are essentially inferred from the value axiom. Hence they are called inferred edges.

Rule 3 (Inferred Edge 1). *If $Reads(L_a^i) = S_a^j$ and $i \neq j$ then for every S_a^i such that $S_a^i ; L_a^i$ add the edge $S_a^i \to S_a^j$. This follows from the value axiom since the alternative global order would mean the load should read the local store.*

Rule 4 (Inferred Edge 2). *If $Reads(L_a^i) = S_a^j$ then for every S_a^k such that $S_a^k \to_P L_a^i$ and $S_a^k \neq S_a^j$, add the edge $S_a^k \to S_a^j$. This follows from the value axiom since the alternative global order would mean that the load should read S_a^k.*

Rule 5 (Inferred Edge 3). *If $Reads(L_a^i) = S_a^j$ then for every S_a^k such that $S_a^j \to_P S_a^k$ add the edge $L_a^i \to S_a^k$. This follows from the value axiom since the alternative global order would mean that the load should read S_a^k.*

3.1 Basic Algorithm

The basic algorithm described in [1] can now be summarized as follows:

1. Compute the $Reads$ function in a preprocessing step.
2. Apply rule 1 to add all possible edges.
3. Apply rule 2 to add all possible edges.
4. Apply rules 3, 4 and 5.
5. If any edges were added in step 4 go back to step 4 else go to step 6
6. Check the graph for cycles. If any are found, flag an error.

An example of this algorithm applied to an execution is shown in Figure 1. We use the notation $S[X]\#V$ for write V to location X, and $L[X] = V$ for read from location X returns value V.

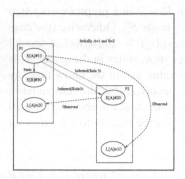

Fig. 1. Example of an incorrect execution with graph edges added

Computing the *Reads* function is $O(n^2)$ since we need to examine all pairs of loads and stores. Steps 2 and 3 are of cost $O(n^2)$ since we examine all pairs of nodes. Step 4 involves determining the relationship $A \rightarrow_P B$ for $O(n)$ nodes. This costs $O(n^2)$ for each node (assuming a depth first search, as one of the obvious options) and hence $O(n^3)$ overall. Since the fixed point iteration imposed by steps 4 and 5 may loop for at most $O(n^2)$ adding one edge on each iteration, we have a worst case complexity of $O(n^5)$. The detailed analysis is in [1]. There has been a subsequent improvement published in [5] that reduces the complexity to $O(kn^3)$. Its correctness requires that there are a constant number of ordered lists on each processor. This is true because all loads and all stores are ordered on a processor in the TSO consistency model that they have considered. Unfortunately this does not hold true for both the IA-32 [8] and Itanium [12] memory models for various memory types (consider WC stores). Hence the formulation in [5] is not general enough.

3.2   Graph Closure

The primary contributor to the $O(n^5)$ complexity is deciding whether $A \rightarrow_P B$ holds. All other operations can be efficiently implemented and do not seem to hold any opportunity for improvement, given our goal of generality. Hence, we decided to focus on the problem of efficiently determining $A \rightarrow_P B$. A solution is to compute the transitive closure of the graph. We first label all the nodes in the directed graph under consideration, $G = (V, E)$ by natural numbers using the bijective mapping function $g : V \rightarrow \{1..n\}$ where $|V| = n$. We can then represent E by the familiar n square adjacency matrix A such that $(U, V) \in E \Leftrightarrow A[g(U), g(V)] = 1$.

For transitive closure of the graph we seek the closed form of the adjacency matrix A such that $U \rightarrow_P V \Leftrightarrow A[g(U), g(V)] = 1$. A well known algorithm for computing the transitive closure of a binary adjacency matrix is Warshall's algorithm[13]. Before giving Warshall's algorithm, we first define some convenient notation and functions to transform the connectivity matrix. $AddEdge(x, y)$ stands for : set $A[x, y] = 1$. $Subsume(x, y)$ is defined as $\forall z$ such that $A[y, z] = 1$, $AddEdge(x, z)$. The subsume function causes all neighbors of node $g^{-1}(y)$ to also become neighbors of node $g^{-1}(x)$ in the adjacency matrix representation.

Incremental Graph Closure: Although Warshall's algorithm will compute the closed form of the adjacency matrix, any edge added by $AddEdge$ will cause the matrix to lose this property since new paths may be available through the added edge. Hence we need an algorithm which when given a closed adjacency matrix and some edges added *efficiently* recomputes the closure.

Warshall's Algorithm:	**Incremental Warshall's Algorithm:**
for all $j \in \{1..N\}$	for all $j \in \{1..N\}$
for all $i \in \{1..N\}$	for all $i \in \{1..N\}$
if($A[i,j] = 1$)	if($A[i,j] = 1$ and
$Subsume(i,j)$	($Changed[j] = 1$ or $Changed[i] = 1$))
end if	$Subsume(i,j)$
end for	end if
end for	end for
	end for

We assume that when adding edges to any node U, we mark that node as changed by setting the corresponding bit in the change vector $Changed[g(U)] = 1$. We can now rerun Warshall's algorithm *restricted* to only those nodes which have either changed themselves, or are connected in the current adjacency matrix to a changed node. This is shown in pseudo-code as incremental Warshall's algorithm. A correctness proof can be found in [14].

Complexity: An important observation is that the complexity of the incremental update is $O(mn^2)$ where the number of changed nodes is $O(m)$. This is because the subsume step takes $O(n)$ and for each node, $Subsume$ can only be called at worst $O(m)$ times, if it is connected to all the changed nodes. At worst all $O(n)$ nodes satisfy the precondition for subsume and hence the $O(mn^2)$ complexity.

3.3 Final Algorithm

We describe algorithms to implement the rules for adding observed and inferred edges in Table 1. Recall that our graph is G=(V, E) and the vertices correspond to memory operations in the test. Also, for ease of specification we have allowed atomic read modify write operations to be treated as both stores $Type(Op) = S$ and loads $Type(Op) = L$.

The ordering of for loops is not arbitrary as it may appear but rather has been carefully chosen to aid in parallelization as we demonstrate in section 4.

We now state the final algorithm used to verify the execution results. A benefit of our approach is that checking the graph for cycles is simply checking whether $\exists i\ A[i,i] = 1$ since a cycle results in a self loop due to the closure. Additionally, note that we have merged the preprocessing step that links loads to the stores they read, into the step to compute observed edges.

1. Apply rule 1 to add all possible edges.
2. Apply rule 2 to add all possible edges.
3. Apply Warshall's algorithm to obtain the closed adjacency matrix.
4. Apply rules 3, 4 and 5.
5. If any edges were added in step 4 go to step 6 else go to step 8.
6. Apply the incremental Warshall's algorithm to recompute closure and reset the changed vector.
7. Go to step 4.
8. Check the graph for cycles. If any are found, flag an error.

Table 1. Pseudcode of Algorithm for Adding Edges

Algorithm for adding edges:
Static Edges:
for all $O_1 \in V$
for all $O_2 \in V$ such that $O_1 \neq O_2$
If O_1 is locally ordered after O_2 as per definition 1then
$AddEdge(g(O_2), g(O_1))$
end for
end for
Observed Edges:
for all $O_1 \in V$ such that $type(O_1) = L$
for all $O_2 \in V$ such that $type(O_2) = S$
If $val(O_1) = val(O_2)$
set $Reads(O_1) = O_2$
If O_2 is on a different CPU from O_1 then $AddEdge(g(O_2), g(O_1))$
end If
end for
If no corresponding store is found for this load then
$AddEdge(g(Sentinel), g(O_1))$ and set $Reads(O_1) = Sentinel$
end for
Inferred Edge 1:
for all $O_1 \in V$ such that $type(O_1) = L$
for all $O_2 \in V$ such that $type(O_2) = S$ and $O_2; O_1$ and $O_2 \neq Reads(O_1)$
If O_2 is on a different CPU from O_1 then
$AddEdge(g(O_2), g(Reads(O_1)))$ and set $Changed[g(O_2)] = 1$
end for
end for
Inferred Edge 2:
for all $O_1 \in V$ such that $type(O_1) = L$
for all $O_2 \in V$ such that $type(O_2) = S$ and $A[g(O_2), g(O_1)] = 1$
and $O_2 \neq Reads(O_1)$
$AddEdge(g(O_2), g(Reads(O_1)))$ and set $Changed[g(O_2)] = 1$
end for
end for
Inferred Edge 3:
for all $O_1 \in V$ such that $type(O_1) = S$
for all $O_2 \in V$ such that $type(O_2) = L$ and $A[g(Reads(O_2)), g(O_1)] = 1$
$AddEdge(g(O_2), g(O_1))$ and set $Changed[g(O_2)] = 1$
end for
end for

3.4 Complexity

The analysis of complexity is straightforward. Each of steps 1 and 2 take $O(n^2)$ since they examine all pairs of nodes. Step 3 takes $O(n^3)$ as is shown in [13]. Each iteration of Step 4 again takes $O(n^2)$ because we examine all pairs of nodes. Note that checking $A \rightarrow_P B$ is now $O(1)$ thanks to the closed adjacency matrix. There are at most $O(n^2)$ edges to be added and hence the worst case complexity for Step 4 is $O(n^4)$. The remaining analysis is step 6. For this we note that the complexity is also $O(mn^2)$ when considered over *all* invocations. Since $m = O(n^2)$ (bounded above by the number of edges we can possibly add and thereby change nodes), we have $O(n^4)$ as the worst case complexity for step 6. Cycle checking in step 8 is simply $O(n)$ due to the closed form of the adjacency matrix. Thus the overall complexity is $O(n^4)$ which meets our stated goal. Our overall space requirements are clearly $\Theta(n^2)$ due to the adjacency matrix.

4 Parallelization

One of the ways to mitigate the expense of an $O(n^4)$ algorithm is parallelization. With a test size of hundreds of memory operation per CPU, result validation time can easily overwhelm the verification process. For example consider a 4 way SMP platform with hyperthreaded processors with a total of 8 threads and hence 800 operations. The way we have arranged the algorithm and data structures allows us to easily do loop parallelization [15].

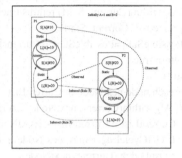

Fig. 2. Example of an actual processor bug

The phases of the algorithm are Warshall's algorithm, incremental graph closure and the rule algorithms given in section 3.3. The key observation is that in each case we always have no more than two nested for loops and there are no data dependences between iterations of the inner loop. The latter is true because no two iterations change the same node in the graph and hence never write to the same element in the adjacency matrix. We are not worried about considering edges added in previous iterations of the inner for loop of step 4 (of the algorithm in 3.3) because such edges are considered in subsequent iterations, since we iterate to a fix point. Also the same element in the *Changed* vector is not accessed by two different inner loop iterations. Hence we can parallelize by distributing different iterations of the inner for loop in each step across processors. Since each inner for loop iterates over all nodes in the graph, this leads to a convenient data partitioning. We allocate each CPU running the verification algorithm a disjoint subset of nodes in the graph. Each CPU executes the inner for loop in each phase only on nodes that it owns. Note that each CPU still needs to synchronize with all other CPUs after completion of the inner for loop in each case (this is similar to the INDEPENDENT FORALL construct in High Performance Fortran).

5 Implementation

Intel's verification environment spans both architecture validation (Pre Silicon on RTL models) as well as extensive testing post silicon with the processor in an actual platform [16]. The algorithm described in this paper has been implemented in an Intel RIT generator, used by verification teams across multiple Intel architectures (Itanium, IA-32

```
Algorithm PrintSomeCycle:
PossibleStart={g⁻¹(i) | A[i,i] = 1}
while PossibleStart is not empty
  StartNode=any node in PossibleStart
  PossibleStart=PossibleStart -{StartNode}
  CurrentList={g⁻¹(i) | A[i,i] = 1} - StartNode
  GetCycleEdge(startNode,startNode)
end while
Function GetCycleEdge:
GetCycleEdge(node Start, node Current)
If Algorithm(Current, Start) returns true
  print edge (Current, Start)
  PossibleStart=PossibleStart -{Current}
  return true
end If
for each node nextNode in CurrentList
  If Algorithm(Current, nextNode) returns true
    CurrentList = CurrentList - {nextNode}
    If GetCycleEdge(Start, nextNode) returns true
      print edge (Current, nextNode)
      PossibleStart=PossibleStart -{Current}
      return true
    end If
  end If
end for
return false
```

Fig. 3. Debug Algorithm

and 64-bit IA-32). Although in the architecture validation (pre silicon on RTL simulators) environment direct visibility into load and store execution allows simpler tools to be built, it has been used in a limited fashion to generate tests that are subsequently run on RTL simulators. The results are then checked by the algorithm to find bugs. The greatest success of the tool has been in the Post Silicon Environment, where the execution speed available (compared to RTL simulations) allows the tool to quickly run a large number of random tests and discover memory ordering issues on processors. In figure 2 we show an example of an incorrect execution corresponding to an actual bug found by this tool. The problem was subsequently traced to incorrect design in the CPU of the locking primitive for certain corner cases.

In the Post Silicon environment the tool has been written to run directly on the Device Under Test(DUT). This was made possible by running it as a process on a deviceless Linux kernel which is booted on the target. The primary advantage of this model is speed and adaptability where the RIT tool directly detects its underlying hardware, generates and executes the appropriate tests and then verifies the result with no communication overhead.Another not so apparent but important advantage is *scaling*. As we anticipate future processors to increase the number of available threads, the tool scales seamlessly by not only running tests on the increased number of threads but also using all available threads to run the checking algorithm itself. This is also the reason why we have paid so much attention to parallelization in this work. That is to allow the algorithm to bootstrap on future generations of multi threaded processors. We point out here that the test generation phase is also parallelized in the tool to make optimal use of resources and achieve the best speedup.

Implementation Environment: The algorithm is implemented in C and architecture dependent assembly that runs on a scaled down version of the Linux kernel. We have chosen to use the Linux process model (avoiding other threading models for simplicity) with shared memory segments for inter process communication. We have hand parallelized the loops using the data distribution concepts described in section 4. This allows us to use off the shelf compilers such as those in standard Linux distributions and work across all the platforms that Linux supports.

Exploiting SIMD: The key kernel used in the iterative phase of our algorithm is *Subsume*. This is called at least once for every edge added to the graph and improving its performance is clearly beneficial. The implementation for $Subsume(x, y)$ is $\forall z \in \{1..n\} A[x, z] = A[x, z] \vee A[y, z]$. Another way of looking at it is as the logical 'OR' of two binary vectors $A[x, .] = A[x, .] \vee A[y, .]$. This could have taken as many as n operations in the most obvious implementation, but we instead chose to use Single Instruction Multiple Data (SIMD) extensions available in both the IA-32 [8] and Itanium [9] instruction sets. These enable us to perform the subsume operation upto 128 bits at a time providing a 128 times speedup to the implementation of *Subsume*. This is also the only place in our tool where we have IA-32 and Itanium specific verification code. The option to use SIMD to speedup the algorithm is really a consequence of the carefully selected data structures and the time consuming graph manipulations being reduced to a single well defined kernel.

Extendibility: We support multiple architectures in our implementation by having as much architecture independent code as possible. This means we need to only recompile the tool to target different architectures. In addition we have made the tool independent of the memory consistency model it is verifying by taking as input to the tool a description of the local ordering rules, as described in definition 1 in a standard format rulefile. This allows us to verify different consistency models (Itanium and different generations of IA-32) and adapt to changes in the consistency models that may happen in the future.

Debug Support: A critical requirement in CPU verification is that failures should be root caused to bugs as soon as possible. Ease of debugging failures is very important in all of Intel's verification methodologies. A failure in our case is a cycle in the graph. The problem with our algorithm formulation is that the final cycle is detected only in terms of *which* nodes are participating in the cycle. There is no way to determine from the closed form adjacency matrix what is the *ordering* of nodes in the cycle. Also the nature of the basic algorithm often leads to more than one cycle in long tests. To work around this problem without sacrificing algorithm efficiency we use a backtracking algorithm described in Figure 3 that prints all the detected cycles. The only change we need to make to the algorithm described in section 3.3 is that it takes as parameter an edge e. Whenever the *AddEdge* function adds the edge e during execution of the algorithm we return true indicating that this edge is actually added by one of the rules in the algorithm. We also return the reason for addition of this edge which allows all edges to be labelled with the corresponding rule, a good aid to debug. Note that the backtrack though costly is only run in case of failure which should be rare.

6 Performance and Scaling

We include some performance data to support our claims of efficient algorithm design. In figure 4(a) we show how the cost of running the algorithm grows with increasing number of nodes. Clearly the algorithm scales well. In figure 4(b) we show how the speedup increases when we use more processors to run the algorithm while keeping the problem size (number of graph nodes) same. The near to linear speedup (ideal) indicates that the parallelization decisions have been correctly made and load balance the problem well among different processors. All the presented scalability data was taken on an 8 way 1.2 Ghz Intel®Xeon®[5] processor platform running Linux.

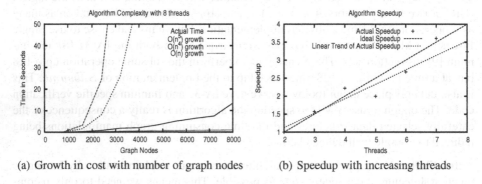

(a) Growth in cost with number of graph nodes   (b) Speedup with increasing threads

Fig. 4. Algorithm Performance

7 Limitations

Although our algorithm is general enough to cover the memory consistency models we need to check for at Intel, it has certain limitations and assumptions stated here. We assume that all stores in the test to the same location write unique values. Thus we are never in a position where we need to reconcile a load with multiple stores for rule 2. This does not affect our coverage of the logic that is responsible for maintaining memory ordering, since that logic has no dependency on the actual data values

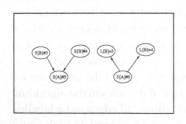

Fig. 5. A missed edge

The algorithm assumes store atomicity, which is necessary for Axiom 3. However it supports slightly relaxed consistency models which allow a load to observe a local store which precedes it in program order, before it is globally observed. Thus we cover all coherence protocols that support the notion of relaxed write atomicity which can be defined as : No store is visible to any *other* processor *before* the execution point of the store. Based on our discussion with Intel microarchitects we determined that all IA-32 and *current* generations of Itanium microprocessors support this due to identifiable and atomic global observation points for any store. This is mostly due to the shared bus and single chipset. For Itanium we can still adapt to the case where stores are not atomically observed by other processors by checking only store releases

---

[5] Intel® Xeon® is a trademark or registered trademark of Intel Corporation or its subsidiaries in the United States and other countries.

[12]. Another approach is to split stores into one for each observing processor and appropriately modify rule 2. This would lead to a worse case degradation of checking performance by a factor equal to the number of processors.

Last, the algorithm does approximate checking only (since it is a polynomial time solution to an NP-Hard problem). It does not completely check for Axiom 3, since it does not attempt to order all stores and thereby find additional inferred edges which could lead to a cycle. An example taken from [1] is shown in 5. The algorithm is unable to deduce the ordering from $S[A]\#6$ to $S[A]\#5$ although that is the only possibility given that the loads to location B read different values. Adding a similar mirrored set of nodes, 2 stores to location C before $S[A]\#6$ and two loads from location C after $S[A]\#5$ give an example violation of the TSO model which is missed by this algorithm. However, we hypothesize that only a small fraction of bugs actually lead to such cases and these are ultimately found by sufficient random testing which will show them up in a form the algorithm can detect, another reason why we place so much emphasis on test tool performance.

8   Conclusion

We have described an algorithm that does efficient polynomial time memory consistency verification. Our algorithm meets its stated goals of efficiency and generality. It is implemented in a tool that is used across multiple groups in Intel to verify increasingly complex microprocessors. It has been appreciated across the corporation for finding a number of bugs that are otherwise hard to find and point to extremely subtle flaws in implementing the memory consistency model. We hope to work further in decreasing the cost of the algorithm by by studying the nature of the graphs generated and considering more fine grained parallelization opportunities.

Acknowledgments. We would like to thank our colleagues Jeffrey Wilson and Sreenivasa Guttal for their contribution to the tool, Mrinal Deo and Harish Kumar for their assistance with memory consistency models and Hemanthkumar Sivaraj for giving valuable feedback during the initial stages of algorithm design.

References

1. Sudheendra Hangal, Durgam Vahia, Chaiyasit Manovit, and Juin-Yeu Joseph Lu. Tsotool: A program for verifying memory systems using the memory consistency model. In *ISCA '04: Proceedings of the 31st annual international symposium on Computer architecture*, page 114, Washington, DC, USA, 2004. IEEE Computer Society.
2. Phillip B. Gibbons and Ephraim Korach. The complexity of sequential consistency. In *SPDP:Proceedings of the Fourth IEEE Symposium on Parallel and Distributed Processing*, pages 317–325, 1992.
3. Jason F. Cantin, Mikko H. Lipasti, and James E. Smith. The complexity of verifying memory coherence. In *SPAA '03: Proceedings of the fifteenth annual ACM symposium on Parallel algorithms and architectures*, pages 254–255, New York, NY, USA, 2003. ACM Press.
4. Cantin, J. F., Lipasti, M. H., and Smith, J. E. "The Complexity of Verifying Memory Coherence". In *Proceedings of the fifteenth annual ACM symposium on Parallel algorithms and architectures (SPAA)*, pages 254 – 255, San Diego, 2003.

5. Chaiyasit Manovit and Sudheendra Hangal. Efficient algorithms for verifying memory consistency. In *SPAA'05: Proceedings of the 17th annual ACM symposium on Parallelism in algorithms and architectures*, pages 245–252, New York, NY, USA, 2005. ACM Press.

6. Sarita V. Adve and Kourosh Gharachorloo. Shared memory consistency models: A tutorial. *Computer*, 29(12):66–76, 1996.

7. Kourosh Gharachorloo, Daniel Lenoski, James Laudon, Phillip B. Gibbons, Anoop Gupta, and John L. Hennessy. Memory consistency and event ordering in scalable shared-memory multiprocessors. In *25 Years ISCA: Retrospectives and Reprints*, pages 376–387, 1998.

8. *IA-32 Intel Architecture Software Developer's Manual, Volume 3: System Programming Guide*. Intel Corporation, 2005. URL: http://www.intel.com/design/pentium4/manuals/index_new.htm.

9. *Intel Itanium Architecture Volume 1:Application Architecture*. Intel Corporation, 2005. URL: http://www.intel.com/design/itanium/manuals/iiasdmanual.htm.

10. Harold W. Cain, Mikko H. Lipasti, and Ravi Nair. Constraint graph analysis of multithreaded programs. In *PACT '03: Proceedings of the 12th International Conference on Parallel Architectures and Compilation Techniques*, page 4, Washington, DC, USA, 2003. IEEE Computer Society.

11. Ganesh Gopalakrishnan, Yue Yang, and Hemanthkumar Sivaraj. Qb or not qb: An efficient execution verification tool for memory orderings. In *CAV*, pages 401–413, 2004.

12. *A Formal Specification of Intel Itanium Processor Family Memory Ordering*. Intel Corporation, 2005. URL: http://www.intel.com/design/itanium/downloads/251429.htm

13. Stephen Warshall. A theorem on boolean matrices. *J. ACM*, 9(1):11–12, 1962.

14. Charles J. Fleckenstein John C. Huang Amitabha Roy, Stephan Zeisset. Fast and Generalized Polynomial Time Memory Consistency Verification. Technical Report arXiv:cs.AR/0605039, May 2006.

15. Utpal K. Banerjee. *Loop Parallelization*. Kluwer Academic Publishers, Norwell, MA, USA, 1994.

16. Bob Bentley. Validating the intel pentium 4 microprocessor. In *DAC '01: Proceedings of the 38th conference on Design automation*, pages 244–248, New York, NY, USA, 2001. ACM Press.

Programs with Lists Are Counter Automata*

Ahmed Bouajjani[2], Marius Bozga[1], Peter Habermehl[2], Radu Iosif[1],
Pierre Moro[2], and Tomáš Vojnar[3]

[1] VERIMAG, 2 av. de Vignate, F-38610 Gières
{iosif, bozga}@imag.fr
[2] LIAFA, Paris University 7, Case 7014, 2, place Jussieu, F-75251 Paris Cedex 05
{Ahmed.Bouajjani, Peter.Habermehl, Pierre.Moro}@liafa.jussieu.fr
[3] FIT, Brno University of Technology, Božetěchova 2, CZ-61266, Brno
vojnar@fit.vutbr.cz

Abstract. We address the verification problem of programs manipulating one-selector linked data structures. We propose a new automated approach for checking safety and termination for these programs. Our approach is based on using counter automata as accurate abstract models: control states correspond to abstract heap graphs where list segments without sharing are collapsed, and counters are used to keep track of the number of elements in these segments. This allows to apply automatic analysis techniques and tools for counter automata in order to verify list programs. We show the effectiveness of our approach, in particular by verifying automatically termination of some sorting programs.

1 Introduction

The design of automatic verification methods for programs manipulating dynamic linked data structures is a challenging problem. Indeed, the analysis of the behaviour of such programs requires reasoning about complex transformations of data structures involving both creation and deletion of objects as well as modifications of the links between them (pointer manipulations). The heap of such programs may have in fact an arbitrary size and shape (a graph structure). There are several approaches for tackling this problem addressing different subclasses of programs and using different kinds of formalisms for representing and reasoning about infinite sets of heap structures, e.g., [19,17,21,8].

We consider in this paper the class of programs manipulating linked data structures with a single data-field selector. It corresponds to programs manipulating linked lists with the possibility of sharing and circularities. We propose a new approach for the automatic verification of such programs which is mainly based on using counter automata as accurate abstract (infinite-state) models. These models can be used for checking both safety properties and termination of the considered programs using techniques such as (abstract) symbolic reachability analysis (for safety and invariance checking) and automatic generation of decreasing ranking functions (for termination checking).

Let us present in more details the proposed approach. We start from the observation that if we do not consider garbage (parts of the heap not reachable from the pointer

---

* This work was supported in part by the French Ministry of Research (ACI project Securité Informatique) and the Czech Grant Agency (projects GA CR 102/04/0780 and 102/03/D211).

variables of the program), the heap graph is always a finite collection of graphs of a special form close to a tree: it is either a tree (where edges are directed towards the root) or a set of trees having all their roots connected to a simple cycle. The number of such graphs is infinite, but it can be proved that for each of them, the number of vertices where sharing occurs is bounded by the number of pointer variables of the program.

Then, for data-insensitive programs (i.e., programs not accessing nor modifying the data stored in lists as, e.g., a list reversal program), a natural abstraction consists in mapping each sequence of elements between two sharing points into an abstract sequence of some (fixed) bounded size. However, for each given value of the bound, this abstraction is obviously not precise in general. In order to define a precise abstraction, we need in fact to reason about the size of each sequence between two sharing points. This leads to the idea of using counters in order to keep this information in the abstract model (and therefore to use counter automata as abstract models).

In fact, considering counter automata-based models has several advantages. Not only does it allow to define accurate abstractions, it allows us also to handle quantitative properties depending on the sizes of some parts of the heap. Thus, we can handle programs with integer variables whose value is somehow related to the contents of the lists (e.g., to their length). Moreover, it provides a powerful way for checking termination which typically requires reasoning about decreasing values (e.g., the size of the part of the list to be treated).

A first contribution of the paper is to define an abstraction mapping from data-insensitive programs to counter automata for which we prove that the (concrete) program and its abstraction are *bisimilar*. This result is interesting since it means that our abstraction preserves all properties of the class of data-insensitive programs. The control states of the built automaton correspond to abstract shapes (heap graphs where sequences between shared points are reduced to single vertices), and each transition corresponds to the execution of a program statement. It represents a modification in the shape together with a modification on the counters (attached to vertices abstracting sequences between sharing nodes).

The control structure of the built counter automata can be arbitrary in general. However, it turns out that these automata have an important property: we prove that if we consider the evolution of the sum of all counters, the effect of executing any control loop is to increment this sum by a constant which depends on the program. We use this fact to establish a new decidability result for list programs: for every given (data-insensitive) list program, if the control structure of the generated counter automaton has no nested loops, the verification problems of safety properties and termination are both decidable.

Subsequently, we go further by considering the issue of data-sensitivity. We consider the class of programs manipulating objects ranging over a potentially infinite data domain supplied with an ordering relation, and we assume that the only allowed operation on these data values is the comparison w.r.t. this ordering relation. This class of programs includes, for instance, sorting programs. We extend our previous abstraction principle to the heap graphs of these programs by taking into account (in addition to the size) some information about the order of the elements in the abstracted sequences between sharing points, and we provide a construction which associates with each program a counter automaton-based abstract model. We show that this abstraction is sound w.r.t. the choice of ordering predicates.

Finally, we show the application of our approach on three examples of programs (list reversal, insertion sort, and bubble sort). We have derived systematically their counter automata models, and then we used (1) our ARMC tool [9] (and some compile-time techniques) for checking safety properties, and (2) the Terminator tool based on [12] for termination.

Related Work. Programs manipulating singly-linked lists have gained a lot of attention within the past two years, as shown by the fairly large number of recent publications on the subject [4,6,18,3,8]. Interestingly, the idea of abstracting away all the list segments with no incoming edges is common to many of these works, even though they are independent and use different approaches and frameworks (e.g., static analysis [18], predicate abstraction [3] symbolic reachability analysis [4] and proof search [6]). The fact that the number of sharing points in abstract heap structures is bounded by the number of variables in the program is also behind the techniques proposed in [18,8].

In [10], the authors use an abstract shape model with counters, but their concerns are mostly related to the decidability of a specification logic. The approach that is the closest to ours is [4]. However, it is rather pointed towards showing particular properties such as absence of segmentation faults and memory leak errors, than checking general safety properties, and the work does not address the problem of verifying termination. Moreover, the work reported in [4] offers less automation of the verification than ours. Recently, the same authors have started independently a work [15] on automatic construction of models based on counter automata similar to our approach. The use of ordering predicates in order to handle sorting programs is similar to the one considered in [14,21] based on the shape analysis approach. Termination is tackled by works such as [22,3]. In all of these works, ranking functions must be given manually, whereas our approach is fully automated.

2   Programs with Lists

In this section we define a model for programs manipulating dynamic list data structures. We consider that lists are implemented using reference (pointer) data types with one selector (next) field, as it is the case in most object-oriented imperative programming languages (e.g., Java, C, C++). For the time being we consider programs without recursion or concurrency constructs, therefore all variables are assumed to be global. In addition to the list data structures, the programs can have integer variables. Examples of such programs include: list reversals, list insertion procedures, sorting procedures, programs counting the elements in a list, etc.

2.1   Syntactic Definitions

We consider imperative programs working with a set of pointer variables *PVar* and a set of integer counter variables *IVar*. The pointer variables refer to list cells. Pointers can be used in assignments such as u := null, u:= w and u := w.next, selector updates u.next := w and u.next := null, and new cell creation u:= new.

Counters can be incremented i := i + 1, decremented i := i - 1 and reset i :=
0. The control structure is composed of iteration (while) statements and conditionals
(if-then-else). The guards of the control constructs are pointer equality u = w, data
comparisons u.data <= v.data, zero tests for counters i = 0 and boolean combinations of the above. A program is said to be *data insensitive* if it does not use guards
of the form u.data <= v.data. A program is said to be *flat* if the body of any of its
while loops does not contain (while) statements nor conditionals (if-then-else).

An example is the list reversal program in Figure 1.
To simplify the definition of the operational semantics
below, we consider that all programs are precompiled
as follows. Each pointer assignment of the form u: =
new, u := w or u := w.next is immediately preceded
by an assignment of the form u := null. A pointer assignment of the form u := u.next is turned into v :=
u; u := null; u := v.next, possibly introducing a
fresh variable v. Each pointer assignment of the form

1:	while i ≠ null do
2:	k := i.next;
3:	i.next := j;
4:	j := i;
5:	i := k;
6:	od

Fig. 1. List Reversing

u.next := w is immediately preceded by u.next := null. In addition, the programs
are allowed to increment, decrement and reset the counter variables that range over integers. Conditional statements involve two kinds of tests: structural tests u = v and u =
null testing for equality and definedness of pointer variables, comparisons of the data
stored in the lists u.data ≤ v.data, and zero tests i = 0.

2.2 Concrete Operational Semantics

In order to define the concrete semantics of programs with lists, we have to formalize
the notion of *heap*. In principle, a heap is a graph in which each node has at most
one successor. In addition, some nodes are designated by special labels (variables from
PVar). If all the edges are reversed, one can imagine a heap as a set of disjoint trees, in
which, for each tree there might be an extra edge from an arbitrary node back to the root.

In the rest of the paper, for a set A we denote by $A_\perp$ the set $A \cup \{\perp\}$. The element $\perp$
is used to denote that a (partial) function is undefined at a given point, e.g., $f(x) = \perp$.
Also, for a function f we denote by $f \downarrow_A$ the projection of f on A i.e. $f \cap A \times A$.

Definition 1. *Let* $\langle \mathfrak{D}, \preceq \rangle$ *be an infinite totally ordered set, and PVar a set of pointer
variables. A heap is a tuple* $H = \langle N, S, V, D \rangle$, *where N is a finite set of nodes,* $S : N \to N_\perp$
is a successor function, $V : PVar \to N_\perp$ *is a function associating nodes with variables,
and* $D : N \to \mathfrak{D}$ *is a function associating each node with a data element.*

The set of all heaps using variables from *PVar* is denoted by $\mathcal{H}(PVar)$. We denote
$S(n_1) = n_2$ in H by $n_1 \xrightarrow{H} n_2$, and $u \xrightarrow{H} n : \exists m . V(u) = m \wedge m \xrightarrow{H} n$. H might be
omitted when it is clear from the context. We denote by $\xrightarrow{*}{H}$ the reflexive and transitive
closure of $\xrightarrow{H}$. A node n is said to be a *cut point* in H, denoted as $cut_H(n)$, if either it has
two predecessors or it is pointed to by a variable. Formally, $cut_H(n) : \exists n_1, n_2 \in N . n_1 \neq
n_2 \wedge S(n_1) = S(n_2) = n \vee \exists u \in Var . V(u) = n$.

The *state* of a program with lists is a triple $\langle l, \iota, H \rangle$ where $l \in Lab$ is the current
program label, $\iota : IVar \to \mathbb{Z}$ is the current valuation of counter variables, and $H \in$

$\mathcal{H}(PVar)$ is the current heap configuration. Each assignment modifies the state as follows: $\langle l, \iota, H \rangle \xrightarrow{l:s;l'} \langle l', \iota', H' \rangle$, where l' is the label of the next statement, ι' is the new valuation of counters, computed as usual, and H' is a heap configuration such that $H \xrightarrow{s} H'$, in conformance with the rules in Figure 2. Due to lack of space, the missing rules are deferred to the extended version of the paper [7].

The semantics described here is based on *garbage collection*. As a result of removing a node from the heap, other nodes might become unreachable from the pointer variables. This set of nodes, whose lifetime *depends exclusively* on $n \in N$, is denoted as $dep_H(n)$. After each step, these nodes are removed.

H_{err} is a special sink heap configuration, attained as the result of a null pointer dereference. A pointer equality test $u = v$ evaluates to true in a heap $H = \langle N, S, V \rangle$ if and only if $V(u) = V(v)$. Also, $u = \text{null}$ is true if and only if $V(u) = \bot$.

$$\frac{V(u) = \bot}{H \xrightarrow{u := \text{null}} H} \; C_1 \qquad \frac{\exists w \in PVar \setminus \{u\} \;.\; w \xrightarrow[H]{*} V(u)}{H \xrightarrow{u := \text{null}} \langle N, S, V[u \to \bot], D \rangle} \; C_2$$

$$\frac{V(u) = n \in N \qquad \forall w \in PVar \setminus \{u\} \;.\; \neg w \xrightarrow[H]{*} n \qquad N' = N \setminus dep_H(n)}{H \xrightarrow{u := \text{null}} \langle N', S\!\downarrow_{N'}, V\!\downarrow_{N'}, D\!\downarrow_{N'} \rangle} \; C_3$$

Fig. 2. Concrete Semantics of Heap Updates

3   Counter Automata

A counter automaton with n counters is a tuple $A = \langle Q, X, \to \rangle$, where Q is a finite set of control states, $X = \{x_1, \ldots, x_n\}$ are the counter variables and $\to \in Q \times \Phi \times Q$ are the transitions, where Φ is the set of Presburger formulae [20] with free variables from $\{x_i, x_i' \mid 1 \le i \le n\}$. A configuration of a counter automaton with n counters is a tuple $\langle q, \nu \rangle$, where ν is a mapping from X to $\mathbb{N}$. The set of all configurations is denoted by C. The transition relation $\xrightarrow{C} \subseteq C \times C$ is defined by $(q, \nu) \xrightarrow{C} (q', \nu')$ iff there exists a transition $q \xrightarrow{\varphi} q'$ such that if σ is an assignment of the free variables of φ ($FV(\varphi)$) where $\sigma(x) = \nu(x)$ and $\sigma(x') = \nu'(x)$, we have that $\varphi(FV(\varphi)\sigma)$ holds and $\nu(x) = \nu'(x)$, for all variables x with $x' \notin FV(\varphi)$. A *run* of A is a sequence of configurations $(q_0, \nu_0), (q_1, \nu_1), (q_2, \nu_2) \ldots$ such that $(q_i, \nu_i) \xrightarrow{C} (q_{i+1}, \nu_{i+1})$, for each $i \ge 0$.

The following definition introduces a novel class of counter automata that is useful for our purposes:

Definition 2. *Let* $A = \langle Q, X, \to \rangle$ *be a counter automaton, where* $X = \{x_1, \ldots, x_n\}$ *are counter variables that range over non-negative integers. A is said to be* linear *if all its transitions are of the form:* $\varphi(X) \wedge \bigwedge_{1 \le i \le n} x_i' = f_i(X)$, *where* φ *is a formula of Presburger arithmetic, and* $f_i = \sum_{j=1}^{n} a_{ij} x_j + b_i$, $1 \le i \le n$ *are linear functions with integer coefficients. Moreover, A is said to be* non-negative *if* $a_{ij} \ge 0$, *for all* $1 \le i, j \le n$.

A is also said to be restrictive *if, there exists a constant* $\alpha \in \mathbb{N}$ *such that for each control state* $q \in Q$, *on each run* π *that visits* q, *the sum of values taken by the counters,* $\sum_{i=1}^{n} x_i$, *increases by at most* α *between any two consecutive times when the control state is* q.

The control graph of a counter automaton A is the graph having as vertices the set Q of control states, and, for any two states q and q', there is an edge between q and q' in the control graph if and only if there exists a transition $q \xrightarrow{\varphi} q'$ in A. A counter automaton is said to be *flat* if its control graph has no nested loops. We can prove:

Theorem 1. *The problems of reachability and termination for flat linear non-negative restrictive counter automata are decidable.*

4   Abstract Semantics of Programs with Lists

A common way of representing heaps compactly, consists in mapping an entire list segment with no incoming edges into a special (abstract) node. This idea constitutes also the basis of our abstraction. Let $\mathcal{N}$ be a set of *abstract nodes* and X be a set of *counter variables*, one for each node. We shall first define the abstract structure of heaps.

Definition 3. *An* abstract structure *is a tuple* $\overline{H} = \langle \overline{N}, \overline{S}, \overline{V} \rangle$, *where:*

- $\overline{N} \subseteq \mathcal{N}$ *is the set of abstract nodes, and*
- $\overline{S} : \overline{N} \to \overline{N}_{\perp}, \overline{V} : PVar \to \overline{N}_{\perp}$, *are the successor and variable mappings,*

An abstract structure is moreover said to be in normal form *if, for each* $n \in \overline{N}$, *there exists* $u \in PVar$ *such that* $u \xrightarrow[\overline{H}]{*} n$, *and* n *is a cut point in* $\overline{H}$.

Intuitively, each abstract node corresponds to a set of concrete nodes, and the counter associated with it in X keeps track of the number of nodes in this set. For abstract structures in normal form, we do not allow sequences of successive abstract node that are neither pointed by a variable, nor have the indegree greater than one. This condition is needed in order to ensure that any such abstract structure defined over a finite set of variables is finite. $\mathcal{H}(PVar)$ denotes the set of all abstract structures with variables from $PVar$. A result similar to the following has been also proved in [4,18]:

Lemma 1. *Let* $PVar = \{u_1, \ldots, u_n\}$ *be a set of variables, and* $\overline{H} = \langle \overline{N}, \overline{S}, \overline{V} \rangle$ *be an abstract structure in normal form such that* $dom(\overline{V}) \subseteq PVar$. *Then,* $\|\overline{N}\| \le 2n$ (*cf. [18]*). *As a consequence, the number of such heaps is bounded asymptotically by* $(2n)^{2n}$, *and the bound is tight.*

Let us define now a first abstraction function, denoted by α_s, that maps concrete heaps into abstract structures. Given a concrete heap $H = \langle N, S, V, D \rangle$, let $\rhd_H \subseteq N \times N$ be a relation on the set of nodes, defined as: $n_1 \rhd_H n_2 : n_1 \xrightarrow[H]{} n_2 \wedge \neg cut(n_2)$. We denote by $\sim_H$ the reflexive, symmetric and transitive closure of $\rhd_H$. The H subscript shall be further omitted for simplicity. For a node $n \in N$, we denote by $[n]$ the equivalence class of n with respect to $\sim$, also referred to as a *list segment*. The *quotient heap* $H_{/\sim} = \langle N_{/\sim}, S_{/\sim}, V_{/\sim} \rangle$ is defined as follows:

- $N_{/\sim} = \{[n] \mid n \in N\}$,
- for all $n, m \in N$, $S_{/\sim}([n]) = [m]$ iff $\exists n_0 \in [n] \; \exists m_0 \in [m] \; . \; S(n_0) = m_0 \wedge cut_H(m_0)$,
- for all $u \in PVar$, $n \in N$, $V_{/\sim}(u) = [n]$ iff $V(u) \in [n]$, and
- $S_{/\sim}$ and $V_{/\sim}$ are undefined, otherwise.

Note that $S_{/\sim}$ and $V_{/\sim}$ are well defined partial functions. For assume that for some $n \in N$, $S_{/\sim}$ maps $[n]$ into two different equivalence classes, call them $[m]$ and $[p]$. This would imply the existence of two nodes $n_1, n_2 \in [n]$ such that $n_1 \xrightarrow{*} m_0$ and $n_2 \xrightarrow{*} p_0$, for some $m_0 \in [m]$ and some $p_0 \in [p]$. Since either $n_1 \xrightarrow{*} n_2$, or $n_2 \xrightarrow{*} n_1$, there must exist a node in $[n]$ with two distinct direct successors, which contradicts the well-formedness of S. The argument for $V_{/\sim}$ is straightforward.

Definition 4. *Let $H = \langle N, S, V, D \rangle$ be a concrete heap and $H_{/\sim} = \langle N_{/\sim}, S_{/\sim}, V_{/\sim} \rangle$ its quotient. An abstract structure $\overline{H} = \langle \overline{N}, \overline{S}, \overline{V} \rangle$ is said to be a* structural abstraction *of H if and only if there exists a bijective function $\beta : N_{/\sim} \cup \{\bot\} \rightarrow \overline{N} \cup \{\bot\}$ such that $\beta(\bot) = \bot$, and for all $u \in PVar$: $\overline{S}(\beta([n])) = \beta(S_{/\sim}([n]))$ and $\overline{V}(u) = \beta(V_{/\sim}(u))$.*

Two abstract structures that differ only in the naming of nodes and counter variables are semantically equivalent, in the sense that they are abstractions of the same set of concrete heaps. In practice, this increases the number of abstract structures generated by a symbolic state exploration tool. This problem can be overcome by choosing a canonical representation of abstract structures, as described in, e.g., [16].

We define the structural abstraction function $\alpha_s : \mathcal{H}(PVar) \rightarrow \overline{\mathcal{H}}(PVar)$, $\alpha_s(H) = \overline{H}$, iff $\overline{H}$ is the canonical representative of a structural abstraction of H. Dually, the *concretisation* of an abstract structure $\overline{H}$ is the set of concrete heaps whose structural abstraction is $\overline{H}$, i.e. $\gamma_s(\overline{H}) = \{H \mid \alpha_s(H) = \overline{H}\}$.

Note that according to Definition 4, $\alpha_s(H)$ is an abstract structure in normal form. For reasons that will become clear later, we need to extend the notion of concretisation to abstract structures not in normal form. Let $\overline{H} = \langle \overline{N}, \overline{S}, \overline{V} \rangle$ be an abstract structure not necessarily in normal form, and $v : \overline{N} \rightarrow \mathbb{N}$ a mapping of nodes to natural numbers. By $v(\overline{H})$ we denote the set of concrete heaps obtained by replacing each node $n \in \overline{N}$ by a list segment of length $v(n)$, and data arbitrarily chosen from $\mathfrak{D}$. In particular, mapping one node into zero makes the node disappear in the concretization, and all its predecessors automatically point to its successor. Then, $\gamma_s(\overline{H}) = \bigcup \{v(\overline{H}) \mid v : \overline{N} \rightarrow \mathbb{N}\}$. Notice that if $\overline{H}$ is in normal form, the two definitions coincide.

4.1 Data Insensitive Programs

This section is devoted to the description of counter automata that abstract the behaviour of the programs with lists. We formalize the correctness of our construction by proving bisimulation between the semantics of a list program and the semantics of a counter automaton. This entails the strong preservation of temporal logic properties. In particular, safety and termination are strongly preserved by the counter automaton, meaning that one can accept and/or refute them based on the behaviour of the latter.

Consider a list program with k pointer variables and l counter variables, i.e. $\|PVar\| = k$ and $\|IVar\| = l$. We construct a counter automaton $A = \langle Q, X, \xrightarrow{s} \rangle$ with $2k + l$ counters as follows. The control states Q of the counter automaton are elements of the set $Lab \times (\overline{\mathcal{H}}(PVar) \cup \{H_{err}\})$. Let $\mathcal{N} = \bigcup \{\overline{N} \mid \langle \overline{N}, \overline{S}, \overline{V} \rangle \in \overline{\mathcal{H}}(PVar)\}$ be the set of nodes used in the structural abstraction. The counters are $X = \{x_n \mid n \in \mathcal{N}\} \cup IVar$, one for each node, and including the counter variables from the original program. The transitions are given by the triples $q \xrightarrow{\varphi} q'$ with $q = \langle l, \overline{H} \rangle$, $q' = \langle l', \overline{H'} \rangle$ such that there is a statement $l : s; l'$ in the program and the relation $\overline{H} \xrightarrow[s]{\varphi} \overline{H'}$ is described by the structural rules in Figure 3. Due to lack of space, the missing rules are deferred to the extended version of the paper [7].

In order to simplify the treatment of the different cases, we have introduced two low-level operations, that perform merging and splitting of abstract nodes (Figure 3). Intuitively, we need to perform merging of two abstract nodes n and m ($\mu(\overline{H}, n, m)$) in order to re-normalize the abstract structure, after a destructive update.

Lemma 2. *If $\overline{H} = \langle \overline{N}, \overline{S}, \overline{V} \rangle$ is an abstract structure, and $n, m \in \overline{N}$ such that $\overline{S}(n) = m$ and m is not a cut point in $\overline{H}$, then $\gamma_s(\overline{H}) = \gamma_s(\mu(\overline{H}, n, m))$.*

$$\frac{\exists w \in Var \setminus \{u\} \quad \overline{V}(w) = \overline{V}(u) \neq \bot}{\overline{H} \xrightarrow[u:=null]{true} \langle \overline{N}, \overline{S}, \overline{V}[u \rightarrow \bot] \rangle} A_2$$

$$\frac{\overline{V}(u) = n \in \overline{N} \quad \forall w \in Var \setminus \{u\} . \overline{V}(w) \neq n}{\exists m, p \in \overline{N} \setminus \{n\} . p \neq m \wedge \overline{S}(m) = \overline{S}(p) = n}{\overline{H} \xrightarrow[u:=null]{true} \langle \overline{N}, \overline{S}, \overline{V}[u \rightarrow \bot] \rangle} A_2'$$

$$\frac{\overline{V}(u) = n \in \overline{N} \quad \forall w \in Var \setminus \{u\} . \overline{V}(w) \neq n \quad \exists m \in \overline{N} \setminus \{n\} . \overline{S}(m) = n \quad \forall p \in \overline{N} \setminus \{n\} . \overline{S}(p) \neq n}{\overline{H} \xrightarrow[u:=null]{x_m' = x_m + x_n} \mu(\langle \overline{N}, \overline{S}, \overline{V}[u \rightarrow \bot] \rangle, m, n)} A_2''$$

$$\frac{\overline{V}(u) = n \in \overline{N} \quad \forall w \in Var \setminus \{u\} . w \xrightarrow[\overline{H}]{*} n \quad \overline{S}(n) \in \{\bot, n\} \quad \overline{N'} = \overline{N} \setminus \{n\}}{\overline{H} \xrightarrow[u:=null]{true} \langle \overline{N'}, \overline{S} \downarrow_{\overline{N'}}, \overline{V} \downarrow_{\overline{N'}} \rangle} A_3$$

$$\frac{\overline{V}(u) = n \in \overline{N} \quad \forall w \in Var \setminus \{u\} . w \xrightarrow[\overline{H}]{*} n \quad \overline{S}(n) = m \in \overline{N} \setminus \{n\} \quad \exists w \in Var \setminus \{u\} . \overline{V}(w) = m \quad \overline{N'} = \overline{N} \setminus \{n\}}{\overline{H} \xrightarrow[u:=null]{true} \langle \overline{N'}, \overline{S} \downarrow_{\overline{N'}}, \overline{V} \downarrow_{\overline{N'}} \rangle} A_3'$$

$$\frac{\overline{V}(u) = n \in \overline{N} \quad \forall w \in Var \setminus \{u\} . w \xrightarrow[\overline{H}]{*} n \quad \overline{S}(n) = m \in \overline{N} \setminus \{n\} \quad \forall w \in Var \setminus \{u\} . \overline{V}(w) \neq m \quad \exists p, q \in \overline{N} \setminus \{n\} . p \neq q \wedge \overline{S}(p) = m \wedge \overline{S}(q) = m \quad \overline{N'} = \overline{N} \setminus \{n\}}{\overline{H} \xrightarrow[u:=null]{true} \langle \overline{N'}, \overline{S} \downarrow_{\overline{N'}}, \overline{V} \downarrow_{\overline{N'}} \rangle} A_3''$$

$$\frac{\overline{V}(u) = n \in \overline{N} \quad \forall w \in Var \setminus \{u\} . w \xrightarrow[\overline{H}]{*} n \quad \overline{S}(n) = m \in \overline{N} \setminus \{n\} \quad \forall w \in Var \setminus \{u\} . \overline{V}(w) \neq m \quad \exists p \in \overline{N} \setminus \{n, m\} . \overline{S}(p) = m \quad \forall q \in \overline{N} \setminus \{n, p\} . \overline{S}(q) \neq m \quad \overline{N'} = \overline{N} \setminus \{n\}}{\overline{H} \xrightarrow[u:=null]{x_p' = x_p + x_m} \mu(\langle \overline{N'}, \overline{S} \downarrow_{\overline{N'}}, \overline{V} \downarrow_{\overline{N'}} \rangle, p, m)} A_3'''$$

$$\frac{\overline{V}(u) = n \in \overline{N} \quad \forall w \in Var \setminus \{u\} . w \xrightarrow[\overline{H}]{*} n \quad \overline{S}(n) = m \in \overline{N} \setminus \{n\} \quad \forall w \in Var \setminus \{u\} . \overline{V}(w) \neq m \quad \forall p \in \overline{N} \setminus \{n, m\} . \overline{S}(p) \neq m \quad \overline{N'} = \overline{N} \setminus \{n, m\}}{\overline{H} \xrightarrow[u:=null]{true} \langle \overline{N'}, \overline{S} \downarrow_{\overline{N'}}, \overline{V} \downarrow_{\overline{N'}} \rangle} A_3''''$$

Fig. 3. Counter Automaton Semantics Let $\overline{H} \triangleq \langle \overline{N}, \overline{S}, \overline{V} \rangle$. The merging function is $\mu : \mathcal{H}(Var) \times \mathcal{N} \times \mathcal{N} \rightarrow \mathcal{H}(Var)$ given by $\mu(\overline{H}, n, m) = \langle \overline{N'}, \overline{S} \downarrow_{\overline{N'}} [n \rightarrow \overline{S}(m)], \overline{V} \rangle$ where $\overline{N'} = \overline{N} \setminus \{m\}$. The splitting function is $\sigma : \mathcal{H}(Var) \times \mathcal{N} \times \mathcal{N} \rightarrow \mathcal{H}(Var)$ given by $\sigma(\overline{H}, n, m) = \langle \overline{N} \cup \{m\}, \overline{S'}, \overline{V} \rangle$ where $\overline{S'} = (\overline{S} \setminus \{(n, p) \mid n \xrightarrow[\overline{H}]{} p\}) \cup \{(m, p) \mid n \xrightarrow[\overline{H}]{} p\} \cup \{(n, m)\}$.

In the case of u := w.next, we need to split $(\sigma(\overline{H},n,m))$ the abstract node n, into two nodes n and m, based on whether the value of its corresponding counter is greater than one or one $(x_n = 1, x_n > 1)$.

Lemma 3. *If $\overline{H} = \langle \overline{N}, \overline{S}, \overline{V} \rangle$ is an abstract structure, and $n \in \overline{N}$, $m \notin \overline{N}$, then $\gamma_s(\overline{H}) = \gamma_s(\sigma(\overline{H},n,m))$.*

The semantics of conditional tests (u = v and u = null) is similar to the concrete case. More details of the translation can be found in the list reversal example in Fig. 4.

Now we can state the main theorem of this section. Given a data insensitive program P, let $\langle S, \xrightarrow{c} \rangle$ be its concrete semantics with set of states $S = Lab \times (IVar \to \mathbb{Z}) \times \mathcal{H}(PVar)$ and $\xrightarrow{c}$ its transition relation. Let $\overline{S} = Q \times (X \to \mathbb{Z})$ be the set of all configurations of the corresponding counter automaton and $\xrightarrow{s}$ its transition relation.

Theorem 2. $\langle S, \xrightarrow{c} \rangle$ *and* $\langle \overline{S}, \xrightarrow{s} \rangle$ *are bisimilar.*

List Reversal Example. Figure 4 shows the counter automaton for the list reversal program from Figure 1, started with a non-circular list pointed to by i, as input. The counter variable corresponding to each abstract node is depicted inside the node itself. For space reasons, only the control states where branching occurs are depicted.

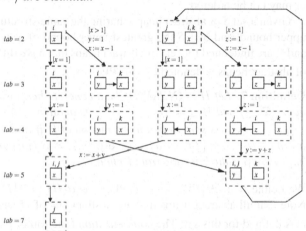

Fig. 4. Non-circular List Reversal

4.2 Ordered Data Programs

In this section we complete the definition of abstraction for programs with lists, by introducing an abstraction for heaps containing data from an ordered domain $\langle \mathcal{D}, \preceq \rangle$. More precisely, we need to abstract the order relations that may occur inside a list segment, and between two list segments.

Definition 5. *Let $H = \langle N, S, V, D \rangle$ be a concrete heap and $H_{/\sim}$ its quotient w.r.t. $\triangleright$ relation. If $R \subseteq N \times N$ is any relation on the set of nodes define, for any $[n], [m] \in N_{/\sim}$:*

- $o^R([n])$ *iff* $\forall n_1, n_2 \in [n] \,.\, n_1 \neq n_2 \,\wedge\, n_1 \triangleright n_2 \Rightarrow n_1 \, R \, n_2$
- $[n] \preceq_{ff}^R [m]$ *iff* $hd([n]) \, R \, hd([m])$
- $[n] \preceq_{fa}^R [m]$ *iff* $\forall n_1 \in [m] \,.\, hd([n]) \, R \, n_1$
- $[n] \preceq_{af}^R [m]$ *iff* $\forall n_1 \in [n] \,.\, n_1 \, R \, hd([n])$
- $[n] \preceq_{aa}^R [m]$ *iff* $\forall n_1 \in [n] \, \forall n_2 \in [m] \,.\, n_1 \, R \, n_2$

For a concrete heap $H = \langle N, S, V, D \rangle$, the relation $c \subseteq N \times N$ is defined as $n_1 \, c \, n_2$: $D(n_1) \preceq D(n_2)$. Then, $o^c([n])$ is true for a list segment $[n]$ iff all its elements are ordered w.r.t. $\preceq$. Similarly, $[n] \preceq^c_\diamond [m]$ for $\diamond \in \{ff, fa, af, aa\}$ iff the first (all) element(s) of $[n]$ is (are) less than the first (all) element(s) of $[m]$.

Definition 6. *An* abstract heap *is a tuple* $\widetilde{H} = \langle \overline{H}, o, \preceq_{ff}, \preceq_{fa}, \preceq_{af}, \preceq_{aa} \rangle$, *where* $\overline{H} = \langle \overline{N}, \overline{S}, \overline{V} \rangle$ *is an abstract structure,* $o \subseteq \overline{N}$ *is a unary ordering predicate, and* $\preceq_{ff, fa, af, aa} \subseteq \overline{N} \times \overline{N}$ *are binary ordering predicates.*

An abstract heap $\widetilde{H} = \langle \overline{H}, o, \preceq_{ff}, \preceq_{fa}, \preceq_{af}, \preceq_{aa} \rangle$ sharing the same structure $\overline{H} = \langle \overline{N}, \overline{S}, \overline{V} \rangle$ as another abstract heap $\widetilde{H'} = \langle \overline{H}, o', \preceq'_{ff}, \preceq'_{fa}, \preceq'_{af}, \preceq'_{aa} \rangle$, is said to be *more precise*, denoted as $\widetilde{H} \sqsubseteq \widetilde{H'}$, if and only if, for each $n, m \in \overline{N}$ we have $o(n) \Leftarrow o'(n)$ and $n \preceq_\diamond m \Leftarrow n \preceq'_\diamond m$, for all $\diamond \in \{ff, fa, af, aa\}$. Intuitively, the absence of a predicate indicates incertitude w.r.t. the concrete ordering configuration. For instance if $o(n)$ does not hold, this means that in the concrete setting, n "represents" a list segment that may or may not be ordered.

Given a set S of abstract heaps sharing the same structure, we denote by $\sqcup S$ the least upper bound, and by $\sqcap S$ the greatest lower bound of S, with respect to $\sqsubseteq$. Note that $\sqcup$ and $\sqcap$ are undefined for sets of abstract heaps that have different structures. The domain of abstract heaps is denoted by $\langle \widetilde{\mathcal{H}}(PVar), \sqsubseteq \rangle$.

Definition 7. *Let* $H = \langle N, S, V, D \rangle$ *be a concrete heap with data from the ordered domain* $\langle \mathfrak{D}, \preceq \rangle$ *and* $H_{/\sim} = \langle N_{/\sim}, S_{/\sim}, V_\sim \rangle$ *its quotient. An abstract heap* $\widetilde{H} = \langle \overline{H}, o, \preceq_{ff}, \preceq_{fa}, \preceq_{af}, \preceq_{aa} \rangle$ *is said to be an* abstraction *of H if and only if* $\alpha_s(H) = \overline{H}$ *and for all* $[n], [m] \in N_{/\sim}, \diamond \in \{ff, fa, af, aa\}$: $o(\beta([n])) \Rightarrow o^c([n])$ *and* $\beta([n]) \preceq_\diamond \beta([m]) \Rightarrow [n] \preceq^c_\diamond [m]$ *where* β *is the bijection from Definition 4.*

We define $\alpha : \mathcal{H}(PVar) \to \widetilde{\mathcal{H}}(PVar)$ as $\alpha(H) = \sqcap \{ \widetilde{H} \mid \widetilde{H}$ is an abstraction of $H \}$. Note that all abstract heaps that are abstractions of H share the same structure, hence $\sqcap$ is defined for this set. The *concretization* function is $\gamma : \widetilde{\mathcal{H}}(PVar) \to \mathcal{P}(\mathcal{H}(PVar))$, defined as $\gamma(\widetilde{H}) = \{ H \mid \alpha(H) \sqsubseteq \widetilde{H} \}$. Clearly, $\gamma(\widetilde{H}_1) \subseteq \gamma(\widetilde{H}_2)$ if $\widetilde{H}_1 \sqsubseteq \widetilde{H}_2$, but the dual does not necessarily hold.

4.3 Counter Automata Semantics with Ordering Predicates

Taking ordering predicates $o, \preceq_{ff, fa, af, aa}$ into account refines our notion of counter automaton, previously introduced. The counter automaton defined in this section keeps track of the ordering information, allowing one to verify properties related to the ordering of lists, as it is the case for sorting programs, e.g., insertsort, bubblesort, etc.

A counter automaton with ordering predicates is $A_a = \langle Q_a, X, \xrightarrow{a} \rangle$. The set of control states is defined now as $Q_a = Lab \times (\widetilde{\mathcal{H}}(PVar) \cup \{H_{err}\})$, and the set of configurations is $S_a = Q_a \times (X \to \mathbb{N})$, with the usual notation. In addition to updating the abstract structure, the transition relation $\xrightarrow{a}$ has to also update the ordering predicates. Our goal is to define the "best transformer" in the sense of [13]. More precisely, our loss of information is only due to the choice of ordering predicates, the definition of $\xrightarrow{a}$ does not introduce further imprecision. Theorem 4 below formalizes this statement.

Weakening

1. $n \preceq_{aa} m \Rightarrow n \preceq_{af} m$

2. $n \preceq_{aa} m \Rightarrow n \preceq_{fa} m$

3. $n \preceq_{af} m \Rightarrow n \preceq_{ff} m$

4. $n \preceq_{fa} m \Rightarrow n \preceq_{ff} m$

Transitivity

5. $n \preceq_{ff} m \land m \preceq_{ff} p \Rightarrow n \preceq_{ff} p$

6. $n \preceq_{af} m \land m \preceq_{ff} p \Rightarrow n \preceq_{af} p$

7. $n \preceq_{ff} m \land m \preceq_{fa} p \Rightarrow n \preceq_{fa} p$

8. $n \preceq_{af} m \land m \preceq_{fa} p \Rightarrow n \preceq_{aa} p$

Reflexivity

9. $n \preceq_{ff} n$

Order

10. $n \preceq_{aa} n \qquad \Rightarrow o(n)$

11. $o(n) \qquad \Rightarrow n \preceq_{fa} n$

Fig. 5. Saturation rules

In order to achieve completeness of the abstract operational semantics, we have designed our abstract state transformer function in two stages. The first stage yields the actual change of the predicates, and the second one is an operation of "saturation" whose goal is to add all the predicates that can be derived from the existing ones, on a given abstract heap, without changing the corresponding set of concrete heaps. For the remainder of this section, we fix an abstract heap $\widetilde{H} = \langle \overline{H}, o, \preceq_{ff}, \preceq_{fa}, \preceq_{af}, \preceq_{aa} \rangle$, with its abstract structure $\overline{H} = \langle \overline{N}, \overline{S}, \overline{V} \rangle$, and let $\widetilde{H}'$ be just like $\widetilde{H}$, except that all the components of the tuples are primed.

Let us begin by the presentation of the second stage. Given an abstract heap $\widetilde{H}$, we define the *saturation* of $\widetilde{H}$ to be the most precise abstract heap whose concretization is the concretization of $\widetilde{H}$. More precisely, $\widetilde{H_0}$ is the saturation of $\widetilde{H}$ if and only if $\widetilde{H_0} = \sqcap \{\widetilde{H'} \mid \gamma(\widetilde{H}) = \gamma(\widetilde{H'})\}$. An abstract heap $\widetilde{H}$ is said to be *saturated* if and only if $\widetilde{H} = \sqcap \{\widetilde{H'} \mid \gamma(\widetilde{H}) = \gamma(\widetilde{H'})\}$. Unfortunately, this definition does not allow one to effectively check that $\widetilde{H'}$ is the saturation of $\widetilde{H}$ for arbitrary abstract heaps. The problem is that the set $\gamma(\widetilde{H})$ is infinite. To overcome this problem, we introduce "syntactical" saturation rules in Fig. 5. The closure of an abstract heap $\widetilde{H}$ w.r.t. these rules is denoted as $sat(\widetilde{H})$.

The saturation rules need to be applied with the following premises. Let $(\widetilde{H}, v)$ be a configuration of the counter automaton, and n an abstract node of $\widetilde{H}$.

- if $v(x_n) = 1$, then it must be the case that $o(n)$ and $n \preceq_\diamond n$, $\diamond \in \{ff, fa, af, aa\}$ all hold in $\widetilde{H}$. The reason is that list segments of size one are ordered and in all possible ordering relations with themselves.
- if $v(x_n) = 2$ and $n \preceq_{fa} n$, then $o(n)$ must also hold in $\widetilde{H}$. In a list segment of size two, if the first element is less than the second, then the segment must be ordered.

The generated counter automaton will test, at each step, for each node $n \in \overline{N}$, that $x_n = 1, 2$ and update the ordering predicates accordingly.

The next Theorem shows the soundness and completeness of the saturation rules.

Theorem 3. *Given an abstract heap* $\widetilde{H}$, *we have* $sat(\widetilde{H}) = \sqcap \{\widetilde{H'} \mid \gamma(\widetilde{H'}) = \gamma(\widetilde{H})\}$.

We define now how the change of abstract predicates is performed. Most of the rules affecting only the abstract structure of the state are very similar with the data insensitive case. To be more precise, all rules from Fig. 3, with the exception of the ones that use the merging (μ) or the splitting (σ) functions, will just maintain the same predicates between the source and destination of the transition. For example, if we had $\overline{V}(u) = \overline{V}(w) = n$ and $n \preceq_{fa} m$, then the result of applying the statement u := null is $\overline{V}' = \overline{V}[u \rightarrow \perp]$ and $n \preceq'_{fa} m$. The remaining rules are dealt with by introducing *ordered* versions of the merging and splitting functions, called μ_o and σ_o, respectively. As a general rule, the new merging and splitting operations are performed on saturated abstract heaps, and another saturation is applied to the result in order to maintain the desired precision.

Let $n, m \in \overline{N}$ be such that $\overline{S}(n) = m$ and m is not a cut point in $\overline{H}$. We recall that the result of $\mu(\overline{H}, n, m)$ in this case is the abstract structure in which n takes the place of both n and m. Then, $\mu_o(\widetilde{H}, n, m) = \langle \mu(\overline{H}, n, m), o', \preceq'_{ff}, \preceq'_{fa}, \preceq'_{af}, \preceq'_{aa} \rangle$ where $o', \preceq'_{ff,fa,af,aa}$ are the (unique) relations on $\overline{N}$ and $\overline{N} \times \overline{N}$ satisfying the following constraints, for all $p \in \overline{N} \setminus \{m\}, q, r \in \overline{N} \setminus \{n\}$ and $\diamond \in \{ff, fa, af, aa\}$:

$$o(n) \wedge o(m) \wedge n \preceq_{aa} m \Leftrightarrow o'(n) \qquad o(q) \Leftrightarrow o'(q) \text{ and } q \preceq_\diamond r \Leftrightarrow q \preceq'_\diamond r$$

$$n \preceq_{ff} p \Leftrightarrow n \preceq'_{ff} p \qquad\qquad p \preceq_{ff} n \Leftrightarrow p \preceq'_{ff} n$$

$$p \preceq_{fa} n \wedge p \preceq_{fa} m \Leftrightarrow p \preceq'_{fa} n \qquad n \preceq_{fa} q \Leftrightarrow n \preceq'_{fa} q$$

$$n \preceq_{af} p \wedge m \preceq_{af} p \Leftrightarrow n \preceq'_{af} p \qquad q \preceq_{af} n \Leftrightarrow q \preceq'_{af} n$$

$$n \preceq_{aa} p \wedge m \preceq_{aa} p \Leftrightarrow n \preceq'_{aa} p \qquad p \preceq_{aa} n \wedge p \preceq_{aa} m \Leftrightarrow p \preceq'_{aa} n$$

Lemma 4. *Let $\widetilde{H} = \langle \overline{H}, o, \preceq_{ff}, \preceq_{fa}, \preceq_{af}, \preceq_{aa} \rangle \in \mathcal{H}(PVar)$ be a saturated abstract heap, where $\overline{H} = \langle \overline{N}, \overline{S}, \overline{V} \rangle \in \mathcal{H}(PVar)$, and $n, m \in \overline{N}$ such that $\overline{S}(n) = m$ and m is not a cut point in $\overline{H}$. Then, $\alpha(\gamma(\widetilde{H})) = \alpha(\gamma(\mu_o(\widetilde{H}, n, m)))$.*

The splitting operation on abstract structures replaces one node n with two nodes n and m, such that m becomes the successor of n and the previous successor of n becomes the successor of m. In addition, the effect of the split operation on the ordering predicates is modeled by the rules given in the following. Formally, $\sigma_o(\widetilde{H}, n, m) = \langle \sigma(\overline{H}, n, m), o', \preceq'_{ff}, \preceq'_{fa}, \preceq'_{af}, \preceq'_{aa} \rangle$, where $o', \preceq'_{ff,fa,af,aa}$ are the (unique) relations on $\overline{N}$ and $\overline{N} \times \overline{N}$ that satisfy the following constraints, for all $p \in \overline{N} \setminus \{n\}, q, r \in \overline{N} \setminus \{p, n\}$, and all $\diamond \in \{ff, fa, af, aa\}$:

$$o'(n), \ n \preceq'_\diamond n, \ \diamond \in \{ff, fa, af, aa\}$$

$$o(n) \Leftrightarrow n \preceq'_{aa} m \wedge o'(m) \qquad n \preceq_{aa} n \Leftrightarrow n \preceq'_{aa} m \wedge m \preceq'_{aa} n \wedge m \preceq'_{aa} m$$

$$n \preceq_{ff} p \Leftrightarrow n \preceq'_{ff} p \qquad\qquad p \preceq_{ff} n \Leftrightarrow p \preceq'_{ff} n$$

$$n \preceq_{fa} p \Leftrightarrow n \preceq'_{fa} p \qquad\qquad p \preceq_{fa} n \Leftrightarrow p \preceq'_{fa} n \wedge p \preceq'_{fa} m$$

$$n \preceq_{af} p \Leftrightarrow n \preceq'_{af} p \wedge m \preceq'_{af} p \qquad p \preceq_{af} n \Leftrightarrow p \preceq'_{af} n$$

$$n \preceq_{aa} p \Leftrightarrow n \preceq'_{aa} p \wedge m \preceq'_{aa} p \qquad p \preceq_{aa} n \Leftrightarrow p \preceq'_{aa} n \wedge p \preceq'_{aa} m$$

$$o(q) \Leftrightarrow o'(q) \qquad\qquad q \preceq_\diamond r \Leftrightarrow q \preceq'_\diamond r$$

The first conditions concerning $o'(n)$ and $n \preceq'_\diamond n$ are due to the fact that the actual size of the list segment represented by n is one, i.e. a split operation separates the head from the tail of a list segment. The following Lemma formalizes the correctness σ_o:

Lemma 5. *Let $\widetilde{H} = \langle \overline{H}, o, \preceq_{ff}, \preceq_{fa}, \preceq_{af}, \preceq_{aa} \rangle \in \mathcal{H}(PVar)$ be a saturated abstract heap, where $\overline{H} = \langle \overline{N}, \overline{S}, \overline{V} \rangle \in \overline{H}(PVar)$, $n \in \overline{N}$ and $m \notin \overline{N}'$. Then, $\alpha(\gamma(\widetilde{H})) = \alpha(\gamma(\sigma_o(\widetilde{H}, n, m)))$.*

A conditional test involving data $u.\mathtt{data} \leq w.\mathtt{data}$ evaluates true in the abstract heap $\tilde{H}$ if and only if $\overline{V}(u) \preceq_{ff} \overline{V}(w)$ holds on $sat(\tilde{H})$. Otherwise, such tests introduce non-determinism in the generated counter automaton. Therefore, the semantics of the counter automaton is a simulation of the semantics of the original program, but not a bisimulation anymore.

Theorem 4. *Let* $\langle l, \iota, H \rangle \in S$ *be a concrete program state. Then, there exists* $\langle l', \iota', H' \rangle \in S$ *such that* $\langle l, \iota, H \rangle \xrightarrow{c} \langle l', \iota', H' \rangle$ *if only if there exists an abstract state* $\langle l, \tilde{H'}, v \rangle \in S_a$ *such that* $\langle l, \alpha(H), v \rangle \xrightarrow{a} \langle l', \tilde{H'}, v' \rangle$ *and* $H' \in \gamma(\tilde{H'})$.

The following is a consequence of Theorems 1, 2 and 4.

Corollary 1. *For every program with lists, if its counter automaton is flat, then safety and termination are decidable properties.*

Notice that the number of objects created by a single loop iteration in a flat list program is always bounded by a constant, therefore its counter automaton is restrictive. The linear and non-negative conditions can be established by inspection of the form of the transitions in the abstract semantics[1]. If this automaton is moreover flat, we can apply Theorem 1. The result does not give us a purely syntactic criterion for decidability of verification of list manipulating programs but still allows us to decide whether the program falls into a significant decidable fragment or not.

5   Experimental Results

In order to obtain experimental evidence about how our techniques behave in practice, we have applied them to several non-trivial procedures manipulating singly-linked lists. In particular, we have considered a procedure for *reversing lists*, whose behaviour we have studied both for an *acyclic* as well as *cyclic* input, and then two procedures for sorting lists, namely *InsertSort* and *BubbleSort*.

For all the examples, we generated (by hand—an implementation of the translation procedure is our future work) the corresponding counter automata. Sizes of the automata—after some trivial simplifications joining sequences of states with no variation in the underlying heap graph—varied as follows: (1) 15 states and 3 counters for reversing acyclic lists (no optimizations were used in this case), (2) 11 states and 3 counters for reversing cyclic lists, (3) 88 states and 6 counters for InsertSort, and (4) 149 states and 7 counters for BubbleSort (we considered the more practical version of the sort with a pointer remembering the already sorted part of the list). For list reversing, no ordering predicates were used.

As for the *safety properties* of the considered programs, we checked that there are no null pointer assignments, no elements are lost, the shape is preserved, and—in the case of the sorting algorithms—that the result is sorted. These properties may be checked by generating a symbolically encoded set of the reachable configurations of the counter automaton corresponding to the program. Using an implementation of the abstract regular

---

[1] Notice that the only negative coefficients in the transition relations are the base coefficients.

model checking technique [9] based on LASH automata libraries [1], the verification took 10 sec for the acyclic list reversion case study and 0.5 sec for cyclic list reversion on a Pentium 4 machine with a 2.6 GHz processor.

Moreover, let us note that all the above properties may often be checked already at the *counter automaton extraction phase*. The checking is mostly straightforward. A slight complication is just checking that no elements of the list are lost via the u.next := w operations. However, even here a simple (fully automatable) heuristic may be used. When we generate a counter automaton state containing a new abstract heap and we can grant that some of its nodes have size one (e.g., after a u := w.next statement), we remember this fact. Later when we again encounter such a heap and we cannot statically guarantee that the appropriate nodes have size one, we may drop the information. Then, when we see that an u.next := w operation is performed on a node for which we remembered that its size is one, we know that we do not loose any list elements. If this is not the case, we have to analyse the dynamic behaviour of the counter automaton and check whether it may actually happen that we loose some elements. In *all* our examples, however, we were able to perform all the checks (and thus verify the described safety properties) statically (i.e. at the counter automaton extraction phase).

In addition to checking safety properties, we have also fully-automatically checked that all the considered programs *terminate*. For checking termination, we analysed the generated counter automata using the tool described in [12]. On the same machine as above, we were able to check termination in 4 sec for reversing acyclic lists, 1.5 sec for reversing cyclic lists, 90 sec for InsertSort, and 150 sec for BubbleSort.

6   Conclusion

We have presented an approach for automatic verification of programs with 1-selector dynamic linked structures. It is based on using counter automata as accurate abstract models for such programs. These infinite-state models can be handled using various advanced techniques and tools which have been designed recently for their automatic analysis (e.g., [1,2,5]), and in particular concerning checking termination and liveness properties (e.g., [12,11]). Indeed, using counters referring to the sizes of parts of the heap structure (e.g., list segments) of a program is a powerful means for dealing with quantitative reasoning about programs, and in particular about their termination. Our future work naturally includes extending this approach to more general linked structures such as doubly linked lists, tree-like structures, etc.

References

1. The LASH toolset. http://www.montefiore.ulg.ac.be/~boigelot/research/lash/.
2. A. Bouajjani A. Annichini and M.Sighireanu. TReX: A Tool for Reachability Analysis of Complex Systems. In *Proc. of CAV'01*, volume 2102 of *LNCS*, 2001.
3. I. Balaban, A. Pnueli, and L. Zuck. Shape Analysis by Predicate Abstraction. In *Proc. of VMCAI'05*, volume 3385 of *LNCS*, 2005.
4. S. Bardin, A.Finkel, and D. Nowak. Toward Symbolic Verification of Programs Handling Pointers. In *Proc. of AVIS'04*, 2004.

5. S. Bardin, A. Finkel, J. Leroux, and L. Petrucci. FAST: Fast Acceleration of Symbolic Transition systems. In *Proc. of CAV'03*, volume 2725 of *LNCS*, 2003.
6. J. Berdine, C. Calcagno, and P. O'Hearn. A Decidable Fragment of Separation Logic. In *Proc. of FSTTCS'04*, volume 3328 of *LNCS*, 2004.
7. A. Bouajjani, M. Bozga, P. Habermehl, R. Iosif, P. Moro, and T. Vojnar. Programs with Lists are Counter Automata. Tech. Rep. TR-2006-3, Verimag, UJF/CNRS/INPG, Grenoble, 2006.
8. A. Bouajjani, P. Habermehl, P. Moro, and T. Vojnar. Verifying Programs with Dynamic 1-Selector-Linked Structures in Regular Model Checking. In *Proc. of TACAS'05*, volume 3440 of *LNCS*, 2005.
9. A. Bouajjani, P. Habermehl, and T. Vojnar. Abstract Regular Model Checking. In *Proc. of CAV'04*, volume 3114 of *LNCS*, 2004.
10. M. Bozga and R. Iosif. Quantitative Verification of Programs with Lists. *VERIMAG TR 2005-2*, http://www-verimag.imag.fr, 2005.
11. A. Bradley, Z. Manna, and H. Sipma. Termination Analysis of Integer Linear Loops. In *Proc. of CONCUR'05*, volume 3653 of *LNCS*, 2005.
12. B. Cook, A. Podelski, and A. Rybalchenko. Abstraction Refinement for Termination. In *Proc. of SAS'05*, volume 3672 of *LNCS*, 2005.
13. P. Cousot and R. Cousot. Abstract Interpretation: A Unified Lattice Model for Static Analysis of Programs by Construction or Approximation of Fixpoints. In *Proc. of POPL'97*, 1977.
14. N. Dor, M. Rodeh, and S. Sagiv. Checking Cleanness in Linked Lists. In *Proc. of SAS'00*, volume 1824 of *LNCS*, 2000.
15. A. Finkel, 2006. Personal communication.
16. R. Iosif. Symmetry Reductions for Model Checking of Concurrent Dynamic Software. *STTT*, pages 302–319, 2004.
17. S. Ishtiaq and P. O'Hearn. BI as an assertion language for mutable data structures. In *Proc. of POPL'01*, 2001.
18. R. Manevich, E. Yahav, G. Ramalingam, and M. Sagiv. Predicate Abstraction and Canonical Abstraction for Singly-Linked Lists. In *Proc. of VMCAI'05*, volume 3385 of *LNCS*, 2005.
19. A. Møller and M.I. Schwartzbach. The Pointer Assertion Logic Engine. In *Proc. of PLDI'01*. ACM Press, 2001.
20. M. Presburger. Über die Vollstandigkeit eines Gewissen Systems der Arithmetik. *Comptes Rendus du I Congrés des Pays Slaves*, 1929.
21. S. Sagiv, T.W. Reps, and R. Wilhelm. Parametric Shape Analysis via 3-Valued Logic. *TOPLAS*, 2002.
22. E. Yahav, T. Reps, M. Sagiv, and R. Wilhelm. Verifying Temporal Heap Properties Specified via Evolution Logic. In *Proc. of ESOP'03*, volume 2618 of *LNCS*, 2003.

Lazy Shape Analysis

Dirk Beyer, Thomas A. Henzinger, and Grégory Théoduloz

EPFL, Switzerland

Abstract. Many software model checkers are based on predicate abstraction. If the verification goal depends on pointer structures, the approach does not work well, because it is difficult to find adequate predicate abstractions for the heap. In contrast, shape analysis, which uses graph-based heap abstractions, can provide a compact representation of recursive data structures. We integrate shape analysis into the software model checker BLAST. Because shape analysis is expensive, we do not apply it globally. Instead, we ensure that, like predicates, shape graphs are computed and stored locally, only where necessary for proving the verification goal. To achieve this, we extend lazy abstraction refinement, which so far has been used only for predicate abstractions, to three-valued logical structures. This approach does not only increase the precision of model checking, but it also increases the efficiency of shape analysis. We implemented the technique by extending BLAST with calls to TVLA.

1 Introduction

Counterexample-guided abstraction refinement [14,6] has dramatically increased the performance of software model checkers in the past few years [2,4]. However, being based on predicate abstractions, current model checkers are not capable of dealing effectively with recursive data structures. Shape analysis [13,5,19] is a static data-flow analysis that models the heap contents using graph-based abstractions. However, shape analysis is among the most expensive static analyses. The contribution of this paper is to show how to increase both the effectiveness of model checking and the efficiency of shape analysis by combining both techniques. By computing both predicate and shape information, we increase the precision of model checking, and thus obtain fewer false positives. The efficiency of shape analysis is improved, because expensive shape computations (such as abstract postconditions) are performed only at those program locations where the shape information is necessary to prove the verification goal. To achieve this, we apply the 'lazy abstraction' paradigm [12] to shapes.

Lazy abstraction involves both lazy (on-the-fly) abstraction construction and lazy (only-where-necessary) abstraction refinement. *Lazy abstraction construction* means that an abstract reachability tree (ART) for the program is computed on-the-fly. Each node of the ART is labeled with both predicate and shape information. The computation of a branch in the ART is terminated when the concrete states represented by the leaf are covered by another node in the tree. *Lazy abstraction refinement* means that predicate and shape information is refined only along branches of the ART that represent spurious counterexamples,

T. Ball and R.B. Jones (Eds.): CAV 2006, LNCS 4144, pp. 532–546, 2006.

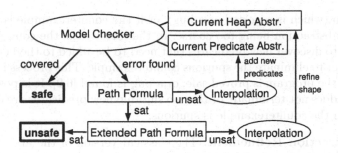

Fig. 1. Abstraction refinement with heap abstraction

in order to remove these false positives. Additional predicates can be discovered automatically using Craig interpolation [18]. This method allows the pinpointing of relevant predicates to individual program locations. In this paper we show how to use interpolation-based predicate discovery to refine also the granularity of the shape analysis. Our algorithm decides, individually for each location along a spurious counterexample, which predicates and pointers to track, and how to refine the local heap abstraction, so that the infeasible error path is removed.

We refer to the predicates used in the predicate abstraction as 'nullary' predicates, because that is how they can be viewed from the shape-analysis perspective. Our interpolation engine discovers not only new nullary predicates (handled by BLAST), but also new unary predicates, which are interpreted over the nodes of a shape graph. To enable the addition of richer, derived predicates (called 'instrumentation' predicates in shape analysis) during refinement, we introduce predefined shape-class generators (SCGs). Consistent with our locality principle, there is an SCG per program location. If an SCG is insufficient for proving the verification goal, then the system proceeds to a finer SCG, which adds additional shape-describing predicates to the local heap abstraction.

We implemented this algorithm in the software model checker BLAST [11], using calls to TVLA [16] for shape operations. We evaluated the method by applying it to several C programs that manipulate list data structures. In these examples, the model checker needs to discover both nullary predicates (to refine the predicate abstraction) and unary predicates (to refine the heap abstraction), in order to automatically prove the program correct.

2   Review

2.1   Software Model Checking by Predicate Abstraction

Counterexample-Guided Abstraction Refinement (CEGAR). The classical CEGAR algorithm starts with an initial (trivial) predicate abstraction, and refines the abstraction iteratively. During each iteration, it explores the states of an abstract boolean program. If the boolean program is safe, then the algorithm stops with the answer 'safe.' If an (abstract) counterexample is found, then the algorithm checks if the counterexample corresponds to a (concrete) error path in the program (which is reported as a bug), or if the counterexample is 'spurious' due to the abstraction being too coarse. In the latter case, the counterexample is analyzed to discover new predicates that need to be added to the boolean program in order to eliminate the spurious counterexample. This process is repeated until either the program is proved safe, or a bug is found [6,2]. It is possible that the process does not terminate, or that no suitable new predicates are discovered even though the counterexample is spurious.

Lazy Abstraction Refinement. The classical version of the abstract-check-refine loop has two drawbacks: first, it is not necessary to represent in the boolean abstraction the part of the state space that is not reachable, and second, it is not necessary to refine the portions of the abstract program that have already been proved safe. Lazy abstraction refinement integrates the steps of the abstract-check-refine loop into an on-the-fly analysis that refines the predicate abstraction locally. Instead of repeatedly building and exploring an abstract boolean program, the lazy algorithm builds an ART. At each node of the ART, the lazy algorithm adds necessary predicates on demand, by refining the abstraction only at locations that occur on a spurious counterexample. As a result, the final abstraction (predicate set) differs from location to location [12].

Craig Interpolation. The crucial measure for the efficiency of the analysis is the number of predicates in the abstraction. To keep the number of predicates per location as small as possible, interpolation-based predicate discovery can be used to produce for each program location the predicates that are needed to eliminate an infeasible error path in the ART. Given an abstract error path, we construct a path formula (PF) such that if the PF is unsatisfiable, then the error path is infeasible. An unsatisfiable PF can be cut, at each location on the path, into two formulas: a prefix formula that leads the program from the initial location to the cut location, and a postfix formula that leads the program from the cut location to the error location. From a Craig interpolant of the two formulas we can extract a suitable set of predicates to be added at the cut location [11,18].

2.2 Shape Analysis by Three-Valued Logic

Shape analysis is a static analysis that represents unbounded instances of recursive data structures on the heap by finite structures, called 'shape graphs.' Following the framework of [19,16], we represent shape graphs as three-valued logical structures.

Figure 2(b) shows an instance of a list structure consisting of five elements, four with data value 1 and one with data value 3. The pointers a and p point to the first list element. Figure 2(c) shows a shape graph that represents all list instances such that the pointers a and p point to the first list element, all elements have data value 1, except the last element, which has data value 3. The concrete list in Fig. 2(b) is an instance of this shape graph. The shape graph is represented by predicates: the unary predicates pt_a, pt_p, $fd_{h=1}$, $fd_{h=3}$, sm, $r_{a,n}$, and $r_{p,n}$, and the binary predicate n. All predicates are interpreted over nodes of the shape graph. The predicate $pt_a(v)$ is true if the pointer variable a

```
 1 typedef struct node {
 2   int h;  struct node *n;
 3 } *List;
 4 void foo(int flag) {
 5   List a = (List) malloc(...);
 6   if (a == NULL) exit(1);
 7   List p = a;
 8   while (random()) {
 9     if (flag)  p->h = 1;
10     else        p->h = 2;
11     p->n = (List) malloc(...);
12     if (p->n == NULL) exit(1);
13     p = p->n;  }
14   p->h = 3;
15   p = a;  /* Now check it. */
16   if (flag)  while (p->h == 1)  p = p->n;
17   else        while (p->h == 2)  p = p->n;
18   assert(p->h == 3);
19 }
```

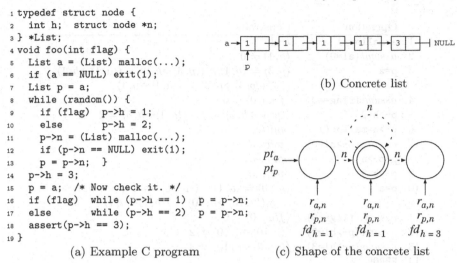

(b) Concrete list

(c) Shape of the concrete list

(a) Example C program

Fig. 2. Example program and two list representations

points to node v (same for pt_p); the predicate $n(v, u)$ is true if the next pointer of node v points to node u; the predicate $fd_{h=1}(v)$ is true if the field h of node v satisfies the assertion h=1 (same for $fd_{h=3}$); the predicate $r_{a,n}(v)$ is true if node v is reachable from pointer a via the next-pointer relation (same for $r_{p,n}$); and the predicate $sm(v)$ has the value $1/2$ if v is a summary node, and the value *false* if v represents a single list element. A summary node (drawn as double-circled) represents one or more list elements. The next pointer of a list element that is abstracted by the second node in Fig. 2(c) may point to itself or to the third node (the value $1/2$ of a predicate is indicated by a dotted edge). The reachability predicates $r_{a,n}$ and $r_{p,n}$ are defined in terms of the other predicates; they are called 'instrumentation' predicates. All other predicates are 'core' predicates.

3   Preview

Lazy CEGAR with Shapes. We define a lazy CEGAR algorithm for abstractions that consist of a predicate abstraction and a heap abstraction (cf. Fig. 1). Moreover, following the lazy abstraction paradigm, both abstractions are refined locally. The initial predicate abstraction is the single predicate *true*, and the initial heap abstraction is the trivial shape graph, which represents every heap. With each program operation, we update both abstractions independently. During lazy abstraction refinement, if the PF is unsatisfiable, then the spurious counterexample is due to the predicate abstraction, and the interpolation procedure discovers new predicates that are added to the predicate abstraction. In this case, the heap abstraction is not changed. However, if the PF is satisfiable, this does not necessarily mean that the error path is feasible. In this case, we construct a more precise extended path formula (EPF), which takes into account also information about the heap. If the EPF is unsatisfiable, then the error path

Operation	Constraint
1 : a=malloc()	$true$
2 : $assume$(a!=0)	$\langle a, 1 \rangle \neq 0$
3 : p=a	$\langle p, 3 \rangle = \langle a, 1 \rangle \wedge \langle\langle p, 3 \rangle \text{->} h, 3 \rangle = \langle\langle a, 1 \rangle \text{->} h, 1 \rangle$
	$\wedge \langle\langle p, 3 \rangle \text{->} n, 3 \rangle = \langle\langle a, 1 \rangle \text{->} n, 1 \rangle$
4 : $assume$(flag==0)	$\langle flag, 0 \rangle = 0$
5 : p->h=2	$\langle\langle p, 3 \rangle \text{->} h, 5 \rangle = 2 \wedge \langle\langle a, 1 \rangle \text{->} h, 5 \rangle = 2$
6 : p->n=malloc()	$omitted$
7 : $assume$(p->n!=0)	$omitted$
8 : p=p->n	$omitted$
9 : p->h=3	$omitted$
10 : p=a	$\langle p, 10 \rangle = \langle a, 1 \rangle \wedge \langle\langle p, 10 \rangle \text{->} h, 10 \rangle = \langle\langle a, 1 \rangle \text{->} h, 5 \rangle$
	$\wedge \langle\langle p, 10 \rangle \text{->} n, 10 \rangle = \langle\langle a, 1 \rangle \text{->} n, 1 \rangle$
11 : $assume$(flag==0)	$\langle flag, 0 \rangle = 0$
12 : $assume$(p->h!=2)	$\langle\langle p, 10 \rangle \text{->} h, 10 \rangle \neq 2$
13 : $assume$(p->h!=3)	$\langle\langle p, 10 \rangle \text{->} h, 10 \rangle \neq 3$
14 : ERROR	

Fig. 3. Extended path formula for the second infeasible error path

(a) Shape before refinement (violating)   (b) Shape after refinement (not viol.)

Fig. 4. Shape graphs before and after the second refinement at program line 18

is guaranteed to be infeasible. We apply the interpolation procedure to the EPF, and use the interpolants to decide how to refine the heap abstraction at the cut locations. For example, from an interpolant of the form p->h=3, we extract the new predicates pt_p and $fd_{h=3}$ to refine the shape graph.

Example. The function in Fig. 2(a) first builds a list that contains a sequence of data values in $\{1, 2\}$ —depending on the variable flag— and ends with data value 3. Then the function verifies that property of the list. Pure predicate abstraction discovers only the nullary predicate np_{flag}, which is insufficient for proving the program safe. The combination of predicate abstraction and heap abstraction tracks both predicate and shape information simultaneously, and automatically discovers the necessary nullary and unary predicates to refine both abstractions. The first infeasible error path that our system reports skips the first while loop, sets p->h=3, assumes flag=0, skips the while loop of the 'else' branch, and violates the assertion. The list consists of one list element, $\langle 3 \rangle$. Pure predicate abstraction would give a false positive, because the PF is satisfiable. However, the EPF is unsatisfiable, and from the interpolant p->h=3 we extract the pointer p and the field assertion h=3. Furthermore, alias analysis indicates that we also need to track the pointer a, which may be aliased to p.

Therefore we locally add the three unary predicates pt_p, pt_a, and $fd_{h=3}$ to the heap abstraction, which removes the infeasible error path.

The second infeasible error path enters the first while loop, assumes flag=0, sets p->h=2, sets p->h=3, assumes flag=0, skips the while loop of the 'else' branch, and violates the assertion. The list now represents the sequence $\langle 2, 3 \rangle$. The abstract state associated with the program location before the assertion is represented by the nullary predicate *true* and the shape graph of Fig. 4(a). The conjuncts of the EPF that show the infeasibility of this error path are given in Fig. 3 (the number annotated to an lvalue in a PF corresponds to the number of the operation that has written this value). The interpolant is p->h=2, and thus we add the field predicate $fd_{h=2}$ to the heap abstraction. When BLAST explores this path again after the refinement, the shape graph in Fig. 4(b) is computed.

The third infeasible error path enters the first while loop, assumes flag=1, sets p->h=1, sets p->h=3, assumes flag=0, skips the while loop of the 'else' branch, and violates the assertion. The list represents the sequence $\langle 1, 3 \rangle$. As the predicate abstraction does not track the predicate flag, this leads to the infeasible situation that in the first while loop the predicate is assumed to be *true*, and in the second part of the program it is assumed to be *false*. The interpolant for the unsatisfiable PF is flag, and we add the nullary predicate np_{flag} to the predicate abstraction. The resulting fourth infeasible error path enters the first while loop, assumes flag=1, sets p->h=1, sets p->h=3, assumes flag=1, skips the while loop of the 'then' branch, and violates the assertion. The list represents the sequence $\langle 1, 3 \rangle$. We discover the field predicate $fd_{h=1}$ from the interpolant p->h=1 for the unsatisfiable EPF, and add it to the heap abstraction.

The last iteration unfolds the remaining states of the ART or marks them as covered. The final ART represents a safety certificate (proof of correctness). The example does not illustrate the 'laziness' of our approach: if the example is only one function of many in a large program, then the generated predicates and shape graphs are tracked only locally within the given function. Similarly, if the program contained a second list that is created but never checked, then the analysis would not track the shape of that list, because the interpolants yield only predicates that are necessary for eliminating the infeasible error paths. Also, the example uses only one of the two ways in which the heap abstraction can be refined: it does not require any instrumentation predicates. To introduce derived predicates, such as reachability, we will add shape-class generators to the heap abstraction; these are not discovered automatically, but need to be predefined.

4   Lazy Abstraction Refinement of Shapes

In the following three subsections, we give the details of our algorithm. First, we explain how we build the ART with abstract states that include both nullary predicates and shape graphs. Second, we explain how we check whether an abstract error path is feasible (i.e., corresponds to a concrete error path). Third, we explain how we refine the predicate and heap abstractions.

4.1   Combining Predicate and Heap Abstractions

Predicate Abstraction. A *nullary predicate* is a predicate over program variables. We write $np_{x=3}$ for the nullary predicate asserting that the value of the program variable x is 3. We denote the set of nullary predicates by $\mathcal{P}$. A *predicate abstraction* for a program is a function $\Pi : L \rightarrow 2^{\mathcal{P}}$ that maps each program location in $L = \{pc_1, \ldots, pc_k\}$ to a set of nullary predicates. We follow the definitions of [11]. For a formula φ over program variables, the abstraction w.r.t. a set $P \subseteq \mathcal{P}$ of nullary predicates is the strongest boolean combination φ' of predicates in P such that φ implies φ'. The semantics of a program path is defined in terms of the strongest-postcondition operator: if the formula φ represents a set of states, and op is an operation, then the formula $\mathsf{SP}.\varphi.\mathsf{op}$ represents the set of successor states. We extend SP to program paths in the natural way. A path t is SP-*infeasible* if $\mathsf{SP}.true.t$ is unsatisfiable. To check if a given path is feasible, we construct a path formula (PF), which is the conjunction of several constraints, one per operation on the path, such that the path is SP-infeasible if the PF is unsatisfiable. For a path $(\mathsf{op}_m : pc_m); \ldots; (\mathsf{op}_n : pc_n)$, the *abstract semantics* SP_Π is the Π-abstraction of the concrete semantics SP, that is, the formula $\mathsf{SP}_\Pi.\varphi.\mathsf{op}_i$ is the abstraction w.r.t. $\Pi(pc_i)$ of the formula $\mathsf{SP}.\varphi.\mathsf{op}_i$.

Shape Classes. The precision of heap abstractions is defined by shape classes. Following [19], a *shape class* $\mathbb{S} = (P_{core}, P_{instr}, P_{abs})$ consists of three sets of predicates over node variables: (1) a set P_{core} of core predicates, (2) a set P_{instr} of instrumentation predicates with $P_{core} \cap P_{instr} = \emptyset$, where each instrumentation predicate $p \in P_{instr}$ has an associated defining formula φ^p over the core predicates, and (3) a set $P_{abs} \subseteq P_{core} \cup P_{instr}$ of abstraction predicates. We denote the set of shape classes by $\mathcal{S}$. A *heap abstraction* for a program is a function $\Psi : L \rightarrow 2^{\mathcal{S}}$ that maps each program location to a set of shape classes (different shape classes can be used to simultaneously track different data structures).

The set of core predicates must contain the special unary predicate sm, which has the value *false* for normal nodes and $1/2$ for summary nodes. Moreover, we distinguish two special subsets of core predicates: the set $P_{pt} \subseteq P_{core}$ of points-to predicates, and the set $P_{fd} \subseteq P_{core}$ of field predicates. A *points-to predicate* $pt_x(v)$ is a unary predicate that indicates if a pointer variable x points to node v. A *field predicate* $fd_\phi(v)$ is a unary predicate that indicates if a field assertion ϕ holds for node v. Each field assertion has a boolean value over the fields of a structure element. Therefore, field predicates represent the data content of a structure, rather than the shape of the structure. A shape class $\mathbb{S}$ *refines* a shape class $\mathbb{S}'$, written $\mathbb{S} \preccurlyeq \mathbb{S}'$, if (1) $P'_{core} \subseteq P_{core}$, (2) $P'_{instr} \subseteq P_{instr}$, and (3) $P'_{abs} \subseteq P_{abs}$. The union of $\mathbb{S}$ and $\mathbb{S}'$ is the shape class $(P_{core} \cup P'_{core}, P_{instr} \cup P'_{instr}, P_{abs} \cup P'_{abs})$ (assuming $P_{core} \cap P'_{instr} = \emptyset$ and $P_{instr} \cap P'_{core} = \emptyset$).

Shape Graphs. The abstract state of the heap is defined as a set of shape regions. A *shape region* $(\mathbb{S}, G)$ consists of a shape class $\mathbb{S}$ and a set G of shape graphs for $\mathbb{S}$. A *shape graph* $g = (V, val)$ for a shape class $\mathbb{S} = (P_{core}, P_{instr}, P_{abs})$ consists of a set V of nodes and a valuation val in three-valued logic of the predicates over V: for a predicate $p \in P_{core} \cup P_{instr}$ of arity n, $val(p) : V^n \to \{0, 1, 1/2\}$. Fig. 2(c) shows an example of a shape graph. Let $\mathbb{S}$ and $\mathbb{S}'$ be two shape classes such that $\mathbb{S} \preccurlyeq \mathbb{S}'$. A shape graph g' for $\mathbb{S}'$ can be extended to a shape graph $g = E_{\mathbb{S}' \triangleright \mathbb{S}}(g')$ for $\mathbb{S}$ such that the set of nodes is unchanged (i.e., $V = V'$), and for each predicate $p \in (P_{core} \cup P_{instr}) \setminus (P'_{core} \cup P'_{instr})$, the value of p is $1/2$ everywhere. We extend the operator E to sets of shape graphs in the natural way. A shape region $(\mathbb{S}, G)$ is *covered* by a shape region $(\mathbb{S}', G')$ if $E_{\mathbb{S} \triangleright (\mathbb{S} \cup \mathbb{S}')}(G) \subseteq E_{\mathbb{S}' \triangleright (\mathbb{S} \cup \mathbb{S}')}(G')$. Consider a program path $(\mathsf{op}_m : pc_m); \ldots; (\mathsf{op}_n : pc_n)$ and a heap abstraction Ψ. The *abstract semantics* SP_Ψ is the Ψ-abstraction of the concrete semantics SP, that is, the formula $\mathsf{SP}_\Psi.(\mathbb{S}, G).\mathsf{op}_i$ is the abstraction w.r.t. $\Psi(pc_i)$ of the formula $\mathsf{SP}.\varphi.\mathsf{op}_i$. The operator SP_Ψ is defined by $\mathsf{SP}_\Psi.(\mathbb{S}, G).\mathsf{op}_i = (\mathbb{S}, [\![\mathsf{op}_i]\!](G))$, where $[\![\cdot]\!]$ is defined as in TVLA [16]. To compute SP_Ψ, we use TVLA's *focus* and *coerce* functions to transform a set of shape graphs. We extend the notion of being covered and the operator SP_Ψ to sets of shape regions in the natural way.

ART Construction. The *abstraction* (Π, Ψ) of a program is a pair consisting of a predicate abstraction Π and a heap abstraction Ψ. Given (Π, Ψ), we construct an ART following [12], but with each vertex of the ART we store not only a program location $pc \in L$, a call stack, and a subset of the (nullary) predicates in $\Pi(pc)$, but also a set of shape regions, one for each shape class in $\Psi(pc)$. Successor vertices in the ART are computed using the SP_Π and SP_Ψ operators independently on the two parts (nullary predicates and shape regions) of the abstract state. We stop expanding the ART at a vertex if (1) both the set of nullary predicates, and the set of shape regions, are covered by some other vertex; or (2) either the predicate set, or the shape set, represents the empty set of concrete states. More sophisticated termination criteria are possible, of course.

4.2   Extracting Interpolants from Extended Path Formulas

Programs. Our formalization of programs is similar to [11]. A program is represented by a set of control flow automata; a path t of length n is a sequence $(\mathsf{op}_1 : pc_1); \ldots; (\mathsf{op}_n : pc_n)$ of operations, which can be either statements or assume predicates. In this paper, we consider flat programs (i.e., program with a single function); our approach can be extended to programs with several functions. The program variables are either integer values or pointers to (possibly recursive) structures with fields that are integers and pointer to structures. We restrict the lvalues that can occur in a program to *ident* and *ident->field*, where *ident* denotes a variable identifier and *field* denotes the name of a structure field. The function F maps an lvalue to the set of fields of the structure pointed to by the lvalue if the lvalue has a pointer type, and to the empty set if the lvalue has an integer type. The operations within a program are limited to the ones listed in the first column of Fig. 5. The expressions that can occur in statements are side-effect free C expressions of linear arithmetic, without pointer dereferences.

Extended Path Formulas. The technique for building PFs from [11] cannot be reused directly, because it does not refer to recursive data structures. However,

Op. op_l	New map θ' and Alloc'	Constraint $\Gamma'(l)$
$s = e$	$\theta'(s) = l$	$\mathsf{sub}.\theta'.s = \mathsf{sub}.\theta.e$
$s_1 = s_2$	$\theta'(s_1) = l$ $\forall f \in \mathsf{F}(s_1) : \theta'(\langle s_1, l\rangle \texttt{->} f) = l$	$\mathsf{eqvar}.(s_1, \theta').(s_2, \theta)$
$s_1 = s_2\texttt{->}f$	$\theta'(s_1) = l$ $\forall f \in \mathsf{F}(s_1) : \theta'(\langle s_1, l\rangle \texttt{->} f) = l$	$\mathsf{sub}.\theta'.s_1 = \mathsf{sub}.\theta.(s_2\texttt{->}f)$ $\wedge \bigwedge\limits_{c \in \mathsf{may}.(l\text{-}1)} \left(\begin{array}{l} \mathsf{sub}.\theta.(s_2\texttt{->}f) = c \\ \Rightarrow \mathsf{eqvar}.(s_1, \theta').(c, \theta) \end{array} \right)$ $.(\mathsf{sub}.\theta.(s_2\texttt{->}f))$
$s_1\texttt{->}f = s_2$	$\theta'(\langle s_1, \theta(s_1)\rangle \texttt{->} f) = l$ $\forall c \in \mathsf{may}.(l\text{-}1).\langle s_1, \theta(s_1)\rangle \texttt{->} f, l\rangle:$ $\quad \forall f \in \mathsf{F}(c) : \theta'(\langle c, l\rangle \texttt{->} f) = l$ $\forall c \in \mathsf{may}.(l\text{-}1).\langle s_1, \theta(s_1)\rangle :$ $\quad \theta'(c\texttt{->}f) = l$	$\mathsf{sub}.\theta'.(s_1\texttt{->}f) = \mathsf{sub}.\theta.s_2$ $\wedge \bigwedge\limits_{c \in \mathsf{may}.(l\text{-}1)} \left(\begin{array}{l} \mathsf{ite}.(c = \mathsf{sub}.\theta'.(s_1\texttt{->}f)) \\ .(\mathsf{eqvar}.(c, \theta').(s_2, \theta)) \\ .(\mathsf{eqvar}.(c, \theta').(c, \theta)) \end{array} \right)$ $.(\mathsf{sub}.\theta'.(s_1\texttt{->}f))$ $\wedge \bigwedge\limits_{c \in \mathsf{may}.(l\text{-}1)} \left(\begin{array}{l} \mathsf{ite}.(c = \mathsf{sub}.\theta'.s_1) \\ .(\mathsf{sub}.\theta'.(c\texttt{->}f) = \mathsf{sub}.\theta.s_2) \\ .(\mathsf{sub}.\theta'.(c\texttt{->}f) = \mathsf{sub}.\theta.(c\texttt{->}f)) \end{array} \right)$ $.(\mathsf{sub}.\theta'.s_1)$
$s = alloc()$	$\theta'(s) = l$ $\forall f \in \mathsf{F}(s) : \theta'(\langle s, l\rangle \texttt{->} f) = l$ $\mathsf{Alloc}' = \mathsf{Alloc} \cup \{\langle s, l\rangle\}$	$\bigwedge\limits_{a \in \mathsf{Alloc}} (\langle s, l\rangle \neq a)$
$assume(p)$		$\mathsf{clos}^*.\theta.true.p$

Fig. 5. Definition of FineCon for each operation: $(\theta', \Gamma') = \mathsf{FineCon}.(\theta, \Gamma).l.\mathsf{op}_l$

since the number of memory cells possibly involved in a PF is bounded, we can produce a finite, sound formula called extended PF (EPF). The address of each heap cell that is accessed on a path must have been previously assigned to a pointer variable (because we consider a restricted set of possible lvalues). To refer to these addresses in the EPF, we use SSA-like renamed lvalues. An *lvalue constant* is either $\langle ident, l\rangle$ (a variable constant), or $\langle\langle ident, l\rangle \texttt{->} field, l'\rangle$ with position labels $l, l' \in [0..n]$ and $l' \geq l$. An *annotated lvalue* is either *ident*, or $\langle ident, l\rangle \texttt{->} field$. The labels l and l' identify the positions on the path where the annotated values may have been modified. An annotated-lvalue map θ is a function from annotated lvalues to labels. The *lvalue-renaming function* $\mathsf{sub}.\theta.v$ is defined by $\mathsf{sub}.\theta.s = \langle s, \theta(s)\rangle$ and $\mathsf{sub}.\theta.(s\texttt{->}f) = \langle(\mathsf{sub}.\theta.s)\texttt{->}f, \theta((\mathsf{sub}.\theta.s)\texttt{->}f)\rangle$, where s is a variable and f is a field.

To simplify the EPF using alias information, the function may maps a label and an lvalue constant to the set of variable constants that may have the same value (i.e., $\langle s, l_s\rangle \in \mathsf{may}.l.c$ if, after the l-th operation of the path, the value of c may be equal to the value of s_1 after the l_1-th operation of the path). The function may is not essential: it is used only to reduce the size of the EPF by taking into account information that two pointers are guaranteed not to be equal.

The function FineCon maps a pair (θ, Γ) consisting of an annotated-lvalue map θ and a constraint map Γ from position labels to first-order logic formulas over lvalue constants, and an operation op_i, to a pair (θ', Γ') consisting of a new annotated-lvalue map and a new constraint map. On the given path, we compute recursively the result of FineCon by computing $(\theta_l, \Gamma_l) = \text{FineCon}.(\theta_{l-1}, \Gamma_{l-1}).\text{op}_l$, where l is the position label of op_l on the path. The map θ_0 is the constant function 0, and Γ_0 is the constant function $\emptyset$. The map θ_l differs from θ_{l-1} only on the annotated lvalues that may be modified by op_l, which are mapped to l by θ_l. The map Γ_l results from extending Γ_{l-1} by mapping l to the constraint derived from op_l. We derive constraints from operations similarly to [11]. An extension is necessary for assignments to pointers: we cannot 'unroll' a recursive data structure and refer to all reachable memory cells, because this would yield an infinite formula. Additionally, we need to add aliasing constraints when several lvalue constants may point to the same memory cell. The formal definition of the function FineCon is given in Fig. 5. The EPF of the path is obtained by taking the conjunction of all formulas in the final constraint map. The EPF is unsatisfiable iff the path is SP-infeasible.

The definition of FineCon uses the following two functions. The function eqvar returns a constraint that expresses the equality of two variables by considering their fields (if any):

$$\text{eqvar}.(s_1, \theta_1).(s_2, \theta_2) = (\text{sub}.\theta_1.s_1 = \text{sub}.\theta_2.s_2)$$
$$\wedge \bigwedge_{f \in F(s_1)} (\text{sub}.\theta_1.(s_1 \rightarrow f) = \text{sub}.\theta_2.(s_2 \rightarrow f))$$

The function $\text{clos*}.\theta.b.p$ returns, given an assume predicate p, the predicate that results from replacing all equalities $x_1 = x_2$ occurring positively (or negatively, depending on the value of the boolean value b) by $\text{eqvar}.(x_1, \theta).(x_2, \theta)$.

Interpolation. We compute the interpolants using the algorithm *Extract* from [11]. We parametrize the algorithm either with the function Con [11] for PFs (written *Extract*[Con]), or with the new function FineCon for EPFs (written *Extract*[FineCon]). The algorithm *Extract* takes as input a program path t and returns a function $\hat{\Pi}$ from position labels (i.e., locations on the path) to sets of nullary predicates. In [11] it was shown that, for a weaker programming language (without recursive data structures), the path t is SP-infeasible iff t is $\text{SP}_{\hat{\Pi}}$-infeasible for $\hat{\Pi} = \textit{Extract}[\text{Con}](t)$. We can prove the analogous statement for our richer programming language: the path t is SP-infeasible iff t is $\text{SP}_{\hat{\Pi}}$-infeasible for $\hat{\Pi} = \textit{Extract}[\text{FineCon}](t)$ [3]. Therefore, our method is sound, that is, we do not report safety when a bug exists.

4.3 Shape-Class Refinement Based on Interpolants

Our refinement procedure first tries to refine the predicate abstraction, by locally adding to the predicate abstraction nullary predicates from the interpolants. If the algorithm does not find new predicates to refine the predicate abstraction, then it tries to refine the heap abstraction, by locally refining the shape classes. In order to specify heap abstractions, we introduce the following data structures.

Tracking Definitions and Shape-Class Generators. A tracking definition represents the pointers and field predicates that we track for analyzing the heap.

A *tracking definition* $D = (T, T_s, \Phi)$ consists of (1) a set T of *tracked pointers*, which is the set of variables that may be pointing to some node in a shape graph; (2) a set $T_s \subseteq T$ of *separating pointers*, which is the set of variables for which we want the corresponding predicates (e.g., points-to, reachability) to be abstraction predicates; and (3) a set Φ of field assertions. A tracking definition $D = (T, T_s, \Phi)$ *refines* a tracking definition $D' = (T', T'_s, \Phi')$, if $T' \subseteq T$, $T'_s \subseteq T_s$ and $\Phi' \subseteq \Phi$. We denote the set of all tracking definitions by $\mathcal{D}$.

A *shape-class generator* (SCG) is a function $m : \mathcal{D} \to \mathcal{S}$ that takes as input a tracking definition and returns a shape class, which consists of core predicates, instrumentation predicates, and abstraction predicates. The tracking definition provides information about which pointers and which field predicates need to be tracked by the program analysis; it is the SCG that determines which predicates are actually added to the shape class. Useful SCGs produce at least the summary predicate sm, a points-to predicate pt_x for each pointer $x \in T$ in the tracking definition, and a field predicate fd_ϕ for each field assertion $\phi \in \Phi$ in the tracking definition. While the pointers and field assertions in the tracking definition are discovered by interpolation (see below), predicates other than sm, pt, and fd predicates need to be added by defining appropriate SCGs.[1] An SCG m *refines* an SCG m' if $m(D) \preccurlyeq m'(D)$ for all tracking definitions D. We require that the set of SCGs contains at least the greatest element m_0, which is a constant function that generates for each tracking definition the shape class $(\emptyset, \emptyset, \emptyset)$. Furthermore, we require each SCG to be monotonic: given an SCG m and two tracking definitions D and D', if $D \preccurlyeq D'$, then $m(D) \preccurlyeq m(D')$.

A *shape type* $\mathbb{T} = (\sigma, m, D)$ consists of a C structure type σ, an SCG m, and a tracking definition D. For example, consider the C type `struct node {int data; struct node *next;}`; and the tracking definition $D = (\{p, q\}, \{p\}, \{data = 0\})$. To form a shape type for a singly-linked list, we can choose an SCG that takes a tracking definition $D = (T, T_s, \Phi)$ and produces a shape class $\mathbb{S} = (P_{core}, P_{instr}, P_{abs})$ with the following components: the set P_{core} of core predicates contains the default unary predicate sm for distinguishing summary nodes, a binary predicate $next$ for representing links between nodes in the list, for each variable in T a unary points-to predicate, and a unary field predicate for each assertion in Φ. The set P_{instr} of instrumentation predicates contains for each variable in T a reachability predicate. The set P_{abs} of abstraction predicates contains all core and instrumentation predicates about separating pointers from T_s. More precise shape types for singly-linked lists can be defined by providing a generator that adds more instrumentation predicates.

A *heap-abstraction specification* is a function $\hat{\Psi}$ that assigns to each program location a set of shape types. The specification $\hat{\Psi}$ defines a heap abstraction in the following way: a pair $(l, \{\mathbb{T}_1, \ldots, \mathbb{T}_k\}) \in \hat{\Psi}$ yields a pair $(l, \{\mathbb{S}_1, \ldots, \mathbb{S}_k\}) \in \Psi$ with $\mathbb{S}_i = \mathbb{T}_i.m(\mathbb{T}_i.D)$ for all $1 \le i \le k$. Technically we do not store the heap abstraction Ψ in our system, but only its specification $\hat{\Psi}$. Whenever a shape class is needed, the algorithm looks it up by applying the current shape type's

---

[1] BLAST uses a predefined set of SCGs, to limit the space of shape classes our algorithm considers. Technically, in BLAST each SCG is given as a code module.

SCG to the shape type's tracking definition. The tracking definition contains information about which pointers and field assertions to track on a syntactic level. Since SCGs are monotonic, shape types can be refined in two different ways: either we refine the shape type's tracking definition, or we refine the shape type's SCG. In both cases, the produced shape class is guaranteed to be finer.

Refinement Algorithm. In the abstract-check-refine loop, predicate abstraction starts with empty set of predicates, and heap abstraction starts with empty shape classes at all program locations. The input to the refinement algorithm is a path t to an error location, which is feasible under the current abstraction (Π, Ψ) (i.e., t is contained in the current ART). Following [11], the algorithm first checks the PF of t for satisfiability. If the PF is unsatisfiable, then the predicate abstraction Π is refined by adding interpolants from $Extract[\mathsf{Con}](t)$ to the locations on the path t. Otherwise, we check the EPF of t for satisfiability. If the EPF is satisfiable, then we report a program bug. Otherwise, we compute new interpolants using $Extract[\mathsf{FineCon}](t)$, and consider each location pc on the path t separately. We either refine the tracking definition of pc in Step 1, or the SCG of pc in Step 2. The algorithm always tries Step 1 first, and only if neither new pointers nor new field assertions are discovered from the corresponding interpolant, it tries Step 2. This interpolation-based analysis identifies the program locations that require more precision to remove the error path from the ART, and we refine the heap abstraction only for those locations.

Step 1: [refine the tracking definition of a location] For every pointer variable p that occurs in the interpolant (e.g., p->h=3), if it matches the C type of the shape type, then we refine the tracking definition of the shape type as follows. We add p to the set of tracked pointers and to the set of separating pointers, and we close the set of tracked pointers under aliasing, by adding also all pointer variables that may be pointing to the newly tracked data structure. Thus the quality of the refinement depends on the quality of the available may-alias information: imprecise information may cause some pt predicates to be added unnecessarily.[2] Moreover, if the pointer p is dereferenced in the interpolant, then we add the corresponding field assertion (e.g., h=3) to the set of tracked field assertions. The same SCG now produces a finer shape class for the refined tracking definition.

Step 2: [refine the SCG of a location] The choice of a finer SCG from the predefined set of SCGs is guided by a refinement relation over the SCGs, which can be used to encode various heuristics that analyze the abstract error path. The finer SCG produces for the same tracking definition a finer shape class, by adding new core, instrumentation, and/or abstraction predicates (e.g., sharing, reachability, cyclicity). If such a finer SCG cannot be found, due to the limitation to a predefined set of SCGs, then the algorithm reports that refinement has not succeeded and terminates. The predefined set of SCGs can be extended in a very flexible way to arbitrary data structures by developers of the model checker, and

---

[2] BLAST currently uses a flow-insensitive may-alias algorithm in which all cells allocated at the same site are represented by one abstract cell.

by experienced users. Given an infeasible program path t and a finite set M of SCGs, it can be proved that the iterative application of the refinement algorithm eventually produces an abstraction (Π', Ψ') that is able to remove t from the ART, provided that M contains an appropriate SCG [3]. Completeness, in this sense, hinges on the use of a sufficiently rich set of SCGs.

5   Implementation

The algorithm presented in this paper is implemented in BLAST 3.0, which integrates TVLA for shape transformations and the foci library [18] of BLAST 2.0 for predicate interpolation. BLAST's abstract states, which were triples consisting of program counter, call stack, and (nullary) predicate set, are extended by a set of shape regions, one for each tracked shape class. TVLA (written in Java) is integrated into BLAST (written in OCaml) as a particular implementation of a shape-analysis module and can be replaced by other shape-analysis tools. We use a simple home-brewed may-alias analysis, but this module can also be changed.

   We used our system to verify several C programs that manipulate list data structures containing integers as data elements; the details about the examples can be found in [3]. None of the programs was successfully verified by BLAST's predicate abstraction without shape analysis. Our examples can also be proved by TVLA, giving as input the abstraction that our system constructs automatically. On the examples we analyzed, BLAST with integrated shape analysis and automatic discovery of relevant points-to and field predicates is never more than 25% slower than TVLA with the given final abstraction. On the other hand, since our system uses different abstractions at different program locations, while TVLA performs a global analysis, there are examples on which our system significantly outperforms TVLA. Also, BLAST uses more efficient data structures (BDDs) for updating the nullary-predicate part of the abstract state. Further experiments are needed to precisely quantify the trade-off between the extra costs caused by the abstraction refinement loop of BLAST versus the global analysis of TVLA.

6   Related Work

Shape analysis based on three-valued logic is a framework that supports a family of abstractions [19,16,15], and from that standpoint, the predicate-abstraction component of our system simply contributes a set of nullary predicates to the shape-abstraction component. Thus our algorithm can be seen as generalizing (1) interpolation-based predicate discovery from nullary predicates to unary points-to and field predicates, and (2) lazy abstraction refinement from predicate abstractions to heap abstractions. We treat field predicates as core predicates, in contrast to [9], where abstractions of the data-structure contents are treated as instrumentation predicates. By relying on a given, fixed set of SCGs, we are still far from a completely automatic lazy implementation of shape analysis, which would require also the automatic discovery of more general instrumentation predicates. However, there are inherent limitations on what first-order theorem provers can deduce about three-valued abstractions that use transitive-closure predicates such as reachability [20]. Instead, one could use learning-based techniques from [17], which generate new instrumentation predicates that are not just boolean combinations of previously used predicates. These could be used in our system to dynamically add new SCGs.

There have also been proposals to encode shape analysis within predicate-abstraction frameworks [1,7]. So far they apply only to restricted settings, such as singly linked lists, or need user help for computing abstractions. Fischer et al. implemented in BLAST a combination of predicate abstraction with a para-metric lattice-based data-flow analysis [8], but they did not consider any auto-matic refinement of the data-flow component. Gulavani and Rajamani proposed a CEGAR method for abstract interpretation and applied it to shape analysis [10], but their refinement is done globally, not lazily.

Acknowledgements. We thank Tom Reps and the anonymous reviewers for many valuable comments. Dirk Beyer was supported in part by the SNSF NCCR on Mobile Information and Communication Systems (MICS).

References

1. I. Balaban, A. Pnueli, and L.D. Zuck. Shape analysis by predicate abstraction. In *Proc. VMCAI*, LNCS 3385, pages 164–180. Springer, 2005.
2. T. Ball and S.K. Rajamani. The SLAM project: Debugging system software via static analysis. In *Proc. POPL*, pages 1–3. ACM, 2002.
3. D. Beyer, T.A. Henzinger, and G. Théoduloz. Lazy shape analysis. Technical Report MTC-REPORT-2005-006, EPFL, 2005.
4. S. Chaki, E.M. Clarke, A. Groce, S. Jha, and H. Veith. Modular verification of software components in C. *IEEE Trans. Software Eng.*, 30(6):388–402, 2004.
5. D.R. Chase, M.N. Wegman, and F.K. Zadeck. Analysis of pointers and structures. In *Proc. PLDI*, pages 296–310. ACM, 1990.
6. E.M. Clarke, O. Grumberg, S. Jha, Y. Lu, and H. Veith. Counterexample-guided abstraction refinement. In *Proc. CAV*, LNCS 1855, pages 154–169. Springer, 2000.
7. D. Dams and K.S. Namjoshi. Shape analysis through predicate abstraction and model checking. In *Proc. VMCAI*, LNCS 2575, pages 310–324. Springer, 2003.
8. J. Fischer, R. Jhala, and R. Majumdar. Joining data flow with predicates. In *Proc. FSE*, pages 227–236. ACM, 2005.
9. D. Gopan, T.W. Reps, and M. Sagiv. A framework for numeric analysis of array operations. In *Proc. POPL*, pages 338–350. ACM, 2005.
10. B.S. Gulavani and S.K. Rajamani. Counterexample-driven refinement for abstract interpretation. In *Proc. TACAS*, LNCS 3920, pages 474–488. Springer, 2006.
11. T.A. Henzinger, R. Jhala, R. Majumdar, and K.L. McMillan. Abstractions from proofs. In *Proc. POPL*, pages 232–244. ACM, 2004.
12. T.A. Henzinger, R. Jhala, R. Majumdar, and G. Sutre. Lazy abstraction. In *Proc. POPL*, pages 58–70. ACM, 2002.
13. N.D. Jones and S.S. Muchnick. A flexible approach to interprocedural data-flow analysis and programs with recursive data structures. In *Proc. POPL*, pages 66–74. ACM, 1982.

14. R.P. Kurshan. *Computer-Aided Verification of Coordinating Processes*. Princeton University Press, 1994.
15. T. Lev-Ami, T.W. Reps, M. Sagiv, and R. Wilhelm. Putting static analysis to work for verification: A case study. In *Proc. ISSTA*, pages 26–38. ACM, 2000.
16. T. Lev-Ami and M. Sagiv. TVLA: A system for implementing static analyses. In *Proc. SAS*, LNCS 2280, pages 280–301. Springer, 2000.
17. A. Loginov, T.W. Reps, and M. Sagiv. Abstraction refinement via inductive learning. In *Proc. CAV*, LNCS 3576, pages 519–533. Springer, 2005.
18. K.L. McMillan. Interpolation and SAT-based model checking. In *Proc. CAV*, LNCS 2725, pages 1–13. Springer, 2003.
19. M. Sagiv, T.W. Reps, and R. Wilhelm. Parametric shape analysis via three-valued logic. *ACM Trans. Program. Lang. Syst.*, 24(3):217–298, 2002.
20. G. Yorsh, T.W. Reps, M. Sagiv, and R. Wilhelm. Logical characterizations of heap abstractions. *ACM Trans. Comput. Log.*, to appear.

Abstraction for Shape Analysis with Fast and Precise Transformers

Tal Lev-Ami[1,*], Neil Immerman[2,**], and Mooly Sagiv[1]

[1] School of Comp. Sci., Tel Aviv Univ.
{tla, msagiv}@post.tau.ac.il
[2] Dept. of Comp. Sci. UMass, Amherst
immerman@cs.umass.edu

Abstract. This paper addresses the problem of proving safety properties of imperative programs manipulating dynamically allocated data structures using destructive pointer updates. We present a new abstraction for linked data structures whose underlying graphs do not contain cycles. The abstraction is simple and allows us to decide reachability between dynamically allocated heap cells.

We present an efficient algorithm that computes the effect of low level heap mutations in the most precise way. The algorithm does not rely on the usage of a theorem prover. In particular, the worst case complexity of computing a single successor abstract state is $O(V \log V)$ where V is the number of program variables. The overall number of successor abstract states can be exponential in V. A prototype of the algorithm was implemented and is shown to be fast.

Our method also handles programs with "simple cycles" such as cyclic singly-linked lists, (cyclic) doubly-linked lists, and trees with parent pointers. Moreover, we allow programs which temporarily violate these restrictions as long as they are restored in loop boundaries.

1 Introduction

Automatically establishing safety properties of programs that permit dynamic storage allocation and low-level pointer manipulations is challenging. Dynamic allocation causes the state space to be infinite; moreover, a program is permitted to mutate a data structure by destructively updating pointer-valued fields of nodes.

It is well understood that reachability is crucial for reasoning about linked data structures. In this work we establish a simple abstraction method for reasoning about reachability that is provably efficient and precise. This provides both a practical analysis method and a theoretical contribution towards the understanding of how precise and efficient shape analysis can be.

1.1 Main Results

We present a method to conservatively verify reachability properties via abstract interpretation [4]. Specifically, we present a new lightweight method for shape analysis (e.g.,

---

* Supported by an Adams Fellowship through the Israel Academy of Sciences and Humanities.
** Supported by NSF grant CCF-0514621.

T. Ball and R.B. Jones (Eds.): CAV 2006, LNCS 4144, pp. 547–561, 2006.
© Springer-Verlag Berlin Heidelberg 2006

see [10,21]) that applies to programs on "regular tree-like" data structures. The method is sound, i.e., whenever it reports that a safety property holds, it indeed holds. Furthermore, we compute **the best abstract transformer** [4] for atomic Java-like statements. A prototype of the algorithm was implemented and is shown to be fast. The system can be seen as a specialization of TVLA [16] to a set of data-structures and a set of properties.

In the rest of the section, we elaborate on the key contributions. Sect. 8 includes more detailed comparison to related work.

New Abstraction of Heap Shape. In Sect. 3, we present our simple abstraction for heaps based on contracting segments of the heap into a single summary-node.

In contrast to existing methods, our abstraction admits the precise and efficient recovery of reachability information concerning the modeled concrete states. For example, every path in the abstraction between "important" nodes is a <u>must-path</u>, i.e., it must exist between the corresponding nodes in each modeled concrete state. Thus, reasoning about reachability between important nodes can be performed efficiently via simple graph traversal.

We show that the abstraction of graphs with no undirected cycles yields a linear number of nodes. Therefore, the size of the abstract state space is bounded for such programs, allowing effective state space exploration. Moreover, this also holds for simple cycles such as cyclic singly-linked lists, (cyclic) doubly-linked lists and trees with parent pointers. Furthermore, it is possible to apply our abstraction only in loop boundaries and thus allowing programs to temporarily violate the data-structure invariants. Full proofs for the theorems in the paper can be found in [15].

Efficient Best Transformers. In Sect. 4, we present an efficient $O(NS * V * \log V)$ algorithm for computing the best abstract transformers for Java-like atomic program statements including destructive pointer manipulation. V is the number of program variables. NS is the number successor abstract states (can be exponential in the number of program variables).

Most existing methods for shape analysis including TVLA do not implement the best transformers and may require exponential time to produce a single abstract state. Also, in contrast to existing methods for generating the best abstract transformers (e.g. [7,22,2]), our method does not employ a theorem prover. Precise reachability information is maintained using our abstraction.

Efficient algorithms for computing the best transformers for predicate abstraction in singly-linked lists were developed in [18]. This paper can be considered as a continuation of [18] that handles more complex data-structures.

Information Extraction. It is important to extract information from an abstract state about the concrete states that it models. For example, we sometimes need to verify disjointness of data structures. For safety properties we check that user-specified assertions hold in every execution leading to a given program point.

In Sect. 5, we provide a conservative and efficient method that extracts such information by evaluating a first-order formula with transitive closure on a given abstract state. Our method is more precise than standard Kleene evaluation (e.g., [21]), although less precise than supervaluational semantics [3,19]. We show that our method is exact for "atomic" reachability properties between important nodes. Our limited experiments indicate that one of our evaluation methods is precise enough in practice.

2   Preliminaries

We call an allocated object on the heap a **heap node**. Shape analysis tracks reference program variables and reference fields, i.e., to which heap node each reference variable points to and for each heap node where each of its reference fields point to. In this paper we assume a fixed set of (reference) program variables denoted by $PVar$ and a fixed set of reference fields denoted by $PRef$.

A **state** (shape graph [10]) is a triple $C \stackrel{\text{def}}{=} (U^C, env^C, ref^C)$. The universe, U^C, is the set of allocated heap nodes; the environment, $env^C \subseteq PVar \times U^C$, is a partial function from program variables to the heap nodes that they point to; and $ref^C : PRef \to \mathcal{P}(U^C \times U^C)$ is a function from each field name f to a relation which pairs each node with the node its f field points to. Since these relations induce a graph on the heap nodes, we will use the term f-**edge** for a pair of nodes in the relation $ref^C(f)$ and call f its **edge type**. In languages such as Java where the program cannot use the memory address of an object directly, the specific names of the nodes in U^C are immaterial. Thus, we define equality between states as isomorphism between them.

2.1   Notations

Fig. 1 lists some notation used throughout. We shorten $E\{\{x\}\}$ to $E\{x\}$.

Symbol	Definition	Meaning
E^*	Reflexive Transitive Closure of E	
$succ(X, E)$	$\{(n, n') \in E \mid n \in X\}$	Restriction of first component
$pred(X, E)$	$\{(n, n') \in E \mid n' \in X\}$	Restriction of second component
$E_1 \circ E_2$	$\{(n, n'') \mid (n, n') \in E_2, (n', n'') \in E_1\}$	Relation composition
$E\{X\}$	$\{n' \mid (n, n') \in succ(X, E)\}$	Relation image
$up_{b \to a}$	$\lambda n.$ if $(n = b)$ then a else n	Updating b to be a
fld^C	$\bigcup_{f \in PRef} ref^C(f)$	Edges of C
$disj(v_1, v_2, v_3)$	$v_1 \neq v_2 \wedge v_1 \neq v_3 \wedge v_2 \neq v_3$	The variables are disjoint

Fig. 1. Notations used in the paper

We define $var(S) \stackrel{\text{def}}{=} env^S\{PVar\}$ to be the set of nodes in S pointed to by program variables and $shared(S)$ to be that set of nodes in S that are pointed to by two or more different heap nodes (ignoring self-loops). We say such a node is **heap-shared**. Formally, $shared(S) \stackrel{\text{def}}{=} \{v \mid (w_1, v) \in fld^S, (w_2, v) \in fld^S, disj(w_1, w_2, v)\}$

3   Abstraction

A state, C, is **concrete** if none of its edges are self loops and if each $ref^C(f)$ is a partial function. The main idea of the abstraction is to keep a set of distinct nodes which are not abstracted and abstract the rest of the graph in such a way that keeps all reachability information for these nodes explicit. The set of distinct nodes we use are those nodes that are either pointed to by variables or heap shared, i.e., $distinct(S) \stackrel{\text{def}}{=} var(S) \cup shared(S)$.

We **contract** an edge (a, b) by replacing each occurrence of b by a, $contract(S, a, b) \stackrel{\text{def}}{=} (U^S - \{b\}, env^S, \lambda f.\{(up_{b\to a}(n_1), up_{b\to a}(n_2) \mid (n_1, n_2) \in ref^S(f)\})$ (note that env^S is not updated because we never contract a node pointed to by a variable). We now define a method $\mathcal{B}(S, D)$ that given a state and a set of nodes D s.t. $distinct(S) \subseteq D \subseteq U^S$, returns the abstract state generated by repeatedly applying contraction on all edges that are not incident to nodes in D until the unique fixpoint is reached. An equivalent way to define $\mathcal{B}(S, D)$ is by collapsing every maximal connected subgraph T_n of S that does not contain nodes in D (the subgraph is a rooted tree) to a single node n (its root). The edge types of the self-loops of n are exactly the types of edges within T_n.

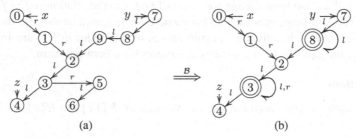

(a)   (b)

Fig. 2. (a) A concrete state C_1, (b) $S_1 = \mathcal{B}(C, distinct(C_1))$

We call the function, M, that maps each node to the node it was collapsed into by $\mathcal{B}$ the **embedding function** (after [21]). When multiple nodes have been embedded into a single node n (i.e., $|M^{-1}(n)| > 1$) we call n a **summary node**. Fig. 2 gives an example of a concrete state C_1 and the result of $\mathcal{B}(C_1, distinct(C_1))$. We mark summary nodes with a double-circle for emphasis.

The abstraction relation, $\beta \stackrel{\text{def}}{=} \{ (S, \mathcal{B}(S, distinct(S))) \mid S$ a state$\}$, maps each state, S, to a state in which every edge not incident to a distinct node has been contracted.

3.1 Data Structures

We limit the class of data structures handled to graphs with no undirected cycles (i.e., when we remove the direction of the edges we get an undirected forest) and no garbage (i.e. all nodes are reachable from program variables). We call such states **admissible states**. This class includes linked lists, trees, and trees with limited amount of sharing (i.e., each pair of nodes has at most one simple path between them and each pair of variables meets at most once). Extensions to support cyclic linked lists, doubly linked lists and trees with parent pointers are described in Sect. 6.

We use a standard relational abstract domain with set-union as join (in Sect. 6 we define a more concise partial-join operator). The concretization relation is defined as

$\gamma \stackrel{\text{def}}{=} \{(S,C)|(C,S) \in \beta$ and C is an admissible concrete state$\}$. We say that an abstract state, S, is **feasible** if $\gamma\{S\} \neq \emptyset$, i.e. S models some admissible concrete state.

3.2 Properties of the Abstraction

We start with some important definitions:

- We say that $(n_1, n_2) \in ref^S(f)$ is an f **must edge** when
  $$\forall C \in \gamma\{S\}, n_1' \in M^{-1}(n_1), n_2' \in M^{-1}(n_2) . (n_1', n_2') \in ref^C(f)$$
- We say that $(n_1, n_2) \in ref^S(f)$ is an f **may edge** when
  $$\forall C \in \gamma\{S\} . \exists n_1' \in M^{-1}(n_1), n_2' \in M^{-1}(n_2) . (n_1', n_2') \in ref^C(f)$$
- We say that $(n_1, n_2) \in ref^S(f)$ is an f **unique may edge** when
  $$\forall C \in \gamma\{S\} . \exists! \, n_1' \in M^{-1}(n_1), n_2' \in M^{-1}(n_2) . (n_1', n_2') \in ref^C(f)$$
- We say there is a **must path** between n_1 and n_2 when
  $$\forall C \in \gamma\{S\}, n_1' \in M^{-1}(n_1), n_2' \in M^{-1}(n_2) . (n_1', n_2') \in (fld^C)^*$$
- We say there is a **may path** between n_1 and n_2 when
  $$\forall C \in \gamma\{S\} . \exists n_1' \in M^{-1}(n_1), n_2' \in M^{-1}(n_2) . (n_1', n_2') \in (fld^C)^*$$

The abstract state S_2 in Fig. 3 models all singly-linked lists of length 4 or more s.t. x points to their head and y to their tail. Note that there are cases in which there is a must path between two nodes (e.g. from 0 to 2) although the path in the abstract state contains may edges (the edges from 0 to 1 and from 1 to 2).

Thm. 1 summarizes some important properties of our abstraction.

Fig. 3. An abstract state S_2

Theorem 1. *For every feasible abstract state S the following hold:*
1. Every f edge in S is an f may edge.
2. Every non self-loop f edge is an f unique may edge.
3. Every f edge between non-summary nodes is an f must edge.
4. A node in S is a summary node iff it has self-loops.
5. For every summary node n the subgraph induced by $M^{-1}(n)$ is a tree and has a unique incoming edge which leads to its root.
6. Let $n_1 \neq n_2$ where n_1 has no self-loops or a single self-loop of the same type as its outgoing edge. A path from n_1 to n_2 is a must path.

Proof: *(sketch)*

1. Immediate from definition of contraction.

2. Analysis of possible contractions reveals that the only case in which two edges are merged by a contraction is if an undirected cycle appeared in the original state.

3. Immediate from 4 and definition of contraction.

4. Contraction always creates a self-loop. Self-loops are preserved by contraction and contraction is the only way to create self-loops.

5. Let T_n be the subgraph induced by $M^{-1}(n)$. Since contraction is done on edges, the nodes in T_n are weakly connected. Shared nodes are never contracted, thus there is no sharing in T_n. Since the original state had no garbage any cycle either has a variable pointing to it, or has a shared node. In any case, an entire cycle cannot be contracted to the same summary node. Thus, T_n is a tree. Furthermore, to avoid sharing and garbage, the one and only incoming edge must be to its root.

6. By 5 and 1, every summary node represents a tree and every edge is a may-edge. Thus, paths between non-summary nodes are must paths. Since a summary node is a tree, all the nodes in it are reachable from the root and so if the target node is a summary node, the path is still a must path. If the source node has a single self-loop it is a singly-linked list. The only outgoing edge from a singly-linked list of the same type as the self-loop is from its last node, thus reachable from all nodes.   □

The last property is of particular importance since it means that the reachability information in the abstract state is explicit. This property is not standard in shape analysis abstractions (e.g., in TVLA it in not always the case). The reason for the limitation on n_1 is that if n_1 has 2 or more self-loops it embeds a tree, thus n_2 is not reachable from some nodes embedded to n_1 (e.g. in Fig. 2 the path in S_1 from node 3 to node 4 is not a must path, since for example in C_1 there is no path from node 5 to node 4).

Lem. 1 defines when an abstract state S is feasible and Lem. 2 bounds its size. Note that the set of admissible concrete states is exactly the set of feasible abstract states with no self-loops.

Lemma 1. (Feasibility) *Abstract state S is feasible iff the following hold:*
1. There are no edges between two different non-distinct nodes.
2. Distinct nodes are never summary nodes.
3. A node that has two outgoing f edges has a self-loop of a different edge type.
4. Deleting all self-loops from S makes it admissible.

Proof: *(sketch)*
(Only If) 1. An edge between two different non-distinct nodes can be contracted, which contradicts that S is in the image of β.

The rest of the properties hold in concrete admissible states and are preserved by contraction.
2. Immediate from definition of contraction.
3. A counterexample would be a node with zero or one self-loops and two outgoing edges of the same type. Since in the original concrete state each edge is a partial function, a node without self-loops cannot have two outgoing edges of the same type. A node with a single self-loop is a linked list, thus the only outgoing edge from it can be from its tail, thus a single edge.
4. It is easy to see that contractions do not introduce garbage or undirected cycles (except for self-loops).

(If) It can be shown that a state that satisfies these properties can always be expanded to a concrete state of finite size.   □

Lemma 2. (MaxSize) *For every feasible abstract state S we have $|U^S| \leq MaxSize$, where $MaxSize \overset{\text{def}}{=} (|PRef| + 1) * (2 * |PVar| - 1)$*

Proof: Let C be an admissible concrete state, D a set s.t. $var(C) \subseteq D \subseteq U^C$, and $S = \mathcal{B}(C, D)$. S has the property that every node is either in D or has a parent in D. Thus, the number of nodes in $|U^S| \leq |D| * (|PRef| + 1)$. Since C has no garbage and no undirected cycles, $|distinct(C)| \leq |PVar| * 2 - 1$. Thus, if $(C, S) \in \beta$ then $|U^S| \leq MaxSize$.   □

4 Best Transformers

Concrete Semantics. Fig. 4 defines the concrete semantics for simple atomic statements in Java-like programs. Most preconditions were added to simplify the presentation. In practice we use temporaries to translate each program statement to a sequence of operations while maintaining the preconditions. Some preconditions such as no null-dereference cannot be removed by a sequence of operations. The analysis detects violations of these preconditions and gives a warning.

The gc operation performs garbage collection by removing all nodes not reachable from any variable. Garbage collection can by executed either after every $x = null$ operation, periodically, or we can run garbage detection instead of garbage collection to detect memory leaks. The semantics of the other operations are straightforward formalizations of standard Java-like operational semantics.

Operation	Precondition	Semantics
gc		let $R = fld^*(var(S))$ in
		$(R, env, \lambda f.succ(R, ref(f)))$
$x \doteq null$		$(U, succ(PVar - \{x\}, env), ref)$
$x = y$	$env\{x\} = \emptyset$	$(U, env \cup \{(x,n)|(y,n) \in env\}, ref)$
$x.f = null$	$env\{x\} \neq \emptyset \wedge$	$(U, env,$
	$ref(f) \circ env\{x\} \subseteq var(S)$	$ref[f := succ(U - env\{x\}, ref(f))])$
$x.f = y$	$env\{x\} \neq \emptyset \wedge$	$(U, env, ref[f := ref(f) \cup \{(n_x, n_y)|$
	$ref(f) \circ env\{x\} = \emptyset$	$(x, n_x) \in env, (y, n_y) \in env\}])$
$x = y.f$	$env\{x\} = \emptyset \wedge$	$(U, env \cup \{(x,n)|(y,n) \in ref(f) \circ env\},$
	$env\{y\} \neq \emptyset$	$ref)$
$x = malloc$	$env\{x\} = \emptyset \wedge n_{malloc} \notin U$	$(U \cup \{n_{malloc}\}, env \cup \{(x, n_{malloc})\}, ref)$
$x == null$		$env\{x\} = \emptyset$
$x == y$		$env\{x\} = env\{y\}$

Fig. 4. The operations supported and their concrete semantics

4.1 Abstract Transformers

We now show how to compute the best abstract transformers (see [4]) for the our abstraction and concrete semantics defined in Fig. 4. The best transformer of an operation st is defined as $st^{best} \stackrel{\text{def}}{=} \beta \circ st \circ \gamma$ (i.e, for each concrete state in $\gamma\{S\}$ apply the concrete semantics and abstract). This definition is not constructive since the number of states in $\gamma\{S\}$ is unbounded and potentially infinite. The main idea is to define a relation $focus[st]$ whose image is a bounded set of states and if $(S, S') \in focus[st]$ there is a representative state $C \in \gamma\{S\}$ s.t. $\beta\{st(S')\} = \beta\{st(C)\}$ and vice versa. Thus, we define the abstract transformer to be $st^\sharp \stackrel{\text{def}}{=} \beta \circ st \circ focus[st]$. Note that the transformer defined in the concrete semantics can be applied to abstract states as well.

The focus operation is similar to the one defined in [21], i.e., it is a partial concretization intended to restore enough information to compute the transformer precisely. Let $D(st, C) \stackrel{\text{def}}{=} distinct(C) \cup distinct(st(C))$. We define focus to be:

Definition 1. $focus[st] \overset{\text{def}}{=} \{(S, \mathcal{B}(C, D(st, C))) \mid C \in \gamma\{S\}\}$

Focus takes all the states in $\gamma\{S\}$ and keeps both the distinct nodes of the state and the nodes that will become distinct after the statement is executed. In Sect. 4.2 we define an algorithm that computes the image of focus.

Lem. 3 gives some important properties for the interaction of β and st. Note that the existence of commutative diagrams is not true in general shape abstraction. Thm. 2 uses Lem. 3 to prove that $st^\sharp$ is the best abstract transformer.

Lemma 3. *For every* $(S, C) \in \gamma$, *let* $D = D(st, C)$ *and* $S' = \mathcal{B}(C, D)$. *Then:*
Idempotence. $\beta\{S'\} = \beta\{S\}$,
Commutative Diagrams. $\mathcal{B}(st(C), D) = \mathcal{B}(st(S'), D)$, *and*
Equivalence under β. $(\beta \circ st)\{C\} = (\beta \circ st)\{S'\}$

Proof: *(sketch)*
Idempotence. It can be shown that contraction induces a confluent derivation relation commutative in the choice of D. Since $\mathcal{B}$ can be seen as the fixed-point of that relation, the statement follows.
Commutative Diagrams. This can be verified by checking the algebraic operations defining the transformer, for each operation in Fig. 4.
Equivalence under β. By commutative diagrams we have $\mathcal{B}(st(C), D) = \mathcal{B}(st(S'), D)$. By Idempotence we have $\beta\{\mathcal{B}(st(C), D)\} = \beta\{st(C)\}$ and $\beta\{\mathcal{B}(st(S'), D)\} = \beta\{st(S')\}$. Thus, $\beta\{st(C)\} = \beta\{st(S')\}$. $\qquad\square$

Theorem 2. $st^\sharp$ *is the best abstract transformer, i.e.,* $st^\sharp = st^{best}$.

Proof: Let $(S, S^\sharp) \in st^\sharp$. There is S' s.t. $(S, S') \in focus[st]$ and $(S', S^\sharp) \in \beta \circ st$. By Def. 1 there is a concrete and admissible state C s.t. $(S, C) \in \gamma$ and $S' = \mathcal{B}(C, D(st, C))$, and by Lem. 3 $(C, S^\sharp) \in (\beta \circ st)$ thus $(S, S^\sharp) \in st^{best}$.

Conversely, let $(S, S^\sharp) \in st^{best}$. There is C s.t. $(S, C) \in \gamma$ and $(C, S^\sharp) \in (\beta \circ st)$. Let $S' = \mathcal{B}(C, D(st, C))$. By Def. 1 we have $(S, S') \in focus[st]$, and by Lem. 3 $(S', S^\sharp) \in \beta \circ st$ thus $(S, S^\sharp) \in st^\sharp$. $\qquad\square$

4.2 Algorithms

In order to compute the best abstract transformer, $st^\sharp$, we must give efficient algorithms for state equality, focus, and β. The total complexity of computing the abstract transformer is $O(NS * V * \log V)$ where NS is the number of successor abstract states (which may be exponential in the number of program variables).

Focus. In Sect. 4.1, we defined focus non-constructively. We now present an algorithm, $Focus(S, st)$, that computes $focus[st]\{S\}$. The first observation is that for all statements, st, except $x = y.f$, $focus[st]$ is the identity relation. This is clear for $x = malloc$, and true for the rest because $distinct(st(S)) \subseteq distinct(S)$,

For $st \overset{\text{def}}{=} x = y.f$, $Focus(S, st)$ enumerates on all states that can be contracted to S by a minimal number of contractions and still have $distinct(st(S)) \subseteq distinct(S)$ as non-summary nodes. Let n_f be the node pointed to by $y.f$ in S. If it is a non-summary node $Focus(S, st) = \{S\}$. Otherwise, let G be the self-loops of n_f in S.

Let $(S, S') \in focus[x = y.f]$, S' can be contracted into S by at most one contraction for each edge type in G. Let N'_f be the subgraph of S' that was contracted into n_f. Since all edges are may-edges, the edges within N'_f are exactly the self-loops of n_f. Furthermore, since all the edges between different nodes are unique may-edges, the edges between N'_f and the rest of the graph are exactly the edges between n_f and the rest of the graph. Finally, since S' is the result of $\mathcal{B}$ on an admissible concrete state the property that a node that has two outgoing g edges has a self-loop of different reference field, is maintained. This gives us an enumeration algorithm to compute $Focus(S, st)$. Lem. 4 summarizes the properties of $Focus(S, st)$.

Lemma 4. $focus[x = y.f]\{S\} = Focus(S, x = y.f)$

Beta. To compute the image of β we perform two tasks, 1) check that the state is admissible and 2) return a state in which all the possible contractions have been made.

Admissibility. Since an admissible state is one without garbage and with no undirected cycles, the check is done by DFS from all nodes pointed to by variables to make sure that there is no garbage. To compute undirected connectivity, we maintain a Union-Find data structure during the DFS, thus detecting undirected cycles. We start with singleton groups for each node and for every edge we encounter we union the groups the two incident nodes belong to. Thus the sets maintain weak reachability. If we find the two incident nodes already belong to the same group we found an undirected cycle and we abort. The complexity for this check is $O(n\alpha(n))$, where n is the size of the input state and α is the inverse Ackerman function.

To compute $\beta\{S\}$ we observe that the edges contracted are exactly the edges between non-distinct nodes. Thus, the algorithm performs two DFS traversals. The first computes $distinct(S)$ by marking nodes that are either pointed to by variables or have an in-degree greater than one (note that self-loops do not contribute to the in-degree). The second traversal simply contracts every non self-loop edge s.t., both its incident nodes are not distinct. The complexity of this algorithm is $O(n)$.

State Equality. We defined state equality as isomorphism between the states. We give an algorithm that computes canonical names for each state. The canonical names of two states are identical iff the two states are isomorphic.

Canonical names are given to nodes by traversing the graph in DFS from program variables (in fixed order) traversing the reference fields in fixed order as well. The name of a node n is composed of the names of the variables pointing to n, n's self loops and for each of n's parents, the parent name and the type of the edge leading from the parent to n. To ensure the traversal order is unique, we only leave a node to its children after all its parents have been visited. Hash-cons is used to store the canonical names, allowing for O(1) amortized time equality checks. The name of a state is the hash-cons of its set of nodes ordered by some fixed order (e.g. memory address of the hash-cons). Thus, the total complexity of the algorithm is $O(V \log V)$.

5   Evaluation

We use a subset of first-order logic with transitive closure as a query logic to extract information from states. Let $[\![\varphi]\!]^S$ denote the boolean value of formula φ in state S.

Definition 2. **(Sound)** *An evaluation function of a formula is* **sound** *iff for every feasible abstract state S,* $\neg\llbracket\varphi\rrbracket^S \Rightarrow \forall C \in \gamma\{S\} . \neg\llbracket\varphi\rrbracket^C$

(Complete) *An evaluation function of a formula is* **complete** *iff for every feasible abstract state S,* $\neg\llbracket\varphi\rrbracket^S \iff \forall C \in \gamma\{S\} . \neg\llbracket\varphi\rrbracket^C$

To compute $\mathtt{assert}(\varphi, S)$, i.e., to verify that all the states in $\gamma\{S\}$ satisfy φ, we will apply a sound evaluation function on $\neg\varphi$ and verify that the result is false.

5.1 Query Logic

The query logic is first order logic in Negation Normal Form (NNF) over the following vocabulary:
- For every $x \in PVar$ a unary predicate symbol; $x(n)$ iff x points to n
- For every $f \in PRef$ a binary predicate symbol; $f(n_1, n_2)$ iff the f field of the n_1 points to the n_2
- Binary predicate symbol TC; $TC(n_1, n_2)$ iff there is any non-empty path from n_1 to n_2
- Equality; $n_1 = n_2$ iff n_1 and n_2 are the same heap node
  Examples:

$$\forall v . \exists w . x(w) \wedge (v = w \vee TC(w, v)) \tag{1}$$

$$\forall v, w . \neg y(w) \vee \neg left(v, w) \tag{2}$$

Formula (1) states that all the nodes in the heap are either pointed to by x or reachable from the node pointed to by x. Formula (2) states that the any node pointed to by y has no incoming $left$ edge.

We will restrict our attention to closed formulas (no free variables). We say that a formula is **guarded** if every quantifier is of the form $(\forall v . x(v) \Rightarrow \psi)$ or $(\exists v . x(v) \wedge \psi)$ where x is some program variable.

To evaluate formula φ in state S we translate S to a standard logical structure $\widehat{S}$ and φ to a FO formula, $TR(\varphi)$, in the vocabulary of $\widehat{S}$. Let $\llbracket\varphi\rrbracket^S \stackrel{\text{def}}{=} \llbracket TR(\varphi)\rrbracket^{\widehat{S}}$ where the right hand side is standard FO Tarskian semantics. Thm. 3 ensures the soundness of the evaluation and guarantees completeness for the guarded fragment of the query logic.

Theorem 3. *For every formula φ, $\lambda S . \llbracket TR(\varphi)\rrbracket^{\widehat{S}}$ is a sound evaluation function. If φ is guarded, it is also a complete evaluation function.*

5.2 Translation

The universe of $\widehat{S}$ is the universe of S. The vocabulary and its interpretation are given in Fig. 5(a). The translation defines for each edge f two predicates, $f^\forall$ and $f^\exists$. If $f^\forall(n_1, n_2)$ then there is an f must edge from n_1 to n_2. If $f^\exists(n_1, n_2)$ then there is an f may edge from n_1 to n_2. Similarly we use $TC^\forall(n_1, n_2)$ to define a must path from n_1 to n_2, and $TC^\exists(n_1, n_2)$ to define a may path from n_1 to n_2. The translation is a formalization of Thm. 1. Fig. 5(b) gives the translation of S_2 defined in Fig. 3. The translation rules for the literals in the query formula are given in Fig. 5(c).

Vocabulary	Interpretation
$x(n)$	$(x,n) \in env^S$
$f^\exists(n_1,n_2)$	$(n_1,n_2) \in ref^S(f)$
$f^\forall(n_1,n_2)$	$f^\exists(n_1,n_2) \wedge \neg sm(n_1) \wedge \neg sm(n_2)$
$TC^\exists(n_1,n_2)$	A (possibly empty) directed path from n_1 to n_2
$TC^\forall(n_1,n_2)$	$TC^\exists(n_1,n_2)$, $n_1 \neq n_2$ and the path satisfies case 6 of Thm. 1
$sm(n)$	$\bigvee_{f\in PRef}(n,n) \in ref^S(f)$

(a)

Predicate	Tuples
x	$\langle 0 \rangle$
y	$\langle 2 \rangle$
$left^\exists$	$\langle 0,1 \rangle, \langle 1,1 \rangle, \langle 1,2 \rangle$
$left^\forall$	
$TC^\exists$	$\langle 0,1 \rangle, \langle 0,2 \rangle,$ $\langle 1,1 \rangle, \langle 1,2 \rangle$
$TC^\forall$	$\langle 0,1 \rangle, \langle 0,2 \rangle, \langle 1,2 \rangle$
sm	$\langle 1 \rangle$

(b)

φ	$TR(\varphi)$	φ	$TR(\varphi)$
$x(v)$	$x(v)$	$TC(v_1,v_2)$	$TC^\exists(v_1,v_2)$
$\neg x(v)$	$\neg x(v)$	$\neg TC(v_1,v_2)$	$\neg TC^\forall(v_1,v_2)$
$f(v_1,v_2)$	$f^\exists(v_1,v_2)$	$n_1 = n_2$	$n_1 = n_2$
$\neg f(v_1,v_2)$	$\neg f^\forall(v_1,v_2)$	$\neg n_1 = n_2$	$\neg n_1 = n_2 \vee sm(n_1)$

(c)

Fig. 5. (a) Translation of an abstract state to a logical structure. (b) $\widehat{S_2}$ - the translation of S_2 from Fig. 3 (c) Rules for translating a query formula to the vocabulary of $\widehat{S}$.

Theorem 3 Proof: *(sketch)*
The evaluation of $TR(\varphi)$ on $\widehat{S}$ simulates the evaluation of a φ on any concrete state C s.t. $(S,C) \in \gamma$. Assume an assignment $v_i \mapsto n_i$ satisfies a literal $L(v_1,...,v_k)$ in S', we shall see that $v_i \mapsto M(n_i)$ satisfies $TR(L)(v_1,...,v_k)$. Most cases are immediate from the definition of $\widehat{S}$ and the properties of the abstraction (Sect. 3.2). The only case requiring further explanation is $L \equiv \neg v_1 = v_2$. Here we may chose $n_1 \neq n_2$ s.t. $M(n_1) = M(n_2)$, but in this case $sm(M(n_1))$ thus $TR(L)(v_1,v_2)$ still evaluates to true. Since an NNF formula has no negation outside of literals this is enough for soundness. □

Examples: The translation of (1) is $\forall v.\exists w.x(w) \wedge (v = w \vee TC^\exists(w,v))$ which evaluates to true in $\widehat{S_2}$ as expected. The translation of (2) is $\forall v,w.\neg y(w) \vee \neg left^\forall(v,w)$ unfortunately this formula also evaluates to true. In some cases, including this one, we can overcome this imprecision by an improved formula translation $TR'(\varphi)$, as described in [15].

6 Extensions

6.1 Loop Boundaries

Some programs temporarily violate the data structure invariants (including admissibility) and restore all within the boundary of a single loop iteration. We can handle such programs with the same level of precision by only performing β on loop boundaries.

6.2 Partial Join

Partial Join [17] replaces union as the join operator of the abstract domain with an operator that merges matching states. We build a variant of the partial join operator by ignoring the self-loops when giving canonical names to states. Matching states are merged by performing union on the self-loops on nodes with the same canonical names. The concretization function is modified to consider that some of the self-loops may not represent concrete edges.

The focus operation needs to be updated according to the changes in the concretization function. There are two changes in the algorithm: 1) There is no need to enumerate the self-loops in the subgraph contracted to the summary node. 2) The case in which the summary node represents a single node needs to be considered.

The experimental results (Sect. 7) show that Partial Join is important for performance, while maintaining precision.

6.3   Cycles

The abstract domain can be extended to support cycles in the following limited way. A directed cycle is admissible if there is a path from a variable that contains the entire cycle and all the outgoing edges from all the nodes of this path are of the same edge type (i.e. the cycle is a part of a singly-linked list). A state is admissible if all its undirected cycles are actually admissible directed cycles. All the properties of the abstraction such as the bounded abstract state size remain true for this extended class.

Focus and β can be easily modified to support these cycles since an entire cycle can never be contracted (since there has to be a node on each cycle that is either pointed to by a variable or heap-shared). The subtleties come from two sources. One is the fact the a self loop can now represent a concrete self-loop and not a summary node. This can be easily solved by adding an extra bit per node indicating whether it is a summary node or not and maintaining it in all the operations.

The second subtlety is in computation of canonical names, since without breaking the cycles we may never be able to give a name to a node before traversing its children. The solution is to mark the back-edges during the first DFS and ignore them in the second DFS. At the end, we add their names to their incoming nodes.

6.4   Parent Pointers

The abstract domain can be extended to allow parent pointers (i.e., doubly linked lists and trees with parent pointers) in the following limited way. Each node can use only a single field as a parent pointer (specified by the user). Parent pointers are not considered for contraction, heap-sharing or garbage (thus every node has to be reachable using non parent-pointer fields). This means that exactly the same nodes will be contracted whether parent pointers exist or not. Either all the nodes contracted to a summary have the same parent pointer (in this case we say that the summary node has that parent pointer) or none of them have it. If two nodes are contracted, all the parent pointers incoming or outgoing from these nodes have to be the inverse of "real" reference fields and the two nodes and the edge between them have to agree on the parent pointer (either none have parent pointers, or all of them have the same parent pointer).

These limitations still allow us to handle doubly-linked lists and trees with parent pointers as long as every node is reachable using "real" reference fields (i.e. there is a pointer from the head of the doubly linked list or from the root of the tree). Specifically we can handle all the doubly-linked list examples of [21].

To support this extension we make the following changes:

Focus. The only problem in the current focus is the fact that we can now traverse a parent pointer into a summary node and, in this case, it does not necessarily lead to the root of the sub-graph contracted to the summary node. The parent pointers within the sub-graph are easy to handle since they are either the inverse of all the reference fields in the sub-graph or none of them.

Beta. Since the contractions ignore the parent pointers we only need to make sure that the state is admissible. We update the current admissibility check to consider the parent pointer limitation described above.

Updating the canonical names algorithm is simple as well.

7 Implementation

We have implemented the abstract transformer detailed above including the extensions of Sect. 6. Focus was implemented only for linked lists and binary trees (i.e., up to two self-loops). The implementation is written in Java and is integrated with the Soot Java Optimization Framework [20] as a front end. The empirical results of running our analysis on some examples are given in Fig. 6. In all cases the analysis also proved absence of memory leaks, acyclicity (where applicable) and absence of null-dereferences. N/A states that the information for the example is not available for that tool and O/S means that it is out of scope for the tool. Max states is the maximum number of states in each program point. The columns marked with "[R]" use the relational join as described in Sect. 4. The columns marked with "[P]" use the partial join extension described in Sect. 6. The TVLA times given for tree manipulating algorithms use partial join as well. The tests were made on an Intel Pentium M, 1.6 GHz with 1.00 GB of RAM.

Programs	Time[R]	Max states[R]	Time[P]	Max states[P]	[2]	TVLA	[18]
deleteSortedTree	2359.70	192355	3.22	520	O/S	47.48	O/S
insertSortedTree	20.85	9365	0.55	264	O/S	1.8	O/S
lindstromScan	1459.63	79673	8.36	1337	O/S	65.86	O/S
insertRedBlack	> 24 hours		38.15	4853	O/S	N/A	O/S
reverse	0.05	15	0.11	8	0.1	0.531	5
reverseCycle	0.24	159	0.26	62	0.1	N/A	2
merge	0.20	96	0.15	36	17.8	4.006	15
delete	0.02	20	0.01	12	0.9	1.242	7
bubbleSort	0.03	36	0.03	21	N/A	11.887	N/A
bubbleSort2	0.08	76	0.08	33	11.4	N/A	N/A
insertSort	0.06	100	0.05	48	N/A	20.219	N/A

Fig. 6. The empirical results from running the abstract transformer implementation

The programs are explained in [15]. The "bubbleSort" and "bubbleSort2" are two variants of an in-place bubble sort for linked lists analyzed by TVLA and [2] respectively.

We can see that our analysis is indeed fast and in some cases up to 100 times faster than the other analyses depicted. We should point out that most examples are small, thus the differences in running times can be partially attributed to engineering issues. Checking the properties detailed above for these examples is done automatically by the system. To check other properties we need a way to extract information from the abstract states. This is done by formula evaluation and is detailed in Sect. 5.

8   Related Work

Shape and heap analysis is a subject of active research with many interesting algorithms including [10,21,13]. The TVLA system generalizes these algorithms and can be utilized to implement our algorithm. Indeed, in this paper we followed the line of research similar to the one in [8,13,12,18] of developing a specialized shape analysis for commonly used data structures.

We are very pleased with the ability of our method to compute the best transformers in an efficient way. In contrast, TVLA can spend a lot of time in order to determine if an abstract state is feasible. Indeed it can spend an exponential time even when there are no resultant abstract states. The abstraction in this paper is tailored for an interesting set of properties. A mechanism to support other properties (such as TVLA's Instrumentation Predicates) remains an interesting open problem.

Connection analysis [6] keeps reachability information between program variables. Our work is more precise as it can perform strong updates for heap manipulation. Grammar based abstraction [13] uses a restricted grammar to annotate summary nodes with their possible shapes. The abstractions are incomparable since the grammar based abstraction can express invariants (such as binomial heap) that cannot be expressed in our abstraction. On the other hand, the grammar based abstraction can deal with only a limited amount of sharing. For example, it cannot represent a tree with parent pointers and a pointer arbitrarily deep into the tree.

The shape analysis of [5] is very similar to [18] both in the properties of the abstraction and in the programs handled.

Decision Procedures for Linked Data Structures. An orthogonal line of research is the development of decision procedures and theorem provers which support transitive closure [1,9,14,2]. Such techniques can be utilized with arbitrary abstractions.

In this paper, we developed direct methods for a specific abstraction. We are encouraged by the fact that our asymptotic complexity is lower than the above mentioned procedures by orders of magnitudes. Moreover, our implementation is also faster by a factor of 100 than the one reported in [2][1]. The MONA System [11] can be used to implement the operations in this paper. However, it has non-elementary complexity and is in our experience infeasible for program with trees.

Acknowledgements. We thank Noam Rinetzky and the anonymous CAV referees for many helpful comments.

---

[1] Our method also allows trees which are beyond the scope of [2].

References

1. I. Balaban, A. Pnueli, and L. D. Zuck. Shape analysis by predicate abstraction. In VMCAI, pages 164–180, 2005.
2. J. Bingham and Z. Rakamaric. A logic and decision procedure for predicate abstraction of heap-manipulating programs. Tech. Rep. TR-2005-19, Dept. of Comp. Sci., Univ. of BC, Canada, 2005.
3. G. Bruns and P. Godefroid. Generalized model checking: Reasoning about partial state spaces. In CONCUR, pages 168–182, 2000.
4. P. Cousot and R. Cousot. Systematic design of program analysis frameworks. In Symp. on Princ. of Prog. Lang., pages 269–282, New York, NY, 1979. ACM Press.
5. D. Distefano, P. W. O'Hearn, and H. Yang. A local shape analysis based on separation logic. In TACAS, pages 287–302, 2006.
6. R. Ghiya and L. Hendren. Putting pointer analysis to work. In Symp. on Princ. of Prog. Lang., New York, NY, 1998. ACM Press.
7. S. Graf and H. Saïdi. Construction of abstract state graphs with PVS. In CAV, 1997.
8. L. Hendren. Parallelizing Programs with Recursive Data Structures. PhD thesis, Cornell Univ., Ithaca, NY, Jan 1990.
9. N. Immerman, A. Rabinovich, T. Reps, M. Sagiv, and G. Yorsh. Verification via structure simulation. In Proc. Computer-Aided Verif., pages 281–294, 2004.
10. N.D. Jones and S.S. Muchnick. Flow analysis and optimization of Lisp-like structures. In S.S. Muchnick and N.D. Jones, editors, Program Flow Analysis: Theory and Applications, chapter 4, pages 102–131. Prentice-Hall, Englewood Cliffs, NJ, 1981.
11. N. Klarlund and A. Møller. MONA Version 1.4 User Manual. BRICS Notes Series NS-01-1, Dept. of Comp. Sci., Univ. of Aarhus, January 2001.
12. S. K. Lahiri and S. Qadeer. Verifying properties of well-founded linked lists. In POPL, 2006.
13. O. Lee, H. Yang, and K. Yi. Automatic verification of pointer programs using grammar-based shape analysis. In ESOP, pages 124–140, 2005.
14. T. Lev-Ami, N. Immerman, T. W. Reps, M. Sagiv, S. Srivastava, and G. Yorsh. Simulating reachability using first-order logic with applications to verification of linked data structures. In CADE, pages 99–115, 2005.
15. T. Lev-Ami, N. Immerman, and M. Sagiv. Fast and precise abstraction for shape analysis. Technical Report TR-2006-01-001221, Tel-Aviv Univ., 2006. Available at http://www.cs.tau.ac.il/~tla/2006/papers/TR-2006-01-001221.pdf.
16. T. Lev-Ami and M. Sagiv. TVLA: A system for implementing static analyses. In Static Analysis Symp., pages 280–301, 2000.
17. R. Manevich, M. Sagiv, G. Ramalingam, and J. Field. Partially disjunctive heap abstraction. In SAS, pages 265–279, 2004.
18. R. Manevich, E. Yahav, G. Ramalingam, and M. Sagiv. Predicate abstraction and canonical abstraction for singly-linked lists. In VMCAI, pages 181–198, 2005.
19. T. Reps, A. Loginov, and M. Sagiv. Semantic minimization of 3-valued propositional formulae. In LICS, pages 40–54, 2002.
20. Cananda Sable Research Group, McGill University. Soot: a java optimization framework. Available at: http://www.sable.mcgill.ca/soot/.
21. M. Sagiv, T. Reps, and R. Wilhelm. Parametric shape analysis via 3-valued logic. Trans. on Prog. Lang. and Syst., 2002.
22. G. Yorsh, T. Reps, and M. Sagiv. Symbolically computing most-precise abstract operations for shape analysis. In TACAS, pages 530–545, 2004.

Author Index

Lecture Notes in Computer Science

For information about Vols. 1–4014

please contact your bookseller or Springer

Vol. 4061: K. Miesenberger, J. Klaus, W. Zagler, A. Karshmer (Eds.), Computers Helping People with Special Needs. XXIX, 1356 pages. 2006.

Vol. 4060: K. Futatsugi, J.-P. Jouannaud, J. Meseguer (Eds.), Algebra, Meaning, and Computation. XXXVIII, 643 pages. 2006.

Vol. 4059: L. Arge, R. Freivalds (Eds.), Algorithm Theory – SWAT 2006. XII, 436 pages. 2006.

Vol. 4058: L.M. Batten, R. Safavi-Naini (Eds.), Information Security and Privacy. XII, 446 pages. 2006.

Vol. 4057: J.P.W. Pluim, B. Likar, F.A. Gerritsen (Eds.), Biomedical Image Registration. XII, 324 pages. 2006.

Vol. 4056: P. Flocchini, L. Gąsieniec (Eds.), Structural Information and Communication Complexity. X, 357 pages. 2006.

Vol. 4055: J. Lee, J. Shim, S.-g. Lee, C. Bussler, S. Shim (Eds.), Data Engineering Issues in E-Commerce and Services. IX, 290 pages. 2006.

Vol. 4054: A. Horváth, M. Telek (Eds.), Formal Methods and Stochastic Models for Performance Evaluation. VIII, 239 pages. 2006.

Vol. 4053: M. Ikeda, K.D. Ashley, T.-W. Chan (Eds.), Intelligent Tutoring Systems. XXVI, 821 pages. 2006.

Vol. 4052: M. Bugliesi, B. Preneel, V. Sassone, I. Wegener (Eds.), Automata, Languages and Programming, Part II. XXIV, 603 pages. 2006.

Vol. 4051: M. Bugliesi, B. Preneel, V. Sassone, I. Wegener (Eds.), Automata, Languages and Programming, Part I. XXIII, 729 pages. 2006.

Vol. 4049: S. Parsons, N. Maudet, P. Moraitis, I. Rahwan (Eds.), Argumentation in Multi-Agent Systems. XIV, 313 pages. 2006. (Sublibrary LNAI).

Vol. 4048: L. Goble, J.-J.C.. Meyer (Eds.), Deontic Logic and Artificial Normative Systems. X, 273 pages. 2006. (Sublibrary LNAI).

Vol. 4047: M. Robshaw (Ed.), Fast Software Encryption. XI, 434 pages. 2006.

Vol. 4046: S.M. Astley, M. Brady, C. Rose, R. Zwiggelaar (Eds.), Digital Mammography. XVI, 654 pages. 2006.

Vol. 4045: D. Barker-Plummer, R. Cox, N. Swoboda (Eds.), Diagrammatic Representation and Inference. XII, 301 pages. 2006. (Sublibrary LNAI).

Vol. 4044: P. Abrahamsson, M. Marchesi, G. Succi (Eds.), Extreme Programming and Agile Processes in Software Engineering. XII, 230 pages. 2006.

Vol. 4043: A.S. Atzeni, A. Lioy (Eds.), Public Key Infrastructure. XI, 261 pages. 2006.

Vol. 4042: D. Bell, J. Hong (Eds.), Flexible and Efficient Information Handling. XVI, 296 pages. 2006.

Vol. 4041: S.-W. Cheng, C.K. Poon (Eds.), Algorithmic Aspects in Information and Management. XI, 395 pages. 2006.

Vol. 4040: R. Reulke, U. Eckardt, B. Flach, U. Knauer, K. Polthier (Eds.), Combinatorial Image Analysis. XII, 482 pages. 2006.

Vol. 4039: M. Morisio (Ed.), Reuse of Off-the-Shelf Components. XIII, 444 pages. 2006.

Vol. 4038: P. Ciancarini, H. Wiklicky (Eds.), Coordination Models and Languages. VIII, 299 pages. 2006.

Vol. 4037: R. Gorrieri, H. Wehrheim (Eds.), Formal Methods for Open Object-Based Distributed Systems. XVII, 474 pages. 2006.

Vol. 4036: O. H. Ibarra, Z. Dang (Eds.), Developments in Language Theory. XII, 456 pages. 2006.

Vol. 4035: T. Nishita, Q. Peng, H.-P. Seidel (Eds.), Advances in Computer Graphics. XX, 771 pages. 2006.

Vol. 4034: J. Münch, M. Vierimaa (Eds.), Product-Focused Software Process Improvement. XVII, 474 pages. 2006.

Vol. 4033: B. Stiller, P. Reichl, B. Tuffin (Eds.), Performability Has its Price. X, 103 pages. 2006.

Vol. 4032: O. Etzion, T. Kuflik, A. Motro (Eds.), Next Generation Information Technologies and Systems. XIII, 365 pages. 2006.

Vol. 4031: M. Ali, R. Dapoigny (Eds.), Advances in Applied Artificial Intelligence. XXIII, 1353 pages. 2006. (Sublibrary LNAI).

Vol. 4029: L. Rutkowski, R. Tadeusiewicz, L.A. Zadeh, J.M. Zurada (Eds.), Artificial Intelligence and Soft Computing – ICAISC 2006. XXI, 1235 pages. 2006. (Sublibrary LNAI).

Vol. 4028: J. Kohlas, B. Meyer, A. Schiper (Eds.), Dependable Systems: Software, Computing, Networks. XII, 295 pages. 2006.

Vol. 4027: H.L. Larsen, G. Pasi, D. Ortiz-Arroyo, T. Andreasen, H. Christiansen (Eds.), Flexible Query Answering Systems. XVIII, 714 pages. 2006. (Sublibrary LNAI).

Vol. 4026: P.B. Gibbons, T. Abdelzaher, J. Aspnes, R. Rao (Eds.), Distributed Computing in Sensor Systems. XIV, 566 pages. 2006.

Vol. 4025: F. Eliassen, A. Montresor (Eds.), Distributed Applications and Interoperable Systems. XI, 355 pages. 2006.

Vol. 4024: S. Donatelli, P.S. Thiagarajan (Eds.), Petri Nets and Other Models of Concurrency - ICATPN 2006. XI, 441 pages. 2006.

Vol. 4021: E. André, L. Dybkjær, W. Minker, H. Neumann, M. Weber (Eds.), Perception and Interactive Technologies. XI, 217 pages. 2006. (Sublibrary LNAI).

Vol. 4020: A. Bredenfeld, A. Jacoff, I. Noda, Y. Takahashi (Eds.), RoboCup 2005: Robot Soccer World Cup IX. XVII, 727 pages. 2006. (Sublibrary LNAI).

Vol. 4019: M. Johnson, V. Vene (Eds.), Algebraic Methodology and Software Technology. XI, 389 pages. 2006.

Vol. 4018: V. Wade, H. Ashman, B. Smyth (Eds.), Adaptive Hypermedia and Adaptive Web-Based Systems. XVI, 474 pages. 2006.

Vol. 4017: S. Vassiliadis, S. Wong, T.D. Hämäläinen (Eds.), Embedded Computer Systems: Architectures, Modeling, and Simulation. XV, 492 pages. 2006.

Vol. 4016: J.X. Yu, M. Kitsuregawa, H.V. Leong (Eds.), Advances in Web-Age Information Management. XVII, 606 pages. 2006.